Official 1986
National Footl

Record & Fact Book

A National Football League Book.

Workman Publishing Co., New York.

National Football League, 1986

410 Park Avenue, New York, N.Y. 10022 (212) 758-1500

Commissioner: Pete Rozelle
Executive Vice President & League Counsel: Jay Moyer
Treasurer: John Schoemer
Executive Director: Don Weiss
Director of Administration: Joe Rhein
Director of Communications: Joe Browne
Director of Operations: Jan Van Duser
Director of Broadcasting: Val Pinchbeck, Jr.
Director of Public Relations: Jim Heffernan
Director of Security: Warren Welsh
Assistant Director of Security: Charles R. Jackson
Director of Player Personnel: Joel Bussert
Supervisor of Officials: Art McNally
Assistant Supervisors of Officials: Jack Reader, Nick Skorich, Joe Gardi, Tony Veteri
Director of Special Events: Jim Steeg
Assistant Director of Special Events: Susan McCann
Assistant Counsel: Jim Noel
Controller: Tom Sullivan
Director of Player Relations: Mel Blount

American Football Conference

President: Lamar Hunt, Kansas City Chiefs
Assistant to President: Al Ward
Director of Information: Pete Abitante

National Football Conference

President: Wellington Mara, New York Giants
Assistant to President: Bill Granholm
Director of Information: Dick Maxwell

Cover Photograph by Vernon Biever.

Printed in the United States of America.

A National Football League Book.
Compiled by the NFL Public Relations Department and Seymour Siwoff, Elias Sports Bureau.
Edited by Pete Abitante, NFL Public Relations and Chuck Garrity, Jr., NFLP Creative Services.
Statistics by Elias Sports Bureau.
Produced by NFL Properties, Inc., Creative Services Division.

Workman Publishing Co.
1 West 39th Street, New York, N.Y. 10018
Manufactured in the United States of America.
First printing, July 1986.

10 9 8 7 6 5 4 3 2 1

Contents

1986 NFL Schedule 4
Important Dates 11
Waivers, Active List, Reserve List, Trades, Annual Player Limits 12
Tie-Breaking Procedures 13
Figuring the 1987 NFL Schedule 14
Instant Replay 16
Active Coaches Career Records 17
Coaches With 100 Career Victories 17
AFC Active Statistical Leaders 18
NFC Active Statistical Leaders 19
Draft List for 1986 20
Look For in 1986 22
American Football Conference
- Buffalo Bills 24
- Cincinnati Bengals 28
- Cleveland Browns 32
- Denver Broncos 36
- Houston Oilers 40
- Indianapolis Colts 44
- Kansas City Chiefs 48
- Los Angeles Raiders 52
- Miami Dolphins 56
- New England Patriots 60
- New York Jets 64
- Pittsburgh Steelers 68
- San Diego Chargers 72
- Seattle Seahawks 76

National Football Conference
- Atlanta Falcons 82
- Chicago Bears 86
- Dallas Cowboys 90
- Detroit Lions 94
- Green Bay Packers 98
- Los Angeles Rams 102
- Minnesota Vikings 106
- New Orleans Saints 110
- New York Giants 114
- Philadelphia Eagles 118
- St. Louis Cardinals 122
- San Francisco 49ers 126
- Tampa Bay Buccaneers 130
- Washington Redskins 134
- 1985-86 Trades 140
- 1985 Preseason Standings and Results 141
- 1985 Regular Season Standings and Results 142
- 1985 Week by Week 144
- 1985 All-Pro Teams 164
- 1985 Professional Football Awards 166
- 1985 Paid Attendance Breakdown 167
- 1985 Ten Best Rushing Performances 168
- 1985 Ten Best Passing Performances 169
- 1985 Ten Best Pass Receiving Performances 170

1985 Statistics
- American Football Conference Team Offense 172
- American Football Conference Team Defense 173
- National Football Conference Team Offense 174
- National Football Conference Team Defense 175
- AFC, NFC, and NFL Team Summary 176
- Club Leaders 177
- Club Rankings by Yards 177
- Individual Scoring 178
- Individual Field Goals 180
- Individual Rushing 182
- Individual Passing 185
- Individual Pass Receiving 187
- Individual Interceptions 190
- Individual Punting 192
- Individual Punt Returns 193
- Individual Kickoff Returns 194
- Individual Fumbles 196
- Individual Sacks 200

Inside the Numbers 204
NFL Statistical Highlights
Pro Football Hall of Fame 214
A Chronology of Professional Football 217
Past Standings 223
All-Time Team vs. Team Results 230
Super Bowl Game Summaries 253
Playoff Game Summaries
- AFC Championship Games 258
- NFC Championship Games 259
- AFC Divisional Playoff Games 261
- NFC Divisional Playoff Games 262
- AFC First-Round Playoff Games 262
- NFC First-Round Playoff Games 262

AFC-NFC Pro Bowl Game Summaries 263
AFC vs. NFC, 1970-1985 267
Monday Night Results 268
Overtime Games 270
Number-One Draft Choices 273
NFL Paid Attendance 274
NFL's 10 Biggest Attendance Weekends 274
NFL's 10 Highest Scoring Weekends 274
Top 10 Televised Sports Events of All Time 274
Ten Most Watched Programs in Television History 274
Chicago All-Star Game 275
NFL Playoff Bowl 275
All-Time Records 278
Outstanding Performers 298
Yearly Statistical Leaders 302
Super Bowl Records 308
Postseason Game Records 315
AFC-NFC Pro Bowl Records 323
1986 Roster of Officials 328
Official Signals 330
Digest of Rules 334

1986 SCHEDULE AND NOTE CALENDAR

All times P.M. local daylight.
Nationally televised games in parentheses. CBS and NBC television doubleheader games in the regular season to be announced.

Preseason/First Week

Saturday, August 2	Hall of Fame Game at Canton, Ohio New England ___ vs. St. Louis ___	(ABC) 2:30
Sunday, August 3	Chicago ___ vs. Dallas ___ at Wembley Stadium, London, England	(NBC) 6:00
Tuesday, August 5	Houston ___ at Los Angeles Rams ___	7:30
Wednesday, August 6	New York Giants ___ at Atlanta ___	7:00
Friday, August 8	Indianapolis ___ at Seattle ___	7:30
	Philadelphia ___ at Detroit ___	8:00
Saturday, August 9	Buffalo ___ at Cleveland ___	7:30
	Chicago ___ at Pittsburgh ___	7:00
	Cincinnati ___ at Kansas City ___	7:30
	Dallas ___ at San Diego ___	6:00
	Miami ___ at Minnesota ___	7:00
	New Orleans ___ at Denver ___	7:00
	New York Jets ___ vs. Green Bay ___ at Madison, Wisconsin	1:00
	St. Louis ___ at Tampa Bay ___	7:00
Sunday, August 10	Los Angeles Raiders ___ at San Francisco ___	(CBS) 12:00
	Washington ___ at New England ___	7:00

Preseason/Second Week

Friday, August 15	Cleveland ___ at Miami ___	(ABC) 8:00
	Pittsburgh ___ at Washington ___	8:00
	Seattle ___ at Detroit ___	8:00
Saturday, August 16	Atlanta ___ at Tampa Bay ___	7:00
	Buffalo ___ at Houston ___	8:00
	Cincinnati ___ at New York Jets ___	8:00
	Dallas ___ at Los Angeles Raiders ___	(NBC) 6:00
	Denver ___ at Minnesota ___	7:00
	Indianapolis ___ at Chicago ___	6:00
	Kansas City ___ at St. Louis ___	7:00
	New England ___ at New Orleans ___	7:00
	New York Giants ___ vs. Green Bay ___ at Milwaukee	7:00
	Philadelphia ___ at San Diego ___	6:00
Monday, August 18	San Francisco ___ at Los Angeles Rams ___	7:30

Preseason/Third Week

Friday, August 22	Minnesota ___ at Seattle ___	7:30
	New England ___ at Los Angeles Raiders ___	7:00
	Pittsburgh ___ at Dallas ___	(ABC) 7:00
Saturday, August 23	Buffalo ___ at Kansas City ___	7:30
	Cleveland ___ at Atlanta ___	8:00
	Detroit ___ at Indianapolis ___	7:30
	Green Bay ___ at Cincinnati ___	7:00
	Miami ___ at Philadelphia ___	7:30
	New Orleans ___ at Houston ___	8:00
	New York Jets ___ at New York Giants ___	8:00
	St. Louis ___ at Chicago ___	(CBS) 8:00
	San Diego ___ at Los Angeles Rams ___	7:00
	San Francisco ___ at Denver ___	7:00
	Washington ___ at Tampa Bay ___	7:00

Preseason/Fourth Week

Thursday, August 28	Cleveland ___ at Los Angeles Raiders ___	7:00
	New York Jets ___ at Philadelphia ___	7:30
Friday, August 29	Atlanta ___ at Washington ___	8:00
	Detroit ___ at Cincinnati ___	8:00
	Los Angeles Rams ___ at Denver ___	(NBC) 6:00
	St. Louis ___ at San Diego ___	7:00
	Seattle ___ at San Francisco ___	6:00
	Tampa Bay ___ at Miami ___	8:00
Saturday, August 30	Chicago ___ vs. Buffalo ___ at South Bend, Indiana	1:30
	Houston ___ at Dallas ___	(CBS) 8:00
	Kansas City ___ at New Orleans ___	7:00
	Minnesota ___ at Indianapolis ___	7:30
	New England ___ at Green Bay ___	7:00
	Pittsburgh ___ at New York Giants ___	8:00

First Week

Sunday, September 7 (NBC-TV doubleheader)	Atlanta ___ at New Orleans ___	12:00
	Cincinnati ___ at Kansas City ___	3:00
	Cleveland ___ at Chicago ___	12:00
	Detroit ___ at Minnesota ___	12:00
	Houston ___ at Green Bay ___	12:00
	Indianapolis ___ at New England ___	4:00
	Los Angeles Raiders ___ at Denver ___	2:00
	Los Angeles Rams ___ at St. Louis ___	12:00
	Miami ___ at San Diego ___	1:00
	New York Jets ___ at Buffalo ___	4:00
	Philadelphia ___ at Washington ___	1:00
	Pittsburgh ___ at Seattle ___	1:00
	San Francisco ___ at Tampa Bay ___	1:00
Monday, September 8	New York Giants ___ at Dallas ___	(ABC) 8:00

Second Week

Thursday, September 11	New England ___ at New York Jets ___	(ABC) 8:00
Sunday, September 14 (CBS-TV doubleheader)	Buffalo ___ at Cincinnati ___	1:00
	Cleveland ___ at Houston ___	12:00
	Dallas ___ at Detroit ___	1:00
	Green Bay ___ at New Orleans ___	12:00
	Indianapolis ___ at Miami ___	4:00
	Kansas City ___ at Seattle ___	1:00
	Los Angeles Raiders ___ at Washington ___	1:00
	Minnesota ___ at Tampa Bay ___	4:00
	Philadelphia ___ at Chicago ___	12:00
	St. Louis ___ at Atlanta ___	1:00
	San Diego ___ at New York Giants ___	1:00
	San Francisco ___ at Los Angeles Rams ___	1:00
Monday, September 15	Denver ___ at Pittsburgh ___	(ABC) 9:00

Third Week

Thursday, September 18	Cincinnati ___ at Cleveland ___	(ABC) 8:00
Sunday, September 21 (CBS-TV doubleheader)	Atlanta ___ at Dallas ___	12:00
	Denver ___ at Philadelphia ___	1:00
	Houston ___ at Kansas City ___	3:00
	Los Angeles Rams ___ at Indianapolis ___	12:00
	Miami ___ at New York Jets ___	1:00
	New Orleans ___ at San Francisco ___	1:00
	New York Giants ___ at Los Angeles Raiders ___	1:00
	Pittsburgh ___ at Minnesota ___	12:00
	St. Louis ___ at Buffalo ___	1:00
	Seattle ___ at New England ___	1:00
	Tampa Bay ___ at Detroit ___	1:00
	Washington ___ at San Diego ___	1:00
Monday, September 22	Chicago ___ at Green Bay ___	(ABC) 8:00

Fourth Week

Sunday, September 28 (NBC-TV doubleheader)	Atlanta ___ at Tampa Bay ___	4:00
	Chicago ___ at Cincinnati ___	1:00
	Detroit ___ at Cleveland ___	1:00
	Green Bay ___ at Minnesota ___	12:00
	Kansas City ___ at Buffalo ___	1:00
	Los Angeles Rams ___ at Philadelphia ___	1:00
	New England ___ at Denver ___	2:00
	New Orleans ___ at New York Giants ___	1:00
	New York Jets ___ at Indianapolis ___	3:00
	Pittsburgh ___ at Houston ___	12:00
	San Diego ___ at Los Angeles Raiders ___	1:00
	San Francisco ___ at Miami ___	1:00
	Seattle ___ at Washington ___	1:00
Monday, September 29	Dallas ___ at St. Louis ___	(ABC) 8:00

Fifth Week

Sunday, October 5 (CBS-TV doubleheader)	Buffalo ___ at New York Jets ___	4:00
	Cincinnati ___ vs. Green Bay ___ at Milwaukee	12:00
	Cleveland ___ at Pittsburgh ___	1:00
	Dallas ___ at Denver ___	2:00
	Houston ___ at Detroit ___	1:00
	Indianapolis ___ at San Francisco ___	1:00
	Los Angeles Raiders ___ at Kansas City ___	12:00
	Miami ___ at New England ___	1:00
	Minnesota ___ at Chicago ___	12:00
	New York Giants ___ at St. Louis ___	12:00
	Philadelphia ___ at Atlanta ___	1:00
	Tampa Bay ___ at Los Angeles Rams ___	1:00
	Washington ___ at New Orleans ___	12:00
Monday, October 6	San Diego ___ at Seattle ___	(ABC) 6:00

Sixth Week

Sunday, October 12 (NBC-TV doubleheader)	Buffalo ___ at Miami ___	1:00
	Chicago ___ at Houston ___	12:00
	Denver ___ at San Diego ___	1:00
	Detroit ___ at Green Bay ___	12:00
	Kansas City ___ at Cleveland ___	1:00
	Los Angeles Rams ___ at Atlanta ___	1:00
	Minnesota ___ at San Francisco ___	1:00
	New Orleans ___ at Indianapolis ___	12:00
	New York Jets ___ at New England ___	1:00
	Philadelphia ___ at New York Giants ___	4:00
	St. Louis ___ at Tampa Bay ___	1:00
	Seattle ___ at Los Angeles Raiders ___	1:00
	Washington ___ at Dallas ___	12:00
Monday, October 13	Pittsburgh ___ at Cincinnati ___	(ABC) 9:00

Seventh Week

Sunday, October 19 (CBS-TV doubleheader)	Chicago ___ at Minnesota ___	12:00
	Dallas ___ at Philadelphia ___	1:00
	Detroit ___ at Los Angeles Rams ___	1:00
	Green Bay ___ at Cleveland ___	1:00
	Houston ___ at Cincinnati ___	1:00
	Indianapolis ___ at Buffalo ___	1:00
	Los Angeles Raiders ___ at Miami ___	1:00
	New England ___ at Pittsburgh ___	1:00
	New York Giants ___ at Seattle ___	1:00
	St. Louis ___ at Washington ___	1:00
	San Diego ___ at Kansas City ___	3:00
	San Francisco ___ at Atlanta ___	1:00
	Tampa Bay ___ at New Orleans ___	12:00
Monday, October 20	Denver ___ at New York Jets ___	(ABC) 9:00

Eighth Week

Sunday, October 26
(NBC-TV doubleheader)

Atlanta ___ at Los Angeles Rams ___	1:00
Cincinnati ___ at Pittsburgh ___	1:00
Cleveland ___ at Minnesota ___	12:00
Detroit ___ at Chicago ___	12:00
Los Angeles Raiders ___ at Houston ___	12:00
Miami ___ at Indianapolis ___	1:00
New England ___ at Buffalo ___	1:00
New Orleans ___ at New York Jets ___	1:00
St. Louis ___ at Dallas ___	3:00
San Diego ___ at Philadelphia ___	1:00
San Francisco ___ vs. Green Bay ___ at Milwaukee	12:00
Seattle ___ at Denver ___	2:00
Tampa Bay ___ at Kansas City ___	12:00

Monday, October 27

Washington ___ at New York Giants ___	(ABC) 9:00

Ninth Week

Sunday, November 2
(NBC-TV doubleheader)

Atlanta ___ at New England ___	1:00
Buffalo ___ at Tampa Bay ___	1:00
Cincinnati ___ at Detroit ___	1:00
Cleveland ___ at Indianapolis ___	1:00
Dallas ___ at New York Giants ___	1:00
Denver ___ at Los Angeles Raiders ___	1:00
Green Bay ___ at Pittsburgh ___	1:00
Houston ___ at Miami ___	1:00
Kansas City ___ at San Diego ___	1:00
Minnesota ___ at Washington ___	4:00
New York Jets ___ at Seattle ___	1:00
Philadelphia ___ at St. Louis ___	12:00
San Francisco ___ at New Orleans ___	12:00

Monday, November 3

Los Angeles Rams ___ at Chicago ___	(ABC) 8:00

Tenth Week

Sunday, November 9
(CBS-TV doubleheader)

Chicago ___ at Tampa Bay ___	1:00
Cincinnati ___ at Houston ___	12:00
Los Angeles Raiders ___ at Dallas ___	3:00
Los Angeles Rams ___ at New Orleans ___	12:00
Minnesota ___ at Detroit ___	1:00
New England ___ at Indianapolis ___	1:00
New York Giants ___ at Philadelphia ___	4:00
New York Jets ___ at Atlanta ___	1:00
Pittsburgh ___ at Buffalo ___	1:00
St. Louis ___ at San Francisco ___	1:00
San Diego ___ at Denver ___	2:00
Seattle ___ at Kansas City ___	12:00
Washington ___ at Green Bay ___	12:00

Monday, November 10

Miami ___ at Cleveland ___	(ABC) 9:00

Eleventh Week

Sunday, November 16
(NBC-TV doubleheader)

Chicago ___ at Atlanta ___	1:00
Cleveland ___ at Los Angeles Raiders ___	1:00
Dallas ___ at San Diego ___	1:00
Detroit ___ at Philadelphia ___	1:00
Houston ___ at Pittsburgh ___	1:00
Indianapolis ___ at New York Jets ___	4:00
Kansas City ___ at Denver ___	2:00
New England ___ at Los Angeles Rams ___	1:00
Miami ___ at Buffalo ___	1:00
New York Giants ___ at Minnesota ___	12:00
New Orleans ___ at St. Louis ___	12:00
Seattle ___ at Cincinnati ___	1:00
Tampa Bay ___ vs. Green Bay ___ at Milwaukee	12:00

Monday, November 17

San Francisco ___ at Washington ___	(ABC) 9:00

Twelfth Week

Thursday, November 20	Los Angeles Raiders ___ at San Diego ___	(ABC) 5:00
Sunday, November 23 (CBS-TV doubleheader)	Atlanta ___ at San Francisco ___	1:00
	Buffalo ___ at New England ___	1:00
	Dallas ___ at Washington ___	1:00
	Denver ___ at New York Giants ___	1:00
	Detroit ___ at Tampa Bay ___	1:00
	Green Bay ___ at Chicago ___	12:00
	Indianapolis ___ at Houston ___	12:00
	Kansas City ___ at St. Louis ___	3:00
	Minnesota ___ at Cincinnati ___	1:00
	New Orleans ___ at Los Angeles Rams ___	1:00
	Philadelphia ___ at Seattle ___	1:00
	Pittsburgh ___ at Cleveland ___	1:00
Monday, November 24	New York Jets ___ at Miami ___	(ABC) 9:00

Thirteenth Week

Thursday, November 27 (Thanksgiving Day)	Green Bay ___ at Detroit ___	(CBS) 12:30
	Seattle ___ at Dallas ___	(NBC) 3:00
Sunday, November 30 (CBS-TV doubleheader)	Atlanta ___ at Miami ___	1:00
	Buffalo ___ at Kansas City ___	12:00
	Cincinnati ___ at Denver ___	2:00
	Houston ___ at Cleveland ___	1:00
	Los Angeles Rams ___ at New York Jets ___	1:00
	New England ___ at New Orleans ___	12:00
	Philadelphia ___ at Los Angeles Raiders ___	1:00
	Pittsburgh ___ at Chicago ___	12:00
	San Diego ___ at Indianapolis ___	1:00
	Tampa Bay ___ at Minnesota ___	12:00
	Washington ___ at St. Louis ___	12:00
Monday, December 1	New York Giants ___ at San Francisco ___	(ABC) 6:00

Fourteenth Week

Sunday, December 7 (NBC-TV doubleheader)	Cincinnati ___ at New England ___	1:00
	Cleveland ___ at Buffalo ___	1:00
	Denver ___ at Kansas City ___	12:00
	Detroit ___ at Pittsburgh ___	1:00
	Houston ___ at San Diego ___	1:00
	Indianapolis ___ at Atlanta ___	1:00
	Miami ___ at New Orleans ___	12:00
	Minnesota ___ at Green Bay ___	12:00
	New York Giants ___ at Washington ___	1:00
	New York Jets ___ at San Francisco ___	1:00
	St. Louis ___ at Philadelphia ___	1:00
	Tampa Bay ___ at Chicago ___	12:00
Sunday Night, December 7	Dallas ___ at Los Angeles Rams ___	(ABC) 6:00
Monday, December 8	Los Angeles Raiders ___ at Seattle ___	(ABC) 6:00

Fifteenth Week

Saturday, December 13	Pittsburgh ___ at New York Jets ___	(NBC) 12:30
	Washington ___ at Denver ___	(CBS) 2:00
Sunday, December 14 (NBC-TV doubleheader)	Buffalo ___ at Indianapolis ___	1:00
	Cleveland ___ at Cincinnati ___	1:00
	Green Bay ___ at Tampa Bay ___	1:00
	Kansas City ___ at Los Angeles Raiders ___	1:00
	Miami ___ at Los Angeles Rams ___	1:00
	Minnesota ___ at Houston ___	3:00
	New Orleans ___ at Atlanta ___	1:00
	Philadelphia ___ at Dallas ___	12:00
	St. Louis ___ at New York Giants ___	1:00
	San Francisco ___ at New England ___	1:00
	Seattle ___ at San Diego ___	1:00
Monday, December 15	Chicago ___ at Detroit ___	(ABC) 9:00

Sixteenth Week

		Network	Time
Friday, December 19	Los Angeles Rams ___ at San Francisco ___	(ABC)	5:00
Saturday, December 20	Denver ___ at Seattle ___	(NBC)	1:00
	Green Bay ___ at New York Giants ___	(CBS)	12:30
Sunday, December 21 (CBS-TV doubleheader)	Atlanta ___ at Detroit ___		1:00
	Buffalo ___ at Houston ___		12:00
	Chicago ___ at Dallas ___		3:00
	Indianapolis ___ at Los Angeles Raiders ___		1:00
	Kansas City ___ at Pittsburgh ___		1:00
	New Orleans ___ at Minnesota ___		12:00
	New York Jets ___ at Cincinnati ___		1:00
	San Diego ___ at Cleveland ___		1:00
	Tampa Bay ___ at St. Louis ___		12:00
	Washington ___ at Philadelphia ___		1:00
Monday, December 22	New England ___ at Miami ___	(ABC)	9:00

First-Round Playoff Games

Sunday, December 28, 1986

American Football Conference

________________ at ________________ (NBC)

National Football Conference

________________ at ________________ (CBS)

Site Priorities

Two wild card teams (fourth- and fifth-best records) from each conference will enter the first round of the playoffs. The wild cards from the same conference will play each other. Home clubs will be the clubs with the best won-lost-tied percentage in the regular season. If tied in record, the tie will be broken by the tie-breaking procedures already in effect.

Divisional Playoff Games

Saturday, January 3, 1987

American Football Conference

________________ at ________________ (NBC)

National Football Conference

________________ at ________________ (CBS)

Sunday, January 4, 1987

American Football Conference

________________ at ________________ (NBC)

National Football Conference

________________ at ________________ (CBS)

Site Priorities

In each conference, the two division winners with the highest won-lost-tied percentage during the regular season will be the home teams. The division winner with the best percentage will be host to the wild card winner from the first-round playoff, and the division winner with the second-best percentage will be host to the third division winner, unless the wild card team is from the same division as the winner with the highest percentage. In that case, the division winner with the best percentage will be host to the third division winner and the second highest division winner will be host to the wild card.

Conference Championship Games, Super Bowl XXI, and AFC-NFC Pro Bowl

Sunday, January 11, 1987

American Football Conference Championship Game

________________ at ________________ (NBC)

National Football Conference Championship Game

________________ at ________________ (CBS)

Sunday, January 25, 1987

Super Bowl XXI at Rose Bowl, Pasadena, California

________________ vs. ________________ (CBS)

Sunday, February 1, 1987

AFC-NFC Pro Bowl at Honolulu, Hawaii

AFC ________________ vs. NFC ________________ (ABC)

Site Priorities for Championship Games

The home teams will be the surviving divisional playoff winners with the best won-lost-tied percentage during the regular season. The wild card team will never be the home team, in either the divisional playoffs or the championship games. Any ties in won-lost-tied percentage will be broken by the tie-breaking procedures already in effect.

Postseason Games

Sunday, December 28	AFC and NFC First-Round Playoffs (NBC and CBS)
Saturday, January 3	AFC and NFC Divisional Playoffs (NBC and CBS)
Sunday, January 4	AFC and NFC Divisional Playoffs (NBC and CBS)
Sunday, January 11	AFC and NFC Championship Games (NBC and CBS)
Sunday, January 25	Super Bowl XXI at Rose Bowl, Pasadena, California (CBS)
Sunday, February 1	AFC-NFC Pro Bowl at Honolulu, Hawaii (ABC)

1986 Nationally Televised Games

(All games carried on NBC Radio Network.)

Regular Season

Monday, September 8	New York Giants at Dallas (night, ABC)
Thursday, September 11	New England at New York Jets (night, ABC)
Monday, September 15	Denver at Pittsburgh (night, ABC)
Thursday, September 18	Cincinnati at Cleveland (night, ABC)
Monday, September 22	Chicago at Green Bay (night, ABC)
Monday, September 29	Dallas at St. Louis (night, ABC)
Monday, October 6	San Diego at Seattle (night, ABC)
Monday, October 13	Pittsburgh at Cincinnati (night, ABC)
Monday, October 20	Denver at New York Jets (night, ABC)
Monday, October 27	Washington at New York Giants (night, ABC)
Monday, November 3	Los Angeles Rams at Chicago (night, ABC)
Monday, November 10	Miami at Cleveland (night, ABC)
Monday, November 17	San Francisco at Washington (night, ABC)
Thursday, November 20	Los Angeles Raiders at San Diego (night, ABC)
Monday, November 24	New York Jets at Miami (night, ABC)
Thursday, November 27 (Thanksgiving)	Green Bay at Detroit (day, CBS) Seattle at Dallas (day, NBC)
Monday, December 1	New York Giants at San Francisco (night, ABC)
Sunday, December 7	Dallas at Los Angeles Rams (night, ABC)
Monday, December 8	Los Angeles Raiders at Seattle (night, ABC)
Saturday, December 13	Pittsburgh at New York Jets (day, NBC) Washington at Denver (day, CBS)
Monday, December 15	Chicago at Detroit (night, ABC)
Friday, December 19	Los Angeles Rams at San Francisco (night, ABC)
Saturday, December 20	Denver at Seattle (day, NBC) Green Bay at New York Giants (day, CBS)
Monday, December 22	New England at Miami (night, ABC)

AFC-NFC Interconference Games

(Sunday unless noted; all times local.)

September 7	Cleveland at Chicago	12:00
	Houston at Green Bay	12:00
September 14	Los Angeles Raiders at Washington	1:00
	San Diego at New York Giants	1:00
September 21	Denver at Philadelphia	1:00
	Los Angeles Rams at Indianapolis	12:00
	New York Giants at Los Angeles Raiders	1:00
	Pittsburgh at Minnesota	12:00
	St. Louis at Buffalo	1:00
	Washington at San Diego	1:00
September 28	Chicago at Cincinnati	1:00
	Detroit at Cleveland	1:00
	San Francisco at Miami	1:00
	Seattle at Washington	1:00
October 5	Cincinnati vs. Green Bay at Milwaukee	12:00
	Dallas at Denver	2:00
	Houston at Detroit	1:00
	Indianapolis at San Francisco	1:00
October 12	Chicago at Houston	12:00
	New Orleans at Indianapolis	12:00
October 19	Green Bay at Cleveland	1:00
	New York Giants at Seattle	1:00
October 26	Cleveland at Minnesota	12:00
	New Orleans at New York Jets	1:00
	San Diego at Philadelphia	1:00
	Tampa Bay at Kansas City	12:00
November 2	Atlanta at New England	1:00
	Buffalo at Tampa Bay	1:00
	Cincinnati at Detroit	1:00
	Green Bay at Pittsburgh	1:00
November 9	Los Angeles Raiders at Dallas	3:00
	New York Jets at Atlanta	1:00
November 16	Dallas at San Diego	1:00
	New England at Los Angeles Rams	1:00
November 23	Denver at New York Giants	1:00
	Kansas City at St. Louis	3:00
	Minnesota at Cincinnati	1:00
	Philadelphia at Seattle	1:00
November 27	Seattle at Dallas (Thanksgiving)	3:00
November 30	Atlanta at Miami	1:00
	Los Angeles Rams at New York Jets	1:00
	New England at New Orleans	12:00
	Philadelphia at Los Angeles Raiders	1:00
	Pittsburgh at Chicago	12:00
December 7	Detroit at Pittsburgh	1:00
	Indianapolis at Atlanta	1:00
	Miami at New Orleans	12:00
	New York Jets at San Francisco	1:00
December 13	Washington at Denver (Saturday)	2:00
December 14	Miami at Los Angeles Rams	1:00
	Minnesota at Houston	3:00
	San Francisco at New England	1:00

Monday Night Games at a Glance

(All times local; televised by ABC and broadcast by NBC Radio Network.)

September 8	New York Giants at Dallas	8:00
September 15	Denver at Pittsburgh	9:00
September 22	Chicago at Green Bay	8:00
September 29	Dallas at St. Louis	8:00
October 6	San Diego at Seattle	6:00
October 13	Pittsburgh at Cincinnati	9:00
October 20	Denver at New York Jets	9:00
October 27	Washington at New York Giants	9:00
November 3	Los Angeles Rams at Chicago	8:00
November 10	Miami at Cleveland	9:00
November 17	San Francisco at Washington	9:00
November 24	New York Jets at Miami	9:00
December 1	New York Giants at San Francisco	6:00
December 8	Los Angeles Raiders at Seattle	6:00
December 15	Chicago at Detroit	9:00
December 22	New England at Miami	9:00

Sunday, Thursday, & Friday Prime Time Night Games at a Glance

(All times local; televised by ABC and broadcast by NBC Radio Network.)

Thursday, September 11	New England at New York Jets	8:00
Thursday, September 18	Cincinnati at Cleveland	8:00
Thursday, November 20	Los Angeles Raiders at San Diego	5:00
Sunday, December 7	Dallas at Los Angeles Rams	6:00
Friday, December 19	Los Angeles Rams at San Francisco	5:00

Important Dates

1986

July 7	Claiming period of 24 hours begins in waiver system. All waivers for the year are no-recall and no-withdrawal.
Mid-July	Team training camps open.
August 2	Hall of Fame Game, Canton, Ohio: New England vs. St. Louis.
August 3	American Bowl, London, England: Chicago vs. Dallas.
August 5-10	First preseason weekend.
August 15-18	Second preseason weekend.
August 19	Roster cutdown to maximum of 60 players.
August 22-23	Third preseason weekend.
August 26	Roster cutdown to maximum of 50 players.
August 28-30	Fourth preseason weekend.
September 1	Roster cutdown to maximum of 45 players.
September 7-8	Regular season opens.
September 23	Priority on multiple waiver claims is now based on the current season's standings.
October 14	Clubs may begin signing free agents for the 1987 season.
October 14	Trading of player contracts/rights ends at 4:00 p.m., E.S.T.
October 14-15	NFL meeting, Chicago, Illinois.
November 22	Deadline for reinstatement of players in Reserve List categories of Retired, Did Not Report, and Veteran Free Agent Asked to Re-Sign.
December 15-16	Balloting for AFC-NFC Pro Bowl.
December 19	Deadline for waiver requests in 1986.
December 24	Deadline for postseason participants to sign free agents for playoffs.
December 28	AFC and NFC First-Round Playoff Games.

1987

January 3-4	AFC and NFC Divisional Playoff Games.
January 11	AFC and NFC Conference Championship Games.
January 25	Super Bowl XXI at Rose Bowl, Pasadena, California.
February 1	AFC-NFC Pro Bowl at Aloha Stadium, Honolulu, Hawaii.
February 2	Waiver system begins for 1987.
February 2	Trading period begins.
March 16-20	NFL annual meeting, Kaanapali Beach, Maui, Hawaii.
April 28	52nd annual NFL selection meeting, New York, New York.
August 8	Hall of Fame Game, Canton, Ohio: Kansas City vs. Los Angeles Rams.
August 14-16	First preseason weekend.
September 13-14	Regular season opens.
December 27-28	Regular season closes.

1988

January 3	AFC and NFC First-Round Playoff Games.
January 9-10	AFC and NFC Divisional Playoff Games.
January 17	AFC and NFC Conference Championship Games.
January 31	Super Bowl XXII at San Diego Jack Murphy Stadium, San Diego, California.
February 7	AFC-NFC Pro Bowl.
March 18-22	NFL annual meeting at Phoenix, Arizona.

1989

January 22	Super Bowl XXIII at Dolphins Stadium, Miami, Florida.
January 29	AFC-NFC Pro Bowl.
March 20-24	NFL annual meeting at Palm Springs, California.

1990

January 28	Super Bowl XXIV at Louisiana Superdome, New Orleans, Louisiana.
February 4	AFC-NFC Pro Bowl.
March 25-30	NFL annual meeting at Maui, Hawaii.

Waivers

The waiver system is a procedure by which player contracts or NFL rights to players are made available by a club to other clubs in the League. During the procedure the 27 other clubs either file claims to obtain the players or waive the opportunity to do so—thus the term "waiver." Claiming clubs are assigned players on a priority based on the inverse of won-and-lost standing. The claiming period normally is 10 days during the offseason and 24 hours from early July through December. In some circumstances another 24 hours is added on to allow the original club to rescind its action (known as a recall of a waiver request) and/or the claiming club to do the same (known as withdrawal of a claim). If a player passes through waivers unclaimed and is not recalled by the original club, he becomes a free agent. All waivers from July through December are no-recall and no withdrawal. Under the Collective Bargaining Agreement, from February 1 through October 14, any veteran who has acquired four years of pension credit may, if about to be assigned to another club through the waiver system, reject such assignment and become a free agent.

Active List

The Active List is the principal status for players participating for a club. It consists of all players under contract, including option, who are eligible for preseason, regular season, and postseason games. Clubs are allowed to open training camp with an unlimited number of players but thereafter must meet a series of mandatory roster reductions prior to the season opener. Teams will be permitted to dress up to 45 players for each regular season and postseason game during the 1986 season. The Active List maximums and dates for 1986 are:

August 19 . . . . 60 players
August 26 . . . . 50 players
September 1 . . . . 45 players

Reserve List

The Reserve List is a status for players who, for reasons of injury, retirement, military service, or other circumstances, are not immediately available for participation with a club. Those players in the category of Reserve/Injured who were physically unable to play football for a minimum of four weeks from the date of going onto Reserve may be re-activated by their clubs upon clearing procedural recall waivers; in addition, each club will have five free re-activations for players meeting the four-week requirement, but only one of the free re-activations can be used for a player placed on Reserve/Injured prior to or concurrent with the final cutdown on September 1. Clubs participating in postseason competition will be granted an additional free re-activation. Players not meeting the four-week requirement may not return in the same season to the Active List of the club which originally placed them on Reserve, but may be assigned through the waiver system to other clubs. Players in the category of Reserve/Retired, Reserve/Did Not Report, or Reserve/Veteran Free Agent Asked to Re-sign, may not be reinstated during the period from 30 days before the end of the regular season on through the postseason.

Trades

Unrestricted trading between the AFC and NFC is allowed in 1986 through October 14, after which trading of player contracts/rights will end until February 2, 1987.

Annual Player Limits

NFL

Year(s)	Limit
1985-86	45
1983-84	49
1982	45†–49
1978–81	45
1975–77	43
1974	47
1964–73	40
1963	37
1961–62	36
1960	38
1959	36
1957–58	35
1951–56	33
1949–50	32
1948	35
1947	35*–34
1945–46	33
1943–44	28
1940–42	33
1938–39	30
1936–37	25
1935	24
1930–34	20
1926–29	18
1925	16

†45 for first two games
*35 for first three games

AFL

Year(s)	Limit
1966–69	40
1965	38
1964	34
1962–63	33
1960–61	35

Tie-Breaking Procedures

The following procedures will be used to break standings ties for postseason playoffs and to determine regular season schedules.

To Break a Tie Within a Division

If, at the end of the regular season, two or more clubs in the same division finish with identical won-lost-tied percentages, the following steps will be taken until a champion is determined.

Two Clubs

1. Head-to-head (best won-lost-tied percentage in games between the clubs).
2. Best won-lost-tied percentage in games played within the division.
3. Best won-lost-tied percentage in games played within the conference.
4. Best won-lost-tied percentage in common games, if applicable.
5. Best net points in division games.
6. Best net points in all games.
7. Strength of schedule.
8. Best net touchdowns in all games.
9. Coin toss.

Three or More Clubs

(Note: If two clubs remain tied after a third club is eliminated during any step, tie-breaker reverts to step 1 of two-club format.)

1. Head-to-head (best won-lost-tied percentage in games among the clubs).
2. Best won-lost-tied percentage in games played within the division.
3. Best won-lost-tied percentage in games played within the conference.
4. Best won-lost-tied percentage in common games.
5. Best net points in division games.
6. Best net points in all games.
7. Strength of schedule.
8. Best net touchdowns in all games.
9. Coin toss.

To Break a Tie for the Wild Card Team

If it is necessary to break ties to determine the two Wild Card clubs from each conference, the following steps will be taken.

1. If the tied clubs are from the same division, apply division tie-breaker.
2. If the tied clubs are from different divisions, apply the following steps.

Two Clubs

1. Head-to-head, if applicable.
2. Best won-lost-tied percentage in games played within the conference.
3. Best won-lost-tied percentage in common games, minimum of four.
4. Best average net points in conference games.
5. Best net points in all games.
6. Strength of schedule.
7. Best net touchdowns in all games.
8. Coin toss.

Three or More Clubs

(Note: If two clubs remain tied after other clubs are eliminated, tie-breaker reverts to step 1 of applicable two-club format.)

1. Head-to-head sweep. (Applicable only if one club has defeated each of the others, or if one club has lost to each of the others.)
2. Best won-lost-tied percentage in games played within the conference.
3. Best won-lost-tied percentage in common games, minimum of four.
4. Best average net points in conference games.
5. Best net points in all games.
6. Strength of schedule.
7. Best net touchdowns in all games.
8. Coin toss.

Tie-Breaking Procedure for Selection Meeting

If two or more clubs are tied for selection order, the conventional strength of schedule tie-breaker will be applied, subject to the following exceptions for playoff teams.

1. The Super Bowl winner will be last and the Super Bowl loser will be next-to-last.
2. Any non-Super Bowl playoff team involved in a tie moves down in drafting priority as follows:
   A. Participation by a club in the playoffs without a victory adds one-half victory to the club's regular season won-lost-tied record.
   B. For each victory in the playoffs, one full victory will be added to the club's regular season won-lost-tied record.
3. Clubs with the best won-lost-tied records after these steps are applied will drop to their appropriate spots at the bottom of the tied segment. In no case will the above process move a club lower than the segment in which it was initially tied.
4. Tied clubs will alternate priority throughout the 12 rounds of the draft. In case of a tie involving three or more teams, the club with priority in the first round will drop to the bottom of the tied segment in the second round and move its way back to the top of the segment in each succeeding round.

Figuring the 1987 NFL Schedule

As soon as the final game of the 1986 NFL regular season (New England at Miami, December 22) has been completed, it will be possible to determine the 1987 opponents of the 28 teams.

Each 1987 team schedule is based on a formula initiated for the 1978 season that uses the team's won-lost-tied percentage from the current season as the primary guide.

For years the NFL had been seeking an easily understood, balanced schedule that would provide for both competitive equality and a variety of opponents. It was easy to segregate groups of teams into tight divisions, have them play the majority of their games within those divisions, and let the division winners emerge into a structured playoff system. But the result was that many attractive teams with star players never appeared in other cities unless those clubs happened to be matched in the playoffs.

The new approach to scheduling gives the fans the best of both systems, a neat competitive format and variety at the same time. It also reduces inequalities in the strength of schedules that popped up too often in the past under the system of rotating opponents over a period of years.

Under the present format, schedules of any NFL team are figured according to one of the following three formulas. (The reference point for the figuring is the final standing. Ties for position in any of the divisions are broken according to the tie-breaking procedures outlined on page 13. The chart on the following page is included for use as you go through each step.)

A. First- through fourth-place teams in a five-team division (AFC East, AFC West, NFC East, NFC Central).

1. Home-and-home round-robin within the division (8 games).
2. One game each with the first- through fourth-place teams in a division of the other conference. In 1987, AFC East will play NFC East, AFC West will play NFC Central, and AFC Central will play NFC West (4 games).
3. The first-place team plays the first- and fourth-place teams in the other divisions within the conference. The second-place team plays the second- and third-place teams in the other divisions within the conference. The third-place team plays the third- and second-place teams in the other divisions within the conference. The fourth-place team plays the fourth- and first-place teams in the other divisions within the conference (4 games).

This completes the 16-game schedule.

B. First- through fourth-place teams in a four-team division (AFC Central, NFC West).

1. Home-and-home round-robin within the division (6 games).
2. One game with each of the fifth-place teams in the conference (2 games).
3. The same procedure that is listed in step A2 (4 games).
4. The same procedure that is listed in step A3 (4 games).

This completes the 16-game schedule.

C. The fifth-place teams in a division (AFC East, AFC West, NFC East, NFC Central).

1. Home-and-home round-robin within the division (8 games).
2. One game with each team in the four-team division of the conference (4 games).
3. A home-and-home with the other fifth-place team in the conference (2 games).
4. One game each with the fifth-place teams in the other conference (2 games).

This completes the 16-game schedule.

The 1987 Opponent Breakdown chart on the following page does not include the round-robin games within the division. Those are automatically on a home-and-away basis.

1986 NFL Standings

AFC

EAST AE

1 __________

2 __________

3 __________

4 __________

5 __________

CENTRAL AC

1 __________

2 __________

3 __________

4 __________

WEST AW

1 __________

2 __________

3 __________

4 __________

5 __________

NFC

EAST NE

1 __________

2 __________

3 __________

4 __________

5 __________

WEST NW

1 __________

2 __________

3 __________

4 __________

CENTRAL NC

1 __________

2 __________

3 __________

4 __________

5 __________

A Team's 1987 Schedule

Team Name

____

1987 Opponent Breakdown

AE — AFC EAST

	HOME	AWAY
AE-1	AC-1	AC-4
	AW-4	AW-1
	NE-1	NE-2
	NE-3	NE-4
AE-2	AC-2	AC-3
	AW-3	AW-2
	NE-2	NE-1
	NE-4	NE-3
AE-3	AC-3	AC-2
	AW-2	AW-3
	NE-1	NE-2
	NE-3	NE-4
AE-4	AC-4	AC-1
	AW-1	AW-4
	NE-2	NE-1
	NE-4	NE-3
AE-5	AC-2	AC-1
	AC-4	AC-3
	AW-5	AW-5
	NC-5	NE-5

AC — AFC CENTRAL

	HOME	AWAY
AC-1	AE-4	AE-1
	AW-1	AW-4
	AE-5	AW-5
	NW-1	NW-2
	NW-3	NW-4
AC-2	AE-3	AE-2
	AW-2	AW-3
	AW-5	AE-5
	NW-2	NW-1
	NW-4	NW-3
AC-3	AE-2	AE-3
	AW-3	AW-2
	AE-5	AW-5
	NW-1	NW-2
	NW-3	NW-4
AC-4	AE-1	AE-4
	AW-4	AW-1
	AW-5	AE-5
	NW-2	NW-1
	NW-4	NW-3

AW — AFC WEST

	HOME	AWAY
AW-1	AE-1	AE-4
	AC-4	AC-1
	NC-1	NC-2
	NC-3	NC-4
AW-2	AE-2	AE-3
	AC-3	AC-2
	NC-2	NC-1
	NC-4	NC-3
AW-3	AE-3	AE-2
	AC-2	AC-3
	NC-1	NC-2
	NC-3	NC-4
AW-4	AE-4	AE-1
	AC-1	AC-4
	NC-2	NC-1
	NC-4	NC-3
AW-5	AC-1	AC-2
	AC-3	AC-4
	AE-5	AE-5
	NE-5	NC-5

NE — NFC EAST

	HOME	AWAY
NE-1	NW-1	NW-4
	NC-4	NC-1
	AE-2	AE-1
	AE-4	AE-3
NE-2	NW-2	NW-3
	NC-3	NC-2
	AE-1	AE-2
	AE-3	AE-4
NE-3	NW-3	NW-2
	NC-2	NC-3
	AE-2	AE-1
	AE-4	AE-3
NE-4	NW-4	NW-1
	NC-1	NC-4
	AE-1	AE-2
	AE-3	AE-4
NE-5	NW-2	NW-1
	NW-4	NW-3
	NC-5	NC-5
	AE-5	AW-5

NC — NFC CENTRAL

	HOME	AWAY
NC-1	NE-1	NE-4
	NW-4	NW-1
	AW-2	AW-1
	AW-4	AW-3
NC-2	NE-2	NE-3
	NW-3	NW-2
	AW-1	AW-2
	AW-3	AW-4
NC-3	NE-3	NE-2
	NW-2	NW-3
	AW-2	AW-1
	AW-4	AW-3
NC-4	NE-4	NE-1
	NW-1	NW-4
	AW-1	AW-2
	AW-3	AW-4
NC-5	NW-1	NW-2
	NW-3	NW-4
	NE-5	NE-5
	AW-5	AE-5

NW — NFC WEST

	HOME	AWAY
NW-1	NE-4	NE-1
	NC-1	NC-4
	NE-5	NC-5
	AC-2	AC-1
	AC-4	AC-3
NW-2	NE-3	NE-2
	NC-2	NC-3
	NC-5	NE-5
	AC-1	AC-2
	AC-3	AC-4
NW-3	NE-2	NE-3
	NC-3	NC-2
	NE-5	NC-5
	AC-2	AC-1
	AC-4	AC-3
NW-4	NE-1	NE-4
	NC-4	NC-1
	NC-5	NE-5
	AC-1	AC-2
	AC-3	AC-4

Limited Instant Replay System to be Used in 1986

At the NFL annual meeting in March 1986, the clubs adopted (23-4-1) a one-year system of limited Instant Replay of officiating calls.

The NFL has discussed Instant Replay in some degree or other since the early 1970s. The League experimented in 1976 and 1978 using two basic frameworks—an independent system using cameras, replay machines, and technicians separate from the network covering the game and a "no-frills" approach using existing TV coverage.

The NFL in 1985 used the network feed of the nine nationally-televised preseason games to experiment with the basic system which later was adopted for 1986. A total of 28 plays (17 confirmed calls, 4 inconclusive, 1 reversed, and 6 no replay shown) were closely examined.

Q—What is the objective of this system?

A—The clubs feel that on certain plays the telecast viewed by the general public should be used to correct an indisputable error. The system will be used to reverse an on-field decision only when the Replay Official has **indisputable visual evidence** available to him that warrants the change.

Q—Who will be involved?

A—The Replay Official (a veteran former NFL official or a member of the League's officiating supervisory staff) will be positioned in a sideline Replay Booth, which will house two TV monitors and two high-speed VCRs plus radio communications to the on-field officials. The Replay Official makes the decision although a Communicator (normally a member of the League Office staff) and a Technician also will be there to lend logistical help.

Q—Why is the system referred to as "limited" Instant Replay?

A—This system will concentrate on plays of **possession** or **touching** (e.g. fumbles, receptions, interceptions, muffs) and most plays governed by the **sidelines, goal lines, end lines,** and **line of scrimmage** (e.g. receiver or runner in or out of bounds, forward or backward passes, breaking the plane of the goal line). It also will be used to determine whether there are more than 11 men on the field.

Q—Why aren't most fouls included in this system?

A—It is recognized that in most circumstances the on-field officials have the best vantage points involving fouls. It is for this reason that Instant Replay **will not review** a list of the following 26 fouls:

1. Clipping
2. Encroachment and offsides
3. Grasp of facemask
4. False start
5. Defensive pass interference
6. Offensive pass interference
7. Offensive holding and illegal use of hands
8. Illegal batting or punching ball
9. Illegal block on free kick or scrimmage kick
10. Illegal crackback
11. Illegal motion
12. Illegal use of forearm or elbow
13. Illegal use of hands by defense
14. Illegally kicking ball
15. Illegally snapping ball
16. Intentional grounding
17. Member of punting team downfield early
18. Illegal formation
19. Palpably unfair act
20. Piling on
21. Roughing the passer
22. Running into/roughing kicker
23. Striking, kicking, or kneeing
24. Unnecessary roughness
25. Unsportsmanlike conduct
26. Use of helmet as a weapon

Q—Is the television network carrying the game part of the review process?

A—No. Although the Replay Official will be viewing the live network feed, there is no communication to television personnel as to what plays to show or not to show.

Q—What is the step-by-step procedure of a play review?

A—The Replay Official will view game action and a play will be replayed immediately on one of the two monitors, while the other one continues to record the live feed.

The Replay Official makes a determination if further study of the play is needed. If not, there is no contact with the field and play continues without interruption.

If the Replay Official believes an error may have been made the Umpire will be contacted (via a paging device worn at the beltline), and he then will use a walkie-talkie for further communication with the Replay Official.

The Replay Official will watch replay(s) on one or both monitors and complete his review within a reasonable period (probably 15-20 seconds) after the play is over. (If there is a time out, the Replay Official would not necessarily be restricted to the 15-20 second period.)

The Replay Official will inform the Umpire of his decision, and the Referee will make the appropriate announcement on the wireless microphone.

Active Coaches' Career Records

Start of 1986 Season

Coach	Team(s)	Regular Season Yrs.	Won	Lost	Tied	Pct.	Postseason Won	Lost	Tied	Pct.	Career Won	Lost	Tied	Pct.
Don Shula	Baltimore Colts, Miami Dolphins	23	239	86	6	.731	16	13	0	.552	255	99	6	.717
Tom Landry	Dallas Cowboys	26	233	132	6	.636	20	16	0	.556	253	148	6	.629
Chuck Noll	Pittsburgh Steelers	17	149	97	1	.605	15	7	0	.682	164	104	1	.612
Chuck Knox	Los Angeles Rams, Buffalo Bills, Seattle Seahawks	13	120	70	1	.631	7	9	0	.438	127	79	1	.616
Don Coryell	St. Louis Cardinals, San Diego Chargers	13	110	76	1	.591	3	6	0	.333	113	82	1	.579
Tom Flores	Los Angeles Raiders	7	70	35	0	.667	8	3	0	.727	78	38	0	.672
Forrest Gregg	Cleveland Browns, Cincinnati Bengals, Green Bay Packers	9	66	64	0	.508	2	2	0	.500	68	66	0	.507
Bill Walsh	San Francisco 49ers	7	59	46	0	.562	7	2	0	.778	66	48	0	.579
Joe Gibbs	Washington Redskins	5	51	22	0	.699	6	2	0	.750	57	24	0	.704
Leeman Bennett	Atlanta Falcons, Tampa Bay Buccaneers	7	48	55	0	.466	1	3	0	.250	49	58	0	.458
Dan Reeves	Denver Broncos	5	45	28	0	.616	0	2	0	.000	45	30	0	.600
Mike Ditka	Chicago Bears	4	36	21	0	.632	4	1	0	.800	40	22	0	.645
John Robinson	Los Angeles Rams	3	30	18	0	.625	2	3	0	.400	32	21	0	.604
Joe Walton	New York Jets	3	25	23	0	.521	0	1	0	.000	25	24	0	.510
Bill Parcells	New York Giants	3	22	25	1	.469	2	2	0	.500	24	27	1	.471
John Mackovic	Kansas City Chiefs	3	20	28	0	.417	0	0	0	.000	20	28	0	.417
Raymond Berry	New England Patriots	2	15	9	0	.625	3	1	0	.750	18	10	0	.643
Dan Henning	Atlanta Falcons	3	15	33	0	.313	0	0	0	.000	15	33	0	.313
Sam Wyche	Cincinnati Bengals	2	15	17	0	.469	0	0	0	.000	15	17	0	.469
Marty Schottenheimer	Cleveland Browns	2	12	12	0	.500	0	1	0	.000	12	13	0	.480
Darryl Rogers	Detroit Lions	1	7	9	0	.438	0	0	0	.000	7	9	0	.438
Rod Dowhower	Indianapolis Colts	1	5	11	0	.313	0	0	0	.000	5	11	0	.313
Hank Bullough	Buffalo Bills	1	2	10	0	.167	0	0	0	.000	2	10	0	.167
Jerry Glanville	Houston Oilers	1	0	2	0	.000	0	0	0	.000	0	2	0	.000
Jerry Burns	Minnesota Vikings	0	0	0	0	.000	0	0	0	.000	0	0	0	.000
Jim Mora	New Orleans Saints	0	0	0	0	.000	0	0	0	.000	0	0	0	.000
Buddy Ryan	Philadelphia Eagles	0	0	0	0	.000	0	0	0	.000	0	0	0	.000
Gene Stallings	St. Louis Cardinals	0	0	0	0	.000	0	0	0	.000	0	0	0	.000

Coaches With 100 Career Victories

Start of 1986 Season

Coach	Team(s)	Regular Season Yrs.	Won	Lost	Tied	Pct.	Postseason Won	Lost	Tied	Pct.	Career Won	Lost	Tied	Pct.
George Halas	Chicago Bears	40	319	148	31	.672	6	3	0	.667	325	151	31	.672
Don Shula	Baltimore Colts, Miami Dolphins	23	239	86	6	.731	16	13	0	.552	255	99	6	.717
Tom Landry	Dallas Cowboys	26	233	132	6	.636	20	16	0	.556	253	148	6	.629
Earl (Curly) Lambeau	Green Bay Packers, Chicago Cardinals, Washington Redskins	33	226	132	22	.623	3	2	0	.600	229	134	22	.623
Paul Brown	Cleveland Browns, Cincinnati Bengals	21	166	100	6	.621	4	8	0	.333	170	108	6	.609
Bud Grant	Minnesota Vikings	18	158	96	5	.620	10	12	0	.455	168	108	5	.607
Chuck Noll	Pittsburgh Steelers	17	149	97	1	.605	15	7	0	.682	164	104	1	.612
Steve Owen	New York Giants	23	151	100	17	.595	2	8	0	.200	153	108	17	.582
Hank Stram	Kansas City Chiefs, New Orleans Saints	17	131	97	10	.571	5	3	0	.625	136	100	10	.573
Weeb Ewbank	Baltimore Colts, New York Jets	20	130	129	7	.502	4	1	0	.800	134	130	7	.507
Chuck Knox	Los Angeles Rams, Buffalo Bills, Seattle Seahawks	13	120	70	1	.631	7	9	0	.438	127	79	1	.616
Sid Gillman	Los Angeles Rams, San Diego Chargers, Houston Oilers	18	122	99	7	.550	1	5	0	.167	123	104	7	.541
George Allen	Los Angeles Rams, Washington Redskins	12	116	47	5	.705	2	7	0	.222	118	54	5	.681
Don Coryell	St. Louis Cardinals, San Diego Chargers	13	110	76	1	.591	3	6	0	.333	113	82	1	.579
John Madden	Oakland Raiders	10	103	32	7	.750	9	7	0	.563	112	39	7	.731
Ray (Buddy) Parker	Chicago Cardinals, Detroit Lions, Pittsburgh Steelers	15	104	75	9	.577	3	1	0	.750	107	76	9	.581
Vince Lombardi	Green Bay Packers, Washington Redskins	10	96	34	6	.728	9	1	0	.900	105	35	6	.740

AFC ACTIVE STATISTICAL LEADERS

LEADING ACTIVE PASSERS, AMERICAN FOOTBALL CONFERENCE

1,000 or more attempts

	Yrs.	Att.	Comp.	Pct. Comp.	Yards	Avg. Gain	TD	Pct. TD	Had Int.	Pct. Int.	Rate Pts.
Dan Marino, Mia.	3	1427	871	61.0	11431	8.01	98	6.9	44	3.1	96.4
Dave Krieg, Sea.	6	1447	821	56.7	10756	7.43	86	5.9	62	4.3	82.3
Ken Anderson, Cin.	15	4452	2643	59.4	32667	7.34	196	4.4	158	3.5	82.0
Dan Fouts, S.D.	13	4810	2839	59.0	37492	7.79	228	4.7	205	4.3	81.8
Bill Kenney, K.C.	6	1735	957	55.2	12699	7.32	77	4.4	61	3.5	78.7
Gary Danielson, Clev.	9	1847	1049	56.8	13159	7.12	77	4.2	77	4.2	75.6
Steve Grogan, N.E.	11	2837	1474	52.0	21581	7.61	146	5.1	167	5.9	69.7
John Elway, Den.	3	1244	664	53.4	8152	6.55	47	3.8	52	4.2	69.0
Jim Plunkett, Raiders	14	3449	1810	52.5	23896	6.93	150	4.3	189	5.5	66.3
Mike Pagel, Clev.	4	1154	587	50.9	7474	6.48	39	3.4	47	4.1	65.8
Marc Wilson, Raiders	6	1160	590	50.9	7969	6.87	53	4.6	63	5.4	65.7
David Woodley, Pitt.	6	1300	687	52.8	8558	6.58	48	3.7	63	4.8	65.7

TOP 10 ACTIVE RUSHERS, AFC

2,000 or more yards

	Yrs.	Att.	Yards	TD
1. Mike Pruitt, K.C.	10	1705	6930	49
2. Marcus Allen, Raiders	4	1081	4638	44
3. Freeman McNeil, N.Y.J.	5	971	4464	17
4. Joe Cribbs, Buff.	5	1082	4445	21
5. Tony Collins, N.E.	5	888	3761	26
6. Curtis Dickey, Clev.	6	802	3496	26
7. Tony Nathan, Mia.	6	701	3320	16
8. Frank Pollard, Pitt.	6	770	3274	17
9. Randy McMillan, Ind.	5	801	3267	21
10. Sammy Winder, Den.	4	758	2883	16
Other Leading Rushers				
James Brooks, Cin.	6	618	2796	21
Charles Alexander, Cin.	7	748	2645	13
Curt Warner, Sea.	3	636	2583	21
Kenny King, Raiders	7	579	2477	7
Ken Anderson, Cin.	15	397	2220	20
Steve Grogan, N.E.	11	397	2090	31
Craig James, N.E.	2	423	2017	6
Walter Abercrombie, Pitt.	4	505	2007	14

TOP 10 ACTIVE PASS RECEIVERS, AFC

225 or more receptions

	Yrs.	No.	Yards	TD
1. Charlie Joiner, S.D.	17	716	11706	63
2. Steve Largent, Sea.	10	624	10059	78
3. Ozzie Newsome, Clev.	8	502	6281	39
4. Cliff Branch, Raiders	14	501	8685	67
5. Nat Moore, Mia.	12	472	7115	67
6. John Stallworth, Pitt.	12	462	7736	60
7. Wes Chandler, S.D.	8	460	7442	50
8. Kellen Winslow, S.D.	7	424	5494	37
9. Henry Marshall, K.C.	10	360	5767	32
10. Stanley Morgan, N.E.	9	351	7201	47
Other Leading Pass Receivers				
Wesley Walker, N.Y.J.	9	346	6460	51
Tony Nathan, Mia.	7	325	3058	14
Cris Collinsworth, Cin.	5	311	4953	25
Todd Christensen, Raiders	7	304	3866	31
Steve Watson, Den.	7	297	5246	32
Dan Ross, Sea.	6	273	3276	18
Jerry Butler, Buff.	6	263	3999	27
Mike Pruitt, K.C.	10	262	1804	5
Marcus Allen, Raiders	4	237	2304	13
Mickey Shuler, N.Y.J.	8	227	2583	25

TOP 10 ACTIVE SCORERS, AFC

250 or more points

	Yrs.	TD	FG	PAT	TP
1. Pat Leahy, N.Y.J.	12	0	184	349	901
2. Chris Bahr, Raiders	10	0	166	361	859
3. Rolf Benirschke, S.D.	9	0	130	289	679
4. Tony Franklin, N.E.	7	0	126	254	632
5. Nick Lowery, K.C.	7	0	136	212	620
6. Jim Breech, Cin.	7	0	120	250	610
7. Matt Bahr, Clev.	7	0	118	238	592
8. Steve Largent, Sea.	10	79	0	1	475
9. Gary Anderson, Pitt.	4	0	94	145	427
10. Nat Moore, Mia.	12	68	0	0	408
Other Leading Scorers					
Cliff Branch, Raiders	14	67	0	0	402
Charlie Joiner, S.D.	17	63	0	0	378
John Stallworth, Pitt.	12	61	0	0	366
Rich Karlis, Den.	40	0	76	127	355
Marcus Allen, Raiders	4	58	0	0	348
Norm Johnson, Sea.	4	0	62	152	338
Mike Pruitt, K.C.	10	54	0	0	324
Wesley Walker, N.Y.J.	9	51	0	0	*308
Wes Chandler, S.D.	8	50	0	0	300
Stanley Morgan, N.E.	9	48	0	0	288

total includes safety scored

TOP 10 ACTIVE INTERCEPTORS, AFC

20 or more interceptions

	Yrs.	No.	Yards	TD
1. Donnie Shell, Pitt.	12	47	411	1
2. Dave Brown, Sea.	11	45	585	4
3. Steve Foley, Den.	10	42	583	1
4. John Harris, Sea.	8	41	425	2
5. Mike Haynes, Raiders	10	39	621	2
6. Lester Hayes, Raiders	9	37	565	4
7. Lyle Blackwood, Mia.	13	34	575	2
8. Terry Jackson, Sea.	8	28	360	3
9. Ray Clayborn, N.E.	9	26	462	1
Kenny Easley, Sea.	5	26	457	3
Other Leading Interceptors				
Charles Romes, Buff.	9	24	470	1
Louis Breeden, Cin.	8	24	437	1
Glenn Blackwood, Mia.	7	24	371	1
Louis Wright, Den.	11	23	304	1
Deron Cherry, K.C.	5	22	331	1
Steve Freeman, Buff.	11	22	329	3
Woodrow Lowe, S.D.	10	21	343	4
Dwayne Woodruff, Pitt.	7	21	322	1
Bobby Jackson, N.Y.J.	8	21	196	2
Tom Jackson, Den.	13	20	340	3
Steve Wilson, Den.	7	20	262	0
Roland James, N.E.	6	20	237	0
Brad Van Pelt, Raiders	13	20	135	0

TOP 10 ACTIVE QUARTERBACK SACKERS, AFC

	No.
1. Mark Gastineau, N.Y.J.	60.5
2. Jacob Green, Sea.	45.5
3. Andre Tippett, N.E.	43.5
4. Howie Long, Raiders	40.5
5. Doug Betters, Mia.	39.5
6. Eddie Edwards, Cin.	36.5
7. Jeff Bryant, Sea.	34.0
8. Bill Pickel, Raiders	31.0
9. Jesse Baker, Hou.	29.5
10. Greg Townsend, Raiders	27.5

TOP 10 ACTIVE PUNT RETURNERS, AFC

40 or more punt returns

	Yrs.	No.	Yards	Avg.	TD
1. Louis Lipps, Pitt.	2	89	1093	12.3	3
2. Irving Fryar, N.E.	2	73	867	11.9	2
3. Mike Martin, Cin.	3	79	871	11.0	0
4. James Brooks, Cin.	6	52	565	10.9	0
5. Tommy Vigorito, Mia.	4	79	830	10.5	2
Kirk Springs, N.Y.J.	5	65	681	10.5	1
7. Mike Haynes, Raiders	10	112	1168	10.4	2
Fulton Walker, Raiders	5	96	997	10.4	0
Stanley Morgan, N.E.	9	92	960	10.4	1
10. Gerald Willhite, Den.	4	42	432	10.3	0
Other Leading Punt Returners					
Robbie Martin, Ind.	5	158	1561	9.9	3
Ricky Smith, Mia.	3	54	537	9.9	0
Mark Clayton, Mia.	3	51	485	9.5	1
Tony Nathan, Mia.	7	51	484	9.5	1
Roland James, N.E.	6	42	400	9.5	1
Donald Wilson, Buff.	2	49	458	9.3	1
Paul Skansi, Sea.	3	90	820	9.1	0
Butch Johnson, Den.	10	146	1313	9.0	0
Cle Montgomery, Raiders	6	70	622	8.9	1
Garcia Lane, K.C.	1	43	381	8.9	0
Nesby Glasgow, Ind.	7	79	651	8.2	1
Brian Brennan, Clev.	2	44	352	8.0	1
Rod Hill, Buff.	4	50	391	7.8	0
Lionel James, S.D.	2	55	421	7.7	1
Jim Smith, Raiders	7	98	737	7.5	0
John Simmons, Cin.	5	42	295	7.0	0
Wes Chandler, S.D.	8	58	387	6.7	0
Robb Riddick, Buff.	3	46	289	6.3	0
Lyle Blackwood, Mia.	13	68	319	4.7	0

TOP 10 ACTIVE KICKOFF RETURNERS, AFC

40 or more kickoff returns

	Yrs.	No.	Yards	Avg.	TD
1. Ray Clayborn, N.E.	9	57	1538	27.0	3
2. Glen Young, Clev.	3	66	1579	23.9	0
3. Fulton Walker, Raiders	5	144	3411	23.7	1
4. Butch Johnson, Den.	10	79	1832	23.2	0
Carlos Carson, K.C.	6	52	1208	23.2	0
6. Nesby Glasgow, Ind.	7	84	1904	22.7	0
Kirk Springs, N.Y.J.	5	49	1112	22.7	0
Lorenzo Hampton, Mia.	1	45	1020	22.7	0
9. Ricky Smith, Mia.	3	67	1505	22.5	1
10. Mike Martin, Cin.	3	68	1509	22.2	0
Other Leading Kickoff Returners					
Lionel James, S.D.	2	79	1738	22.0	0
Wes Chandler, S.D.	8	47	1021	21.7	0
James Brooks, Cin.	6	115	2487	21.6	0
Tony Nathan, Mia.	7	53	1133	21.4	0
Stephen Starring, N.E.	3	48	1012	21.1	0
Rich Erenberg, Pitt.	2	49	1016	20.7	0
Tony Collins, N.E.	5	64	1317	20.6	0
Cle Montgomery, Raiders	6	132	2706	20.5	0
Drew Hill, Hou.	6	172	3460	20.1	1
Anthony Hancock, K.C.	4	64	1281	20.0	0
Robb Riddick, Buff.	3	42	825	19.6	0
Steve Wilson, Den.	7	58	1107	19.1	0
Kurt Sohn, N.Y.J.	4	44	834	19.0	0
Robbie Martin, Ind.	5	91	1699	18.7	0
Donald Wilson, Buff.	2	56	1041	18.6	0

TOP 10 ACTIVE PUNTERS, AFC

50 or more punts

	Yrs.	No.	Avg.	LG
1. Rohn Stark, Ind.	4	313	45.2	72
2. Reggie Roby, Mia.	3	184	43.7	69
3. Rich Camarillo, N.E.	5	317	43.2	76
4. Ray Guy, Raiders	13	959	42.6	74
5. Ralf Mojsiejenko, S.D.	1	68	42.4	67
6. Jim Arnold, K.C.	3	284	42.0	64
7. Pat McInally, Cin.	10	700	41.9	67
8. John Kidd, Buff.	2	180	41.7	67
Lee Johnson, Hou.	1	83	41.7	65
10. Dave Jennings, N.Y.J.	12	1005	41.6	73
Other Leading Punters				
Jeff Gossett, Clev.	4	213	40.5	64
Chris Norman, Den.	2	188	40.5	83
John Misko, N.Y.J.	3	201	40.4	67
David Finzer, Sea.	2	151	40.4	87
Harry Newsome, Pitt.	1	78	39.6	59
Joe Prokop, N.Y.J.	1	56	39.5	66

NFC ACTIVE STATISTICAL LEADERS

LEADING ACTIVE PASSERS, NATIONAL FOOTBALL CONFERENCE

1,000 or more attempts

	Yrs.	Att.	Comp.	Pct. Comp.	Yards	Avg. Gain	TD	Pct. TD	Had Int.	Pct. Int.	Rate Pts.
Joe Montana, S.F.	7	2571	1627	63.3	19262	7.49	133	5.2	67	2.6	92.4
Neil Lomax, St.L.	5	1826	1047	57.3	13406	7.34	79	4.3	55	3.0	82.3
Danny White, Dall.	10	2393	1422	59.4	17911	7.48	130	5.4	107	4.5	82.3
Joe Theismann, Wash.	12	3602	2044	56.7	25206	7.00	160	4.4	138	3.8	77.4
Steve Bartkowski, Rams	11	3330	1871	56.2	23470	7.05	154	4.6	142	4.2	76.0
Ron Jaworski, Phil.	12	3797	2014	53.0	26277	6.92	168	4.4	153	4.0	73.1
Phil Simms, N.Y.G.	6	2024	1067	52.7	14098	6.97	83	4.1	81	4.0	72.0
Tommy Kramer, Minn.	9	2886	1603	55.5	19153	6.64	119	4.1	128	4.4	71.3
Lynn Dickey, G.B.	13	3125	1747	55.9	23322	7.46	141	4.5	179	5.7	70.9
Steve Fuller, Chi.	6	1002	571	57.0	6705	6.69	26	2.6	37	3.7	70.7
Vince Ferragamo, G.B.	8	1575	879	55.8	11053	7.02	75	4.8	88	5.6	70.4
Steve DeBerg, T.B.	8	2626	1489	56.7	17081	6.50	97	3.7	120	4.6	69.7
Joe Ferguson, Det.	13	4220	2219	52.6	27954	6.62	183	4.3	193	4.6	68.9
Eric Hipple, Det.	6	1196	619	51.8	8544	7.14	46	3.8	56	4.7	68.3
Richard Todd, N.O.	10	2967	1610	54.3	20610	6.95	124	4.2	161	5.4	67.6
Jim Zorn, G.B.	10	3113	1649	53.0	20916	6.72	111	3.6	139	4.5	67.5
Scott Brunner, St.L.	5	1046	512	48.9	6457	6.17	29	2.8	54	5.2	56.3

TOP 10 ACTIVE RUSHERS, NFC

2,000 or more yards

	Yrs.	Att.	Yards	TD
1. Walter Payton, Chi.	11	3371	14860	98
2. Tony Dorsett, Dall.	9	2441	10832	66
3. Earl Campbell, N.O.	8	2187	9407	74
4. Ottis Anderson, St.L.	7	1807	7843	44
5. Wendell Tyler, S.F.	9	1313	6251	50
6. William Andrews, Atl.	5	1263	5772	29
7. George Rogers, Wash.	5	1226	5360	30
8. Eric Dickerson, Rams	3	1061	5147	44
9. Billy Sims, Det.	5	1131	5106	42
10. Joe Washington, Atl.	9	1195	4839	12
Other Leading Rushers				
Rob Carpenter, N.Y.G.	9	1170	4360	29
Ted Brown, Minn.	7	1054	4295	36
James Wilder, T.B.	5	1123	4178	34
Gerald Riggs, Atl.	4	928	3941	36
Tony Galbreath, N.Y.G.	10	1005	3937	34
Gerry Ellis, G.B.	6	752	3481	23
Eddie Lee Ivery, G.B.	7	663	2908	23
Wayne Wilson, N.O.	7	656	2457	16
Roger Craig, S.F.	3	545	2424	24
Matt Suhey, Chi.	6	630	2348	15
Earnest Jackson, Phil.	3	589	2246	13
Ron Springs, T.B.	7	620	2234	28
Stump Mitchell, St.L.	5	402	2177	20
Darrin Nelson, Minn.	4	478	2077	9
Joe Morris, N.Y.G.	4	477	2039	26

TOP 10 ACTIVE PASS RECEIVERS, NFC

225 or more receptions

	Yrs.	No.	Yards	TD
1. James Lofton, G.B.	8	466	8816	45
2. Pat Tilley, St.L.	10	465	6954	37
3. Tony Galbreath, N.Y.G.	10	431	3550	9
4. Tony Hill, Dall.	9	430	7218	48
5. Walter Payton, Chi.	11	422	3939	11
6. Dwight Clark, S.F.	7	421	5666	41
7. Joe Washington, Atl.	9	395	3413	18
8. Sammy White, Minn.	10	393	6400	50
Art Monk, Wash.	6	393	5482	24
10. Tony Dorsett, Dall.	9	338	2988	11
Other Leading Pass Receivers				
David Hill, Rams	10	333	3905	27
Ted Brown, Minn.	7	324	2718	13
Billy Johnson, Atl.	11	323	4070	25
Paul Coffman, G.B.	8	322	4223	39
Russ Francis, S.F.	10	319	4394	39
James Wilder, T.B.	5	296	2379	4
Ottis Anderson, St.L.	7	289	2404	5
Jimmie Giles, T.B.	9	278	4269	33
Kevin House, T.B.	6	275	4722	31
Roy Green, St.L.	7	272	4651	38
William Andrews, Atl.	5	272	2612	11
Mike Renfro, Dall.	8	255	3721	21
Leonard Thompson, Det.	11	252	4362	30
Earnest Gray, St.L.	7	246	3790	27
Gerry Ellis, G.B.	6	243	2256	10
Preston Dennard, G.B.	8	232	3565	30
Ron Springs, T.B.	7	225	2072	10

TOP 10 ACTIVE SCORERS, NFC

250 or more points

	Yrs.	TD	FG	PAT	TP
1. Mark Moseley, Wash.	15	0	288	457	1321
2. Ray Wersching, S.F.	13	0	184	371	923
3. Rafael Septien, Dall.	9	0	165	377	872
4. Walter Payton, Chi.	11	109	0	0	654
5. Ed Murray, Det.	6	0	134	197	599
6. Tony Dorsett, Dall.	9	78	0	0	468
7. Mick Luckhurst, Atl.	5	0	92	175	451
8. Earl Campbell, N.O.	8	74	0	0	444
9. Wendell Tyler, S.F.	9	66	0	0	396
10. Morten Andersen, N.O.	4	0	71	104	317
Other Leading Scorers					
Sammy White, Minn.	10	50	0	0	300
Ottis Anderson, St.L.	7	49	0	0	294
Ted Brown, Minn.	7	49	0	0	294
Mike Lansford, Rams	4	0	62	107	293
Tony Hill, Dall.	9	48	0	0	288
Billy Sims, Det.	5	47	0	0	282
Eric Dickerson, Rams	3	46	0	0	276
James Lofton, G.B.	8	46	0	0	276
Tony Galbreath, N.Y.G.	10	43	2	1	265

TOP 10 ACTIVE INTERCEPTORS, NFC

20 or more interceptions

	Yrs.	No.	Yards	TD
1. Dennis Thurman, Dall.	8	36	562	4
2. Gary Fencik, Chi.	10	35	451	1
3. Everson Walls, Dall.	5	34	307	0
4. Gary Green, Rams	9	33	502	2
Herman Edwards, Phil.	9	33	98	1
6. Dwight Hicks, S.F.	7	30	586	3
Nolan Cromwell, Rams	9	30	542	3
8. Tim Fox, Rams	10	26	376	0
9. John Turner, Minn.	8	24	270	1
10. Ronnie Lott, S.F.	5	23	328	4
Other Leading Interceptors				
Michael Downs, Dall.	5	22	320	1
Tom Pridemore, Atl.	8	21	372	1
Eric Harris, Rams	6	21	329	1
John Anderson, G.B.	8	21	141	1
LeRoy Irvin, Rams	6	20	389	3
Leslie Frazier, Chi.	5	20	343	2
Vernon Dean, Wash.	4	20	238	2
Bobby Watkins, Det.	4	20	85	0

TOP 10 ACTIVE QUARTERBACK SACKERS, NFC

	No.
1. Dexter Manley, Wash.	46.0
2. Curtis Greer, St.L.	44.5
3. Greg Brown, Phil.	41.5
4. Lawrence Taylor, N.Y.G.	41.0
5. Rickey Jackson, N.O.	39.5
6. Randy White, Dall.	38.0
7. Richard Dent, Chi.	37.5
8. Dennis Harrison, Rams	37.0
9. Ezra Johnson, G.B.	36.5
10. William Gay, Det.	36.0

TOP 10 ACTIVE PUNT RETURNERS, NFC

40 or more punt returns

	Yrs.	No.	Yards	Avg.	TD
1. Henry Ellard, Rams	3	83	1121	13.5	4
2. Billy Johnson, Atl.	11	250	3036	12.1	6
3. J.T. Smith, St.L.	8	246	2605	10.6	4
4. Dana McLemore, S.F.	4	121	1266	10.5	3
5. LeRoy Irvin, Rams	6	144	1448	10.1	4
Kenneth Jenkins, Wash.	3	50	503	10.1	0
Pete Mandley, Det.	2	40	403	10.1	1
8. Dennis McKinnon, Chi.	3	43	422	9.8	1
9. Stump Mitchell, St.L.	5	156	1377	8.8	1
10. James Jones, Dall.	5	87	736	8.5	0
Other Leading Punt Returners					
Jeff Groth, N.O.	7	105	887	8.4	0
Phillip Epps, G.B.	4	100	819	8.2	1
Phil McConkey, N.Y.G.	2	99	748	7.6	0
Dwight Hicks, S.F.	7	54	403	7.5	0
Evan Cooper, Phil.	2	83	614	7.4	0
Ron Fellows, Dall.	5	46	308	6.7	0

TOP 10 ACTIVE KICKOFF RETURNERS, NFC

40 or more kickoff returns

	Yrs.	No.	Yards	Avg.	TD
1. Buster Rhymes, Minn.	1	53	1345	25.4	0
2. Billy Johnson, Atl.	11	123	2941	23.9	2
3. Brian Baschnagel, Chi.	9	89	2102	23.6	1
4. Roy Green, St.L.	7	83	1917	23.1	1
Kenneth Jenkins, Wash.	3	81	1873	23.1	0
6. Wayne Wilson, N.O.	7	68	1565	23.0	0
Darrin Nelson, Minn.	4	66	1519	23.0	0
8. Carl Monroe, S.F.	3	63	1430	22.7	1
9. Stump Mitchell, St.L.	5	161	3633	22.6	0
Phil Freeman, T.B.	1	48	1085	22.6	0
Other Leading Kickoff Returners					
Alvin Hall, Det.	5	122	2714	22.2	1
Willie Tullis, N.O.	5	61	1356	22.2	1
James Rogers, S.F.	5	77	1678	21.8	0
Herman Hunter, Phil.	1	48	1047	21.8	0
Barry Redden, Rams	4	64	1390	21.7	0
Dennis Gentry, Chi.	4	45	966	21.5	1
David Verser, T.B.	5	65	1371	21.1	0
Kenny Duckett, Dall.	4	73	1511	20.7	0
James Jones, Dall.	5	70	1444	20.6	0
Ron Springs, T.B.	7	44	905	20.6	0
Dana McLemore, S.F.	4	53	1085	20.5	0
Cliff Austin, Atl.	3	50	1027	20.5	1
Ron Fellows, Dall.	5	73	1478	20.2	0
Phil McConkey, N.Y.G.	2	40	775	19.4	0
Mark Lee, G.B.	6	45	859	19.1	0
Harlan Huckleby, G.B.	6	70	1300	18.6	0

TOP 10 ACTIVE PUNTERS, NFC

50 or more punts

	Yrs.	No.	Avg.	LG
1. Rick Donnelly, Atl.	1	59	43.6	68
2. Dale Hatcher, Rams	1	87	43.2	67
3. Brian Hansen, N.O.	2	158	42.9	66
Sean Landeta, N.Y.G.	1	81	42.9	68
5. Maury Buford, Chi.	4	218	42.5	71
6. Frank Garcia, T.B.	4	242	42.0	64
7. Steve Cox, Wash.	5	242	41.9	69
Mike Saxon, Dall.	1	81	41.9	57
9. Mike Horan, Phil.	2	183	41.8	75
10. Mike Black, Det.	3	220	41.5	63
Other Leading Punters				
Carl Birdsong, St.L.	5	360	41.4	75
Ralph Giacomarro, Atl.	3	167	40.9	58
Greg Coleman, Minn.	9	669	40.7	73
Max Runager, S.F.	7	457	40.4	64
Danny White, Dall.	10	610	40.2	73
Jeff Hayes, Wash.	4	211	39.0	59

DRAFT LIST FOR 1986

51st Annual NFL Draft, April 29-30, 1986

Atlanta Falcons

1. Tony Casillas—2, NT, Oklahoma
   Tim Green—17, LB, Syracuse, from Washington
2. Choice to Washington
3. Choice to Cincinnati
4. Choice to Los Angeles Raiders
5. Choice to Washington
6. Choice to Kansas City through Washington
   Floyd Dixon—154, WR, Stephen F. Austin, from Cleveland through Buffalo
   Keith Williams—159, RB, Southwest Missouri, from Washington
7. Choice to Philadelphia
8. Kevin Hudgens—197, DE, Idaho State
9. Kevin Starks—224, TE, Minnesota
10. Tony Baker—252, RB, East Carolina
11. Chris Hegg—280, QB, Northeast Missouri
12. Steve Griffin—308, WR, Purdue

Buffalo Bills

1. Choice exercised in 1985 Supplemental Draft by Cleveland for Bernie Kosar, QB, Miami
   Ronnie Harmon—16, RB, Iowa, from Cleveland
   Will Wolford—20, T, Vanderbilt, from Dallas through San Francisco
2. Choice to Detroit through San Francisco
3. Choice to San Francisco
   Leonard Burton—77, C, South Carolina, from Los Angeles Rams
4. Choice to Green Bay
5. Carl Byrum—111, RB, Mississippi Valley State
6. Choice to Dallas
7. Choice to Cleveland
   Bob Williams—168, TE, Penn State, from Tampa Bay
   Mark Pike—178, DT, Georgia Tech, from Detroit
   Butch Rolle—180, TE, Michigan State, from Seattle
8. Choice to Kansas City
   Tony Furjanic—202, LB, Notre Dame, from Kansas City
9. Reggie Bynum—222, WR, Oregon State
10. Guy Teafatiller—251, NT, Illinois
11. Tony Garbarczyk—278, NT, Wake Forest
    Billy Witt—282, DE, North Alabama from Indianapolis
12. Choice to Dallas
    Brian McClure—313, QB, Bowling Green, from Kansas City
    Derek Christian—331, LB, West Virginia, from Green Bay

Chicago Bears

1. Neal Anderson—27, RB, Florida
2. Vestee Jackson—55, DB, Washington
3. David Williams—82, WR, Illinois
4. Paul Blair—110, T, Oklahoma State
5. Lew Barnes—138, WR, Oregon
6. Jeff Powell—166, RB, Tennessee
7. Bruce Jones—194, DB, North Alabama
8. Maurice Douglass—221, DB, Kentucky
9. John Teltschik—249, P, Texas
10. Barton Hundley—277, DB, Kansas State
11. Glen Kozlowski—305, WR, Brigham Young
12. Choice to San Diego

Cincinnati Bengals

1. Joe Kelly—11, LB, Washington
2. Tim McGee—21, WR, Tennessee, from Denver
   Lewis Billups—38, DB, North Alabama
3. Jim Skow—58, DE, Nebraska, from Atlanta
   Mike Hammerstein—65, DT, Michigan
   David Fulcher—78, DB, Arizona State, from Denver
4. Eric Kattus—91, TE, Michigan
   Doug Gaynor—99, QB, Long Beach State, from Seattle
5. Leon White—123, LB, Brigham Young
6. Gary Hunt—152, DB, Memphis State
7. Pat Franklin—177, RB, Southwest Texas State
8. David Douglas—204, G, Tennessee
9. Cary Whittingham—230, LB, Brigham Young
10. Jeff Shaw—262, NT, Salem, West Virginia
11. Tim Stone—289, T, Kansas State
    Tom Flaherty—294, LB, Northwestern, from Green Bay
12. Steve Bradley—316, QB, Indiana

Cleveland Browns

1. Choice from Buffalo exercised in 1985 Supplemental Draft for Bernie Kosar, QB, Miami
   Choice to Buffalo
2. Webster Slaughter—43, WR, San Diego State
3. Choice to Detroit
4. Choice to San Francisco through Los Angeles Rams
5. Nick Miller—127, LB, Arkansas
6. Choice to Atlanta through Buffalo
7. Jim Meyer—167, T, Illinois State, from Buffalo
   Mike Norseth—174, QB, Kansas, from Kansas City
   Choice to Seattle
8. Choice to Philadelphia
9. Danny Taylor—238, DB, Texas-El Paso
10. Willie Smith—265, TE, Miami
11. Randy Dausin—292, G, Texas A&M
12. King Simmons—319, DB, Texas Tech

Dallas Cowboys

1. Mike Sherrard—18, WR, UCLA, from San Francisco
2. Darryl Clack—33, RB, Arizona State, from Indianapolis
   Choice to Indianapolis
3. Mark Walen—74, DT, UCLA
4. Max Zendejas—100, K, Arizona
5. Choice to San Francisco
6. Thornton Chandler—140, TE, Alabama, from Buffalo
   Stan Gelbaugh—150, QB, Maryland, from Detroit
   Lloyd Yancey—158, G, Temple
7. Johnny Holloway—185, WR, Kansas
8. Topper Clemons—212, RB, Wake Forest
9. John Ionata—242, G, Florida State
10. Bryan Chester—269, G, Texas
11. Garth Jax—296, LB, Florida State
12. Chris Duliban—307, LB, Texas, from Buffalo
    Tony Flack—322, DB, Georgia

Denver Broncos

1. Choice to Cincinnati
2. Choice to New York Giants
3. Choice to Cincinnati
4. Jim Juriga—104, T, Illinois
5. Tony Colorito—134, NT, Southern California
6. Orson Mobley—151, TE, Salem, West Virginia, from Green Bay
   Mark Jackson, 161, WR, Purdue
7. Raymond Phillips—188, LB, North Carolina State
8. Bruce Klosterman—217, LB, South Dakota State
9. Joe Thomas—244, WR, Mississippi Valley State
10. Victor Hall—271, TE, Jackson State
11. Thomas Dendy—301, RB, South Carolina
12. Choice to Los Angeles Rams

Detroit Lions

1. Chuck Long—12, QB, Iowa
2. Garry James—29, RB, Louisiana State, from Buffalo through San Francisco
   Choice to San Francisco
3. Joe Milinichik—69, T, North Carolina State, from Cleveland
   Choice to Los Angeles Rams through San Francisco
4. Devon Mitchell—92, DB, Iowa
5. Oscar Smith—119, RB, Nicholls State
6. Choice to Dallas
7. Choice to Buffalo
8. Allyn Griffin—205, WR, Wyoming
9. Lyle Pickens—231, DB, Colorado
10. Tracy Johnson—258, LB, Morningside
11. Leland Melvin—290, WR, Richmond
12. Allan Durden—317, DB, Arizona

Green Bay Packers

1. Choice to Minnesota through San Diego
2. Kenneth Davis—41, RB, Texas Christian
3. Robbie Bosco—72, QB, Brigham Young
4. Tim Harris—84, LB, Memphis State, from Buffalo
   Dan Knight—98, T, San Diego State
5. Matt Koart—125, DT, Southern California
6. Burnell Dent—143, LB, Tulane, from St. Louis
   Choice to Denver
7. Ed Berry—183, DB, Utah State
8. Michael Cline—210, NT, Arkansas State
9. Brent Moore—236, DT, Southern California
10. Gary Spann—263, LB, Texas Christian
11. Choice to Cincinnati
12. Choice to Buffalo

Houston Oilers

1. Jim Everett—3, QB, Purdue
2. Ernest Givins—34, WR, Louisville
3. Allen Pinkett—61, RB, Notre Dame
4. Choice to Kansas City
5. Jeff Parks—114, TE, Auburn
6. Ray Wallace—145, RB, Purdue
7. Choice to Indianapolis through Los Angeles Rams
8. Larry Griffin—199, DB, North Carolina
9. Bob Sebring—225, LB, Illinois
10. Don Sommer—256, G, Texas-El Paso
11. Mark Cochran—283, T, Baylor
12. Chuck Banks—310, RB, West Virginia Tech

Indianapolis Colts

1. Jon Hand—4, DE, Alabama, from New Orleans
   Choice to New Orleans
2. Choice to Dallas
   Jack Trudeau—47, QB, Illinois, from Dallas
3. Choice to New Orleans
4. Bill Brooks—86, WR, Boston University
5. Scott Kellar—117, DE, Northern Illinois
   Gary Walker—124, C, Boston University, from San Diego
6. Choice to Los Angeles Rams
7. Steve O'Malley—171, NT, Northern Illinois
   Chris White—172, K, Illinois, from Houston through Los Angeles Rams
   Tommy Sims—190, DB, Tennessee, from Los Angeles Rams
8. Trell Hooper—198, DB, Memphis State
9. Bob Brotzki—228, T, Syracuse
10. Choice to St. Louis
    Pete Anderson—266, G, Georgia, from San Diego
11. Choice to Buffalo
12. Steve Wade—309, DT, Vanderbilt
    Isaac Williams—326, DT, Florida State, from Los Angeles Rams

Kansas City Chiefs

1. Brian Jozwiak—7, T, West Virginia
2. Dino Hackett—35, LB, Appalachian State
3. Leonard Griffin—63, DE, Grambling
4. Tom Baugh—87, C, Southern Illinois, from Houston
   Chas Fox—90, WR, Furman
5. Choice to San Diego
6. Kent Hagood—141, RB, South Carolina, from Atlanta through Washington
   Choice to Washington
7. Choice to Cleveland
8. Lewis Colbert—196, P, Auburn, from Buffalo
   Choice to Buffalo
9. Gary Baldinger—229, DE, Wake Forest
10. Ike Readon—257, NT, Hampton Institute
11. Aaron Pearson—285, LB, Mississippi State
12. Choice to Buffalo

Los Angeles Raiders

1. Bob Buczowski—24, DE, Pittsburgh
2. Choice to New York Giants through Minnesota
3. Brad Cochran—80, DB, Michigan
4. Mike Wise—85, DE, Cal-Davis, from Atlanta
   Vance Mueller—103, RB, Occidental, from New York Giants
   Napoleon McCallum—108, RB, Navy
5. Choice to Pittsburgh
6. Doug Marrone—164, T, Syracuse
7. Bill Lewis—191, C, Nebraska
8. Joe Mauntel—219, LB, Eastern Kentucky
9. Zeph Lee—246, RB, Southern California
10. Jeff Reinke—275, DE, Mankato State
11. Randell Webster—302, LB, Southwestern Oklahoma
12. Larry Shepherd—330, WR, Houston

Los Angeles Rams

1. Mike Schad—23, T, Queen's (Canada) University
2. Tom Newberry—50, G, Wisconsin-La Crosse
3. Hugh Millen—71, QB, Washington, from Detroit through San Francisco
   Choice to Buffalo
4. Choice to Philadelphia
5. Choice to San Diego
6. Robert Cox—144, T, UCLA, from Indianapolis
   Lynn Williams—160, RB, Kansas
7. Choice to Indianapolis
8. Steve Jarecki—195, LB, UCLA, from Tampa Bay
   Hank Goebel—216, T, Cal State-Fullerton
9. Elbert Watts—243, DB, Southern California
10. Garrett Breeland—273, LB, Southern California
11. Chul Schwanke—300, RB, South Dakota
12. Choice to Indianapolis
   Marcus Dupree—327, RB, Oklahoma, from Denver

Miami Dolphins

1. Choice to Tampa Bay
2. John Offerdahl—52, LB, Western Michigan
3. T.J. Turner—81, DT, Houston
4. James Pruitt—107, WR, Cal State-Fullerton
5. Kevin Wyatt—136, DB, Arkansas
6. Brent Sowell—163, DT, Alabama
7. Larry Kolic—193, LB, Ohio State
8. John Stuart—218, T, Texas
9. Reyna Thompson—247, DB, Baylor
10. Jeff Wickersham—274, QB, Louisiana State
11. Arnold Franklin—303, TE, North Carolina
12. Rickey Isom—329, RB, North Carolina State

Minnesota Vikings

1. Choice to San Diego
   Gerald Robinson—14, DE, Auburn, from Green Bay through San Diego
2. Choice to Tampa Bay through Miami
3. Choice to San Diego
4. Joe Phillips—93, DT, Southern Methodist
5. Hassan Jones—120, WR, Florida State
6. Thomas Rooks—147, RB, Illinois
7. Carl Hilton—179, TE, Houston
8. Gary Schippang—206, T, West Chester State
9. Mike Slaton—232, DB, South Dakota
10. Joe Cormier—259, WR, Southern California
11. John Armstrong—286, DB, Richmond
12. Jesse Solomon—318, LB, Florida State

New England Patriots

1. Reggie Dupard—26, RB, Southern Methodist
2. Mike Ruth—42, NT, Boston College, from Seattle
   Vencie Glenn—54, DB, Indiana State
3. Forfeited
4. Scott Gieselman—109, TE, Boston College
5. Greg Robinson—137, G, Cal State-Sacramento
6. Choice to Tampa Bay
7. Ray McDonald—187, WR, Florida, from San Francisco
   Brent Williams—192, DE, Toledo
8. Greg Baty—220, TE, Stanford
9. George Colton—248, G, Maryland
10. Cletis Jones—276, RB, Florida State
11. Gene Thomas—304, WR, Pacific
12. Don McAulay—332, K, Syracuse

New Orleans Saints

1. Choice to Indianapolis
   Jim Dombrowski—6, T, Virginia, from Indianapolis
2. Dalton Hilliard—31, RB, Louisiana State
3. Rueben Mayes—57, RB, Washington State, from Tampa Bay
   Pat Swilling—60, LB, Georgia Tech, from Indianapolis
   Barry Word—62, RB, Virginia
4. Kelvin Edwards—88, WR, Liberty Baptist
5. Reggie Sutton—115, DB, Miami
6. Robert Thompson—142, WR, Youngstown State
7. Gill Fenerty—173, RB, Holy Cross
8. Filipo Mokofisi—200, LB, Utah
9. Merlon Jones—226, LB, Florida A&M
10. Jon Dumbauld—253, DE, Kentucky
11. Pat Swoopes—284, NT, Mississippi State
12. Sebastian Brown—311, WR, Bethune-Cookman

New York Giants

1. Eric Dorsey—19, DE, Notre Dame
2. Mark Collins—44, DB, Cal State-Fullerton, from San Diego through Minnesota
   Erik Howard—46, NT, Washington State
   Pepper Johnson—51, LB, Ohio State, from Denver
   Greg Lasker—53, DB, Arkansas, from Los Angeles Raiders through Minnesota
3. John Washington—73, DE, Oklahoma State
4. Choice to Los Angeles Raiders
5. Vince Warren—130, WR, San Diego State
6. Ron Brown—139, WR, Colorado, from Tampa Bay through Denver
   Solomon Miller—157, WR, Utah State
7. Jon Francis—184, RB, Boise State
8. Steve Cisowski—214, T, Santa Clara
9. Jim Luebbers—241, DE, Iowa State
10. Jerry Kimmel—268, LB, Syracuse
11. Len Lynch—295, G, Maryland
12. Choice to Philadelphia

New York Jets

1. Mike Haight—22, T, Iowa
2. Doug Williams—49, T, Texas A&M
3. Tim Crawford—79, LB, Texas Tech
4. Rogers Alexander—105, LB, Penn State
5. Ron Hadley—132, LB, Washington
6. Choice to San Francisco
7. Bob White—189, T, Rhode Island
8. Robert Ducksworth—215, DB, Southern Mississippi
9. Nuu Faaola—245, RB, Hawaii
10. Carl Carr—272, LB, North Carolina
11. Vince Amoia—299, RB, Arizona State
12. Sal Cesario—328, T, Cal Poly-San Luis Obispo

Philadelphia Eagles

1. Keith Byars—10, RB, Ohio State
2. Anthony Toney—37, RB, Texas A&M
   Alonzo Johnson—48, LB, Florida, from Washington through Los Angeles Raiders
3. Choice to San Francisco
4. Choice to San Diego
   Matt Darwin—106, C, Texas A&M, from Los Angeles Rams
5. Ray Criswell—121, P, Florida
   Dan McMillen—128, DE, Colorado, from Washington through Atlanta
6. Bob Landsee—149, C, Wisconsin
7. Corn Redick—169, WR, Cal State-Fullerton, from Atlanta
   Byron Lee—176, LB, Ohio State
8. Choice to San Francisco
   Seth Joyner—208, LB, Texas-El Paso, from Cleveland
9. Clyde Simmons—233, DE, Western Carolina
10. Junior Tautalatasi—261, RB, Washington State
11. Steve Bogdalek—288, G, Michigan State
12. Reggie Singletary—315, DE, North Carolina State
   Bobby Howard—325, RB, Indiana, from New York Giants

Pittsburgh Steelers

1. John Rienstra—9, G, Temple
2. Gerald Williams—36, DE, Auburn
3. Walter Brister—67, QB, Northeast Louisiana
4. Bill Callahan—94, DB, Pittsburgh
5. Erroll Tucker—122, DB, Utah
   Brent Jones—135, TE, Santa Clara, from Los Angeles Raiders
6. Domingo Bryant—148, DB, Texas A&M
7. Rodney Carter—175, RB, Purdue
8. Cap Boso—207, TE, Illinois
9. Anthony Henton—234, LB, Troy State
10. Warren Seitz—260, WR, Missouri
11. Larry Station—287, LB, Iowa
12. Mike Williams—314, LB, Tulsa

St. Louis Cardinals

1. Anthony Bell—5, LB, Michigan State
2. John Lee—32, K, UCLA
3. Gene Chilton—59, C, Texas
4. Carl Carter—89, DB, Texas Tech
5. Jeff Tupper—116, DE, Oklahoma
6. Choice to Green Bay
7. Eric Swanson—170, WR, Tennessee
8. Ray Brown—201, G, Arkansas State
9. Kent Kafentzis—227, DB, Hawaii
10. Vai Sikahema—254, RB, Brigham Young
   Wes Smith—255, WR, East Texas State, from Indianapolis
11. Wayne Dillard—281, LB, Alcorn State
12. Kent Austin—312, QB, Mississippi

San Diego Chargers

1. Leslie O'Neal—8, DE, Oklahoma State, from Minnesota
   James FitzPatrick—13, T, Southern California
2. Choice to New York Giants through Minnesota
3. Terry Unrein—66, DE, Colorado State, from Minnesota
   Jeff Walker—70, T, Memphis State
4. Ty Allert—95, LB, Texas, from Philadelphia
   Tommy Taylor—97, LB, UCLA
5. Doug Landry—118, LB, Louisiana Tech, from Kansas City
   Choice to Indianapolis
   Donald Brown—129, DB, Maryland, from San Francisco
   Matt Johnson—133, DB, Southern California, from Los Angeles Rams
6. Curt Pardridge—155, WR, Northern Illinois
7. Fred Smalls—182, LB, West Virginia
8. Mike Perrino—209, T, Notre Dame
9. Mike Zordich—235, DB, Penn State
10. Choice to Indianapolis
11. Chuck Sanders—293, RB, Slippery Rock
   Drew Smetana—298, T, Oregon, from San Francisco
12. Jeff Sprowls—320, DB, Brigham Young
   Mike Travis—333, DB, Georgia Tech, from Chicago

San Francisco 49ers

1. Choice to Dallas
2. Larry Roberts—39, DE, Alabama, from Detroit
   Choice to Washington
3. Tom Rathman—56, RB, Nebraska, from Buffalo
   Tim McKyer—64, DB, Texas-Arlington, from Philadelphia
   John Taylor—76, WR, Delaware State
4. Charles Haley—96, LB, James Madison, from Cleveland through Los Angeles Rams
   Steve Wallace—101, T, Auburn, from Washington through Los Angeles Rams
   Kevin Fagan—102, DT, Miami
5. Choice to San Diego
   Patrick Miller—131, LB, Florida, from Dallas
6. Choice to Washington
   Don Griffin—162, DB, Middle Tennessee State, from New York Jets
7. Choice to New England
8. Jim Popp—203, TE, Vanderbilt, from Philadelphia
   Choice exercised in 1985 Supplemental Draft for Roosevelt Snipes, RB, Florida State
9. Tony Cherry—240, RB, Oregon
10. Elliston Stinson—267, WR, Rice
   Harold Hallman—270, LB, Auburn, from Washington
11. Choice to San Diego
12. Choice to Tampa Bay

Seattle Seahawks

1. John L. Williams—15, RB, Florida
2. Choice to New England
3. Patrick Hunter—68, DB, Nevada-Reno
4. Choice to Cincinnati
5. Bobby Joe Edmonds—126, WR, Arkansas
6. Eddie Anderson—153, DB, Fort Valley State
7. Choice to Buffalo
   Paul Miles—181, RB, Nebraska, from Cleveland
8. Alonzo Mitz—211, DE, Florida
9. Mike Black—237, T, Cal State-Sacramento
10. Don Fairbanks—264, DE, Colorado
11. David Norrie—291, QB, UCLA
12. John McVeigh—321, LB, Miami

Tampa Bay Buccaneers

1. Bo Jackson—1, RB, Auburn
   Roderick Jones—25, DB, Southern Methodist, from Miami
2. Jackie Walker—28, LB, Jackson State
   Kevin Murphy—40, LB, Oklahoma, from Minnesota through Miami
3. Choice to New Orleans
4. Craig Swoope—83, DB, Illinois
5. J.D. Maarleveld—112, T, Maryland
6. Choice to New York Giants through Denver
   Kevin Walker—165, DB, East Carolina, from New England
7. Choice to Buffalo
8. Choice to Los Angeles Rams
9. Tommy Barnhardt—223, P, North Carolina
10. Benton Reed—250, DE, Mississippi
11. Mark Drenth—279, T, Purdue
12. Clay Miller—306, G, Michigan
   Mike Crawford—324, RB, Arizona State, from San Francisco

Washington Redskins

1. Choice to Atlanta
2. Markus Koch—30, DE, Boise State, from Atlanta
   Walter Murray—45, WR, Hawaii, from San Francisco
   Choice to Philadelphia through Los Angeles Raiders
3. Alvin Walton—75, DB, Kansas
4. Choice to San Francisco through Los Angeles Rams
5. Ravin Caldwell—113, LB, Arkansas, from Atlanta
   Choice to Philadelphia through Atlanta
6. Mark Rypien—146, QB, Washington State, from Kansas City
   Jim Huddleston—156, G, Virginia, from San Francisco
   Choice to Atlanta
7. Rick Badanjek—186, RB, Maryland
8. Kurt Gouveia—213, LB, Brigham Young
9. Wayne Asberry—239, DB, Texas A&M
10. Choice to San Francisco
11. Kenny Fells—297, RB, Henderson State
12. Eric Yarber—323, WR, Idaho

Look for in 1986

Things that could happen in 1986:

• Walter Payton, Chicago, needs 662 combined yards to become the first player in NFL history to reach 20,000 yards via rushing, receiving, and returns. He starts the season with 19,338 combined yards; an NFL-record 14,860 by rushing, 3,939 on receptions, and 539 on kick-off returns.

• With 109 career touchdowns, Payton needs five to pass Lenny Moore (113) for third place on the all-time NFL list. Jim Brown holds the record of 126 and John Riggins stands second with 116.

• Of Payton's total, 98 touchdowns have come by rushing; he needs nine more to break Brown's career record for rushing touchdowns (106). Riggins is in second place with 104 rushing touchdowns.

• Marcus Allen, Los Angeles Raiders, needs to rush for 100-or-more yards in his first game of 1986 to break the NFL record for consecutive 100-yard rushing games. The record of nine was established last season by Payton, and was tied by Allen in his final nine games of 1985.

• Tony Dorsett, Dallas, needs 405 yards rushing to move past O.J. Simpson into fourth place in NFL history. Dorsett, who has had eight 1,000-yard rushing seasons (one short of Payton's record), has gained 10,832 yards; Simpson had 11,236.

• Earl Campbell, New Orleans, needs 593 yards rushing to become the seventh NFL player to accumulate 10,000 yards rushing. He starts the season with 9,407.

• Ottis Anderson, St. Louis, needs 239 rushing yards to crack the NFL's all-time top 10 in that category. Anderson starts the season in eleventh place with 7,843 yards; Larry Csonka stands tenth with 8,081.

• Dan Marino, Miami, needs to throw 73 passes to reach the 1,500 mark for his career, the minimum number needed for inclusion in career rankings. At that time, he will likely become the NFL's all-time passing leader. He starts the season with a career rating of 96.4, comfortably ahead of the current qualifying leader, Joe Montana (92.4).

• Dan Fouts, San Diego, needs 161 completions to become only the second NFL player to complete 3,000 passes. He starts the season with 2,839; the record of 3,686 is held by Fran Tarkenton.

• Fouts also needs 2,508 passing yards to become the third player to pass for 40,000 yards in his career. Fran Tarkenton (47,003) and Johnny Unitas (40,239) are the others.

• If Fouts passes for more than 3,000 yards, it will be his sixth such season, breaking a tie with Sonny Jurgensen for most 3,000-yard seasons in an NFL career.

• Charlie Joiner, San Diego, needs 129 yards on receptions to break Don Maynard's all-time record of 11,834 yards. Joiner, entering his eighteenth season, has gained 11,706 yards on a record 716 receptions.

• Steve Largent, Seattle, needs to catch at least one pass in his next five games in order to break Harold Carmichael's league record of 127 consecutive regular-season games catching at least one pass. Largent's streak is at 123 entering the 1986 season.

• Largent starts the 1986 season with 624 career receptions. When he accumulates 26 more, he would pass Raymond Berry (631), Maynard (633), and Charley Taylor (649) and move into second place on the all-time list behind Joiner.

• Largent needs one more season of 1,000-or-more yards on receptions to break the record of seven such seasons, which he currently shares with Lance Alworth.

• James Lofton, Green Bay, needs 1,184 yards on receptions to reach the 10,000-yard mark for his career, a level reached by only five players in NFL history: Maynard, Joiner, Harold Jackson, Alworth, and Largent.

• Ozzie Newsome, Cleveland, needs 40 receptions to crack the NFL's all-time top 10 in that category. He starts the season with 502 receptions; Alworth stands in tenth place with 542.

• John Stallworth, Pittsburgh, has a team record 462 receptions, 38 from becoming the fifteenth NFL player to catch 500 passes in a career.

• Donnie Shell, Pittsburgh, the leading active interceptor in the NFL, needs three interceptions to become the twenty-first player in the NFL to collect 50.

• Mark Moseley, Washington, needs 12 field goals to become the fourth kicker to accumulate 300 career field goals. The others: Jan Stenerud (373), George Blanda (335), and Jim Turner (304).

• Ray Wersching, San Francisco, and Pat Leahy, New York Jets, are within reach of 1,000-career points, a total achieved by only 11 players in NFL history. Wersching starts 1986 with 923 points, Leahy has 901.

• Rohn Stark, Indianapolis, needs to average approximately 45 yards per punt to maintain his status as the record holder for career punting average. Stark begins 1986 with an average of 45.16 yards per punt. Sammy Baugh stands second at 45.10.

• Dave Jennings, New York Jets, needs 79 punts to break the NFL record of 1,083, held by John James. Jennings starts 1986 with 1,005 punts, trailing only James and Jerrel Wilson (1,072).

• Henry Ellard, Los Angeles Rams, needs to average nearly 11 yards per punt return to maintain his status as the record holder for career punt-return average. Ellard began the season with an average of 13.51 yards per return. George McAfee stands second at 12.78.

• Chuck Noll, Pittsburgh, becomes the fourth head coach in NFL history to lead a team for 18 consecutive seasons, the others being Curly Lambeau (31), Tom Landry (27), and Steve Owen (23).

• The Cowboys can extend their NFL record of consecutive winning seasons to 21. Dallas's current 20 straight winning seasons is the longest active streak in pro team sports and third longest all-time behind the New York Yankees' 39 straight (1926-64) and the Montreal Canadians' 32 in a row (1951-52 to 1982-83).

THE AFC

Buffalo Bills
Cincinnati Bengals
Cleveland Browns
Denver Broncos
Houston Oilers
Indianapolis Colts
Kansas City Chiefs
Los Angeles Raiders
Miami Dolphins
New England Patriots
New York Jets
Pittsburgh Steelers
San Diego Chargers
Seattle Seahawks

American Football Conference
Eastern Division

Team Colors: Royal Blue, Scarlet Red, and White

One Bills Drive
Orchard Park, New York 14127
Telephone: (716) 648-1800

Club Officials

President: Ralph C. Wilson, Jr.
Executive Vice President: David N. Olsen
General Manager and Vice President-Administration: Bill Polian
Assistant General Manager: Bill Munson
Treasurer: Jeffery Littmann
Vice President-Head Coach: Hank Bullough
Vice President-Player Personnel: Norm Pollom
Vice President-Media Relations: L. Budd Thalman
Ticket Director: Jim Cipriano
Administrative Assistant to Head Coach: Jim Valek
Assistant Ticket Director: Adam Ziccardi
Assistant Media Relations Director: Dave Senko
Assistant Director of Player Personnel: Bob Ferguson
Trainers: Ed Abramoski, Bud Carpenter
Equipment Manager: Dave Hojnowski
Assistant Equipment Manager: Randy Ribbeck
Strength and Conditioning Coordinator: Rusty Jones

Stadium: Rich Stadium • **Capacity:** 80,290
One Bills Drive
Orchard Park, New York 14127

Playing Surface: AstroTurf

Training Camp: Fredonia State University
Fredonia, New York 14063

1986 SCHEDULE

Preseason

Aug. 9	at Cleveland	7:30
Aug. 16	at Houston	8:00
Aug. 23	at Kansas City	7:30
Aug. 30	vs. Chicago at South Bend, Ind.	1:30

Regular Season

Sept. 7	**New York Jets**	4:00
Sept. 14	at Cincinnati	1:00
Sept. 21	**St. Louis**	1:00
Sept. 28	**Kansas City**	1:00
Oct. 5	at New York Jets	4:00
Oct. 12	at Miami	1:00
Oct. 19	**Indianapolis**	1:00
Oct. 26	**New England**	1:00
Nov. 2	at Tampa Bay	1:00
Nov. 9	**Pittsburgh**	1:00
Nov. 16	**Miami**	1:00
Nov. 23	at New England	1:00
Nov. 30	at Kansas City	12:00
Dec. 7	**Cleveland**	1:00
Dec. 14	at Indianapolis	1:00
Dec. 21	at Houston	12:00

BILLS COACHING HISTORY

(156-217-8)

1960-61	Buster Ramsey	11-16-1
1962-65	Lou Saban	38-18-3
1966-68	Joe Collier*	13-17-1
1968	Harvey Johnson	1-10-1
1969-70	John Rauch	7-20-1
1971	Harvey Johnson	1-13-0
1972-76	Lou Saban**	32-29-1
1976-77	Jim Ringo	3-20-0
1978-82	Chuck Knox	38-38-0
1983-84	Kay Stephenson***	10-26-0
1985	Hank Bullough	2-10-0

*Released after two games in 1968
**Resigned after five games in 1976
***Released after four games in 1985

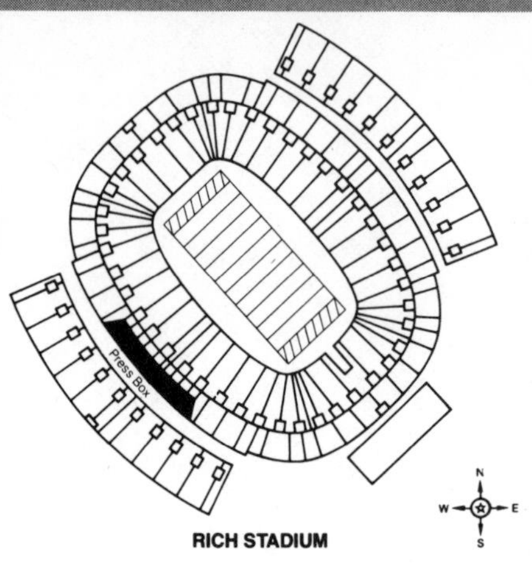

RICH STADIUM

RECORD HOLDERS

Individual Records—Career

Category	Name	Performance
Rushing (Yds.)	O.J. Simpson, 1969-1977	10,183
Passing (Yds.)	Joe Ferguson, 1973-1984	27,590
Passing (TDs)	Joe Ferguson, 1973-1984	181
Receiving (No.)	Elbert Dubenion, 1960-67	296
Receiving (Yds.)	Elbert Dubenion, 1960-67	5,304
Interceptions	George (Butch) Byrd, 1964-1970	40
Punting (Avg.)	Paul Maguire, 1964-1970	42.1
Punt Return (Avg.)	Keith Moody, 1976-79	10.5
Kickoff Return (Avg.)	Wallace Francis, 1973-74	27.2
Field Goals	John Leypoldt, 1971-76	74
Touchdowns (Tot.)	O.J. Simpson, 1969-1977	70
Points	O.J. Simpson, 1969-1977	420

Individual Records—Single Season

Category	Name	Performance
Rushing (Yds.)	O.J. Simpson, 1973	2,003
Passing (Yds.)	Joe Ferguson, 1981	3,652
Passing (TDs)	Joe Ferguson, 1983	26
Receiving (No.)	Frank Lewis, 1981	70
Receiving (Yds.)	Frank Lewis, 1981	1,244
Interceptions	Billy Atkins, 1961	10
	Tom Janik, 1967	10
Punting (Avg.)	Billy Atkins, 1961	44.5
Punt Return (Avg.)	Keith Moody, 1977	13.1
Kickoff Return (Avg.)	Ed Rutkowski, 1963	30.2
Field Goals	Pete Gogolak, 1965	28
Touchdowns (Tot.)	O.J. Simpson, 1975	23
Points	O.J. Simpson, 1975	138

Individual Records—Single Game

Category	Name	Performance
Rushing (Yds.)	O.J. Simpson, 11-25-76	273
Passing (Yds.)	Joe Ferguson, 10-9-83	419
Passing (TDs)	Joe Ferguson, 9-23-79	5
	Joe Ferguson, 10-9-83	5
Receiving (No.)	Greg Bell, 9-8-85	13
Receiving (Yds.)	Jerry Butler, 9-23-79	255
Interceptions	Many times	3
	Last time by Jeff Nixon, 9-7-80	
Field Goals	Pete Gogolak, 12-5-65	5
Touchdowns (Tot.)	Cookie Gilchrist, 12-8-63	5
Points	Cookie Gilchrist, 12-8-63	30

1985 TEAM STATISTICS

	Buffalo	Opp.
Total First Downs	256	320
Rushing	86	142
Passing	151	159
Penalty	19	19
Third Down: Made/Att.	68/208	100/226
Fourth Down: Made/Att.	7/17	8/14
Total Net Yards	4595	5540
Avg. Per Game	287.2	346.3
Total Plays	971	1071
Avg. Per Play	4.7	5.2
Net Yards Rushing	1611	2462
Avg. Per Game	100.7	153.9
Total Rushes	412	569
Net Yards Passing	2984	3078
Avg. Per Game	186.5	192.4
Tackled/Yards Lost	42/347	25/223
Gross Yards	3331	3301
Att./Completions	517/263	477/265
Completion Pct.	50.9	55.6
Had Intercepted	31	20
Punts/Avg.	92/41.5	81/40.5
Net Punting Avg.	35.9	34.0
Penalties/Yards Lost	132/965	107/870
Fumbles/Ball Lost	36/21	36/15
Touchdowns	23	50
Rushing	13	20
Passing	9	24
Returns	1	6
Avg. Time of Possession	28:21	31:39

1985 TEAM RECORD

Preseason (0-3-1)

Date	Buffalo		Opponents
8/10	10	Detroit (OT)	10
8/17	17	Miami	27
8/24	28	*Cleveland	31
8/31	14	Chicago	45
	69		113

Regular Season (2-14)

Date	Buffalo		Opp.	Att.
9/8	9	*San Diego	14	67,597
9/15	3	N.Y. Jets	42	63,449
9/22	14	*New England	17	40,334
9/29	20	*Minnesota	27	45,667
10/6	17	Indianapolis	49	60,003
10/13	3	New England	14	40,462
10/20	21	*Indianapolis	9	28,430
10/27	17	Philadelphia	21	60,987
11/3	17	*Cincinnati	23	25,640
11/10	20	*Houston	0	21,881
11/17	7	Cleveland	17	44,915
11/24	14	*Miami	23	50,474
12/1	7	San Diego	40	45,487
12/8	7	*N.Y. Jets	27	23,122
12/15	24	Pittsburgh	30	35,953
12/22	0	Miami	28	64,811

*Home Game (OT) Overtime

Score by Periods

Buffalo	58	63	41	38	0	—	200
Opponents	51	144	78	108	0	—	381

Attendance

Home 303,145 Away 416,067 Total 719,212
Single game home record, 79,933 (10-3-83)
Single season home record, 601,712 (1981)

1985 INDIVIDUAL STATISTICS

Rushing

Rushing	Att.	Yds.	Avg.	LG	TD
Bell	223	883	4.0	77t	8
Cribbs	122	399	3.3	16	1
Mathison	27	231	8.6	22	1
Steels, S.D.-Buff.	10	38	3.8	22	0
Steels, Buff.	4	26	6.5	22	0
Pruitt	7	24	3.4	7	0
Moore	15	23	1.5	4	1
Ferragamo	8	15	1.9	5	1
Hutchison	2	11	5.5	7	0
B. Smith	1	0	0.0	0	0
Reed	3	−1	−0.3	14t	1
Bills	412	1611	3.9	77t	13
Opponents	569	2462	4.3	69	20

Passing

Passing	Att.	Comp.	Pct.	Yds.	TD	Int.	Tkld.	Rate
Ferragamo	287	149	51.9	1677	5	17	19/135	50.8
Mathison	228	113	49.6	1635	4	14	22/203	53.5
Reich	1	1	100.0	19	0	0	0/0	118.8
Bell	1	0	0.0	0	0	0	0/0	39.6
Kidd	0	0	—	0	0	0	1/9	0.0
Bills	517	263	50.9	3331	9	31	42/347	52.1
Opponents	477	265	55.6	3301	24	20	25/223	76.5

Receiving

Receiving	No.	Yds.	Avg.	LG	TD
Bell	58	576	9.9	49	1
Reed	48	637	13.3	32	4
Butler	41	770	18.8	60t	2
Ramson	37	369	10.0	43	1
Burkett	21	371	17.7	38	0
Cribbs	18	142	7.9	23	0
Richardson	12	201	16.8	27	0
Metzelaars	12	80	6.7	13	1
Moore	7	44	6.3	9	0
Brookins	3	71	23.7	46	0
Norris	2	30	15.0	18	0
Steels	2	9	4.5	6	0
Teal	1	24	24.0	24	0
V. Williams	1	7	7.0	7	0
Bills	263	3331	12.7	60t	9
Opponents	265	3301	12.5	96t	24

Interceptions

Interceptions	No.	Yds.	Avg.	LG	TD
Romes	7	56	8.0	21	0
Bellinger	2	64	32.0	41	0
D. Wilson	2	23	11.5	23	0
Hill	2	17	8.5	17	0
Bayless	2	10	5.0	10	0
Burroughs	2	7	3.5	7	0
Haslett	1	40	40.0	40	0
Frazier	1	8	8.0	8	0
Johnson	1	0	0.0	0	0
Bills	20	225	11.3	41	0
Opponents	31	418	13.5	75t	4

Punting

Punting	No.	Yds.	Avg.	In 20	LG
Kidd	92	3818	41.5	33	67
Bills	92	3818	41.5	33	67
Opponents	81	3284	40.5	21	64

Punt Returns

Punt Returns	No.	FC	Yds.	Avg.	LG	TD
D. Wilson	16	5	161	10.1	30	0
Hill	16	1	120	7.5	25	0
Reed	5	0	12	2.4	5	0
E. Wilson	1	0	0	0.0	0	0
Steels, S.D.-Buff.	0	1	0	—	0	0
Bills	38	6	293	7.7	30	0
Opponents	49	15	438	8.9	85t	1

Kickoff Returns

Kickoff Returns	No.	Yds.	Avg.	LG	TD
D. Wilson	22	465	21.1	37	0
Steels, S.D.-Buff.	30	561	18.7	54	0
Steels, Buff.	20	338	16.9	35	0
Hutchison	12	239	19.9	36	0
Brookins	6	152	25.3	39	0
Richardson	3	69	23.0	31	0
Moore	3	31	10.3	15	0
Teal	1	20	20.0	20	0
V. Williams	1	20	20.0	20	0
Bills	68	1334	19.6	39	0
Opponents	41	798	19.5	53	0

Scoring

Scoring	TD R	TD P	TD Rt	PAT	FG	Saf	TP
Norwood	0	0	0	23/23	13/17	0	62
Bell	8	1	0	0/0	0/0	0	54
Reed	1	4	0	0/0	0/0	0	30
Butler	0	2	0	0/0	0/0	0	12
Cribbs	1	0	0	0/0	0/0	0	6
Ferragamo	1	0	0	0/0	0/0	0	6
Mathison	1	0	0	0/0	0/0	0	6
Metzelaars	0	1	0	0/0	0/0	0	6
Moore	1	0	0	0/0	0/0	0	6
Ramson	0	1	0	0/0	0/0	0	6
D. Wilson	0	0	1	0/0	0/0	0	6
Bills	13	9	1	23/23	13/17	0	200
Opponents	20	24	6	45/50	12/15	0	381

FIRST-ROUND SELECTIONS

(If club had no first-round selection, first player drafted is listed with round in parentheses.)

Year	Player, College, Position
1960	Richie Lucas, Penn State, QB
1961	Ken Rice, Auburn, T
1962	Ernie Davis, Syracuse, RB
1963	Dave Behrman, Michigan State, C
1964	Carl Eller, Minnesota, DE
1965	Jim Davidson, Ohio State, T
1966	Mike Dennis, Mississippi, RB
1967	John Pitts, Arizona State, S
1968	Haven Moses, San Diego State, WR
1969	O.J. Simpson, Southern California, RB
1970	Al Cowlings, Southern California, DE
1971	J. D. Hill, Arizona State, WR
1972	Walt Patulski, Notre Dame, DE
1973	Paul Seymour, Michigan, TE
	Joe DeLamielleure, Michigan State, G
1974	Reuben Gant, Oklahoma State, TE
1975	Tom Ruud, Nebraska, LB
1976	Mario Clark, Oregon, DB
1977	Phil Dokes, Oklahoma State, DT
1978	Terry Miller, Oklahoma State, RB
1979	Tom Cousineau, Ohio State, LB
	Jerry Butler, Clemson, WR
1980	Jim Ritcher, North Carolina State, C
1981	Booker Moore, Penn State, RB
1982	Perry Tuttle, Clemson, WR
1983	Tony Hunter, Notre Dame, TE
	Jim Kelly, Miami, QB
1984	Greg Bell, Notre Dame, RB
1985	Bruce Smith, Virginia Tech, DE
	Derrick Burroughs, Memphis State, DB
1986	Ronnie Harmon, Iowa, RB
	Will Wolford, Vanderbilt, T

BUFFALO BILLS 1986 VETERAN ROSTER

No.	Name	Pos.	Ht.	Wt.	Birth-date	NFL Exp.	College	Hometown	How Acq.	'85 Games/ Starts
43	Bayless, Martin	S	6-2	195	10/11/62	3	Bowling Green	Dayton, Ohio	W(StL)-'84	12/11
28	Bell, Greg	RB	5-10	210	8/1/62	3	Notre Dame	Columbus, Ohio	D1-'84	16/15
36	Bellinger, Rodney	CB	5-8	189	6/4/62	3	Miami	Coral Gables, Fla.	D3a-'84	16/0
81	Brookins, Mitchell	WR	5-11	196	12/10/60	3	Illinois	Chicago, Ill.	D4-'84	5/1
85	Burkett, Chris	WR	6-4	198	8/21/62	2	Jackson State	Collins, Miss.	D2b-'85	16/1
29	Burroughs, Derrick	CB	6-1	180	5/18/62	2	Memphis State	Mobile, Ala.	D1b-'85	14/8
80	Butler, Jerry	WR	6-0	178	10/2/57	7	Clemson	Ware Shoals, S.C.	D1b-'79	16/13
67	Caldwell, Darryl	T	6-5	252	2/2/60	2	Tennessee State	Birmingham, Ala.	FA-'86	0*
69	Christy, Greg	G	6-4	279	4/29/62	2	Pittsburgh	Freeport, Pa.	FA-'85	7/0
20	Cribbs, Joe	RB	5-11	193	1/5/58	6	Auburn	Sulligent, Ala.	D2a-'80	10/5
63	†Cross, Justin	T	6-6	265	4/29/59	5	Western State, Colo.	Portsmouth, N.H.	D10-'81	3/2
59	David, Stan	LB	6-3	210	2/17/62	2	Texas Tech	Tucumcari, N.M.	D7-'84	0*
70	Devlin, Joe	T	6-5	267	2/23/54	10	Iowa	Frazer, Pa.	D2b-'76	16/16
58	Dickerson, Anthony	LB	6-2	222	6/9/57	7	Southern Methodist	Houston, Tex.	T(Dall)-'85	16/0
52	Frazier, Guy	LB	6-2	217	7/20/59	6	Wyoming	Detroit, Mich.	W(NE)-'85	16/16
22	Freeman, Steve	S	5-11	185	5/8/53	12	Mississippi State	Memphis, Tenn.	W(Cin)-'85	16/16
99	Garner, Hal	LB	6-5	220	1/18/62	2	Utah State	Logan, Utah	D3b-'85	13/0
53	Grant, Will	C	6-3	264	3/7/54	9	Kentucky	Milton, Mass.	D10-'78	16/15
55	Haslett, Jim	LB	6-3	228	12/9/57	8	Indiana, Pa.	Pittsburgh, Pa.	D2b-'79	16/16
71	Hellestrae, Dale	T	6-5	261	7/11/62	2	Southern Methodist	Scottsdale, Ariz.	D4b-'85	4/0
25	Hill, Rod	CB	6-0	188	3/14/59	4	Kentucky State	Detroit, Mich.	T(Dall)-'85	10/5
30	Hutchison, Anthony	RB	5-10	186	2/4/61	4	Texas Tech	Converse, Tex.	W(Chi)-'85	5/0
48	Johnson, Lawrence	CB	5-11	202	9/11/57	7	Wisconsin	Gary, Ind.	T(Clev)-'84	16/3
72	Jones, Ken	T	6-5	279	12/1/52	11	Arkansas State	Bridgeton, Mo.	D2a-'76	16/14
4	Kidd, John	P	6-3	208	8/22/61	3	Northwestern	Findlay, Ohio	D5-'84	16/0
90	Maidlow, Steve	LB	6-2	238	6/6/60	4	Michigan State	East Lansing, Mich.	W(Cin)-'85	16/2
54	Marve, Eugene	LB	6-2	240	8/14/56	5	Saginaw Valley State	Flint, Mich.	D3-'82	14/14
7	Mathison, Bruce	QB	6-3	205	4/25/59	4	Nebraska	Superior, Wis.	FA-'85	10/7
95	McNanie, Sean	DE	6-5	265	9/9/61	3	San Diego State	Mundelein, Ill.	D3b-'84	16/0
88	Metzelaars, Pete	TE	6-7	243	5/24/60	5	Wabash	Portage, Mich.	T(Sea)-'85	16/8
34	Moore, Booker	RB	5-11	222	6/23/59	5	Penn State	Flint, Mich.	D1-'82	16/6
11	Norwood, Scott	K	6-0	205	7/17/60	2	James Madison	Alexandria, Va.	FA-'85	16/0
10	Osiecki, Sandy	QB	6-5	205	5/18/60	2	Arizona State	Ansonia, Calif.	FA-'86	0*
23	Perryman, Jim	S	6-0	175	12/23/60	2	Millikin	Pittsburgh, Pa.	FA-'85	11/0
79	Prater, Dean	DE	6-4	256	9/28/58	5	Oklahoma State	Wichita Falls, Tex.	FA-'85	16/0
87	†Ramson, Eason	TE	6-2	234	4/30/56	8	Washington State	Sacramento, Calif.	W(Hou)-'85	16/12
83	Reed, Andre	WR	6-0	186	1/29/65	2	Kutztown State	Allentown, Pa.	D4a-'85	16/15
14	Reich, Frank	QB	6-3	208	12/4/61	2	Maryland	Lebanon, Pa.	D3a-'85	1/0
82	Richardson, Eric	WR	6-1	185	4/18/62	2	San Jose State	Novato, Calif.	D2-'84	16/1
40	Riddick, Robb	RB	6-0	195	4/26/57	4	Millersville State	Perkasie, Pa.	D9-'81	0*
51	†Ritcher, Jim	G	6-3	258	5/21/58	7	North Carolina State	Medina, Ohio	D1-'80	16/16
26	Romes, Charles	CB	6-1	188	12/16/54	10	North Carolina Central	Durham, N.C.	D12-'77	16/16
57	Sanford, Lucius	LB	6-2	220	2/14/56	9	Georgia Tech	Atlanta, Ga.	D4-'78	11/11
76	Smerlas, Fred	NT	6-3	268	4/8/57	8	Boston College	Waltham, Mass.	D2a-'79	16/16
78	Smith, Bruce	DE	6-4	279	6/18/63	2	Virginia Tech	Norfolk, Va.	D1-'85	16/13
74	Smith, Don	NT	6-5	262	5/9/57	8	Miami	Tarpon Springs, Fla.	T(Atl)-'85	16/3
45	Steels, Anthony	RB	5-9	200	1/8/59	2	Nebraska	Zaragoza, Spain	W(SD)-'85	15/0*
56	Talley, Darryl	LB	6-4	227	7/10/60	4	West Virginia	Cleveland, Ohio	D2-'83	16/5
86	Teal, Jimmy	WR	5-10	170	8/18/62	2	Texas A&M	Diboll, Tex.	D5-'85	3/0
62	Traynowicz, Mark	G	6-5	272	11/20/62	2	Nebraska	Omaha, Neb.	D2a-'85	14/0
65	Vogler, Tim	G	6-1	267	10/2/56	8	Ohio State	Covington, Ohio	FA-'79	14/14
77	†Williams, Ben	DE	6-3	266	9/1/54	11	Mississippi	Yazoo City, Miss.	D3-'76	16/16
21	Wilson, Don	S	6-2	190	7/21/61	3	North Carolina State	Washington, D.C.	FA-'84	16/5
50	Wilson, Eric	LB	6-1	247	10/17/62	2	Maryland	Charlottesville, Va.	FA-'85	14/0

* Caldwell last active with Buffalo in '83; David and Riddick missed '85 season due to injury; Osiecki last active with Kansas City in '84. Steels played 6 games with San Diego, 9 with Buffalo in '85.

†Option playout; subject to developments.

Also played with Bills in '85—G Joe DeLamielleure (10 games), QB Joe Dufek (active for 1 game, but did not play), QB Vince Ferragamo (10), LB Larry Kubin (2), TE Ulysses Norris (2), RB Mike Pruitt (4), RB Van Williams (2).

COACHING STAFF

Head Coach, Hank Bullough

Pro Career: Begins his first full season as head coach of the Bills. Was appointed to succeed Kay Stephenson on October 1, 1985, and guided the club to a 2-10 mark in the final twelve weeks of the regular season. Bullough has coached in professional football since 1970 when he joined the staff of the late Don McCafferty in Baltimore. He experienced instantaneous success, going to Super Bowl V with the Colts in his first season and defeating the Dallas Cowboys 16-13. Bullough moved to New England in 1973, serving for five seasons as defensive line coach and for two more as assistant head coach and defensive coordinator. Named defensive coordinator and linebacker coach of the Cincinnati Bengals in 1980, Bullough went to Super Bowl XVI with the AFC champion Bengals, who lost to the 49ers in the NFL title game. Named head coach of the USFL Pittsburgh Maulers in 1984, he was to have coached the team in the spring of 1985 only to see the franchise fold before the season began. He was named assistant head coach and defensive coordinator of the Bills in January, 1985. He was an offensive guard for the Green Bay Packers in 1955 and 1958 around a two-year stint in the military. Career record: 2-10.

Background: A college standout at Michigan State where he won All-Big Ten mention as a guard in 1953-54, Bullough played with the Spartans in the 1954 Rose Bowl. An assistant coach at Michigan State from 1959-70, Bullough spent several seasons as the Spartans' defensive coordinator.

Personal: Born January 24, 1934, in Scranton, Pa. Hank and his wife, Lou Ann, live in Orchard Park, N.Y., and have three children— Cheryl, Shane, and Chuck.

Assistant Coaches

Ted Cottrell, defensive line; born June 13, 1947, Chester, Pa., lives in Orchard Park, N.Y. Linebacker Delaware Valley 1966-68. Pro linebacker Atlanta Falcons 1969-70, Winnipeg Blue Bombers (CFL) 1971. College coach: Rutgers 1973-80, 1983. Pro coach: Kansas City Chiefs 1981-82, New Jersey Generals (USFL) 1983-84, first year with Bills.

Joe Daniels, receivers; born November 15, 1942, Bethel Park, Pa., lives in Orchard Park, N.Y. No college or pro playing experience. College coach: East Stroudsburg State 1966, New Hampshire 1967-68, Boston College 1969-76, West Virginia 1977-79, Pittsburgh 1980-82. Pro coach: Cleveland Browns 1983-84, first year with Bills.

Joe Faragalli, tight ends-offensive assignments; born April 18, 1929, Philadelphia, Pa., lives in Orchard Park, N.Y. Offensive-defensive tackle Villanova 1950-53. No pro playing experience. College coach: Villanova 1962-66, Brown 1970-72, Marshall 1973. Pro coach: Winnipeg Blue Bombers (CFL) 1967-69, 1974-76, Edmonton Eskimos (CFL) 1977-80, Saskatchewan Roughriders (CFL) 1980-82 (head coach), Cincinnati Bengals 1984, Houston Oilers 1985, first year with Bills.

Rusty Jones, strength and conditioning; born August 14, 1953, Berwick, Maine, lives in Orchard Park, N.Y. No college or pro playing experience. College coach: Springfield 1978-79. Pro coach: Pittsburgh Maulers (USFL) 1983-84, joined Bills in 1985.

Bob Leahy, quarterbacks-passing game; born September 5, 1946, Passaic, N.J., lives in West Seneca, N.Y. Quarterback Emporia State 1967-69. Pro quarterback Pittsburgh Steelers 1970-71. College coach: Pittsburgh 1973-75, 1977, Washington State 1976, California 1978, Oklahoma State 1979-82. Pro coach: Michigan Panthers (USFL) 1983-84, Minnesota Vikings 1984, joined Bills in 1985.

Dick Moseley, defensive backs, born August 1, 1933, Detroit, Mich., lives in Orchard Park, N.Y. Offensive-defensive back Eastern Michigan 1951-54. No pro playing experience. College coach: Eastern Michigan 1968-70, Wichita State 1971, Minnesota 1972-78, Colorado 1979-82. Pro coach: New Jersey Generals (USFL) 1983, Pittsburgh Maulers (USFL) 1984, joined Bills in 1985.

BUFFALO BILLS 1986 FIRST-YEAR ROSTER

Name	Pos.	Ht.	Wt.	Birth-date	College	Hometown	How Acq.
Albright, Ira (1)	RB	6-0	245	1/2/59	Northeastern State	Dallas, Tex.	FA
Babyar, Chris (1)	G	6-4	264	6/1/62	Illinois	Roselle, Ill.	D10-'85
Bowers, James (1)	S	6-2	195	8/8/62	Memphis State	Memphis, Tenn.	FA
Burton, Leonard	C	6-3	252	6/18/64	South Carolina	Memphis, Tenn.	D3
Bynum, Reggie	WR	6-1	185	2/10/64	Oregon State	San Jose, Calif.	D9
Byrum, Carl	RB	6-0	232	6/29/63	Mississippi Valley St.	Southave, Miss.	D5
Carter, Alex (1)	DE	6-3	255	9/6/63	Tennessee State	Miami, Fla.	FA
Cattage, Ray (1)	DE	6-3	261	9/22/60	Washington	Spokane, Wash.	FA
Christian, Derek	LB	6-2	231	4/30/63	West Virginia	St. Albans, W. Va.	D12b
Cook, Kelly (1)	RB	5-11	210	8/20/62	Oklahoma State	Midwest City, Okla.	FA
Ford, Herman	CB	5-8	170	5/11/61	No college	Norfolk, Va.	FA
Furjanic, Tony	LB	6-1	228	2/26/64	Notre Dame	Chicago, Ill.	D8
Garbarczyk, Tony	NT	6-4	251	1/20/64	Wake Forest	Hauppauge, N.Y.	D11a
Hamby, Mike (1)	NT	6-4	253	11/2/62	Utah State	Lehi, Utah	D6-'85
Harbison, Charles (1)	S	6-1	195	10/27/59	Gardner-Webb	Boiling Springs, N.C.	FA
Harmon, Ronnie	RB	5-11	192	5/7/64	Iowa	Queens, N.Y.	D1a
Harris, Leslie (1)	G	6-2	285	11/7/61	Mississippi State	Water Valley, Miss.	FA
Howard, Joe	WR	5-9	175	12/21/62	Notre Dame	Clinton, Md.	FA
Kelso, Mark (1)	S	5-11	177	7/23/63	William & Mary	Pittsburgh, Pa.	FA
Kidd, Keith (1)	WR	6-1	198	9/10/62	Arkansas	Crossett, Ark.	FA
Knight, Danny (1)	WR	5-11	205	5/30/60	Mississippi State	Natchez, Miss.	FA
Krerowicz, Mark (1)	G	6-3	285	3/1/63	Ohio State	Toledo, Ohio	FA
Lamar, Kevin (1)	C	6-3	268	11/29/61	Stanford	Louisville, N.Y.	FA
Lester, Keith (1)	TE	6-5	245	5/28/62	Murray State	Clearwater, Fla.	FA
McClure, Brian	QB	6-6	233	12/28/63	Bowling Green	Rootstown, Ohio	D12a
Melka, James (1)	LB	6-1	228	1/15/62	Wisconsin	West Allis, Wis.	FA
Moore, Ricky (1)	RB	5-11	234	4/7/63	Alabama	Huntsville, Ala.	FA
Napolitan, Mark (1)	C	6-2	260	2/9/62	Michigan State	Trenton, Mich.	FA
Pike, Mark	LB	6-4	257	12/27/63	Georgia Tech	Villa Hills, Ky.	D7b
Pitts, Ron (1)	S	5-10	175	10/14/62	UCLA	Orchard Park, N.Y.	D7-'85
Ponder, David (1)	NT	6-3	267	6/27/62	Florida State	Cairo, Ga.	FA
Potts, Shawn (1)	WR	5-10	170	9/6/60	Bowling Green	Kalamazoo, Mich.	FA
Rolle, Butch	TE	6-3	242	8/19/64	Michigan State	Hallandale, Fla.	D7c
Seawright, James (1)	LB	6-2	219	3/30/62	South Carolina	Simpsonville, S.C.	D11-'85
Teafatiller, Guy	NT	6-2	260	5/10/64	Illinois	Cerritos, Calif.	D10
Williams, Bob	TE	6-3	231	9/22/63	Penn State	Easton, Pa.	D7a
Wilson, Mark (1)	S	6-0	195	10/8/60	Abilene Christian	Throckmorton, Tex.	FA
Wojciechowski, John	G	6-4	265	7/30/63	Michigan State	Warren, Mich.	FA
Wolford, Will	T	6-5	276	5/18/64	Vanderbilt	Louisville, Ky.	D1b
Witt, Billy	DE	6-5	258	4/15/64	North Alabama	Russellville, Ala.	D11b

The term NFL Rookie is defined as a player who is in his first season of professional football and has not been on the roster of another professional football team for any regular season or postseason games. A Rookie is designated by an "R" on NFL rosters. Players who have been active in another professional football league or players who have NFL experience, including either preseason training camp or being on an active roster for fewer than three regular season or postseason games, are termed NFL First-Year Players. An NFL First-Year Player is designated by a "1" on NFL rosters. Thereafter, a player on an NFL active roster for at least three regular season or postseason games is credited with an additional year of NFL playing experience.

NOTES

Herb Paterra, defensive coordinator-inside linebackers; born November 8, 1940, Glassport, Pa., lives in Orchard Park, N.Y. Offensive guard-linebacker Michigan State 1960-62. Pro linebacker Buffalo Bills 1963-64, Hamilton Tiger-Cats (CFL) 1965-68. College coach: Michigan State 1969-71, Wyoming 1972-74. Pro coach: Charlotte Hornets (WFL) 1975, Hamilton Tiger-Cats (CFL) 1978-79, Los Angeles Rams 1980-82, Edmonton Eskimos (CFL) 1983, Green Bay Packers 1984-85, first year with Bills.

Elijah Pitts, running backs-special teams coordinator; born February 3, 1938, Mayflower, Ark., lives in Orchard Park, N.Y. Running back Philander Smith 1957-60. Pro running back Green Bay Packers 1961-69, 1971, Los Angeles Rams 1970, Chicago Bears 1970, New Orleans Saints 1970. Pro coach: Los Angeles Rams 1974-77, Buffalo Bills 1978-80, Houston Oilers 1981-83, Hamilton Tiger-Cats (CFL) 1984, rejoined Bills in 1985.

Jim Ringo, offensive coordinator-running game-offensive line; born November 21, 1932, Orange, N.J., lives in Orchard Park, N.Y. Center Syracuse 1950-52. Pro center Green Bay Packers 1953-63, Philadelphia Eagles 1964-66. Pro coach: Chicago Bears 1969-71, Buffalo Bills 1972-77 (head coach 1976-77), New England Patriots 1978-81, Los Angeles Rams 1982, New York Jets 1983-84, rejoined Bills in 1985. Member of Pro Football Hall of Fame.

Ardell Wiegandt, outside linebackers; born June 28, 1940, in Lakota, N.D., lives in Orchard Park, N.Y. Guard-linebacker North Dakota State 1963-65. No pro playing experience. College coach: North Dakota State 1969-74, Wyoming 1983-84. Pro coach: Birmingham Americans (WFL) 1975-76, Calgary Stampeders (CFL) 1977-81 (head coach 1980-81), Montreal Concordes (CFL) 1982, joined Bills in 1985.

American Football Conference
Central Division

Team Colors: Black, Orange, and White

200 Riverfront Stadium
Cincinnati, Ohio 45202
Telephone: (513) 621-3550

Club Officials

President: John Sawyer
General Manager: Paul E. Brown
Assistant General Manager: Michael Brown
Business Manager: Bill Connelly
Director of Public Relations: Allan Heim
Director of Player Personnel: Pete Brown
Ticket Manager: Paul Kelly
Consultant: John Murdough
Trainer: Marv Pollins
Equipment Managers: Tom Gray, Al Davis

Stadium: Riverfront Stadium • **Capacity:** 59,754
200 Riverfront Stadium
Cincinnati, Ohio 45202

Playing Surface: AstroTurf

Training Camp: Wilmington College
Wilmington, Ohio 45177

1986 SCHEDULE

Preseason

Aug. 9	at Kansas City	7:30
Aug. 16	at New York Jets	8:00
Aug. 23	**Green Bay**	7:00
Aug. 29	**Detroit**	8:00

Regular Season

Sept. 7	at Kansas City	3:00
Sept. 14	**Buffalo**	1:00
Sept. 18	at Cleveland (Thursday)	8:00
Sept. 28	**Chicago**	1:00
Oct. 5	vs. Green Bay at Milwaukee	12:00
Oct. 13	**Pittsburgh** (Monday)	9:00
Oct. 19	**Houston**	1:00
Oct. 26	at Pittsburgh	1:00
Nov. 2	at Detroit	1:00
Nov. 9	at Houston	12:00
Nov. 16	**Seattle**	1:00
Nov. 23	**Minnesota**	1:00
Nov. 30	at Denver	2:00
Dec. 7	at New England	1:00
Dec. 14	**Cleveland**	1:00
Dec. 21	**New York Jets**	1:00

BENGALS COACHING HISTORY

(130-137-1)

1968-75	Paul Brown	55-59-1
1976-78	Bill Johnson*	18-15-0
1978-79	Homer Rice	8-19-0
1980-83	Forrest Gregg	34-27-0
1984-85	Sam Wyche	15-17-0

*Resigned after five games in 1978

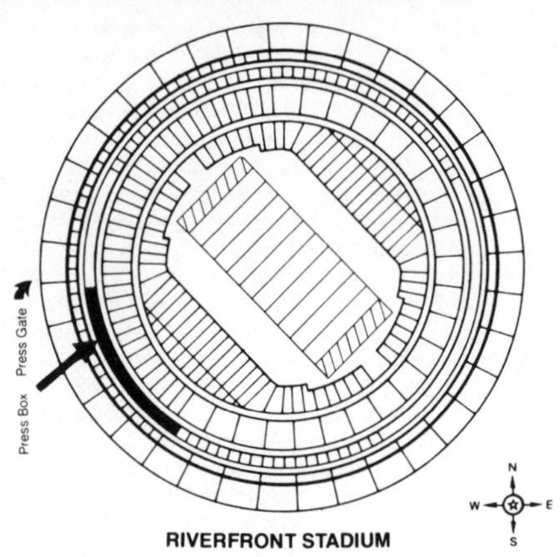

RIVERFRONT STADIUM

RECORD HOLDERS

Individual Records—Career

Category	Name	Performance
Rushing (Yds.)	Pete Johnson, 1977-1983	5,421
Passing (Yds.)	Ken Anderson, 1973-1985	32,667
Passing (TDs)	Ken Anderson, 1973-1985	196
Receiving (No.)	Isaac Curtis, 1973-1984	420
Receiving (Yds.)	Isaac Curtis, 1973-1984	7,106
Interceptions (No.)	Ken Riley, 1969-1983	63
Punting (Avg.)	Dave Lewis, 1970-73	43.9
Punt Return (Avg.)	Mike Martin, 1983-85	12.8
Kickoff Return (Avg.)	Lemar Parrish, 1970-78	24.7
Field Goals	Horst Muhlmann, 1969-1974	120
Touchdowns (Tot.)	Pete Johnson, 1977-1983	70
Points	Horst Muhlmann, 1969-1974	549

Individual Records—Single Season

Category	Name	Performance
Rushing (Yds.)	Pete Johnson, 1981	1,077
Passing (Yds.)	Ken Anderson, 1981	3,754
Passing (TDs)	Ken Anderson, 1981	29
Receiving (No.)	Dan Ross, 1981	71
Receiving (Yds.)	Cris Collinsworth, 1983	1,130
Interceptions	Ken Riley, 1976	9
Punting (Avg.)	Dave Lewis, 1970	46.2
Punt Return (Avg.)	Mike Martin, 1984	15.7
Kickoff Return (Avg.)	Lemar Parrish, 1980	30.2
Field Goals	Horst Muhlmann, 1972	27
Touchdowns (Tot.)	Pete Johnson, 1981	16
Points	Jim Breech, 1985	120

Individual Records—Single Game

Category	Name	Performance
Rushing (Yds.)	Pete Johnson, 12-17-78	160
Passing (Yds.)	Ken Anderson, 11-17-75	447
Passing (TDs)	Many times Last time by Ken Anderson, 11-29-81	4
Receiving (No.)	Many times Last time by Cris Collinsworth, 9-22-85	10
Receiving (Yds.)	Cris Collinsworth, 10-2-83	216
Interceptions	Many times Last time by Ken Riley, 11-28-83	3
Field Goals	Horst Muhlmann, 11-8-70, 9-24-72	5
Touchdowns (Tot.)	Larry Kinnebrew, 10-28-84	4
Points	Larry Kinnebrew, 10-28-84	24

1985 TEAM STATISTICS

	Cincinnati	Opp.
Total First Downs	344	337
Rushing	125	118
Passing	191	194
Penalty	28	25
Third Down: Made/Att.	82/208	85/197
Fourth Down: Made/Att.	9/19	8/12
Total Net Yards	5900	5663
Avg. Per Game	368.8	353.9
Total Plays	1062	1019
Avg. Per Play	5.6	5.6
Net Yards Rushing	2183	1999
Avg. Per Game	136.4	124.9
Total Rushes	503	461
Net Yards Passing	3717	3664
Avg. Per Game	232.3	229.0
Tackled/Yards Lost	41/365	40/334
Gross Yards	4082	3998
Att./Completions	518/302	518/297
Completion Pct.	58.3	57.3
Had Intercepted	13	19
Punts/Avg.	63/40.7	60/41.3
Net Punting Avg.	29.7	34.5
Penalties/Yards Lost	110/795	84/731
Fumbles/Ball Lost	35/16	34/19
Touchdowns	53	51
Rushing	20	23
Passing	31	26
Returns	2	2
Avg. Time of Possession	31:18	28:42

1985 TEAM RECORD

Preseason (2-2)

Date	Cincinnati		Opponents
8/10	27	*Kansas City	35
8/17	24	*N.Y. Jets	20
8/23	17	Detroit	31
8/30	31	Indianapolis	21
	99		107

Regular Season (7-9)

Date	Cincinnati		Opp.	Att.
9/8	24	*Seattle	28	51,625
9/15	27	St. Louis	41	46,321
9/22	41	*San Diego	44	52,270
9/30	37	Pittsburgh	24	59,541
10/6	20	*N.Y. Jets	29	51,785
10/13	35	*N.Y. Giants	30	53,112
10/20	27	Houston	44	35,590
10/27	26	*Pittsburgh	21	55,421
11/3	23	Buffalo	17	25,640
11/10	27	*Cleveland	10	57,293
11/17	6	L.A. Raiders	13	52,501
11/24	6	Cleveland	24	69,439
12/1	45	*Houston	27	46,140
12/8	50	*Dallas	24	56,936
12/15	24	Washington	27	50,544
12/22	23	New England	34	57,953

*Home Game

Score by Periods

Cincinnati	115	106	119	101	0	—	441
Opponents	61	131	107	138	0	—	437

Attendance

Home 424,582 Away 397,529 Total 822,111
Single game home record, 60,284 (10-17-71)
Single season home record, 424,582 (1985)

1985 INDIVIDUAL STATISTICS

Rushing	Att.	Yds.	Avg.	LG	TD
Brooks	192	929	4.8	39	7
Kinnebrew	170	714	4.2	29	9
Alexander	44	156	3.5	18	2
Brown	14	129	9.2	35	0
Jennings	31	92	3.0	19	1
Esiason	33	79	2.4	20	1
Johnson	8	44	5.5	15	0
Schonert	8	39	4.9	17	0
Collinsworth	1	3	3.0	3	0
Anderson	1	0	0.0	0	0
McInally	1	−2	−2.0	−2	0
Bengals	503	2183	4.3	39	20
Opponents	461	1999	4.3	56t	23

Passing	Att.	Comp.	Pct.	Yds.	TD	Int.	Tkld.	Rate
Esiason	431	251	58.2	3443	27	12	32/289	93.2
Schonert	51	33	64.7	460	1	0	6/54	100.1
Anderson	32	16	50.0	170	2	0	2/16	86.7
Brooks	1	1	100.0	8	1	0	0/0	139.6
Kreider	1	1	100.0	1	0	0	0/0	79.2
Collinsworth	1	0	0.0	0	0	1	0/0	0.0
McInally	1	0	0.0	0	0	0	0/0	39.6
Brown	0	0	—	0	0	0	1/6	0.0
Bengals	518	302	58.3	4082	31	13	41/365	93.0
Opponents	518	297	57.3	3998	26	19	40/334	83.5

Receiving	No.	Yds.	Avg.	LG	TD
Collinsworth	65	1125	17.3	71	5
Brooks	55	576	10.5	57t	5
Brown	53	942	17.8	68t	8
Holman	38	479	12.6	64t	7
Kinnebrew	22	187	8.5	29t	1
Alexander	15	110	7.3	19	0
Martin	14	187	13.4	28	0
Jennings	12	101	8.4	24	3
Kreider	10	184	18.4	56	1
Harris	10	123	12.3	22t	1
Ross	6	63	10.5	20	0
Blados	1	4	4.0	4	0
Munoz	1	1	1.0	1	0
Bengals	302	4082	13.5	71	31
Opponents	297	3998	13.5	72t	26

Interceptions	No.	Yds.	Avg.	LG	TD
Griffin	7	116	16.6	33	1
Jackson	6	100	16.7	57t	1
Breeden	2	24	12.0	30	0
Horton	2	3	1.5	3	0
Turner	1	40	40.0	40	0
Kemp	1	0	0.0	0	0
Bengals	19	283	14.9	57t	2
Opponents	13	199	15.3	58	0

Punting	No.	Yds.	Avg.	In 20	LG
McInally	57	2410	42.3	8	64
Breech	5	153	30.6	2	43
Bengals	63	2563	40.7	10	64
Opponents	60	2477	41.3	11	63

Punt Returns	No.	FC	Yds.	Avg.	LG	TD
Martin	32	8	268	8.4	26	0
Bengals	32	8	268	8.4	26	0
Opponents	42	0	554	13.2	62t	1

Kickoff Returns	No.	Yds.	Avg.	LG	TD
Martin	48	1104	23.0	45	0
Jennings	13	218	16.8	26	0
Brooks	3	38	12.7	15	0
Washington, Pitt-Cin.	3	34	11.3	14	0
Zander	1	19	19.0	19	0
Brown	1	6	6.0	6	0
Griffin	1	0	0.0	0	0
Bengals	67	1385	20.7	45	0
Opponents	81	1734	21.4	58	0

Scoring	TD R	TD P	TD Rt	PAT	FG	Saf	TP
Breech	0	0	0	48/50	24/33	0	120
Brooks	7	5	0	0/0	0/0	0	72
Kinnebrew	9	1	0	0/0	0/0	0	60
Brown	0	8	0	0/0	0/0	0	48
Holman	0	7	0	0/0	0/0	0	42
Collinsworth	0	5	0	0/0	0/0	0	30
Jennings	1	3	0	0/0	0/0	0	24
Alexander	2	0	0	0/0	0/0	0	12
Kreider	0	1	0	1/1	0/0	0	7
Esiason	1	0	0	0/0	0/0	0	6
Griffin	0	0	1	0/0	0/0	0	6
Harris	0	1	0	0/0	0/0	0	6
Jackson	0	0	1	0/0	0/0	0	6
Browner	0	0	0	0/0	0/0	1	2
Bengals	20	31	2	49/53	24/33	1	441
Opponents	23	26	2	51/51	26/34	1	437

FIRST-ROUND SELECTIONS

(If club had no first-round selection, first player drafted is listed with round in parentheses.)

Year	Player, College, Position
1968	Bob Johnson, Tennessee, C
1969	Greg Cook, Cincinnati, QB
1970	Mike Reid, Penn State, DT
1971	Vernon Holland, Tennessee State, T
1972	Sherman White, California, DE
1973	Isaac Curtis, San Diego State, WR
1974	Bill Kollar, Montana State, DT
1975	Glenn Cameron, Florida, LB
1976	Billy Brooks, Oklahoma, WR
	Archie Griffin, Ohio State, RB
1977	Eddie Edwards, Miami, DT
	Wilson Whitley, Houston, DT
	Mike Cobb, Michigan State, TE
1978	Ross Browner, Notre Dame, DT
	Blair Bush, Washington, C
1979	Jack Thompson, Washington State, QB
	Charles Alexander, Louisiana State, RB
1980	Anthony Muñoz, Southern California, T
1981	David Verser, Kansas, WR
1982	Glen Collins, Mississippi State, DE
1983	Dave Rimington, Nebraska, C
1984	Ricky Hunley, Arizona, LB
	Pete Koch, Maryland, DE
	Brian Blados, North Carolina, T
1985	Eddie Brown, Miami, WR
	Emanuel King, Alabama, LB
1986	Joe Kelly, Washington, LB
	Tim McGee, Tennessee, WR

CINCINNATI BENGALS 1986 VETERAN ROSTER

No.	Name	Pos.	Ht.	Wt.	Birth-date	NFL Exp.	College	Hometown	How Acq.	'85 Games/ Starts
40	Alexander, Charles	RB	6-1	226	7/28/57	8	Louisiana State	Galveston, Tex.	D1a-'79	16/5
14	Anderson, Ken	QB	6-3	212	2/15/49	16	Augustana, Ill.	Batavia, Ill.	D3-'71	3/2
53	Barker, Leo	LB	6-1	221	11/7/59	3	New Mexico State	Cristobal, Panama	D7-'84	16/2
74	Blados, Brian	T	6-4	295	1/11/62	3	North Carolina	Arlington, Va.	D1b-'84	16/16
61	†Boyarsky, Jerry	NT	6-3	290	5/15/59	6	Pittsburgh	Scott, Pa.	FA-'82	16/0
3	†Breech, Jim	K	5-6	161	4/11/56	8	California	Sacramento, Calif.	FA-'80	16/0
34	Breeden, Louis	CB	5-11	185	10/26/53	9	North Carolina Central	Hamlet, N.C.	D7-'77	16/16
21	Brooks, James	RB	5-10	182	12/28/58	6	Auburn	Warner Robins, Ga.	T(SD)-'84	16/16
81	Brown, Eddie	WR	6-0	185	12/17/62	2	Miami	Miami, Fla.	D1-'85	16/16
79	Browner, Ross	DE	6-3	265	3/22/54	9	Notre Dame	Warren, Ohio	D1-'78	16/16
80	Collinsworth, Cris	WR	6-5	192	1/27/59	6	Florida	Titusville, Fla.	D2-'81	16/16
73	Edwards, Eddie	DE	6-5	256	4/25/54	10	Miami	Sumter, S.C.	D1-'77	16/16
7	Esiason, Boomer	QB	6-4	220	4/17/61	3	Maryland	East Islip, N.Y.	D2-'84	15/14
22	Griffin, James	S	6-2	197	9/7/61	4	Middle Tennessee State	Camilla, Ga.	D7-'83	16/11
83	Harris, M. L.	TE	6-5	238	1/16/54	7	Kansas	Columbus, Ohio	FA-'80	10/0
82	†Holman, Rodney	TE	6-3	232	4/20/60	5	Tulane	Ypsilanti, Mich.	D3-'82	16/16
20	Horton, Ray	CB	5-11	190	4/12/60	4	Washington	Tacoma, Wash.	D2-'83	16/16
37	Jackson, Robert	S	5-10	186	10/10/58	5	Central Michigan	Allendale, Mich.	D11-'81	16/5
36	Jennings, Stanford	RB	6-1	205	3/12/62	3	Furman	Summerville, S.C.	D3-'84	16/0
30	Johnson, Bill	RB	6-2	230	10/31/60	2	Arkansas	Millerton, N.Y.	SD2-'85	13/0
26	Kemp, Bobby	S	6-0	192	5/29/59	6	Cal State-Fullerton	Pomona, Calif.	D8-'81	16/16
89	Kern, Don	TE	6-4	225	8/25/62	3	Arizona State	Los Gatos, Calif.	D6-'84	8/0
90	King, Emanuel	LB	6-4	245	8/15/63	2	Alabama	Leroy, Ala.	D1a-'85	16/2
28	Kinnebrew, Larry	RB	6-1	255	6/11/59	4	Tennessee State	Rome, Ga.	D6a-'83	12/11
64	Kozerski, Bruce	C	6-4	275	4/2/62	3	Holy Cross	Plains, Pa.	D9-'84	14/0
86	Kreider, Steve	WR	6-4	192	5/12/58	8	Lehigh	Reading, Pa.	D6-'79	16/0
69	Krumrie, Tim	NT	6-2	262	5/20/60	4	Wisconsin	Eau Claire, Wis.	D10-'83	16/16
88	†Martin, Mike	WR	5-10	186	11/18/60	4	Illinois	Washington, D.C.	D8-'83	16/0
87	McInally, Pat	P	6-6	212	5/7/53	11	Harvard	Villa Park, Calif.	D5-'75	16/0
65	Montoya, Max	G	6-5	275	5/12/56	8	UCLA	La Puente, Calif.	D7-'79	16/16
78	Muñoz, Anthony	T	6-6	278	8/19/58	7	Southern California	Ontario, Calif.	D1-'80	16/16
42	Pickering, Clay	WR	6-5	215	6/2/61	2	Maine	Akron, Ohio	FA-'84	1/0
75	Reimers, Bruce	T	6-7	280	9/18/60	3	Iowa State	Humboldt, Iowa	D8-'84	14/0
52	Rimington, Dave	C	6-3	288	8/13/62	4	Nebraska	Omaha, Neb.	D1-'83	16/16
59	†Schuh, Jeff	LB	6-3	234	5/22/58	6	Minnesota	Minneapolis, Minn.	D7-'81	16/14
25	Simmons, John	CB	5-11	192	12/1/58	6	Southern Methodist	Little Rock, Ark.	D3-'81	9/0
56	Simpkins, Ron	LB	6-1	235	4/2/58	6	Michigan	Detroit, Mich.	D7-'80	16/9
62	Smith, Gary	G	6-2	265	1/27/60	2	Virginia Tech	Hampton, Va.	FA-'85	0*
35	†Turner, Jimmy	CB	6-0	187	6/15/59	4	UCLA	Sherman, Tex.	D3-'83	16/0
63	Walter, Joe	T	6-6	290	6/18/63	2	Texas Tech	Dallas, Tex.	D7a-'85	14/0
41	Washington, Sam	CB	5-9	180	3/7/60	5	Mississippi Valley State	Tampa, Fla.	FA-'85	15/0*
57	Williams, Reggie	LB	6-0	228	9/19/54	11	Dartmouth	Flint, Mich.	D3a-'76	16/15
77	Wilson, Mike	T	6-5	271	5/28/55	9	Georgia	Gainesville, Ga.	D4-'77	16/16
91	Zander, Carl	LB	6-2	235	3/23/64	2	Tennessee	Mendham, N.J.	D2-'85	16/7

* Smith last active with Cincinnati in '84; Washington played 7 games with Pittsburgh, 8 with Cincinnati in '85.

†Option playout; subject to developments.

Traded—Defensive end Glen Collins to Green Bay; Quarterback Turk Schonert to Atlanta.

Also played with Bengals in '85—LB Glenn Cameron (16 games); CB Lee Davis (7), LB Tom Dinkel (13), TE Dan Ross (6), CB-S Sean Thomas (5).

COACHING STAFF

Head Coach, Sam Wyche

Pro Career: Became the fifth head coach in Cincinnati history when he was named to lead the Bengals on December 28, 1983. Played quarterback with Bengals 1968-70, Washington Redskins 1971-73, Detroit Lions 1974-75, St. Louis 1976, and Buffalo 1977. Quarterback coach with the San Francisco 49ers 1979-82. Career record: 15-17.

Background: Attended North Fulton High School in Atlanta and Furman University where he was the quarterback from 1962-66. Assistant coach at South Carolina in 1967. Head coach at Indiana University in 1983.

Personal: Born January 5, 1945, in Atlanta, Ga. Sam and his wife, Jane, have two children—Zak and Kerry. They live in Cincinnati.

Assistant Coaches

Jim Anderson, running backs; born March 27, 1948, Harrisburg, Pa., lives in Cincinnati. Linebacker-defensive end Cal Western (U.S. International) 1969-70. No pro playing experience. College coach: Cal Western 1970-71, Scottsdale Community College 1973, Nevada-Las Vegas 1974-75, Southern Methodist 1977-80, Stanford 1981-83. Pro coach: Joined Bengals in 1984.

Bruce Coslet, offensive coordinator; born August 5, 1946, Oakdale, Calif., lives in Cincinnati. Tight end University of the Pacific 1967-69. Pro tight end Cincinnati Bengals 1969-76. Pro coach: San Francisco 49ers 1980, joined Bengals in 1981.

Bill Johnson, tight ends; born July 14, 1926, Tyler, Tex., lives in Cincinnati. Center Texas A&M 1944-46. Pro center San Francisco 49ers 1948-55. Pro coach: San Francisco 49ers 1956-67, Cincinnati Bengals 1968-78 (head coach 1976-78), Tampa Bay Buccaneers 1979-82, Detroit Lions 1983-84, rejoined Bengals in 1985.

Dick LeBeau, defensive coordinator-defensive backs; born September 9, 1937, London, Ohio, lives in Cincinnati. Halfback Ohio State 1957-59. Pro defensive back Detroit Lions 1959-72. Pro coach: Philadelphia Eagles 1973-75, Green Bay Packers 1976-79, joined Bengals in 1980.

Jim McNally, offensive line-running game; born December 13, 1943, Buffalo, N.Y., lives in Cincinnati. Guard Buffalo 1961-65. No pro playing experience. College coach: Buffalo 1966-69, Marshall 1973-75, Boston College 1976-78, Wake Forest 1979. Pro coach: Joined Bengals in 1980.

Dick Selcer, linebackers; born August 22, 1937, Cincinnati, Ohio, lives in Cincinnati. Running back Notre Dame 1955-58. No pro playing experience. College coach: Xavier, Ohio 1962-64, 1970-71 (head coach), Cincinnati 1965-66, Brown 1967-69, Wisconsin 1972-74, Kansas State 1975-77, Southwestern Louisiana 1978-80. Pro coach: Houston Oilers 1981-83, joined Bengals in 1984.

Bill Urbanik, defensive line; born December 27, 1946, Donora, Pa., lives in Cincinnati. Lineman Ohio State 1965-68. No pro playing experience. College coach: Marshall 1971-73, 1975, Northern Illinois 1976-78, Wake Forest 1979-83. Pro coach: Joined Bengals in 1984.

Kim Wood, strength; born July 12, 1945, Barrington, Ill., lives in Cincinnati. Running back Wisconsin 1965-68. No pro playing experience. Pro coach: Joined Bengals in 1975.

CINCINNATI BENGALS 1986 FIRST-YEAR ROSTER

Name	Pos.	Ht.	Wt.	Birth-date	College	Hometown	How Acq.
Aikens, Carl (1)	WR	6-1	190	6/5/62	Northern Illinois	Chicago, Ill.	FA
Anderson, Ricky (1)	P-K	6-2	195	1/24/63	Vanderbilt	St. Petersburg, Fla.	FA
Armstrong, Keith	DE	6-9	250	9/28/64	Pittsburgh	Ypsilanti, Mich.	FA
Billups, Lewis	CB	5-11	190	10/10/63	North Alabama	Ft. Walton Beach, Fla.	D2
Bradley, Steve	QB	6-2	210	7/16/63	Indiana	Knox, Ind.	D12
Brown, Richard	NT	6-1	270	9/1/64	Tennessee	Riviera Beach, Fla.	FA
Cruise, Keith (1)	DE	6-3	270	1/17/63	Northwestern	Cahokia, Ill.	FA
Dimaggio, Tony	TE	6-4	230	8/21/63	Rhode Island	New Milford, N.J.	FA
Douglas, David	T	6-4	280	3/20/63	Tennessee	Evansville, Tenn.	D8
Flaherty, Tom	LB	6-3	235	9/24/64	Northwestern	Chicago, Ill.	D11b
Foley, Skip	LB	6-0	230	6/2/62	Maine	Kents Hill, Maine	FA
Franklin, Pat	RB	6-0	232	8/16/63	Southwest Texas St.	Bay City, Tex.	D7
Fulcher, David	S	6-3	228	9/28/64	Arizona State	Los Angeles, Calif.	D3c
Gaynor, Doug	QB	6-2	205	7/5/63	Long Beach State	Fresno, Calif.	D4b
Grant, Wayne	NT	6-1	290	6/12/63	Akron	Cleveland, Ohio	FA
Hammerstein, Mike	DE	6-4	270	3/29/63	Michigan	Wapakoneta, Ohio	D3b
Herrmann, James (1)	DE	6-6	266	10/20/62	Brigham Young	Hartland, Wis.	FA
Hillary, Ira (1)	WR	5-11	190	11/13/62	South Carolina	Johnston, S.C.	FA
Hunt, Gary	CB-S	5-11	178	10/28/63	Memphis State	Texarkana, Tex.	D6
Johnson, Mark	C	6-2	260	11/3/62	VPI	Winston-Salem, N.C.	FA
Johnson, Stan (1)	WR	6-2	195	9/16/63	Wisconsin-La Crosse	Pewaukee, Wis.	FA
Kattus, Eric	TE	6-5	232	3/4/63	Michigan	Cincinnati, Ohio	D4a
Kelly, Joe	LB	6-2	224	12/11/64	Washington	Los Angeles, Calif.	D1a
Knight, Chris	TE	6-4	235	2/1/63	Maryland	Stevensville, Md.	FA
McGee, Tim	WR	5-10	175	8/7/64	Tennessee	Cleveland, Ohio	D1b
Palozzolo, Mike	WR	6-0	190	11/19/63	Rhodes	Memphis, Tenn.	FA
Partridge, Jeff	P	6-1	180	9/13/61	Washington	Tustin, Calif.	FA
Richey, Tom	T-G	6-4	275	6/13/61	Kentucky	Lexington, Ky.	FA
Russell, Mike	TE	6-2	230	4/20/62	Kansas State	Marysville, Ky.	FA
Schwartzburg, Dodge (1)	K	5-7	165	5/6/62	Kansas	Ocala, Ill.	FA
Shaw, Jeff	NT	6-1	280	2/27/62	Salem College	Matawan, N.J.	D10
Skow, Jim	DE	6-3	250	6/29/63	Nebraska	Omaha, Neb.	D3a
Stone, Tim	T	6-6	285	11/24/60	Kansas State	Tioga, Pa.	D11a
Turner, Craig	RB	5-10	229	2/19/63	Alabama	Damascus, Md.	FA
Wade, Michael (1)	WR	5-9	190	2/4/61	Iowa State	Chicago, Ill.	FA
Ward, Rick (1)	P-K	6-3	220	4/5/62	Eastern Oregon	Roseburg, Ore.	FA
White, Leon	LB	6-2	225	10/4/63	Brigham Young	La Mesa, Calif.	D5
Whittingham, Cary	LB	6-2	236	5/30/63	Brigham Young	Provo, Utah	D9

The term NFL Rookie is defined as a player who is in his first season of professional football and has not been on the roster of another professional football team for any regular season or postseason games. A Rookie is designated by an "R" on NFL rosters. Players who have been active in another professional football league or players who have NFL experience, including either preseason training camp or being on an active roster for fewer than three regular season or postseason games, are termed NFL First-Year Players. An NFL First-Year Player is designated by a "1" on NFL rosters. Thereafter, a player on an NFL active roster for at least three regular season or postseason games is credited with an additional year of NFL playing experience.

NOTES

CLEVELAND BROWNS

American Football Conference
Central Division

Team Colors: Seal Brown, Orange, and White

Tower B
Cleveland Stadium
Cleveland, Ohio 44114
Telephone: (216) 696-5555

Club Officials

President: Arthur B. Modell
Executive Vice President/Legal and Administrative: Jim Bailey
Executive Vice President/Football Operations: Ernie Accorsi
Vice President/Finance: Mike Poplar
Vice President/Player Personnel: Bill Davis
Vice President/Public Relations: Kevin Byrne
Director of Player Relations: Paul Warfield
Director of Marketing: David Modell
Director of Pro Personnel: Chip Falivene
Director of Security: Ted Chappelle
Area Scouts: Dom Anile, Dave Beckman, Tom Heckert, Tom Miner
Video Director: John Wuehrmann
Ticket Director: Bill Breit
Head Trainer: Bill Tessendorf
Equipment Manager: Charley Cusick

Stadium: Cleveland Stadium • **Capacity:** 80,098
West 3rd Street
Cleveland, Ohio 44114

Playing Surface: Grass

Training Camp: Lakeland Community College
Mentor, Ohio 44060

1986 SCHEDULE

Preseason

Aug. 9	**Buffalo**	7:30
Aug. 15	at Miami	8:00
Aug. 23	at Atlanta	8:00
Aug. 28	at Los Angeles Raiders	7:00

Regular Season

Sept. 7	at Chicago	12:00
Sept. 14	at Houston	12:00
Sept. 18	**Cincinnati** (Thursday)	8:00
Sept. 28	**Detroit**	1:00
Oct. 5	at Pittsburgh	1:00
Oct. 12	**Kansas City**	1:00
Oct. 19	**Green Bay**	1:00
Oct. 26	at Minnesota	12:00
Nov. 2	at Indianapolis	1:00
Nov. 10	**Miami** (Monday)	9:00
Nov. 16	at Los Angeles Raiders	1:00
Nov. 23	**Pittsburgh**	1:00
Nov. 30	**Houston**	1:00
Dec. 7	at Buffalo	1:00
Dec. 14	at Cincinnati	1:00
Dec. 21	**San Diego**	1:00

BROWNS COACHING HISTORY

(301-202-9)

1950-62	Paul Brown	115-49-5
1963-70	Blanton Collier	79-38-2
1971-74	Nick Skorich	30-26-2
1975-77	Forrest Gregg*	18-23-0
1977	Dick Modzelewski	0-1-0
1978-84	Sam Rutigliano**	47-52-0
1984-85	Marty Schottenheimer	12-13-0

*Resigned after 13 games in 1977
**Released after eight games in 1984

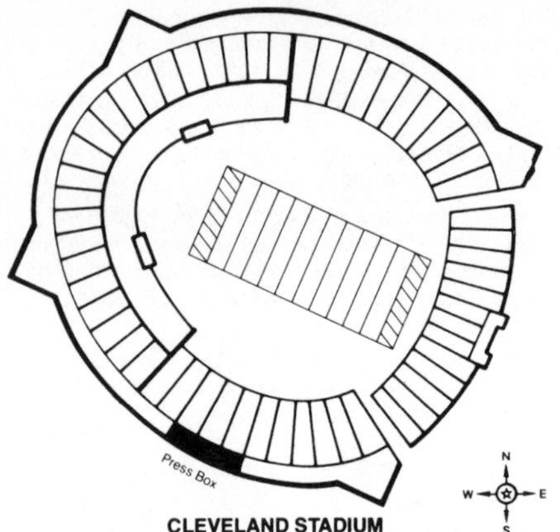

CLEVELAND STADIUM

RECORD HOLDERS

Individual Records—Career

Category	Name	Performance
Rushing (Yds.)	Jim Brown, 1957-1965	12,312
Passing (Yds.)	Brian Sipe, 1974-1983	23,713
Passing (TDs)	Brian Sipe, 1974-1983	154
Receiving (No.)	Ozzie Newsome, 1978-1985	502
Receiving (Yds.)	Ozzie Newsome, 1978-1985	6,281
Interceptions	Thom Darden, 1972-74, 1976-1981	45
Punting (Avg.)	Horace Gillom, 1950-56	43.8
Punt Return (Avg.)	Greg Pruitt, 1973-1981	11.8
Kickoff Return (Avg.)	Greg Pruitt, 1973-1981	26.3
Field Goals	Lou Groza, 1950-59, 1961-67	234
Touchdowns (Tot.)	Jim Brown, 1957-1965	126
Points	Lou Groza, 1950-59, 1961-67	1,349

Individual Records—Single Season

Category	Name	Performance
Rushing (Yds.)	Jim Brown, 1963	1,863
Passing (Yds.)	Brian Sipe, 1980	4,132
Passing (TDs)	Brian Sipe, 1980	30
Receiving (No.)	Ozzie Newsome, 1983, 1984	89
Receiving (Yds.)	Paul Warfield, 1968	1,067
Interceptions	Thom Darden, 1978	10
Punting (Avg.)	Gary Collins, 1965	46.7
Punt Return (Avg.)	Leroy Kelly, 1965	15.6
Kickoff Return (Avg.)	Billy Reynolds, 1954	29.5
Field Goals	Matt Bahr, 1984	24
Touchdowns (Tot.)	Jim Brown, 1965	21
Points	Jim Brown, 1965	126

Individual Records—Single Game

Category	Name	Performance
Rushing (Yds.)	Jim Brown, 11-24-57	237
	Jim Brown, 11-19-61	237
Passing (Yds.)	Brian Sipe, 10-25-81	444
Passing (TDs)	Frank Ryan, 12-12-64	5
	Bill Nelsen, 11-2-69	5
	Brian Sipe, 10-7-79	5
Receiving (No.)	Ozzie Newsome, 10-14-84	14
Receiving (Yds.)	Ozzie Newsome, 10-14-84	191
Interceptions	Many times	3
	Last time by Hanford Dixon, 12-19-82	
Field Goals	Don Cockroft, 10-19-75	5
Touchdowns (Tot.)	Dub Jones, 11-25-51	6
Points	Dub Jones, 11-25-51	36

1985 TEAM STATISTICS

	Cleveland	Opp.
Total First Downs	271	297
Rushing	119	106
Passing	128	172
Penalty	24	19
Third Down: Made/Att.	79/216	83/228
Fourth Down: Made/Att.	12/21	7/15
Total Net Yards	4921	4958
Avg. Per Game	307.6	309.9
Total Plays	983	1050
Avg. Per Play	5.0	4.7
Net Yards Rushing	2285	1851
Avg. Per Game	142.8	115.7
Total Rushes	533	497
Net Yards Passing	2636	3107
Avg. Per Game	164.8	194.2
Tackled/Yards Lost	36/249	44/353
Gross Yards	2885	3460
Att./Completions	414/222	509/289
Completion Pct.	53.6	56.8
Had Intercepted	13	18
Punts/Avg.	81/40.3	91/42.2
Net Punting Avg.	34.5	34.6
Penalties/Yards Lost	99/753	102/773
Fumbles/Ball Lost	40/23	28/9
Touchdowns	35	34
Rushing	16	14
Passing	17	18
Returns	2	2
Avg. Time of Possession	28:53	31:07

1985 TEAM RECORD

Preseason (2-2)

Date	Cleveland		Opponents
8/10	7	San Diego	12
8/17	28	*Philadelphia	14
8/24	31	Buffalo	28
8/31	7	*L.A. Raiders	26
	73		80

Regular Season (8-8)

Date	Cleveland		Opp.	Att.
9/8	24	*St. Louis (OT)	27	62,107
9/16	17	*Pittsburgh	7	76,042
9/22	7	Dallas	20	61,456
9/29	21	San Diego	7	52,107
10/6	24	*New England	20	60,639
10/13	21	Houston	6	38,386
10/20	20	*L.A. Raiders	21	77,928
10/27	7	*Washington	14	75,540
11/3	9	Pittsburgh	10	51,976
11/10	10	Cincinnati	27	57,293
11/17	17	*Buffalo	7	44,915
11/24	24	*Cincinnati	6	69,439
12/1	35	N.Y. Giants	33	66,482
12/8	13	Seattle	31	58,477
12/15	28	*Houston	21	40,793
12/22	10	N.Y. Jets	37	59,073

Postseason (0-1)

Date	Cleveland		Opp.	Att.
1/4/86	21	Miami	24	74,667

*Home Game (OT) Overtime

Score by Periods

Cleveland	44	68	78	97	0	—	287
Opponents	75	81	50	85	3	—	294

Attendance

Home 507,403 Away 445,250 Total 952,653
Single game home record, 85,703 (9-21-70)
Single season home record, 620,496 (1980)

1985 INDIVIDUAL STATISTICS

Rushing	Att.	Yds.	Avg.	LG	TD
Mack	222	1104	5.0	61	7
Byner	244	1002	4.1	36	8
Danielson	25	126	5.0	28	0
Dickey, Ind.-Clev.	11	40	3.6	11	0
Dickey, Clev.	2	6	3.0	5	0
Allen	8	32	4.0	8	0
Cl. Weathers	1	18	18.0	18	0
Davis	4	9	2.3	5	0
Baab	1	0	0.0	0	0
Kosar	26	−12	−0.5	10	1
Browns	533	2285	4.3	61	16
Opponents	497	1851	3.7	58t	14

Passing	Att.	Comp.	Pct.	Yds.	TD	Int.	Tkld.	Rate
Kosar	248	124	50.0	1578	8	7	19/121	69.3
Danielson	163	97	59.5	1274	8	6	17/128	85.3
Brennan	1	1	100.0	33	1	0	0/0	158.3
Fontenot	1	0	0.0	0	0	0	0/0	39.6
Gossett	1	0	0.0	0	0	0	0/0	39.6
Browns	414	222	53.6	2885	17	13	36/249	76.4
Opponents	509	289	56.8	3460	18	18	44/353	74.8

Receiving	No.	Yds.	Avg.	LG	TD
Newsome	62	711	11.5	38	5
Byner	45	460	10.2	31	2
Brennan	32	487	15.2	57	0
Mack	29	297	10.2	43	3
Cl. Weathers	16	449	28.1	72t	3
Adams	10	132	13.2	22	0
Holt	10	95	9.5	23	1
Young	5	111	22.2	45t	1
F. Banks	5	62	12.4	17t	2
Dickey, Ind.-Clev.	3	30	10.0	11	0
Jefferson	3	30	10.0	17	0
Tucker	2	20	10.0	10	0
Fontenot	2	19	9.5	17	0
Langhorne	1	12	12.0	12	0
Browns	222	2885	13.0	72t	17
Opponents	289	3460	12.0	54t	18

Interceptions	No.	Yds.	Avg.	LG	TD
Gross	5	109	21.8	37t	1
Dixon	3	65	21.7	37	0
Braziel	2	40	20.0	40	0
Wright	2	11	5.5	10	0
Cu. Weathers	1	9	9.0	9	0
Rockins	1	8	8.0	8	0
Johnson	1	6	6.0	6	0
Minnifield	1	3	3.0	3	0
Rogers	1	3	3.0	3	0
Cousineau	1	0	0.0	0	0
Browns	18	254	14.1	40	1
Opponents	13	217	16.7	48t	1

Punting	No.	Yds.	Avg.	In 20	LG
Gossett	81	3261	40.3	18	64
Browns	81	3261	40.3	18	64
Opponents	91	3842	42.2	23	64

Punt Returns	No.	FC	Yds.	Avg.	LG	TD
Cl. Weathers	28	4	218	7.8	16	0
Brennan	19	4	153	8.1	37t	1
Browns	47	8	371	7.9	37t	1
Opponents	36	14	304	8.4	38	0

Kickoff Returns	No.	Yds.	Avg.	LG	TD
Young	35	898	25.7	63	0
Fontenot	8	215	26.9	81	0
Langhorne	3	46	15.3	19	0
Green	2	20	10.0	13	0
Puzzuoli	2	8	4.0	8	0
Cl. Weathers	1	17	17.0	17	0
Nicolas	1	9	9.0	9	0
Allen	1	4	4.0	4	0
Browns	53	1217	23.0	81	0
Opponents	51	884	17.3	37	0

Scoring	TD R	TD P	TD Rt	PAT	FG	Saf	TP
Bahr	0	0	0	35/35	14/18	0	77
Byner	8	2	0	0/0	0/0	0	60
Mack	7	3	0	0/0	0/0	0	60
Newsome	0	5	0	0/0	0/0	0	30
Cl. Weathers	0	3	0	0/0	0/0	0	18
F. Banks	0	2	0	0/0	0/0	0	12
Brennan	0	0	1	0/0	0/0	0	6
Gross	0	0	1	0/0	0/0	0	6
Holt	0	1	0	0/0	0/0	0	6
Kosar	1	0	0	0/0	0/0	0	6
Young	0	1	0	0/0	0/0	0	6
Browns	16	17	2	35/35	14/18	0	287
Opponents	14	18	2	33/34	19/29	0	294

FIRST-ROUND SELECTIONS

(If club had no first-round selection, first player drafted is listed with round in parentheses.)

Year	Player, College, Position
1950	Ken Carpenter, Oregon State, B
1951	Ken Konz, Louisiana State, B
1952	Bert Rechichar, Tennessee, DB
	Harry Agganis, Boston U., QB
1953	Doug Atkins, Tennessee, DE
1954	Bobby Garrett, Stanford, QB
	John Bauer, Illinois, G
1955	Kurt Burris, Oklahoma, C
1956	Preston Carpenter, Arkansas, B
1957	Jim Brown, Syracuse, B
1958	Jim Shofner, Texas Christian, DB
1959	Rich Kreitling, Illinois, DE
1960	Jim Houston, Ohio State, DE
1961	Bobby Crespino, Mississippi, TE
1962	Gary Collins, Maryland, WR
	Leroy Jackson, Western Illinois, RB
1963	Tom Hutchinson, Kentucky, WR
1964	Paul Warfield, Ohio State, WR
1965	James Garcia, Purdue, T (2)
1966	Milt Morin, Massachusetts, TE
1967	Bob Matheson, Duke, LB
1968	Marvin Upshaw, Trinity, Texas, DT-DE
1969	Ron Johnson, Michigan, RB
1970	Mike Phipps, Purdue, QB
	Bob McKay, Texas, T
1971	Clarence Scott, Kansas State, CB
1972	Thom Darden, Michigan, DB
1973	Steve Holden, Arizona State, WR
	Pete Adams, Southern California, T
1974	Billy Corbett, Johnson C. Smith, T (2)
1975	Mack Mitchell, Houston, DE
1976	Mike Pruitt, Purdue, RB
1977	Robert Jackson, Texas A&M, LB
1978	Clay Matthews, Southern California, LB
	Ozzie Newsome, Alabama, TE
1979	Willis Adams, Houston, WR
1980	Charles White, Southern California, RB
1981	Hanford Dixon, Southern Mississippi, DB
1982	Chip Banks, Southern California, LB
1983	Ron Brown, Arizona State, WR (2)
1984	Don Rogers, UCLA, DB
1985	Greg Allen, Florida State, RB (2)
1986	Webster Slaughter, San Diego State, WR (2)

CLEVELAND BROWNS 1986 VETERAN ROSTER

No.	Name	Pos.	Ht.	Wt.	Birth-date	NFL Exp.	College	Hometown	How Acq.	'85 Games/ Starts
80	†Adams, Willis	WR	6-2	200	8/22/56	7	Houston	Schulenburg, Tex.	D1-'79	3/3
26	Allen, Greg	RB	5-11	200	6/4/63	2	Florida State	Milton, Fla.	D2-'85	7/0
61	Baab, Mike	C	6-4	270	12/6/59	5	Texas	Euless, Tex.	D5-'82	16/16
9	Bahr, Matt	K	5-10	175	7/6/56	8	Penn State	Neshaminy, Pa.	T(SF)-'81	16/0
99	†Baldwin, Keith	DE	6-4	270	10/13/60	5	Texas A&M	Houston, Tex.	D2-'82	10/0
56	Banks, Chip	LB	6-4	233	9/18/59	5	Southern California	Augusta, Ga.	D1-'82	16/16
83	Banks, Fred	WR	5-10	177	5/26/62	2	Liberty Baptist	Columbus, Ga.	D8-'85	10/5
36	Bell, Bobby	LB	6-2	220	2/7/62	2	Missouri	Kansas City, Mo.	FA-'86	0*
77	Bolden, Rickey	T-G	6-6	280	9/8/61	3	Southern Methodist	Dallas, Tex.	D4a-'84	16/9
47	†Braziel, Larry	CB	6-0	184	9/25/54	8	Southern California	Ft. Worth, Tex.	FA-'82	16/0
86	Brennan, Brian	WR	5-9	178	2/15/62	3	Boston College	Bloomfield, Mich.	D4b-'84	12/10
49	†Burrell, Clinton	S	6-1	192	9/4/56	6	Louisiana State	Franklin, La.	D6-'79	0*
44	Byner, Earnest	RB	5-10	215	9/15/62	3	East Carolina	Milledgeville, Ga.	D10-'84	16/13
96	†Camp, Reggie	DE	6-4	270	2/28/61	4	California	So. San Francisco, Calif.	D3-'83	16/16
91	Clancy, Sam	DE	6-7	260	5/29/58	3	Pittsburgh	Pittsburgh, Pa.	T(Sea)-'85	14/0
75	†Contz, Bill	T	6-5	270	5/12/61	4	Penn State	Belle Vernon, Pa.	D5-'83	5/0
50	Cousineau, Tom	LB	6-3	225	5/6/57	5	Ohio State	Lakewood, Ohio	T(Buff)-'82	16/15
18	†Danielson, Gary	QB	6-2	196	9/10/51	10	Purdue	Dearborn, Mich.	T(Det)-'85	8/6
38	Davis, Johnny	RB	6-1	235	7/17/56	9	Alabama	Montgomery, Ala.	FA-'82	16/0
33	Dickey, Curtis	RB	6-1	220	11/27/56	7	Texas A&M	Bryan, Tex.	W(Ind)-'85	7/0*
29	Dixon, Hanford	CB	5-11	186	12/25/58	6	Southern Mississippi	Theodore, Ala.	D1-'81	16/16
47	Fantetti, Ken	LB	6-2	230	4/7/57	8	Wyoming	Rochester, Mich.	FA-'86	8/4*
74	Farren, Paul	T	6-5	270	12/24/60	4	Boston University	Cohasset, Mass.	D12-'83	13/13
69	Fike, Dan	G-T	6-7	280	6/16/61	2	Florida	Pensacola, Fla.	FA-'85	13/13
28	Fontenot, Herman	RB-KR	6-0	206	9/12/63	2	Louisiana State	Beaumont, Tex.	FA-'85	9/0
79	†Golic, Bob	NT	6-2	260	10/26/57	7	Notre Dame	Cleveland, Ohio	W(NE)-'82	16/16
7	Gossett, Jeff	P	6-2	200	1/25/57	5	Eastern Illinois	Charleston, Ill.	FA-'85	16/0
53	t-Griggs, Anthony	LB	6-3	230	2/12/60	5	Ohio State	Somerville, N.J.	T(Phil)-'86	16/16
27	†Gross, Al	S	6-3	195	1/4/61	4	Arizona	Stockton, Calif.	W(Dall)-'83	16/16
78	†Hairston, Carl	DE	6-4	260	12/15/52	11	Maryland-East. Shore	Martinsville, Va.	T(Phil)-'84	16/16
81	†Holt, Harry	TE	6-4	230	12/29/57	4	Arizona	Harlingen, Tex.	FA-'83	11/2
68	Jackson, Robert	G	6-5	260	4/1/53	12	Duke	Huntersville, N.C.	FA-'75	15/1
51	†Johnson, Eddie	LB	6-1	225	2/3/59	6	Louisville	Albany, Ga.	D7-'81	16/16
19	Kosar, Bernie	QB	6-5	210	11/25/63	2	Miami	Boardman, Ohio	SD1-'85	12/10
88	Langhorne, Reginald	WR	6-2	195	4/7/63	2	Elizabeth City State	Smithfield, Va.	D7-'85	16/3
62	†Lilja, George	G-C	6-4	270	3/3/58	5	Michigan	Orland Park, Ill.	FA-'84	16/16
34	Mack, Kevin	RB	6-0	212	8/9/62	2	Clemson	Kings Mountain, N.C.	SD1-'84	16/15
57	Matthews, Clay	LB	6-2	235	3/15/56	9	Southern California	Los Angeles, Calif.	D1a-'78	14/14
16	McDonald, Paul	QB	6-2	185	2/23/58	7	Southern California	La Puente, Calif.	D4b-'80	16/0
31	Minnifield, Frank	CB	5-9	180	1/1/60	3	Louisville	Lexington, Ky.	FA-'84	16/16
82	Newsome, Ozzie	TE	6-2	232	3/16/56	9	Alabama	Muscle Shoals, Ala.	D1b-'78	16/16
58	†Nicolas, Scott	LB	6-3	226	8/7/60	5	Miami	Clearwater, Fla.	D12-'82	16/1
10	t-Pagel, Mike	QB	6-2	211	9/13/60	5	Arizona State	Phoenix, Ariz.	T(Ind)-'86	16/14
72	Puzzuoli, Dave	NT	6-3	260	1/12/61	4	Pittsburgh	Stamford, Conn.	D6b-'83	16/0
63	Risien, Cody	T	6-7	280	3/22/57	7	Texas A&M	Cypress, Tex.	D7-'79	12/12
37	Rockins, Chris	S	6-0	195	5/18/62	3	Oklahoma State	Sherman, Tex.	D2a-'84	16/0
20	Rogers, Don	S	6-1	206	9/17/62	3	UCLA	Sacramento, Calif.	D1-'84	16/16
87	Tucker, Travis	TE	6-3	227	9/19/63	2	So. Connecticut State	Brooklyn, N.Y.	D11-'85	16/2
85	Weathers, Clarence	WR-KR	5-9	170	1/10/62	4	Delaware State	Fort Pierce, Fla.	W(NE)-'85	13/7
55	Weathers, Curtis	LB	6-5	230	9/16/56	8	Mississippi	Memphis, Tenn.	D9b-'79	16/2
22	Wright, Felix	CB-S	6-2	190	6/22/59	2	Drake	Carthage, Mo.	FA-'85	16/0
84	†Young, Glen	WR-KR	6-2	205	10/11/60	4	Mississippi State	Greenwood, Miss.	FA-'84	15/2

* Bell last active with N.Y. Jets in '84; Burrell missed '85 season due to injury; Dickey played 6 games with Indianapolis, 1 with Cleveland in '85; Fantetti played 8 games with Detroit in '85.

†Option playout; subject to developments.

t-Browns traded for Griggs (Philadelphia), Pagel (Indianapolis).

Traded—Running back Boyce Green to Kansas City.

Retired—Robert Jackson, 11-year guard, 15 games in '85.

Also played with Browns in '85—G Scott Bolzan (active for 1 game, but did not play), CB D.D. Hoggard (2 games), WR John Jefferson (7), G Mark Krerowicz (active for 6 games but did not play), DE James White (active for 1 game but did not play).

COACHING STAFF

Head Coach, Marty Schottenheimer

Pro Career: Became the sixth head coach in Cleveland history on October 22, 1984, when he was promoted from defensive coordinator. Replaced Sam Rutigliano at midseason and guided Browns to a 4-4 finish. Joined the Cleveland staff in 1980 as defensive coordinator. Served as an assistant coach with Portland Storm (WFL) in 1974, was linebacker coach and defensive coordinator with New York Giants 1975-77, and linebacker coach with Detroit Lions 1978-79. Drafted in the seventh round of the 1965 draft by the Buffalo Bills. Played linebacker for Bills 1965-68 and for Boston Patriots 1969-70. Career record: 12-13.

Background: All-America linebacker at University of Pittsburgh 1962-64. Following retirement from pro football, worked as a real estate developer in both Miami and Denver from 1971-74.

Personal: Born September 23, 1943, Canonsburg, Pa. Marty and his wife, Patricia, live in Strongsville, Ohio, and have two children—Kristen and Brian.

Assistant Coaches

Dave Adolph, defensive coordinator; born June 6, 1937, Akron, Ohio, lives in Berea, Ohio. Guard-linebacker Akron 1955-58. No pro playing experience. College coach: Akron 1963-64, Connecticut 1965-68, Kentucky 1969-72, Illinois 1973-76, Ohio State 1977-78. Pro coach: Cleveland Browns 1979-84, San Diego Chargers 1985, rejoined Browns in 1986.

Bill Cowher, special teams; born May 8, 1957, Pittsburgh, Pa., lives in Strongsville, Ohio. Linebacker North Carolina State 1975-78. Pro linebacker Cleveland Browns 1980-82, Philadelphia Eagles 1983-84. Pro coach: Joined Browns in 1985.

Charlie Davis, tight ends; born August 7, 1944, San Diego, Calif., lives in Middleburg Heights, Ohio. Linebacker UCLA 1962-64. No pro playing experience. College coach: San Francisco State 1967-70, Xavier 1971-73, Ball State 1974-75, Tulane 1976-80. Pro coach: Jacksonville Bulls (USFL) 1984-85, first year with Browns.

Lindy Infante, offensive coordinator-quarterbacks; born May 27, 1940, Miami, Fla., lives in Berea, Ohio. Running back-defensive back Florida 1960-62. Pro running back Hamilton Tiger-Cats (CFL) 1963. College coach: Florida 1966-71, Memphis State 1972-73, Tulane 1976, 1979. Pro coach: Charlotte Hornets (WFL) 1975, New York Giants 1977-78, Cincinnati Bengals 1980-82, Jacksonville Bulls (USFL, head coach) 1984-85, first year with Browns.

Richard Mann, receivers; born April 20, 1947, Aliquippa, Pa., lives in Strongsville, Ohio. Wide receiver Arizona State 1966-68. No pro playing experience. College coach: Arizona State 1974-79, Louisville 1980-81. Pro coach: Indianapolis Colts 1982-84, joined Browns in 1985.

Howard Mudd, offensive line; born February 10, 1942, Midland, Mich., lives in Medina, Ohio. Guard Hillsdale 1961-63. Pro guard San Francisco 49ers 1964-69, Chicago Bears 1970-71. College coach: California 1972-73. Pro coach: San Diego Chargers 1974-76, San Francisco 49ers 1977, Seattle Seahawks 1978-82, joined Browns in 1983.

Tom Olivadotti, secondary; born September 22, 1945, Long Branch, N.J., lives in Strongsville, Ohio. Defensive end-wide receiver Upsala 1963-66. No pro playing experience. College coach: Princeton 1975-77, Boston College 1978-79, Miami 1980-83. Pro coach: Joined Browns in 1985.

Joe Pendry, running backs; born August 5, 1947, Matheny, W. Va., lives in Strongsville, Ohio. Tight end West Virginia 1966-67. No pro playing experience. College coach: West Virginia 1967-74, 1976-77, Kansas State 1975, Pittsburgh 1978-79, Michigan State 1980-81. Pro coach: Philadelphia Stars (USFL) 1983, Pittsburgh Maulers (USFL, head coach) 1984, joined Browns in 1985.

Tom Pratt, defensive line; born June 21, 1935, Edgerton, Wis., lives in Medina, Ohio. Linebacker Miami 1954-56. No pro playing experience. College coach: Miami 1957-59, Southern Mississippi 1960-62. Pro coach: Kansas City Chiefs 1963-77, New Orleans Saints 1978-80, joined Browns in 1981.

Dave Redding, strength and conditioning; born June 14, 1952, North Platte, Neb., lives in Medina, Ohio. Defensive end Nebraska 1972-75. No pro playing experience. College coach: Nebraska 1976, Washington State 1977, Missouri 1978-81. Pro coach: Joined Browns in 1982.

Darvin Wallis, special assistant-defense; born February 14, 1949, Ft. Branch, Ind., lives in Middleburg Heights, Ohio. Defensive end Arizona 1970-71. No pro playing experience. College coach: Adams State 1976-77, Tulane 1978-79, Mississippi 1980-81. Pro coach: Joined Browns in 1982.

CLEVELAND BROWNS 1986 FIRST-YEAR ROSTER

Name	Pos.	Ht.	Wt.	Birth-date	College	Hometown	How Acq.
Alexis, Alton (1)	WR	5-11	182	11/16/57	Tulane	Jacksonville, Fla.	FA
Anderson, Greg (1)	WR	5-10	170	5/20/59	Alabama State	North Olmsted, Ohio	FA
Apke, Joe (1)	C	6-5	230	8/12/62	Cincinnati	Cincinnati, Ohio	FA
Baylor, Valdez	RB	5-11	205	9/3/63	Minnesota	Harrisburg, Pa.	FA
Bolzan, Scott (1)	T	6-3	270	7/25/62	Northern Illinois	Andover, Mass.	FA
Boyd, Jeff (1)	WR	6-2	185	4/17/58	Chapman, Calif.	Berea, Ohio	FA
Brooks, Mark (1)	RB	6-0	235	5/15/63	Notre Dame	Cincinnati, Ohio	FA
Brooks, Terrance (1)	G-C	6-1	245	12/12/63	Towson State	Union Bridge, Md.	FA
Cade, Jon	DE	6-5	240	6/13/63	Louisville	Cleveland, Ohio	FA
Carr, Reginald	NT	6-2	290	2/17/63	Jackson State	Meridian, Miss.	FA
Carter, Mansel	NT	6-5	230	1/7/62	Notre Dame	Winfield, Mo.	FA
Coleman, Eddie	WR	5-10	175	5/3/63	Fairmont State	Fairmont, W. Va.	FA
Collins, Kyle	RB	5-10	195	5/15/63	Auburn	Gadsden, Ala.	FA
Colson, Eddie (1)	RB	5-10	228	9/8/63	North Carolina	Berea, Ohio	FA
Costello, Joe	LB	6-3	250	6/1/60	Central Conn. St.	Stratford, Conn.	FA
Curtin, Mike	S	6-2	195	3/20/64	Yale	Salt Lake City, Utah	FA
Dausin, Randy	G-C	6-4	265	9/17/63	Texas A&M	San Antonio, Tex.	D11
Driver, Stacy	RB	5-6	185	3/4/64	Clemson	Griffin, Ga.	FA
Emmons, Tom	T	6-4	261	10/23/62	Oregon State	Ventura, Calif.	FA
Gann, Ricky	K	5-8	182	9/11/61	Texas Tech	Weatherford, Tex.	FA
Greer, Terry	WR	6-2	197	9/27/57	Alabama State	Memphis, Tenn.	T(Rams)-'86
Hanna, Paul	NT	6-3	255	12/14/59	Purdue	Westlake, Ohio	FA
Harper, Mark	CB	5-9	174	11/5/61	Alcorn State	Memphis, Tenn.	FA
Harrison, Marck (1)	RB	5-7	186	4/20/61	Wisconsin	Columbus, Ohio	FA
Hestera, Dave (1)	TE	6-3	240	5/15/61	Colorado	Arvada, Colo.	FA
Hill, Troy	CB-S	5-11	174	2/18/62	Pittsburgh	Pittsburgh, Pa.	FA
Hoggard, D.D. (1)	CB	6-0	188	5/20/61	North Carolina State	Falls Church, Va.	FA
Jackson, Enis	CB	5-9	180	5/16/63	Memphis State	Helena, Ark.	FA
Kalis, Gary	G	6-3	270	5/31/63	Akron	Lakewood, Ohio	FA
Malone, Ralph	DE	6-5	225	1/12/64	Georgia Tech	Atlanta, Ga.	FA
Marek, Marcus (1)	LB	6-0	220	1/8/61	Ohio State	Masury, Ohio	FA
McBride, Adrian	S-WR	6-0	195	3/23/63	Missouri	Zanesville, Ohio	FA
Meyer, Jim	T	6-5	295	6/9/63	Illinois State	Normal, Ill.	D7a
Miller, Nick	LB	6-2	238	10/26/63	Arkansas	Fayetteville, Ark.	D5
Morrill, David	NT	6-2	260	4/27/63	Ohio State	Dayton, Ohio	FA
Norman, Kurt	LB	6-2	230	8/12/63	Hillsdale	Clarkston, Mich.	FA
Norseth, Mike	QB	6-2	205	8/22/64	Kansas	Lawrence, Kan.	D7b
Reid, Cliff	RB	5-10	205	11/25/63	Appalachian State	Granite Falls, N.C.	FA
Russo, Tony	T	6-4	275	3/16/64	Texas-El Paso	Mahopac, N.Y.	FA
Schick, Bill	C	6-5	280	10/22/63	Wisconsin	Black River Falls, Wis.	FA
Shakespeare, Stanley (1)	WR	6-0	180	2/5/63	Miami	North Olmsted, Ohio	FA
Siano, Mike	TE-WR	6-4	215	11/29/63	Syracuse	Springfield, Pa.	FA
Simmons, King	CB	6-2	197	2/12/63	Texas Tech	Lubbock, Tex.	D12
Skipper, Harry	CB	5-11	175	4/2/60	South Carolina	Columbia, S.C.	FA
Slaughter, Webster	WR	6-0	170	10/19/64	San Diego State	El Cajon, Calif.	D2
Smith, Willie	TE	6-2	230	8/6/64	Miami	Miami, Fla.	D10
Snowden, Jeremiah	RB	5-11	214	2/25/62	Mississippi Valley St.	Bay Minette, Ala.	FA
Tait, Jim	TE	6-4	228	9/12/62	Syracuse	Shaker Heights, Ohio	FA
Talley, Stan (1)	P	6-5	225	9/5/58	Texas Christian	Dana Point, Calif.	FA
Tatum, Rowland (1)	LB	6-0	235	11/20/62	Ohio State	Columbus, Ohio	FA
Taylor, Danny	CB	5-9	177	9/19/64	Texas-El Paso	El Paso, Tex.	D9
Watson, Louis	WR	5-11	175	1/11/63	Mississippi Valley St.	Mobile, Ala.	FA
White, James (1)	DE	6-3	245	7/5/62	Louisiana State	Rayville, La.	FA
Williams, Larry (1)	G	6-5	269	7/3/63	Notre Dame	Berea, Ohio	D10-'85
Wilson, Clint	TE	6-3	225	9/20/63	Pittsburgh	Pahokee, Fla.	FA
Wilson, Othell	CB-S	6-2	180	10/26/61	Virginia	Alexandria, Va.	FA
Wiska, Jeff (1)	G	6-3	260	10/17/59	Michigan State	Novi, Mich.	FA

The term NFL Rookie is defined as a player who is in his first season of professional football and has not been on the roster of another professional football team for any regular season or postseason games. A Rookie is designated by an "R" on NFL rosters. Players who have been active in another professional football league or players who have NFL experience, including either preseason training camp or being on an active roster for fewer than three regular season or postseason games, are termed NFL First-Year Players. An NFL First-Year Player is designated by a "1" on NFL rosters. Thereafter, a player on an NFL active roster for at least three regular season or postseason games is credited with an additional year of NFL playing experience.

NOTES

DENVER BRONCOS

American Football Conference
Western Division

Team Colors: Orange, Royal Blue, and White

5700 Logan Street
Denver, Colorado 80216
Telephone: (303) 296-1982

Club Officials

President-Chief Executive Officer: Patrick D. Bowlen
Vice President-Head Coach: Dan Reeves
General Manager: John Beake
Chief Financial Officer-Treasurer: Robert M. Hurley
Director of Administration: Sandy Waters
Director of Player Personnel: Reed Johnson
Director of Pro Personnel: Carroll Hardy
Director of Media Relations: Jim Saccomano
Ticket Manager: Gail Stuckey
Director of Player and Community Relations: Charlie Lee
Equipment Manager: Dan Bill
Trainer: Steve Antonopulos

Stadium: Denver Mile High Stadium • **Capacity:** 75,100
1900 West Eliot
Denver, Colorado 80204

Playing Surface: Grass (PAT)

Training Camp: University of Northern Colorado
Greeley, Colorado 80639

1986 SCHEDULE

Preseason

Aug. 9	**New Orleans**	7:00
Aug. 16	at Minnesota	7:00
Aug. 23	**San Francisco**	7:00
Aug. 29	**Los Angeles Rams**	6:00

Regular Season

Sept. 7	**Los Angeles Raiders**	2:00
Sept. 15	at Pittsburgh (Monday)	9:00
Sept. 21	at Philadelphia	1:00
Sept. 28	**New England**	2:00
Oct. 5	**Dallas**	2:00
Oct. 12	at San Diego	1:00
Oct. 20	at New York Jets (Monday)	9:00
Oct. 26	**Seattle**	2:00
Nov. 2	at Los Angeles Raiders	1:00
Nov. 9	**San Diego**	2:00
Nov. 16	**Kansas City**	2:00
Nov. 23	at New York Giants	1:00
Nov. 30	**Cincinnati**	2:00
Dec. 7	at Kansas City	12:00
Dec. 13	**Washington** (Saturday)	2:00
Dec. 20	at Seattle (Saturday)	1:00

BRONCOS COACHING HISTORY

(169-202-9)

1960-61	Frank Filchock	7-20-1
1962-64	Jack Faulkner*	9-22-1
1964-66	Mac Speedie**	6-19-1
1966	Ray Malavasi	4-8-0
1967-71	Lou Saban***	20-42-3
1971	Jerry Smith	2-3-0
1972-76	John Ralston	34-33-3
1977-80	Robert (Red) Miller	42-25-0
1981-85	Dan Reeves	45-30-0

*Released after four games in 1964
**Resigned after two games in 1966
***Resigned after nine games in 1971

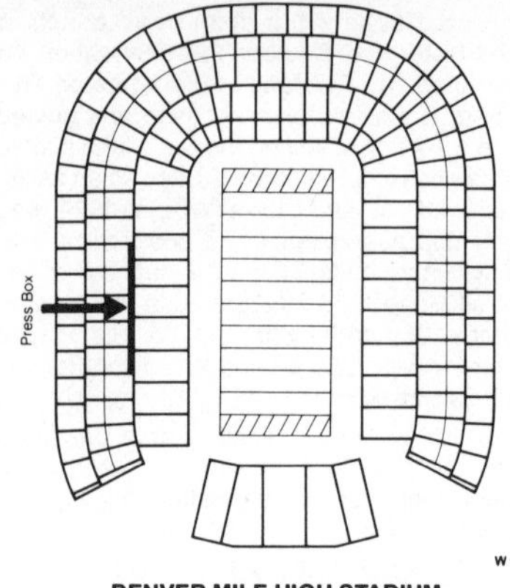

DENVER MILE HIGH STADIUM

RECORD HOLDERS

Individual Records—Career

Category	Name	Performance
Rushing (Yds.)	Floyd Little, 1967-1975	6,323
Passing (Yds.)	Craig Morton, 1977-1982	11,895
Passing (TDs)	Craig Morton, 1977-1982	74
Receiving (No.)	Lionel Taylor, 1960-66	543
Receiving (Yds.)	Lionel Taylor, 1960-66	6,872
Interceptions	Goose Gonsoulin, 1960-66	43
Punting (Avg.)	Jim Fraser, 1962-64	45.2
Punt Return (Avg.)	Rick Upchurch, 1975-1983	12.1
Kickoff Return (Avg.)	Abner Haynes, 1965-66	26.3
Field Goals	Jim Turner, 1971-79	151
Touchdowns (Tot.)	Floyd Little, 1967-1975	54
Points	Jim Turner, 1971-79	742

Individual Records—Single Season

Category	Name	Performance
Rushing (Yds.)	Otis Armstrong, 1974	1,407
Passing (Yds.)	John Elway, 1985	3,891
Passing (TDs)	Frank Tripucka, 1960	24
Receiving (No.)	Lionel Taylor, 1961	100
Receiving (Yds.)	Steve Watson, 1981	1,244
Interceptions	Goose Gonsoulin, 1960	11
Punting (Avg.)	Jim Fraser, 1963	46.1
Punt Return (Avg.)	Floyd Little, 1967	16.9
Kickoff Return (Avg.)	Bill Thompson, 1969	28.5
Field Goals	Gene Mingo, 1962	27
Touchdowns (Tot.)	Floyd Little, 1972, 1973	13
	Steve Watson, 1981	13
Points	Gene Mingo, 1962	137

Individual Records—Single Game

Category	Name	Performance
Rushing (Yds.)	Otis Armstrong, 12-8-74	183
Passing (Yds.)	Frank Tripucka, 9-15-62	447
Passing (TDs)	Frank Tripucka, 10-28-62	5
	John Elway, 11-18-84	5
Receiving (No.)	Lionel Taylor, 11-29-64	13
	Bobby Anderson, 9-30-73	13
Receiving (Yds.)	Lionel Taylor, 11-27-60	199
Interceptions	Goose Gonsoulin, 9-18-60	4
	Willie Brown, 11-15-64	4
Field Goals	Gene Mingo, 10-6-63	5
	Rich Karlis, 11-20-83	5
Touchdowns (Tot.)	Many times	3
	Last time by Steve Watson, 9-20-81	
Points	Gene Mingo, 12-10-60	21

1985 TEAM STATISTICS

	Denver	Opp.
Total First Downs	339	290
Rushing	113	103
Passing	192	168
Penalty	34	19
Third Down: Made/Att.	102/253	73/229
Fourth Down: Made/Att.	6/10	8/20
Total Net Yards	5496	5179
Avg. Per Game	343.5	323.7
Total Plays	1152	1069
Avg. Per Play	4.8	4.8
Net Yards Rushing	1851	1973
Avg. Per Game	115.7	123.3
Total Rushes	497	475
Net Yards Passing	3645	3206
Avg. Per Game	227.8	200.4
Tackled/Yards Lost	38/307	47/378
Gross Yards	3952	3584
Att./Completions	617/329	547/277
Completion Pct.	53.3	50.6
Had Intercepted	23	24
Punts/Avg.	94/40.0	94/41.1
Net Punting Avg.	34.0	34.2
Penalties/Yards Lost	85/677	91/953
Fumbles/Ball Lost	24/8	22/12
Touchdowns	45	36
Rushing	20	10
Passing	23	22
Returns	2	4
Avg. Time of Possession	31:19	28:41

1985 TEAM RECORD

Preseason (2-2)

Date	Denver		Opponents
8/10	20	*N.Y. Giants	30
8/19	20	San Francisco	13
8/24	20	*Indianapolis	3
8/30	9	*Minnesota	13
	69		59

Regular Season (11-5)

Date	Denver		Opp.	Att.
9/8	16	L.A. Rams	20	52,522
9/15	34	*New Orleans	23	74,488
9/22	44	Atlanta	28	37,903
9/29	26	*Miami	30	73,614
10/6	31	*Houston	20	74,699
10/13	15	Indianapolis	10	60,128
10/20	13	*Seattle (OT)	10	74,899
10/27	30	Kansas City	10	68,248
11/3	10	San Diego	30	57,312
11/11	17	*San Francisco	16	73,173
11/17	30	*San Diego (OT)	24	74,376
11/24	28	L.A. Raiders (OT)	31	63,161
12/1	31	Pittsburgh	23	56,797
12/8	14	*L.A. Raiders (OT)	17	75,042
12/14	14	*Kansas City	13	69,209
12/20	27	Seattle	24	56,283

*Home Game (OT) Overtime

Score by Periods

Denver	82	142	39	108	9	—	380
Opponents	48	89	102	84	6	—	329

Attendance

Home 589,500 Away 452,354 Total 1,041,854
Single game home record, 75,042 (12-8-85)
Single season home record, 589,500 (1985)

1985 INDIVIDUAL STATISTICS

Rushing	Att.	Yds.	Avg.	LG	TD
Winder	199	714	3.6	42	8
Lang	84	318	3.8	26	5
Sewell	81	275	3.4	16	4
Elway	51	253	5.0	22	0
Willhite	66	237	3.6	14	3
V. Johnson	10	36	3.6	14	0
Poole	4	12	3.0	6	0
Kubiak	1	6	6.0	6	0
Norman	1	0	0.0	0	0
Broncos	497	1851	3.7	42	20
Opponents	475	1973	4.2	61t	10

Passing	Att.	Comp.	Pct.	Yds.	TD	Int.	Tkld.	Rate
Elway	605	327	54.0	3891	22	23	38/307	70.2
Kubiak	5	2	40.0	61	1	0	0/0	125.8
Willhite	3	0	0.0	0	0	0	0/0	39.6
V. Johnson	1	0	0.0	0	0	0	0/0	39.6
Norman	1	0	0.0	0	0	0	0/0	39.6
Sewell	1	0	0.0	0	0	0	0/0	39.6
Winder	1	0	0.0	0	0	0	0/0	39.6
Broncos	617	329	53.3	3952	23	23	38/307	70.1
Opponents	547	277	50.6	3584	22	24	47/378	66.7

Receiving	No.	Yds.	Avg.	LG	TD
Watson	61	915	15.0	60	5
V. Johnson	51	721	14.1	63t	3
Willhite	35	297	8.5	21	1
Winder	31	197	6.4	24	0
Kay	29	339	11.7	27	3
J. Wright	28	246	8.8	30	1
Sampson	26	432	16.6	46	4
Sewell	24	224	9.3	54t	1
Lang	23	180	7.8	24	2
B. Johnson	19	380	20.0	65t	3
Barber, Rams-Den.	2	37	18.5	29	0
Barber, Den.	1	8	8.0	8	0
Cooper	1	13	13.0	13	0
Broncos	329	3952	12.0	65t	23
Opponents	277	3584	12.9	73	22

Interceptions	No.	Yds.	Avg.	LG	TD
Harden	5	100	20.0	42t	1
L. Wright	5	44	8.8	24	0
Foley	3	47	15.7	29	0
Smith	3	46	15.3	39	0
Wilson	3	8	2.7	8	0
Lilly	2	4	2.0	4	0
Hunter	1	20	20.0	20	0
Woodard	1	18	18.0	18	0
Robbins	1	3	3.0	3	0
Broncos	24	290	12.1	42t	1
Opponents	23	332	14.4	53	2

Punting	No.	Yds.	Avg.	In 20	LG
Norman	92	3764	40.9	16	61
Broncos	94	3764	40.0	16	61
Opponents	94	3868	41.1	19	68

Punt Returns	No.	FC	Yds.	Avg.	LG	TD
V. Johnson	30	6	260	8.7	38	0
Willhite	16	5	169	10.6	18	0
Broncos	46	11	429	9.3	38	0
Opponents	38	17	325	8.6	30	0

Kickoff Returns	No.	Yds.	Avg.	LG	TD
V. Johnson	30	740	24.7	39	0
Lang	17	361	21.2	33	0
Willhite	2	40	20.0	20	0
Hunter	2	33	16.5	18	0
Sewell	1	29	29.0	29	0
Broncos	52	1203	23.1	39	0
Opponents	64	1346	21.0	98t	1

Scoring	TD R	TD P	TD Rt	PAT	FG	Saf	TP
Karlis	0	0	0	41/44	23/38	0	110
Winder	8	0	0	0/0	0/0	0	48
Lang	5	2	0	0/0	0/0	0	42
Sewell	4	1	0	0/0	0/0	0	30
Watson	0	5	0	0/0	0/0	0	30
Sampson	0	4	0	0/0	0/0	0	24
Willhite	3	1	0	0/0	0/0	0	24
B. Johnson	0	3	0	0/0	0/0	0	18
V. Johnson	0	3	0	0/0	0/0	0	18
Kay	0	3	0	0/0	0/0	0	18
Harden	0	0	1	0/0	0/0	0	6
J. Wright	0	1	0	0/0	0/0	0	6
L. Wright	0	0	1	0/0	0/0	0	6
Broncos	20	23	2	41/44	23/38	0	380
Opponents	10	22	4	35/36	26/33	0	329

FIRST-ROUND SELECTIONS

(If club had no first-round selection, first player drafted is listed with round in parentheses.)

Year	Player, College, Position
1960	Roger LeClerc, Trinity, Connecticut, C
1961	Bob Gaiters, New Mexico State, RB
1962	Merlin Olsen, Utah State, DT
1963	Kermit Alexander, UCLA, CB
1964	Bob Brown, Nebraska, T
1965	Dick Butkus, Illinois, LB (2)
1966	Jerry Shay, Purdue, DT
1967	Floyd Little, Syracuse, RB
1968	Curley Culp, Arizona State, DE (2)
1969	Grady Cavness, Texas-El Paso, DB (2)
1970	Bob Anderson, Colorado, RB
1971	Marv Montgomery, Southern California, T
1972	Riley Odoms, Houston, TE
1973	Otis Armstrong, Purdue, RB
1974	Randy Gradishar, Ohio State, LB
1975	Louis Wright, San Jose State, DB
1976	Tom Glassic, Virginia, G
1977	Steve Schindler, Boston College, G
1978	Don Latimer, Miami, DT
1979	Kelvin Clark, Nebraska, T
1980	Rulon Jones, Utah State, DE (2)
1981	Dennis Smith, Southern California, DB
1982	Gerald Willhite, San Jose State, RB
1983	Chris Hinton, Northwestern, G
1984	Andre Townsend, Mississippi, DE (2)
1985	Steve Sewell, Oklahoma, RB
1986	Jim Juriga, Illinois, T (4)

DENVER BRONCOS 1986 VETERAN ROSTER

No.	Name	Pos.	Ht.	Wt.	Birth-date	NFL Exp.	College	Hometown	How Acq.	'85 Games/ Starts
85	†Barber, Mike	TE	6-3	237	6/4/53	10	Louisiana Tech	White Oak, Tex.	T(Rams)-'85	15/6*
54	Bishop, Keith	C-G	6-3	265	3/10/57	6	Baylor	Midland, Tex.	D6-'80	14/14
65	Bowyer, Walt	DE	6-4	252	9/8/60	4	Arizona State	Wilkinsburg, Pa.	D10-'83	0*
64	Bryan, Billy	C	6-2	255	9/21/55	9	Duke	Burlington, N.C.	D4-'77	16/16
58	Busick, Steve	LB	6-4	227	12/10/58	6	Southern California	Temple City, Calif.	D7-'81	16/16
68	Carter, Rubin	NT	6-0	256	12/12/52	12	Miami	Fort Lauderdale, Fla.	D5b-'75	16/16
79	Chavous, Barney	DE	6-3	258	3/22/51	14	South Carolina State	Aiken, S.C.	D2-'73	16/15
59	†Comeaux, Darren	LB	6-1	227	4/15/60	5	Arizona State	San Diego, Calif.	FA-'82	11/0
63	Cooper, Mark	G-T	6-5	267	2/14/60	4	Miami	Miami, Fla.	D2-'83	15/2
55	Dennison, Rick	LB	6-3	220	6/22/58	5	Colorado State	Fort Collins, Colo.	FA-'82	15/7
7	Elway, John	QB	6-3	210	6/28/60	4	Stanford	Los Angeles, Calif.	T(Ind)-'83	16/16
73	Fletcher, Simon	DE	6-5	240	2/18/62	2	Houston	Bay City, Tex.	D2b-'85	16/1
43	†Foley, Steve	S	6-3	190	11/11/53	10	Tulane	New Orleans, La.	D8-'75	12/11
62	Freeman, Mike	G	6-3	256	10/13/61	2	Arizona	Fountain Valley, Calif.	FA-'84	0*
72	Graves, Marsharne	T	6-3	272	7/8/62	2	Arizona	San Francisco, Calif.	FA-'84	0*
31	Harden, Mike	CB	6-1	192	2/16/58	7	Michigan	Detroit, Mich.	D5a-'80	16/16
36	t-Haynes, Mark	CB	5-11	195	11/6/58	7	Colorado	Kansas City, Kan.	T(NYG)-'86	5/1
74	Hood, Winford	T	6-3	262	3/29/62	3	Georgia	Atlanta, Ga.	D8a-'84	16/3
60	Howard, Paul	G	6-3	260	9/12/50	13	Brigham Young	Central Valley, Calif.	D3a-'73	16/15
98	Hunley, Ricky	LB	6-2	238	11/11/61	3	Arizona	Petersburg, Va.	T(Cin)-'84	16/2
25	Hunter, Daniel	CB	5-11	175	9/1/62	2	Henderson State	Arkadelphia, Ark.	FA-'85	16/0
57	Jackson, Tom	LB	5-11	220	4/4/51	14	Louisville	Cleveland, Ohio	D4-'73	12/5
86	†Johnson, Butch	WR	6-1	187	5/28/54	11	Cal-Riverside	Los Angeles, Calif.	T(Hou)-'84	16/8
82	Johnson, Vance	WR-KR	5-11	185	3/13/63	2	Arizona	Tucson, Ariz.	D2a-'85	16/7
75	Jones, Rulon	DE	6-6	260	3/25/58	7	Utah State	Ogden, Utah	D2-'80	16/16
3	†Karlis, Rich	K	6-0	180	5/23/59	5	Cincinnati	Salem, Ohio	FA-'82	16/0
88	Kay, Clarence	TE	6-2	237	7/30/61	3	Georgia	Seneca, S.C.	D7-'84	16/16
71	Kragen, Greg	NT	6-3	245	3/4/62	2	Utah State	Pleasanton, Calif.	FA-'85	16/1
8	Kubiak, Gary	QB	6-0	192	8/15/61	4	Texas A&M	Houston, Tex.	D8-'83	16/0
33	Lang, Gene	RB	5-10	196	3/15/62	3	Louisiana State	Pass Christian, Miss.	D11-'84	12/2
76	Lanier, Ken	T	6-3	269	7/8/59	6	Florida State	Columbus, Ohio	D5-'81	16/16
22	Lilly, Tony	S	6-0	199	2/16/62	3	Florida	Woodbridge, Va.	D3-'84	16/5
77	Mecklenburg, Karl	LB	6-3	230	9/1/60	4	Minnesota	Edina, Minn.	D12-'83	16/9
	t-Mills, Jim	T	6-9	281	9/23/61	3	Hawaii	Vancouver, B.C.,Canada	T(Ind)-'86	0*
67	Miraldi, Dean	T	6-5	285	4/8/58	4	Utah	Rosemead, Calif.	FA-'85	10/0
1	†Norman, Chris	P	6-2	198	5/25/62	3	South Carolina	Albany, Ga.	FA-'84	16/0
34	Poole, Nathan	RB	5-9	212	12/17/56	6	Louisville	Alexander City, Ala.	FA-'85	3/0
48	Robbins, Randy	S	6-2	189	9/14/62	3	Arizona	Casa Grande, Ariz.	D4-'84	10/1
50	Ryan, Jim	LB	6-1	218	5/18/57	8	William & Mary	Pennsauken, N.J.	FA-'79	16/14
84	Sampson, Clint	WR	5-11	183	1/4/61	4	San Diego State	Los Angeles, Calif.	D3-'83	16/0
83	†Sawyer, John	TE	6-2	230	7/26/53	11	Southern Mississippi	Baker, La.	FA-'83	0*
30	Sewell, Steve	RB	6-3	210	4/2/63	2	Oklahoma	San Francisco, Calif.	D1-'85	16/2
56	Smith, Aaron	LB	6-2	225	8/10/62	2	Utah State	Playa Del Rey, Calif.	D6-'84	0*
49	Smith, Dennis	S	6-3	200	2/3/59	6	Southern California	Santa Monica, Calif.	D1-'81	13/12
14	Stankavage, Scott	QB	6-1	194	7/5/62	2	North Carolina	Buckingham, Pa.	FA-'84	0*
70	Studdard, Dave	T	6-4	260	11/22/55	8	Texas	Pearsall, Tex.	FA-'79	16/15
61	Townsend, Andre	DE-NT	6-3	265	10/8/62	3	Mississippi	Aberdeen, Miss.	D2-'84	16/1
81	Watson, Steve	WR	6-4	195	5/28/57	8	Temple	Wilmington, Del.	FA-'79	16/15
47	Willhite, Gerald	RB	5-10	200	5/30/59	5	San Jose State	Cordova, Calif.	D1-'82	15/4
45	Wilson, Steve	CB	5-10	195	8/25/57	8	Howard	Durham, N.C.	FA-'82	14/4
23	Winder, Sammy	RB	5-11	203	7/15/59	5	Southern Mississippi	Madison, Miss.	D5-'82	14/12
52	Woodard, Ken	LB	6-1	218	1/22/60	5	Tuskegee Institute	Detroit, Mich.	D10-'82	16/9
87	Wright, James	TE	6-3	240	9/1/56	7	Texas Christian	Brenham, Tex.	FA-'80	16/12
20	Wright, Louis	CB	6-3	200	1/31/53	12	San Jose State	Bakersfield, Calif.	D1-'75	15/15

* Barber played 5 games with L.A. Rams, 10 with Denver in '85; Bowyer and Stankavage last active with Denver in '84; Freeman, Graves, Sawyer, and A. Smith missed '85 season due to injury; Mills last active with Indianapolis in '84.

†Option playout; subject to developments.

t-Broncos traded for Haynes (New York Giants), Mills (Indianapolis).

Also played with Broncos in '85—G-C Glenn Hyde (11 games), S Roger Jackson (9), TE Keli McGregor (2), TE Don Summers (2).

COACHING STAFF

Head Coach, Dan Reeves

Pro Career: Became ninth head coach in Broncos history on February 28, 1981, after spending entire pro career as both player and coach with Dallas Cowboys. Led Denver to an 11-5 record in 1985, barely missing a playoff berth. Guided Broncos to AFC West championship with a 13-3 record in 1984, and a 9-7 mark and playoff berth in 1983. His teams were 10-6 in 1981 and 2-7 in 1982. He joined the Cowboys as a free agent running back in 1965 and became a member of the coaching staff in 1970 when he undertook the dual role of player-coach for two seasons. Was Cowboys offensive backfield coach from 1972-76 and became offensive coordinator in 1977. Was an all-purpose running back during his eight seasons as a player, rushing for 1,990 yards and catching 129 passes for 1,693. Career record: 45-30.

Background: Quarterback at South Carolina from 1962-64 and was inducted into the school's Hall of Fame in 1978.

Personal: Born January 19, 1944, Rome, Ga. Dan and his wife, Pam, live in Denver and have three children—Dana, Laura, and Lee.

Assistant Coaches

Marvin Bass, special assistant; born August 28, 1919, Norfolk, Va., lives in Denver. Tackle William & Mary 1940-42. No pro playing experience. College coach: William & Mary 1944-48, 1950-51 (head coach), North Carolina 1949, 1953-55, South Carolina 1956-59, 1961-65, Georgia Tech 1960, Richmond 1973. Pro coach: Washington Redskins 1952, Montreal Beavers (Continental League) 1966-67, Montreal Alouettes (CFL) 1968, Buffalo Bills 1969-71, Birmingham Americans (WFL) 1974-75, joined Broncos in 1982.

Joe Collier, assistant head coach, defense; born June 7, 1932, Rock Island, Ill., lives in Denver. End Northwestern 1950-53. No pro playing experience. College coach: Western Illinois 1957-59. Pro coach: Boston Patriots 1960-62, Buffalo Bills 1963-68 (head coach 1966-68), joined Broncos in 1969.

Chan Gailey, special teams, tight ends; born January 5, 1952, Americus, Ga., lives in Denver. Quarterback Florida 1971-74. No pro playing experience. College coach: Troy State 1976-77, 1983-84 (head coach), Air Force Academy 1978-82. Pro coach: Joined Broncos in 1985.

Alex Gibbs, head offensive line, running game; born February 11, 1941, Morganton, N.C., lives in Denver. Running back-defensive back Davidson 1959-63. No pro playing experience. College coach: Duke 1969-70, Kentucky 1971-72, West Virginia 1973-74, Ohio State 1975-78, Auburn 1979-81, Georgia 1982-83. Pro coach: Joined Broncos in 1984.

Stan Jones, defensive line; born November 24, 1931, Altoona, Pa., lives in Denver. Tackle Maryland 1950-53. Pro lineman Chicago Bears 1954-65, Washington Redskins 1966. Pro coach: Denver Broncos 1967-71, Buffalo Bills 1972-75, rejoined Broncos in 1976.

Al Miller, strength and conditioning; born August 29, 1947, El Dorado, Ark., lives in Denver. Wide receiver Northeast Louisiana 1966-69. No pro playing experience. College coach: Northwestern Louisiana 1974-78, Mississippi State 1980, Northeast Louisiana 1981, Alabama 1982-84. Pro coach: Joined Broncos in 1985.

Myrel Moore, linebackers; born March 9, 1934, Sebastopol, Calif., lives in Denver. Receiver California-Davis 1955-57. Pro defensive back Washington Redskins 1958. College coach: Santa Ana, Calif., J.C. 1959-62, California 1963-71. Pro coach: Denver Broncos 1972-77, Oakland Raiders 1978-79, rejoined Broncos in 1982.

DENVER BRONCOS 1986 FIRST-YEAR ROSTER

Name	Pos.	Ht.	Wt.	Birth-date	College	Hometown	How Acq.
Banks, Larry	DE-NT	6-3	265	12/9/58	Wisconsin-Superior	Superior, Wis.	FA
Baran, Dave	G-T	6-6	275	6/28/63	UCLA	Franklin, N.J.	FA
Boddie, Tony (1)	RB	5-11	198	11/11/60	Montana State	Bremerton, Wash.	FA
Cameron, Dallas	LB	6-2	250	11/6/63	Miami	Melbourne, Fla.	FA
Chesley, John (1)	TE	6-5	235	7/2/62	Oklahoma State	Washington, D.C.	FA
Clendenen, Michael (1)	K	6-0	190	6/12/63	Houston	LaPorte, Tex.	FA
Colorito, Tony	NT	6-5	260	9/8/64	Southern California	Brooklyn, N.Y.	D5
Davis, Kent	S	6-2	205	3/1/62	Colorado	Miami, Fla.	FA
Dendy, Thomas	RB	5-10	187	3/10/63	South Carolina	Columbia, S.C.	D11
Field, Tom	K	6-0	175	10/10/61	Colorado	River Falls, Wis.	FA
Geier, Mitch (1)	G-T	6-4	290	3/15/62	Troy State	Tarpon Springs, Fla.	FA
Hall, Victor	TE	6-3	234	11/8/63	Jackson State	Columbus, Miss.	D10
Hill, Al (1)	WR	6-3	205	7/17/60	Arizona	Mesa, Ariz.	FA
Hinson, Billy (1)	G-T	6-1	278	1/8/63	Florida	Hilliard, Fla.	D5-'85
Jackson, Mark	WR	5-9	174	7/23/63	Purdue	Terre Haute, Ind.	D6b
Juriga, Jim	T	6-6	269	9/12/64	Illinois	Wheaton, Ill.	D4
Keyton, James (1)	G-T	6-4	275	9/9/62	Arizona State	Lansing, Mich.	FA
Klostermann, Bruce	LB	6-4	225	4/17/63	South Dakota State	Dyersville, Iowa	D8
Lobenstein, Bill (1)	DE	6-3	275	5/11/61	Wisconsin-Whitewater	Deerfield, Wis.	FA
Massie, Rick (1)	WR	6-1	193	1/16/60	Kentucky	Paris, Ky.	SD2-'84
Mobley, Orson	TE	6-5	256	3/4/63	Salem College	Miami, Fla.	D6a
Nelson, Byron (1)	T	6-5	290	5/8/62	Arizona	Glendale, Ariz.	FA
Noble, Ray (1)	CB-S	6-0	175	12/19/62	California	Monterey, Calif.	FA
Phillips, Ray	DE	6-3	240	7/24/64	North Carolina State	Charlotte, N.C.	D7
Remsberg, Daniel (1)	G-T	6-6	275	4/7/62	Abilene Christian	Temple, Tex.	FA
Riley, Eric (1)	CB	6-0	170	8/15/62	Florida State	Fort Myers, Fla.	D8-'85
Rolle, Gary (1)	WR	5-11	174	2/16/62	Florida	Miami, Fla.	FA
Scissum, Willard (1)	G-T	6-3	278	10/28/62	Alabama	Huntsville, Ala.	FA
Short, Stan (1)	G-T	6-4	269	9/20/63	Penn State	Sierra Vista, Ariz.	FA
Texeira, David (1)	K	5-9	212	3/2/61	American Int'l.	Westfield, Mass.	FA
Thomas, Joe	WR	5-11	167	3/25/62	Mississippi Valley St.	Franklin, La.	D9
Weil, Jack (1)	P	5-11	175	3/16/62	Wyoming	Northglenn, Colo.	FA
Willis, Larry (1)	WR	5-10	170	7/13/63	Fresno State	Santa Monica, Calif.	FA
Woodard, Raymond (1)	T	6-6	290	8/20/61	Texas	Corrigan, Tex.	FA

The term NFL Rookie is defined as a player who is in his first season of professional football and has not been on the roster of another professional football team for any regular season or postseason games. A Rookie is designated by an "R" on NFL rosters. Players who have been active in another professional football league or players who have NFL experience, including either preseason training camp or being on an active roster for fewer than three regular season or postseason games, are termed NFL First-Year Players. An NFL First-Year Player is designated by a "1" on NFL rosters. Thereafter, a player on an NFL active roster for at least three regular season or postseason games is credited with an additional year of NFL playing experience.

NOTES

Nick Nicolau, running backs, play-action passing game; born May 5, 1933, New York, N.Y., lives in Denver. Running back Southern Connecticut 1957-59. No pro playing experience. College coach: Southern Connecticut 1960, Springfield 1961, Bridgeport 1962-69 (head coach 1965-69), Massachusetts 1970, Connecticut 1971-72, Kentucky 1973-75, Kent State 1976. Pro coach: Hamilton Tiger-Cats (CFL) 1977, Montreal Alouettes (CFL) 1978-79, New Orleans Saints 1980, joined Broncos in 1981.

Mike Shanahan, offensive coordinator, wide receivers; born August 24, 1952, Oak Park, Ill., lives in Denver. Quarterback Eastern Illinois 1970-73. No pro playing experience. College coach: Oklahoma 1975-76, Northern Arizona 1977, Eastern Illinois 1978, Minnesota 1979, Florida 1980-83. Pro coach: Joined Broncos in 1984.

Charlie West, defensive backs; born August 31, 1946, Big Spring, Tex., lives in Denver. Defensive back Texas-El Paso 1963-67. Pro defensive back Minnesota Vikings 1968-73, Detroit Lions 1974-77, Denver Broncos 1978-79. College coach: MacAlister 1981, California 1982. Pro coach: Joined Broncos in 1983.

HOUSTON OILERS

American Football Conference
Central Division

Team Colors: Columbia Blue, Scarlet, and White

Box 1516
Houston, Texas 77001
Telephone: (713) 797-9111

Club Officials

President: K. S. (Bud) Adams, Jr.
Executive Vice President-General Manager: Ladd K. Herzeg
Vice President-Player Personnel: Mike Holovak
Director of Administration: Rick Nichols
Media Relations Director: Chip Namias
Public Relations Director: Gregg Stengel
Ticket Manager: David Fuqua
Head Trainer: Jerry Meins
Assistant Trainer: Mark Chisum
Equipment Manager: Gordon Batty

Stadium: Astrodome • **Capacity:** 50,496
Loop 610, Kirby and Fannin Streets
Houston, Texas 77054

Playing Surface: AstroTurf

Training Camp: Angelo State University
San Angelo, Texas 76901

1986 SCHEDULE

Preseason

Aug. 5	at Los Angeles Rams	7:30
Aug. 16	**Buffalo**	8:00
Aug. 23	**New Orleans**	8:00
Aug. 30	at Dallas	8:00

Regular Season

Sept. 7	at Green Bay	12:00
Sept. 14	**Cleveland**	12:00
Sept. 21	at Kansas City	3:00
Sept. 28	**Pittsburgh**	12:00
Oct. 5	at Detroit	1:00
Oct. 12	**Chicago**	12:00
Oct. 19	at Cincinnati	1:00
Oct. 26	**Los Angeles Raiders**	12:00
Nov. 2	at Miami	1:00
Nov. 9	**Cincinnati**	12:00
Nov. 16	at Pittsburgh	1:00
Nov. 23	**Indianapolis**	12:00
Nov. 30	at Cleveland	1:00
Dec. 7	at San Diego	1:00
Dec. 14	**Minnesota**	3:00
Dec. 21	**Buffalo**	12:00

OILERS COACHING HISTORY

(165-214-6)

1960-61	Lou Rymkus*	12-7-1
1961	Wally Lemm	10-0-0
1962-63	Frank (Pop) Ivy	17-12-0
1964	Sammy Baugh	4-10-0
1965	Hugh Taylor	4-10-0
1966-70	Wally Lemm	28-40-4
1971	Ed Hughes	4-9-1
1972-73	Bill Peterson**	1-18-0
1973-74	Sid Gillman	8-15-0
1975-80	O.A. (Bum) Phillips	59-38-0
1981-83	Ed Biles***	8-23-0
1983	Chuck Studley	2-8-0
1984-85	Hugh Campbell****	8-22-0
1985	Jerry Glanville	0-2-0

*Released after five games in 1961
**Released after five games in 1973
***Resigned after six games in 1983
****Released after 14 games in 1985

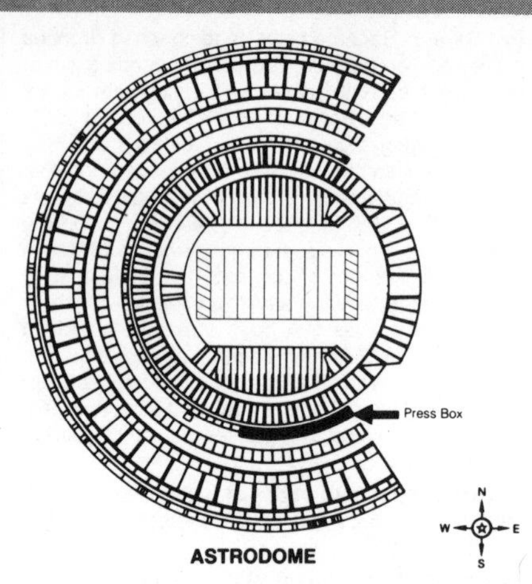

RECORD HOLDERS

Individual Records—Career

Category	Name	Performance
Rushing (Yds.)	Earl Campbell, 1978-1984	8,574
Passing (Yds.)	George Blanda, 1960-66	19,149
Passing (TDs)	George Blanda, 1960-66	165
Receiving (No.)	Charley Hennigan, 1960-66	410
Receiving (Yds.)	Ken Burrough, 1971-1982	6,907
Interceptions	Jim Norton, 1960-68	45
Punting (Avg.)	Jim Norton, 1960-68	42.3
Punt Return (Avg.)	Billy Johnson, 1974-1980	13.2
Kickoff Return (Avg.)	Bobby Jancik, 1962-67	26.4
Field Goals	George Blanda, 1960-66	91
Touchdowns (Tot.)	Earl Campbell, 1978-1984	73
Points	George Blanda, 1960-66	596

Individual Records—Single Season

Category	Name	Performance
Rushing (Yds.)	Earl Campbell, 1980	1,934
Passing (Yds.)	Warren Moon, 1984	3,338
Passing (TDs)	George Blanda, 1961	36
Receiving (No.)	Charley Hennigan, 1964	101
Receiving (Yds.)	Charley Hennigan, 1961	1,746
Interceptions	Fred Glick, 1963	12
	Mike Reinfeldt, 1979	12
Punting (Avg.)	Jim Norton, 1965	44.2
Punt Return (Avg.)	Billy Johnson, 1977	15.4
Kickoff Return (Avg.)	Ken Hall, 1960	31.2
Field Goals	Toni Fritsch, 1979	21
	Tony Zendejas, 1985	21
Touchdowns (Tot.)	Earl Campbell, 1979	19
Points	George Blanda, 1960	115

Individual Records—Single Game

Category	Name	Performance
Rushing (Yds.)	Billy Cannon, 12-10-61	216
Passing (Yds.)	George Blanda, 10-29-61	464
Passing (TDs)	George Blanda, 11-19-61	7
Receiving (No.)	Charley Hennigan, 10-13-61	13
Receiving (Yds.)	Charley Hennigan, 10-13-61	272
Interceptions	Many times	3
	Last time by Willie Alexander, 11-14-71	
Field Goals	Skip Butler, 10-12-75	6
Touchdowns (Tot.)	Billy Cannon, 12-10-61	5
Points	Billy Cannon, 12-10-61	30

1985 TEAM STATISTICS

	Houston	Opp.
Total First Downs	270	356
Rushing	96	150
Passing	149	158
Penalty	25	48
Third Down: Made/Att.	74/218	84/213
Fourth Down: Made/Att.	8/20	10/15
Total Net Yards	4652	6155
Avg. Per Game	290.8	384.7
Total Plays	998	1091
Avg. Per Play	4.7	5.6
Net Yards Rushing	1570	2814
Avg. Per Game	98.1	175.9
Total Rushes	428	588
Net Yards Passing	3082	3341
Avg. Per Game	192.6	208.8
Tackled/Yards Lost	58/441	41/313
Gross Yards	3523	3654
Att./Completions	512/277	462/260
Completion Pct.	54.1	56.3
Had Intercepted	22	15
Punts/Avg.	84/41.5	68/39.4
Net Punting Avg.	35.5	33.3
Penalties/Yards Lost	127/1150	121/908
Fumbles/Ball Lost	41/15	35/20
Touchdowns	32	51
Rushing	13	21
Passing	18	29
Returns	1	1
Avg. Time of Possession	28:07	31:53

1985 TEAM RECORD

Preseason (1-4)

Date	Houston		Opponents
8/3	20	N.Y. Giants	21
8/10	3	L.A. Rams	7
8/17	23	New Orleans	20
8/24	19	*Kansas City	24
8/31	10	Dallas	20
	75		92

Regular Season (5-11)

Date	Houston		Opp.	Att.
9/8	26	*Miami	23	47,656
9/15	13	Washington	16	53,553
9/22	0	Pittsburgh	20	58,752
9/29	10	*Dallas	17	49,686
10/6	20	Denver	31	74,699
10/13	6	*Cleveland	21	38,386
10/20	44	*Cincinnati	27	35,590
10/27	20	St. Louis	10	43,190
11/3	23	*Kansas City	20	41,238
11/10	0	Buffalo	20	21,881
11/17	7	*Pittsburgh	30	45,977
11/24	37	*San Diego	35	34,336
12/1	27	Cincinnati	45	46,140
12/8	14	*N.Y. Giants	35	36,576
12/15	21	Cleveland	28	40,793
12/22	16	Indianapolis	34	55,818

*Home Game

Score by Periods

Houston	24	90	63	107	0	—	284
Opponents	126	94	112	80	0	—	412

Attendance

Home 329,445 Away 394,826 Total 724,271
Single game home record, 55,293 (12-10-79)
Single season home record, 400,156 (1980)

1985 INDIVIDUAL STATISTICS

Rushing	Att.	Yds.	Avg.	LG	TD
Rozier	133	462	3.5	30	8
Woolfolk	103	392	3.8	43	1
Moriarty	106	381	3.6	18	3
Moon	39	130	3.3	17	0
Edwards	25	96	3.8	19	1
Luck	15	95	6.3	17	0
Tasker	2	16	8.0	13	0
Moroski	2	2	1.0	2	0
L. Johnson	1	0	0.0	0	0
Drewrey	2	−4	−2.0	5	0
Oilers	428	1570	3.7	43	13
Opponents	588	2814	4.8	67	21

Passing	Att.	Comp.	Pct.	Yds.	TD	Int.	Tkld.	Rate
Moon	377	200	53.1	2709	15	19	46/366	68.5
Luck	100	56	56.0	572	2	2	8/50	70.9
Moroski	34	20	58.8	249	1	1	4/25	79.2
Zendejas	1	1	100.0	−7	0	0	0/0	79.2
Oilers	512	277	54.1	3523	18	22	58/441	69.7
Opponents	462	260	56.3	3654	29	15	41/313	89.3

Receiving	No.	Yds.	Avg.	LG	TD
Woolfolk	80	814	10.2	80t	4
Hill	64	1169	18.3	57t	9
T. Smith	46	660	14.3	33	2
Williams	39	444	11.4	29	1
Moriarty	17	112	6.6	16	0
Rozier	9	96	10.7	52	0
Edwards	7	71	10.1	31	0
McCloskey	4	29	7.3	24t	1
Dressel	3	17	5.7	12	1
Akiu	2	32	16.0	24	0
Drewrey	2	28	14.0	19	0
Tasker	2	19	9.5	14	0
Holston	1	25	25.0	25	0
Walls	1	7	7.0	7	0
Oilers	277	3523	12.7	80t	18
Opponents	260	3654	14.1	68t	29

Interceptions	No.	Yds.	Avg.	LG	TD
Brown	5	41	8.2	22	0
Eason	3	55	18.3	55	0
Bostic	3	28	9.3	26	0
Kush	2	6	3.0	6	0
Riley	1	14	14.0	14	0
Stensrud	1	0	0.0	0	0
Oilers	15	144	9.6	55	0
Opponents	22	267	12.1	61t	1

Punting	No.	Yds.	Avg.	In 20	LG
L. Johnson	83	3464	41.7	22	65
T. Smith	1	26	26.0	1	26
Oilers	84	3490	41.5	23	65
Opponents	68	2677	39.4	19	56

Punt Returns	No.	FC	Yds.	Avg.	LG	TD
Drewrey	24	10	215	9.0	23	0
Donaldson	6	1	35	5.8	13	0
Oilers	30	11	250	8.3	23	0
Opponents	45	7	345	7.7	31	0

Kickoff Returns	No.	Yds.	Avg.	LG	TD
Drewrey	26	642	24.7	50	0
Tasker	17	447	26.3	52	0
Walls	12	234	19.5	42	0
Donaldson	5	93	18.6	22	0
Brown	2	45	22.5	28	0
Williams	2	21	10.5	12	0
Hill	1	22	22.0	22	0
Lyday	1	6	6.0	6	0
Briehl	1	5	5.0	5	0
Oilers	67	1515	22.6	52	0
Opponents	39	970	24.9	81	0

Scoring	TD R	TD P	TD Rt	PAT	FG	Saf	TP
Zendejas	0	0	0	29/31	21/27	0	92
Hill	0	9	0	0/0	0/0	0	54
Rozier	8	0	0	0/0	0/0	0	48
Woolfolk	1	4	0	0/0	0/0	0	30
Moriarty	3	0	0	0/0	0/0	0	18
T. Smith	0	2	0	0/0	0/0	0	12
Akiu	0	0	1	0/0	0/0	0	6
Dressel	0	1	0	0/0	0/0	0	6
Edwards	1	0	0	0/0	0/0	0	6
McCloskey	0	1	0	0/0	0/0	0	6
Williams	0	1	0	0/0	0/0	0	6
Oilers	13	18	1	29/32	21/27	0	284
Opponents	21	29	1	49/51	19/34	0	412

FIRST-ROUND SELECTIONS

(If club had no first-round selection, first player drafted is listed with round in parentheses.)

Year	Player, College, Position
1960	Billy Cannon, Louisiana State, RB
1961	Mike Ditka, Pittsburgh, E
1962	Ray Jacobs, Howard Payne, DT
1963	Danny Brabham, Arkansas, LB
1964	Scott Appleton, Texas, DT
1965	Lawrence Elkins, Baylor, WR
1966	Tommy Nobis, Texas, LB
1967	George Webster, Michigan State, LB
	Tom Regner, Notre Dame, G
1968	Mac Haik, Mississippi, WR (2)
1969	Ron Pritchard, Arizona State, LB
1970	Doug Wilkerson, N. Carolina Central, G
1971	Dan Pastorini, Santa Clara, QB
1972	Greg Sampson, Stanford, DE
1973	John Matuszak, Tampa, DE
	George Amundson, Iowa State, RB
1974	Steve Manstedt, Nebraska, LB (4)
1975	Robert Brazile, Jackson State, LB
	Don Hardeman, Texas A&I, RB
1976	Mike Barber, Louisiana Tech, TE (2)
1977	Morris Towns, Missouri, T
1978	Earl Campbell, Texas, RB
1979	Mike Stensrud, Iowa State, DE (2)
1980	Angelo Fields, Michigan State, T (2)
1981	Michael Holston, Morgan State, WR (3)
1982	Mike Munchak, Penn State, G
1983	Bruce Matthews, Southern California, T
1984	Dean Steinkuhler, Nebraska, T
1985	Ray Childress, Texas A&M, DE
	Richard Johnson, Wisconsin, DB
1986	Jim Everett, Purdue, QB

HOUSTON OILERS 1986 VETERAN ROSTER

No.	Name	Pos.	Ht.	Wt.	Birth-date	NFL Exp.	College	Hometown	How Acq.	'85 Games/ Starts
56	Abraham, Robert	LB	6-1	230	7/13/60	5	North Carolina State	Myrtle Beach, S.C.	D3c-'82	16/15
86	†Akiu, Mike	WR	5-9	185	2/12/62	2	Hawaii	Kailua, Hawaii	D7-'85	9/0
29	Allen, Patrick	CB	5-10	185	8/26/61	3	Utah State	Seattle, Wash.	D4b-'84	16/16
75	Baker, Jesse	DE	6-5	271	7/10/57	8	Jacksonville State	Conyers, Ga.	D2b-'79	16/16
25	Bostic, Keith	S	6-1	210	1/17/61	4	Michigan	Ann Arbor, Mich.	D2b-'83	16/16
92	Briehl, Tom	LB	6-3	247	9/8/62	2	Stanford	Phoenix, Ariz.	D4-'85	16/0
24	Brown, Steve	CB	5-11	189	3/20/60	4	Oregon	Sacramento, Calif.	D3c-'83	15/14
94	Bush, Frank	LB	6-1	218	1/10/63	2	North Carolina State	Athens, Ga.	D5b-'85	16/11
71	Byrd, Richard	NT	6-3	255	3/20/62	2	Southern Mississippi	Jackson, Miss.	D2b-'85	15/0
79	Childress, Ray	DE	6-6	267	10/20/62	2	Texas A&M	Richardson, Tex.	D1a-'85	16/16
42	†Crutchfield, Dwayne	RB	6-0	245	9/30/59	4	Iowa State	Cincinnati, Ohio	W(Mia)-'85	0*
31	Donaldson, Jeff	S	6-0	193	4/19/62	3	Colorado	Ft. Collins, Colo.	D9a-'84	16/0
88	Dressel, Chris	TE	6-4	238	2/7/61	4	Stanford	Placentia, Calif.	D3b-'83	16/0
15	Drewrey, Willie	WR-KR	5-7	158	4/28/63	2	West Virginia	Columbus, N.J.	D11-'85	14/0
21	Eason, Bo	S	6-2	200	3/10/61	3	California-Davis	Walnut Grove, Calif.	D2b-'84	16/16
32	Edwards, Stan	RB	6-0	210	5/20/60	5	Michigan	Detroit, Mich.	D3b-'82	15/0
59	Grimsley, John	LB	6-2	232	2/25/62	3	Kentucky	Canton, Ohio	D6a-'83	15/1
85	Hill, Drew	WR	5-9	170	10/5/56	7	Georgia Tech	Newman, Ga.	T(Rams)-'85	16/16
66	Howell, Pat	G	6-6	265	3/12/57	8	Southern California	Fresno, Calif.	FA-'83	2/0
84	Jefferson, John	WR	6-1	204	2/3/56	9	Arizona State	Dallas, Tex.	FA-'86	7/2*
11	Johnson, Lee	P-K	6-1	204	11/27/61	2	Brigham Young	The Woodlands, Tex.	D5c-'85	16/0
97	†Johnson, Mike	DE	6-5	253	4/24/62	2	Illinois	Chicago, Ill.	D9b-'84	0*
23	Johnson, Richard	CB	6-1	195	9/16/63	2	Wisconsin	Harvey, Ill.	D1b-'85	16/2
58	Kelley, Mike	C-G	6-5	266	8/27/62	2	Notre Dame	Westfield, Mass.	D3c-'85	16/0
37	Kush, Rod	S	6-1	195	12/29/56	7	Nebraska-Omaha	Gretna, Neb.	FA-'85	16/0
10	Luck, Oliver	QB	6-2	196	4/5/60	5	West Virginia	Cleveland, Ohio	D2b-'82	5/2
28	Lyday, Allen	S	5-10	186	10/16/60	3	Nebraska	Wichita, Kan.	FA-'84	13/0
93	Lyles, Robert	LB	6-1	223	3/21/61	3	Texas Christian	Los Angeles, Calif.	D5-'84	16/16
74	Matthews, Bruce	T	6-4	280	8/8/61	4	Southern California	Arcadia, Calif.	D1-'83	16/16
89	McCloskey, Mike	TE	6-5	246	2/2/61	4	Penn State	Philadelphia, Pa.	D4b-'83	16/0
26	McMillian, Audrey	S-CB	6-0	190	8/13/62	2	Houston	Carthage, Tex.	W(NE)-'85	16/0
91	†Meads, Johnny	LB	6-2	225	6/25/61	3	Nicholls State	Napoleonville, La.	D3-'84	5/5
1	Moon, Warren	QB	6-3	208	11/18/56	3	Washington	Los Angeles, Calif.	FA-'84	14/14
76	Moran, Eric	T	6-5	282	6/10/60	3	Washington	Pleasanton, Calif.	FA-'84	15/3
30	Moriarty, Larry	RB	6-1	240	8/24/58	4	Notre Dame	Santa Barbara, Calif.	D5a-'83	15/12
63	Munchak, Mike	G	6-3	286	3/5/60	5	Penn State	Scranton, Pa.	D1-'82	16/16
53	Riley, Avon	LB	6-3	236	2/10/58	6	UCLA	Savannah, Ga.	D9-'81	15/15
55	Romano, Jim	C	6-3	255	9/27/59	5	Penn State	Glen Cove, N.Y.	T(Raiders)-'84	16/16
33	Rozier, Mike	RB	5-10	198	3/1/61	2	Nebraska	Camden, N.J.	SD1-'84	14/6
73	Salem, Harvey	T	6-6	285	1/15/61	4	California	El Cerrito, Calif.	D2a-'83	14/13
62	Schuhmacher, John	G	6-3	277	9/23/55	6	Southern California	Arcadia, Calif.	D12-'78	16/16
99	Smith, Doug	NT	6-4	285	6/6/60	2	Auburn	Bayboro, N.C.	D2a-'84	11/1
83	Smith, Tim	WR	6-2	206	3/20/57	7	Nebraska	San Diego, Calif.	D3-'80	16/16
72	Sochia, Brian	NT	6-3	254	7/21/61	4	Northwest Oklahoma St.	Brasher Falls, N.Y.	FA-'83	16/0
70	Steinkuhler, Dean	G	6-3	273	1/27/61	3	Nebraska	Burr, Neb.	D1-'84	0*
67	Stensrud, Mike	NT	6-5	280	2/19/56	8	Iowa State	Lake Mills, Iowa	D2a-'79	16/16
80	†Tasker, Steve	KR	5-9	185	4/10/62	2	Northwestern	Leoti, Kan.	D9-'85	7/0
84	Walls, Herkie	WR-KR	5-8	160	7/18/61	4	Texas	Garland, Tex.	D7-'83	6/0
87	Williams, Jamie	TE	6-4	232	2/25/60	4	Nebraska	Davenport, Iowa	W(TB)-'84	16/16
40	Woolfolk, Butch	RB	6-1	212	3/1/60	5	Michigan	Westfield, N.J.	T(NYG)-'85	16/14
7	Zendejas, Tony	K	5-8	160	3/15/60	2	Nevada-Reno	Chino, Calif.	T(Wash)-'85	14/0

* Crutchfield and M. Johnson missed entire '85 season due to injury; Jefferson played 7 games with Cleveland in '85; Steinkuhler active for 6 games but did not play.

†Option playout; subject to developments.

Also played with Oilers in '85—WR Steve Bryant (4 games), WR Mike Holston (3), QB Mike Moroski (4), QB Brian Ransom (active for 1 game, but did not play).

COACHING STAFF

Head Coach, Jerry Glanville

Pro Career: Named Houston's head coach on January 20, 1986, after spending the last two games of the 1985 season as interim head coach of the Oilers. Glanville was Houston's defensive coordinator in 1984 and 1985 and has over 20 years of coaching experience. He coached in the NFL for the Detroit Lions 1974-76, was the defensive coordinator with the Atlanta Falcons 1977-82, and was an assistant at Buffalo in 1983. Career record: 0-2.

Background: Glanville played collegiately at Montana State and Northern Michigan 1961-63, where he was a linebacker. Glanville was an assistant coach at Western Kentucky 1967 and Georgia Tech 1968-73.

Personal: Born October 14, 1941, in Detroit, Michigan. Jerry and wife, Brenda, live in Houston and have one son—Justin.

Assistant Coaches

Tom Bettis, secondary; born March 17, 1933, Chicago, Ill., lives in Missouri City, Tex. Linebacker-offensive guard Purdue 1951-54. Pro linebacker Green Bay Packers 1955-61, Pittsburgh Steelers 1962, Chicago Bears 1963. Pro coach: Kansas City Chiefs 1966-77 (head coach for final seven games of 1977), St. Louis 1978-84, Cleveland 1985, first year with Oilers.

Gary Huff, quarterbacks; born April 27, 1951, lives in Missouri City, Tex. Quarterback Florida State 1971-73. Pro quarterback Chicago Bears 1973-76, San Francisco 1977, Tampa Bay 1977-78. College coach: Indiana 1983. Pro coach: Memphis Showboats (USFL) 1984-85, first year with Oilers.

Dick Jamieson, offensive coordinator-running backs; born November 13, 1937, Streator, Ill., lives in Missouri City, Tex. Quarterback Bradley 1955-58. Pro quarterback Baltimore Colts 1959, New York Titans 1960. College coach: Bradley 1962-64, Missouri 1972-77, Indiana State 1978-79. Pro coach: St. Louis Cardinals 1980-85, first year with Oilers.

Milt Jackson, receivers; born October 16, 1943, Groesbeck, Tex., lives in Missouri City, Tex. Defensive back Tulsa 1965-66. Pro defensive back San Francisco 49ers 1967. College coach: Oregon State 1973, Rice 1974, California 1975-76, Oregon 1977-78, UCLA 1979. Pro coach: San Francisco 49ers 1980-82, Buffalo Bills 1983-84, Philadelphia Eagles 1985, first year with Oilers.

Miller McCalmon, special teams; born January 9, 1947, Denver, Colo., lives in Missouri City, Tex. Defensive back Tulsa 1968-69. No pro playing experience. College coach: Tulsa 1970, Colorado State 1971-72. Pro coach: Baltimore Colts 1978-79, Buffalo Bills 1980-84, first year with Oilers.

Floyd Reese, linebackers; born August 8, 1948, Springfield, Mo., lives in Missouri City, Tex. Defensive tackle UCLA 1967-69. Pro lineman Montreal Alouettes (CFL) 1970. College coach: UCLA 1970-73, Georgia Tech 1974. Pro coach: Detroit Lions 1975-77, San Francisco 49ers 1978, Minnesota Vikings 1979-85, first year with Oilers.

Doug Shively, defensive line; born March 18, 1938, Lexington, Ky., lives in Sugar Land, Tex. End Kentucky 1955-58. No pro playing experience. College coach: Virginia Tech 1961-66, Kentucky 1967-69, Clemson 1970-72, North Carolina 1973. Pro coach: New Orleans Saints 1974-76, Atlanta Falcons 1977-82, Arizona Wranglers (USFL, head coach) 1983, San Diego Chargers 1984, Tampa Bay Buccaneers 1985, first year with Oilers.

Bill Walsh, offensive line; born September 8, 1927, Phillipsburg, N.J., lives in Houston, Tex. Center Notre Dame 1945-48. Pro center Pittsburgh Steelers 1949-54. College coach: Notre Dame 1955-58, Kansas State 1959. Pro coach: Dallas Texans-Kansas City Chiefs 1960-74, Atlanta Falcons 1975-82, joined Oilers in 1983.

HOUSTON OILERS 1986 FIRST-YEAR ROSTER

Name	Pos.	Ht.	Wt.	Birth-date	College	Hometown	How Acq.
Banks, Chuck	RB	6-0	219	1/4/64	West Virginia Tech	Baltimore, Md.	D12
Cochran, Mark	T	6-5	281	5/6/63	Baylor	Pasadena, Tex.	D11
Everett, Jim	QB	6-5	212	1/3/63	Purdue	Albuquerque, N.M.	D1
Givins, Ernest	WR	5-10	168	9/3/64	Louisville	St. Petersburg, Fla.	D2
Griffin, Larry	CB	5-11	195	1/11/63	North Carolina	Chesapeake, Va.	D8
Harlien, Matt (1)	T	6-4	280	9/16/60	Texas Tech	Pasadena, Tex.	FA
Parks, Jeff	TE	6-3	240	9/14/64	Auburn	Gardendale, Ala.	D5
Pinkett, Allen	RB	5-8	181	1/25/64	Notre Dame	Sterling Park, Va.	D3
Robinson, Melvin	WR	5-8	169	9/4/62	Rice	Garland, Tex.	FA
Sebring, Bob	LB	6-1	236	4/10/63	Illinois	Villa Park, Calif.	D9
Sommer, Don	G	6-4	260	2/1/64	Texas-El Paso	Houston, Tex.	D10
Wallace, Ray	RB	6-0	217	12/3/63	Purdue	Indianapolis, Ind.	D6

The term NFL Rookie is defined as a player who is in his first season of professional football and has not been on the roster of another professional football team for any regular season or postseason games. A Rookie is designated by an "R" on NFL rosters. Players who have been active in another professional football league or players who have NFL experience, including either preseason training camp or being on an active roster for fewer than three regular season or postseason games, are termed NFL First-Year Players. An NFL First-Year Player is designated by a "1" on NFL rosters. Thereafter, a player on an NFL active roster for at least three regular season or postseason games is credited with an additional year of NFL playing experience.

NOTES

INDIANAPOLIS COLTS

American Football Conference
Eastern Division

Team Colors: Royal Blue, White, and Silver

P.O. Box 24100
Indianapolis, Indiana 46224-0100
Telephone: (317) 297-2658

Club Officials

President-Treasurer: Robert Irsay
Vice President-General Manager: James Irsay
Vice President-General Counsel: Michael G. Chernoff
Assistant General Manager: Bob Terpening
Director of Player Personnel: Jack Bushofsky
Director of Pro Personnel: Clyde Powers
Controller: Kurt Humphrey
Director of Operations: Pete Ward
Director of Public Relations: Bob Eller
Ticket Manager: Larry Hall
Assistant Director of Public Relations: Craig Kelley
Purchasing Administrator: David Filar
Equipment Manager: Jon Scott
Director of Video Operations: Marty Heckscher
Assistant Director of Video Operations: John Starliper
Cheerleader Director: Meg Irsay

Stadium: Hoosier Dome • **Capacity:** 60,127
100 South Capitol Avenue
Indianapolis, Indiana 46225

Playing Surface: AstroTurf

Training Camp: Anderson College
Anderson, Indiana 46011

1986 SCHEDULE

Preseason

Aug. 8	at Seattle	7:30
Aug. 16	at Chicago	6:00
Aug. 23	**Detroit**	7:30
Aug. 30	**Minnesota**	7:30

Regular Season

Sept. 7	at New England	4:00
Sept. 14	at Miami	4:00
Sept. 21	**Los Angeles Rams**	12:00
Sept. 28	**New York Jets**	3:00
Oct. 5	at San Francisco	1:00
Oct. 12	**New Orleans**	12:00
Oct. 19	at Buffalo	1:00
Oct. 26	**Miami**	1:00
Nov. 2	**Cleveland**	1:00
Nov. 9	**New England**	1:00
Nov. 16	at New York Jets	4:00
Nov. 23	at Houston	12:00
Nov. 30	**San Diego**	1:00
Dec. 7	at Atlanta	1:00
Dec. 14	**Buffalo**	1:00
Dec. 21	at Los Angeles Raiders	1:00

COLTS COACHING HISTORY

(238-224-7)

1953	Keith Molesworth	3-9-0
1954-62	Weeb Ewbank	61-52-1
1963-69	Don Shula	73-26-4
1970-72	Don McCafferty*	26-11-1
1972	John Sandusky	4-5-0
1973-74	Howard Schnellenberger**	4-13-0
1974	Joe Thomas	2-9-0
1975-79	Ted Marchibroda	41-36-0
1980-81	Mike McCormack	9-23-0
1982-84	Frank Kush***	11-28-1
1984	Hal Hunter	0-1-0
1985	Rod Dowhower	5-11-0

*Released after five games in 1972
**Released after three games in 1974
***Resigned after 15 games in 1984

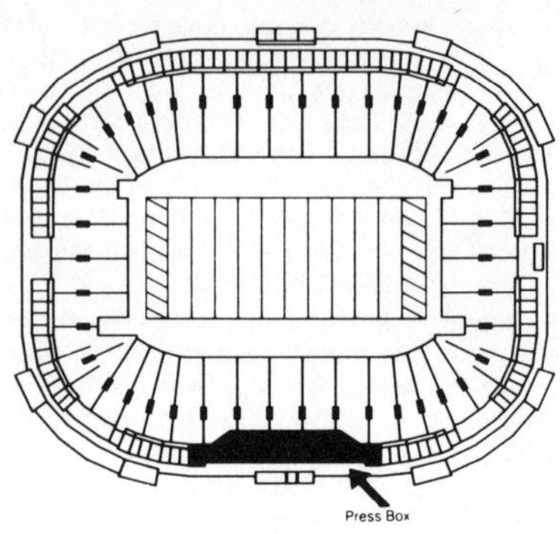

HOOSIER DOME

RECORD HOLDERS

Individual Records—Career

Category	Name	Performance
Rushing (Yds.)	Lydell Mitchell, 1972-77	5,487
Passing (Yds.)	Johnny Unitas, 1956-1972	39,768
Passing (TDs)	Johnny Unitas, 1956-1972	287
Receiving (No.)	Raymond Berry, 1955-1967	631
Receiving (Yds.)	Raymond Berry, 1955-1967	9,275
Interceptions	Bob Boyd, 1960-68	57
Punting (Avg.)	Rohn Stark, 1982-85	45.2
Punt Return (Avg.)	Wendell Harris, 1964	12.6
Kickoff Return (Avg.)	Jim Duncan, 1969-1971	32.5
Field Goals	Lou Michaels, 1964-69	107
Touchdowns (Tot.)	Lenny Moore, 1956-1967	113
Points	Lenny Moore, 1956-1967	678

Individual Records—Single Season

Category	Name	Performance
Rushing (Yds.)	Lydell Mitchell, 1976	1,200
Passing (Yds.)	Johnny Unitas, 1963	3,481
Passing (TDs)	Johnny Unitas, 1959	32
Receiving (No.)	Joe Washington, 1979	82
Receiving (Yds.)	Raymond Berry, 1960	1,298
Interceptions	Tom Keane, 1953	11
Punting (Avg.)	Rohn Stark, 1985	45.9
Punt Return (Avg.)	Wendell Harris, 1964	12.6
Kickoff Return (Avg.)	Jim Duncan, 1970	35.4
Field Goals	Raul Allegre, 1983	30
Touchdowns (Tot.)	Lenny Moore, 1964	20
Points	Lenny Moore, 1964	120

Individual Records—Single Game

Category	Name	Performance
Rushing (Yds.)	Norm Bulaich, 9-19-71	198
Passing (Yds.)	Johnny Unitas, 9-17-67	401
Passing (TDs)	Gary Cuozzo, 11-14-65	5
Receiving (No.)	Lydell Mitchell, 12-15-74	13
	Joe Washington, 9-2-79	13
Receiving (Yds.)	Raymond Berry, 11-10-57	224
Interceptions	Many times	3
	Last time by Eugene Daniel, 10-27-85	
Field Goals	Many times	5
	Last time by Raul Allegre, 10-30-83	
Touchdowns (Tot.)	Many times	4
	Last time by Lydell Mitchell, 10-12-75	
Points	Many times	24
	Last time by Lydell Mitchell, 10-12-75	

1985 TEAM STATISTICS

	Indianapolis	Opp.
Total First Downs	282	330
Rushing	131	124
Passing	130	192
Penalty	21	14
Third Down: Made/Att.	81/215	103/230
Fourth Down: Made/Att.	12/17	10/14
Total Net Yards	5006	5599
Avg. Per Game	312.9	349.9
Total Plays	988	1079
Avg. Per Play	5.1	5.2
Net Yards Rushing	2439	2145
Avg. Per Game	152.4	134.1
Total Rushes	485	539
Net Yards Passing	2567	3454
Avg. Per Game	160.4	215.9
Tackled/Yards Lost	35/244	36/267
Gross Yards	2811	3721
Att./Completions	468/235	504/275
Completion Pct.	50.2	54.6
Had Intercepted	20	16
Punts/Avg.	80/44.8	72/41.4
Net Punting Avg.	34.2	33.0
Penalties/Yards Lost	87/678	90/699
Fumbles/Ball Lost	27/14	32/17
Touchdowns	39	45
Rushing	22	20
Passing	15	24
Returns	2	1
Avg. Time of Possession	28:49	31:11

1985 TEAM RECORD

Preseason (2-2)

Date	Indianapolis		Opponents
8/10	19	*Seattle	7
8/17	24	Chicago	13
8/24	3	Denver	20
8/30	21	*Cincinnati	31
	67		71

Regular Season (5-11)

Date	Indianapolis		Opp.	Att.
9/8	3	Pittsburgh	45	57,279
9/15	13	Miami	30	53,693
9/22	14	*Detroit	6	60,042
9/29	20	N.Y. Jets	25	61,987
10/6	49	*Buffalo	17	60,003
10/13	10	*Denver	15	60,128
10/20	9	Buffalo	21	28,430
10/27	37	*Green Bay	10	59,708
11/3	17	*N.Y. Jets	35	59,683
11/10	15	New England	34	53,824
11/17	20	*Miami	34	59,666
11/24	7	Kansas City	20	19,762
12/1	31	*New England	38	56,740
12/8	10	Chicago	17	59,997
12/15	31	Tampa Bay	23	25,577
12/22	34	*Houston	16	55,818

*Home Game

Score by Periods

Indianapolis	65	98	52	105	0	—	320
Opponents	81	145	64	96	0	—	386

Attendance

Home 471,788 Away 360,549 Total 832,337
Single game home record, 61,479 (11-11-83)
Single season home record, 481,305 (1984)

1985 INDIVIDUAL STATISTICS

Rushing	Att.	Yds.	Avg.	LG	TD
McMillan	190	858	4.5	38	7
Wonsley	138	716	5.2	36	6
Bentley	54	288	5.3	26t	2
Gill	45	262	5.8	67	2
Pagel	25	160	6.4	29	2
Middleton	13	35	2.7	13	1
Dickey	9	34	3.8	11	0
Kofler	4	33	8.3	23	1
Martin	1	23	23.0	23	0
Capers	3	18	6.0	20t	1
Schlichter	2	13	6.5	9	0
Butler	1	−1	−1.0	−1	0
Colts	485	2439	5.0	67	22
Opponents	539	2145	4.0	28t	20

Passing	Att.	Comp.	Pct.	Yds.	TD	Int.	Tkld.	Rate
Pagel	393	199	50.6	2414	14	15	25/180	65.8
Kofler	48	23	47.9	284	1	3	8/58	47.6
Schlichter	25	12	48.0	107	0	2	2/6	26.6
Bentley	1	1	100.0	6	0	0	0/0	91.7
Stark	1	0	0.0	0	0	0	0/0	39.6
Colts	468	235	50.2	2811	15	20	35/244	61.8
Opponents	504	275	54.6	3721	24	16	36/267	81.0

Receiving	No.	Yds.	Avg.	LG	TD
Beach	36	376	10.4	30	6
Wonsley	30	257	8.6	26	0
Bouza	27	381	14.1	40	2
Capers	25	438	17.5	80t	4
Boyer	25	274	11.0	33	0
McMillan	22	115	5.2	17	0
Butler	19	345	18.2	72t	2
Bentley	11	85	7.7	16	0
Martin	10	128	12.8	22	0
O. Williams	9	175	19.4	30	1
Sherwin	5	64	12.8	29	0
Middleton	5	54	10.8	34	0
Gill	5	52	10.4	20	0
Dickey	3	30	10.0	11	0
Henry	2	31	15.5	16	0
Pagel	1	6	6.0	6	0
Colts	235	2811	12.0	80t	15
Opponents	275	3721	13.5	59	24

Interceptions	No.	Yds.	Avg.	LG	TD
Daniel	8	53	6.6	29	0
Davis	2	14	7.0	14	0
Cooks	1	7	7.0	7	0
Anderson	1	1	1.0	1	0
Bickett	1	0	0.0	0	0
Krauss	1	0	0.0	0	0
Randle	1	0	0.0	0	0
Young	1	0	0.0	0	0
Colts	16	75	4.7	29	0
Opponents	20	232	11.6	41	0

Punting	No.	Yds.	Avg.	In 20	LG
Stark	78	3584	45.9	12	68
Colts	80	3584	44.8	12	68
Opponents	72	2982	41.4	18	64

Punt Returns	No.	FC	Yds.	Avg.	LG	TD
Martin	40	7	443	11.1	70t	1
Daniel	1	1	6	6.0	6	0
Lowry	1	0	0	0.0	0	0
Young	0	1	0	—	0	0
Colts	42	9	449	10.7	70t	1
Opponents	43	8	572	13.3	77t	1

Kickoff Returns	No.	Yds.	Avg.	LG	TD
Bentley	27	674	25.0	48	0
Martin	32	638	19.9	36	0
O. Williams	3	44	14.7	21	0
Young	2	15	7.5	17	0
Middleton	1	20	20.0	20	0
Gill	1	6	6.0	6	0
Lee	1	6	6.0	6	0
Colts	67	1403	20.9	48	0
Opponents	59	1189	20.2	47	0

Scoring	TD R	TD P	TD Rt	PAT	FG	Saf	TP
Allegre	0	0	0	36/39	16/26	0	84
McMillan	7	0	0	0/0	0/0	0	42
Beach	0	6	0	0/0	0/0	0	36
Wonsley	6	0	0	0/0	0/0	0	36
Capers	1	4	0	0/0	0/0	0	30
Bentley	2	0	0	0/0	0/0	0	12
Bouza	0	2	0	0/0	0/0	0	12
Butler	0	2	0	0/0	0/0	0	12
Gill	2	0	0	0/0	0/0	0	12
Pagel	2	0	0	0/0	0/0	0	12
Kofler	1	0	0	0/0	0/0	0	6
Martin	0	0	1	0/0	0/0	0	6
Middleton	1	0	0	0/0	0/0	0	6
O. Williams	0	1	0	0/0	0/0	0	6
Young	0	0	1	0/0	0/0	0	6
Randle	0	0	0	0/0	0/0	1	2
Colts	22	15	2	36/39	16/26	1	320
Opponents	20	24	1	41/45	25/31	0	386

FIRST-ROUND SELECTIONS

(If club had no first-round selection, first player drafted is listed with round in parentheses.)

Year	Player, College, Position
1953	Billy Vessels, Oklahoma, B
1954	Cotton Davidson, Baylor, B
1955	George Shaw, Oregon, B
	Alan Ameche, Wisconsin, FB
1956	Lenny Moore, Penn State, B
1957	Jim Parker, Ohio State, G
1958	Lenny Lyles, Louisville, B
1959	Jackie Burkett, Auburn, C
1960	Ron Mix, Southern California, T
1961	Tom Matte, Ohio State, RB
1962	Wendell Harris, Louisiana State, S
1963	Bob Vogel, Ohio State, T
1964	Marv Woodson, Indiana, CB
1965	Mike Curtis, Duke, LB
1966	Sam Ball, Kentucky, T
1967	Bubba Smith, Michigan State, DT
	Jim Detwiler, Michigan, RB
1968	John Williams, Minnesota, G
1969	Eddie Hinton, Oklahoma, WR
1970	Norman Bulaich, Texas Christian, RB
1971	Don McCauley, North Carolina, RB
	Leonard Dunlap, North Texas State, DB
1972	Tom Drougas, Oregon, T
1973	Bert Jones, Louisiana State, QB
	Joe Ehrmann, DT, Syracuse
1974	John Dutton, Nebraska, DE
	Roger Carr, Louisiana Tech, WR
1975	Ken Huff, North Carolina, G
1976	Ken Novak, Purdue, DT
1977	Randy Burke, Kentucky, WR
1978	Reese McCall, Auburn, TE
1979	Barry Krauss, Alabama, LB
1980	Curtis Dickey, Texas A&M, RB
	Derrick Hatchett, Texas, DB
1981	Randy McMillan, Pittsburgh, RB
	Donnell Thompson, North Carolina, DT
1982	Johnie Cooks, Mississippi State, LB
	Art Schlichter, Ohio State, QB
1983	John Elway, Stanford, QB
1984	Leonard Coleman, Vanderbilt, DB
	Ron Solt, Maryland, G
1985	Duane Bickett, Southern California, LB
1986	Jon Hand, Alabama, DE

INDIANAPOLIS COLTS 1986 VETERAN ROSTER

No.	Name	Pos.	Ht.	Wt.	Birth-date	NFL Exp.	College	Hometown	How Acq.	'85 Games/ Starts
57	†Ahrens, Dave	LB	6-3	245	12/5/58	6	Wisconsin	Oregon, Wis.	T(StL)-'85	16/0
2	Allegre, Raul	K	5-10	167	6/15/59	4	Texas	Shelton, Wash.	T(Dall)-'83	16/0
36	Anderson, Don	CB	5-10	197	7/8/63	2	Purdue	Detroit, Mich.	D2-'85	5/0
61	†Bailey, Don	C	6-4	268	3/24/61	3	Miami	Miami, Fla.	FA-'84	12/0
72	†Baldischwiler, Karl	T	6-5	276	1/19/56	8	Oklahoma	Okmulgee, Okla.	T(Det)-'83	16/16
	t-Barnes, Roosevelt	LB	6-2	228	8/3/58	5	Purdue	Ft. Wayne, Ind.	T(Det)-'86	16/0
81	†Beach, Pat	TE	6-4	244	12/28/59	4	Washington State	Pullman, Wash.	D6-'82	16/16
97	Benson, Charles	DE	6-3	267	11/21/60	3	Baylor	Houston, Tex.	FA-'85	1/0
20	Bentley, Albert	RB	5-11	215	8/15/60	2	Miami	Immokalee, Fla.	SD2-'84	15/1
50	Bickett, Duane	LB	6-5	244	12/1/62	2	Southern California	Los Angeles, Calif.	D1-'85	16/16
85	Bouza, Matt	WR	6-3	215	4/8/59	5	California	Sacramento, Calif.	FA-'82	12/5
84	Boyer, Mark	TE	6-4	232	9/16/62	2	Southern California	Huntington Beach, Calif.	D9-'85	16/7
68	Broughton, Willie	DE	6-5	282	9/9/64	2	Miami	Fort Pierce, Fla.	D4-'85	15/1
72	Call, Kevin	T	6-7	288	11/13/61	3	Colorado State	Boulder, Colo.	D5b-'84	13/0
87	Capers, Wayne	WR	6-2	203	5/17/61	4	Kansas	Miami, Fla.	W(Pitt)-'85	14/10
67	Caron, Roger	T	6-5	292	6/3/62	2	Harvard	Norwell, Mass.	D5-'85	7/1
31	Coleman, Leonard	S	6-2	211	1/30/62	2	Vanderbilt	Boynton Beach, Fla.	D1-'84	12/0
98	Cooks, Johnie	LB	6-4	243	11/23/58	5	Mississippi State	Leland, Miss.	D1a-'82	16/16
38	Daniel, Eugene	CB	5-11	184	5/4/61	3	Louisiana State	Baton Rouge, La.	D8-'84	16/16
27	Davis, Preston	CB	5-11	180	3/10/62	3	Baylor	Lubbock, Tex.	FA-'84	16/16
53	Donaldson, Ray	C	6-4	281	5/17/58	7	Georgia	Rome, Ga.	D2a-'80	16/16
44	Gill, Owen	RB	6-1	230	2/19/62	2	Iowa	Brooklyn, N.Y.	W(Sea)-'85	15/0
25	Glasgow, Nesby	S	5-10	191	4/15/57	8	Washington	Los Angeles, Calif.	D8a-'79	16/16
75	Hinton, Chris	G	6-4	285	7/31/61	4	Northwestern	Chicago, Ill.	T(Den)-'83	16/16
7	t-Hogeboom, Gary	QB	6-4	207	8/21/58	7	Central Michigan	Grand Rapids, Mich.	D5-'80	16/2
56	Hunley, Lamonte	LB	6-2	238	1/31/63	2	Arizona	Petersburg, Va.	FA-'85	16/0
63	†Kirchner, Mark	T	6-3	265	10/19/59	3	Baylor	Houston, Tex.	FA-'84	0*
12	Kofler, Matt	QB	6-3	203	8/30/59	5	San Diego State	San Diego, Calif.	T(Buff)-'85	5/1
55	Krauss, Barry	LB	6-3	253	3/17/57	8	Alabama	Pompano Beach, Fla.	D1-'79	16/16
42	Lee, Keith	CB-S	5-11	200	12/22/57	6	Colorado State	Los Angeles, Calif.	FA-'85	14/0
59	Lowry, Orlando	LB	6-4	238	8/14/61	2	Ohio State	Shaker Heights, Ohio	FA-'85	16/0
88	Martin, Robbie	WR	5-8	187	12/3/58	6	Cal Poly-SLO	Villa Park, Calif.	T(Det)-'85	16/5
49	McGregor, Keli	TE	6-6	253	1/23/63	2	Colorado State	Lakewood, Colo.	FA-'85	8/0*
32	McMillan, Randy	RB	6-0	220	12/17/58	6	Pittsburgh	Jarrettsville, Md.	D1a-'81	14/14
80	Nichols, Ricky	WR	5-10	176	7/27/62	2	East Carolina	Chesapeake, Va.	D8-'85	3/0
93	†Odom, Cliff	LB	6-2	241	9/15/58	6	Texas-Arlington	Beaumont, Tex.	W(Raiders)-'82	16/16
35	†Randle, Tate	S	6-0	204	8/15/59	5	Texas Tech	Fort Stockton, Tex.	FA-'83	16/4
95	Scott, Chris	DE	6-5	271	12/11/61	3	Purdue	Berea, Ohio	D3-'84	16/12
83	Sherwin, Tim	TE	6-6	246	5/4/58	6	Boston College	Watervliet, N.Y.	D4-'81	9/0
91	Smith, Byron	DE	6-5	271	12/21/62	3	California	Inglewood, Calif.	SD3-'84	16/7
66	Solt, Ron	G	6-3	283	5/19/62	3	Maryland	Wilkes-Barre, Pa.	D1b-'84	15/15
3	Stark, Rohn	P	6-3	212	6/4/59	5	Florida State	Minneapolis, Minn.	D2b-'82	16/0
99	Thompson, Donnell	DE	6-5	269	10/27/58	6	North Carolina	Lumberton, N.C.	D1b-'81	14/12
64	†Utt, Ben	G	6-5	281	6/13/59	5	Georgia Tech	Visalia, Calif.	FA-'82	16/16
94	Virkus, Scott	DE	6-5	283	9/7/59	4	San Francisco C.C.	Rochester, N.Y.	FA-'85	15/0
92	†White, Brad	NT	6-2	261	8/18/58	6	Tennessee	Idaho Falls, Idaho	FA-'84	16/15
86	Williams, Oliver	WR	6-3	192	10/17/60	2	Illinois	Los Angeles, Calif.	FA-'85	8/1
96	Winter, Blaise	DE	6-3	274	1/31/62	2	Syracuse	Blauvelt, N.Y.	D2-'84	0*
69	Wisniewski, Leo	NT	6-1	259	11/6/59	4	Penn State	Pittsburgh, Pa.	D2a-'82	0*
34	Wonsley, George	RB	6-0	221	11/23/60	3	Mississippi State	Moss Point, Miss.	D4b-'84	16/9
37	Young, Anthony	S	5-11	196	10/8/63	2	Temple	Pemberton, N.J.	D3-'85	13/12

* Kirchner, Winter, and Wisniewski missed '85 season due to injury; McGregor played 2 games with Denver, 6 with Indianapolis in '85.

†Option playout; subject to developments.

t-Colts traded for Barnes (Detroit), Hogeboom (Dallas).

Traded—Tackle Jim Mills to Denver, quarterback Mike Pagel to Cleveland.

Also played with Colts in '85—NT George Achica (4 games), WR Ray Butler (11), RB Curtis Dickey (6), WR Bernard Henry (1), RB Frank Middleton (6), CB-S George Radachowsky (3), QB Art Schlichter (1).

COACHING STAFF

Head Coach, Rod Dowhower

Pro Career: Named Colts' eleventh head coach on January 28, 1985. In first season as NFL head coach, Dowhower guided Colts to 5-11 mark. No pro playing experience. Career record: 5-11.

Background: Began coaching career as a graduate assistant at San Diego State under Don Coryell in 1966 as quarterback and receivers coach. He was elevated to offensive coordinator in 1968, and served in that capacity until 1972. Dowhower joined the St. Louis Cardinals with Coryell in 1973 as quarterbacks and receivers coach. He moved to UCLA from 1974-75 as offensive coordinator under Dick Vermeil. Following a season as offensive coordinator at Boise State in 1976, Dowhower joined Bill Walsh's staff at Stanford as quarterback coach. He landed his first head coaching job at Stanford in 1979, posting a 5-5-1 record. Dowhower moved back to the NFL from 1980-82 as the offensive coordinator with Denver. He moved to the St. Louis Cardinals, where he was offensive coordinator from 1983-84.

Personal: Born April 15, 1943, Ord, Nebraska. Rod and his wife, Nancy, have two sons, Brian and Deron. They live in Indianapolis.

Assistant Coaches

John Becker, quarterbacks; born February 16, 1943, Alexandria, Va., lives in Indianapolis. Cal State-Northridge 1965. No college or pro playing experience. College coach: UCLA 1970, New Mexico State 1971, New Mexico 1972-73, Los Angeles Valley College 1974-76 (head coach), Oregon 1977-79. Pro coach: Philadelphia Eagles 1980-83, Buffalo Bills 1984, joined Colts in 1985.

George Catavolos, secondary; born May 8, 1945, Cleveland, Ohio, lives in Indianapolis. Defensive back Purdue 1965-67. No pro playing experience. College coach: Purdue 1967-68, 1971-76, Middle Tennessee State 1969, Louisville 1970, Kentucky 1977-81, Tennessee 1982-83. Pro coach: Joined Colts in 1984.

George Hill, defensive coordinator; born April 28, 1933, Bay Village, Ohio, lives in Indianapolis. Tackle-fullback Denison 1954-57. No pro playing experience. College coach: Findlay 1959, Denison 1960-64. Cornell 1965, Duke 1966-70, Ohio State 1971-78. Pro coach: Philadelphia Eagles 1979-84, joined Colts in 1985.

Tom Lovat, offensive line-assistant head coach; born December 28, 1938, Bingham, Utah, lives in Indianapolis. Guard-linebacker Utah 1958-60. No pro playing experience. College coach: Utah 1967, 1972-76 (head coach 1974-76), Idaho State 1968-70, Stanford 1977-79. Pro coach: Saskatchewan Roughriders (CFL) 1971, Green Bay Packers 1980, St. Louis Cardinals 1981-84, joined Colts in 1985.

John Marshall, defensive line; born October 2, 1945, Arroyo Grande, Calif., lives in Indianapolis. Linebacker Washington State 1964. No pro playing experience. College coach: Oregon 1970-76, Southern California 1977-79. Pro coach: Green Bay Packers 1980-82, Atlanta Falcons 1983-85, first year with Colts.

Billie Matthews, offensive coordinator-running backs; born March 15, 1930, Houston, Tex., lives in Indianapolis. Quarterback Southern University 1948-51. No pro playing experience. College coach: Kansas 1970, UCLA 1971-78. Pro coach: San Francisco 49ers 1979-82, Philadelphia Eagles 1983-84, joined Colts in 1985.

Chip Myers, receivers; born July 9, 1945, Panama City, Fla., lives in Indianapolis. Receiver Northwest Oklahoma 1964-66. Pro receiver San Francisco 49ers 1967, Cincinnati Bengals 1969-76. College coach: Illinois 1980-82. Pro coach: Tampa Bay Buccaneers 1983-84, joined Colts in 1985.

Keith Rowen, special teams-assistant offensive line; born September 2, 1952, New York, N.Y., lives in Indianapolis. Stanford. No college or pro playing experience. College coach: Stanford 1975-76, Long Beach State 1977-78, Arizona 1979-82. Pro coach: Boston/New Orleans Breakers (USFL) 1983-84, Cleveland Browns 1984, joined Colts in 1985.

Rick Venturi, linebackers; born February 23, 1946, Taylorville, Ill., lives in Indianapolis. Quarterback Northwestern 1965-67. No pro playing experience. College coach: Northwestern 1968-72, 1978-80 (head coach), Purdue 1973-76, Illinois 1977. Pro coach: Joined Colts in 1982.

Tom Zupancic, strength; born September 14, 1955, Indianapolis, Ind., lives in Indianapolis. Defensive-offensive tackle Indiana Central 1975-78. No pro playing experience. Pro coach: Joined Colts in 1984.

INDIANAPOLIS COLTS 1986 FIRST-YEAR ROSTER

Name	Pos.	Ht.	Wt.	Birth-date	College	Hometown	How Acq.
Anderson, Pete	C	6-3	254	10/20/63	Georgia	Glen Ridge, N.J.	D10
Biggers, Keith (1)	LB	6-0	204	3/31/61	Southern California	Los Angeles, Calif.	FA
Brewster, Tim (1)	TE	6-4	232	10/13/60	Illinois	Champaign, Ill.	FA
Brooks, Bill	WR	6-1	187	4/6/64	Boston University	Milton, Mass.	D4
Brotzki, Bob	T	6-4	266	12/24/62	Syracuse	Portsmouth, N.H.	D9
Chatman, Ricky (1)	LB	6-2	222	1/4/62	Louisiana State	Winnfield, La.	FA
Davis, Russell (1)	TE	6-4	217	6/16/60	Maryland	Silver Spring, Md.	FA
Hand, Jon	NT	6-6	283	11/13/63	Alabama	Sylacauga, Ala.	D1
Holmes, Don (1)	WR	5-10	180	4/1/61	Mesa College	Grand Junction, Colo.	FA
Hooper, Trell	CB-S	5-11	190	12/22/61	Memphis State	Jackson, Tenn.	D8
Kellar, Scott	DE	6-2	260	12/31/63	Northern Illinois	Roselle, Ill.	D5a
Locklin, Kim (1)	RB	6-0	210	11/21/63	New Mexico State	Rockdale, Tex.	FA
Martin, Ed (1)	LB	6-3	225	5/29/62	Indiana State	Chicago, Ill.	FA
McIntyre, Marlon (1)	RB	6-0	220	8/28/62	Pittsburgh	Pricedale, Pa.	FA
O'Malley, Steve	NT	6-2	257	12/3/62	Northern Illinois	Oak Forest, Ill.	D7a
Robertson, John (1)	T	6-6	280	9/26/61	East Carolina	Cherry Hill, N.J.	FA
Rockford, Jim (1)	CB-S	6-0	220	8/28/62	Oklahoma	Norman, Okla.	FA
Sims, Tommy	CB-S	6-0	190	9/29/62	Tennessee	Americus, Ga.	D7c
Trudeau, Jack	QB	6-3	211	11/13/63	Illinois	Livermore, Calif.	D2
Wade, Steve	NT	6-3	270	7/10/64	Vanderbilt	Chattanooga, Tenn.	D12a
Walker, Gary	C	6-3	269	10/15/63	Boston University	Portsmouth, N.H.	D5b
White, Chris	K	5-11	168	6/17/62	Illinois	Champaign, Ill.	D7b
Williams, Isaac	NT	6-1	260	10/9/64	Florida State	Sanford, Fla.	D12b
Wood, Tony (1)	K	5-8	195	3/20/63	Tulane	River Ridge, La.	FA
Wright, Frank (1)	NT	6-3	280	11/25/61	South Carolina	Columbia, S.C.	FA

The term NFL Rookie is defined as a player who is in his first season of professional football and has not been on the roster of another professional football team for any regular season or postseason games. A Rookie is designated by an "R" on NFL rosters. Players who have been active in another professional football league or players who have NFL experience, including either preseason training camp or being on an active roster for fewer than three regular season or postseason games, are termed NFL First-Year Players. An NFL First-Year Player is designated by a "1" on NFL rosters. Thereafter, a player on an NFL active roster for at least three regular season or postseason games is credited with an additional year of NFL playing experience.

NOTES

KANSAS CITY CHIEFS

American Football Conference
Western Division

Team Colors: Red, Gold, and White

One Arrowhead Drive
Kansas City, Missouri 64129
Telephone: (816) 924-9300

Club Officials

Owner: Lamar Hunt
President: Jack Steadman
Vice President-General Manager: Jim Schaaf
Assistant to General Manager: Dennis Thum
Vice President-Administration: Don Steadman
Treasurer: Randy Cooper
Secretary: Jim Seigfreid
Director of Player Personnel: Les Miller
Director of Public Relations and Community Relations: Bob Sprenger
Media Services Manager: Gary Heise
Community Relations Manager: Brenda Boatright
Director of Sales and Promotions: Mitch Wheeler
Director of Arrowhead Stadium: David Smith
Stadium Operations: Bob Wachter
Ticket Manager: Joe Mazza
Manager of Information Systems: Andy Sawyer
Trainer: Dave Kendall
Equipment Coordinator: John Phillips

Stadium: Arrowhead Stadium • **Capacity:** 78,067
One Arrowhead Drive
Kansas City, Missouri 64129

Playing Surface: AstroTurf-8

Training Camp: William Jewell College
Liberty, Missouri 64068

1986 SCHEDULE

Preseason

Aug. 9	**Cincinnati**	7:30
Aug. 16	at St. Louis	7:00
Aug. 23	**Buffalo**	7:30
Aug. 30	at New Orleans	7:00

Regular Season

Sept. 7	**Cincinnati**	3:00
Sept. 14	at Seattle	1:00
Sept. 21	**Houston**	3:00
Sept. 28	at Buffalo	1:00
Oct. 5	**Los Angeles Raiders**	12:00
Oct. 12	at Cleveland	1:00
Oct. 19	**San Diego**	3:00
Oct. 26	**Tampa Bay**	12:00
Nov. 2	at San Diego	1:00
Nov. 9	**Seattle**	12:00
Nov. 16	at Denver	2:00
Nov. 23	at St. Louis	3:00
Nov. 30	**Buffalo**	12:00
Dec. 7	**Denver**	12:00
Dec. 14	at Los Angeles Raiders	1:00
Dec. 21	at Pittsburgh	1:00

CHIEFS COACHING HISTORY

Dallas Texans 1960-62
(192-179-10)

1960-74	Hank Stram	129-79-10
1975-77	Paul Wiggin*	11-24-0
1977	Tom Bettis	1-6-0
1978-82	Marv Levy	31-42-0
1983-85	John Mackovic	20-28-0

*Released after seven games in 1977

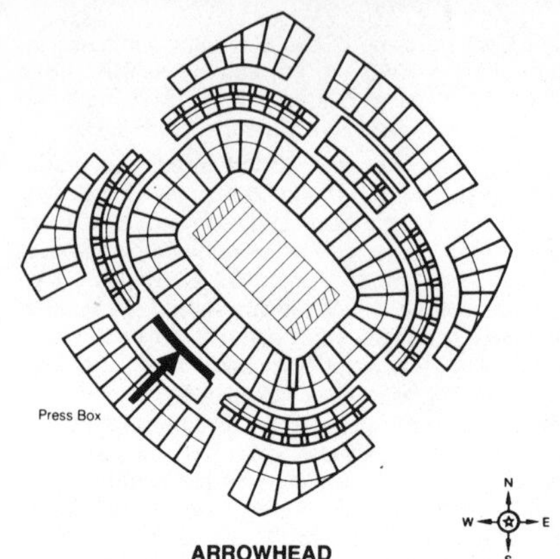

ARROWHEAD

RECORD HOLDERS

Individual Records—Career

Category	Name	Performance
Rushing (Yds.)	Ed Podolak, 1969-1977	4,451
Passing (Yds.)	Len Dawson, 1962-1975	28,507
Passing (TDs)	Len Dawson, 1962-1975	237
Receiving (No.)	Otis Taylor, 1965-1975	410
Receiving (Yds.)	Otis Taylor, 1965-1975	7,306
Interceptions	Emmitt Thomas, 1966-1978	58
Punting (Avg.)	Jerrel Wilson, 1963-1977	43.5
Punt Return (Avg.)	J.T. Smith, 1979-1984	10.6
Kickoff Return (Avg.)	Noland Smith, 1967-69	26.8
Field Goals	Jan Stenerud, 1967-1979	279
Touchdowns (Tot.)	Otis Taylor, 1965-1975	60
Points	Jan Stenerud, 1967-1979	1,231

Individual Records—Single Season

Category	Name	Performance
Rushing (Yds.)	Joe Delaney, 1981	1,121
Passing (Yds.)	Bill Kenney, 1983	4,348
Passing (TDs)	Len Dawson, 1964	30
Receiving (No.)	Carlos Carson, 1983	80
Receiving (Yds.)	Carlos Carson, 1983	1,351
Interceptions	Emmitt Thomas, 1974	12
Punting (Avg.)	Jerrel Wilson, 1965	46.0
Punt Return (Avg.)	Abner Haynes, 1960	15.4
Kickoff Return (Avg.)	Dave Grayson, 1962	29.7
Field Goals	Jan Stenerud, 1968, 1970	30
Touchdowns (Tot.)	Abner Haynes, 1962	19
Points	Jan Stenerud, 1968	129

Individual Records—Single Game

Category	Name	Performance
Rushing (Yds.)	Joe Delaney, 11-15-81	193
Passing (Yds.)	Len Dawson, 11-1-64	435
Passing (TDs)	Len Dawson, 11-1-64	6
Receiving (No.)	Ed Podolak, 10-7-73	12
Receiving (Yds.)	Stephone Paige, 12-22-85	309
Interceptions	Bobby Ply, 12-16-62	4
	Bobby Hunt, 12-4-64	4
Field Goals	Jan Stenerud, 11-2-69	5
	Jan Stenerud, 12-7-69	5
	Jan Stenerud, 12-19-71	5
Touchdowns (Tot.)	Abner Haynes, 11-26-61	5
Points	Abner Haynes, 11-26-61	30

1985 TEAM STATISTICS

	Kansas City	Opp.
Total First Downs	258	336
Rushing	79	129
Passing	158	184
Penalty	21	23
Third Down: Made/Att.	76/225	99/239
Fourth Down: Made/Att.	8/16	10/20
Total Net Yards	4877	5658
Avg. Per Game	304.8	353.6
Total Plays	982	1126
Avg. Per Play	5.0	5.0
Net Yards Rushing	1486	2169
Avg. Per Game	92.9	135.6
Total Rushes	428	513
Net Yards Passing	3391	3489
Avg. Per Game	211.9	218.1
Tackled/Yards Lost	43/335	37/263
Gross Yards	3726	3752
Att./Completions	511/267	576/332
Completion Pct.	52.3	57.6
Had Intercepted	23	27
Punts/Avg.	95/40.3	75/41.2
Net Punting Avg.	32.4	34.2
Penalties/Yards Lost	87/666	89/777
Fumbles/Ball Lost	22/11	25/14
Touchdowns	35	41
Rushing	10	18
Passing	23	22
Returns	2	1
Avg. Time of Possession	28:06	31:54

1985 TEAM RECORD

Preseason (3-1)

Date	Kansas City		Opponents
8/10	35	Cincinnati	27
8/17	13	*New England	31
8/24	24	Houston	19
8/31	17	*St. Louis	13
	89		90

Regular Season (6-10)

Date	Kansas City		Opp.	Att.
9/8	47	New Orleans	27	57,760
9/12	36	*L.A. Raiders	20	72,686
9/22	0	Miami	31	70,244
9/29	28	*Seattle	7	50,485
10/6	10	L.A. Raiders	19	55,133
10/13	20	San Diego	31	50,067
10/20	0	*L.A. Rams	16	64,474
10/27	10	*Denver	30	68,248
11/3	20	Houston	23	41,238
11/10	28	*Pittsburgh	36	46,126
11/17	3	San Francisco	31	56,447
11/24	20	*Indianapolis	7	19,762
12/1	6	Seattle	24	52,655
12/8	38	*Atlanta	10	18,199
12/14	13	Denver	14	69,209
12/22	38	*San Diego	34	18,178

*Home Game

Score by Periods

Kansas City	77	111	66	63	0	—	317
Opponents	39	135	65	121	0	—	360

Attendance

Home 358,158 Away 452,753 Total 810,911
Single game home record, 82,094 (11-5-72)
Single season home record, 509,291 (1972)

1985 INDIVIDUAL STATISTICS

Rushing	Att.	Yds.	Avg.	LG	TD
Heard	164	595	3.6	33	4
Pruitt, Buff.-K.C.	112	390	3.5	54	2
Pruitt, K.C.	105	366	3.5	54	2
Horton	48	146	3.0	19t	3
Smith	30	118	3.9	27	0
Blackledge	17	97	5.7	25	0
King	28	83	3.0	9	0
Carson	3	25	8.3	13	0
Lacy	6	21	3.5	6	0
Jones	12	19	1.6	7	0
Paige	1	15	15.0	15	0
Kenney	14	1	0.1	5	1
Chiefs	428	1486	3.5	54	10
Opponents	513	2169	4.2	50	18

Passing	Att.	Comp.	Pct.	Yds.	TD	Int.	Tkld.	Rate
Kenney	338	181	53.6	2536	17	9	28/223	83.6
Blackledge	172	86	50.0	1190	6	14	15/112	50.3
Horton	1	0	0.0	0	0	0	0/0	39.6
Chiefs	511	267	52.3	3726	23	23	43/335	72.3
Opponents	576	332	57.6	3752	22	27	37/263	70.5

Receiving	No.	Yds.	Avg.	LG	TD
Carson	47	843	17.9	37t	4
Paige	43	943	21.9	84t	10
Heard	31	257	8.3	27	2
W. Arnold	28	339	12.1	38	1
Horton	28	185	6.6	22	1
Marshall	25	446	17.8	50	0
Smith	18	157	8.7	45t	2
Hancock	15	286	19.1	48	2
King	7	45	6.4	8	0
Pruitt	7	43	6.1	9	0
Holston, Hou.-K.C.	6	76	12.7	25	0
Holston, K.C.	5	51	10.2	17	0
Scott	5	61	12.2	21	0
Hayes	5	39	7.8	12	1
Jones	3	31	10.3	15	0
Chiefs	267	3726	14.0	84t	23
Opponents	332	3752	11.3	56t	22

Interceptions	No.	Yds.	Avg.	LG	TD
Lewis	8	59	7.4	16	0
Cherry	7	87	12.4	47t	1
Ross	3	47	15.7	27	0
Hill	3	37	12.3	37	0
Cocroft	3	27	9.0	27	0
Radecic	1	21	21.0	21	0
Robinson	1	20	20.0	20	0
Burruss	1	0	0.0	0	0
Chiefs	27	298	11.0	47t	1
Opponents	23	251	10.9	47	0

Punting	No.	Yds.	Avg.	In 20	LG
J. Arnold	93	3827	41.2	15	62
Chiefs	95	3827	40.3	15	62
Opponents	75	3088	41.2	17	60

Punt Returns	No.	FC	Yds.	Avg.	LG	TD
Lane	43	7	381	8.9	57	0
Chiefs	43	7	381	8.9	57	0
Opponents	48	15	530	11.0	71t	1

Kickoff Returns	No.	Yds.	Avg.	LG	TD
Smith	33	654	19.8	39	0
Lane	13	269	20.7	37	0
Hancock	6	125	20.8	40	0
Paige	2	36	18.0	23	0
W. Arnold	2	9	4.5	9	0
King	1	13	13.0	13	0
Shorthose	1	11	11.0	11	0
Hayes	1	0	0.0	0	0
Chiefs	59	1117	18.9	40	0
Opponents	69	1626	23.6	69	0

Scoring	TD R	TD P	TD Rt	PAT	FG	Saf	TP
Lowery	0	0	0	35/35	24/27	0	107
Paige	0	10	0	0/0	0/0	0	60
Heard	4	2	0	0/0	0/0	0	36
Carson	0	4	0	0/0	0/0	0	24
Horton	3	1	0	0/0	0/0	0	24
Hancock	0	2	0	0/0	0/0	0	12
Pruitt	2	0	0	0/0	0/0	0	12
Smith	0	2	0	0/0	0/0	0	12
W. Arnold	0	1	0	0/0	0/0	0	6
Cherry	0	0	1	0/0	0/0	0	6
Hayes	0	1	0	0/0	0/0	0	6
Kenney	1	0	0	0/0	0/0	0	6
Lewis	0	0	1	0/0	0/0	0	6
Chiefs	10	23	2	35/35	24/27	0	317
Opponents	18	22	1	39/41	25/30	0	360

FIRST-ROUND SELECTIONS

(If club had no first-round selection, first player drafted is listed with round in parentheses.)

Year	Player, College, Position
1960	Don Meredith, Southern Methodist, QB
1961	E.J. Holub, Texas Tech, C
1962	Ronnie Bull, Baylor, RB
1963	Buck Buchanan, Grambling, DT
	Ed Budde, Michigan State, G
1964	Pete Beathard, Southern California, QB
1965	Gale Sayers, Kansas, RB
1966	Aaron Brown, Minnesota, DE
1967	Gene Trosch, Miami, DE-DT
1968	Mo Moorman, Texas A&M, G
	George Daney, Texas-El Paso, G
1969	Jim Marsalis, Tennessee State, CB
1970	Sid Smith, Southern California, T
1971	Elmo Wright, Houston, WR
1972	Jeff Kinney, Nebraska, RB
1973	Gary Butler, Rice, TE (2)
1974	Woody Green, Arizona State, RB
1975	Elmore Stephens, Kentucky, TE (2)
1976	Rod Walters, Iowa, G
1977	Gary Green, Baylor, DB
1978	Art Still, Kentucky, DE
1979	Mike Bell, Colorado State, DE
	Steve Fuller, Clemson, QB
1980	Brad Budde, Southern California, G
1981	Willie Scott, South Carolina, TE
1982	Anthony Hancock, Tennessee, WR
1983	Todd Blackledge, Penn State, QB
1984	Bill Maas, Pittsburgh, DT
	John Alt, Iowa, T
1985	Ethan Horton, North Carolina, RB
1986	Brian Jozwiak, West Virginia, T

KANSAS CITY CHIEFS 1986 VETERAN ROSTER

No.	Name	Pos.	Ht.	Wt.	Birth-date	NFL Exp.	College	Hometown	How Acq.	'85 Games/ Starts
76	Alt, John	T	6-7	282	5/30/62	3	Iowa	Columbia Heights, Minn.	D1b-'78	13/6
6	Arnold, Jim	P	6-2	220	1/31/61	4	Vanderbilt	Dalton, Ga.	D5-'83	16/0
87	Arnold, Walt	TE	6-3	221	8/31/58	7	New Mexico	Los Alamos, N.M.	FA-'84	16/16
68	Auer, Scott	G-T	6-5	255	10/4/61	3	Michigan State	Fort Wayne, Ind.	D9a-'84	7/6
77	Baldinger, Rich	G-T	6-4	281	12/31/59	4	Wake Forest	Long Island, N.Y.	FA-'83	16/5
99	Bell, Mike	DE	6-4	259	8/30/57	7	Colorado State	Wichita, Kan.	D1a-'79	11/11
14	Blackledge, Todd	QB	6-3	225	2/25/61	4	Penn State	Canton, Ohio	D1-'83	12/6
57	Blanton, Jerry	LB	6-1	229	12/10/56	8	Kentucky	Toledo, Ohio	FA-'79	16/3
66	Budde, Brad	G	6-4	271	5/9/58	7	Southern California	Kansas City, Mo.	D1-'80	7/7
34	Burruss, Lloyd	S	6-0	209	10/31/57	6	Maryland	Charlottesville, N.C.	D3c-'81	15/14
88	Carson, Carlos	WR	5-11	182	12/28/58	7	Louisiana State	Lake Worth, Fla.	D5a-'80	15/14
20	Cherry, Deron	S	5-11	196	9/12/59	6	Rutgers	Palmyra, N.J.	FA-'81	16/16
22	Cocroft, Sherman	S	6-1	188	8/29/61	2	San Jose State	Mobile, Ala.	FA-'85	16/0
55	Cooper, Louis	LB	6-2	235	8/5/63	2	Western Carolina	Marion, S.C.	FA-'85	8/0
50	Daniels, Calvin	LB	6-3	241	12/26/58	5	North Carolina	Goldsboro, N.C.	D2-'82	16/16
51	t-Donnalley, Rick	C-G	6-2	257	12/11/58	5	North Carolina	Raleigh, N.C.	T(Wash)-'86	13/12
65	Fada, Rob	G	6-2	259	5/7/61	4	Pittsburgh	Fairborn, Ohio	FA-'85	5/0
40	t-Green, Boyce	RB	5-11	215	6/24/60	4	Carson-Newman	Beaufort, S.C.	T(Clev)-'86	13/0
90	Hamm, Bob	DE	6-4	257	4/24/59	4	Nevada-Reno	Mountain View, Calif.	T(Hou)-'85	14/5
82	Hancock, Anthony	WR-KR	6-0	204	6/10/60	5	Tennessee	Cleveland, Ohio	D1-'82	16/1
85	Hayes, Jonathan	TE	6-5	234	8/11/62	2	Iowa	Pittsburgh, Pa.	D2-'85	16/0
44	Heard, Herman	RB	5-10	182	11/24/61	3	Southern Colorado	Denver, Colo.	D3-'84	16/12
60	†Herkenhoff, Matt	T	6-4	286	4/2/51	11	Minnesota	Melrose, Minn.	D4-'74	10/10
23	†Hill, Greg	CB	6-1	199	2/12/61	4	Oklahoma State	Orange, Tex.	W(Hou)-'84	16/1
93	Holle, Eric	DE-NT	6-5	258	9/5/60	3	Texas	Austin, Tex.	D5a-'84	16/5
32	Horton, Ethan	RB	6-3	228	12/19/62	2	North Carolina	Kannapolis, N.C.	D1-'85	16/0
52	†Jolly, Ken	LB	6-2	220	2/28/62	3	Mid-America Nazarene	Dallas, Tex.	FA-'84	16/12
9	Kenney, Bill	QB	6-4	211	1/20/55	8	Northern Colorado	San Clemente, Calif.	FA-'79	16/10
46	King, Bruce	RB	6-1	219	1/7/63	2	Purdue	Lincoln City, Ind.	D5-'85	16/6
74	Koch, Pete	DE	6-6	265	1/23/62	3	Maryland	Manhasset, N.Y.	FA-'85	16/0
41	Lane, Garcia	CB-KR	5-9	180	12/31/61	2	Ohio State	Youngstown, Ohio	FA-'85	16/0
29	†Lewis, Albert	CB	6-2	192	10/6/60	4	Grambling	Mansfield, La.	D3-'83	16/16
71	Lindstrom, Dave	DE	6-6	258	11/16/54	9	Boston College	Weymouth, Mass.	W(SD)-'78	16/2
62	†Lingner, Adam	C-G	6-4	260	11/2/60	4	Illinois	Rock Island, Ill.	D9-'83	16/0
8	Lowery, Nick	K	6-4	189	5/27/56	7	Dartmouth	Washington, D.C.	FA-'80	16/0
72	Lutz, Dave	T	6-5	287	12/30/59	4	Georgia Tech	Peachland, N.C.	D2-'83	16/16
63	Maas, Bill	NT-DE	6-5	259	3/2/62	3	Pittsburgh	Newtown Square, Pa.	D1-'84	16/16
89	†Marshall, Henry	WR	6-2	213	8/9/54	11	Missouri	Dalzell, S.C.	D3d-'76	11/9
94	McAlister, Ken	LB	6-5	220	4/15/60	4	San Francisco	Oakland, Calif.	FA-'84	0*
64	Olderman, Bob	G	6-5	262	6/5/62	2	Virginia	Atlanta, Ga.	D4-'85	16/14
83	Paige, Stephone	WR	6-2	191	10/15/61	4	Fresno State	Long Beach, Calif.	FA-'83	16/8
95	Paine, Jeff	LB	6-2	224	8/19/61	3	Texas A&M	Richardson, Tex.	D5b-'84	12/4
43	Pruitt, Mike	RB	6-0	225	4/3/54	11	Purdue	Chicago, Ill.	FA-'85	13/10*
97	Radecic, Scott	LB	6-3	246	6/14/62	3	Penn State	Pittsburgh, Pa.	D2-'84	16/16
30	Robinson, Mark	S	5-11	206	9/13/62	3	Penn State	Pittsburgh, Pa.	D4-'84	11/1
31	Ross, Kevin	CB	5-9	182	1/16/62	3	Temple	Paulsboro, N.J.	D7-'84	16/15
53	†Rush, Bob	C	6-5	270	2/27/55	9	Memphis State	Clarksville, Tenn.	T(SD)-'83	16/16
81	†Scott, Willie	TE	6-4	254	2/13/59	6	South Carolina	Newberry, S.C.	D1-'81	16/5
80	Shorthose, George	WR-KR	6-0	198	12/22/61	2	Missouri	Stanton, Calif.	FA-'85	3/0
42	Smith, Jeff	RB-KR	5-9	201	3/22/62	2	Nebraska	Wichita, Kan.	D10-'85	13/1
59	Spani, Gary	LB	6-2	229	1/9/56	9	Kansas State	Manhattan, Kan.	D3-'78	14/13
92	Stephens, Hal	DE	6-4	252	4/14/61	2	East Carolina	Whiteville, N.C.	FA-'85	2/0*
67	Still, Art	DE	6-7	254	12/5/55	9	Kentucky	Camden, N.J.	D1-'78	9/9

* McAlister missed '85 season due to injury; Pruitt played 4 games with Buffalo, 9 with Kansas City in '85; Stephens played 1 game with Detroit, 1 with Kansas City.

†Option playout; subject to developments.

t-Chiefs traded for Donnalley (Washington), Green (Cleveland).

Also played with Chiefs in '85—WR Mike Holston (4 games), RB E.J. Jones (5), RB Ken Lacy (2), S Odis McKinney (5), T Billy Shields (2).

COACHING STAFF

Head Coach, John Mackovic

Pro Career: Begins fourth season as Chiefs head coach. Came to the Chiefs after serving as quarterback coach with Dallas Cowboys in 1981-82. No pro playing experience. Career record: 20-28.

Background: Played quarterback for Wake Forest 1961-64. Was freshman coach at Army in 1967-68 before joining San Jose State as offensive coordinator 1969-70. Returned to Army as an assistant 1971-72, then to Arizona 1973-76, and Purdue 1977. Became head coach at Wake Forest 1978-80 before going to the Cowboys.

Personal: Born October 1, 1943, Barberton, Ohio. John and his wife, Arlene, live in Kansas City, and have two children—Aimee and John III.

Assistant Coaches

David Brazil, defensive assistant; born March 25, 1936, Detroit, Mich., lives in Kansas City. No college or pro playing experience. College coach: Holy Cross 1968-69, Tulsa 1970-71, Eastern Michigan 1972-74, Boston College 1978-79. Pro coach: Detroit Wheels (WFL) 1975, Chicago Fire (WFL) 1976, joined Chiefs in 1984.

Walt Corey, defensive coordinator-linebackers; born May 9, 1938, Latrobe, Pa., lives in Kansas City. Defensive end Miami 1957-59. Pro linebacker Kansas City Chiefs 1960-66. College coach: Utah State 1967-69, Miami 1970-71. Pro coach: Kansas City Chiefs 1971-74, Cleveland Browns 1975-77, rejoined Chiefs in 1978.

Frank Gansz, assistant head coach-kicking teams; born November 22, 1938, Altoona, Pa., lives in Kansas City. Center Navy 1957-59. No pro playing experience. College coach: Air Force 1964-66, Colgate 1968, Navy 1969-72, Oklahoma State 1973, 1975, Army 1974, UCLA 1976-77. Pro coach: San Francisco 49ers 1978, Cincinnati Bengals 1979-80, Kansas City Chiefs 1981-82, Philadelphia Eagles 1983-85, rejoined Chiefs 1986.

Doug Graber, defensive backs; born September 26, 1944, Detroit, Mich., lives in Kansas City. Defensive back Wayne State 1963-66. No pro playing experience. College coach: Michigan Tech 1969-71, Eastern Michigan 1972-75, Ball State 1976-77, Wisconsin 1978-81, Montana State 1982 (head coach). Pro coach: Joined Chiefs in 1983.

J. D. Helm, offensive assistant; born December 27, 1940, El Dorado Springs, Mo., lives in Overland Park, Kan. Running back Kansas 1959-60. No pro playing experience. College coach: Brigham Young 1969-75. Pro coach: Joined Chiefs in 1976.

C. T. Hewgley, offensive and defensive lines-coordinator of strength and conditioning program; born August 22, 1925, Nashville, Tenn., lives in Kansas City. Tackle Wyoming 1947-50. No pro playing experience. College coach: Miami 1968-70, Wyoming 1971-73, Nebraska-Omaha 1974 (head coach), Michigan State 1976-79, Arizona State 1980-82. Pro coach: Joined Chiefs in 1983.

Carl Mauck, offensive line; born July 7, 1947, McLeansboro, Ill., lives in Kansas City. Center Southern Illinois 1965-68. Pro center San Diego Chargers 1969-74, Houston Oilers 1975-80. Pro coach: New Orleans Saints 1982-85, first year with Chiefs.

Pete McCulley, quarterbacks; born November 29, 1931, Franklin, Miss., lives in Kansas City. Quarterback Louisiana Tech 1954-56. No pro playing experience. College coach: Stephen F. Austin 1959, Houston 1960-61, Baylor 1963-69, Navy 1970-72. Pro coach: Baltimore Colts 1973-75, Washington Redskins 1976-77, San Francisco 49ers 1978 (head coach nine games), New York Jets 1979-82, joined Chiefs in 1983.

Willie Peete, offensive backs; born September 14, 1937, Mesa, Ariz., lives in Kansas City. Wide receiver Arizona 1956-59. No pro playing experience. College coach: Arizona 1970-82. Pro coach: Joined Chiefs in 1983.

Richard Williamson, receivers; born April 13, 1941, Fort Deposit, Ala., lives in Kansas City. Wide receiver Alabama 1959-62. No pro playing experience. College coach: Alabama 1963-67, 1970-71, Arkansas 1968-69, 1972-74, Memphis State 1975-80. Pro coach: Joined Chiefs in 1983.

John Paul Young, defensive line; born December 31, 1939, Dallas, Tex., lives in Kansas City. Linebacker Texas-El Paso 1959-61. No pro playing experience. College coach: Texas-El Paso 1962-63, Southern Methodist 1967-68, Oklahoma State 1969, Texas A&M 1970-77. Pro coach: Houston Oilers 1978-80, New Orleans Saints 1981-85, first year with Chiefs.

KANSAS CITY CHIEFS 1986 FIRST-YEAR ROSTER

Name	Pos.	Ht.	Wt.	Birth-date	College	Hometown	How Acq.
Addison, John	TE	6-5	233	12/15/61	William Jewell	Independence, Mo.	FA
Adickes, Mark (1)	T	6-4	274	4/22/61	Baylor	Waco, Tex.	SD1-84
Albert, Mark	CB	6-0	205	4/10/62	Sacramento State	Mobile, Ala.	FA
Atterberry, Greg	CB	5-10	180	7/19/62	Central Florida	Denmark, S.C.	FA
Baldinger, Gary	NT-DE	6-2	260	10/4/63	Wake Forest	Winston-Salem, N.C.	D9
Baugh, Tom	C	6-3	274	12/1/63	Southern Illinois	North Riverside, Ill.	D4a
Bergmann, Paul (1)	TE	6-2	235	3/30/61	UCLA	Carlsbad, Calif.	FA
Brinkley, Tony	RB	5-8	220	6/1/62	Rice	Wharton, Tex.	FA
Brown, Byron (1)	RB	5-8	182	10/28/61	Nevada-Las Vegas	Las Vegas, Nev.	FA
Cofield, Tim	LB	6-2	235	5/18/63	Elizabeth City State	Murfreesboro, N.C.	FA
Colbert, Lewis	P	5-11	179	8/23/63	Auburn	Phenix City, Ala.	D8
Drake, Ron	C	6-2	250	8/10/62	Nevada-Las Vegas	Upland, Calif.	FA
Eggleston, Kevin	T	6-7	320	12/18/62	Iowa State	Memphis, Mo.	FA
Epps, Jack	CB	6-0	195	3/20/63	Kansas State	Overland Park, Kan.	FA
Estell, Richard	WR	6-2	208	10/13/63	Kansas	Kansas City, Kan.	FA
Federico, Creig	WR	6-2	200	5/7/63	Illinois State	Schaumburg, Ill.	FA
Fleming, Bruce	LB	6-2	226	10/8/63	Miami	Monaca, Pa.	FA
Fox, Charles	WR	5-11	180	10/3/63	Furman	Rapid City, S.D	D4b
Garron, Andre	RB	5-11	193	2/6/64	New Hampshire	Framingham, Mass.	FA
Goodburn, Kelly	P	6-2	210	4/14/62	Emporia State	Cushing, Iowa	FA
Griffin, Leonard	DE	6-4	252	9/22/62	Grambling	Lake Providence, La.	D3
Hackett, Dino	LB	6-3	220	6/28/64	Appalachian State	Greensboro, N.C.	D2
Hagood, Kent	RB	5-11	218	3/10/63	South Carolina	Piedmont, S.C.	D6a
Happel, Bill	WR	5-11	187	12/17/63	Iowa	Cedar Rapids, Iowa	FA
Harris, James	LB	6-2	213	2/3/63	Grambling	Monroe, La.	FA
Harry, Emile (1)	WR	5-11	175	4/5/63	Stanford	Fountain Valley, Calif.	FA
Heath, Jeff	K	5-11	185	5/11/63	East Carolina	Virginia Beach, Va.	FA
Hopkins, Brendel	DE	6-4	235	3/8/63	Grambling	Lake Providence, La.	FA
Ivemeyer, John	T	6-3	272	7/20/64	Georgia Tech	Clayton, Ga.	FA
James, Angelo	S	6-0	180	6/13/62	Sacramento State	Mobile, Ala.	FA
Jozwiak, Brian	T	6-5	309	6/20/63	West Virginia	Catonsville, Md.	D1
Knapp, Greg	QB	6-4	202	3/5/63	Sacramento State	Seal Beach, Calif.	FA
Ledenko, Rob	S	6-2	196	5/28/63	Brigham Young	Chelan, Wash.	FA
Lilleberg, Jon	T	6-5	266	9/26/62	Minnesota	Atwater, Minn.	FA
Mark, Bruce	DE	6-3	258	2/7/63	Wake Forest	Cedarhurst, N.Y.	FA
McAllister, Darren	DE	6-7	290	3/6/63	Prairie View A&M	Brooklyn, N.Y.	FA
McCarthy, Tom (1)	P	6-2	200	6/25/62	Hawaii	Honolulu, Hawaii	FA
Moran, Matt (1)	T	6-4	270	5/14/62	Stanford	Palo Alto, Calif.	FA
Murray, Lloyd	RB	6-0	225	3/11/63	Mid-Amer. Nazarene	Boise, Idaho	FA
Oliver, Ken	WR	6-2	195	8/25/63	Miami	Miami, Fla.	FA
Ozee, Ken	K	5-10	185	9/7/63	Texas Christian	Amarillo, Tex.	FA
Pearson, Aaron	LB	6-0	236	8/22/64	Mississippi State	Gadsden, Ala.	D11
Pearson, J.C. (1)	CB-S	5-11	183	8/17/63	Washington	Oceanside, Calif.	FA
Pickens, Jerry	CB	5-10	190	5/2/62	North Texas State	San Augustine, Tex.	FA
Pippens, Woodie (1)	RB	5-11	225	2/7/63	Thiel College	Cleveland, Ohio	FA
Readon, Isaac	NT	6-0	273	5/16/63	Hampton Institute	Miami, Fla.	D10
Scott, Tony	LB	6-2	243	8/23/63	Wake Forest	Lancaster, S.C.	FA
Seurer, Frank (1)	QB	6-1	195	8/16/62	Kansas	Huntington Beach, Calif.	FA
Shehan, Tom	T	6-3	280	10/24/62	Texas Christian	Irving, Tex.	FA
Smith, Chris (1)	RB	6-0	222	6/1/63	Notre Dame	Cincinnati, Ohio	FA
Smith, Dave	T	6-4	277	2/12/63	Tulsa	Kirkwood, Mo.	FA
Thomas, Lavale	RB	5-11	205	12/12/63	Fresno State	Fresno, Calif.	FA
Tuiasosopo, Ana	LB	6-1	255	11/7/63	Hawaii	San Jose, Calif.	FA
Walczak, Mark	TE	6-6	252	4/26/62	Arizona	Rochester, N.Y.	FA

The term NFL Rookie is defined as a player who is in his first season of professional football and has not been on the roster of another professional football team for any regular season or postseason games. A Rookie is designated by an "R" on NFL rosters. Players who have been active in another professional football league or players who have NFL experience, including either preseason training camp or being on an active roster for fewer than three regular season or postseason games, are termed NFL First-Year Players. An NFL First-Year Player is designated by a "1" on NFL rosters. Thereafter, a player on an NFL active roster for at least three regular season or postseason games is credited with an additional year of NFL playing experience.

NOTES

LOS ANGELES RAIDERS

American Football Conference
Western Division

Team Colors: Silver and Black

332 Center Street
El Segundo, California 90245
Telephone: (213) 322-3451

Club Officials

Managing General Partner: Al Davis
Executive Assistant: Al LoCasale
Player Personnel: Ron Wolf
Business Manager: Ken LaRue
Senior Administrators: Tom Grimes, Irv Kaze, John Herrera
Finance: Michael Reinfeldt
Marketing/Promotions: Mike Ornstein
Community Relations: Gil Hernandez, Calvin Peterson
Publications: Steve Hartman
Ticket Operations: Peter Eiges
Trainers: George Anderson, H. Rod Martin
Equipment Manager: Richard Romanski

Stadium: Los Angeles Memorial Coliseum • **Capacity:** 92,516
3911 South Figueroa Street
Los Angeles, California 90037

Playing Surface: Grass

Training Camp: Hilton Hotel
Oxnard, California 93030

1986 SCHEDULE

Preseason

Aug. 10	at San Francisco	12:00
Aug. 16	**Dallas**	6:00
Aug. 22	**New England**	7:00
Aug. 28	**Cleveland**	7:00

Regular Season

Sept. 7	at Denver	2:00
Sept. 14	at Washington	1:00
Sept. 21	**New York Giants**	1:00
Sept. 28	**San Diego**	1:00
Oct. 5	at Kansas City	12:00
Oct. 12	**Seattle**	1:00
Oct. 19	at Miami	1:00
Oct. 26	at Houston	12:00
Nov. 2	**Denver**	1:00
Nov. 9	at Dallas	3:00
Nov. 16	**Cleveland**	1:00
Nov. 20	at San Diego (Thursday)	5:00
Nov. 30	**Philadelphia**	1:00
Dec. 8	at Seattle (Monday)	6:00
Dec. 14	**Kansas City**	1:00
Dec. 21	**Indianapolis**	1:00

RAIDERS COACHING HISTORY

Oakland 1960-81
(257-136-11)

1960-61	Eddie Erdelatz*	6-10-0
1961-62	Marty Feldman**	2-15-0
1962	Red Conkright	1-8-0
1963-65	Al Davis	23-16-3
1966-68	John Rauch	35-10-1
1969-78	John Madden	112-39-7
1979-85	Tom Flores	78-38-0

*Released after two games in 1961
**Released after five games in 1962

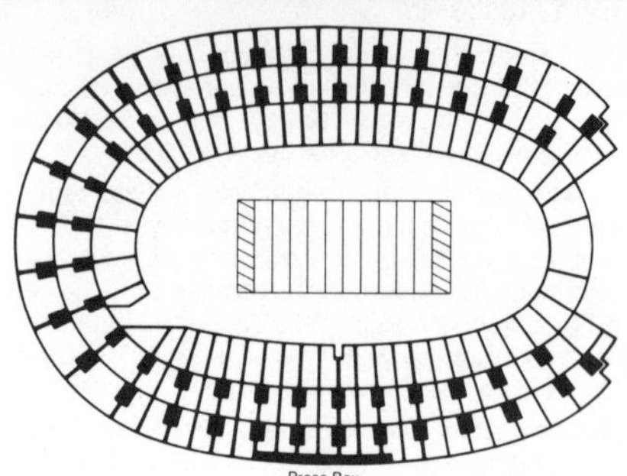

MEMORIAL COLISEUM

RECORD HOLDERS

Individual Records—Career

Category	Name	Performance
Rushing (Yds.)	Mark van Eeghen, 1974-1981	5,907
Passing (Yds.)	Ken Stabler, 1970-79	19,078
Passing (TDs)	Ken Stabler, 1970-79	150
Receiving (No.)	Fred Biletnikoff, 1965-1978	589
Receiving (Yds.)	Fred Biletnikoff, 1965-1978	8,974
Interceptions	Willie Brown, 1967-1978	39
Punting (Avg.)	Ray Guy, 1973-1985	42.6
Punt Return (Avg.)	Claude Gibson, 1963-65	12.6
Kickoff Return (Avg.)	Jack Larscheid, 1960-61	28.4
Field Goals	George Blanda, 1967-1975	156
Touchdowns (Tot.)	Fred Biletnikoff, 1965-1978	77
Points	George Blanda, 1967-1975	863

Individual Records—Single Season

Category	Name	Performance
Rushing (Yds.)	Marcus Allen, 1985	1,759
Passing (Yds.)	Ken Stabler, 1979	3,615
Passing (TDs)	Daryle Lamonica, 1969	34
Receiving (No.)	Todd Christensen, 1983	92
Receiving (Yds.)	Art Powell, 1964	1,361
Interceptions	Lester Hayes, 1980	13
Punting (Avg.)	Ray Guy, 1973	45.3
Punt Return (Avg.)	Claude Gibson, 1963	14.4
Kickoff Return (Avg.)	Harold Hart, 1975	30.5
Field Goals	George Blanda, 1973	23
Touchdowns (Tot.)	Marcus Allen, 1984	18
Points	George Blanda, 1968	117

Individual Records—Single Game

Category	Name	Performance
Rushing (Yds.)	Clem Daniels, 10-20-63	200
Passing (Yds.)	Cotton Davidson, 10-25-64	427
Passing (TDs)	Tom Flores, 12-22-63	6
	Daryle Lamonica, 10-19-69	6
Receiving (No.)	Dave Casper, 10-3-76	12
Receiving (Yds.)	Art Powell, 12-22-63	247
Interceptions	Many times	3
	Last time by Charles Phillips, 12-8-75	
Field Goals	Many times	4
	Last time by Chris Bahr, 10-6-85	
Touchdowns (Tot.)	Art Powell, 12-22-63	4
	Marcus Allen, 9-24-84	4
Points	Art Powell, 12-22-63	24
	Marcus Allen, 9-24-84	24

1985 TEAM STATISTICS

	L.A. Raiders	Opp.
Total First Downs	304	273
Rushing	111	73
Passing	167	166
Penalty	26	34
Third Down: Made/Att.	87/229	79/238
Fourth Down: Made/Att.	7/14	6/10
Total Net Yards	5408	4603
Avg. Per Game	338.0	287.7
Total Plays	1081	1037
Avg. Per Play	5.0	4.4
Net Yards Rushing	2262	1605
Avg. Per Game	141.4	100.3
Total Rushes	532	461
Net Yards Passing	3146	2998
Avg. Per Game	196.6	187.4
Tackled/Yards Lost	43/335	65/488
Gross Yards	3481	3486
Att./Completions	506/269	511/251
Completion Pct.	53.2	49.1
Had Intercepted	24	17
Punts/Avg.	89/40.8	104/41.9
Net Punting Avg.	36.3	33.0
Penalties/Yards Lost	116/962	109/856
Fumbles/Ball Lost	27/14	27/13
Touchdowns	42	34
Rushing	18	7
Passing	20	22
Returns	4	5
Avg. Time of Possession	30:26	29:34

1985 TEAM RECORD

Preseason (1-3)

Date	Los Angeles Raiders		Opponents
8/10	21	*San Francisco	28
8/18	9	*Washington	14
8/24	17	*Miami	23
8/30	26	Cleveland	7
	73		72

Regular Season (12-4)

Date	Los Angeles Raiders		Opp.	Att.
9/8	31	*N.Y. Jets	0	57,123
9/12	20	Kansas City	36	72,686
9/22	10	*San Francisco	34	87,006
9/29	35	New England	20	60,893
10/6	19	*Kansas City	10	55,133
10/13	23	*New Orleans	13	48,152
10/20	21	Cleveland	20	77,928
10/28	34	*San Diego	21	69,297
11/3	3	Seattle	33	64,060
11/10	34	San Diego (OT)	40	58,566
11/17	13	*Cincinnati	6	52,501
11/24	31	*Denver (OT)	28	63,161
12/1	34	Atlanta	24	20,585
12/8	17	Denver (OT)	14	75,042
12/15	13	*Seattle	3	77,425
12/23	16	L.A. Rams	6	66,676

Postseason (0-1)

Date	Los Angeles Raiders		Opp.	Att.
1/5/86	20	*New England	27	87,163

*Home Game (OT) Overtime

Score by Periods

L.A. Raiders	79	93	76	100	6	—	354
Opponents	73	93	67	69	6	—	308

Attendance

Home 509,798 Away 496,436 Total 1,006,234
Single game home record, 90,334 (1-1-84)
Single season home record, 557,881 (1972; Oakland Coliseum), 512,520 (1984; L.A. Coliseum).

1985 INDIVIDUAL STATISTICS

Rushing	Att.	Yds.	Avg.	LG	TD
Allen	380	1759	4.6	61t	11
Hawkins	84	269	3.2	21t	4
Wilson	24	98	4.1	17	2
King	16	67	4.2	19	0
D. Jensen	16	35	2.2	8	0
Hester	1	13	13.0	13t	1
Plunkett	5	12	2.4	7	0
Hilger	3	8	2.7	4	0
Strachan	2	1	0.5	1	0
Guy	1	0	0.0	0	0
Raiders	532	2262	4.3	61t	18
Opponents	461	1605	3.5	23	7

Passing	Att.	Comp.	Pct.	Yds.	TD	Int.	Tkld.	Rate
Wilson	388	193	49.7	2608	16	21	27/202	62.7
Plunkett	103	71	68.9	803	3	3	13/101	89.6
Hilger	13	4	30.8	54	1	0	3/32	70.7
Allen	2	1	50.0	16	0	0	0/0	77.1
Raiders	506	269	53.2	3481	20	24	43/335	68.5
Opponents	511	251	49.1	3486	22	17	65/488	71.9

Receiving	No.	Yds.	Avg.	LG	TD
Christensen	82	987	12.0	48	6
Allen	67	555	8.3	44	3
D. Williams	48	925	19.3	55	5
Hester	32	665	20.8	59	4
Hawkins	27	174	6.4	20	0
Moffett	5	90	18.0	34	0
King	3	49	16.3	37	0
Smith	3	28	9.3	14	1
Junkin	2	8	4.0	5	1
Raiders	269	3481	12.9	59	20
Opponents	251	3486	13.9	62t	22

Interceptions	No.	Yds.	Avg.	LG	TD
Hayes	4	27	6.8	27t	1
Haynes	4	8	2.0	8	0
McElroy	2	23	11.5	23	0
Toran	1	76	76.0	76t	1
Seale	1	38	38.0	38t	1
McKinney	1	22	22.0	22	0
Van Pelt	1	22	22.0	22	0
Martin	1	16	16.0	16	0
Squirek	1	3	3.0	3	0
Barnes	1	0	0.0	0	0
Raiders	17	235	13.8	76t	3
Opponents	24	365	15.2	75t	1

Punting	No.	Yds.	Avg.	In 20	LG
Guy	89	3627	40.8	32	68
Raiders	89	3627	40.8	32	68
Opponents	104	4356	41.9	12	58

Punt Returns	No.	FC	Yds.	Avg.	LG	TD
Walker	62	6	692	11.2	32	0
Montgomery	8	2	84	10.5	32	0
Haynes	1	0	9	9.0	9	0
Raiders	71	8	785	11.1	32	0
Opponents	26	14	159	6.1	25	0

Kickoff Returns	No.	Yds.	Avg.	LG	TD
Walker	21	467	22.2	57	0
Seale	23	482	21.0	36	0
Montgomery	7	150	21.4	30	0
D. Williams	1	19	19.0	19	0
Hawkins	1	14	14.0	14	0
Hayes	1	0	0.0	0	0
Raiders	54	1132	21.0	57	0
Opponents	59	1165	19.7	38	0

Scoring	TD R	TD P	TD Rt	PAT	FG	Saf	TP
Bahr	0	0	0	40/42	20/32	0	100
Allen	11	3	0	0/0	0/0	0	84
Christensen	0	6	0	0/0	0/0	0	36
Hester	1	4	0	0/0	0/0	0	30
D. Williams	0	5	0	0/0	0/0	0	30
Hawkins	4	0	0	0/0	0/0	0	24
Wilson	2	0	0	0/0	0/0	0	12
Alzado	0	0	1	0/0	0/0	1	8
Hayes	0	0	1	0/0	0/0	0	6
Junkin	0	1	0	0/0	0/0	0	6
Seale	0	0	1	0/0	0/0	0	6
Smith	0	1	0	0/0	0/0	0	6
Toran	0	0	1	0/0	0/0	0	6
Raiders	18	20	4	40/42	20/32	1	354
Opponents	7	22	5	32/33	24/35	0	308

FIRST-ROUND SELECTIONS

(If club had no first-round selection, first player drafted is listed with round in parentheses.)

Year	Player, College, Position
1960	Dale Hackbart, Wisconsin, CB
1961	Joe Rutgens, Illinois, DT
1962	Roman Gabriel, North Carolina State, QB
1963	George Wilson, Alabama, RB (6)
1964	Tony Lorick, Arizona State, RB
1965	Harry Schuh, Memphis State, T
1966	Rodger Bird, Kentucky, S
1967	Gene Upshaw, Texas A&I, G
1968	Eldridge Dickey, Tennessee State, QB
1969	Art Thoms, Syracuse, DT
1970	Raymond Chester, Morgan State, TE
1971	Jack Tatum, Ohio State, S
1972	Mike Siani, Villanova, WR
1973	Ray Guy, Southern Mississippi, K-P
1974	Henry Lawrence, Florida A&M, T
1975	Neal Colzie, Ohio State, DB
1976	Charles Philyaw, Texas Southern, DT (2)
1977	Mike Davis, Colorado, DB (2)
1978	Dave Browning, Washington, DE (2)
1979	Willie Jones, Florida State, DE (2)
1980	Marc Wilson, Brigham Young, QB
1981	Ted Watts, Texas Tech, DB
	Curt Marsh, Washington, T
1982	Marcus Allen, Southern California, RB
1983	Don Mosebar, Southern California, T
1984	Sean Jones, Northeastern, DE (2)
1985	Jessie Hester, Florida State, WR
1986	Bob Buczkowski, Pittsburgh, DE

LOS ANGELES RAIDERS 1986 VETERAN ROSTER

No.	Name	Pos.	Ht.	Wt.	Birth-date	NFL Exp.	College	Hometown	How Acq.	'85 Games/Starts
32	Allen, Marcus	RB	6-2	205	3/22/60	5	Southern California	San Diego, Calif.	D1-'82	16/16
10	†Bahr, Chris	K	5-10	170	2/3/53	11	Penn State	Feasterville, Pa.	FA-'80	16/0
56	Barnes, Jeff	LB	6-2	230	3/1/55	10	California	Hayward, Calif.	D5-'77	16/1
49	Barnett, Buster	TE	6-5	240	11/24/58	5	Jackson State	Jackson, Miss.	FA-'86	0*
76	Belcher, Kevin	G	6-5	285	11/9/61	2	Wisconsin	Bridgeport, Conn.	D7-'85	4/0
21	Branch, Cliff	WR	5-11	170	8/1/48	15	Colorado	Houston, Tex.	D4-'72	4/0
46	Christensen, Todd	TE	6-3	230	8/3/56	8	Brigham Young	Eugene, Ore.	FA-'79	16/16
	t-Cooper, Earl	TE	6-2	232	9/17/57	7	Rice	Lexington, Tex.	T(SF)-'86	15/0
50	Dalby, Dave	C	6-3	250	10/19/50	15	UCLA	Whittier, Calif.	D4-'72	16/2
79	Davis, Bruce	T	6-6	280	6/21/56	8	UCLA	Marbury, Md.	D11-'79	16/16
80	Davis, Bruce	WR	5-8	160	2/25/63	2	Baylor	Dallas, Tex.	FA-'86	0*
45	Davis, James	CB	6-0	200	6/12/57	5	Southern	Los Angeles, Calif.	D5-'81	15/0
36	Davis, Mike	S	6-3	205	4/15/56	9	Colorado	Los Angeles, Calif.	D2-'77	11/10
94	Franks, Elvis	DE	6-4	270	7/9/57	7	Morgan State	Woodville, Tex.	FA-'85	3/1
8	Guy, Ray	P	6-3	200	12/22/49	14	Southern Mississippi	Thomson, Ga.	D1-'73	16/0
73	†Hannah, Charley	G	6-5	260	7/26/55	10	Alabama	Chattanooga, Tenn.	T(TB)-'83	15/15
27	†Hawkins, Frank	RB	5-9	210	7/3/59	6	Nevada-Reno	Las Vegas, Nev.	D10-'81	16/16
37	Hayes, Lester	CB	6-0	200	1/22/55	10	Texas A&M	Houston, Tex.	D5-'77	16/15
22	Haynes, Mike	CB	6-2	190	7/1/53	11	Arizona State	Los Angeles, Calif.	T(NE)-'83	16/16
84	Hester, Jessie	WR	5-11	170	1/21/63	2	Florida State	Belle Glade, Fla.	D1-'85	16/16
12	Hilger, Rusty	QB	6-4	200	5/9/62	2	Oklahoma State	Oklahoma City, Okla.	D6-'85	4/0
31	Jensen, Derrick	RB	6-1	220	4/27/56	8	Texas-Arlington	Osawatomie, Kan.	D3-'78	16/0
99	Jones, Sean	DE	6-7	275	12/19/62	3	Northeastern	Montclair, N.J.	D2-'84	15/4
74	Jordan, Shelby	T	6-7	280	1/23/52	11	Washington, Mo.	East St. Louis, Ill.	T(NE)-'83	16/2
87	Junkin, Trey	TE	6-2	225	1/23/61	4	Louisiana Tech	Winfield, La.	FA-'85	16/0
33	King, Kenny	RB	5-11	205	3/7/57	8	Oklahoma	Clarendon, Tex.	T(Hou)-'80	16/0
70	Lawrence, Henry	T	6-4	275	9/26/51	13	Florida A&M	Palmetto, Fla.	D1-'74	16/16
75	Long, Howie	DE	6-4	270	1/6/60	6	Villanova	Charlestown, Mass.	D2-'81	16/16
60	†Marsh, Curt	G	6-5	275	8/25/59	5	Washington	Snohomish, Wash.	D1-'81	7/0
53	Martin, Rod	LB	6-2	225	4/7/54	10	Southern California	Los Angeles, Calif.	D12-'77	16/16
65	Marvin, Mickey	G	6-4	265	10/5/55	10	Tennessee	Hendersonville, N.C.	D4-'77	15/15
26	McElroy, Vann	S	6-2	195	1/13/60	5	Baylor	Uvalde, Tex.	D3-'82	12/12
54	McKenzie, Reggie	LB	6-1	240	2/8/63	2	Tennessee	Knoxville, Tenn.	D10-'85	16/16
23	McKinney, Odis	S	6-2	190	5/19/57	9	Colorado	Reseda, Calif.	FA-'85	15/4*
35	McSwain, Chuck	RB	6-0	195	2/21/63	3	Clemson	Caroleen, N.C.	FA-'86	0*
55	Millen, Matt	LB	6-2	245	3/12/58	7	Penn State	Hokendauqua, Pa.	D2-'80	16/16
83	Moffett, Tim	WR	6-1	180	2/28/62	2	Mississippi	Taylorsville, Miss.	D3-'85	13/0
28	Montgomery, Cle	WR	5-8	180	7/1/56	7	Abilene Christian	Greenville, Miss.	FA-'81	4/0
72	Mosebar, Don	C	6-6	270	9/11/61	4	Southern California	Visalia, Calif.	D1-'83	16/14
51	Nelson, Bob	LB	6-4	235	6/30/53	8	Nebraska	Stillwater, Minn.	FA-'80	0*
81	Parker, Andy	TE	6-5	240	9/8/61	3	Utah	Ramona, Calif.	D5-'84	16/0
71	Pickel, Bill	DT	6-5	260	11/5/59	4	Rutgers	Brooklyn, N.Y.	D2-'83	16/16
16	Plunkett, Jim	QB	6-2	225	12/5/47	16	Stanford	San Jose, Calif.	FA-'78	3/3
57	Robinson, Jerry	LB	6-2	225	12/18/56	8	UCLA	Santa Rosa, Calif.	T(Phil)-'85	11/0
69	Russell, Rusty	T	6-5	290	8/16/63	2	South Carolina	Orangeburg, S.C.	FA-'86	0*
43	Seale, Sam	CB	5-9	175	10/6/62	3	Western State, Colo.	East Orange, N.J.	D8-'84	16/0
86	Smith, Jim	WR	6-2	195	7/20/55	8	Michigan	Harvey, Ill.	T(Pitt)-'85	6/0
58	Squirek, Jack	LB	6-4	235	2/16/59	5	Illinois	Cleveland, Ohio	D2-'82	16/0
39	Strachan, Steve	RB	6-1	215	3/22/63	2	Boston College	Burlington, Mass.	D11-'85	4/0
30	Toran, Stacey	S	6-2	200	11/10/61	3	Notre Dame	Indianapolis, Ind.	D6-'84	16/10
93	Townsend, Greg	DE	6-3	250	11/3/61	4	Texas Christian	Compton, Calif.	D4-'83	16/0
68	Van Divier, Randy	T	6-5	290	6/5/58	3	Washington	Anaheim, Calif.	FA-'82	0*
91	Van Pelt, Brad	LB	6-5	235	4/5/51	14	Michigan State	Owosso, Mich.	T(Minn)-'84	16/15
41	Walker, Fulton	S	5-11	200	4/30/58	6	West Virginia	Martinsburg, W. Va.	FA-'85	15/0*
67	Wheeler, Dwight	C	6-3	275	1/3/55	7	Tennessee State	Memphis, Tenn.	FA-'84	0*
85	Williams, Dokie	WR	5-11	180	8/25/60	4	UCLA	Oceanside, Calif.	D5-'83	16/16
98	Willis, Mitch	DT	6-7	275	3/16/62	2	Southern Methodist	Arlington, Tex.	D7-'84	11/0
6	Wilson, Marc	QB	6-6	205	2/15/57	7	Brigham Young	Seattle, Wash.	D1-'80	16/13

* Barnett last active with Buffalo in '84; WR Bruce Davis last played with Cleveland in '84; McKinney played five games with Kansas City, 10 with L.A. Raiders in '85; McSwain last played with Dallas in '84; Nelson and Van Divier missed '85 season due to injury; Russell last played with Philadelphia in '84; Walker played two games with Miami, 13 with L.A. Raiders in '85; Wheeler last played with L.A. Raiders in '84.

†Option playout; subject to developments.

t-Raiders traded for Cooper (San Francisco).

Retired—Lyle Alzado, 14-year defensive end, 11 games in '85.

Also played with Raiders in '85—S Don Bessillieu (4 games), LB Tony Caldwell (3), QB Russ Jensen (active for 1 game, but did not play), DT Dave Stalls (4), CB Ricky Williams (2).

COACHING STAFF

Head Coach, Tom Flores

Pro Career: Begins eighth year as head coach. Guided Raiders to 38-9 victory over Redskins in Super Bowl XVIII and 27-10 win over Eagles in Super Bowl XV. Has been with Raiders' organization as either a player or coach for 21 years. Played six years at quarterback for Raiders 1960-61, 1963-66. After spending two years (1967-68) with the Buffalo Bills and two seasons (1969-70) with the Kansas City Chiefs, Flores returned to Oakland as receivers coach in February, 1972. Ranks as Raiders number-three all-time passer with 11,635 yards and 92 touchdowns. He also passed for a club-record six touchdowns in one game in 1963. Career record: 78-38.

Background: Quarterback at Fresno, Calif., J.C. 1954-55 and Pacific 1956-57. Coached at his alma mater in 1959 before joining Raiders as a quarterback in 1960.

Personal: Born March 21, 1937, in Fresno, Calif. Tom and his wife, Barbara, live in Manhattan Beach, Calif. They have twin sons, Mark and Scott, and a daughter, Kimberly.

Assistant Coaches

Sam Boghosian, offensive line; born December 22, 1931, Fresno, Calif., lives in El Segundo, Calif. Guard UCLA 1951-54. No pro playing experience. College coach: UCLA 1955-64, Oregon State 1965-73. Pro coach: Houston Oilers 1974-75, Seattle Seahawks 1976-77, joined Raiders in 1979.

Willie Brown, defensive backfield; born December 2, 1940, Yazoo City, Miss., lives in Rancho Palos Verdes, Calif. Defensive back Grambling 1959-62. Pro cornerback Denver Broncos 1963-66, Oakland Raiders 1967-78. Pro coach: Joined Raiders in 1979.

Chet Franklin, defensive backfield; born March 19, 1935, Ontario, Ore., lives in Los Angeles. Guard Utah 1954-56. No pro playing experience. College coach: Stanford 1959, Oklahoma 1960-62, Colorado 1963-70. Pro coach: San Francisco 49ers 1971-74, Kansas City Chiefs 1975-77, New Orleans Saints 1978-79, joined Raiders in 1980.

Larry Kennan, quarterbacks; born June 13, 1944, Pomona, Calif., lives in Rancho Palos Verdes, Calif. Quarterback LaVerne College 1962-65. College coach: Colorado 1969-72, Nevada-Las Vegas 1973-75, Southern Methodist 1976-78, Lamar 1979-81. Pro coach: Joined Raiders in 1982.

Earl Leggett, defensive line; born May 5, 1933, Jacksonville, Fla., lives in Fountain Valley, Calif. Tackle Hinds J.C. 1953-54, Louisiana State 1955-56. Pro defensive tackle Chicago Bears 1957-65, Los Angeles Rams 1966, New Orleans Saints 1967-68. College coach: Nicholls State 1971, Texas Christian 1972-73. Pro coach: Southern California Sun (WFL) 1974-75, Seattle Seahawks 1976-77, San Francisco 49ers 1978, joined Raiders in 1980.

Bob Mischak, tight ends, strength and conditioning; born October 25, 1932, Newark, N.J., lives in El Segundo, Calif. Guard Army 1951-53. Pro guard New York Giants 1958, New York Titans 1960-62, Oakland Raiders 1963-65. College coach: Army 1966-72. Pro coach: Joined Raiders in 1973.

Steve Ortmayer, football operations and special teams; born February 13, 1944, Painesville, Ohio, lives in Rancho Palos Verdes, Calif. LaVerne College 1966. No college or pro playing experience. College coach: Colorado 1967-73, Georgia Tech 1974. Pro coach: Kansas City Chiefs 1975-77, joined Raiders in 1978.

Art Shell, offensive line; born November 26, 1946, Charleston, S.C., lives in Rancho Palos Verdes, Calif. Tackle Maryland State 1965-67. Pro offensive tackle Oakland Raiders 1968-81, Los Angeles Raiders 1982. Pro coach: Joined Raiders in 1983.

Tom Walsh, receivers; born April 16, 1949, Vallejo, Calif., lives in Manhattan Beach, Calif. UC-Santa Barbara 1971. No college or pro playing experience. College coach: University of San Diego 1972-76, U.S. International 1979, Murray State 1980, Cincinnati 1981. Pro coach: Joined Raiders in 1982.

LOS ANGELES RAIDERS 1986 FIRST-YEAR ROSTER

Name	Pos.	Ht.	Wt.	Birth-date	College	Hometown	How Acq.
Adams, Stefon (1)	CB	5-10	190	8/11/63	East Carolina	High Point, N.C.	D3a-'85
Alphin, Gerald	WR	6-3	210	5/21/64	Kansas State	University City, Mo.	FA
Avery, Todd	CB	6-0	185	7/26/64	Illinois	Los Angeles, Calif.	FA
Barbero, Ed	RB	6-1	220	10/4/63	California	San Francisco, Calif.	FA
Barksdale, Rod (1)	WR	6-1	185	9/8/62	Arizona	Compton, Calif.	FA
Barrett, Joel	TE	6-3	250	7/26/62	Baylor	Corpus Christi, Tex.	FA
Bean, Gerald	RB	5-11	205	7/25/62	Texas Tech	Houston, Tex.	FA
Benn, Rennie	WR	6-3	190	3/3/63	Lehigh	Short Hills, N.J.	FA
Blakeney, Lee (1)	LB	6-0	240	9/18/61	Washington State	Concord, Calif.	FA
Buckley, Fred	QB	6-1	195	8/22/63	Stanford	Ft. Lauderdale, Fla.	FA
Buczkowski, Bob	DE	6-4	270	5/5/64	Pittsburgh	Monroeville, Pa.	D1
Buenafe, Kevin (1)	P	6-0	195	4/19/62	UCLA	Tulare, Calif.	FA
Cochran, Brad	CB	6-3	200	6/17/63	Michigan	Royal Oak, Mich.	D3
Corley, Chris (1)	TE	6-3	248	10/24/63	South Carolina	Irmo, S.C.	FA
Deaton, Jeff (1)	G	6-3	270	4/26/62	Stanford	St. Cloud, Minn.	FA
Dickey, Charlie (1)	G	6-2	275	12/31/62	Arizona	Scottsdale, Ariz.	FA
Dixon, Joe	DT	6-2	270	1/8/64	Tulsa	Pocola, Okla.	FA
Dozier, Cornelius	S	6-0	190	2/5/64	Southern Methodist	Dallas, Tex.	FA
Gibson, Steve (1)	DT	6-3	260	5/5/62	Cal Poly-SLO	Oxnard, Calif.	FA
Greene, Dwayne (1)	S	6-0	190	12/3/60	North Carolina State	Raleigh, N.C.	FA
Haden, Nick (1)	C	6-2	270	11/7/62	Penn State	McKees Rocks, Pa.	D7b-'85
Hopper, Darrell (1)	CB	6-1	190	3/14/63	Southern California	Carson, Calif.	FA
Howell, Glenn	DE	6-3	245	11/15/63	Arizona	Castro Valley, Calif.	FA
James, Ronnie (1)	RB	6-1	240	1/2/61	Grambling	Houston, Tex.	FA
Jensen, Russ (1)	QB	6-2	215	7/13/61	California Lutheran	La Mirada, Calif.	FA
Kearney, Robert	S	5-11	195	4/10/63	N. Carolina Central	Norfolk, Va.	FA
Kimmel, Jamie (1)	LB	6-3	235	3/28/62	Syracuse	Conklin, N.Y.	D4-'85
Lee, Zeph	RB	6-3	215	6/17/63	Southern California	San Francisco, Calif.	D9
Lewis, Bill	C	6-6	275	7/12/63	Nebraska	Sioux City, Iowa	D7
Marrone, Doug	G	6-5	270	7/25/64	Syracuse	Bronx, N.Y.	D6
Mauntel, Joe	LB	6-4	225	11/1/62	Eastern Kentucky	Cincinnati, Ohio	D8
McCallum, Napolean	RB	6-2	215	10/6/63	Navy	Milford, Ohio	D4c
Mueller, Vance	RB	6-0	210	5/5/64	Occidental	Jackson, Calif.	D4b
Murphy, Greg	QB	6-3	210	4/5/63	Pacific	Sacramento, Calif.	FA
Oce, Rastee (1)	CB	6-0	165	6/8/62	Northern Illinois	Miami, Fla.	FA
O'Neill, Brian	DT	6-4	265	12/31/62	New Hampshire	Waterville, Maine	FA
Osborn, Kelly (1)	DE	6-5	250	7/25/62	Sacramento State	Angels Camp, Calif.	FA
Pattison, Mark (1)	WR	6-2	195	12/13/61	Washington	Seattle, Wash.	D7a-'85
Pope, Damon (1)	TE	6-2	225	1/30/63	East Carolina	Atlanta, Ga.	FA
Potter, Ken (1)	K	6-1	195	8/23/62	UCLA	Alta Loma, Calif.	FA
Reinke, Jeff	DE	6-5	275	9/12/62	Mankato State	Sacred Heart, Minn.	D10
Sartin, Martin	RB	5-10	195	3/9/63	Long Beach State	Camden, N.J.	FA
Scarcelli, Jim	LB	6-5	220	5/2/63	Michigan	Warren, Mich.	FA
Scott, Ed	S	5-11	180	2/15/61	Grambling	New Orleans, La.	FA
Shepherd, Larry	WR	6-3	195	4/9/63	Houston	Kilgore, Tex.	D12
Sloan, Rick	QB	6-2	215	5/12/63	Idaho	Post Falls, Idaho	FA
Swanson, Gary (1)	LB	6-1	235	8/17/61	Cal Poly-SLO	Big Creek, Calif.	FA
Tatko, Ken (1)	DE	6-6	275	7/23/62	Elon	Endicott, N.Y.	FA
Trainor, Mike (1)	LB	6-0	235	9/19/61	Louisville	Bayonne, N.J.	FA
Tubbs, Bradley (1)	WR	6-4	205	3/14/63	St. Mary's, Calif.	Pleasant Hill, Calif.	FA
Walker, Carlton (1)	T	6-3	280	1/17/62	Utah	Tampa, Fla.	FA
Webster, Darrell	LB	6-2	225	8/22/63	S.W. Oklahoma	Durant, Miss.	D11
Williams, Gardner (1)	S	6-2	195	12/11/61	St. Mary's, Calif.	Oakland, Calif.	FA
Williams, Tim (1)	S	6-1	200	2/21/63	North Carolina A&T	Greensboro, N.C.	FA
Wise, Mike	DE	6-6	275	6/5/64	California-Davis	Novato, Calif.	D4a
Wong, Louis (1)	T	6-4	280	1/5/63	Brigham Young	Kaneohe, Hawaii	FA
Zogg, Jon (1)	C	6-3	280	11/19/60	Boise State	Aromas, Calif.	FA

The term NFL Rookie is defined as a player who is in his first season of professional football and has not been on the roster of another professional football team for any regular season or postseason games. A Rookie is designated by an "R" on NFL rosters. Players who have been active in another professional football league or players who have NFL experience, including either preseason training camp or being on an active roster for fewer than three regular season or postseason games, are termed NFL First-Year Players. An NFL First-Year Player is designated by a "1" on NFL rosters. Thereafter, a player on an NFL active roster for at least three regular season or postseason games is credited with an additional year of NFL playing experience.

NOTES

Ray Willsey, offensive backfield; born September 30, 1929, Regina, Saskatchewan, lives in Playa del Rey, Calif. Quarterback-defensive back California 1951-52. Pro back Edmonton Eskimos (CFL) 1953. College coach: California 1954-55, 1964-71 (head coach), Washington 1956, Texas 1957-59. Pro coach: St. Louis Cardinals 1960-61, 1973-77, Washington Redskins 1962-63, joined Raiders in 1978.

Bob Zeman, linebackers; born February 22, 1937, Wheaton, Ill., lives in Manhattan Beach, Calif. Fullback-halfback Wisconsin 1957-59. Pro defensive back Los Angeles-San Diego Chargers 1960-61, 1965-66, Denver Broncos 1962-63. College coach: Northwestern 1968-69, Wisconsin 1970. Pro coach: Oakland Raiders 1971-77, Denver Broncos 1978-82, Buffalo Bills 1983, rejoined Raiders in 1984.

MIAMI DOLPHINS

American Football Conference
Eastern Division

Team Colors: Aqua, Coral, and White

4770 Biscayne Boulevard
Suite 1440
Miami, Florida 33137
Telephone: (305) 576-1000

Club Officials

President: Joseph Robbie
Vice President/General Manager: J. Michael Robbie
Vice President/Head Coach: Don Shula
Vice President/Public Affairs: Joe Abrell
Director of Pro Personnel: Charley Winner
Director of Player Personnel: Chuck Connor
Director of Publicity: Eddie White
Ticket Director: Kevin Fitzgerald
Controller: Howard Rieman
Traveling Secretary: Bryan Wiedmeier
Trainer: Bob Lundy
Equipment Manager: Bob Monica

Stadium: Orange Bowl • **Capacity:** 75,206
1501 N.W. Third Street
Miami, Florida 33125

Playing Surface: Grass

Training Camp: St. Thomas University
16400-D N.W. 32nd Avenue
Miami, Florida 33054

1986 SCHEDULE

Preseason

Aug. 9	at Minnesota	7:00
Aug. 15	**Cleveland**	8:00
Aug. 23	at Philadelphia	7:30
Aug. 29	**Tampa Bay**	8:00

Regular Season

Sept. 7	at San Diego	1:00
Sept. 14	**Indianapolis**	4:00
Sept. 21	at New York Jets	1:00
Sept. 28	**San Francisco**	1:00
Oct. 5	at New England	1:00
Oct. 12	**Buffalo**	1:00
Oct. 19	**Los Angeles Raiders**	1:00
Oct. 26	at Indianapolis	1:00
Nov. 2	**Houston**	1:00
Nov. 10	at Cleveland (Monday)	9:00
Nov. 16	at Buffalo	1:00
Nov. 24	**New York Jets** (Monday)	9:00
Nov. 30	**Atlanta**	1:00
Dec. 7	at New Orleans	12:00
Dec. 14	at Los Angeles Rams	1:00
Dec. 22	**New England** (Monday)	9:00

DOLPHINS COACHING HISTORY

(197-112-4)

1966-69	George Wilson	15-39-2
1970-85	Don Shula	182-73-2

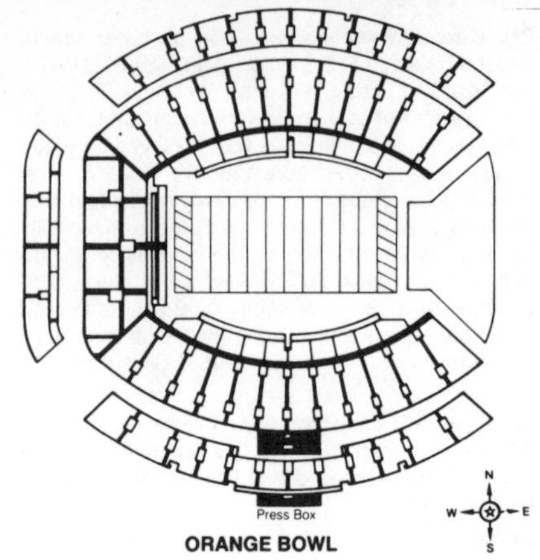

ORANGE BOWL

RECORD HOLDERS

Individual Records—Career

Category	Name	Performance
Rushing (Yds.)	Larry Csonka, 1968-1974, 1979	6,737
Passing (Yds.)	Bob Griese, 1967-1980	25,092
Passing (TDs)	Bob Griese, 1967-1980	192
Receiving (No.)	Nat Moore, 1974-1985	472
Receiving (Yds.)	Nat Moore, 1974-1985	7,116
Interceptions	Jake Scott, 1970-75	35
Punting (Avg.)	Reggie Roby, 1983-85	43.7
Punt Return (Avg.)	Freddie Solomon, 1975-77	11.4
Kickoff Return (Avg.)	Mercury Morris, 1969-1975	26.5
Field Goals	Garo Yepremian, 1970-78	165
Touchdowns (Tot.)	Nat Moore, 1974-1985	68
Points	Garo Yepremian, 1970-78	830

Individual Records—Single Season

Category	Name	Performance
Rushing (Yds.)	Delvin Williams, 1978	1,258
Passing (Yds.)	Dan Marino, 1984	5,084
Passing (TDs)	Dan Marino, 1984	48
Receiving (No.)	Mark Clayton, 1984	73
Receiving (Yds.)	Mark Clayton, 1984	1,389
Interceptions	Dick Westmoreland, 1967	10
Punting (Avg.)	Reggie Roby, 1984	44.7
Punt Return (Avg.)	Freddie Solomon, 1975	12.3
Kickoff Return (Avg.)	Duriel Harris, 1976	32.9
Field Goals	Garo Yepremian, 1971	28
Touchdowns (Tot.)	Mark Clayton, 1984	18
Points	Garo Yepremian, 1971	117

Individual Records—Single Game

Category	Name	Performance
Rushing (Yds.)	Mercury Morris, 9-30-73	197
Passing (Yds.)	Dan Marino, 12-2-84	470
Passing (TDs)	Bob Griese, 11-24-77	6
Receiving (No.)	Duriel Harris, 10-28-79	10
Receiving (Yds.)	Mark Duper, 11-10-85	217
Interceptions	Dick Anderson, 12-3-73	4
Field Goals	Garo Yepremian, 9-26-71	5
Touchdowns (Tot.)	Paul Warfield, 12-15-73	4
Points	Paul Warfield, 12-15-73	24

1985 TEAM STATISTICS

	Miami	Opp.
Total First Downs	361	314
Rushing	116	135
Passing	218	160
Penalty	27	19
Third Down: Made/Att.	88/193	88/216
Fourth Down: Made/Att.	8/11	8/13
Total Net Yards	5843	5767
Avg. Per Game	365.2	360.4
Total Plays	1039	1034
Avg. Per Play	5.6	5.6
Net Yards Rushing	1729	2256
Avg. Per Game	108.1	141.0
Total Rushes	444	509
Net Yards Passing	4114	3511
Avg. Per Game	257.1	219.4
Tackled/Yards Lost	19/164	38/278
Gross Yards	4278	3789
Att./Completions	576/343	487/257
Completion Pct.	59.5	52.8
Had Intercepted	21	23
Punts/Avg.	59/43.7	73/40.7
Net Punting Avg.	34.7	34.2
Penalties/Yards Lost	77/637	112/854
Fumbles/Ball Lost	31/20	36/18
Touchdowns	52	38
Rushing	19	15
Passing	31	21
Returns	2	2
Avg. Time of Possession	30:17	29:43

1985 TEAM RECORD

Preseason (2-2)

Date	Miami		Opponents
8/10	13	*Minnesota (OT)	16
8/17	27	*Buffalo	17
8/24	23	L.A. Raiders	17
8/30	17	Atlanta	19
	80		69

Regular Season (12-4)

Date	Miami		Opp.	Att.
9/8	23	Houston	26	47,656
9/15	30	*Indianapolis	13	53,693
9/22	31	*Kansas City	0	70,244
9/29	30	Denver	26	73,614
10/6	24	*Pittsburgh	20	72,820
10/14	7	N.Y. Jets	23	73,807
10/20	41	*Tampa Bay	38	62,335
10/27	21	Detroit	31	75,291
11/3	13	New England	17	58,811
11/10	21	*N.Y. Jets	17	73,965
11/17	34	Indianapolis	20	59,666
11/24	23	Buffalo	14	50,474
12/2	38	*Chicago	24	75,594
12/8	34	Green Bay	24	52,671
12/16	30	*New England	27	69,489
12/22	28	*Buffalo	0	64,811

Postseason (1-1)

Date	Miami		Opp.	Att.
1/4/86	24	*Cleveland	21	74,667
1/12/86	14	*New England	31	75,662

*Home game (OT) Overtime

Score by Periods

Miami	88	136	95	109	0	—	428
Opponents	44	96	78	102	0	—	320

Attendance

Home 542,951 Away 491,990 Total 1,034,941
Single game home record, 78,939 (1-2-72)
Single season home record, 542,951 (1985)

1985 INDIVIDUAL STATISTICS

Rushing	Att.	Yds.	Avg.	LG	TD
Nathan	143	667	4.7	22	5
Davenport	98	370	3.8	33	11
Hampton	105	369	3.5	15	3
Bennett	54	256	4.7	17	0
Carter	14	76	5.4	19	0
N. Moore	1	11	11.0	11	0
Clayton	1	10	10.0	10	0
Strock	2	−6	−3.0	−3	0
Marino	26	−24	−0.9	6	0
Dolphins	444	1729	3.9	33	19
Opponents	509	2256	4.4	32	15

Passing	Att.	Comp.	Pct.	Yds.	TD	Int.	Tkld.	Rate
Marino	567	336	59.3	4137	30	21	18/157	84.1
Strock	9	7	77.8	141	1	0	0/0	155.8
Clayton	0	0	—	0	0	0	1/7	0.0
Dolphins	576	343	59.5	4278	31	21	19/164	85.4
Opponents	487	257	52.8	3789	21	23	38/278	73.2

Receiving	No.	Yds.	Avg.	LG	TD
Nathan	72	651	9.0	73	1
Clayton	70	996	14.2	45	4
N. Moore	51	701	13.7	69t	7
Hardy	39	409	10.5	31	4
Duper	35	650	18.6	67t	3
Rose	19	306	16.1	42	4
Johnson	13	192	14.8	61t	3
Davenport	13	74	5.7	17t	2
Bennett	10	101	10.1	27t	1
Hampton	8	56	7.0	15	0
Heflin	6	98	16.3	46t	1
Harris	3	24	8.0	11	0
Carter	2	7	3.5	4	0
Vigorito	1	9	9.0	9	0
Jensen	1	4	4.0	4t	1
Dolphins	343	4278	12.5	73	31
Opponents	257	3789	14.7	80t	21

Interceptions	No.	Yds.	Avg.	LG	TD
G. Blackwood	6	36	6.0	17	0
Judson	4	88	22.0	61t	1
Lankford	4	10	2.5	6	0
B. Brown	2	40	20.0	26	0
Brophy	1	41	41.0	41	0
H. Green	1	28	28.0	28	0
Shipp	1	7	7.0	7	0
Brudzinski	1	6	6.0	6	0
M. Brown	1	5	5.0	5	0
Moyer	1	4	4.0	4	0
L. Blackwood	1	0	0.0	0	0
Dolphins	23	265	11.5	61t	1
Opponents	21	100	4.8	40	0

Punting	No.	Yds.	Avg.	In 20	LG
Roby	59	2576	43.7	19	63
Dolphins	59	2576	43.7	19	63
Opponents	73	2972	40.7	13	67

Punt Returns	No.	FC	Yds.	Avg.	LG	TD
Vigorito	22	5	197	9.0	21	0
Kozlowski	7	2	65	9.3	17	0
Lockett	5	0	23	4.6	8	0
G. Blackwood	3	3	20	6.7	18	0
Clayton	2	0	14	7.0	11	0
L. Blackwood	0	4	0	—	0	0
Dolphins	39	14	319	8.2	21	0
Opponents	27	6	371	13.7	70t	1

Kickoff Returns	No.	Yds.	Avg.	LG	TD
Hampton	45	1020	22.7	46	0
Carter	4	82	20.5	25	0
L. Blackwood	2	32	16.0	17	0
Hardy	1	11	11.0	11	0
Kozlowski	0	32	—	32	0
Dolphins	52	1177	22.6	46	0
Opponents	63	1370	21.7	50	0

Scoring	TD R	TD P	TD Rt	PAT	FG	Saf	TP
Reveiz	0	0	0	50/52	22/27	0	116
Davenport	11	2	0	0/0	0/0	0	78
N. Moore	0	7	0	0/0	0/0	0	42
Nathan	5	1	0	0/0	0/0	0	36
Clayton	0	4	0	0/0	0/0	0	24
Hardy	0	4	0	0/0	0/0	0	24
Rose	0	4	0	0/0	0/0	0	24
Duper	0	3	0	0/0	0/0	0	18
Hampton	3	0	0	0/0	0/0	0	18
Johnson	0	3	0	0/0	0/0	0	18
Bennett	0	1	0	0/0	0/0	0	6
Brudzinski	0	0	1	0/0	0/0	0	6
Heflin	0	1	0	0/0	0/0	0	6
Jensen	0	1	0	0/0	0/0	0	6
Judson	0	0	1	0/0	0/0	0	6
Dolphins	19	31	2	50/52	22/27	0	428
Opponents	15	21	2	35/38	19/28	0	320

FIRST-ROUND SELECTIONS

(If club had no first-round selection, first player drafted is listed with round in parentheses.)

Year	Player, College, Position
1966	Jim Grabowski, Illinois, RB
	Rick Norton, Kentucky, QB
1967	Bob Griese, Purdue, QB
1968	Larry Csonka, Syracuse, RB
	Doug Crusan, Indiana, T
1969	Bill Stanfill, Georgia, DE
1970	Jim Mandich, Michigan, TE (2)
1971	Otto Stowe, Iowa State, WR (2)
1972	Mike Kadish, Notre Dame, DT
1973	Chuck Bradley, Oregon, C (2)
1974	Donald Reese, Jackson State, DE
1975	Darryl Carlton, Tampa, T
1976	Larry Gordon, Arizona State, LB
	Kim Bokamper, San Jose State, LB
1977	A.J. Duhe, Louisiana State, DT
1978	Guy Benjamin, Stanford, QB (2)
1979	Jon Giesler, Michigan, T
1980	Don McNeal, Alabama, DB
1981	David Overstreet, Oklahoma, RB
1982	Roy Foster, Southern California, G
1983	Dan Marino, Pittsburgh, QB
1984	Jackie Shipp, Oklahoma, LB
1985	Lorenzo Hampton, Florida, RB
1986	John Offerdahl, Western Michigan, LB (2)

MIAMI DOLPHINS 1986 VETERAN ROSTER

No.	Name	Pos.	Ht.	Wt.	Birth-date	NFL Exp.	College	Hometown	How Acq.	'85 Games/ Starts
70	†Barnett, Bill	DE-NT	6-4	260	5/10/56	7	Nebraska	Stillwater, Minn.	D3-'80	16/1
73	Baumhower, Bob	NT	6-5	265	8/4/55	9	Alabama	Palm Beach Gardens, Fla.	D2-'77	0*
34	Bennett, Woody	RB	6-2	225	3/24/55	8	Miami	York, Pa.	W(NYJ)-'80	16/13
75	†Betters, Doug	DE	6-7	265	6/11/56	9	Nevada-Reno	Arlington Heights, Ill.	D6-'78	14/14
47	Blackwood, Glenn	S	6-0	190	2/23/57	8	Texas	San Antonio, Tex.	D8b-'79	14/14
42	Blackwood, Lyle	S	6-1	190	5/24/51	14	Texas Christian	San Antonio, Tex.	FA-'81	16/0
58	Bokamper, Kim	DE	6-6	255	9/25/54	10	San Jose State	Milpitas, Calif.	D1b-'76	16/12
56	Bowser, Charles	LB	6-3	235	10/2/59	5	Duke	Plymouth, N.C.	D4-'82	2/2
53	Brophy, Jay	LB	6-3	233	7/27/60	3	Miami	Akron, Ohio	D2-'84	16/6
43	Brown, Bud	S	6-0	194	4/19/61	3	Southern Mississippi	DeKalb, Miss.	D11-'84	16/16
51	Brown, Mark	LB	6-2	225	7/18/61	4	Purdue	Inglewood, Calif.	D9-'83	15/15
59	Brudzinski, Bob	LB	6-4	223	1/1/55	10	Ohio State	Fremont, Ohio	T(Rams)-'81	14/13
23	Carter, Joe	RB	5-11	198	6/23/62	3	Alabama	Starkville, Miss.	D4-'84	10/0
71	Charles, Mike	NT	6-4	285	9/23/62	4	Syracuse	Newark, N.J.	D2-'83	16/16
76	†Clark, Steve	G	6-4	255	8/2/60	5	Utah	Salt Lake City, Utah	D9a-'82	16/5
83	Clayton, Mark	WR	5-9	175	4/8/61	4	Louisville	Indianapolis, Ind.	D8b-'83	16/16
30	Davenport, Ron	RB	6-2	230	12/22/62	2	Louisville	Atlanta, Ga.	D6b-'85	16/1
65	Dellenbach, Jeff	T	6-6	280	2/14/63	2	Wisconsin	Wausau, Wis.	D4b-'85	11/1
85	Duper, Mark	WR	5-9	187	1/25/59	5	Northwestern State, La.	Moreauville, La.	D2-'82	9/8
61	Foster, Roy	G	6-4	275	5/24/60	5	Southern California	Los Angeles, Calif.	D1-'82	16/16
79	Giesler, Jon	T	6-5	260	12/23/56	8	Michigan	Woodville, Ohio	D1-'79	13/13
74	Green, Cleveland	T	6-3	262	9/11/57	8	Southern	Bolton, Miss.	FA-'79	12/11
55	Green, Hugh	LB	6-2	225	7/27/59	6	Pittsburgh	Natchez, Miss.	T(TB)-'85	16/16*
27	Hampton, Lorenzo	RB	6-0	212	3/12/62	2	Florida	Lake Wales, Fla.	D1-'85	16/1
84	Hardy, Bruce	TE	6-5	232	6/1/56	9	Arizona State	Bingham, Utah	D9-'78	16/16
88	Heflin, Vince	WR	6-0	185	7/7/59	5	Central State, Ohio	Dayton, Ohio	FA-'82	5/0
11	Jensen, Jim	WR	6-4	215	11/14/58	6	Boston University	Doylestown, Pa.	D11-'81	16/1
87	Johnson, Dan	TE	6-3	240	5/17/60	4	Iowa State	New Hope, Minn.	D7a-'82	12/1
49	Judson, William	CB	6-1	190	3/26/59	5	South Carolina State	Atlanta, Ga.	D8-'81	16/16
40	Kozlowski, Mike	S	6-1	198	2/24/56	7	Colorado	Encinitas, Calif.	D10b-'79	5/2
44	Lankford, Paul	CB	6-2	184	6/15/58	5	Penn State	Farmingdale, N.Y.	D3-'82	16/15
63	Lee, Larry	G-C	6-2	263	9/10/59	6	UCLA	Dayton, Ohio	W(Det)-'85	11/0*
72	Lee, Ronnie	G	6-4	265	12/24/56	8	Baylor	Tyler, Tex.	T(Atl)-'84	15/13
99	Little, George	NT	6-4	278	6/27/63	2	Iowa	Duquesne, Pa.	D3a-'85	14/3
13	Marino, Dan	QB	6-4	214	9/15/61	4	Pittsburgh	Pittsburgh, Pa.	D1-'83	16/16
28	McNeal, Don	CB	5-11	192	5/6/58	6	Alabama	Atmore, Ala.	D1-'80	10/0
91	Moore, Mack	DE	6-4	258	3/4/59	2	Texas A&M	Monroe, La.	D6a-'81	16/2
89	Moore, Nat	WR	5-9	188	9/19/51	13	Florida	Miami, Fla.	D3-'74	15/7
54	Moyer, Alex	LB	6-1	221	10/25/63	2	Northwestern	Detroit, Mich.	D3b-'85	10/0
22	Nathan, Tony	RB	6-0	206	12/14/56	8	Alabama	Birmingham, Ala.	D3a-'79	16/15
64	†Newman, Ed	G	6-2	255	6/4/51	13	Duke	Syosset, N.Y.	D6-'73	0*
9	Pisarcik, Joe	QB	6-4	220	7/2/52	9	New Mexico State	Kingston, Pa.	FA-'85	0*
7	Reveiz, Fuad	K	5-11	222	2/24/63	2	Tennessee	Bogota, Colombia	D7-'85	16/0
4	Roby, Reggie	P	6-2	243	7/30/61	4	Iowa	Waterloo, Iowa	D6-'83	16/0
80	Rose, Joe	TE	6-3	230	6/24/57	7	California	Marysville, Calif.	D7-'80	16/1
52	Sendlein, Robin	LB	6-3	225	12/1/58	6	Texas	Las Vegas, Nev.	T(Minn)-'85	16/3
50	Shipp, Jackie	LB	6-2	236	3/19/62	3	Oklahoma	Stillwater, Okla.	D1-'84	16/11
18	Smith, Mike	CB	6-0	171	10/24/62	2	Texas-El Paso	Houston, Tex.	D4a-'85	7/0
45	Sowell, Robert	CB	5-11	175	6/23/61	4	Howard	Columbus, Ohio	FA-'83	10/1
57	Stephenson, Dwight	C	6-2	255	11/20/57	7	Alabama	Hampton, Va.	D2-'80	16/16
10	Strock, Don	QB	6-5	220	11/27/50	13	Virginia Tech	Pottstown, Pa.	D5-'73	16/0
60	Toews, Jeff	G-C	6-3	255	11/4/57	8	Washington	San Jose, Calif.	D2-'79	11/5
32	†Vigorito, Tom	WR-RB	5-10	190	10/23/59	4	Virginia	Wayne, N.J.	D5b-'81	9/0

* Baumhower, Newman, and Pisarcik missed '85 season due to injury; H. Green played 5 games with Tampa Bay, 11 with Miami in '85; L. Lee played 6 games with Detroit, 5 with Miami.

†Option playout; subject to developments.

Also played with Dolphins in '85—WR Duriel Harris (6 games), WR Frank Lockett (3), LB Sanders Shiver (6), CB John Swain (6), CB-KR Fulton Walker (2).

COACHING STAFF

Head Coach, Don Shula

Pro Career: Begins his twenty-fourth season as an NFL head coach, and seventeenth with the Dolphins. Miami has won or shared first place in the AFC East in 13 of his 16 years. Has highest overall winning percentage (.717) among active NFL coaches with 100 or more wins. Captured back-to-back NFL championships, defeating Washington 14-7 in Super Bowl VII and Minnesota 24-7 in Super Bowl VIII. Lost to Dallas 24-3 in Super Bowl VI, to Washington 27-17 in Super Bowl XVII, and to San Francisco 38-16 in Super Bowl XIX. His 1972 17-0 club is the only team in NFL history to go undefeated throughout the regular season and postseason. Started his pro playing career with Cleveland Browns as defensive back in 1951. After two seasons with Browns, spent 1953-56 with Baltimore Colts and 1957 with Washington Redskins. Joined Detroit Lions as defensive coach in 1960 and was named head coach of the Colts in 1963. Baltimore had a 13-1 record in 1968 and captured NFL championship before losing to New York Jets in Super Bowl III. Career record: 255-99-6.

Background: Outstanding offensive player at John Carroll University in Cleveland before becoming defensive specialist as a pro. His alma mater gave him doctorate in humanities, May 1973. Served as assistant coach at Virginia in 1958 and at Kentucky in 1959.

Personal: Born January 4, 1930, in Painesville, Ohio. Don and his wife, Dorothy, live in Miami Lakes and have five children—David, Donna, Sharon, Annie, and Mike.

Assistant Coaches

Bob Matheson, linebackers; born November 25, 1944, Boone, N.C., lives in Hollywood, Fla. Linebacker Duke 1964-66. Pro linebacker Cleveland Browns 1967-70, Miami Dolphins 1971-79. College coach: Duke 1981-82. Pro coach: Joined Dolphins in 1983.

Mel Phillips, defensive backfield; born January 6, 1942, Shelby, N.C., lives in North Miami. Defensive back-running back North Carolina A&T 1964-65. Pro defensive back San Francisco 49ers 1966-77. Pro coach: Detroit Lions 1980-84, joined Dolphins in 1985.

John Sandusky, offense-offensive line; born December 28, 1925, Philadelphia, Pa., lives in Cooper City, Fla. Tackle Villanova 1946-49. Pro tackle Cleveland Browns 1950-55, Green Bay Packers 1956. College coach: Villanova 1957-58. Pro coach: Baltimore Colts 1959-72 (head coach 1972), Philadelphia Eagles 1973-75, joined Dolphins in 1976.

Dan Sekanovich, defensive line; born July 27, 1933, West Hazleton, Pa., lives in Miami. Defensive end-tight end Tennessee 1951-53. Pro defensive end Montreal Alouettes (CFL) 1954. College coach: Susquehanna 1961-63, Connecticut 1964-67, Pittsburgh 1968, Navy 1969-70, Kentucky 1971-72. Pro coach: Montreal Alouettes (CFL) 1973-76, New York Jets 1977-82, Atlanta Falcons 1983-85, first year with Dolphins.

David Shula, assistant head coach-receivers and quarterbacks; born May 28, 1959, Lexington, Ky., lives in Miami Lakes. Wide receiver Dartmouth 1977-80. Pro receiver Baltimore Colts 1981. Pro coach: Joined Dolphins in 1982.

Chuck Studley, defense; born January 17, 1929, Maywood, Ill., lives in Miami Lakes. Guard Illinois 1949-51. No pro playing experience. College coach: Illinois 1955-59, Massachusetts 1960 (head coach), Cincinnati 1961-68 (head coach). Pro coach: Cincinnati Bengals 1969-78, San Francisco 49ers 1979-82, Houston Oilers 1983 (interim head coach for last 10 games), joined Dolphins in 1984.

Carl Taseff, offensive backfield; born September 28, 1928, Cleveland, Ohio, lives in Pembroke Pines, Fla. Back John Carroll 1947-50. Pro defensive back Cleveland Browns 1951, Baltimore Colts 1953-61, Philadelphia Eagles 1961, Buffalo Bills 1962. Pro coach: Boston Patriots 1964, Detroit Lions 1965-66, joined Dolphins in 1970.

Junior Wade, strength-conditioning; born February 2, 1947, Bath, S.C., lives in Hialeah, Fla. South Carolina State 1969. No college or pro playing experience. Pro coach: Joined Dolphins in 1975, coach since 1983.

Mike Westhoff, special teams-tight ends; born January 10, 1948, Pittsburgh, Pa., lives in Miami. Center-linebacker Wichita State 1967-69. No pro playing experience. College coach: Indiana 1974-75, Dayton 1976, Indiana State 1977, Northwestern 1978-80, Texas Christian 1981. Pro coach: Baltimore/Indianapolis Colts 1982-84, Arizona Outlaws (USFL) 1985, first year with Dolphins.

MIAMI DOLPHINS 1986 FIRST-YEAR ROSTER

Name	Pos.	Ht.	Wt.	Birth-date	College	Hometown	How Acq.
Franklin, Arnold	TE	6-3	253	12/6/63	North Carolina	Lincoln Heights, Ohio	D11
Hendel, Andy	LB	6-1	230	3/4/61	North Carolina State	Rochester, N.Y.	FA
Isom, Rickey	RB	6-0	225	11/30/63	North Carolina State	Harrisburg, Pa.	D12
Kolic, Larry	LB	6-1	248	8/31/63	Ohio State	Smithville, Ohio	D7
Mielke, David	G	6-4	263	7/14/62	Wisconsin	Merrill, Wis.	FA
Offerdahl, John	LB	6-2	232	8/17/64	Western Michigan	Fort Atkinson, Wis.	D2
Petty, Gregory (1)	WR	5-11	171	11/15/62	Tulsa	Miami, Fla.	FA
Pruitt, James	WR	6-2	199	1/29/64	Cal State-Fullerton	Los Angeles, Calif.	D4
Robinson, Jacque (1)	RB	6-0	225	3/5/63	Washington	San Jose, Calif.	FA
Robinson, Larry (1)	CB-S	5-10	195	4/30/62	Northwestern St., La.	Natchitoches, La.	FA
Schuchts, Wayne (1)	QB	6-3	209	3/25/61	Virginia	Hollywood, Fla.	FA
Sowell, Brent	NT	6-5	256	3/27/63	Alabama	Clearwater, Fla.	D6
Stuart, John	T	6-4	280	2/25/63	Texas	Clear Lake, Tex.	D8
Taylor, Tom (1)	C-G	6-3	265	9/14/62	Georgia Tech	Palmdale, Calif.	FA
Thompson, Reyna	S	5-11	194	8/28/63	Baylor	Dallas, Tex.	D9
Turner, T.J.	NT	6-4	265	5/16/63	Houston	Lufkin, Tex.	D3
White, Marc	RB	6-0	210	10/15/63	Utah State	Oakland, Calif.	FA
Wray, Stephen (1)	QB	6-2	215	1/29/60	Franklin College	Plainfield, Ind.	FA
Wickersham, Jeff	QB	6-2	195	12/5/63	Louisiana State	Merrit Island, Fla.	D10
Wyatt, Kevin	CB	5-10	190	3/14/64	Arkansas	Kansas City, Mo.	D5

The term NFL Rookie is defined as a player who is in his first season of professional football and has not been on the roster of another professional football team for any regular season or postseason games. A Rookie is designated by an "R" on NFL rosters. Players who have been active in another professional football league or players who have NFL experience, including either preseason training camp or being on an active roster for fewer than three regular season or postseason games, are termed NFL First-Year Players. An NFL First-Year Player is designated by a "1" on NFL rosters. Thereafter, a player on an NFL active roster for at least three regular season or postseason games is credited with an additional year of NFL playing experience.

NOTES

NEW ENGLAND PATRIOTS

American Football Conference
Eastern Division

Team Colors: Red, White, and Blue

Sullivan Stadium
Route 1
Foxboro, Massachusetts 02035
Telephone: (617) 543-7911, 262-1776

Club Officials

President: William H. Sullivan, Jr.
Executive Vice President: Charles W. Sullivan
Vice President: Francis J. (Bucko) Kilroy
General Manager: Patrick J. Sullivan
Director of Player Development: Dick Steinberg
Director of Pro Scouting: Bill McPeak
Director of College Scouting: Joe Mendes
Executive Director of Player Personnel: Darryl Stingley
Personnel Scouts: George Blackburn, Larry Cook, Charlie Garcia, Pat Naughton, Bob Teahan
Director of Public Relations: Dave Wintergrass
Director of Publicity: Jim Greenidge
Assistant Publicity Director: Mike Loftus
Box Office Manager: Ken Sternfeld
Trainer: Ron O'Neil
Equipment Manager: George Luongo
Video Manager: Ken Deininger

Stadium: Sullivan Stadium • **Capacity:** 61,000
Route 1
Foxboro, Massachusetts 02035

Playing Surface: SuperTurf

Training Camp: Bryant College
Smithfield, Rhode Island 02917

1986 SCHEDULE

Preseason

Aug. 2	vs. St. Louis at Canton, Ohio	2:30
Aug. 10	**Washington**	7:00
Aug. 16	at New Orleans	7:00
Aug. 22	at Los Angeles Raiders	7:00
Aug. 30	at Green Bay	7:00

Regular Season

Sept. 7	**Indianapolis**	4:00
Sept. 11	at New York Jets (Thursday)	8:00
Sept. 21	**Seattle**	1:00
Sept. 28	at Denver	2:00
Oct. 5	**Miami**	1:00
Oct. 12	**New York Jets**	1:00
Oct. 19	at Pittsburgh	1:00
Oct. 26	at Buffalo	1:00
Nov. 2	**Atlanta**	1:00
Nov. 9	at Indianapolis	1:00
Nov. 16	at Los Angeles Rams	1:00
Nov. 23	**Buffalo**	1:00
Nov. 30	at New Orleans	12:00
Dec. 7	**Cincinnati**	1:00
Dec. 14	**San Francisco**	1:00
Dec. 22	at Miami (Monday)	9:00

PATRIOTS COACHING HISTORY

Boston 1960-70
(178-195-9)

1960-61	Lou Saban*	7-12-0
1961-68	Mike Holovak	53-47-9
1969-70	Clive Rush**	5-16-0
1970-72	John Mazur***	9-21-0
1972	Phil Bengtson	1-4-0
1973-78	Chuck Fairbanks****	46-41-0
1978	Hank Bullough-Ron Erhardt#	0-1-0
1979-81	Ron Erhardt	21-27-0
1982-84	Ron Meyer##	18-16-0
1984-85	Raymond Berry	18-10-0

*Released after five games in 1961
**Released after seven games in 1970
***Released after nine games in 1972
****Resigned after 15 games in 1978
#Co-coaches
##Released after eight games in 1984

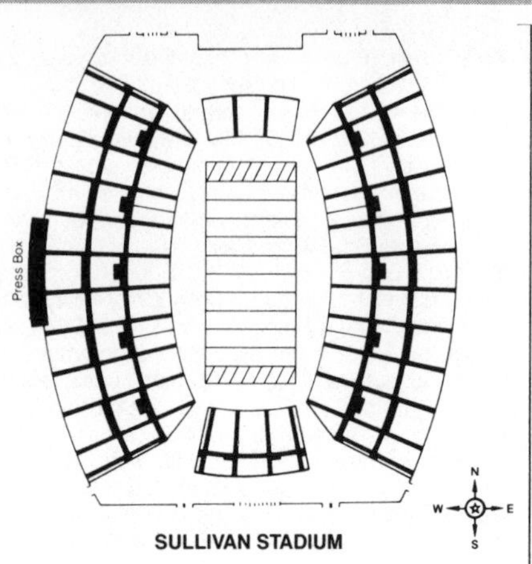

SULLIVAN STADIUM

RECORD HOLDERS

Individual Records—Career

Category	Name	Performance
Rushing (Yds.)	Sam Cunningham, 1973-79, 1981-82	5,453
Passing (Yds.)	Steve Grogan, 1975-1985	21,581
Passing (TDs)	Steve Grogan, 1975-1985	146
Receiving (No.)	Stanley Morgan, 1977-1985	351
Receiving (Yds.)	Stanley Morgan, 1977-1985	7,201
Interceptions	Ron Hall, 1961-67	29
Punting (Avg.)	Rich Camarillo, 1981-85	43.2
Punt Return (Avg.)	Mack Herron, 1973-75	12.0
Kickoff Return (Avg.)	Horace Ivory, 1977-1981	27.6
Field Goals	Gino Cappelletti, 1960-1970	176
Touchdowns (Tot.)	Sam Cunningham, 1973-79, 1981-82	49
Points	Gino Cappelletti, 1960-1970	1,130

Individual Records—Single Season

Category	Name	Performance
Rushing (Yds.)	Jim Nance, 1966	1,458
Passing (Yds.)	Vito (Babe) Parilli, 1964	3,465
Passing (TDs)	Vito (Babe) Parilli, 1964	31
Receiving (No.)	Derrick Ramsey, 1984	66
Receiving (Yds.)	Stanley Morgan, 1981	1,029
Interceptions	Ron Hall, 1964	11
Punting (Avg.)	Rich Camarillo, 1983	44.6
Punt Return (Avg.)	Mack Herron, 1974	14.8
Kickoff Return (Avg.)	Raymond Clayborn, 1977	31.0
Field Goals	John Smith, 1980	26
Touchdowns (Tot.)	Steve Grogan, 1976	13
	Stanley Morgan, 1979	13
Points	Gino Cappelletti, 1964	155

Individual Records—Single Game

Category	Name	Performance
Rushing (Yds.)	Tony Collins, 9-18-83	212
Passing (Yds.)	Vito (Babe) Parilli, 10-16-64	400
Passing (TDs)	Vito (Babe) Parilli, 11-15-64	5
	Vito (Babe) Parilli, 10-15-67	5
	Steve Grogan, 9-9-79	5
Receiving (No.)	Art Graham, 11-20-66	11
Receiving (Yds.)	Stanley Morgan, 11-8-81	182
Interceptions	Many times	3
	Last time by Roland James, 10-23-83	
Field Goals	Gino Cappelletti, 10-4-64	6
Touchdowns (Tot.)	Many times	3
	Last time by Derrick Ramsey, 11-18-84	
Points	Gino Cappelletti, 12-18-65	28

1985 TEAM STATISTICS

	New England	Opp.
Total First Downs	294	284
Rushing	126	92
Passing	153	168
Penalty	15	24
Third Down: Made/Att.	82/224	74/227
Fourth Down: Made/Att.	4/10	5/15
Total Net Yards	5499	4714
Avg. Per Game	343.7	294.6
Total Plays	1061	1042
Avg. Per Play	5.2	4.5
Net Yards Rushing	2331	1655
Avg. Per Game	145.7	103.4
Total Rushes	565	466
Net Yards Passing	3168	3059
Avg. Per Game	198.0	191.2
Tackled/Yards Lost	39/315	51/334
Gross Yards	3483	3393
Att./Completions	457/255	525/262
Completion Pct.	55.8	49.9
Had Intercepted	22	23
Punts/Avg.	92/43.0	97/40.5
Net Punting Avg.	33.6	32.6
Penalties/Yards Lost	114/842	83/699
Fumbles/Ball Lost	37/20	36/24
Touchdowns	41	32
Rushing	15	15
Passing	20	14
Returns	6	3
Avg. Time of Possession	31:07	28:53

1985 TEAM RECORD

Preseason (1-3)

Date	New England		Opponents
8/10	20	*New Orleans	32
8/17	31	Kansas City	13
8/23	36	Washington	37
8/31	13	L.A. Rams	14
	100		96

Regular Season (11-5)

Date	New England		Opp.	Att.
9/8	26	*Green Bay	20	49,488
9/15	7	Chicago	20	60,533
9/22	17	Buffalo	14	40,334
9/29	20	*L.A. Raiders	35	60,893
10/6	20	Cleveland	24	60,639
10/13	14	*Buffalo	3	40,462
10/20	20	*N.Y. Jets	13	58,163
10/27	32	Tampa Bay	14	34,661
11/3	17	*Miami	13	58,811
11/10	34	*Indianapolis	15	53,824
11/17	20	Seattle	13	60,345
11/24	13	N.Y. Jets (OT)	16	74,100
12/1	38	Indianapolis	31	56,740
12/8	23	*Detroit	6	59,078
12/16	27	Miami	30	69,489
12/22	34	*Cincinnati	23	57,953

Postseason (3-1)

Date	New England		Opp.	Att.
12/28/85	26	N.Y. Jets	14	75,945
1/5/86	27	L.A. Raiders	20	87,163
1/12/86	31	Miami	14	75,662
1/26/86	10	*Chicago	46	73,818

*Home Game (OT) Overtime

Score by Periods

New England	54	115	44	149	0	—	362
Opponents	75	64	56	92	3	—	290

Attendance

Home 438,672 Away 456,841 Total 895,513
Single game home record, 61,457 (12-5-71)
Single season home record, 475,081 (1978)

1985 INDIVIDUAL STATISTICS

Rushing	Att.	Yds.	Avg.	LG	TD
C. James	263	1227	4.7	65t	5
Collins	163	657	4.0	28	3
Weathers	41	174	4.2	42t	1
Tatupu	47	152	3.2	11	2
Eason	22	70	3.2	23	1
Grogan	20	29	1.5	12	2
Fryar	7	27	3.9	13	1
Morgan	1	0	0.0	0	0
Franklin	1	−5	−5.0	−5	0
Patriots	565	2331	4.1	65t	15
Opponents	466	1655	3.6	24	15

Passing	Att.	Comp.	Pct.	Yds.	TD	Int.	Tkld.	Rate
Eason	299	168	56.2	2156	11	17	28/229	67.5
Grogan	156	85	54.5	1311	7	5	11/86	84.1
C. James	2	2	100.0	16	2	0	0/0	139.6
Patriots	457	255	55.8	3483	20	22	39/315	74.9
Opponents	525	262	49.9	3393	14	23	51/334	61.2

Receiving	No.	Yds.	Avg.	LG	TD
Collins	52	549	10.6	49	2
Morgan	39	760	19.5	50t	5
Fryar	39	670	17.2	56	7
D. Ramsey	28	285	10.2	26	1
C. James	27	360	13.3	90t	2
Jones	21	237	11.3	29t	2
Dawson	17	148	8.7	26	0
Starring	16	235	14.7	40	0
D. Williams	9	163	18.1	30	0
Hawthorne	3	42	14.0	28t	1
Weathers	2	18	9.0	13	0
Tatupu	2	16	8.0	15	0
Patriots	255	3483	13.7	90t	20
Opponents	262	3393	13.0	88t	14

Interceptions	No.	Yds.	Avg.	LG	TD
Marion	7	189	27.0	83	0
Clayborn	6	80	13.3	38	1
R. James	4	51	12.8	39	0
Lippett	3	93	31.0	58	0
Blackmon	1	14	14.0	14	0
McGrew	1	0	0.0	0	0
McSwain	1	0	0.0	0	0
Patriots	23	427	18.6	83	1
Opponents	22	243	11.0	38t	2

Punting	No.	Yds.	Avg.	In 20	LG
Camarillo	92	3953	43.0	16	75
Patriots	92	3953	43.0	16	75
Opponents	97	3933	40.5	25	64

Punt Returns	No.	FC	Yds.	Avg.	LG	TD
Fryar	37	15	520	14.1	85t	2
R. James	2	0	13	6.5	13	0
Starring	2	0	0	0.0	0	0
Bowman	1	0	−3	−3.0	−3	0
Marion	0	1	0	—	0	0
Patriots	42	16	530	12.6	85t	2
Opponents	56	7	598	10.7	46	0

Kickoff Returns	No.	Yds.	Avg.	LG	TD
Starring	48	1012	21.1	53	0
Fryar	3	39	13.0	24	0
Jones	3	37	12.3	20	0
Weathers	1	18	18.0	18	0
Hawthorne	1	13	13.0	13	0
C. James	1	0	0.0	0	0
Patriots	57	1119	19.6	53	0
Opponents	76	1434	18.9	58	0

Scoring	TD R	TD P	TD Rt	PAT	FG	Saf	TP
Franklin	0	0	0	40/41	24/30	0	112
Fryar	1	7	2	0/0	0/0	0	60
C. James	5	2	0	0/0	0/0	0	42
Collins	3	2	0	0/0	0/0	0	30
Morgan	0	5	0	0/0	0/0	0	30
Jones	0	2	1	0/0	0/0	0	18
Grogan	2	0	0	0/0	0/0	0	12
Tatupu	2	0	0	0/0	0/0	0	12
Clayborn	0	0	1	0/0	0/0	0	6
Eason	1	0	0	0/0	0/0	0	6
Hawthorne	0	1	0	0/0	0/0	0	6
D. Ramsey	0	1	0	0/0	0/0	0	6
Rembert	0	0	1	0/0	0/0	0	6
Tippett	0	0	1	0/0	0/0	0	6
Weathers	1	0	0	0/0	0/0	0	6
Blackmon	0	0	0	0/0	0/0	2	4
Patriots	15	20	6	40/41	24/30	2	362
Opponents	15	14	3	30/32	22/25	1	290

FIRST-ROUND SELECTIONS

(If club had no first-round selection, first player drafted is listed with round in parentheses.)

Year	Player, College, Position
1960	Ron Burton, Northwestern, RB
1961	Tommy Mason, Tulane, RB
1962	Gary Collins, Maryland, WR
1963	Art Graham, Boston College, WR
1964	Jack Concannon, Boston College, QB
1965	Jerry Rush, Michigan State, DE
1966	Karl Singer, Purdue, T
1967	John Charles, Purdue, S
1968	Dennis Byrd, North Carolina State, DE
1969	Ron Sellers, Florida State, WR
1970	Phil Olsen, Utah State, DE
1971	Jim Plunkett, Stanford, QB
1972	Tom Reynolds, San Diego State, WR (2)
1973	John Hannah, Alabama, G
	Sam Cunningham, Southern California, RB
	Darryl Stingley, Purdue, WR
1974	Steve Corbett, Boston College, G (2)
1975	Russ Francis, Oregon, TE
1976	Mike Haynes, Arizona State, DB
	Pete Brock, Colorado, C
	Tim Fox, Ohio State, DB
1977	Raymond Clayborn, Texas, DB
	Stanley Morgan, Tennessee, WR
1978	Bob Cryder, Alabama, G
1979	Rick Sanford, South Carolina, DB
1980	Roland James, Tennessee, DB
	Vagas Ferguson, Notre Dame, RB
1981	Brian Holloway, Stanford, T
1982	Kenneth Sims, Texas, DT
	Lester Williams, Miami, DT
1983	Tony Eason, Illinois, QB
1984	Irving Fryar, Nebraska, WR
1985	Trevor Matich, Brigham Young, C
1986	Reggie Dupard, Southern Methodist, RB

NEW ENGLAND PATRIOTS 1986 VETERAN ROSTER

No.	Name	Pos.	Ht.	Wt.	Birth-date	NFL Exp.	College	Hometown	How Acq.	'85 Games/ Starts
55	Blackmon, Don	LB	6-3	235	3/14/58	6	Tulsa	Land-O-Lakes, Fla.	D4-'81	14/14
28	Bowman, Jim	S	6-2	210	10/26/63	2	Central Michigan	Cadillac, Mich.	D2b-'85	16/0
58	†Brock, Pete	C	6-5	275	7/14/54	11	Colorado	Portland, Ore.	D1b-'76	9/8
3	Camarillo, Rich	P	5-11	185	11/29/59	6	Washington	Pico Rivera, Calif.	FA-'81	16/0
26	Clayborn, Raymond	CB	6-0	186	1/2/55	10	Texas	Ft. Worth, Tex.	D1a-'77	16/16
33	Collins, Tony	RB	5-11	212	5/27/59	6	East Carolina	Penn Yan, N.Y.	D2-'81	16/16
92	†Creswell, Smiley	DE	6-4	251	12/11/59	2	Michigan State	Monroe, Wash.	D5a-'83	3/0*
87	Dawson, Lin	TE	6-3	240	6/24/59	6	North Carolina State	Kinston, N.C.	D8b-'81	16/13
59	Doig, Steve	LB	6-3	240	3/28/60	4	New Hampshire	North Reading, Mass.	FA-'86	0*
11	Eason, Tony	QB	6-4	212	10/8/59	4	Illinois	Walnut Grove, Calif.	D1-'83	16/10
66	Fairchild, Paul	G	6-4	270	9/14/61	3	Kansas	Glidden, Iowa	D5-'84	16/2
1	Franklin, Tony	K	5-8	182	11/18/56	8	Texas A&M	Big Spring, Tex.	T(Phil)-'84	16/0
80	Fryar, Irving	WR-KR	6-0	200	9/28/62	3	Nebraska	Mt. Holly, N.J.	D1-'84	16/14
43	Gibson, Ernest	CB	5-10	185	10/3/61	3	Furman	Jacksonville, Fla.	D6-'84	9/0
14	†Grogan, Steve	QB	6-4	210	7/24/53	12	Kansas State	Ottawa, Kan.	D5a-'75	7/6
68	Haley, Darryl	T	6-4	265	2/16/61	4	Utah	Los Angeles, Calif.	D2c-'82	0*
73	Hannah, John	G	6-3	265	4/4/51	14	Alabama	Canton, Ga.	D1a-'73	14/14
27	†Hawthorne, Greg	WR-RB	6-2	225	9/5/56	8	Baylor	Ft. Worth, Tex.	T(Pitt)-'84	15/0
76	Holloway, Brian	T	6-7	288	7/25/59	6	Stanford	Potomac, Md.	D1-'81	16/16
51	†Ingram, Brian	LB	6-4	235	10/31/59	5	Tennessee	Memphis, Tenn.	D4b-'82	15/0
32	James, Craig	RB	6-0	215	1/2/61	3	Southern Methodist	Houston, Tex.	D7-'83	16/14
38	†James, Roland	S	6-2	191	2/18/58	7	Tennessee	Xenia, Ohio	D1a-'80	16/16
83	Jones, Cedric	WR	6-1	184	6/1/60	5	Duke	Weldon, N.C.	D3a-'82	16/3
42	†Lippett, Ronnie	CB	5-11	180	12/10/60	4	Miami	Sebring, Fla.	D8-'83	16/16
31	†Marion, Fred	S	6-2	191	8/2/59	5	Miami	Gainesville, Fla.	D5-'82	16/16
64	Matich, Trevor	C	6-4	270	10/9/61	2	Brigham Young	Sacramento, Calif.	D1a-'85	1/0
50	McGrew, Larry	LB	6-5	233	7/23/57	6	Southern California	Berkeley, Calif.	D2-'80	13/13
23	McSwain, Rod	CB	6-1	198	1/28/62	3	Clemson	Caroleen, N.C.	T(Atl)-'84	16/0
67	Moore, Steve	G-T	6-4	285	10/1/60	4	Tennessee State	Memphis, Tenn.	D3b-'83	16/16
86	Morgan, Stanley	WR	5-11	181	2/17/55	10	Tennessee	Easley, S.C.	D1b-'77	15/13
75	†Morriss, Guy	C-G	6-4	255	5/13/51	14	Texas Christian	Arlington, Tex.	FA-'84	16/10
57	†Nelson, Steve	LB	6-2	230	4/26/51	13	North Dakota State	Anoka, Minn.	D2b-'74	15/15
98	Owens, Dennis	NT	6-1	258	2/24/60	5	North Carolina State	Clinton, N.C.	FA-'82	14/13
70	†Plunkett, Art	T	6-7	260	3/8/59	6	Nevada-Las Vegas	Salt Lake City, Utah	FA-'85	15/0
88	Ramsey, Derrick	TE	6-5	235	12/23/56	9	Kentucky	Hastings, Fla.	T(Raiders)-'83	16/3
12	†Ramsey, Tom	QB	6-1	189	7/9/61	2	UCLA	Encino, Calif.	D10c-'83	0*
52	Rembert, Johnny	LB	6-3	234	1/19/61	4	Clemson	Arcadia, Fla.	D4-'83	16/6
95	†Reynolds, Ed	LB	6-5	230	9/23/61	4	Virginia	Ridgeway, Va.	FA-'83	12/0
41	Robinson, Bo	TE-RB	6-2	225	5/27/59	7	West Texas State	LaMesa, Tex.	FA-'84	0*
77	Sims, Kenneth	DE	6-5	271	10/31/59	5	Texas	Kosse, Tex.	D1a-'82	13/13
81	Starring, Stephen	WR-KR	5-10	172	7/30/61	4	McNeese State	Vinton, La.	D3a-'83	16/1
30	Tatupu, Mosi	RB	6-0	227	4/26/55	9	Southern California	Honolulu, Hawaii	D8b-'78	16/2
99	Thomas, Ben	DE	6-4	280	7/2/61	2	Auburn	Ashburn, Ga.	D2c-'85	15/0
56	Tippett, Andre	LB	6-3	241	12/27/59	5	Iowa	Newark, N.J.	D2b-'82	16/16
60	Veris, Garin	DE	6-4	255	2/27/63	2	Stanford	Chillocothe, Ohio	D2a-'85	16/4
24	Weathers, Robert	RB	6-2	222	9/13/60	5	Arizona State	Ft. Pierce, Fla.	D2a-'82	16/0
53	Weishuhn, Clayton	LB	6-1	218	10/7/59	3	Angelo State	San Angelo, Tex.	D3b-'82	0*
82	Williams, Derwin	WR	6-0	170	5/6/61	2	New Mexico	Brownwood, Tex.	D7b-'84	16/0
54	Williams, Ed	LB	6-4	244	8/9/61	3	Texas	Ector, Tex.	D2-'84	13/0
44	Williams, Jon	RB	5-9	190	6/1/61	2	Penn State	Somerville, N.J.	D3-'84	0*
72	Williams, Lester	NT	6-3	272	1/19/59	5	Miami	Carol City, Fla.	D1b-'82	9/3
90	†Williams, Toby	DE	6-3	254	11/19/59	4	Nebraska	Washington, D.C.	D10b-'83	5/3
61	†Wooten, Ron	G	6-3	273	6/28/59	5	North Carolina	Kinston, N.C.	D6-'81	14/14

* Creswell played 3 games for Philadelphia and was active for 3 games with New England but did not play in '85; Doig last active with Detroit in '84; Haley, Robinson, Weishuhn, and J. Williams missed '85 season due to injury; T. Ramsey active for 11 games but did not play.

†Option playout; subject to developments.

Retired—Julius Adams, 14-year defensive end 16 games in '85

Also played with Patriots in '85—G Tom Condon (1 game).

COACHING STAFF

Head Coach, Raymond Berry

Pro Career: Became ninth head coach in Patriots history when he was named to replace Ron Meyer on October 25, 1984, after eighth game of the season. Led team to Super Bowl in first full season last year. The Patriots became the first team to reach the Super Bowl by winning three road playoff games. Played receiver for the Baltimore Colts 1955-67. Made 631 catches for 9,275 yards and 68 touchdowns in his playing career. His number of career catches is presently fourth best in NFL history, while his receiving yardage is fifth best ever, and his career touchdown catches fourteenth. Helped Colts to two world championships (1958 and 1959) and to NFL Championship Game (1964). Named all-pro three times (1958-60) and played in five Pro Bowl games. Led NFL in receiving 1958-60. Holds NFL Championship Game records for yardage (178) and receptions (12), set in 1958 sudden-death title game vs. New York Giants. Was inducted into the Pro Football Hall of Fame on July 29, 1973, six years after his retirement. Was receivers coach with Dallas Cowboys in 1968-69, Detroit Lions 1973-75, Cleveland Browns 1976-77, and New England Patriots 1978-81. Career record: 18-10.

Background: Attended Paris (Texas) High School and Southern Methodist 1951-54, where he played receiver. Coached receivers at Arkansas 1970-72.

Personal: Born February 27, 1933, in Corpus Christi, Tex. Raymond and his wife, Sally, live in Medfield, Mass., with their children—Mark, Suzanne, and Ashley.

Assistant Coaches

Dean Brittenham, strength-conditioning; born June 25, 1931, Brady, Neb., lives in Foxboro, Mass. 1957 graduate of Nebraska. No college or pro playing experience. College coach: Kansas 1962-64, Occidental 1965-67, Nebraska 1968-71, Colorado 1972-81. Pro coach: Kansas City Chiefs 1969-70, New Orleans Saints 1977-78, Denver Broncos 1982-83, Minnesota Vikings 1984, joined Patriots in 1985.

Jim Carr, defensive backs; born March 25, 1933, Kayford, W. Va., lives in North Attleboro, Mass. Running back-defensive back-linebacker Morris Harvey (now Univ. of Charleston, W. Va.) 1951-54. Pro running back-defensive back-linebacker Chicago Cardinals 1955-57, Montreal Alouettes (CFL) 1958, Philadelphia Eagles 1959-63, Washington Redskins 1964-65. Pro coach: Minnesota Vikings 1966-68, 1979-81, Chicago Bears 1969, 1973-74, Philadelphia Eagles 1970-72, Detroit Lions 1975-76, Buffalo Bills 1977, San Francisco 49ers 1978, Denver Gold (USFL) 1983-84, joined Patriots in 1985.

Bobby Grier, offensive backs; born November 10, 1942, Detroit, Mich., lives in Holliston, Mass. Running back Iowa 1961-64. No pro playing experience. College coach: Eastern Michigan 1974-77, Boston College 1978-80. Pro coach: Joined Patriots in 1981. Moved to team's scouting department 1982-84. Rejoined Patriots as coach in 1985.

Ray Hamilton, assistant, defensive line; born January 20, 1951, Omaha, Neb., lives in Sharon, Mass. Defensive tackle Oklahoma 1970-72. Nose tackle New England Patriots 1973-81. Pro coach: Joined Patriots in 1985.

Rod Humenuik, assistant head coach-offense, offensive line; born June 17, 1938, Detroit, Mich., lives in Foxboro, Mass. Guard Southern California 1956-58. Pro guard Winnipeg Blue Bombers (CFL) 1960-62. College coach: Fullerton, Calif., J.C. 1964-65, Southern California 1966-70, Cal State-Northridge 1971-72 (head coach). Pro coach: Toronto Argonauts (CFL) 1973-74, Cleveland Browns 1975-82, Kansas City Chiefs 1983-84, joined Patriots in 1985.

Harold Jackson, assistant, receivers; born January 6, 1946, Hattiesburg, Miss., lives in Foxboro, Mass. Receiver Jackson State 1964-67. Pro wide receiver Los Angeles Rams 1968, 1973-77, Philadelphia Eagles 1969-72, New England Patriots 1978-81, Seattle Seahawks 1983. Pro coach: Joined Patriots in 1985.

NEW ENGLAND PATRIOTS 1986 FIRST-YEAR ROSTER

Name	Pos.	Ht.	Wt.	Birth-date	College	Hometown	How Acq.
Baty, Greg	TE	6-5	241	8/28/64	Stanford	Sparta, N.J.	D8
Calabria, Steve (1)	QB	6-4	210	6/20/63	Colgate	Carle Place, N.Y.	FA
Colton, George	G	6-4	279	7/28/63	Maryland	Lindenhurst, N.Y.	D9
Conner, John (1)	QB	6-3	205	5/9/61	Arizona	Tucson, Ariz.	FA
Dupard, Reggie	RB	5-11	205	10/30/63	Southern Methodist	New Orleans, La.	D1
Gieselman, Scott	TE	6-6	243	4/3/63	Boston College	Weston, Mass.	D4
Glenn, Vencie	CB-S	6-0	183	10/26/64	Indiana State	Silver Spring, Md.	D2b
Hodge, Milford (1)	NT	6-3	275	3/11/61	Washington State	San Bruno, Calif.	FA
Jones, Cletis	RB	5-11	217	8/6/64	Florida State	Tallahassee, Fla.	D10
Jordan, Eric (1)	RB-KR	6-0	190	11/17/61	Purdue	Las Vegas, Nev.	SD2-'84
McAulay, Don	K	5-10	198	1/30/64	Syracuse	East Islip, N.Y.	D12
McDonald, Ray	WR	5-11	181	8/25/64	Florida	Belle Glade, Fla.	D7a
Mills, David (1)	TE	6-2	225	11/17/61	Brigham Young	American Fork, Utah	FA
Moog, Aaron (1)	DE	6-4	262	2/3/62	Nevada-Las Vegas	Las Vegas, Nev.	FA
Napier, Scott (1)	RB	6-1	250	6/11/62	Nebraska	Sherman Oaks, Calif.	FA
Phelan, Gerard (1)	WR	6-0	190	1/20/63	Boston College	Rosemont, Pa.	D4a-'85
Robinson, Greg	G-T	6-5	284	12/25/62	Cal St.-Sacramento	Elk Grove, Calif.	D5
Ruth, Mike	NT	6-1	266	6/25/64	Boston College	Norristown, Pa.	D2a
Thomas, Greg	WR	5-11	157	6/7/62	Pacific	San Diego, Calif.	D11
Toth, Tom (1)	T	6-5	275	5/23/62	Western Michigan	Orland Park, Ill.	D4b-'85
Williams, Brent	DE	6-4	278	10/23/64	Toledo	Flint, Mich.	D7b
Wingate, Leonard (1)	NT	6-4	270	11/3/61	South Carolina State	Charleston, S.C.	FA

The term NFL Rookie is defined as a player who is in his first season of professional football and has not been on the roster of another professional football team for any regular season or postseason games. A Rookie is designated by an "R" on NFL rosters. Players who have been active in another professional football league or players who have NFL experience, including either preseason training camp or being on an active roster for fewer than three regular season or postseason games, are termed NFL First-Year Players. An NFL First-Year Player is designated by a "1" on NFL rosters. Thereafter, a player on an NFL active roster for at least three regular season or postseason games is credited with an additional year of NFL playing experience.

NOTES

Ed Khayat, defensive line; born September 14, 1935, Moss Point, Miss., lives in Foxboro, Mass. Offensive-defensive end Millsaps 1953, Perkinston J.C. 1954, Tulane 1955-56. Pro defensive end-defensive tackle Washington Redskins 1957, 1962-63, Philadelphia Eagles 1958-61, 1964-65, Boston Patriots 1966. Pro coach: New Orleans Saints 1967-70, Philadelphia Eagles 1971-72 (head coach), Detroit Lions 1973-74, Atlanta Falcons 1975-76, Baltimore Colts 1977-81, Detroit Lions 1982-84, joined Patriots in 1985.

John Polonchek, special assistant to head coach; born January 1, 1928, in Granastrov, Czechoslovakia, lives in Foxboro, Mass. Running back-defensive back Michigan State 1947-49. No pro playing experience. College coach: Michigan State 1950, 1955-57, Colorado 1959-61. Pro coach: Oakland Raiders 1967-71, Green Bay Packers 1972-74, New England Patriots 1975-81, New Jersey Generals (USFL) 1982-83, rejoined Patriots in 1985.

Rod Rust, defensive coordinator; born August 2, 1928, Webster City, Iowa, lives in Foxboro, Mass. Center-linebacker Iowa State 1947-49. No pro playing experience. College coach: New Mexico 1960-62, Stanford 1963-66, North Texas State 1967-72 (head coach). Pro coach: Montreal Alouettes (CFL) 1973-75, Philadelphia Eagles 1976-77, Kansas City Chiefs 1978-82, joined Patriots in 1983.

Dante Scarnecchia, special teams-tight ends; born February 15, 1948, Los Angeles, Calif., lives in Wrentham, Mass. Center Taft, Calif., J.C. 1966-67, California Western 1968-69. No pro playing experience. College coach: California Western 1970-72, Iowa State 1973-74, Southern Methodist 1975-76, 1980-81, Pacific 1977-78, Northern Arizona 1979. Pro coach: Joined Patriots in 1982.

Don Shinnick, linebackers; born May 15, 1935, Kansas City, Mo., lives in Walpole, Mass. Guard-defensive back-running back-linebacker UCLA 1954-56. Pro linebacker Baltimore Colts 1957-69. College coach: Central Methodist College (Fayette, Missouri; head coach) 1979-81. Pro coach: Chicago Bears 1970-71, St. Louis Cardinals 1972, Oakland Raiders 1973-77, joined Patriots in 1985.

Les Steckel, quarterbacks-receivers; born July 1, 1946, Whitehall, Pa., lives in Foxboro, Mass. Running back Kansas 1964-68. No pro playing experience. College coach: Colorado 1972-76, Navy 1977. Pro coach: San Francisco 49ers 1978, Minnesota Vikings 1979-84 (head coach 1984), joined Patriots in 1985.

NEW YORK JETS

American Football Conference
Eastern Division

Team Colors: Kelly Green and White

598 Madison Avenue
New York, New York 10022
Telephone: (212) 421-6600

Club Officials

Chairman of the Board: Leon Hess
President-Chief Operating Officer: Jim Kensil
Secretary and Administrative Manager: Steve Gutman
Director of Player Personnel: Mike Hickey
Pro Personnel Director: Jim Royer
Talent Scouts: Joe Collins, Don Grammer, Sid Hall, Marv Sunderland
Director of Public Relations: Frank Ramos
Assistant Director of Public Relations: Ron Cohen
Director of Operations: Tim Davey
Traveling Secretary: Mike Kensil
Ticket Manager: Bob Parente
Video Director: Jim Pons
Trainer: Bob Reese
Assistant Trainers: Pepper Burruss, Joe Patten
Equipment Manager: Bill Hampton

Stadium: Giants Stadium • **Capacity:** 76,891
East Rutherford, New Jersey 07073

Playing Surface: AstroTurf

Training Center: 1000 Fulton Avenue
Hempstead, New York 11550
(516) 538-6600

1986 SCHEDULE

Preseason

Aug. 9	vs. Green Bay at Madison, Wis.	1:00
Aug. 16	**Cincinnati**	8:00
Aug. 23	at New York Giants	8:00
Aug. 28	at Philadelphia	7:30

Regular Season

Sept. 7	at Buffalo	4:00
Sept. 11	**New England** (Thursday)	8:00
Sept. 21	**Miami**	1:00
Sept. 28	at Indianapolis	3:00
Oct. 5	**Buffalo**	4:00
Oct. 12	at New England	1:00
Oct. 20	**Denver** (Monday)	9:00
Oct. 26	**New Orleans**	1:00
Nov. 2	at Seattle	1:00
Nov. 9	at Atlanta	1:00
Nov. 16	**Indianapolis**	4:00
Nov. 24	at Miami (Monday)	9:00
Nov. 30	**Los Angeles Rams**	1:00
Dec. 7	at San Francisco	1:00
Dec. 13	**Pittsburgh** (Saturday)	12:30
Dec. 21	at Cincinnati	1:00

JETS COACHING HISTORY

New York Titans 1960-62
(171-203-7)

1960-61	Sammy Baugh	14-14-0
1962	Clyde (Bulldog) Turner	5-9-0
1963-73	Weeb Ewbank	73-78-6
1974-75	Charley Winner*	9-14-0
1975	Ken Shipp	1-4-0
1976	Lou Holtz**	3-10-0
1976	Mike Holovak	0-1-0
1977-82	Walt Michaels	41-49-1
1983-85	Joe Walton	25-24-0

*Released after nine games in 1975
**Resigned after 13 games in 1976

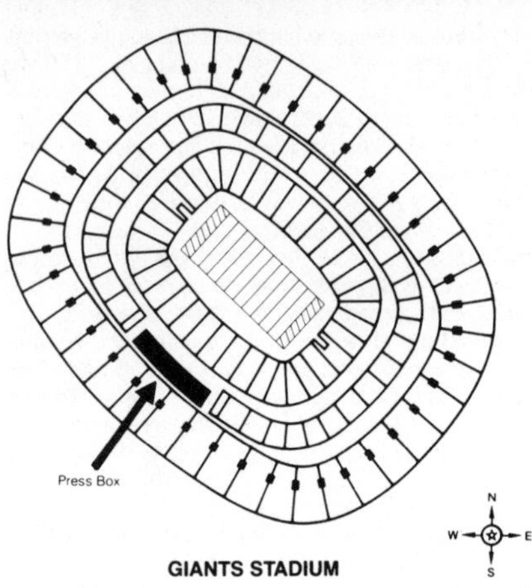

GIANTS STADIUM

RECORD HOLDERS

Individual Records—Career

Category	Name	Performance
Rushing (Yds.)	Emerson Boozer, 1966-1975	5,104
Passing (Yds.)	Joe Namath, 1965-1976	27,057
Passing (TDs)	Joe Namath, 1965-1976	170
Receiving (No.)	Don Maynard, 1960-1972	627
Receiving (Yds.)	Don Maynard, 1960-1972	11,732
Interceptions	Bill Baird, 1963-69	34
Punting (Avg.)	Curley Johnson, 1961-68	42.8
Punt Return (Avg.)	Dick Christy, 1961-63	16.2
Kickoff Return (Avg.)	Bobby Humphery, 1984-85	26.6
Field Goals	Pat Leahy, 1974-1985	184
Touchdowns (Tot.)	Don Maynard, 1960-1972	88
Points	Pat Leahy, 1974-1985	901

Individual Records—Single Season

Category	Name	Performance
Rushing (Yds.)	Freeman McNeil, 1985	1,331
Passing (Yds.)	Joe Namath, 1967	4,007
Passing (TDs)	Al Dorow, 1960	26
	Joe Namath, 1967	26
Receiving (No.)	Mickey Shuler, 1985	76
Receiving (Yds.)	Don Maynard, 1967	1,434
Interceptions	Dainard Paulson, 1964	12
Punting (Avg.)	Curley Johnson, 1965	45.3
Punt Return (Avg.)	Dick Christy, 1961	21.3
Kickoff Return (Avg.)	Bobby Humphery, 1984	30.7
Field Goals	Jim Turner, 1968	34
Touchdowns (Tot.)	Art Powell, 1960	14
	Don Maynard, 1965	14
	Emerson Boozer, 1972	14
Points	Jim Turner, 1968	145

Individual Records—Single Game

Category	Name	Performance
Rushing (Yds.)	Freeman McNeil, 9-15-85	192
Passing (Yds.)	Joe Namath, 9-24-72	496
Passing (TDs)	Joe Namath, 9-24-72	6
Receiving (No.)	Clark Gaines, 9-21-80	17
Receiving (Yds.)	Don Maynard, 11-17-68	228
Interceptions	Dainard Paulson, 9-28-63	3
	Bill Baird, 10-31-64	3
	Rich Sowells, 9-23-73	3
Field Goals	Jim Turner, 11-3-68	6
	Bobby Howfield, 12-3-72	6
Touchdowns (Tot.)	Many times	3
	Last time by Mickey Shuler, 11-17-85	
Points	Jim Turner, 11-3-68	19
	Pat Leahy, 9-16-84	19

1985 TEAM STATISTICS

	N.Y. Jets	Opp.
Total First Downs	344	276
Rushing	121	85
Passing	201	154
Penalty	22	37
Third Down: Made/Att.	99/237	68/208
Fourth Down: Made/Att.	12/19	7/16
Total Net Yards	5896	4772
Avg. Per Game	368.5	298.3
Total Plays	1123	989
Avg. Per Play	5.3	4.8
Net Yards Rushing	2312	1516
Avg. Per Game	144.5	94.8
Total Rushes	564	433
Net Yards Passing	3584	3256
Avg. Per Game	224.0	203.5
Tackled/Yards Lost	62/399	49/370
Gross Yards	3983	3626
Att./Completions	497/303	507/267
Completion Pct.	61.0	52.7
Had Intercepted	8	22
Punts/Avg.	74/40.2	88/41.8
Net Punting Avg.	33.8	35.1
Penalties/Yards Lost	119/907	113/868
Fumbles/Ball Lost	35/21	42/20
Touchdowns	45	30
Rushing	18	10
Passing	25	17
Returns	2	3
Avg. Time of Possession	31:11	28:49

1985 TEAM RECORD

Preseason (1-3)

Date	New York Jets		Opponents
8/10	17	*Philadelphia	37
8/17	20	Cincinnati	24
8/24	31	N.Y. Giants (OT)	34
8/31	30	Green Bay	20
	98		115

Regular Season (11-5)

Date	New York Jets		Opp.	Att.
9/8	0	L.A. Raiders	31	57,123
9/15	42	*Buffalo	3	63,449
9/22	24	Green Bay	3	53,667
9/29	25	*Indianapolis	20	61,987
10/6	29	Cincinnati	20	51,785
10/14	23	*Miami	7	73,807
10/20	13	New England	20	58,163
10/27	17	*Seattle	14	69,320
11/3	35	Indianapolis	17	59,683
11/10	17	Miami	21	73,965
11/17	62	*Tampa Bay	28	65,344
11/24	16	*New England (OT)	13	74,100
11/28	20	Detroit	31	65,531
12/8	27	Buffalo	7	23,122
12/14	6	*Chicago	19	74,752
12/22	37	*Cleveland	10	59,073

Postseason (0-1)

Date	New York Jets		Opp.	Att.
12/28	14	*New England	26	75,945

*Home Game (OT) Overtime

Score by Periods

New York Jets	70	128	111	81	3	—	393
Opponents	50	91	59	64	0	—	264

Attendance

Home 541,832 Away 443,039 Total 984,871

Single game home record, 74,975 (12-2-84)

Single season home record, 541,832 (1985)

1985 INDIVIDUAL STATISTICS

Rushing	Att.	Yds.	Avg.	LG	TD
McNeil	294	1331	4.5	69	3
Hector	145	572	3.9	22	6
Paige	55	158	2.9	30	8
Bligen	22	107	4.9	28t	1
O'Brien	25	58	2.3	22	0
Barber	9	41	4.6	10	0
Minter	8	23	2.9	11	0
Sohn	1	12	12.0	12	0
Humphery	1	10	10.0	10	0
Toon	1	5	5.0	5	0
Ryan	3	−5	−1.7	−1	0
N.Y. Jets	564	2312	4.1	69	18
Opponents	433	1516	3.5	57	10

Passing	Att.	Comp.	Pct.	Yds.	TD	Int.	Tkld.	Rate
O'Brien	488	297	60.9	3888	25	8	62/399	96.2
Ryan	9	6	66.7	95	0	0	0/0	101.6
N.Y. Jets	497	303	61.0	3983	25	8	62/399	96.3
Opponents	507	267	52.7	3626	17	22	49/370	68.9

Receiving	No.	Yds.	Avg.	LG	TD
Shuler	76	879	11.6	35	7
Toon	46	662	14.4	78t	3
Sohn	39	534	13.7	39t	4
McNeil	38	427	11.2	25	2
Walker	34	725	21.3	96t	5
Paige	18	120	6.7	19	2
Hector	17	164	9.6	28	0
Klever	14	183	13.1	23	2
Townsell	12	187	15.6	36	0
Bligen	5	43	8.6	14	0
Barber	3	46	15.3	22	0
Minter	1	13	13.0	13	0
N.Y. Jets	303	3983	13.1	96t	25
Opponents	267	3626	13.6	72t	17

Interceptions	No.	Yds.	Avg.	LG	TD
Glenn	4	15	3.8	15t	1
B. Jackson	4	8	2.0	8	0
Mehl	3	33	11.0	18	0
Mullen	3	14	4.7	14	0
Clifton	3	10	3.3	10	0
Hamilton	2	14	7.0	14	0
Miano	2	9	4.5	6	0
Lynn	1	24	24.0	24	0
N.Y. Jets	22	127	5.8	24	1
Opponents	8	101	12.6	76t	1

Punting	No.	Yds.	Avg.	In 20	LG
Jennings	74	2978	40.2	23	66
N.Y. Jets	74	2978	40.2	23	66
Opponents	88	3679	41.8	21	74

Punt Returns	No.	FC	Yds.	Avg.	LG	TD
Sohn	16	5	149	9.3	46	0
Springs	14	4	147	10.5	40	0
Townsell	6	1	65	10.8	22	0
Minter	2	4	25	12.5	20	0
Humphery	1	0	0	0.0	0	0
N.Y. Jets	39	14	386	9.9	46	0
Opponents	36	10	319	8.9	37t	1

Kickoff Returns	No.	Yds.	Avg.	LG	TD
Humphery	17	363	21.4	56	0
Hector	11	274	24.9	47	0
Springs	10	227	22.7	58	0
Glenn	5	71	14.2	20	0
Elder	3	42	14.0	25	0
Sohn	3	7	2.3	4	0
Townsell	2	42	21.0	23	0
Klever	1	3	3.0	3	0
Minter	1	14	14.0	14	0
N.Y. Jets	53	1043	19.7	58	0
Opponents	58	1135	19.6	45	0

Scoring	TD R	TD P	TD Rt	PAT	FG	Saf	TP
Leahy	0	0	0	43/45	26/34	0	121
Paige	8	2	0	0/0	0/0	0	60
Shuler	0	7	0	0/0	0/0	0	42
Hector	6	0	0	0/0	0/0	0	36
Walker	0	5	0	0/0	0/0	1	32
McNeil	3	2	0	0/0	0/0	0	30
Sohn	0	4	0	0/0	0/0	0	24
Toon	0	3	0	0/0	0/0	0	18
Klever	0	2	0	0/0	0/0	0	12
Baldwin	0	0	1	0/0	0/0	0	6
Bligen	1	0	0	0/0	0/0	0	6
Glenn	0	0	1	0/0	0/0	0	6
N.Y. Jets	18	25	2	43/45	26/34	1	393
Opponents	10	17	3	30/30	18/25	0	264

FIRST-ROUND SELECTIONS

(If club had no first-round selection, first player drafted is listed with round in parentheses.)

Year	Player, College, Position
1960	George Izo, Notre Dame, QB
1961	Tom Brown, Minnesota, G
1962	Sandy Stephens, Minnesota, QB
1963	Jerry Stovall, Louisiana State, S
1964	Matt Snell, Ohio State, RB
1965	Joe Namath, Alabama, QB
	Tom Nowatzke, Indiana, RB
1966	Bill Yearby, Michigan, DT
1967	Paul Seiler, Notre Dame, T
1968	Lee White, Weber State, RB
1969	Dave Foley, Ohio State, T
1970	Steve Tannen, Florida, CB
1971	John Riggins, Kansas, RB
1972	Jerome Barkum, Jackson State, WR
	Mike Taylor, Michigan, LB
1973	Burgess Owens, Miami, DB
1974	Carl Barzilauskas, Indiana, DT
1975	Anthony Davis, Southern California, RB (2)
1976	Richard Todd, Alabama, QB
1977	Marvin Powell, Southern California, T
1978	Chris Ward, Ohio State, T
1979	Marty Lyons, Alabama, DE
1980	Johnny (Lam) Jones, Texas, WR
1981	Freeman McNeil, UCLA, RB
1982	Bob Crable, Notre Dame, LB
1983	Ken O'Brien, Cal-Davis, QB
1984	Russell Carter, Southern Methodist, DB
	Ron Faurot, Arkansas, DE
1985	Al Toon, Wisconsin, WR
1986	Mike Haight, Iowa, T

NEW YORK JETS 1986 VETERAN ROSTER

No.	Name	Pos.	Ht.	Wt.	Birth-date	NFL Exp.	College	Hometown	How Acq.	'85 Games/ Starts
60	Alexander, Dan	G	6-4	260	6/17/55	10	Louisiana State	Houston, Tex.	D8a-'77	16/16
95	Baldwin, Tom	DT	6-4	275	5/13/61	3	Tulsa	Lansing, Ill.	D9-'84	16/0
63	Banker, Ted	T-G-C	6-2	255	2/17/61	3	Southeast Missouri	Belleville, Ill.	FA-'84	16/4
31	Barber, Marion	RB	6-2	224	12/6/59	5	Minnesota	Detroit, Mich.	D2-'81	9/1
78	Bennett, Barry	DE-DT	6-4	260	12/10/55	9	Concordia	St. Paul, Minn.	W(Minn)-'82	16/16
64	Bingham, Guy	T-G-C	6-3	255	2/25/58	7	Montana	Aberdeen, Wash.	D10-'80	16/2
23	Bligen, Dennis	RB	5-11	209	3/3/62	3	St. John's	Queen's Village, N.Y.	FA-'84	9/0
22	Bruckner, Nick	WR	5-11	185	5/19/61	4	Syracuse	Selden, N.Y.	FA-'83	9/0
27	Carter, Russell	CB-S	6-2	195	2/10/62	3	Southern Methodist	Ardmore, Pa.	D1a-'84	8/8
59	Clifton, Kyle	LB	6-4	233	8/23/62	3	Texas Christian	Bridgeport, Tex.	D3-'84	16/16
50	Crable, Bob	LB	6-3	228	9/22/59	5	Notre Dame	Cincinnati, Ohio	D1-'82	10/2
86	Dennison, Glenn	TE	6-3	225	11/17/61	2	Miami	Beaver Falls, Pa.	D2b-'84	0*
37	Elder, Donnie	CB	5-9	175	12/13/62	2	Memphis State	Chattanooga, Tenn.	D3-'85	10/0
65	Fields, Joe	C	6-2	253	11/14/53	12	Widener	Deptford, N.J.	D14-'75	15/15
38	†Flowers, Larry	S	6-1	190	4/19/58	6	Texas Tech	Temple, Tex.	FA-'85	15/0*
99	Gastineau, Mark	DE	6-5	265	11/20/56	8	East Central Oklahoma	Springerville, Ariz.	D2-'79	16/12
35	Glenn, Kerry	CB	5-9	175	3/31/62	2	Minnesota	East St. Louis, Ill.	D10-'85	16/6
81	Griggs, Billy	TE	6-3	230	8/4/62	2	Virginia	Pennsauken, N.J.	D8a-'84	16/3
94	Guilbeau, Rusty	LB	6-4	237	11/20/58	5	McNeese State	Sunset, La.	FA-'82	14/7
39	Hamilton, Harry	S	6-0	193	11/29/62	3	Penn State	Wilkes-Barre, Pa.	D7-'84	11/11
34	Hector, Johnny	RB	5-11	197	11/26/60	4	Texas A&M	New Iberia, La.	D2-'83	14/6
28	Howard, Carl	CB	6-2	177	9/20/61	3	Rutgers	Irvington, N.J.	FA-'85	7/0*
84	Humphery, Bobby	WR-KR	5-10	180	8/23/61	3	New Mexico State	Lubbock, Tex.	D9-'83	12/0
40	Jackson, Bobby	CB	5-10	180	12/23/56	9	Florida State	Albany, Ga.	D6a-'78	12/11
55	Jackson, Charles	LB	6-2	224	3/22/55	9	Washington	Berkeley, Calif.	T(KC)-'85	16/14
13	Jennings, Dave	P	6-4	200	6/8/52	13	St. Lawrence	Garden City, N.Y.	W(NYG)-'85	16/0
80	Jones, Johnny "Lam"	WR	5-11	180	4/4/58	6	Texas	Lampasas, Tex.	D1-'80	0*
73	Klecko, Joe	DT-DE	6-3	263	10/15/53	10	Temple	Chester, Pa.	D6-'77	16/16
89	Klever, Rocky	TE	6-3	225	7/10/59	4	Montana	Anchorage, Alaska	D9-'82	16/6
5	Leahy, Pat	K	6-0	193	3/19/51	13	St. Louis	St. Louis, Mo.	FA-'74	16/0
26	Lyles, Lester	S-LB	6-3	209	12/27/62	2	Virginia	Washington, D.C.	D2-'85	6/0
29	Lynn, Johnny	CB-S	6-0	198	12/19/56	7	UCLA	Pasadena, Calif.	D4b-'79	14/12
93	Lyons, Marty	DE-DT	6-5	269	1/15/57	8	Alabama	St. Petersburg, Fla.	D1-'79	16/8
68	†McElroy, Reggie	T	6-6	270	3/4/60	4	West Texas State	Beaumont, Tex.	D2-'82	13/11
24	McNeil, Freeman	RB	5-11	212	4/22/59	6	UCLA	Carson, Calif.	D1-'81	14/13
56	Mehl, Lance	LB	6-3	233	2/14/58	7	Penn State	Bellaire, Ohio	D4-'80	16/16
36	Miano, Rich	S	6-0	200	9/3/62	2	Hawaii	Honolulu, Hawaii	D6b-'85	16/1
25	Minter, Cedric	RB-KR	5-10	200	11/13/58	3	Boise State	Boise, Idaho	FA-'84	3/0
6	Misko, John	P	6-5	207	10/1/54	4	Oregon State	Porterville, Calif.	FA-'86	0*
58	Monger, Matt	LB	6-1	235	11/15/61	2	Oklahoma State	Miami, Okla.	D8-'85	15/0
20	Mullen, Davlin	CB-KR	6-1	177	2/17/60	4	Western Kentucky	Clairton, Pa.	D8-'83	11/1
7	O'Brien, Ken	QB	6-4	208	11/27/60	4	California-Davis	Sacramento, Calif.	D1-'83	16/16
49	Paige, Tony	RB	5-10	220	10/14/62	3	Virginia Tech	Washington, D.C.	D6-'84	16/8
11	Prokop, Joe	P	6-3	225	7/7/60	2	Cal Poly-Pomona	St. Paul, Minn.	FA-'86	9/0*
76	Rudolph, Ben	DE	6-5	271	8/29/57	6	Long Beach State	Fairhope, Ala.	D3-'81	16/1
10	Ryan, Pat	QB	6-3	210	9/16/55	9	Tennessee	Oklahoma City, Okla.	D11-'78	16/0
82	Shuler, Mickey	TE	6-3	231	8/21/56	9	Penn State	Enola, Pa.	D3-'78	16/13
87	Sohn, Kurt	WR	5-11	180	6/26/57	5	Fordham	Huntington, N.Y.	FA-'81	15/6
21	Springs, Kirk	S-KR	6-0	197	8/10/58	6	Miami, Ohio	Cincinnati, Ohio	FA-'81	16/14
53	Sweeney, Jim	G-T-C	6-4	266	8/8/62	3	Pittsburgh	Pittsburgh, Pa.	D2a-'84	16/16
88	Toon, Al	WR	6-4	200	4/30/63	2	Wisconsin	Newport News, Va.	D1-'85	15/8
83	Townsell, JoJo	WR	5-9	180	11/4/60	2	UCLA	Reno, Nev.	D3-'83	16/6
70	Waldemore, Stan	G-C-T	6-4	269	2/20/55	8	Nebraska	Belleville, N.J.	FA-'78	0*
85	Walker, Wesley	WR	6-0	182	5/26/55	10	California	Carson, Calif.	D2-'77	12/10
57	Woodring, John	LB	6-2	232	4/4/59	6	Brown	Erdenheim, Pa.	D6-'81	2/0

* Dennison, Jones, and Waldemore missed '85 season due to injury; Flowers played 8 games with N.Y. Giants, 7 with N.Y. Jets in '85; Howard played 4 games with Tampa Bay, 3 with N.Y. Jets; Misko last active with L.A. Rams in '84; Prokop played 9 games with Green Bay.

†Option playout; subject to developments.

Traded—Tackle Marvin Powell to Tampa Bay.

Retired—Ken Schroy, 8-year safety, injured reserve in '85.

Also played with Jets in '85—T Sid Abramowitz (1 game), WR Chy Davidson (1), LB Jim Eliopulos (8), LB Ron Faurot (5), T Billy Shields (3), DE Mark Shumate (4).

COACHING STAFF

Head Coach, Joe Walton

Pro Career: Begins fourth year as head coach of the Jets. Entered pro coaching ranks as an assistant with the New York Giants in 1969-73. Joined the Washington Redskins' staff in 1974 and became the Redskins' offensive coordinator in 1978. Originally came to the Jets as the offensive coordinator in 1981. Career record: 25-24.

Background: Played tight end for the University of Pittsburgh 1953-56, before playing professionally for the Washington Redskins 1957-60 and the New York Giants 1961-63. Walton did some radio work before joining the Giants' staff as a scout in 1967-68.

Personal: Born December 15, 1935, Beaver Falls, Pa. Joe and his wife, Ginger, have three children—Jodi, Stacy, and Joseph, Jr. They live in Long Island.

Assistant Coaches

Zeke Bratkowski, quarterbacks; born October 20, 1931, Danville, Ill., lives in Long Island. Quarterback Georgia 1951-53. Pro quarterback Chicago Bears 1954, 1957-60, Los Angeles Rams 1961-63, Green Bay Packers 1963-68, 1971. Pro coach: Green Bay Packers 1969-70, 1975-81, Chicago Bears 1972-74, Indianapolis Colts 1982-84, joined Jets in 1985.

Ray Callahan, defensive line; born April 28, 1933, Lebanon, Ky., lives in Long Island. Guard-linebacker Kentucky 1952-56. No pro playing experience. College coach: Kentucky 1963-67, Cincinnati 1968-72 (head coach 1969-72). Pro coach: Baltimore Colts 1973, Florida Blazers (WFL) 1974, Chicago Bears 1975-77, Houston Oilers 1981-82, joined Jets in 1983.

Bud Carson, defensive coordinator; born April 28, 1931, Brackenridge, Pa., lives in Long Island. Defensive back North Carolina 1948-52. No pro playing experience. College coach: North Carolina 1957-64, South Carolina 1965, Georgia Tech 1966-71 (head coach). Pro coach: Pittsburgh Steelers 1972-77, Los Angeles Rams 1978-81, Baltimore Colts 1982, Kansas City Chiefs 1983-84, joined Jets in 1985.

Mike Faulkiner, special assistant to the head coach; born March 27, 1947, Cameron, W. Va., lives in Long Island. Quarterback-defensive back West Virginia Tech 1967-70. No pro playing experience. College coach: Eastern Illinois 1981. Pro coach: Toronto Argonauts (CFL) 1979, New York Giants 1980, Montreal Alouettes (CFL) 1982, joined Jets in 1983.

Bobby Hammond, running backs; born February 20, 1952, Orangeburg, S.C., lives in New York. Running back Morgan State 1973-75. Pro running back New York Giants 1976-79, Washington Redskins 1979-80. Pro coach: Joined Jets in 1983.

Rich Kotite, offensive coordinator-receivers; born October 13, 1942, Brooklyn, N.Y., lives in Long Island. End Wagner 1963-65. Pro tight end New York Giants 1967, 1969-72, Pittsburgh Steelers 1968. College coach: Tennessee-Chattanooga 1973-76. Pro coach: New Orleans Saints 1977, Cleveland Browns 1978-82, joined Jets in 1983.

Larry Pasquale, special teams; born April 21, 1941, Brooklyn, N.Y., lives in New York. Quarterback Bridgeport 1961-63. No pro playing experience. College coach: Slippery Rock State 1967, Boston University 1968, Navy 1969-70, Massachusetts 1971-75, Idaho State 1976. Pro coach: Montreal Alouettes (CFL) 1977-78, Detroit Lions 1979, joined Jets in 1980.

Dan Radakovich, linebackers; born November 27, 1935, Duquesne, Pa., lives in Long Island. Center-linebacker Penn State 1954-56. No pro playing experience. College coach: Penn State 1960-69, Cincinnati 1970, Colorado 1972-73, North Carolina State 1982. Pro coach: Pittsburgh Steelers 1971, 1974-77, San Francisco 49ers 1978, Los Angeles Rams 1979-81, Denver Broncos 1983, Minnesota Vikings 1984, joined Jets in 1985.

Jim Vechiarella, linebackers; born February 20, 1937, Youngstown, Ohio, lives in Long Island. Linebacker Youngstown State 1955-57. No pro playing experience. College coach: Youngstown State 1964-74, Southern Illinois 1976-77, Tulane 1978-80. Pro coach: Charlotte Hornets (WFL) 1975, Los Angeles Rams 1981-82, Kansas City Chiefs 1983-85, first year with Jets.

NEW YORK JETS 1986 FIRST-YEAR ROSTER

Name	Pos.	Ht.	Wt.	Birth-date	College	Hometown	How Acq.
Alexander, Rogers	LB	6-3	219	8/11/64	Penn State	Riverdale, Md.	D4
Amoia, Vince	RB	5-11	220	3/30/63	Arizona State	Buffalo, N.Y.	D11
Benson, Troy (1)	LB	6-2	235	7/30/63	Pittsburgh	Altoona, Pa.	D5a-'85
Buckley, John	TE	6-6	242	5/16/63	Concordia	Massapequa, N.Y.	FA
Burnette, Dave (1)	T	6-7	280	3/24/61	Central Arkansas	Parkin, Ark.	FA
Carr, Carl	LB	6-3	228	3/26/64	North Carolina	Alexandria, Va.	D10
Cesario, Sal	T	6-5	260	7/4/63	Cal Poly-SLO	San Jose, Calif.	D12
Courtney, Matthew (1)	CB-S	5-11	188	12/21/61	Idaho State	Littleton, Colo.	FA
Crawford, Tim	LB	6-4	230	12/17/62	Texas Tech	Houston, Tex.	D3
Ducksworth, Robert	CB	5-11	200	1/5/63	Southern Mississippi	Biloxi, Miss.	D8
Dunham, David	T-G	6-5	285	5/22/62	Central State	Toledo, Ohio	FA
Ehrhardt, Tom	QB	6-2	210	10/11/63	Rhode Island	Flushing, N.Y.	FA
Estes, Robert (1)	S	6-0	202	4/9/62	Tulsa	Tyler, Tex.	FA
Faaola, Nuu	RB	5-11	215	1/15/64	Hawaii	Honolulu, Hawaii	D9
Francis, Andre	CB	5-10	170	10/5/61	New Mexico State	Miami, Fla.	FA
Geist, Donald (1)	P	6-1	200	12/4/62	Northern Colorado	Fort Morgan, Colo.	FA
Glascoe, Keith	LB	6-3	226	12/9/62	Delaware State	Brooklyn, N.Y.	FA
Hadley, Ron	LB	6-2	241	11/9/63	Washington	Boise, Idaho	D5
Haight, Mike	T-G	6-4	270	10/6/62	Iowa	Dyersville, Iowa	D1
Harper, Michael (1)	WR	5-10	180	5/11/61	Southern California	Kansas City, Mo.	FA
Harrison, Phil (1)	LB	6-5	230	12/21/60	Hampton Institute	Ardmore, Pa.	FA
Kepano, Tony (1)	C-G	6-2	264	5/24/63	Georgia Tech	Woodbridge, Va.	FA
Kilgo, John (1)	G	6-3	267	10/8/61	Boise State	Mountain Home, Idaho	FA
Luft, Brian (1)	DT	6-6	270	9/5/63	Southern California	Fresno, Calif.	D5b-'85
Mazzu, Anthony	RB	6-1	210	11/25/63	North Dakota	Bloomington, Minn.	FA
McArthur, Kevin (1)	LB	6-2	230	5/11/62	Lamar	Lake Charles, La.	FA
Metter, Jeff (1)	LB	6-3	225	3/8/60	Eastern Washington	San Mateo, Calif.	FA
Mooney, Timothy (1)	DT	6-2	265	1/25/62	Western Kentucky	Evansville, Ind.	FA
Moore, Roderick (1)	RB	6-0	230	10/17/61	Temple	Hammond, Ind.	FA
Proffitt, Loyal (1)	QB	6-3	205	1/12/63	Abilene Christian	Abilene, Tex.	FA
Smith, Tony (1)	WR	5-11	170	6/28/62	San Jose State	San Diego, Calif.	FA
Stokes, Eric (1)	G	6-3	287	1/13/62	Northeastern	Ansonia, Conn.	FA
White, Bob	T	6-5	255	4/9/63	Rhode Island	Lunenberg, Mass.	D7
Will, Kevin (1)	LB	6-3	230	1/25/62	St. Mary's	Santa Maria, Calif.	FA
Williams, Doug	T	6-5	290	10/1/62	Texas A&M	Cincinnati, Ohio	D2

The term NFL Rookie is defined as a player who is in his first season of professional football and has not been on the roster of another professional football team for any regular season or postseason games. A Rookie is designated by an "R" on NFL rosters. Players who have been active in another professional football league or players who have NFL experience, including either preseason training camp or being on an active roster for fewer than three regular season or postseason games, are termed NFL First-Year Players. An NFL First-Year Player is designated by a "1" on NFL rosters. Thereafter, a player on an NFL active roster for at least three regular season or postseason games is credited with an additional year of NFL playing experience.

NOTES

PITTSBURGH STEELERS

American Football Conference
Central Division

Team Colors: Black and Gold

Three Rivers Stadium
300 Stadium Circle
Pittsburgh, Pennsylvania 15212
Telephone: (412) 323-1200

Club Officials

Chairman of the Board: Arthur J. Rooney, Sr.
President: Daniel M. Rooney
Vice President: John R. McGinley
Vice President: Arthur J. Rooney, Jr.
Traveling Secretary: Jim Boston
Controller: Dennis P. Thimons
Assistant Controller: Dan Ferens
Publicity Director: Joe Gordon
Assistant Publicity Director: Dan Edwards
Director of Player Personnel: Dick Haley
Assistant Director of Player Personnel: William Nunn, Jr.
Pro Talent Scout: Tom Modrak
Talent Scout-West Coast: Bob Schmitz
College Talent Scout: Joe Krupa
Director of Ticket Sales: Geraldine R. Glenn
Trainer: Ralph Berlin
Equipment Manager: Anthony Parisi

Stadium: Three Rivers Stadium • **Capacity:** 59,000
300 Stadium Circle
Pittsburgh, Pennsylvania 15212

Playing Surface: AstroTurf

Training Camp: St. Vincent College
Latrobe, Pennsylvania 15650

1986 SCHEDULE

Preseason

Aug. 9	**Chicago**	7:00
Aug. 15	at Washington	8:00
Aug. 22	at Dallas	7:00
Aug. 30	at New York Giants	8:00

Regular Season

Sept. 7	at Seattle	1:00
Sept. 15	**Denver** (Monday)	9:00
Sept. 21	at Minnesota	12:00
Sept. 28	at Houston	12:00
Oct. 5	**Cleveland**	1:00
Oct. 13	at Cincinnati (Monday)	9:00
Oct. 19	**New England**	1:00
Oct. 26	**Cincinnati**	1:00
Nov. 2	**Green Bay**	1:00
Nov. 9	at Buffalo	1:00
Nov. 16	**Houston**	1:00
Nov. 23	at Cleveland	1:00
Nov. 30	at Chicago	12:00
Dec. 7	**Detroit**	1:00
Dec. 13	at New York Jets (Saturday)	12:30
Dec. 21	**Kansas City**	1:00

STEELERS COACHING HISTORY

(325-359-20)

1933	Forrest (Jap) Douds	3-6-2
1934	Luby DiMelio	2-10-0
1935-36	Joe Bach	10-14-0
1937-39	Johnny Blood (McNally)*	6-19-0
1939-40	Walter Kiesling	3-13-3
1941	Bert Bell**	0-2-0
	Aldo (Buff) Donelli***	0-5-0
1941-44	Walter Kiesling****	13-20-2
1945	Jim Leonard	2-8-0
1946-47	Jock Sutherland	13-10-1
1948-51	Johnny Michelosen	20-26-2
1952-53	Joe Bach	11-13-0
1954-56	Walter Kiesling	14-22-0
1957-64	Raymond (Buddy) Parker	51-47-6
1965	Mike Nixon	2-12-0
1966-68	Bill Austin	11-28-3
1969-85	Chuck Noll	164-104-1

*Released after three games in 1939
**Released after two games in 1941
***Released after five games in 1941
****Co-coach with Earl (Greasy) Neale in Philadelphia-Pittsburgh merger in 1943 and with Phil Handler in Chicago Cardinals-Pittsburgh merger in 1944.

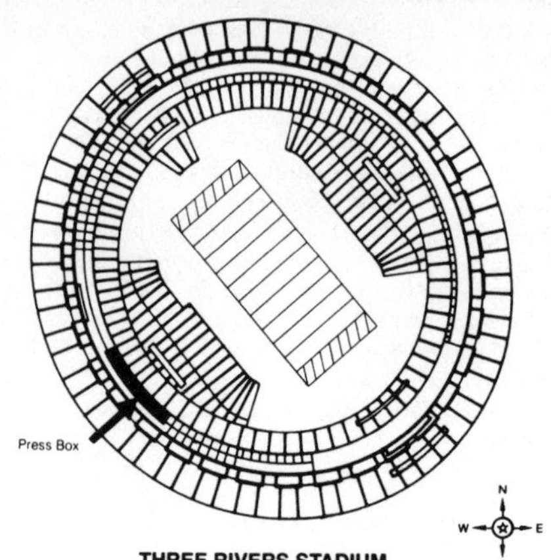

THREE RIVERS STADIUM

RECORD HOLDERS

Individual Records—Career

Category	Name	Performance
Rushing (Yds.)	Franco Harris, 1972-1983	11,950
Passing (Yds.)	Terry Bradshaw, 1970-1983	27,989
Passing (TDs)	Terry Bradshaw, 1970-1983	212
Receiving (No.)	John Stallworth, 1974-1985	462
Receiving (Yds.)	John Stallworth, 1974-1985	7,736
Interceptions	Mel Blount, 1971-1983	57
Punting (Avg.)	Bobby Joe Green, 1960-61	45.7
Punt Return (Avg.)	Bobby Gage, 1949-1950	14.9
Kickoff Return (Avg.)	Lynn Chandnois, 1950-56	29.6
Field Goals	Roy Gerela, 1971-78	146
Touchdowns (Tot.)	Franco Harris, 1972-1983	100
Points	Roy Gerela, 1971-78	731

Individual Records—Single Season

Category	Name	Performance
Rushing (Yds.)	Franco Harris, 1975	1,246
Passing (Yds.)	Terry Bradshaw, 1979	3,724
Passing (TDs)	Terry Bradshaw, 1978	28
Receiving (No.)	John Stallworth, 1984	80
Receiving (Yds.)	John Stallworth, 1984	1,395
Interceptions	Mel Blount, 1975	11
Punting (Avg.)	Bobby Joe Green, 1961	47.0
Punt Return (Avg.)	Bobby Gage, 1949	16.0
Kickoff Return (Avg.)	Lynn Chandnois, 1952	35.2
Field Goals	Gary Anderson, 1985	33
Touchdowns (Tot.)	Louis Lipps, 1985	15
Points	Gary Anderson, 1985	139

Individual Records—Single Game

Category	Name	Performance
Rushing (Yds.)	John Fuqua, 12-20-70	218
Passing (Yds.)	Bobby Layne, 12-3-58	409
Passing (TDs)	Terry Bradshaw, 11-15-81	5
	Mark Malone, 9-8-85	5
Receiving (No.)	J.R. Wilburn, 10-22-67	12
Receiving (Yds.)	Buddy Dial, 10-22-61	235
Interceptions	Jack Butler, 12-13-53	4
Field Goals	Gary Anderson, 11-10-85	5
Touchdowns (Tot.)	Ray Mathews, 10-17-54	4
	Roy Jefferson, 11-3-68	4
Points	Ray Mathews, 10-17-54	24
	Roy Jefferson, 11-3-68	24

1985 TEAM STATISTICS

	Pittsburgh	Opp.
Total First Downs	315	273
Rushing	125	105
Passing	165	144
Penalty	25	24
Third Down: Made/Att.	91/236	71/209
Fourth Down: Made/Att.	7/13	5/12
Total Net Yards	5350	4659
Avg. Per Game	334.4	291.2
Total Plays	1086	990
Avg. Per Play	4.9	4.7
Net Yards Rushing	2177	1876
Avg. Per Game	136.1	117.3
Total Rushes	541	470
Net Yards Passing	3173	2783
Avg. Per Game	198.3	173.9
Tackled/Yards Lost	33/224	36/305
Gross Yards	3397	3088
Att./Completions	512/254	484/287
Completion Pct.	49.6	59.3
Had Intercepted	27	20
Punts/Avg.	79/39.1	86/40.9
Net Punting Avg.	32.5	32.9
Penalties/Yards Lost	85/665	89/679
Fumbles/Ball Lost	31/9	34/14
Touchdowns	40	43
Rushing	14	19
Passing	23	18
Returns	3	6
Avg. Time of Possession	30:52	29:08

1985 TEAM RECORD

Preseason (1-3)

Date	Pittsburgh		Opponents
8/10	42	Tampa Bay	27
8/17	34	Minnesota	41
8/23	6	St. Louis	14
8/30	14	*N.Y. Giants	24
	96		106

Regular Season (7-9)

Date	Pittsburgh		Opp.	Att.
9/8	45	*Indianapolis	3	57,279
9/16	7	Cleveland	17	76,042
9/22	20	*Houston	0	58,752
9/30	24	*Cincinnati	37	59,541
10/6	20	Miami	24	72,820
10/13	13	Dallas	27	62,932
10/20	23	*St. Louis	10	56,478
10/27	21	Cincinnati	26	55,421
11/3	10	*Cleveland	9	51,976
11/10	36	Kansas City	28	46,126
11/17	30	Houston	7	45,977
11/24	23	*Washington	30	59,293
12/1	23	*Denver	31	56,797
12/8	44	San Diego	54	52,098
12/15	30	*Buffalo	24	35,953
12/21	10	N.Y. Giants	28	66,785

*Home Game

Score by Periods

Pittsburgh	58	134	83	104	0	—	379
Opponents	72	129	53	101	0	—	355

Attendance

Home 436,069 Away 478,201 Total 914,270
Single game home record, 59,541 (9-30-85)
Single season home record, 462,567 (1983)

1985 INDIVIDUAL STATISTICS

Rushing	Att.	Yds.	Avg.	LG	TD
Pollard	233	991	4.3	56	3
Abercrombie	227	851	3.7	32t	7
Malone	15	80	5.3	25	1
Woodley	17	71	4.2	13	2
Erenberg	17	67	3.9	12	0
Spencer	13	56	4.3	11	0
Campbell	9	28	3.1	14	0
Morse	8	17	2.1	9	0
Lipps	2	16	8.0	15t	1
Steelers	541	2177	4.0	56	14
Opponents	470	1876	4.0	77t	19

Passing	Att.	Comp.	Pct.	Yds.	TD	Int.	Tkld.	Rate
Malone	233	117	50.2	1428	13	7	10/80	75.5
Woodley	183	94	51.4	1357	6	14	13/84	54.8
Campbell	96	43	44.8	612	4	6	10/60	53.8
Steelers	512	254	49.6	3397	23	27	33/224	64.1
Opponents	484	287	59.3	3088	18	20	36/305	73.3

Receiving	No.	Yds.	Avg.	LG	TD
Stallworth	75	937	12.5	41	5
Lipps	59	1134	19.2	51	12
Erenberg	33	326	9.9	35	3
Pollard	24	250	10.4	20	0
Abercrombie	24	209	8.7	27	2
Sweeney	16	234	14.6	69	0
Thompson	8	138	17.3	42	1
Gothard	6	83	13.8	24	0
Cunningham	6	61	10.2	17	0
Spencer	3	25	8.3	13	0
Steelers	254	3397	13.4	69	23
Opponents	287	3088	10.8	75t	18

Interceptions	No.	Yds.	Avg.	LG	TD
Woodruff	5	80	16.0	33	0
Williams	4	47	11.8	29	0
Shell	4	40	10.0	26	0
Merriweather	2	36	18.0	35t	1
Swain	2	4	2.0	4	0
Little	2	0	0.0	3	0
Cole	1	4	4.0	4	0
Winston, N.O-Pitt.	0	8	—	8	0
Steelers	20	211	10.6	35t	1
Opponents	27	409	15.1	57t	5

Punting	No.	Yds.	Avg.	In 20	LG
Newsome	78	3088	39.6	17	59
Steelers	79	3088	39.1	17	59
Opponents	86	3515	40.9	17	65

Punt Returns	No.	FC	Yds.	Avg.	LG	TD
Lipps	36	2	437	12.1	71t	2
Woods	13	2	46	3.5	10	0
Steelers	49	4	483	9.9	71t	2
Opponents	43	8	380	8.8	31	0

Kickoff Returns	No.	Yds.	Avg.	LG	TD
Spencer	27	617	22.9	40	0
Erenberg	21	441	21.0	35	0
Lipps	13	237	18.2	26	0
Washington	3	34	11.3	14	0
Tuggle	1	8	8.0	8	0
Steelers	65	1337	20.6	40	0
Opponents	65	1566	24.1	95	0

Scoring	TD R	TD P	TD Rt	PAT	FG	Saf	TP
Anderson	0	0	0	40/40	33/42	0	139
Lipps	1	12	2	0/0	0/0	0	90
Abercrombie	7	2	0	0/0	0/0	0	54
Stallworth	0	5	0	0/0	0/0	0	30
Erenberg	0	3	0	0/0	0/0	0	18
Pollard	3	0	0	0/0	0/0	0	18
Woodley	2	0	0	0/0	0/0	0	12
Malone	1	0	0	0/0	0/0	0	6
Merriweather	0	0	1	0/0	0/0	0	6
Thompson	0	1	0	0/0	0/0	0	6
Steelers	14	23	3	40/40	33/42	0	379
Opponents	19	18	6	40/43	19/25	0	355

FIRST-ROUND SELECTIONS

(If club had no first-round selection, first player drafted is listed with round in parentheses.)

Year	Player, College, Position
1936	Bill Shakespeare, Notre Dame, B
1937	Mike Basrak, Duquesne, C
1938	Byron (Whizzer) White, Colorado, B
1939	Bill Patterson, Baylor, B (3)
1940	Kay Eakin, Arkansas, B
1941	Chet Gladchuk, Boston College, C (2)
1942	Bill Dudley, Virginia, B
1943	Bill Daley, Minnesota, B
1944	Johnny Podesto, St. Mary's, California, B
1945	Paul Duhart, Florida, B
1946	Felix (Doc) Blanchard, Army, B
1947	Hub Bechtol, Texas, E
1948	Dan Edwards, Georgia, E
1949	Bobby Gage, Clemson, B
1950	Lynn Chandnois, Michigan State, B
1951	Butch Avinger, Alabama, B
1952	Ed Modzelewski, Maryland, B
1953	Ted Marchibroda, St. Bonaventure, B
1954	Johnny Lattner, Notre Dame, B
1955	Frank Varrichione, Notre Dame, T
1956	Gary Glick, Colorado A&M, B
	Art Davis, Mississippi State, B
1957	Len Dawson, Purdue, B
1958	Larry Krutko, West Virginia, B (2)
1959	Tom Barnett, Purdue, B (8)
1960	Jack Spikes, Texas Christian, RB
1961	Myron Pottios, Notre Dame, LB (2)
1962	Bob Ferguson, Ohio State, RB
1963	Frank Atkinson, Stanford, T (8)
1964	Paul Martha, Pittsburgh, S
1965	Roy Jefferson, Utah, WR (2)
1966	Dick Leftridge, West Virginia, RB
1967	Don Shy, San Diego State, RB (2)
1968	Mike Taylor, Southern California, T
1969	Joe Greene, North Texas State, DT
1970	Terry Bradshaw, Louisiana Tech, QB
1971	Frank Lewis, Grambling, WR
1972	Franco Harris, Penn State, RB
1973	J.T. Thomas, Florida State, DB
1974	Lynn Swann, Southern California, WR
1975	Dave Brown, Michigan, DB
1976	Bennie Cunningham, Clemson, TE
1977	Robin Cole, New Mexico, LB
1978	Ron Johnson, Eastern Michigan, DB
1979	Greg Hawthorne, Baylor, RB
1980	Mark Malone, Arizona State, QB
1981	Keith Gary, Oklahoma, DE
1982	Walter Abercrombie, Baylor, RB
1983	Gabriel Rivera, Texas Tech, DT
1984	Louis Lipps, Southern Mississippi, WR
1985	Darryl Sims, Wisconsin, DE
1986	John Rienstra, Temple, G

PITTSBURGH STEELERS 1986 VETERAN ROSTER

No.	Name	Pos.	Ht.	Wt.	Birth-date	NFL Exp.	College	Hometown	How Acq.	'85 Games/ Starts
34	†Abercrombie, Walter	RB	6-0	208	9/26/59	5	Baylor	Waco, Tex.	D1-'82	16/16
1	Anderson, Gary	K	5-11	174	7/16/59	5	Syracuse	Durban, South Africa	W(Buff)-'82	16/0
71	Boures, Emil	G-C	6-1	260	1/29/60	5	Pittsburgh	Norristown, Pa.	D7-'82	6/5
23	Brown, Chris	CB	6-0	205	4/11/62	3	Notre Dame	Owensboro, Ky.	D6-'84	6/0
10	Campbell, Scott	QB	6-0	194	4/15/62	3	Purdue	Hershey, Pa.	D7-'84	16/2
91	Carr, Gregg	LB	6-1	216	3/31/62	2	Auburn	Birmingham, Ala.	D6-'85	16/2
78	Catano, Mark	NT-DT	6-3	267	1/26/62	3	Valdosta State	Montrose, N.Y.	FA-'84	15/6
33	†Clayton, Harvey	CB	5-9	179	4/4/61	4	Florida State	Florida City, Fla.	FA-'83	14/14
56	Cole, Robin	LB	6-2	225	9/11/55	10	New Mexico	Compton, Calif.	D1-'77	16/16
89	Cunningham, Bennie	TE	6-5	260	12/23/54	11	Clemson	Seneca, S.C.	D1-'76	11/11
67	Dunn, Gary	NT	6-3	275	8/24/53	10	Miami	Coral Gables, Fla.	D6-'76	10/7
42	Edwards, Dave	S	6-0	192	3/31/62	2	Illinois	Decatur, Ga.	FA-'85	14/0
24	Erenberg, Rich	RB-KR	5-10	195	4/17/62	3	Colgate	Chappaqua, N.Y.	D9-'84	14/0
92	Gary, Keith	DE	6-3	265	9/14/59	4	Oklahoma	Fairfax, Va.	D1-'81	12/7
95	Goodman, John	DE-NT	6-6	258	11/12/58	6	Oklahoma	Garland, Tex.	D2-'80	12/6
86	Gothard, Preston	TE	6-4	237	2/23/62	2	Alabama	Montgomery, Ala.	FA-'85	16/0
53	Hinkle, Bryan	LB	6-2	218	6/4/59	5	Oregon	Silverdale, Wash.	D6-'81	14/14
62	Ilkin, Tunch	T	6-3	262	9/23/57	7	Indiana State	Highland Park, Ill.	D6-'80	16/16
90	Kohrs, Bob	LB	6-3	235	11/8/58	6	Arizona State	Phoenix, Ariz.	D2-'80	11/0
83	Lipps, Louis	WR-KR	5-10	185	8/9/62	3	Southern Mississippi	Reserve, La.	D1-'84	16/16
50	Little, David	LB	6-1	238	1/3/59	6	Florida	Miami, Fla.	D7-'81	16/16
74	Long, Terry	G	5-11	265	7/21/59	3	East Carolina	Columbia, S.C.	D4-'84	15/14
16	†Malone, Mark	QB	6-4	220	11/22/58	7	Arizona State	El Cajon, Calif.	D1-'80	10/8
57	Merriweather, Mike	LB	6-2	216	11/26/60	5	Pacific	Vallejo, Calif.	D3-'82	16/16
47	Morse, Steve	RB	5-11	211	5/28/63	2	Virginia	Eight-Mile, Ala.	FA-'85	16/0
64	Nelson, Edmund	DE-DT	6-3	277	4/30/60	5	Auburn	Tampa, Fla.	D7-'82	6/6
18	Newsome, Harry	P	6-0	185	1/25/63	2	Wake Forest	Cheraw, S.C.	D8-'85	16/0
65	Pinney, Ray	T-C	6-4	262	6/29/54	8	Washington	Seattle, Wash.	D2-'76	15/11
80	Pokorny, Frank	WR	6-0	205	5/13/63	2	Youngstown State	Monaca, Pa.	FA-'85	4/0
30	Pollard, Frank	RB	5-10	223	6/15/57	7	Baylor	Meridian, Tex.	D11-'80	16/16
60	Rasmussen, Randy	G-C	6-1	254	9/27/60	3	Minnesota	Irondale, Minn.	D8-'84	11/0
63	†Rostosky, Pete	T	6-4	252	7/21/61	3	Connecticut	Monongahela, Pa.	FA-'83	16/5
31	Shell, Donnie	S	5-11	198	8/26/52	13	South Carolina State	Whitmire, S.C.	FA-'74	16/16
99	Sims, Darryl	DE	6-3	265	7/23/61	2	Wisconsin	Bridgeport, Conn.	D1-'85	16/0
54	Small, Fred	LB	5-11	230	7/15/63	2	Washington	Fremont, Calif.	D9-'85	16/0
82	Stallworth, John	WR	6-2	202	7/15/52	13	Alabama A&M	Tuscaloosa, Ala.	D4-'74	16/16
26	Swain, John	CB	6-1	192	9/4/59	6	Miami	Miami, Fla.	W(Mia)-'85	15/1*
85	Sweeney, Calvin	WR	6-2	202	1/12/55	7	Southern California	Santa Monica, Calif.	D4-'79	16/0
87	Thompson, Weegie	WR	6-6	209	3/21/61	3	Florida State	Midlothian, Va.	D4-'84	16/0
52	Webster, Mike	C	6-1	260	3/18/52	13	Wisconsin	Tomahawk, Wis.	D5-'74	16/16
21	Williams, Eric	S	6-1	190	2/21/60	4	North Carolina State	Garner, N.C.	D6-'83	14/14
93	Willis, Keith	DE	6-1	258	7/29/59	5	Northeastern	Newark, N.J.	FA-'82	16/16
55	Winston, Dennis	LB	6-0	238	10/25/55	10	Arkansas	Marianna, Ark.	FA-'85	12/0*
73	Wolfley, Craig	G	6-1	265	5/19/58	7	Syracuse	Orchard Park, N.Y.	D5-'80	13/13
19	Woodley, David	QB	6-2	211	10/25/58	7	Louisiana State	Shreveport, La.	T(Mia)-'84	9/6
49	Woodruff, Dwayne	CB	6-0	198	2/18/57	8	Louisville	New Richmond, Ohio	D6-'79	12/10
22	Woods, Rick	S-CB	6-1	195	11/16/59	5	Boise State	Boise, Idaho	D4-'82	16/9

* Swain played 6 games with Miami, 9 with Pittsburgh in '85; Winston played 2 games with New Orleans, 10 with Pittsburgh.

†Option playout; subject to developments.

Also played with Steelers in '85—T Glen Howe (2 games), TE Darrell Nelson (5), T Ray Snell (5), RB-KR Todd Spencer (16), CB Sam Washington (7), G Blake Wingle (3).

COACHING STAFF

Head Coach, Chuck Noll

Pro Career: Became first NFL coach to win four Super Bowls when Steelers defeated Los Angeles Rams 31-19 in Super Bowl XIV. Put together 13 consecutive non-losing seasons and has guided Steelers into postseason play 11 of last 14 years. Led Steelers to consecutive NFL championships twice (1974-75, 1978-79). With 164 career wins is third among active NFL coaches behind Don Shula (255) and Tom Landry (253). Has eighth-highest winning percentage (.612) among active coaches and ranks seventh among the NFL's all-time winningest coaches with a 164-104-1 career record. Noll is one of only four all-time NFL head coaches to lead a team for 18 consecutive seasons—Curly Lambeau (29), Landry (25), and Steve Owen (23). Played pro ball as guard-linebacker for Cleveland Browns from 1953-59. At age 28, he started coaching career as defensive coach with Los Angeles (San Diego) Chargers in 1960. Left after 1965 season to become Don Shula's defensive backfield assistant in Baltimore. Remained with Colts until taking over Pittsburgh reins as head coach in 1969. Career record: 164-104-1.

Background: Was an all-state star at Benedictine High in Cleveland. Captained the University of Dayton team, playing both tackle and linebacker. He was drafted by the Browns in 1953.

Personal: Born in Cleveland on January 5, 1932. He and his wife, Marianne, live in Pittsburgh and have one son—Chris.

Assistant Coaches

Ron Blackledge, offensive line-tackles/tight ends; born April 15, 1938, Canton, Ohio, lives in Pittsburgh. Tight end-defensive end Bowling Green 1957-59. No pro playing experience. College coach: Ashland 1968-69, Cincinnati 1970-72, Kentucky 1973-75, Princeton 1976, Kent State 1977-81 (head coach 1979-81). Pro coach: Joined Steelers in 1982.

Tony Dungy, defensive coordinator; born October 6, 1955, Jackson, Mich., lives in Pittsburgh. Quarterback Minnesota 1973-76. Pro safety Pittsburgh Steelers 1977-78, San Francisco 49ers 1979. College coach: Minnesota 1980. Pro coach: Joined Steelers in 1981.

Walt Evans, conditioning and training; born May 15, 1951, Pittsburgh, Pa., lives in Pittsburgh. Marietta College 1974. No college or pro playing experience. Pro coach: Joined Steelers in 1983.

Dennis Fitzgerald, inside linebackers; born March 13, 1936, Ann Arbor, Mich., lives in Pittsburgh. Running back Michigan 1958-60. No pro playing experience. College coach: Michigan 1961-68, Kentucky 1969-70, Kent State 1971-77 (head coach 1975-77), Syracuse 1978-80, Tulane 1981. Pro coach: Joined Steelers in 1982.

Dick Hoak, offensive backfield; born December 8, 1939, Jeannette, Pa., lives in Greenburg, Pa. Halfback-quarterback Penn State 1958-60. Pro running back Pittsburgh Steelers 1961-70. Pro coach: Joined Steelers in 1972.

Jed Hughes, outside linebackers; born November 14, 1947, New York, N.Y., lives in Pittsburgh. Linebacker Springfield 1966-68, tight end Gettysburg 1969-70. No pro playing experience. College coach: Stanford 1971-72, Michigan 1973-75, UCLA 1976-81. Pro coach: Minnesota Vikings 1982-83, joined Steelers in 1984.

Hal Hunter, offensive line-guards/centers; born June 3, 1934, Canonsburg, Pa., lives in Pittsburgh. Linebacker-guard Pittsburgh 1955-57. No pro playing experience. College coach: Richmond 1958-61, West Virginia 1962-63, Maryland 1964-65, Duke 1966-70, Kentucky 1971-72, Indiana 1973-76, California State (Pa.) 1977-80 (head coach). Pro coach: Hamilton Tiger-Cats (CFL) 1981, Indianapolis Colts 1982-84, joined Steelers in 1985.

Jon Kolb, defensive line; born August 30, 1947, Ponca City, Okla., lives in Pittsburgh. Center-linebacker Oklahoma State 1966-68. Pro tackle Pittsburgh Steelers 1969-81. Pro coach: Joined Steelers in 1982.

Tom Moore, offensive coordinator; born November 7, 1938, Owatonna, Minn., lives in Pittsburgh. Quarterback Iowa 1957-60. No pro playing experience. College coach: Iowa 1961-62, Dayton 1965-68, Wake Forest 1969, Georgia Tech 1970-71, Minnesota 1972-73, 1975-76. Pro coach: New York Stars (WFL) 1974, joined Steelers in 1977.

PITTSBURGH STEELERS 1986 FIRST-YEAR ROSTER

Name	Pos.	Ht.	Wt.	Birth-date	College	Hometown	How Acq.
Andrews, Alan (1)	TE	6-5	240	2/15/62	Rutgers	Succasunna, N.J.	D7-'85
Baker, Andrew (1)	WR	6-1	193	12/17/62	Rutgers	Tucson, Ariz.	FA
Behning, Mark (1)	T	6-6	275	9/26/61	Nebraska	Denton, Tex.	D2-'85
Blankenship, Brian	G	6-1	286	4/7/63	Nebraska	Omaha, Neb.	FA
Boso, Cap	TE	6-3	224	9/10/62	Illinois	Indianapolis, Ind.	D8
Brister, Walter	QB	6-2	184	8/15/62	Northeast Louisiana	Monroe, La.	D3
Britt, Jessie	WR	6-3	198	3/3/63	North Carolina A&T	Greensboro, N.C.	FA
Bryant, Domingo	CB-S	6-3	178	12/8/63	Texas A&M	Garrison, Tex.	D6
Callahan, Bill	S	5-10	192	4/11/64	Pittsburgh	New Kensington, Pa.	D4
Carter, Rodney	RB	5-11	199	10/30/64	Purdue	Elizabeth, N.J.	D7
Henton, Anthony	LB	6-1	218	7/27/63	Troy State	Bessemer, Ala.	D9
Holmes, Russell (1)	LB	6-3	213	3/1/63	Akron	Mansfield, Ohio	FA
Jacobs, Cam (1)	LB	6-1	225	3/10/62	Kentucky	Coral Gables, Fla.	D5-'85
Jones, Brent	TE	6-3	221	2/12/63	Santa Clara	San Jose, Calif.	D5b
Long, Peter	NT	6-1	238	8/7/61	Waynesburg	Orange, Va.	FA
Reeder, Dan (1)	RB	5-11	235	3/18/61	Delaware	Newark, Del.	FA
Rienstra, John	G	6-4	273	3/22/63	Temple	Colorado Springs, Colo.	D1
Seitz, Warren	WR	6-4	223	9/29/62	Missouri	Topeka, Kan.	D10
Sheffield, Chris	CB	6-1	180	1/9/63	Albany State	Cairo, Ga.	FA
Station, Larry	LB	5-11	227	12/5/63	Iowa	Omaha, Neb.	D11
Stephens, Mark	T-G	6-5	280	4/2/63	California	Arcadia, Calif.	FA
Tucker, Erroll	CB-KR	5-7	169	7/5/64	Utah	Long Beach, Calif.	D5a
Tuggle, Anthony (1)	S-CB	6-1	210	9/16/63	Nicholls State	Baton Rouge, La.	FA
Turk, Dan (1)	C	6-4	270	6/25/62	Wisconsin	Pittsburgh, Pa.	D4-'85
Walls, Jay	DT-NT	6-3	260	1/28/63	Valdosta State	Valdosta, Ga.	FA
Williams, Gerald	DT-NT	6-3	262	9/8/63	Auburn	Lanett, Ala.	D2
Williams, Mike	LB	6-0	221	10/8/63	Tulsa	Oklahoma City, Okla.	D12

The term NFL Rookie is defined as a player who is in his first season of professional football and has not been on the roster of another professional football team for any regular season or postseason games. A Rookie is designated by an "R" on NFL rosters. Players who have been active in another professional football league or players who have NFL experience, including either preseason training camp or being on an active roster for fewer than three regular season or postseason games, are termed NFL First-Year Players. An NFL First-Year Player is designated by a "1" on NFL rosters. Thereafter, a player on an NFL active roster for at least three regular season or postseason games is credited with an additional year of NFL playing experience.

NOTES

American Football Conference
Western Division

Team Colors: Blue, Gold, and White

San Diego Jack Murphy Stadium
P.O. Box 20666
San Diego, California 92120
Telephone: (619) 280-2111

Club Officials

Chairman of the Board/President: Alex G. Spanos
General Manager: John R. Sanders
Assistant General Manager: Paul (Tank) Younger
Assistant to the President: Jack Teele
Director of Scouting: Ron Nay
Director of Public Relations: Rick Smith
Business Manager: Pat Curran
Director of Marketing: Rich Israel
Director of Ticket Operations: Joe Scott
Assistant Director of Public Relations: Bill Johnston
Chief Financial Officer: Jerry Murphy
Head Trainer: Mark Howard
Equipment Manager: Sid Brooks

Stadium: San Diego Jack Murphy Stadium • **Capacity:** 60,100
9449 Friars Road
San Diego, California 92108

Playing Surface: Grass

Training Camp: University of California-San Diego
Third College
La Jolla, California 92037

1986 SCHEDULE

Preseason

Aug. 9	**Dallas**	6:00
Aug. 16	**Philadelphia**	6:00
Aug. 23	at Los Angeles Rams	7:00
Aug. 29	**St. Louis**	7:00

Regular Season

Sept. 7	**Miami**	1:00
Sept. 14	at New York Giants	1:00
Sept. 21	**Washington**	1:00
Sept. 28	at Los Angeles Raiders	1:00
Oct. 6	at Seattle (Monday)	6:00
Oct. 12	**Denver**	1:00
Oct. 19	at Kansas City	3:00
Oct. 26	at Philadelphia	1:00
Nov. 2	**Kansas City**	1:00
Nov. 9	at Denver	2:00
Nov. 16	**Dallas**	1:00
Nov. 20	**L.A. Raiders** (Thursday)	5:00
Nov. 30	at Indianapolis	1:00
Dec. 7	**Houston**	1:00
Dec. 14	**Seattle**	1:00
Dec. 21	at Cleveland	1:00

CHARGERS COACHING HISTORY

Los Angeles 1960
(196-178-11)

1960-69	Sid Gillman*	83-51-6
1969-70	Charlie Waller	9-7-3
1971	Sid Gillman**	4-6-0
1971-73	Harland Svare***	7-17-2
1973	Ron Waller	1-5-0
1974-78	Tommy Prothro****	21-39-0
1978-85	Don Coryell	71-53-0

*Retired after nine games in 1969
**Released after 10 games in 1971
***Resigned after eight games in 1973
****Resigned after four games in 1978

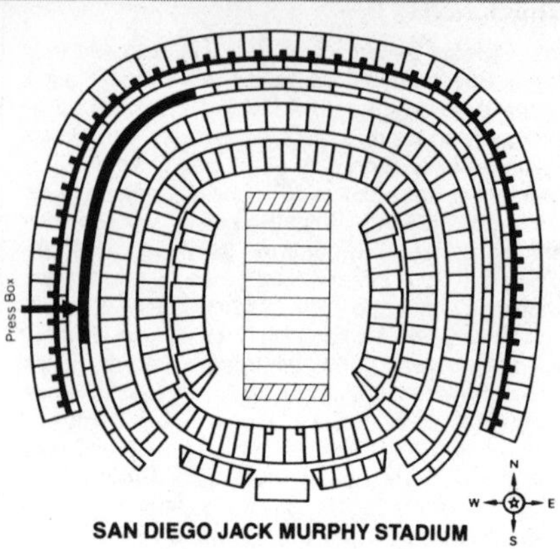

SAN DIEGO JACK MURPHY STADIUM

RECORD HOLDERS

Individual Records—Career

Category	Name	Performance
Rushing (Yds.)	Paul Lowe, 1960-67	4,963
Passing (Yds.)	Dan Fouts, 1973-1985	37,492
Passing (TDs)	Dan Fouts, 1973-1985	228
Receiving (No.)	Charlie Joiner, 1976-1985	552
Receiving (Yds.)	Lance Alworth, 1962-1970	9,585
Interceptions	Dick Harris, 1960-65	29
Punting (Avg.)	Maury Buford, 1982-84	42.7
Punt Return (Avg.)	Leslie (Speedy) Duncan, 1964-1970	12.3
Kickoff Return (Avg.)	Leslie (Speedy) Duncan, 1964-1970	25.2
Field Goals	Rolf Benirschke, 1977-1985	130
Touchdowns	Lance Alworth, 1962-1970	83
Points	Rolf Benirschke, 1977-1985	679

Individual Records—Single Season

Category	Name	Performance
Rushing (Yds.)	Earnest Jackson, 1984	1,179
Passing (Yds.)	Dan Fouts, 1981	4,802
Passing (TDs)	Dan Fouts, 1981	33
Receiving (No.)	Kellen Winslow, 1980	89
Receiving (Yds.)	Lance Alworth, 1965	1,602
Interceptions	Charlie McNeil, 1961	9
Punting (Avg.)	Dennis Partee, 1969	44.6
Punt Return (Avg.)	Leslie (Speedy) Duncan, 1965	15.5
Kickoff Return (Avg.)	Keith Lincoln, 1962	28.4
Field Goals	Rolf Benirschke, 1980	24
Touchdowns	Chuck Muncie, 1981	19
Points	Rolf Benirschke, 1980	118

Individual Records—Single Game

Category	Name	Performance
Rushing (Yds.)	Keith Lincoln, 1-5-64	206
Passing (Yds.)	Dan Fouts, 10-19-80	444
	Dan Fouts, 12-11-82	444
Passing (TDs)	Dan Fouts, 11-22-81	6
Receiving (No.)	Kellen Winslow, 10-7-84	15
Receiving (Yds.)	Wes Chandler, 12-20-82	260
Interceptions	Many times	3
	Last time by Pete Shaw, 11-2-80	
Field Goals	Many times	4
	Last time by Rolf Benirschke, 12-22-80	
Touchdowns (Tot.)	Kellen Winslow, 11-22-81	5
Points	Kellen Winslow, 11-22-81	30

1985 TEAM STATISTICS

	San Diego	Opp.
Total First Downs	380	364
Rushing	92	122
Passing	259	218
Penalty	29	24
Third Down: Made/Att.	86/208	89/209
Fourth Down: Made/Att.	6/10	8/12
Total Net Yards	6535	6265
Avg. Per Game	408.4	391.6
Total Plays	1111	1105
Avg. Per Play	5.9	5.7
Net Yards Rushing	1665	1972
Avg. Per Game	104.1	123.3
Total Rushes	440	470
Net Yards Passing	4870	4293
Avg. Per Game	304.4	268.3
Tackled/Yards Lost	39/305	40/304
Gross Yards	5175	4597
Att./Completions	632/386	595/357
Completion Pct.	61.1	60.0
Had Intercepted	30	26
Punts/Avg.	68/42.4	70/38.8
Net Punting Avg.	35.7	33.5
Penalties/Yards Lost	100/937	86/703
Fumbles/Ball Lost	44/19	37/16
Touchdowns	60	55
Rushing	20	25
Passing	37	28
Returns	3	2
Avg. Time of Possession	29:21	30:39

1985 TEAM RECORD

Preseason (2-2)

Date	San Diego		Opponents
8/10	12	*Cleveland	7
8/17	24	*Dallas (OT)	27
8/24	10	San Francisco	25
8/30	21	*New Orleans	20
	67		79

Regular Season (8-8)

Date	San Diego		Opp.	Att.
9/8	14	Buffalo	9	67,597
9/15	35	*Seattle	49	54,420
9/22	44	Cincinnati	41	52,270
9/29	7	*Cleveland	21	52,107
10/6	21	Seattle	26	61,300
10/13	31	*Kansas City	20	50,067
10/20	17	Minnesota	21	61,670
10/28	21	L.A. Raiders	34	69,297
11/3	30	*Denver	10	57,312
11/10	40	*L.A. Raiders (OT)	34	58,566
11/17	24	Denver (OT)	30	74,376
11/24	35	Houston	37	34,336
12/1	40	*Buffalo	7	45,487
12/8	54	*Pittsburgh	44	52,098
12/15	20	*Philadelphia	14	45,569
12/22	34	Kansas City	38	18,178

*Home Game (OT) Overtime

Score by Periods

San Diego	86	134	96	145	6	—	467
Opponents	82	124	114	109	6	—	435

Attendance

Home 415,626 Away 439,024 Total 854,650
Single game home record, 58,566 (11-10-85)
Single season home record, 415,626 (1985)

1985 INDIVIDUAL STATISTICS

Rushing	Att.	Yds.	Avg.	LG	TD
James	105	516	4.9	56t	2
Spencer	124	478	3.9	24	10
Anderson	116	429	3.7	27	4
McGee	42	181	4.3	44	3
Adams	16	49	3.1	14	1
Steels	6	12	2.0	5	0
Chandler	1	9	9.0	9	0
Mojsiejenko	1	0	0.0	0	0
Fouts	11	−1	−0.1	7	0
Herrmann	18	−8	−0.4	11	0
Chargers	440	1665	3.8	56t	20
Opponents	470	1972	4.2	61	25

Passing	Att.	Comp.	Pct.	Yds.	TD	Int.	Tkld.	Rate
Fouts	430	254	59.1	3638	27	20	18/135	88.1
Herrmann	201	132	65.7	1537	10	10	19/157	84.5
Holohan	1	0	0.0	0	0	0	1/8	39.6
Anderson	0	0	—	0	0	0	1/5	0.0
Chargers	632	386	61.1	5175	37	30	39/305	86.8
Opponents	595	357	60.0	4597	28	26	40/304	81.8

Receiving	No.	Yds.	Avg.	LG	TD
James	86	1027	11.9	67t	6
Chandler	67	1199	17.9	75t	10
Joiner	59	932	15.8	39t	7
Holohan	42	458	10.9	23	3
Sievers	41	438	10.7	30t	6
Anderson	35	422	12.1	52t	2
Winslow	25	318	12.7	26	0
Bendross	11	156	14.2	54t	2
Spencer	11	135	12.3	43	0
Johnson	4	51	12.8	20t	1
McGee	3	15	5.0	7	0
Adams	1	12	12.0	12	0
Faulkner	1	12	12.0	12	0
Chargers	386	5175	13.4	75t	37
Opponents	357	4597	12.9	84t	28

Interceptions	No.	Yds.	Avg.	LG	TD
Walters	5	71	14.2	30	0
Hendy	4	139	34.8	75t	1
Lowe	3	6	2.0	4	0
Dale	2	83	41.5	47t	1
Bradley	2	36	18.0	18	0
Davis	2	29	14.5	28	0
Green	2	17	8.5	12	0
L. King	2	8	4.0	5	0
McPherson	1	30	30.0	30	0
Byrd	1	25	25.0	25	0
Williams	1	17	17.0	17	0
B. Smith	1	0	0.0	0	0
Chargers	26	461	17.7	75t	2
Opponents	30	268	8.9	27	0

Punting	No.	Yds.	Avg.	In 20	LG
Mojsiejenko	68	2881	42.4	15	67
Chargers	68	2881	42.4	15	67
Opponents	70	2717	38.8	21	61

Punt Returns	No.	FC	Yds.	Avg.	LG	TD
James	25	8	213	8.5	24	0
McPherson	0	2	0	—	0	0
Steels	0	1	0	—	0	0
Chargers	25	11	213	8.5	24	0
Opponents	36	1	274	7.6	20	0

Kickoff Returns	No.	Yds.	Avg.	LG	TD
James	36	779	21.6	46	0
Anderson	13	302	23.2	98t	1
Steels	10	223	22.3	54	0
McGee	7	135	19.3	33	0
Adams	2	50	25.0	26	0
Bendross	1	2	2.0	2	0
Holohan	1	0	0.0	0	0
Sievers	1	3	3.0	3	0
Chargers	71	1494	21.0	98t	1
Opponents	68	1363	20.0	51	0

Scoring	TD R	TD P	TD Rt	PAT	FG	Saf	TP
Thomas	0	0	0	51/55	18/28	0	105
Chandler	0	10	0	0/0	0/0	0	60
Spencer	10	0	0	0/0	0/0	0	60
James	2	6	0	0/0	0/0	0	48
Anderson	4	2	1	0/0	0/0	0	42
Joiner	0	7	0	0/0	0/0	0	42
Sievers	0	6	0	0/0	0/0	0	36
Holohan	0	3	0	0/0	0/0	0	18
McGee	3	0	0	0/0	0/0	0	18
Bendross	0	2	0	0/0	0/0	0	12
Adams	1	0	0	0/0	0/0	0	6
Dale	0	0	1	0/0	0/0	0	6
Hendy	0	0	1	0/0	0/0	0	6
Johnson	0	1	0	0/0	0/0	0	6
Benirschke	0	0	0	2/2	0/0	0	2
Chargers	20	37	3	53/59	18/28	0	467
Opponents	25	28	2	51/54	18/30	0	435

FIRST-ROUND SELECTIONS

(If club had no first-round selection, first player drafted is listed with round in parentheses.)

Year	Player, College, Position
1960	Monty Stickles, Notre Dame, E
1961	Earl Faison, Indiana, DE
1962	Bob Ferguson, Ohio State, RB
1963	Walt Sweeney, Syracuse, G
1964	Ted Davis, Georgia Tech, LB
1965	Steve DeLong, Tennessee, DE
1966	Don Davis, Cal State-Los Angeles, DT
1967	Ron Billingsley, Wyoming, DE
1968	Russ Washington, Missouri, DT
	Jimmy Hill, Texas A&I, DB
1969	Marty Domres, Columbia, QB
	Bob Babich, Miami, Ohio, LB
1970	Walker Gillette, Richmond, WR
1971	Leon Burns, Long Beach State, RB
1972	Pete Lazetich, Stanford, DE (2)
1973	Johnny Rodgers, Nebraska, WR
1974	Bo Matthews, Colorado, RB
	Don Goode, Kansas, LB
1975	Gary Johnson, Grambling, DT
	Mike Williams, Louisiana State, DB
1976	Joe Washington, Oklahoma, RB
1977	Bob Rush, Memphis State, C
1978	John Jefferson, Arizona State, WR
1979	Kellen Winslow, Missouri, TE
1980	Ed Luther, San Jose State, QB (4)
1981	James Brooks, Auburn, RB
1982	Hollis Hall, Clemson, DB (7)
1983	Billy Ray Smith, Arkansas, LB
	Gary Anderson, Arkansas, WR
	Gill Byrd, San Jose State, DB
1984	Mossy Cade, Texas, DB
1985	Jim Lachey, Ohio State, G
1986	Leslie O'Neal, Oklahoma State, DE
	James FitzPatrick, Southern California, T

SAN DIEGO CHARGERS 1986 VETERAN ROSTER

No.	Name	Pos.	Ht.	Wt.	Birth-date	NFL Exp.	College	Hometown	How Acq.	'85 Games/ Starts
40	Anderson, Gary	RB	6-0	190	4/8/61	2	Arkansas	Columbia, Mo.	D1b-'83	12/6
6	Benirschke, Rolf	K	6-1	183	2/7/55	9	California-Davis	La Jolla, Calif.	FA-'77	1/0
59	Bingham, Craig	LB	6-2	220	9/29/59	5	Syracuse	Stamford, Conn.	FA-'85	8/0
50	Bradley, Carlos	LB	6-0	222	4/27/60	6	Wake Forest	Germantown, Pa.	D11b-'81	10/2
22	Byrd, Gill	S	5-10	201	2/20/61	4	San Jose State	San Francisco, Calif.	D1c-'83	16/16
89	Chandler, Wes	WR	6-0	182	8/22/56	9	Florida	New Smyrna Beach, Fla.	T(NO)-'81	15/13
77	†Claphan, Sam	T	6-6	282	10/10/56	6	Oklahoma	Stillwell, Okla.	FA-'81	12/12
37	Dale, Jeff	S	6-3	214	10/6/62	2	Louisiana State	Winnfield, La.	D2b-'85	16/16
69	Dallafior, Ken	G	6-4	262	8/26/59	2	Minnesota	Madison Heights, Mich.	FA-'85	3/0
20	Davis, Wayne	CB	5-11	175	7/17/63	2	Indiana State	Mt. Healthy, Ohio	D2a-'85	16/6
65	Doerger, Jerry	C-T	6-5	270	7/18/60	3	Wisconsin	Cincinnati, Ohio	FA-'85	8/0
12	†Dufek, Joe	QB	6-4	215	8/23/61	4	Yale	Kent, Michigan	FA-'85	0*
78	Ehin, Chuck	NT	6-4	265	7/1/61	4	Brigham Young	Leyton, Utah	D12b-'83	16/15
84	Faulkner, Chris	TE	6-4	250	4/13/60	3	Florida	Arcadia, Ind.	FA-'85	9/0
79	Faurot, Ron	DE	6-7	262	1/27/62	3	Arkansas	Bedford, Tex.	FA-'85	5/0*
14	Fouts, Dan	QB	6-3	205	6/10/51	14	Oregon	San Francisco, Calif.	D3-'73	14/12
92	Garnett, Scott	NT	6-2	271	12/3/62	3	Washington	Pasadena, Calif.	FA-'85	8/0*
53	Guendling, Mike	LB	6-3	238	6/18/62	2	Northwestern	Elk Grove, Ill.	D2-'84	9/0
29	Hendy, John	CB	5-10	196	10/9/62	2	Long Beach State	Santa Clara, Calif.	D3-'85	16/10
9	Herrmann, Mark	QB	6-4	209	1/8/59	6	Purdue	Carmel, Ind.	T(Ind)-'85	9/4
88	Holohan, Pete	TE	6-4	244	7/25/59	6	Notre Dame	Liverpool, N.Y.	D7-'81	15/3
26	James, Lionel	RB-KR	5-6	170	5/25/62	3	Auburn	Albany, Ga.	D5-'84	16/7
83	Johnson, Trumaine	WR	6-1	196	1/16/60	2	Grambling	Baker, La.	D6-'83	11/2
18	Joiner, Charlie	WR	5-11	177	10/14/47	18	Grambling	Lake Charles, La.	T(Cinn)-'76	16/14
57	King, Linden	LB	6-4	247	6/28/55	9	Colorado State	Colorado Springs, Colo.	D3-'77	16/16
68	†Kowalski, Gary	T	6-5	290	7/2/60	3	Boston College	Clinton, Conn.	T(Rams)-'85	13/1
74	Lachey, Jim	T	6-6	288	6/4/63	2	Ohio State	St. Henry, Ohio	D1-'85	16/16
63	Leonard, Jim	C	6-3	260	10/19/57	6	Santa Clara	Santa Cruz, Calif.	FA-'85	7/3
32	Lewis, Terry	CB	5-11	193	12/9/61	2	Michigan State	Highland Park, Mich.	D6-'85	10/0
51	Lowe, Woodrow	LB	6-0	229	6/9/54	11	Alabama	Phenix City, Ala.	D5-'75	16/14
62	Macek, Don	C	6-2	260	7/2/54	11	Boston College	Manchester, N.H.	D2-'76	15/15
21	McGee, Buford	RB	6-0	203	8/16/60	3	Mississippi	Durant, Miss.	D11-'84	11/1
60	McKnight, Dennis	C-G	6-3	273	9/12/59	5	Drake	Staten Island, N.Y.	FA-'82	16/16
24	McPherson, Miles	S	5-11	186	3/30/60	5	New Haven, Conn.	Long Island, N.Y.	FA-'82	9/0
47	Micho, Bob	TE	6-3	240	3/7/62	2	Texas	Austin, Tex.	W(Den)-'84	0*
2	Mojsiejenko, Ralf	P-K	6-3	198	1/28/63	2	Michigan	Bridgman, Mich.	D4-'85	16/0
55	†Nelson, Derrie	LB	6-2	234	2/8/58	4	Nebraska	Fairmont, Neb.	FA-'82	16/1
59	Nelson, Shane	LB	6-0	238	5/25/55	6	Baylor	Mathis, Tex.	FA-'85	0*
27	O'Bard, Ronnie	CB	5-9	190	6/11/58	2	Brigham Young	Spring Valley, Calif.	FA-'85	16/0
56	Osby, Vince	LB	5-11	221	7/8/61	3	Illinois	Lynwood, Calif.	FA-'84	7/0
90	Robinson, Fred	DE	6-5	242	10/22/61	3	Miami	Miami, Fla.	FA-'84	16/1
85	Sievers, Eric	TE	6-3	236	11/9/58	6	Maryland	Arlington, Va.	D4b-'81	16/11
97	Simmons, Tony	DE	6-4	270	12/18/62	2	Tennessee	Oakland, Calif.	D12a-'85	13/0
54	Smith, Billy Ray	LB	6-3	231	8/10/61	4	Arkansas	Plano, Tex.	D1a-'83	15/15
33	†Smith, Lucious	CB	5-10	190	1/17/57	7	Cal State-Fullerton	San Diego, Calif.	FA-'84	5/0
43	Spencer, Tim	RB	6-1	220	12/10/60	2	Ohio State	St. Clairsville, Ohio	D11b-'83	16/15
16	†Thomas, Bob	K	5-10	177	8/7/57	11	Notre Dame	Rochester, N.Y.	FA-'85	15/0
66	Umphrey, Rich	C-G	6-3	270	12/3/58	5	Colorado	Tustin, Calif.	FA-'85	11/1
23	†Walters, Danny	CB	6-1	180	11/4/60	4	Arkansas	Chicago, Ill.	D4-'83	16/16
67	White, Ed	G	6-2	284	4/4/47	18	California	Coachella, Calif.	T(Minn)-'78	16/16
99	Williams, Lee	DE	6-6	273	10/15/62	3	Bethune-Cookman	Ft. Lauderdale, Fla.	D1-'84	16/16
93	Wilson, Earl	DE	6-4	267	9/13/58	2	Kentucky	Atlantic City, N.J.	FA-'85	16/9
80	Winslow, Kellen	TE	6-5	242	11/5/57	8	Missouri	St. Louis, Mo.	D1-'79	10/6

* Dufek active for 1 game with Buffalo in '85 but did not play, active for 4 games with San Diego but did not play; Faurot played 5 games with N.Y. Jets in '85; Garnett played 3 games with San Francisco in '85, 5 with San Diego; Micho and S. Nelson missed '85 season due to injury.

†Option playout; subject to developments.

Traded—Wide receiver Jesse Bendross to Tampa Bay.

Retired—Andrew Gissinger, 3-year center-tackle, injured reserve in '85.

Also played with Chargers in '85—NT Tony Chickillo (4 games), RB Anthony Corley (4), CB-S David Croudip (2), DE Keith Ferguson (10), LB Mike Green (15), QB Babe Laufenberg (active for 2 games but did not play), CB-S Jim Rockford (1), RB Anthony Steels (6).

COACHING STAFF

Head Coach, Don Coryell

Pro Career: Begins ninth year as San Diego's head coach. Became head coach of the Chargers after fourth game of 1978 season and led them to 8 wins in final 12 games. Before coming to Chargers was St. Louis Cardinals head coach for five seasons, compiling a 42-29-1 record and leading Cardinals to NFC East titles in 1974-75. Career record: 113-82-1.

Background: Played defensive back for University of Washington 1947-49. Assistant coach Punahou Academy, Honolulu, 1951. Head coach Farrington High School, Honolulu, 1952. Head coach University of British Columbia 1953-54. Head coach, Fort Ord, California, army team 1956. Head coach Whittier College 1957-59 (23-5-1). Offensive backfield coach at Southern California 1960. Head coach at San Diego State from 1961-72 where he compiled a 104-19-2 record.

Personal: Born October 17, 1924, in Seattle, Washington. Graduated from Lincoln High School, Seattle, in 1943. Served in United States Army 1943-46, released as first lieutenant. Don and his wife, Aliisa, live in El Cajon, Calif., and have two children—Mike and Mindy (Mrs. Michael Lewis).

Assistant Coaches

Hank Bauer, special teams; born July 15, 1954, Scottsbluff, Neb., lives in San Diego. Running back California Lutheran College 1972-75. Pro running back San Diego 1977-82. Pro coach: Joined Chargers in 1983.

Gunther Cunningham, defensive line; born June 19, 1946, Munich, Germany, lives in San Diego. Linebacker Oregon 1965-67. No pro playing experience. College coach: Oregon 1969-71, Arkansas 1972, Stanford 1973-76, California 1977-80. Pro coach: Hamilton Tiger-Cats (CFL) 1981, Indianapolis Colts 1982-84, joined Chargers in 1985.

Earnel Durden, offensive backfield; born January 24, 1937, Los Angeles, Calif., lives in La Mesa, Calif. Halfback Oregon State 1956-58. No pro playing experience. College coach: Compton, Calif., J.C. 1966-67, Long Beach State 1968, UCLA 1969-70. Pro coach: Los Angeles Rams 1971-72, Houston Oilers 1973, joined Chargers in 1974.

Mike Haluchak, linebackers; born November 28, 1949, Concord, Calif., lives in San Diego. Linebacker Southern California 1967-70. No pro playing experience. College coach: Southern California 1976-77, Cal State-Fullerton 1978, Pacific 1979-80, California 1981, North Carolina State 1982. Pro coach: Oakland Invaders (USFL) 1983-85, first year with Chargers.

Dave Levy, offensive line; born October 25, 1932, Carrollton, Mo., lives in Solana Beach, Calif. Guard UCLA 1952-53. No pro playing experience. College coach: UCLA 1954, Long Beach City College 1955, Southern California 1960-75. Pro coach: Joined Chargers in 1980.

Ron Lynn, defensive coordinator; born December 6, 1944, Youngstown, Ohio, lives in San Diego. Quarterback-defensive back Mount Union (Ohio) 1963-65. College coach: Toledo 1966, Mount Union 1967-73, Kent State 1974-76, San Jose State 1977-78, Pacific 1979, California 1980-82. Pro coach: Oakland Invaders (USFL) 1983-85, first year with Chargers.

Al Saunders, assistant head coach; born February 1, 1947, London, England, lives in San Diego. Defensive back San Jose State 1966-68. No pro playing experience. College coach: Southern California 1970-71, Missouri 1972, Utah State 1973-75, California 1976-81, Tennessee 1982. Pro coach: Joined Chargers in 1983.

Ernie Zampese, offensive coordinator; born March 12, 1936, Santa Barbara, Calif., lives in San Diego. Halfback Southern California 1956-58. No pro playing experience. College coach: Hancock, Calif., J.C. 1962-65, Cal Poly-SLO 1966, San Diego State 1967-75. Pro coach: San Diego Chargers 1976, scout N.Y. Jets 1977-78, rejoined Chargers in 1979.

SAN DIEGO CHARGERS 1986 FIRST-YEAR ROSTER

Name	Pos.	Ht.	Wt.	Birth-date	College	Hometown	How Acq.
Adams, Curtis (1)	RB	5-11	198	4/30/62	Central Michigan	Muskegon, Mich.	D8-'85
Allert, Ty	LB	6-1	228	7/7/63	Texas	Houston, Tex.	D4a
Brown, Casey	RB	6-1	215	5/2/63	San Diego State	La Jolla, Calif.	FA
Brown, Donald	CB	5-11	192	11/28/63	Maryland	Annapolis, Md.	D5b
Collier, Steve (1)	T	6-7	305	4/19/63	Bethune-Cookman	Chicago, Ill.	FA
Dralle, James	C	6-3	280	7/17/62	Vanderbilt	Torrance, Calif.	FA
Fellows, Mark (1)	LB	6-1	222	2/22/63	Montana State	Choteau, Mont.	D7-'85
FitzPatrick, James	T	6-8	295	2/1/64	Southern California	Beaverton, Ore.	D1b
Johnson, Juan (1)	S	6-0	193	2/21/62	Langston	Okmulgee, Okla.	FA
Johnson, Matt	S	6-3	205	9/10/62	Southern California	Chula Vista, Calif.	D5c
King, David (1)	CB	5-8	176	5/19/63	Auburn	Fairhope, Ala.	D10-'85
Landry, Doug	LB	6-1	217	4/21/64	Louisiana Tech	New Orleans, La.	D5a
Lockette, James (1)	DE	6-4	260	4/7/60	Missouri	St. Louis, Mo.	FA
Miller, Mike	RB	6-0	225	9/2/62	North Carolina State	Greensboro, N.C.	FA
Milus, Ron	CB	5-9	177	11/25/63	Washington	Tacoma, Wash.	FA
Moore, Malcolm (1)	TE	6-5	225	6/24/61	Southern California	San Fernando, Calif.	FA
Nielsen, Jim	K	5-11	198	7/9/64	Oregon State	Beaverton, Ore.	FA
O'Neal, Leslie	DE	6-3	252	5/7/64	Oklahoma State	Little Rock, Ark.	D1a
Pardridge, Curtis	WR	5-9	169	3/13/64	Northern Illinois	DeKalb, Ill.	D6
Pate, Carl	WR	6-3	195	6/21/63	Humboldt State	Seaside, Calif.	FA
Peace, Wayne (1)	QB	6-2	215	11/3/61	Florida	Lakeland, Fla.	FA
Perrino, Mike	T	6-4	278	3/2/64	Notre Dame	Elmhurst, Ill.	D8
Rodgers, James	S	6-0	200	1/25/62	Washington	Aloha, Ore.	FA
Sanders, Chuck	RB	6-1	223	4/24/64	Slippery Rock	Penn Hills, Pa.	D11a
Searcey, Bill (1)	G	6-1	281	3/3/59	Alabama	Savannah, Ga.	FA
Schwab, Greg	T	6-7	280	7/5/63	Oregon	The Dalles, Ore.	FA
Smalls, Fred	LB	6-1	215	1/7/63	West Virginia	Beaufort, S.C.	D7
Smetana, Drew	T	6-8	277	3/4/63	Oregon	South Salem, Ore.	D11b
Smith, Steve (1)	QB	6-0	200	12/19/61	Michigan	Grand Blanc, Mich.	SD3-'84
Sprowls, Jeff	S	6-1	179	2/19/63	Brigham Young	La Canada, Calif.	D12a
Taylor, Tommy	LB	6-1	233	11/23/62	UCLA	Chattanooga, Tenn.	D4b
Trimble, David	WR	5-10	182	6/7/62	Washington	Yakima, Wash.	FA
Travis, Mike	CB	6-0	192	12/22/63	Georgia Tech	Marietta, Ga.	D12b
Tyler, Jerome	CB-S	6-1	185	9/30/63	Southern California	Riverside, Calif.	FA
Unrein, Terry	DE	6-5	285	10/24/62	Colorado State	Fort Lupton, Colo.	D3a
Walker, Jeff	G	6-4	280	1/22/63	Memphis State	Olive Branch, Miss.	D3b
Ware, Timmy (1)	WR	5-10	178	4/2/63	Southern California	Compton, Calif.	FA
Zordich, Mike	S	5-11	207	10/12/64	Penn State	Youngstown, Ohio	D9

The term NFL Rookie is defined as a player who is in his first season of professional football and has not been on the roster of another professional football team for any regular season or postseason games. A Rookie is designated by an "R" on NFL rosters. Players who have been active in another professional football league or players who have NFL experience, including either preseason training camp or being on an active roster for fewer than three regular season or postseason games, are termed NFL First-Year Players. An NFL First-Year Player is designated by a "1" on NFL rosters. Thereafter, a player on an NFL active roster for at least three regular season or postseason games is credited with an additional year of NFL playing experience.

NOTES

SEATTLE SEAHAWKS

American Football Conference
Western Division

Team Colors: Blue, Green, and Silver

11220 N.E. 53rd Street
Kirkland, Washington 98033
Telephone: (206) 827-9777

Club Officials

President-General Manager: Mike McCormack
Assistant General Manager: Chuck Allen
Player Personnel Director: Mike Allman
Public Relations Director: Gary Wright
Assistant Public Relations Director: Dave Neubert
Business Manager: Mickey Loomis
Data Processing Director: Tom Monroe
Ticket Manager: James Nagaoka
Trainer: Jim Whitesel
Equipment Manager: Walt Loeffler

Stadium: Kingdome • **Capacity:** 64,984
201 South King Street
Seattle, Washington 98104

Playing Surface: AstroTurf

Training Camp: 11220 N.E. 53rd Street
Kirkland, Washington 98033

1986 SCHEDULE

Preseason

Aug. 8	**Indianapolis**	7:30
Aug. 15	at Detroit	8:00
Aug. 22	**Minnesota**	7:30
Aug. 29	at San Francisco	6:00

Regular Season

Sept. 7	**Pittsburgh**	1:00
Sept. 14	**Kansas City**	1:00
Sept. 21	at New England	1:00
Sept. 28	at Washington	1:00
Oct. 6	**San Diego** (Monday)	6:00
Oct. 12	at Los Angeles Raiders	1:00
Oct. 19	**New York Giants**	1:00
Oct. 26	at Denver	2:00
Nov. 2	**New York Jets**	1:00
Nov. 9	at Kansas City	12:00
Nov. 16	at Cincinnati	1:00
Nov. 23	**Philadelphia**	1:00
Nov. 27	at Dallas (Thanksgiving)	3:00
Dec. 8	**L.A. Raiders** (Monday)	6:00
Dec. 14	at San Diego	1:00
Dec. 20	**Denver** (Saturday)	1:00

SEAHAWKS COACHING HISTORY

(71-83-0)

1976-82	Jack Patera*	35-59-0
1982	Mike McCormack	4-3-0
1983-85	Chuck Knox	32-21-0

*Released after two games in 1982

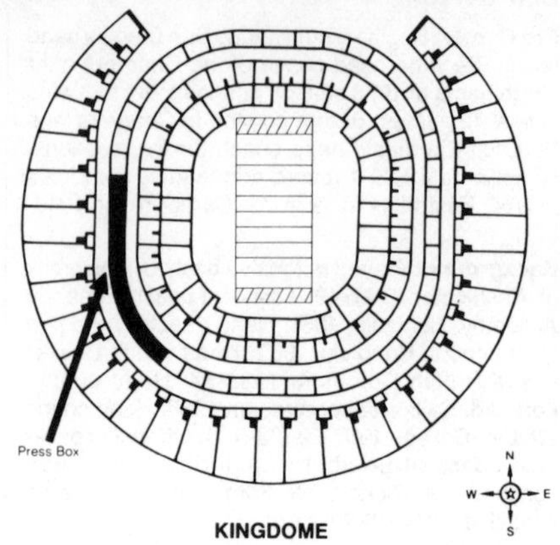

RECORD HOLDERS

Individual Records—Career

Category	Name	Performance
Rushing (Yds.)	Sherman Smith, 1976-1982	3,429
Passing (Yds.)	Jim Zorn, 1976-1984	20,042
Passing (TDs)	Jim Zorn, 1976-1984	107
Receiving (No.)	Steve Largent, 1976-1985	624
Receiving (Yds.)	Steve Largent, 1976-1985	10,059
Interceptions	Dave Brown, 1976-1985	45
Punting (Avg.)	Herman Weaver, 1977-1980	40.0
Punt Return (Avg.)	Paul Johns, 1981-84	11.2
Kickoff Return (Avg.)	Zachary Dixon, 1983-84	23.4
Field Goals	Efren Herrera, 1978-1981	64
Touchdowns (Tot.)	Steve Largent, 1976-1985	79
Points	Steve Largent, 1976-1985	475

Individual Records—Single Season

Category	Name	Performance
Rushing (Yds.)	Curt Warner, 1983	1,449
Passing (Yds.)	Dave Krieg, 1984	3,671
Passing (TDs)	Dave Krieg, 1984	32
Receiving (No.)	Steve Largent, 1985	79
Receiving (Yds.)	Steve Largent, 1985	1,287
Interceptions	John Harris, 1981	10
	Kenny Easley, 1984	10
Punting (Avg.)	Herman Weaver, 1980	41.8
Punt Return (Avg.)	Kenny Easley, 1984	12.1
Kickoff Return (Avg.)	Al Hunter, 1978	24.1
Field Goals	Efren Herrera, 1980	20
	Norm Johnson, 1984	20
Touchdowns (Tot.)	David Sims, 1978	15
	Sherman Smith, 1979	15
Points	Norm Johnson, 1984	110

Individual Records—Single Game

Category	Name	Performance
Rushing (Yds.)	Curt Warner, 11-27-83	207
Passing (Yds.)	Dave Krieg, 11-20-83	418
Passing (TDs)	Dave Krieg, 12-2-84	5
	Dave Krieg, 9-15-85	5
Receiving (No.)	David Hughes, 9-27-81	12
	Steve Largent, 11-25-84	12
Receiving (Yds.)	Steve Largent, 11-25-84	191
Interceptions	Kenny Easley, 9-3-84	3
Field Goals	Efren Herrera, 10-5-80	4
	Norm Johnson, 9-3-84	4
Touchdowns (Tot.)	Daryl Turner, 9-15-85	4
Points	Daryl Turner, 9-15-85	24

1985 TEAM STATISTICS

	Seattle	Opp.
Total First Downs	299	290
Rushing	96	90
Passing	179	179
Penalty	24	21
Third Down: Made/Att.	96/244	72/218
Fourth Down: Made/Att.	10/17	9/13
Total Net Yards	5007	5160
Avg. Per Game	312.9	322.5
Total Plays	1090	1030
Avg. Per Play	4.6	5.0
Net Yards Rushing	1644	1837
Avg. Per Game	102.8	114.8
Total Rushes	462	473
Net Yards Passing	3363	3323
Avg. Per Game	210.2	207.7
Tackled/Yards Lost	53/457	61/464
Gross Yards	3820	3787
Att./Completions	575/304	496/273
Completion Pct.	52.9	55.0
Had Intercepted	23	24
Punts/Avg.	91/40.3	97/42.1
Net Punting Avg.	33.8	34.6
Penalties/Yards Lost	102/827	106/840
Fumbles/Ball Lost	34/18	39/20
Touchdowns	44	35
Rushing	9	12
Passing	28	22
Returns	7	1
Avg. Time of Possession	30:13	29:47

1985 TEAM RECORD

Preseason (2-2)

Date	Seattle		Opponents
8/10	7	Indianapolis	19
8/16	28	*Detroit	3
8/24	27	Minnesota	10
8/30	21	*San Francisco	23
	83		55

Regular Season (8-8)

Date	Seattle		Opp.	Att.
9/8	28	Cincinnati	24	51,625
9/15	49	San Diego	35	54,420
9/23	24	*L.A Rams	35	63,292
9/29	7	Kansas City	28	50,485
10/6	26	*San Diego	21	61,300
10/13	30	*Atlanta	26	60,430
10/20	10	Denver (OT)	13	74,899
10/27	14	N.Y. Jets	17	69,320
11/3	33	*L.A. Raiders	3	64,060
11/10	27	New Orleans	3	47,365
11/17	13	*New England	20	60,345
11/25	6	San Francisco	19	57,482
12/1	24	*Kansas City	6	52,655
12/8	31	*Cleveland	13	58,477
12/15	3	L.A. Raiders	13	77,425
12/20	24	*Denver	27	56,283

*Home Game (OT) Overtime

Score by Periods

Seattle	43	116	90	100	0	—	349
Opponents	47	78	63	112	3	—	303

Attendance

Home 476,842 Away 483,021 Total 959,863
Single game home record, 64,411 (12-15-84)
Single season home record, 493,657 (1984)

1985 INDIVIDUAL STATISTICS

Rushing	Att.	Yds.	Avg.	LG	TD
Warner	291	1094	3.8	38	8
Morris	55	236	4.3	21	0
Hughes	40	128	3.2	9	0
Krieg	35	121	3.5	17	1
Williams, Dall.-Sea.	14	42	3.0	9	0
Williams, Sea.	1	2	2.0	2	0
Lane	14	32	2.3	12	0
Parros	8	19	2.4	6	0
Franklin	1	5	5.0	5	0
Hardy	5	5	1.0	4	0
Gilbert	7	4	0.6	8	0
Doornink	4	0	0.0	3	0
R. Butler, Ind.-Sea.	1	−1	−1.0	−1	0
Finzer	1	−2	−2.0	−2	0
Seahawks	462	1644	3.6	38	9
Opponents	473	1837	3.9	43	12

Passing	Att.	Comp.	Pct.	Yds.	TD	Int.	Tkld.	Rate
Krieg	532	285	53.6	3602	27	20	52/448	76.2
Gilbert	40	19	47.5	218	1	2	1/9	51.9
Finzer	1	0	0.0	0	0	1	0/0	0.0
Largent	1	0	0.0	0	0	0	0/0	39.6
Morris	1	0	0.0	0	0	0	0/0	39.6
Seahawks	575	304	52.9	3820	28	23	53/457	73.4
Opponents	496	273	55.0	3787	22	24	61/464	74.4

Receiving	No.	Yds.	Avg.	LG	TD
Largent	79	1287	16.3	43	6
Warner	47	307	6.5	27t	1
Turner	34	670	19.7	54	13
C. Young	28	351	12.5	32t	2
Skansi	21	269	12.8	32	1
R. Butler, Ind.-Sea.	19	345	18.2	72t	2
Walker	19	285	15.0	28t	2
Hughes	19	184	9.7	26	0
Ross, Cin.-Sea.	16	135	8.4	20	2
Ross, Sea.	10	72	7.2	12	2
Lane	15	153	10.2	20	0
Franklin	10	119	11.9	28	0
Doornink	8	52	6.5	19	0
Morris	6	14	2.3	6	0
Hardy	3	7	2.3	3	0
Tice	2	13	6.5	7	0
Greene	2	10	5.0	7	1
Parros	1	27	27.0	27	0
Seahawks	304	3820	12.6	54	28
Opponents	273	3787	13.9	71	22

Interceptions	No.	Yds.	Avg.	LG	TD
Harris	7	20	2.9	17	0
Brown	6	58	9.7	28t	1
Taylor	4	75	18.8	75t	1
Robinson	2	47	23.5	47	0
K. Butler	2	31	15.5	31	0
Easley	2	22	11.0	16	0
Green	1	19	19.0	19t	1
Seahawks	24	272	11.3	75t	3
Opponents	23	389	16.9	83	1

Punting	No.	Yds.	Avg.	In 20	LG
Finzer	68	2766	40.7	12	61
Colquitt	12	481	40.1	3	55
West	11	420	38.2	0	52
Seahawks	91	3667	40.3	15	61
Opponents	97	4081	42.1	22	62

Punt Returns	No.	FC	Yds.	Avg.	LG	TD
Skansi	31	7	312	10.1	32	0
Greene	11	3	60	5.5	13	0
Easley	8	0	87	10.9	25	0
Harris	3	1	24	8.0	12	0
Seahawks	53	11	483	9.1	32	0
Opponents	47	14	374	8.0	19	0

Kickoff Returns	No.	Yds.	Avg.	LG	TD
Morris	31	636	20.5	58	0
Skansi	19	358	18.8	35	0
Williams, Dall.-Sea.	6	129	21.5	30	0
Greene	5	144	28.8	52	0
Lane	1	1	1.0	1	0
Robinson	1	10	10.0	10	0
Tice	1	17	17.0	17	0
Seahawks	58	1166	20.1	58	0
Opponents	47	918	19.5	63	0

Scoring	TD R	TD P	TD Rt	PAT	FG	Saf	TP
Johnson	0	0	0	40/41	14/25	0	82
Turner	0	13	0	0/0	0/0	0	78
Warner	8	1	0	0/0	0/0	0	54
Largent	0	6	0	1/1	0/0	0	37
Walker	0	2	1	0/0	0/0	0	18
R. Butler, Ind.-Sea.	0	2	0	0/0	0/0	0	12
Green	0	0	2	0/0	0/0	0	12
Ross	0	2	0	0/0	0/0	0	12
Taylor	0	0	2	0/0	0/0	0	12
C. Young	0	2	0	0/0	0/0	0	12
Brown	0	0	1	0/0	0/0	0	6
Greene	0	1	0	0/0	0/0	0	6
Krieg	1	0	0	0/0	0/0	0	6
Merriman	0	0	1	0/0	0/0	0	6
Skansi	0	1	0	0/0	0/0	0	6
Seahawks	9	28	7	41/44	14/25	1	349
Opponents	12	22	1	31/35	20/28	1	303

FIRST-ROUND SELECTIONS

(If club had no first-round selection, first player drafted is listed with round in parentheses.)

Year	Player, College, Position
1976	Steve Niehaus, Notre Dame, DT
1977	Steve August, Tulsa, G
1978	Keith Simpson, Memphis State, DB
1979	Manu Tuiasosopo, UCLA, DT
1980	Jacob Green, Texas A&M, DE
1981	Ken Easley, UCLA, DB
1982	Jeff Bryant, Clemson, DE
1983	Curt Warner, Penn State, RB
1984	Terry Taylor, Southern Illinois, DB
1985	Owen Gill, Iowa, RB (2)
1986	John L. Williams, Florida, RB

SEATTLE SEAHAWKS 1986 VETERAN ROSTER

No.	Name	Pos.	Ht.	Wt.	Birth-date	NFL Exp.	College	Hometown	How Acq.	'85 Games/ Starts
65	†Bailey, Edwin	G	6-4	265	5/15/59	6	South Carolina State	Savannah, Ga.	D5-'81	16/16
76	†Borchardt, Jon	G	6-5	270	8/13/57	8	Montana State	Minneapolis, Minn.	T(Buff)-'85	14/0
22	Brown, Dave	CB	6-1	197	1/16/53	12	Michigan	Akron, Ohio	VA-'76	16/16
77	†Bryant, Jeff	DE	6-5	270	5/22/60	5	Clemson	Decatur, Ga.	D1-'82	16/16
59	Bush, Blair	C	6-3	257	11/25/56	9	Washington	Palos Verdes, Calif.	T(Cin)-'83	16/16
53	†Butler, Keith	LB	6-4	238	5/16/56	9	Memphis State	Huntsville, Ala.	D2-'78	16/16
83	†Butler, Ray	WR	6-3	203	6/28/57	7	Southern California	Sweeny, Tex.	FA-'85	13/9*
92	Caldwell, Tony	LB	6-1	220	4/1/61	4	Washington	Carson, Calif.	FA-'85	3/0*
52	Cameron, Glenn	LB	6-2	228	2/21/53	12	Florida	Gainesville, Fla.	FA-'86	16/15*
79	†Cryder, Bob	T	6-4	286	9/7/56	9	Alabama	O'Fallon, Ill.	T(NE)-'84	16/15
35	Davis, Lee	CB	5-11	195	12/18/62	2	Mississippi	Okalona, Miss.	FA-'86	7/0
31	Dixon, Zachary	RB	6-1	204	3/5/57	7	Temple	Dorchester, Mass.	FA-'83	0*
33	Doornink, Dan	RB	6-3	210	2/1/56	9	Washington State	Wapato, Wash.	T(NYG)-'79	6/1
45	Easley, Kenny	S	6-3	206	1/15/59	6	UCLA	Chesapeake, Va.	D1-'81	13/13
68	Edwards, Randy	DE	6-4	266	3/9/61	3	Alabama	Atlanta, Ga.	FA-'84	16/0
64	†Essink, Ron	T	6-6	279	7/30/58	7	Grand Valley State	Zeeland, Mich.	D10-'80	12/12
15	†Finzer, Dave	P	6-0	196	2/3/59	3	DePauw	Wilmette, Ill.	FA-'85	12/0
88	Franklin, Byron	WR	6-1	181	9/4/58	5	Auburn	Sheffield, Ala.	T(Buff)-'85	13/0
56	Gaines, Greg	LB	6-3	222	10/16/58	5	Tennessee	Heritage, Tex.	FA-'81	16/0
7	Gilbert, Gale	QB	6-3	206	12/20/61	2	California	Red Bluff, Calif.	FA-'84	9/0
79	Green, Jacob	DE	6-3	257	1/21/57	7	Texas A&M	Houston, Tex.	D1-'80	16/16
84	Greene, Danny	WR	5-11	191	12/26/61	2	Washington	Compton, Calif.	D3-'85	4/0
44	†Harris, John	S	6-2	204	6/13/56	9	Arizona State	Miami, Fla.	D7-'78	16/16
46	Hughes, David	RB	6-0	220	6/1/59	6	Boise State	Honolulu, Hawaii	D2-'81	12/10
55	Jackson, Michael	LB	6-1	228	7/15/57	8	Washington	Pasco, Wash.	D3-'79	16/16
24	Jackson, Terry	CB	5-11	197	12/9/56	9	San Diego State	San Diego, Calif.	T(NYG)-'84	16/0
9	Johnson, Norm	K	6-2	194	5/31/60	5	UCLA	Garden Grove, Calif.	FA-'82	16/0
54	†Kaiser, John	LB	6-3	227	6/6/62	3	Arizona	Hartland, Wis.	D6-'84	16/0
62	Kauahi, Kani	C	6-2	254	9/6/59	5	Hawaii	Honolulu, Hawaii	FA-'82	16/0
63	Kinlaw, Reggie	NT	6-2	249	1/9/57	7	Oklahoma	Miami, Fla.	W(Raiders)-'85	16/0
17	†Krieg, Dave	QB	6-1	196	10/20/58	7	Milton	Schofield, Wis.	FA-'80	16/16
37	†Lane, Eric	RB	6-0	197	1/6/59	6	Brigham Young	Hayward, Calif.	D8-'81	16/3
80	Largent, Steve	WR	5-11	191	9/28/54	11	Tulsa	Oklahoma City, Okla.	T(Hou)-'76	16/16
51	†Merriman, Sam	LB	6-3	229	5/5/61	4	Idaho	Tucson, Ariz.	D7-'83	14/0
71	Millard, Bryan	G	6-5	273	12/2/60	3	Texas	Dumas, Tex.	FA-'84	16/9
43	†Morris, Randall	RB	6-0	199	4/22/61	3	Tennessee	Long Beach, Calif.	D10-'84	16/0
21	Moyer, Paul	S	6-1	201	7/26/61	4	Arizona State	Villa Park, Calif.	FA-'83	11/3
72	Nash, Joe	NT	6-2	257	10/11/60	5	Boston College	Boston, Mass.	FA-'82	16/16
29	†Parros, Rick	RB	5-11	202	6/14/58	6	Utah State	Salt Lake City, Utah	W(Den)-'85	4/0
41	Robinson, Eugene	S	6-0	186	5/28/63	2	Colgate	Hartford, Conn.	FA-'85	16/0
57	Robinson, Shelton	LB	6-2	236	9/14/60	5	North Carolina	Pikeville, N.C.	FA-'82	15/3
85	†Ross, Dan	TE	6-4	234	2/9/57	7	Northeastern	Everett, Mass.	T(Cin)-'85	16/5*
58	†Scholtz, Bruce	LB	6-6	240	9/26/58	5	Texas	Austin, Tex.	D2-'82	16/16
42	†Simpson, Keith	CB	6-1	195	3/9/56	9	Memphis State	Memphis, Tenn.	D1-'78	15/0
82	Skansi, Paul	WR	5-11	183	1/11/61	4	Washington	Gig Harbor, Wash.	FA-'85	12/0
20	Taylor, Terry	CB	5-10	188	7/18/61	3	Southern Illinois	Youngstown, Ohio	D1-'84	16/16
86	Tice, Mike	TE	6-7	247	2/2/59	6	Maryland	Central Islip, N.Y.	FA-'81	9/2
81	Turner, Daryl	WR	6-3	191	12/15/61	3	Michigan	Flint, Mich.	D2-'84	16/12
89	†Walker, Byron	WR	6-4	188	7/28/60	5	Citadel	Warner Robbins, Ga.	FA-'82	16/0
28	Warner, Curt	RB	5-11	205	3/18/61	3	Penn State	Pineville, W. Va.	D1-'83	16/16
40	Williams, John	RB	5-11	219	10/26/60	2	Wisconsin	Muskegon, Mich.	FA-'85	10/0*
50	Young, Fredd	LB	6-1	233	11/14/61	3	New Mexico State	Dallas, Tex.	D3-'84	16/13

* R. Butler played 11 games with Indianapolis, 2 with Seattle in '85; Caldwell played 3 games with L.A. Raiders in '85; Cameron played 16 games with Cincinnati in '85; Dixon missed '85 season due to injury; Ross played 6 games with Cincinnati, 10 with Seattle in '85; Williams played 8 games with Dallas, 2 with Seattle in '85.

†Option playout; subject to developments.

Retired—Robert Pratt, 12-year guard, 12 games in '85; Charle Young, 13-year tight end, 14 games in '85.

Also played with Seahawks in '85—P Jimmy Colquitt (2 games), RB Andre Hardy (3), S Rick Sanford (5), P Jeff West (2).

COACHING STAFF

Head Coach, Chuck Knox

Pro Career: Named head coach of Seahawks on January 26, 1983, after five seasons as head coach of Buffalo where he led Bills to AFC East title in 1980. Led Los Angeles Rams to five straight NFC West titles before taking over Bills in 1978. Pro assistant with New York Jets 1963-66, coaching offensive line, before moving to Detroit in 1967. Served Lions in same capacity until named head coach of Rams in 1973. No pro playing experience. Career record: 127-79-1.

Background: Played tackle for Juniata College in Huntingdon, Pa., 1950-53. Was assistant coach at his alma mater in 1954, then spent 1955 season as line coach at Ellwood City High School in Pennsylvania. Moved to Wake Forest as an assistant coach in 1959-60, then Kentucky in 1961-62.

Personal: Born April 27, 1932, Sewickley, Pa. Chuck and his wife, Shirley, live in Bellevue, Wash., and have four children—Chris, Kathy, Colleen, and Chuck.

Assistant Coaches

Tom Catlin, assistant head coach-defensive coordinator-linebackers; born September 8, 1931, Ponca City, Okla., lives in Redmond, Wash. Center-linebacker Oklahoma 1950-52. Pro linebacker Cleveland Browns 1953-54, 1957-58, Philadelphia Eagles 1959. College coach: Army 1956. Pro coach: Dallas Texans-Kansas City Chiefs 1960-65, Los Angeles Rams 1966-77, Buffalo Bills 1978-82, joined Seahawks in 1983.

George Dyer, defensive line; born May 4, 1940, Alhambra, Calif., lives in Redmond, Wash. Center-linebacker U.C. Santa Barbara 1961-63. No pro playing experience. College coach: Humboldt State 1964-66, Coalinga, Calif., J.C. 1967 (head coach), Portland State 1968-71, Idaho 1972, San Jose State 1973, Michigan State 1977-79, Arizona State 1980-81. Pro coach: Winnipeg Blue Bombers (CFL) 1974-76 (head coach), Buffalo Bills 1982, joined Seahawks in 1983.

Chick Harris, offensive backfield; born September 21, 1945, Durham, N.C., lives in Redmond, Wash. Running back Northern Arizona 1966-69. No pro playing experience. College coach: Colorado State 1970-72, Long Beach State 1973-74, Washington 1975-80. Pro coach: Buffalo Bills 1981-82, joined Seahawks in 1983.

Ralph Hawkins, defensive backfield; born May 4, 1935, Washington, D.C., lives in Redmond, Wash. Quarterback-defensive back Maryland 1953-55. Pro defensive back New York Titans (AFL) 1960. College coach: Maryland 1959, 1967, Southern Methodist 1961, Kentucky 1962-65, Army 1966, Cincinnati 1968. Pro coach: Buffalo Bills 1969-71, 1981-82, Washington Redskins 1973-77, Baltimore Colts 1978, New York Giants 1979-80, joined Seahawks in 1983.

Ken Meyer, quarterbacks; born July 14, 1926, Erie, Pa., lives in Bellevue, Wash. Quarterback Denison 1947-50. No pro playing experience. College coach: Denison 1952-57, Wake Forest 1958-59, Florida State 1960-62, Alabama 1963-67, Tulane 1981-82. Pro coach: San Francisco 49ers 1968, 1977 (head coach), New York Jets 1969-72, Los Angeles Rams 1973-76, Chicago Bears 1978-80, joined Seahawks in 1983.

Steve Moore, offensive coordinator-receivers; born August 19, 1947, Los Angeles, Calif., lives in Bellevue, Wash. Running back U.C. Santa Barbara 1968-69. No pro playing experience. College coach: U.C. Santa Barbara 1970-71, Army 1975, Rice 1976-77. Pro coach: Buffalo Bills 1978-82, joined Seahawks in 1983.

Kent Stephenson, offensive line; born February 4, 1942, Anita, Iowa, lives in Redmond, Wash. Guard-nose tackle Northern Iowa 1962-64. No pro playing experience. College coach: Wayne State 1965-68, North Dakota 1969-71, Southern Methodist 1972-73, Iowa 1974-76, Oklahoma State 1977-78, Kansas 1979-82. Pro coach: Michigan Panthers (USFL) 1983-84, joined Seahawks in 1985.

Rusty Tillman, tight ends-special teams; born February 27, 1948, Beloit, Wis., lives in Bellevue, Wash. Linebacker Northern Arizona 1967-69. Pro linebacker Washington Redskins 1970-77. Pro coach: Joined Seahawks in 1979.

Joe Vitt, special assignments; born August 23, 1954, Camden, N.J., lives in Redmond, Wash. Linebacker Towson State 1973-75. No pro playing experience. Pro coach: Baltimore Colts 1979-81, joined Seahawks in 1982.

SEATTLE SEAHAWKS 1986 FIRST-YEAR ROSTER

Name	Pos.	Ht.	Wt.	Birth-date	College	Hometown	How Acq.
Anderson, Eddie	S	6-1	191	7/22/63	Fort Valley State	Warner Robins, Ga.	D6
Barns, John	T	6-7	285	1/5/63	Stanford	Dallas, Tex.	FA
Belk, Veno	TE	6-3	224	3/7/63	Michigan State	Tifton, Ga.	FA
Black, Michael	G	6-4	290	8/24/64	Sacramento State	Auburn, Calif.	D9
Burnham, Tim	G	6-5	264	5/6/63	Washington	Redding, Calif.	FA
Cartwright, Jeff	LB	6-2	246	6/10/63	Vanderbilt	Cleveland, Tenn.	FA
Conway, Earl	NT	6-4	262	11/25/63	Mississippi College	Gulfport, Miss.	FA
Davis, Tony (1)	TE	6-5	248	2/11/62	Missouri	Santa Ana, Calif.	D4-'85
Dilulo, Angelo (1)	NT	6-1	254	5/11/62	Oregon State	Boise, Idaho	FA
Edmonds, Bobby Joe	RB	5-11	175	9/26/64	Arkansas	Nashville, Tenn.	D5
Eisenhooth, Stan	C	6-6	278	7/8/63	Towson State	Harrisburg, Pa.	FA
Eldridge, Maurice	G	6-4	251	9/14/63	Kent State	Buffalo, N.Y.	FA
Fairbanks, Don	DE	6-3	260	2/13/64	Colorado	Wheatridge, Colo.	D10
Gamache, Vince (1)	P	5-11	174	11/18/61	Cal State-Fullerton	Los Angeles, Calif.	FA
Graves, Rory	T	6-6	280	7/21/63	Ohio State	Decatur, Ga.	FA
Haeusler, Greg (1)	LB	6-2	223	8/12/62	Southern Mississippi	South Hampton, N.Y.	FA
Hoffman, Jeff (1)	C	6-2	255	11/14/62	Sacramento State	Sacramento, Calif.	FA
Howell, Leroy (1)	DE	6-4	260	11/4/62	Appalachian State	Columbia, S.C.	FA
Hudson, Gordon (1)	TE	6-3	230	6/22/62	Brigham Young	Everett, Wash.	SD1-'84
Hunter, Patrick	CB	5-11	180	10/29/64	Nevada-Reno	San Francisco, Calif.	D3
Jackson, Charles	S	6-5	187	3/12/63	Texas Tech	Fort Gaines, Ga.	FA
Kartz, Keith	G	6-3	256	5/5/63	California	Las Vegas, Nev.	FA
Lewis, Paul (1)	RB	5-8	197	9/12/62	Boston University	Boston, Mass.	FA
Mattes, Ron (1)	T	6-6	290	8/8/63	Virginia	Shenandoah, Va.	D7-'85
McVeigh, John	LB	6-1	226	10/19/62	Miami	Coral Gables, Fla.	D12
Miles, Paul	RB	5-10	198	7/11/63	Nebraska	Orange, N.J.	D7b
Mitz, Alonzo	NT	6-3	270	6/5/63	Florida	Henderson, N.C.	D8
Najarian, Peter	LB	6-1	208	2/18/64	Minnesota	San Francisco, Calif.	FA
Nelson, Dirk (1)	P	6-0	195	7/23/62	Montana State	Wichita, Kan.	FA
Norrie, David	QB	6-4	211	11/30/63	UCLA	Boston, Mass.	D11
Parker, Ken	DE	6-5	240	9/5/64	Georgia Tech	Huntsville, Ala.	FA
Pearson, Rik (1)	K	5-8	172	9/22/60	Whitworth	San Diego, Calif.	FA
Pollard, Darryl	CB	5-11	183	5/11/64	Weber State	Ellsworth, Maine	FA
Rovito, John	NT	6-4	275	5/22/63	Lehigh	Shamokin, Pa.	FA
Salisbury, Sean	QB	6-5	210	3/9/63	Southern California	Long Beach, Calif.	FA
Schlopy, Todd (1)	K	5-10	165	6/17/61	Michigan	Bradford, Pa.	FA
Sikora, Pat	LB	6-3	235	3/17/62	Montana State	Weirton, W. Va.	FA
Sims, Jack (1)	G	6-3	242	4/2/62	Hawaii	San Mateo, Calif.	FA
Singer, Curt (1)	T	6-5	275	11/4/61	Tennessee	Aliquippa, Pa.	FA
Stacy, Curtis	CB	5-10	180	9/7/64	Florida	Gainesville, Fla.	FA
Storay, Dwight	CB	5-11	180	6/11/64	Utah State	Compton, Calif.	FA
Summerfield, Terry	QB	6-2	188	12/2/62	Portland State	Portland, Ore.	FA
Tolbert, William	LB	6-3	240	9/10/63	Alabama State	Memphis, Tenn.	FA
Warren, Jimmie	CB	5-11	180	2/25/63	Auburn	Birmingham, Ala.	FA
White, Chris	S	6-3	200	3/1/62	Tennessee	Cleveland, Tenn.	FA
Williams, John L.	RB	5-11	225	11/23/64	Florida	Palatka, Fla.	D1
Winfield, Earl	WR	6-0	187	3/10/61	North Carolina	Richmond, Va.	FA
Winn, Bryant (1)	LB	6-3	231	1/7/62	Houston	Memphis, Tenn.	FA

The term NFL Rookie is defined as a player who is in his first season of professional football and has not been on the roster of another professional football team for any regular season or postseason games. A Rookie is designated by an "R" on NFL rosters. Players who have been active in another professional football league or players who have NFL experience, including either preseason training camp or being on an active roster for fewer than three regular season or postseason games, are termed NFL First-Year Players. An NFL First-Year Player is designated by a "1" on NFL rosters. Thereafter, a player on an NFL active roster for at least three regular season or postseason games is credited with an additional year of NFL playing experience.

NOTES

THE NFC

Atlanta Falcons
Chicago Bears
Dallas Cowboys
Detroit Lions
Green Bay Packers
Los Angeles Rams
Minnesota Vikings
New Orleans Saints
New York Giants
Philadelphia Eagles
St. Louis Cardinals
San Francisco 49ers
Tampa Bay Buccaneers
Washington Redskins

ATLANTA FALCONS

National Football Conference
Western Division

Team Colors: Red, Black, White, and Silver

Suwanee Road at I-85
Suwanee, Georgia 30174
Telephone: (404) 945-1111

Club Officials

Chairman of the Board: Rankin M. Smith, Sr.
President: Rankin Smith, Jr.
Corporate Secretary: Taylor Smith
Director of College Scouting: Tom Braatz
Chief Financial Officer: Jim Hay
Director of Pro Personnel: Bill Jobko
Scouts: Bob Cegelski, Bob Fry, John Jelacic, Bob Riggle, Bill Striegel
Ticket Manager: Jack Ragsdale
Assistant Ticket Manager: Lucy Bailey
Director of Marketing: Tommy Nobis
Director of Public Relations: Charlie Dayton
Assistant Director of Public Relations: Bob Dickinson
Assistant Director of Community Affairs: Carol Henderson
Head Trainer: Jerry Rhea
Assistant Trainer: Billy Brooks
Equipment Manager: Whitey Zimmerman
Assistant Equipment Manager: Horace Daniel

Stadium: Atlanta-Fulton County Stadium • **Capacity:** 60,748
521 Capitol Avenue, S.W.
Atlanta, Georgia 30312

Playing Surface: Grass

Training Camp: Suwanee Road at I-85
Suwanee, Georgia 30174

1986 SCHEDULE

Preseason

Aug. 6	**New York Giants**	7:00
Aug. 16	at Tampa Bay	7:00
Aug. 23	**Cleveland**	8:00
Aug. 29	at Washington	8:00

Regular Season

Sept. 7	at New Orleans	12:00
Sept. 14	**St. Louis**	1:00
Sept. 21	at Dallas	12:00
Sept. 28	at Tampa Bay	4:00
Oct. 5	**Philadelphia**	1:00
Oct. 12	**Los Angeles Rams**	1:00
Oct. 19	**San Francisco**	1:00
Oct. 26	at Los Angeles Rams	1:00
Nov. 2	at New England	1:00
Nov. 9	**New York Jets**	1:00
Nov. 16	**Chicago**	1:00
Nov. 23	at San Francisco	1:00
Nov. 30	at Miami	1:00
Dec. 7	**Indianapolis**	1:00
Dec. 14	**New Orleans**	1:00
Dec. 21	at Detroit	1:00

FALCONS COACHING HISTORY

(112-177-4)

1966-68	Norb Hecker*	4-26-1
1968-74	Norm Van Brocklin**	37-49-3
1974-76	Marion Campbell***	6-19-0
1976	Pat Peppler	3-6-0
1977-82	Leeman Bennett	47-44-0
1983-85	Dan Henning	15-33-0

*Released after three games in 1968
**Released after eight games in 1974
***Released after five games in 1976

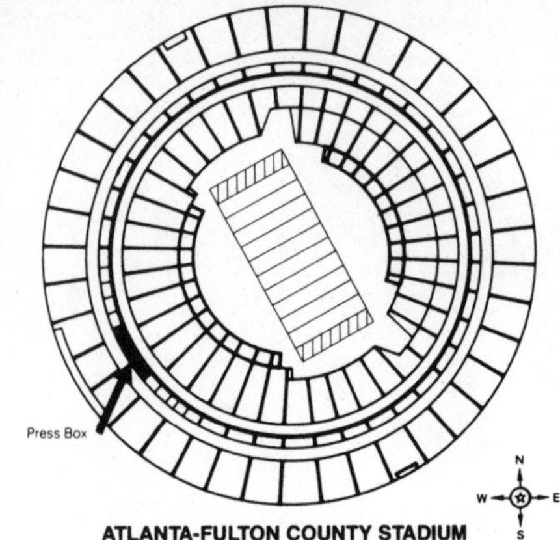

ATLANTA-FULTON COUNTY STADIUM

RECORD HOLDERS

Individual Records—Career

Category	Name	Performance
Rushing (Yds.)	William Andrews, 1979-1983	5,772
Passing (Yds.)	Steve Bartkowski, 1975-1985	23,468
Passing (TDs)	Steve Bartkowski, 1975-1985	154
Receiving (No.)	Alfred Jenkins, 1975-1983	359
Receiving (Yds.)	Alfred Jenkins, 1975-1983	6,257
Interceptions	Rolland Lawrence, 1973-1981	39
Punting (Avg.)	Billy Lothridge, 1966-1971	41.3
Punt Return (Avg.)	Al Dodd, 1973-74	11.8
Kickoff Return (Avg.)	Ron Smith, 1966-67	24.3
Field Goals	Mick Luckhurst, 1981-85	92
Touchdowns (Tot.)	Alfred Jenkins, 1975-1983	40
	William Andrews, 1979-1983	40
Points	Mick Luckhurst, 1981-85	451

Individual Records—Single Season

Category	Name	Performance
Rushing (Yds.)	Gerald Riggs, 1985	1,719
Passing (Yds.)	Steve Bartkowski, 1981	3,830
Passing (TDs)	Steve Bartkowski, 1980	31
Receiving (No.)	William Andrews, 1981	81
Receiving (Yds.)	Alfred Jenkins, 1981	1,358
Interceptions	Rolland Lawrence, 1975	9
Punting (Avg.)	Billy Lothridge, 1968	44.3
Punt Return (Avg.)	Gerald Tinker, 1974	13.9
Kickoff Return (Avg.)	Dennis Pearson, 1978	26.7
Field Goals	Nick Mike-Mayer, 1973	26
Touchdowns (Tot.)	Alfred Jenkins, 1981	13
	Gerald Riggs, 1984	13
Points	Mick Luckhurst, 1981	114

Individual Records—Single Game

Category	Name	Performance
Rushing (Yds.)	Gerald Riggs, 9-2-84	202
Passing (Yds.)	Steve Bartkowski, 11-15-81	416
Passing (TDs)	Randy Johnson, 11-16-69	4
	Steve Bartkowski, 10-19-80	4
	Steve Bartkowski, 10-18-81	4
Receiving (No.)	William Andrews, 11-15-81	15
Receiving (Yds.)	Alfred Jackson, 12-2-84	193
Interceptions	Many times	2
	Last time by Bobby Butler, 9-2-84	
Field Goals	Nick Mike-Mayer, 11-4-73	5
	Tim Mazzetti, 10-30-78	5
Touchdowns (Tot.)	Many times	3
	Last time by Gerald Riggs, 11-17-85	
Points	Many times	18
	Last time by Gerald Riggs, 11-17-85	

1985 TEAM STATISTICS

	Atlanta	Opp.
Total First Downs	296	329
Rushing	149	112
Passing	132	181
Penalty	15	36
Third Down: Made/Att.	86/236	100/217
Fourth Down: Made/Att.	12/24	9/16
Total Net Yards	4960	5850
Avg. Per Game	310.0	365.6
Total Plays	1091	1014
Avg. Per Play	4.5	5.8
Net Yards Rushing	2466	2052
Avg. Per Game	154.1	128.3
Total Rushes	560	437
Net Yards Passing	2494	3798
Avg. Per Game	155.9	237.4
Tackled/Yards Lost	69/531	42/331
Gross Yards	3025	4129
Att./Completions	462/254	535/289
Completion Pct.	55.0	54.0
Had Intercepted	20	22
Punts/Avg.	89/42.2	69/42.0
Net Punting Avg.	36.0	35.6
Penalties/Yards Lost	126/1149	97/738
Fumbles/Ball Lost	23/10	18/12
Touchdowns	30	57
Rushing	14	24
Passing	13	32
Returns	3	1
Avg. Time of Possession	33:11	26:49

1985 TEAM RECORD

Preseason (2-2)

Date	Atlanta		Opponents
8/10	14	*Washington	17
8/17	23	Tampa Bay	17
8/24	24	Green Bay	28
8/30	19	*Miami	17
	80		79

Regular Season (4-12)

Date	Atlanta		Opp.	Att.
9/8	27	*Detroit	28	37,785
9/15	16	San Francisco	35	58,923
9/22	28	*Denver	44	37,903
9/29	6	L.A. Rams	17	49,870
10/6	17	*San Francisco	38	44,740
10/13	26	Seattle	30	60,430
10/20	31	*New Orleans	24	44,784
10/27	10	Dallas	24	57,941
11/3	10	*Washington	44	42,209
11/10	17	Philadelphia (OT)	23	63,694
11/17	30	*L.A. Rams	14	29,960
11/24	0	Chicago	36	61,769
12/1	24	*L.A. Raiders	34	20,585
12/8	10	Kansas City	38	18,199
12/15	14	*Minnesota	13	14,167
12/22	16	New Orleans	10	37,717

*Home Game (OT) Overtime

Score by Periods

Atlanta	68	90	33	91	0	—	282
Opponents	45	153	89	159	6	—	452

Attendance

Home 272,133 Away 408,543 Total 680,676
Single game home record, 59,257 (10-30-77)
Single season home record, 442,457 (1980)

1985 INDIVIDUAL STATISTICS

Rushing	Att.	Yds.	Avg.	LG	TD
Riggs	397	1719	4.3	50	10
Archer	70	347	5.0	29t	2
J. Washington	52	210	4.0	14	1
Austin	20	110	5.5	17	0
Pridemore	1	48	48.0	48	0
Holly	3	36	12.0	20t	1
Bartkowski	5	9	1.8	5	0
Whisenhunt	1	3	3.0	3	0
Bailey	1	-3	-3.0	-3	0
Donnelly	2	-5	-2.5	0	0
B. Johnson	8	-8	-1.0	6	0
Falcons	560	2466	4.4	50	14
Opponents	437	2052	4.7	66t	24

Passing	Att.	Comp.	Pct.	Yds.	TD	Int.	Tkld.	Rate
Archer	312	161	51.6	1992	7	17	43/312	56.5
Bartkowski	111	69	62.2	738	5	1	18/158	92.8
Holly	39	24	61.5	295	1	2	8/61	72.1
Falcons	462	254	55.0	3025	13	20	69/531	66.5
Opponents	535	289	54.0	4129	32	22	42/331	82.1

Receiving	No.	Yds.	Avg.	LG	TD
B. Johnson	62	830	13.4	62t	5
J. Washington	37	328	8.9	34	1
Cox	33	454	13.8	62t	2
Riggs	33	267	8.1	44	0
Bailey	30	364	12.1	31	0
Brown	24	412	17.2	48	2
Allen	14	207	14.8	37t	2
C. Benson	10	37	3.7	6	0
Matthews	7	57	8.1	15	1
Whisenhunt	3	48	16.0	29	0
Austin	1	21	21.0	21	0
Falcons	254	3025	11.9	62t	13
Opponents	289	4129	14.3	99t	32

Interceptions	No.	Yds.	Avg.	LG	TD
Butler	5	-4	-0.8	0	0
Case	4	78	19.5	47	0
Cason	3	30	10.0	22	0
Pridemore	2	45	22.5	36	0
Rade	2	42	21.0	38t	1
Greene	2	27	13.5	27	0
Frye	1	20	20.0	20	0
Britt	1	8	8.0	8	0
Pitts	1	1	1.0	1	0
Curry	1	0	0.0	0	0
Falcons	22	247	11.2	47	1
Opponents	20	172	8.6	32	0

Punting	No.	Yds.	Avg.	In 20	LG
Donnelly	59	2574	43.6	18	68
Giacomarro	29	1157	39.9	1	52
Luckhurst	1	26	26.0	1	26
Falcons	89	3757	42.2	20	68
Opponents	69	2899	42.0	10	75

Punt Returns	No.	FC	Yds.	Avg.	LG	TD
Allen	21	8	141	6.7	23	0
B. Johnson	10	0	82	8.2	18	0
Falcons	31	8	223	7.2	23	0
Opponents	52	10	417	8.0	32	0

Kickoff Returns	No.	Yds.	Avg.	LG	TD
Austin	39	838	21.5	94t	1
Wagoner	13	262	20.2	34	0
Allen	8	140	17.5	26	0
Stamps	4	89	22.3	32	0
Whisenhunt	4	33	8.3	14	0
K. Johnson	1	20	20.0	20	0
Matthews	1	11	11.0	11	0
Tyrrell	1	13	13.0	13	0
R. Washington	1	0	0.0	0	0
Falcons	72	1406	19.5	94t	1
Opponents	62	1135	18.3	37	0

Scoring	TD R	TD P	TD Rt	PAT	FG	Saf	TP
Luckhurst	0	0	0	29/29	24/31	0	101
Riggs	10	0	0	0/0	0/0	0	60
B. Johnson	0	5	0	0/0	0/0	0	30
Allen	0	2	0	0/0	0/0	0	12
Archer	2	0	0	0/0	0/0	0	12
Brown	0	2	0	0/0	0/0	0	12
Cox	0	2	0	0/0	0/0	0	12
J. Washington	1	1	0	0/0	0/0	0	12
Austin	0	0	1	0/0	0/0	0	6
Gann	0	0	1	0/0	0/0	0	6
Holly	1	0	0	0/0	0/0	0	6
Matthews	0	1	0	0/0	0/0	0	6
Rade	0	0	1	0/0	0/0	0	6
Bryan	0	0	0	1/1	0/0	0	1
Falcons	14	13	3	30/30	24/31	0	282
Opponents	24	32	1	55/56	17/23	2	452

FIRST-ROUND SELECTIONS

(If club had no first-round selection, first player drafted is listed with round in parentheses.)

Year	Player, College, Position
1966	Tommy Nobis, Texas, LB
	Randy Johnson, Texas A&I, QB
1967	Leo Carroll, San Diego State, DE (2)
1968	Claude Humphrey, Tennessee State, DE
1969	George Kunz, Notre Dame, T
1970	John Small, Citadel, LB
1971	Joe Profit, Northeast Louisiana, RB
1972	Clarence Ellis, Notre Dame, DB
1973	Greg Marx, Notre Dame, DT (2)
1974	Gerald Tinker, Kent State, WR (2)
1975	Steve Bartkowski, California, QB
1976	Bubba Bean, Texas A&M, RB
1977	Warren Bryant, Kentucky, T
	Wilson Faumuina, San Jose State, DT
1978	Mike Kenn, Michigan, T
1979	Don Smith, Miami, DE
1980	Junior Miller, Nebraska, TE
1981	Bobby Butler, Florida State, DB
1982	Gerald Riggs, Arizona State, RB
1983	Mike Pitts, Alabama, DE
1984	Rick Bryan, Oklahoma, DT
1985	Bill Fralic, Pittsburgh, T
1986	Tony Casillas, Oklahoma, NT
	Tim Green, Syracuse, LB

ATLANTA FALCONS 1986 VETERAN ROSTER

No.	Name	Pos.	Ht.	Wt.	Birth-date	NFL Exp.	College	Hometown	How Acq.	'85 Games/ Starts
85	Allen, Anthony	WR	5-11	182	6/29/59	2	Washington	Seattle, Wash.	D6-'83	16/2
31	Andrews, William	RB	6-0	213	12/25/55	6	Auburn	Thomasville, Ga.	D3b-'79	0*
16	†Archer, Dave	QB	6-2	203	2/15/62	3	Iowa State	Soda Springs, Idaho	FA-'84	16/11
39	Austin, Cliff	RB	6-0	207	3/2/60	4	Clemson	Avondale, Ga.	FA-'84	14/0
82	Bailey, Stacey	WR	6-0	157	2/10/60	5	San Jose State	San Rafael, Calif.	D3-'82	15/13
69	Benish, Dan	DT	6-5	280	11/21/61	4	Clemson	Youngstown, Ohio	FA-'83	16/16
87	Benson, Cliff	TE	6-4	238	8/28/61	3	Purdue	Chicago, Ill.	D5-'84	16/14
53	Benson, Thomas	LB	6-2	235	9/6/61	3	Oklahoma	Ardmore, Okla.	D2b-'84	16/1
26	Britt, James	CB	6-0	185	9/12/60	3	Louisiana State	Minden, La.	D2-'83	2/2
89	Brown, Charlie	WR	5-10	184	10/29/58	5	South Carolina State	St. John's Island, S.C.	T(Wash)-'85	13/9
77	Bryan, Rick	DE	6-4	270	3/20/62	3	Oklahoma	Coweta, Okla.	D1-'84	16/16
23	Butler, Bobby	CB	5-11	170	5/28/59	6	Florida State	Delray Beach, Fla.	D1-'81	16/16
25	Case, Scott	S	6-0	178	5/17/62	3	Oklahoma	Edmond, Okla.	D2a-'84	14/13
20	Cason, Wendell	CB	5-11	183	1/22/63	2	Oregon	Carson, Calif.	FA-'85	14/14
88	Cox, Arthur	TE	6-2	255	2/5/61	4	Texas Southern	Plant City, Fla.	FA-'83	16/16
30	Croudip, David	CB-S	5-8	180	1/25/59	3	San Diego State	Compton, Calif.	FA-'85	13/0*
50	Curry, Buddy	LB	6-4	222	6/4/58	7	North Carolina	Danville, Va.	D2-'80	16/14
3	Donnelly, Rick	P	6-0	184	5/17/62	2	Wyoming	Long Island, N.Y.	FA-'85	11/0
79	Fralic, Bill	G-T	6-5	280	10/31/62	2	Pittsburgh	Penn Hills, Pa.	D1-'85	15/14
58	†Frye, David	LB	6-2	218	6/21/61	4	Purdue	Cincinnati, Ohio	FA-'83	14/5
76	Gann, Mike	DE	6-5	265	10/19/63	2	Notre Dame	Lakewood, Colo.	D2-'85	16/16
1	Giacomarro, Ralph	P	6-1	194	1/17/61	4	Penn State	Saddle Brook, N.J.	FA-'85	5/0
70	Goff, Willard	DT	6-3	265	10/17/61	2	West Texas State	Springfield, Colo.	FA-'85	7/0
33	†Greene, Tiger	CB	5-10	184	2/15/62	2	Western Carolina	Flat Rock, N.C.	FA-'85	10/7
8	Holly, Bob	QB	6-2	190	6/1/60	5	Princeton	Clifton, N.J.	FA-'85	4/0
71	Howe, Glen	T	6-6	292	10/18/61	2	Southern Mississippi	New Albany, Miss.	FA-'85	9/1*
51	Jackson, Jeff	LB	6-1	228	10/9/61	3	Auburn	Griffin, Ga.	D8-'84	11/1
81	Johnson, Billy	WR-KR	5-9	170	1/27/52	11	Widener	Chichester, Pa.	FA-'82	16/8
37	Johnson, Kenny	S	5-11	167	1/7/58	7	Mississippi State	Moss Point, Miss.	D5a-'80	5/3
78	Kenn, Mike	T	6-7	277	2/9/56	9	Michigan	Evanston, Ill.	D1-'78	11/11
63	†Kiewel, Jeff	G	6-4	265	9/27/60	2	Arizona	Tucson, Ariz.	FA-'85	16/9
80	†Landrum, Mike	TE	6-2	231	11/6/61	2	Southern Mississippi	Columbia, Miss.	FA-'84	0*
18	Luckhurst, Mick	K	6-2	183	3/31/58	6	California	Redbourn, England	FA-'81	16/0
52	Malancon, Rydell	LB	6-1	227	1/20/62	2	Louisiana State	Vacherie, La.	D4-'84	0*
49	†Matthews, Allama	TE	6-2	230	3/24/61	4	Vanderbilt	Jacksonville, Fla.	D12-'83	15/2
62	Miller, Brett	T	6-7	290	10/2/58	4	Iowa	Glendale, Calif.	D5-'83	12/12
64	Pellegrini, Joe	G-C	6-4	264	4/8/57	5	Harvard	Braintree, Mass.	FA-'84	5/2
74	Pitts, Mike	DT	6-5	277	9/25/60	4	Alabama	Baltimore, Md.	D1-'83	16/16
27	†Pridemore, Tom	S	5-11	186	4/29/56	9	West Virginia	Andstead, W. Va.	D9-'78	16/5
72	Provence, Andrew	DE	6-3	267	3/8/61	4	South Carolina	Savannah, Ga.	D3-'83	16/0
59	Rade, John	LB	6-1	220	8/31/60	4	Boise State	Sierra Vista, Ariz.	D8-'83	16/14
55	Radloff, Wayne	C-G	6-5	263	5/17/61	2	Georgia	Winter Park, Fla.	FA-'85	16/0
56	Richardson, Al	LB	6-3	222	9/23/57	7	Georgia Tech	Miami, Fla.	D8-'80	16/11
42	Riggs, Gerald	RB	6-1	232	11/6/60	5	Arizona State	Las Vegas, Nev.	D1-'82	16/16
67	Sanders, Eric	T	6-7	280	10/22/58	6	Nevada-Reno	Reno, Nev.	D5-'81	16/7
14	t-Schonert, Turk	QB	6-1	190	1/15/57	7	Stanford	Placentia, Calif.	T(Cin)-'86	7/0
61	Scully, John	G	6-6	265	8/2/58	6	Notre Dame	Huntington, N.Y.	D4-'81	8/8
29	Stamps, Sylvester	RB	5-7	166	2/24/61	2	Jackson State	Vicksburg, Miss.	FA-'85	2/0
96	†Taylor, Johnny	LB	6-4	235	6/21/60	2	Hawaii	Seattle, Wash.	FA-'84	15/5
66	Thomas, Chuck	C-G	6-3	277	12/24/60	2	Oklahoma	Houston, Tex.	FA-'85	4/0
22	Thomas, Sean	CB-S	5-11	190	4/12/62	2	Texas Christian	Sacramento, Calif.	FA-'85	6/0
32	Tyrrell, Tim	RB	6-1	201	2/19/61	3	Northern Illinois	Hoffman Estates, Ill.	FA-'84	16/0
57	Van Note, Jeff	C	6-2	264	2/7/46	18	Kentucky	Bardstown, Ky.	D11-'69	16/16
36	Wagoner, Dan	CB-S	5-10	180	12/12/59	4	Kansas	High Point, N.C.	FA-'85	14/0
24	Washington, Joe	RB	5-10	179	9/24/53	11	Oklahoma	Port Arthur, Tex.	T(Wash)-'85	16/0
92	Washington, Ronnie	LB	6-1	236	7/29/63	2	Northeast Louisiana	Richwood, La.	D8b-'85	16/1
45	†Whisenhunt, Ken	TE	6-2	233	2/28/62	2	Georgia Tech	Augusta, Ga.	D12-'85	16/0
51	t-Wilkes, Reggie	LB	6-4	242	5/27/56	9	Georgia Tech	Atlanta, Ga.	T(Phil)-'86	16/16
54	t-Williams, Joel	LB	6-1	227	12/13/56	8	Wisconsin-La Crosse	Miami, Fla.	T(Phil)-'86	7/0

* Andrews, Landrum, and Malancon missed '85 season due to injury; Croudip played 2 games with San Diego, 11 with Atlanta in '85; Howe played 4 games with Pittsburgh, 5 with Atlanta in '85.

†Option playout; subject to developments.

t-Falcons traded for Schonert (Cincinnati), Wilkes (Philadelphia), and Williams (Philadelphia).

Also played with Falcons in '85—QB Steve Bartkowski (5 games), DT Roy Harris (5), DE Lawrence Pillers (9), CB Reggie Pleasant (3).

COACHING STAFF

Head Coach, Dan Henning

Pro Career: Begins fourth season as Falcons head coach. Came from the Washington Redskins where he was assistant head coach under Joe Gibbs, helping the Redskins to a 20-9 record in 1981 and 1982 and a Super Bowl victory in 1983. Also was an assistant with the Houston Oilers 1972, New York Jets 1976-78, and Miami Dolphins 1979-80. Played quarterback for the San Diego Chargers 1964-67. Career record: 15-33.

Background: Played quarterback for William & Mary 1960-63. Began college coaching career with Florida State 1968-70, 1974, Virginia Tech 1971, 1973.

Personal: Born June 21, 1942, Bronx, N.Y. Dan and his wife, Sandy, have five children—Mary K., Patty, Danny, Terry, and Mike. They live in Roswell, Ga.

Assistant Coaches

Larry Beightol, offensive line; born November 21, 1942, Pittsburgh, Pa., lives in Atlanta. Guard-linebacker Catawba College 1965-67. No pro playing experience. College coach: William & Mary 1968-71, North Carolina State 1972-75, Auburn 1976, Arkansas 1977-78, Louisiana Tech 1979, Missouri 1980-84. Pro coach: Joined Falcons in 1985.

Tommy Brasher, defensive line; born December 30, 1940, El Dorado, Ark., lives in Dunwoody, Ga. Linebacker Arkansas 1961-63. No pro playing experience. College coach: Arkansas 1970, Virginia Tech 1971-73, Northeast Louisiana 1974, 1976, Southern Methodist 1977-81. Pro coach: Shreveport Steamer (WFL) 1975, New England Patriots 1982-84, Philadelphia Eagles 1985, first year with Falcons.

Fred Bruney, defensive backfield; born December 30, 1931, Martins Ferry, Ohio, lives in Atlanta. Back Ohio State 1949-52. Pro defensive back San Francisco 49ers 1953-56, Pittsburgh Steelers 1957, Washington Redskins 1958, Boston Patriots 1960-62. College coach: Ohio State 1959. Pro coach: Boston Patriots 1963, Philadelphia Eagles 1964-68, 1977-85, Atlanta Falcons 1969-76, rejoined Falcons in 1986.

Marion Campbell, defensive coordinator; born May 25, 1929, Chester, S.C., lives in Atlanta. Tackle Georgia 1948-51. Pro defensive tackle San Francisco 49ers 1954-55, Philadelphia Eagles 1956-61. Pro coach: Boston Patriots 1962-63, Minnesota Vikings 1964-66, Los Angeles Rams 1967-68, Atlanta Falcons 1969-76 (head coach 1975-76), Philadelphia Eagles 1977-85 (head coach 1983-85), rejoined Falcons in 1986.

Chuck Clausen, linebackers; born June 23, 1940, Anamosa, Iowa, lives in Roswell, Ga. Defensive lineman New Mexico 1961-63. No pro playing experience. College coach: William & Mary 1969-70, Ohio State 1971-75. Pro coach: Philadelphia Eagles 1976-85, first year with Falcons.

George Dostal, strength and conditioning; born October 25, 1934, Cleveland, Ohio, lives in Lawrenceville, Ga. Fullback-linebacker Kent State 1964-67. No pro playing experience. College coach: Clemson 1977-82. Pro coach: Joined Falcons in 1983.

Sam Elliott, running backs; born August 3, 1946, Huntington, W. Va., lives in Alpharetta, Ga. Quarterback-defensive back Ohio State 1965-67. No pro playing experience. College coach: Ohio State 1968, Florida State 1969-70, 1974, Kent State 1971-73. Pro coach: Joined Falcons in 1983.

Ted Fritsch, special teams; born August 26, 1950, Green Bay, Wis., lives in Marietta, Ga. Center St. Norbert 1969-71. Pro center Atlanta Falcons 1972-75, Washington Redskins 1976-79. Pro coach: Joined Falcons in 1983.

Bob Harrison, receivers; born September 9, 1941, Cleveland, Ohio, lives in Roswell, Ga. End Kent State 1961-64. No pro playing experience. College coach: Kent State 1969-70, Iowa 1971-73, Cornell 1974, North Carolina State 1975-76, Tennessee 1977-82. Pro coach: Joined Falcons in 1983.

ATLANTA FALCONS 1986 FIRST-YEAR ROSTER

Name	Pos.	Ht.	Wt.	Birth-date	College	Hometown	How Acq.
Adams, David	T	6-5	266	4/24/64	Duke	Stone Mountain, Ga.	FA
Allen, Earl	CB	5-9	183	10/24/61	Houston	Houston, Tex.	FA
Ayres, John (1)	CB	5-11	192	9/6/63	Illinois	Oakland, Calif.	D11-'85
Baker, Tony	RB	5-10	175	6/11/64	East Carolina	High Point, N.C.	D10
Baroncelli, Andy	C	6-3	256	11/5/63	San Diego State	Chevy Chase, Md.	FA
Branaman, Lance	NT	6-3	270	7/15/64	Wisconsin	Oak Creek, Wis.	FA
Busch, Michael	QB	6-3	218	2/8/63	South Dakota State	Huron, S.D.	FA
Butler, Jerry	RB	5-11	193	12/7/62	East Tennessee State	Decatur, Ga.	FA
Caravello, Joe	NT	6-2	266	6/6/63	Tulane	Ann Arbor, Mich.	FA
Casillas, Tony	NT	6-3	280	10/26/63	Oklahoma	Norman, Okla.	D1a
Clark, Bret	S	6-3	195	2/24/61	Nebraska	Neb. City, Neb.	T(Raiders)-'86
Dixon, Floyd	WR	5-9	170	4/9/64	Stephen F. Austin	Beaumont, Tex.	D6a
Dukes, Jamie	G	6-1	280	6/14/64	Florida State	Orlando, Fla.	FA
Fulton, Charles	CB-S	6-1	179	10/14/63	Northwest Louisiana	Bunkie, La.	FA
Green, Tim	LB	6-2	249	12/16/64	Syracuse	Liverpool, N.Y.	D1b
Griffin, Steve	WR	6-0	190	12/24/64	Purdue	Miami, Fla.	D12
Hegg, Chris	QB	6-3	201	1/5/64	Northeast Missouri	Hudson, Iowa	D11
Hudgens, Kevin	NT	6-4	266	6/14/64	Idaho State	Caldwell, Idaho	D8
Kniptash, David	T	6-5	287	9/6/63	Missouri	Chesterfield, Mo.	FA
Mangram, Tony	RB	5-10	187	9/22/64	Georgia	Brunswick, Ga.	FA
Martin, Brent (1)	C	6-3	263	6/5/63	Stanford	Madera, Calif.	D10-'85
Massey, Timothy	CB-S	5-11	180	1/22/64	Valdosta State	Woodbine, Ga.	FA
McInnis, Michael (1)	DE	6-6	272	3/22/62	Arkansas-Pine Bluff	Jackson, Miss.	SD2-'84
Middleton, Ron	TE	6-2	252	7/17/65	Auburn	Atmore, Ala.	FA
Nielson, James	NT	6-3	287	8/24/63	Idaho State	Pocatello, Idaho	FA
Price, Arthur (1)	LB	6-3	227	5/17/62	Wisconsin	Newport News, Va.	FA
Sawyer, Bob	P	6-1	200	11/18/62	Baylor	Joshua, Tex.	FA
Sharp, Dan (1)	TE	6-2	235	2/5/62	Texas Christian	Ft. Worth, Tex.	FA
Sharron, Scott	TE	6-2	232	12/5/63	Wisconsin	Madison, Wis.	FA
Shepherd, Darryl	WR	6-4	190	11/11/63	Pittsburgh	Pittsburgh, Pa.	FA
Smith, Jeffrey	TE	6-3	240	12/28/62	Tennessee	Knoxville, Tenn.	FA
Starks, Kevin	TE	6-4	224	9/4/63	Minnesota	Robbins, Ill.	D9
Thompson, James	CB	5-10	170	7/1/60	E. Cent. Oklahoma	Marlin, Tex.	FA
Tweet, Rodney	WR	6-2	189	2/20/64	South Dakota	Austin, Minn.	FA
Upchurch, Andy	C	6-2	257	9/11/62	Arkansas	Ft. Smith, Ark.	FA
Wilkes, Del	G	6-3	275	12/21/61	South Carolina	Columbia, S.C.	FA
Williams, Keith	RB	5-10	173	9/30/64	Southwest Missouri	Springfield, Mo.	D6b

The term NFL Rookie is defined as a player who is in his first season of professional football and has not been on the roster of another professional football team for any regular season or postseason games. A Rookie is designated by an "R" on NFL rosters. Players who have been active in another professional football league or players who have NFL experience, including either preseason training camp or being on an active roster for fewer than three regular season or postseason games, are termed NFL First-Year Players. An NFL First-Year Player is designated by a "1" on NFL rosters. Thereafter, a player on an NFL active roster for at least three regular season or postseason games is credited with an additional year of NFL playing experience.

NOTES

Bobby Jackson, tight ends-H-Backs; born February 16, 1940, Forsyth, Ga., lives in Roswell, Ga. Linebacker-running back Samford 1959-62. No pro playing experience. College coach: Florida State 1965-69, Kansas State 1970-74, Louisville 1975-76, Tennessee 1977-82. Pro coach: Joined Falcons in 1983.

Joe Madden, defensive assistant-research and development; born March 5, 1935, Washington, D.C., lives in Atlanta. Back Maryland 1954-56. No pro playing experience. College coach: Mississippi State 1962, Morehead State 1963, Wake Forest 1964-67, Iowa State 1968-71, Kansas State 1972, Pittsburgh 1973-76, Tennessee 1977-79. Pro coach: Detroit Lions 1980-84, joined Falcons in 1985.

CHICAGO BEARS

National Football Conference
Central Division

Team Colors: Navy Blue, Orange, and White

Corporate Headquarters:
Halas Hall
250 North Washington
Lake Forest, Illinois 60045
Telephone: (312) 295-6600

Club Officials

Chairman of the Board: Edward W. McCaskey
President and Chief Executive Officer: Michael B. McCaskey
Vice President and General Manager, Treasurer: Jerome R. Vainisi
Vice President: Charles A. Brizzolara
Secretary: Virginia H. McCaskey
Dir., Player Personnel: Bill Tobin
Dir., Community Involvement: Pat McCaskey
Dir., Marketing/Communications: Bill McGrane
Dir., Media Relations: Ken Valdiserri
Media Relations Assistant: Bryan Harlan
Ticket Manager: Gary Christenson
Trainer: Fred Caito
Assistant Trainer: Brian McCaskey
Strength Coordinator: Clyde Emrich
Equipment Manager: Ray Earley
Assistant Equipment Manager: Gary Haeger
Scouts: Jim Parmer, Rod Graves, Don King

Stadium: Soldier Field • **Capacity:** 65,790
425 McFetridge Place
Chicago, Illinois 60605

Playing Surface: AstroTurf

Training Camp: Wisconsin-Platteville
Platteville, Wisconsin 53818

1986 SCHEDULE

Preseason

Aug. 3	vs. Dallas at London, Eng.	6:00
Aug. 9	at Pittsburgh	7:00
Aug. 16	**Indianapolis**	6:00
Aug. 23	**St. Louis**	8:00
Aug. 30	vs. Buffalo at South Bend, Ind.	1:30

Regular Season

Sept. 7	**Cleveland**	12:00
Sept. 14	**Philadelphia**	12:00
Sept. 22	at Green Bay (Monday)	8:00
Sept. 28	at Cincinnati	1:00
Oct. 5	**Minnesota**	12:00
Oct. 12	at Houston	12:00
Oct. 19	at Minnesota	12:00
Oct. 26	**Detroit**	12:00
Nov. 3	**L.A. Rams** (Monday)	8:00
Nov. 9	at Tampa Bay	1:00
Nov. 16	at Atlanta	1:00
Nov. 23	**Green Bay**	12:00
Nov. 30	**Pittsburgh**	12:00
Dec. 7	**Tampa Bay**	12:00
Dec. 15	at Detroit (Monday)	9:00
Dec. 21	at Dallas	3:00

BEARS COACHING HISTORY

Chicago Staleys 1921
(507-329-42)

1920-29	George Halas	84-31-19
1930-32	Ralph Jones	24-10-7
1933-42	George Halas*	89-24-4
1942-45	Hunk Anderson-Luke Johnsos**	23-12-2
1946-55	George Halas	76-43-2
1956-57	John (Paddy) Driscoll	14-10-1
1958-67	George Halas	76-53-6
1968-71	Jim Dooley	20-36-0
1972-74	Abe Gibron	11-30-1
1975-77	Jack Pardee	20-23-0
1978-81	Neill Armstrong	30-35-0
1982-85	Mike Ditka	40-22-0

*Retired November 1 to re-enter Navy
**Co-coaches

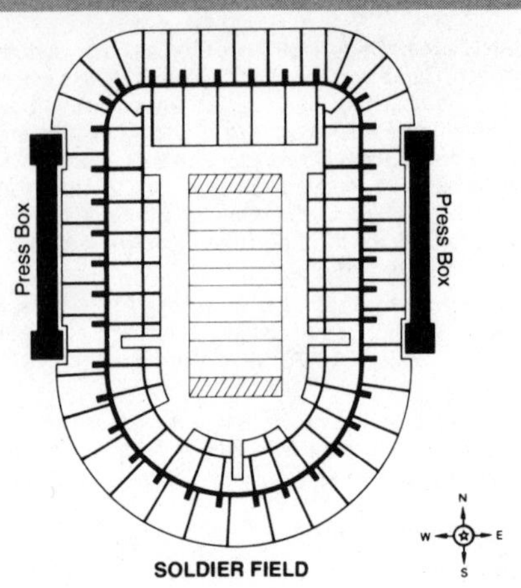

SOLDIER FIELD

RECORD HOLDERS

Individual Records—Career

Category	Name	Performance
Rushing (Yds.)	Walter Payton, 1975-1985	14,860
Passing (Yds.)	Sid Luckman, 1939-1950	14,686
Passing (TDs)	Sid Luckman, 1939-1950	137
Receiving (No.)	Walter Payton, 1975-1985	422
Receiving (Yds.)	Walter Payton, 1975-1985	5,099
Interceptions	Richie Petitbon, 1959-1968	37
Punting (Avg.)	George Gulyanics, 1947-1952	44.5
Punt Return (Avg.)	Ray (Scooter) McLean, 1940-47	14.8
Kickoff Return (Avg.)	Gale Sayers, 1965-1971	30.6
Field Goals	Bob Thomas, 1975-1984	128
Touchdowns (Tot.)	Walter Payton, 1975-1985	109
Points	Walter Payton, 1975-1985	654

Individual Records—Single Season

Category	Name	Performance
Rushing (Yds.)	Walter Payton, 1977	1,852
Passing (Yds.)	Bill Wade, 1962	3,172
Passing (TDs)	Sid Luckman, 1943	28
Receiving (No.)	Johnny Morris, 1964	93
Receiving (Yds.)	Johnny Morris, 1964	1,200
Interceptions	Roosevelt Taylor, 1963	9
Punting (Avg.)	Bobby Joe Green, 1963	46.4
Punt Return (Avg.)	Harry Clark, 1943	15.8
Kickoff Return (Avg.)	Gale Sayers, 1967	37.7
Field Goals	Kevin Butler, 1985	31
Touchdowns (Tot.)	Gale Sayers, 1965	22
Points	Kevin Butler, 1985	144

Individual Records—Single Game

Category	Name	Performance
Rushing (Yds.)	Walter Payton, 11-20-77	275
Passing (Yds.)	Johnny Lujack, 12-11-49	468
Passing (TDs)	Sid Luckman, 11-14-43	7
Receiving (No.)	Jim Keane, 10-23-49	14
Receiving (Yds.)	Harlon Hill, 10-31-54	214
Interceptions	Many times	3
	Last time by Ross Brupbacher, 12-12-76	
Field Goals	Roger LeClerc, 12-3-61	5
	Mac Percival, 10-20-68	5
Touchdowns (Tot.)	Gale Sayers, 12-12-65	6
Points	Gale Sayers, 12-12-65	36

1985 TEAM STATISTICS

	Chicago	Opp.
Total First Downs	343	236
Rushing	176	74
Passing	145	141
Penalty	22	21
Third Down: Made/Att.	84/218	61/206
Fourth Down: Made/Att.	5/13	6/16
Total Net Yards	5837	4135
Avg. Per Game	364.8	258.4
Total Plays	1085	945
Avg. Per Play	5.4	4.4
Net Yards Rushing	2761	1319
Avg. Per Game	172.6	82.4
Total Rushes	610	359
Net Yards Passing	3076	2816
Avg. Per Game	192.3	176.0
Tackled/Yards Lost	43/227	64/483
Gross Yards	3303	3299
Att./Completions	432/237	522/249
Completion Pct.	54.9	47.7
Had Intercepted	16	34
Punts/Avg.	69/41.6	90/40.4
Net Punting Avg.	34.6	33.5
Penalties/Yards Lost	104/912	118/944
Fumbles/Ball Lost	24/15	30/20
Touchdowns	51	23
Rushing	27	6
Passing	17	16
Returns	7	1
Avg. Time of Possession	34:33	25:27

1985 TEAM RECORD

Preseason (1-3)

Date	Chicago		Opponents
8/9	3	St. Louis	10
8/17	13	*Indianapolis	24
8/26	13	Dallas	15
8/31	45	*Buffalo	14
	74		63

Regular Season (15-1)

Date	Chicago		Opp.	Att.
9/8	38	*Tampa Bay	28	57,828
9/15	20	*New England	7	60,533
9/19	33	Minnesota	24	61,242
9/29	45	*Washington	10	63,708
10/6	27	Tampa Bay	19	51,795
10/13	26	San Francisco	10	60,523
10/21	23	*Green Bay	7	65,095
10/27	27	*Minnesota	9	63,815
11/3	16	Green Bay	10	56,895
11/10	24	*Detroit	3	53,467
11/17	44	Dallas	0	63,750
11/24	36	*Atlanta	0	61,769
12/2	24	Miami	38	75,594
12/8	17	*Indianapolis	10	59,997
12/14	19	N.Y. Jets	6	74,752
12/22	37	Detroit	17	74,042

Postseason (3-0)

Date	Chicago		Opp.	Att.
1/5/86	21	*N.Y. Giants	0	65,670
1/12/86	24	*L.A. Rams	0	66,030
1/26/86	46	New England	10	73,818

*Home Game

Score by Periods

Chicago	67	144	123	122	0	—	456
Opponents	50	77	34	37	0	—	198

Attendance

Home 486,212 Away 518,593 Total 1,004,805
Single game home record, 80,259 (11-24-66)
Single season home record, 486,212 (1985)

1985 INDIVIDUAL STATISTICS

Rushing	Att.	Yds.	Avg.	LG	TD
Payton	324	1551	4.8	40t	9
Suhey	115	471	4.1	17	1
McMahon	47	252	5.4	19	3
Gentry	30	160	5.3	21	2
Thomas	31	125	4.0	17	4
Sanders	25	104	4.2	28	1
Fuller	24	77	3.2	13	5
Gault	5	18	3.6	11	0
Perry	5	7	1.4	2	2
Tomczak	2	3	1.5	3	0
McKinnon	1	0	0.0	0	0
Margerum	1	−7	−7.0	−7	0
Bears	610	2761	4.5	40t	27
Opponents	359	1319	3.7	37	6

Passing	Att.	Comp.	Pct.	Yds.	TD	Int.	Tkld.	Rate
McMahon	313	178	56.9	2392	15	11	26/125	82.6
Fuller	107	53	49.5	777	1	5	17/102	57.3
Tomczak	6	2	33.3	33	0	0	0/0	52.8
Payton	5	3	60.0	96	1	0	0/0	143.8
Buford	1	1	100.0	5	0	0	0/0	87.5
Bears	432	237	54.9	3303	17	16	43/227	77.3
Opponents	522	249	47.7	3299	16	34	64/483	51.2

Receiving	No.	Yds.	Avg.	LG	TD
Payton	49	483	9.9	65	2
Moorehead	35	481	13.7	25	1
Gault	33	704	21.3	70t	1
Suhey	33	295	8.9	35	1
McKinnon	31	555	17.9	48	7
Wrightman	24	407	17.0	49	1
Margerum	17	190	11.2	20	2
Gentry	5	77	15.4	30	0
Thomas	5	45	9.0	15	0
Maness	1	34	34.0	34	0
McMahon	1	13	13.0	13t	1
Sanders	1	9	9.0	9	0
Anderson	1	6	6.0	6	0
Perry	1	4	4.0	4t	1
Bears	237	3303	13.9	70t	17
Opponents	249	3299	13.2	90t	16

Interceptions	No.	Yds.	Avg.	LG	TD
Frazier	6	119	19.8	33	1
Duerson	5	53	10.6	20	0
Fencik	5	43	8.6	22	0
Richardson	4	174	43.5	90	1
Marshall	4	23	5.8	14	0
Wilson	3	35	11.7	23t	1
Taylor	3	28	9.3	18	0
Dent	2	10	5.0	9	1
Singletary	1	23	23.0	23	0
Rivera	1	4	4.0	4	0
Bears	34	512	15.1	90	4
Opponents	16	99	6.2	43t	1

Punting	No.	Yds.	Avg.	In 20	LG
Buford	68	2870	42.2	18	69
Bears	69	2870	41.6	18	69
Opponents	90	3639	40.4	12	75

Punt Returns	No.	FC	Yds.	Avg.	LG	TD
Taylor	25	8	198	7.9	21	0
Ortego	17	2	158	9.3	23	0
Duerson	6	0	47	7.8	11	0
McKinnon	4	0	44	11.0	17	0
Maness	2	0	9	4.5	5	0
Gentry	0	0	47	—	47	0
Bears	54	10	503	9.3	47	0
Opponents	23	9	203	8.8	29	0

Kickoff Returns	No.	Yds.	Avg.	LG	TD
Gault	22	577	26.2	99t	1
Gentry	18	466	25.9	94t	1
McKinnon	1	16	16.0	16	0
Sanders	1	10	10.0	10	0
Taylor	1	18	18.0	18	0
Marshall	0	2	—	2	0
Bears	43	1089	25.3	99t	2
Opponents	78	1827	23.4	58	0

Scoring	TD R	TD P	TD Rt	PAT	FG	Saf	TP
Butler	0	0	0	51/51	31/37	0	144
Payton	9	2	0	0/0	0/0	0	66
McKinnon	0	7	0	0/0	0/0	0	42
Fuller	5	0	0	0/0	0/0	0	30
McMahon	3	1	0	0/0	0/0	0	24
Thomas	4	0	0	0/0	0/0	0	24
Gentry	2	0	1	0/0	0/0	0	18
Perry	2	1	0	0/0	0/0	0	18
Gault	0	1	1	0/0	0/0	0	12
Margerum	0	2	0	0/0	0/0	0	12
Suhey	1	1	0	0/0	0/0	0	12
Wilson	0	0	1	0/0	0/0	1	8
Dent	0	0	1	0/0	0/0	0	6
Frazier	0	0	1	0/0	0/0	0	6
Moorehead	0	1	0	0/0	0/0	0	6
Richardson	0	0	1	0/0	0/0	0	6
Rivera	0	0	1	0/0	0/0	0	6
Sanders	1	0	0	0/0	0/0	0	6
Wrightman	0	1	0	0/0	0/0	0	6
McMichael	0	0	0	0/0	0/0	1	2
Waechter	0	0	0	0/0	0/0	1	2
Bears	27	17	7	51/51	31/37	3	456
Opponents	6	16	1	22/23	12/19	1	198

FIRST-ROUND SELECTIONS

(If club had no first-round selection, first player drafted is listed with round in parentheses.)

Since 1949

Year	Player, College, Position
1949	Dick Harris, Texas, C
1950	Chuck Hunsinger, Florida, B
	Fred Morrison, Ohio State, B
1951	Bob Williams, Notre Dame, B
	Billy Stone, Bradley, B
	Gene Schroeder, Virginia, E
1952	Jim Dooley, Miami, B
1953	Billy Anderson, Compton (Calif.) JC, B
1954	Stan Wallace, Illinois, B
1955	Ron Drzewiecki, Marquette, B
1956	Menan (Tex) Schriewer, Texas, E
1957	Earl Leggett, Louisiana State, T
1958	Chuck Howley, West Virginia, G
1959	Don Clark, Ohio State, B
1960	Roger Davis, Syracuse, G
1961	Mike Ditka, Pittsburgh, E
1962	Ronnie Bull, Baylor, RB
1963	Dave Behrman, Michigan State, C
1964	Dick Evey, Tennessee, DT
1965	Dick Butkus, Illinois, LB
	Gale Sayers, Kansas, RB
	Steve DeLong, Tennessee, T
1966	George Rice, Louisiana State, DT
1967	Loyd Phillips, Arkansas, DE
1968	Mike Hull, Southern California, RB
1969	Rufus Mayes, Ohio State, T
1970	George Farmer, UCLA, WR (3)
1971	Joe Moore, Missouri, RB
1972	Lionel Antoine, Southern Illinois, T
	Craig Clemons, Iowa, DB
1973	Wally Chambers, Eastern Kentucky, DE
1974	Waymond Bryant, Tennessee State, LB
	Dave Gallagher, Michigan, DT
1975	Walter Payton, Jackson State, RB
1976	Dennis Lick, Wisconsin, T
1977	Ted Albrecht, California, T
1978	Brad Shearer, Texas, DT (3)
1979	Dan Hampton, Arkansas, DT
	Al Harris, Arizona State, DE
1980	Otis Wilson, Louisville, LB
1981	Keith Van Horne, Southern California, T
1982	Jim McMahon, Brigham Young, QB
1983	Jimbo Covert, Pittsburgh, T
	Willie Gault, Tennessee, WR
1984	Wilber Marshall, Florida, LB
1985	William Perry, Clemson, DT
1986	Neal Anderson, Florida, RB

CHICAGO BEARS 1986 VETERAN ROSTER

No.	Name	Pos.	Ht.	Wt.	Birth-date	NFL Exp.	College	Hometown	How Acq.	'85 Games/ Starts
86	Anderson, Brad	WR	6-2	198	1/21/61	3	Arizona	Glendale, Ariz.	D8-'84	14/0
60	Andrews, Tom	C	6-4	267	1/11/62	3	Louisville	Parma, Ohio	D4-'84	14/0
84	Baschnagel, Brian	WR	5-11	193	1/8/54	10	Ohio State	Kingston, N.Y.	D3-'76	0*
25	†Bell, Todd	S	6-1	205	11/28/58	5	Ohio State	Middletown, Ohio	D4-'81	0*
79	Becker, Kurt	G	6-5	270	12/22/58	5	Michigan	Aurora, Ill.	D6-'82	3/3
62	†Bortz, Mark	G	6-6	269	2/12/61	4	Iowa	Pardeeville, Wis.	D8-'83	16/16
8	Buford, Maury	P	6-1	191	2/18/60	5	Texas Tech	Port Arthur, Tex.	T(SD)-'85	16/0
6	Butler, Kevin	K	6-1	204	7/24/62	2	Georgia	Atlanta, Ga.	D4-'85	16/0
54	Cabral, Brian	LB	6-1	227	6/23/56	8	Colorado	Ft. Benning, Ga.	FA-'81	1/0
74	Covert, Jim	T	6-4	271	3/22/60	4	Pittsburgh	Conway, Pa.	D1-'83	15/15
95	Dent, Richard	DE	6-5	263	12/13/60	4	Tennessee State	Atlanta, Ga.	D8-'83	16/16
22	†Duerson, Dave	S	6-1	203	11/28/60	4	Notre Dame	Muncie, Ind.	D3-'83	15/15
88	†Dunsmore, Pat	TE	6-3	237	10/2/59	3	Drake	Duluth, Minn.	D4-'83	0*
45	†Fencik, Gary	S	6-1	196	6/11/54	11	Yale	Chicago, Ill.	FA-'76	16/16
21	†Frazier, Leslie	CB	6-0	187	4/3/59	6	Alcorn State	Columbus, Miss.	FA-'81	16/16
71	Frederick, Andy	T	6-6	265	7/25/54	10	New Mexico	Oak Park, Ill.	T(Clev)-'83	16/1
4	†Fuller, Steve	QB	6-4	195	1/5/57	8	Clemson	Enid, Okla.	T(Rams)-'84	16/5
83	Gault, Willie	WR	6-1	183	9/5/60	4	Tennessee	Griffin, Ga.	D1-'83	16/16
23	Gayle, Shaun	CB	5-11	193	3/8/62	3	Ohio State	Hampton, Va.	D10-'84	16/0
29	Gentry, Dennis	RB	5-8	181	2/10/59	5	Baylor	Lubbock, Tex.	D4-'82	16/0
99	Hampton, Dan	DT	6-5	267	9/19/57	8	Arkansas	Oklahoma City, Okla.	D1-'79	16/15
90	†Harris, Al	LB	6-5	253	12/31/56	7	Arizona State	Bangor, Maine	D1-'79	0*
73	Hartenstine, Mike	DE	6-3	254	7/27/53	12	Penn State	Allentown, Pa.	D2-'75	16/8
63	Hilgenberg, Jay	C	6-3	258	3/21/59	6	Iowa	Iowa City, Iowa	FA-'81	16/16
75	Humphries, Stefan	G	6-3	263	1/20/62	3	Michigan	Broward, Fla.	D3-'84	11/0
98	Keys, Tyrone	DE	6-7	267	10/24/59	4	Mississippi State	Brookhaven, Miss.	T(NYJ)-'83	16/0
89	Krenk, Mitch	TE	6-2	233	11/19/59	2	Nebraska	Crete, Neb.	FA-'84	0*
82	Margerum, Ken	WR	6-0	180	10/5/58	5	Stanford	Fountain Valley, Calif.	D3-'81	16/2
58	Marshall, Wilber	LB	6-1	225	4/18/62	3	Florida	Titusville, Fla.	D1-'84	16/15
85	McKinnon, Dennis	WR	6-1	185	8/22/61	4	Florida State	Quitman, Ga.	FA-'83	14/13
9	McMahon, Jim	QB	6-1	190	8/21/59	5	Brigham Young	Jersey City, N.J.	FA-'82	13/11
76	McMichael, Steve	DT	6-2	260	10/17/57	7	Texas	Houston, Tex.	FA-'81	16/16
87	Moorehead, Emery	TE	6-2	220	3/22/54	10	Colorado	Evanston, Ill.	FA-'81	15/14
51	Morrissey, Jim	LB	6-3	215	12/24/62	2	Michigan State	Flint, Mich.	D11-'85	15/0
89	Ortego, Keith	WR	6-0	180	8/30/63	2	McNeese State	Eunice, Tex.	FA-'85	7/0
34	Payton, Walter	RB	5-10	202	7/25/54	12	Jackson State	Columbia, Miss.	D1-'75	16/16
72	Perry, William	DT	6-2	308	12/16/62	2	Clemson	Aiken, S.C.	D1-'85	16/9
48	Phillips, Reggie	CB-S	5-10	170	12/12/60	2	Southern Methodist	Houston, Tex.	D2-'85	16/1
53	Rains, Dan	LB	6-1	229	4/26/56	3	Cincinnati	Rochester, Pa.	FA-'82	0*
27	Richardson, Mike	CB	6-0	188	5/23/61	4	Arizona State	Compton, Calif.	D2-'83	14/14
59	Rivera, Ron	LB	6-3	239	1/7/62	3	California	Monterey, Calif.	D2-'84	16/0
20	Sanders, Thomas	RB	5-11	203	1/4/62	2	Texas A&M	Giddings, Tex.	D9-'85	15/0
50	Singletary, Mike	LB	6-0	228	10/9/58	6	Baylor	Houston, Tex.	D2-'81	16/16
26	Suhey, Matt	RB	5-11	216	7/7/58	7	Penn State	State College, Pa.	D2-'80	16/16
31	Taylor, Ken	CB	6-1	185	9/2/63	2	Oregon State	San Jose, Calif.	FA-'85	16/1
57	Thayer, Tom	G-C	6-4	261	8/16/61	2	Notre Dame	Joliet, Ill.	FA-'85	16/13
33	Thomas, Calvin	RB	5-11	245	1/7/60	5	Illinois	St. Louis, Mo.	FA-'80	13/0
52	†Thrift, Cliff	LB	6-1	230	5/3/56	8	East Central Oklahoma	Dallas, Tex.	T(SD)-'85	16/2
18	Tomczak, Mike	QB	6-1	195	10/23/62	2	Ohio State	Calumet City, Ill.	FA-'85	6/0
78	Van Horne, Keith	T	6-6	280	11/6/57	6	Southern California	Mt. Lebanon, Pa.	D1-'81	16/16
70	Waechter, Henry	DT	6-5	275	2/13/59	5	Nebraska	Dubuque, Iowa	FA-'84	13/0
55	Wilson, Otis	LB	6-2	232	9/15/57	7	Louisville	New York, N.Y.	D1-'80	16/16
80	Wrightman, Tim	TE	6-3	237	3/27/60	2	UCLA	Harbor City, Calif.	FA-'85	16/3

* Baschnagel, Dunsmore, Krenk, and Rains missed '85 season due to injury; Bell and Harris last active with Chicago in '84.

†Option playout; subject to developments.

Also played with Bears in '85—WR James Maness (8 games).

COACHING STAFF

Head Coach, Mike Ditka

Pro Career: Became tenth head coach of Bears on January 20, 1982, after serving nine years as an offensive assistant with Dallas. Led Bears to first Super Bowl title following 15-1 1985 season. Bears shut out Giants and Rams in playoffs before routing Patriots, 46-10 in Super Bowl XX. His 11-7 1984 record included trip to NFC Championship Game at San Francisco (23-0 loss). The 46-year-old Ditka owns a 40-22 record since taking over the coaching reins and has won 34 of his last 43 games. Ditka is a 25-year veteran of the NFL as both a player and a coach. Had 12-year playing career as a tight end with Chicago (1961-66), Philadelphia (1967-68), and Dallas (1969-72). A first-round draft choice by Chicago in 1961, Ditka was NFL rookie of the year, all-NFL (1961-64), and played in five Pro Bowls (1962-66). He joined Cowboys coaching staff in 1973. In addition to working with Dallas special teams, he coached Cowboys' receivers. During his NFL career, he has been in the playoffs 14 seasons and been a member of five NFC champions and three NFL champions. Career record: 40-22.

Background: Played at Pittsburgh from 1958-60 and was a unanimous All-America his senior year. A two-way performer, he played both tight end and linebacker. He also was one of the nation's leading punters with a 40-plus yard average over three years.

Personal: Born October 18, 1939, Carnegie, Pa. Mike and his wife, Diana, live in Grayslake, Ill., and have four children—Michael, Mark, Megan, and Matt.

Assistant Coaches

Jim Dooley, research and quality control; born February 8, 1930, Stoutsville, Mo., lives in Chicago. End Miami 1949-51. Pro receiver Chicago Bears 1952-61. Pro coach: Chicago Bears 1962-71 (head coach 1968-71), Buffalo Bills 1972, rejoined Bears in 1981.

Ed Hughes, offensive coordinator; born October 23, 1927, Buffalo, N.Y., lives in Libertyville, Ill. Halfback Tulsa 1952-53. Pro defensive back Los Angeles Rams 1954-55, New York Giants 1956-58. Pro coach: Dallas Texans 1960-62, Denver Broncos 1963, Washington Redskins 1964-67, San Francisco 49ers 1968-70, Houston Oilers 1971 (head coach), St. Louis Cardinals 1972, Dallas Cowboys 1973-76, Detroit Lions 1977, New Orleans Saints 1978-80, Philadelphia Eagles 1981, joined Bears in 1982.

Steve Kazor, special teams; born February 24, 1948, New Kensington, Pa., lives in Vernon Hills, Ill. Nose tackle Westminister College 1967-70. No pro playing experience. College coach: Colorado State 1975, Wyoming 1976, Texas-El Paso 1979-80, Emporia State 1981 (head coach). Pro coach: Joined Bears in 1983.

Greg Landry, quarterbacks-receivers; born December 18, 1946, Nashua, N.H., lives in Libertyville, Ill. Quarterback Massachusetts 1965-67. Pro quarterback Detroit Lions 1968-78, Baltimore Colts 1979-81, Arizona Wranglers/Chicago Blitz (USFL) 1983-84, Chicago Bears 1984. Pro coach: Cleveland Browns 1985, first year with Bears.

Jim LaRue, defensive backfield; born August 11, 1925, Clinton, Okla., lives in Libertyville, Ill. Halfback Carson-Newman 1943, Duke 1944-45, Maryland 1947-49. No pro playing experience. College coach: Maryland 1950, Kansas State 1951-54, Houston 1955-56, Southern Methodist 1957-58, Arizona 1959-66 (head coach), Utah 1967-73, Wake Forest 1974-75. Pro coach: Buffalo Bills 1976-77, joined Bears in 1978.

John Levra, defensive line; born October 2, 1937, Arma, Kan., lives in Libertyville, Ill. Guard-linebacker Pittsburgh (Kansas) State 1963-65. No pro playing experience. College coach: Stephen F. Austin 1971-74, Kansas 1975-78, North Texas State 1979. Pro coach: British Columbia Lions (CFL) 1980, New Orleans Saints 1981-85, first year with Bears.

CHICAGO BEARS 1986 FIRST-YEAR ROSTER

Name	Pos.	Ht.	Wt.	Birth-date	College	Hometown	How Acq.
Anderson, Neal	RB	5-11	210	8/14/64	Florida	Graceville, Fla.	D1
Barnes, Lew	WR	5-8	163	12/27/62	Oregon	Long Beach, Calif.	D5
Blair, Paul	T	6-4	290	8/3/63	Oklahoma State	Edmond, Okla.	D4
Douglass, Maurice	CB-S	5-11	200	2/12/64	Kentucky	Trotwood, Ohio	D8
Hundley, Barton	S	5-11	187	9/19/63	Kansas State	Clay Center, Kan.	D10
Jackson, Vestee	CB	6-0	186	8/14/63	Washington	Fresno, Calif.	D2
Jones, Bruce	S	6-1	195	12/26/62	North Alabama	Courtland, Ala.	D7
Kindt, Don (1)	TE	6-7	258	3/9/61	Wisconsin-La Crosse	Milwaukee, Wis.	FA
Kozlowski, Glen	WR	6-1	193	12/31/62	Brigham Young	Honolulu, Hawaii	D11
Powell, Jeff	RB	5-10	170	5/27/63	Tennessee	Nashville, Tenn.	D6
Spivak, Joe (1)	G	6-0	284	2/19/62	Illinois State	Chicago, Ill.	FA
Teltschik, John	P	6-1	207	3/8/64	Texas	Floresville, Tex.	D9
Williams, David	WR	6-3	187	6/10/63	Illinois	Los Angeles, Calif.	D3

The term NFL Rookie is defined as a player who is in his first season of professional football and has not been on the roster of another professional football team for any regular season or postseason games. A Rookie is designated by an "R" on NFL rosters. Players who have been active in another professional football league or players who have NFL experience, including either preseason training camp or being on an active roster for fewer than three regular season or postseason games, are termed NFL First-Year Players. An NFL First-Year Player is designated by a "1" on NFL rosters. Thereafter, a player on an NFL active roster for at least three regular season or postseason games is credited with an additional year of NFL playing experience.

NOTES

David McGinnis, defensive assistant; born August 7, 1951, Independence, Kan., lives in Lake Forest, Ill. Defensive back Texas Christian 1970-72. No pro playing experience. College coach: Texas Christian 1973-74, 1982, Missouri 1975-77, Indiana State 1978-81, Kansas State 1983-85. Pro coach: First year with Bears.

Johnny Roland, offensive backs; born May 21, 1943, Corpus Christi, Tex., lives in Vernon Hills, Ill. Running back Missouri 1963-65. Pro running back St. Louis Cardinals 1966-72, New York Giants 1973. College coach: Notre Dame 1975. Pro coach: Green Bay Packers 1974, Philadelphia Eagles 1976-78, joined Bears in 1983.

Dick Stanfel, offensive line; born July 20, 1927, San Francisco, Calif., lives in Libertyville, Ill. Guard San Francisco 1948-51. Pro guard Detroit Lions 1952-55, Washington Redskins 1956-58. College coach: Notre Dame 1959-62, California 1963. Pro coach: Philadelphia Eagles 1964-70, San Francisco 49ers 1971-75, New Orleans Saints 1976-80 (head coach, 4 games in 1980), joined Bears in 1981.

Vince Tobin, defensive coordinator; born September 29, 1943, in Burlington Junction, Mo., lives in Libertyville, Ill. Defensive back-running back Missouri 1961-64. No pro playing experience. College coach: Missouri 1967-76. Pro coach: British Columbia Lions (CFL) 1977-82; Philadelphia/Baltimore Stars (USFL) 1983-85, first year with Bears.

DALLAS COWBOYS

National Football Conference
Eastern Division

Team Colors: Royal Blue, Metallic Silver Blue, and White

Cowboys Center
One Cowboys Parkway
Irving, Texas 75063
Telephone: (214) 556-9900

Club Officials

General Partner: H.R. Bright
President-General Manager: Texas E. Schramm
Vice President-Personnel Development: Gil Brandt
Vice President-Treasurer: Don Wilson
Vice President-Administration: Joe Bailey
Public Relations Director: Doug Todd
Media Relations-Marketing: Greg Aiello
Business Manager: Dan Werner
Ticket Manager: Steve Orsini
Trainers: Don Cochren, Ken Locker
Equipment Manager: William T. (Buck) Buchanan
Cheerleaders Director: Suzanne Mitchell

Stadium: Texas Stadium • **Capacity:** 63,749
Irving, Texas 75062

Playing Surface: Texas Turf

Training Camp: California Lutheran University
Thousand Oaks, California 91360

1986 SCHEDULE

Preseason

Aug. 3	vs. Chicago at London, Eng.	6:00
Aug. 9	at San Diego	6:00
Aug. 16	at Los Angeles Raiders	6:00
Aug. 22	**Pittsburgh**	7:00
Aug. 30	**Houston**	8:00

Regular Season

Sept. 8	**New York Giants** (Monday)	8:00
Sept. 14	at Detroit	1:00
Sept. 21	**Atlanta**	12:00
Sept. 29	at St. Louis (Monday)	8:00
Oct. 5	at Denver	2:00
Oct. 12	**Washington**	12:00
Oct. 19	at Philadelphia	1:00
Oct. 26	**St. Louis**	3:00
Nov. 2	at New York Giants	1:00
Nov. 9	**Los Angeles Raiders**	3:00
Nov. 16	at San Diego	1:00
Nov. 23	at Washington	1:00
Nov. 27	**Seattle** (Thanksgiving)	3:00
Dec. 7	at Los Angeles Rams	6:00
Dec. 14	**Philadelphia**	12:00
Dec. 21	**Chicago**	3:00

COWBOYS COACHING HISTORY

(253-148-6)

1960-85 Tom Landry 253-148-6

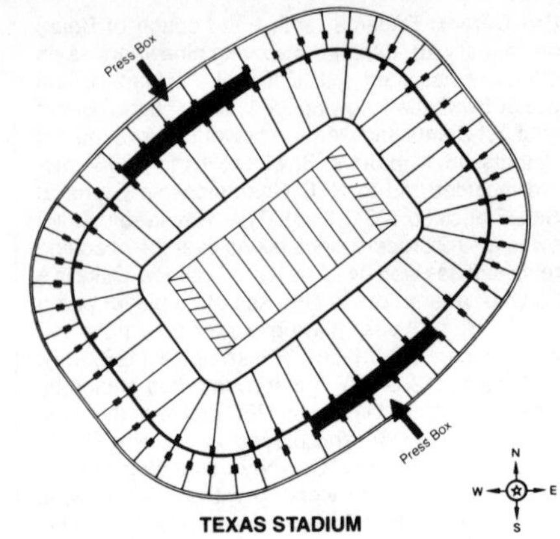

TEXAS STADIUM

RECORD HOLDERS

Individual Records—Career

Category	Name	Performance
Rushing (Yds.)	Tony Dorsett, 1977-1985	10,832
Passing (Yds.)	Roger Staubach, 1969-1979	22,700
Passing (TDs)	Roger Staubach, 1969-1979	153
Receiving (No.)	Drew Pearson, 1973-1983	489
Receiving (Yds.)	Drew Pearson, 1973-1983	7,822
Interceptions	Mel Renfro, 1964-1977	52
Punting (Avg.)	Sam Baker, 1962-63	45.1
Punt Return (Avg.)	Bob Hayes, 1965-1974	11.1
Kickoff Return (Avg.)	Mel Renfro, 1964-1977	26.4
Field Goals	Rafael Septien, 1978-1985	147
Touchdowns (Tot.)	Tony Dorsett, 1977-1985	79
Points	Rafael Septien, 1978-1985	786

Individual Records—Single Season

Category	Name	Performance
Rushing (Yds.)	Tony Dorsett, 1981	1,646
Passing (Yds.)	Danny White, 1983	3,980
Passing (TDs)	Danny White, 1983	29
Receiving (No.)	Tony Hill, 1985	74
Receiving (Yds.)	Bob Hayes, 1966	1,232
Interceptions	Everson Walls, 1981	11
Punting (Avg.)	Sam Baker, 1962	45.4
Punt Return (Avg.)	Bob Hayes, 1968	20.8
Kickoff Return (Avg.)	Mel Renfro, 1965	30.0
Field Goals	Rafael Septien, 1981	27
Touchdowns (Tot.)	Dan Reeves, 1966	16
Points	Rafael Septien, 1983	123

Individual Records—Single Game

Category	Name	Performance
Rushing (Yds.)	Tony Dorsett, 12-4-77	206
Passing (Yds.)	Don Meredith, 11-10-63	460
Passing (TDs)	Many times	5
	Last time by Danny White, 10-30-83	
Receiving (No.)	Lance Rentzel, 11-19-67	13
Receiving (Yds.)	Bob Hayes, 11-13-66	246
Interceptions	Herb Adderley, 9-26-71	3
	Lee Roy Jordan, 11-4-73	3
	Dennis Thurman, 12-13-81	3
Field Goals	Many times	4
	Last time by Rafael Septien, 9-21-81	
Touchdowns (Tot.)	Many times	4
	Last time by Duane Thomas, 12-18-71	
Points	Many times	24
	Last time by Duane Thomas, 12-18-71	

1985 TEAM STATISTICS

	Dallas	Opp.
Total First Downs	336	312
Rushing	95	98
Passing	208	193
Penalty	33	21
Third Down: Made/Att.	96/227	87/228
Fourth Down: Made/Att.	5/9	7/17
Total Net Yards	5602	5608
Avg. Per Game	350.1	350.5
Total Plays	1093	1076
Avg. Per Play	5.1	5.2
Net Yards Rushing	1741	1853
Avg. Per Game	108.8	115.8
Total Rushes	462	465
Net Yards Passing	3861	3755
Avg. Per Game	241.3	234.7
Tackled/Yards Lost	44/375	62/459
Gross Yards	4236	4214
Att./Completions	587/344	549/279
Completion Pct.	58.6	50.8
Had Intercepted	25	33
Punts/Avg.	83/41.4	78/41.3
Net Punting Avg.	35.3	36.7
Penalties/Yards Lost	100/759	108/990
Fumbles/Ball Lost	29/16	24/15
Touchdowns	43	40
Rushing	11	18
Passing	27	20
Returns	5	2
Avg. Time of Possession	30:34	29:26

1985 TEAM RECORD

Preseason (4-0)

Date	Dallas		Opponents
8/10	27	*Green Bay	3
8/17	27	San Diego (OT)	24
8/26	15	*Chicago	13
8/31	20	*Houston	10
	89		50

Regular Season (10-6)

Date	Dallas		Opp.	Att.
9/9	44	*Washington	14	61,543
9/15	21	Detroit	26	72,985
9/22	20	*Cleveland	7	61,456
9/29	17	Houston	10	49,686
10/6	30	N.Y. Giants	29	74,981
10/13	27	*Pittsburgh	13	62,932
10/20	14	Philadelphia	16	70,114
10/27	24	*Atlanta	10	57,941
11/4	10	St. Louis	21	49,347
11/10	13	Washington	7	55,750
11/17	0	*Chicago	44	63,750
11/24	34	*Philadelphia	17	54,047
11/28	35	*St. Louis	17	54,125
12/8	24	Cincinnati	50	56,936
12/15	28	*N.Y. Giants	21	62,310
12/22	16	San Francisco	31	60,114

Postseason (0-1)

Date	Dallas		Opp.	Att.
1/4/86	0	L.A. Rams	20	66,581

*Home Game (OT) Overtime

Score by Periods

Dallas	55	122	78	102	0	—	357
Opponents	66	73	98	96	0	—	333

Attendance

Home 478,104 Away 489,913 Total 968,017
Single game home record, 80,259 (11-24-66)
Single season home record, 511,541 (1981)

1985 INDIVIDUAL STATISTICS

Rushing	Att.	Yds.	Avg.	LG	TD
Dorsett	305	1307	4.3	60t	7
Newsome	88	252	2.9	15	2
Hogeboom	8	48	6.0	15	1
D. White	22	44	2.0	21	1
Williams	13	40	3.1	9	0
Lavette	13	34	2.6	10	0
Fowler	7	25	3.6	6	0
J. Jones	1	0	0.0	0	0
Banks	1	−1	−1.0	−1	0
Pelluer	3	−2	−0.7	1	0
Hill	1	−6	−6.0	−6	0
Cowboys	462	1741	3.8	60t	11
Opponents	465	1853	4.0	74t	18

Passing	Att.	Comp.	Pct.	Yds.	TD	Int.	Tkld.	Rate
D. White	450	267	59.3	3157	21	17	30/257	80.6
Hogeboom	126	70	55.6	978	5	7	14/118	70.8
Pelluer	8	5	62.5	47	0	0	0/0	78.6
J. Jones	2	1	50.0	12	1	1	0/0	68.8
Hill	1	1	100.0	42	0	0	0/0	118.8
Cowboys	587	344	58.6	4236	27	25	44/375	78.6
Opponents	549	279	50.8	4214	20	33	62/459	63.5

Receiving	No.	Yds.	Avg.	LG	TD
Hill	74	1113	15.0	53t	7
Cosbie	64	793	12.4	42	6
Renfro	60	955	15.9	58t	8
Dorsett	46	449	9.8	56t	3
Newsome	46	361	7.8	24	1
J. Jones	24	179	7.5	35	0
Powe	14	237	16.9	34	0
Cornwell	6	77	12.8	32	1
Fowler	5	24	4.8	10	0
Gonzalez	3	28	9.3	13	0
D. White	1	12	12.0	12t	1
Lavette	1	8	8.0	8	0
Cowboys	344	4236	12.3	58t	27
Opponents	279	4214	15.1	70t	20

Interceptions	No.	Yds.	Avg.	LG	TD
Walls	9	31	3.4	19	0
Thurman	5	21	4.2	21t	1
Fellows	4	52	13.0	29	0
Bates	4	15	3.8	8	0
Clinkscale	3	16	5.3	11	0
Downs	3	11	3.7	11	0
Scott	2	26	13.0	26t	1
Jeffcoat	1	65	65.0	65t	1
Lockhart	1	19	19.0	19t	1
Hegman	1	7	7.0	7	0
Cowboys	33	263	8.0	65t	4
Opponents	25	319	12.8	47	2

Punting	No.	Yds.	Avg.	In 20	LG
Saxon	81	3396	41.9	20	57
D. White	1	43	43.0	0	43
Cowboys	83	3439	41.4	20	57
Opponents	78	3218	41.3	25	60

Punt Returns	No.	FC	Yds.	Avg.	LG	TD
Bates	22	6	152	6.9	21	0
Gonzalez	15	5	58	3.9	13	0
Banks	3	3	27	9.0	28	0
Cowboys	40	14	237	5.9	28	0
Opponents	44	10	286	6.5	19	0

Kickoff Returns	No.	Yds.	Avg.	LG	TD
Lavette	34	682	20.1	34	0
Duckett	9	173	19.2	25	0
J. Jones	9	161	17.9	26	0
Williams	6	129	21.5	30	0
Fowler	3	48	16.0	20	0
Powe	1	17	17.0	17	0
Cowboys	62	1210	19.5	34	0
Opponents	68	1310	19.3	43	0

Scoring	TD R	TD P	TD Rt	PAT	FG	Saf	TP
Septien	0	0	0	42/43	19/28	0	99
Dorsett	7	3	0	0/0	0/0	0	60
Renfro	0	8	0	0/0	0/0	0	48
Hill	0	7	0	0/0	0/0	0	42
Cosbie	0	6	0	0/0	0/0	0	36
Newsome	2	1	0	0/0	0/0	0	18
D. White	1	1	0	0/0	0/0	0	12
Cornwell	0	1	0	0/0	0/0	0	6
Hogeboom	1	0	0	0/0	0/0	0	6
Jeffcoat	0	0	1	0/0	0/0	0	6
Lockhart	0	0	1	0/0	0/0	0	6
Penn	0	0	1	0/0	0/0	0	6
Scott	0	0	1	0/0	0/0	0	6
Thurman	0	0	1	0/0	0/0	0	6
Cowboys	11	27	5	42/43	19/28	0	357
Opponents	18	20	2	37/40	18/27	1	333

FIRST-ROUND SELECTIONS

(If club had no first-round selection, first player drafted is listed with round in parentheses.)

Year	Player, College, Position
1960	None
1961	Bob Lilly, Texas Christian, DT
1962	Sonny Gibbs, Texas Christian, QB (2)
1963	Lee Roy Jordan, Alabama, LB
1964	Scott Appleton, Texas, DT
1965	Craig Morton, California, QB
1966	John Niland, Iowa, G
1967	Phil Clark, Northwestern, DB (3)
1968	Dennis Homan, Alabama, WR
1969	Calvin Hill, Yale, RB
1970	Duane Thomas, West Texas State, RB
1971	Tody Smith, Southern California, DE
1972	Bill Thomas, Boston College, RB
1973	Billy Joe DuPree, Michigan State, TE
1974	Ed (Too Tall) Jones, Tennessee State, DE
	Charley Young, North Carolina State, RB
1975	Randy White, Maryland, LB
	Thomas Henderson, Langston, LB
1976	Aaron Kyle, Wyoming, DB
1977	Tony Dorsett, Pittsburgh, RB
1978	Larry Bethea, Michigan State, DE
1979	Robert Shaw, Tennessee, C
1980	Bill Roe, Colorado, LB (3)
1981	Howard Richards, Missouri, T
1982	Rod Hill, Kentucky State, DB
1983	Jim Jeffcoat, Arizona State, DE
1984	Billy Cannon, Jr., Texas A&M, LB
1985	Kevin Brooks, Michigan, DE
1986	Mike Sherrard, UCLA, WR

DALLAS COWBOYS 1986 VETERAN ROSTER

No.	Name	Pos.	Ht.	Wt.	Birth-date	NFL Exp.	College	Hometown	How Acq.	'85 Games/ Starts
36	Albritton, Vince	LB	6-2	213	7/23/62	3	Washington	Oakland, Calif.	FA-'84	7/1
76	Aughtman, Dowe	G	6-2	259	1/28/61	2	Auburn	Brewton, Ala.	D11-'84	0*
62	Baldinger, Brian	G	6-4	261	1/7/59	4	Duke	Massapequa, N.Y.	FA-'82	0*
87	Banks, Gordon	WR	5-10	173	3/12/58	4	Stanford	Los Angeles, Calif.	FA-'85	2/0
40	Bates, Bill	S	6-1	199	6/6/61	4	Tennessee	Knoxville, Tenn.	FA-'83	16/2
99	Brooks, Kevin	DE	6-6	270	2/9/63	2	Michigan	Detroit, Mich.	D1-'85	11/0
47	Clinkscale, Dextor	S	5-11	195	4/13/58	6	South Carolina State	Greenville, S.C.	FA-'80	16/16
61	Cooper, Jim	T	6-5	274	9/28/55	10	Temple	Philadelphia, Pa.	D6-'77	15/15
85	Cornwell, Fred	TE	6-6	233	8/7/61	3	Southern California	Saugus, Calif.	D3-'84	16/1
84	Cosbie, Doug	TE	6-6	245	2/27/56	8	Santa Clara	Mountain View, Calif.	D3-'79	16/16
55	DeOssie, Steve	LB	6-2	245	11/22/62	3	Boston College	Roslindale, Mass.	D4-'84	16/0
33	Dorsett, Tony	RB	5-11	185	4/7/54	10	Pittsburgh	Aliquippa, Pa.	D1-'77	16/16
26	Downs, Michael	S	6-3	204	6/9/59	6	Rice	Dallas, Tex.	FA-'81	16/16
86	Duckett, Kenny	WR	5-11	183	10/1/59	5	Wake Forest	Winston-Salem, N.C.	FA-'85	4/0*
78	Dutton, John	DT	6-7	268	2/6/51	13	Nebraska	Rapid City, S.D.	T(Balt)-'79	16/15
27	Fellows, Ron	CB	6-0	180	11/7/58	6	Missouri	South Bend, Ind.	D7a-'81	13/11
46	Fowler, Todd	RB	6-3	218	6/19/62	2	Stephen F. Austin	Van, Tex.	SD1-'84	8/0
83	Gonzales, Leon	WR	5-10	162	9/21/63	2	Bethune-Cookman	Jacksonville, Fla.	D8-'85	11/0
28	Granger, Norm	RB	5-10	220	9/14/61	2	Iowa	Newark, N.J.	FA-'86	0*
58	Hegman, Mike	LB	6-1	228	1/17/53	11	Tennessee State	Memphis, Tenn.	D7-'75	16/15
80	Hill, Tony	WR	6-2	202	6/23/56	10	Stanford	Long Beach, Calif.	D3a-'77	15/14
77	Jeffcoat, Jim	DE	6-5	263	4/1/61	4	Arizona State	Cliffwood, N.J.	D1-'83	16/16
72	Jones, Ed	DE	6-9	287	2/23/51	12	Tennessee State	Jackson, Tenn.	D1a-'74	16/16
23	Jones, James	RB	5-10	203	12/6/58	6	Mississippi State	Starkville, Miss.	D3b-'80	16/2
68	Ker, Crawford	G	6-3	293	5/5/62	2	Florida	Dunedin, Fla.	D3-'85	5/0
29	Lavette, Robert	RB	5-11	199	9/8/63	2	Georgia Tech	Cartersville, Ga.	D4-'85	12/0
56	Lockhart, Eugene	LB	6-2	234	3/8/61	3	Houston	Crockett, Tex.	D6a-'84	16/15
30	Newsome, Timmy	RB	6-1	237	5/17/58	7	Winston-Salem State	Ahoskie, N.C.	D6-'80	14/14
79	Patten, Joel	G-T	6-6	240	2/7/58	2	Duke	Fairfax, Va.	FA-'86	0*
16	Pelluer, Steve	QB	6-4	208	7/29/62	3	Washington	Bellevue, Wash.	D5a-'84	2/0
59	Penn, Jesse	LB	6-3	217	9/6/62	2	Virginia Tech	Martinsville, Va.	D2-'85	16/1
65	Petersen, Kurt	G	6-4	278	6/17/57	7	Missouri	St. Louis, Mo.	D4-'80	16/16
81	Powe, Karl	WR	6-2	175	1/17/62	2	Alabama State	Mobile, Ala.	D7a-'85	15/1
75	Pozderac, Phil	T	6-9	282	12/19/59	5	Notre Dame	Garfield Heights, Ohio	D5-'82	14/8
64	†Rafferty, Tom	C	6-3	264	8/2/54	11	Penn State	Fayetteville, N.Y.	D4-'76	16/16
82	Renfro, Mike	WR	6-0	189	6/19/55	9	Texas Christian	Fort Worth, Tex.	T(Hou)-'84	16/16
70	†Richards, Howard	G-T	6-6	262	8/7/59	6	Missouri	St. Louis, Mo.	D1-'81	7/0
50	Rohrer, Jeff	LB	6-2	230	12/25/58	5	Yale	Manhattan Beach, Calif.	D2-'82	15/12
89	Salonen, Brian	LB	6-3	226	7/29/61	3	Montana	Great Falls, Mont.	D10-'84	16/0
4	Saxon, Mike	P	6-3	187	7/10/62	2	San Diego State	Arcadia, Calif.	FA-'85	16/0
66	Schultz, Chris	T	6-8	288	2/16/60	3	Arizona	Burlington, Ontario	D7-'83	16/9
22	Scott, Victor	CB-S	6-0	196	6/1/62	3	Colorado	East St. Louis, Ill.	D2-'84	16/3
1	Septien, Rafael	K	5-10	179	12/12/53	10	Southwest Louisiana	Mexico City, Mex.	FA-'78	16/0
60	Smerek, Don	DT	6-7	265	12/20/57	5	Nevada-Reno	Henderson, Nev.	FA-'80	10/1
67	Thompson, Broderick	G	6-5	280	8/14/60	2	Kansas	Cerritos, Calif.	FA-'85	11/0
32	Thurman, Dennis	S	5-11	179	4/13/56	9	Southern California	Los Angeles, Calif.	D11-'78	16/3
63	Titensor, Glen	G	6-4	261	2/21/58	6	Brigham Young	Garden Grove, Calif.	D3-'81	16/16
71	Tuinei, Mark	C	6-5	270	3/31/60	4	Hawaii	Honolulu, Hawaii	FA-'83	16/0
24	Walls, Everson	CB	6-1	194	12/28/59	6	Grambling	Dallas, Tex.	FA-'81	16/16
11	White, Danny	QB	6-3	196	2/9/52	11	Arizona State	Mesa, Ariz.	D3a-'74	14/14
54	White, Randy	DT	6-4	272	1/15/53	12	Maryland	Wilmington, Del.	D1a-'75	16/16

* Aughtman and Baldinger missed '85 season due to injury; Duckett played 1 game with New Orleans, 3 with Dallas in '85; Granger last active with Dallas in '84; Patten last active with Cleveland in '80.

†Option playout; subject to developments.

Traded—Quarterback Gary Hogeboom to Indianapolis.

Also played with Cowboys in '85—CB-S Ricky Easmon (8 games), DT David Ponder (4), RB John Williams (8).

COACHING STAFF

Head Coach, Tom Landry

Pro Career: Landry, the Cowboys' only head coach in their 26-year history, has compiled 20 winning seasons in succession and his overall record of 253-148-6 is second only to Don Shula among active coaches. Cowboys became the fourth team in NFL to win a second Super Bowl. They defeated Denver 27-10 in Super Bowl XII on January 15, 1978, at Louisiana Superdome. Dallas has played in four other Super Bowls (V, VI, X, and XIII), winning Game VI 24-3 over Miami. Pro defensive back with New York Yanks (AAFC) 1949, New York Giants 1950-55. Player-coach with Giants 1954-55, named all-pro in 1954. Defensive assistant coach with Giants 1956-59 before moving to Dallas as head coach in 1960. Career record: 253-148-6.

Background: Halfback, University of Texas 1947-48, and played in Longhorns' victories over Alabama in 1948 Sugar Bowl and Georgia in 1949 Orange Bowl.

Personal: Born September 11, 1924, Mission, Tex. A World War II bomber pilot. Tom and his wife, Alicia, live in Dallas and have three children—Tom Jr., Kitty, and Lisa.

Assistant Coaches

Neill Armstrong, research and development; born March 9, 1926, Tishomingo, Okla., lives in Dallas. End Oklahoma State 1943-46. Pro end-defensive back Philadelphia Eagles 1947-51, Winnipeg Blue Bombers (CFL) 1951, 1953-54. College coach: Oklahoma State 1955-61. Pro coach: Houston Oilers 1962-63, Edmonton Eskimos (CFL) 1964-69 (head coach), Minnesota Vikings 1970-77, Chicago Bears 1978-81 (head coach), joined Cowboys in 1982.

Paul Hackett, pass offense coordinator; born July 5, 1947, Burlington, Vt., lives in Roanoke, Tex. Quarterback Cal-Davis 1965-68. No pro playing experience. College coach: Cal-Davis 1970-71, California 1972-75, Southern California 1976-80. Pro coach: Cleveland Browns 1981-82, San Francisco 49ers 1983-85, first year with Cowboys.

Al Lavan, running backs; born September 13, 1946, Pierce, Fla., lives in Dallas. Defensive back Colorado State 1965-67. Pro defensive back Philadelphia Eagles 1968, Atlanta Falcons 1969-70. College coach: Colorado State 1972, Louisville 1973, Iowa State 1974, Georgia Tech 1977-78, Stanford 1979. Pro coach: Atlanta Falcons 1975-76, joined Cowboys in 1980.

Alan Lowry, special teams; born November 21, 1950, Irving, Tex., lives in Dallas. Defensive back-quarterback Texas 1970-72. No pro playing experience. College coach: Virginia Tech 1974, Wyoming 1975, Texas 1976-81. Pro coach: Joined Cowboys in 1982.

Jim Myers, assistant head coach-offensive line; born November 12, 1921, Madison, W. Va., lives in Dallas. Guard Tennessee 1941-42, 1946, Duke 1943. No pro playing experience. College coach: Wofford 1947, Vanderbilt 1948, UCLA 1949-56, Iowa State 1957 (head coach), Texas A&M 1958-61 (head coach). Pro coach: Joined Cowboys in 1962.

Dick Nolan, defensive backs; born March 26, 1932, Pittsburgh, Pa., lives in Dallas. Offensive-defensive back Maryland 1951-53. Pro defensive back New York Giants 1954-57, 1959-61, St. Louis Cardinals 1958, Dallas player-coach 1962. Pro coach: Dallas Cowboys 1963-67, San Francisco 49ers 1968-75 (head coach), New Orleans Saints 1977-80 (head coach), Houston Oilers 1981, rejoined Cowboys in 1982.

Ernie Stautner, defensive coordinator-defensive line; born April 2, 1925, Cham, Bavaria, lives in Dallas. Tackle Boston College 1946-49. Pro defensive tackle Pittsburgh Steelers 1950-63. Pro coach: Pittsburgh Steelers 1963-64, Washington Redskins 1965, joined Cowboys in 1966.

Jerry Tubbs, linebackers; born January 23, 1935, Breckenridge, Tex., lives in Dallas. Center-linebacker Oklahoma 1954-56. Pro linebacker Chicago Cardinals 1957, San Francisco 49ers 1958-59, Dallas Cowboys 1960-67. Pro coach: Joined Cowboys in 1966 (player-coach 1966-67).

Bob Ward, conditioning; born July 4, 1933, Huntington Park, Calif., lives in Dallas. Fullback-quarterback Whitworth College 1952-54. Doctorate in physical education, Indiana University. No pro playing experience. College coach: Fullerton, Calif., J.C. (track) 1965-75. Pro coach: Joined Cowboys in 1975.

DALLAS COWBOYS 1986 FIRST-YEAR ROSTER

Name	Pos.	Ht.	Wt.	Birth-date	College	Hometown	How Acq.
Chandler, Thornton	TE	6-5	238	11/27/63	Alabama	Jacksonville, Fla.	D6a
Chester, Bryan	G	6-4	260	2/2/63	Texas	Houston, Tex.	D10
Clack, Darryl	RB	5-10	207	10/29/63	Arizona State	Security, Colo.	D2
Clemons, Topper	RB	5-11	205	9/16/63	Wake Forest	Cinnaminson, N.J.	D8
Collier, Reggie (1)	QB	6-3	207	5/14/61	Southern Mississippi	Biloxi, Miss.	D6-'83
Duliban, Chris	LB	6-2	216	1/9/63	Texas	Houston, Tex.	D12a
Flack, Tony	CB-S	6-1	184	8/31/64	Georgia	Greensboro, N.C.	D12b
Gelbaugh, Stan	QB	6-3	207	12/4/62	Maryland	Carlisle, Pa.	D6b
Haynes, Tommy (1)	S	6-0	190	2/6/63	Southern California	Covina, Calif.	FA
Holloway, Johnny	CB	5-11	181	11/8/63	Kansas	Houston, Tex.	D7
Ionata, John	G	6-2	280	12/26/63	Florida State	Dunedin, Fla.	D9
Jax, Garth	LB	6-2	225	9/16/63	Florida State	Houston, Tex.	D11
Otto, Bob (1)	DE	6-6	250	12/16/62	Idaho State	Sacramento, Calif.	FA
Ploeger, Kurt (1)	DE	6-5	259	12/1/62	Gustavus Adolphus	LeSuer, Minn.	D6a-'85
Potter, Kelly (1)	K	5-11	165	5/22/62	Middle Tennessee St.	Franklin, Tenn.	FA
Roby, Wayne	WR	6-2	190	1/10/62	Wisconsin	Sycamore, Ill.	FA
Sherrard, Mike	WR	6-2	185	6/21/63	UCLA	Chico, Calif.	D1
Strasburger, Scott (1)	LB	6-1	220	2/14/63	Nebraska	Holdrege, Neb.	FA
Walen, Mark	DT	6-5	265	3/10/63	UCLA	Burlingame, Calif.	D3
Waltman, Chris (1)	TE	6-7	255	11/25/61	Oregon State	Elgin, Minn.	FA
Yancey, Lloyd	G	6-4	275	12/8/62	Temple	Philadelphia, Pa.	D6c
Zendejas, Max	K	5-11	184	9/2/63	Arizona	Chino, Calif.	D4

The term NFL Rookie is defined as a player who is in his first season of professional football and has not been on the roster of another professional football team for any regular season or postseason games. A Rookie is designated by an "R" on NFL rosters. Players who have been active in another professional football league or players who have NFL experience, including either preseason training camp or being on an active roster for fewer than three regular season or postseason games, are termed NFL First-Year Players. An NFL First-Year Player is designated by a "1" on NFL rosters. Thereafter, a player on an NFL active roster for at least three regular season or postseason games is credited with an additional year of NFL playing experience.

NOTES

National Football Conference
Central Division

Team Colors: Honolulu Blue and Silver

Pontiac Silverdome
1200 Featherstone Road — Box 4200
Pontiac, Michigan 48057
Telephone: (313) 335-4131

Club Officials

President-Owner: William Clay Ford
Executive Vice President-General Manager: Russell Thomas
Director of Football Operations-Head Coach: Darryl Rogers
Director of Player Personnel: Joe Bushofsky
Controller: Charles Schmidt
Scouts: Dirk Dierking, Ron Hughes, Jim Owen, Jerry Neri
Director of Public Relations: George Heddleston
Assistant Director of Public Relations: Bill Keenist
Public and Community Relations: Tim Pendell
Ticket Manager: Fred Otto
Trainer: Kent Falb
Strength and Conditioning: Don Clemons
Equipment Manager: Dan Jaroshewich

Stadium: Pontiac Silverdome • **Capacity:** 80,638
1200 Featherstone Road
Pontiac, Michigan 48057

Playing Surface: AstroTurf

Training Camp: Oakland University
Rochester, Michigan 48063

1986 SCHEDULE

Preseason

Aug. 8	**Philadelphia**	8:00
Aug. 15	**Seattle**	8:00
Aug. 23	at Indianapolis	7:30
Aug. 29	at Cincinnati	8:00

Regular Season

Sept. 7	at Minnesota	12:00
Sept. 14	**Dallas**	1:00
Sept. 21	**Tampa Bay**	1:00
Sept. 28	at Cleveland	1:00
Oct. 5	**Houston**	1:00
Oct. 12	at Green Bay	12:00
Oct. 19	at Los Angeles Rams	1:00
Oct. 26	at Chicago	12:00
Nov. 2	**Cincinnati**	1:00
Nov. 9	**Minnesota**	1:00
Nov. 16	at Philadelphia	1:00
Nov. 23	at Tampa Bay	1:00
Nov. 27	**Green Bay** (Thanksgiving)	12:30
Dec. 7	at Pittsburgh	1:00
Dec. 15	**Chicago** (Monday)	9:00
Dec. 21	**Atlanta**	1:00

LIONS COACHING HISTORY

Portsmouth Spartans 1930-33
(355-345-32)

1930-36	George (Potsy) Clark	54-26-9
1937-38	Earl (Dutch) Clark	14-8-0
1939	Gus Henderson	6-5-0
1940	George (Potsy) Clark	5-5-1
1941-42	Bill Edwards*	4-9-1
1942	John Karcis	0-8-0
1943-47	Charles (Gus) Dorais	20-31-2
1948-50	Alvin (Bo) McMillin	12-24-0
1951-56	Raymond (Buddy) Parker	50-24-2
1957-64	George Wilson	55-45-6
1965-66	Harry Gilmer	10-16-2
1967-72	Joe Schmidt	43-35-7
1973	Don McCafferty	6-7-1
1974-76	Rick Forzano**	15-17-0
1976-77	Tommy Hudspeth	11-13-0
1978-84	Monte Clark	43-63-1
1985	Darryl Rogers	7-9-0

*Resigned after three games in 1942
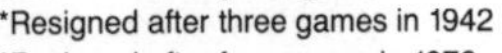
**Resigned after four games in 1976

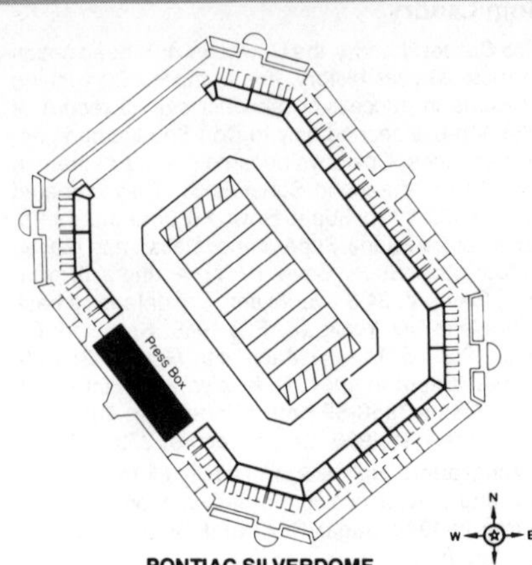

PONTIAC SILVERDOME

RECORD HOLDERS

Individual Records—Career

Category	Name	Performance
Rushing (Yds.)	Billy Sims, 1980-1984	5,106
Passing (Yds.)	Bobby Layne, 1950-58	15,710
Passing (TDs)	Bobby Layne, 1950-58	118
Receiving (No.)	Charlie Sanders, 1968-1977	336
Receiving (Yds.)	Gail Cogdill, 1960-68	5,220
Interceptions	Dick LeBeau, 1959-1972	62
Punting (Avg.)	Yale Lary, 1952-53, 1956-1964	44.3
Punt Return (Avg.)	Jack Christiansen, 1951-58	12.8
Kickoff Return (Avg.)	Pat Studstill, 1961-67	25.7
Field Goals	Errol Mann, 1969-1976	141
Touchdowns (Tot.)	Billy Sims, 1980-84	47
Points	Errol Mann, 1969-1976	636

Individual Records—Single Season

Category	Name	Performance
Rushing (Yds.)	Billy Sims, 1981	1,437
Passing (Yds.)	Gary Danielson, 1980	3,223
Passing (TDs)	Bobby Layne, 1951	26
Receiving (No.)	James Jones, 1984	77
Receiving (Yds.)	Pat Studstill, 1966	1,266
Interceptions	Don Doll, 1950	12
	Jack Christiansen, 1953	12
Punting (Avg.)	Yale Lary, 1963	48.9
Punt Return (Avg.)	Jack Christiansen, 1952	21.5
Kickoff Return (Avg.)	Tom Watkins, 1965	34.4
Field Goals	Ed Murray, 1980	27
Touchdowns (Tot.)	Billy Sims, 1980	16
Points	Doak Walker, 1950	128

Individual Records—Single Game

Category	Name	Performance
Rushing (Yds.)	Bob Hoernschemeyer, 11-23-50	198
Passing (Yds.)	Bobby Layne, 11-5-50	374
Passing (TDs)	Gary Danielson, 12-9-78	5
Receiving (No.)	Cloyce Box, 12-3-50	12
Receiving (Yds.)	Cloyce Box, 12-3-50	302
Interceptions	Don Doll, 10-23-49	4
Field Goals	Garo Yepremian, 11-13-66	6
Touchdowns (Tot.)	Cloyce Box, 12-3-50	4
Points	Cloyce Box, 12-3-50	24

1985 TEAM STATISTICS

	Detroit	Opp.
Total First Downs	259	359
Rushing	89	179
Passing	150	156
Penalty	20	24
Third Down: Made/Att.	81/211	67/196
Fourth Down: Made/Att.	2/8	10/18
Total Net Yards	4476	5591
Avg. Per Game	279.8	349.4
Total Plays	967	1083
Avg. Per Play	4.6	5.2
Net Yards Rushing	1538	2685
Avg. Per Game	96.1	167.8
Total Rushes	452	560
Net Yards Passing	2938	2906
Avg. Per Game	183.6	181.6
Tackled/Yards Lost	53/378	45/336
Gross Yards	3316	3242
Att./Completions	462/254	478/283
Completion Pct.	55.0	59.2
Had Intercepted	21	18
Punts/Avg.	73/41.8	64/40.2
Net Punting Avg.	34.7	30.8
Penalties/Yards Lost	104/741	105/729
Fumbles/Ball Lost	36/20	35/18
Touchdowns	33	40
Rushing	13	19
Passing	19	16
Returns	1	5
Avg. Time of Possession	27:30	32:30

1985 TEAM RECORD

Preseason (1-2-1)

Date	Detroit		Opponents
8/10	10	*Buffalo (OT)	10
8/16	3	Seattle	28
8/25	31	*Cincinnati	17
8/29	16	Philadelphia	20
	60		75

Regular Season (7-9)

Date	Detroit		Opp.	Att.
9/8	28	Atlanta	27	37,785
9/15	26	*Dallas	21	72,985
9/22	6	Indianapolis	14	60,042
9/29	30	*Tampa Bay	9	45,023
10/6	10	Green Bay	43	55,914
10/13	3	Washington	24	52,845
10/20	23	*San Francisco	21	67,715
10/27	31	*Miami	21	75,291
11/3	13	Minnesota	16	58,012
11/10	3	Chicago	24	53,467
11/17	41	*Minnesota	21	54,647
11/24	16	Tampa Bay (OT)	19	43,471
11/28	31	*N.Y. Jets	20	65,531
12/8	6	New England	23	59,078
12/15	23	*Green Bay	26	49,379
12/22	17	*Chicago	37	74,042

*Home Game (OT) Overtime

Score by Periods

Detroit	76	95	79	57	0	—	307
Opponents	68	96	85	114	3	—	366

Attendance

Home 504,613 Away 420,614 Total 925,227
Single game home record, 80,444 (12-20-81)
Single season home record, 622,593 (1980)

1985 INDIVIDUAL STATISTICS

Rushing	Att.	Yds.	Avg.	LG	TD
J. Jones	244	886	3.6	29	6
Montgomery	75	251	3.3	22	0
Moore	80	221	2.8	18	4
Hipple	32	89	2.8	26	2
Kane	11	44	4.0	7	0
Meade	3	18	6.0	9	0
Nichols	1	15	15.0	15	0
J. Ferguson	4	12	3.0	15	1
A. Jones	1	2	2.0	2	0
Black	1	0	0.0	0	0
Lions	452	1538	3.4	29	13
Opponents	560	2685	4.8	37t	19

Passing	Att.	Comp.	Pct.	Yds.	TD	Int.	Tkld.	Rate
Hipple	406	223	54.9	2952	17	18	49/343	73.6
J. Ferguson	54	31	57.4	364	2	3	4/35	67.2
J. Jones	1	0	0.0	0	0	0	0/0	39.6
Moore	1	0	0.0	0	0	0	0/0	39.6
Lions	462	254	55.0	3316	19	21	53/378	72.6
Opponents	478	283	59.2	3242	16	18	45/336	75.1

Receiving	No.	Yds.	Avg.	LG	TD
Thompson	51	736	14.4	48	5
J. Jones	45	334	7.4	36	3
Nichols	36	592	16.4	43	4
Lewis	28	354	12.6	40	3
Chadwick	25	478	19.1	56	3
Moore	19	154	8.1	14	1
Mandley	18	316	17.6	37	0
Bland	12	157	13.1	24	0
Montgomery	7	55	7.9	28	0
Kane	5	56	11.2	18	0
McDonald	3	23	7.7	9	0
Rubick	2	33	16.5	18	0
Meade	2	21	10.5	14	0
McCall	1	7	7.0	7	0
Lions	254	3316	13.1	56	19
Opponents	283	3242	11.5	50	16

Interceptions	No.	Yds.	Avg.	LG	TD
Watkins	5	15	3.0	8	0
Johnson	3	39	13.0	19	0
Graham	3	22	7.3	22	0
McNorton	2	14	7.0	10	0
Harrell	1	20	20.0	20	0
Bunz	1	17	17.0	17	0
Gay	1	7	7.0	7	0
Frizzell	1	3	3.0	3	0
Barnes	1	−1	−1.0	−1	0
Lions	18	136	7.6	22	0
Opponents	21	247	11.8	80t	1

Punting	No.	Yds.	Avg.	In 20	LG
Black	73	3054	41.8	17	60
Lions	73	3054	41.8	17	60
Opponents	64	2572	40.2	12	57

Punt Returns	No.	FC	Yds.	Avg.	LG	TD
Mandley	38	5	403	10.6	63t	1
Lions	38	5	403	10.6	63t	1
Opponents	44	12	420	9.5	47	0

Kickoff Returns	No.	Yds.	Avg.	LG	TD
Hall	39	886	22.7	54	0
Moore	13	230	17.7	24	0
A. Jones	10	226	22.6	30	0
Mandley	6	152	25.3	35	0
Lions	68	1494	22.0	54	0
Opponents	60	1313	21.9	94t	1

Scoring	TD R	TD P	TD Rt	PAT	FG	Saf	TP
Murray	0	0	0	31/33	26/31	0	109
J. Jones	6	3	0	0/0	0/0	0	54
Moore	4	1	0	0/0	0/0	0	30
Thompson	0	5	0	0/0	0/0	0	30
Nichols	0	4	0	0/0	0/0	0	24
Chadwick	0	3	0	0/0	0/0	0	18
Lewis	0	3	0	0/0	0/0	0	18
Hipple	2	0	0	0/0	0/0	0	12
J. Ferguson	1	0	0	0/0	0/0	0	6
Mandley	0	0	1	0/0	0/0	0	6
Lions	13	19	1	31/33	26/31	0	307
Opponents	19	16	5	40/40	28/36	1	366

FIRST-ROUND SELECTIONS

(If club had no first-round selection, first player drafted is listed with round in parentheses.)

Year	Player, College, Position
1936	Sid Wagner, Michigan State, G
1937	Lloyd Cardwell, Nebraska, B
1938	Alex Wojciechowicz, Fordham, C
1939	John Pingel, Michigan State, B
1940	Doyle Nave, Southern California, B
1941	Jim Thomason, Texas A&M, B
1942	Bob Westfall, Michigan, B
1943	Frank Sinkwich, Georgia, B
1944	Otto Graham, Northwestern, B
1945	Frank Szymanski, Notre Dame, C
1946	Bill Dellastatious, Missouri, B
1947	Glenn Davis, Army, B
1948	Y.A. Tittle, Louisiana State, B
1949	John Rauch, Georgia, B
1950	Leon Hart, Notre Dame, E
	Joe Watson, Rice, C
1951	Dick Stanfel, San Francisco, G (2)
1952	Yale Lary, Texas A&M, B (3)
1953	Harley Sewell, Texas, G
1954	Dick Chapman, Rice, T
1955	Dave Middleton, Auburn, B
1956	Hopalong Cassady, Ohio State, B
1957	Bill Glass, Baylor, G
1958	Alex Karras, Iowa, T
1959	Nick Pietrosante, Notre Dame, B
1960	John Robinson, Louisiana State, S
1961	Danny LaRose, Missouri, T (2)
1962	John Hadl, Kansas, QB
1963	Daryl Sanders, Ohio State, T
1964	Pete Beathard, Southern California, QB
1965	Tom Nowatzke, Indiana, RB
1966	Nick Eddy, Notre Dame, RB (2)
1967	Mel Farr, UCLA, RB
1968	Greg Landry, Massachusetts, QB
	Earl McCullouch, Southern California, WR
1969	Altie Taylor, Utah State, RB (2)
1970	Steve Owens, Oklahoma, RB
1971	Bob Bell, Cincinnati, DT
1972	Herb Orvis, Colorado, DE
1973	Ernie Price, Texas A&I, DE
1974	Ed O'Neil, Penn State, LB
1975	Lynn Boden, South Dakota State, G
1976	James Hunter, Grambling, DB
	Lawrence Gaines, Wyoming, RB
1977	Walt Williams, New Mexico State, DB (2)
1978	Luther Bradley, Notre Dame, DB
1979	Keith Dorney, Penn State, T
1980	Billy Sims, Oklahoma, RB
1981	Mark Nichols, San Jose State, WR
1982	Jimmy Williams, Nebraska, LB
1983	James Jones, Florida, RB
1984	David Lewis, California, TE
1985	Lomas Brown, Florida, T
1986	Chuck Long, Iowa, QB

DETROIT LIONS 1986 VETERAN ROSTER

No.	Name	Pos.	Ht.	Wt.	Birth-date	NFL Exp.	College	Hometown	How Acq.	'85 Games/ Starts
95	Allerman, Kurt	LB	6-3	231	8/30/55	10	Penn State	Kinnelon, N.J.	FA-'85	10/7
68	Baack, Steve	NT-DE	6-4	265	11/16/60	3	Oregon	John Day, Ore.	D3c-'84	16/1
11	Black, Mike	P	6-2	197	1/18/61	4	Arizona State	Glendale, Calif.	D7-'83	16/0
80	†Bland, Carl	WR	5-11	182	8/17/61	3	Virginia Union	Richmond, Va.	FA-'84	8/2
42	Bostic, John	CB	5-10	178	10/6/62	2	Bethune-Cookman	Jacksonville, Fla.	FA-'85	13/0
83	Brammer, Mark	TE	6-3	236	5/3/58	6	Michigan State	Traverse City, Mich.	FA-'86	0*
23	Brown, Arnold	CB	5-10	185	8/27/62	2	North Carolina Central	Wilmington, N.C.	FA-'85	7/0
75	Brown, Lomas	T	6-4	282	3/30/63	2	Florida	Miami, Fla.	D1-'85	16/16
89	Chadwick, Jeff	WR	6-3	190	12/16/60	4	Grand Valley State	Dearborn, Mich.	FA-'83	7/5
55	Cofer, Michael	LB	6-5	245	4/7/60	4	Tennessee	Knoxville, Tenn.	D3-'83	7/7
91	Collins, Dwight	WR	6-2	210	8/23/61	2	Pittsburgh	Beaver Falls, Pa.	FA-'86	0*
50	Curley, August	LB	6-3	226	1/24/60	4	Southern California	Atlanta, Ga.	D4-'83	16/14
44	D'Addio, Dave	RB	6-2	229	7/13/61	2	Maryland	Union, N.J.	D4-'84	0*
72	†Dieterich, Chris	G-T	6-3	260	7/27/58	7	North Carolina State	East Setauket, N.Y.	D6-'80	9/7
93	†Dodge, Kirk	LB	6-1	231	6/4/62	2	Nevada-Las Vegas	San Francisco, Calif.	FA-'84	0*
70	Dorney, Keith	G-T	6-5	270	12/3/57	8	Penn State	Emmaus, Pa.	D1-'79	16/16
66	Evans, Leon	DE	6-5	282	10/12/61	2	Miami	Silver Spring, Md.	FA-'85	8/0
12	Ferguson, Joe	QB	6-1	195	4/23/50	14	Arkansas	Shreveport, La.	T(Buff)-'85	8/1
77	Ferguson, Keith	DE	6-5	260	4/3/59	6	Ohio State	Miami, Fla.	W(SD)-'85	15/11*
26	Frizzell, William	S	6-3	198	9/8/62	3	North Carolina Central	Greenville, N.C.	D10-'84	8/0
79	Gay, William	DE	6-5	260	5/28/55	9	Southern California	San Diego, Calif.	T(Den)-'78	16/16
53	Glover, Kevin	C-G	6-2	267	6/17/63	2	Maryland	Upper Marlboro, Md.	D2-'85	10/0
33	†Graham, William	S	5-11	191	9/27/59	5	Texas	Silsbee, Tex.	D5-'82	16/16
67	Greco, Don	G	6-3	265	4/1/59	5	Western Illinois	St. Louis, Mo.	D3-'81	8/6
62	Green, Curtis	NT-DE	6-3	258	6/3/57	6	Alabama State	Quincy, Fla.	D2-'81	15/8
35	†Hall, Alvin	S-KR	5-10	184	8/12/58	6	Miami, Ohio	Dayton, Ohio	FA-'81	16/0
58	†Harrell, James	LB	6-1	230	7/19/57	7	Florida	Tampa, Fla.	W(Den)-'79	7/2
17	Hipple, Eric	QB	6-2	198	9/16/57	7	Utah State	Downey, Calif.	D4-'80	16/15
96	James, June	LB	6-1	218	12/2/62	2	Texas	Kansas City, Mo.	D9-'85	16/0
21	Johnson, Demetrious	S	5-11	190	7/21/61	4	Missouri	St. Louis, Mo.	D5a-'83	16/16
34	Jones, A.J.	RB-KR	6-1	215	5/30/59	5	Texas	Youngstown, Ohio	FA-'85	9/0*
51	Jones, David	C-G	6-3	260	10/25/61	3	Texas	Austin, Tex.	D8-'84	9/8
30	Jones, James	RB	6-2	229	3/21/61	4	Florida	Pompano Beach, Fla.	D1-'83	14/13
92	†King, Angelo	LB	6-1	222	2/10/58	6	South Carolina State	Columbia, S.C.	T(Dall)-'84	16/9
73	Laster, Don	T	6-4	278	12/13/58	3	Tennessee State	Dougherty, Ga.	FA-'84	0*
87	Lewis, David	TE	6-3	235	6/8/61	3	California	Portland, Ore.	D1-'84	15/15
82	Mandley, Pete	WR-KR	5-10	191	7/29/61	3	Northern Arizona	Mesa, Ariz.	D2-'84	16/0
98	†Maxwell, Vernon	LB	6-2	235	10/25/61	4	Arizona State	Los Angeles, Calif.	FA-'85	9/2
81	†McCall, Reese	TE	6-6	245	6/16/56	9	Auburn	Bessemer, Ala.	W(TB)-'83	16/2
29	McNorton, Bruce	CB	5-11	175	2/28/59	5	Georgetown, Ky.	Daytona Beach, Fla.	D4-'82	16/16
36	Meade, Mike	RB	5-11	227	2/12/60	5	Penn State	Dover, Del.	W(GB)-'84	16/0
24	†Moore, Alvin	RB	6-0	194	5/3/59	4	Arizona State	Coolidge, Ariz.	T(Ind)-'85	16/5
52	Mott, Steve	C	6-3	265	3/24/61	4	Alabama	New Orleans, La.	D5b-'83	16/16
3	†Murray, Ed	K	5-10	175	8/29/56	7	Tulane	Victoria, British Columbia	D7-'80	16/0
86	Nichols, Mark	WR	6-2	208	10/29/59	6	San Jose State	Bakersfield, Calif.	D1-'81	14/12
84	Rubick, Rob	TE	6-3	234	9/27/60	5	Grand Valley State	Newberry, Mich.	D12b-'82	9/4
20	Sims, Billy	RB	6-0	212	9/18/55	6	Oklahoma	Hooks, Tex.	D1-'80	0*
65	Stevenson, Mark	G-C	6-3	285	2/24/58	2	Western Illinois	Rock Island, Ill.	FA-'85	2/0
71	Strenger, Rich	T	6-7	276	3/10/60	3	Michigan	Grafton, Wis.	D2-'83	13/6
39	Thompson, Leonard	WR	5-11	192	7/28/52	12	Oklahoma State	Tucson, Ariz.	D8-'75	16/13
60	†Turnure, Tom	C-G	6-4	253	7/9/57	6	Washington	Seattle, Wash.	D3-'80	6/0
27	Watkins, Bobby	CB	5-10	184	5/31/60	5	Southwest Texas State	Dallas, Tex.	D2-'82	16/16
76	Williams, Eric	NT	6-4	280	2/24/62	3	Washington State	Stockton, Calif.	D3a-'84	12/12
59	Williams, Jimmy	LB	6-3	230	11/15/60	5	Nebraska	Washington, D.C.	D1-'82	16/16
18	Witkowski, John	QB	6-1	205	6/18/62	2	Columbia	Lindenhurst, N.Y.	D6-'84	0*

* Brammer last active with Buffalo in '84; Collins last active with Minnesota in '84; D'Addio, Dodge, Laster, and Sims missed '85 season due to injury; K. Ferguson played 10 games with San Diego, 5 with Detroit in '85; A.J. Jones played 1 game with L.A. Rams, 8 games with Detroit in '85; Witkowski last active with Detroit in '84.

†Option playout; subject to developments.

Traded—Linebacker Roosevelt Barnes to Indianapolis.

Retired—Doug English, 10-year defensive tackle, 10 games in '85; Wilbert Montgomery, 9-year running back, 7 games in '85.

Also played with Lions in '85—LB Dan Bunz (2 games), CB-S Clarence Chapman (3), LB Ken Fantetti (8), CB Duane Galloway (2), RB Rick Kane (16), G-C Larry Lee (6), TE James McDonald (6), DE Martin Moss (6), G Ray Snell (2), NT Hal Stephens (1).

COACHING STAFF

Head Coach, Darryl Rogers

Pro Career: Became Lions' sixteenth head coach and director of football operations on February 6, 1985. No pro playing experience. Career record: 7-9.

Background: Wide receiver who gained all-West Coast honors while playing at Fresno State. Served in U.S. Marine Corps and later earned his master's degree in physical education from Fresno State. Spent twenty years coaching in the collegiate ranks at Hayward State 1965, Fresno State 1966-72, San Jose State 1973-75 (head coach), Michigan State 1976-79 (head coach), Arizona State 1980-84 (head coach). Named national college coach of the year in 1978 while at Michigan State. Ranked as one of the winningest active coaches in the college ranks with a 129-84-7 mark.

Personal: Born May 28, 1935, Los Angeles, Calif. Darryl and his wife, Marsha, live in Rochester, Mich., and have three daughters—Jamie, Keely, and Stacy.

Assistant Coaches

Bob Baker, offensive coordinator; born November 28, 1927, Lima, Ohio, lives in Rochester Hills, Mich. Quarterback Ball State 1947-51. No pro playing experience. College coach: Indiana 1966-73, Michigan State 1977-79, Arizona State 1980-82. Pro coach: Calgary Stampeders (CFL) 1974-76 (head coach 1976), Los Angeles Rams 1983-84, joined Lions in 1985.

Carl Battershell, special teams-secondary; born November 5, 1948, Alliance, Ohio, lives in Rochester, Mich. Offensive tackle Bowling Green 1966-69. No pro playing experience. College coach: Bowling Green 1973-76, Syracuse 1977-79, West Virginia 1980-82, Arizona State 1983-84. Pro coach: Joined Lions in 1985.

Don Doll, administrative assistant to coaching staff-tight ends; born August 29, 1926, Los Angeles, Calif., lives in Birmingham, Mich. Defensive back Southern California 1944, 1946-48. Pro defensive back Detroit Lions 1949-52, Washington Redskins 1953, Los Angeles Rams 1954. College coach: Washington 1955, Contra Costa, Calif., J.C. 1956, Southern California 1957-58, Notre Dame 1959-62. Pro coach: Detroit Lions 1963-64, Los Angeles Rams 1965, Washington Redskins 1966-70, Green Bay Packers 1971-73, Baltimore Colts 1974, Miami Dolphins, 1975-76, rejoined Lions in 1978.

Wayne Fontes, defensive coordinator; born February 17, 1940, New Bedford, Mass., lives in Rochester, Mich. Defensive back Michigan State 1959-62. Pro defensive back New York Titans (AFL) 1962. College coach: Dayton 1967-68, Iowa 1969-70, Southern California 1971-75. Pro coach: Tampa Bay Buccaneers 1976-84, joined Lions in 1985.

Paul Lanham, receivers; born July 31, 1935, Ripley, W. Va., lives in Pontiac, Mich. Linebacker Glenville State, W. Va. 1957-59. No pro playing experience. College coach: Dayton 1961, Colorado State 1962-69, Arkansas 1970-71. Pro coach: Washington Redskins 1973-77, Los Angeles Rams 1978-82, Chicago Blitz (USFL) 1983, Arizona Wranglers (USFL) 1984, joined Lions in 1985.

Bill Muir, offensive line; born October 26, 1942, Pittsburgh, Pa., lives in Rochester Hills, Mich. Tackle Susquehanna 1962-64. No pro playing experience. College coach: Susquehanna 1965, Delaware Valley 1966-67, Rhode Island 1970-71, Idaho State 1972-73, Southern Methodist 1976-77. Pro coach: Orlando (Continental Football League) 1968-69, Houston-Shreveport (WFL) 1975, New England Patriots 1982-84, joined Lions in 1985.

Mike Murphy, linebackers; born September 25, 1944, New York, N.Y., lives in Rochester, Mich. Guard-linebacker Huron, S.D., College 1962-65. No pro playing experience. College coach: Vermont 1970-73, Idaho State 1974-76, Western Illinois 1977-78. Pro coach: Saskatchewan Roughriders (CFL) 1979-83, Chicago Blitz (USFL) 1984, joined Lions in 1985.

DETROIT LIONS 1986 FIRST-YEAR ROSTER

Name	Pos.	Ht.	Wt.	Birth-date	College	Hometown	How Acq.
Barrows, Scott (1)	G	6-2	278	3/31/63	West Virginia	Marietta, Ohio	FA
Beauford, Clayton (1)	WR	5-10	173	3/1/63	Auburn	Palatka, Fla.	D10-'85
Bosley, Keith	T	6-4	340	6/19/63	Eastern Kentucky	Richmond, Ky.	FA
Caldwell, Scotty (1)	RB	5-10	200	2/8/63	Texas-Arlington	Grand Prairie, Tex.	FA
Callahan, Mitch	NT	6-2	268	2/19/61	Arizona State	Phoenix, Ariz.	FA
Durden, Allan	S	5-11	167	11/25/63	Arizona	Los Angeles, Calif.	D12
Galloway, Duane (1)	CB-S	5-8	181	11/7/61	Arizona State	Los Angeles, Calif.	FA
Gancitano, Nick	K	5-8	182	5/14/63	Penn State	Coral Springs, Fla.	FA
Griffin, Allyn	WR	6-2	189	4/4/63	Wyoming	Casper, Wyo.	D8
Hancock, Kevin (1)	LB	6-2	223	1/6/62	Baylor	Texas City, Tex.	D4-'85
Heffernan, Dave (1)	G-C	6-4	267	10/28/62	Miami	Miami, Fla.	FA
Hillman, Scott	DE	6-3	250	5/13/63	Virginia	Roanoke, Va.	FA
Hughes, Allen (1)	DE	6-3	254	9/8/59	Western Michigan	Detroit, Mich.	FA
James, Garry	RB	5-10	204	9/4/62	Louisiana State	Gretna, La.	D2
Johnson, James (1)	LB	6-2	236	6/21/62	San Diego State	Lake Elsinore, Calif.	D3-'85
Johnson, Tracy	LB	6-1	244	4/3/62	Morningside	Omaha, Neb.	D10
Long, Chuck	QB	6-4	211	2/18/63	Iowa	Wheaton, Ill.	D1
Luckett, Ken	S	6-2	195	1/9/64	Western Michigan	Detroit, Mich.	FA
Melvin, Leland	WR	5-11	175	2/15/64	Richmond	Lynchburg, Va.	D11
Milinichik, Joe	G-T	6-5	300	3/30/63	North Carolina State	Macungie, Pa.	D3
Mitchell, Devon	S	6-1	194	12/30/62	Iowa	Brooklyn, N.Y.	D4
Muehling, Burt (1)	TE	6-4	220	6/11/62	Kearney State	Lincoln, Neb.	FA
Pickens, Lyle	CB	5-10	165	9/5/64	Colorado	Reseda, Calif.	D9
Smith, Oscar	RB	5-9	203	4/5/63	Nicholls State	Tampa, Fla.	D5
Weaver, Mike (1)	NT-G	6-1	325	12/15/62	Georgia	Haines City, Fla.	FA
Wells, Mike (1)	TE	6-3	235	1/22/62	San Diego State	Quincy, Calif.	FA
West, Bernard	LB	6-0	225	3/13/58	North Texas State	Conroe, Tex.	FA
Williams, Scott (1)	RB-TE	6-2	234	7/21/62	Georgia	Charlotte, N.C.	FA
Wilson, Farrell (1)	C	6-4	260	1/25/62	Arkansas State	Cabot, Ark.	FA
Wright, Brett (1)	P	6-3	200	1/5/62	S.E. Louisiana	Ponchatoula, La.	FA

The term NFL Rookie is defined as a player who is in his first season of professional football and has not been on the roster of another professional football team for any regular season or postseason games. A Rookie is designated by an "R" on NFL rosters. Players who have been active in another professional football league or players who have NFL experience, including either preseason training camp or being on an active roster for fewer than three regular season or postseason games, are termed NFL First-Year Players. An NFL First-Year Player is designated by a "1" on NFL rosters. Thereafter, a player on an NFL active roster for at least three regular season or postseason games is credited with an additional year of NFL playing experience.

NOTES

Rex Norris, defensive line; born December 10, 1939, Tipton, Ind., lives in Bloomfield Hills, Mich. Linebacker East Texas State 1964. No pro playing experience. College coach: Navarro, Tex., J.C. 1970-71, Texas A&M 1972, Oklahoma 1973-83, Arizona State 1984. Pro coach: Joined Lions in 1985.

Willie Shaw, defensive backs; born January 11, 1944, Glenmora, La., lives in Rochester, Mich. Defensive back New Mexico 1966-68. No pro playing experience. College coach: San Diego City College 1970-72, Stanford 1973-76, Long Beach State 1977-78, Oregon 1979, Arizona State 1980-84. Pro coach: Joined Lions in 1985.

Ivy Williams, offensive backs; born August 12, 1949, New York, N.Y., lives in Rochester Hills, Mich. Running back Xavier (Ohio) 1968-72. No pro playing experience. College coach: Marshall 1974, Kansas State 1975-77, New Mexico State 1978, Kansas 1979-81, Arizona State 1982-84. Pro coach: Joined Lions in 1985.

National Football Conference
Central Division

Team Colors: Dark Green, Gold, and White

1265 Lombardi Avenue
Green Bay, Wisconsin 54307-0628
Telephone: (414) 494-2351

Club Officials

Chairman of the Board: Dominic Olejniczak
President, CEO: Robert Parins
Vice President: Tony Canadeo
Secretary: Peter M. Platten III
Treasurer: Phil Hendrickson
Assistant to the President: Bob Harlan
Assistant to the President: Tom Miller
Green Bay Ticket Director: Mark Wagner
Public Relations Director: Lee Remmel
Assistant Director of Public Relations: Scott Berchtold
Director of Player Personnel: Dick Corrick
Director of Player Procurement: Chuck Hutchison
Video Director: Al Treml
Trainer: Domenic Gentile
Equipment Manager: Bob Noel

Stadium: Lambeau Field • **Capacity:** 57,063
P.O. Box 10628
1265 Lombardi Avenue
Green Bay, Wisconsin 54307-0628

Milwaukee County Stadium • **Capacity:** 55,976
Highway I-94
Milwaukee, Wisconsin 53214

Playing Surfaces: Grass

Training Camp: St. Norbert College
DePere, Wisconsin 54115

1986 SCHEDULE

Preseason

Aug. 9	**N.Y. Jets** at Madison, Wis.	1:00
Aug. 16	**N.Y. Giants** at Milwaukee	7:00
Aug. 23	at Cincinnati	7:00
Aug. 30	**New England**	7:00

Regular Season

Sept. 7	**Houston**	12:00
Sept. 14	at New Orleans	12:00
Sept. 22	**Chicago** (Monday)	8:00
Sept. 28	at Minnesota	12:00
Oct. 5	**Cincinnati** at Milwaukee	12:00
Oct. 12	**Detroit**	12:00
Oct. 19	at Cleveland	1:00
Oct. 26	**San Francisco** at Milw.	12:00
Nov. 2	at Pittsburgh	1:00
Nov. 9	**Washington**	12:00
Nov. 16	**Tampa Bay** at Milwaukee	12:00
Nov. 23	at Chicago	12:00
Nov. 27	at Detroit (Thanksgiving)	12:30
Dec. 7	**Minnesota**	12:00
Dec. 14	at Tampa Bay	1:00
Dec. 20	at N.Y. Giants (Saturday)	12:30

PACKERS COACHING HISTORY

(456-352-35)

1921-49	Earl (Curly) Lambeau	212-106-21
1950-53	Gene Ronzani*	14-31-1
1953	Hugh Deyone-Ray (Scooter) McLean**	0-2-0
1954-57	Lisle Blackbourn	17-31-0
1958	Ray (Scooter) McLean	1-10-1
1959-67	Vince Lombardi	98-30-4
1968-70	Phil Bengtson	20-21-1
1971-74	Dan Devine	25-28-4
1975-83	Bart Starr	53-77-3
1984-85	Forrest Gregg	16-16-0

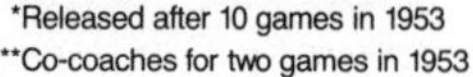

*Released after 10 games in 1953
**Co-coaches for two games in 1953

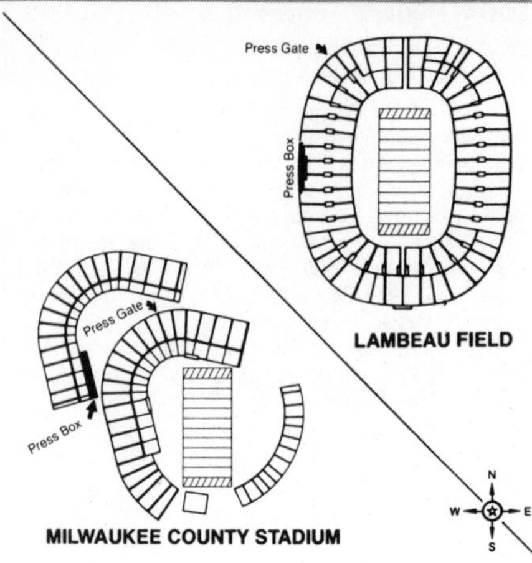

RECORD HOLDERS

Individual Records—Career

Category	Name	Performance
Rushing (Yds.)	Jim Taylor, 1958-1966	8,207
Passing (Yds.)	Bart Starr, 1956-1971	23,718
Passing (TDs)	Bart Starr, 1956-1971	152
Receiving (No.)	Don Hutson, 1935-1945	488
Receiving (Yds.)	James Lofton, 1978-1985	8,816
Interceptions	Bobby Dillon, 1952-59	52
Punting (Avg.)	Bucky Scribner, 1983-84	42.0
Punt Return (Avg.)	Billy Grimes, 1950-52	13.2
Kickoff Return (Avg.)	Dave Hampton, 1970-71	28.9
Field Goals	Chester Marcol, 1972-1980	120
Touchdowns (Tot.)	Don Hutson, 1935-1945	105
Points	Don Hutson, 1935-1945	823

Individual Records—Single Season

Category	Name	Performance
Rushing (Yds.)	Jim Taylor, 1962	1,407
Passing (Yds.)	Lynn Dickey, 1983	4,458
Passing (TDs)	Lynn Dickey, 1983	32
Receiving (No.)	Don Hutson, 1942	74
Receiving (Yds.)	James Lofton, 1984	1,361
Interceptions	Irv Comp, 1943	10
Punting (Avg.)	Jerry Norton, 1963	44.7
Punt Return (Avg.)	Billy Grimes, 1950	19.1
Kickoff Return (Avg.)	Travis Williams, 1967	41.1
Field Goals	Chester Marcol, 1972	33
Touchdowns (Tot.)	Jim Taylor, 1962	19
Points	Paul Hornung, 1960	176

Individual Records—Single Game

Category	Name	Performance
Rushing (Yds.)	Jim Taylor, 12-3-61	186
Passing (Yds.)	Lynn Dickey, 10-12-80	418
Passing (TDs)	Many times	5
	Last time by Lynn Dickey, 9-4-83	
Receiving (No.)	Don Hutson, 11-22-42	14
Receiving (Yds.)	Bill Howton, 10-21-56	257
Interceptions	Bobby Dillon, 11-26-53	4
	Willie Buchanon, 9-24-78	4
Field Goals	Many times	4
	Last time by Al Del Greco, 12-15-85	
Touchdowns (Tot.)	Paul Hornung, 12-12-65	5
Points	Paul Hornung, 10-8-61	33

1985 TEAM STATISTICS

	Green Bay	Opp.
Total First Downs	318	310
Rushing	114	111
Passing	172	178
Penalty	32	21
Third Down: Made/Att.	66/200	80/213
Fourth Down: Made/Att.	6/12	6/15
Total Net Yards	5371	5173
Avg. Per Game	335.7	323.3
Total Plays	1033	1051
Avg. Per Play	5.2	4.9
Net Yards Rushing	2208	2047
Avg. Per Game	138.0	127.9
Total Rushes	470	494
Net Yards Passing	3163	3126
Avg. Per Game	197.7	195.4
Tackled/Yards Lost	50/389	48/383
Gross Yards	3552	3509
Att./Completions	513/267	509/295
Completion Pct.	52.0	58.0
Had Intercepted	27	15
Punts/Avg.	82/39.8	77/42.7
Net Punting Avg.	32.8	35.3
Penalties/Yards Lost	101/798	102/797
Fumbles/Ball Lost	39/18	44/25
Touchdowns	40	43
Rushing	16	17
Passing	21	22
Returns	3	4
Avg. Time of Possession	28:59	31:01

1985 TEAM RECORD

Preseason (1-3)

Date	Green Bay		Opponents
8/10	3	Dallas	27
8/17	2	N.Y. Giants	10
8/24	28	*Atlanta	24
8/31	20	*N.Y. Jets	30
	53		91

Regular Season (8-8)

Date	Green Bay		Opp.	Att.
9/8	20	New England	26	49,488
9/15	23	*N.Y. Giants	20	56,149
9/22	3	*N.Y. Jets	24	53,667
9/29	28	St. Louis	43	48,598
10/6	43	*Detroit	10	55,914
10/13	20	*Minnesota	17	54,674
10/21	7	Chicago	23	65,095
10/27	10	Indianapolis	37	59,708
11/3	10	*Chicago	16	56,895
11/10	27	Minnesota	17	59,970
11/17	38	*New Orleans	14	52,104
11/24	17	L.A. Rams	34	52,710
12/1	21	*Tampa Bay	0	19,856
12/8	24	*Miami	34	52,671
12/15	26	Detroit	23	49,379
12/22	20	Tampa Bay	17	33,992

*Home Game

Score by Periods

Green Bay	50	82	89	116	0	—	337
Opponents	68	109	66	112	0	—	355

Attendance

Home 401,930 Away 418,940 Total 820,870
Single game home record, 56,895 (11-3-85; Lambeau Field), 56,258 (9-28-80; Milwaukee County Stadium)
Single season home record, 435,521 (1980)

1985 INDIVIDUAL STATISTICS

Rushing	Att.	Yds.	Avg.	LG	TD
Ivery	132	636	4.8	34	2
Clark	147	633	4.3	80	5
Ellis	104	571	5.5	39t	5
Ellerson	32	205	6.4	37t	2
Epps	5	103	20.6	34	1
Huckleby	8	41	5.1	15	0
Ferragamo, Buff.-GB	8	15	1.9	5	1
Lofton	4	14	3.5	21	0
Zorn	10	9	0.9	8	0
Wright	8	8	1.0	8	0
Prather	1	0	0.0	0	0
West	1	0	0.0	0	0
Dickey	18	−12	−0.7	3	1
Packers	470	2208	4.7	80	16
Opponents	494	2047	4.1	65t	17

Passing	Att.	Comp.	Pct.	Yds.	TD	Int.	Tkld.	Rate
Dickey	314	172	54.8	2206	15	17	30/226	70.4
Ferragamo, Buff.-GB	287	149	51.9	1677	5	17	19/135	50.8
Zorn	123	56	45.5	794	4	6	11/89	57.4
Wright	74	39	52.7	552	2	4	8/67	63.6
Ellis	1	0	0.0	0	0	0	0/0	39.6
Ivery	1	0	0.0	0	0	0	1/7	39.6
Packers	513	267	52.0	3552	21	27	50/389	66.0
Opponents	509	295	58.0	3509	22	15	48/383	81.2

Receiving	No.	Yds.	Avg.	LG	TD
Lofton	69	1153	16.7	56t	4
Coffman	49	666	13.6	32	6
Epps	44	683	15.5	63	3
Ivery	28	270	9.6	24	2
Clark	24	252	10.5	55t	2
Ellis	24	206	8.6	35	0
Dennard	13	182	14.0	34	2
West	8	95	11.9	30	1
Huckleby	5	27	5.4	8	0
Ellerson	2	15	7.5	11	0
Moore	1	3	3.0	3t	1
Packers	267	3552	13.3	63	21
Opponents	295	3509	11.9	61t	22

Interceptions	No.	Yds.	Avg.	LG	TD
Lewis	4	4	1.0	4	0
Douglass	2	126	63.0	80t	1
Murphy	2	50	25.0	50t	1
Scott	2	50	25.0	30	0
Anderson	2	2	1.0	2	0
Lee	1	23	23.0	23	0
Flynn	1	7	7.0	7	0
Cade	1	0	0.0	0	0
Packers	15	262	17.5	80t	2
Opponents	27	326	12.1	67	1

Punting	No.	Yds.	Avg.	In 20	LG
Bracken	26	1052	40.5	1	54
Prokop	56	2210	39.5	9	66
Packers	82	3262	39.8	10	66
Opponents	77	3290	42.7	24	68

Punt Returns	No.	FC	Yds.	Avg.	LG	TD
Epps	15	3	146	9.7	46	0
Stanley	14	3	179	12.8	27	0
Flynn	7	4	41	5.9	13	0
Hayes	1	0	0	0.0	0	0
Murphy	1	0	4	4.0	4	0
Packers	38	10	370	9.7	46	0
Opponents	46	10	411	8.9	47	0

Kickoff Returns	No.	Yds.	Avg.	LG	TD
Ellerson	29	521	18.0	32	0
Ellis	13	247	19.0	40	0
Epps	12	279	23.3	48	0
Stanley	9	212	23.6	36	0
Turner, Minn.-G.B.	4	61	15.3	18	0
Anderson	1	14	14.0	14	0
Flynn	1	20	20.0	20	0
Jones	1	11	11.0	11	0
Stills	1	14	14.0	14	0
Packers	67	1318	19.7	48	0
Opponents	71	1570	22.1	98t	2

Scoring	TD R	TD P	TD Rt	PAT	FG	Saf	TP
Del Greco	0	0	0	38/40	19/26	0	95
Clark	5	2	0	0/0	0/0	0	42
Coffman	0	6	0	0/0	0/0	0	36
Ellis	5	0	0	0/0	0/0	0	30
Epps	1	3	0	0/0	0/0	0	24
Ivery	2	2	0	0/0	0/0	0	24
Lofton	0	4	0	0/0	0/0	0	24
Dennard	0	2	0	0/0	0/0	0	12
Ellerson	2	0	0	0/0	0/0	0	12
Dickey	1	0	0	0/0	0/0	0	6
Douglass	0	0	1	0/0	0/0	0	6
Ferragamo, Buff-GB	1	0	0	0/0	0/0	0	6
Lewis	0	0	1	0/0	0/0	0	6
Moore	0	1	0	0/0	0/0	0	6
Murphy	0	0	1	0/0	0/0	0	6
West	0	1	0	0/0	0/0	0	6
Brown	0	0	0	0/0	0/0	1	2
Packers	16	21	3	38/40	19/26	1	337
Opponents	17	22	4	41/43	16/31	4	355

FIRST-ROUND SELECTIONS

(If club had no first-round selection, first player drafted is listed with round in parentheses.)

Since 1946

Year	Player, College, Position
1946	Johnny (Strike) Strzykalski, Marquette, B
1947	Ernie Case, UCLA, B
1948	Earl (Jug) Girard, Wisconsin, B
1949	Stan Heath, Nevada, B
1950	Clayton Tonnemaker, Minnesota, C
1951	Bob Gain, Kentucky, T
1952	Babe Parilli, Kentucky, QB
1953	Al Carmichael, Southern California, B
1954	Art Hunter, Notre Dame, T
	Veryl Switzer, Kansas State, B
1955	Tom Bettis, Purdue, G
1956	Jack Losch, Miami, B
1957	Paul Hornung, Notre Dame, B
	Ron Kramer, Michigan, E
1958	Dan Currie, Michigan State, C
1959	Randy Duncan, Iowa, B
1960	Tom Moore, Vanderbilt, RB
1961	Herb Adderley, Michigan State, CB
1962	Earl Gros, Louisiana State, RB
1963	Dave Robinson, Penn State, LB
1964	Lloyd Voss, Nebraska, DT
1965	Donny Anderson, Texas Tech, RB
	Larry Elkins, Baylor, E
1966	Jim Grabowski, Illinois, RB
	Gale Gillingham, Minnesota, T
1967	Bob Hyland, Boston College, C
	Don Horn, San Diego State, QB
1968	Fred Carr, Texas-El Paso, LB
	Bill Lueck, Arizona, G
1969	Rich Moore, Villanova, DT
1970	Mike McCoy, Notre Dame, DT
	Rich McGeorge, Elon, TE
1971	John Brockington, Ohio State, RB
1972	Willie Buchanon, San Diego State, DB
	Jerry Tagge, Nebraska, QB
1973	Barry Smith, Florida State, WR
1974	Barty Smith, Richmond, RB
1975	Bill Bain, Southern California, G (2)
1976	Mark Koncar, Colorado, T
1977	Mike Butler, Kansas, DE
	Ezra Johnson, Morris Brown, DE
1978	James Lofton, Stanford, WR
	John Anderson, Michigan, LB
1979	Eddie Lee Ivery, Georgia Tech, RB
1980	Bruce Clark, Penn State, DE
	George Cumby, Oklahoma, LB
1981	Rich Campbell, California, QB
1982	Ron Hallstrom, Iowa, G
1983	Tim Lewis, Pittsburgh, DB
1984	Alphonso Carreker, Florida State, DE
1985	Ken Ruettgers, Southern California, T
1986	Kenneth Davis, Texas Christian, RB (2)

GREEN BAY PACKERS 1986 VETERAN ROSTER

No.	Name	Pos.	Ht.	Wt.	Birth-date	NFL Exp.	College	Hometown	How Acq.	'85 Games/ Starts
59	†Anderson, John	LB	6-3	229	2/14/56	9	Michigan	Waukesha, Wis.	D1b-'78	16/16
17	Bracken, Don	P	6-0	205	2/16/62	2	Michigan	Thermopolis, Wyo.	FA-'85	7/0
93	Brown, Robert	DE	6-2	250	5/21/60	5	Virginia Tech	Edenton, N.C.	D4-'82	16/4
39	Burgess, Ronnie	CB-S	5-11	175	3/7/63	2	Wake Forest	Sumter, S.C.	D10-'85	11/0
77	Butler, Mike	DE	6-5	269	4/4/54	8	Kansas	Washington, D.C.	D1-'77	12/2
24	Cade, Mossy	CB	6-1	195	12/26/61	2	Texas	Eloy, Ariz.	T(SD)-'85	14/3
58	†Cannon, Mark	C	6-3	258	6/14/62	3	Texas-Arlington	Austin, Tex.	D11-'84	16/16
76	Carreker, Alphonso	DE	6-6	260	5/25/62	3	Florida State	Columbus, Ohio	D1-'84	16/16
23	Clanton, Chuck	CB-S	5-11	192	5/15/62	2	Auburn	Pensacola, Fla.	SD2-'84	3/0
33	Clark, Jessie	RB	6-0	233	1/3/60	4	Arkansas	Crossett, Ark.	D7-'83	16/14
82	†Coffman, Paul	TE	6-3	225	3/29/56	9	Kansas State	Chase, Kan.	FA-'78	16/16
	t-Collins, Glen	DE	6-6	265	7/10/59	5	Mississippi State	Jackson, Miss.	T(Cin)-'85	16/0
52	Cumby, George	LB	6-0	224	7/5/56	7	Oklahoma	LaRue, Tex.	D1b-'80	16/1
10	†Del Greco, Al	K	5-10	195	3/2/62	3	Auburn	Coral Gables, Fla.	FA-'84	16/0
88	Dennard, Preston	WR	6-1	183	11/28/55	9	New Mexico	Phoenix, Ariz.	T(Buff)-'85	16/0
12	†Dickey, Lynn	QB	6-4	203	10/19/49	14	Kansas State	Osawatomie, Kan.	T(Hou)-'76	12/10
99	Dorsey, John	LB	6-2	235	8/31/60	3	Connecticut	Leonardtown, Md.	D4-'84	16/0
42	Ellerson, Gary	RB	5-11	220	7/17/63	2	Wisconsin	Albany, Ga.	D7b-'85	15/0
31	Ellis, Gerry	RB	5-11	225	11/12/57	7	Missouri	Columbia, Mo.	FA-'80	16/7
85	†Epps, Phillip	WR	5-10	165	11/11/59	5	Texas Christian	Atlanta, Tex.	D12-'82	16/16
5	Ferragamo, Vince	QB	6-3	217	4/24/54	9	Nebraska	Wilmington, Calif.	FA-'85	9/9*
41	Flynn, Tom	S	6-0	195	3/24/62	3	Pittsburgh	Verona, Pa.	D5-'84	15/15
65	Hallstrom, Ron	G	6-6	283	6/11/59	5	Iowa	Moline, Ill.	D1-'82	16/15
27	Hayes, Gary	CB-S	5-10	180	8/19/57	3	Fresno State	Richmond, Calif.	FA-'84	16/0
25	Huckleby, Harlan	RB	6-1	201	12/30/57	7	Michigan	Detroit, Mich.	FA-'80	11/0
79	Humphrey, Donnie	DE	6-3	275	4/20/61	3	Auburn	Huntsville, Ala.	D3-'84	16/6
40	Ivery, Eddie Lee	RB	6-0	214	7/30/57	6	Georgia Tech	Thomson, Ga.	D1-'79	15/10
90	Johnson, Ezra	DE	6-4	259	10/2/55	10	Morris Brown	Shreveport, La.	D1b-'77	16/16
43	Jones, Daryll	CB-S	6-0	190	3/23/62	3	Georgia	Columbus, Ga.	D7-'84	8/1
68	†Koch, Greg	T	6-4	276	6/14/55	10	Arkansas	Houston, Tex.	D2-'77	16/16
22	†Lee, Mark	CB-S	5-11	188	3/20/58	7	Washington	Hanford, Calif.	D2-'80	14/14
26	Lewis, Tim	CB-S	5-11	191	12/18/61	4	Pittsburgh	Perkasie, Pa.	D1-'83	16/16
80	Lofton, James	WR	6-3	197	7/5/56	9	Stanford	Los Angeles, Calif.	D1-'78	16/16
94	Martin, Charles	DE	6-4	270	8/31/59	3	Livingston	Canton, Ga.	FA-'84	16/10
28	†McLeod, Mike	CB-S	6-0	180	5/4/58	3	Montana State	Cheyenne, Wyo.	FA-'84	8/0
60	†Moore, Blake	C-G	6-5	272	5/8/58	7	Wooster	Chattanooga, Tenn.	FA-'84	16/0
57	Moran, Rich	C-G	6-2	272	3/19/62	2	San Diego State	Pleasanton, Calif.	D3-'85	16/9
37	†Murphy, Mark	S	6-2	201	4/22/58	6	West Liberty State	Canton, Ohio	FA-'80	14/14
91	Noble, Brian	LB	6-3	237	9/6/62	2	Arizona State	Anaheim, Calif.	D5-'85	16/15
78	Obrovac, Mike	G-T	6-6	275	10/11/55	4	Bowling Green	Canton, Ohio	T(Cin)-'85	0*
51	Prather, Guy	LB	6-2	229	3/28/58	6	Grambling	Gaithersburg, Md.	FA-'81	16/1
75	Ruettgers, Ken	T	6-5	267	8/20/62	2	Southern California	Bakersfield, Calif.	D1-'85	16/2
55	Scott, Randy	LB	6-1	222	1/31/59	6	Alabama	Decatur, Ga.	FA-'81	16/16
71	Shumate, Mark	NT	6-5	265	3/30/60	2	Wisconsin	Poynette, Wis.	FA-'85	7/0*
87	Stanley, Walter	WR-KR	5-9	180	11/5/62	2	Mesa College	Chicago, Ill.	D4-'85	14/0
29	Stills, Ken	CB-S	5-10	185	9/6/63	2	Wisconsin	Oceanside, Calif.	D8-'85	8/1
67	†Swanke, Karl	T-C	6-6	262	12/29/57	7	Boston College	Newington, Conn.	D6-'80	15/15
70	Uecker, Keith	G-T	6-5	270	6/29/60	5	Auburn	Hollywood, Fla.	W(Den)-'84	8/7
86	West, Ed	TE	6-1	242	8/2/61	3	Auburn	Leighton, Ala.	FA-'84	16/0
61	Wingle, Blake	G	6-2	260	4/17/60	4	UCLA	Oxnard, Calif.	FA-'85	5/0*
16	Wright, Randy	QB	6-2	194	1/12/61	3	Wisconsin	St. Charles, Ill.	D6-'84	7/1
18	†Zorn, Jim	QB	6-2	200	5/10/53	11	Cal Poly-Pomona	Cerritos, Calif.	FA-'85	13/5

* Ferragamo played 9 games with Buffalo, active for 2 games with Green Bay in '85 but did not play; Obrovac last active with Cincinnati in '83; Shumate played 4 games with N.Y. Jets, 3 with Green Bay in '85; Wingle played 3 games with Pittsburgh, 2 with Green Bay in '85.

†Option playout; subject to developments.

t-Packers traded for Collins (Cincinnati).

Also played with Packers in '85—DE Tony Degrate (1 game), LB Mike Douglass (16), T Tim Huffman (2), P Joe Prokop (9), QB Joe Shield (active for 3 games but did not play), RB Maurice Turner (3).

COACHING STAFF

Head Coach, Forrest Gregg

Pro Career: Registered 8-8 mark in each of first two seasons at Green Bay. Named Packers head coach on December 26, 1983, after compiling 34-27 record as Cincinnati's coach from 1980-83, including 1981 AFC Central title and Super Bowl XVI appearance. Was previously head coach of Cleveland Browns, where he compiled an 18-23 record from 1975-77, including 9-5 record in 1976. Also was head coach of Toronto Argonauts (CFL) in 1979 before signing to take over Bengals. Served as an NFL assistant coach from 1972-74. He was offensive line coach with San Diego Chargers in 1972-73 before joining Cleveland Browns in same capacity in 1974. Had outstanding 15-year playing career in NFL as a guard-tackle with Green Bay Packers 1956-70 (he played in the Packers' two Super Bowl wins) and as a player-coach with Dallas Cowboys in Super Bowl championship season of 1971. Inducted into the Pro Football Hall of Fame in 1977. Career record: 68-66.

Background: Tackle at Southern Methodist 1953-55. Twice named to the All-Southwest Conference team. Captain of the SMU team his senior year. Spent 1957 in military service.

Personal: Born October 18, 1933, in Birthright, Tex. Attended Sulphur Springs (Tex.) High School. He and his wife, Barbara, live in Green Bay and have two children—Forrest, Jr., and Karen.

Assistant Coaches

Tom Coughlin, passing game-wide receivers; born August 31, 1946, Waterloo, N.Y., lives in Green Bay. Halfback Syracuse 1965-67. No pro playing experience. College coach: Rochester Tech (head coach) 1969-73, Syracuse 1974-80, Boston College 1981-83. Pro coach: Philadelphia Eagles 1984-85, first year with Packers.

Forrest Gregg, Jr., administrative assistant-defense; born February 23, 1962, Dallas, Tex., lives in Green Bay. Center Southern Methodist 1984. No pro playing experience. Pro coach: First year with Packers.

John Hilton, offensive backfield-special teams; born March 12, 1942, Albany, N.Y., lives in Green Bay. Wide receiver Richmond 1961-64. Pro tight end Pittsburgh Steelers 1965-69, Green Bay Packers 1970, Minnesota Vikings 1971, Detroit Lions 1972-73, Florida Blazers (WFL) 1974. Pro coach: Chicago Bears 1975-77, Washington Redskins 1978-80, first year with Packers.

Dick Jauron, defensive backfield; born October 7, 1950, Swampscott, Mass., lives in Green Bay. Defensive back Yale 1970-73. Pro defensive back Detroit Lions 1974-77, Cincinnati Bengals 1978-80. Pro coach: Buffalo Bills 1985, first year with Packers.

Virgil Knight, strength-conditioning; born January 30, 1948, Clarksville, Ark., lives in Green Bay. Tight end Northeastern Oklahoma 1968-70. No pro playing experience. College coach: Arkansas Tech 1975-78, Florida 1979-80, Auburn 1981-83. Pro coach: Joined Packers in 1985.

Dale Lindsey, linebackers; born January 18, 1943, Bowling Green, Ky., lives in Green Bay. Linebacker Western Kentucky 1961-64. Pro linebacker Cleveland Browns 1965-73. Pro coach: Cleveland Browns 1974, Portland Storm (WFL) 1975, Toronto Argonauts (CFL) 1979-82, Boston Breakers (USFL) 1983, New Jersey Generals (USFL) 1984-85, first year with Packers.

Dick Modzelewski, defensive coordinator-defensive line; born January 16, 1931, West Natrona, Pa., lives in Green Bay. Tackle Maryland 1950-52. Pro defensive tackle Washington Redskins 1953-54, Pittsburgh Steelers 1955, New York Giants 1956-63, Cleveland Browns 1964-66. Pro coach: Cleveland Browns 1968-77, New York Giants 1978, Cincinnati Bengals 1979-83, joined Packers in 1984.

GREEN BAY PACKERS 1986 FIRST-YEAR ROSTER

Name	Pos.	Ht.	Wt.	Birth-date	College	Hometown	How Acq.
Abernathy, Kirk	WR	5-11	182	9/18/62	Drake	Cedar Rapids, Iowa	FA
Berry, Ed	CB-S	5-10	176	9/28/63	Utah State	San Francisco, Calif.	D7
Boerema, Kim	WR	5-10	185	5/28/63	Northern Colorado	Denver, Colo.	FA
Bosco, Robbie	QB	6-2	188	1/11/63	Brigham Young	Roseville, Calif.	D3
Bowens, Nat (1)	LB	6-4	233	6/9/62	Southwest Oklahoma	Mahwah, N.J.	FA
Buxton, Steve (1)	T-G	6-6	270	12/23/61	Indiana State	Sullivan, Ill.	FA
Cherry, Bill	C-G	6-4	275	1/5/61	Middle Tennessee St.	Dover, Tenn.	FA
Cline, Michael	NT	6-3	265	7/28/63	Arkansas State	Pine Bluff, Ark.	D8
Davis, Ken	RB	5-10	212	4/16/62	Texas Christian	Temple, Tex.	D2
Dent, Burnell	LB	6-1	230	3/16/63	Tulane	New Orleans, La.	D6a
Dimido, Dean	TE	6-3	227	2/6/64	Penn State	West Chester, Pa.	FA
Fitzgerald, Pat	WR	6-3	200	10/13/63	Boise State	Boise, Idaho	FA
Gruner, Paul	G-T	6-5	271	10/20/62	Wisconsin-Platteville	Mequon, Wis.	FA
Harris, Tim	LB	6-5	238	9/10/64	Memphis State	Birmingham, Ala.	D4a
Hausauer, Ron (1)	G-T	6-3	275	8/16/59	Jamestown College	Beulah, N.D.	FA
Johnson, Morris (1)	G	6-4	295	6/25/62	Alabama A&M	Detroit, Mich.	D9-'85
Jones, Jessie	RB	6-0	220	3/5/64	Montana State	Tacoma, Wash.	FA
Jones, Mike	WR	6-0	173	6/13/62	Wisconsin	Chicago, Ill.	FA
Keever, Carl (1)	LB	6-2	235	8/17/61	Boise State	Boise, Idaho	FA
Koart, Matt	DE	6-5	256	9/28/63	Southern California	Goleta, Calif.	D5
Knight, Dan	T	6-5	280	7/19/63	San Diego State	Bonita, Calif.	D4b
Koenning, Vic (1)	LB	6-3	230	2/26/60	Kansas State	Owasso, Okla.	FA
Latham, Matt (1)	S	6-0	193	2/9/63	Connecticut	Stonington, Conn.	FA
Mallory, Mike	LB	6-0	228	11/16/62	Michigan	DeKalb, Ill.	FA
Moffitt, Mike	TE	6-4	215	7/28/63	Fresno State	Los Angeles, Calif.	FA
Moore, Brent	LB	6-5	242	1/9/63	Southern California	Novato, Calif.	D9
Neville, Tom (1)	T-G	6-5	280	9/4/61	Fresno State	Great Falls, Mont.	FA
Newell, Daryl	G-T	6-4	282	10/5/63	Northwestern	Gary, Ind.	FA
Parker, Freddie	RB	5-10	215	7/6/62	Mississippi Valley St.	Heidelberg, Miss.	FA
Rafferty, Vince (1)	C-G	6-4	280	8/6/61	Colorado	Longmont, Colo.	FA
Regent, Shawn	G-T	6-4	280	4/14/63	Boston College	Cheektowaga, N.Y.	FA
Roche, John	WR	6-1	194	11/30/62	Widener	Enola, Pa.	FA
Sellenriek, Brad	T-G	6-6	273	7/1/63	S.W. Missouri State	St. Louis, Mo.	FA
Spann, Gary	LB	6-2	220	2/3/63	Texas Christian	Dallas, Tex.	D10
Stevens, Tim	K	6-2	219	5/30/62	Southern Oregon St.	Salem, Ore.	FA
Stewart, Russell	LB	6-2	283	7/2/64	Sioux Falls College	Long Island, N.Y.	FA
Stokes, Randy	T-G	6-4	278	7/4/64	Auburn	Tallahassee, Fla.	FA
Thompson, Lawrence (1)	WR	5-11	176	1/6/61	Miami	Wauchula, Fla.	FA
Turpin, Miles	LB	6-4	230	5/15/64	California	Fremont, Calif.	FA
Vasquez, Gilbert	CB-S	6-0	186	11/26/62	Weber State	Magna, Utah	FA
Veingrad, Alan (1)	T-G	6-5	275	7/24/63	East Texas State	Miami, Fla.	FA
Ware, Willie	WR	5-8	165	9/9/63	Mississippi Valley St.	Carrollton, Miss.	FA
Zubradt, Tim	CB-S	6-0	201	12/19/63	Colorado State	Ft. Collins, Colo.	FA

The term NFL Rookie is defined as a player who is in his first season of professional football and has not been on the roster of another professional football team for any regular season or postseason games. A Rookie is designated by an "R" on NFL rosters. Players who have been active in another professional football league or players who have NFL experience, including either preseason training camp or being on an active roster for fewer than three regular season or postseason games, are termed NFL First-Year Players. An NFL First-Year Player is designated by a "1" on NFL rosters. Thereafter, a player on an NFL active roster for at least three regular season or postseason games is credited with an additional year of NFL playing experience.

NOTES

George Sefcik, quarterbacks; born December 27, 1939, Cleveland, Ohio, lives in Green Bay. Halfback Notre Dame 1959-61. No pro playing experience. College coach: Notre Dame 1963-68, Kentucky 1969-72. Pro coach: Baltimore Colts 1973-74, Cleveland Browns 1975-77, Cincinnati Bengals 1978-83, joined Packers in 1984.

Jerry Wampfler, offensive line; born August 6, 1932, New Philadelphia, Ohio, lives in Green Bay. Tackle Miami, Ohio 1951-54. No pro playing experience. College coach: Presbyterian 1955, Miami, Ohio 1963-65, Notre Dame 1966-69, Colorado State 1970-72 (head coach). Pro coach: Philadelphia Eagles 1973-75, 1979-83, Buffalo Bills 1976-77, New York Giants 1978, joined Packers in 1984.

National Football Conference
Western Division

Team Colors: Royal Blue, Gold, and White

Business Address:
2327 West Lincoln Avenue
Anaheim, California 92801

Ticket Office:
Anaheim Stadium
1900 State College Boulevard
Anaheim, California 92806
Telephone: (714) 535-7267
or (213) 585-5400

Club Officials

President: Georgia Frontiere
Vice President, Finance: John Shaw
General Counsel: Jay Zygmunt
Administrator, Football Operations: Jack Faulkner
Director of Operations: Dick Beam
Director of Player Personnel: John Math
Director of Public Relations: Pete Donovan
Assistant Director of Public Relations: John Oswald
Director of Community Relations: Marshall Klein
Trainers: George Menefee, Jim Anderson, Garrett Giemont
Equipment Manager: Don Hewitt
Assistant Equipment Manager: Todd Hewitt

Stadium: Anaheim Stadium • **Capacity:** 69,007
Anaheim, California 92806

Playing Surface: Grass

Training Camp: California State University
Fullerton, California 92634

1986 SCHEDULE

Preseason

Aug. 5	**Houston**	7:30
Aug. 18	**San Francisco**	7:30
Aug. 23	**San Diego**	7:00
Aug. 29	at Denver	6:00

Regular Season

Sept. 7	at St. Louis	12:00
Sept. 14	**San Francisco**	1:00
Sept. 21	at Indianapolis	12:00
Sept. 28	at Philadelphia	1:00
Oct. 5	**Tampa Bay**	1:00
Oct. 12	at Atlanta	1:00
Oct. 19	**Detroit**	1:00
Oct. 26	**Atlanta**	1:00
Nov. 3	at Chicago (Monday)	8:00
Nov. 9	at New Orleans	12:00
Nov. 16	**New England**	1:00
Nov. 23	**New Orleans**	1:00
Nov. 30	at New York Jets	1:00
Dec. 7	**Dallas**	6:00
Dec. 14	**Miami**	1:00
Dec. 19	at San Francisco (Friday)	5:00

RAMS COACHING HISTORY

Cleveland 1937-45
(349-283-20)

1937-38	Hugo Bezdek*	1-13-0
1938	Art Lewis	4-4-0
1939-42	Earl (Dutch) Clark	16-26-2
1944	Aldo (Buff) Donelli	4-6-0
1945-46	Adam Walsh	16-5-1
1947	Bob Snyder	6-6-0
1948-49	Clark Shaughnessy	14-8-3
1950-52	Joe Stydahar**	19-9-0
1952-54	Hamp Pool	23-11-2
1955-59	Sid Gillman	28-32-1
1960-62	Bob Waterfield***	9-24-1
1962-65	Harland Svare	14-31-3
1966-70	George Allen	49-19-4
1971-72	Tommy Prothro	14-12-2
1973-77	Chuck Knox	57-20-1
1978-82	Ray Malavasi	43-36-0
1983-85	John Robinson	32-21-0

*Released after three games in 1938
**Resigned after one game in 1952
***Resigned after eight games in 1962

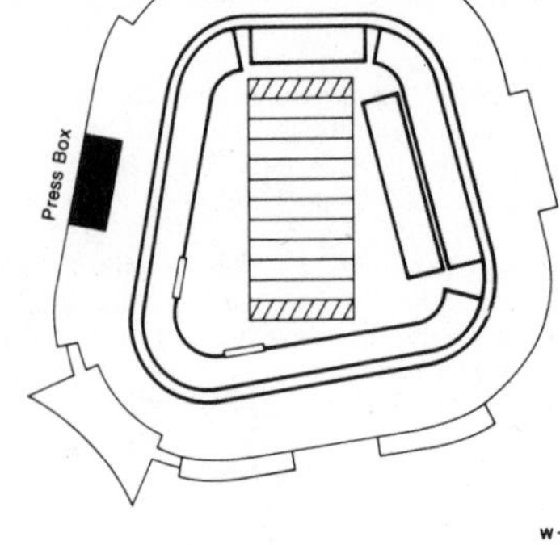

ANAHEIM STADIUM

RECORD HOLDERS

Individual Records—Career

Category	Name	Performance
Rushing (Yds.)	Lawrence McCutcheon, 1973-79	6,186
Passing (Yds.)	Roman Gabriel, 1962-1972	22,223
Passing (TDs)	Roman Gabriel, 1962-1972	154
Receiving (No.)	Tom Fears, 1948-1956	400
Receiving (Yds.)	Elroy Hirsch, 1949-1957	6,289
Interceptions	Ed Meador, 1959-1970	46
Punting (Avg.)	Danny Villanueva, 1960-64	44.2
Punt Return (Avg.)	Henry Ellard, 1983-85	13.5
Kickoff Return (Avg.)	Ron Brown, 1984-85	32.8
Field Goals	Bruce Gossett, 1964-69	120
Touchdowns (Tot.)	Elroy Hirsch, 1949-1957	55
Points	Bob Waterfield, 1946-1952	573

Individual Records—Single Season

Category	Name	Performance
Rushing (Yds.)	Eric Dickerson, 1984	2,105
Passing (Yds.)	Vince Ferragamo, 1983	3,276
Passing (TDs)	Vince Ferragamo, 1980	30
Receiving (No.)	Tom Fears, 1950	84
Receiving (Yds.)	Elroy Hirsch, 1951	1,425
Interceptions	Dick (Night Train) Lane, 1952	14
Punting (Avg.)	Danny Villanueva, 1962	45.5
Punt Return (Avg.)	Woodley Lewis, 1952	18.5
Kickoff Return (Avg.)	Verda (Vitamin T) Smith, 1950	33.7
Field Goals	David Ray, 1973	30
Touchdowns (Tot.)	Eric Dickerson, 1983	20
Points	David Ray, 1973	130

Individual Records—Single Game

Category	Name	Performance
Rushing (Yds.)	Eric Dickerson, 1-4-86	248
Passing (Yds.)	Norm Van Brocklin, 9-28-51	554
Passing (TDs)	Many times	5
	Last time by Vince Ferragamo, 10-23-83	
Receiving (No.)	Tom Fears, 12-3-50	18
Receiving (Yds.)	Jim Benton, 11-22-45	303
Interceptions	Many times	3
	Last time by Pat Thomas, 10-7-79	
Field Goals	Bob Waterfield, 12-9-51	5
Touchdowns (Tot.)	Bob Shaw, 12-11-49	4
	Elroy Hirsch, 9-28-51	4
	Harold Jackson, 10-14-73	4
Points	Bob Shaw, 12-11-49	24
	Elroy Hirsch, 9-28-51	24
	Harold Jackson, 10-14-73	24

1985 TEAM STATISTICS

	L.A. Rams	Opp.
Total First Downs	258	281
Rushing	115	104
Passing	131	155
Penalty	12	22
Third Down: Made/Att.	69/205	86/236
Fourth Down: Made/Att.	7/13	12/19
Total Net Yards	4520	4648
Avg. Per Game	282.5	290.5
Total Plays	963	1048
Avg. Per Play	4.7	4.4
Net Yards Rushing	2057	1586
Avg. Per Game	128.6	99.1
Total Rushes	503	444
Net Yards Passing	2463	3062
Avg. Per Game	153.9	191.4
Tackled/Yards Lost	57/409	56/421
Gross Yards	2872	3483
Att./Completions	403/234	548/296
Completion Pct.	58.1	54.0
Had Intercepted	14	29
Punts/Avg.	88/42.7	89/42.0
Net Punting Avg.	38.0	34.6
Penalties/Yards Lost	97/730	72/529
Fumbles/Ball Lost	35/21	30/17
Touchdowns	39	30
Rushing	15	9
Passing	16	19
Returns	8	2
Avg. Time of Possession	29:51	30:09

1985 TEAM RECORD

Preseason (3-1)

Date	Los Angeles Rams		Opponents
8/10	7	*Houston	3
8/15	39	*St. Louis	7
8/23	12	Philadelphia	14
8/31	14	*New England	13
	72		37

Regular Season (11-5)

Date	Los Angeles Rams		Opp.	Att.
9/8	20	*Denver	16	52,522
9/15	17	Philadelphia	6	60,920
9/23	35	Seattle	24	63,292
9/29	17	*Atlanta	6	49,870
10/6	13	*Minnesota	10	61,139
10/13	31	Tampa Bay	27	39,607
10/20	16	Kansas City	0	64,474
10/27	14	*San Francisco	28	65,939
11/3	28	*New Orleans	10	49,030
11/10	19	N.Y. Giants	24	74,603
11/17	14	Atlanta	30	29,960
11/24	34	*Green Bay	17	52,710
12/1	3	New Orleans	29	44,122
12/9	27	San Francisco	20	60,581
12/15	46	*St. Louis	14	52,052
12/23	6	*L.A. Raiders	16	66,676

Postseason (1-1)

Date	Los Angeles Rams		Opp.	Att.
1/4/86	20	*Dallas	0	66,581
1/12/86	0	Chicago	24	66,030

*Home Game

Score by Periods

L.A. Rams	54	102	82	102	0	—	340
Opponents	47	99	53	78	0	—	277

Attendance

Home 449,938 Away 437,559 Total 887,497
Single game home record, 102,368 (11-10-57; L.A. Coliseum), 67,037 (12-23-84; Anaheim Stadium)
Single season home record, 519,175 (1973; L.A. Coliseum), 500,403 (1980; Anaheim Stadium)

1985 INDIVIDUAL STATISTICS

Rushing	Att.	Yds.	Avg.	LG	TD
Dickerson	292	1234	4.2	43	12
Redden	87	380	4.4	41	0
White	70	310	4.4	32	3
Cain	11	46	4.2	9	0
Brock	20	38	1.9	13	0
Guman	11	32	2.9	6	0
Brown	2	13	6.5	9	0
Ellard	3	8	2.7	16	0
Kemp	5	0	0.0	3	0
Dils	2	−4	−2.0	−2	0
L.A. Rams	503	2057	4.1	43	15
Opponents	444	1586	3.6	36	9

Passing	Att.	Comp.	Pct.	Yds.	TD	Int.	Tkld.	Rate
Brock	365	218	59.7	2658	16	13	51/351	82.0
Kemp	38	16	42.1	214	0	1	6/58	49.7
L.A. Rams	403	234	58.1	2872	16	14	57/409	78.9
Opponents	548	296	54.0	3483	19	29	56/421	63.1

Receiving	No.	Yds.	Avg.	LG	TD
Ellard	54	811	15.0	64t	5
Hunter	50	562	11.2	47t	4
D. Hill	29	271	9.3	37	1
Duckworth	25	422	16.9	42	3
Dickerson	20	126	6.3	33	0
Redden	16	162	10.1	32	0
Brown	14	215	15.4	43t	3
Young	14	157	11.2	23	0
McDonald, Det.-Rams	5	81	16.2	35	0
McDonald, Rams	2	58	29.0	35	0
Cain	5	24	4.8	13	0
Guman	3	23	7.7	11	0
Barber	1	29	29.0	29	0
White	1	12	12.0	12	0
L.A. Rams	234	2872	12.3	64t	16
Opponents	296	3483	11.8	73	19

Interceptions	No.	Yds.	Avg.	LG	TD
Green	6	84	14.0	41t	1
Irvin	6	83	13.8	34t	1
Johnson	5	96	19.2	46	1
Newsome	3	20	6.7	20	0
Ekern	2	55	27.5	33t	1
Collins	2	8	4.0	4	0
Fox	2	8	4.0	8	0
Cromwell	2	5	2.5	5	0
Wilcher	1	0	0.0	0	0
L.A. Rams	29	359	12.4	46	4
Opponents	14	138	9.9	30	1

Punting	No.	Yds.	Avg.	In 20	LG
Hatcher	87	3761	43.2	32	67
L.A. Rams	88	3761	42.7	32	67
Opponents	89	3738	42.0	24	61

Punt Returns	No.	FC	Yds.	Avg.	LG	TD
Ellard	37	9	501	13.5	80t	1
White	1	0	0	0.0	0	0
Johnson	0	7	0	—	0	0
L.A. Rams	38	16	501	13.2	80t	1
Opponents	43	22	297	6.9	23	0

Kickoff Returns	No.	Yds.	Avg.	LG	TD
Brown	28	918	32.8	98t	3
White	17	300	17.6	32	0
Cain	6	115	19.2	28	0
Guman	2	30	15.0	17	0
Cromwell	1	3	3.0	3	0
Miller	1	10	10.0	10	0
Slaton	1	18	18.0	18	0
L.A. Rams	56	1394	24.9	98t	3
Opponents	66	1253	19.0	62	0

Scoring	TD R	TD P	TD Rt	PAT	FG	Saf	TP
Lansford	0	0	0	38/39	22/29	0	104
Dickerson	12	0	0	0/0	0/0	0	72
Brown	0	3	3	0/0	0/0	0	36
Ellard	0	5	1	0/0	0/0	0	36
Hunter	0	4	0	0/0	0/0	0	24
Duckworth	0	3	0	0/0	0/0	0	18
White	3	0	0	0/0	0/0	0	18
Ekern	0	0	1	0/0	0/0	0	6
Green	0	0	1	0/0	0/0	0	6
D. Hill	0	1	0	0/0	0/0	0	6
Irvin	0	0	1	0/0	0/0	0	6
Johnson	0	0	1	0/0	0/0	0	6
Doss	0	0	0	0/0	0/0	1	2
L.A. Rams	15	16	8	38/39	22/29	1	340
Opponents	9	19	2	28/30	23/29	0	277

FIRST-ROUND SELECTIONS

(If club had no first-round selection, first player drafted is listed with round in parentheses.)

Year	Player, College, Position
1937	Johnny Drake, Purdue, B
1938	Corbett Davis, Indiana, B
1939	Parker Hall, Mississippi, B
1940	Ollie Cordill, Rice, B
1941	Rudy Mucha, Washington, C
1942	Jack Wilson, Baylor, B
1943	Mike Holovak, Boston College, B
1944	Tony Butkovich, Illinois, B
1945	Elroy (Crazylegs) Hirsch, Wisconsin, B
1946	Emil Sitko, Notre Dame, B
1947	Herman Wedemeyer, St. Mary's, Cal., B
1948	Tom Keane, West Virginia, B (2)
1949	Bobby Thomason, Virginia Military, B
1950	Ralph Pasquariello, Villanova, B
	Stan West, Oklahoma, G
1951	Bud McFadin, Texas, G
1952	Bill Wade, Vanderbilt, QB
	Bob Carey, Michigan State, E
1953	Donn Moomaw, UCLA, C
	Ed Barker, Washington State, E
1954	Ed Beatty, Cincinnati, C
1955	Larry Morris, Georgia Tech, C
1956	Joe Marconi, West Virginia, B
	Charles Horton, Vanderbilt, B
1957	Jon Arnett, Southern California, B
	Del Shofner, Baylor, E
1958	Lou Michaels, Kentucky, T
	Jim Phillips, Auburn, E
1959	Dick Bass, Pacific, B
	Paul Dickson, Baylor, T
1960	Billy Cannon, Louisiana State, RB
1961	Marlin McKeever, Southern California, E-LB
1962	Roman Gabriel, North Carolina State, QB
	Merlin Olsen, Utah State, DT
1963	Terry Baker, Oregon State, QB
	Rufus Guthrie, Georgia Tech, G
1964	Bill Munson, Utah State, QB
1965	Clancy Williams, Washington State, CB
1966	Tom Mack, Michigan, G
1967	Willie Ellison, Texas Southern, RB (2)
1968	Gary Beban, UCLA, QB (2)
1969	Larry Smith, Florida, RB
	Jim Seymour, Notre Dame, WR
	Bob Klein, Southern California, TE
1970	Jack Reynolds, Tennessee, LB
1971	Isiah Robertson, Southern, LB
	Jack Youngblood, Florida, DE
1972	Jim Bertelsen, Texas, RB (2)
1973	Cullen Bryant, Colorado, DB (2)
1974	John Cappelletti, Penn State, RB
1975	Mike Fanning, Notre Dame, DT
	Dennis Harrah, Miami, T
	Doug France, Ohio State, T
1976	Kevin McLain, Colorado State, LB
1977	Bob Brudzinski, Ohio State, LB
1978	Elvis Peacock, Oklahoma, RB
1979	George Andrews, Nebraska, LB
	Kent Hill, Georgia Tech, T
1980	Johnnie Johnson, Texas, DB
1981	Mel Owens, Michigan, LB
1982	Barry Redden, Richmond, RB
1983	Eric Dickerson, Southern Methodist, RB
1984	Hal Stephens, East Carolina, DE (5)
1985	Jerry Gray, Texas, DB
1986	Mike Schad, Queen's University, Canada, T

LOS ANGELES RAMS 1986 VETERAN ROSTER

No.	Name	Pos.	Ht.	Wt.	Birth-date	NFL Exp.	College	Hometown	How Acq.	'85 Games/ Starts
52	Andrews, George	LB	6-3	225	11/28/55	7	Nebraska	Omaha, Neb.	D1-'79	0*
10	Bartkowski, Steve	QB	6-4	218	11/12/52	12	California	Santa Clara, Calif.	FA-'86	5/5*
90	†Brady, Ed	LB	6-2	235	6/17/60	3	Illinois	Morris, Ill.	D8-'84	16/0
5	Brock, Dieter	QB	6-1	195	2/12/51	2	Jacksonville State	Birmingham, Ala.	FA-'85	15/15
89	Brown, Ron	WR	5-11	181	3/31/61	3	Arizona State	Baldwin Park, Calif.	T(Clev)-'84	13/9
50	†Collins, Jim	LB	6-2	230	6/11/58	6	Syracuse	Mendham, N.J.	D2-'81	16/16
21	Cromwell, Nolan	S	6-1	200	1/30/55	10	Kansas	Ransom, Kan.	D2-'77	16/16
70	†DeJurnett, Charles	NT	6-4	260	6/17/52	10	San Jose State	Picayune, Mich.	FA-'82	15/14
29	Dickerson, Eric	RB	6-3	220	9/2/60	4	Southern Methodist	Sealy, Tex.	D1-'83	14/14
8	Dils, Steve	QB	6-1	191	12/8/55	7	Stanford	Vancouver, Wash.	T(Minn)-'84	15/0
71	†Doss, Reggie	DE	6-4	263	12/7/56	9	Hampton Institute	San Antonio, Tex.	D7-'78	16/15
82	Duckworth, Bobby	WR	6-3	196	11/27/58	5	Arkansas	Crossett, Ark.	T(SD)-'85	14/6
55	†Ekern, Carl	LB	6-3	230	5/27/54	10	San Jose State	Sunnyvale, Calif.	D5-'76	16/16
80	†Ellard, Henry	WR	5-11	175	7/21/61	4	Fresno State	Fresno, Calif.	D2-'83	16/16
48	Fox, Tim	S	5-11	186	11/1/53	11	Ohio State	Foxboro, Mass.	FA-'85	6/0
25	Gray, Jerry	CB	6-0	185	12/2/62	2	Texas	Lubbock, Tex.	D1-'85	16/1
27	Green, Gary	CB	5-11	191	10/2/55	10	Baylor	San Antonio, Tex.	T(KC)-'84	16/16
91	Greene, Kevin	LB	6-3	238	7/31/62	2	Auburn	Anderson, Ala.	D5-'85	15/0
44	Guman, Mike	RB	6-2	218	4/21/58	7	Penn State	Bethlehem, Pa.	D6-'80	8/1
60	†Harrah, Dennis	G	6-5	265	3/9/53	12	Miami	Charleston, W. Va.	D1-'75	10/10
26	Harris, Eric	CB	6-3	202	8/11/55	7	Memphis State	Memphis, Tenn.	T(KC)-'83	9/0
68	Harrison, Dennis	DE	6-8	280	7/13/56	9	Vanderbilt	Nashville, Tenn.	T(Phil)-'85	12/0
3	Hatcher, Dale	P	6-2	200	4/5/63	2	Clemson	Cheraw, S.C.	D3-'85	16/0
81	Hill, David	TE	6-2	240	1/1/54	11	Texas A&I	San Antonio, Tex.	T(Det)-'83	16/16
72	Hill, Kent	G	6-5	260	3/7/57	8	Georgia Tech	Americus, Ga.	D1-'79	16/16
87	Hunter, Tony	TE	6-4	237	5/22/60	4	Notre Dame	Cincinnati, Ohio	T(Buff)-'85	16/9
47	Irvin, LeRoy	CB	5-11	184	9/15/57	7	Kansas	Augusta, Ga.	D5-'80	16/16
59	†Jerue, Mark	LB	6-3	232	1/15/60	4	Washington	Seattle, Wash.	T(Ind)-'83	16/0
77	Jeter, Gary	DE	6-4	260	3/24/55	10	Southern California	Cleveland, Ohio	T(NYG)-'83	16/1
20	Johnson, Johnnie	S	6-1	183	10/8/56	7	Texas	LaGrange, Tex.	D1-'80	16/15
1	Lansford, Mike	K	6-0	183	7/20/58	5	Washington	Arcadia, Calif.	FA-'82	16/0
57	†Laughlin, Jim	LB	6-1	222	7/5/58	7	Ohio State	Cleveland, Ohio	FA-'84	10/0
67	Love, Duval	G	6-3	263	6/24/63	2	UCLA	Fountain Valley, Calif.	D10-'85	6/0
83	McDonald, James	TE	6-5	230	3/29/61	4	Southern California	Long Beach, Calif.	T(Det)-'85	15/0*
69	Meisner, Greg	NT	6-3	253	4/23/59	6	Pittsburgh	New Kensington, Pa.	D3-'81	14/0
98	†Miller, Shawn	NT	6-4	255	3/14/61	3	Utah State	Ogden, Utah	FA-'84	16/3
22	Newsome, Vince	S	6-1	179	1/22/61	4	Washington	Vacaville, Calif.	D4-'83	16/1
58	†Owens, Mel	LB	6-2	224	12/7/58	6	Michigan	Detroit, Mich.	D1-'81	16/15
75	Pankey, Irv	T	6-4	267	12/15/58	6	Penn State	Aberdeen, Pa.	D2-'80	16/12
43	†Pleasant, Mike	CB	6-1	195	8/16/58	2	Oklahoma	Muskogee, Okla.	FA-'84	0*
30	Redden, Barry	RB	5-10	205	7/21/60	5	Richmond	Sarasota, Fla.	D1-'82	14/2
93	†Reed, Doug	DE	6-3	262	7/16/60	3	San Diego State	San Diego, Calif.	D4-'83	16/16
78	Slater, Jackie	T	6-4	271	5/27/54	11	Jackson State	Meridian, Mich.	D3-'76	16/16
61	Slaton, Tony	C	6-3	265	4/12/61	3	Southern California	Merced, Calif.	FA-'84	13/5
56	†Smith, Doug	C	6-3	260	11/25/56	9	Bowling Green	Columbus, Ohio	FA-'78	13/13
51	Vann, Norwood	LB	6-2	225	2/18/62	3	East Carolina	Magnolia, S.C.	D10-'84	8/0
33	White, Charles	RB	5-10	190	1/22/58	6	Southern California	San Fernando, Calif.	FA-'85	16/0
54	Wilcher, Mike	LB	6-3	240	3/20/60	4	North Carolina	Washington, D.C.	D2-'83	16/15
88	Young, Michael	WR	6-1	185	2/2/62	2	UCLA	Visalia, Calif.	D6-'85	15/1

* Andrews and Pleasant missed '85 season due to injury; Bartkowski played 5 games with Atlanta, active for 2 games with Washington, but did not play in '85; McDonald played 6 games with Detroit, 9 with L.A. Rams in '85.

†Option playout; subject to developments.

Traded—Quarterback Jeff Kemp to San Francisco.

Retired—Russ Bolinger, 9-year guard, 6 games in '85.

Also played with Rams in '85—T Bill Bain (15 games), TE Mike Barber (5), RB Lynn Cain (7), RB A.J. Jones (1), DE Booker Reese (2).

COACHING STAFF

Head Coach, John Robinson

Pro Career: Begins fourth season as Rams head coach. Guided Rams to an 11-5 record and berth in NFC Championship Game in 1985. Has taken Rams to playoffs three straight years. Became seventeenth head coach in Rams history on February 14, 1983. Arrived with 23 years of coaching experience, including one on the professional level with the Raiders in 1975. No pro playing experience. Career record: 32-21.

Background: Played end at Oregon 1955-58. Began coaching career with his alma mater from 1960-71. Became an assistant at Southern California from 1972-74. Returned as head coach in 1976 before resigning after the 1982 season. Compiled seven-year .819 winning percentage at Southern California with 67 wins, 14 losses, and 2 ties.

Personal: Born July 25, 1935, in Chicago, Ill. John and his wife, Barbara, live in Fullerton, Calif., and have four children—Teresa, Lynn, David, and Christopher.

Assistant Coaches

Dick Coury, quarterbacks; born September 29, 1929, Athens, Ohio, lives in Anaheim, Calif. No college or pro playing experience. College coach: Southern California 1965-67, Cal State-Fullerton 1968-70 (head coach). Pro coach: Denver Broncos 1971-73, Portland Storm (WFL) 1974 (head coach), San Diego Chargers 1975, Philadelphia Eagles 1976-81, Boston-Portland Breakers (USFL) 1983-85 (head coach), first year with Rams.

Lew Erber, wide receivers; born May 27, 1934, Clifton, N.J., lives in Corona del Mar, Calif. Wing back Montclair, N.J., State, 1954-55. No pro playing experience. College coach: Iowa State 1967-68, California Western 1969-72, San Diego State 1973, California 1974. Pro coach: San Francisco 49ers 1975, Oakland Raiders 1976-81, New England Patriots 1982-84, joined Rams in 1985.

Marv Goux, defensive line; born September 8, 1932, Santa Barbara, Calif., lives in Long Beach, Calif. Linebacker Southern California 1952, 1954-55. No pro playing experience. College coach: Southern California 1957-82. Pro coach: Joined Rams in 1983.

Gil Haskell, special teams; born September 24, 1943, San Francisco, Calif., lives in Diamond Bar, Calif. Defensive back San Francisco State 1961, 1963-65. No pro playing experience. College coach: Southern California 1978-82. Pro coach: Joined Rams in 1983.

Hudson Houck, offensive line; born January 7, 1943, Los Angeles, Calif., lives in Long Beach, Calif. Center Southern California 1962-64. No pro playing experience. College coach: Southern California 1970-72, 1976-82, Stanford 1973-75. Pro coach: Joined Rams in 1983.

Steve Shafer, defensive backs; born December 8, 1940, Glendale, Calif., lives in Anaheim, Calif. Quarterback-defensive back Utah State 1961-62. Pro defensive back British Columbia Lions (CFL) 1963-67. College coach: San Mateo, Calif., J.C. 1968-74 (head coach 1973-74), San Diego State 1975-82. Pro coach: Joined Rams in 1983.

Fritz Shurmur, defensive coordinator-inside linebackers; born July 15, 1932, Riverview, Mich., lives in Diamond Bar, Calif. Center Albion 1951-53. No pro playing experience. College coach: Albion 1956-61, Wyoming 1962-74 (head coach 1971-74). Pro coach: Detroit Lions 1975-77, New England Patriots 1978-81, joined Rams in 1982.

Bruce Snyder, running backs-running game coordinator; born March 14, 1940, Santa Monica, Calif., lives in Anaheim, Calif. Fullback Oregon 1960-62. No pro playing experience. College coach: Oregon 1966-72, Utah State 1973, 1976-82 (head coach), Southern California 1974-75. Pro coach: Joined Rams in 1983.

Norval Turner, tight ends-U-backs; born May 17, 1952, Martinez, Calif., lives in Long Beach, Calif. Quarterback Oregon 1972-74. No pro playing experience. College coach: Oregon 1975, Southern California 1976-84. Pro coach: Joined Rams in 1985.

LOS ANGELES RAMS 1986 FIRST-YEAR ROSTER

Name	Pos.	Ht.	Wt.	Birth-date	College	Hometown	How Acq.
Bradley, Danny (1)	WR	5-9	178	3/2/63	Oklahoma	Pine Bluff, Ark.	D7-'85
Breeland, Garrett	LB	6-1	230	5/31/63	Southern California	Fullerton, Calif.	D10
Cox, Robert	T	6-5	258	12/30/63	UCLA	Dublin, Calif.	D6a
Dupree, Marcus	RB	6-3	235	5/22/64	Oklahoma	Philadelphia, Miss.	D12
Edwards, Dennis (1)	DE	6-4	253	10/6/59	Southern California	Stockton, Calif.	FA
Goebel, Hank	T	6-7	270	11/1/64	Cal State-Fullerton	Newport Beach, Calif.	D8b
Jarecki, Steve	LB	6-2	217	7/13/63	UCLA	Napa, Calif.	D8a
Johnson, Damone (1)	TE	6-4	230	3/2/62	Cal Poly-SLO	Santa Monica, Calif.	D6-'85
Long, Darren (1)	TE	6-3	240	7/12/59	Long Beach State	Exeter, Calif.	FA
McAdoo, Howard (1)	LB	6-2	230	1/14/62	Michigan State	Rolling Hills, Calif.	FA
McDonald, Keith (1)	WR	5-8	170	11/7/63	San Jose State	Wilmington, Calif.	FA
McNeil, Mark	CB	6-0	195	8/25/61	Houston	San Antonio, Tex.	FA
Millen, Hugh	QB	6-4	216	11/22/63	Washington	Seattle, Wash.	D3
Newberry, Tom	G	6-2	279	12/20/62	Wisconsin-La Crosse	Onalaska, Wis.	D2
Pembrook, Mark (1)	S	6-0	195	9/17/63	Cal State-Fullerton	Paramount, Calif.	FA
Richard, Darryl (1)	WR	5-9	173	1/22/58	Azusa Pacific	Sun Valley, Calif.	FA
Richardson, Paul	WR	5-11	175	2/3/61	San Diego State	Visalia, Calif.	FA
Schad, Mike	T	6-5	290	10/4/63	Queen's Univ. (Can.)	Belleville, Canada	D1
Schwanke, Chul	RB	5-11	213	4/2/63	South Dakota	Hutchinson, Minn.	D11
Schamel, Duke (1)	LB	6-2	220	11/3/63	South Dakota	Tulelake, Calif.	FA
Scott, Chuck (1)	WR	6-2	202	5/24/63	Vanderbilt	Maitland, Fla.	D2-'85
Shiner, Mike (1)	T	6-8	285	1/27/61	Notre Dame	Sunnyvale, Calif.	FA
Stone, William (1)	RB	5-10	201	2/25/63	Adams State	Covina, Calif.	FA
Toub, Dave (1)	C	6-3	280	6/1/62	Texas-El Paso	Mahopac, N.Y.	FA
Watts, Elbert	CB	6-2	205	3/20/63	Southern California	Carson, Calif.	D9
Williams, Lynn	RB	6-2	215	12/19/62	Kansas	Carson, Calif.	D6b
Wright, Alvin (1)	NT	6-2	265	2/5/61	Jacksonville State	Nedonee, Ala.	FA

The term NFL Rookie is defined as a player who is in his first season of professional football and has not been on the roster of another professional football team for any regular season or postseason games. A Rookie is designated by an "R" on NFL rosters. Players who have been active in another professional football league or players who have NFL experience, including either preseason training camp or being on an active roster for fewer than three regular season or postseason games, are termed NFL First-Year Players. An NFL First-Year Player is designated by a "1" on NFL rosters. Thereafter, a player on an NFL active roster for at least three regular season or postseason games is credited with an additional year of NFL playing experience.

NOTES

Fred Whittingham, outside linebackers; born February 4, 1942, Boston, Mass., lives in Anaheim, Calif. Linebacker Cal Poly-SLO 1960-62. Pro linebacker Los Angeles Rams 1964, Philadelphia Eagles 1965-66, 1971, New Orleans Saints 1967-68, Dallas Cowboys 1969-70. College coach: Brigham Young 1973-81. Pro coach: Joined Rams in 1982.

National Football Conference
Central Division

Team Colors: Purple, Gold, and White

9520 Viking Drive
Eden Prairie, Minnesota 55344
Telephone: (612) 828-6500

Club Officials

Chairman of the Board: John Skoglund
President: Max Winter
Senior Vice President: Jack Steele
Secretary/Treasurer: Sheldon Kaplan
Executive Vice President/General Manager: Mike Lynn
Assistant to the General Manager/Director of Operations: Jeff Diamond
Director of Administration: Harley Peterson
Director of Football Operations: Jerry Reichow
Director of Player Personnel: Frank Gilliam
Head Scout: Ralph Kohl
Assistant Head Scout: Don Deisch
Regional Scout: John Carson
Director of Public Relations: Merrill Swanson
Director of Communications and Community Relations: Kernal Buhler
Public Relations Assistant: Katie Hogan
Public Relations Assistant: Daniel Endy
Trainer: Fred Zamberletti
Equipment Manager: Dennis Ryan

Stadium: Hubert H. Humphrey Metrodome • **Capacity:** 62,345
500 11th Avenue So.
Minneapolis, Minnesota 55415

Playing Surface: SuperTurf

Training Camp: Mankato State University
Mankato, Minnesota 56001

1986 SCHEDULE

Preseason

Aug. 9	**Miami**	7:00
Aug. 16	**Denver**	7:00
Aug. 22	at Seattle	7:30
Aug. 30	at Indianapolis	7:30

Regular Season

Sept. 7	**Detroit**	12:00
Sept. 14	at Tampa Bay	4:00
Sept. 21	**Pittsburgh**	12:00
Sept. 28	**Green Bay**	12:00
Oct. 5	at Chicago	12:00
Oct. 12	at San Francisco	1:00
Oct. 19	**Chicago**	12:00
Oct. 26	**Cleveland**	12:00
Nov. 2	at Washington	4:00
Nov. 9	at Detroit	1:00
Nov. 16	**New York Giants**	12:00
Nov. 23	at Cincinnati	1:00
Nov. 30	**Tampa Bay**	12:00
Dec. 7	at Green Bay	12:00
Dec. 14	at Houston	3:00
Dec. 21	**New Orleans**	12:00

VIKINGS COACHING HISTORY

(200-172-9)

1961-66	Norm Van Brocklin	29-51-4
1967-83	Bud Grant	161-99-5
1984	Les Steckel	3-13-0
1985	Bud Grant	7-9-0

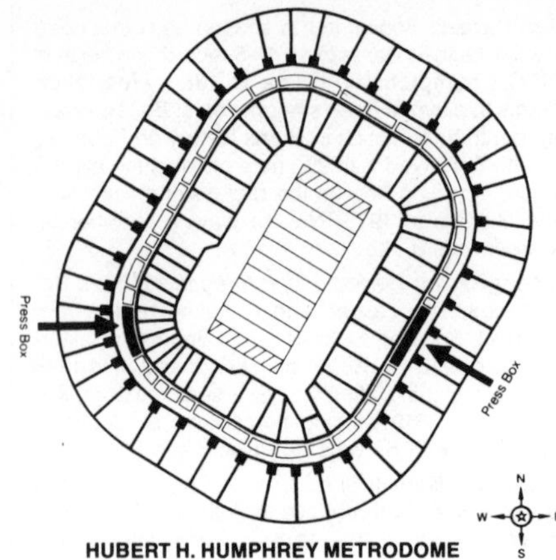

HUBERT H. HUMPHREY METRODOME

RECORD HOLDERS

Individual Records—Career

Category	Name	Performance
Rushing (Yds.)	Chuck Foreman, 1973-79	5,879
Passing (Yds.)	Fran Tarkenton, 1961-66, 1972-78	33,098
Passing (TDs)	Fran Tarkenton, 1961-66, 1972-78	239
Receiving (No.)	Ahmad Rashad, 1976-1982	400
Receiving (Yds.)	Sammy White, 1976-1985	5,925
Interceptions	Paul Krause, 1968-1979	53
Punting (Avg.)	Bobby Walden, 1964-67	42.9
Punt Return (Avg.)	Tommy Mason, 1961-66	10.5
Kickoff Return (Avg.)	Bob Reed, 1962-63	27.1
Field Goals	Fred Cox, 1963-1977	282
Touchdowns (Tot.)	Bill Brown, 1962-1974	76
Points	Fred Cox, 1963-1977	1,365

Individual Records—Single Season

Category	Name	Performance
Rushing (Yds.)	Chuck Foreman, 1976	1,155
Passing (Yds.)	Tommy Kramer, 1981	3,912
Passing (TDs)	Tommy Kramer, 1981	26
Receiving (No.)	Rickey Young, 1978	88
Receiving (Yds.)	Ahmad Rashad, 1979	1,156
Interceptions	Paul Krause, 1975	10
Punting (Avg.)	Bobby Walden, 1964	46.4
Punt Return (Avg.)	Billy Butler, 1963	10.5
Kickoff Return (Avg.)	John Gilliam, 1972	26.3
Field Goals	Fred Cox, 1970	30
Touchdowns (Tot.)	Chuck Foreman, 1975	22
Points	Chuck Foreman, 1975	132

Individual Records—Single Game

Category	Name	Performance
Rushing (Yds.)	Chuck Foreman, 10-24-76	200
Passing (Yds.)	Tommy Kramer, 12-14-80	456
Passing (TDs)	Joe Kapp, 9-28-69	7
Receiving (No.)	Rickey Young, 12-16-79	15
Receiving (Yds.)	Sammy White, 11-7-76	210
Interceptions	Many times	3
	Last time by Willie Teal, 11-28-82	
Field Goals	Fred Cox, 9-23-73	5
	Jan Stenerud, 9-23-84	5
Touchdowns (Tot.)	Chuck Foreman, 12-20-75	4
	Ahmad Rashad, 9-2-79	4
Points	Chuck Foreman, 12-20-75	24
	Ahmad Rashad, 9-2-79	24

1985 TEAM STATISTICS

	Minnesota	Opp.
Total First Downs	317	324
Rushing	95	139
Passing	189	163
Penalty	33	22
Third Down: Made/Att.	81/206	97/223
Fourth Down: Made/Att.	9/13	8/13
Total Net Yards	5151	5464
Avg. Per Game	321.9	341.5
Total Plays	1027	1065
Avg. Per Play	5.0	5.1
Net Yards Rushing	1516	2223
Avg. Per Game	94.8	138.9
Total Rushes	406	542
Net Yards Passing	3635	3241
Avg. Per Game	227.2	202.6
Tackled/Yards Lost	45/296	33/223
Gross Yards	3931	3464
Att./Completions	576/311	490/280
Completion Pct.	54.0	57.1
Had Intercepted	29	22
Punts/Avg.	67/42.8	65/41.4
Net Punting Avg.	36.7	34.2
Penalties/Yards Lost	88/690	123/1000
Fumbles/Ball Lost	27/18	37/22
Touchdowns	43	39
Rushing	19	16
Passing	22	20
Returns	2	3
Avg. Time of Possession	28:07	31:53

1985 TEAM RECORD

Preseason (3-1)

Date	Minnesota		Opponents
8/10	16	Miami (OT)	13
8/17	41	*Pittsburgh	34
8/24	10	*Seattle	27
8/30	13	Denver	9
	80		83

Regular Season (7-9)

Date	Minnesota		Opp.	Att.
9/8	28	*San Francisco	21	57,375
9/15	31	Tampa Bay	16	46,188
9/19	24	*Chicago	33	61,242
9/29	27	Buffalo	20	45,667
10/6	10	L.A. Rams	13	61,139
10/13	17	Green Bay	20	54,674
10/20	21	*San Diego	17	61,670
10/27	9	Chicago	27	63,815
11/3	16	*Detroit	13	58,012
11/10	17	*Green Bay	27	59,970
11/17	21	Detroit	41	54,647
11/24	23	*New Orleans	30	54,117
12/1	28	Philadelphia	23	54,688
12/8	26	*Tampa Bay	7	51,593
12/15	13	Atlanta	14	14,167
12/22	35	*Philadelphia	37	49,722

*Home Game (OT) Overtime

Score by Periods

Minnesota	44	91	83	128	0	—	346
Opponents	81	92	96	90	0	—	359

Attendance

Home 453,701 Away 394,985 Total 848,686
Single game home record, 61,670 (10-20-85)
Single season home record, 464,902 (1983)

1985 INDIVIDUAL STATISTICS

Rushing	Att.	Yds.	Avg.	LG	TD
Nelson	200	893	4.5	37	5
Brown	93	336	3.6	30	7
Anderson	50	121	2.4	10	4
Rice	31	104	3.4	15	3
Kramer	27	54	2.0	11	0
Jones	2	6	3.0	6	0
Lewis	1	2	2.0	2	0
Coleman	2	0	0.0	0	0
Vikings	406	1516	3.7	37	19
Opponents	542	2223	4.1	59	16

Passing	Att.	Comp.	Pct.	Yds.	TD	Int.	Tkld.	Rate
Kramer	506	277	54.7	3522	19	26	39/255	67.8
Wilson	60	33	55.0	404	3	3	4/28	71.8
Bono	10	1	10.0	5	0	0	2/13	39.6
Vikings	576	311	54.0	3931	22	29	45/296	67.3
Opponents	490	280	57.1	3464	20	22	33/223	74.1

Receiving	No.	Yds.	Avg.	LG	TD
Jordan	68	795	11.7	32	0
Jones	46	641	13.9	44t	4
Carter	43	821	19.1	57t	8
Nelson	43	301	7.0	25t	1
Brown	30	291	9.7	54t	3
Lewis	29	442	15.2	43t	3
Anderson	16	175	10.9	54t	1
Mularkey	13	196	15.1	51t	1
Rice	9	61	6.8	13	1
White	8	76	9.5	15	0
Rhymes	5	124	24.8	36	0
Carroll	1	8	8.0	8	0
Vikings	311	3931	12.6	57t	22
Opponents	280	3464	12.4	70t	20

Interceptions	No.	Yds.	Avg.	LG	TD
J. Turner	5	62	12.4	25	0
Lee	3	68	22.7	35	0
Teal	3	6	2.0	6	0
Newton	2	63	31.5	63	0
Bess	2	27	13.5	27	0
Studwell	2	20	10.0	13	0
Browner	2	17	8.5	15t	1
Mullaney	1	15	15.0	15	0
Doleman	1	5	5.0	5	0
Holt	1	0	0.0	0	0
Vikings	22	283	12.9	63	1
Opponents	29	311	10.7	50t	2

Punting	No.	Yds.	Avg.	In 20	LG
Coleman	67	2867	42.8	12	62
Vikings	67	2867	42.8	12	62
Opponents	65	2694	41.4	10	65

Punt Returns	No.	FC	Yds.	Avg.	LG	TD
Nelson	16	3	133	8.3	21	0
Carter	9	5	117	13.0	41	0
Vikings	25	8	250	10.0	41	0
Opponents	36	3	328	9.1	21	0

Kickoff Returns	No.	Yds.	Avg.	LG	TD
Rhymes	53	1345	25.4	88	0
Rice	4	70	17.5	27	0
M. Turner	4	61	15.3	18	0
Nelson	3	51	17.0	26	0
Bess	2	33	16.5	22	0
Brown	1	7	7.0	7	0
Browner	1	0	0.0	0	0
Mularkey	0	9	—	9	0
Vikings	68	1576	23.2	88	0
Opponents	68	1491	21.9	48	0

Scoring	TD R	TD P	TD Rt	PAT	FG	Saf	TP
Stenerud	0	0	0	41/43	15/26	0	86
Brown	7	3	0	0/0	0/0	0	60
Carter	0	8	0	0/0	0/0	0	48
Nelson	5	1	0	0/0	0/0	0	36
Anderson	4	1	0	0/0	0/0	0	30
Jones	0	4	0	0/0	0/0	0	24
Rice	3	1	0	0/0	0/0	0	24
Lewis	0	3	0	0/0	0/0	0	18
Browner	0	0	1	0/0	0/0	0	6
Mularkey	0	1	0	0/0	0/0	0	6
Teal	0	0	1	0/0	0/0	0	6
Elshire	0	0	0	0/0	0/0	1	2
Vikings	19	22	2	41/43	15/26	1	346
Opponents	16	20	3	38/39	29/37	0	359

FIRST-ROUND SELECTIONS

(If club had no first-round selection, first player drafted is listed with round in parentheses.)

Year	Player, College, Position
1961	Tommy Mason, Tulane, RB
1962	Bill Miller, Miami, WR (3)
1963	Jim Dunaway, Mississippi, T
1964	Carl Eller, Minnesota, DE
1965	Jack Snow, Notre Dame, WR
1966	Jerry Shay, Purdue, DT
1967	Clinton Jones, Michigan State, RB
	Gene Washington, Michigan State, WR
	Alan Page, Notre Dame, DT
1968	Ron Yary, Southern California, T
1969	Ed White, California, G (2)
1970	John Ward, Oklahoma State, DT
1971	Leo Hayden, Ohio State, RB
1972	Jeff Siemon, Stanford, LB
1973	Chuck Foreman, Miami, RB
1974	Fred McNeill, UCLA, LB
	Steve Riley, Southern California, T
1975	Mark Mullaney, Colorado State, DE
1976	James White, Oklahoma State, DT
1977	Tommy Kramer, Rice, QB
1978	Randy Holloway, Pittsburgh, DE
1979	Ted Brown, North Carolina State, RB
1980	Doug Martin, Washington, DT
1981	Mardye McDole, Mississippi State, WR (2)
1982	Darrin Nelson, Stanford, RB
1983	Joey Browner, Southern California, DB
1984	Keith Millard, Washington State, DE
1985	Chris Doleman, Pittsburgh, LB
1986	Gerald Robinson, Auburn, DE

MINNESOTA VIKINGS 1986 VETERAN ROSTER

No.	Name	Pos.	Ht.	Wt.	Birth-date	NFL Exp.	College	Hometown	How Acq.	'85 Games/ Starts
46	Anderson, Alfred	RB	6-1	219	8/4/61	3	Baylor	Waco, Tex.	D3-'84	12/6
58	Ashley, Walker Lee	LB	6-0	240	7/28/60	3	Penn State	Jersey City, N.J.	D3-'83	0*
21	†Bess, Rufus	CB	5-9	187	3/13/56	8	South Carolina State	Hartsville, S.C.	W(Buff)-'82	11/11
59	Blair, Matt	LB	6-5	242	9/20/50	13	Iowa State	Dayton, Ohio	D2b-'74	6/2
13	Bono, Steve	QB	6-3	216	5/11/62	2	UCLA	Norristown, Pa.	D6a-'85	1/0
62	†Boyd, Brent	G	6-3	276	3/23/57	6	UCLA	La Habra, Calif.	D3-'80	15/14
23	Brown, Ted	RB	5-10	212	2/2/57	8	North Carolina State	High Point, N.C.	D1-'79	14/9
47	Browner, Joey	S	6-2	212	5/15/60	4	Southern California	Warren, Ohio	D1-'83	16/16
84	Carroll, Jay	TE	6-4	232	11/8/61	3	Minnesota	Winona, Minn.	W(TB)-'85	16/0
81	Carter, Anthony	WR	5-11	166	9/17/60	2	Michigan	Riviera Beach, Fla.	T (Mia)-'85	16/15
	Cephous, Frank	RB	5-10	205	7/14/61	2	UCLA	Wilmington, Del.	FA-'86	0*
8	Coleman, Greg	P	6-0	181	9/9/54	10	Florida A&M	Jacksonville, Fla.	FA-'78	16/0
56	Doleman, Chris	LB	6-5	250	10/16/61	2	Pittsburgh	York, Pa.	D1-'85	16/13
73	Elshire, Neil	DE	6-6	270	3/8/58	6	Oregon	Albany, Ore.	W(Wash)-'81	16/3
50	†Fowlkes, Dennis	LB	6-2	234	3/11/61	4	West Virginia	Columbus, Ohio	FA-'83	15/8
61	Hamilton, Wes	G	6-3	271	4/24/53	10	Tulsa	Flossmoor, Ill.	D3-'76	0*
30	Holt, Issiac	CB	6-1	197	10/4/62	2	Alcorn State	Birmingham, Ala.	D2-'85	15/1
51	Hough, Jim	G	6-2	276	8/4/56	9	Utah State	La Mirada, Calif.	D4-'78	4/1
99	Howard, David	LB	6-2	228	12/8/61	2	Long Beach State	Long Beach, Calif.	SD3-'84	16/4
72	†Huffman, David	G	6-6	283	4/4/57	7	Notre Dame	Dallas, Tex.	D2-'79	15/2
76	Irwin, Tim	T	6-6	289	12/13/58	6	Tennessee	Knoxville, Tenn.	D3-'81	16/16
89	Jones, Mike	WR	5-11	183	4/14/60	4	Tennessee State	Chattanooga, Tenn.	D6-'83	16/8
83	†Jordan, Steve	TE	6-3	236	1/10/61	5	Brown	Phoenix, Ariz.	D7-'82	16/16
9	Kramer, Tommy	QB	6-2	207	3/7/55	10	Rice	San Antonio, Tex.	D1-'77	15/15
39	†Lee, Carl	CB-S	5-11	184	4/6/61	4	Marshall	South Charleston, W. Va.	D7-'83	15/5
87	Lewis, Leo	WR	5-8	171	9/17/56	6	Missouri	Columbia, Mo.	FA-'81	10/10
63	Lowdermilk, Kirk	C	6-3	263	4/10/63	2	Ohio State	Salem, Ohio	D3a-'85	16/2
71	MacDonald, Mark	G	6-4	267	4/30/61	2	Boston College	West Roxbury, Mass.	D5-'85	16/3
56	Martin, Chris	LB	6-2	233	12/19/60	4	Auburn	Huntsville, Ala.	W(NO)-'84	12/12
79	Martin, Doug	DE	6-3	270	5/22/57	7	Washington	Fairfield, Calif.	D1-'80	16/15
53	Meamber, Tim	LB	6-3	231	10/29/62	2	Washington	Yreka, Calif.	D3b-'85	4/0
75	Millard, Keith	DE	6-6	260	3/18/62	2	Washington State	Pullman, Wash.	D1-'84	16/5
86	†Mularkey, Mike	TE	6-4	238	11/19/61	4	Florida	Ft. Lauderdale, Fla.	W(SF)-'83	15/5
77	Mullaney, Mark	DE	6-6	246	4/30/53	12	Colorado State	Denver, Colo.	D1-'75	15/13
20	†Nelson, Darrin	RB	5-9	183	1/2/59	5	Stanford	Downey, Calif.	D1-'82	16/10
96	Newton, Tim	NT	6-0	283	3/23/63	2	Florida	Orlando, Fla.	D6b-'85	16/14
49	†Nord, Keith	S	6-0	192	3/13/57	7	St. Cloud State	Minnetonka, Minn.	FA-'79	16/13
88	Rhymes, Buster	WR-KR	6-1	216	1/27/62	2	Oklahoma	Miami, Fla.	D4a-'85	15/0
36	Rice, Allen	RB-S	5-10	203	4/5/62	3	Baylor	Houston, Tex.	D5-'84	14/1
28	Rosnagle, Ted	S	6-3	207	9/29/61	2	Portland State	Tustin, Calif.	FA-'85	6/0
68	Rouse, Curtis	G	6-3	322	7/13/60	5	Tenn.-Chattanooga	Augusta, Ga.	D11-'82	16/13
74	Smith, Robert	DE	6-5	255	12/3/62	2	Grambling	Bogalusa, La.	SD2-'84	16/0
55	Studwell, Scott	LB	6-2	228	8/27/54	10	Illinois	Evansville, Ind.	D9-'77	14/12
67	†Swilley, Dennis	C	6-3	257	6/28/55	9	Texas A&M	Pine Bluff, Ark.	D2-'77	16/13
66	†Tausch, Terry	T	6-5	275	2/5/59	5	Texas	New Braunfels, Tex.	D2-'82	16/15
37	Teal, Willie	CB	5-10	190	12/20/57	6	Louisiana State	Texarkana, Tex.	D2-'80	16/16
27	Turner, John	CB	6-0	196	2/22/56	9	Miami	Miami, Fla.	FA-'85	15/4
85	White, Sammy	WR	5-11	210	3/16/54	11	Grambling	Monroe, La.	D2-'76	6/0
11	Wilson, Wade	QB	6-3	208	2/1/59	6	East Texas State	Commerce, Tex.	D8-'81	4/1

* Ashley and Hamilton missed '85 season due to injury; Cephous last active with N.Y. Giants in '84.

†Option playout; subject to developments.

Retired—Jan Stenerud, 19-year kicker, 16 games in '85.

Also played with Vikings in '85—LB Dennis Johnson (8 games), LB Fred McNeill (10), RB Maurice Turner (10).

COACHING STAFF

Head Coach, Jerry Burns

Pro Career: Named fourth head coach in Vikings' history on January 6, 1986. Served as Vikings' assistant head coach and offensive coordinator under Bud Grant in 1985. Since his arrival in Minnesota as offensive coordinator in 1968, became known as an innovator and was credited with popularizing such changes as the one-back offense and short passing game. Has coached in six Super Bowls. Directed Vikings offense in Super Bowls IV, VIII, IX, XI and coached defensive backs for Vince Lombardi on Green Bay's Super Bowl champions in Super Bowls I and II.

Background: Quarterback at University of Michigan 1948-50. No pro playing experience. Began coaching career at University of Hawaii in 1951 as backfield coach for football team and head baseball coach. Moved to Whittier (Calif.) College in 1952 as backfield coach before returning to native Detroit in 1953 as head football coach at St. Mary's of Redford High School. Assistant coach at Iowa from 1954-60 before being named Hawkeyes head coach in 1961. Hawkeyes were 16-27-2 in five seasons under Burns. He coached with the Packers in 1966-67 before joining the Vikings in 1968.

Personal: Born January 24, 1927, in Detroit, Mich. Graduated from Michigan with bachelor of science degree in physical education. Jerry and his wife, Marlyn, have five children—Michael, Erin, Kelly, Kathy, and Kerry and live in Eden Prairie, Minn.

Assistant Coaches

Tom Batta, tight ends-special teams; born October 6, 1942, Youngstown, Ohio, lives in Bloomington, Minn. Offensive-defensive lineman Kent State 1961-63. No pro playing experience. College coach: Akron 1973, Colorado 1974-78, Kansas 1979-82, North Carolina State 1983. Pro coach: Joined Vikings in 1984.

Pete Carroll, secondary; born September 15, 1951, San Francisco, Calif., lives in Bloomington, Minn. Defensive back Pacific 1969-72. No pro playing experience. College coach: Arkansas 1977, Iowa State 1978, Ohio State 1979, North Carolina State 1980-82, Pacific 1983. Pro coach: Buffalo Bills 1984, joined Vikings in 1985.

Bob Hollway, special assistant-football operations; born January 29, 1926, Ann Arbor, Mich., lives in Edina, Minn. End Michigan 1947-49. No pro playing experience. College coach: Maine 1951-52, Eastern Michigan 1953, Michigan 1954-66. Pro coach: Minnesota Vikings 1967-70, St. Louis Cardinals 1971-72 (head coach), Detroit Lions 1973-74, San Francisco 49ers 1975, Seattle Seahawks 1976-77, rejoined Vikings in 1978.

Monte Kiffin, linebackers; born February 29, 1940, Lexington, Neb., lives in Bloomington, Minn. Defensive end Nebraska 1961-63. Pro defensive end Winnipeg Blue Bombers (CFL) 1965-66. College coach: Nebraska 1966-76, Arkansas 1977-79, North Carolina State 1980-82 (head coach). Pro coach: Green Bay Packers 1983, Buffalo Bills 1984-85, first year with Vikings.

John Michels, offensive line; born February 15, 1931, Philadelphia, Pa., lives in Bloomington, Minn. Guard Tennessee 1949-52. Pro guard Philadelphia Eagles 1953, 1956, Winnipeg Blue Bombers (CFL) 1957. College coach: Texas A&M 1958. Pro coach: Winnipeg Blue Bombers (CFL) 1959-66, joined Vikings in 1967.

Floyd Peters, defensive coordinator; born May 21, 1936, Council Bluffs, Iowa, lives in Bloomington, Minn. Defensive tackle-guard San Francisco State 1954-57. Pro defensive lineman Baltimore Colts 1958, Cleveland Browns 1959-62, Detroit Lions 1963, Philadelphia Eagles 1964-69, Washington Redskins 1970 (player/coach). Pro scout: Miami Dolphins 1971-73. Pro coach: New York Giants 1974-75, San Francisco 49ers 1976-77, Detroit Lions 1978-81, St. Louis Cardinals 1982-85, first year with Vikings.

Dick Rehbein, receivers; born November 22, 1955, Green Bay, Wis., lives in Edina, Minn. Center Ripon 1973-77. No pro playing experience. Pro coach: Green Bay Packers 1979-83, Los Angeles Express (USFL) 1984, joined Vikings in 1984.

Bob Schnelker, offensive-coordinator; born October 17, 1928, Galion, Ohio, lives in Bloomington, Minn. Tight end Bowling Green 1946-49. Pro tight end Cleveland Browns 1953, New York Giants 1954-59, Minnesota Vikings 1961, Pittsburgh Steelers 1961. Pro coach: Los Angeles Rams 1963-65, Green Bay Packers 1966-71, 1982-85, San Diego Chargers 1972-73, Miami Dolphins 1974, Kansas City Chiefs 1975-77, Detroit Lions 1978-81, first year with Vikings.

Marc Trestman, running backs; born January 15, 1956, Minneapolis, Minn., lives in Minneapolis. Quarterback Minnesota 1976-78. No pro playing experience. College coach: Miami 1981-84. Pro coach: Joined Vikings in 1985.

Paul Wiggin, defensive line; born November 18, 1934, Modesto, Calif., lives in Eden Prairie, Minn. Offensive-defensive tackle Stanford 1953-56. Pro defensive end Cleveland Browns 1957-67. College coach: Stanford 1980-83 (head coach). Pro coach: San Francisco 49ers 1968-74, Kansas City Chiefs 1975-77 (head coach), New Orleans Saints 1978-79, joined Vikings in 1985.

MINNESOTA VIKINGS 1986 FIRST-YEAR ROSTER

Name	Pos.	Ht.	Wt.	Birth-date	College	Hometown	How Acq.
Armstrong, John	WR	5-9	190	7/7/63	Richmond	Pittsboro, Miss.	D11
Brockhaus, Jeff (1)	K	6-2	205	4/15/59	Missouri	St. Louis, Mo.	FA
Cormier, Joe	TE-WR	6-5	223	5/3/63	Southern California	Gardena, Calif.	D10
Evans, Vince	RB	5-10	204	9/8/63	North Carolina State	Fayetteville, N.C.	FA
Guggemos, Neal	CB-WR	6-0	191	6/14/64	St. Thomas	Winstead, Minn.	FA
Gustafson, Jim (1)	WR	6-1	185	3/16/61	St. Thomas	Bloomington, Minn.	FA
Hechinger, Rick (1)	G	6-5	255	6/18/62	Memphis State	Memphis, Tenn.	FA
Hilton, Carl	TE	6-3	229	2/28/64	Houston	Galveston, Tex.	D7
Jones, Hassan	WR	6-0	198	7/2/64	Florida State	Clearwater, Fla.	D5
Long, Tim (1)	T	6-5	305	4/20/63	Memphis State	Cleveland, Tenn.	D3c-'85
Morrell, Kyle (1)	S	6-1	189	10/9/63	Brigham Young	Bountiful, Utah	D4b-'85
Palumbis, Gary	NT	6-1	278	4/28/63	Portland State	Lake Oswego, Ore.	FA
Phillips, Joe	NT	6-4	280	7/15/63	Southern Methodist	Vancouver, Wash.	D4
Robinson, Gerald	DE	6-3	253	5/4/63	Auburn	Notasulga, Ala.	D1
Rooks, Thomas	RB	6-1	209	11/26/63	Illinois	St. Louis, Mo.	D6
Schippang, Gary	T	6-4	254	4/16/63	West Chester	Bethlehem, Pa.	D8
Slaton, Mike	CB-S	6-1	191	9/25/64	South Dakota	Bellevue, Neb.	D9
Solomon, Jesse	LB	6-0	249	11/4/63	Florida State	Madison, Fla.	D12
Zendejas, Luis (1)	K	5-8	186	10/22/61	Arizona State	Chino, Calif.	FA
Zimmerman, Gary (1)	T	6-5	280	12/13/61	Oregon	Walnut, Calif.	T(NYG)-'86

The term NFL Rookie is defined as a player who is in his first season of professional football and has not been on the roster of another professional football team for any regular season or postseason games. A Rookie is designated by an "R" on NFL rosters. Players who have been active in another professional football league or players who have NFL experience, including either preseason training camp or being on an active roster for fewer than three regular season or postseason games, are termed NFL First-Year Players. An NFL First-Year Player is designated by a "1" on NFL rosters. Thereafter, a player on an NFL active roster for at least three regular season or postseason games is credited with an additional year of NFL playing experience.

NOTES

NEW ORLEANS SAINTS

National Football Conference
Western Division

Team Colors: Old Gold, Black, and White

1500 Poydras Street
New Orleans, Louisiana 70112
Telephone: (504) 522-1500

Club Officials

Owner/General Partner: Tom Benson, Jr.
President/General Manager: Jim Finks
Head Coach: Jim Mora
Director of Administration: Bruce Broussard
Director of Public Relations: Greg Suit
Assistant Director of Public Relations: Rusty Kasmiersky
Public Relations Assistant: Sylvia Alfortish
Ticket Manager: Sandy King
Marketing Director: Barra Birrcher
Trainer: Dean Kleinschmidt
Equipment Manager: Dan Simmons

Stadium: Louisiana Superdome • **Capacity:** 69,723
1500 Poydras Street
New Orleans, Louisiana 70112

Playing Surface: AstroTurf

Training Camp: Southeastern Louisiana University
Hammond, Louisiana 70402

1986 SCHEDULE

Preseason

Aug. 9	at Denver	7:00
Aug. 16	**New England**	7:00
Aug. 23	at Houston	8:00
Aug. 30	**Kansas City**	7:00

Regular Season

Sept. 7	**Atlanta**	12:00
Sept. 14	**Green Bay**	1:00
Sept. 21	at San Francisco	1:00
Sept. 28	at New York Giants	1:00
Oct. 5	**Washington**	12:00
Oct. 12	at Indianapolis	12:00
Oct. 19	**Tampa Bay**	12:00
Oct. 26	at New York Jets	1:00
Nov. 2	**San Francisco**	12:00
Nov. 9	**Los Angeles Rams**	12:00
Nov. 16	at St. Louis	12:00
Nov. 23	at Los Angeles Rams	1:00
Nov. 30	**New England**	12:00
Dec. 7	**Miami**	12:00
Dec. 14	at Atlanta	1:00
Dec. 21	at Minnesota	12:00

SAINTS COACHING HISTORY

(83-187-5)

1967-70	Tom Fears*	13-34-2
1970-72	J.D. Roberts	7-25-3
1973-75	John North**	11-23-0
1975	Ernie Hefferle	1-7-0
1976-77	Hank Stram	7-21-0
1978-80	Dick Nolan***	15-29-0
1980	Dick Stanfel	1-3-0
1981-85	O.A. (Bum) Phillips****	27-42-0
1985	Wade Phillips	1-3-0

*Released after seven games in 1970
**Released after six games in 1975
***Released after 12 games in 1980
****Resigned after 12 games in 1985

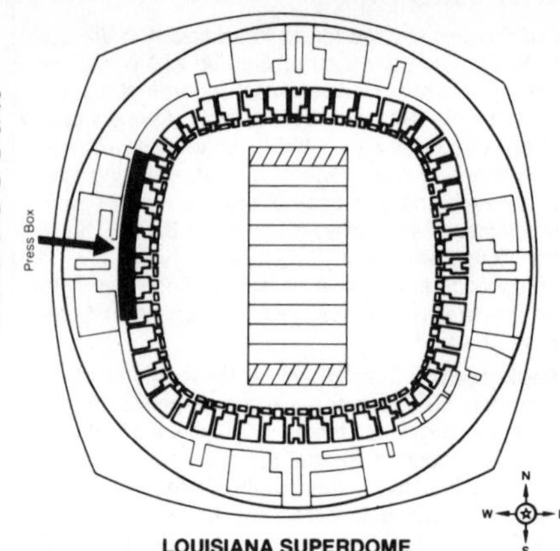

LOUISIANA SUPERDOME

RECORD HOLDERS

Individual Records—Career

Category	Name	Performance
Rushing (Yds.)	George Rogers, 1981-84	4,267
Passing (Yds.)	Archie Manning, 1971-1982	21,734
Passing (TDs)	Archie Manning, 1971-1982	115
Receiving (No.)	Dan Abramowicz, 1967-1973	309
Receiving (Yds.)	Dan Abramowicz, 1967-1973	4,875
Interceptions	Tommy Myers, 1972-1982	36
Punting (Avg.)	Tom McNeill, 1967-69	42.3
Punt Return (Avg.)	Gil Chapman, 1975	12.2
Kickoff Return (Avg.)	Walt Roberts, 1967	26.3
Field Goals	Morten Andersen, 1982-85	71
Touchdowns (Tot.)	Dan Abramowicz, 1967-1973	37
Points	Morten Andersen, 1982-85	317

Individual Records—Single Season

Category	Name	Performance
Rushing (Yds.)	George Rogers, 1981	1,674
Passing (Yds.)	Archie Manning, 1980	3,716
Passing (TDs)	Archie Manning, 1980	23
Receiving (No.)	Tony Galbreath, 1978	74
Receiving (Yds.)	Wes Chandler, 1979	1,069
Interceptions	Dave Whitsell, 1967	10
Punting (Avg.)	Brian Hansen, 1984	43.8
Punt Return (Avg.)	Gil Chapman, 1975	12.2
Kickoff Return (Avg.)	Don Shy, 1969	27.9
Field Goals	Morten Andersen, 1985	31
Touchdowns (Tot.)	George Rogers, 1981	13
Points	Morten Andersen, 1985	120

Individual Records—Single Game

Category	Name	Performance
Rushing (Yds.)	George Rogers, 9-4-83	206
Passing (Yds.)	Archie Manning, 12-7-80	377
Passing (TDs)	Billy Kilmer, 11-2-69	6
Receiving (No.)	Tony Galbreath, 9-10-78	14
Receiving (Yds.)	Wes Chandler, 9-2-79	205
Interceptions	Tommy Myers, 9-3-78	3
Field Goals	Morten Andersen, 12-1-85	5
Touchdowns (Tot.)	Many times Last time by Wayne Wilson, 1-2-83	3
Points	Many times Last time by Wayne Wilson, 1-2-83	18

1985 TEAM STATISTICS

	New Orleans	Opp.
Total First Downs	250	335
Rushing	83	125
Passing	148	188
Penalty	19	22
Third Down: Made/Att.	66/221	96/228
Fourth Down: Made/Att.	8/16	7/13
Total Net Yards	4479	5815
Avg. Per Game	279.9	363.4
Total Plays	997	1083
Avg. Per Play	4.5	5.4
Net Yards Rushing	1683	2162
Avg. Per Game	105.2	135.1
Total Rushes	431	508
Net Yards Passing	2796	3653
Avg. Per Game	174.8	228.3
Tackled/Yards Lost	58/461	46/322
Gross Yards	3257	3975
Att./Completions	508/260	529/306
Completion Pct.	51.2	57.8
Had Intercepted	23	21
Punts/Avg.	89/42.3	81/42.2
Net Punting Avg.	36.5	37.8
Penalties/Yards Lost	96/805	108/837
Fumbles/Ball Lost	23/13	24/16
Touchdowns	29	48
Rushing	4	19
Passing	20	26
Returns	5	3
Avg. Time of Possession	28:33	31:27

1985 TEAM RECORD

Preseason (1-3)

Date	New Orleans		Opponents
8/10	32	New England	20
8/17	20	*Houston	23
8/24	10	*Tampa Bay	14
8/30	20	San Diego	21
	82		78

Regular Season (5-11)

Date	New Orleans		Opp.	Att.
9/8	27	*Kansas City	47	57,760
9/15	23	Denver	34	74,488
9/22	20	*Tampa Bay	13	45,320
9/29	20	San Francisco	17	58,053
10/6	23	*Philadelphia	21	56,364
10/13	13	L.A. Raiders	23	48,152
10/20	24	Atlanta	31	44,784
10/27	13	*N.Y. Giants	21	54,082
11/3	10	L.A. Rams	28	49,030
11/10	3	*Seattle	27	47,365
11/17	14	Green Bay	38	52,104
11/24	30	Minnesota	23	54,117
12/1	29	*L.A. Rams	3	44,122
12/8	16	St. Louis	28	29,527
12/15	19	*San Francisco	31	46,065
12/22	10	*Atlanta	16	37,717

*Home Game

Score by Periods

New Orleans	46	77	43	128	0	—	294
Opponents	55	142	51	153	0	—	401

Attendance

Home 388,795 Away 410,255 Total 799,050
Single game home record, 76,490 (11-4-79)
Single season home record, 557,530 (1979)

1985 INDIVIDUAL STATISTICS

Rushing	Att.	Yds.	Avg.	LG	TD
W. Wilson	168	645	3.8	41t	1
Campbell	158	643	4.1	45	1
Gajan	50	251	5.0	26	2
Anthony	17	65	3.8	13	0
Wattelet	2	42	21.0	23	0
Hebert	12	26	2.2	8	0
D. Wilson	18	7	0.4	17	0
Fowler	2	4	2.0	3	0
Goodlow	1	3	3.0	3	0
Martin	2	–1	–0.5	11	0
Merkens	1	–2	–2.0	–2	0
Saints	431	1683	3.9	45	4
Opponents	508	2162	4.3	48	19

Passing	Att.	Comp.	Pct.	Yds.	TD	Int.	Tkld.	Rate
D. Wilson	293	145	49.5	1843	11	15	39/291	60.7
Hebert	181	97	53.6	1208	5	4	17/150	74.6
Todd	32	16	50.0	191	3	4	1/10	60.3
Hansen	1	1	100.0	8	0	0	0/0	100.0
Merkens	1	1	100.0	7	1	0	1/10	135.4
Saints	508	260	51.2	3257	20	23	58/461	65.7
Opponents	529	306	57.8	3975	26	21	46/322	81.4

Receiving	No.	Yds.	Avg.	LG	TD
Brenner	42	652	15.5	30	3
W. Wilson	38	228	6.0	21	2
Martin	35	522	14.9	50	4
Goodlow	32	603	18.8	76t	3
Anthony	28	185	6.6	36	0
Tice	24	266	11.1	39t	2
Groth	15	238	15.9	56t	2
Hardy	15	208	13.9	31	2
Gajan	8	87	10.9	22	0
Scott	7	61	8.7	15	0
Campbell	6	88	14.7	39	0
Fowler	5	43	8.6	11	0
Merkens	3	61	20.3	39t	1
Barnwell, Wash.-N.O.	3	28	9.3	13	0
Haynes	1	8	8.0	8	0
Hebert	1	7	7.0	7t	1
Saints	260	3257	12.5	76t	20
Opponents	306	3975	13.0	65t	26

Interceptions	No.	Yds.	Avg.	LG	TD
Waymer	6	49	8.2	28	0
Hoage	4	79	19.8	52t	1
Poe	3	63	21.0	40t	1
Tullis	2	22	11.0	22	0
Del Rio	2	13	6.5	11	0
Wattelet	2	0	0.0	0	0
Kovach	1	53	53.0	53	0
Redd	1	25	25.0	25	0
Winston	0	8	—	8	0
Saints	21	312	14.9	53	2
Opponents	23	251	10.9	33	1

Punting	No.	Yds.	Avg.	In 20	LG
Hansen	89	3763	42.3	14	58
Saints	89	3763	42.3	14	58
Opponents	81	3417	42.2	24	61

Punt Returns	No.	FC	Yds.	Avg.	LG	TD
Tullis	17	6	141	8.3	17	0
Martin	8	10	53	6.6	13	0
Roaches	4	2	21	5.3	10	0
Groth	1	0	0	0.0	0	0
Saints	30	18	215	7.2	17	0
Opponents	45	17	397	8.8	46	0

Kickoff Returns	No.	Yds.	Avg.	LG	TD
Anthony	23	476	20.7	52	0
Tullis	23	470	20.4	62	0
Martin	15	384	25.6	69	0
Fowler	4	78	19.5	23	0
Roaches	4	76	19.0	23	0
Merkens	1	0	0.0	0	0
Rackley	1	63	63.0	63	0
Saints	71	1547	21.8	69	0
Opponents	43	968	22.5	94t	1

Scoring	TD R	TD P	TD Rt	PAT	FG	Saf	TP
Andersen	0	0	0	27/29	31/35	0	120
Martin	0	4	0	0/0	0/0	0	24
Brenner	0	3	0	0/0	0/0	0	18
Goodlow	0	3	0	0/0	0/0	0	18
W. Wilson	1	2	0	0/0	0/0	0	18
Gajan	2	0	0	0/0	0/0	0	12
Groth	0	2	0	0/0	0/0	0	12
Hardy	0	2	0	0/0	0/0	0	12
Tice	0	2	0	0/0	0/0	0	12
Warren	0	0	2	0/0	0/0	0	12
Campbell	1	0	0	0/0	0/0	0	6
Del Rio	0	0	1	0/0	0/0	0	6
Hebert	0	1	0	0/0	0/0	0	6
Hoage	0	0	1	0/0	0/0	0	6
Merkens	0	1	0	0/0	0/0	0	6
Poe	0	0	1	0/0	0/0	0	6
Saints	4	20	5	27/29	31/35	0	294
Opponents	19	26	3	48/48	21/28	1	401

FIRST-ROUND SELECTIONS

(If club had no first-round selection, first player drafted is listed with round in parentheses.)

Year	Player, College, Position
1967	Les Kelley, Alabama, RB
1968	Kevin Hardy, Notre Dame, DE
1969	John Shinners, Xavier, G
1970	Ken Burrough, Texas Southern, WR
1971	Archie Manning, Mississippi, QB
1972	Royce Smith, Georgia, G
1973	Derland Moore, Oklahoma, DE (2)
1974	Rick Middleton, Ohio State, LB
1975	Larry Burton, Purdue, WR
	Kurt Schumacher, Ohio State, T
1976	Chuck Muncie, California, RB
1977	Joe Campbell, Maryland, DE
1978	Wes Chandler, Florida, WR
1979	Russell Erxleben, Texas, P-K
1980	Stan Brock, Colorado, T
1981	George Rogers, South Carolina, RB
1982	Lindsay Scott, Georgia, WR
1983	Steve Korte, Arkansas, G (2)
1984	James Geathers, Wichita State, DE
1985	Alvin Toles, Tennessee, LB
1986	Jim Dombrowski, Virginia, T

NEW ORLEANS SAINTS 1986 VETERAN ROSTER

No.	Name	Pos.	Ht.	Wt.	Birth-date	NFL Exp.	College	Hometown	How Acq.	'85 Games/ Starts
7	Andersen, Morten	K	6-2	205	8/19/60	5	Michigan State	Indianapolis, Ind.	D4-'82	16/0
22	Anthony, Tyrone	RB	5-11	212	3/3/62	3	North Carolina	Pfafftown, N.C.	D3b-'84	16/0
85	Brenner, Hoby	TE	6-4	245	6/2/59	6	Southern California	Fullerton, Calif.	D3b-'81	16/16
67	Brock, Stan	T	6-6	288	6/8/58	7	Colorado	Beaverton, Ore.	D1-'80	16/16
35	†Campbell, Earl	RB	5-11	233	3/29/55	9	Texas	Tyler, Tex.	T(Hou)-'84	16/12
75	Clark, Bruce	DE	6-3	281	3/31/58	5	Penn State	New Castle, Pa.	T(GB)-'82	16/16
68	†Clark, Kelvin	G	6-3	273	1/30/56	8	Nebraska	Odessa, Tex.	T(Den)-'82	2/2
50	Del Rio, Jack	LB	6-4	235	4/4/63	2	Southern California	Castro Valley, Calif.	D3-'85	16/9
63	Edelman, Brad	G	6-6	262	9/3/60	5	Missouri	Creve Coeur, Mo.	D2-'82	8/8
99	Elliott, Tony	NT	6-2	300	4/23/59	5	North Texas State	Bridgeport, Conn.	D5-'82	16/16
43	Fowler, Bobby	RB	6-2	230	9/11/60	2	Louisiana Tech	Temple, Tex.	FA-'85	10/0
46	Gajan, Hokie	RB	5-11	226	9/6/59	5	Louisiana State	Baker, La.	D10-'81	8/6
20	Gary, Russell	S	5-11	196	7/31/59	6	Nebraska	Minneapolis, Minn.	D2a-'81	6/6
97	Geathers, James	DE	6-7	267	6/26/60	3	Wichita State	Georgetown, S.C.	D2-'84	16/0
77	Gilbert, Daren	T	6-6	285	10/3/63	2	Cal State-Fullerton	Compton, Calif.	D2-'85	16/0
88	Goodlow, Eugene	WR	6-2	181	12/19/58	4	Kansas State	Rochester, N.Y.	D3b-'82	12/11
86	Groth, Jeff	WR	5-10	181	7/2/57	8	Bowling Green	Chagrin Falls, Ohio	FA-'81	12/2
10	Hansen, Brian	P	6-3	218	10/26/60	3	Sioux Falls	Hawarden, Iowa	D9-'84	16/0
87	†Hardy, Larry	TE	6-3	246	7/9/56	9	Jackson State	Mendenhall, Miss.	D12-'78	16/0
92	Haynes, James	LB	6-2	227	8/9/60	3	Mississippi Valley State	Tallulah, La.	FA-'84	16/5
3	Hebert, Bobby	QB	6-4	215	8/19/60	2	Northwest Louisiana	Galliano, La.	FA-'85	6/6
61	Hilgenberg, Joel	C-G	6-3	253	7/10/62	3	Iowa	Iowa City, Iowa	D4-'84	15/5
24	Hoage, Terry	S	6-3	199	4/11/62	3	Georgia	Huntsville, Tex.	D3a-'84	16/13
57	Jackson, Rickey	LB	6-2	239	3/20/58	6	Pittsburgh	Pahokee, Fla.	D2b-'81	16/16
55	Kohlbrand, Joe	LB	6-4	242	3/18/63	2	Miami	Merritt Island, Fla.	D8-'85	12/0
60	†Korte, Steve	C	6-2	271	1/15/60	4	Arkansas	Littleton, Colo.	D2-'83	12/12
64	Lafary, Dave	T	6-7	285	1/13/55	9	Purdue	Cincinnati, Ohio	D5a-'77	11/11
84	Martin, Eric	WR	6-1	195	11/8/61	2	Louisiana State	Van Vleck, Tex.	D7-'85	16/11
39	Maxie, Brett	CB-S	6-2	190	1/13/62	2	Texas Southern	Dallas, Tex.	FA-'85	16/1
19	Merkens, Guido	QB-WR	6-1	197	8/14/55	9	Sam Houston State	San Antonio, Tex.	FA-'80	16/0
80	Miller, Mike	WR	6-0	183	12/29/59	3	Tennessee	Flint, Mich.	FA-'85	3/0
74	Moore, Derland	NT	6-4	273	10/7/51	14	Oklahoma	Poplar Bluff, Mo.	D2-'73	6/0
51	Paul, Whitney	LB	6-3	218	10/8/55	11	Colorado	Galveston, Tex.	T(KC)-'82	14/8
53	†Pelluer, Scott	LB	6-2	227	4/28/59	6	Washington State	Bellevue, Wash.	W(Dall)-'81	11/5
71	†Perot, Petey	G	6-2	271	1/28/57	7	Northwest Louisiana	Natchitoches, La.	FA-'85	7/7
25	Poe, Johnnie	CB	6-1	194	8/29/59	6	Missouri	East St. Louis, Ill.	D6b-'81	16/16
47	Rackley, David	CB	5-9	172	2/2/61	2	Texas Southern	Miami, Fla.	FA-'85	7/0
58	Redd, Glen	LB	6-1	231	6/17/58	5	Brigham Young	Ogden, Utah	D6c-'81	16/16
70	†Rourke, Jim	T	6-5	263	2/10/57	7	Boston College	Boston, Mass.	FA-'85	13/5
65	Schreiber, Adam	G	6-4	270	2/20/62	3	Texas	Huntsville, Ala.	FA-'85	1/0
82	Tice, John	TE	6-5	243	6/22/60	4	Maryland	Central Islip, N.Y.	D3a-'83	16/9
14	Todd, Richard	QB	6-2	212	11/19/53	11	Alabama	Mobile, Ala.	T(NYJ)-'84	2/0
54	Toles, Alvin	LB	6-1	211	3/23/63	2	Tennessee	Forsythe, Ga.	D1-'85	16/2
26	†Tullis, Willie	CB	6-0	190	4/5/58	6	Troy State	Headland, Ala.	FA-'85	14/1
42	Walker, Dwight	WR	5-9	189	1/10/59	4	Nicholls State	Metairie, La.	FA-'86	0*
73	†Warren, Frank	DE	6-4	278	9/14/59	6	Auburn	Birmingham, Ala.	D3a-'81	16/0
49	Wattelet, Frank	S	6-0	185	10/25/58	6	Kansas	Abilene, Kan.	FA-'81	16/16
44	†Waymer, Dave	CB	6-1	188	7/1/58	7	Notre Dame	Charlotte, N.C.	D2-'80	16/15
94	Wilks, Jim	DE	6-5	265	3/12/58	6	San Diego State	Pasadena, Calif.	D12-'81	16/16
79	Williams, Ralph	T	6-3	270	3/27/58	4	Southern	West Monroe, La.	FA-'85	16/14
18	Wilson, Dave	QB	6-3	211	4/27/59	5	Illinois	Anaheim, Calif.	SD1-'81	10/10
30	†Wilson, Wayne	RB	6-3	220	9/4/57	8	Shepherd	Ellicott City, Md.	FA-'79	16/10
89	†Young, Tyrone	WR	6-6	192	4/29/60	3	Florida	Ocala, Fla.	FA-'83	0*

* Walker last active with Cleveland in '84; Young missed '85 season due to injury.

†Option playout; subject to developments.

Also played with Saints in '85—WR Malcolm Barnwell (2 games), C-G David Carter (4), WR Kenny Duckett (1), CB Earl Johnson (2), LB Jim Kovach (2), G Charles Pitcock (1), WR Lindsay Scott (10), LB Dennis Winston (4).

COACHING STAFF

Head Coach, Jim Mora

Pro Career: Begins first season as an NFL head coach following a three-year tenure as head coach of USFL Philadelphia/Baltimore Stars. Directed Stars to championship game in each of his three seasons as head coach and won league championship in 1984 and 1985. He was named coach-of-the-year following the 1984 season. Mora began his pro coaching career in 1978 as defensive line coach of the Seattle Seahawks. In 1982, he became defensive coordinator for the New England Patriots and played a vital role in the Patriots' march to the playoffs that year. No pro playing experience.

Background: Played tight end and defensive end at Occidental College. Assistant coach at Occidental 1957-60 and head coach 1961-63. Linebacker coach at Stanford in 1967 under head coach John Ralston on a staff that included former Eagles' head coach Dick Vermeil. Defensive assistant at Colorado 1968-73. Linebacker coach under Vermeil at UCLA 1974. Defensive coordinator at University of Washington 1975-77. Received bachelor's degree in physical education from Occidental College in 1957. Also holds master's degree in education from Southern California.

Personal: Born May 24, 1935, in Glendale, Calif. Jim and his wife, Connie, live in New Orleans and have three sons—Jim, Michael, and Stephen.

Assistant Coaches

Dom Capers, defensive backs; born August 7, 1950, Cambridge, Ohio, lives in Metairie, La. Defensive back Mount Union College 1968-71. No pro playing experience. College coach: Hawaii 1975-76, San Jose State 1977, California 1978-79, Tennessee 1980-81, Ohio State 1982-83. Pro coach: Philadelphia/Baltimore Stars (USFL) 1984-85, first year with Saints.

Jim Erkenbeck, offensive line; born September 10, 1931, Los Angeles, Calif., lives in Destrehan, La. Fullback San Diego State 1949-52. No pro playing experience. College coach: San Diego State 1960-63, Grossmont, Calif., J.C. 1964-67, Utah State 1968, Washington State 1969-71, California 1972-76. Pro coach: Winnipeg Blue Bombers (CFL) 1977, Montreal Alouettes (CFL) 1978-81, Calgary Stampeders (CFL) 1982, Philadelphia/Baltimore Stars (USFL) 1983-85, first year with Saints.

Vic Fangio, linebackers; born August 22, 1958, Dunmore, Pa., lives in Metairie, La. Defensive back East Stroudsburg State 1976-78. No pro playing experience. College coach: North Carolina 1983. Pro coach: Philadelphia/Baltimore Stars (USFL) 1983-85, first year with Saints.

Joe Marciano, tight ends-special teams; born February 10, 1954, Scranton, Pa., lives in Metairie, La. Quarterback Temple 1972-75. No pro playing experience. College coach: East Stroudsburg State 1977, Rhode Island 1978-79, Villanova 1980, Penn State 1981, Temple 1982. Pro coach: Philadelphia/Baltimore Stars (USFL) 1983-85, first year with Saints.

Russell Paternostro, strength and conditioning; born July 21, 1940, New Orleans, La., lives in Jefferson, La. San Diego State. No college or pro playing experience. Pro coach: Joined Saints in 1981.

John Pease, defensive line; born October 14, 1943, Pittsburgh, Pa., lives in Kenner, La. Wingback Utah 1963-64. No pro playing experience. College coach: Fullerton, Calif., J.C. 1970-73, Long Beach State 1974-76, Utah 1977, Washington 1978-83. Pro coach: Philadelphia/Baltimore Stars (USFL) 1983-85, first year with Saints.

Steve Sidwell, defensive coordinator-linebackers; born August 30, 1944, Winfield, Kan., lives in Destrehan, La. Linebacker Colorado 1962-65. No pro playing experience. College coach: Colorado 1966-73, Nevada-Las Vegas 1974-75, Southern Methodist 1976-81. Pro coach: New England Patriots 1982-84, Indianapolis Colts 1985, first year with Saints.

Jim Skipper, running backs; born January 23, 1949, Breaux Bridge, La., lives in Metairie, La. Defensive back Whittier College 1971-72. No pro playing experience. College coach: Cal Poly-Pomona 1974-76, San Jose State 1977-78, Pacific 1979, Oregon 1980-82. Pro coach: Philadelphia/Baltimore Stars (USFL) 1983-85, first year with Saints.

Carl Smith, offensive coordinator-quarterbacks; born April 26, 1948, Wasco, Calif., lives in Metairie, La. Defensive back Cal Poly-San Luis Obispo 1968-70. No pro playing experience. College coach: Cal Poly-San Luis Obispo 1971, Colorado 1972-73, Southwestern Louisiana 1974-78, Lamar 1979-81, North Carolina State 1982. Pro coach: Philadelphia/Baltimore Stars (USFL) 1983-85, first year with Saints.

Steve Walters, wide receivers; born June 16, 1948, Jonesboro, Ark., lives in Metairie, La. Quarterback-defensive back Arkansas 1967-70. No pro playing experience. College coach: Tampa 1973, Northeast Louisiana 1974-75, Morehead State 1976, Tulsa 1977-78, Memphis State 1979, Southern Methodist 1980-81, Alabama 1985. Pro coach: New England Patriots 1982-84, first year with Saints.

NEW ORLEANS SAINTS 1986 FIRST-YEAR ROSTER

Name	Pos.	Ht.	Wt.	Birth-date	College	Hometown	How Acq.
Bennett, Rob (1)	TE	6-5	250	8/4/63	West Virginia	Morgantown, W. Va.	FA
Brown, Sebastian	WR	6-0	181	3/22/63	Bethune-Cookman	Lakeland, Fla.	D12
Dombrowski, Jim	T	6-5	289	10/19/63	Virginia	Charlottesville, Va.	D1
Dumbauld, Jonathan	DE	6-4	259	2/14/63	Kentucky	Lexington, Ky.	D10
Edwards, Kelvin	WR	6-2	192	7/19/64	Liberty Baptist	Lynchburg, Va.	D4
Fenerty, Gill	RB	6-0	193	8/24/63	Holy Cross	Worcester, Mass.	D7
Harris, Herbert (1)	WR	6-1	200	5/4/61	Lamar	Houston, Tex.	FA
Hilliard, Dalton	RB	5-8	196	1/21/64	Louisiana State	Patterson, La.	D2
Johnson, Earl (1)	CB	6-0	190	10/20/63	South Carolina	Daytona Beach, Fla.	D9-'85
Jones, Merlon	LB	6-2	222	9/25/64	Florida A&M	Gainesville, Fla.	D9
Jordan, Buford (1)	RB	6-0	218	6/26/62	McNeese State	Kenner, La.	FA
Mayes, Rueben	RB	5-11	201	6/6/63	Washington State	Pullman, Wash.	D3a
Mokofisi, Filipo	LB	6-1	232	10/22/62	Utah	Salt Lake City, Utah	D8
Sutton, Reggie	CB-S	5-10	175	2/16/65	Miami	Miami, Fla.	D5
Swilling, Pat	LB	6-3	243	10/25/64	Georgia Tech	Atlanta, Ga.	D3b
Swoopes, Patrick	NT	6-3	262	3/4/64	Mississippi State	Starkville, Miss.	D11
Thompson, Robert	WR	5-9	174	9/9/62	Youngstown State	Youngstown, Ohio	D6
Wheeler, Jerry (1)	WR	6-0	190	2/28/61	N.W. Louisiana	West Monroe, La.	FA
Word, Barry	RB	6-2	220	7/17/64	Virginia	Charlottesville, Va.	D3c

The term NFL Rookie is defined as a player who is in his first season of professional football and has not been on the roster of another professional football team for any regular season or postseason games. A Rookie is designated by an "R" on NFL rosters. Players who have been active in another professional football league or players who have NFL experience, including either preseason training camp or being on an active roster for fewer than three regular season or postseason games, are termed NFL First-Year Players. An NFL First-Year Player is designated by a "1" on NFL rosters. Thereafter, a player on an NFL active roster for at least three regular season or postseason games is credited with an additional year of NFL playing experience.

NOTES

National Football Conference
Eastern Division

Team Colors: Blue, Red, and White

Giants Stadium
East Rutherford, New Jersey 07073
Telephone: (201) 935-8111

Club Officials

President: Wellington T. Mara
Vice President-Treasurer: Timothy J. Mara
Vice President-Secretary: Raymond J. Walsh
Vice President-General Manager: George Young
Assistant General Manager: Harry Hulmes
Controller: John Pasquali
Director of Player Personnel: Tom Boisture
Director of Pro Personnel: Tim Rooney
Director of Media Services: Ed Croke
Director of Promotions: Tom Power
Director of Special Projects: Victor Del Guercio
Box Office Treasurer: Jim Gleason
Trainer Emeritus: John Dziegiel
Head Trainer: Ronnie Barnes
Assistant Trainers: John Johnson, Jim Madaleno
Equipment Manager: Ed Wagner, Jr.

Stadium: Giants Stadium • **Capacity:** 76,891
East Rutherford, New Jersey 07073

Playing Surface: AstroTurf

Training Camp: Pace University
Pleasantville, New York 10570

1986 SCHEDULE

Preseason

Aug. 6	at Atlanta	7:00
Aug. 16	vs. Green Bay at Milwaukee	7:00
Aug. 23	**New York Jets**	8:00
Aug. 30	**Pittsburgh**	8:00

Regular Season

Sept. 8	at Dallas (Monday)	8:00
Sept. 14	**San Diego**	1:00
Sept. 21	at Los Angeles Raiders	1:00
Sept. 28	**New Orleans**	1:00
Oct. 5	at St. Louis	12:00
Oct. 12	**Philadelphia**	4:00
Oct. 19	at Seattle	1:00
Oct. 27	**Washington** (Monday)	9:00
Nov. 2	**Dallas**	1:00
Nov. 9	at Philadelphia	4:00
Nov. 16	at Minnesota	12:00
Nov. 23	**Denver**	1:00
Dec. 1	at San Francisco (Monday)	6:00
Dec. 7	at Washington	1:00
Dec. 14	**St. Louis**	1:00
Dec. 20	**Green Bay** (Saturday)	12:30

GIANTS COACHING HISTORY

(420-365-32)

1925	Bob Folwell	8-4-0
1926	Joe Alexander	8-4-1
1927-28	Earl Potteiger	15-8-3
1929-30	LeRoy Andrews	26-5-1
1931-53	Steve Owen	154-108-17
1954-60	Jim Lee Howell	54-29-4
1961-68	Allie Sherman	57-54-4
1969-73	Alex Webster	29-40-1
1974-76	Bill Arnsparger*	7-28-0
1976-78	John McVay	14-23-0
1979-82	Ray Perkins	24-35-0
1983-85	Bill Parcells	24-27-1

*Released after seven games in 1976

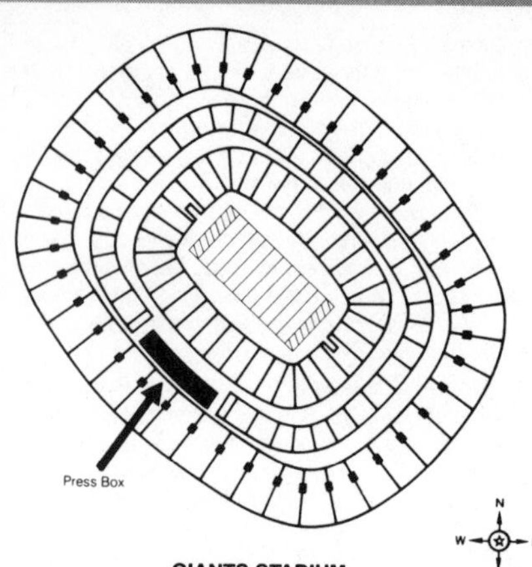

GIANTS STADIUM

RECORD HOLDERS

Individual Records—Career

Category	Name	Performance
Rushing (Yds.)	Alex Webster, 1955-1964	4,638
Passing (Yds.)	Charlie Conerly, 1948-1961	19,488
Passing (TDs)	Charlie Conerly, 1948-1961	173
Receiving (No.)	Joe Morrison, 1959-1972	395
Receiving (Yds.)	Frank Gifford, 1952-1960, 1962-64	5,434
Interceptions	Emlen Tunnell, 1948-1958	74
Punting (Avg.)	Don Chandler, 1956-1964	43.8
Punt Return (Avg.)	Bob Hammond, 1976-78	9.1
Kickoff Return (Avg.)	Rocky Thompson, 1971-72	27.2
Field Goals	Pete Gogolak, 1966-1974	126
Touchdowns (Tot.)	Frank Gifford, 1952-1960, 1962-64	78
Points	Pete Gogolak, 1966-1974	646

Individual Records—Single Season

Category	Name	Performance
Rushing (Yds.)	Joe Morris, 1985	1,336
Passing (Yds.)	Phil Simms, 1984	4,044
Passing (TDs)	Y.A. Tittle, 1963	36
Receiving (No.)	Earnest Gray, 1983	78
Receiving (Yds.)	Homer Jones, 1967	1,209
Interceptions	Otto Schnellbacher, 1951	11
	Jim Patton, 1958	11
Punting (Avg.)	Don Chandler, 1959	46.6
Punt Return (Avg.)	Merle Hapes, 1942	15.5
Kickoff Return (Avg.)	John Salscheider, 1949	31.6
Field Goals	Ali Haji-Sheikh, 1983	35
Touchdowns (Tot.)	Joe Morris, 1985	21
Points	Ali Haji-Sheikh, 1983	127

Individual Records—Single Game

Category	Name	Performance
Rushing (Yds.)	Gene Roberts, 11-12-50	218
Passing (Yds.)	Phil Simms, 10-13-85	513
Passing (TDs)	Y.A. Tittle, 10-28-62	7
Receiving (No.)	Mark Bavaro, 10-13-85	12
Receiving (Yds.)	Del Shofner, 10-28-62	269
Interceptions	Many times	3
	Last time by Carl Lockhart, 12-4-66	
Field Goals	Joe Danelo, 10-18-81	6
Touchdowns (Tot.)	Ron Johnson, 10-2-72	4
	Earnest Gray, 9-7-80	4
Points	Ron Johnson, 10-2-72	24
	Earnest Gray, 9-7-80	24

1985 TEAM STATISTICS

	N.Y. Giants	Opp.
Total First Downs	356	258
Rushing	138	77
Passing	192	163
Penalty	26	18
Third Down: Made/Att.	95/230	66/228
Fourth Down: Made/Att.	4/11	5/16
Total Net Yards	5884	4320
Avg. Per Game	367.8	270.0
Total Plays	1130	1022
Avg. Per Play	5.2	4.2
Net Yards Rushing	2451	1482
Avg. Per Game	153.2	92.6
Total Rushes	581	419
Net Yards Passing	3433	2838
Avg. Per Game	214.6	177.4
Tackled/Yards Lost	52/396	68/539
Gross Yards	3829	3377
Att./Completions	497/275	535/278
Completion Pct.	55.3	52.0
Had Intercepted	20	24
Punts/Avg.	81/42.9	107/40.8
Net Punting Avg.	36.4	33.7
Penalties/Yards Lost	80/781	106/821
Fumbles/Ball Lost	36/18	36/13
Touchdowns	48	33
Rushing	24	9
Passing	22	20
Returns	2	4
Avg. Time of Possession	31:49	28:11

1985 TEAM RECORD

Preseason (5-0)

Date	New York Giants		Opponents
8/3	21	Houston	20
8/10	30	Denver	20
8/17	10	*Green Bay	2
8/24	34	*N.Y. Jets (OT)	31
8/30	24	Pittsburgh	14
	119		87

Regular Season (10-6)

Date	New York Giants		Opp.	Att.
9/8	21	*Philadelphia	0	76,141
9/15	20	Green Bay	23	56,149
9/22	27	*St. Louis	17	74,987
9/29	16	Philadelphia (OT)	10	66,696
10/6	29	*Dallas	30	74,981
10/13	30	Cincinnati	35	53,112
10/20	17	*Washington	3	74,389
10/27	21	New Orleans	13	54,082
11/3	22	*Tampa Bay	20	72,031
11/10	24	*L.A. Rams	19	74,603
11/18	21	Washington	23	53,371
11/24	34	St. Louis	3	41,248
12/1	33	*Cleveland	35	66,482
12/8	35	Houston	14	36,576
12/15	21	Dallas	28	62,310
12/21	28	*Pittsburgh	10	66,785

Postseason (1-1)

Date	New York Giants		Opp.	Att.
12/29/85	17	*San Francisco	3	75,131
1/5/86	0	Chicago	21	65,670

*Home Game (OT) Overtime

Score by Periods

New York Giants	62	118	118	95	6	—	399
Opponents	75	85	34	89	0	—	283

Attendance

Home 580,399 Away 423,544 Total 1,003,943
Single game home record, 76,490 (11-4-79)
Single season home record, 583,945 (1984)

1985 INDIVIDUAL STATISTICS

Rushing	Att.	Yds.	Avg.	LG	TD
Morris	294	1336	4.5	65t	21
Adams	128	498	3.9	39	2
Carpenter	60	201	3.4	46	0
Galbreath	29	187	6.4	18	0
Simms	37	132	3.6	28	0
Carthon	27	70	2.6	12	0
B. Williams	2	18	9.0	17	0
Atkinson	1	14	14.0	14t	1
Rouson	1	1	1.0	1	0
Rutledge	2	−6	−3.0	−2	0
N.Y. Giants	581	2451	4.2	65t	24
Opponents	419	1482	3.5	42t	9

Passing	Att.	Comp.	Pct.	Yds.	TD	Int.	Tkld.	Rate
Simms	495	275	55.6	3829	22	20	52/396	78.6
Adams	1	0	0.0	0	0	0	0/0	39.6
Landeta	1	0	0.0	0	0	0	0/0	39.6
N.Y. Giants	497	275	55.3	3829	22	20	52/396	78.3
Opponents	535	278	52.0	3377	20	24	68/539	65.5

Receiving	No.	Yds.	Avg.	LG	TD
Manuel	49	859	17.5	51t	5
Bavaro	37	511	13.8	32	4
Johnson	33	533	16.2	42	8
Adams	31	389	12.5	70t	2
Galbreath	30	327	10.9	49	1
McConkey	25	404	16.2	48	1
Morris	22	212	9.6	17	0
Carpenter	20	162	8.1	23	0
B. Williams	15	280	18.7	45	0
Carthon	8	81	10.1	22	0
Hasselbeck	5	71	14.2	30	1
N.Y. Giants	275	3829	13.9	70t	22
Opponents	278	3377	12.1	58t	20

Interceptions	No.	Yds.	Avg.	LG	TD
Patterson	6	88	14.7	29t	1
Kinard	5	100	20.0	31	0
Hill	2	30	15.0	30	0
P. Williams	2	28	14.0	28	0
Welch	2	8	4.0	8	0
Headen	2	7	3.5	7	0
Martin	1	56	56.0	56t	1
Reasons	1	10	10.0	10	0
Currier	1	9	9.0	9	0
Marshall	1	3	3.0	3	0
Watts	1	0	0.0	0	0
N.Y. Giants	24	339	14.1	56t	2
Opponents	20	285	14.3	65t	4

Punting	No.	Yds.	Avg.	In 20	LG
Landeta	81	3472	42.9	20	68
N.Y. Giants	81	3472	42.9	20	68
Opponents	107	4363	40.8	19	58

Punt Returns	No.	FC	Yds.	Avg.	LG	TD
McConkey	53	18	442	8.3	37	0
N.Y. Giants	53	18	442	8.3	37	0
Opponents	29	20	247	8.5	28	0

Kickoff Returns	No.	Yds.	Avg.	LG	TD
Adams	14	241	17.2	29	0
McConkey	12	234	19.5	43	0
Hill	11	186	16.9	27	0
Galbreath	7	120	17.1	37	0
Morris	2	25	12.5	18	0
Rouson	2	35	17.5	26	0
Hasselbeck	1	21	21.0	21	0
Sally	1	4	4.0	4	0
N.Y. Giants	50	866	17.3	43	0
Opponents	79	1697	21.5	89	0

Scoring	TD R	TD P	TD Rt	PAT	FG	Saf	TP
Morris	21	0	0	0/0	0/0	0	126
Schubert	0	0	0	26/27	10/13	0	56
Atkinson	1	0	0	14/15	10/15	0	50
Johnson	0	8	0	0/0	0/0	0	48
Manuel	0	5	0	0/0	0/0	0	30
Adams	2	2	0	0/0	0/0	0	24
Bavaro	0	4	0	0/0	0/0	0	24
Haji-Sheikh	0	0	0	5/5	2/5	0	11
Galbreath	0	1	0	0/0	0/0	0	6
Hasselbeck	0	1	0	0/0	0/0	0	6
Martin	0	0	1	0/0	0/0	0	6
McConkey	0	1	0	0/0	0/0	0	6
Patterson	0	0	1	0/0	0/0	0	6
N.Y. Giants	24	22	2	45/47	22/33	0	399
Opponents	9	20	4	31/33	18/21	0	283

FIRST-ROUND SELECTIONS

(If club had no first-round selection, first player drafted is listed with round in parentheses.)

Year	Player, College, Position
1936	Art Lewis, Ohio U., T
1937	Ed Widseth, Minnesota, T
1938	George Karamatic, Gonzaga, B
1939	Walt Neilson, Arizona, B
1940	Grenville Lansdell, Southern California, B
1941	George Franck, Minnesota, B
1942	Merle Hapes, Mississippi, B
1943	Steve Filipowicz, Fordham, B
1944	Billy Hillenbrand, Indiana, B
1945	Elmer Barbour, Wake Forest, B
1946	George Connor, Notre Dame, T
1947	Vic Schwall, Northwestern, B
1948	Tony Minisi, Pennsylvania, B
1949	Paul Page, Southern Methodist, B
1950	Travis Tidwell, Auburn, B
1951	Kyle Rote, Southern Methodist, B
	Jim Spavital, Oklahoma A&M, B
1952	Frank Gifford, Southern California, B
1953	Bobby Marlow, Alabama, B
1954	Ken Buck, Pacific, C (2)
1955	Joe Heap, Notre Dame, B
1956	Henry Moore, Arkansas, B (2)
1957	Sam DeLuca, South Carolina, T (2)
1958	Phil King, Vanderbilt, B
1959	Lee Grosscup, Utah, B
1960	Lou Cordileone, Clemson, G
1961	Bruce Tarbox, Syracuse, G (2)
1962	Jerry Hillebrand, Colorado, LB
1963	Frank Lasky, Florida, T (2)
1964	Joe Don Looney, Oklahoma, RB
1965	Tucker Frederickson, Auburn, RB
1966	Francis Peay, Missouri, T
1967	Louis Thompson, Alabama, DT (4)
1968	Dick Buzin, Penn State, T (2)
1969	Fred Dryer, San Diego State, DE
1970	Jim Files, Oklahoma, LB
1971	Rocky Thompson, West Texas State, WR
1972	Eldridge Small, Texas A&I, DB
	Larry Jacobson, Nebraska, DE
1973	Brad Van Pelt, Michigan State, LB (2)
1974	John Hicks, Ohio State, G
1975	Al Simpson, Colorado State, T (2)
1976	Troy Archer, Colorado, DE
1977	Gary Jeter, Southern California, DT
1978	Gordon King, Stanford, T
1979	Phil Simms, Morehead State, QB
1980	Mark Haynes, Colorado, DB
1981	Lawrence Taylor, North Carolina, LB
1982	Butch Woolfolk, Michigan, RB
1983	Terry Kinard, Clemson, DB
1984	Carl Banks, Michigan State, LB
	Bill Roberts, Ohio State, T
1985	George Adams, Kentucky, RB
1986	Eric Dorsey, Notre Dame, DE

NEW YORK GIANTS 1986 VETERAN ROSTER

No.	Name	Pos.	Ht.	Wt.	Birth-date	NFL Exp.	College	Hometown	How Acq.	'85 Games/ Starts
33	Adams, George	RB	6-1	225	12/22/62	2	Kentucky	Lexington, Ky.	D1-'85	16/0
67	Ard, Bill	G	6-3	270	3/12/59	6	Wake Forest	Watchung, N.J.	D8c-'81	16/16
58	Banks, Carl	LB	6-4	235	8/29/62	3	Michigan State	Flint, Mich.	D1-'84	12/5
89	Bavaro, Mark	TE	6-4	245	4/28/63	2	Notre Dame	Danvers, Mass.	D4-'85	16/16
60	Benson, Brad	T	6-3	270	11/25/55	9	Penn State	Altoona, Pa.	FA-'77	16/16
64	Burt, Jim	NT	6-1	260	6/7/59	6	Miami	Orchard Park, N.Y.	FA-'81	16/15
26	†Carpenter, Rob	RB	6-1	226	4/20/55	10	Miami, Ohio	Lancaster, Ohio	T(Hou)-'81	14/8
53	Carson, Harry	LB	6-2	240	11/26/53	11	South Carolina State	Florence, S.C.	D4-'76	16/16
44	Carthon, Maurice	RB	6-1	225	4/24/61	2	Arkansas State	Osceola, Ark.	FA-'85	16/8
24	Daniel, Kenny	CB	5-10	180	6/1/60	2	San Jose State	Richmond, Calif.	FA-'84	0*
39	Davis, Tyrone	CB	6-1	190	11/16/61	2	Clemson	Athens, Ga.	D3-'85	7/0
30	†Galbreath, Tony	RB	6-0	228	1/29/54	11	Missouri	Fulton, Mo.	T(Minn)-'84	16/0
61	Godfrey, Chris	G	6-3	265	5/17/58	4	Michigan	Detroit, Mich.	FA-'84	16/16
62	Goode, Conrad	T-C	6-6	285	1/19/62	3	Missouri	Creve Coeur, Mo.	D4-'84	16/2
6	†Haji-Sheikh, Ali	K	6-0	170	1/11/61	3	Michigan	Arlington, Tex.	D9-'83	2/0
79	Hardison, Dee	DE	6-4	274	5/2/56	9	North Carolina	Newton Grove, N.C.	FA-'81	13/0
85	†Hasselbeck, Don	TE	6-7	245	4/1/55	10	Colorado	Cincinnati, Ohio	FA-'85	7/0
54	Headen, Andy	LB	6-5	242	7/8/60	4	Clemson	Asheboro, N.C.	D8-'83	16/1
48	†Hill, Kenny	S	6-0	195	7/25/58	6	Yale	Oak Grove, La.	T(Raiders)-'84	12/11
15	Hostetler, Jeff	QB	6-3	212	4/22/61	3	West Virginia	Johnstown, Pa.	D3-'84	5/0
57	Hunt, Byron	LB	6-5	242	12/17/58	6	Southern Methodist	Longview, Tex.	D9-'81	16/11
88	Johnson, Bob	WR	5-11	171	12/14/61	3	Kansas	East St. Louis, Ill.	FA-'84	16/15
51	Jones, Robbie	LB	6-2	230	12/25/59	3	Alabama	Demopolis, Ala.	D12-'83	16/0
69	Jordan, David	G	6-6	276	7/14/62	3	Auburn	Vestavia Hills, Ala.	D10-'84	16/0
82	†Kab, Vyto	TE	6-5	240	12/23/59	5	Penn State	Wayne, N.J.	T(Phil)-'85	12/0*
43	Kinard, Terry	S	6-1	200	11/24/59	4	Clemson	Sumter, S.C.	D1-'83	16/16
72	King, Gordon	T	6-6	275	2/3/56	8	Stanford	Fair Oaks, Calif.	D1-'78	15/0
5	Landeta, Sean	P	6-0	200	1/6/62	2	Towson State	Baltimore, Md.	FA-'85	16/0
86	Manuel, Lionel	WR	5-11	175	4/13/62	3	Pacific	La Puente, Calif.	D7-'84	12/12
70	Marshall, Leonard	DE	6-3	285	10/22/61	4	Louisiana State	Franklin, La.	D2-'83	16/16
75	Martin, George	DE	6-4	255	2/16/53	12	Oregon	Fairfield, Calif.	D11-'75	16/0
80	McConkey, Phil	WR-KR	5-10	170	2/24/57	3	Navy	Buffalo, N.Y.	FA-'84	16/0
76	McGriff, Curtis	DE	6-5	276	5/17/58	7	Alabama	Cottonwood, Ala.	FA-'80	16/16
71	Merrill, Casey	DE	6-4	260	7/16/57	8	Cal-Davis	Danville, Calif.	FA-'83	11/0
20	Morris, Joe	RB	5-7	195	9/15/60	5	Syracuse	Ayer, Mass.	D2-'82	16/16
84	Mowatt, Zeke	TE	6-3	240	3/5/61	3	Florida State	Wauchula, Fla.	FA-'83	0*
63	Nelson, Karl	T	6-6	285	6/14/60	3	Iowa State	Dekalb, Ill.	D3-'83	16/16
65	Oates, Bart	C	6-3	265	12/16/58	2	Brigham Young	Albany, Ga.	FA-'85	16/14
34	Patterson, Elvis	CB	5-11	188	10/21/60	3	Kansas	Houston, Tex.	FA-'84	16/15
55	Reasons, Gary	LB	6-4	234	2/18/62	3	Northwest Louisiana	Crowley, Tex.	D4a-'84	16/15
66	Roberts, William	T	6-5	280	8/5/62	2	Ohio State	Miami, Fla.	D1a-'84	0*
81	Robinson, Stacy	WR	5-11	186	2/19/62	2	North Dakota State	St. Paul, Minn.	D2-'85	4/0
22	Rouson, Lee	RB	6-1	210	10/18/62	2	Colorado	Greensboro, N.C.	D8-'85	2/0
17	Rutledge, Jeff	QB	6-1	195	1/22/57	8	Alabama	Birmingham, Ala.	T(Rams)-'82	16/0
78	Sally, Jerome	NT	6-3	270	2/24/59	5	Missouri	Maywood, Ill.	FA-'82	16/1
3	Schubert, Eric	K	5-8	193	5/28/62	2	Pittsburgh	Greenwood, N.J.	FA-'85	8/0
11	Simms, Phil	QB	6-3	214	11/3/56	7	Morehead State	Louisville, Ky.	D1-'79	16/16
56	Taylor, Lawrence	LB	6-3	243	2/4/59	6	North Carolina	Williamsburg, Va.	D1-'81	16/16
21	Watts, Ted	CB	6-0	190	5/29/58	6	Texas Tech	Tarpon Springs, Fla.	T(Raiders)-'85	16/3
27	Welch, Herb	CB-S	5-11	180	1/12/61	2	UCLA	Downey, Calif.	D12-'85	16/0
87	†Williams, Byron	WR	6-2	183	10/31/60	4	Texas-Arlington	Texarkana, Tex.	FA-'83	16/5
23	Williams, Perry	CB	6-2	203	5/12/61	3	North Carolina State	Hamlet, N.C.	D7-'83	16/16

* Daniel, Mowatt, and Roberts missed '85 season due to injury; Kab played 1 game with Philadelphia, 11 with N.Y. Giants in '85.

†Option playout; subject to developments.

Traded—Cornerback Mark Haynes to Denver.

Retired—Bill Currier, 9-year safety, 2 games in '85.

Also played with Giants in '85—K Jess Atkinson (6 games), S Larry Flowers (9).

COACHING STAFF

Head Coach, Bill Parcells

Pro Career: Became twelfth head coach in New York Giants history on December 15, 1982. Parcells begins fourth campaign as head coach after spending two seasons as the Giants' defensive coordinator and linebacker coach. He has led Giants to Wild Card playoff berth each of the last two seasons. Started pro coaching career in 1980 as linebacker coach with New England. Career record: 24-27-1.

Background: Linebacker at Wichita State 1961-63. College assistant Hastings (Neb.) 1964, Wichita State 1965, Army 1966-69, Florida State 1970-72, Vanderbilt 1973-74, Texas Tech 1975-77, Air Force 1978 (head coach).

Personal: Born August 22, 1941, Englewood, N.J. Bill and his wife, Judy, live in Upper Saddle River, N.J., and have three daughters—Suzy, Jill, and Dallas.

Assistant Coaches

Bill Belichick, defensive coordinator; born April 16, 1952, Nashville, Tenn., lives in Chatham, N.J. Center-tight end Wesleyan 1972-74. No pro playing experience. Pro coach: Baltimore Colts 1975, Detroit Lions 1976-77, Denver Broncos 1978, joined Giants in 1979.

Romeo Crennell, special teams; born June 18, 1947, Lynchburg, Va., lives in Montvale, N.J. Defensive lineman Western Kentucky 1966-69. No pro playing experience. College coach: Western Kentucky 1970-74, Texas Tech 1975-77, Mississippi 1978-79, Georgia Tech 1980. Pro coach: Joined Giants in 1981.

Ron Erhardt, offensive coordinator; born February 27, 1932, Mandan, N.D., lives in Wykoff, N.J. Quarterback Jamestown (N.D.) College 1951-54. No pro playing experience. College coach: North Dakota State 1963-72 (head coach 1966-72). Pro coach: New England Patriots 1973-81 (head coach 1979-81), joined Giants in 1982.

Len Fontes, defensive backfield; born March 8, 1938, New Bedford, Mass., lives in Dover, N.J. Defensive back Ohio State 1958-59. No pro playing experience. College coach: Eastern Michigan 1968, Dayton 1969-72, Navy 1973-76, Miami 1977-79. Pro coach: Cleveland Browns 1980-82, joined Giants in 1983.

Ray Handley, running backs; born October 8, 1944, Artesia, N.M., lives in West Orange, N.J. Running back Stanford 1963-65. No pro playing experience. College coach: Stanford 1967, 1971-74, 1979-83, Army 1968-69, Air Force 1975-78. Pro coach: Joined Giants in 1984.

Fred Hoaglin, offensive line; born January 28, 1944, Alliance, Ohio, lives in Sparta, N.J. Center Pittsburgh 1962-65. Pro center Cleveland Browns 1966-72, Baltimore Colts 1973, Houston Oilers 1974-75, Seattle Seahawks 1976. Pro coach: Detroit Lions 1978-84, joined Giants in 1985.

Pat Hodgson, receivers; born January 30, 1944, Columbus, Ga., lives in East Rutherford, N.J. Tight end Georgia 1963-65. Pro tight end Washington Redskins 1966, Minnesota Vikings 1967. College coach: Georgia 1968-70, 1972-77, Florida State 1971, Texas Tech 1978. Pro coach: San Diego Chargers 1978, joined Giants in 1979.

Lamar Leachman, defensive line; born August 7, 1934, Cartersville, Ga., lives in Ridgewood, N.J. Center-linebacker Tennessee 1952-55. No pro playing experience. College coach: Richmond 1966-67, Georgia Tech 1968-71, Memphis State 1972, South Carolina 1973. Pro coach: New York Stars (WFL) 1974, Toronto Argonauts (CFL) 1975-77, Montreal Alouettes (CFL) 1978-79, joined Giants in 1980.

Johnny Parker, strength and conditioning; born February 1, 1947, Greenville, S.C., lives in Montvale, N.J. No pro playing experience. Graduate of Mississippi, master's degree from Delta State University. College coach: South Carolina 1974-76, Indiana 1977-79, Louisiana State 1980, Mississippi 1981-83. Pro coach: Joined Giants in 1984.

Mike Pope, tight ends; born March 15, 1942, Monroe, N.C., lives in River Vale, N.J. Quarterback Lenoir Rhyne 1962-64. No pro playing experience. College coach: Florida State 1970-74, Texas Tech 1975-77, Mississippi 1978-82. Pro coach: Joined Giants in 1983.

Mike Sweatman, assistant special teams; born October 23, 1946, Kansas City, Mo., lives in Wayne, N.J. Linebacker Kansas 1964-67. No pro playing experience. College coach: Kansas 1973-74, 1979-82, Tulsa 1977-78, Tennessee 1983. Pro coach: Minnesota Vikings 1984, joined Giants in 1985.

NEW YORK GIANTS 1986 FIRST-YEAR ROSTER

Name	Pos.	Ht.	Wt.	Birth-date	College	Hometown	How Acq.
Bailey, Eric (1)	TE	6-5	240	5/12/63	Kansas State	Ft. Worth, Tex.	FA
Brown, Ron	WR	5-10	186	1/11/63	Colorado	Pasadena, Calif.	D6a
Butler, Doug	QB	6-0	185	8/29/64	Princeton	Anaheim, Calif.	FA
Cisowski, Steve	T	6-5	275	1/23/63	Santa Clara	Campbell, Calif.	D8
Collins, Mark	CB	5-10	190	1/16/64	Cal State-Fullerton	San Bernardino, Calif.	D2a
Corbin, Mark	RB	5-10	208	4/13/63	Central State	Brooklyn, N.Y.	FA
Covington, Al	S	5-11	200	6/17/63	Maryland	Danville, Va.	FA
Dorsey, Eric	DE	6-5	280	8/5/64	Notre Dame	McLean, Va.	D1
DuFault, Paul	C	6-4	270	2/15/64	New Hampshire	Rochester, N.H.	FA
Francis, Jon	RB	5-11	205	6/21/64	Boise State	Corvallis, Ore.	D7
Hamilton, Lance	S	5-11	185	10/21/64	Penn State	Wilkes-Barre, Pa.	FA
Holinka, Jeff	G	6-3	270	9/19/63	Maryland	Pottstown, Pa.	FA
Howard, Erik	NT	6-4	268	11/12/64	Washington State	San Jose, Calif.	D2b
Johnson, Thomas	LB	6-3	248	7/29/64	Ohio State	Detroit, Mich.	D2c
Kimmel, Jerry	LB	6-2	250	7/18/63	Syracuse	Kirkwood, N.Y.	D10
Lasker, Greg	S	6-0	200	9/28/64	Arkansas	Conway, Ark.	D2d
Lewis, Tony	RB	6-1	215	10/28/63	Nevada-Las Vegas	Las Vegas, Nev.	FA
Luebbers, Jim	DE	6-5	255	5/20/63	Iowa State	Shellrock, Iowa	D9
Lynch, Len	G	6-2	270	4/6/62	Maryland	Levittown, Pa.	D11
McKinney, James (1)	LB	6-3	240	10/3/63	Texas	Austin, Tex.	FA
Miller, Solomon	WR	6-1	185	12/6/64	Utah State	Los Angeles, Calif.	D6b
Pontiakos, Steve	TE	6-5	230	4/23/63	Delaware	Livingston, N.J.	FA
Pounds, Cleve	S	6-0	195	6/28/64	Georgia Tech	Winston, Ga.	FA
Ramseur, Mike	RB	5-10	184	4/3/64	Wake Forest	Durham, N.C.	FA
Santos, Henry	QB	6-1	197	9/25/64	Columbia	Edison, N.J.	FA
Scott, Stanley	DE	6-3	250	1/30/64	Florida State	Tampa, Fla.	FA
Smith, Al	RB	5-10	219	1/25/63	Rutgers	Union, N.J.	FA
Soule, Glen	WR	5-9	165	2/13/62	Angelo State	Darrow, La.	FA
Swoapu, Roy (1)	LB	6-2	222	5/17/63	Western Michigan	Kalamazoo, Mich.	FA
Warren, Vince	WR	6-0	180	2/18/63	San Diego State	Albuquerque, N.M.	D5
Washington, John	DE	6-4	275	2/20/63	Oklahoma State	Houston, Tex.	D3

The term NFL Rookie is defined as a player who is in his first season of professional football and has not been on the roster of another professional football team for any regular season or postseason games. A Rookie is designated by an "R" on NFL rosters. Players who have been active in another professional football league or players who have NFL experience, including either preseason training camp or being on an active roster for fewer than three regular season or postseason games, are termed NFL First-Year Players. An NFL First-Year Player is designated by a "1" on NFL rosters. Thereafter, a player on an NFL active roster for at least three regular season or postseason games is credited with an additional year of NFL playing experience.

NOTES

PHILADELPHIA EAGLES

National Football Conference
Eastern Division

Team Colors: Kelly Green, Silver, and White

Veterans Stadium
Broad Street and Pattison Avenue
Philadelphia, Pennsylvania 19148
Telephone: (215) 463-2500

Club Officials

Owner: Norman Braman
Co-owner: Ed Leibowitz
Vice President-General Manager: Harry Gamble
Assistant to the Vice President-General Manager: Patrick Forte
Assistant to the Vice President-General Manager: George Azar
Director of Player Personnel: Joe Woolley
Talent Scouts: Bill Baker, Lou Blumling
Director of Communications: Ed Wisneski
Assistant Director of Public Relations: Ron Howard
Executive Director of Marketing and Promotions: Decker Uhlhorn
Associate Director of Sales and Marketing: Jim Gallagher
Ticket Manager: Leo Carlin
Business Manager: Mimi Box
Director of Penthouse Sales: Lou Scheinfeld
Trainer: Otho Davis
Assistant Trainer: David Price
Strength and Conditioning Coordinator: Tim Jorgensen
Equipment Manager: Rusty Sweeney
Video Director: Mike Dougherty

Stadium: Veterans Stadium •
Capacity: 69,417
Broad Street and Pattison Avenue
Philadelphia, Pennsylvania 19148

Playing Surface: AstroTurf

Training Camp: West Chester University
West Chester, Pennsylvania
19380

1986 SCHEDULE

Preseason

Aug. 8	at Detroit	8:00
Aug. 16	at San Diego	6:00
Aug. 23	**Miami**	7:30
Aug. 28	**New York Jets**	7:30

Regular Season

Sept. 7	at Washington	1:00
Sept. 14	at Chicago	12:00
Sept. 21	**Denver**	1:00
Sept. 28	**Los Angeles Rams**	1:00
Oct. 5	at Atlanta	1:00
Oct. 12	at New York Giants	4:00
Oct. 19	**Dallas**	1:00
Oct. 26	**San Diego**	1:00
Nov. 2	at St. Louis	12:00
Nov. 9	**New York Giants**	4:00
Nov. 16	**Detroit**	1:00
Nov. 23	at Seattle	1:00
Nov. 30	at Los Angeles Raiders	1:00
Dec. 7	**St. Louis**	1:00
Dec. 14	at Dallas	12:00
Dec. 21	**Washington**	1:00

EAGLES COACHING HISTORY

(290-376-23)

1933-35	Lud Wray	9-21-1
1936-40	Bert Bell	10-44-2
1941-50	Earle (Greasy) Neale*	66-44-5
1951	Alvin (Bo) McMillin**	2-0-0
1951	Wayne Millner	2-8-0
1952-55	Jim Trimble	25-20-3
1956-57	Hugh Devore	7-16-1
1958-60	Lawrence (Buck) Shaw	20-16-1
1961-63	Nick Skorich	15-24-3
1964-68	Joe Kuharich	28-41-1
1969-71	Jerry Williams***	7-22-2
1971-72	Ed Khayat	8-15-2
1973-75	Mike McCormack	16-25-1
1976-82	Dick Vermeil	57-51-0
1983-85	Marion Campbell****	17-29-1
1985	Fred Bruney	1-0-0

*Co-coach with Walt Kiesling in Philadelphia-Pittsburgh merger in 1943
**Retired after two games in 1951
***Released after three games in 1971
****Released after 15 games in 1985

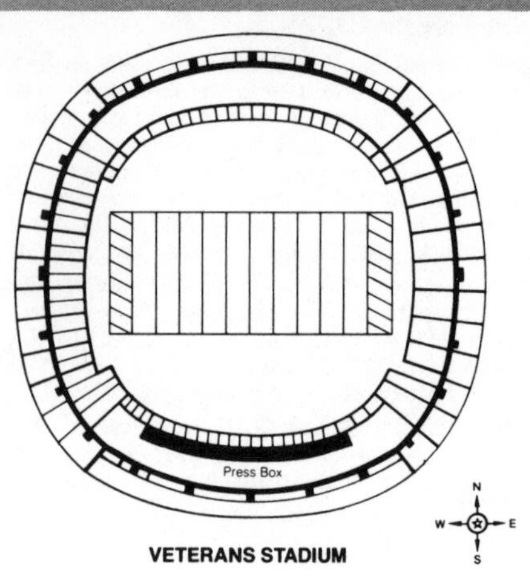

VETERANS STADIUM

RECORD HOLDERS

Individual Records—Career

Category	Name	Performance
Rushing (Yds.)	Wilbert Montgomery, 1977-1984	6,538
Passing (Yds.)	Ron Jaworski, 1977-1985	25,558
Passing (TDs)	Ron Jaworski, 1977-1985	167
Receiving (No.)	Harold Carmichael, 1971-1983	589
Receiving (Yds.)	Harold Carmichael, 1971-1983	8,978
Interceptions	Bill Bradley, 1969-1976	34
Field Goals	Sam Baker, 1964-69	90
Touchdowns (Tot.)	Harold Carmichael, 1971-1983	79
Points	Bobby Walston, 1951-1962	881

Individual Records—Single Season

Category	Name	Performance
Rushing (Yds.)	Wilbert Montgomery, 1979	1,512
Passing (Yds.)	Sonny Jurgensen, 1961	3,723
Passing (TDs)	Sonny Jurgensen, 1961	32
Receiving (No.)	Mike Quick, 1985	71
Receiving (Yds.)	Mike Quick, 1983	1,409
Interceptions	Bill Bradley, 1971	11
Field Goals	Paul McFadden, 1984	30
Touchdowns (Tot.)	Steve Van Buren, 1945	18
Points	Paul McFadden, 1984	116

Individual Records—Single Game

Category	Name	Performance
Rushing (Yds.)	Steve Van Buren, 11-27-49	205
Passing (Yds.)	Bobby Thomason, 11-18-53	437
Passing (TDs)	Adrian Burk, 10-17-54	7
Receiving (No.)	Don Looney, 12-1-40	14
Receiving (Yds.)	Tommy McDonald, 12-10-60	237
Interceptions	Russ Craft, 9-24-50	4
Field Goals	Tom Dempsey, 11-12-72	6
Touchdowns (Tot.)	Many times Last time by Wilbert Montgomery, 10-7-79	4
Points	Bobby Walston, 10-17-54	25

1985 TEAM STATISTICS

	Philadelphia	Opp.
Total First Downs	292	307
Rushing	82	122
Passing	188	160
Penalty	22	25
Third Down: Made/Att.	82/231	91/234
Fourth Down: Made/Att.	7/13	5/8
Total Net Yards	5216	5135
Avg. Per Game	326.0	320.9
Total Plays	1050	1057
Avg. Per Play	5.0	4.9
Net Yards Rushing	1630	2205
Avg. Per Game	101.9	137.8
Total Rushes	428	526
Net Yards Passing	3586	2930
Avg. Per Game	224.1	183.1
Tackled/Yards Lost	55/450	53/359
Gross Yards	4036	3289
Att./Completions	567/290	478/251
Completion Pct.	51.1	52.5
Had Intercepted	28	18
Punts/Avg.	91/41.5	92/42.6
Net Punting Avg.	34.2	36.6
Penalties/Yards Lost	98/736	99/834
Fumbles/Ball Lost	25/12	27/14
Touchdowns	30	39
Rushing	8	17
Passing	19	18
Returns	3	4
Avg. Time of Possession	29:13	30:47

1985 TEAM RECORD

Preseason (3-1)

Date	Philadelphia		Opponents
8/10	37	N.Y. Jets	17
8/17	14	Cleveland	28
8/23	14	L.A. Rams	12
8/29	20	*Detroit	16
	85		73

Regular Season (7-9)

Date	Philadelphia		Opp.	Att.
9/8	0	N.Y. Giants	21	76,141
9/15	6	*L.A. Rams	17	60,920
9/22	19	Washington	6	53,748
9/29	10	*N.Y. Giants (OT)	16	66,696
10/6	21	New Orleans	23	56,364
10/13	30	*St. Louis	7	48,186
10/20	16	*Dallas	14	70,114
10/27	21	*Buffalo	17	60,987
11/3	13	San Francisco	24	58,383
11/10	23	*Atlanta (OT)	17	63,694
11/17	24	St. Louis	14	39,032
11/24	17	Dallas	34	54,047
12/1	23	*Minnesota	28	54,688
12/8	12	*Washington	17	60,737
12/15	14	San Diego	20	45,569
12/22	37	Minnesota	35	49,722

*Home Game (OT) Overtime

Score by Periods

Philadelphia	60	72	56	92	6	—	286
Opponents	69	67	76	92	6	—	310

Attendance

Home 486,022 Away 433,006 Total 919,028
Single game home record, 72,111 (11-1-81)
Single season home record, 557,325 (1980)

1985 INDIVIDUAL STATISTICS

Rushing	Att.	Yds.	Avg.	LG	TD
E. Jackson	282	1028	3.6	59	5
Haddix	67	213	3.2	12	0
Cunningham	29	205	7.1	37	0
Hunter	27	121	4.5	74t	1
Jaworski	17	35	2.1	31	2
Everett	4	13	3.3	8	0
Horan	1	12	12.0	12	0
Oliver	1	3	3.0	3	0
Eagles	428	1630	3.8	74t	8
Opponents	526	2205	4.2	60	17

Passing	Att.	Comp.	Pct.	Yds.	TD	Int.	Tkld.	Rate
Jaworski	484	255	52.7	3450	17	20	34/289	70.2
Cunningham	81	34	42.0	548	1	8	20/150	29.8
Hunter	2	1	50.0	38	1	0	1/11	135.4
Eagles	567	290	51.1	4036	19	28	55/450	65.0
Opponents	478	251	52.5	3289	18	18	53/359	71.4

Receiving	No.	Yds.	Avg.	LG	TD
Quick	73	1247	17.1	99t	11
Spagnola	64	772	12.1	35	5
Haddix	43	330	7.7	17	0
K. Jackson	40	692	17.3	54	1
Hunter	28	405	14.5	43	1
Johnson	11	186	16.9	37	0
E. Jackson	10	126	12.6	25	1
Garrity	7	142	20.3	34	0
Little	7	82	11.7	28	0
Everett	4	25	6.3	11	0
K. Baker	2	25	12.5	20	0
Oliver	1	4	4.0	4	0
Eagles	290	4036	13.9	99t	19
Opponents	251	3289	13.1	46	18

Interceptions	No.	Yds.	Avg.	LG	TD
Hopkins	6	36	6.0	24t	1
Ellis	4	32	8.0	18	0
Edwards	3	8	2.7	3t	1
Cooper	2	13	6.5	13	0
Kraynak	1	26	26.0	26	0
Reichenbach	1	10	10.0	10	0
Young	1	0	0.0	0	0
Eagles	18	125	6.9	26	2
Opponents	28	474	16.9	46	2

Punting	No.	Yds.	Avg.	In 20	LG
Horan	91	3777	41.5	20	75
Eagles	91	3777	41.5	20	75
Opponents	92	3918	42.6	32	68

Punt Returns	No.	FC	Yds.	Avg.	LG	TD
Cooper	43	10	364	8.5	56	0
Hunter	1	0	6	6.0	6	0
Waters	1	0	23	23.0	23	0
Eagles	45	10	393	8.7	56	0
Opponents	41	16	462	11.3	80t	1

Kickoff Returns	No.	Yds.	Avg.	LG	TD
Hunter	48	1047	21.8	51	0
Waters	4	74	18.5	23	0
Cooper	3	32	10.7	13	0
Foules	1	7	7.0	7	0
Eagles	56	1160	20.7	51	0
Opponents	65	1293	19.9	88	0

Scoring	TD R	TD P	TD Rt	PAT	FG	Saf	TP
McFadden	0	0	0	29/29	25/30	0	104
Quick	0	11	0	0/0	0/0	0	66
E. Jackson	5	1	0	0/0	0/0	0	36
Spagnola	0	5	0	0/0	0/0	0	30
Hunter	1	1	0	0/0	0/0	0	12
Jaworski	2	0	0	0/0	0/0	0	12
Edwards	0	0	1	0/0	0/0	0	6
Hopkins	0	0	1	0/0	0/0	0	6
K. Jackson	0	1	0	0/0	0/0	0	6
Little	0	0	1	0/0	0/0	0	6
Eagles	8	19	3	29/29	25/30	1	286
Opponents	17	18	4	37/38	13/29	0	310

FIRST-ROUND SELECTIONS

(If club had no first-round selection, first player drafted is listed with round in parentheses.)

Year	Player, College, Position
1936	Jay Berwanger, Chicago, B
1937	Sam Francis, Nebraska, B
1938	Jim McDonald, Ohio State, B
1939	Davey O'Brien, Texas Christian, B
1940	George McAfee, Duke, B
1941	Art Jones, Richmond, B (2)
1942	Pete Kmetovic, Stanford, B
1943	Joe Muha, Virginia Military, B
1944	Steve Van Buren, Louisiana State, B
1945	John Yonaker, Notre Dame, E
1946	Leo Riggs, Southern California, B
1947	Neill Armstrong, Oklahoma A&M, E
1948	Clyde (Smackover) Scott, Arkansas, B
1949	Chuck Bednarik, Pennsylvania, C
	Frank Tripucka, Notre Dame, B
1950	Harry (Bud) Grant, Minnesota, E
1951	Ebert Van Buren, Louisiana State, B
	Chet Mutryn, Xavier, B
1952	Johnny Bright, Drake, B
1953	Al Conway, Army, B (2)
1954	Neil Worden, Notre Dame, B
1955	Dick Bielski, Maryland, B
1956	Bob Pellegrini, Maryland, C
1957	Clarence Peaks, Michigan State, B
1958	Walt Kowalczyk, Michigan State, B
1959	J.D. Smith, Rice, T (2)
1960	Ron Burton, Northwestern, RB
1961	Art Baker, Syracuse, RB
1962	Pete Case, Georgia, G (2)
1963	Ed Budde, Michigan State, G
1964	Bob Brown, Nebraska, T
1965	Ray Rissmiller, Georgia, T (2)
1966	Randy Beisler, Indiana, DE
1967	Harry Jones, Arkansas, RB
1968	Tim Rossovich, Southern California, DE
1969	Leroy Keyes, Purdue, RB
1970	Steve Zabel, Oklahoma, TE
1971	Richard Harris, Grambling, DE
1972	John Reaves, Florida, QB
1973	Jerry Sisemore, Texas, T
	Charle Young, Southern California, TE
1974	Mitch Sutton, Kansas, DT (3)
1975	Bill Capraun, Miami, T (7)
1976	Mike Smith, Florida, DE (4)
1977	Skip Sharp, Kansas, DB (5)
1978	Reggie Wilkes, Georgia Tech, LB (3)
1979	Jerry Robinson, UCLA, LB
1980	Roynell Young, Alcorn State, DB
1981	Leonard Mitchell, Houston, DE
1982	Mike Quick, North Carolina State, WR
1983	Michael Haddix, Mississippi State, RB
1984	Kenny Jackson, Penn State, WR
1985	Kevin Allen, Indiana, T
1986	Keith Byars, Ohio State, RB

PHILADELPHIA EAGLES 1986 VETERAN ROSTER

No.	Name	Pos.	Ht.	Wt.	Birth-date	NFL Exp.	College	Hometown	How Acq.	'85 Games/ Starts
72	Allen, Kevin	T	6-5	284	6/21/63	2	Indiana	Cincinnati, Ohio	D1-'85	16/4
80	Baker, Keith	WR	5-10	185	6/4/57	2	Texas Southern	Dallas, Tex.	T(SF)-'85	8/1
63	Baker, Ron	G	6-4	274	11/19/54	9	Oklahoma State	Gary, Ind.	T(Ind)-'80	15/15
98	Brown, Greg	DE	6-5	265	1/5/57	6	Kansas State	Washington, D.C.	FA-'81	16/16
6	t-Cavanaugh, Matt	QB	6-2	212	10/27/56	9	Pittsburgh	Youngstown, Ohio	T(SF)-'86	16/1
71	†Clarke, Ken	DT	6-2	272	8/28/56	9	Syracuse	Boston, Mass.	FA-'78	16/16
50	Cobb, Garry	LB	6-2	228	3/16/57	8	Southern California	Stamford, Conn.	T(Det)-'85	16/16
21	Cooper, Evan	CB-S-KR	5-11	184	6/28/62	3	Michigan	Miami, Fla.	D4-'84	16/0
12	Cunningham, Randall	QB-P	6-4	192	3/27/63	2	Nevada-Las Vegas	Santa Barbara, Calif.	D2-'85	6/4
94	Darby, Byron	DE	6-4	262	6/4/60	4	Southern California	Inglewood, Calif.	D5-'83	10/1
65	Dennard, Mark	C	6-1	262	11/2/55	8	Texas A&M	Bay City, Tex.	T(Mia)-'84	16/16
99	Drake, Joe	DT	6-2	290	5/28/63	2	Arizona	San Francisco, Calif.	D9b-'85	16/0
46	†Edwards, Herman	CB	6-0	194	4/27/54	10	San Diego State	Monterey, Calif.	FA-'77	16/16
24	Ellis, Ray	S	6-1	196	4/27/59	6	Ohio State	Canton, Ohio	D12-'81	16/16
39	Everett, Major	RB	5-11	218	1/4/60	4	Mississippi College	New Hebron, Miss.	FA-'83	15/0
67	Feehery, Gerry	C	6-2	270	3/9/60	4	Syracuse	Springfield, Pa.	FA-'83	15/0
29	†Foules, Elbert	CB	5-11	185	7/4/61	4	Alcorn State	Greenville, Miss.	FA-'83	16/3
86	Garrity, Gregg	WR	5-10	169	11/24/60	4	Penn State	Pittsburgh, Pa.	FA-'84	12/1
84	†Goode, John	TE	6-2	243	11/5/62	3	Youngstown State	Cleveland, Ohio	FA-'85	14/0
26	Haddix, Michael	RB	6-2	227	12/27/61	4	Mississippi State	Walnut, Miss.	D1-'83	16/15
48	Hopkins, Wes	S	6-1	212	9/26/61	4	Southern Methodist	Birmingham, Ala.	D2a-'83	15/15
2	Horan, Michael	P	5-11	190	2/1/59	3	Long Beach State	Fullerton, Calif.	FA-'84	16/0
36	Hunter, Herman	RB-KR	6-1	193	2/14/61	2	Tennessee State	Columbus, Ga.	D11-'85	16/5
41	Jackson, Earnest	RB	5-9	208	12/18/59	4	Texas A&M	Rosenberg, Tex.	T(SD)-'85	16/10
81	Jackson, Kenny	WR	6-0	177	2/15/62	3	Penn State	South River, N.J.	D1-'84	16/16
7	†Jaworski, Ron	QB	6-2	199	3/23/51	13	Youngstown State	Lackawanna, N.Y.	T(Rams)-'77	16/12
77	Jelesky, Tom	T	6-6	275	10/4/60	2	Purdue	Merrillville, Ind.	FA-'84	16/0
53	Jiles, Dwayne	LB	6-4	242	11/23/63	2	Texas Tech	Linden, Tex.	D5-'85	10/0
85	Johnson, Ron	WR	6-3	186	9/21/58	2	Long Beach State	Monterey, Calif.	FA-'85	8/0
73	Kenney, Steve	G	6-4	274	12/26/55	7	Clemson	Raleigh, N.C.	FA-'79	16/16
54	Kimmel, Jon	LB	6-4	240	7/21/60	2	Colgate	Kirkwood, N.Y.	FA-'85	4/0
52	†Kraynak, Rich	LB	6-1	230	1/20/61	4	Pittsburgh	Phoenixville, Pa.	D8-'83	16/0
89	Little, Dave	TE	6-2	232	4/18/61	3	Middle Tennessee State	Fresno, Calif.	FA-'85	15/0
8	McFadden, Paul	K	5-11	163	9/24/61	3	Youngstown State	Euclid, Ohio	D12-'84	16/0
74	Mitchell, Leonard	T	6-7	295	10/12/58	6	Houston	Houston, Tex.	D1-'81	16/16
38	†Penaranda, Jairo	RB	6-0	218	6/15/58	3	UCLA	Burbank, Calif.	FA-'85	4/0
82	Quick, Mike	WR	6-2	190	5/14/59	5	North Carolina State	Richmond, N.C.	D1-'82	16/15
66	Reeves, Ken	T-G	6-5	268	10/4/61	2	Texas A&M	Pittsburg, Tex.	D6b-'85	15/13
55	†Reichenbach, Mike	LB	6-2	238	9/14/61	3	East Stroudsburg State	Bethlehem, Pa.	FA-'84	16/16
95	Schulz, Jody	LB	6-3	240	8/17/60	3	East Carolina	Centreville, Md.	D2b-'83	0*
88	†Spagnola, John	TE	6-4	238	8/1/57	7	Yale	Bethlehem, Pa.	FA-'79	16/16
93	†Strauthers, Thomas	DE	6-4	264	4/6/61	4	Jackson State	Brookhaven, Miss.	D10-'83	16/3
20	†Waters, Andre	CB	5-11	185	3/10/62	3	Cheyney State	Pahokee, Fla.	FA-'84	16/0
91	White, Reggie	DT	6-5	285	12/19/61	2	Tennessee	Chattanooga, Tenn.	SD1-'84	13/12
22	Wilson, Brenard	S-CB	6-0	185	8/15/55	8	Vanderbilt	Daytona Beach, Fla.	FA-'79	16/1
43	Young, Roynell	CB	6-1	185	12/1/57	7	Alcorn State	New Orleans, La.	D1-'80	14/13

* Schulz missed '85 season due to injury.

†Option playout; subject to developments.

t-Eagles traded for Cavanaugh (San Francisco).

Traded—Linebacker Anthony Griggs to Cleveland; linebacker Reggie Wilkes to Atlanta; linebacker Joel Williams to Atlanta.

Also played with Eagles in '85—LB Aaron Brown (7 games), QB Jeff Christensen (1), DE Smiley Creswell (3), LB Tim Golden (2), TE Vyto Kab (1), NT Dwaine Morris (1), RB Hubie Oliver (1), LB Tom Polley (2).

COACHING STAFF

Head Coach, Buddy Ryan

Pro Career: Ryan was named head coach of the Eagles on January 29, 1986, after eight seasons as the defensive coordinator of the Chicago Bears. An NFL assistant coach for 18 years, Ryan has been on the staffs of three Super Bowl teams: Jets, 1968; Vikings, 1976; Bears, 1985. He served as defensive line coach under Bud Grant with the Minnesota Vikings in 1976 and 1977 before joining Chicago. From 1968-75, he was on the defensive staff of the New York Jets under coach Weeb Ewbank. In Ryan's eight seasons as defensive coordinator with Chicago, his defenses ranked among the NFL's top 10 six times. He devised the "46 defense" with its multiple variations of alignments and coverages.

Background: Ryan was a four-year letterman at Oklahoma State from 1952-55 as an offensive guard. While serving in the U.S. Army in Korea, Ryan played on the Fourth Army championship team in Japan. He served as an assistant at the University of Buffalo from 1961-65, Vanderbilt 1966, and the University of the Pacific 1967. Ryan has a master's degree in education from Middle Tennessee State.

Personal: Born James Ryan on February 17, 1934, in Frederick, Okla. Buddy and his wife, Joan, live in Cherry Hill, N.J., and have three sons: Jimmy, Jr., Rex, and Robert. They own a horse farm in Kentucky.

Assistant Coaches

Dave Atkins, offensive backfield; born May 18, 1949, Victoria, Tex., lives in Philadelphia. Running back Texas-El Paso 1970-72. Pro running back San Francisco 49ers 1973, Honolulu Hawaiians (WFL) 1974, San Diego Chargers 1975. College coach: Texas-El Paso 1979-80, San Diego State 1981-85. Pro coach: First year with Eagles.

Jeff Fisher, defensive backs; born February 25, 1958, Culver City, Calif., lives in Cherry Hill, N.J. Defensive back Southern California 1978-1980. Pro defensive back-punt returner Chicago Bears 1981-85. No college or pro coaching experience. First year with Eagles.

Dale Haupt, defensive line; born April 12, 1929, Manitowoc, Wis., lives in Cherry Hill, N.J. Defensive lineman-linebacker Wyoming 1950-53. No pro playing experience. College coach: Tennessee 1960-63, Iowa State 1964-65, Richmond 1966-71, North Carolina State 1972-76, Duke 1977. Pro coach: Chicago Bears 1978-85, first year with Eagles.

Ken Iman, offensive line; born February 8, 1939, St. Louis, Mo., lives in Springfield, Pa. Center-linebacker Southeast Missouri State 1956-59. Pro center Green Bay Packers 1960-63, Los Angeles Rams 1964-74. Pro coach: Joined Eagles in 1976.

Dan Neal, special teams; born August 30, 1949, Corbin, Ky., lives in Philadelphia. Center Kentucky 1970-72. Pro center Baltimore Colts 1973-74, Chicago Bears 1975-83. No college or pro coaching experience. First year with Eagles.

Wade Phillips, defensive coordinator-linebackers; born June 21, 1947, Orange, Tex., lives in Philadelphia. Linebacker Houston 1966-68. No pro playing experience. College coach: Houston 1969, Oklahoma State 1973-74, Kansas 1975. Pro coach: Houston Oilers 1976-80, New Orleans Saints 1981-85 (head coach last four games of 1985), first year with Eagles.

Ted Plumb, assistant head coach-offense; born August 20, 1939, Reno, Nev., lives in Cherry Hill, N.J. Wide receiver Baylor 1960-61. Pro wide receiver Buffalo Bills 1962. College coach: Cerritos, Calif., J.C. 1966-67, Texas Christian 1968-70, Tulsa 1971, Kansas 1972-73. Pro coach: New York Giants 1974-76, Atlanta Falcons 1977-79, Chicago Bears 1980-85, first year with Eagles.

Doug Scovil, quarterbacks; born July 1, 1927, Anacortes, Wash., lives in Philadelphia. Quarterback Stockton, Calif., J.C. and Pacific, 1948-51. No pro playing experience. College coach: San Mateo, Calif., J.C. 1958-62 (head coach), Navy 1963-65, Pacific 1966-69 (head coach), Brigham Young 1976-77, 1979-80, San Diego State 1981-85 (head coach). Pro coach: San Francisco 49ers 1970-75, Chicago Bears 1978, first year with Eagles.

PHILADELPHIA EAGLES 1986 FIRST-YEAR ROSTER

Name	Pos.	Ht.	Wt.	Birth-date	College	Hometown	How Acq.
Bogdalek, Steve	G	6-4	270	11/13/64	Michigan State	Naperville, Ill.	D11
Bond, Thomas	CB	5-11	175	12/14/62	Cheyney State	Camden, N.J.	FA
Brown, Cedrick	CB	5-10	178	9/6/64	Washington State	Compton, Calif.	FA
Byars, Keith	RB	6-1	230	10/14/63	Ohio State	Dayton, Ohio	D1
Criswell, Ray	P	6-0	182	8/16/63	Florida	Orange Park, Fla.	D5a
Darwin, Matt	C	6-4	260	3/11/63	Texas A&M	Spring, Tex.	D4
Fazio, Ron (1)	TE	6-4	242	6/5/62	Maryland	Willingboro, N.J.	FA
Gilmore, Jim	T	6-5	262	12/19/62	Ohio State	Philadelphia, Pa.	FA
Howard, Bobby	RB	6-0	210	6/1/64	Indiana	Pittsburgh, Pa.	D12b
Johnson, Alonzo	LB	6-3	217	4/4/63	Florida	Panama City, Fla.	D2b
Jones, Rennie	WR	6-3	215	9/9/63	Liberty Baptist	Newark, Del.	FA
Joyner, Seth	LB	6-2	230	11/18/64	Texas-El Paso	Spring Valley, N.Y.	D8
Kilkenny, Tom (1)	LB	6-3	242	8/27/58	Temple	Philadelphia, Pa.	FA
Landsee, Bob	C-G	6-4	270	3/21/64	Wisconsin	Iron Mountain, Mich.	D6
Lee, Byron	LB	6-2	230	9/8/64	Ohio State	Columbus, Ohio	D7b
Major, Doran	CB-S	5-11	178	5/20/61	Memphis State	Biloxi, Miss.	FA
McInerny, Sean	DT	6-3	250	12/27/60	Frostburg State	McLean, Va.	FA
McMillen, Dan	DE	6-4	240	2/23/64	Colorado	Colorado Springs, Colo.	D5b
Miller, Bob (1)	C	6-2	248	3/2/62	Illinois	Itasca, Ill.	FA
Moore, Dana (1)	P-K	5-10	185	9/7/61	Mississippi State	Baton Rouge, La.	FA
Morris, Dwaine (1)	DT	6-2	255	8/24/63	Southwest Louisiana	Greenburg, La.	FA
Morris, Raymond (1)	LB	5-11	234	6/8/61	Texas-El Paso	Odessa, Tex.	FA
Naron, Greg (1)	G	6-4	270	10/21/63	North Carolina	Randleman, N.C.	D4-'85
Polley, Tom (1)	LB	6-3	242	2/17/62	Nevada-Las Vegas	St. Louis Park, Minn.	D8-'85
Redick, Cornelius	WR-KR	5-11	185	1/7/64	Cal State-Fullerton	Los Angeles, Calif.	D7a
Roehlk, Jon (1)	G	6-2	255	6/25/61	Iowa	Durant, Iowa	FA
Simmons, Clyde	DE	6-6	247	8/4/64	Western Carolina	Wilmington, N.C.	D9
Singletary, Reggie	DT	6-3	255	1/17/64	North Carolina State	Whiteville, N.C.	D12a
Tautalatasi, Junior	RB	5-10	198	3/24/62	Washington State	Alameda, Calif.	D10
Thompson, Emmuel (1)	CB-S	5-11	175	11/15/59	Texas A&I	Houston, Tex.	FA
Toney, Anthony	RB	6-0	227	9/23/62	Texas A&M	Salinas, Calif.	D2a
Waters, Mike (1)	RB	6-2	225	3/15/62	San Diego State	Ridgecrest, Calif.	FA
Webb, Jim	T	6-4	248	8/2/63	Colorado	St. Louis, Mo.	FA

The term NFL Rookie is defined as a player who is in his first season of professional football and has not been on the roster of another professional football team for any regular season or postseason games. A Rookie is designated by an "R" on NFL rosters. Players who have been active in another professional football league or players who have NFL experience, including either preseason training camp or being on an active roster for fewer than three regular season or postseason games, are termed NFL First-Year Players. An NFL First-Year Player is designated by a "1" on NFL rosters. Thereafter, a player on an NFL active roster for at least three regular season or postseason games is credited with an additional year of NFL playing experience.

NOTES

ST. LOUIS CARDINALS

National Football Conference
Eastern Division

Team Colors: Cardinal Red, Black, and White

Busch Stadium, Box 888
St. Louis, Missouri 63188
Telephone: (314) 421-0777

Club Officials

Chairman/President: William V. Bidwill
Vice President/Administration: Curt Mosher
Secretary and General Counsel: Thomas J. Guilfoil
Treasurer: Charley Schlegel
Director of Pro Personnel: Larry Wilson
Director of Player Personnel: George Boone
Public Relations Director: Bob Rose
Media Coordinator: Greg Gladysiewski
Director of Community Relations: Adele Harris
Ticket Manager: Steve Walsh
Trainer: John Omohundro
Assistant Trainers: Jim Shearer, Ed Fleming
Equipment Manager: Bill Simmons
Assistant Equipment Manager: Mark Ahlemeier

Stadium: Busch Stadium •
Capacity: 51,392
200 Stadium Plaza
St. Louis, Missouri 63102

Playing Surface: AstroTurf-8

Training Camp: Eastern Illinois University
Charleston, Illinois 61920

1986 SCHEDULE

Preseason

Aug. 2	vs. New England at Canton, Ohio	2:30
Aug. 9	at Tampa Bay	7:00
Aug. 16	**Kansas City**	7:00
Aug. 23	at Chicago	8:00
Aug. 29	at San Diego	7:00

Regular Season

Sept. 7	**Los Angeles Rams**	12:00
Sept. 14	at Atlanta	1:00
Sept. 21	at Buffalo	1:00
Sept. 29	**Dallas** (Monday)	8:00
Oct. 5	**New York Giants**	12:00
Oct. 12	at Tampa Bay	1:00
Oct. 19	at Washington	1:00
Oct. 26	at Dallas	3:00
Nov. 2	**Philadelphia**	12:00
Nov. 9	at San Francisco	1:00
Nov. 16	**New Orleans**	12:00
Nov. 23	**Kansas City**	3:00
Nov. 30	**Washington**	12:00
Dec. 7	at Philadelphia	1:00
Dec. 14	at New York Giants	1:00
Dec. 21	**Tampa Bay**	12:00

CARDINALS COACHING HISTORY

Chicago 1920-59
(339-442-37)

1920-22	John (Paddy) Driscoll	17-8-4
1923-24	Arnold Horween	13-8-1
1925-26	Norman Barry	16-8-2
1927	Guy Chamberlin	3-7-1
1928	Fred Gillies	1-5-0
1929	Dewey Scanlon	6-6-1
1930	Ernie Nevers	5-6-2
1931	LeRoy Andrews*	0-2-0
1931	Ernie Nevers	5-2-0
1932	Jack Chevigny	2-6-2
1933-34	Paul Schissler	6-15-1
1935-38	Milan Creighton	16-26-4
1939	Ernie Nevers	1-10-0
1940-42	Jimmy Conzelman	8-22-3
1943-45	Phil Handler**	1-29-0
1946-48	Jimmy Conzelman	27-10-0
1949	Phil Handler-Buddy Parker***	2-4-0
1950-51	Earl (Curly) Lambeau	8-16-0
1952	Joe Kuharich	4-8-0
1953-54	Joe Stydahar	3-20-1
1955-57	Ray Richards	14-21-1
1958-61	Frank (Pop) Ivy****	17-29-2
1961	Chuck Drulis-Ray Prochaska-Ray Willsey#	2-0-0
1962-65	Wally Lemm	27-26-3
1966-70	Charley Winner	35-30-5
1971-72	Bob Hollway	8-18-2
1973-77	Don Coryell	42-29-1
1978-79	Bud Wilkinson##	9-20-0
1979	Larry Wilson	2-1-0
1980-85	Jim Hanifan	39-50-1

*Resigned after two games in 1931
**Co-coach with Walt Kiesling of 1944 Card-Pitt team
***Co-coaches for first six games in 1949
****Resigned after 12 games in 1961
#Co-coaches
##Released after 13 games in 1979

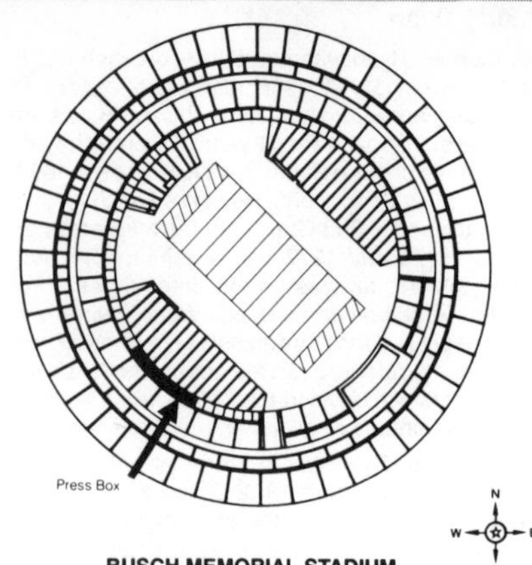

BUSCH MEMORIAL STADIUM

RECORD HOLDERS

Individual Records—Career

Category	Name	Performance
Rushing (Yds.)	Ottis Anderson, 1979-1985	7,845
Passing (Yds.)	Jim Hart, 1966-1983	34,639
Passing (TDs)	Jim Hart, 1966-1983	209
Receiving (No.)	Jackie Smith, 1963-1977	480
Receiving (Yds.)	Jackie Smith, 1963-1977	7,918
Interceptions	Larry Wilson, 1960-1972	52
Punting (Avg.)	Jerry Norton, 1959-1961	44.9
Punt Return (Avg.)	Charley Trippi, 1947-1955	13.7
Kickoff Return (Avg.)	Ollie Matson, 1952, 1954-58	28.5
Field Goals	Jim Bakken, 1962-1978	282
Touchdowns (Tot.)	Sonny Randle, 1959-1966	60
Points	Jim Bakken, 1962-1978	1,380

Individual Records—Single Season

Category	Name	Performance
Rushing (Yds.)	Ottis Anderson, 1979	1,605
Passing (Yds.)	Neil Lomax, 1984	4,614
Passing (TDs)	Charley Johnson, 1963	28
	Neil Lomax, 1984	28
Receiving (No.)	Roy Green, 1983, 1984	78
Receiving (Yds.)	Roy Green, 1984	1,555
Interceptions	Bob Nussbaumer, 1949	12
Punting (Avg.)	Jerry Norton, 1960	45.6
Punt Return (Avg.)	John (Red) Cochran, 1949	20.9
Kickoff Return (Avg.)	Ollie Matson, 1958	35.5
Field Goals	Jim Bakken, 1967	27
Touchdowns (Tot.)	John David Crow, 1962	17
Points	Jim Bakken, 1967	117
	Neil O'Donoghue, 1984	117

Individual Records—Single Game

Category	Name	Performance
Rushing (Yds.)	John David Crow, 12-18-60	203
Passing (Yds.)	Neil Lomax, 12-16-84	468
Passing (TDs)	Jim Hardy, 10-2-50	6
	Charley Johnson, 9-26-65	6
	Charley Johnson, 11-2-69	6
Receiving (No.)	Sonny Randle, 11-4-62	16
Receiving (Yds.)	Sonny Randle, 11-4-62	256
Interceptions	Bob Nussbaumer, 11-13-49	4
	Jerry Norton, 11-20-60	4
Field Goals	Jim Bakken, 9-24-67	7
Touchdowns (Tot.)	Ernie Nevers, 11-28-29	6
Points	Ernie Nevers, 11-28-29	40

1985 TEAM STATISTICS

	St. Louis	Opp.
Total First Downs	301	314
Rushing	108	115
Passing	171	169
Penalty	22	30
Third Down: Made/Att.	68/208	83/214
Fourth Down: Made/Att.	5/12	10/12
Total Net Yards	5086	5381
Avg. Per Game	317.9	336.3
Total Plays	1016	1045
Avg. Per Play	5.0	5.1
Net Yards Rushing	1974	2378
Avg. Per Game	123.4	148.6
Total Rushes	417	552
Net Yards Passing	3112	3003
Avg. Per Game	194.5	187.7
Tackled/Yards Lost	65/469	32/254
Gross Yards	3581	3257
Att./Completions	534/296	461/253
Completion Pct.	55.4	54.9
Had Intercepted	18	13
Punts/Avg.	87/40.7	75/40.9
Net Punting Avg.	33.7	34.3
Penalties/Yards Lost	101/816	88/742
Fumbles/Ball Lost	38/16	28/14
Touchdowns	34	47
Rushing	14	11
Passing	19	34
Returns	1	2
Avg. Time of Possession	29:22	30:38

1985 TEAM RECORD

Preseason (2-2)

Date	St. Louis		Opponents
8/9	10	*Chicago	3
8/15	7	L.A. Rams	39
8/23	14	*Pittsburgh	6
8/31	13	Kansas City	17
	44		65

Regular Season (5-11)

Date	St. Louis		Opp.	Att.
9/8	27	Cleveland (OT)	24	62,107
9/15	41	*Cincinnati	27	46,321
9/22	17	N.Y. Giants	27	74,987
9/29	43	*Green Bay	28	48,598
10/7	10	Washington	27	53,134
10/13	7	Philadelphia	30	48,186
10/20	10	Pittsburgh	23	56,478
10/27	10	*Houston	20	43,190
11/4	21	*Dallas	10	49,347
11/10	0	Tampa Bay	16	34,736
11/17	14	*Philadelphia	24	39,032
11/24	3	*N.Y. Giants	34	41,248
11/28	17	Dallas	35	54,125
12/8	28	*New Orleans	16	29,527
12/15	14	L.A. Rams	46	52,052
12/21	16	*Washington	27	28,090

*Home Game (OT) Overtime

Score by Periods

St. Louis	67	73	48	87	3	—	278
Opponents	78	122	77	137	0	—	414

Attendance

Home 325,353 Away 435,805 Total 761,158
Single game home record, 51,010 (11-4-84)
Single season home record, 384,375 (1981)

1985 INDIVIDUAL STATISTICS

Rushing	Att.	Yds.	Avg.	LG	TD
Mitchell	183	1006	5.5	64	7
Anderson	117	479	4.1	38	4
Ferrell	46	208	4.5	30	2
Lomax	32	125	3.9	23	0
Wolfley	24	64	2.7	11	0
Harrington	7	42	6.0	22	1
J. Smith	3	36	12.0	30	0
Atkinson, NYG-St.L	1	14	14.0	14t	1
Brunner	3	8	2.7	8	0
Love	1	4	4.0	4	0
Green	1	2	2.0	2	0
Cardinals	417	1974	4.7	64	14
Opponents	552	2378	4.3	80	11

Passing	Att.	Comp.	Pct.	Yds.	TD	Int.	Tkld.	Rate
Lomax	471	265	56.3	3214	18	12	61/442	79.5
Brunner	60	30	50.0	336	1	6	4/27	33.1
Mitchell	2	1	50.0	31	0	0	0/0	95.8
Birdsong	1	0	0.0	0	0	0	0/0	39.6
Cardinals	534	296	55.4	3581	19	18	65/469	74.0
Opponents	461	253	54.9	3257	34	13	32/254	90.1

Receiving	No.	Yds.	Avg.	LG	TD
Green	50	693	13.9	47	5
Tilley	49	726	14.8	46t	6
Mitchell	47	502	10.7	46	3
J. Smith	43	581	13.5	34	1
Marsh	37	355	9.6	23	1
Ferrell	25	277	11.1	30	2
Anderson	23	225	9.8	43	0
LaFleur	9	119	13.2	24	0
Duncan	4	39	9.8	14	1
Gray	3	22	7.3	12	0
Wolfley	2	18	9.0	17	0
Love	2	4	2.0	3	0
Mack	1	16	16.0	16	0
Novacek	1	4	4.0	4	0
Cardinals	296	3581	12.1	47	19
Opponents	253	3257	12.9	53t	34

Interceptions	No.	Yds.	Avg.	LG	TD
Junior	5	109	21.8	53	0
Young	3	0	0.0	0	0
Le. Smith	2	73	36.5	67	0
Mack	2	10	5.0	10	0
Washington	1	48	48.0	48t	1
Cardinals	13	240	18.5	67	1
Opponents	18	245	13.6	56t	1

Punting	No.	Yds.	Avg.	In 20	LG
Birdsong	85	3545	41.7	20	67
Cardinals	87	3545	40.7	20	67
Opponents	75	3069	40.9	12	64

Punt Returns	No.	FC	Yds.	Avg.	LG	TD
J. Smith	26	10	283	10.9	31	0
Mitchell	11	2	97	8.8	21	0
Nelson	2	0	14	7.0	8	0
Tilley	1	0	−1	−1.0	−1	0
Cardinals	40	12	393	9.8	31	0
Opponents	51	12	456	8.9	26	0

Kickoff Returns	No.	Yds.	Avg.	LG	TD
Duncan	28	550	19.6	34	0
Mitchell	19	345	18.2	35	0
Wolfley	13	234	18.0	28	0
Le. Smith	5	68	13.6	26	0
Harrington	4	77	19.3	35	0
J. Smith	4	59	14.8	33	0
Nelson	3	49	16.3	26	0
Mumford	1	19	19.0	19	0
Novacek	1	20	20.0	20	0
Cardinals	78	1421	18.2	35	0
Opponents	56	1150	20.5	40	0

Scoring	TD R	TD P	TD Rt	PAT	FG	Saf	TP
Mitchell	7	3	0	0/0	0/0	0	60
Atkinson, NYG-St.L.	1	0	0	17/18	10/18	0	53
Atkinson, St.L.	0	0	0	3/3	0/3	0	3
O'Donoghue	0	0	0	19/19	10/18	0	49
Tilley	0	6	0	0/0	0/0	0	36
Green	0	5	0	0/0	0/0	0	30
Anderson	4	0	0	0/0	0/0	0	24
Ferrell	2	2	0	0/0	0/0	0	24
Bojovic	0	0	0	11/12	3/7	0	20
Duncan	0	1	0	0/0	0/0	0	6
Harrington	1	0	0	0/0	0/0	0	6
Marsh	0	1	0	0/0	0/0	0	6
J. Smith	0	1	0	0/0	0/0	0	6
Washington	0	0	1	0/0	0/0	0	6
Cardinals	14	19	1	33/34	13/28	1	278
Opponents	11	34	2	46/47	28/38	1	414

FIRST-ROUND SELECTIONS

(If club had no first-round selection, first player drafted is listed with round in parentheses.)

Year	Player, College, Position
1936	Jim Lawrence, Texas Christian, B
1937	Ray Buivid, Marquette, B
1938	Jack Robbins, Arkansas, B
1939	Charles (Ki) Aldrich, Texas Christian, C
1940	George Cafego, Tennessee, B
1941	John Kimbrough, Texas A&M, B
1942	Steve Lach, Duke, B
1943	Glenn Dobbs, Tulsa, B
1944	Pat Harder, Wisconsin, B
1945	Charley Trippi, Georgia, B
1946	Dub Jones, Louisiana State, B
1947	DeWitt (Tex) Coulter, Army, T
1948	Jim Spavital, Oklahoma A&M, B
1949	Bill Fischer, Notre Dame, G
1950	Jack Jennings, Ohio State, T (2)
1951	Jerry Groom, Notre Dame, C
1952	Ollie Matson, San Francisco, B
1953	Johnny Olszewski, California, B
1954	Lamar McHan, Arkansas, B
1955	Max Boydston, Oklahoma, E
1956	Joe Childress, Auburn, B
1957	Jerry Tubbs, Oklahoma, C
1958	King Hill, Rice, B
	John David Crow, Texas A&M, B
1959	Bill Stacy, Mississippi State, B
1960	George Izo, Notre Dame, QB
1961	Ken Rice, Auburn, T
1962	Fate Echols, Northwestern, DT
	Irv Goode, Kentucky, C
1963	Jerry Stovall, Louisiana State, S
	Don Brumm, Purdue, DE
1964	Ken Kortas, Louisville, DT
1965	Joe Namath, Alabama, QB
1966	Carl McAdams, Oklahoma, LB
1967	Dave Williams, Washington, WR
1968	MacArthur Lane, Utah State, RB
1969	Roger Wehrli, Missouri, DB
1970	Larry Stegent, Texas A&M, RB
1971	Norm Thompson, Utah, CB
1972	Bobby Moore, Oregon, RB-WR
1973	Dave Butz, Purdue, DT
1974	J.V. Cain, Colorado, TE
1975	Tim Gray, Texas A&M, DB
1976	Mike Dawson, Arizona, DT
1977	Steve Pisarkiewicz, Missouri, QB
1978	Steve Little, Arkansas, K
	Ken Greene, Washington State, DB
1979	Ottis Anderson, Miami, RB
1980	Curtis Greer, Michigan, DE
1981	E. J. Junior, Alabama, LB
1982	Luis Sharpe, UCLA, T
1983	Leonard Smith, McNeese State, DB
1984	Clyde Duncan, Tennessee, WR
1985	Freddie Joe Nunn, Mississippi, LB
1986	Anthony Bell, Michigan State, LB

ST. LOUIS CARDINALS 1986 VETERAN ROSTER

No.	Name	Pos.	Ht.	Wt.	Birth-date	NFL Exp.	College	Hometown	How Acq.	'85 Games/ Starts
32	Anderson, Ottis	RB	6-2	225	11/19/57	8	Miami	Forest Hill, Fla.	D1-'79	9/8
60	†Baker, Al	DE	6-6	270	12/9/56	9	Colorado State	Newark, N.J.	T(Det)-'83	16/16
52	†Baker, Charlie	LB	6-2	234	9/26/57	7	New Mexico	Odessa, Tex.	D3b-'80	15/3
74	Bergold, Scott	T	6-7	263	11/19/61	2	Wisconsin	Wauwatosa, Wis.	D2-'85	16/0
18	Birdsong, Carl	P	6-0	192	1/1/59	6	S.W. Oklahoma State	Amarillo, Tex.	W(Buff)-'81	16/0
71	Bostic, Joe	G	6-3	268	4/20/57	8	Clemson	Greensboro, N.C.	D3-'79	16/16
12	Brunner, Scott	QB	6-5	215	3/24/57	6	Delaware	Lawrenceville, N.J.	T(GB)-'85	16/0
64	Clark, Randy	C	6-4	270	7/27/57	7	Northern Illinois	Mt. Prospect, Ill.	FA-'80	16/16
66	Dawson, Doug	G	6-3	267	12/27/61	3	Texas	Houston, Tex.	D2-'84	16/16
73	†Duda, Mark	DT	6-3	279	2/4/61	4	Maryland	Plymouth, Pa.	D4a-'83	16/16
86	Duncan, Clyde	WR	6-2	211	2/5/61	3	Tennessee	Oxon Hill, Md.	D1-'84	11/0
31	Ferrell, Earl	RB	6-0	224	3/27/58	5	East Tennessee State	Halifax, Va.	D5b-'82	11/9
65	Galloway, David	DT	6-3	279	2/16/59	5	Florida	Brandon, Fla.	D2-'82	16/16
87	Gray, Earnest	WR	6-3	195	3/2/57	8	Memphis State	Greenwood, Miss.	W(NYG)-'85	5/0
81	Green, Roy	WR	6-0	195	6/30/57	8	Henderson State	Magnolia, Ark.	D4-'79	13/13
75	Greer, Curtis	DE	6-4	258	11/10/57	7	Michigan	Detroit, Mich.	D1-'80	16/14
35	†Griffin, Jeff	CB	6-0	185	7/19/58	6	Utah	Carson, Calif.	D3-'81	12/0
78	†Grooms, Elois	DT	6-4	250	5/20/53	12	Tennessee Tech	Tompkinsville, Ky.	T(NO)-'82	5/0
36	†Harrington, Perry	RB	5-11	216	3/13/58	7	Jackson State	Jackson, Miss.	FA-'84	11/0
50	†Harris, Bob	LB	6-2	223	11/11/60	4	Auburn	Ellenwood, Ga.	D8-'83	10/0
59	†Howard, Thomas	LB	6-2	220	8/18/54	10	Texas Tech	Lubbock, Tex.	T(KC)-'84	3/2
42	†Johnson, Bobby	S	6-0	187	9/1/60	4	Texas	LaGrange, Tex.	FA-'85	11/0
54	Junior, E.J.	LB	6-3	235	12/8/59	6	Alabama	Nashville, Tenn.	D1-'81	16/16
89	LaFleur, Greg	TE	6-4	236	9/16/58	6	Louisiana State	Ville Platte, La.	W(Phil)-'81	16/4
15	Lomax, Neil	QB	6-3	215	2/17/59	6	Portland State	Portland, Ore.	D2-'81	16/16
40	†Love, Randy	RB	6-1	224	9/30/56	8	Houston	Garland, Tex.	FA-'79	12/0
47	†Mack, Cedric	CB	6-0	194	9/14/60	4	Baylor	Freeport, Tex.	D2-'83	16/14
80	Marsh, Doug	TE	6-3	238	6/18/58	7	Michigan	Akron, Ohio	D2-'80	16/16
76	†Mays, Stafford	DE	6-2	255	3/13/58	7	Washington	Tacoma, Wash.	D9-'80	16/2
14	McIvor, Rick	QB	6-4	210	9/26/60	3	Texas	Fort Davis, Tex.	D3-'84	2/0
30	†Mitchell, Stump	RB	5-9	188	3/15/59	6	Citadel	St. Mary's, Ga.	D9-'81	16/8
51	Monaco, Rob	C	6-3	283	9/5/61	2	Vanderbilt	Hamden, Conn.	D8-'85	6/0
34	Mumford, Tony	RB	6-0	215	6/14/63	2	Penn State	Yeadon, Pa.	FA-'85	2/0
38	Nelson, Lee	S	5-10	185	1/30/54	11	Florida State	Kissimmee, Fla.	D15-'76	13/0
57	Noga, Niko	LB	6-1	235	3/2/62	3	Hawaii	Honolulu, Hawaii	D8a-'84	16/11
85	Novacek, Jay	WR	6-4	217	10/24/62	2	Wyoming	Gothenburg, Neb.	D6-'85	16/0
53	Nunn, Freddie Joe	LB	6-4	228	4/9/62	2	Mississippi	Louisville, Miss.	D1-'85	16/16
23	Perrin, Benny	S	6-2	175	10/20/59	5	Alabama	Decatur, Ala.	D3a-'82	7/6
63	†Robbins, Tootie	T	6-5	302	6/2/58	5	East Carolina	Windsor, N.C.	D4-'82	12/11
72	Ralph, Dan	DT	6-4	260	3/9/61	2	Oregon	Denver, Colo.	FA-'84	0*
56	†Scott, Carlos	T-C	6-4	285	7/2/60	4	Texas-El Paso	Hempstead, Tex.	D7-'83	16/0
67	Sharpe, Luis	T	6-4	260	6/16/60	5	UCLA	Detroit, Mich.	D1-'82	16/16
84	Smith, J.T.	WR-KR	6-2	185	10/29/55	9	North Texas State	Leonard, Tex.	FA-'85	14/5
61	Smith, Lance	G	6-2	262	1/1/63	2	Louisiana State	Kannapolis, N.C.	D3-'85	14/5
45	Smith, Leonard	S	5-11	202	9/2/60	4	McNeese State	Baton Rouge, La.	D1-'83	16/16
44	Smith, Wayne	CB	6-0	170	5/9/57	7	Purdue	Chicago, Ill.	W(Det)-'82	16/16
83	†Tilley, Pat	WR	5-10	178	2/15/53	11	Louisiana Tech	Shreveport, La.	D4-'76	16/16
33	Walker, Quentin	RB	6-1	201	8/27/61	2	Virginia	Teaneck, N.J.	D7-'84	0*
48	Washington, Lionel	CB	6-0	188	10/21/60	4	Tulane	New Orleans, La.	D4b-'83	5/2
24	Wolfley, Ron	RB	6-0	222	10/14/62	2	West Virginia	Orchard Park, N.Y.	D4-'85	16/1
43	Young, Lonnie	CB-S	6-1	182	7/18/63	2	Michigan State	Flint, Mich.	D12-'85	16/10

* Ralph and Walker missed '85 season due to injury.

†Option playout; subject to developments.

Also played with Cardinals in '85—K Jess Atkinson (2 games), K Novo Bojovic (6), S Liffort Hobley (5), K Neil O'Donoghue (8), LB Danny Spradlin (8).

COACHING STAFF

Head Coach, Gene Stallings

Pro Career: Named head coach on February 10, 1986, and becomes the ninth head coach since the team's move to St. Louis in 1960, and thirtieth in the history of the franchise dating back to 1920. Defensive backfield coach with Dallas from 1972-85.

Background: End Texas A&M 1954-57. No pro playing experience. College coach: Texas A&M 1957, 1965-71 (head coach), Alabama 1958-64. Assistant under just two coaches in career: Paul "Bear" Bryant at Alabama, and Tom Landry at Dallas. Was All-SWC receiver at Texas A&M under Bryant and tri-captain on undefeated 1956 team.

Personal: Born March 2, 1935, in Paris, Texas. Gene and his wife, Ruth Ann, live in St. Louis, and have five children: Anna Lee, Laurie, John Mark, Jacklyn, and Martha Kate.

Assistant Coaches

Marv Braden, special teams; born January 25, 1938, Kansas City, Mo., lives in Manchester, Mo. Linebacker Southwest Missouri State 1956-59. No pro playing experience. College coach: Parsons 1963-66, Northeast Missouri State 1967-68 (head coach), U.S. International 1969-72, Iowa State 1973, Southern Methodist 1974-75, Michigan State 1976. Pro coach: Denver Broncos 1977-80, San Diego Chargers 1981-85, first year with Cardinals.

Tom Bresnahan, offensive line; born January 21, 1935, Springfield, Mass., lives in St. Louis. Tackle Holy Cross 1953-55. No pro playing experience. College coach: Williams 1963-67, Columbia 1968-72, Navy 1973-80. Pro coach: Kansas City Chiefs 1981-82, New York Giants 1983-84, first year with Cardinals.

LeBaron Caruthers, strength and conditioning; born April 20, 1954, Nashville, Tenn., lives in St. Louis. Tackle East Carolina 1972-73. No pro playing experience. College coach: Auburn 1978-79, Southern Methodist 1980-81. Pro coach: New England Patriots 1982-84, first year with Cardinals.

Jim Johnson, defensive line; born May 26, 1941, Maywood, Ill., lives in St. Louis. Quarterback Missouri 1959-62. Pro tight end Buffalo Bills 1963-64. College coach: Missouri Southern 1967-68 (head coach), Drake 1969-72, Indiana 1973-76, Notre Dame 1977-80. Pro coach: Oklahoma Outlaws (USFL) 1984, Jacksonville Bulls (USFL) 1985, first year with Cardinals.

Hank Kuhlmann, running backs; born October 6, 1937, St. Louis, Mo., lives in St. Louis. Running back Missouri 1956-59. No pro playing experience. College coach: Missouri 1963-71, Notre Dame 1975-77. Pro coach: Green Bay Packers 1972-74, Chicago Bears 1978-82, Birmingham Stallions (USFL) 1983-85, first year with Cardinals.

Leon McLaughlin, special assistant-quality control; born May 30, 1925, San Diego, Calif., lives in St. Louis. Center-linebacker UCLA 1946-49. Pro center Los Angeles Rams 1951-55. College coach: Washington State 1956, Stanford 1959-65, San Fernando Valley State 1969-70 (head coach). Pro coach: Pittsburgh Steelers 1966-68, Los Angeles Rams 1971-72, Detroit Lions 1973-74, Green Bay Packers 1975-76, New England Patriots 1977, joined Cardinals in 1978.

Mal Moore, receivers; born December 19, 1939, Dozier, Ala., lives in St. Louis. Quarterback-defensive back Alabama 1958-62. No pro playing experience. College coach: Montana State 1963, Alabama 1964-82, Notre Dame 1983-85. Pro coach: First year with Cardinals.

Joe Pascale, linebackers; born April 4, 1946, New York, N.Y., lives in St. Louis. Linebacker Connecticut 1963-66. No pro playing experience. College coach: Connecticut 1967-68, Rhode Island 1969-73, Idaho State 1974-76 (head coach, 1976), Princeton 1977-79. Pro coach: Montreal Alouettes (CFL) 1980-81, Ottawa Rough Riders (CFL) 1982-83, New Jersey Generals (USFL) 1984-85, first year with Cardinals.

ST. LOUIS CARDINALS 1986 FIRST-YEAR ROSTER

Name	Pos.	Ht.	Wt.	Birth-date	College	Hometown	How Acq.
Austin, Kent	QB	6-1	195	6/25/63	Mississippi	Natick, Miss.	D12
Bell, Anthony	LB	6-3	231	7/2/64	Michigan State	Miami, Fla.	D1
Brown, Ray	G-T	6-5	257	12/12/62	Arkansas State	Marion, Ark.	D8
Carter, Carl	CB	5-11	180	3/7/64	Texas Tech	Fort Worth, Tex.	D4
Chilton, Gene	C	6-3	271	3/27/64	Texas	Houston, Tex.	D3
Dillard, Wayne	LB	6-2	232	1/11/64	Alcorn State	Indianola, Miss.	D11
Kafentzis, Kent	S	6-1	205	12/31/62	Hawaii	Richland, Wash.	D9
Lee, John	K	5-11	182	5/19/64	UCLA	Downey, Calif.	D2
Newton, James (1)	CB	6-1	200	5/6/62	San Jose State	Barstow, Calif.	FA
Sikahema, Vai	RB	5-9	191	8/29/62	Brigham Young	American Samoa	D10a
Smith, Wes	WR	5-11	194	6/24/63	East Texas State	Garland, Tex.	D10b
Swanson, Eric	WR	5-11	186	8/25/63	Tennessee	San Bernardino, Calif.	D7
Tupper, John	DE	6-5	263	12/26/62	Oklahoma	Joplin, Mo.	D5

The term NFL Rookie is defined as a player who is in his first season of professional football and has not been on the roster of another professional football team for any regular season or postseason games. A Rookie is designated by an "R" on NFL rosters. Players who have been active in another professional football league or players who have NFL experience, including either preseason training camp or being on an active roster for fewer than three regular season or postseason games, are termed NFL First-Year Players. An NFL First-Year Player is designated by a "1" on NFL rosters. Thereafter, a player on an NFL active roster for at least three regular season or postseason games is credited with an additional year of NFL playing experience.

NOTES

Mel Renfro, defensive backs; born December 30, 1941, Houston, Tex., lives in St. Louis. Running back Oregon 1961-63. Pro defensive back Dallas Cowboys 1964-77. Pro coach: Los Angeles Express (USFL) 1984, first year with Cardinals.

Jim Shofner, offensive coordinator; born December 18, 1935, Grapevine, Tex., lives in Chesterfield, Mo. Running back Texas Christian 1955-57. Pro defensive back Cleveland Browns 1958-63. College coach: Texas Christian 1964-66, 1974-76 (head coach). Pro coach: San Francisco 49ers 1967-73, 1977, Cleveland Browns 1978-80, Houston Oilers 1981-82, Dallas Cowboys 1983-85, first year with Cardinals.

SAN FRANCISCO 49ERS

National Football Conference
Western Division

Team Colors: Forty Niners Gold and Scarlet

711 Nevada Street
Redwood City, California 94061
Telephone (415) 365-3420

Club Officials

Owner, Chairman of the Board: Edward J. DeBartolo, Jr.
President, Head Coach: Bill Walsh
Vice President, General Manager: John McVay
Vice President of Marketing and Community Affairs: Ken Flower
Director of Pro Scouting: Alan Webb
Director of College Scouting: Tony Razzano
Director of Public Relations: Jerry Walker
Publications Coordinator: Rodney Knox
Business Manager: Keith Simon
Ticket Manager: Ken Dargel
Trainer: Lindsy McLean
Equipment Manager: Bronco Hinek
Equipment Manager Emeritus: Chico Norton

Stadium: Candlestick Park • **Capacity:** 61,499
San Francisco, California 94124

Playing Surface: Grass

Training Camp: Sierra Community College
Rocklin, California 95677

1986 SCHEDULE

Preseason

Aug. 10	**Los Angeles Raiders**	12:00
Aug. 18	at Los Angeles Rams	7:30
Aug. 23	at Denver	7:00
Aug. 29	**Seattle**	6:00

Regular Season

Sept. 7	at Tampa Bay	1:00
Sept. 14	at Los Angeles Rams	1:00
Sept. 21	**New Orleans**	1:00
Sept. 28	at Miami	1:00
Oct. 5	**Indianapolis**	1:00
Oct. 12	**Minnesota**	1:00
Oct. 19	at Atlanta	1:00
Oct. 26	vs. Green Bay at Milw.	12:00
Nov. 2	at New Orleans	12:00
Nov. 9	**St. Louis**	1:00
Nov. 17	at Washington (Monday)	9:00
Nov. 23	**Atlanta**	1:00
Dec. 1	**New York Giants** (Monday)	6:00
Dec. 7	**New York Jets**	1:00
Dec. 14	at New England	1:00
Dec. 19	**Los Angeles Rams** (Friday)	5:00

49ERS COACHING HISTORY

(246-248-12)

1950-54	Lawrence (Buck) Shaw	33-25-2
1955	Norman (Red) Strader	4-8-0
1956-58	Frankie Albert	19-17-1
1959-63	Howard (Red) Hickey*	27-27-1
1963-67	Jack Christiansen	26-38-3
1968-75	Dick Nolan	56-56-5
1976	Monte Clark	8-6-0
1977	Ken Meyer	5-9-0
1978	Pete McCulley**	1-8-0
1978	Fred O'Connor	1-6-0
1979-85	Bill Walsh	66-48-0

*Resigned after three games in 1963
**Released after nine games in 1978

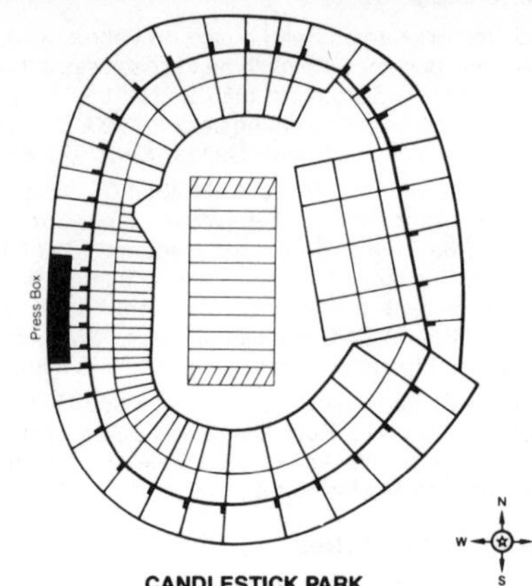

CANDLESTICK PARK

RECORD HOLDERS

Individual Records—Career

Category	Name	Performance
Rushing (Yds.)	Joe Perry, 1950-1960, 1963	7,344
Passing (Yds.)	John Brodie, 1957-1973	31,548
Passing (TDs)	John Brodie, 1957-1973	214
Receiving (No.)	Dwight Clark, 1979-1985	421
Receiving (Yds.)	Gene Washington, 1969-1977	6,664
Interceptions	Jimmy Johnson, 1961-1976	47
Punting (Avg.)	Tommy Davis, 1959-1969	44.7
Punt Return (Avg.)	Manfred Moore, 1974-75	14.7
Kickoff Return (Avg.)	Abe Woodson, 1958-1964	29.4
Field Goals	Ray Wersching, 1977-1985	160
Touchdowns (Tot.)	Ken Willard, 1965-1973	61
Points	Ray Wersching, 1977-1985	780

Individual Records—Single Season

Category	Name	Performance
Rushing (Yds.)	Wendell Tyler, 1984	1,262
Passing (Yds.)	Joe Montana, 1983	3,910
Passing (TDs)	John Brodie, 1965	30
Receiving (No.)	Roger Craig, 1985	92
Receiving (Yds.)	Dave Parks, 1965	1,344
Interceptions	Dave Baker, 1960	10
Punting (Avg.)	Tommy Davis, 1965	45.8
Punt Return (Avg.)	Dana McLemore, 1982	22.3
Kickoff Return (Avg.)	Joe Arenas, 1953	34.4
Field Goals	Bruce Gossett, 1973	26
Touchdowns (Tot.)	Roger Craig, 1985	15
Points	Ray Wersching, 1984	131

Individual Records—Single Game

Category	Name	Performance
Rushing (Yds.)	Delvin Williams, 10-31-76	194
Passing (Yds.)	Joe Montana, 10-6-85	429
Passing (TDs)	John Brodie, 11-23-65	5
	Steve Spurrier, 11-19-72	5
	Joe Montana, 10-6-85	5
Receiving (No.)	Bernie Casey, 11-13-66	12
	Dwight Clark, 12-11-82	12
	Roger Craig, 10-6-85	12
Receiving (Yds.)	Jerry Rice, 12-9-85	241
Interceptions	Dave Baker, 12-4-60	4
Field Goals	Ray Wersching, 10-16-83	6
Touchdowns (Tot.)	Billy Kilmer, 10-15-61	4
Points	Gordy Soltau, 10-27-51	26

1985 TEAM STATISTICS

	San Francisco	Opp.
Total First Downs	340	293
Rushing	137	89
Passing	179	183
Penalty	24	21
Third Down: Made/Att.	83/214	80/245
Fourth Down: Made/Att.	6/14	8/22
Total Net Yards	5920	5191
Avg. Per Game	370.0	324.4
Total Plays	1069	1116
Avg. Per Play	5.5	4.7
Net Yards Rushing	2232	1683
Avg. Per Game	139.5	105.2
Total Rushes	477	435
Net Yards Passing	3688	3508
Avg. Per Game	230.5	219.3
Tackled/Yards Lost	42/299	60/457
Gross Yards	3987	3965
Att./Completions	550/331	621/346
Completion Pct.	60.2	55.7
Had Intercepted	14	18
Punts/Avg.	87/39.3	92/39.6
Net Punting Avg.	33.9	35.3
Penalties/Yards Lost	105/868	106/778
Fumbles/Ball Lost	29/20	31/17
Touchdowns	53	26
Rushing	20	10
Passing	28	11
Returns	5	5
Avg. Time of Possession	28:45	31:15

1985 TEAM RECORD

Preseason (3-1)

Date	San Francisco		Opponents
8/10	28	L.A. Raiders	21
8/19	13	*Denver	20
8/24	25	*San Diego	10
8/30	23	Seattle	21
	89		72

Regular Season (10-6)

Date	San Francisco		Opp.	Att.
9/8	21	Minnesota	28	57,375
9/15	35	*Atlanta	16	58,923
9/22	34	L.A. Raiders	10	87,006
9/29	17	*New Orleans	20	58,053
10/6	38	Atlanta	17	44,740
10/13	10	*Chicago	26	60,523
10/20	21	Detroit	23	67,715
10/27	28	L.A. Rams	14	65,939
11/3	24	*Philadelphia	13	58,383
11/11	16	Denver	17	73,173
11/17	31	*Kansas City	3	56,447
11/25	19	*Seattle	6	57,482
12/1	35	Washington	8	51,321
12/9	20	*L.A. Rams	27	60,581
12/15	31	New Orleans	19	46,065
12/22	31	*Dallas	16	60,114

Postseason (0-1)

Date	San Francisco		Opp.	Att.
12/29	3	N.Y. Giants	17	75,131

*Home Game

Score by Periods

San Francisco	69	111	102	129	0	—	411
Opponents	53	65	47	98	0	—	263

Attendance

Home 470,506 Away 493,840 Total 964,346
Single game home record, 61,214 (4 times, 1972)
Single season home record, 470,506 (1985)

1985 INDIVIDUAL STATISTICS

Rushing	Att.	Yds.	Avg.	LG	TD
Craig	214	1050	4.9	62t	9
Tyler	171	867	5.1	30	6
Montana	42	153	3.6	16	3
Harmon	28	92	3.3	17	0
Rice	6	26	4.3	15t	1
Ring	8	23	2.9	9t	1
Cooper	2	12	6.0	14	0
Cavanaugh	4	5	1.3	13	0
Solomon	2	4	2.0	6	0
49ers	477	2232	4.7	62t	20
Opponents	435	1683	3.9	41	10

Passing	Att.	Comp.	Pct.	Yds.	TD	Int.	Tkld.	Rate
Montana	494	303	61.3	3653	27	13	35/246	91.3
Cavanaugh	54	28	51.9	334	1	1	7/53	69.5
Harmon	1	0	0.0	0	0	0	0/0	39.6
Solomon	1	0	0.0	0	0	0	0/0	39.6
49ers	550	331	60.2	3987	28	14	42/299	88.8
Opponents	621	346	55.7	3965	11	18	60/457	68.9

Receiving	No.	Yds.	Avg.	LG	TD
Craig	92	1016	11.0	73	6
Clark	54	705	13.1	49t	10
Rice	49	927	18.9	66t	3
Francis	44	478	10.9	25	3
Solomon	25	259	10.4	39	1
Tyler	20	154	7.7	16	2
Harmon	14	123	8.8	42	0
Wilson	10	165	16.5	52t	2
Monroe	10	51	5.1	9	0
Frank	7	50	7.1	14	1
Cooper	4	45	11.3	20	0
Ring	2	14	7.0	8	0
49ers	331	3987	12.0	73	28
Opponents	346	3965	11.5	82t	11

Interceptions	No.	Yds.	Avg.	LG	TD
Lott	6	68	11.3	25	0
Hicks	4	68	17.0	25	0
Williamson	3	137	45.7	82	1
Kovach, N.O.-S.F.	1	53	53.0	53	0
Shell	1	33	33.0	33	0
Fuller	1	4	4.0	4	0
McLemore	1	0	0.0	0	0
Walter	1	0	0.0	0	0
Wright	1	0	0.0	0	0
49ers	18	310	17.2	82	1
Opponents	14	80	5.7	41t	1

Punting	No.	Yds.	Avg.	In 20	LG
Runager	86	3422	39.8	30	57
49ers	87	3422	39.3	30	57
Opponents	92	3644	39.6	24	58

Punt Returns	No.	FC	Yds.	Avg.	LG	TD
McLemore	38	14	258	6.8	22	0
49ers	38	14	258	6.8	22	0
Opponents	33	6	294	8.9	63t	1

Kickoff Returns	No.	Yds.	Avg.	LG	TD
Monroe	28	717	25.6	95t	1
Harmon	23	467	20.3	37	0
McLemore	4	76	19.0	26	0
Frank	1	1	1.0	1	0
Lott	1	2	2.0	2	0
Rice	1	6	6.0	6	0
49ers	58	1269	21.9	95t	1
Opponents	72	1485	20.6	86t	1

Scoring	TD R	TD P	TD Rt	PAT	FG	Saf	TP
Wersching	0	0	0	52/53	13/21	0	91
Craig	9	6	0	0/0	0/0	0	90
Clark	0	10	0	0/0	0/0	0	60
Tyler	6	2	0	0/0	0/0	0	48
Rice	1	3	0	0/0	0/0	0	24
Francis	0	3	0	0/0	0/0	0	18
Montana	3	0	0	0/0	0/0	0	18
Wilson	0	2	0	0/0	0/0	0	12
Frank	0	1	0	0/0	0/0	0	6
McColl	0	0	1	0/0	0/0	0	6
McIntyre	0	0	1	0/0	0/0	0	6
Monroe	0	0	1	0/0	0/0	0	6
Ring	1	0	0	0/0	0/0	0	6
Solomon	0	1	0	0/0	0/0	0	6
Turner	0	0	1	0/0	0/0	0	6
Williamson	0	0	1	0/0	0/0	0	6
Harty	0	0	0	0/0	0/0	1	2
49ers	20	28	5	52/53	13/21	1	411
Opponents	10	11	5	24/26	27/35	1	263

FIRST-ROUND SELECTIONS

(If club had no first-round selection, first player drafted is listed with round in parentheses.)

Year	Player, College, Position
1950	Leo Nomellini, Minnesota, T
1951	Y.A. Tittle, Louisiana State, B
1952	Hugh McElhenny, Washington, B
1953	Harry Babcock, Georgia, E
	Tom Stolhandske, Texas, E
1954	Bernie Faloney, Maryland, B
1955	Dickie Moegle, Rice, B
1956	Earl Morrall, Michigan State, B
1957	John Brodie, Stanford, B
1958	Jim Pace, Michigan, B
	Charlie Krueger, Texas A&M, T
1959	Dave Baker, Oklahoma, B
	Dan James, Ohio State, C
1960	Monty Stickles, Notre Dame, E
1961	Jimmy Johnson, UCLA, CB
	Bernie Casey, Bowling Green, WR
	Bill Kilmer, UCLA, QB
1962	Lance Alworth, Arkansas, WR
1963	Kermit Alexander, UCLA, CB
1964	Dave Parks, Texas Tech, WR
1965	Ken Willard, North Carolina, RB
	George Donnelly, Illinois, DB
1966	Stan Hindman, Mississippi, DE
1967	Steve Spurrier, Florida, QB
	Cas Banaszek, Northwestern, T
1968	Forrest Blue, Auburn, C
1969	Ted Kwalick, Penn State, TE
	Gene Washington, Stanford, WR
1970	Cedrick Hardman, North Texas State, DE
	Bruce Taylor, Boston U., DB
1971	Tim Anderson, Ohio State, DB
1972	Terry Beasley, Auburn, WR
1973	Mike Holmes, Texas Southern, DB
1974	Wilbur Jackson, Alabama, RB
	Bill Sandifer, UCLA, DT
1975	Jimmy Webb, Mississippi State, DT
1976	Randy Cross, UCLA, C (2)
1977	Elmo Boyd, Eastern Kentucky, WR (3)
1978	Ken MacAfee, Notre Dame, TE
	Dan Bunz, Cal State-Long Beach, LB
1979	James Owens, UCLA, WR (2)
1980	Earl Cooper, Rice, RB
	Jim Stuckey, Clemson, DT
1981	Ronnie Lott, Southern California, DB
1982	Bubba Paris, Michigan, T (2)
1983	Roger Craig, Nebraska, RB (2)
1984	Todd Shell, Brigham Young, LB
1985	Jerry Rice, Mississippi Valley State, WR
1986	Larry Roberts, Alabama, DE (2)

SAN FRANCISCO 49ERS 1986 VETERAN ROSTER

No.	Name	Pos.	Ht.	Wt.	Birth-date	NFL Exp.	College	Hometown	How Acq.	'85 Games/ Starts
68	†Ayers, John	G	6-5	265	4/14/53	10	West Texas State	Carrizo Springs, Tex.	D8-'76	16/16
76	†Board, Dwaine	DE	6-5	248	11/29/56	7	North Carolina A&T	Rocky Mount, Va.	FA-'79	16/16
95	Carter, Michael	NT	6-2	285	10/29/60	3	Southern Methodist	Dallas, Tex.	D5a-'84	12/9
87	Clark, Dwight	WR	6-4	215	1/8/57	8	Clemson	Charlotte, N.C.	D10a-'79	16/14
69	Collie, Bruce	T	6-6	275	6/27/62	2	Texas-Arlington	San Antonio, Tex.	D5-'85	16/0
33	Craig, Roger	RB	6-0	224	7/10/60	4	Nebraska	Davenport, Iowa	D2-'83	16/16
51	Cross, Randy	G	6-3	265	4/25/54	11	UCLA	Encino, Calif.	D2-'76	15/15
74	Dean, Fred	DE	6-2	232	2/24/52	12	Louisiana Tech	Ruston, La.	T(SD)-'81	16/0
50	†Ellison, Riki	LB	6-2	225	8/15/60	4	Southern California	Tucson, Ariz.	D5-'83	16/16
55	Fahnhorst, Jim	LB	6-4	230	11/8/58	3	Minnesota	St. Cloud, Minn.	FA-'84	15/2
71	†Fahnhorst, Keith	T	6-6	273	2/6/52	13	Minnesota	St. Cloud, Minn.	D2a-'74	16/15
54	Ferrari, Ron	LB	6-0	215	7/30/59	5	Illinois	Moweaqua, Ill.	D7-'82	16/0
81	Francis, Russ	TE	6-6	242	4/3/53	11	Oregon	Pleasant Hill, Ore.	T(NE)-'82	16/16
86	Frank, John	TE	6-3	225	4/17/62	3	Ohio State	Mt. Lebanon, Pa.	D2-'84	16/3
49	Fuller, Jeff	S-LB	6-2	216	8/8/62	3	Texas A&M	Dallas, Tex.	D5b-'84	16/0
24	Harmon, Derrick	RB-KR	5-10	202	4/26/63	3	Cornell	Queens, N.Y.	D9b-'84	15/3
75	†Harty, John	DE	6-4	260	12/17/58	5	Iowa	Sioux City, Iowa	D2a-'81	7/4
22	†Hicks, Dwight	CB-S	6-1	192	4/5/56	8	Michigan	Pennsauken, N.J.	FA-'79	16/16
28	Holmoe, Tom	S	6-2	180	3/7/60	3	Brigham Young	La Crescenta, Calif.	D4-'83	0*
97	†Johnson, Gary	DT	6-2	261	8/31/52	12	Grambling	Shreveport, La.	T(SD)-'84	11/0
9	t-Kemp, Jeff	QB	6-0	201	7/11/59	6	Dartmouth	Bethesda, Md.	T(Rams)-'86	5/1
66	Kennedy, Allan	T	6-7	275	1/8/58	4	Washington State	Woodland Hills, Calif.	FA-'81	0*
57	†Kovach, Jim	LB	6-2	239	5/1/56	8	Kentucky	Parma Heights, Ohio	FA-'85	6/0*
42	Lott, Ronnie	S-CB	6-0	200	5/8/59	6	Southern California	Rialto, Calif.	D1-'81	16/16
53	McColl, Milt	LB	6-6	230	8/28/59	6	Stanford	Covina, Calif.	FA-'81	16/4
62	McIntyre, Guy	G	6-3	264	2/17/61	3	Georgia	Thomasville, Ga.	D3-'84	15/3
43	†McLemore, Dana	CB-KR	5-10	183	7/1/60	5	Hawaii	Venice, Calif.	D10a-'82	16/0
32	Monroe, Carl	RB-KR	5-8	180	2/20/60	4	Utah	San Jose, Calif.	FA-'83	14/0
16	Montana, Joe	QB	6-2	195	6/11/56	8	Notre Dame	Monongahela, Pa.	D3-'79	15/15
20	Nixon, Tory	CB	5-11	186	2/24/62	2	San Diego State	Phoenix, Ariz.	T(Wash)-'85	16/0
77	Paris, Bubba	T	6-6	299	10/6/60	4	Michigan	Louisville, Ky.	D2-'82	16/16
56	Quillan, Fred	C	6-5	266	1/27/56	9	Oregon	Portland, Ore.	D7-'78	15/15
80	Rice, Jerry	WR	6-2	200	10/13/62	2	Mississippi Valley State	Crawford, Miss.	D1-'85	16/4
30	Ring, Bill	RB	5-10	205	12/13/56	6	Brigham Young	Belmont, Calif.	FA-'81	10/0
4	†Runager, Max	P	6-1	189	3/24/56	8	South Carolina	Orangeburg, S.C.	FA-'84	16/0
61	Sapolu, Jesse	G-C	6-4	260	3/10/61	2	Hawaii	Honolulu, Hawaii	D11-'83	0*
90	Shell, Todd	LB	6-4	225	6/24/62	3	Brigham Young	Mesa, Ariz.	D1-'84	15/13
72	Stover, Jeff	DE	6-5	275	5/22/58	5	Oregon	Corning, Calif.	FA-'82	16/11
79	†Stuckey, Jim	DE	6-4	253	6/21/58	7	Clemson	Columbia, S.C.	FA-'85	15/1
78	Tuiasosopo, Manu	NT	6-3	262	8/30/57	8	UCLA	Long Beach, Calif.	T(Sea)-'84	15/7
58	Turner, Keena	LB	6-2	222	10/22/58	7	Purdue	Chicago, Ill.	D2-'80	15/15
26	†Tyler, Wendell	RB	5-10	207	5/20/55	9	UCLA	Los Angeles, Calif.	T(Rams)-'83	13/12
99	Walter, Michael	LB	6-3	238	11/30/60	4	Oregon	Eugene, Ore.	FA-'84	14/14
14	Wersching, Ray	K	5-11	215	8/21/50	14	California	Downey, Calif.	FA-'77	16/0
27	Williamson, Carlton	S	6-0	204	6/12/58	6	Pittsburgh	Atlanta, Ga.	D3-'81	16/16
85	Wilson, Mike	WR	6-3	215	12/19/58	6	Washington State	Carson, Calif.	FA-'81	16/0
21	Wright, Eric	CB	6-1	185	4/18/59	6	Missouri	East St. Louis, Ill.	D2b-'81	16/16

* Holmoe, Kennedy, and Sapolu missed '85 season due to injury; Kovach played 2 games with New Orleans, 4 with San Francisco in '85.

†Option playout; subject to developments.

t-49ers traded for Kemp (Los Angeles Rams).

Traded—Quarterback Matt Cavanaugh to Philadelphia, tight end Earl Cooper to Los Angeles Raiders.

Retired—Freddie Solomon, 11-year wide receiver, 16 games in '85.

Also played with 49ers in '85—NT Scott Garnett (3 games), C John Hill (2), LB Fulton Kuykendall (1), C Jim Leonard (9).

COACHING STAFF

Head Coach, Bill Walsh

Pro Career: Begins eighth season as an NFL head coach. Directed 49ers to NFC championship in 1981 and 1984 and to victories in Super Bowl XVI (26-21 over Cincinnati) and Super Bowl XIX (38-16 over Miami). Started pro coaching career in 1966 as offensive backfield coach for the Oakland Raiders. He then spent eight seasons (1968-75) in Cincinnati, where he was responsible for coaching the Bengals' quarterbacks and receivers. His tenure in Cincinnati was followed by a season with the San Diego Chargers as offensive coordinator. While at Cincinnati he tutored Ken Anderson, who became the first NFL quarterback to lead the league in passing two straight years. At San Diego, he helped develop the talents of quarterback Dan Fouts. No pro playing experience. Career record: 66-48.

Background: End at San Jose State in 1953-54. Started college coaching career at California, where he served under Marv Levy from 1960-62. In 1963, he joined John Ralston's Stanford staff and worked with the defensive backfield for three seasons. Returned to Stanford as head coach in 1977 and directed Cardinals to a two-year record of 17-7, including wins in the Sun and Bluebonnet Bowls. Received his master's degree in history from San Jose State in 1959.

Personal: Born November 30, 1931, in Los Angeles, Calif. He and his wife, Geri, live in Menlo Park, Calif., and have three children—Steve, Craig, and Elizabeth.

Assistant Coaches

Jerry Attaway, conditioning; born January 3, 1946, Susanville, Calif., lives in San Carlos, Calif. Defensive back Yuba, Calif., J.C. 1964-65, Cal-Davis 1967. No pro playing experience. College coach: Cal-Davis 1970-71, Idaho 1972-74, Utah State 1975-77, Southern California 1978-82. Pro coach: Joined 49ers in 1983.

Norb Hecker, linebackers; born May 26, 1927, Berea, Ohio, lives in San Francisco. End Baldwin-Wallace 1947-50. Pro end-defensive back Los Angeles Rams 1951-53, Toronto Argonauts (CFL) 1954, Washington Redskins 1955-57. College coach: Stanford 1972-78. Pro coach: Hamilton Tiger-Cats (CFL) 1958, Green Bay Packers 1959-65, Atlanta Falcons 1966-68 (head coach), New York Giants 1969-71, joined 49ers in 1979.

Sherman Lewis, running backs, born June 29, 1942, Louisville, Ky., lives in Redwood City, Calif. Running back Michigan State 1961-63. Pro running back Toronto Argonauts (CFL) 1964-65, New York Jets 1966. College coach: Michigan State 1969-82. Pro coach: Joined 49ers in 1983.

Bobb McKittrick, offensive line; born December 29, 1935, Baker, Ore., lives in San Mateo, Calif. Guard Oregon State 1955-57. No pro playing experience. College coach: Oregon State 1961-64, UCLA 1965-70. Pro coach: Los Angeles Rams 1971-72, San Diego Chargers 1974-78, joined 49ers in 1979.

Bill McPherson, defensive line; born October 24, 1931, Santa Clara, Calif., lives in San Jose, Calif. Tackle Santa Clara 1950-52. No pro playing experience. College coach: Santa Clara 1963-74, UCLA 1975-77. Pro coach: Philadelphia Eagles 1978, joined 49ers in 1979.

Ray Rhodes, defensive backfield; born October 20, 1950, Mexia, Tex., lives in Fremont, Calif. Running back-receiver Texas Christian 1969-70, Tulsa 1972-73. Pro defensive back New York Giants 1974-79, San Francisco 49ers 1980. Pro coach: Joined 49ers in 1981.

George Seifert, defensive coordinator; born January 22, 1940, San Francisco, Calif., lives in Sunnyvale, Calif. Linebacker Utah 1960-62. No pro playing experience. College coach: Westminster 1965 (head coach), Iowa 1966, Oregon 1967-71, Stanford 1972-74, 1977-79, Cornell 1975-76 (head coach). Pro coach: Joined 49ers in 1980.

SAN FRANCISCO 49ERS 1986 FIRST-YEAR ROSTER

Name	Pos.	Ht.	Wt.	Birth-date	College	Hometown	How Acq.
Allen, Douglas (1)	WR	5-10	180	4/22/63	Arizona State	Baldwin Park, Calif.	FA
Bowman, Kevin (1)	WR	6-3	205	2/23/62	San Jose State	Sacramento, Calif.	FA
Cherry, Tony	RB	5-7	187	2/8/63	Oregon	Victorville, Calif.	D9
Dubroc, Gregg (1)	LB	6-3	230	1/15/62	Louisiana State	Baton Rouge, La.	FA
Durrett, Michael (1)	G	6-4	280	8/11/57	West Virginia	Van Nuys, Calif.	FA
Fagan, Kevin	NT	6-3	260	4/25/63	Miami	Lake Worth, Fla.	D4c
Gabrish, James	G	6-4	265	6/12/63	Citadel	Canfield, Ohio	FA
Glover, Clyde (1)	DE	6-5	266	7/16/60	Fresno State	Las Vegas, Nev.	FA
Griffin, Don	S	6-0	176	3/17/64	Middle Tennessee St.	Pelham, Ga.	D6
Haley, Charles	LB	6-5	230	1/6/64	James Madison	Campbell County, Va.	D4a
Hallman, Harold	LB	5-11	234	12/12/62	Auburn	Macon, Ga.	D10b
Henderson, Wymon (1)	CB	5-10	190	12/15/61	Nevada-Las Vegas	La Habra, Calif.	FA
Hoffman, Gary (1)	T	6-7	285	9/28/61	Santa Clara	Sacramento, Calif.	FA
Inglesby, Patrick (1)	P	6-2	198	2/26/60	California-Davis	Pleasanton, Calif.	FA
Jones, Joseph (1)	TE	6-4	250	6/26/62	Virginia Tech	Windber, Pa.	FA
King, Lorenzo (1)	NT-DE	6-4	265	2/17/62	Alcorn State	Memphis, Tenn.	FA
Kott, Kevin	QB	6-2	206	3/16/62	Eastern New Mexico	Danville, Calif.	FA
Mancini, Michael	P	5-10	175	4/3/63	Fresno State	Mountain View, Calif.	FA
Martin, Derrick (1)	CB	5-11	185	5/31/57	San Jose State	San Leandro, Calif.	FA
Marvin, Albert (1)	DE	6-4	295	5/20/59	Alabama State	Andalusia, Ala.	FA
McIntosh, Joe (1)	RB	5-11	197	12/9/62	North Carolina State	Lexington, N.C.	FA
McKyer, Tim	CB	6-0	174	9/5/63	Texas-Arlington	Lincoln, Neb.	D3b
Miller, Pat	LB	6-1	220	6/24/64	Florida	Panama City, Fla.	D5
Patterson, Reno (1)	NT	6-3	275	4/22/61	Bethune-Cookman	Chicago, Ill.	FA
Popp, Jim	TE	6-5	239	11/13/63	Vanderbilt	Libertyville, Ill.	D8
Rathman, Tom	RB	6-1	232	10/7/62	Nebraska	Grand Island, Neb.	D3a
Roberts, Larry	DE	6-3	264	6/2/63	Alabama	Dothan, Ala.	D2
Stinson, Elliston	WR	5-10	175	10/3/62	Rice	Galveston, Tex.	D10a
Taylor, John	WR	6-1	185	3/31/62	Delaware State	Pennsauken, N.J.	D3c
Wallace, Steve	T	6-5	276	12/27/64	Auburn	Atlanta, Ga.	D4b
Williams, Cecil	WR	6-3	204	2/4/62	Sacramento State	Sacramento, Calif.	FA
Wood, David (1)	DE	6-4	265	5/12/62	Arizona	Tucson, Ariz.	FA

The term NFL Rookie is defined as a player who is in his first season of professional football and has not been on the roster of another professional football team for any regular season or postseason games. A Rookie is designated by an "R" on NFL rosters. Players who have been active in another professional football league or players who have NFL experience, including either preseason training camp or being on an active roster for fewer than three regular season or postseason games, are termed NFL First-Year Players. An NFL First-Year Player is designated by a "1" on NFL rosters. Thereafter, a player on an NFL active roster for at least three regular season or postseason games is credited with an additional year of NFL playing experience.

NOTES

Fred von Appen, special teams; born March 22, 1942, Eugene, Ore., lives in Cupertino, Calif. Lineman Linfield College 1960-63. No pro playing experience. College coach: Linfield 1967-68, Arkansas 1969, 1981, UCLA 1970, Virginia Tech 1971, Oregon 1972-76, Stanford 1977-78, 1982. Pro coach: Green Bay Packers 1979-80, joined 49ers in 1983.

National Football Conference Central Division

Team Colors: Florida Orange, White, and Red

One Buccaneer Place
Tampa, Florida 33607
Telephone: (813) 870-2700

Club Officials

Owner-President: Hugh F. Culverhouse
Vice President: Joy Culverhouse
Vice President-Head Coach: Leeman Bennett
Vice President-Community Relations: Gay Culverhouse Gold
Secretary-Treasurer: Ward Holland
Director of Administration: Herbert M. Gold
Assistant to the President: Phil Krueger
Director of Player Personnel: Jim Gruden
Director of Pro Personnel: Erik Widmark
Director of Ticket Operations: Terry Wooten
Director of Public Relations: Rick Odioso
Director of Marketing & Advertising: Bob Passwaters
Assistant Director-Community Involvement: Sandy Cottrell
Assistant Director-Media Relations: John Gerdes
College Personnel: Gary Horton, Leland Kendall, Dean Rossi
Controller: Ed Easom
Consultant-Player and Community Relations: Theo Bell
Trainer: Jay Shoop
Assistant Trainer: Scott Anderson
Equipment Manager: Frank Pupello
Assistant Equipment Manager: Carl Melchior

Stadium: Tampa Stadium • **Capacity:** 74,315
North Dale Mabry
Tampa, Florida 33607

Playing Surface: Grass

Training Camp: One Buccaneer Place
Tampa, Florida 33607

1986 SCHEDULE

Preseason

Aug. 9	**St. Louis**	7:00
Aug. 16	**Atlanta**	7:00
Aug. 23	**Washington**	7:00
Aug. 29	at Miami	8:00

Regular Season

Sept. 7	**San Francisco**	1:00
Sept. 14	**Minnesota**	4:00
Sept. 21	at Detroit	1:00
Sept. 28	**Atlanta**	4:00
Oct. 5	at Los Angeles Rams	1:00
Oct. 12	**St. Louis**	1:00
Oct. 19	at New Orleans	12:00
Oct. 26	at Kansas City	12:00
Nov. 2	**Buffalo**	1:00
Nov. 9	**Chicago**	1:00
Nov. 16	vs. Green Bay at Milw.	12:00
Nov. 23	**Detroit**	1:00
Nov. 30	at Minnesota	12:00
Dec. 7	at Chicago	12:00
Dec. 14	**Green Bay**	1:00
Dec. 21	at St. Louis	12:00

BUCCANEERS COACHING HISTORY

(47-105-1)

1976-84	John McKay	45-91-1
1985	Leeman Bennett	2-14-0

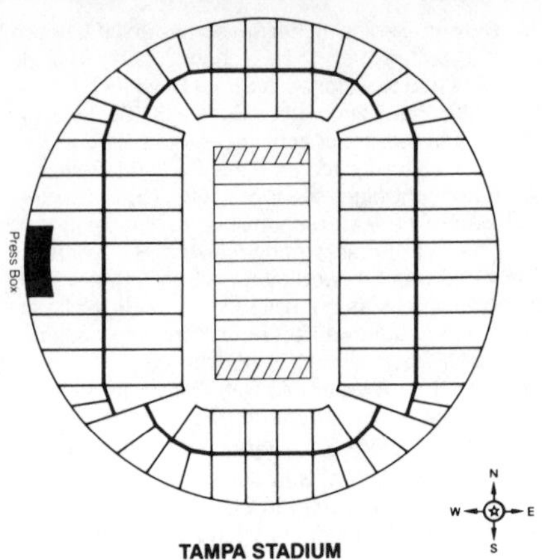

TAMPA STADIUM

RECORD HOLDERS

Individual Records—Career

Category	Name	Performance
Rushing (Yds.)	James Wilder, 1981-85	4,178
Passing (Yds.)	Doug Williams, 1978-1982	12,648
Passing (TDs)	Doug Williams, 1978-1982	73
Receiving (No.)	James Wilder, 1981-85	296
Receiving (Yds.)	Kevin House, 1980-85	4,722
Interceptions	Cedric Brown, 1977-1984	29
Punting (Avg.)	Frank Garcia, 1983-85	42.0
Punt Return (Avg.)	John Holt, 1981-83	7.5
Kickoff Ret. (Avg.)	Phil Freeman, 1985	22.6
Field Goals	Bill Capece, 1981-83	43
Touchdowns (Tot.)	James Wilder, 1981-85	38
Points	James Wilder, 1981-85	228

Individual Records—Single Season

Category	Name	Performance
Rushing (Yds.)	James Wilder, 1984	1,544
Passing (Yds.)	Doug Williams, 1981	3,563
Passing (TDs)	Doug Williams, 1980	20
Receiving (No.)	James Wilder, 1984	85
Receiving (Yds.)	Kevin House, 1981	1,176
Interceptions	Cedric Brown, 1981	9
Punting (Avg.)	Larry Swider, 1981	42.7
Punt Return (Avg.)	Leon Bright, 1985	10.3
Kickoff Return (Avg.)	Isaac Hagins, 1977	23.5
Field Goals	Donald Igwebuike, 1985	22
Touchdowns (Tot.)	James Wilder, 1984	13
Points	Donald Igwebuike, 1985	96

Individual Records—Single Game

Category	Name	Performance
Rushing (Yds.)	James Wilder, 11-6-83	219
Passing (Yds.)	Doug Williams, 11-16-80	486
Passing (TDs)	Many times	4
	Last time by Steve DeBerg, 10-20-85	
Receiving (No.)	James Wilder, 9-15-85	13
Receiving (Yds.)	Kevin House, 10-18-81	178
Interceptions	Many times	2
	Last time by David Greenwood, 10-6-85	
Field Goals	Bill Capece, 10-30-83	4
	Bill Capece, 1-2-83	4
	Donald Igwebuike, 11-24-85	4
Touchdowns	Jimmie Giles, 10-20-85	4
Points	Jimmie Giles, 10-20-85	24

1985 TEAM STATISTICS

	Tampa Bay	Opp.
Total First Downs	291	351
Rushing	95	146
Passing	162	185
Penalty	34	20
Third Down: Made/Att.	69/212	89/214
Fourth Down: Made/Att.	11/17	4/7
Total Net Yards	4766	6108
Avg. Per Game	297.9	381.8
Total Plays	982	1087
Avg. Per Play	4.9	5.6
Net Yards Rushing	1644	2430
Avg. Per Game	102.8	151.9
Total Rushes	434	547
Net Yards Passing	3122	3678
Avg. Per Game	195.1	229.9
Tackled/Yards Lost	40/301	35/277
Gross Yards	3423	3955
Att./Completions	508/269	505/318
Completion Pct.	53.0	63.0
Had Intercepted	26	18
Punts/Avg.	79/40.9	59/44.4
Net Punting Avg.	32.8	37.8
Penalties/Yards Lost	103/751	114/945
Fumbles/Ball Lost	37/22	37/22
Touchdowns	33	50
Rushing	11	28
Passing	22	18
Returns	0	4
Avg. Time of Possession	27:55	32:05

1985 TEAM RECORD

Preseason (1-3)

Date	Tampa Bay		Opponents
8/10	27	*Pittsburgh	42
8/17	17	*Atlanta	23
8/24	14	New Orleans	10
8/30	7	*Washington	20
	65		95

Regular Season (2-14)

Date	Tampa Bay		Opp.	Att.
9/8	28	Chicago	38	57,828
9/15	16	*Minnesota	31	46,188
9/22	13	New Orleans	20	45,320
9/29	9	Detroit	30	45,023
10/6	19	*Chicago	27	51,795
10/13	27	*L.A. Rams	31	39,607
10/20	38	Miami	41	62,335
10/27	14	*New England	32	34,661
11/3	20	N.Y. Giants	22	72,031
11/10	16	*St. Louis	0	34,736
11/17	28	N.Y. Jets	62	65,344
11/24	19	*Detroit (OT)	16	43,471
12/1	0	Green Bay	21	19,856
12/8	7	Minnesota	26	51,593
12/15	23	*Indianapolis	31	25,577
12/22	17	*Green Bay	20	33,992

*Home Game (OT) Overtime

Score by Periods

Tampa Bay	71	109	31	80	3	—	294
Opponents	75	144	110	119	0	—	448

Attendance

Home 310,027 Away 419,330 Total 729,357
Single game home record, 72,033 (1-6-80)
Single season home record, 545,980 (1979)

1985 INDIVIDUAL STATISTICS

Rushing	Att.	Yds.	Avg.	LG	TD
Wilder	365	1300	3.6	28	10
Young	40	233	5.8	20	1
Springs	16	54	3.4	11	0
DeBerg	9	28	3.1	13	0
Carter	1	13	13.0	13	0
Risher	1	10	10.0	10	0
Armstrong	2	6	3.0	8	0
Buccaneers	434	1644	3.8	28	11
Opponents	547	2430	4.4	38	28

Passing	Att.	Comp.	Pct.	Yds.	TD	Int.	Tkld.	Rate
DeBerg	370	197	53.2	2488	19	18	19/143	71.3
Young	138	72	52.2	935	3	8	21/158	56.9
Buccaneers	508	269	53.0	3423	22	26	40/301	67.4
Opponents	505	318	63.0	3955	18	18	35/277	84.2

Receiving	No.	Yds.	Avg.	LG	TD
Wilder	53	341	6.4	20	0
House	44	803	18.3	59	5
Giles	43	673	15.7	44	8
J. Bell	43	496	11.5	27	2
Carter	40	557	13.9	40	3
Magee	26	288	11.1	35	3
T. Bell	12	189	15.8	24	0
Springs	3	44	14.7	22	0
Witte	3	28	9.3	13	0
Armstrong	2	4	2.0	3	1
Buccaneers	269	3423	12.7	59	22
Opponents	318	3955	12.4	78t	18

Interceptions	No.	Yds.	Avg.	LG	TD
Castille	7	49	7.0	20	0
Greenwood	5	15	3.0	7	0
Browner	1	25	25.0	25	0
Davis	1	22	22.0	22	0
Sully	1	20	20.0	20	0
C. Johnson	1	12	12.0	12	0
Holt	1	3	3.0	3	0
Randle	1	0	0.0	0	0
Buccaneers	18	146	8.1	25	0
Opponents	26	368	14.2	46	4

Punting	No.	Yds.	Avg.	In 20	LG
Garcia	77	3233	42.0	12	61
Buccaneers	79	3233	40.9	12	61
Opponents	59	2617	44.4	16	69

Punt Returns	No.	FC	Yds.	Avg.	LG	TD
Prior	13	7	105	8.1	19	0
Bright	12	2	124	10.3	29	0
Buccaneers	25	9	229	9.2	29	0
Opponents	47	7	519	11.0	28	0

Kickoff Returns	No.	Yds.	Avg.	LG	TD
Freeman	48	1085	22.6	58	0
Bright	11	213	19.4	47	0
Prior	10	131	13.1	27	0
Springs	5	112	22.4	34	0
Verser	4	61	15.3	18	0
Magee	2	20	10.0	15	0
Buccaneers	80	1622	20.3	58	0
Opponents	51	1187	23.3	51	0

Scoring	TD R	TD P	TD Rt	PAT	FG	Saf	TP
Igwebuike	0	0	0	30/32	22/32	0	96
Wilder	10	0	0	0/0	0/0	0	60
Giles	0	8	0	0/0	0/0	0	48
House	0	5	0	0/0	0/0	0	30
Carter	0	3	0	0/0	0/0	0	18
Magee	0	3	0	0/0	0/0	0	18
J. Bell	0	2	0	0/0	0/0	0	12
Armstrong	0	1	0	0/0	0/0	0	6
Young	1	0	0	0/0	0/0	0	6
Buccaneers	11	22	0	30/33	22/32	0	294
Opponents	28	18	4	50/50	32/43	1	448

FIRST-ROUND SELECTIONS

(If club had no first-round selection, first player drafted is listed with round in parentheses.)

Year	Player, College, Position
1976	Lee Roy Selmon, Oklahoma, DT
1977	Ricky Bell, Southern California, RB
1978	Doug Williams, Grambling, QB
1979	Greg Roberts, Oklahoma, G (2)
1980	Ray Snell, Wisconsin, G
1981	Hugh Green, Pittsburgh, LB
1982	Sean Farrell, Penn State, G
1983	Randy Grimes, Baylor, C (2)
1984	Keith Browner, Southern California, LB (2)
1985	Ron Holmes, Washington, DE
1986	Bo Jackson, Auburn, RB
	Roderick Jones, Southern Methodist, DB

TAMPA BAY BUCCANEERS 1986 VETERAN ROSTER

No.	Name	Pos.	Ht.	Wt.	Birth-date	NFL Exp.	College	Hometown	How Acq.	'85 Games/ Starts
40	†Armstrong, Adger	RB	6-0	230	6/21/57	7	Texas A&M	Houston, Tex.	FA-'83	16/0
82	Bell, Jerry	TE	6-5	230	3/7/59	5	Arizona State	Richmond, Calif.	D3-'82	9/9
52	†Brantley, Scot	LB	6-1	230	2/24/58	7	Florida	Ocala, Fla.	D3-'80	13/13
57	Browner, Keith	LB	6-5	240	1/24/62	3	Southern California	Atlanta, Ga.	D2-'84	16/5
78	Cannon, John	DE	6-5	260	7/30/60	5	William & Mary	Long Branch, N.J.	D3-'82	16/16
87	†Carter, Gerald	WR	6-1	190	6/19/57	7	Texas A&M	Bryan, Tex.	D9-'80	16/16
23	†Castille, Jeremiah	CB	5-10	175	1/15/61	4	Alabama	Phenix City, Ala.	D3-'83	16/16
72	Courson, Steve	G	6-1	275	10/1/55	9	South Carolina	Gettysburg, Pa.	T(Pitt)-'84	16/13
31	†Curry, Craig	S	6-0	190	7/20/61	3	Texas	Houston, Tex.	FA-'84	16/6
58	Davis, Jeff	LB	6-0	230	1/26/60	5	Clemson	Greensboro, N.C.	D5-'82	16/16
17	DeBerg, Steve	QB	6-3	210	1/19/54	10	San Jose State	Anaheim, Calif.	T(Den)-'84	11/11
80	Dunn, K.D.	TE	6-3	235	4/28/63	2	Clemson	Decatur, Ga.	FA-'85	7/0
26	Easmon, Ricky	CB	5-10	160	7/20/63	2	Florida	Dunnellon, Fla.	FA-'85	14/0*
62	†Farrell, Sean	G	6-3	260	5/25/60	5	Penn State	Westhampton Beach, N.Y.	D1-'82	14/14
65	Fielder, Don	DE	6-3	260	10/20/59	2	Kentucky	Garden Grove, Calif.	FA-'85	11/0
81	Freeman, Phil	WR	5-11	185	12/9/62	2	Arizona	Los Angeles, Calif.	D8-'85	14/0
5	Garcia, Frank	P	6-0	210	6/5/57	4	Arizona	Tucson, Ariz.	FA-'83	16/0
88	Giles, Jimmie	TE	6-3	240	11/8/54	10	Alcorn State	Greenville, Miss.	T(Hou)-'78	16/16
30	Greenwood, David	S	6-3	210	3/25/60	2	Wisconsin	Park Falls, Wis.	T(NO)-'85	16/10
60	†Grimes, Randy	C	6-4	270	7/20/60	4	Baylor	Tyler, Tex.	D2-'83	16/16
73	Heller, Ron	T	6-6	280	8/25/62	3	Penn State	Farmingdale, N.Y.	D4-'84	16/16
90	Holmes, Ron	DE	6-4	255	8/26/63	2	Washington	Lacey, Wash.	D1-'85	16/14
21	Holt, John	CB	5-11	180	5/14/59	6	West Texas State	Enid, Okla.	D4-'81	16/16
89	House, Kevin	WR	6-1	185	12/20/57	7	Southern Illinois	St. Louis, Mo.	D2-'80	16/16
1	Igwebuike, Donald	K	5-9	185	12/27/60	2	Clemson	Anambra, Nigeria	D10-'85	16/0
91	Janata, John	T	6-7	275	4/10/61	2	Illinois	Las Vegas, Nev.	FA-'85	0*
55	†Johnson, Dennis	LB	6-3	235	6/19/58	7	Southern California	Flint, Mich.	W(Minn)-'85	16/6*
79	†Kaplan, Ken	T	6-4	275	1/12/60	3	New Hampshire	Brockton, Mass.	D6-'83	16/0
75	Lindstrom, Chris	DE	6-7	260	8/3/60	3	Boston University	Weymouth, Mass.	FA-'85	13/2
76	Logan, David	NT	6-2	250	10/25/62	8	Pittsburgh	Pittsburgh, Pa.	D12-'79	16/16
86	Magee, Calvin	TE	6-3	240	4/23/63	2	Southern	New Orleans, La.	FA-'85	16/7
68	†Mallory, Rick	G	6-2	260	10/21/60	2	Washington	Renton, Wash.	D9-'84	13/8
	Middleton, Frank	RB	5-11	210	10/28/60	3	Florida A&M	Savannah, Ga.	FA-'86	5/0*
67	Morgan, Karl	NT	6-1	255	2/23/61	3	UCLA	Houma, La.	FA-'84	16/0
	Pleasant, Reggie	CB	5-9	175	5/2/62	2	Clemson	Sumter, S.C.	FA-'86	3/0*
74	t-Powell, Marvin	T	6-5	270	8/30/55	9	Southern California	Fayetteville, N.C.	T(NYJ)-'86	14/14
24	Prior, Mike	S	6-0	200	11/14/63	2	Illinois State	Chicago Heights, Ill.	D7-'85	16/0
54	Randle, Ervin	LB	6-1	250	10/12/62	2	Baylor	Mumford, Tex.	D3-'85	16/7
7	Risher, Alan	QB	6-2	190	5/6/61	2	Louisiana State	Slidell, La.	FA-'85	16/0
74	Sanders, Gene	T	6-3	285	11/10/56	7	Texas A&M	Harvey, La.	D8-'79	2/0
64	†Shearin, Joe	G	6-4	250	4/16/60	4	Texas	Dallas, Tex.	FA-'85	10/0
20	†Springs, Ron	RB	6-2	225	11/4/56	8	Ohio State	Williamsburg, Va.	FA-'85	12/0
71	Studaway, Mark	DE	6-4	275	9/20/60	3	Tennessee	Memphis, Tenn.	FA-'85	6/0
44	†Sully, Ivory	S	6-0	200	1/20/57	8	Delaware	Leonia, N.J.	T(Rams)-'85	16/16
84	Verser, David	WR	6-1	200	3/1/58	5	Kansas	Kansas City, Kan.	FA-'85	1/0
51	Washington, Chris	LB	6-4	230	3/6/62	3	Iowa State	Chicago, Ill.	D6-'84	16/16
32	Wilder, James	RB	6-3	225	5/12/58	6	Missouri	Sikeston, Mo.	D2-'81	16/16
85	†Witte, Mark	TE	6-3	235	12/3/59	4	North Texas State	San Marcos, Tex.	D11-'83	16/0
66	†Yarno, George	G-T	6-2	265	8/12/57	7	Washington State	Spokane, Wash.	FA-'79	12/12
8	Young, Steve	QB	6-2	200	10/11/61	2	Brigham Young	Greenwich, Conn.	SD1-'84	5/5

* Easmon played 8 games with Dallas, 6 with Tampa Bay in '85; Janata missed '85 season due to injury; Johnson played 8 games with Minnesota, 8 with Tampa Bay in '85; Middleton played 5 games with Indianapolis in '85; Pleasant played 3 games with Atlanta in '85.

†Option playout; subject to developments.

t-Buccaneers traded for Powell (New York Jets).

Retired—Theo Bell, 9-year wide receiver, 15 games in '85; Mark Cotney, 9-year safety, injured reserve in '85; Lee Roy Selmon, 9-year defensive end, injured reserve in '85; Steve Wilson, 10-year center, 5 games in '85.

Also played with Buccaneers in '85—TE Gene Branton (3 games), RB Leon Bright (8), RB Melvin Carver (2), S Paul Dombroski (6), LB Hugh Green (5), CB Carl Howard (4), LB Cecil Johnson (16), T Wally Kersten (active for 3 games but did not play), LB Larry Kubin (4), RB George Peoples (2).

COACHING STAFF

Head Coach, Leeman Bennett

Pro Career: Became only the second head coach in the 10-year history of the franchise when named to the post on January 23, 1985. Previously head coach of the Atlanta Falcons 1977-82. During that time, Bennett had a record of 47-44 and led the Falcons to postseason playoffs in 1978, 1980, and 1982. NFC coach of the year following 1980 season in which Falcons were 12-4 and NFC Western Division champions. Served seven years as a pro assistant coaching offensive backs with St. Louis Cardinals 1970-71 and Detroit Lions 1972 and receivers with Los Angeles Rams 1973-76. No pro playing experience. Career record: 49-58.

Background: College quarterback and defensive back Kentucky 1958-60. College coach Kentucky 1961-62, 1965, Pittsburgh 1966, Cincinnati 1967-68, and Navy 1969.

Personal: Born June 20, 1938, in Paducah, Kentucky. Leeman and his wife, Pat, live in Tampa and have two sons—Paul and Greg.

Assistant Coaches

Greg Brown, offensive-video assistant; born October 10, 1957, Denver, Colo., lives in Tampa. Defensive back Glendale Community College 1976-77, Texas-El Paso 1978-79. No pro playing experience. Pro coach: Denver Gold (USFL) 1983-84, joined Buccaneers in 1985.

Joe Diange, strength; born April 24, 1956, Massapequa Park, N.Y., lives in Tampa. Linebacker Penn State 1976-77. No pro playing experience. College coach: Penn State 1978-81; Navy 1982-83. Pro coach: Joined Buccaneers in 1984.

Kim Helton, offensive line; born July 28, 1948, Pensacola, Fla., lives in Tampa. Center Florida 1967-69. No pro playing experience. College coach: Florida 1972-78, Miami 1979-82. Pro coach: Joined Buccaneers in 1983.

Don Lawrence, defensive line; born June 4, 1937, Cleveland, Ohio, lives in Tampa. Tackle Notre Dame 1953-55. Pro tackle Washington Redskins 1956-61. College coach: Notre Dame 1963-67, Kansas State 1968-69, Cincinnati 1970, Virginia 1971-73 (head coach), Texas Christian 1974-75, Missouri 1976-77. Pro coach: British Columbia Lions (CFL) 1978-79, Kansas City Chiefs 1980-82, Buffalo Bills 1983-84, joined Buccaneers in 1985.

Vic Rapp, running backs; born December 23, 1935, Marionville, Mo., lives in Tampa. Running back Southwest Missouri State 1954-57. No pro playing experience. College coach: Missouri 1967-71. Pro coach: Edmonton Eskimos (CFL) 1972-76, British Columbia Lions (CFL) 1977-82 (head coach), Houston Oilers 1983, Los Angeles Rams 1984, joined Buccaneers in 1985.

Jimmy Raye, offensive coordinator-quarterbacks; born July 3, 1945, Fayetteville, N.C., lives in Tampa. Quarterback Michigan State 1965-67. Pro defensive back Philadelphia Eagles 1969. College coach: Michigan State 1971-75, Wyoming 1976. Pro coach: San Francisco 49ers 1977, Detroit Lions 1978-79, Atlanta Falcons 1980-82, Los Angeles Rams 1983-84, joined Buccaneers in 1985.

Dick Roach, defensive backs; born August 23, 1937, Rapid City, S.D., lives in Tampa. Defensive back Black Hills State 1952-55. No pro playing experience. College coach: Montana State 1966-69, Oregon State 1970, Wyoming 1971-72, Fresno State 1973, Washington State 1974-75. Pro coach: Montreal Alouettes (CFL) 1976-77, Kansas City Chiefs 1978-80, New England Patriots 1981, Michigan Panthers (USFL) 1983-84, joined Buccaneers in 1985.

Larry Seiple, receivers; born February 14, 1945, Allentown, Pa., lives in Tampa. Punter-tight end Kentucky 1964-66. Pro punter Miami Dolphins 1967-77. College coach: Miami 1979. Pro coach: Detroit Lions 1980-84, joined Buccaneers in 1985.

Jim Stanley, defensive coordinator; born June 19, 1934, Dunham, Ky., lives in Tampa. Offensive-defensive lineman Texas A&M 1955-57. No pro playing experience. College coach: Southern Methodist 1961, Texas-El Paso 1962, Oklahoma State 1963-68, 1972, 1973-78 (head coach), Navy 1969-70. Pro coach: Winnipeg Blue Bombers (CFL) 1971, New York Giants 1979, Atlanta Falcons 1980-82, Michigan Panthers (USFL) 1983-84 (head coach), first year with Buccaneers.

Howard Tippett, special teams-linebackers; born September 23, 1938, Tallassee, Ala., lives in Tampa. Quarterback-safety East Tennessee State 1955-57. No pro playing experience. College coach: Tulane 1963-65, West Virginia 1966, 1971, Houston 1967-70, Mississippi State 1972-73, 1979, Washington State 1976, Oregon 1977-78, UCLA 1980. Pro coach: Jacksonville Sharks (WFL) 1974-75, joined Buccaneers in 1981.

TAMPA BAY BUCCANEERS 1986 FIRST-YEAR ROSTER

Name	Pos.	Ht.	Wt.	Birthdate	College	Hometown	How Acq.
Aldredge, Corwyn (1)	TE	6-5	225	9/6/63	Mississippi State	Natchitoches, La.	FA
Barnhardt, Tommy	P	6-2	205	6/11/63	North Carolina	China Grove, N.C.	D9
Colquitt, Jimmy (1)	P	6-4	210	1/17/63	Tennessee	Knoxville, Tenn.	FA
Crawford, Mike	RB	5-10	200	1/1/64	Arizona State	Thousand Oaks, Calif.	D12b
Degrate, Anthony (1)	NT	6-3	290	4/25/62	Texas	Snyder, Tex.	FA
Drenth, Mark	G	6-5	280	2/12/64	Purdue	Kalamazoo, Mich.	D11
Futrell, Bobby	CB-S	5-11	185	8/4/62	Elizabeth City State	Ahoskie, N.C.	FA
Jackson, Bo	RB	6-2	225	11/30/62	Auburn	Bessemer, Ala.	D1a
Jones, Roderick	CB-S	5-11	175	3/31/64	Southern Methodist	Dallas, Tex.	D1b
Lampley, Deverick (1)	WR	6-0	190	6/18/62	Milikin	Oakland, Calif.	FA
Maarleveld, J.D.	T	6-6	300	10/24/61	Maryland	Rutherford, N.J.	D5
Miller, Clay	G	6-4	280	8/27/63	Michigan	Norman, Okla.	D12a
Murphy, Kevin	LB	6-2	230	9/8/63	Oklahoma	Plano, Tex.	D2b
Nelson, Bob (1)	NT	6-3	265	3/3/59	Miami	Baltimore, Md.	FA
Polk, Ray (1)	CB-S	5-11	195	6/10/62	Oklahoma State	Sherman, Tex.	FA
Reed, Ben	DE	6-5	270	5/7/63	Mississippi	Baton Rouge, La.	D10
Scott, Ed (1)	WR	6-0	190	12/29/62	Idaho State	San Diego, Calif.	FA
Swoope, Craig	CB-S	6-1	195	2/3/64	Illinois	Ft. Pierce, Fla.	D4
Taylor, Rob (1)	T	6-6	285	11/14/60	Northwestern	Kettering, Ohio	FA
Turner, Bill (1)	P	6-2	210	12/26/62	California Lutheran	Westlake Village, Calif.	FA
Vogel, Paul (1)	LB	6-1	220	2/2/61	South Carolina	Greenville, S.C.	FA
Walker, Jackie	LB	6-5	245	11/3/62	Jackson State	Monroe, La.	D2a
Walker, Kevin	CB-S	5-11	180	10/20/63	East Carolina	Greensboro, N.C.	D6
Williams, Carl (1)	WR	6-2	175	1/21/63	Louisville	Atlanta, Ga.	FA
Young, Almon (1)	G	6-4	270	8/27/63	Bethune-Cookman	Umatilla, Fla.	FA

The term NFL Rookie is defined as a player who is in his first season of professional football and has not been on the roster of another professional football team for any regular season or postseason games. A Rookie is designated by an "R" on NFL rosters. Players who have been active in another professional football league or players who have NFL experience, including either preseason training camp or being on an active roster for fewer than three regular season or postseason games, are termed NFL First-Year Players. An NFL First-Year Player is designated by a "1" on NFL rosters. Thereafter, a player on an NFL active roster for at least three regular season or postseason games is credited with an additional year of NFL playing experience.

NOTES

WASHINGTON REDSKINS

National Football Conference
Eastern Division

Team Colors: Burgundy and Gold

Redskin Park
P.O. Box 17247
Dulles International Airport
Washington, D.C. 20041
Telephone: (703) 471-9100

Club Officials

Chairman of the Board-Chief Operating Executive: Jack Kent Cooke
Executive Vice President: John Kent Cooke
Senior Vice President: Gerard T. Gabrys
Secretary: Robert N. Eisman
Board of Directors: Jack Kent Cooke, John Kent Cooke, James Lacher, William A. Shea, Esq., The Honorable John W. Warner
General Manager: Bobby Beathard
Assistant General Managers: Bobby Mitchell, Charles Casserly
Director of Player Personnel: Dick Daniels
Director of Pro Scouting: Kirk Mee
Talent Scouts: Billy Devaney, George Saimes
Director of Public Relations: Charles M. Taylor
Director of Media Relations: John C. Konoza
Director of Publications: Ronn Levine
Director of Marketing: Paul Denfeld
Director of Stadium Operations: Dale Morris
Director of Photography: Nate Fine
Ticket Manager: Sue Barton
Head Trainer: Lamar (Bubba) Tyer
Assistant Trainers: Joe Kuczo, Keoki Kamau
Equipment Manager: Jay Brunetti

Stadium: Robert F. Kennedy Stadium • **Capacity:** 55,750
East Capitol Street
Washington, D.C. 20003

Playing Surface: Grass (PAT)

Training Camp: Dickinson College
Carlisle, Pennsylvania 17013

1986 SCHEDULE

Preseason

Aug. 10	at New England	7:00
Aug. 15	**Pittsburgh**	8:00
Aug. 23	at Tampa Bay	7:00
Aug. 29	**Atlanta**	8:00

Regular Season

Sept. 7	**Philadelphia**	1:00
Sept. 14	**Los Angeles Raiders**	1:00
Sept. 21	at San Diego	1:00
Sept. 28	**Seattle**	1:00
Oct. 5	at New Orleans	12:00
Oct. 12	at Dallas	12:00
Oct. 19	**St. Louis**	1:00
Oct. 27	at N.Y. Giants (Monday)	9:00
Nov. 2	**Minnesota**	4:00
Nov. 9	at Green Bay	12:00
Nov. 17	**San Francisco** (Monday)	9:00
Nov. 23	**Dallas**	1:00
Nov. 30	at St. Louis	12:00
Dec. 7	**New York Giants**	1:00
Dec. 13	at Denver (Saturday)	2:00
Dec. 21	at Philadelphia	1:00

REDSKINS COACHING HISTORY

Boston 1932-36
(363-324-26)

1932	Lud Wray	4-4-2
1933-34	William (Lone Star) Dietz	11-11-2
1935	Eddie Casey	2-8-1
1936-42	Ray Flaherty*	56-23-3
1943	Arthur (Dutch) Bergman	7-4-1
1944-45	Dudley DeGroot	14-6-1
1946-48	Glen (Turk) Edwards	16-18-1
1949	John (Billick) Whelchel**	2-4-1
1949-51	Herman Ball***	5-15-0
1951	Dick Todd	5-4-0
1952-53	Earl (Curly) Lambeau	10-13-1
1954-58	Joe Kuharich	26-32-2
1959-60	Mike Nixon	4-18-2
1961-65	Bill McPeak	21-46-3
1966-68	Otto Graham	17-22-3
1969	Vince Lombardi	7-5-2
1970	Bill Austin	6-8-0
1971-77	George Allen	69-35-1
1978-80	Jack Pardee	24-24-0
1981-85	Joe Gibbs	57-24-0

*Retired to enter Navy
**Released after seven games in 1949
***Released after three games in 1951

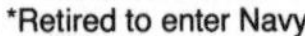

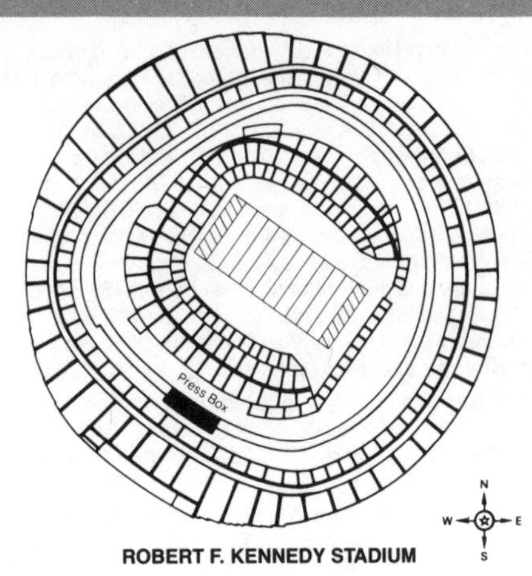

ROBERT F. KENNEDY STADIUM

RECORD HOLDERS

Individual Records—Career

Category	Name	Performance
Rushing (Yds.)	John Riggins, 1976-79, 1981-85	7,472
Passing (Yds.)	Joe Theismann, 1974-1985	25,206
Passing (TDs)	Sonny Jurgensen, 1964-1974	209
Receiving (No.)	Charley Taylor, 1964-1977	649
Receiving (Yds.)	Charley Taylor, 1964-1977	9,140
Interceptions	Brig Owens, 1966-1977	36
Punting (Avg.)	Sammy Baugh, 1937-1952	45.1
Punt Return (Avg.)	Johnny Williams, 1952-53	12.8
Kickoff Return (Avg.)	Bobby Mitchell, 1962-68	28.5
Field Goals	Mark Moseley, 1974-1985	257
Touchdowns (Tot.)	Charley Taylor, 1964-1977	90
Points	Mark Moseley, 1974-1985	1,176

Individual Records—Single Season

Category	Name	Performance
Rushing (Yds.)	John Riggins, 1983	1,347
Passing (Yds.)	Sonny Jurgensen, 1967	3,747
Passing (TDs)	Sonny Jurgensen, 1967	31
Receiving (No.)	Art Monk, 1984	106
Receiving (Yds.)	Bobby Mitchell, 1963	1,436
Interceptions	Dan Sandifer, 1948	13
Punting (Avg.)	Sammy Baugh, 1940	51.4
Punt Return (Avg.)	Johnny Williams, 1952	15.3
Kickoff Return (Avg.)	Mike Nelms, 1981	29.7
Field Goals	Mark Moseley, 1983	33
Touchdowns (Tot.)	John Riggins, 1983	24
Points	Mark Moseley, 1983	161

Individual Records—Single Game

Category	Name	Performance
Rushing (Yds.)	George Rogers, 12-21-85	206
Passing (Yds.)	Sammy Baugh, 10-31-48	446
Passing (TDs)	Sammy Baugh, 10-31-43	6
	Sammy Baugh, 11-23-47	6
Receiving (No.)	Art Monk, 12-15-85	13
Receiving (Yds.)	Art Monk, 12-15-85	230
Interceptions	Sammy Baugh, 11-14-43	4
	Dan Sandifer, 10-31-48	4
Field Goals	Many times	5
	Last time by Mark Moseley, 10-26-80	
Touchdowns (Tot.)	Dick James, 12-17-61	4
	Larry Brown, 12-4-73	4
Points	Dick James, 12-17-61	24
	Larry Brown, 12-4-73	24

1985 TEAM STATISTICS

	Washington	Opp.
Total First Downs	319	244
Rushing	147	94
Passing	157	134
Penalty	15	16
Third Down: Made/Att.	107/247	73/211
Fourth Down: Made/Att.	9/19	6/15
Total Net Yards	5338	4480
Avg. Per Game	333.6	280.0
Total Plays	1135	941
Avg. Per Play	4.7	4.8
Net Yards Rushing	2523	1734
Avg. Per Game	157.7	108.4
Total Rushes	571	424
Net Yards Passing	2815	2746
Avg. Per Game	175.9	171.6
Tackled/Yards Lost	52/428	52/378
Gross Yards	3243	3124
Att./Completions	512/280	465/239
Completion Pct.	54.7	51.4
Had Intercepted	21	23
Punts/Avg.	73/40.7	85/43.8
Net Punting Avg.	32.4	36.2
Penalties/Yards Lost	74/596	89/699
Fumbles/Ball Lost	27/19	28/11
Touchdowns	33	35
Rushing	20	11
Passing	13	19
Returns	0	5
Avg. Time of Possession	33:17	26:43

1985 TEAM RECORD

Preseason (4-0)

Date	Washington		Opponents
8/10	17	Atlanta	14
8/18	14	L.A. Raiders	9
8/23	37	*New England	36
8/30	20	Tampa Bay	7
	88		66

Regular Season (10-6)

Date	Washington		Opp.	Att.
9/9	14	Dallas	44	61,543
9/15	16	*Houston	13	53,553
9/22	6	*Philadelphia	19	53,748
9/29	10	Chicago	45	63,708
10/7	27	*St. Louis	10	53,134
10/13	24	*Detroit	3	52,845
10/20	3	N.Y. Giants	17	74,389
10/27	14	Cleveland	7	75,540
11/3	44	Atlanta	10	42,209
11/10	7	*Dallas	13	55,750
11/18	23	*N.Y. Giants	21	53,371
11/24	30	Pittsburgh	23	59,293
12/1	8	*San Francisco	35	51,321
12/8	17	Philadelphia	12	60,737
12/15	27	*Cincinnati	24	50,544
12/21	27	St. Louis	16	28,090

*Home Game

Score by Periods

Washington	81	105	44	67	0	—	297
Opponents	59	107	78	68	0	—	312

Attendance

Home 424,266 Away 465,509 Total 889,775
Single game home record, 55,750 (11-10-85)
Single season home record, 427,651 (1979)

1985 INDIVIDUAL STATISTICS

Rushing	Att.	Yds.	Avg.	LG	TD
Rogers	231	1093	4.7	35	7
Riggins	176	677	3.8	51	8
Griffin	102	473	4.6	66t	3
Theismann	25	115	4.6	25	2
Monk	7	51	7.3	16	0
Jenkins	2	39	19.5	37	0
Schroeder	17	30	1.8	14	0
Walker	3	16	5.3	9	0
Clark	2	10	5.0	7	0
Bartkowski, Atl.-Wash.	5	9	1.8	5	0
Wonsley	4	8	2.0	5	0
Green	1	6	6.0	6	0
Warren	1	5	5.0	5	0
Redskins	571	2523	4.4	66t	20
Opponents	424	1734	4.1	64	11

Passing	Att.	Comp.	Pct.	Yds.	TD	Int.	Tkld.	Rate
Theismann	301	167	55.5	1774	8	16	37/314	59.6
Schroeder	209	112	53.6	1458	5	5	15/114	73.8
Bartkowski, Atl.-Wash.	111	69	62.2	738	5	1	18/158	92.8
Cox	1	1	100.0	11	0	0	0/0	112.5
Riggins	1	0	0.0	0	0	0	0/0	39.6
Redskins	512	280	54.7	3243	13	21	52/428	65.4
Opponents	465	239	51.4	3124	19	23	52/378	65.9

Receiving	No.	Yds.	Avg.	LG	TD
Monk	91	1226	13.5	53	2
Clark	72	926	12.9	55	5
Didier	41	433	10.6	29	4
Griffin	37	285	7.7	28	0
Warren	15	163	10.9	19	1
Muhammad	9	116	12.9	32	1
Riggins	6	18	3.0	8	0
Rogers	4	29	7.3	23	0
Barnwell	3	28	9.3	13	0
Cherry	1	11	11.0	11	0
Walker	1	8	8.0	8	0
Redskins	280	3243	11.6	55	13
Opponents	239	3124	13.1	69	19

Interceptions	No.	Yds.	Avg.	LG	TD
Jordan	5	88	17.6	36	0
Dean	5	8	1.6	8	0
Kaufman	3	10	3.3	10	0
Milot	2	33	16.5	22	0
Cherry	2	29	14.5	22	0
Peters	2	21	10.5	12	0
Green	2	0	0.0	0	0
Olkewicz	1	21	21.0	21	0
Wilburn	1	10	10.0	10	0
Redskins	23	220	9.6	36	0
Opponents	21	215	10.2	90	2

Punting	No.	Yds.	Avg.	In 20	LG
Cox	52	2175	41.8	14	57
Hayes	16	665	41.6	4	55
Schroeder	4	132	33.0	0	44
Theismann	1	1	1.0	0	1
Redskins	73	2973	40.7	18	57
Opponents	85	3723	43.8	24	68

Punt Returns	No.	FC	Yds.	Avg.	LG	TD
Jenkins	26	9	272	10.5	28	0
Green	16	0	214	13.4	37	0
Cherry	4	1	22	5.5	9	0
Dean	1	0	0	0.0	0	0
Clark	0	1	0	—	0	0
Redskins	47	11	508	10.8	37	0
Opponents	32	11	285	8.9	56	0

Kickoff Returns	No.	Yds.	Avg.	LG	TD
Jenkins	41	1018	24.8	95	0
Griffin	7	142	20.3	35	0
Morton	6	131	21.8	27	0
Wonsley	2	26	13.0	19	0
Cherry	1	9	9.0	9	0
Hamel	1	14	14.0	14	0
Jones	1	0	0.0	0	0
Keating	1	9	9.0	9	0
Redskins	60	1349	22.5	95	0
Opponents	53	1186	22.4	99t	2

Scoring	TD R	TD P	TD Rt	PAT	FG	Saf	TP
Moseley	0	0	0	31/33	22/34	0	97
Riggins	8	0	0	0/0	0/0	0	48
Rogers	7	0	0	0/0	0/0	0	42
Clark	0	5	0	0/0	0/0	0	30
Didier	0	4	0	0/0	0/0	0	24
Griffin	3	0	0	0/0	0/0	0	18
Monk	0	2	0	0/0	0/0	0	12
Theismann	2	0	0	0/0	0/0	0	12
Muhammad	0	1	0	0/0	0/0	0	6
Warren	0	1	0	0/0	0/0	0	6
Redskins	20	13	0	31/33	22/35	1	297
Opponents	11	19	5	34/35	22/28	1	312

FIRST-ROUND SELECTIONS

(If club had no first-round selection, first player drafted is listed with round in parentheses.)

Year	Player, College, Position
1936	Riley Smith, Alabama, B
1937	Sammy Baugh, Texas Christian, B
1938	Andy Farkas, Detroit, B
1939	I.B. Hale, Texas Christian, T
1940	Ed Boell, New York U., B
1941	Forest Evashevski, Michigan, B
1942	Orban (Spec) Sanders, Texas, B
1943	Jack Jenkins, Missouri, B
1944	Mike Micka, Colgate, B
1945	Jim Hardy, Southern California, B
1946	Cal Rossi, UCLA, B*
1947	Cal Rossi, UCLA, B
1948	Harry Gilmer, Alabama, B
	Lowell Tew, Alabama, B
1949	Rob Goode, Texas A&M, B
1950	George Thomas, Oklahoma, B
1951	Leon Heath, Oklahoma, B
1952	Larry Isbell, Baylor, B
1953	Jack Scarbath, Maryland, B
1954	Steve Meilinger, Kentucky, E
1955	Ralph Guglielmi, Notre Dame, B
1956	Ed Vereb, Maryland, B
1957	Don Bosseler, Miami, B
1958	M. Sommer, George Washington, B (2)
1959	Don Allard, Boston College, B
1960	Richie Lucas, Penn State, QB
1961	Norman Snead, Wake Forest, QB
	Joe Rutgens, Illinois, DT
1962	Ernie Davis, Syracuse, RB
1963	Pat Richter, Wisconsin, TE
1964	Charley Taylor, Arizona State, RB-WR
1965	Bob Breitenstein, Tulsa, T (2)
1966	Charlie Gogolak, Princeton, K
1967	Ray McDonald, Idaho, RB
1968	Jim Smith, Oregon, DB
1969	Eugene Epps, Texas-El Paso, DB (2)
1970	Bill Brundige, Colorado, DT (2)
1971	Cotton Speyrer, Texas, WR (2)
1972	Moses Denson, Maryland State, RB (8)
1973	Charles Cantrell, Lamar, G (5)
1974	Jon Keyworth, Colorado, TE (6)
1975	Mike Thomas, Nevada-Las Vegas, RB (6)
1976	Mike Hughes, Baylor, G (5)
1977	Duncan McColl, Stanford, DE (4)
1978	Tony Green, Florida, RB (6)
1979	Don Warren, San Diego State, TE (4)
1980	Art Monk, Syracuse, WR
1981	Mark May, Pittsburgh, T
1982	Vernon Dean, San Diego State, DB (2)
1983	Darrell Green, Texas A&I, DB
1984	Bob Slater, Oklahoma, DT (2)
1985	Tory Nixon, San Diego State, DB (2)
1986	Markus Koch, Boise State, DE (2)

Choice lost due to ineligibility.

WASHINGTON REDSKINS 1986 VETERAN ROSTER

No.	Name	Pos.	Ht.	Wt.	Birth-date	NFL Exp.	College	Hometown	How Acq.	'85 Games/ Starts
58	Anderson, Stuart	LB	6-1	255	12/25/59	5	Virginia	Cardinal, Va.	FA-'85	16/0
4	Atkinson, Jess	K	5-9	168	12/11/61	2	Maryland	Temple Hills, Md.	W(StL)-'86	8/0*
67	Beasley, Tom	DT-DE	6-5	248	8/11/54	9	Virginia Tech	Northfolk, W. Va.	FA-'84	12/0
53	Bostic, Jeff	C-G	6-2	260	9/18/58	7	Clemson	Greensboro, N.C.	FA-'80	10/6
30	Branch, Reggie	RB	5-11	227	10/22/62	2	East Carolina	Sanford, Fla.	FA-'85	8/0
65	Butz, Dave	DT	6-7	295	6/23/50	13	Purdue	Park Ridge, Ill.	FA-'75	16/16
37	Cherry, Raphel	S	6-0	194	12/19/61	2	Hawaii	Los Angeles, Calif.	D5-'85	16/5
84	Clark, Gary	WR	5-9	173	5/1/62	2	James Madison	Dublin, Va.	FA-'85	16/10
48	†Coffey, Ken	S	6-0	198	11/7/60	3	Southwest Texas State	Big Spring, Tex.	D9-'82	0*
51	†Coleman, Monte	LB	6-2	230	11/4/57	8	Central Arkansas	Pine Bluff, Ark.	D11-'79	11/1
12	†Cox, Steve	P	6-4	195	5/11/58	6	Arkansas	Charleston, Ark.	FA-'85	12/0
32	Dean, Vernon	CB	5-11	178	5/5/59	5	San Diego State	Los Angeles, Calif.	D2-'82	16/16
86	†Didier, Clint	TE	6-5	240	4/4/59	5	Portland State	Pasco, Wash.	D12-'81	16/14
77	Grant, Darryl	DT	6-1	275	11/22/59	6	Rice	San Antonio, Tex.	D9-'81	8/8
28	Green, Darrell	CB	5-8	170	2/15/60	4	Texas A&I	Houston, Tex.	D1-'83	16/16
35	Griffin, Keith	RB	5-8	185	10/26/61	3	Miami	Eastmoor, Ohio	D10-'84	16/0
68	Grimm, Russ	G	6-3	275	5/2/59	6	Pittsburgh	Southmoreland, Pa.	D3-'81	16/16
78	Hamel, Dean	DT	6-3	275	7/7/61	2	Tulsa	Warren, Mich.	D12-'85	16/8
64	Hamilton, Steve	DE	6-4	255	9/28/61	2	East Carolina	Williamsville, N.Y.	D2-'84	7/0
5	Hayes, Jeff	P	5-11	175	8/19/59	5	North Carolina	Elkin, N.C.	FA-'82	4/0
61	Huff, Ken	G	6-4	265	2/21/53	12	North Carolina	Deerfield, Mass.	FA-'83	16/15
66	Jacoby, Joe	T	6-7	305	7/6/59	6	Louisville	Louisville, Ky.	FA-'81	11/11
31	Jenkins, Ken	RB-KR	5-8	185	5/8/59	4	Bucknell	Bethesda, Md.	FA-'85	13/0
82	Jones, Anthony	TE	6-3	248	5/16/60	3	Wichita State	Baltimore, Md.	D11-'84	16/2
22	Jordan, Curtis	S	6-2	205	1/25/54	10	Texas Tech	Lubbock, Tex.	FA-'81	16/16
55	Kaufman, Mel	LB	6-2	218	2/24/58	6	Cal Poly-SLO	Santa Monica, Calif.	FA-'81	15/15
16	Laufenberg, Babe	QB	6-2	195	12/5/59	3	Indiana	Burbank, Calif.	FA-'85	0*
72	†Manley, Dexter	DE	6-3	250	2/2/59	6	Oklahoma State	Houston, Tex.	D5-'81	16/16
71	Mann, Charles	DE	6-6	260	4/12/61	4	Nevada-Reno	Sacramento, Calif.	D3-'83	16/16
73	May, Mark	T	6-6	295	11/2/59	6	Pittsburgh	Oneonta, N.Y.	D1-'81	16/16
83	McGrath, Mark	WR	5-11	175	12/17/57	5	Montana State	Seattle, Wash.	FA-'84	5/0
63	McKenzie, Raleigh	G	6-2	262	2/8/63	2	Tennessee	Knoxville, Tenn.	D11-'85	6/0
60	†McQuaid, Dan	T	6-7	278	10/4/60	2	Nevada-Las Vegas	Clarksburg, Calif.	T(Rams)-'85	16/3
57	Milot, Rich	LB	6-4	237	5/28/57	8	Penn State	Coraopolis, Pa.	D7-'79	16/16
81	Monk, Art	WR	6-3	209	12/5/57	7	Syracuse	White Plains, N.Y.	D1-'80	15/14
3	Moseley, Mark	K	6-0	204	3/12/48	15	Stephen F. Austin	Livingston, Tex.	FA-'74	16/0
89	Muhammad, Calvin	WR	6-0	190	12/10/58	5	Texas Southern	Jacksonville, Fla.	T(Raiders)-'84	12/5
52	Olkewicz, Neal	LB	6-0	233	1/30/57	8	Maryland	Phoenixville, Pa.	FA-'79	16/16
80	Phillips, Joe	WR	5-9	188	4/12/63	2	Kentucky	Franklin, Ky.	FA-'85	4/0
38	†Rogers, George	RB	6-2	229	12/8/58	6	South Carolina	Duluth, Ga.	T(NO)-'85	15/5
10	Schroeder, Jay	QB	6-4	215	6/28/61	3	UCLA	Pacific Palisades, Calif.	D3-'84	9/5
7	Theismann, Joe	QB	6-0	198	9/9/49	13	Notre Dame	South River, N.J.	T(Mia)-'74	11/11
69	Thielemann, R.C.	G	6-4	262	8/12/55	10	Arkansas	Houston, Tex.	T(Atl)-'85	3/1
88	Walker, Rick	TE	6-4	245	5/28/55	10	UCLA	Santa Ana, Calif.	FA-'80	16/0
85	Warren, Don	TE	6-4	242	5/5/56	8	San Diego State	Covina, Calif.	D4-'79	16/16
45	Wilburn, Barry	CB	6-3	186	12/9/63	2	Mississippi	Memphis, Tenn.	D8-'85	16/1
47	Williams, Greg	S	5-11	185	8/1/59	5	Mississippi State	Greenville, Miss.	FA-'82	16/0
34	Williams, Kevin	CB	5-9	169	11/28/61	2	Iowa State	San Diego, Calif.	FA-'85	12/0
39	Wonsley, Otis	RB	5-10	214	8/13/57	6	Alcorn State	Moss Point, Miss.	FA-'81	16/1

* Atkinson played 6 games with N.Y. Giants, 2 with St. Louis in '85; Coffey missed '85 season due to injury; Laufenberg active for 5 games in '85, but did not play.

†Option playout; subject to developments.

Traded—Center-guard Rick Donnalley to Kansas City.

Also played with Redskins in '85—DE Doug Barnett (2 games), WR Malcolm Barnwell (7), QB Steve Bartkowski (active for 2 games but did not play), LB Peter Cronan (4), LB Chris Keating (10), DE Todd Liebenstein (4), RB Michael Morton (1), RB John Riggins (12).

COACHING STAFF

Head Coach, Joe Gibbs

Pro Career: Enters sixth year as Redskins coach. Led Washington to a 10-6 record in 1985. Named head coach on January 13, 1981, after spending eight years as an NFL assistant coach and nine years on the college level. Came to Redskins from the San Diego Chargers where he was offensive coordinator in 1979 and 1980. Prior to that, he was offensive coordinator for the Tampa Bay Buccaneers in 1978 and offensive backfield coach for the St. Louis Cardinals from 1973-77. While he was with San Diego, the Chargers won the AFC West title and led the NFL in passing two straight years. No pro playing experience. Career record: 57-24.

Background: Played tight end, linebacker, and guard under Don Coryell at San Diego State in 1961 and 1962 after spending two years at Cerritos, Calif., J.C. 1959-60. Started his college coaching career at San Diego State 1964-66, followed by stints at Florida State 1967-68, Southern California 1969-70, and Arkansas 1971-72.

Personal: Born November 25, 1940, in Mocksville, N.C. Graduated from Santa Fe Springs, Calif., High School. Two-time national racquetball champion and ranked second in the over-35 category in 1978. He and his wife, Pat, live in Vienna, Va., and have two sons—J.D. and Coy.

Assistant Coaches

Don Breaux, offensive backs; born August 3, 1940, Jennings, La., lives in Centerville, Va. Quarterback McNeese State 1959-61. Pro quarterback Denver Broncos 1963, San Diego Chargers 1964-65. College coach: Florida State 1966-67, Arkansas 1968-71, 1977-80, Florida 1973-74, Texas 1975-76. Pro coach: Joined Redskins in 1981.

Joe Bugel, assistant head coach-offense; born March 10, 1940, Pittsburgh, Pa., lives in Oakton, Va. Guard Western Kentucky 1960-62. No pro playing experience. College coach: Western Kentucky 1964-68, Navy 1969-72, Iowa State 1973, Ohio State 1974. Pro coach: Detroit Lions 1975-76, Houston Oilers 1977-80, joined Redskins in 1981.

Bill Hickman, administrative assistant; born June 21, 1923, Baltimore, Md., lives in Leesburg, Va. Halfback Virginia 1946-48. No pro playing experience. College coach: Virginia 1949, Duke 1950, North Carolina State 1951, Vanderbilt 1953, North Carolina 1966-72. Pro coach: Washington Redskins 1973-77, Los Angeles Rams 1978-80, rejoined Redskins in 1981.

Larry Peccatiello, defensive coordinator; born December 21, 1935, Newark, N.J., lives in Warrenton, Va. Receiver William & Mary 1955-58. No pro playing experience. College coach: William & Mary 1961-68, Navy 1969-70, Rice 1971. Pro coach: Houston Oilers 1972-75, Seattle Seahawks 1976-80, joined Redskins in 1981.

Richie Petitbon, assistant head coach-defense; born April 18, 1938, New Orleans, La., lives in Vienna, Va. Back Tulane 1955-58. Pro defensive back Chicago Bears 1959-67, Los Angeles Rams 1969-70, Washington Redskins 1971-73. Pro coach: Houston Oilers 1974-77, joined Redskins in 1978.

Jerry Rhome, quarterbacks; born March 6, 1942, Dallas, Tex., lives in Herndon, Va. Quarterback Southern Methodist 1960-61, Tulsa 1963-64. Pro quarterback Dallas Cowboys 1965-68, Cleveland Browns 1969, Houston Oilers 1970, Los Angeles Rams 1971-72. College coach: Tulsa 1973-75. Pro coach: Seattle Seahawks 1976-82, joined Redskins in 1983.

Dan Riley, conditioning; born October 19, 1949, Syracuse, N.Y., lives in Herndon, Va. No college or pro playing experience. College coach: Army 1973-76, Penn State 1977-81. Pro coach: Joined Redskins in 1982.

Wayne Sevier, special teams; born July 3, 1941, San Diego, Calif., lives in Centerville, Va. Quarterback Chaffey, Calif., J.C. 1960, San Diego State 1961-62. No pro playing experience. College coach: California Western 1968-69. Pro coach: St. Louis Cardinals 1974-75, Atlanta Falcons 1976, San Diego Chargers 1979-80, joined Redskins in 1981.

Warren Simmons, tight ends; born February 25, 1942, Poughkeepsie, N.Y., lives in Centerville, Va. Center San Diego State 1963-65. No pro playing experience. College coach: Cal State-Fullerton 1972-75, Cerritos, Calif., J.C. 1976-80. Pro coach: Joined Redskins in 1981.

Charley Taylor, wide receivers; born September 28, 1942, Grand Prairie, Tex., lives in Sterling, Va. Running back Arizona State 1961-63. Pro wide receiver Washington Redskins 1964-76. Pro coach: Joined Redskins in 1982.

Emmitt Thomas, research and development; born June 4, 1943, Angleton, Tex., lives in Reston, Va. Quarterback-wide receiver Bishop (Tex.) College 1963-65. Pro defensive back Kansas City Chiefs 1966-78. College coach: Central Missouri State 1979-80. Pro coach: St. Louis Cardinals 1981-85, first year with Redskins.

LaVern Torgeson, defensive line; born February 28, 1929, LaCrosse, Wash., lives in Fairfax, Va. Center-linebacker Washington State 1948-50. Pro linebacker Detroit Lions 1951-54, Washington Redskins 1955-58. Pro coach: Washington Redskins 1959-61, 1971-77, Pittsburgh Steelers 1962-68, Los Angeles Rams 1969-70, 1978-80, rejoined Redskins in 1981.

WASHINGTON REDSKINS 1986 FIRST-YEAR ROSTER

Name	Pos.	Ht.	Wt.	Birth-date	College	Hometown	How Acq.
Adams, Ricky	LB	6-1	238	3/31/64	Oklahoma State	Junction City, Kan.	FA
Asberry, Wayne	CB	5-10	185	10/14/62	Texas A&M	Palestine, Tex.	D9
Asmus, Jim (1)	K	6-1	190	12/2/58	Hawaii	La Puente, Calif.	FA
Badanjek, Rick	RB	5-8	217	3/25/62	Maryland	West Farmington, Ohio	D7
Bartlett, Mark	T	6-6	281	4/1/63	North Texas State	Gatesville, Tex.	FA
Bentley, Kenneth	G	6-4	265	9/17/63	Southern Mississippi	Birmingham, Ala.	FA
Bodner, Glenn	TE	6-5	245	1/3/63	William & Mary	Clark, N.J.	FA
Bowles, Todd	S	6-2	203	11/18/63	Temple	Elizabeth, N.J.	FA
Bunch, Gordon	S	5-11	188	1/2/64	Arizona	Pacoima, Calif.	FA
Burks, Shawn	LB	6-1	230	2/10/63	Louisiana State	Baton Rouge, La.	FA
Caldwell, Ravin	LB	6-3	229	8/4/63	Arkansas	Ft. Smith, Ark.	D5
Cobble, Eric	RB	5-9	200	4/11/64	S.W. Texas State	Austin, Tex.	FA
Cole, Nathaniel	WR-RB	5-10	185	1/3/62	Morningside College	Chicago, Ill.	FA
Copeland, Anthony	LB	6-2	230	4/14/63	Louisville	East Point, Ga.	FA
Costello, Rocky (1)	K	5-10	164	10/31/61	Fresno State	La Mirada, Calif.	FA
DeYoung, Donnie	C-G	6-2	270	9/14/63	New Mexico	Colorado Springs, Colo.	FA
Fells, Kenny	RB	6-0	190	1/9/64	Henderson State	Little Rock, Ark.	D11
Fonoti, David	T	6-4	274	8/17/63	Arizona State	Aiea, Hawaii	FA
Frain, Todd	TE	6-2	235	1/31/62	Nebraska	Treynor, Iowa	FA
Gardner, Dwight	RB-KR	5-8	183	10/25/64	California	Oakland, Calif.	FA
Gouveia, Kurt	LB	6-1	227	9/14/64	Brigham Young	Waianae, Hawaii	D8
Gunn, Duane (1)	WR	6-0	185	11/17/61	Indiana	Indianapolis, Ind.	FA
Guzik, John	DE	6-3	250	9/25/62	Ohio	Middleburg Hts., Ohio	FA
Hairston, Stanley	WR	5-10	176	11/25/62	Elon	Eden, N.C.	FA
Harris, Nathaniel	WR-CB-S	5-9	172	9/28/62	Tulsa	Longview, Tex.	FA
Huddleston, James	G	6-4	266	9/22/62	Virginia	Alexandria, Va.	D6b
Koch, Markus	DE-DT	6-5	262	2/13/63	Boise State	Ontario, Canada	D2a
Krakoski, Joe (1)	LB	6-1	224	11/11/62	Washington	San Jose, Calif.	FA
Lee, Danziel (1)	TE	6-2	232	3/16/63	Lamar	Corsicana, Tex.	D6-'85
Lovelady, Edwin	WR	5-9	172	4/23/63	Memphis State	Chattanooga, Tenn.	FA
McHale, Joseph	LB	6-2	225	9/26/63	Delaware	Denville, N.J.	FA
Medley, Biddle	CB	5-11	190	10/17/62	Grambling	Salem, N.J.	FA
Morrison, Tim	S	6-1	195	4/3/63	North Carolina	Fayetteville, N.C.	FA
Murray, Walter	WR	6-3	200	12/13/62	Hawaii	Berkeley, Calif.	D2b
Nelson, Jeffrey	WR	5-9	165	9/25/64	Texas A&M	Beaumont, Tex.	FA
Noble, James	WR	6-0	193	8/14/63	Stephen F. Austin	Jacksonville, Tex.	FA
Orr, Terry (1)	TE	6-3	227	9/27/61	Texas	Abilene, Tex.	D10-'85
Osswald, Chris (1)	C-G	6-4	268	11/13/62	Wisconsin	Scofield, Wis.	FA
Pearson, Dale	DT	6-1	270	2/29/64	Stephen F. Austin	Woodlands, Tex.	FA
Pruitt, Glenn	WR	6-0	198	9/23/62	Baylor	Waxahachie, Tex.	FA
Ray, Ted	CB-WR	5-11	180	3/26/64	Montana	Stevensville, Mont.	FA
Reese, Steve	G	6-2	275	8/17/64	Clemson	Thomson, Ga.	FA
Rypien, Mark	QB	6-4	234	10/2/62	Washington State	Spokane, Wash.	D6a
Sagnella, Anthony	DT	6-5	260	2/28/64	Rutgers	Hamden, Conn.	FA
Slater, Bob (1)	DT	6-4	265	11/14/60	Oklahoma	Tulsa, Okla.	D2a-'84
Smith, Allanda (1)	S	6-1	195	3/7/62	Texas Christian	Houston, Tex.	FA
Smith, Roosevelt	DT	6-4	261	9/19/62	Southern Mississippi	Vicksburg, Miss.	FA
Thomas, Troy	T	6-7	285	9/29/63	Northern Iowa	Cedarburg, Iowa	FA
Tilton, Ron	G	6-4	250	8/9/63	Tulane	Tampa, Fla.	FA
Vital, Lionel (1)	RB	5-9	195	7/15/63	Nicholls State	Loreauville, La.	D7a-'85
Walton, Alvin	S	6-0	180	3/14/64	Kansas	Banning, Calif.	D3
Wardell, Leroy	CB	5-11	185	5/7/64	San Diego State	Stockton, Calif.	FA
White, Richie	RB	5-11	193	4/25/64	Central Arkansas	Alma, Ark.	FA
Williams, Robert	WR	5-10	195	10/2/62	Baylor	Galveston, Tex.	FA
Willis, Steve (1)	K	6-2	200	4/28/62	Kansas State	Shawnee, Kan.	FA
Wimberly, Derek	DE-DT	6-5	270	1/4/64	Purdue	Miami, Fla.	FA
Woodside, Paul (1)	K	5-11	170	9/2/63	West Virginia	Falls Church, Va.	FA
Yagiello, Stan	QB	6-0	198	5/4/63	William & Mary	Livingston, N.J.	FA
Yarber, Eric	WR	5-8	156	9/22/63	Idaho	Los Angeles, Calif.	D12

The term NFL Rookie is defined as a player who is in his first season of professional football and has not been on the roster of another professional football team for any regular season or postseason games. A Rookie is designated by an "R" on NFL rosters. Players who have been active in another professional football league or players who have NFL experience, including either preseason training camp or being on an active roster for fewer than three regular season or postseason games, are termed NFL First-Year Players. An NFL First-Year Player is designated by a "1" on NFL rosters. Thereafter, a player on an NFL active roster for at least three regular season or postseason games is credited with an additional year of NFL playing experience.

1985 SEASON IN REVIEW

Trades

Preseason Standings and Results

Regular Season Standings and Results

Week by Week Game Summaries

All-Pro Teams

Pro Football Awards

Paid Attendance Breakdown

Rushing, Passing, and Receiving Leaders

Team and Individual Statistics

Trades

1985 Interconference Trades

Wide receiver **Drew Hill** from the L.A. Rams to Houston for two draft choices (7/3).

Tight end **Tony Hunter** from Buffalo to the L.A. Rams for quarterback **Vince Ferragamo** and a draft choice (7/20).

Running back **Chuck Muncie** from San Diego to Minnesota for a draft choice (7/20).

Tight end **Eddie McGill** from St. Louis to Indianapolis for a draft choice (7/23).

Wide receiver **Robbie Martin** from Detroit to Indianapolis for running back **Alvin Moore** (7/25).

Tackle **Billy Shields** from San Francisco to the N.Y. Jets for a draft choice (8/2).

Linebacker **Blanchard Montgomery** from San Francisco to Buffalo for a draft choice (8/13).

Selection rights to wide receiver **Anthony Carter** from Miami to Minnesota for linebacker **Robin Sendlein** and a draft choice (8/15).

Wide receiver **Preston Dennard** from Buffalo to Green Bay for a draft choice (8/20).

Punter **Maury Buford** from San Diego to Chicago for a draft choice (8/20).

Defensive tackle **Don Smith** from Atlanta to Buffalo for a draft choice (8/21).

Wide receiver **David Verser** from Cincinnati to Green Bay for a draft choice (8/26).

Wide receiver **Malcolm Barnwell** from the L.A. Raiders to Washington for a draft choice (8/26).

Kicker **Tony Zendejas** from Washington to Houston for a draft choice (8/27).

Linebacker **Anthony Dickerson** from Dallas to Buffalo for a draft choice (8/27).

Linebacker **Dave Ahrens** from St. Louis to Indianapolis for a draft choice (8/28).

Defensive back **Ted Watts** from the L.A. Raiders to the N.Y. Giants for a draft choice (8/31).

Linebacker **Larry Kubin** from Washington to Buffalo for a draft choice (9/2).

Running back **Earnest Jackson** from San Diego to Philadelphia for a draft choice (9/2).

Wide receiver **Bobby Duckworth** from San Diego to the L.A. Rams for tackle **Gary Kowalski** and a draft choice (9/2).

Guard **Mike Obrovac** from Cincinnati to Green Bay for a draft choice (9/4).

Selection rights to defensive back **Mossy Cade** from San Diego to Green Bay for a draft choice (9/6).

Wide receiver **John Jefferson** from Green Bay to Cleveland for the selection rights to tackle **Tommy Robinson** and a draft choice (9/20).

Linebacker **Jerry Robinson** from Philadelphia to the L.A. Raiders for a draft choice (9/30).

Linebacker **Hugh Green** from Tampa Bay to Miami for draft choices (10/9).

Tight end **Mike Barber** from the L.A. Rams to Denver for a draft choice (10/9).

1986 Interconference Trades

Quarterback **Turk Schonert** from Cincinnati to Atlanta for the Falcons' third-round choice in 1986. (4/7). Cincinnati selected defensive end **Jim Skow** (Nebraska).

New Orleans traded its first-round choice in 1986 to Indianapolis for the Colts' first- and third-round choices in 1986. (4/17). Indianapolis selected defensive end **Jon Hand** (Alabama). New Orleans selected tackle **Jim Dombrowski** (Virginia) and linebacker **Pat Swilling** (Georgia Tech).

Dallas traded quarterback **Gary Hogeboom** and its second-round choice in 1986 to Indianapolis for the Colts' second-round choice in 1986. (4/28). Dallas selected running back **Darryl Clack** (Arizona State). Indianapolis selected quarterback **Jack Trudeau** (Illinois).

Minnesota traded its first- and third-round choices in 1986 to San Diego for Green Bay's first-round choice which was owned by San Diego and the Chargers' second-round choice in 1986. San Diego selected defensive end **Leslie O'Neal** (Oklahoma State) and defensive tackle **Terry Unrein** (Colorado State). Minnesota selected defensive end **Gerald Robinson** (Auburn) and traded San Diego's second choice in 1986 to the N.Y. Giants (4/29).

San Francisco traded Dallas's first-round choice which it owned and its own tenth-round choice in 1987 to Buffalo for the Bills' second- and third-round choices in 1986. Buffalo selected tackle **Will Wolford** (Vanderbilt). San Francisco traded Buffalo's second-round choice in 1986 to Detroit and selected running back **Tom Rathman** (Nebraska) with the Bills' third-round pick (4/29).

N.Y. Giants traded cornerback **Mark Haynes** to Denver for the Broncos' second-round choice in 1986 and Tampa Bay's sixth-round choice in 1986 which was owned by Denver and the Broncos' second-round choice in 1987. N.Y. Giants selected linebacker **Pepper Johnson** (Ohio State) and wide receiver **Ron Brown** (Colorado) (4/29).

L.A. Raiders traded the rights to defensive back **Bret Clark** (Nebraska) to Atlanta for the Falcons' fourth-round choice in 1986. L.A. Raiders selected defensive tackle **Mike Wise** (Cal-Davis) (4/29).

Philadelphia traded linebacker **Anthony Griggs** to Cleveland for the Browns' eighth-round choice in 1986. Philadelphia selected linebacker **Seth Joiner** (Utah) (4/29).

Indianapolis traded its sixth-round choice in 1986 to the L.A. Rams for the Rams' seventh- and twelfth-round choices in 1986 and Houston's seventh-round choice in 1986 which was owned by the Rams. L.A. Rams selected tackle **Robert Cox** (UCLA). Indianapolis selected kicker **Chris White** (Illinois) with the Houston choice, defensive back **Tommy Sims** (Tennessee), and defensive tackle **Isaac Williams** (Florida State) (4/29).

Washington traded center **Rick Donnelly** to Kansas City for the Chiefs' sixth-round choice in 1986. Washington selected quarterback **Mark Rypien** (Washington State) (4/29).

New England traded its sixth-round choice in 1986 for Tampa Bay's fifth-round choice in 1987. Tampa Bay selected defensive back **Kevin Walker** (East Carolina) (4/29).

1985 AFC Trades

Linebacker **Vernon Maxwell** from Indianapolis to San Diego for a draft choice (8/1).

Linebacker **Tim Golden** from New England to Indianapolis for a draft choice (8/3).

Quarterback **Matt Kofler** from Buffalo to Indianapolis for a draft choice (8/14).

Wide receiver **Byron Franklin** from Buffalo to Seattle for tight end **Pete Metzelaars** (8/20).

Defensive end **Sam Clancy** from Seattle to Cleveland for a draft choice (8/28).

Wide receiver **Jim Smith** from Pittsburgh to the L.A. Raiders for a draft choice (8/31).

Tight end **Dan Ross** from Cincinnati to Seattle for a draft choice (10/15).

1986 AFC Trades

Cleveland traded running back **Boyce Green** to Kansas City for the Chiefs' seventh-round choice in 1986. Cleveland selected quarterback **Mike Norseth** (Kansas) (4/29).

Kansas City traded its eighth- and twelfth-round choices in 1986 to Buffalo for the Bills' eighth-round choice in 1986. Kansas City selected punter **Louis Colbert** (Auburn). Buffalo selected linebacker **Tony Furjanic** (Notre Dame) and quarterback **Brian McClure** (Bowling Green) (4/29).

1985 NFC Trades

Linebacker **Fulton Kuykendall** from Atlanta to San Francisco for defensive end **Lawrence Pillars** (7/19).

Tackle **Kelly Thomas** from Tampa Bay to Washington for defensive back **Anthony Washington** (8/2).

Defensive back **Ivory Sully** from the L.A. Rams to Tampa Bay for a draft choice (8/2).

Center **Jim Leonard** from Tampa Bay to San Francisco for a draft choice. (8/9).

Linebacker **Garry Cobb** from Detroit to Philadelphia for running back **Wilbert Montgomery** (8/22).

Tackle **Dan McQuaid** from the L.A. Rams to Washington for a draft choice (8/23).

Guard **R.C. Thielemann** from Atlanta to Washington for wide receiver **Charlie Brown** (8/26).

Quarterback **Scott Brunner** from Green Bay to St. Louis for a draft choice (8/26).

Wide receiver **Keith Baker** from San Francisco to Philadelphia for a draft choice (8/30).

Selection rights to defensive back **David Greenwood** from New Orleans to Tampa Bay for a draft choice (8/30).

Defensive back **Tory Nixon** from Washington to San Francisco for a draft choice (9/2).

Defensive end **Dennis Harrison** from Philadelphia to the L.A. Rams for a draft choice (9/28).

Tight end **James McDonald** from Detroit to L.A. Rams for a draft choice (10/15).

1986 NFC Trades

N.Y. Giants traded their twelfth-round choice in 1986 to Philadelphia for past considerations. (2/5). Philadelphia selected running back **Bobby Howard** (Indiana).

N.Y. Giants traded the rights to guard **Gary Zimmermann** (Oregon) to Minnesota for San Diego's second-round choice in 1986 which was owned by Minnesota and the L.A. Raiders' second-round choice in 1986 also held by the Vikings. N.Y. Giants selected defensive back **Mark Collins** (Cal State-Fullerton) and defensive back **Greg Lasker** (Arkansas) (4/29).

San Francisco traded its first-round choice in 1986 to Dallas for the Cowboys' first- and fifth-round choices in 1986. Dallas selected wide receiver **Mike Sherrard** (UCLA). San Francisco selected linebacker **Pat Miller** (Florida) with the Cowboys' fifth pick and traded Dallas's first-round choice in 1986 and its own tenth-round choice in 1987 to Buffalo (4/29).

San Francisco traded Buffalo's second-round choice in 1986 which it owned to Detroit for the Lions' second- and third-round choices in 1986. Detroit selected running back **Garry James** (Louisiana State). San Francisco selected defensive end **Larry Roberts** (Alabama) (4/29).

San Francisco traded its second-round choice in 1986 to Washington for the Redskins' tenth-round choice in 1986 and first-round choice in 1987. Washington selected receiver **Walter Murray** (Hawaii). San Francisco selected linebacker **Harold Hallman** (Auburn) (4/29).

San Francisco traded quarterback **Matt Cavanaugh** to Philadelphia for the Eagles' third-round choice in 1986 and second-round choice in 1987. San Francisco selected defensive back **Tim McKyer** (Texas-Arlington) (4/29).

San Francisco traded Detroit's third-round choice in 1986 which it owned to the L.A. Rams for Cleveland's fourth-round choice in 1986 and Washington's fourth-round choice in 1986, both owned by the Rams. L.A. Rams selected quarterback **Hugh Millen** (Washington). San Francisco selected linebacker **Charlie Haley** (James Madison) and tackle **Steve Wallace** (Auburn) (4/29).

Atlanta traded its fifth-round choice in 1986 to Washington for the Redskins' fifth- and sixth-round choices in 1986. Atlanta traded Washington's fifth-round choice in 1986 to Philadelphia and selected running back **Keith Williams** (Southwest Missouri). Washington selected linebacker **Ravin Caldwell** (Arkansas) (4/29).

Philadelphia traded linebacker **Joel Williams** to Atlanta for Washington's fifth-round choice in 1986 which was owned by Atlanta. Philadelphia selected defensive end **Dan Millen** (Colorado) (4/29).

1985 PRESEASON STANDINGS

American Football Conference

EASTERN DIVISION

	W	L	T	Pct.	Pts.	OP
Indianapolis	2	2	0	.500	67	71
Miami	2	2	0	.500	80	69
New England	1	3	0	.250	100	96
N.Y. Jets	1	3	0	.250	98	115
Buffalo	0	3	1	.125	69	113

CENTRAL DIVISION

	W	L	T	Pct.	Pts.	OP
Cincinnati	2	2	0	.500	99	107
Cleveland	2	2	0	.500	73	80
Pittsburgh	1	3	0	.250	96	106
Houston*	1	4	0	.200	75	92

WESTERN DIVISION

	W	L	T	Pct.	Pts.	OP
Kansas City	3	1	0	.750	89	90
Denver	2	2	0	.500	69	59
San Diego	2	2	0	.500	67	79
Seattle	2	2	0	.500	83	55
L.A. Raiders	1	3	0	.250	73	72

*Includes Hall of Fame Game

National Football Conference

EASTERN DIVISION

	W	L	T	Pct.	Pts.	OP
N.Y. Giants*	5	0	0	1.000	119	87
Dallas	4	0	0	1.000	89	50
Washington	4	0	0	1.000	88	66
Philadelphia	3	1	0	.750	85	73
St. Louis	2	2	0	.500	44	65

CENTRAL DIVISION

	W	L	T	Pct.	Pts.	OP
Minnesota	3	1	0	.750	80	83
Detroit	1	2	1	.375	60	75
Chicago	1	3	0	.250	74	63
Green Bay	1	3	0	.250	53	91
Tampa Bay	1	3	0	.250	65	95

WESTERN DIVISION

	W	L	T	Pct.	Pts.	OP
L.A. Rams	3	1	0	.750	72	37
San Francisco	3	1	0	.750	89	72
Atlanta	2	2	0	.500	80	79
New Orleans	1	3	0	.250	82	78

AFC Preseason Records—Team By Team

EASTERN DIVISION

BUFFALO (0-3-1)

10	Detroit (OT)	10
17	Miami	27
28	*Cleveland	31
14	Chicago	45
69		113

INDIANAPOLIS (2-2)

19	*Seattle	7
24	Chicago	13
3	Denver	20
21	*Cincinnati	31
67		71

MIAMI (2-2)

13	*Minnesota (OT)	16
27	*Buffalo	17
23	L.A. Raiders	17
17	Atlanta	19
80		69

NEW ENGLAND (1-3)

20	*New Orleans	32
31	Kansas City	13
36	Washington	37
13	L.A. Rams	14
100		96

N.Y. JETS (1-3)

17	*Philadelphia	37
20	Cincinnati	24
31	N.Y. Giants (OT)	34
30	Green Bay	20
98		115

CENTRAL DIVISION

CINCINNATI (2-2)

27	*Kansas City	35
24	*N.Y. Jets	20
17	Detroit	31
31	Indianapolis	21
99		107

CLEVELAND (2-2)

7	San Diego	12
28	*Philadelphia	14
31	Buffalo	28
7	*L.A. Raiders	26
73		80

HOUSTON (1-4)

20	N.Y. Giants (HOF)	21
3	L.A. Rams	7
23	New Orleans	20
19	*Kansas City	24
10	Dallas	20
75		92

PITTSBURGH (1-3)

42	Tampa Bay	27
34	Minnesota	41
6	St. Louis	14
14	*N.Y. Giants	24
96		106

WESTERN DIVISION

DENVER (2-2)

20	*N.Y. Giants	30
20	San Francisco	13
20	*Indianapolis	3
9	*Minnesota	13
69		59

KANSAS CITY (3-1)

35	Cincinnati	27
13	*New England	31
24	Houston	19
17	*St. Louis	13
89		90

L.A. RAIDERS (1-3)

21	*San Francisco	28
9	*Washington	14
17	*Miami	23
26	Cleveland	7
73		72

SAN DIEGO (2-2)

12	*Cleveland	7
24	*Dallas (OT)	27
10	San Francisco	25
21	*New Orleans	20
67		79

SEATTLE (2-2)

7	Indianapolis	19
28	*Detroit	3
27	Minnesota	10
21	*San Francisco	23
83		55

NFC Preseason Records—Team By Team

EASTERN DIVISION

DALLAS (4-0)

27	*Green Bay	3
27	San Diego (OT)	24
15	*Chicago	13
20	*Houston	10
89		50

N.Y. GIANTS (5-0)

21	Houston (HOF)	20
30	Denver	20
10	*Green Bay	2
34	*N.Y. Jets (OT)	31
24	Pittsburgh	14
119		87

PHILADELPHIA (3-1)

37	N.Y. Jets	17
14	Cleveland	28
14	L.A. Rams	12
20	*Detroit	16
85		73

ST. LOUIS (2-2)

10	*Chicago	3
7	L.A. Rams	39
14	*Pittsburgh	6
13	Kansas City	17
44		65

WASHINGTON (4-0)

17	Atlanta	14
14	L.A. Raiders	9
37	*New England	36
20	Tampa Bay	7
88		66

CENTRAL DIVISION

CHICAGO (1-3)

3	St. Louis	10
13	*Indianapolis	24
13	Dallas	15
45	*Buffalo	14
74		63

DETROIT (1-2-1)

10	*Buffalo (OT)	10
3	Seattle	28
31	*Cincinnati	17
16	Philadelphia	20
60		75

GREEN BAY (1-3)

3	Dallas	27
2	N.Y. Giants	10
28	*Atlanta	24
20	*N.Y. Jets	30
53		91

MINNESOTA (3-1)

16	Miami (OT)	13
41	*Pittsburgh	34
10	*Seattle	27
13	Denver	9
80		83

TAMPA BAY (1-3)

27	*Pittsburgh	42
17	*Atlanta	23
14	New Orleans	10
7	*Washington	20
65		95

WESTERN DIVISION

ATLANTA (2-2)

14	*Washington	17
23	Tampa Bay	17
24	Green Bay	28
19	*Miami	17
80		79

L.A. RAMS (3-1)

7	*Houston	3
39	*St. Louis	7
12	Philadelphia	14
14	*New England	13
72		37

NEW ORLEANS (1-3)

32	New England	20
20	*Houston	23
10	*Tampa Bay	14
20	San Diego	21
82		78

SAN FRANCISCO (3-1)

28	L.A. Raiders	21
13	*Denver	20
25	*San Diego	10
23	Seattle	21
89		72

1985 NFL STANDINGS

American Football Conference

EASTERN DIVISION

	W	L	T	Pct.	Pts.	OP
Miami	12	4	0	.750	428	320
N.Y. Jets*	11	5	0	.688	393	264
New England*	11	5	0	.688	362	290
Indianapolis	5	11	0	.313	320	386
Buffalo	2	14	0	.125	200	381

CENTRAL DIVISION

	W	L	T	Pct.	Pts.	OP
Cleveland	8	8	0	.500	287	294
Cincinnati	7	9	0	.438	441	437
Pittsburgh	7	9	0	.438	379	355
Houston	5	11	0	.313	284	412

WESTERN DIVISION

	W	L	T	Pct.	Pts.	OP
L.A. Raiders	12	4	0	.750	354	308
Denver	11	5	0	.688	380	329
Seattle	8	8	0	.500	349	303
San Diego	8	8	0	.500	467	435
Kansas City	6	10	0	.375	317	360

National Football Conference

EASTERN DIVISION

	W	L	T	Pct.	Pts.	OP
Dallas	10	6	0	.625	357	333
N.Y. Giants*	10	6	0	.625	399	283
Washington	10	6	0	.625	297	312
Philadelphia	7	9	0	.438	286	310
St. Louis	5	11	0	.313	278	414

CENTRAL DIVISION

	W	L	T	Pct.	Pts.	OP
Chicago	15	1	0	.938	456	198
Green Bay	8	8	0	.500	337	355
Minnesota	7	9	0	.438	346	359
Detroit	7	9	0	.438	307	366
Tampa Bay	2	14	0	.125	294	448

WESTERN DIVISION

	W	L	T	Pct.	Pts.	OP
L.A. Rams	11	5	0	.688	340	277
San Francisco*	10	6	0	.625	411	263
New Orleans	5	11	0	.313	294	401
Atlanta	4	12	0	.250	282	452

**Wild Card qualifiers for playoffs*

New York Jets gained first AFC Wild Card position on better conference record (9-3) over New England (8-4) and Denver (8-4). New England gained second AFC Wild Card position based on better record vs. common opponents (4-2) than Denver (3-3). Dallas won NFC Eastern Division title based on better record (3-1) vs. New York Giants (1-3) and Washington (1-3). New York Giants gained first NFC Wild Card position based on better conference record (8-4) over San Francisco (7-5) and Washington (6-6). San Francisco gained second NFC Wild Card position based on head-to-head victory over Washington.

FIRST-ROUND PLAYOFFS

AFC.............. New England 26, New York Jets 14, December 28, at East Rutherford

NFC............. New York Giants 17, San Francisco 3, December 29 at East Rutherford

DIVISIONAL PLAYOFFS

AFC .... Miami 24, Cleveland 21, January 4 at Miami
New England 27, Los Angeles Raiders 20, January 5 at Los Angeles

NFC........................... Los Angeles Rams 20, Dallas 0, January 4 at Anaheim
Chicago 21, New York Giants 0, January 5 at Chicago

CHAMPIONSHIP GAMES

AFC................................. New England 31, Miami 14, January 12 at Miami

NFC .... Chicago 24, Los Angeles Rams 0, January 12 at Chicago

SUPER BOWL XX .... Chicago 46, New England 10, January 26 at Louisiana Superdome, New Orleans, Louisiana

AFC-NFC PRO BOWL . NFC 28, AFC 24, February 2 at Aloha Stadium, Honolulu, Hawaii

AFC Season Records—Team by Team

BUFFALO (2-14)

9	*San Diego	14
3	at N.Y. Jets	42
14	*New England	17
20	*Minnesota	27
17	at Indianapolis	49
3	at New England	14
21	*Indianapolis	9
17	at Philadelphia	21
17	*Cincinnati	23
20	*Houston	0
7	at Cleveland	17
14	*Miami	23
7	at San Diego	40
7	*N.Y. Jets	27
24	at Pittsburgh	30
0	at Miami	28
200		381

CINCINNATI (7-9)

24	*Seattle	28
27	at St. Louis	41
41	*San Diego	44
37	at Pittsburgh	24
20	*N.Y. Jets	29
35	*N.Y. Giants	30
27	at Houston	44
26	*Pittsburgh	21
23	at Buffalo	17
27	*Cleveland	10
6	at L.A. Raiders	13
6	at Cleveland	24
45	*Houston	27
50	*Dallas	24
24	at Washington	27
23	at New England	34
441		437

CLEVELAND (8-8)

24	*St. Louis (OT)	27
17	*Pittsburgh	7
7	at Dallas	20
21	at San Diego	7
24	*New England	20
21	at Houston	6
20	*L.A. Raiders	21
7	*Washington	14
9	at Pittsburgh	10
10	at Cincinnati	27
17	*Buffalo	7
24	*Cincinnati	6
35	at N.Y. Giants	33
13	at Seattle	31
28	*Houston	21
10	at N.Y. Jets	37
287		294

DENVER (11-5)

16	at L.A. Rams	20
34	*New Orleans	23
44	at Atlanta	28
26	*Miami	30
31	*Houston	20
15	at Indianapolis	10
13	*Seattle (OT)	10
30	at Kansas City	10
10	at San Diego	30
17	*San Francisco	16
30	*San Diego (OT)	24
28	at L.A. Raid. (OT)	31
31	at Pittsburgh	23
14	*L.A. Raiders (OT)	17
14	*Kansas City	13
27	at Seattle	24
380		329

HOUSTON (5-11)

26	*Miami	23
13	at Washington	16
0	at Pittsburgh	20
10	*Dallas	17
20	at Denver	31
6	*Cleveland	21
44	*Cincinnati	27
20	at St. Louis	10
23	*Kansas City	20
0	at Buffalo	20
7	*Pittsburgh	30
37	*San Diego	35
27	at Cincinnati	45
14	*N.Y. Giants	35
21	at Cleveland	28
16	at Indianapolis	34
284		412

INDIANAPOLIS (5-11)

3	at Pittsburgh	45
13	at Miami	30
14	*Detroit	6
20	at N.Y. Jets	25
49	*Buffalo	17
10	*Denver	15
9	at Buffalo	21
37	*Green Bay	10
17	*N.Y. Jets	35
15	at New England	34
20	*Miami	34
7	at Kansas City	20
31	*New England	38
10	at Chicago	17
31	at Tampa Bay	23
34	*Houston	16
320		386

KANSAS CITY (6-10)

47	at New Orleans	27
36	*L.A. Raiders	20
0	at Miami	31
28	*Seattle	7
10	at L.A. Raiders	19
20	at San Diego	31
0	*L.A. Rams	16
10	*Denver	30
20	at Houston	23
28	*Pittsburgh	36
3	at San Francisco	31
20	*Indianapolis	7
6	at Seattle	24
38	*Atlanta	10
13	at Denver	14
38	*San Diego	34
317		360

L.A. RAIDERS (12-4)

31	*N.Y. Jets	0
20	at Kansas City	36
10	*San Francisco	34
35	at New England	20
19	*Kansas City	10
23	*New Orleans	13
21	at Cleveland	20
34	*San Diego	21
3	at Seattle	33
34	at San Diego (OT)	40
13	*Cincinnati	6
31	*Denver (OT)	28
34	at Atlanta	24
17	at Denver (OT)	14
13	*Seattle	3
16	at L.A. Rams	6
354		308

MIAMI (12-4)

23	at Houston	26
30	*Indianapolis	13
31	*Kansas City	0
30	at Denver	26
24	*Pittsburgh	20
7	at N.Y. Jets	23
41	*Tampa Bay	38
21	at Detroit	31
13	at New England	17
21	*N.Y. Jets	17
34	at Indianapolis	20
23	at Buffalo	14
38	*Chicago	24
34	at Green Bay	24
30	*New England	27
28	*Buffalo	0
428		320

NEW ENGLAND (11-5)

26	*Green Bay	20
7	at Chicago	20
17	at Buffalo	14
20	*L.A. Raiders	35
20	at Cleveland	24
14	*Buffalo	3
20	*N.Y. Jets	13
32	at Tampa Bay	14
17	*Miami	13
34	*Indianapolis	15
20	at Seattle	13
13	at N.Y. Jets (OT)	16
38	at Indianapolis	31
23	*Detroit	6
27	at Miami	30
34	*Cincinnati	23
362		290

N.Y. JETS (11-5)

0	at L.A. Raiders	31
42	*Buffalo	3
24	at Green Bay	3
25	*Indianapolis	20
29	at Cincinnati	20
23	*Miami	7
13	at New England	20
17	*Seattle	14
35	at Indianapolis	17
17	at Miami	21
62	*Tampa Bay	28
16	*New England (OT)	13
20	at Detroit	31
27	at Buffalo	7
6	*Chicago	19
37	*Cleveland	10
393		264

PITTSBURGH (7-9)

45	*Indianapolis	3
7	at Cleveland	17
20	*Houston	0
24	*Cincinnati	37
20	at Miami	24
13	at Dallas	27
23	*St. Louis	10
21	at Cincinnati	26
10	*Cleveland	9
36	at Kansas City	28
30	at Houston	7
23	*Washington	30
23	*Denver	31
44	at San Diego	54
30	*Buffalo	24
10	at N.Y. Giants	28
379		355

SAN DIEGO (8-8)

14	at Buffalo	9
35	*Seattle	49
44	at Cincinnati	41
7	*Cleveland	21
21	at Seattle	26
31	*Kansas City	20
17	at Minnesota	21
21	at L.A. Raiders	34
30	*Denver	10
40	*L.A. Raiders (OT)	34
24	at Denver (OT)	30
35	at Houston	37
40	*Buffalo	7
54	*Pittsburgh	44
20	*Philadelphia	14
34	at Kansas City	38
467		435

SEATTLE (8-8)

28	at Cincinnati	24
49	at San Diego	35
24	*L.A. Rams	35
7	at Kansas City	28
26	*San Diego	21
30	*Atlanta	26
10	at Denver (OT)	13
14	at N.Y. Jets	17
33	*L.A. Raiders	3
27	at New Orleans	3
13	*New England	20
6	at San Francisco	19
24	*Kansas City	6
31	*Cleveland	13
3	at L.A. Raiders	13
24	*Denver	27
349		303

**Denotes Home Game*
(OT) Denotes Overtime

NFC Season Records—Team by Team

ATLANTA (4-12)		
27	*Detroit	28
16	at San Francisco	35
28	*Denver	44
6	at L.A. Rams	17
17	*San Francisco	38
26	at Seattle	30
31	*New Orleans	24
10	at Dallas	24
10	*Washington	44
17	at Phil. (OT)	23
30	*L.A. Rams	14
0	at Chicago	36
24	*L.A. Raiders	34
10	at Kansas City	38
14	*Minnesota	13
16	at New Orleans	10
282		452

CHICAGO (15-1)		
38	*Tampa Bay	28
20	*New England	7
33	at Minnesota	24
45	*Washington	10
27	at Tampa Bay	19
26	at San Francisco	10
23	*Green Bay	7
27	*Minnesota	9
16	at Green Bay	10
24	*Detroit	3
44	at Dallas	0
36	*Atlanta	0
24	at Miami	38
17	*Indianapolis	10
19	at N.Y. Jets	6
37	at Detroit	17
456		198

DALLAS (10-6)		
44	*Washington	14
21	at Detroit	26
20	*Cleveland	7
17	at Houston	10
30	at N.Y. Giants	29
27	*Pittsburgh	13
14	at Philadelphia	16
24	*Atlanta	10
10	at St. Louis	21
13	at Washington	7
0	*Chicago	44
34	*Philadelphia	17
35	*St. Louis	17
24	at Cincinnati	50
28	*N.Y. Giants	21
16	at San Francisco	31
357		333

DETROIT (7-9)		
28	at Atlanta	27
26	*Dallas	21
6	at Indianapolis	14
30	*Tampa Bay	9
10	at Green Bay	43
3	at Washington	24
23	*San Francisco	21
31	*Miami	21
13	at Minnesota	16
3	at Chicago	24
41	*Minnesota	21
16	at Tampa Bay (OT)	19
31	*N.Y. Jets	20
6	at New England	23
23	*Green Bay	26
17	*Chicago	37
307		366

GREEN BAY (8-8)		
20	at New England	26
23	*N.Y. Giants	20
3	*N.Y Jets	24
28	at St. Louis	43
43	*Detroit	10
20	*Minnesota	17
7	at Chicago	23
10	at Indianapolis	37
10	*Chicago	16
27	at Minnesota	17
38	*New Orleans	14
17	at L.A. Rams	34
21	*Tampa Bay	0
24	*Miami	34
26	at Detroit	23
20	at Tampa Bay	17
337		355

L.A. RAMS (11-5)		
20	*Denver	16
17	at Philadelphia	6
35	at Seattle	24
17	*Atlanta	6
13	*Minnesota	10
31	at Tampa Bay	27
16	at Kansas City	0
14	*San Francisco	28
28	*New Orleans	10
19	at N.Y. Giants	24
14	at Atlanta	30
34	*Green Bay	17
3	at New Orleans	29
27	at San Francisco	20
46	*St. Louis	14
6	*L.A. Raiders	16
340		277

MINNESOTA (7-9)		
28	*San Francisco	21
31	at Tampa Bay	16
24	*Chicago	33
27	at Buffalo	20
10	at L.A. Rams	13
17	at Green Bay	20
21	*San Diego	17
9	at Chicago	27
16	*Detroit	13
17	*Green Bay	27
21	at Detroit	41
23	*New Orleans	30
28	at Philadelphia	23
26	*Tampa Bay	7
13	at Atlanta	14
35	*Philadelphia	37
346		359

NEW ORLEANS (5-11)		
27	*Kansas City	47
23	at Denver	34
20	*Tampa Bay	13
20	at San Francisco	17
23	*Philadelphia	21
13	at L.A. Raiders	23
24	at Atlanta	31
13	*N.Y. Giants	21
10	at L.A. Rams	28
3	*Seattle	27
14	at Green Bay	38
30	at Minnesota	23
29	*L.A. Rams	3
16	at St. Louis	28
19	*San Francisco	31
10	*Atlanta	16
294		401

N.Y. GIANTS (10-6)		
21	*Philadelphia	0
20	at Green Bay	23
27	*St. Louis	17
16	at Phil. (OT)	10
29	*Dallas	30
30	at Cincinnati	35
17	*Washington	3
21	at New Orleans	13
22	*Tampa Bay	20
24	*L.A. Rams	19
21	at Washington	23
34	at St. Louis	3
33	*Cleveland	35
35	at Houston	14
21	at Dallas	28
28	*Pittsburgh	10
399		283

PHILADELPHIA (7-9)		
0	at N.Y. Giants	21
6	*L.A. Rams	17
19	at Washington	6
10	*N.Y. Giants (OT)	16
21	at New Orleans	23
30	*St. Louis	7
16	*Dallas	14
21	*Buffalo	17
13	at San Francisco	24
23	*Atlanta (OT)	17
24	at St. Louis	14
17	at Dallas	34
23	*Minnesota	28
12	*Washington	17
14	at San Diego	20
37	at Minnesota	35
286		310

ST. LOUIS (5-11)		
27	at Cleveland (OT)	24
41	*Cincinnati	27
17	at N.Y. Giants	27
43	*Green Bay	28
10	at Washington	27
7	at Philadelphia	30
10	at Pittsburgh	23
10	*Houston	20
21	*Dallas	10
0	at Tampa Bay	16
14	*Philadelphia	24
3	*N.Y. Giants	34
17	at Dallas	35
28	*New Orleans	16
14	at L.A. Rams	46
16	*Washington	27
278		414

SAN FRANCISCO (10-6)		
21	at Minnesota	28
35	*Atlanta	16
34	at L.A. Raiders	10
17	*New Orleans	20
38	at Atlanta	17
10	*Chicago	26
21	at Detroit	23
28	at L.A. Rams	14
24	*Philadelphia	13
16	at Denver	17
31	*Kansas City	3
19	*Seattle	6
35	at Washington	8
20	*L.A. Rams	27
31	at New Orleans	19
31	*Dallas	16
411		263

TAMPA BAY (2-14)		
28	at Chicago	38
16	*Minnesota	31
13	at New Orleans	20
9	at Detroit	30
19	*Chicago	27
27	*L.A. Rams	31
38	at Miami	41
14	*New England	32
20	at N.Y. Giants	22
16	*St. Louis	0
28	at N.Y. Jets	62
19	*Detroit (OT)	16
0	at Green Bay	21
7	at Minnesota	26
23	*Indianapolis	31
17	*Green Bay	20
294		448

WASHINGTON (10-6)		
14	at Dallas	44
16	*Houston	13
6	*Philadelphia	19
10	at Chicago	45
27	*St. Louis	10
24	*Detroit	3
3	at N.Y. Giants	17
14	at Cleveland	7
44	at Atlanta	10
7	*Dallas	13
23	*N.Y. Giants	21
30	at Pittsburgh	23
8	*San Francisco	35
17	at Philadelphia	12
27	*Cincinnati	24
27	at St. Louis	16
297		312

**Denotes Home Game*
(OT) Denotes Overtime

Attendances as they appear in the following, and in the club-by-club sections starting on page 24, are turnstile counts and not paid attendance. Paid attendance totals are on page 167.

FIRST WEEK SUMMARIES

STANDINGS

American Football Conference

Eastern Division	W	L	T	Pct.	Pts.	OP
New England	1	0	0	1.000	26	20
Buffalo	0	1	0	.000	9	14
Indianapolis	0	1	0	.000	3	45
Miami	0	1	0	.000	23	26
N.Y. Jets	0	1	0	.000	0	31
Central Division						
Houston	1	0	0	1.000	26	23
Pittsburgh	1	0	0	1.000	45	3
Cincinnati	0	1	0	.000	24	28
Cleveland	0	1	0	.000	24	27
Western Division						
Kansas City	1	0	0	1.000	47	27
L.A. Raiders	1	0	0	1.000	31	0
San Diego	1	0	0	1.000	14	9
Seattle	1	0	0	1.000	28	24
Denver	0	1	0	.000	16	20

National Football Conference

Eastern Division	W	L	T	Pct.	Pts.	OP
Dallas	1	0	0	1.000	44	14
St. Louis	1	0	0	1.000	27	24
N.Y. Giants	1	0	0	1.000	21	0
Philadelphia	0	1	0	.000	0	21
Washington	0	1	0	.000	14	44
Central Division						
Chicago	1	0	0	1.000	38	28
Detroit	1	0	0	1.000	28	27
Minnesota	1	0	0	1.000	28	21
Green Bay	0	1	0	.000	20	26
Tampa Bay	0	1	0	.000	28	38
Western Division						
L.A. Rams	1	0	0	1.000	20	16
Atlanta	0	1	0	.000	27	28
New Orleans	0	1	0	.000	27	47
San Francisco	0	1	0	.000	21	28

NOTE: The 659 points scored this opening day weekend was the highest of any opening day in NFL history.

SUNDAY, SEPTEMBER 8

Los Angeles Rams 20, Denver 16—At Anaheim Stadium, attendance 52,522. Charles White's eight-yard touchdown run with 2:07 remaining sealed the Rams' comeback win. The Broncos led 16-10 at halftime on a pair of John Elway touchdown passes, but the Rams responded with 10 unanswered points. White, replacing holdout Eric Dickerson and injured Barry Redden, rushed for 83 yards on 18 carries in the second half. Dieter Brock, playing in his first NFL game after 11 seasons in the Canadian Football League, completed 16 of 29 passes for 174 yards and one touchdown.

Denver	0	16	0	0	— 16
L.A. Rams	3	7	0	10	— 20

Rams —FG Lansford 37
Den —FG Karlis 24
Rams —D. Hill 2 pass from Brock (Lansford kick)
Den —B. Johnson 28 pass from Elway (kick failed)
Den —Sampson 25 pass from Elway (Karlis kick)
Rams —FG Lansford 33
Rams —White 8 run (Lansford kick)

Detroit 28, Atlanta 27—At Atlanta-Fulton County Stadium, attendance 37,785. Detroit's Eric Hipple survived a rough first quarter to throw three scoring passes and help Darryl Rogers record his first head coaching victory in the NFL. A pair of interceptions thrown by Hipple helped Atlanta build a 21-14 halftime lead. A nine-yard scoring pass from Hipple to Jeff Chadwick, and James Jones's 21-yard scoring run put the Lions ahead 28-21. Two fourth-quarter field goals by Mick Luckhurst brought Atlanta to within a point of the Lions, but that is as close as the Falcons got. Atlanta's Billy (White Shoes) Johnson returned five punts for 58 yards to become the NFL's all-time leader in punt return yardage with 3,012, surpassing Rick Upchurch with 3,008 yards.

Detroit	0	14	14	0	— 28
Atlanta	14	7	0	6	— 27

Atl —Riggs 1 run (Luckhurst kick)
Atl —Brown 12 pass from Bartkowski (Bryan pass from Archer)
Det —J. Jones 8 pass from Hipple (Murray kick)
Det —Chadwick 15 pass from Hipple (Murray kick)
Atl —B. Johnson 35 pass from Bartkowski (Luckhurst kick)
Det —Chadwick 9 pass from Hipple (Murray kick)
Det —J. Jones 21 run (Murray kick)
Atl —FG Luckhurst 46
Atl —FG Luckhurst 31

New England 26, Green Bay 20—At Sullivan Stadium, attendance 49,488. Craig James's 65-yard scoring run with 6:23 left proved to be the winning margin as the Patriots' defense held on to thwart a late Packers rally. Don Blackmon and Andre Tippett each had three sacks as New England's defense limited Green Bay to 206 total yards. Tony Eason completed 21 of 28 passes for 241 yards as the Patriots' offense compiled 410 total yards. James finished with 99 yards rushing on 12 carries. First-year man Derwin Williams topped all receivers in the game with five receptions for 99 yards.

Green Bay	0	6	0	14	— 20
New England	7	12	0	7	— 26

NE —Collins 11 run (Franklin kick)
NE —FG Franklin 34
NE —Safety, Blackmon tackled Dickey in end zone
GB —Ellis 1 run (kick failed)
NE —Jones 3 pass from Eason (Franklin kick)
NE —C. James 65 run (Franklin kick)
GB —Coffman 8 pass from Dickey (Del Greco kick)
GB —Clark 23 run (Del Greco kick)

Pittsburgh 45, Indianapolis 3—At Three Rivers Stadium, attendance 57,279. Mark Malone completed 21 of 30 passes for 287 yards and five touchdowns to lead the Steelers over the Colts. Malone's five scoring passes to Louis Lipps (7, 11, and 16 yards), Rich Erenberg (11), and John Stallworth (6) tied Terry Bradshaw's club record and earned him AFC player of the week honors. Lipps finished with nine receptions for 154 yards. The Steelers' defense limited the Colts to 159 total yards.

Indianapolis	3	0	0	0	— 3
Pittsburgh	7	17	7	14	— 45

Pitt —Lipps 7 pass from Malone (Anderson kick)
Ind —FG Allegre 39
Pitt —Lipps 11 pass from Malone (Anderson kick)
Pitt —FG Anderson 31
Pitt —Erenberg 11 pass from Malone (Anderson kick)
Pitt —Stallworth 6 pass from Malone (Anderson kick)
Pitt —Malone 1 run (Anderson kick)
Pitt —Lipps 16 pass from Malone (Anderson kick)

Kansas City 47, New Orleans 27—At Louisiana Superdome, attendance 57,760. Bill Kenney completed 22 of 34 passes for 397 yards and three touchdowns to lead the Chiefs to victory. Kansas City scored on six of its first eight possessions to take a 26-3 halftime lead. Kenney threw scoring passes to Walt Arnold (31 yards) and Carlos Carson (37 and 19), who finished with 173 yards on eight receptions. The Chiefs generated 504 yards total offense compared to the Saints' 304.

Kansas City	10	16	7	14	— 47
New Orleans	3	0	0	24	— 27

KC —Arnold 31 pass from Kenney (Lowery kick)
KC —FG Lowery 48
NO —FG Andersen 50
KC —FG Lowery 52
KC —Carson 37 pass from Kenney (Lowery kick)
KC —FG Lowery 52
KC —FG Lowery 34
KC —Heard 3 run (Lowery kick)
NO —Brenner 5 pass from Todd (Andersen kick)
NO —W. Wilson 6 pass from Todd (Andersen kick)
NO —FG Andersen 36
KC —Carson 19 pass from Kenney (Lowery kick)
KC —Horton 19 run (Lowery kick)
NO —Groth 56 pass from Todd (Andersen kick)

Houston 26, Miami 23—At Astrodome, attendance 47,656. Mike Rozier's one-yard scoring run with 25 seconds left lifted Houston over defending AFC champion Miami. Rozier's run gave the Oilers the lead for good. The Dolphins had taken a 23-19 lead on a 67-yard scoring pass from Don Strock to Mark Duper. Oilers running back Butch Woolfolk had 120 yards on three receptions, including an 80-yard scoring pass from Warren Moon. Steve Brown, who set up a Houston field goal with one interception and ended a Miami drive in the fourth quarter with another, was named AFC defensive player of the week.

Miami	10	3	3	7	— 23
Houston	0	9	3	14	— 26

Mia —FG Reveiz 33
Mia —Judson 61 interception return (Reveiz kick)
Mia —FG Reveiz 36
Hou —Woolfolk 80 pass from Moon (kick blocked)
Hou —FG Zendejas 35
Mia —FG Reveiz 23
Hou —FG Zendejas 46
Hou —Rozier 3 run (Zendejas kick)
Mia —Duper 67 pass from Strock (Reveiz kick)
Hou —Rozier 1 run (Zendejas kick)

Los Angeles Raiders 31, New York Jets 0—At Memorial Coliseum, attendance 57,123. A pair of Marcus Allen touchdown runs and an aggressive defense helped the Raiders down the Jets 31-0. Allen's scoring runs of one and three yards, along with Jim Plunkett's 41-yard touchdown pass to Dokie Williams, enabled the Raiders to open a 21-0 halftime lead. Los Angeles outgained the Jets 356 to 193 yards and the defense recorded 10 sacks. Safety Stacey Toran returned a third-quarter interception 76 yards for his first NFL touchdown.

N.Y. Jets	0	0	0	0	— 0
L.A. Raiders	7	14	7	3	— 31

Raiders —Allen 1 run (Bahr kick)
Raiders —Williams 41 pass from Plunkett (Bahr kick)
Raiders —Allen 3 run (Bahr kick)
Raiders —Toran 76 interception return (Bahr kick)
Raiders —FG Bahr 20

New York Giants 21, Philadelphia 0—At Giants Stadium, attendance 76,141. The Giants recorded their first shutout since November 23, 1983, in defeating the Eagles 21-0. Two Joe Morris scoring runs (11 and 8 yards) and a Phil Simms to Lionel Manuel 23-yard scoring pass were all the Giants needed as their defense limited the Eagles to 168 total yards. George Martin had three of the Giants' eight sacks. Morris led all rushers with 88 yards on 19 carries. Manuel topped all receivers with four receptions for 92 yards.

Philadelphia	0	0	0	0	— 0
N.Y. Giants	14	0	0	7	— 21

NYG —Manuel 23 pass from Simms (Haji-Sheikh kick)
NYG —Morris 11 run (Haji-Sheikh kick)
NYG —Morris 8 run (Haji-Sheikh kick)

St. Louis 27, Cleveland 24—At Cleveland Stadium, attendance 62,107. Neil O'Donoghue's 35-yard field goal with 5:27 elapsed in overtime, lifted the Cardinals over the Browns. Cleveland had taken a 24-17 lead with 38 seconds left in regulation play on Gary Danielson's 25-yard scoring pass to Ozzie Newsome. St. Louis forced overtime when Neil Lomax completed a five-yard touchdown pass to Pat Tilley with only four seconds left in the fourth quarter. Newsome led all receivers with six receptions for 79 yards.

St. Louis	7	0	3	14	3	— 27
Cleveland	0	3	0	21	0	— 24

StL —Anderson 4 run (O'Donoghue kick)
Clev —FG Bahr 33
StL —FG O'Donoghue 37
StL —Washington 48 interception return (O'Donoghue kick)
Clev —Mack 13 run (Bahr kick)
Clev —Holt 17 pass from Danielson (Bahr kick)
Clev —Newsome 25 pass from Danielson (Bahr kick)
StL —Tilley 5 pass from Lomax (O'Donoghue kick)
StL —FG O'Donoghue 35

San Diego 14, Buffalo 9—At Rich Stadium, attendance 67, 597. Dan Fouts's 30-yard touchdown pass to Eric Sievers and Curtis Adams's one-yard scoring run were all the Chargers needed as the defense held its opponent without a touchdown for the first time in three years. The win upstaged the performance of Buffalo quarterback Vince Ferragamo, who completed 31 of 46 passes for 377 yards. The Bills penetrated the Chargers' 25-yard line five times, but had to settle for three Scott Norwood field goals from 27, 34, and 29 yards. Buffalo's Jerry Butler caught four passes for 160 yards in his first game since October 30, 1983.

San Diego	7	7	0	0	— 14
Buffalo	3	6	0	0	— 9

SD —Adams 1 run (Benirschke kick)
Buff —FG Norwood 27
Buff —FG Norwood 34
SD —Sievers 30 pass from Fouts (Benirschke kick)
Buff —FG Norwood 29

Minnesota 28, San Francisco 21—At Metrodome, attendance 57,375. Ted Brown's 10-yard scoring run with 1:49 remaining in the game capped the Vikings' comeback win over the defending NFL champions. San Francisco took a 21-14 fourth-quarter lead on Joe Montana's 19-yard scoring pass to Roger Craig. However, the Vikings capitalized on two 49ers turnovers within a 1:07 span of the fourth quarter to set up Alfred Anderson's one-yard scoring dive and Brown's go-ahead touchdown. The Vikings' aggressive defense caused seven turnovers to end the 49ers' nine-game regular-season win streak.

San Francisco	7	0	0	14	— 21
Minnesota	0	0	7	21	— 28

SF —Craig 10 run (Wersching kick)
Minn —Rice 1 run (Stenerud kick)
SF —Craig 18 pass from Montana (Wersching kick)
Minn —Jones 44 pass from Kramer (Stenerud kick)
SF —Craig 19 pass from Montana (Wersching kick)
Minn —Anderson 1 run (Stenerud kick)
Minn —Brown 10 run (Stenerud kick)

Seattle 28, Cincinnati 24—At Riverfront Stadium, attendance 51,625. Curt Warner's 11-yard scoring run with 7:07 left in the game lifted the Seahawks over the Bengals. Warner, who was returning to action for the first time since suffering a season-ending knee injury in the first game of the 1984 season, gained 66 yards on 17 carries. Dave Krieg threw scoring passes to Byron Walker (28 yards), Daryl Turner (6), and Charle Young (19) to give the Seahawks a 21-10 halftime edge. But the Bengals, led by running back Larry Kinnebrew who finished with 101 yards on 18 carries, rallied in the third quarter to take a 24-21 lead.

Seattle	7	14	0	7 —	28
Cincinnati	0	10	14	0 —	24

Sea —Walker 28 pass from Krieg (Johnson kick)
Cin —Brooks 15 run (Breech kick)
Sea —Turner 6 pass from Krieg (Johnson kick)
Sea —C. Young 19 pass from Krieg (Johnson kick)
Cin —FG Breech 22
Cin —Brooks 17 pass from Schonert (Breech kick)
Cin —Kinnebrew 9 run (Breech kick)
Sea —Warner 11 run (Johnson kick)

Chicago 38, Tampa Bay 28—At Soldier Field, attendance 57,828. Jim McMahon passed for two touchdowns and rushed for two more as the Bears defeated the Buccaneers. Steve DeBerg's three first-half touchdown passes gave the Buccaneers a 28-17 halftime edge. Chicago took the lead late in the third quarter on McMahon's nine-yard touchdown pass to Matt Suhey. McMahon's decisive one-yard scoring run with 12:32 left in the game, followed a blocked punt by Shaun Gayle. Tampa Bay's James Wilder gained 166 yards on 27 carries, while Chicago's Walter Payton recorded his sixty-fourth career 100-yard rushing game with 120 yards on 17 carries.

Tampa Bay	14	14	0	0 —	28
Chicago	7	10	14	7 —	38

TB —Magee 1 pass from DeBerg (Igwebuike kick)
Chi —McKinnon 21 pass from McMahon (Butler kick)
TB —House 44 pass from DeBerg (Igwebuike kick)
TB —Bell 11 pass from DeBerg (Igwebuike kick)
Chi —McMahon 1 run (Butler kick)
Chi —FG Butler 38
TB —Wilder 3 run (Igwebuike kick)
Chi —Frazier 29 interception return (Butler kick)
Chi —Suhey 9 pass from McMahon (Butler kick)
Chi —McMahon 1 run (Butler kick)

MONDAY, SEPTEMBER 9
Dallas 44, Washington 14—At Texas Stadium, attendance 62,292. Dallas capitalized on seven Washington turnovers to post their largest margin of victory (30 points) ever over the Redskins. Rafael Septien's 53-yard field goal tied his career best and gave the Cowboys a first-period lead they never relinquished. The Cowboys scored 27 points as a result of a fumble recovery and a club-record six interceptions, including two returned for touchdowns by Victor Scott (26 yards) and Dennis Thurman (21).

Washington	0	7	0	7 —	14
Dallas	3	14	13	14 —	44

Dall —FG Septien 53
Dall —Newsome 1 run (Septien kick)
Wash —Riggins 1 run (Moseley kick)
Dall —Renfro 55 pass from D. White (Septien kick)
Dall —FG Septien 39
Dall —FG Septien 43
Dall —Dorsett 9 run (Septien kick)
Dall —Scott 26 interception return (Septien kick)
Wash —Didier 19 pass from Theismann (Moseley kick)
Dall —Thurman 21 interception return (Septien kick)

SECOND WEEK SUMMARIES

STANDINGS

American Football Conference

Eastern Division	W	L	T	Pct.	Pts.	OP
Miami	1	1	0	.500	53	39
New England	1	1	0	.500	33	40
N.Y. Jets	1	1	0	.500	42	34
Buffalo	0	2	0	.000	12	56
Indianapolis	0	2	0	.000	16	75
Central Division						
Cleveland	1	1	0	.500	41	34
Houston	1	1	0	.500	39	39
Pittsburgh	1	1	0	.500	52	20
Cincinnati	0	2	0	.000	51	69
Western Division						
Kansas City	2	0	0	1.000	83	47
Seattle	2	0	0	1.000	77	59
Denver	1	1	0	.500	50	43
L.A. Raiders	1	1	0	.500	51	36
San Diego	1	1	0	.500	49	58

National Football Conference

Eastern Division	W	L	T	Pct.	Pts.	OP
St. Louis	2	0	0	1.000	68	51
Dallas	1	1	0	.500	65	40
N.Y. Giants	1	1	0	.500	41	23
Washington	1	1	0	.500	30	57
Philadelphia	0	2	0	.000	6	38
Central Division						
Chicago	2	0	0	1.000	58	35
Detroit	2	0	0	1.000	54	48
Minnesota	2	0	0	1.000	59	37
Green Bay	1	1	0	.500	43	46
Tampa Bay	0	2	0	.000	44	69
Western Division						
L.A. Rams	2	0	0	1.000	37	22
San Francisco	1	1	0	.500	56	44
Atlanta	0	2	0	.000	43	63
New Orleans	0	2	0	.000	50	81

NOTE: Paid attendance of 880,013 this weekend was the tenth-highest weekend in NFL history.

THURSDAY, SEPTEMBER 12
Kansas City 36, Los Angeles Raiders 20—At Arrowhead Stadium, attendance 72,686. Bill Kenney passed for two touchdowns and Nick Lowery kicked five field goals to lead the Chiefs over the Raiders. Trailing 14-12 at halftime, Kansas City scored 17 points in the third quarter on Lowery's 21-yard field goal and Kenney scoring passes to Carlos Carson (25 yards) and Stephone Paige (5) to take a 29-14 lead. Lowery's other field goals were from 39, 22, 42, and 58 yards. Kenney connected on 18 of 38 passes for 259 yards, including five to Carson for 118 yards. Cornerback Albert Lewis recovered a Raiders fumble in the end zone to finish the Chiefs' scoring.

L.A. Raiders	7	7	0	6 —	20
Kansas City	3	9	17	7 —	36

Raiders —Hawkins 1 run (Bahr kick)
KC —FG Lowery 39
KC —FG Lowery 22
KC —FG Lowery 42
Raiders —Christensen 3 pass from Plunkett (Bahr kick)
KC —FG Lowery 58
KC —FG Lowery 21
KC —Carson 25 pass from Kenney (Lowery kick)
KC —Paige 5 pass from Kenney (Lowery kick)

SUNDAY, SEPTEMBER 15
San Francisco 35, Atlanta 16—At Candlestick Park, attendance 58,923. Roger Craig rushed for 107 yards and a pair of touchdowns as the 49ers overpowered the Falcons. Trailing 10-0 at halftime, Craig scored on a nine-yard run and Joe Montana added a one-yard dive to give the 49ers a 14-10 advantage. Montana completed 19 of 26 passes for 206 yards and a touchdown to move into second place in passing yards (16,078) and touchdown passes (109) on the 49ers' all-time list. Craig's efforts marked his first 100-yard rushing game in the NFL and earned him NFC offensive player of the week honors.

Atlanta	7	3	3	3 —	16
San Francisco	0	0	14	21 —	35

Atl —Allen 17 pass from Bartkowski (Luckhurst kick)
Atl —FG Luckhurst 24
SF —Craig 9 run (Wersching kick)
Atl —FG Luckhurst 48
SF —Montana 1 run (Wersching kick)
SF —Clark 9 pass from Montana (Wersching kick)
SF —Craig 62 run (Wersching kick)
Atl —FG Luckhurst 29
SF —Tyler 4 run (Wersching kick)

New York Jets 42, Buffalo 3—At Giants Stadium, attendance 63,449. Freeman McNeil rushed for a club-record 192 yards on 18 carries and Ken O'Brien threw two touchdown passes to highlight the Jets' victory. New York scored 21 unanswered points in the second quarter after Buffalo had taken a 3-0 lead on Scott Norwood's 32-yard field goal. A pair of McNeil scoring runs from 6 and 13 yards and O'Brien's seven-yard scoring pass to Kurt Sohn, were all the points the Jets needed as they recorded their third straight win over the Bills. Kerry Glenn returned a third-quarter interception 15 yards for his first NFL touchdown.

Buffalo	3	0	0	0 —	3
N.Y. Jets	0	21	14	7 —	42

Buff —FG Norwood 32
NYJ —McNeil 6 run (Leahy kick)
NYJ —Sohn 7 pass from O'Brien (Leahy kick)
NYJ —McNeil 13 run (Leahy kick)
NYJ —Paige 2 pass from O'Brien (Leahy kick)
NYJ —Glenn 15 interception return (Leahy kick)
NYJ —Paige 2 run (Leahy kick)

St. Louis 41, Cincinnati 27—At Busch Memorial Stadium, attendance 46,321. Neil Lomax completed 17 of 31 passes for 250 yards and two touchdowns as the Cardinals overpowered the Bengals. St. Louis took a 17-14 halftime lead on the last play of the second quarter on Neil O'Donoghue's 46-yard field goal. Perry Harrington's one-yard scoring run with 2:57 remaining in the game clinched the Cardinals' first-ever victory over the Bengals. Roy Green finished with six catches for 68 yards to extend his consecutive games streak with at least one reception to 58.

Cincinnati	7	7	3	10 —	27
St. Louis	7	10	10	14 —	41

Cin —Jennings 4 pass from Anderson (Breech kick)
StL —Ferrell 27 pass from Lomax (O'Donoghue kick)
Cin —Brown 44 pass from Anderson (Breech kick)
StL —Anderson 1 run (O'Donoghue kick)
StL —FG O'Donoghue 46
StL —Green 25 pass from Lomax (O'Donoghue kick)
Cin —FG Breech 33
StL —FG O'Donoghue 49
Cin —FG Breech 47
StL —Mitchell 1 run (O'Donoghue kick)
StL —Harrington 1 run (O'Donoghue kick)
Cin —Kinnebrew 29 pass from Esiason (Breech kick)

Detroit 26, Dallas 21—At Pontiac Silverdome, attendance 72,985. William Gay and James Harrell spearheaded a tenacious Detroit defense which held Dallas scoreless the first three quarters en route to victory. Gay's first-half interception and fumble recovery set up two scores to give Detroit a 13-0 halftime lead. Harrell's third-period interception set up James Jones's two-yard scoring run to put Detroit ahead 26-0. The Cowboys outgained the Lions in total yards 545 to 200, but turned the ball over five times.

Dallas	0	0	0	21 —	21
Detroit	10	3	13	0 —	26

Det —FG Murray 34
Det —Chadwick 21 pass from Hipple (Murray kick)
Det —FG Murray 46
Det —Hipple 1 run (kick failed)
Det —J. Jones 2 run (Murray kick)
Dall —Hill 11 pass from Hogeboom (Septien kick)
Dall —Hill 44 pass from Hogeboom (Septien kick)
Dall —Hogeboom 2 run (Septien kick)

Washington 16, Houston 13—At Robert F. Kennedy Stadium, attendance 53,553. John Riggins and George Rogers combined for 162 yards rushing to enable the Redskins to squeak by the Oilers. Washington opened a 16-0 first-quarter lead on Joe Theismann's 17-yard touchdown pass to Calvin Muhammad, Rogers's 31-yard scoring run, and Mark Moseley's 34-yard field goal. The Oilers responded with 13 straight points. They then pulled within three points on Tony Zendejas's 35-yard field goal with 9:45 remaining in the third quarter, but never got any closer.

Houston	0	10	3	0 —	13
Washington	13	3	0	0 —	16

Wash —Muhammad 17 pass from Theismann (Moseley kick)
Wash —Rogers 31 run (kick failed)
Wash —FG Moseley 34
Hou —FG Zendejas 44
Hou —Hill 2 pass from Moon (Zendejas kick)
Hou —FG Zendejas 35

Miami 30, Indianapolis 13—At Orange Bowl, attendance 53,693. Dan Marino completed 29 of 48 passes for 329 yards and two touchdowns to lead the Dolphins over the Colts. Miami took a 13-7 halftime lead on Marino's six-yard scoring pass to Mark Clayton. Tony Nathan's 21-yard touchdown run early in the fourth quarter gave the Dolphins a 23-7 lead and clinched their tenth consecutive win over the Colts. Miami outgained the Colts 486 to 298 total yards.

Indianapolis	0	7	0	6 —	13
Miami	3	10	3	14 —	30

Mia —FG Reveiz 22
Mia —FG Reveiz 25
Ind —Beach 2 pass from Pagel (Allegre kick)
Mia —Clayton 6 pass from Marino (Reveiz kick)
Mia —FG Reveiz 40
Mia —Nathan 21 run (Reveiz kick)
Mia —Moore 3 pass from Marino (Reveiz kick)
Ind —Wonsley 1 run (kick blocked)

Los Angeles Rams 17, Philadelphia 6—At Veterans Stadium, attendance 60,920. Charles White's 17-yard touchdown run with 9:39 left helped lift the Rams over the Eagles. Henry Ellard's 80-yard punt return for a touchdown just 2:09 into the game gave the Rams a lead they never relinquished. White, who gained 144 yards on 36 carries for his first NFL 100-yard rushing game, broke Eric Dickerson's club single-game record of 34 rushing attempts. The Rams' defense victimized the Eagles for seven turnovers.

L.A. Rams	10	0	0	7 —	17
Philadelphia	3	3	0	0 —	6

Rams —Ellard 80 punt return (Lansford kick)
Rams —FG Lansford 33
Phil —FG McFadden 50
Phil —FG McFadden 45
Rams —White 17 run (Lansford kick)

Minnesota 31, Tampa Bay 16—At Tampa Stadium, attendance 46,188. The Vikings capitalized on four Buccaneers turnovers to post their second victory. Joey Browner's 15-yard interception return for a touchdown gave the Vikings a 17-3 first-half advantage. Following the Buccaneers' fourth-quarter score, Tommy Kramer hooked up with Ted Brown on a 54-yard touchdown pass to clinch the win. James Wilder rushed for 113 yards on 22 carries to become the Buccaneers' all-time leading rusher with 3,157 yards.

Minnesota	7	10	7	7 —	31
Tampa Bay	0	3	7	6 —	16

Minn —Rice 2 run (Stenerud kick)
Minn —FG Stenerud 31
TB —FG Igwebuike 25
Minn —J. Browner 15 interception return (Stenerud kick)
Minn —Anderson 1 run (Stenerud kick)
TB —Wilder 1 run (Igwebuike kick)
TB —J. Bell 12 pass from DeBerg (kick failed)
Minn —T. Brown 54 pass from Kramer (Stenerud kick)

Chicago 20, New England 7—At Soldier Field, attendance 60,533. The Bears took advantage of four Patriots miscues to defeat New England and maintain a share of first place in the NFC Central. Jim McMahon's 32-yard touchdown pass to Dennis McKinnon and Kevin Butler's 21-yard field goal gave the Bears a 10-0 halftime edge. Mike Singletary registered three of the Bears' six sacks. Patriots quarterback Tony Eason's 90-yard scoring strike to Craig James in the fourth quarter prevented a Bears shutout. Chicago held a 37:25 to 22:35 time of possession advantage over New England.

New England	0	0	0	7	— 7
Chicago	7	3	10	0	— 20

Chi — McKinnon 32 pass from McMahon (Butler kick)
Chi — FG Butler 21
Chi — Suhey 1 run (Butler kick)
Chi — FG Butler 28
NE — James 90 pass from Eason (Franklin kick)

Denver 34, New Orleans 23—At Mile High Stadium, attendance 74,488. John Elway completed 28 of 40 passes for 353 yards and four touchdowns as the Broncos cruised past the Saints. Denver took a 24-6 first-half lead behind three Elway scoring passes to Butch Johnson (65 yards), Clint Sampson (26), and Gene Lang (10). Karl Mecklenburg led the defense with four of the team's six sacks. Rich Karlis kicked two field goals from 43 and 48 yards to extend his consecutive game streak to seven.

New Orleans	0	6	10	7	— 23
Denver	7	17	7	3	— 34

Den — B. Johnson 65 pass from Elway (Karlis kick)
Den — Sampson 26 pass from Elway (Karlis kick)
Den — Lang 10 pass from Elway (Karlis kick)
NO — Groth 39 pass from D. Wilson (kick failed)
Den — FG Karlis 43
NO — FG Andersen 55
Den — Kay 2 pass from Elway (Karlis kick)
NO — Hardy 13 pass from D. Wilson (Andersen kick)
Den — FG Karlis 48
NO — Gajan 3 run (Andersen kick)

Green Bay 23, N.Y. Giants 20—At Lambeau Field, attendance 56,144. Lynn Dickey completed 15 of 26 passes for 188 yards to guide the Packers to a 23-20 comeback win over the Giants. Eddie Lee Ivery's one-yard run with 3:07 left capped a 75-yard drive and put the Packers ahead for good. Dickey, harassed for most of the game by the Giants' outstanding defense, completed passes of 22 yards to Phillip Epps and 34 yards to James Lofton in the final drive to set up the decisive score. Ezra Johnson had two of the Packers' five sacks. Ali Haji-Sheikh's 47-yard field-goal attempt to tie the game with 1:07 left fell short.

N.Y. Giants	0	6	7	7	— 20
Green Bay	10	7	0	6	— 23

GB — FG Del Greco 40
GB — Clark 1 run (Del Greco kick)
NYG — FG Haji-Sheikh 23
NYG — FG Haji-Sheikh 52
GB — Coffman 1 pass from Dickey (Del Greco kick)
NYG — Hasselbeck 20 pass from Simms (Haji-Sheikh kick)
NYG — Manuel 5 pass from Simms (Haji-Sheikh kick)
GB — Ivery 1 run (kick failed)

Seattle 49, San Diego 35—At San Diego Jack Murphy Stadium, attendance 54,420. Dave Krieg completed 22 of 32 passes for 307 yards and five touchdowns to lead the Seahawks over the Chargers. Seattle came back from a 23-14 halftime deficit by scoring 28 third-quarter points. Daryl Turner's third touchdown of the day, a 30-yard pass from Krieg, gave the Seahawks a 35-29 lead with 2:22 remaining in the third period. Turner also had scoring catches of 34, 15, and 7 yards and finished with seven catches for 121 yards and four touchdowns. He shared AFC offensive player of the week honors with teammate Krieg, whose five scoring passes tied his club record.

Seattle	7	7	28	7	— 49
San Diego	10	13	6	6	— 35

SD — James 7 pass from Fouts (Thomas kick)
SD — FG Thomas 21
Sea — Turner 34 pass from Krieg (Johnson kick)
Sea — Warner 3 run (Johnson kick)
SD — Joiner 18 pass from Fouts (kick blocked)
SD — Chandler 20 pass from Fouts (Thomas kick)
Sea — Largent 6 pass from Krieg (Johnson kick)
SD — Sievers 5 pass from Fouts (kick failed)
Sea — Turner 15 pass from Krieg (Johnson kick)
Sea — Turner 30 pass from Krieg (Johnson kick)
Sea — Warner 1 run (Johnson kick)
Sea — Turner 7 pass from Krieg (Johnson kick)
SD — Joiner 1 pass from Herrmann (kick blocked)

MONDAY, SEPTEMBER 16

Cleveland 17, Pittsburgh 7—At Cleveland Stadium, attendance 79,042. Gary Danielson completed 18 of 30 passes for 206 yards and a touchdown to guide the Browns past the Steelers. Danielson's 17-yard scoring strike to rookie Fred Banks gave Cleveland a 7-0 halftime advantage. Matt Bahr extended his consecutive field goals streak to 14 with an 18-yarder in the third quarter. Earnest Byner's 21-yard touchdown run with 2:37 left sealed the win. Cleveland's defense held Pittsburgh to 54 yards rushing.

Pittsburgh	0	0	0	7	— 7
Cleveland	0	7	3	7	— 17

Clev — Banks 17 pass from Danielson (Bahr kick)
Clev — FG Bahr 18
Pitt — Stallworth 6 pass from Malone (Anderson kick)
Clev — Byner 21 run (Bahr kick)

THIRD WEEK SUMMARIES

STANDINGS

American Football Conference

Eastern Division	W	L	T	Pct.	Pts.	OP
Miami	2	1	0	.667	84	39
New England	2	1	0	.667	50	54
N.Y. Jets	2	1	0	.667	66	37
Indianapolis	1	2	0	.333	30	81
Buffalo	0	3	0	.000	26	73
Central Division						
Pittsburgh	2	1	0	.667	72	20
Cleveland	1	2	0	.333	48	54
Houston	1	2	0	.333	39	59
Cincinnati	0	3	0	.000	92	113
Western Division						
Denver	2	1	0	.667	94	71
Kansas City	2	1	0	.667	83	78
San Diego	2	1	0	.667	93	99
Seattle	2	1	0	.667	101	94
L.A. Raiders	1	2	0	.333	61	70

National Football Conference

Eastern Division	W	L	T	Pct.	Pts.	OP
Dallas	2	1	0	.667	85	47
N.Y. Giants	2	1	0	.667	68	40
St. Louis	2	1	0	.667	85	78
Philadelphia	1	2	0	.333	25	44
Washington	1	2	0	.333	36	76
Central Division						
Chicago	3	0	0	1.000	91	59
Detroit	2	1	0	.667	60	62
Minnesota	2	1	0	.667	83	70
Green Bay	1	2	0	.333	46	70
Tampa Bay	0	3	0	.000	57	89
Western Division						
L.A. Rams	3	0	0	1.000	72	46
San Francisco	2	1	0	.667	90	54
New Orleans	1	2	0	.333	70	94
Atlanta	0	3	0	.000	71	107

THURSDAY, SEPTEMBER 19

Chicago 33, Minnesota 24—At Metrodome, attendance 61,242. With Chicago trailing Minnesota 17-9 midway through the third quarter, Jim McMahon came off the bench and threw three touchdown passes within a span of 6:40 to highlight the Bears' victory. McMahon's scoring passes to Willie Gault (70 yards) and Dennis McKinnon (25 and 43) gave the Bears a 30-17 advantage going into the fourth period. Chicago's defense then stiffened to secure the win. Gault finished with six catches for a career-high 146 yards. Wilber Marshall had two (an interception and fumble recovery) of the Bears' five takeaways.

Chicago	3	3	24	3	— 33
Minnesota	3	7	7	7	— 24

Chi — FG Butler 24
Minn — FG Stenerud 25
Chi — FG Butler 19
Minn — Carter 14 pass from Kramer (Stenerud kick)
Chi — FG Butler 34
Minn — Jones 9 pass from Kramer (Stenerud kick)
Chi — Gault 70 pass from McMahon (Butler kick)
Chi — McKinnon 25 pass from McMahon (Butler kick)
Chi — McKinnon 43 pass from McMahon (Butler kick)
Minn — Carter 57 pass from Kramer (Stenerud kick)
Chi — FG Butler 31

SUNDAY, SEPTEMBER 22

Dallas 20, Cleveland 7—At Texas Stadium, attendance 61,456. Danny White passed for one touchdown and caught another in the Cowboys' 20-7 win over the Browns. Leading 3-0, White passed 10 yards to Doug Cosbie for a score and with 10 seconds remaining in the third period, running back James Jones lofted a 12-yard scoring pass to White to give the Cowboys a commanding 17-0 advantage. Rafael Septien added a pair of field goals (from 39 and 33 yards) to extend his consecutive game scoring streak to 121.

Cleveland	0	0	0	7	— 7
Dallas	3	7	7	3	— 20

Dall — FG Septien 39
Dall — Cosbie 10 pass from D. White (Septien kick)
Dall — D. White 12 pass from J. Jones (Septien kick)
Dall — FG Septien 33
Clev — Byner 1 run (Bahr kick)

Denver 44, Atlanta 28—At Atlanta-Fulton County Stadium, attendance 37,903. John Elway threw for three touchdowns and Rich Karlis kicked three field goals from 42, 25, and 47 yards to power the Broncos over the Falcons. Elway completed 19 of 38 passes for 291 yards, including scoring tosses to Vance Johnson (63 yards), Clint Sampson (17), and Butch Johnson (31). Gene Lang finished a four-play, 67-yard drive with a two-yard scoring run to give the Broncos a 34-28 lead with 13:32 left. Atlanta's Billy (White Shoes) Johnson caught seven passes for 110 yards and two touchdowns (6 and 62 yards).

Denver	7	14	6	17	— 44
Atlanta	7	7	14	0	— 28

Den — V. Johnson 63 pass from Elway (Karlis kick)
Atl — Rade 38 interception return (Luckhurst kick)
Den — Sampson 17 pass from Elway (Karlis kick)
Atl — Riggs 1 run (Luckhurst kick)
Den — Winder 1 run (Karlis kick)
Atl — B. Johnson 62 pass from Bartkowski (Luckhurst kick)
Den — FG Karlis 42
Den — FG Karlis 25
Atl — B. Johnson 6 pass from Bartkowski (Luckhurst kick)
Den — Lang 2 run (Karlis kick)
Den — FG Karlis 47
Den — B. Johnson 31 pass from Elway (Karlis kick)

Indianapolis 14, Detroit 6—At Hoosier Dome, attendance 60,042. George Wonsley, making his first NFL start, rushed for 170 yards to lead the Colts over the Lions. Frank Middleton's one-yard scoring run with 46 seconds left sealed the victory for Indianapolis. The Colts controlled the tempo of the game as they outgained the Lions 355 to 204 total yards and maintained a 35:08 to 24:52 time of possession advantage. Wonsley's 170-yard total was the fifth-highest single-game rushing total in Colts history.

Detroit	0	3	3	0	— 6
Indianapolis	7	0	0	7	— 14

Ind — Gill 1 run (Allegre kick)
Det — FG Murray 37
Det — FG Murray 35
Ind — Middleton 1 run (Allegre kick)

Pittsburgh 20, Houston 0—At Three Rivers Stadium, attendance 58,752. Mark Malone threw two touchdown passes to Louis Lipps (25 and 5 yards), and Gary Anderson kicked a pair of field goals from 37 and 38 yards as the Steelers blanked the Oilers. Pittsburgh rushed for 233 yards to give it a 335 to 134 total yardage advantage. Lipps finished with six receptions for 98 yards. The shutout marked the Steelers' first since November 29, 1981.

Houston	0	0	0	0	— 0
Pittsburgh	14	3	3	0	— 20

Pitt — Lipps 25 pass from Malone (Anderson kick)
Pitt — Lipps 5 pass from Malone (Anderson kick)
Pitt — FG Anderson 37
Pitt — FG Anderson 38

Miami 31, Kansas City 0—At Orange Bowl, attendance 69,791. Dan Marino fired two third-quarter touchdown passes to lead the Dolphins over the Chiefs. After a scoreless first half, Marino completed scoring strikes to Bruce Hardy (nine yards) and Woody Bennett (27) on Miami's first two series of the second half. The Dolphins' defense shut down the Chiefs' offense, which was averaging 41.5 points per game, to record their first shutout since blanking the Colts 37-0 on November 20, 1983. Ron Davenport scored his first two NFL touchdowns on a pair of fourth-period runs from one and three yards.

Kansas City	0	0	0	0	— 0
Miami	0	0	14	17	— 31

Mia — Hardy 9 pass from Marino (Reveiz kick)
Mia — Bennett 27 pass from Marino (Reveiz kick)
Mia — Davenport 1 run (Reveiz kick)
Mia — Davenport 3 run (Reveiz kick)
Mia — FG Reveiz 37

New England 17, Buffalo 14—At Rich Stadium, attendance 45,320. Irving Fryar's 85-yard punt return early in the third quarter proved to be the decisive score as the Patriots downed the Bills. Craig James's five-yard option pass to Tony Collins gave New England a 10-7 halftime lead. The Patriots' defense held the Bills to 55 rushing yards. Fryar's punt return for a touchdown was the Patriots' first since November 2, 1980.

New England	3	7	7	0	— 17
Buffalo	0	7	0	7	— 14

NE — FG Franklin 32
Buff — Bell 16 pass from Ferragamo (Norwood kick)
NE — Collins 5 pass from C. James (Franklin kick)
NE — Fryar 85 punt return (Franklin kick)
Buff — Reed 18 pass from Ferragamo (Norwood kick)

New York Jets 24, Green Bay 3—At Milwaukee County Stadium, attendance 53,667. Running back Tony Paige ran for one touchdown and caught a pass for another as the Jets overpowered the Packers. New York took command of the game on Ken O'Brien's five-yard scoring pass to Paige with 8:01 left in the first period. The Jets' defense, led by linebacker Lance Mehl, registered five sacks and had three turnovers. Nose tackle Tom Baldwin returned a fumble nine yards for a touchdown in the fourth quarter to finish the Jets' scoring.

N.Y. Jets	7	0	10	7	— 24
Green Bay	3	0	0	0	— 3

NYJ — Paige 5 pass from O'Brien (Leahy kick)
GB — FG Del Greco 39
NYJ — FG Leahy 25
NYJ — Paige 11 run (Leahy kick)
NYJ — Baldwin 9 fumble recovery return (Leahy kick)

Philadelphia 19, Washington 6—At Robert F. Kennedy Stadium, attendance 53,748. Rookie quarterback Randall Cunningham passed for 187 yards and rushed for 60 more to lead the Eagles over the Redskins. Wes Hopkins's 42-yard fourth-quarter fumble recovery set up Cunningham's 17-yard touchdown pass to Earnest Jackson, which gave the Eagles a commanding 17-6 lead. The Redskins were held without a touchdown for the first time since December 12, 1982.

Philadelphia	3	3	3	10	—	19
Washington	0	6	0	0	—	6

Phil —FG McFadden 41
Phil —FG McFadden 36
Wash —FG Moseley 41
Wash —FG Moseley 26
Phil —FG McFadden 37
Phil —E. Jackson 17 pass from Cunningham (McFadden kick)
Phil —FG McFadden 34

New York Giants 27, St. Louis 17—At Giants Stadium, attendance 74,987. Phil Simms completed 10 of 23 passes for 167 yards and three touchdowns to lift the Giants over the Cardinals. New York answered a 10-10 halftime tie with Jess Atkinson's 19-yard field goal and a pair of Simms scoring passes to Phil McConkey (20 yards) and Bobby Johnson (16) to take a 27-10 lead. Johnson also had an eight-yard scoring catch for his first two receptions of the season. McConkey's touchdown was the first of his career.

St. Louis	7	3	0	7	—	17
N.Y. Giants	7	3	10	7	—	27

NYG —Johnson 8 pass from Simms (Atkinson kick)
StL —Green 39 pass from Lomax (O'Donoghue kick)
NYG —FG Atkinson 20
StL —FG O'Donoghue 21
NYG —FG Atkinson 19
NYG —McConkey 20 pass from Simms (Atkinson kick)
NYG —Johnson 16 pass from Simms (Atkinson kick)
StL —Ferrell 15 pass from Lomax (O'Donoghue kick)

San Diego 44, Cincinnati 41—At Riverfront Stadium, attendance 52,270. Lionel James became the sixteenth player in NFL history to rush (127 yards on 12 carries) and receive (118 yards on 5 catches) for over 100 yards in the same game, as the Chargers defeated Cincinnati in a shootout, 44-41. Dan Fouts connected with James on a 60-yard touchdown to tie the game 41-41 with 3:45 left. Following a Chuck Ehin fumble recovery, Bob Thomas kicked a 34-yard field goal with four seconds left to provide the margin of victory.

San Diego	3	17	14	10	—	44
Cincinnati	7	6	21	7	—	41

SD —FG Thomas 20
Cin —Collinsworth 18 pass from Esiason (Breech kick)
SD —Sievers 4 pass from Fouts (Thomas kick)
SD —Sievers 5 pass from Fouts (Thomas kick)
Cin —Brooks 1 run (kick failed)
SD —FG Thomas 28
Cin —Collinsworth 16 pass from Esiason (Breech kick)
SD —Holohan 3 pass from Fouts (Thomas kick)
Cin —Kinnebrew 4 run (Breech kick)
Cin —Jennings 11 pass from Esiason (Breech kick)
SD —James 56 run (Thomas kick)
Cin —Kinnebrew 8 run (Breech kick)
SD —James 60 pass from Fouts (Thomas kick)
SD —FG Thomas 34

San Francisco 34, Los Angeles Raiders 10—At Memorial Coliseum, attendance 87,006. Joe Montana threw for two touchdowns and the 49ers' defense shut down the Raiders' explosive attack en route to victory. Montana's 14-yard scoring pass to Dwight Clark with 2:27 left in the third period gave the 49ers a 20-3 edge to put the game away. San Francisco's defense finished with nine sacks; Dwaine Board accounted for four. Milt McColl scored his first NFL touchdown on a 28-yard fumble recovery. Raiders quarterback Jim Plunkett had to leave the game with an injured shoulder.

San Francisco	10	3	14	7	—	34
L.A. Raiders	3	0	0	7	—	10

SF —Craig 20 pass from Montana (Wersching kick)
Raiders —FG Bahr 24
SF —FG Wersching 22
SF —FG Wersching 26
SF —Clark 14 pass from Montana (Wersching kick)
SF —McColl 28 fumble recovery return (Wersching kick)
Raiders —Wilson 1 run (Bahr kick)
SF —Ring 9 run (Wersching kick)

New Orleans 20, Tampa Bay 13—At Louisiana Superdome, attendance 45,320. The Saints won their first game of the season behind the passing of Dave Wilson, who completed 16 of 25 for 246 yards and two touchdowns. Wilson's two scoring passes to Larry Hardy (23 yards) and Hoby Brenner (three) gave the Saints a 17-6 halftime lead. Morten Andersen kicked a 40-yard field goal and Frank Wattelet's interception clinched the win for the Saints. Tampa Bay's James Wilder finished with 114 yards on 26 carries.

Tampa Bay	0	6	0	7	—	13
New Orleans	7	10	3	0	—	20

NO —Hardy 23 pass from D. Wilson (Andersen kick)
TB —FG Igwebuike 38
NO —Brenner 3 pass from D. Wilson (Andersen kick)
TB —FG Igwebuike 51
NO —FG Andersen 37
NO —FG Andersen 40
TB —Carter 22 pass from DeBerg (Igwebuike kick)

MONDAY, SEPTEMBER 23

Los Angeles Rams 35, Seattle 24—At Kingdome, attendance 63,292. Eric Dickerson, appearing in his first game after a 47-day contract holdout, rushed for 150 yards on 31 carries and scored three touchdowns to lead the Rams over the Seahawks. Dickerson's third scoring run of the game, a 15-yarder with 3:24 left, gave the Rams a 28-17 advantage. Johnnie Johnson returned an interception 27 yards for a score to conclude the Rams' scoring. Los Angeles's defense recorded seven sacks and had two interceptions.

L.A. Rams	7	0	14	14	—	35
Seattle	0	7	3	14	—	24

Rams —Dickerson 1 run (Lansford kick)
Sea —Brown 28 interception return (Johnson kick)
Rams —Duckworth 19 pass from Brock (Lansford kick)
Rams —Dickerson 2 run (Lansford kick)
Sea —FG Johnson 26
Sea —Greene 21 pass from Krieg (Johnson kick)
Rams —Dickerson 15 run (Lansford kick)
Rams —Johnson 27 interception return (Lansford kick)
Sea —Turner 37 pass from Gilbert (Johnson kick)

FOURTH WEEK SUMMARIES

STANDINGS

American Football Conference

Eastern Division	W	L	T	Pct.	Pts.	OP
Miami	3	1	0	.750	114	65
N.Y. Jets	3	1	0	.750	91	57
New England	2	2	0	.500	70	89
Indianapolis	1	3	0	.250	50	106
Buffalo	0	4	0	.000	46	100
Central Division						
Cleveland	2	2	0	.500	69	61
Pittsburgh	2	2	0	.500	96	57
Cincinnati	1	3	0	.250	129	137
Houston	1	3	0	.250	49	76
Western Division						
Kansas City	3	1	0	.750	111	85
Denver	2	2	0	.500	120	101
L.A. Raiders	2	2	0	.500	96	90
San Diego	2	2	0	.500	100	120
Seattle	2	2	0	.500	108	122

National Football Conference

Eastern Division	W	L	T	Pct.	Pts.	OP
Dallas	3	1	0	.750	102	57
N.Y. Giants	3	1	0	.750	84	50
St. Louis	3	1	0	.750	128	106
Philadelphia	1	3	0	.250	35	60
Washington	1	3	0	.250	46	121
Central Division						
Chicago	4	0	0	1.000	136	69
Detroit	3	1	0	.750	90	71
Minnesota	3	1	0	.750	110	90
Green Bay	1	3	0	.250	74	113
Tampa Bay	0	4	0	.000	66	119
Western Division						
L.A. Rams	4	0	0	1.000	89	52
New Orleans	2	2	0	.500	90	111
San Francisco	2	2	0	.500	107	74
Atlanta	0	4	0	.000	77	124

SUNDAY, OCTOBER 6

Los Angeles Rams 17, Atlanta 6—At Anaheim Stadium, attendance 49,870. Dieter Brock completed 16 of 20 passes for 216 yards and two touchdowns to lead the Rams over the Falcons. Brock's 64-yard touchdown pass to Henry Ellard and Mike Lansford's career-best 52-yard field goal gave the Rams a 10-3 first-half lead. Ellard finished with five catches for 123 yards. Brock was named NFC offensive player of the week.

Atlanta	0	3	3	0	—	6
L.A. Rams	0	10	7	0	—	17

Atl —FG Luckhurst 44
Rams —Ellard 64 pass from Brock (Lansford kick)
Rams —FG Lansford 52
Atl —FG Luckhurst 47
Rams —Duckworth 13 pass from Brock (Lansford kick)

Cleveland 21, San Diego 7—At San Diego Jack Murphy Stadium, attendance 52,107. Kevin Mack rushed for 130 yards on 16 carries and Gary Danielson threw for two touchdowns as the Browns defeated the Chargers. San Diego took a 7-0 lead on Dan Fouts's 54-yard scoring pass to Jesse Bendross. Mack then countered for the Browns with a 10-yard scoring run in the second period to tie the score at 7-7. Danielson hooked up with Earnest Byner (11 yards) and Mack (10) to complete the Browns' scoring. Cleveland gained a season-high 275 yards rushing to outgain San Diego in total yards 440 to 275. Reggie Camp had three sacks to lead the Browns' defense.

Cleveland	0	7	7	7	—	21
San Diego	7	0	0	0	—	7

SD —Bendross 54 pass from Fouts (Thomas kick)
Clev —Mack 10 run (Bahr kick)
Clev —Byner 11 pass from Danielson (Bahr kick)
Clev —Mack 10 pass from Danielson (Bahr kick)

Dallas 17, Houston 10—At Astrodome, attendance 39,686. Tony Dorsett ran for 159 yards and Danny White fired a pair of touchdown passes to lead the Cowboys past the Oilers. Dallas took a 7-0 halftime advantage on White's seven-yard strike to Timmy Newsome. White's one-yard scoring pass to Fred Cornwell with 1:47 left capped a five-play, 75-yard drive to give the Cowboys the lead for good. Dallas' defense victimized the Oilers for an NFL record-tying 12 sacks and four interceptions.

Dallas	7	0	3	7	—	17
Houston	0	0	10	0	—	10

Dall —Newsome 7 pass from D. White (Septien kick)
Dall —FG Septien 35
Hou —Hill 57 pass from Moon (Zendejas kick)
Hou —FG Zendejas 33
Dall —Cornwell 1 pass from D. White (Septien kick)

St. Louis 43, Green Bay 28—At Busch Memorial Stadium, attendance 48,598. Neil Lomax threw three touchdown passes and Ottis Anderson ran for 104 yards on 20 carries as the Cardinals overpowered the Packers. St. Louis took a 19-0 halftime lead on Earl Ferrell's three-yard run, Anderson's one-yard plunge, Neil O'Donoghue's 22-yard field goal, and a safety. Lomax connected with Stump Mitchell (39 yards), Pat Tilley (11), and Roy Green (37) on second-half scoring passes to further the onslaught. The Packers' Jessie Clark registered his first NFL 100-yard rushing game with 112 yards on nine carries, while Anderson's 100-yard effort was the thirty-fourth of his career.

Green Bay	0	0	7	21	—	28
St. Louis	0	19	14	10	—	43

StL —Ferrell 3 run (O'Donoghue kick)
StL —Safety, McCarren snapped ball into end zone
StL —Anderson 1 run (O'Donoghue kick)
StL —FG O'Donoghue 22
StL —Mitchell 39 pass from Lomax (O'Donoghue kick)
GB —Ellis 39 run (Del Greco kick)
StL —Tilley 11 pass from Lomax (O'Donoghue kick)
GB —Lofton 10 pass from Dickey (Del Greco kick)
StL —FG O'Donoghue 36
GB —Coffman 19 pass from Dickey (Del Greco kick)
StL —Green 37 pass from Lomax (O'Donoghue kick)
GB —Coffman 3 pass from Dickey (Del Greco kick)

New York Jets 25, Indianapolis 20—At Giants Stadium, attendance 61,987. AFC rushing leader Freeman McNeil ran for 115 yards on 25 carries and Pat Leahy kicked four field goals to lead the Jets to a 25-20 victory. New York opened an 18-10 halftime lead on Ken O'Brien's 39-yard scoring pass to Kurt Sohn and Leahy's field goals of 22, 35, 48, and 45 yards. The Jets' lone second-half score, a one-yard run by Tony Paige, proved decisive as the Colts rallied with 10 second-half points.

Indianapolis	0	10	7	3	—	20
N.Y. Jets	6	12	7	0	—	25

NYJ —FG Leahy 22
NYJ —FG Leahy 35
NYJ —Sohn 39 pass from O'Brien (kick failed)
Ind —FG Allegre 40
NYJ —FG Leahy 48
Ind —Butler 72 pass from Pagel (Allegre kick)
NYJ —FG Leahy 45
Ind —Beach 16 pass from Pagel (Allegre kick)
NYJ —Paige 1 run (Leahy kick)
Ind —FG Allegre 29

Los Angeles Raiders 35, New England 20—At Sullivan Stadium, attendance 60,686. The Raiders turned three New England miscues into 21 points to win 35-20. Los Angeles overcame a 20-14 halftime deficit when Lyle Alzado recovered teammate Rod Martin's fumble, following a three-yard fumble return, in the end zone for a touchdown. Interception returns by Lester Hayes (27 yards) and Sam Seale (38) accounted for the other Raiders defensive scores. Rookie quarterback Rusty Hilger, replacing an injured Marc Wilson in the second half, connected with Todd Christensen on a two-yard pass to record his first NFL touchdown completion.

L.A. Raiders	14	0	7	14	—	35
New England	10	10	0	0	—	20

NE —FG Franklin 47
Raiders —Hayes 27 interception return (Bahr kick)
NE —Fryar 40 pass from Eason (Franklin kick)
Raiders —Williams 38 pass from Wilson (Bahr kick)
NE —FG Franklin 20
NE —Tippett 25 fumble recovery return (Franklin kick)
Raiders —Alzado fumble recovery in end zone (Bahr kick)
Raiders —Christensen 2 pass from Hilger (Bahr kick)
Raiders —Seale 38 interception return (Bahr kick)

Miami 30, Denver 26—At Mile High Stadium, attendance 73,614. Dan Marino passed for three touchdowns and Fuad Reveiz kicked three field goals to lead the Dolphins' win. Marino's third-quarter 46-yard strike to Vince Heflin proved to be the winning score as the defense limited the Broncos to a field goal the rest of the way. Marino completed 25 of 43 passes for 390 yards to earn AFC offensive player of the week honors.

Miami	7	13	7	3	—	30
Denver	7	10	6	3	—	26

Den — Lang 10 run (Karlis kick)
Mia — Moore 69 pass from Marino (Reveiz kick)
Mia — FG Reveiz 40
Den — Winder 7 run (Karlis kick)
Mia — FG Reveiz 24
Mia — Rose 24 pass from Marino (Reveiz kick)
Den — FG Karlis 43
Den — Winder 1 run (kick failed)
Mia — Heflin 46 pass from Marino (Reveiz kick)
Mia — FG Reveiz 27
Den — FG Karlis 33

Minnesota 27, Buffalo 20—At Rich Stadium, attendance 45,667. Ted Brown ran 22 yards for a touchdown with 2:57 remaining to give the Vikings a 27-20 win. Tommy Kramer hooked up with Leo Lewis (10 yards), Brown (15), and Anthony Carter (43) on first-half scoring passes to give the Vikings a 20-3 lead. After Buffalo closed the gap to 20-13, Kramer engineered a seven-play, 82-yard drive to set up Brown's decisive touchdown. John Turner's 25-yard interception return in the final minutes sealed the Vikings' victory.

Minnesota	7	13	0	7	—	27
Buffalo	0	3	10	7	—	20

Minn — Lewis 10 pass from Kramer (Stenerud kick)
Minn — Brown 15 pass from Kramer (kick blocked)
Buff — FG Norwood 49
Minn — Carter 43 pass from Kramer (Stenerud kick)
Buff — FG Norwood 28
Buff — Ferragamo 1 run (Norwood kick)
Buff — Bell 1 run (Norwood kick)
Minn — Brown 22 run (Stenerud kick)

New Orleans 20, San Francisco 17—At Candlestick Park, attendance 58,053. Running back Wayne Wilson rushed for 108 yards on 24 carries as the Saints snapped a four-game losing streak to the 49ers. Hokie Gajan's five-yard run and Morten Andersen's 39-yard field goal gave the Saints a 10-7 halftime lead. Trailing 17-13 in the fourth quarter, Dave Wilson climaxed a three-play, 80-yard drive with a 43-yard scoring pass to Eugene Goodlow to provide the winning score. The Saints outgained the 49ers 354 yards to 231.

New Orleans	0	10	3	7	—	20
San Francisco	0	7	3	7	—	17

SF — Tyler 8 run (Wersching kick)
NO — Gajan 5 run (Andersen kick)
NO — FG Andersen 39
SF — FG Wersching 42
NO — FG Andersen 39
SF — Craig 2 run (Wersching kick)
NO — Goodlow 43 pass from D. Wilson (Andersen kick)

New York Giants 16, Philadelphia 10—At Veterans Stadium, attendance 66,696. Elvis Patterson's 29-yard interception return with 55 seconds remaining in overtime gave the Giants a season sweep of the Eagles for the first time since 1982. New York took a 10-3 third-quarter lead on Jess Atkinson's 49-yard field goal and Phil Simms's 26-yard scoring pass to Mark Bavaro. The game was forced into overtime by the Eagles' Herman Edwards, who intercepted a tipped pass out of the air and returned it three yards for the tying score with 3:02 left. Leonard Marshall led the Giants' defense with three of the team's seven sacks.

N.Y. Giants	0	0	10	0	6	—	16
Philadelphia	0	0	3	7	0	—	10

Phil — FG McFadden 41
NYG — FG Atkinson 49
NYG — Bavaro 26 pass from Simms (Atkinson kick)
Phil — Edwards 3 interception return (McFadden kick)
NYG — Patterson 29 interception return (no kick)

Kansas City 28, Seattle 7—At Arrowhead Stadium, attendance 50,485. The Chiefs' defense victimized the Seahawks for seven turnovers, three of which set up touchdowns, as Kansas City gained sole possession of first place in the AFC West. The Chiefs took a 21-0 first-half lead on Herman Heard's two-yard scoring run, Bill Kenney's 34-yard touchdown pass to Stephone Paige, and Kenney's one-yard run. Deron Cherry's NFL record-tying four interceptions earned him AFC defensive player of the week honors.

Seattle	0	0	7	0	—	7
Kansas City	14	7	7	0	—	28

KC — Heard 2 run (Lowery kick)
KC — Paige 34 pass from Kenney (Lowery kick)
KC — Kenney 1 run (Lowery kick)
KC — Paige 8 pass from Kenney (Lowery kick)
Sea — Turner 35 pass from Krieg (Johnson kick)

Detroit 30, Tampa Bay 9—At Pontiac Silverdome, attendance 45,023. Eric Hipple threw a pair of touchdown passes and ran for another to help the Lions hand the Buccaneers their fourteenth straight road defeat. Detroit led 16-9 after three quarters on three Ed Murray field goals and Hipple's four-yard scoring pass to Mark Nichols. Hipple, who completed 19 of 31 passes for 250 yards, added to the Lions' scoring in the final period with a nine-yard completion to Nichols and a one-yard run. Detroit safety Demetrious Johnson was named NFC defensive player of the week for his two forced fumbles, a fumble recovery, and an interception.

Tampa Bay	3	3	3	0	—	9
Detroit	0	10	6	14	—	30

TB — FG Igwebuike 21
Det — FG Murray 22
TB — FG Igwebuike 32
Det — Nichols 4 pass from Hipple (Murray kick)
TB — FG Igwebuike 20
Det — FG Murray 33
Det — FG Murray 39
Det — Nichols 9 pass from Hipple (Murray kick)
Det — Hipple 1 run (Murray kick)

Chicago 45, Washington 10—At Soldier Field, attendance 63,708. The Bears overcame a 10-0 deficit by exploding for a team-record 31 second-quarter points in defeating the Redskins. Willie Gault ignited Chicago's scoring with a 99-yard kickoff return. Jim McMahon then threw a pair of touchdown passes to Dennis McKinnon (14 yards) and Emery Moorehead (10), and caught a 13-yarder from Walter Payton for another score. Kevin Butler finished off the record-setting period with a 28-yard field goal to give the Bears a 31-10 first-half lead. The loss was the Redskins' worst since being shut out 53-0 by the Giants on November 5, 1961.

Washington	7	3	0	0	—	10
Chicago	0	31	7	7	—	45

Wash — Riggins 7 run (Moseley kick)
Wash — FG Moseley 32
Chi — Gault 99 kickoff return (Butler kick)
Chi — McKinnon 14 pass from McMahon (Butler kick)
Chi — Moorehead 10 pass from McMahon (Butler kick)
Chi — McMahon 13 pass from Payton (Butler kick)
Chi — FG Butler 28
Chi — Payton 33 pass from McMahon (Butler kick)
Chi — Gentry 1 run (Butler kick)

MONDAY, SEPTEMBER 30

Cincinnati 37, Pittsburgh 24—At Three Rivers Stadium, attendance 59,541. James Brooks rushed for 133 yards and two touchdowns, and Boomer Esiason threw three scoring passes to highlight the Bengals' win. Cincinnati rallied in the fourth quarter to overcome a 24-21 deficit on Esiason's four-yard scoring pass to Rodney Holman, Jim Breech's 32-yard field goal, and Brooks's 32-yard run. Esiason also had scoring passes of 26 yards to Holman and eight yards to Eddie Brown. The win overshadowed the performance of the Steelers' Mark Malone, who completed 26 of 44 passes for 374 yards and three touchdowns.

Cincinnati	0	14	7	16	—	37
Pittsburgh	0	10	14	0	—	24

Pitt — Lipps 15 pass from Malone (Anderson kick)
Cin — Brooks 14 run (Breech kick)
Cin — Holman 26 pass from Esiason (Breech kick)
Pitt — FG Anderson 29
Cin — Brown 8 pass from Esiason (Breech kick)
Pitt — Stallworth 17 pass from Malone (Anderson kick)
Pitt — Erenberg 4 pass from Malone (Anderson kick)
Cin — Holman 4 pass from Esiason (Breech kick)
Cin — FG Breech 32
Cin — Brooks 32 run (pass failed)

FIFTH WEEK SUMMARIES

STANDINGS

American Football Conference

Eastern Division	W	L	T	Pct.	Pts.	OP
Miami	4	1	0	.800	138	85
N.Y. Jets	4	1	0	.800	120	77
Indianapolis	2	3	0	.400	99	123
New England	2	3	0	.400	90	113
Buffalo	0	5	0	.000	63	149
Central Division						
Cleveland	3	2	0	.600	93	81
Pittsburgh	2	3	0	.400	116	81
Cincinnati	1	4	0	.200	149	166
Houston	1	4	0	.200	69	107
Western Division						
Denver	3	2	0	.600	151	121
Kansas City	3	2	0	.600	121	104
L.A. Raiders	3	2	0	.600	115	100
Seattle	3	2	0	.600	134	143
San Diego	2	3	0	.400	121	146

National Football Conference

Eastern Division	W	L	T	Pct.	Pts.	OP
Dallas	4	1	0	.800	132	86
N.Y. Giants	3	2	0	.600	113	80
St. Louis	3	2	0	.600	138	133
Washington	2	3	0	.400	73	131
Philadelphia	1	4	0	.200	56	83
Central Division						
Chicago	5	0	0	1.000	163	88
Detroit	3	2	0	.600	100	114
Minnesota	3	2	0	.600	120	103
Green Bay	2	3	0	.400	117	123
Tampa Bay	0	5	0	.000	85	146
Western Division						
L.A. Rams	5	0	0	1.000	102	62
New Orleans	3	2	0	.600	113	132
San Francisco	3	2	0	.600	145	91
Atlanta	0	5	0	.000	94	162

SUNDAY, OCTOBER 6

Indianapolis 49, Buffalo 17—At Hoosier Dome, attendance 60,003. Randy McMillan ran for 112 yards and a pair of touchdowns to lead the Colts over the winless Bills. Indianapolis opened a 28-10 halftime lead behind touchdown runs by Mike Pagel (two yards) and George Wonsley (seven and three) and Pagel's 18-yard touchdown pass to Raymond Butler. McMillan and Albert Bentley (100 yards) became only the third pair of backs in Colts history to rush for 100 yards in the same game. Indianapolis outgained Buffalo 464 total yards to 252.

Buffalo	7	3	0	7	—	17
Indianapolis	7	21	14	7	—	49

Buff — Bell 18 run (Norwood kick)
Ind — Pagel 2 run (Allegre kick)
Ind — Wonsley 7 run (Allegre kick)
Buff — FG Norwood 45
Ind — Wonsley 3 run (Allegre kick)
Ind — Butler 18 pass from Pagel (Allegre kick)
Ind — McMillan 6 run (Allegre kick)
Ind — Young 28 fumble recovery return (Allegre kick)
Ind — McMillan 2 run (Allegre kick)
Buff — Reed 10 pass from Ferragamo (Norwood kick)

Chicago 27, Tampa Bay 19—At Tampa Stadium, attendance 51,795. Jim McMahon completed 22 of 34 passes for 292 yards and a touchdown to guide the Bears past the Buccaneers. Trailing 12-3 at halftime, McMahon hooked up with Dennis McKinnon on a 21-yard scoring pass and Kevin Butler kicked a 31-yard field goal to give the Bears a 13-12 third-quarter lead. Walter Payton rushed for a pair of touchdowns to become the sixth player in NFL history to score 100 touchdowns. Chicago tight end Emery Moorehead had a career-high eight catches for 118 yards.

Chicago	0	3	10	14	—	27
Tampa Bay	0	12	0	7	—	19

TB — FG Igwebuike 19
TB — House 21 pass from DeBerg (kick failed)
TB — FG Igwebuike 36
Chi — FG Butler 30
Chi — McKinnon 21 pass from McMahon (Butler kick)
Chi — FG Butler 31
Chi — Payton 4 run (Butler kick)
TB — Carter 25 pass from DeBerg (Igwebuike kick)
Chi — Payton 9 run (Butler kick)

Dallas 30, New York Giants 29—At Giants Stadium, attendance 74,981. Rafael Septien's game-winning field goal, a 31-yarder with 2:19 remaining, gave Dallas the victory and lifted the Cowboys into sole possession of first place in the NFC East. A pair of Danny White eight-yard scoring passes to Tony Hill and Mike Renfro gave Dallas a 14-6 halftime lead. The Giants battled back in the third quarter behind three Phil Simms touchdown passes to take a 26-21 lead. However, two costly fumbles by Simms set up two of Septien's three fourth-period field goals that put the Cowboys ahead 27-26. Renfro finished with a career-high 10 receptions for 141 yards and two touchdowns.

Dallas	7	7	7	9	—	30
N.Y. Giants	3	3	20	3	—	29

Dall — Hill 8 pass from D. White (Septien kick)
NYG — FG Atkinson 23
Dall — Renfro 8 pass from D. White (Septien kick)
NYG — FG Atkinson 37
NYG — Manuel 51 pass from Simms (kick failed)
NYG — Manuel 23 pass from Simms (Atkinson kick)
NYG — Adams 70 pass from Simms (Atkinson kick)
Dall — Renfro 24 pass from D. White (Septien kick)
Dall — FG Septien 22
Dall — FG Septien 29
NYG — FG Atkinson 47
Dall — FG Septien 31

Green Bay 43, Detroit 10—At Lambeau Field, attendance 55,914. Lynn Dickey and Randy Wright each fired a pair of touchdown passes as the Packers easily defeated the Lions. Two Al Del Greco field goals from 33 and 21 yards, coupled with Dickey's two-yard scoring pass to Eddie Lee Ivery and Jessie Clark's six-yard touchdown run, gave Green Bay a 20-3 halftime lead. The Packers capitalized on six Lions turnovers to set up 31 of their points. James Lofton finished with 10 receptions for 151 yards to become Green Bay's all-time receiving leader with 8,050 career yards, passing Hall of Famer Don Hutson.

Detroit	3	0	0	7	—	10
Green Bay	7	13	23	0	—	43

Det — FG Murray 22
GB — Ivery 2 pass from Dickey (Del Greco kick)
GB — FG Del Greco 33
GB — Clark 6 run (Del Greco kick)
GB — FG Del Greco 21
GB — Epps 9 pass from Dickey (Del Greco kick)
GB — West 7 pass from Wright (Del Greco kick)

GB —Epps 28 pass from Wright (Del Greco kick)
GB —Safety, Brown tackled Ferguson in end zone
Det —Moore 13 pass from Ferguson (Murray kick)

Denver 31, Houston 20—At Mile High Stadium, attendance 74,699. John Elway completed 17 of 35 passes for 256 yards and three touchdowns as the Broncos cruised past the Oilers 31-20. Rich Karlis's 37-yard field goal, Sammy Winder's one-yard scoring run, and Elway's 41-yard touchdown pass to Steve Watson gave the Broncos a 17-3 halftime lead. Elway also hooked up with Clarence Kay (six yards) and Vance Johnson (29) in the third quarter to clinch the win. Karlis's first-half field goal tied the club record of 13 straight.

Houston	0	3	10	7	— 20
Denver	10	7	14	0	— 31

Den —FG Karlis 37
Den —Winder 1 run (Karlis kick)
Hou —FG Zendejas 27
Den —Watson 41 pass from Elway (Karlis kick)
Den —Kay 6 pass from Elway (Karlis kick)
Hou —Woolfolk 67 pass from Moon (Zendejas kick)
Den —V. Johnson 29 pass from Elway (Karlis kick)
Hou —FG Zendejas 25
Hou —Hill 7 pass from Moroski (Zendejas kick)

Los Angeles Raiders 19, Kansas City 10—At Memorial Coliseum, attendance 55,133. Marcus Allen gained 126 yards on 29 carries and Chris Bahr kicked four field goals to lead the Raiders over the Chiefs. Marc Wilson's six-yard touchdown pass to Jim Smith and Bahr's 37-yard field goal helped Los Angeles to a 10-3 second-quarter advantage. Bahr added second-half field goals of 25, 41, and 41 yards to insure the victory and give him four field goals in a single game for the third time in his career. Allen's 100-yard effort was the eighth of his career and first in 1985.

Kansas City	3	0	0	7	— 10
L.A. Raiders	0	10	3	6	— 19

KC —FG Lowery 36
Raiders —Smith 6 pass from Wilson (Bahr kick)
Raiders —FG Bahr 37
Raiders —FG Bahr 25
KC —Hancock 41 pass from Kenney (Lowery kick)
Raiders —FG Bahr 41
Raiders —FG Bahr 41

Los Angeles Rams 13, Minnesota 10—At Anaheim Stadium, attendance 61,139. Linebacker Jim Collins spearheaded the Rams' defense, which stopped the Vikings on a critical goal-line stand with time running out to keep Los Angeles undefeated. The Rams took a 6-0 halftime lead on a pair of Mike Lansford field goals from 43 and 33 yards. Eric Dickerson's two-yard scoring run at the beginning of the third quarter proved decisive as the Vikings battled back with 10 second-half points. Minnesota opted to try for the win rather than force overtime with a tying field goal with one second left. Darrin Nelson attempted to go over the top and was stopped by Collins and Los Angeles's top-rated rushing defense.

Minnesota	0	0	7	3	— 10
L.A. Rams	0	6	7	0	— 13

Rams —FG Lansford 43
Rams —FG Lansford 33
Rams —Dickerson 2 run (Lansford kick)
Minn —Brown 1 run (Stenerud kick)
Minn —FG Stenerud 24

Cleveland 24, New England 20—At Cleveland Stadium, attendance 62,139. Kevin Mack ran for 115 yards on 20 carries and scored the go-ahead touchdown in the fourth quarter on a 10-yard run to lead the Browns to a comeback win. Earnest Byner's nine-yard run and wide receiver Brian Brennan's 33-yard scoring pass to Ozzie Newsome gave the Browns a 14-13 halftime advantage. The Browns' defense, ranked second in the AFC against the run, held the Patriots on a fourth-and-goal situation from their own six-inch line late in the fourth quarter to preserve the victory.

New England	0	13	7	0	— 20
Cleveland	7	7	3	7	— 24

Clev —Byner 9 run (Bahr kick)
NE —Rembert fumble recovery in end zone (Franklin kick)
Clev —Newsome 33 pass from Brennan (Bahr kick)
NE —FG Franklin 29
NE —FG Franklin 33
Clev —FG Bahr 44
NE —Morgan 22 pass from Eason (Franklin kick)
Clev —Mack 10 run (Bahr kick)

New York Jets 29, Cincinnati 20—At Riverfront Stadium, attendance 51,785. Ken O'Brien completed 19 of 28 passes for 211 yards and a touchdown to spark the Jets' 29-20 win. New York gained a 14-13 halftime advantage on scoring runs by Tony Paige (two yards) and Johnny Hector (one). Pat Leahy kicked a 30-yard field goal and the Jets scored a safety and a touchdown within a 1:57 span of the third quarter to take a 26-13 lead. Wesley Walker tackled Louis Breeden in the end zone for a safety following Breeden's interception at the six-yard line.

N.Y. Jets	7	7	12	3	— 29
Cincinnati	7	6	0	7	— 20

Cin —Esiason 11 run (Breech kick)
NYJ —Paige 2 run (Leahy kick)
Cin —FG Breech 53
Cin —FG Breech 29
NYJ —Hector 1 run (Leahy kick)
NYJ —FG Leahy 30
NYJ —Safety, Breeden tackled in end zone
NYJ —Shuler 7 pass from O'Brien (Leahy kick)
NYJ —FG Leahy 33
Cin —Jennings 1 run (Breech kick)

New Orleans 23, Philadelphia 21—At Louisiana Superdome, attendance 56,364. The Saints' defense forced five turnovers and Morten Andersen kicked three field goals to lead New Orleans to their third straight victory. The Saints took a 20-7 halftime lead on two Andersen field goals (40 and 33 yards), Dave Wilson's 31-yard touchdown pass to Eugene Goodlow, and Johnnie Poe's 40-yard interception return. The win overshadowed the comeback effort of Eagles quarterback Ron Jaworski, who came off the bench to throw three touchdowns. Dave Waymer had three interceptions to tie a Saints' record, the third with 1:24 remaining in the game to thwart the Eagles' final scoring threat.

Philadelphia	0	7	0	14	— 21
New Orleans	10	10	0	3	— 23

NO —FG Andersen 40
NO —Goodlow 31 pass from D. Wilson (Andersen kick)
NO —FG Andersen 33
NO —Poe 40 interception return (Andersen kick)
Phil —Spagnola 7 pass from Jaworski (McFadden kick)
Phil —Spagnola 14 pass from Jaworski (McFadden kick)
NO —FG Andersen 43
Phil —Quick 20 pass from Jaworski (McFadden kick)

Miami 24, Pittsburgh 20—At Orange Bowl, attendance 72,820. Rookie running back Lorenzo Hampton scored his first career touchdown on a two-yard run with 47 seconds remaining to give the Dolphins their fourth straight win. Fuad Reveiz's 35-yard field goal six minutes into the third quarter tied the score at 17-17. The Steelers regained the lead 20-17 on Gary Anderson's 33-yard field goal with 8:25 left in the game. The Dolphins generated 399 yards total offense compared to the Steelers' 282.

Pittsburgh	0	17	0	3	— 20
Miami	7	7	3	7	— 24

Mia —Nathan 1 run (Reveiz kick)
Pitt —Abercrombie 1 run (Anderson kick)
Pitt —FG Anderson 48
Mia —Johnson 2 pass from Marino (Reveiz kick)
Pitt —Thompson 1 pass from Malone (Anderson kick)
Mia —FG Reveiz 35
Pitt —FG Anderson 33
Mia —Hampton 2 run (Reveiz kick)

Seattle 26, San Diego 21—At Kingdome, attendance 61,300. Curt Warner ran for 94 yards and a pair of touchdowns and Norm Johnson kicked two field goals from 28 and 46 yards to give the Seahawks a 26-21 win and a share of first place in the AFC West. Seattle overcame a 7-6 halftime deficit as Warner scored on runs of 1 and 18 yards to take a 19-7 lead. Dave Krieg's 14-yard touchdown pass to Steve Largent with 3:15 left was decisive as the Chargers rebounded in the fourth period to score 14 points.

San Diego	0	7	0	14	— 21
Seattle	3	3	7	13	— 26

Sea —FG Johnson 28
Sea —FG Johnson 46
SD —Chandler 3 pass from Herrmann (Benirschke kick)
Sea —Warner 1 run (Johnson kick)
Sea —Warner 18 run (kick failed)
SD —Chandler 6 pass from Herrmann (Benirschke kick)
Sea —Largent 14 pass from Krieg (Johnson kick)
SD —Joiner 9 pass from Herrmann (Benirschke kick)

San Francisco 38, Atlanta 17—At Atlanta-Fulton County Stadium, attendance 44,740. Joe Montana completed 37 of 57 passes for 429 yards and five touchdowns to power the 49ers over the Falcons. Montana's 46-yard scoring strike to Roger Craig and Ray Wersching's 37-yard field goal gave San Francisco a 10-3 lead it never relinquished. Montana, the NFC offensive player of the week, completed scoring passes to Wendell Tyler (14 yards), Jerry Rice (25), John Frank (5), and Dwight Clark (32) in the second half to tie a 49ers record for touchdown passes. Craig's 12 catches for 167 yards tied the 49ers' single-game record for receptions.

San Francisco	7	3	7	21	— 38
Atlanta	0	3	0	14	— 17

SF —Craig 46 pass from Montana (Wersching kick)
Atl —FG Luckhurst 45
SF —FG Wersching 37
SF —Tyler 14 pass from Montana (Wersching kick)
Atl —Archer 29 run (Luckhurst kick)
SF —Rice 25 pass from Montana (Wersching kick)
SF —Frank 5 pass from Montana (Wersching kick)
Atl —Holly 20 run (Luckhurst kick)
SF —Clark 32 pass from Montana (Wersching kick)

MONDAY, OCTOBER 7

Washington 27, St. Louis 10—At Robert F. Kennedy Stadium, attendance 53,134. John Riggins and George Rogers each rushed for over 100 yards and the Washington defense intercepted five passes as the Redskins overpowered the Cardinals. Washington opened up a 17-3 halftime lead on Mark Moseley's 33-yard field goal and Joe Theismann's 14-yard touchdown run and 10-yard scoring pass to Gary Clark. Riggins rushed for 103 yards on 17 carries and Rogers finished with 104 yards on 25 carries to become the first pair of backs in club history to rush for over 100 yards in the same game.

St. Louis	0	3	0	7	— 10
Washington	10	7	3	7	— 27

Wash —Theismann 14 run (Moseley kick)
Wash —FG Moseley 33
StL —FG O'Donoghue 22
Wash —Clark 10 pass from Theismann (Moseley kick)
Wash —FG Moseley 29
StL —Anderson 10 run (O'Donoghue kick)
Wash —Didier 12 pass from Theismann (Moseley kick)

SIXTH WEEK SUMMARIES

STANDINGS

American Football Conference

Eastern Division	W	L	T	Pct.	Pts.	OP
N.Y. Jets	5	1	0	.833	143	84
Miami	4	2	0	.667	145	108
New England	3	3	0	.500	104	116
Indianapolis	2	4	0	.333	109	138
Buffalo	0	6	0	.000	66	163
Central Division						
Cleveland	4	2	0	.667	114	87
Cincinnati	2	4	0	.333	184	196
Pittsburgh	2	4	0	.333	129	108
Houston	1	5	0	.167	75	128
Western Division						
Denver	4	2	0	.667	166	131
L.A. Raiders	4	2	0	.667	138	113
Seattle	4	2	0	.667	164	169
Kansas City	3	3	0	.500	141	135
San Diego	3	3	0	.500	152	166

National Football Conference

Eastern Division	W	L	T	Pct.	Pts.	OP
Dallas	5	1	0	.833	159	99
N.Y. Giants	3	3	0	.500	143	115
St. Louis	3	3	0	.500	145	163
Washington	3	3	0	.500	97	134
Philadelphia	2	4	0	.333	86	90
Central Division						
Chicago	6	0	0	1.000	189	98
Detroit	3	3	0	.500	103	138
Green Bay	3	3	0	.500	137	140
Minnesota	3	3	0	.500	137	123
Tampa Bay	0	6	0	.000	112	177
Western Division						
L.A. Rams	6	0	0	1.000	133	89
New Orleans	3	3	0	.500	126	155
San Francisco	3	3	0	.500	155	117
Atlanta	0	6	0	.000	120	192

SUNDAY, OCTOBER 13

Seattle 30, Atlanta 26—At Kingdome, attendance 60,430. Dave Krieg completed 33 of 51 passes for 405 yards and four touchdowns to rally the Seahawks to a 30-26 victory. Trailing 26-21 late in the fourth quarter, Krieg completed a 12-yard scoring pass to Paul Skansi with 35 seconds left to give the Seahawks a 28-26 lead. Krieg's other touchdown passes were to Steve Largent (12 yards), Charle Young (32), and Byron Walker (24). His 405-yard output was the third 400-yard passing game of his career and extended his consecutive games streak with at least one touchdown pass to 24.

Atlanta	0	6	3	17	— 26
Seattle	7	0	7	16	— 30

Sea —Largent 12 pass from Krieg (Johnson kick)
Atl —FG Luckhurst 25
Atl —FG Luckhurst 52
Atl —FG Luckhurst 48
Sea —Young 32 pass from Krieg (Johnson kick)
Sea —Walker 24 pass from Krieg (Johnson kick)
Atl —B. Johnson 12 pass from Archer (Luckhurst kick)
Atl —Allen 37 pass from Archer (Luckhurst kick)
Atl —FG Luckhurst 40
Sea —Skansi 12 pass from Krieg (Johnson kick)
Sea —Safety, fumble rolled out of end zone

New England 14, Buffalo 3—At Sullivan Stadium, attendance 40,462. Steve Grogan came off the bench to throw a touchdown pass and lead the Patriots to a 14-3 win over the Bills. In a game played in fog and drizzle, Grogan replaced injured Tony Eason (shoulder) in the second quarter and capped an eight-play, 80-yard drive with a 16-yard scoring pass to Irving Fryar to give New England a 7-3 third-quarter lead. Ray Clayborn's 27-yard interception return with 8:12 left finished the Patriots' scoring. Fryar had his first 100-yard receiving game in the NFL, finishing with six catches for 132 yards.

Buffalo	0	3	0	0	— 3
New England	0	0	7	7	— 14

Buff —FG Norwood 47
NE —Fryar 16 pass from Grogan (Franklin kick)
NE —Clayborn 27 interception return (Franklin kick)

Chicago 26, San Francisco 10—At Candlestick Park, attendance 60,523. Walter Payton ran for two touchdowns and Kevin Butler kicked four field goals to help the Bears avenge last season's NFC Championship Game loss to the 49ers. Chicago took a 16-10 lead on Payton's three-yard scoring run and Butler's three field goals from 34, 38, and 27 yards. San Francisco's scoring came from Carlton Williamson's 43-yard interception return and Ray Wersching's 32-yard field goal. The Bears' defense held the 49ers in check, sacking quarterback Joe Montana seven times and holding San Francisco's offense without a touchdown for the first time since November 27, 1983 (versus Chicago). Payton had his sixty-fifth career 100-yard rushing game with 132 yards on 24 carries.

Chicago	13	3	0	10	— 26
San Francisco	0	10	0	0	— 10

Chi —Payton 3 run (Butler kick)
Chi —FG Butler 34
Chi —FG Butler 38
Chi —FG Butler 27
SF —Williamson 43 interception return (Wersching kick)
SF —FG Wersching 32
Chi —FG Butler 29
Chi —Payton 17 run (Butler kick)

Cleveland 21, Houston 6—At Astrodome, attendance 38,386. Bernie Kosar completed 8 of 19 passes for 208 yards and had his first NFL touchdown pass to lead the Browns' second-half rally. Trailing 6-0 at halftime, Kosar hooked up with Clarence Weathers on a 68-yard scoring pass in the third quarter to put Cleveland ahead for good 7-6. The Browns increased their lead to 21-6 on scoring runs by Kevin Mack (four yards) and Earnest Byner (five). Chip Banks had two of the Browns' seven sacks. Weathers had his finest game in the NFL with three catches for 146 yards.

Cleveland	0	0	14	7	— 21
Houston	3	3	0	0	— 6

Hou —FG Zendejas 50
Hou —FG Zendejas 27
Clev —Weathers 68 pass from Kosar (Bahr kick)
Clev —Mack 4 run (Bahr kick)
Clev —Byner 5 run (Bahr kick)

Denver 15, Indianapolis 10—At Hoosier Dome, attendance 60,128. Rich Karlis's two second-half field goals from 30 and 18 yards were the difference as the Broncos downed the Colts 15-10. John Elway's 45-yard pass to Clint Sampson set up Denver's only touchdown, a two-yard run in the first quarter by Sammy Winder. Karlis's 32-yard second-quarter field goal gave the Broncos a 9-3 halftime lead. Elway generated 288 yards (17 of 36 passes for 239 yards), including a career-high 49 yards rushing.

Denver	6	3	3	3	— 15
Indianapolis	0	3	0	7	— 10

Den —Winder 2 run (kick failed)
Ind —FG Allegre 28
Den —FG Karlis 32
Den —FG Karlis 30
Den —FG Karlis 18
Ind —Bouza 19 pass from Pagel (Allegre kick)

Washington 24, Detroit 3—At Robert F. Kennedy Stadium, attendance 52,845. John Riggins ran for 114 yards and scored the one-hundredth rushing touchdown of his career in the Redskins' win over the Lions. After Mark Moseley's 24-yard field goal and his own one-yard touchdown run, Riggins powered his way 21 yards for the milestone score. Later, the 14-year veteran finished the Redskins' scoring with a five-yard touchdown run to give him 101 career rushing touchdowns, second in NFL history to Jim Brown's 106. Overall, his 113 career scores tied him with Lenny Moore, behind only Brown's record total 126. Vernon Dean's fumble recovery and Tony Peters's nine-yard interception return set up Riggins's first two touchdowns.

Detroit	3	0	0	0	— 3
Washington	3	14	7	0	— 24

Det —FG Murray 33
Wash —FG Moseley 24
Wash —Riggins 1 run (Moseley kick)
Wash —Riggins 21 run (Moseley kick)
Wash —Riggins 5 run (Moseley kick)

San Diego 31, Kansas City 20—At San Diego Jack Murphy Stadium, attendance 50,067. Mark Herrmann, replacing injured Dan Fouts, threw for 320 yards and two touchdowns to lead the Chargers to a 31-20 win over the Chiefs. Nick Lowery's 34-yard field goal snapped a 17-17 halftime tie but Herrmann came right back for San Diego with a 10-yard strike to Eric Sievers to put the Chargers ahead 24-20. San Diego's final score came on Tim Spencer's one-yard run with 6:17 left. Wayne Davis's interception with 3:45 left stymied Kansas City's final drive and secured the win for the Chargers. Charlie Joiner finished with six catches for 118 yards, including a 39-yard scoring reception.

Kansas City	3	14	3	0	— 20
San Diego	0	17	0	14	— 31

KC —FG Lowery 41
KC —Horton 2 pass from Kenney (Lowery kick)
SD —Joiner 39 pass from Herrmann (Thomas kick)
KC —Carson 18 pass from Kenney (Lowery kick)
SD —Anderson 6 run (Thomas kick)
SD —FG Thomas 30
KC —FG Lowery 34
SD —Sievers 10 pass from Herrmann (Thomas kick)
SD —Spencer 1 run (Thomas kick)

Los Angeles Rams 31, Tampa Bay 27—At Tampa Stadium, attendance 39,607. Two second-half interception returns for touchdowns by Carl Ekern (33 yards) and LeRoy Irvin (34) propelled Los Angeles to its sixth straight win. Trailing 20-14 at halftime, the Rams' defense outscored the Buccaneers' offense 17-7 in the second half to spark the comeback win. In addition to intercepting four passes, the Los Angeles defense limited Buccaneers' running back James Wilder, the NFC's leading rusher, to 49 yards on 24 carries.

L.A. Rams	0	14	10	7	— 31
Tampa Bay	7	13	0	7	— 27

TB —Wilder 1 run (Igwebuike kick)
Rams —Duckworth 23 pass from Brock (Lansford kick)
Rams —Dickerson 6 run (Lansford kick)
TB —FG Igwebuike 34
TB —House 17 pass from DeBerg (Igwebuike kick)
TB —FG Igwebuike 49
Rams —FG Lansford 27
Rams —Ekern 33 interception return (Lansford kick)
TB —Carter 13 pass from DeBerg (Igwebuike kick)
Rams —Irvin 34 interception return (Lansford kick)

Green Bay 20, Minnesota 17—At Milwaukee County Stadium, attendance 54,647. Al Del Greco kicked a 22-yard field goal with seven seconds left to hand the Vikings their second straight last-minute loss. Tim Lewis's six-yard fumble return for a touchdown snapped a 7-7 halftime tie to put Green Bay ahead 14-7. Following Tommy Kramer's 43-yard scoring pass to Leo Lewis, Del Greco kicked a 45-yard field goal to give the Packers a 17-14 lead. The Vikings responded with an 18-yard field goal by Jan Stenerud to tie the score at 17-17 with 1:24 left. Green Bay quarterback Lynn Dickey directed a 66-yard, nine-play drive to set up Del Greco's winning field goal.

Minnesota	0	7	7	3	— 17
Green Bay	0	7	7	6	— 20

GB —Clark 5 pass from Dickey (Del Greco kick)
Minn —Jones 14 pass from Kramer (Stenerud kick)
GB —T. Lewis 6 fumble recovery return (Del Greco kick)
Minn —L. Lewis 43 pass from Kramer (Stenerud kick)
GB —FG Del Greco 45
Minn —FG Stenerud 18
GB —FG Del Greco 22

Los Angeles Raiders 23, New Orleans 13—At Memorial Coliseum, attendance 48,152. Marcus Allen rushed for 107 yards and two touchdowns to highlight the Raiders' victory. Los Angeles took a 14-7 halftime lead on Allen's two scoring runs from 11 and 8 yards. The Saints battled back with two Morten Andersen field goals before the Raiders clinched the win on Marc Wilson's 15-yard scoring pass to Dokie Williams with 6:32 left. Defensive end Howie Long recorded two of Los Angeles's four sacks.

New Orleans	0	7	3	3	— 13
L.A. Raiders	7	7	0	9	— 23

Raiders —Allen 11 run (Bahr kick)
Raiders —Allen 8 run (Bahr kick)
NO —Merkens 39 pass from D. Wilson (Andersen kick)
NO —FG Andersen 34
NO —FG Andersen 33
Raiders —Williams 15 pass from Wilson (Bahr kick)
Raiders —Safety, Alzado tackled D. Wilson in end zone

Cincinnati 35, New York Giants 30—At Riverfront Stadium, attendance 53,112. Boomer Esiason completed three touchdown passes and the Bengals' defense forced four New York turnovers en route to victory. The Bengals opened a 21-3 first-half lead on Esiason's scoring passes to Cris Collinsworth (16 yards) and James Brooks (27), and Brooks's five-yard touchdown run. New York responded with 17 straight points to pull within one 21-20, before James Griffin returned an interception 24 yards for a touchdown to put the Bengals ahead 28-20. Reggie Williams's fumble recovery set up Cincinnati's final score, a five-yard scoring pass from Esiason to Rodney Holman. The win upstaged the performance of the Giants' Phil Simms, who passed for 513 yards, the second-best passing yardage performance in NFL history behind Norm Van Brocklin's 554 in 1951.

N.Y. Giants	0	3	17	10	— 30
Cincinnati	14	7	7	7	— 35

Cin —Collinsworth 16 pass from Esiason (Breech kick)
Cin —Brooks 27 pass from Esiason (Breech kick)
Cin —Brooks 5 run (Breech kick)
NYG —FG Atkinson 33
NYG —Morris 1 run (Atkinson kick)
NYG —Atkinson 14 run (Atkinson kick)
NYG —FG Atkinson 37
Cin —Griffin 24 interception return (Breech kick)
Cin —Holman 5 pass from Esiason (Breech kick)
NYG —FG Atkinson 46
NYG —Adams 24 pass from Simms (Atkinson kick)

Philadelphia 30, St. Louis 7—At Veterans Stadium, attendance 48,186. Ron Jaworski passed for three touchdowns and Earnest Jackson ran for 103 yards to lead the Eagles past the Cardinals. Philadelphia outscored St. Louis 23-0 in the first three quarters on three Paul McFadden field goals (39, 21, and 52 yards) and two Jaworski scoring passes to John Spagnola (10 yards) and Mike Quick (17). Jaworski's 32-yard completion to Herman Hunter in the fourth period finished the Eagles' scoring. Cardinals' backup quarterback Scott Brunner prevented a shutout late in the fourth quarter with a 40-yard touchdown pass to Pat Tilley.

St. Louis	0	0	0	7	— 7
Philadelphia	3	10	10	7	— 30

Phil —FG McFadden 39
Phil —FG McFadden 21
Phil —Spagnola 10 pass from Jaworski (McFadden kick)
Phil —Quick 17 pass from Jaworski (McFadden kick)
Phil —FG McFadden 52
Phil —Hunter 32 pass from Jaworski (McFadden kick)
StL —Tilley 40 pass from Brunner (O'Donoghue kick)

Dallas 27, Pittsburgh 13—At Texas Stadium, attendance 62,932. Tony Dorsett rushed for 113 yards to become the sixth player in NFL history to go over the 10,000-yard mark as the Cowboys snapped a five-game losing streak to the Steelers. Danny White fired a 56-yard touchdown pass to Dorsett and Rafael Septien kicked a 38-yard field goal to give the Cowboys a 10-3 halftime lead. Dallas increased the margin to 20-3 in the third quarter with another Septien field goal (39 yards) and Eugene Lockhart's 19-yard interception return for a touchdown. Dorsett completed the Cowboys' scoring with a 35-yard run, to total 10,082 career yards.

Pittsburgh	0	3	0	10	— 13
Dallas	0	10	10	7	— 27

Pitt —FG Anderson 48
Dall —Dorsett 56 pass from D. White (Septien kick)
Dall —FG Septien 38
Dall —FG Septien 39
Dall —Lockhart 19 interception return (Septien kick)
Pitt —FG Anderson 34
Pitt —Abercrombie 1 run (Anderson kick)
Dall —Dorsett 35 run (Septien kick)

MONDAY, OCTOBER 14

New York Jets 23, Miami 7—At Giants Stadium, attendance 73,807. Freeman McNeil rushed for 173 yards and Pat Leahy kicked three field goals as the Jets overpowered the Dolphins to take sole possession of first place in the AFC East. Leahy connected on field goals of 22 and 18 yards to give New York a 6-0 halftime advantage. McNeil, the AFC offensive player of the week, also caught three passes for 46 yards to pace the Jets with 219 combined yards. New York outgained the Dolphins 476 to 200 in total yards.

Miami	0	0	7	0	— 7
N.Y. Jets	0	6	10	7	— 23

NYJ —FG Leahy 22
NYJ —FG Leahy 18
NYJ —Sohn 15 pass from O'Brien (Leahy kick)
Mia —Davenport 3 run (Reveiz kick)
NYJ —FG Leahy 18
NYJ —Paige 1 run (Leahy kick)

SEVENTH WEEK SUMMARIES

STANDINGS

American Football Conference

Eastern Division	W	L	T	Pct.	Pts.	OP
Miami	5	2	0	.714	186	146
N.Y. Jets	5	2	0	.714	156	104
New England	4	3	0	.571	124	129
Indianapolis	2	5	0	.286	118	159
Buffalo	1	6	0	.143	87	172
Central Division						
Cleveland	4	3	0	.571	134	108
Pittsburgh	3	4	0	.429	152	118
Cincinnati	2	5	0	.286	211	240
Houston	2	5	0	.286	119	155
Western Division						
Denver	5	2	0	.714	179	141
L.A. Raiders	5	2	0	.714	159	133
Seattle	4	3	0	.571	174	182
Kansas City	3	4	0	.429	141	151
San Diego	3	4	0	.429	169	187

National Football Conference

Eastern Division	W	L	T	Pct.	Pts.	OP
Dallas	5	2	0	.714	173	115
N.Y. Giants	4	3	0	.571	160	118
Philadelphia	3	4	0	.429	102	104
St. Louis	3	4	0	.429	155	186
Washington	3	4	0	.429	100	151

Central Division

Chicago	7	0	0	1.000	212	105
Detroit	4	3	0	.571	126	159
Minnesota	4	3	0	.571	158	140
Green Bay	3	4	0	.429	144	163
Tampa Bay	0	7	0	.000	150	218

Western Division

L.A Rams	7	0	0	1.000	149	89
New Orleans	3	4	0	.429	150	186
San Francisco	3	4	0	.429	176	140
Atlanta	1	6	0	.143	151	216

SUNDAY, OCTOBER 20

Houston 44, Cincinnati 27—At Astrodome, attendance 35,590. Warren Moon completed two touchdown passes and Tony Zendejas kicked three field goals from 34, 28, and 32 yards to help the Oilers snap a five-game losing streak. Moon connected on 20 of 31 passes for 266 yards, including a pair of scoring passes to Drew Hill (34 yards) and Mike McCloskey (24). Leading 17-13 at halftime, Houston put the game out of reach by converting four of Cincinnati's five second-half turnovers into 24 points. The 44 points were the most scored by the Oilers since they shut out the Bears 47-0 on November 6, 1977.

Cincinnati	0	13	0	14	— 27
Houston	7	10	10	17	— 44

Hou —Moriarty 6 run (Zendejas kick)
Hou —FG Zendejas 34
Cin —FG Breech 47
Hou —Rozier 3 run (Zendejas kick)
Cin —Brown 20 pass from Esiason (Kreider run)
Cin —FG Breech 22
Hou —Edwards 1 run (Zendejas kick)
Hou —FG Zendejas 28
Hou —Hill 34 pass from Moon (Zendejas kick)
Hou —FG Zendejas 32
Hou —McCloskey 24 pass from Moon (Zendejas kick)
Cin —Brooks 23 pass from Esiason (Breech kick)
Cin —Jennings 9 pass from Esiason (Breech kick)

Philadelphia 16, Dallas 14—At Veterans Stadium, attendance 70,114. Ron Jaworski's fourth-quarter touchdown pass of 36 yards to Kenny Jackson proved decisive and the defense held on to preserve the Eagles' win. Trailing 14-6 after three periods, Philadelphia battled back on Paul McFadden's third field goal of the game (36 yards) and Jaworski's scoring pass to Jackson. Philadelphia safety Wes Hopkins ended two Dallas drives deep in Eagles' territory with an interception in the first quarter and a fumble recovery in the fourth quarter and was named NFC defensive player of the week.

Dallas	7	0	7	0	— 14
Philadelphia	0	3	3	10	— 16

Dall —Dorsett 7 pass from Hogeboom (Septien kick)
Phil —FG McFadden 39
Phil —FG McFadden 33
Dall —Dorsett 10 run (Septien kick)
Phil —FG McFadden 36
Phil —K. Jackson 36 pass from Jaworski (McFadden kick)

Buffalo 21, Indianapolis 9—At Rich Stadium, attendance 28,430. Greg Bell rushed for two touchdowns to lead the Bills to their first win of the season. Bell's first-half touchdown runs of seven and one yards gave the Bills a 14-6 halftime lead. Vince Ferragamo added a three-yard touchdown pass to tight end Pete Metzelaars in the fourth quarter to complete Buffalo's scoring. The win snapped the Bills' eight-game losing streak. Bell was named AFC offensive player of the week.

Indianapolis	3	3	3	0	— 9
Buffalo	7	7	0	7	— 21

Buff —Bell 7 run (Norwood kick)
Ind —FG Allegre 41
Ind —FG Allegre 27
Buff —Bell 1 run (Norwood kick)
Ind —FG Allegre 38
Buff —Metzelaars 3 pass from Ferragamo (Norwood kick)

Los Angeles Raiders 21, Cleveland 20—At Cleveland Stadium, attendance 77,928. Marc Wilson's eight-yard touchdown pass to Todd Christensen on fourth down with 29 seconds left rallied the Raiders to their fifth straight win. Los Angeles led 14-7 at halftime on Frank Hawkins's 21-yard touchdown run and Wilson's 11-yard scoring pass to Marcus Allen. The Browns responded with 13 straight points to take a 20-14 lead before Wilson moved the Raiders 60 yards in 13 plays for the winning score.

L.A. Raiders	7	7	0	7	— 21
Cleveland	7	0	3	10	— 20

Raiders —Hawkins 21 run (C. Bahr kick)
Clev —Byner 1 run (M. Bahr kick)
Raiders —Allen 11 pass from Wilson (C. Bahr kick)
Clev —FG M. Bahr 31
Clev —FG M. Bahr 31
Clev —Mack 7 pass from Kosar (M. Bahr kick)
Raiders —Christensen 8 pass from Wilson (C. Bahr kick)

Los Angeles Rams 16, Kansas City 0—At Arrowhead Stadium, attendance 64,474. Eric Dickerson ran for one touchdown and Mike Lansford kicked three field goals as the Rams remained unbeaten by blanking the Chiefs. Dickerson's scoring run covered one yard, while Lansford connected on field goals from 33, 37, and 30 yards. LeRoy Irvin's two interceptions paced Los Angeles's defense as they picked off six Todd Blackledge passes. It was the Rams' first shutout since defeating the Buccaneers 9-0 in the 1979 NFC Championship Game.

L.A. Rams	0	13	3	0	— 16
Kansas City	0	0	0	0	— 0

Rams —Dickerson 1 run (Lansford kick)
Rams —FG Lansford 33
Rams —FG Lansford 37
Rams —FG Lansford 30

Atlanta 31, New Orleans 24—At Atlanta-Fulton County Stadium, attendance 44,784. Cliff Austin's 94-yard kickoff return with 4:13 left helped the Falcons post their first win. Touchdown runs by Gerald Riggs (three yards) and Dave Archer (18), and Mike Gann's 42-yard fumble return for a score put Atlanta ahead 21-10 going into the final quarter. Austin's return, following a Saints' touchdown, sealed the victory for the Falcons. Atlanta's defense forced five turnovers and recorded four sacks.

New Orleans	0	10	0	14	— 24
Atlanta	7	7	7	10	— 31

Atl —Riggs 3 run (Luckhurst kick)
NO —W. Wilson 11 pass from D. Wilson (Andersen kick)
Atl —Gann 42 fumble recovery return (Luckhurst kick)
NO —FG Andersen 33
Atl —Archer 18 run (Luckhurst kick)
Atl —FG Luckhurst 31
NO —Brenner 28 pass from D. Wilson (Andersen kick)
Atl —Austin 94 kickoff return (Luckhurst kick)
NO —Del Rio 50 fumble recovery return (Andersen kick)

New England 20, New York Jets 13—At Sullivan Stadium, attendance 58,163. Steve Grogan passed for one touchdown and ran for another to spark the Patriots' fourth-quarter rally and win over the Jets. Grogan's 36-yard scoring pass to Irving Fryar early in the fourth period gave New England a 13-6 lead. Playing without NFL rushing leader Freeman McNeil (rib injury), the Jets bounced back on Tony Paige's two-yard touchdown run to tie the game 13-13. The Patriots scored their final touchdown on Grogan's three-yard bootleg with 3:27 left to put the game away. New England linebacker Andre Tippett finished with three sacks to earn AFC defensive player of the week honors. The loss snapped the Jets' five-game win streak.

N.Y. Jets	0	3	3	7	— 13
New England	3	3	0	14	— 20

NE —FG Franklin 19
NYJ —FG Leahy 53
NE —FG Franklin 44
NYJ —FG Leahy 52
NE —Fryar 36 pass from Grogan (Franklin kick)
NYJ —Paige 2 run (Leahy kick)
NE —Grogan 3 run (Franklin kick)

Pittsburgh 23, St. Louis 10—At Three Rivers Stadium, attendance 56,478. Gary Anderson's three field goals helped the Steelers snap a three-game losing streak. Mark Malone completed a 45-yard touchdown pass to Louis Lipps with three minutes remaining in the first quarter to give Pittsburgh the lead for good 7-3. Anderson's two field goals in the third period clinched the win as the defense shut down the Cardinals' offense by forcing three turnovers and accumulating six sacks.

St. Louis	3	0	0	7	— 10
Pittsburgh	14	3	6	0	— 23

StL —FG O'Donoghue 19
Pitt —Lipps 45 pass from Malone (Anderson kick)
Pitt —Pollard 14 run (Anderson kick)
Pitt —FG Anderson 33
Pitt —FG Anderson 18
Pitt —FG Anderson 26
StL —Mitchell 5 pass from Lomax (O'Donoghue kick)

Minnesota 21, San Diego 17—At Metrodome, attendance 61,670. Tommy Kramer's 26-yard touchdown pass to Leo Lewis with 19 seconds left in the game highlighted the Vikings' comeback win. Trailing 10-7 in the fourth quarter, Kramer found tight end Mike Mularkey on a 51-yard scoring pass to give Minnesota a 14-10 lead. But the Chargers rebounded on Tim Spencer's second touchdown run of the game from one yard to take a 17-14 lead with 6:13 remaining. Lewis's scoring catch finished a 13-play, 76-yard drive. Kramer completed 31 of 46 passes for 311 yards, while Darrin Nelson had a career-high 12 catches for 67 yards.

San Diego	7	3	0	7	— 17
Minnesota	0	7	0	14	— 21

SD —Spencer 2 run (Thomas kick)
Minn —Rice 1 run (Stenerud kick)
SD —FG Thomas 42
Minn —Mularkey 51 pass from Kramer (Stenerud kick)
SD —Spencer 1 run (Thomas kick)
Minn —Lewis 26 pass from Kramer (Stenerud kick)

Detroit 23, San Francisco 21—At Pontiac Silverdome, attendance 67,715. James Jones ran for 116 yards on 30 carries and Ed Murray kicked three field goals to lead the Lions over the 49ers. Pete Mandley's 63-yard punt return, Jones's two-yard touchdown run, and two Murray field goals from 24 and 41 yards gave Detroit a 20-14 halftime lead. Murray's third field goal late in the third quarter from 45 yards proved decisive as the defense held off a late San Francisco rally. Jones's 100-yard effort was the first of his career.

San Francisco	14	0	0	7	— 21
Detroit	7	13	3	0	— 23

Det —Mandley 63 punt return (Murray kick)
SF —Montana 1 run (Wersching kick)
SF —McIntyre recovered fumble in end zone (Wersching kick)
Det —J. Jones 2 run (Murray kick)
Det —FG Murray 24
Det —FG Murray 41
Det —FG Murray 45
SF —Craig 11 run (Wersching kick)

Denver 13, Seattle 10—At Mile High Stadium, attendance 74,899. Rich Karlis's 24-yard field goal 9:19 into overtime helped the Broncos to a 13-10 win and a share of first place in the AFC West. Sammy Winder's first-quarter 36-yard touchdown run and Karlis's 45-yard field goal provided Denver with a 10-0 lead midway through the third quarter. Seattle forced overtime by scoring 10 straight points. Dave Krieg connected with Steve Largent on a nine-yard touchdown pass and Norm Johnson's 39-yard field goal tied the game up. Rookie defensive back Daniel Hunter's 20-yard interception return to the Seahawks' 15-yard line set up Karlis's deciding field goal. Seattle's Curt Warner led all rushers with 136 yards on 27 carries.

Seattle	0	0	7	3	0	— 10
Denver	7	0	3	0	3	— 13

Den —Winder 36 run (Karlis kick)
Den —FG Karlis 45
Sea —Largent 9 pass from Krieg (Johnson kick)
Sea —FG Johnson 39
Den —FG Karlis 24

Miami 41, Tampa Bay 38—At Orange Bowl, attendance 62,335. Fuad Reveiz's 43-yard field goal with six seconds left lifted the Dolphins over the Buccaneers. Down 24-14 at halftime, the Buccaneers scored 24 points in the second half to tie the score at 38-38 with 48 seconds left. Dan Marino, who finished with 302 yards passing and three touchdowns, moved the Dolphins 49 yards in 42 seconds to set up Reveiz's winning field goal. The win overshadowed the performances of Tampa Bay's Steve DeBerg, who passed for a career-high 365 yards (19 of 32), and Jimmie Giles, who caught a team-record four touchdown passes (seven catches for 116 yards).

Tampa Bay	0	14	7	17	— 38
Miami	14	10	14	3	— 41

Mia —Moore 16 pass from Marino (Reveiz kick)
Mia —Jensen 4 pass from Marino (Reveiz kick)
TB —Wilder 10 run (Igwebuike kick)
Mia —Davenport 1 run (Reveiz kick)
Mia —FG Reveiz 20
TB —Giles 15 pass from DeBerg (Igwebuike kick)
Mia —Nathan 1 run (Reveiz kick)
TB —Giles 39 pass from DeBerg (Igwebuike kick)
Mia —Hardy 3 pass from Marino (Reveiz kick)
TB —Giles 7 pass from DeBerg (Igwebuike kick)
TB —Giles 16 pass from DeBerg (Igwebuike kick)
TB —FG Igwebuike 38
Mia —FG Reveiz 43

New York Giants 17, Washington 3—At Giants Stadium, attendance 74,389. Two Giants rookies, George Adams and Mark Bavaro, each accounted for touchdowns as New York's defense shut down the Redskins' offense to register a 17-3 win. Phil Simms's 29-yard scoring pass to Bavaro opened the Giants' scoring. Adams then followed with his first NFL rushing score, a two-yard run 5:48 into the second half to give New York a 14-0 lead. Mark Moseley's 47-yard field goal with 4:30 left prevented a shutout. Lawrence Taylor had two of the Giants' seven sacks to earn NFC defensive player of the week honors. New York's defense stopped three Washington drives deep in Giants territory with three interceptions and limited the Redskins' league-leading rushing attack to 69 yards.

Washington	0	0	0	3	— 3
N.Y. Giants	0	7	7	3	— 17

NYG —Bavaro 29 pass from Simms (Atkinson kick)
NYG —Adams 2 run (Atkinson kick)
NYG —FG Atkinson 47
Wash —FG Moseley 47

MONDAY, OCTOBER 21

Chicago 23, Green Bay 7—At Soldier Field, attendance 65,095. Three second-quarter touchdown runs by Walter Payton and defensive tackle William Perry helped the Bears down the Packers. In a game plagued by turnovers, Chicago took advantage of three Green Bay miscues to open up a 21-7 lead. Payton, who rushed for over 100 yards for the sixty-sixth time (112 yards), surpassed former kicker Bob Thomas (629 points) to become the Bears' all-time leading scorer with 630 points. Perry, the rookie sensation, scored his first NFL touchdown playing fullback in a short-yardage situation.

Green Bay	7	0	0	0	— 7
Chicago	0	21	0	2	— 23

GB —Lofton 27 pass from Dickey (Del Greco kick)
Chi —Payton 2 run (Butler kick)
Chi —Perry 1 run (Butler kick)
Chi —Payton 1 run (Butler kick)
Chi —Safety, Wilson sacked Zorn in end zone

EIGHTH WEEK SUMMARIES

STANDINGS

American Football Conference

Eastern Division

	W	L	T	Pct.	Pts.	OP
N.Y. Jets	6	2	0	.750	173	118
Miami	5	3	0	.625	207	177
New England	5	3	0	.625	156	143
Indianapolis	3	5	0	.375	155	169
Buffalo	1	7	0	.125	104	193

Central Division

	W	L	T	Pct.	Pts.	OP
Cleveland	4	4	0	.500	141	122
Cincinnati	3	5	0	.375	237	261
Houston	3	5	0	.375	139	165
Pittsburgh	3	5	0	.375	173	144

Western Division

	W	L	T	Pct.	Pts.	OP
Denver	6	2	0	.750	209	151
L.A. Raiders	6	2	0	.750	193	154
Seattle	4	4	0	.500	188	199
Kansas City	3	5	0	.375	151	181
San Diego	3	5	0	.375	190	221

National Football Conference

Eastern Division

	W	L	T	Pct.	Pts.	OP
Dallas	6	2	0	.750	197	125
N.Y. Giants	5	3	0	.625	181	131
Philadelphia	4	4	0	.500	123	121
Washington	4	4	0	.500	114	158
St. Louis	3	5	0	.375	165	206

Central Division

	W	L	T	Pct.	Pts.	OP
Chicago	8	0	0	1.000	239	114
Detroit	5	3	0	.625	157	180
Minnesota	4	4	0	.500	167	167
Green Bay	3	5	0	.375	154	200
Tampa Bay	0	8	0	.000	164	250

Western Division

	W	L	T	Pct.	Pts.	OP
L.A. Rams	7	1	0	.875	163	117
San Francisco	4	4	0	.500	204	154
New Orleans	3	5	0	.375	163	207
Atlanta	1	7	0	.125	161	240

NOTE: The record-total 902,657 paid attendance this weekend marked the first time in the 66-year history of the NFL that over 900,000 tickets were sold for a single weekend.

SUNDAY, OCTOBER 27

Dallas 24, Atlanta 10—At Texas Stadium, attendance 57,941. Danny White passed for one touchdown and ran for another to help the Cowboys defeat the Falcons. White's 35-yard touchdown completion to Tony Hill, followed by Tony Dorsett's 60-yard scoring run and Rafael Septien's 28-yard field goal, gave Dallas a 17-10 halftime lead. White, who connected on 27 of 47 passes for 362 yards, scored on a one-yard touchdown dive to clinch the win for the Cowboys. The Cowboys' defense was instrumental in the win shutting out the Falcons in the second half. Dallas outgained Atlanta 461 total yards to 253.

Atlanta	7	3	0	0	—	10
Dallas	0	17	0	7	—	24

Atl —Matthews 3 pass from Archer (Luckhurst kick)
Atl —FG Luckhurst 38
Dall —Hill 35 pass from D. White (Septien kick)
Dall —Dorsett 60 run (Septien kick)
Dall —FG Septien 28
Dall —D. White 1 run (Septien kick)

Philadelphia 21, Buffalo 17—At Veterans Stadium, attendance 60,987. Ron Jaworski's 32-yard touchdown pass to Mike Quick with 1:55 remaining in the game climaxed the Eagles' 21-17 win. Trailing 17-0 in the final period, Philadelphia rallied to pull within three, 17-14, on Jaworski's three-yard touchdown run and Wes Hopkins's 24-yard interception return for a score. Jaworski completed 21 of 42 passes for 258 yards to pace the Eagles' offensive attack, which was limited to 38 rushing yards by the Bills. Quick led all receivers with 117 yards on eight catches.

Buffalo	7	3	7	0	—	17
Philadelphia	0	0	0	21	—	21

Buff —Reed 14 run (Norwood kick)
Buff —FG Norwood 26
Buff —Reed 7 pass from Ferragamo (Norwood kick)
Phil —Jaworski 3 run (McFadden kick)
Phil —Hopkins 24 interception return (McFadden kick)
Phil —Quick 32 pass from Jaworski (McFadden kick)

Denver 30, Kansas City 10—At Arrowhead Stadium, attendance 68,246. Gerald Willhite rushed for a pair of touchdowns and Rich Karlis kicked three field goals to power the Broncos to their fourth straight win. Denver took a commanding 27-7 second-quarter lead by scoring on Willhite touchdown runs of one and three yards, plus Gene Lang's one-yard scoring plunge, and Karlis's two field goals from 24 and 23 yards. Rulon Jones paced the Broncos' defense with two sacks.

Denver	10	17	0	3	—	30
Kansas City	0	7	3	0	—	10

Den —Willhite 1 run (Karlis kick)
Den —FG Karlis 24
Den —Lang 1 run (Karlis kick)
Den —Willhite 3 run (Karlis kick)
KC —Horton 1 run (Lowery kick)
Den —FG Karlis 23
KC —FG Lowery 33
Den —FG Karlis 19

Indianapolis 37, Green Bay 10—At Hoosier Dome, attendance 59,708. Randy McMillan ran for 126 yards on 24 carries and Wayne Capers scored three touchdowns to help the Colts over the Packers. Capers scored on a 20-yard run and had touchdown receptions of 33 and 39 yards to earn AFC offensive player of the week honors. He finished with five catches for 117 yards. Teammate Matt Bouza caught six passes for 109 yards to become the first two Colts receivers to total 100 receiving yards in a game since Raymond Chester (122) and Glenn Doughty (110) in 1977. Eugene Daniel, who set up two Colts scores with two of his three interceptions, was named AFC defensive player of the week.

Green Bay	7	3	0	0	—	10
Indianapolis	14	6	7	10	—	37

Ind —Capers 20 run (Allegre kick)
Ind —McMillan 21 run (Allegre kick)
GB —Coffman 8 pass from Dickey (Del Greco kick)
Ind —FG Allegre 24
GB —FG Del Greco 29
Ind —FG Allegre 26
Ind —Capers 39 pass from Pagel (Allegre kick)
Ind —FG Allegre 22
Ind —Capers 33 pass from Kofler (Allegre kick)

Houston 20, St. Louis 10—At Busch Memorial Stadium, attendance 43,190. Fourth-quarter touchdowns by Drew Hill and Mike Akiu highlighted the Oilers' comeback win. Trailing 10-6 early in the fourth quarter, Warren Moon completed a 37-yard touchdown pass to Hill and Akiu returned a blocked punt 20 yards for the final margin of victory. Tony Zendejas's two second-quarter field goals from 39 and 38 yards kept the Oilers within striking distance at halftime. Hill finished with six catches for 132 yards to lead all receivers, while St. Louis's reserve running back Stump Mitchell rushed for 148 yards on 21 carries to top all rushers.

Houston	0	6	0	14	—	20
St. Louis	10	0	0	0	—	10

StL —Tilley 12 pass from Lomax (O'Donoghue kick)
StL —FG O'Donoghue 30
Hou —FG Zendejas 39
Hou —FG Zendejas 38
Hou —Hill 37 pass from Moon (Zendejas kick)
Hou —Akiu 20 blocked punt return (Zendejas kick)

Detroit 31, Miami 21—At Pontiac Silverdome, attendance 75,291. Eric Hipple passed for three touchdowns to lead the Lions past the Dolphins. Detroit took a 24-14 halftime lead on Ed Murray's 50-yard field goal and Hipple's scoring passes to James Jones (6 yards), Leonard Thompson (28), and Mark Nichols (30). Jones's one-yard touchdown run early in the fourth quarter clinched the win for the Lions. Hipple, who completed 14 of 19 passes for 239 yards, was named NFC offensive player of the week. Jones had 114 yards rushing for Detroit.

Miami	0	14	7	0	—	21
Detroit	10	14	0	7	—	31

Det —J. Jones 6 pass from Hipple (Murray kick)
Det —FG Murray 50
Mia —Rose 19 pass from Marino (Reveiz kick)
Det —Thompson 28 pass from Hipple (Murray kick)
Mia —Moore 5 pass from Marino (Reveiz kick)
Det —Nichols 30 pass from Hipple (Murray kick)
Mia —Brudzinski 7 fumble recovery return (Reveiz kick)
Det —J. Jones 1 run (Murray kick)

Chicago 27, Minnesota 9—At Soldier Field, attendance 63,815. Walter Payton rushed for 118 yards and Jim McMahon completed a pair of touchdown passes as the Bears defeated the Vikings 27-9. Leading 13-7 at halftime, Chicago pulled away in the third quarter when linebacker Otis Wilson intercepted a Tommy Kramer pass and returned it 23 yards for a score. McMahon's 20-yard scoring pass to Payton put the game out of reach. The Bears' offense amassed 413 total yards, while the defense yielded just 236 and picked off five Vikings passes.

Minnesota	0	7	0	2	—	9
Chicago	10	3	7	7	—	27

Chi —McKinnon 33 pass from McMahon (Butler kick)
Chi —FG Butler 40
Minn —Nelson 1 run (Stenerud kick)
Chi —FG Butler 29
Chi —Wilson 23 interception return (Butler kick)
Chi —Payton 20 pass from McMahon (Butler kick)
Minn —Safety, Elshire tackled Fuller in end zone

New England 32, Tampa Bay 14—At Tampa Stadium, attendance 34,661. Running back Craig James ran for two touchdowns and threw another to help the Patriots defeat the Buccaneers for their third straight win. James connected with running mate Tony Collins on an 11-yard scoring play in the second period to pull New England within 14-13 at halftime. James's second-half scoring runs of 8 and 22 yards put the Patriots ahead for good. Collins finished with six catches for 109 yards. New England outgained Tampa Bay 420 total yards to 209.

New England	0	13	3	16	—	32
Tampa Bay	14	0	0	0	—	14

TB —Giles 16 pass from DeBerg (Igwebuike kick)
TB —Wilder 1 run (Igwebuike kick)
NE —FG Franklin 35
NE —FG Franklin 50
NE —Collins 11 pass from C. James (Franklin kick)
NE —FG Franklin 49
NE —C. James 8 run (Franklin kick)
NE —C. James 22 run (Franklin kick)
NE —Safety, Blackmon tackled DeBerg in end zone

New York Giants 21, New Orleans 13—At Louisiana Superdome, attendance 54,082. Joe Morris rushed for over 100 yards for the second straight week (104 yards on 20 carries) to lead the Giants past the Saints. New York, which had a slim 7-6 edge in the fourth quarter, took a commanding 21-6 lead when Morris ran for two scores within a span of 4:03 of the final period. Elvis Patterson had an interception and a fumble recovery to account for two of the Giants' four takeaways.

N.Y. Giants	0	7	0	14	—	21
New Orleans	3	0	0	10	—	13

NO —FG Andersen 33
NYG —Johnson 6 pass from Simms (Atkinson kick)
NO —FG Andersen 43
NYG —Morris 5 run (Atkinson kick)
NYG —Morris 1 run (Atkinson kick)
NO —Martin 17 pass from D. Wilson (Andersen kick)

Cincinnati 26, Pittsburgh 21—At Riverfront Stadium, attendance 55,421. Boomer Esiason completed 18 of 29 passes for 235 yards and a touchdown as the Bengals held off a Steelers' fourth-quarter rally to register their first season-sweep of Pittsburgh since 1981. Jim Breech kicked three third-period field goals from 39, 40, and 32 yards to help Cincinnati to a 26-7 lead. Safety Robert Jackson's two interceptions, including one for a 57-yard touchdown, accounted for two of the six Bengals takeaways.

Pittsburgh	0	7	0	14	—	21
Cincinnati	3	14	9	0	—	26

Cin —FG Breech 37
Cin —Holman 11 pass from Esiason (Breech kick)
Cin —Jackson 57 interception return (Breech kick)
Pitt —Lipps 49 pass from Woodley (Anderson kick)
Cin —FG Breech 39
Cin —FG Breech 40
Cin —FG Breech 32
Pitt —Lipps 62 punt return (Anderson kick)
Pitt —Abercrombie 1 run (Anderson kick)

San Francisco 28, Los Angeles Rams 14—At Anaheim Stadium, attendance 65,939. Joe Montana completed 22 of 30 passes for 306 yards and three touchdowns as the 49ers handed the Rams their first loss of the season. San Francisco jumped out to a 28-0 halftime lead on Montana's scoring passes to Wendell Tyler (9 yards), Dwight Clark (8), and Roger Craig (35), and Craig's 14-yard touchdown run. Craig accounted for 195 (63 rushing, 132 receiving) of the 49ers' 429 yards of offense. Three interceptions by the 49ers' defense ended three Rams' drives in the second half.

San Francisco	14	14	0	0	—	28
L.A. Rams	0	0	7	7	—	14

SF —Craig 14 run (Wersching kick)
SF —Tyler 9 pass from Montana (Wersching kick)
SF —Clark 8 pass from Montana (Wersching kick)
SF —Craig 35 pass from Montana (Wersching kick)
Rams —Ellard 23 pass from Brock (Lansford kick)
Rams —Hunter 3 pass from Brock (Lansford kick)

New York Jets 17, Seattle 14—At Giants Stadium, attendance 69,320. Freeman McNeil rushed for 151 yards and Ken O'Brien passed for two touchdowns as the Jets overcame a 14-0 first-half deficit to defeat the Seahawks for the first time ever. New York trailed 14-10 early in the fourth period on O'Brien's 16-yard scoring strike to McNeil and Pat Leahy's 41-yard field goal. O'Brien then concluded a seven-play, 91-yard drive with a 15-yard scoring pass to Wesley Walker to put the Jets ahead for good 17-14 with 5:11 left. New York's defense excelled in the second half as it forced three turnovers while limiting the Seahawks' offense to 68 yards.

Seattle	0	14	0	0	—	14
N.Y. Jets	0	0	7	10	—	17

Sea —Turner 45 pass from Krieg (Johnson kick)
Sea —Green 79 fumble recovery return (Johnson kick)
NYJ —McNeil 16 pass from O'Brien (Leahy kick)
NYJ —FG Leahy 41
NYJ —Walker 15 pass from O'Brien (Leahy kick)

Washington 14, Cleveland 7—At Cleveland Stadium, attendance 78,540. John Riggins ran for 112 yards and a touchdown to lead the Redskins over the Browns. Riggins's one-yard touchdown run and Joe Theismann's 19-yard touchdown pass to Gary Clark in the first quarter were all the points the Redskins needed as the defense forced four Browns turnovers. Theismann connected on 16 of 23 passes for 166 yards in Washington's ball-control offense. Cleveland's Ozzie Newsome caught nine passes for 92 yards and a touchdown to extend his consecutive games streak with at least one reception to 90.

Washington	14	0	0	0	—	14
Cleveland	0	0	7	0	—	7

Wash — Riggins 1 run (Moseley kick)
Wash — Clark 19 pass from Theismann (Moseley kick)
Clev — Newsome 14 pass from Danielson (Bahr kick)

MONDAY, OCTOBER 28

Los Angeles Raiders 34, San Diego 21—At Memorial Coliseum, attendance 69,297. Marcus Allen scored three touchdowns and rushed for 111 yards on 30 carries to power the Raiders past the Chargers. Los Angeles took a 24-7 halftime lead on scoring runs by Allen (three and one yards) and Jessie Hester (13), and Chris Bahr's 20-yard field goal. Allen added a four-yard touchdown run in the third quarter. Todd Christensen had seven catches for 134 yards. Linebacker Rod Martin had two of the Raiders' six sacks.

San Diego	0	7	7	7	— 21
L.A. Raiders	10	14	7	3	— 34

Raiders — FG Bahr 20
Raiders — Hester 13 run (Bahr kick)
SD — Anderson 52 pass from Fouts (Thomas kick)
Raiders — Allen 3 run (Bahr kick)
Raiders — Allen 1 run (Bahr kick)
SD — Anderson 4 run (Thomas kick)
Raiders — Allen 4 run (Bahr kick)
Raiders — FG Bahr 35
SD — Bendross 1 pass from Fouts (Thomas kick)

NINTH WEEK SUMMARIES

STANDINGS

American Football Conference

Eastern Division	W	L	T	Pct.	Pts.	OP
N.Y. Jets	7	2	0	.778	208	135
New England	6	3	0	.667	173	156
Miami	5	4	0	.556	220	194
Indianapolis	3	6	0	.333	172	204
Buffalo	1	8	0	.111	121	216
Central Division						
Cincinnati	4	5	0	.444	260	278
Cleveland	4	5	0	.444	150	132
Houston	4	5	0	.444	162	185
Pittsburgh	4	5	0	.444	183	153
Western Division						
Denver	6	3	0	.667	219	181
L.A. Raiders	6	3	0	.667	196	187
Seattle	5	4	0	.556	221	202
San Diego	4	5	0	.444	220	231
Kansas City	3	6	0	.333	171	204

National Football Conference

Eastern Division	W	L	T	Pct.	Pts.	OP
Dallas	6	3	0	.667	207	146
N.Y. Giants	6	3	0	.667	203	151
Washington	5	4	0	.556	158	168
Philadelphia	4	5	0	.444	136	145
St. Louis	4	5	0	.444	186	216
Central Division						
Chicago	9	0	0	1.000	255	124
Detroit	5	4	0	.556	170	196
Minnesota	5	4	0	.556	183	180
Green Bay	3	6	0	.333	164	216
Tampa Bay	0	9	0	.000	184	272
Western Division						
L.A. Rams	8	1	0	.889	191	127
San Francisco	5	4	0	.556	228	167
New Orleans	3	6	0	.333	173	235
Atlanta	1	8	0	.111	171	284

SUNDAY, NOVEMBER 3

Chicago 16, Green Bay 10—At Lambeau Field, attendance 55,343. Walter Payton ran for 192 yards and a touchdown and William Perry caught his first NFL touchdown pass as the Bears squeaked by the Packers to remain unbeaten. Chicago overcame a 10-7 deficit in the fourth quarter on Payton's 27-yard scoring run and Steve McMichael's safety. Jim McMahon's four-yard touchdown pass to Perry gave the Bears a 7-0 halftime lead. Chicago was held to a season-low 58 yards passing.

Chicago	0	7	0	9	— 16
Green Bay	3	0	7	0	— 10

GB — FG Del Greco 40
Chi — Perry 4 pass from McMahon (Butler kick)
GB — Clark 55 pass from Zorn (Del Greco kick)
Chi — Safety, McMichael sacked Zorn in end zone
Chi — Payton 27 run (Butler kick)

Cincinnati 23, Buffalo 17—At Rich Stadium, attendance 25,640. Larry Kinnebrew rushed for a career-high 128 yards on 30 carries and Boomer Esiason threw two touchdown passes to highlight the Bengals' victory. Cincinnati came back from a 10-6 halftime deficit on Esiason's 22-yard scoring pass to M.L. Harris in the third quarter. Kinnebrew's three-yard run with 8:38 left and Jim Breech's 31-yard field goal finished the Bengals' scoring. Esiason completed 11 of 21 passes for 193 yards as Cincinnati's offense compiled 389 total yards.

Cincinnati	0	6	7	10	— 23
Buffalo	7	3	0	7	— 17

Buff — Bell 14 run (Norwood kick)
Buff — FG Norwood 43
Cin — Brown 68 pass from Esiason (kick blocked)
Cin — Harris 22 pass from Esiason (Breech kick)
Cin — Kinnebrew 3 run (Breech kick)
Cin — FG Breech 31
Buff — Ramson 5 pass from Mathison (Norwood kick)

Pittsburgh 10, Cleveland 9—At Three Rivers Stadium, attendance 51,976. Gary Anderson's 25-yard field goal with nine seconds left lifted the Steelers over the Browns for the sixteenth straight time at Three Rivers Stadium. The win put all four AFC Central teams into an unprecedented four-way tie for first place. Walter Abercrombie scored the game's only touchdown on a 32-yard run, which gave Pittsburgh a 7-6 lead 4:59 into the second half. Cleveland regained the lead in the fourth quarter 9-7 on Matt Bahr's third field goal. Anderson's winning kick completed a 10-play, 73-yard drive. Cleveland's offense was held to a season-low 153 total yards.

Cleveland	0	6	0	3	— 9
Pittsburgh	0	0	7	3	— 10

Clev — FG Bahr 34
Clev — FG Bahr 45
Pitt — Abercrombie 32 run (Anderson kick)
Clev — FG Bahr 30
Pitt — FG Anderson 25

San Diego 30, Denver 10—At San Diego Jack Murphy Stadium, attendance 57,312. Dan Fouts passed for two touchdowns and Gary Anderson ran 16 yards for another as the Chargers easily beat the Broncos. Fouts and Wes Chandler combined on first-half touchdowns of 19 and 9 yards and Bob Thomas kicked a 36-yard field goal to give San Diego a 17-3 halftime lead. Anderson finished with 116 yards rushing, which marked his first career 100-yard game. Fouts completed 23 of 34 passes for 302 of the Chargers' 430 total yards. San Diego's defense limited the Broncos to 295 total yards, including only 64 yards rushing.

Denver	0	3	0	7	— 10
San Diego	7	10	7	6	— 30

SD — Chandler 19 pass from Fouts (Thomas kick)
SD — FG Thomas 36
SD — Chandler 9 pass from Fouts (Thomas kick)
Den — FG Karlis 36
SD — Anderson 16 run (Thomas kick)
SD — FG Thomas 35
Den — Sewell 54 pass from Kubiak (Karlis kick)
SD — FG Thomas 18

Minnesota 16, Detroit 13—At Metrodome, attendance 58,012. Jan Stenerud's third field goal of the game, a 28-yarder with one second left, gave the Vikings a win over the Lions. Minnesota took a 13-3 third-quarter lead on Ted Brown's one-yard touchdown run following Stenerud's second-quarter field goals of 26 and 49 yards. Darrin Nelson ran for 122 yards on 25 carries as the Vikings gained 301 total yards. Minnesota's defense limited Detroit to 153 yards.

Detroit	3	0	7	3	— 13
Minnesota	0	6	7	3	— 16

Det — FG Murray 32
Minn — FG Stenerud 26
Minn — FG Stenerud 49
Minn — Brown 1 run (Stenerud kick)
Det — Ferguson 1 run (Murray kick)
Det — FG Murray 20
Minn — FG Stenerud 28

Houston 23, Kansas City 20—At Astrodome, attendance 41,238. Tony Zendejas's 38-yard field goal with 14 seconds left led the Oilers to their third straight win and a share of first place in the AFC Central for the first time since 1981. Butch Woolfolk ran for 101 yards on 14 carries, including a third-quarter four-yard touchdown run which gave Houston a 20-6 lead. The Chiefs tied the score 20-20 on a pair of Bill Kenney touchdown passes. Warren Moon completed 24 of 35 passes for 255 yards, including touchdown passes to Drew Hill (23 yards) and Chris Dressel (three).

Kansas City	0	3	3	14	— 20
Houston	0	6	14	3	— 23

Hou — Hill 23 pass from Moon (kick failed)
KC — FG Lowery 35
Hou — Dressel 3 pass from Moon (Zendejas kick)
KC — FG Lowery 39
Hou — Woolfolk 4 run (Zendejas kick)
KC — Heard 6 pass from Kenney (Lowery kick)
KC — Paige 18 pass from Kenney (Lowery kick)
Hou — FG Zendejas 38

Seattle 33, Los Angeles Raiders 3—At Kingdome, attendance 64,060. Terry Taylor led a fierce Seahawks defense that intercepted four passes and recorded six sacks en route to defeating the Raiders. Taylor's 75-yard interception return for a touchdown capped a 26-point first-half scoring spree that also included touchdown passes from Dave Krieg to Curt Warner (27 yards) and Byron Walker's 56-yard blocked field goal return for a touchdown. Walker's return for a score was the first in club history. It was Los Angeles's worst defeat since November 22, 1981, when the Raiders were beaten by San Diego 55-21.

L.A. Raiders	0	0	3	0	— 3
Seattle	3	23	7	0	— 33

Sea — FG Johnson 39
Sea — Warner 27 pass from Krieg (kick failed)
Sea — FG Johnson 31
Sea — Walker 56 blocked field goal return (Johnson kick)
Sea — Taylor 75 interception return (Johnson kick)
Raiders — FG Bahr 30
Sea — Turner 38 pass from Krieg (Johnson kick)

New England 17, Miami 13—At Sullivan Stadium, attendance 58,811. Steve Grogan ran for one touchdown and threw for another on a flea-flicker play to rally the Patriots past the Dolphins. Trailing 13-3 in the fourth quarter, Grogan handed off to running back Mosi Tatupu, who pitched back to Grogan, who then threw a 28-yard scoring pass to Greg Hawthorne to pull New England within three of Miami at 13-10. Grogan's one-yard touchdown run with 3:03 left gave the Patriots their first lead of the day and sealed the win. Led by Craig James's 119 rushing yards, New England outgained the Dolphins 380 to 236. The victory was the Patriots' fourth straight.

Miami	7	3	3	0	— 13
New England	0	3	0	14	— 17

Mia — Davenport 3 run (Reveiz kick)
Mia — FG Reveiz 26
NE — FG Franklin 38
Mia — FG Reveiz 32
NE — Hawthorne 28 pass from Grogan (Franklin kick)
NE — Grogan 1 run (Franklin kick)

Los Angeles Rams 28, New Orleans 10—At Anaheim Stadium, attendance 49,030. Eric Dickerson ran for 108 yards and Dieter Brock completed a pair of touchdown passes to lead the Rams over the Saints. Dickerson's 11-yard run and Brock's 17-yard scoring pass to Henry Ellard gave Los Angeles a 14-0 halftime lead. Tony Hunter's career-high 113 yards on six receptions included a 29-yard touchdown. Charles White's five-yard run finished Los Angeles's scoring in the fourth quarter. The Rams' defense intercepted three passes, recorded nine sacks, and held the Saints' offense to 65 yards rushing.

New Orleans	0	0	7	3	— 10
L.A. Rams	7	7	7	7	— 28

Rams — Dickerson 11 run (Lansford kick)
Rams — Ellard 17 pass from Brock (Lansford kick)
NO — Martin 3 pass from D. Wilson (Andersen kick)
Rams — Hunter 29 pass from Brock (Lansford kick)
NO — FG Andersen 51
Rams — White 5 run (Lansford kick)

New York Jets 35, Indianapolis 17—At Hoosier Dome, attendance 59,683. The Jets exploded for 35 first-half points, including three touchdown passes by Ken O'Brien, en route to their victory over the Colts. O'Brien threw scoring passes to Al Toon (17 yards), Wesley Walker (seven), and Rocky Klever (nine). Freeman McNeil carried 26 times for 149 yards and a touchdown (15 yards) to increase his league-leading total to 945 yards. Kerry Glenn paced the defense with three (two fumble recoveries and one interception) of the Jets' five steals. The defense registered six sacks, while limiting the Colts to 51 yards rushing.

N.Y. Jets	14	21	0	0	— 35
Indianapolis	0	3	7	7	— 17

NYJ — Toon 17 pass from O'Brien (Leahy kick)
NYJ — McNeil 15 run (Leahy kick)
Ind — FG Allegre 23
NYJ — Walker 7 pass from O'Brien (Leahy kick)
NYJ — Klever 9 pass from O'Brien (Leahy kick)
NYJ — Bligen 28 run (Leahy kick)
Ind — Beach 2 pass from Pagel (Allegre kick)
Ind — Kofler 1 run (Allegre kick)

San Francisco 24, Philadelphia 13—At Candlestick Park, attendance 58,383. Wendell Tyler ran for a pair of touchdowns and Matt Cavanaugh threw a 14-yard scoring pass to Jerry Rice as the 49ers snapped the Eagles' three-game win streak. Cavanaugh, who replaced injured starter Joe Montana, completed 20 of 32 passes for 255 yards and one touchdown. Roger Craig, the league leader in total yards from scrimmage, totalled 167 yards (91 rushing, 76 receiving) to total 1,213. Philadelphia's Ron Jaworski was 24 of 48 for 394 yards. Mike Quick caught six passes for 146 yards, including an 82-yard touchdown from Jaworski for the Eagles' only touchdown.

Philadelphia	3	0	10	0	— 13
San Francisco	7	7	10	0	— 24

SF — Tyler 2 run (Wersching kick)
Phil — FG McFadden 36
SF — Rice 14 pass from Cavanaugh (Wersching kick)
SF — Tyler 3 run (Wersching kick)
Phil — Quick 82 pass from Jaworski (McFadden kick)
Phil — FG McFadden 44
SF — FG Wersching 36

New York Giants 22, Tampa Bay 20—At Giants Stadium, attendance 72,031. Eric Schubert became the first player in NFL history to kick five field goals in his first game, as the Giants edged the Buccaneers. Schubert's field goals were from 24, 36, 24, 41, and 33 yards. Joe Morris also helped lead New York by running for a career-high 132 yards on 26 carries, including a three-yard touchdown run. Giants quarterback Phil Simms directed a ball-control offense that generated 342 total yards. Safety Terry Kinard's interception in the closing minutes sealed New York's win.

Tampa Bay	3	10	0	7	— 20
N.Y. Giants	3	3	10	6	— 22

NYG — FG Schubert 24
TB — FG Igwebuike 53
TB — Giles 25 pass from DeBerg (Igwebuike kick)
NYG — FG Schubert 36
TB — FG Igwebuike 20
NYG — Morris 3 run (Schubert kick)
NYG — FG Schubert 24
NYG — FG Schubert 41
NYG — FG Schubert 33
TB — Giles 1 pass from DeBerg (Igwebuike kick)

Washington 44, Atlanta 10—At Atlanta-Fulton County Stadium, attendance 42,209. George Rogers and Keith Griffin combined for 288 yards rushing to lead the Redskins to a 44-10 victory over the Falcons. Griffin's five-yard touchdown run in the second quarter snapped a 3-3 tie as the Redskins reeled off a club-record 28 straight points. Griffin gained 164 yards on 16 carries, including a 66-yarder for Washington's final score. Rogers added 124 yards on 16 carries. Art Monk caught six passes for 106 yards to top all receivers. Washington's 307 yards rushing was the second highest in club history to the 352 gained versus the Los Angeles Rams on November 25, 1951.

Washington	3	28	3	10	— 44
Atlanta	3	0	0	7	— 10

Atl — FG Luckhurst 28
Wash — FG Moseley 39
Wash — Griffin 5 run (Moseley kick)
Wash — Theismann 11 run (Moseley kick)
Wash — Rogers 1 run (Moseley kick)
Wash — Monk 34 pass from Theismann (Moseley kick)
Wash — FG Moseley 40
Wash — FG Moseley 48
Wash — Griffin 66 run (Moseley kick)
Atl — Cox 14 pass from Holly (Luckhurst kick)

MONDAY, NOVEMBER 4

St. Louis 21, Dallas 10—At Busch Memorial Stadium, attendance 49,347. Neil Lomax passed for two second-half touchdowns to help spark the Cardinals' comeback win. Trailing 10-0 at halftime, St. Louis battled back in the third quarter to take a 14-10 lead on Lomax's 46-yard scoring pass to Pat Tilley and Earl Ferrell's eight-yard touchdown run. Lomax's nine-yard pass to J.T. Smith in the fourth quarter finished the Cardinals' scoring. Tilley finished with six receptions for 113 yards. Safety Leonard Smith had an interception and one of the Cardinals' four sacks to earn NFC defensive player of the week honors.

Dallas	0	10	0	0	— 10
St. Louis	0	0	14	7	— 21

Dall — Hill 8 pass from D. White (Septien kick)
Dall — FG Septien 19
StL — Tilley 46 pass from Lomax (Atkinson kick)
StL — Ferrell 8 run (Atkinson kick)
StL — J.T. Smith 9 pass from Lomax (Atkinson kick)

TENTH WEEK SUMMARIES

STANDINGS

American Football Conference

Eastern Division	W	L	T	Pct.	Pts.	OP
New England	7	3	0	.700	207	171
N.Y. Jets	7	3	0	.700	225	156
Miami	6	4	0	.600	241	211
Indianapolis	3	7	0	.300	187	238
Buffalo	2	8	0	.200	141	216
Central Division						
Cincinnati	5	5	0	.500	287	288
Pittsburgh	5	5	0	.500	219	181
Cleveland	4	6	0	.400	160	159
Houston	4	6	0	.400	162	205
Western Division						
Denver	7	3	0	.700	236	197
L.A. Raiders	6	4	0	.600	230	227
Seattle	6	4	0	.600	248	205
San Diego	5	5	0	.500	260	265
Kansas City	3	7	0	.300	199	240

National Football Conference

Eastern Division	W	L	T	Pct.	Pts.	OP
Dallas	7	3	0	.700	220	153
N.Y. Giants	7	3	0	.700	227	170
Philadelphia	5	5	0	.500	159	162
Washington	5	5	0	.500	165	181
St. Louis	4	6	0	.400	186	232
Central Division						
Chicago	10	0	0	1.000	279	127
Detroit	5	5	0	.500	173	220
Minnesota	5	5	0	.500	200	207
Green Bay	4	6	0	.400	191	233
Tampa Bay	1	9	0	.100	200	272
Western Division						
L.A. Rams	8	2	0	.800	210	151
San Francisco	5	5	0	.500	244	184
New Orleans	3	7	0	.300	176	262
Atlanta	1	9	0	.100	188	307

SUNDAY, NOVEMBER 10

Philadelphia 23, Atlanta 17—At Veterans Stadium, attendance 63,694. Ron Jaworski hit Mike Quick with a 99-yard touchdown pass 1:49 into overtime to give the Eagles a 23-17 win. Philadelphia took a 17-0 third-quarter lead on runs by Jaworski (one yard) and Earnest Jackson (eight), and Paul McFadden's 30-yard field goal. However, Atlanta stormed back with 17 straight fourth-quarter points to force the extra period. Thomas Strauthers had two of the Eagles' seven sacks as the defense held the Falcons to 91 passing yards. Quick finished with three catches for 145 yards, his third straight 100-yard game.

Atlanta	0	0	0	17	0	— 17
Philadelphia	0	14	3	0	6	— 23

Phil — E. Jackson 8 run (McFadden kick)
Phil — Jaworski 1 run (McFadden kick)
Phil — FG McFadden 30
Atl — Washington 18 pass from Archer (Luckhurst kick)
Atl — Riggs 1 run (Luckhurst kick)
Atl — FG Luckhurst 27
Phil — Quick 99 pass from Jaworski (no kick)

Cincinnati 27, Cleveland 10—At Riverfront Stadium, attendance 57,293. Boomer Esiason completed 23 of 33 passes for 262 yards and a touchdown to guide the Bengals over the Browns. Esiason's eight-yard scoring pass to James Brooks with 3:40 left in the first quarter gave Cincinnati a 7-0 lead. Charles Alexander and Larry Kinnebrew added touchdown runs to finish the Bengals' scoring. Cris Collinsworth finished with eight catches for 135 yards.

Cleveland	0	7	3	0	— 10
Cincinnati	7	7	3	10	— 27

Cin — Brooks 8 pass from Esiason (Breech kick)
Clev — Byner 27 pass from Kosar (Bahr kick)
Cin — Alexander 1 run (Breech kick)
Cin — FG Breech 28
Clev — FG Bahr 39
Cin — FG Breech 33
Cin — Kinnebrew 3 run (Breech kick)

Dallas 13, Washington 7—At Robert F. Kennedy Stadium, attendance 55,750. Danny White threw a 48-yard touchdown pass to Tony Dorsett and Everson Walls intercepted two passes to help the Cowboys sweep the Redskins for the first time since 1981. Dorsett's scoring catch with 5:12 left in the third quarter followed 40- and 36-yard field goals by Rafael Septien to give Dallas a 13-0 lead. Tony Hill had seven receptions for 136 yards. Jim Jeffcoat registered five of the Cowboys' six sacks to earn NFC defensive player of the week honors.

Dallas	0	3	10	0	— 13
Washington	0	0	0	7	— 7

Dall — FG Septien 40
Dall — FG Septien 36
Dall — Dorsett 48 pass from D. White (Septien kick)
Wash — Clark 11 pass from Theismann (Moseley kick)

Chicago 24, Detroit 3—At Soldier Field, attendance 53,467. Walter Payton and Matt Suhey combined for 209 yards rushing and backup quarterback Steve Fuller ran for two scores (one and five yards) to pace the Bears' victory. The win extended Chicago's unbeaten string to 10. Behind Payton's 107 yards on 26 carries and Suhey's 102 on 16, the Bears grounded out a season-high 250 yards rushing and 360 total yards. Detroit was limited to only 106 total yards. Chicago held a 41:02 to 18:58 time of possession advantage.

Detroit	0	0	3	0	— 3
Chicago	7	7	7	3	— 24

Chi — Fuller 1 run (Butler kick)
Chi — Thomas 7 run (Butler kick)
Det — FG Murray 34
Chi — Fuller 5 run (Butler kick)
Chi — FG Butler 39

Green Bay 27, Minnesota 17—At Metrodome, attendance 59,970. Safety Mark Murphy's 50-yard interception return for a touchdown highlighted a 21-point fourth-quarter blitz as the Packers rallied to down the Vikings. Gerry Ellis's one-yard touchdown run and Lynn Dickey's one-yard scoring pass to Eddie Lee Ivery within a span of 2:04 of the final period, gave Green Bay a 20-17 lead. Ivery finished with 111 yards on 15 carries to pace the Packers' rushing attack, while Darrin Nelson carried 21 times for a career-high 146 yards for the Vikings. Phillip Epps had a personal-best 118 yards on six receptions.

Green Bay	3	3	0	21	— 27
Minnesota	7	0	7	3	— 17

Minn — Brown 1 run (Stenerud kick)
GB — FG Del Greco 46
GB — FG Del Greco 28
Minn — Nelson 4 run (Stenerud kick)
Minn — FG Stenerud 24
GB — Ellis 1 run (Del Greco kick)
GB — Ivery 1 pass from Dickey (Del Greco kick)
GB — Murphy 50 interception return (Del Greco kick)

Buffalo 20, Houston 0—At Rich Stadium, attendance 21,831. The Bills' defense forced six turnovers and limited the Oilers to 31 passing yards en route to registering their first shutout since December 12, 1982, when they blanked the Steelers 13-0. Buffalo built a 10-0 lead on Scott Norwood's 24-yard field goal and Greg Bell's two-yard touchdown run. Quarterback Bruce Mathison, making his first NFL start for the Bills, directed a ball-control offense, which held a 39:04 to 20:56 time of possession advantage. Mathison's five-yard touchdown run with 6:36 left in the third quarter concluded Buffalo's scoring.

Houston	0	0	0	0	— 0
Buffalo	10	0	10	0	— 20

Buff — FG Norwood 24
Buff — Bell 2 run (Norwood kick)
Buff — FG Norwood 23
Buff — Mathison 5 run (Norwood kick)

New England 34, Indianapolis 15—At Sullivan Stadium, attendance 54,176. Irving Fryar scored two touchdowns in the Patriots' 27-point second half to lead New England to its fifth straight win. Fryar scored on a five-yard touchdown reception and 77-yard punt return. Steve Grogan completed 13 of 22 passes for 190 yards, including Fryar's touchdown and a 19-yard scoring pass to Stanley Morgan (seven catches for 120 yards). Three Colts fumbles set up 17 of the Patriots' 27 second-half points. Andre Tippett had three of New England's seven sacks.

Indianapolis	0	6	0	9	— 15
New England	0	7	17	10	— 34

Ind — Beach 18 pass from Pagel (kick failed)
NE — Morgan 19 pass from Grogan (Franklin kick)
NE — FG Franklin 41
NE — Fryar 5 pass from Grogan (Franklin kick)
NE — Fryar 77 punt return (Franklin kick)
NE — Collins 2 run (Franklin kick)
NE — FG Franklin 30
Ind — Gill 1 run (Allegre kick)
Ind — Safety, Randle tackled Fryar in end zone

San Diego 40, Los Angeles Raiders 34—At San Diego Jack Murphy Stadium, attendance 58,566. Lionel James's 17-yard touchdown run with 3:44 elapsed in overtime lifted the Chargers over the Raiders. James's score capped a seven-play, 80-yard drive. San Diego forced overtime when Dan Fouts threw a 14-yard touchdown pass to Charlie Joiner with 53 seconds left. Fouts (26 of 41 for 436 yards) passed for over 400 yards for an NFL-record sixth time. James's 345 combined yards (51 rushing, 168 receiving, and 126 on five kickoff returns) was the second-highest single-game total in NFL history to Billy Cannon's 373 in 1961. Los Angeles's Marcus Allen ran for 119 yards and one touchdown, and rookie wide receiver Jessie Hester had two touchdown receptions (35 and 54 yards). The Chargers outgained the Raiders 593 total yards to 454.

L.A. Raiders	7	6	14	7	0	— 34
San Diego	7	3	10	14	6	— 40

SD — Chandler 10 pass from Fouts (Thomas kick)
Raiders — Hester 35 pass from Wilson (Bahr kick)
SD — FG Thomas 34
Raiders — Hawkins 1 run (kick blocked)
SD — FG Thomas 23
Raiders — Allen 1 run (Bahr kick)
SD — James 34 pass from Fouts (Thomas kick)
Raiders — Hester 54 pass from Wilson (Bahr kick)
SD — Anderson 21 pass from Fouts (Thomas kick)
Raiders — Christensen 24 pass from Wilson (Bahr kick)
SD — Joiner 14 pass from Fouts (Thomas kick)
SD — James 17 run (no kick)

New York Giants 24, Los Angeles Rams 19—At Giants Stadium, attendance 74,663. Joe Morris ran for two touchdowns and Phil Simms passed for another to help the Giants defeat the Rams and retain a share of first place in the NFC East. Simms's 36-yard scoring pass to Bobby Johnson, 16 seconds before halftime, narrowed the Rams' lead to 13-7. Morris's scoring runs of one and three yards proved decisive as the defense held the Rams to a pair of Mike Lansford field goals and 68 total yards in the second half. Leonard Marshall added another sack to increase his league-leading total to 12½.

L.A. Rams	7	6	3	3	— 19
N.Y. Giants	0	7	10	7	— 24

Rams — Dickerson 1 run (Lansford kick)
Rams — FG Lansford 31
Rams — FG Lansford 40
NYG — Johnson 36 pass from Simms (Schubert kick)
Rams — FG Lansford 26
NYG — FG Schubert 40
NYG — Morris 1 run (Schubert kick)
NYG — Morris 3 run (Schubert kick)
Rams — FG Lansford 25

Miami 21, New York Jets 17—At Orange Bowl, attendance 73,965. Dan Marino's 50-yard scoring pass to Mark Duper with 41 seconds left highlighted the Dolphins' comeback win as they snapped a two-game losing streak. Duper, playing in his first game since week two, broke Nat Moore's single-game club receiving record of 210 yards with eight catches for 217 yards, including a 60-yard touchdown from Marino in the second quarter. Marino connected on 21 of 37 passes for 365 yards for his sixteenth career 300-yard passing game. Ken O'Brien directed New York's 491-yard attack by completing 26 of 43 passes for a career-high 393 yards and two touchdowns. Miami's offense accumulated 400 total yards.

N.Y. Jets	0	3	7	7	— 17
Miami	0	7	7	7	— 21

NYJ — FG Leahy 21
Mia — Duper 60 pass from Marino (Reveiz kick)
Mia — Clayton 22 pass from Marino (Reveiz kick)
NYJ — McNeil 14 pass from O'Brien (Leahy kick)
NYJ — Klever 20 pass from O'Brien (Leahy kick)
Mia — Duper 50 pass from Marino (Reveiz kick)

Pittsburgh 36, Kansas City 28—At Arrowhead Stadium, attendance 46,126. Louis Lipps returned a punt 71 yards for a touchdown and Gary Anderson set a team record by kicking five field goals to lead the Steelers past the Chiefs. Anderson connected on field goals of 35, 31, 27, 36, and 28 yards to surpass his own single-game record of four. David Woodley, replacing injured Mark Malone, completed 13 of 25 passes for 258 yards as Pittsburgh's offense rolled for 396 total yards. John Stallworth caught seven passes for 126 yards, including a 13-yarder from Woodley for Pittsburgh's first score. Kansas City gained 295 yards, but was held to only 36 rushing yards.

Pittsburgh	10	17	3	6	— 36
Kansas City	7	7	0	14	— 28

KC —Cherry 47 interception return (Lowery kick)
Pitt —Stallworth 13 pass from Woodley (Anderson kick)
Pitt —FG Anderson 35
Pitt —FG Anderson 31
KC —Smith 45 pass from Kenney (Lowery kick)
Pitt —Lipps 71 punt return (Anderson kick)
Pitt —Abercrombie 2 run (Anderson kick)
Pitt —FG Anderson 27
KC —Smith 13 pass from Kenney (Lowery kick)
Pitt —FG Anderson 36
Pitt —FG Anderson 28
KC —Hancock 13 pass from Kenney (Lowery kick)

Tampa Bay 16, St. Louis 0—At Tampa Stadium, attendance 34,736. Steve DeBerg threw for one touchdown and Donald Igwebuike kicked three field goals to help the Buccaneers to their first win of the season. Igwebuike preceded DeBerg's one-yard scoring pass to Adger Armstrong with a 47-yard field goal, and then he added 46- and 50-yarders to finish the scoring. James Wilder ran for 120 yards on 29 carries, while tight end Jimmie Giles accumulated 134 yards on six catches. It was the first time the Cardinals had been shut out since being blanked 28-0 by the Redskins on January 2, 1982.

St. Louis	0	0	0	0	— 0
Tampa Bay	3	7	0	6	— 16

TB —FG Igwebuike 47
TB —Armstrong 1 pass from DeBerg (Igwebuike kick)
TB —FG Igwebuike 46
TB —FG Igwebuike 50

Seattle 27, New Orleans 3—At Louisiana Superdome, attendance 47,365. Dave Krieg completed 21 of 28 passes for 282 yards and a touchdown to power the Seahawks over the Saints. Seattle increased a 7-3 fourth-quarter lead to 27-3 with two Norm Johnson field goals (32 and 26 yards), Krieg's 15-yard scoring pass to Daryl Turner, and defensive end Jacob Green's 19-yard interception return for a score. Steve Largent caught five passes for 110 yards to move ahead of Harold Carmichael (590 receptions) into fifth place on the NFL all-time reception list with 592. Seattle outgained New Orleans 346 total yards to 183.

Seattle	0	7	0	20	— 27
New Orleans	3	0	0	0	— 3

NO —FG Andersen 20
Sea —Warner 1 run (Johnson kick)
Sea —FG Johnson 32
Sea —Green 19 interception return (Johnson kick)
Sea —Turner 15 pass from Krieg (Johnson kick)
Sea —FG Johnson 26

MONDAY, NOVEMBER 11

Denver 17, San Francisco 16—At Mile High Stadium, attendance 73,173. Rich Karlis's 24-yard field goal with 1:27 left lifted the Broncos past the 49ers and into sole possession of first place in the AFC West. Denver opened up a 14-3 halftime lead on a pair of John Elway touchdown passes to Gene Lang (three yards) and Steve Watson (six). The 49ers stormed ahead 16-14 on Joe Montana's 13-yard touchdown pass to Mike Wilson and field goals by Ray Wersching of 22 and 45 yards. San Francisco's Roger Craig ran for 117 yards on 22 carries to pace all rushers. The loss dropped the 49ers three games back of the NFC West-leading Rams.

San Francisco	0	3	10	3	— 16
Denver	7	7	0	3	— 17

Den —Lang 3 pass from Elway (Karlis kick)
SF —FG Wersching 26
Den —Watson 6 pass from Elway (Karlis kick)
SF —Wilson 13 pass from Montana (Wersching kick)
SF —FG Wersching 22
SF —FG Wersching 45
Den —FG Karlis 24

ELEVENTH WEEK SUMMARIES

STANDINGS

American Football Conference

Eastern Division	W	L	T	Pct.	Pts.	OP
New England	8	3	0	.727	227	184
N.Y. Jets	8	3	0	.727	287	184
Miami	7	4	0	.636	275	231
Indianapolis	3	8	0	.273	207	272
Buffalo	2	9	0	.182	148	233
Central Division						
Pittsburgh	6	5	0	.545	249	188
Cincinnati	5	6	0	.455	293	301
Cleveland	5	6	0	.455	177	166
Houston	4	7	0	.364	169	235
Western Division						
Denver	8	3	0	.727	266	221
L.A. Raiders	7	4	0	.636	243	233
Seattle	6	5	0	.545	261	225
San Diego	5	6	0	.455	284	295
Kansas City	3	8	0	.273	202	271

National Football Conference

Eastern Division	W	L	T	Pct.	Pts.	OP
Dallas	7	4	0	.636	220	197
N.Y. Giants	7	4	0	.636	248	193
Philadelphia	6	5	0	.545	183	176
Washington	6	5	0	.545	188	202
St. Louis	4	7	0	.364	200	256
Central Division						
Chicago	11	0	0	1.000	323	127
Detroit	6	5	0	.545	214	241
Green Bay	5	6	0	.455	229	247
Minnesota	5	6	0	.455	221	248
Tampa Bay	1	10	0	.091	228	334
Western Division						
L.A. Rams	8	3	0	.727	224	181
San Francisco	6	5	0	.545	275	187
New Orleans	3	8	0	.273	190	300
Atlanta	2	9	0	.182	218	321

SUNDAY, NOVEMBER 17

Cleveland 17, Buffalo 7—At Cleveland Stadium, attendance 50,764. Earnest Byner and Kevin Mack combined for 203 yards rushing as the Browns defeated the Bills 17-7. Matt Bahr's 40-yard field goal, followed by Byner's four-yard touchdown run, gave Cleveland the lead for good in the third quarter 10-7. Bernie Kosar hit tight end Ozzie Newsome with an 11-yard scoring pass with 2:11 left to secure the victory. Byner gained 109 yards on 15 carries and Mack had 94 yards on 21 attempts. Cleveland held Buffalo to only 55 yards rushing.

Buffalo	7	0	0	0	— 7
Cleveland	3	0	7	7	— 17

Clev —FG Bahr 40
Buff —Moore 1 run (Norwood kick)
Clev —Byner 4 run (Bahr kick)
Clev —Newsome 11 pass from Kosar (Bahr kick)

Chicago 44, Dallas 0—At Texas Stadium, attendance 63,855. Richard Dent and Mike Richardson each returned interceptions for touchdowns and Kevin Butler kicked three field goals as the Bears handed the Cowboys their worst defeat in franchise history. Chicago took a 24-0 halftime lead on Steve Fuller's one-yard touchdown run, Butler's 44-yard field goal, and interception returns by Dent (one yard) and Richardson (36). Walter Payton gained 132 yards on 22 carries to set a club record with his sixth-straight 100-yard game. The Bears' defense had six sacks and four interceptions, while limiting the Cowboys to a season-low 52 yards rushing.

Chicago	7	17	3	17	— 44
Dallas	0	0	0	0	— 0

Chi —Dent 1 interception return (Butler kick)
Chi —FG Butler 44
Chi —Richardson 36 interception return (Butler kick)
Chi —Fuller 1 run (Butler kick)
Chi —FG Butler 46
Chi —FG Butler 22
Chi —Thomas 17 run (Butler kick)
Chi —Gentry 16 run (Butler kick)

Los Angeles Raiders 13, Cincinnati 6—At Memorial Coliseum, attendance 52,501. Marc Wilson completed a seven-yard touchdown pass to Marcus Allen with 2:50 left to rally the Raiders to a 13-6 win. Allen's decisive score was the only touchdown of the game as the Raiders' Chris Bahr (38 and 20 yards) and the Bengals' Jim Breech (39 and 37) traded field goals throughout. Allen carried 31 times for 135 yards for his club-record sixth 100-yard game of the season. The loss snapped Cincinnati's three-game win streak.

Cincinnati	3	0	3	0	— 6
L.A. Raiders	3	3	0	7	— 13

Raiders —FG Bahr 38
Cin —FG Breech 39
Raiders —FG Bahr 20
Cin —FG Breech 37
Raiders —Allen 7 pass from Wilson (Bahr kick)

San Francisco 31, Kansas City 3—At Candlestick Park, attendance 56,447. Joe Montana threw for two touchdowns and ran for another as the 49ers handed the Chiefs their seventh straight loss. San Francisco built a 17-3 halftime lead on Ray Wersching's 41-yard field goal and one-yard scoring runs by Roger Craig and Montana. Montana completed 23 of 34 passes for 235 yards, including touchdown passes to Dwight Clark (22 yards) and Russ Francis (eight). The 49ers generated 417 total yards, including 111 rushing by Wendell Tyler.

Kansas City	3	0	0	0	— 3
San Francisco	3	14	7	7	— 31

SF —FG Wersching 41
KC —FG Lowery 46
SF —Craig 1 run (Wersching kick)
SF —Montana 1 run (Wersching kick)
SF —Clark 22 pass from Montana (Wersching kick)
SF —Francis 8 pass from Montana (Wersching kick)

Atlanta 30, Los Angeles Rams 14—At Atlanta-Fulton County Stadium, attendance 29,960. Gerald Riggs scored three touchdowns and Mick Luckhurst kicked three field goals as the Falcons defeated the Rams. The victory snapped Atlanta's three-game losing streak. Riggs set club records for attempts (41) and consecutive 100-yard games (four) as he ran for 123 yards, including scoring runs of one, one, and three yards. Riggs's efforts earned him NFC offensive player of the week honors. Luckhurst added field goals of 39, 27, and 38 yards to finish the Falcons' scoring. Atlanta's defense stopped Eric Dickerson and shut down Los Angeles's running game, holding the Rams to 45 yards rushing.

L.A. Rams	0	0	0	14	— 14
Atlanta	10	10	3	7	— 30

Atl —FG Luckhurst 39
Atl —Riggs 3 run (Luckhurst kick)
Atl —Riggs 1 run (Luckhurst kick)
Atl —FG Luckhurst 27
Atl —FG Luckhurst 38
Rams —Dickerson 1 run (Lansford kick)
Rams —Brown 43 pass from Brock (Lansford kick)
Atl —Riggs 1 run (Luckhurst kick)

Miami 34, Indianapolis 20—At Hoosier Dome, attendance 59,666. Rookie running backs Lorenzo Hampton and Ron Davenport each scored two touchdowns as the Dolphins beat the Colts for the eleventh straight time. Miami broke open a 13-13 third-quarter tie with one-yard scoring runs by Hampton and Davenport. Dan Marino completed 22 of 37 passes for 330 yards, including a 17-yard touchdown to Davenport in the fourth quarter to clinch the win. Glenn Blackwood led the Dolphins' defense with three (two interceptions and a fumble recovery) of Miami's five takeaways.

Miami	3	10	14	7	— 34
Indianapolis	10	3	7	0	— 20

Ind —FG Allegre 28
Ind —Martin 70 punt return (Allegre kick)
Mia —FG Reveiz 45
Mia —Hampton 4 run (Reveiz kick)
Ind —FG Allegre 32
Mia —FG Reveiz 44
Mia —Davenport 1 run (Reveiz kick)
Mia —Hampton 1 run (Reveiz kick)
Ind —Capers 80 pass from Pagel (Allegre kick)
Mia —Davenport 17 pass from Marino (Reveiz kick)

Detroit 41, Minnesota 21—At Pontiac Silverdome, attendance 54,647. Three Eric Hipple touchdown passes led the Lions to 31 first-half points as Detroit downed the Vikings to remain unbeaten at home. Hipple completed scoring passes to James Jones (five yards) and David Lewis (four and three) as Detroit jumped out to a 31-7 halftime lead. Ed Murray added field goals of 49 and 51 yards. The Lions capitalized on four Minnesota turnovers to score 24 of their points. Detroit maintained a 40:49 to 19:11 time of possession advantage. Safety William Graham had two interceptions for the Lions.

Minnesota	0	7	7	7	— 21
Detroit	17	14	7	3	— 41

Det —Jones 5 pass from Hipple (Murray kick)
Det —Moore 1 run (Murray kick)
Det —FG Murray 49
Det —Lewis 4 pass from Hipple (Murray kick)
Det —Lewis 3 pass from Hipple (Murray kick)
Minn —Carter 10 pass from Kramer (Stenerud kick)
Det —Moore 2 run (Murray kick)
Minn —Carter 38 pass from Kramer (Stenerud kick)
Det —FG Murray 51
Minn —Anderson 1 run (Stenerud kick)

New England 20, Seattle 13—At Kingdome, attendance 60,345. Steve Grogan completed a 13-yard touchdown pass to Irving Fryar with 2:39 left to clinch the Patriots' comeback win. Trailing 13-7 in the fourth quarter, New England tied the score on Grogan's 23-yard touchdown pass to Craig James. Fred Marion's second interception of the game, which he returned 83 yards, set up Grogan's decisive scoring pass to Fryar. Seattle's Steve Largent had eight receptions for 130 yards to increase his season total to 55 and become the first NFL player to post eight, 50-plus reception seasons.

New England	0	7	0	13	— 20
Seattle	0	3	10	0	— 13

NE —Fryar 5 run (Franklin kick)
Sea —FG Johnson 32
Sea —FG Johnson 31
Sea —Krieg 3 run (Johnson kick)
NE —James 23 pass from Grogan (kick failed)
NE —Fryar 13 pass from Grogan (Franklin kick)

Green Bay 38, New Orleans 14—At Milwaukee County Stadium, attendance 52,104. Lynn Dickey completed 22 of 35 passes for 302 yards and two touchdowns to lead the Packers to victory. Green Bay took a commanding 17-0 halftime lead on two second-quarter Dickey scoring passes to center Blake Moore (three yards) and Phillip

Epps (11), and Al Del Greco's 27-yard field goal. Gerry Ellis and Gary Ellerson added touchdown runs of 15 and one yards, respectively, and Jim Zorn threw an eight-yard strike to Preston Dennard to finish Green Bay's scoring. John Anderson had two of the Packers' six sacks. Green Bay gained 433 total yards and yielded 207.

New Orleans	0	0	7	7	— 14
Green Bay	0	17	7	14	— 38

GB —FG Del Greco 27
GB —Moore 3 pass from Dickey (Del Greco kick)
GB —Epps 11 pass from Dickey (Del Greco kick)
GB —Ellis 15 run (Del Greco kick)
NO —Hoage 52 interception return (Andersen kick)
GB —Ellerson 1 run (Del Greco kick)
NO —Hebert 7 pass from Merkens (Andersen kick)
GB —Dennard 8 pass from Zorn (Del Greco kick)

Pittsburgh 30, Houston 7—At Astrodome, attendance 45,977. Frank Pollard and Walter Abercrombie each rushed for over 100 yards and a touchdown to power the Steelers over the Oilers. Pollard (123 yards on 23 carries) and Abercrombie (107 on 23) became the first pair of Pittsburgh backs to go over the 100-yard mark in the same game since Rocky Bleier (107) and Franco Harris (104) did it on December 11, 1976, versus Houston. Pollard scored on a two-yard run in the second quarter, while Abercrombie finished the Steelers' scoring in the final period with a five-yard run. Behind a season-high 248 yards rushing, Pittsburgh outgained Houston 378 to 162 (56 passing yards) in total yards.

Pittsburgh	3	7	13	7	— 30
Houston	0	0	7	0	— 7

Pitt —FG Anderson 52
Pitt —Pollard 2 run (Anderson kick)
Hou —Rozier 15 run (Zendejas kick)
Pitt —FG Anderson 31
Pitt —Woodley 1 run (Anderson kick)
Pitt —FG Anderson 34
Pitt —Abercrombie 5 run (Anderson kick)

Philadelphia 24, St. Louis 14—At Busch Memorial Stadium, attendance 39,032. Earnest Jackson rushed for a career-high 162 yards on 34 carries and Mike Quick caught two touchdown passes to help the Eagles defeat the Cardinals. Quick's first-quarter scoring receptions came on a halfback option pass from running back Herman Hunter (38 yards) and quarterback Ron Jaworski (five). Stump Mitchell (22 carries for 179 yards) led a St. Louis comeback by scoring on second-quarter touchdown runs of three and one yards. Jackson's 51-yard touchdown run completed the Eagles' scoring. Reggie White had three sacks to lead Philadelphia's defense.

Philadelphia	14	0	0	10	— 24
St. Louis	0	14	0	0	— 14

Phil —Quick 38 pass from Hunter (McFadden kick)
Phil —Quick 5 pass from Jaworski (McFadden kick)
StL —Mitchell 3 run (Bojovic kick)
StL —Mitchell 1 run (Bojovic kick)
Phil —FG McFadden 20
Phil —E. Jackson 51 run (McFadden kick)

Denver 30, San Diego 24—At Mile High Stadium, attendance 74,376. Dennis Smith blocked Bob Thomas's 47-yard field goal attempt and Louis Wright returned it 60 yards for the winning touchdown 4:55 into overtime to give Denver a 30-24 win and sole possession of first place in the AFC West. The Broncos took a 21-14 fourth-quarter lead on Gene Lang's scoring runs of two and four yards. Tim Spencer's two-yard blast gave San Diego a brief 24-21 lead with 1:18 left. Rich Karlis's 34-yard field goal 73 seconds later forced the extra period. Karlis's game-tying field goal extended his consecutive games streak with at least one field goal to 15.

San Diego	7	7	0	10	0	— 24
Denver	7	0	0	17	6	— 30

SD —Anderson 98 kickoff return (Thomas kick)
Den —Watson 4 pass from Elway (Karlis kick)
SD —James 6 pass from Fouts (Thomas kick)
Den —Lang 2 run (Karlis kick)
Den —Lang 4 run (Karlis kick)
SD —FG Thomas 36
SD —Spencer 2 run (Thomas kick)
Den —FG Karlis 34
Den —L. Wright 60 blocked field goal return (no kick)

New York Jets 62, Tampa Bay 28—At Giants Stadium, attendance 65,344. Ken O'Brien threw five touchdown passes and Johnny Hector ran for two more to lead the Jets in a 62-28 rout of the Buccaneers. O'Brien completed 23 of 30 passes for 367 yards, including touchdown completions to Wesley Walker (22 yards) and Al Toon (78). Tight end Mickey Shuler became the fifth Jets player to score three touchdowns in a game by catching three O'Brien scores (11, 10, and 8 yards) in the second quarter. The Jets outgained Tampa Bay 581 total yards to 212 as the defense held James Wilder and the Buccaneers' offense to 22 yards rushing. It was the most points scored by an NFL team since Atlanta defeated New Orleans 62-7 in 1973.

Tampa Bay	14	7	7	0	— 28
N.Y. Jets	17	24	14	7	— 62

TB —House 39 pass from DeBerg (Igwebuike kick)
TB —Magee 7 pass from DeBerg (Igwebuike kick)
NYJ —Hector 2 run (Leahy kick)
NYJ —Walker 22 pass from O'Brien (Leahy kick)
NYJ —FG Leahy 23
NYJ —Shuler 11 pass from O'Brien (Leahy kick)
NYJ —Shuler 10 pass from O'Brien (Leahy kick)
TB —Wilder 2 run (Igwebuike kick)
NYJ —Shuler 8 pass from O'Brien (Leahy kick)
NYJ —FG Leahy 27
NYJ —Toon 78 pass from O'Brien (Leahy kick)
NYJ —Hector 7 run (Leahy kick)
TB —Wilder 1 run (Igwebuike kick)
NYJ —Paige 1 run (Leahy kick)

MONDAY, NOVEMBER 18

Washington 23, New York Giants 21—At Robert F. Kennedy Stadium, attendance 53,371. The Redskins recovered two onside kicks and capitalized on a fake punt to set up three touchdowns as they defeated the Giants to move to within a game of division-leading New York and Dallas. Punter Steve Cox's 11-yard pass to Raphael Cherry on fourth down set up Washington's first touchdown, Joe Theismann's 10-yard pass to Don Warren. Jay Schroeder replaced an injured Theismann in the second quarter, and completed 13 of 21 passes for 221 yards and the game-winning touchdown to Clint Didier with 8:21 left. Joe Morris (17 carries for 118 yards) accounted for all three of New York's scores on runs of 56, 41, and 8 yards. The Redskins dominated the Giants, controlling the ball for 38:38 compared to New York's 21:22.

N.Y. Giants	7	0	14	0	— 21
Washington	7	0	7	9	— 23

Wash —Warren 10 pass from Theismann (Moseley kick)
NYG —Morris 56 run (Schubert kick)
Wash —Riggins 1 run (Moseley kick)
NYG —Morris 41 run (Schubert kick)
NYG —Morris 8 run (Schubert kick)
Wash —FG Moseley 28
Wash —Didier 14 pass from Schroeder (kick failed)

TWELFTH WEEK SUMMARIES

STANDINGS

American Football Conference

Eastern Division	W	L	T	Pct.	Pts.	OP
N.Y. Jets	9	3	0	.750	303	197
Miami	8	4	0	.667	298	245
New England	8	4	0	.667	240	200
Indianapolis	3	9	0	.273	214	292
Buffalo	2	10	0	.167	162	256
Central Division						
Cleveland	6	6	0	.500	201	172
Pittsburgh	6	6	0	.500	272	218
Cincinnati	5	7	0	.417	299	325
Houston	5	7	0	.417	206	270
Western Division						
Denver	8	4	0	.667	294	252
L.A. Raiders	8	4	0	.667	274	261
Seattle	6	6	0	.500	267	244
San Diego	5	7	0	.417	319	332
Kansas City	4	8	0	.333	222	278

National Football Conference

Eastern Division	W	L	T	Pct.	Pts.	OP
Dallas	8	4	0	.667	254	214
N.Y. Giants	8	4	0	.667	282	196
Washington	7	5	0	.583	218	225
Philadelphia	6	6	0	.500	200	210
St. Louis	4	8	0	.333	203	290
Central Division						
Chicago	12	0	0	1.000	359	127
Detroit	6	6	0	.500	230	260
Green Bay	5	7	0	.417	246	281
Minnesota	5	7	0	.417	244	278
Tampa Bay	2	10	0	.167	247	350
Western Division						
L.A. Rams	9	3	0	.750	258	198
San Francisco	7	5	0	.583	294	193
New Orleans	4	8	0	.333	220	323
Atlanta	2	10	0	.167	218	357

SUNDAY, NOVEMBER 24

Chicago 36, Atlanta 0—At Soldier Field, attendance 61,769. Walter Payton ran for his seventh straight 100-yard game (102 yards on 20 carries) to tie the NFL record (held by O. J. Simpson and Earl Campbell) and lead the unbeaten Bears over the Falcons. Chicago erupted for 20 second-quarter points on a pair of Kevin Butler field goals (35 and 32 yards) and touchdown runs by Payton (40 yards) and William Perry (one). Led by Henry Waechter, who had three sacks and a safety, the Bears' defense held the Falcons to 119 total yards (minus 22 passing). Atlanta's Gerald Riggs rushed for his fifth straight 100-yard game with 110 yards on 30 attempts.

Atlanta	0	0	0	0	— 0
Chicago	0	20	7	9	— 36

Chi —FG Butler 35
Chi —FG Butler 32
Chi —Payton 40 run (Butler kick)
Chi —Perry 1 run (Butler kick)
Chi —Thomas 2 run (Butler kick)
Chi —Safety, Waechter tackled Holly in end zone
Chi —Sanders 1 run (Butler kick)

Cleveland 24, Cincinnati 6—At Cleveland Stadium, attendance 74,439. Kevin Mack rushed for 117 yards and a pair of touchdowns to lead the Browns to a 24-6 win over the Bengals. Mack's scoring runs of two and 35 yards, sandwiched around Gary Danielson's 72-yard scoring bomb to Clarence Weathers, were all the points Cleveland needed as its defense held the high-scoring Bengals to only a pair of field goals. The Browns' defense registered five sacks, while limiting Cincinnati to a season-low 90 yards passing.

Cincinnati	0	3	3	0	— 6
Cleveland	3	7	14	0	— 24

Clev —FG Bahr 29
Clev —Mack 2 run (Bahr kick)
Cin —FG Breech 30
Clev —Cl. Weathers 72 pass from Danielson (Bahr kick)
Cin —FG Breech 29
Clev —Mack 35 run (Bahr kick)

Los Angeles Raiders 31, Denver 28—At Memorial Coliseum, attendance 63,131. Chris Bahr's 32-yard field goal 2:42 into overtime gave the Raiders a 31-28 win and a share of first place in the AFC West. Marc Wilson accounted for three of the Raiders' touchdowns with a one-yard run and scoring passes to Todd Christensen (17 yards) and Trey Junkin (three). Marcus Allen ran for a career-high 173 yards on 24 carries, including a 61-yard touchdown to open Los Angeles's scoring. The Raiders outgained the Broncos 424 total yards to 291.

Denver	7	14	0	7	0	— 28
L.A. Raiders	7	7	14	0	3	— 31

Den —Watson 16 pass from Elway (Karlis kick)
Raiders —Allen 61 run (Bahr kick)
Den —Willhite 9 pass from Elway (Karlis kick)
Raiders —Christensen 17 pass from Wilson (Bahr kick)
Den —Kay 6 pass from Elway (Karlis kick)
Raiders —Junkin 3 pass from Wilson (Bahr kick)
Raiders —Wilson 1 run (Bahr kick)
Den —Sewell 3 run (Karlis kick)
Raiders —FG Bahr 32

Tampa Bay 19, Detroit 16—At Tampa Stadium, attendance 43,471. Donald Igwebuike's fourth field goal, a 24-yarder with 2:29 left in overtime, lifted the Buccaneers over the Lions. Trailing 16-6 in the fourth quarter, Tampa Bay rallied behind James Wilder's six-yard touchdown run and Igwebuike's 36-yard field goal to force the extra period. Igwebuike's other field goals came from 33 and 48 yards. His winning kick completed an 11-play, 56-yard drive. Wilder ran for 96 yards to go over the 1,000-yard mark (1,039) for the second time in his career.

Detroit	0	7	6	3	0	— 16
Tampa Bay	3	3	0	10	3	— 19

TB —FG Igwebuike 33
Det —J. Jones 1 run (Murray kick)
TB —FG Igwebuike 48
Det —FG Murray 47
Det —FG Murray 38
Det —FG Murray 39
TB —Wilder 6 run (Igwebuike kick)
TB —FG Igwebuike 36
TB —FG Igwebuike 24

Los Angeles Rams 34, Green Bay 17—At Anaheim Stadium, attendance 52,710. Ron Brown returned a pair of kickoffs for touchdowns and Eric Dickerson rushed for 150 yards on 31 carries to highlight the Rams' win. Brown became the third player in NFL history to return two kickoffs (98 and 86 yards) for scores in a single game. Brown's returns helped Los Angeles post a 14-10 first-half advantage. Following a Green Bay touchdown, the Rams opened up a 28-17 lead on Dickerson's 14-yard scoring run and Dieter Brock's 39-yard touchdown pass to Brown. Brown's efforts earned him NFC offensive player of the week honors.

Green Bay	0	10	7	0	— 17
L.A. Rams	7	7	7	13	— 34

Rams —Brown 98 kickoff return (Lansford kick)
GB —Coffman 15 pass from Dickey (Del Greco kick)
Rams —Brown 86 kickoff return (Lansford kick)
GB —FG Del Greco 38
GB —Lofton 21 pass from Dickey (Del Greco kick)
Rams —Dickerson 14 run (Lansford kick)
Rams —Brown 39 pass from Brock (Lansford kick)
Rams —FG Lansford 43
Rams —FG Lansford 32

Kansas City 20, Indianapolis 7—At Arrowhead Stadium, attendance 21,762. Todd Blackledge completed 16 of 31 passes for 246 yards and a touchdown to help the Chiefs snap a seven-game losing streak. Kansas City opened a 17-0 halftime lead as Blackledge threw for 190 yards, including a 22-yard touchdown to Stephone Paige. Mike Pruitt's two-yard run and Nick Lowery's 29- and 42-yard field goals finished the Chiefs' scoring. Indianapolis's George Wonsley ran 14 yards for a touchdown with 2:22 left to prevent a shutout.

Indianapolis	0	0	0	7	— 7
Kansas City	7	10	3	0	— 20

KC —Paige 22 pass from Blackledge (Lowery kick)
KC —Pruitt 2 run (Lowery kick)

KC —FG Lowery 29
KC —FG Lowery 42
Ind —Wonsley 14 run (Allegre kick)

Miami 23, Buffalo 14—At Rich Stadium, attendance 50,474. Dan Marino passed for two touchdowns and Tony Nathan ran for another to help the Dolphins defeat the Bills. Marino completed 22 of 31 passes for 233 yards, including scoring passes of seven yards to Ron Davenport and 15 yards to Dan Johnson to give Miami a 14-7 halftime lead. Davenport's touchdown, his eighth of the season, broke the Dolphins' rookie record of seven held by Larry Csonka and Andra Franklin.

Miami	7	7	3	6	—	23
Buffalo	0	7	7	0	—	14

Mia —Davenport 7 pass from Marino (Reveiz kick)
Mia —Johnson 15 pass from Marino (Reveiz kick)
Buff —Reed 11 pass from Mathison (Norwood kick)
Buff —Butler 60 pass from Mathison (Norwood kick)
Mia —FG Reveiz 22
Mia —Nathan 4 run (kick failed)

New York Jets 16, New England 13—At Giants Stadium, attendance 74,100. Pat Leahy's 32-yard field goal 10:05 into overtime lifted the Jets past the Patriots and into sole possession of first place in the AFC East. Ken O'Brien completed 20 of 33 passes for 311 yards, including an 88-yard touchdown pass to Wesley Walker (six catches for 168 yards). Leahy's winning field goal was set up by Kurt Sohn's 46-yard punt return. Tony Eason, who replaced injured Steve Grogan, rallied the Patriots to 10 fourth-quarter points to force the extra period. New England's Craig James ran for 108 yards on 14 carries.

New England	0	3	0	10	0	—	13
N.Y. Jets	6	0	7	0	3	—	16

NYJ —FG Leahy 21
NYJ —FG Leahy 21
NE —FG Franklin 23
NYJ —Walker 88 pass from O'Brien (Leahy kick)
NE —Jones 29 pass from Eason (Franklin kick)
NE —FG Franklin 28
NYJ —FG Leahy 32

New Orleans 30, Minnesota 23—At Metrodome, attendance 54,117. Bobby Hebert's 39-yard touchdown pass to John Tice with 50 seconds left helped the Saints beat Minnesota and snap a six-game losing streak. New Orleans took a 23-10 third-quarter lead on scoring runs by Wayne Wilson (41 yards) and Earl Campbell (four), and Morten Andersen's three field goals from 26, 47, and 45 yards. Campbell carried the ball a team-record 35 times for his first 100-yard game of the season (160) as the Saints outrushed the Vikings 234 to 59. New Orleans controlled the ball for 38:14 compared to Minnesota's 21:46.

New Orleans	14	6	3	7	—	30
Minnesota	7	3	3	10	—	23

NO —W. Wilson 41 run (Andersen kick)
Minn —Anderson 54 pass from Kramer (Stenerud kick)
NO —Campbell 4 run (Andersen kick)
NO —FG Andersen 26
NO —FG Andersen 47
Minn —FG Stenerud 22
NO —FG Andersen 45
Minn —FG Stenerud 22
Minn —FG Stenerud 37
Minn —Jones 6 pass from Kramer (Stenerud kick)
NO —Tice 39 pass from Hebert (Andersen kick)

New York Giants 34, St. Louis 3—At Busch Memorial Stadium, attendance 41,248. Rookie George Adams ran for his first 100-yard game and defensive end George Martin scored his sixth career touchdown as the Giants overpowered the Cardinals. New York opened up a 20-3 third-quarter lead on two Eric Schubert field goals from 27 and 34 yards, and a pair of Phil Simms scoring passes to Lionel Manuel (31 yards) and Mark Bavaro (12). Adams gained 113 yards on 25 carries, including a 37-yard touchdown. Martin returned an interception 56 yards to conclude New York's scoring. He had three of the Giants' season-high eight sacks as they held St. Louis to 40 yards rushing.

N.Y. Giants	0	10	10	14	—	34
St. Louis	3	0	0	0	—	3

StL —FG Bojovic 40
NYG —FG Schubert 27
NYG —Manuel 31 pass from Simms (Schubert kick)
NYG —FG Schubert 34
NYG —Bavaro 12 pass from Simms (Schubert kick)
NYG —Adams 37 run (Schubert kick)
NYG —Martin 56 interception return (Schubert kick)

Dallas 34, Philadelphia 17—At Texas Stadium, attendance 54,047. Danny White completed 20 of 28 passes for 243 yards and three touchdowns to lead the Cowboys over the Eagles. White's second-quarter scoring passes of 2 and 23 yards to Doug Cosbie helped Dallas take a 21-10 halftime lead. Tony Dorsett opened and closed the Cowboys' scoring with runs of 2 and 10 yards. Dallas's defense intercepted three of Philadelphia quarterback Ron Jaworski's passes.

Philadelphia	10	0	0	7	—	17
Dallas	7	14	0	13	—	34

Phil —FG McFadden 26
Dall —Dorsett 2 run (Septien kick)
Phil —Hunter 74 run (McFadden kick)
Dall —Cosbie 2 pass from D. White (Septien kick)
Dall —Cosbie 23 pass from D. White (Septien kick)
Dall —Renfro 19 pass from D. White (kick failed)
Phil —Quick 11 pass from Jaworski (McFadden kick)
Dall —Dorsett 10 run (Septien kick)

Houston 37, San Diego 35—At Astrodome, attendance 34,336. Tony Zendejas connected on his third field goal of the game, a 51-yarder with two seconds left, to help the Oilers squeak by the Chargers. Trailing 21-20 after three quarters, Houston took a 34-28 lead behind Mike Rozier's scoring runs of three and two yards. Following a San Diego score, Oliver Luck moved the Oilers' offense 45 yards in six plays to set up Zendejas's game-winning kick. Zendejas also kicked field goals from 46 and 52 yards.

San Diego	0	7	14	14	—	35
Houston	14	3	3	17	—	37

Hou —Moriarty 16 run (Zendejas kick)
Hou —Hill 8 pass from Luck (Zendejas kick)
Hou —FG Zendejas 46
SD —Spencer 1 run (Thomas kick)
SD —James 67 pass from Fouts (Thomas kick)
Hou —FG Zendejas 52
SD —McGee 2 run (Thomas kick)
Hou —Rozier 3 run (Zendejas kick)
SD —Spencer 15 run (Thomas kick)
Hou —Rozier 2 run (Zendejas kick)
SD —Chandler 11 pass from Fouts (Thomas kick)
Hou —FG Zendejas 51

Washington 30, Pittsburgh 23—At Three Rivers Stadium, attendance 59,293. Jay Schroeder, making his first NFL start, threw for one touchdown and Mark Moseley kicked three field goals as the Redskins downed the Steelers. Ken Jenkins returned the opening kickoff 95 yards to set up Washington's first touchdown, a one-yard run by George Rogers. Following a blocked punt by Otis Wonsley, Schroeder threw an 18-yard scoring pass to Clint Didier. Moseley connected on field goals from 20, 39, and 42 yards. Washington's John Riggins scored his 116th career touchdown on a one-yard run in the third quarter.

Washington	14	6	7	3	—	30
Pittsburgh	3	14	0	6	—	23

Wash —Rogers 1 run (Moseley kick)
Pitt —FG Anderson 22
Wash —Didier 18 pass from Schroeder (Moseley kick)
Wash —FG Moseley 20
Pitt —Lipps 5 pass from Campbell (Anderson kick)
Pitt —Erenberg 9 pass from Campbell (Anderson kick)
Wash —FG Moseley 39
Wash —Riggins 1 run (Moseley kick)
Pitt —FG Anderson 37
Wash —FG Moseley 42
Pitt —FG Anderson 27

MONDAY, NOVEMBER 25

San Francisco 19, Seattle 6—At Candlestick Park, attendance 57,482. Joe Montana completed 17 of 33 passes for 237 yards and two touchdowns to lead the 49ers over the Seahawks. Montana rebounded from three first-half interceptions to throw scoring passes of 27 yards to Freddie Solomon and 22 yards to Dwight Clark. Clark's touchdown catch, his 408th career reception, surpassed Billy Wilson's club mark of 407. San Francisco kicker Ray Wersching extended his streak of extra points without a miss to 144. He also kicked a 32-yard field goal.

Seattle	0	0	0	6	—	6
San Francisco	0	12	0	7	—	19

SF —Solomon 27 pass from Montana (Wersching kick)
SF —Safety, Harty tackled Warner in end zone
SF —FG Wersching 32
SF —Clark 22 pass from Montana (Wersching kick)
Sea —Merriman recovered blocked punt in end zone (kick failed)

THIRTEENTH WEEK SUMMARIES

STANDINGS

American Football Conference

Eastern Division	W	L	T	Pct.	Pts.	OP
Miami	9	4	0	.692	336	269
New England	9	4	0	.692	278	231
N.Y. Jets	9	4	0	.692	323	228
Indianapolis	3	10	0	.231	245	330
Buffalo	2	11	0	.154	169	296
Central Division						
Cleveland	7	6	0	.538	236	205
Cincinnati	6	7	0	.462	344	352
Pittsburgh	6	7	0	.462	295	249
Houston	5	8	0	.385	233	315
Western Division						
Denver	9	4	0	.692	325	275
L.A. Raiders	9	4	0	.692	308	285
Seattle	7	6	0	.538	291	250
San Diego	6	7	0	.462	359	339
Kansas City	4	9	0	.308	228	302

National Football Conference

Eastern Division	W	L	T	Pct.	Pts.	OP
Dallas	9	4	0	.692	289	231
N.Y. Giants	8	5	0	.615	315	231
Washington	7	6	0	.538	226	260
Philadelphia	6	7	0	.462	223	238
St. Louis	4	9	0	.308	220	325
Central Division						
Chicago	12	1	0	.923	383	165
Detroit	7	6	0	.538	261	280
Green Bay	6	7	0	.462	267	281
Minnesota	6	7	0	.462	272	301
Tampa Bay	2	11	0	.154	247	371
Western Division						
L.A. Rams	9	4	0	.692	261	227
San Francisco	8	5	0	.615	329	201
New Orleans	5	8	0	.385	249	326
Atlanta	2	11	0	.154	242	391

NOTE: The Chicago at Miami Monday Night game this weekend produced the highest rating, 29.6, and highest share, 46, of any prime-time game in NFL history.

THURSDAY, NOVEMBER 28

Detroit 31, New York Jets 20—at Pontiac Silverdome, attendance 65,531. Eric Hipple passed for four touchdowns, including three to wide receiver Leonard Thompson, as the Lions downed the Jets to remain unbeaten at home. Hipple's two first-half scoring passes to Thompson (25 yards) and Mark Nichols (38) helped Detroit take a commanding 17-3 halftime lead. Thompson (seven catches for 115 yards) caught touchdowns of eight and 44 yards in the second half to complete Detroit's scoring. William Gay had three of the Lions' season-high seven sacks. New York's Johnny Hector, subbing for an injured Freeman McNeil, had his first 100-yard rushing game when he gained 114 on 23 carries.

N.Y. Jets	0	3	7	10	—	20
Detroit	3	14	7	7	—	31

Det —FG Murray 19
Det —Thompson 25 pass from Hipple (Murray kick)
NYJ —FG Leahy 29
Det —Nichols 38 pass from Hipple (Murray kick)
Det —Thompson 8 pass from Hipple (Murray kick)
NYJ —Toon 35 pass from O'Brien (Leahy kick)
NYJ —FG Leahy 27
Det —Thompson 44 pass from Hipple (Murray kick)
NYJ —Shuler 8 pass from O'Brien (Leahy kick)

Dallas 35, St. Louis 17—At Texas Stadium, attendance 54,125. Danny White threw for four touchdowns as the Cowboys downed the Cardinals to take sole possession of first place in the NFC East. Ahead 21-17 at the half, Dallas pulled away in the third quarter on White's 53-yard scoring pass to Tony Hill and Tony Dorsett's three-yard touchdown run. White completed 14 of 26 passes for 235 yards, including first-half scoring passes to Mike Renfro (18 yards), Doug Cosbie (19), and Hill (16). Cosbie had five receptions for 111 yards. St. Louis's Neil Lomax completed 28 of 43 passes for 319 yards and a touchdown, but was sacked five times by the Dallas defense.

St. Louis	7	10	0	0	—	17
Dallas	7	14	14	0	—	35

Dall —Renfro 18 pass from D. White (Septien kick)
StL —Mitchell 2 run (Bojovic kick)
StL —FG Bojovic 38
Dall —Cosbie 19 pass from D. White (Septien kick)
StL —Green 5 pass from Lomax (Bojovic kick)
Dall —Hill 16 pass from D. White (Septien kick)
Dall —Hill 53 pass from D. White (Septien kick)
Dall —Dorsett 3 run (Septien kick)

SUNDAY, DECEMBER 1

San Diego 40, Buffalo 7—At San Diego Jack Murphy Stadium, attendance 45,487. Dan Fouts passed for three touchdowns and Bob Thomas kicked a pair of field goals to lead the Chargers over the Bills. Fouts threw scoring passes to Charlie Joiner (38 yards), Eric Sievers (23), and Pete Holohan (13). Rookie cornerback John Hendy paced San Diego's defense with two interceptions, including a 75-yard return for a touchdown. Thomas's field goals were from 24 and 28 yards. Buffalo scored its only touchdown on a two-yard run by Joe Cribbs in the second quarter.

Buffalo	0	7	0	0	—	7
San Diego	7	17	10	6	—	40

SD —Joiner 38 pass from Fouts (Thomas kick)
SD —FG Thomas 24
SD —Hendy 75 interception return (Thomas kick)
SD —Spencer 1 run (Thomas kick)
Buff —Cribbs 2 run (Norwood kick)
SD —FG Thomas 28
SD —Sievers 23 pass from Fouts (Thomas kick)
SD —Holohan 13 pass from Fouts (kick failed)

Cleveland 35, New York Giants 33—At Giants Stadium, attendance 66,482. Gary Danielson came off the bench to lead the Browns' comeback win over the Giants. Trailing 33-21 with 8:52 left, Danielson completed a 65-yard drive with a 25-yard scoring pass to Clarence Weathers to bring Cleveland to within a touchdown. Seven minutes later, Earnest Byner ran nine yards for the go-ahead touchdown. The Browns held a 21-20 halftime lead on scoring runs by

Kevin Mack (42 yards) and Byner (two), and Al Gross's 37-yard interception return for a touchdown. New York's Joe Morris gained 131 yards on 22 carries, and scored three touchdowns from 3, 58, and 5 yards.

Cleveland	7	14	0	14 —	35
N.Y. Giants	7	13	3	10 —	33

NYG — Morris 3 run (Schubert kick)
Clev — Mack 42 run (Bahr kick)
Clev — Byner 2 run (Bahr kick)
Clev — Gross 37 interception return (Bahr kick)
NYG — Morris 58 run (kick failed)
NYG — Johnson 29 pass from Simms (Schubert kick)
NYG — FG Schubert 35
NYG — Morris 5 run (Schubert kick)
NYG — FG Schubert 40
Clev — Weathers 25 pass from Danielson (Bahr kick)
Clev — Byner 9 run (Bahr kick)

Denver 31, Pittsburgh 23—At Three Rivers Stadium, attendance 56,797. A pair of touchdown runs by Steve Sewell and Mike Harden's 42-yard interception return for a touchdown highlighted the Broncos' victory. Denver led 10-9 after three quarters on John Elway's 24-yard scoring pass to Clint Sampson and Rich Karlis's 42-yard field goal. Following Sewell's 12-yard touchdown run, Pittsburgh rallied for two scores to take a 23-17 lead. Sewell's game-winning two-yard touchdown run was set up by Vance Johnson's 39-yard kickoff return. Steve Wilson had two interceptions and Karl Mecklenburg four sacks to pace the Broncos' defense.

Denver	0	10	0	21 —	31
Pittsburgh	0	6	3	14 —	23

Pitt — FG Anderson 25
Den — Sampson 24 pass from Elway (Karlis kick)
Den — FG Karlis 42
Pitt — FG Anderson 34
Pitt — FG Anderson 24
Den — Sewell 12 run (Karlis kick)
Pitt — Lipps 31 pass from Woodley (Anderson kick)
Pitt — Merriweather 35 interception return (Anderson kick)
Den — Sewell 2 run (Karlis kick)
Den — Harden 42 interception return (Karlis kick)

Cincinnati 45, Houston 27—At Riverfront Stadium, attendance 46,140. Boomer Esiason passed for three touchdowns and Larry Kinnebrew ran for three more as the Bengals routed the Oilers 45-27. Cincinnati scored on its first four possessions of the game to open a 28-10 first-half lead on Kinnebrew scoring runs of one, three, and seven yards and Esiason's 57-yard scoring pass to James Brooks. Esiason connected on 18 of 24 passes for 320 yards and had two other touchdown passes, 64 yards to Rodney Holman and 19 yards to Eddie Brown. Cincinnati amassed 555 total yards, the second-highest total in the club's history.

Houston	0	10	3	14 —	27
Cincinnati	21	7	14	3 —	45

Cin — Kinnebrew 7 run (Breech kick)
Cin — Kinnebrew 1 run (Breech kick)
Cin — Brooks 57 pass from Esiason (Breech kick)
Cin — Kinnebrew 3 run (Breech kick)
Hou — FG Zendejas 25
Hou — Woolfolk 46 pass from Luck (Zendejas kick)
Hou — FG Zendejas 26
Cin — Holman 64 pass from Esiason (Breech kick)
Cin — Brown 19 pass from Esiason (Breech kick)
Cin — FG Breech 29
Hou — Rozier 1 run (Zendejas kick)
Hou — Moriarty 1 run (Zendejas kick)

Seattle 24, Kansas City 6—At Kingdome, attendance 52,655. Dave Krieg completed 21 of 34 passes for 254 yards and two touchdowns to lead the Seahawks past the Chiefs. Krieg's 11-yard scoring pass to Dan Ross snapped a 3-3 tie. Curt Warner's five-yard touchdown run 2:04 later, following Eugene Robinson's 47-yard interception return, increased Seattle's lead to 17-3 at halftime. Krieg finished the Seahawks' scoring in the second half with a 17-yard completion to Steve Largent, who caught seven passes for 101 yards. Jacob Green and Randy Edwards led Seattle's defense with a pair of sacks each.

Kansas City	3	0	3	0 —	6
Seattle	3	14	7	0 —	24

Sea — FG Johnson 23
KC — FG Lowery 25
Sea — Ross 11 pass from Krieg (Johnson kick)
Sea — Warner 5 run (Johnson kick)
KC — FG Lowery 35
Sea — Largent 17 pass from Krieg (Johnson kick)

Los Angeles Raiders 34, Atlanta 24—At Atlanta-Fulton County Stadium, attendance 20,585. Marcus Allen ran for his sixth straight 100-yard game and Marc Wilson threw three touchdown passes to highlight the Raiders' win. With Atlanta leading 17-13 at halftime, Wilson threw scoring passes to Allen (four yards) and Dokie Williams (seven), and Frank Hawkins scored on a one-yard run to give Los Angeles a commanding 34-17 lead with eight minutes remaining. Wilson also completed a 37-yard scoring pass to Jessie Hester to open the Raiders' scoring. Allen gained 156 yards on 28 carries to increase his league-leading total to 1,392.

L.A. Raiders	7	6	7	14 —	34
Atlanta	10	7	0	7 —	24

Atl — FG Luckhurst 39
Raiders — Hester 37 pass from Wilson (Bahr kick)
Atl — Cox 62 pass from Archer (Luckhurst kick)
Raiders — FG Bahr 35
Atl — Riggs 11 run (Luckhurst kick)
Raiders — FG Bahr 49
Raiders — Allen 4 pass from Wilson (Bahr kick)
Raiders — Hawkins 1 run (Bahr kick)
Raiders — Williams 7 pass from Wilson (Bahr kick)
Atl — B. Johnson 25 pass from Archer (Luckhurst kick)

New Orleans 29, Los Angeles Rams 3—At Louisiana Superdome, attendance 44,122. Morten Andersen kicked a career-high five field goals and the defense compiled a team-record nine sacks as the Saints made Wade Phillips's head coaching debut a successful one. Leading 9-3 after three quarters, New Orleans exploded for 20 unanswered points within a span of six minutes to clinch the victory. Andersen kicked a 27-yard field goal and Johnnie Poe's interception set up Bobby Hebert's 43-yard scoring pass to Eric Martin to give the Saints a 19-3 lead. Jack Del Rio returned a fumble 22 yards for one score and set up Andersen's 35-yard field goal with another. Andersen's other field goals were from 47, 42, and 35 yards. New Orleans held the Rams to a season-low 164 total yards.

L.A. Rams	0	3	0	0 —	3
New Orleans	6	3	0	20 —	29

NO — FG Andersen 47
NO — FG Andersen 42
NO — FG Andersen 35
Rams — FG Lansford 41
NO — FG Andersen 27
NO — Martin 43 pass from Hebert (Andersen kick)
NO — Del Rio 22 fumble recovery return (Andersen kick)
NO — FG Andersen 35

Minnesota 28, Philadelphia 23—At Veterans Stadium, attendance 54,688. Wade Wilson passed for three touchdowns and Willie Teal returned a fumble for another score to highlight the Vikings' dramatic comeback win. Trailing 23-0 with 8:27 left, Wilson fired a seven-yard scoring pass to Allen Rice. Teal then returned a fumble 65 yards for a score to cut the deficit to 23-14. Following a Joey Browner fumble recovery, Wilson hooked up with Anthony Carter on a 36-yard touchdown pass to pull Minnesota to within two points 23-21. Carter finished with five catches for 124 yards, including the game-winning score (a 42-yarder from Wilson) with 1:11 left.

Minnesota	0	0	0	28 —	28
Philadelphia	10	10	3	0 —	23

Phil — FG McFadden 29
Phil — Spagnola 28 pass from Jaworski (McFadden kick)
Phil — FG McFadden 33
Phil — Quick 9 pass from Jaworski (McFadden kick)
Phil — FG McFadden 25
Minn — Rice 7 pass from Wilson (Stenerud kick)
Minn — Teal 65 fumble recovery return (Stenerud kick)
Minn — Carter 36 pass from Wilson (Stenerud kick)
Minn — Carter 42 pass from Wilson (Stenerud kick)

New England 38, Indianapolis 31—At Hoosier Dome, attendance 56,740. Tony Eason, making his first start in seven weeks, completed 20 of 28 passes for 293 yards and three touchdowns to help the Patriots maintain a share of first place in the AFC East. New England took a 24-17 first-half lead on Eason's touchdown passes to Irving Fryar (six yards) and Stanley Morgan (14), Tony Franklin's 35-yard field goal, and Craig James's four-yard touchdown run. Eason's 25-yard scoring pass to Morgan increased the Patriots' lead to 31-17. Mosi Tatupu's one-yard scoring run with 5:21 left proved decisive after the Colts rallied for two fourth-quarter touchdowns.

New England	7	17	0	14 —	38
Indianapolis	7	10	0	14 —	31

NE — Fryar 6 pass from Eason (Franklin kick)
Ind — McMillan 1 run (Allegre kick)
NE — FG Franklin 35
NE — Morgan 14 pass from Eason (Franklin kick)
Ind — FG Allegre 25
Ind — McMillan 6 run (Allegre kick)
NE — C. James 4 run (Franklin kick)
NE — Morgan 25 pass from Eason (Franklin kick)
Ind — McMillan 6 run (Allegre kick)
NE — Tatupu 1 run (Franklin kick)
Ind — Bouza 10 pass from Pagel (Allegre kick)

San Francisco 35, Washington 8—At Robert F. Kennedy Stadium, attendance 51,321. San Francisco's Carl Monroe returned the opening kickoff 95 yards for a touchdown and the defense capitalized on five Redskins' turnovers en route to a 35-8 victory. Dwight Hicks's interception set up Wendell Tyler's one-yard scoring run and Keena Turner returned a fumble 65 yards for another score to put San Francisco ahead 21-8 at halftime. Tyler's four-yard run, set up by a Ronnie Lott interception, and Joe Montana's eight-yard touchdown pass to Russ Francis, completed the 49ers' scoring. Washington's Jay Schroeder connected on 30 of a club-record 58 passes for 348 yards as the Redskins outgained the 49ers 398 total yards to 224.

San Francisco	7	14	7	7 —	35
Washington	3	5	0	0 —	8

SF — Monroe 95 kickoff return (Wersching kick)
Wash — FG Moseley 25
Wash — Safety, Montana called for intentional grounding in end zone
SF — Tyler 1 run (Wersching kick)
SF — Turner 65 fumble recovery return (Wersching kick)
Wash — FG Moseley 21
SF — Tyler 4 run (Wersching kick)
SF — Francis 8 pass from Montana (Wersching kick)

Green Bay 21, Tampa Bay 0—At Lambeau Field, attendance 19,856. Eddie Lee Ivery and Gerry Ellis combined for 210 yards rushing to help the Packers blank the Buccaneers. The game was played in a swirling snowstorm. Green Bay scored in each of the final three quarters on runs by Lynn Dickey (one yard), Ellis (35), and Jessie Clark (three). Ivery gained 109 yards on 13 carries, while Ellis had 101 on nine. Dickey completed 22 of 36 passes for 299 yards, including six to James Lofton for 106 yards. Green Bay compiled a season-high 512 total yards, while the Packers' defense limited Tampa Bay to a club-record low 65 total yards.

Tampa Bay	0	0	0	0 —	0
Green Bay	0	7	7	7 —	21

GB — Dickey 1 run (Del Greco kick)
GB — Ellis 35 run (Del Greco kick)
GB — Clark 3 run (Del Greco kick)

MONDAY, DECEMBER 2

Miami 38, Chicago 24—At Orange Bowl, attendance 75,594. Dan Marino threw three touchdown passes and Ron Davenport ran for two more as the Dolphins handed the Bears their first loss of the season. Davenport's pair of one-yard scoring runs and Marino's two scoring passes to Nat Moore (33 and 6 yards) highlighted Miami's first-half explosion as it scored on its first five possessions to take a 31-10 lead. Marino finished with 14 completions in 27 attempts for 270 yards, including a 42-yard touchdown pass to Mark Clayton. Chicago's Walter Payton ran for 121 yards on 23 carries for his NFL-record eighth straight 100-yard rushing game. The loss snapped the Bears' 13-game regular-season win streak and helped the Dolphins maintain a share of the lead in the AFC East.

Chicago	7	3	14	0 —	24
Miami	10	21	7	0 —	38

Mia — Moore 33 pass from Marino (Reveiz kick)
Chi — Fuller 1 run (Butler kick)
Mia — FG Reveiz 47
Mia — Davenport 1 run (Reveiz kick)
Chi — FG Butler 30
Mia — Davenport 1 run (Reveiz kick)
Mia — Moore 6 pass from Marino (Reveiz kick)
Chi — Fuller 1 run (Butler kick)
Mia — Clayton 42 pass from Marino (Reveiz kick)
Chi — Margerum 19 pass from Fuller (Butler kick)

FOURTEENTH WEEK SUMMARIES

STANDINGS

American Football Conference

Eastern Division

	W	L	T	Pct.	Pts.	OP
Miami	10	4	0	.714	370	293
New England	10	4	0	.714	301	237
N.Y. Jets	10	4	0	.714	350	235
Indianapolis	3	11	0	.214	255	347
Buffalo	2	12	0	.143	176	323

Central Division

	W	L	T	Pct.	Pts.	OP
Cincinnati	7	7	0	.500	394	376
Cleveland	7	7	0	.500	249	236
Pittsburgh	6	8	0	.429	339	303
Houston	5	9	0	.357	247	350

Western Division

	W	L	T	Pct.	Pts.	OP
L.A. Raiders	10	4	0	.714	325	299
Denver	9	5	0	.643	339	292
Seattle	8	6	0	.571	322	263
San Diego	7	7	0	.500	413	383
Kansas City	5	9	0	.357	266	312

National Football Conference

Eastern Division

	W	L	T	Pct.	Pts.	OP
Dallas	9	5	0	.643	313	281
N.Y. Giants	9	5	0	.643	350	245
Washington	8	6	0	.571	243	272
Philadelphia	6	8	0	.429	235	255
St. Louis	5	9	0	.357	248	341

Central Division

	W	L	T	Pct.	Pts.	OP
Chicago	13	1	0	.929	400	175
Detroit	7	7	0	.500	267	303
Minnesota	7	7	0	.500	298	308
Green Bay	6	8	0	.429	291	315
Tampa Bay	2	12	0	.143	254	397

Western Division

	W	L	T	Pct.	Pts.	OP
L.A. Rams	10	4	0	.714	288	247
San Francisco	8	6	0	.571	349	228
New Orleans	5	9	0	.357	265	354
Atlanta	2	12	0	.143	252	429

SUNDAY, DECEMBER 8

Kansas City 38, Atlanta 10—At Arrowhead Stadium, attendance 18,199. Todd Blackledge passed for three touchdowns and Mike Pruitt became the first Kansas City player to rush for over 100 yards since 1981, as the Chiefs cruised past the Falcons 38-10. Kansas City opened a 14-0 first-quarter lead on scoring runs by Ethan Horton (one yard) and Herman Heard (six). Blackledge added scoring passes to Stephone Paige (70 and 14 yards) and Heard (15). Cornerback Albert Lewis had three interceptions to lead the Kansas City defense. Pruitt gained 102 yards on 16 carries to become the first Chiefs back to go over the 100-yard mark since Billy Jackson gained 102 yards against the Vikings on December 20, 1981. Atlanta's Gerald Riggs ran for 197 yards on 26 carries and a touchdown.

Atlanta	0	10	0	0 —	10
Kansas City	14	10	14	0 —	38

KC —Horton 1 run (Lowery kick)
KC —Heard 6 run (Lowery kick)
Atl —Riggs 1 run (Luckhurst kick)
KC —Paige 70 pass from Blackledge (Lowery kick)
KC —FG Lowery 49
Atl —FG Luckhurst 37
KC —Heard 15 pass from Blackledge (Lowery kick)
KC —Paige 14 pass from Blackledge (Lowery kick)

Seattle 31, Cleveland 13—At Kingdome, attendance 58,477. Dave Krieg completed four touchdown passes, including two to Daryl Turner, to help the Seahawks defeat the Browns. Seattle built a commanding 17-3 halftime lead on Norm Johnson's 51-yard field goal and Krieg's scoring passes to Dan Ross (four yards) and Turner (eight). Following a 32-yard field goal by Cleveland's Matt Bahr, Krieg hooked up with Turner (15 yards) and Steve Largent (nine) to put the game out of reach. The Seahawks recorded six sacks, including two by Jacob Green, to snap the Browns' three-game winning streak.

Cleveland	3	0	3	7 —	13
Seattle	3	14	7	7 —	31

Sea —FG Johnson 51
Clev —FG Bahr 27
Sea —Ross 4 pass from Krieg (Johnson kick)
Sea —Turner 8 pass from Krieg (Johnson kick)
Clev —FG Bahr 32
Sea —Turner 15 pass from Krieg (Johnson kick)
Sea —Largent 9 pass from Krieg (Johnson kick)
Clev —Young 45 pass from Kosar (Bahr kick)

Cincinnati 50, Dallas 24—At Riverfront Stadium, attendance 56,936. James Brooks ran for two touchdowns and Boomer Esiason threw for three more as the Bengals easily beat the Cowboys 50-24. Cincinnati scored 22 points in the first nine minutes and never looked back. Brooks gained 109 yards on 13 carries, including scoring runs of 27 and 18 yards. Esiason (15 of 25 for 265 yards) completed scoring passes to Eddie Brown (45 yards), Steve Kreider (29), and Cris Collinsworth (58). The Bengals outgained the Cowboys 570 total yards to 260. Collinsworth had seven catches for 123 yards to go over the 1,000-yard mark (1,016) for the third time in his career.

Dallas	0	3	7	14 —	24
Cincinnati	22	0	21	7 —	50

Cin —Safety, Browner tackled D. White in end zone
Cin —Kinnebrew 3 run (Breech kick)
Cin —Brown 45 pass from Esiason (Breech kick)
Cin —Brooks 27 run (pass failed)
Dall —FG Septien 21
Cin —Kreider 29 pass from Esiason (Breech kick)
Cin —Brooks 18 run (Breech kick)
Dall —Renfro 9 pass from D. White (Septien kick)
Cin —Collinsworth 58 pass from Esiason (Breech kick)
Cin —Alexander 5 run (Breech kick)
Dall —Cosbie 1 pass from D. White (Septien kick)
Dall —Penn 46 blocked punt return (Septien kick)

New England 23, Detroit 6—At Sullivan Stadium, attendance 59,078. Craig James rushed for 115 yards on 26 carries and Tony Franklin kicked three field goals to help lead the Patriots past the Lions. Tony Eason ran 16 yards for New England's first score and passed six yards to Derrick Ramsey for another to help the Patriots to a 17-3 halftime advantage. Franklin's field goals came from 38, 50, and 22 yards. James became the fourth Patriots' player to rush for over 1,000 yards in a season (1,027).

Detroit	3	0	3	0 —	6
New England	7	10	0	6 —	23

NE —Eason 16 run (Franklin kick)
Det —FG Murray 26
NE —D. Ramsey 6 pass from Eason (Franklin kick)
NE —FG Franklin 38
Det —FG Murray 37
NE —FG Franklin 50
NE —FG Franklin 22

Chicago 17, Indianapolis 10—At Soldier Field, attendance 59,997. Touchdown runs by Walter Payton and Calvin Thomas helped the Bears snap a seven-game losing streak to the Colts. Payton's 16-yard scoring run with 1:53 left in the third quarter, finished off a 63-yard drive to give Chicago a 10-3 edge. Thomas's three-yard touchdown run proved decisive as Indianapolis battled back on Mike Pagel's 61-yard scoring pass to Wayne Capers. Payton gained 111 yards on 26 carries to extend his NFL-record consecutive 100-yard games streak to nine.

Indianapolis	0	3	0	7 —	10
Chicago	0	3	7	7 —	17

Chi —FG Butler 20
Ind —FG Allegre 30
Chi —Payton 16 run (Butler kick)
Chi —Thomas 3 run (Butler kick)
Ind —Capers 61 pass from Pagel (Allegre kick)

Los Angeles Raiders 17, Denver 14—At Mile High Stadium, attendance 75,042. Chris Bahr's 26-yard field goal 4:55 into overtime gave the Raiders their second overtime win over the Broncos this season and sole possession of first place in the AFC West. The Raiders came back from a 14-0 halftime deficit when Marc Wilson threw to Todd Christensen for a three-yard touchdown and Marcus Allen ran 15 yards for another score to tie the game 14-14. Allen rushed 25 times for 135 yards for his seventh straight 100-yard game. Bahr's winning kick was set up by Greg Townsend's fumble recovery on the Broncos' 8-yard line.

L.A. Raiders	0	0	14	0	3 —	17
Denver	7	7	0	0	0 —	14

Den —J. Wright 5 pass from Elway (Karlis kick)
Den —Winder 1 run (Karlis kick)
Raiders —Christensen 3 pass from Wilson (Bahr kick)
Raiders —Allen 15 run (Bahr kick)
Raiders —FG Bahr 26

Miami 34, Green Bay 24—At Lambeau Field, attendance 52,671. Dan Marino completed a career-record-tying five touchdown passes to power the Dolphins past the Packers. Miami opened a 20-3 advantage on Marino scoring passes to Tony Nathan (10 yards), Mark Clayton (21), and Nat Moore (16). Green Bay rallied to take a 24-20 lead behind a pair of Jim Zorn touchdown passes and Eddie Lee Ivery's one-yard scoring run. Marino, who completed 30 of 44 passes for 345 yards, came right back with scoring passes to Joe Rose (two yards) and Dan Johnson (61) to put the game out of reach. Fuad Reveiz became the first Dolphins rookie to score 100 points in a season.

Miami	6	14	0	14 —	34
Green Bay	3	0	14	7 —	24

GB —FG Del Greco 22
Mia —Nathan 10 pass from Marino (kick blocked)
Mia —Clayton 21 pass from Marino (Reveiz kick)
Mia —Moore 16 pass from Marino (Reveiz kick)
GB —Dennard 29 pass from Zorn (Del Greco kick)
GB —Lofton 56 pass from Zorn (Del Greco kick)
GB —Ivery 1 run (Del Greco kick)
Mia —Rose 2 pass from Marino (Reveiz kick)
Mia —D. Johnson 61 pass from Marino (Reveiz kick)

St. Louis 28, New Orleans 16—At Busch Memorial Stadium, attendance 29,527. Stump Mitchell ran for two touchdowns and Neil Lomax threw for two more as the Cardinals upended the Saints. St. Louis opened a 21-6 halftime lead on scoring runs of 5 and 16 yards by Mitchell and Lomax's seven-yard touchdown pass to Pat Tilley. Mitchell, who finished the Cardinals' scoring with a five-yard touchdown reception, gained 158 yards on 28 carries to lead all rushers. Safety Lonnie Young had two interceptions for the St. Louis defense.

New Orleans	0	6	0	10 —	16
St. Louis	7	14	0	7 —	28

StL —Mitchell 5 run (Bojovic kick)
NO —FG Andersen 31
StL —Mitchell 16 run (Bojovic kick)
StL —Tilley 7 pass from Lomax (Bojovic kick)
NO —FG Andersen 30
StL —Mitchell 5 pass from Lomax (Bojovic kick)
NO —FG Andersen 42
NO —Tice 2 pass from Hebert (Andersen kick)

New York Giants 35, Houston 14—At Astrodome, attendance 36,576. Joe Morris became only the second player in Giants' history to gain more than 1,000 yards rushing in a season (1,004) when he ran for 129 yards on 25 carries to help New York defeat the Oilers. New York opened a 14-0 first-quarter lead on scoring runs of 12 and 2 yards by Morris. Following a pair of Oilers touchdowns, the Giants erupted for three touchdowns in the final 3:36 of the first half to take a 35-14 lead. Morris scored on another two-yard touchdown run and Simms completed scoring passes of 10 yards to Mark Bavaro and 22 yards to Bobby Johnson. Morris's club-record-tying fifth 100-yard game allowed him to join Ron Johnson as the only other 1,000-yard rusher in Giants' history.

N.Y. Giants	14	21	0	0 —	35
Houston	0	14	0	0 —	14

NYG —Morris 12 run (Schubert kick)
NYG —Morris 2 run (Schubert kick)
Hou —Williams 3 pass from Moon (Zendejas kick)
Hou —Smith 27 pass from Moon (Zendejas kick)
NYG —Bavaro 10 pass from Simms (Schubert kick)
NYG —Morris 2 run (Schubert kick)
NYG —Johnson 22 pass from Simms (Schubert kick)

New York Jets 27, Buffalo 7—At Rich Stadium, attendance 23,122. Ken O'Brien completed 25 of 40 passes for 370 yards and three touchdowns as the Jets defeated the Bills to maintain a share of first place in the AFC East. New York opened a 21-0 halftime lead on Johnny Hector's 12-yard scoring run and touchdown passes from Ken O'Brien of 96 yards to Wesley Walker (a club record) and 20 yards to Mickey Shuler. O'Brien completed the Jets' scoring with a two-yard pass to Shuler in the final period. Buffalo penetrated New York's 10-yard line on four separate occasions, but came away with just seven points.

N.Y. Jets	0	21	0	6 —	27
Buffalo	0	0	7	0 —	7

NYJ —Shuler 20 pass from O'Brien (Leahy kick)
NYJ —Walker 96 pass from O'Brien (Leahy kick)
NYJ —Hector 12 run (Leahy kick)
Buff —Bell 8 run (Norwood kick)
NYJ —Shuler 2 pass from O'Brien (kick blocked)

San Diego 54, Pittsburgh 44—At San Diego Jack Murphy Stadium, attendance 52,098. Dan Fouts completed 21 of 33 passes for 372 yards and three touchdowns as the Chargers outdistanced the Steelers in the fourth-highest scoring game in NFL history. Fouts completed scoring passes of 36 and 75 yards to Wes Chandler and 20 yards to Pete Holohan as San Diego built a 34-20 halftime advantage. Buford McGee's second touchdown, a seven-yard run, gave the Chargers a 41-34 lead going into the final quarter, but Pittsburgh countered with 10 straight points. The Chargers regained the lead for good on Gary Anderson's two-yard touchdown dive. Jeff Dale's 47-yard interception return for a score with 2:09 remaining sealed the win.

Pittsburgh	7	13	14	10 —	44
San Diego	21	13	7	13 —	54

SD —Spencer 12 run (Thomas kick)
Pitt —Abercrombie 15 pass from Woodley (Anderson kick)
SD —Chandler 36 pass from Fouts (Thomas kick)
SD —Holohan 20 pass from Fouts (Thomas kick)
Pitt —Lipps 8 pass from Woodley (Anderson kick)
Pitt —FG Anderson 45
SD —Chandler 75 pass from Fouts (Thomas kick)
SD —McGee 3 run (kick failed)
Pitt —FG Anderson 41
Pitt —Woodley 1 run (Anderson kick)
Pitt —Abercrombie 25 pass from Woodley (Anderson kick)
SD —McGee 7 run (Thomas kick)
Pitt —Lipps 15 run (Anderson kick)
Pitt —FG Anderson 26
SD —Anderson 2 run (kick failed)
SD —Dale 47 interception return (Thomas kick)

Minnesota 26, Tampa Bay 7—At Metrodome, attendance 51,593. Jan Stenerud kicked four field goals and the defense forced six turnovers to lead the Vikings over the Buccaneers. Tommy Kramer completed 21 of 36 passes for 309 yards, including four to Mike Jones for 104 yards. While Stenerud was successful from 24, 24, 25, and 35 yards out, Minnesota's Darrin Nelson and Ted Brown added scoring runs of one and eight yards, respectively. Rookie Chris Doleman had an interception and a fumble recovery for the Vikings.

Tampa Bay	0	0	7	0 —	7
Minnesota	6	10	3	7 —	26

Minn —FG Stenerud 24
Minn —FG Stenerud 24
Minn —Nelson 1 run (Stenerud kick)
Minn —FG Stenerud 25
Minn —FG Stenerud 35
TB —Magee 7 pass from Young (Igwebuike kick)
Minn —Brown 8 run (Stenerud kick)

Washington 17, Philadelphia 12—At Veterans Stadium, attendance 60,373. George Rogers ran for 150 yards and a touchdown to spark the Redskins to a 17-12 win over the Eagles. Philadelphia led 12-3 late in the third quarter, before Rogers scored on a 28-yard run, which narrowed the margin to 12-10. The Redskins took their first lead, 17-12, on Jay Schroeder's five-yard scoring pass to Gary Clark. Rogers rushed a club-record 36 times as the Redskins maintained a 38:23 to 21:37 time of possession advantage. Washington's defense held Philadelphia to 26 yards rushing.

Washington	0	3	7	7 —	17
Philadelphia	0	5	7	0 —	12

Phil —Safety, Schroeder called for intentionally grounding in end zone
Phil —FG McFadden 44
Wash —FG Moseley 32
Phil —E. Jackson 1 run (McFadden kick)
Wash —Rogers 28 run (Moseley kick)
Wash —Clark 5 pass from Schroeder (Moseley kick)

MONDAY, DECEMBER 9

Los Angeles Rams 27, San Francisco 20—At Candlestick Park, attendance 60,581. Gary Green's 41-yard interception return for a touchdown with 3:22 left climaxed the Rams' fourth-quarter rally which secured their third straight playoff berth. Ron Brown returned the opening kickoff of the second half 86 yards for a touchdown to give Los Angeles a 10-7 lead. The 49ers rallied to take a 20-13 lead with 5:38 left. Dieter Brock's 39-yard touchdown pass to Henry Ellard tied the score at 20-20. Gary Jeter's sack and fumble recovery in the final minutes sealed the win. San Francisco's rookie wide receiver Jerry Rice caught 10 passes for a club-record 241 yards, including a 66-yard touchdown, to capture NFC offensive player of the week honors.

L.A. Rams	0	3	7	17 —	27
San Francisco	0	7	6	7 —	20

SF —Clark 7 pass from Montana (Wersching kick)
Rams —FG Lansford 25
Rams —Brown 86 kickoff return (Lansford kick)
SF —Rice 66 pass from Montana (kick failed)
Rams —FG Lansford 29

SF — Craig 1 pass from Montana (Wersching kick)
Rams — Ellard 39 pass from Brock (Lansford kick)
Rams — Green 41 interception return (Lansford kick)

FIFTEENTH WEEK SUMMARIES

STANDINGS

American Football Conference

Eastern Division	W	L	T	Pct.	Pts.	OP
Miami	11	4	0	.733	400	320
New England	10	5	0	.667	328	267
N.Y. Jets	10	5	0	.667	356	254
Indianapolis	4	11	0	.267	286	370
Buffalo	2	13	0	.133	200	353
Central Division						
Cleveland	8	7	0	.533	277	257
Cincinnati	7	8	0	.467	418	403
Pittsburgh	7	8	0	.467	369	327
Houston	5	10	0	.333	268	378
Western Division						
L.A. Raiders	11	4	0	.733	338	302
Denver	10	5	0	.667	353	305
San Diego	8	7	0	.533	433	397
Seattle	8	7	0	.533	325	276
Kansas City	5	10	0	.333	279	326

National Football Conference

Eastern Division	W	L	T	Pct.	Pts.	OP
Dallas	10	5	0	.667	341	302
N.Y. Giants	9	6	0	.600	371	273
Washington	9	6	0	.600	270	296
Philadelphia	7	8	0	.467	249	275
St. Louis	5	10	0	.333	262	387
Central Division						
Chicago	14	1	0	.933	419	181
Detroit	7	8	0	.467	290	329
Green Bay	7	8	0	.467	317	338
Minnesota	7	8	0	.467	311	322
Tampa Bay	2	13	0	.133	277	428
Western Division						
L.A. Rams	11	4	0	.733	334	261
San Francisco	9	6	0	.600	380	247
New Orleans	5	10	0	.333	284	385
Atlanta	3	12	0	.200	266	442

SATURDAY, DECEMBER 14

Chicago 19, New York Jets 6—At Giants Stadium, attendance 74,752. Kevin Butler kicked four field goals to lead the Bears over the Jets. Chicago opened a 10-3 halftime lead on Butler's 18-yard field goal and Jim McMahon's seven-yard scoring pass to Tim Wrightman. Butler added second-half field goals of 31, 37, and 21 yards to complete the Bears' scoring. Walter Payton's consecutive 100-yard rushing games streak was stopped at nine as New York's defense held him to 53 yards on 28 carries. The Jets' Dave Jennings became the third player in NFL history to punt 1,000 times (1,002) with six punts for 221 yards. Chicago outgained New York 319 to 159 total yards, while maintaining a 39:36 to 20:24 time of possession advantage.

Chicago	3	7	3	6	— 19
N.Y. Jets	3	0	3	0	— 6

Chi — FG Butler 18
NYJ — FG Leahy 23
Chi — Wrightman 7 pass from McMahon (Butler kick)
NYJ — FG Leahy 55
Chi — FG Butler 31
Chi — FG Butler 37
Chi — FG Butler 21

Denver 14, Kansas City 13—At Mile High Stadium, attendance 69,209. Sammy Winder's one-yard touchdown run with 22 seconds remaining lifted the Broncos over the Chiefs and helped Denver remain in contention for a playoff berth. John Elway completed 22 of 37 passes for 301 yards, including an 11-yard scoring pass to Vance Johnson. The Broncos struggled throughout as Kansas City intercepted Elway five times, including one by cornerback Albert Lewis which set up its lone touchdown, a seven-yard pass from Todd Blackledge to Stephone Paige.

Kansas City	3	0	3	7	— 13
Denver	0	7	0	7	— 14

KC — FG Lowery 32
Den — V. Johnson 11 pass from Elway (Karlis kick)
KC — FG Lowery 41
KC — Paige 7 pass from Blackledge (Lowery kick)
Den — Winder 1 run (Karlis kick)

SUNDAY, DECEMBER 15

Pittsburgh 30, Buffalo 24—At Three Rivers Stadium, attendance 35,953. Backup quarterback Scott Campbell came off the bench to rally the Steelers over the Bills. Trailing 21-0 in the second quarter, Campbell, who followed David Woodley and Mark Malone into the game, completed a 13-yard scoring pass to Louis Lipps. Frank Pollard followed with a four-yard touchdown run to narrow the halftime margin to 21-14. Gary Anderson kicked field goals of 26, 31, and 45 yards, and Walter Abercrombie scored on a two-yard run with 47 seconds left to conclude Pittsburgh's comeback. Campbell completed 18 of 38 passes for 275 yards, including four to Lipps for 116 yards.

Buffalo	7	14	0	3	— 24
Pittsburgh	0	14	6	10	— 30

Buff — Bell 77 run (Norwood kick)
Buff — Butler 33 pass from Mathison (Norwood kick)
Buff — Wilson 61 fumble recovery return (Norwood kick)
Pitt — Lipps 13 pass from Campbell (Anderson kick)
Pitt — Pollard 4 run (Anderson kick)
Pitt — FG Anderson 26
Pitt — FG Anderson 31
Buff — FG Norwood 24
Pitt — FG Anderson 45
Pitt — Abercrombie 2 run (Anderson kick)

Washington 27, Cincinnati 24—At Robert F. Kennedy Stadium, attendance 50,544. Two touchdown runs by George Rogers and a pair of Mark Moseley field goals helped the Redskins keep their playoff hopes alive. Boomer Esiason, who completed 22 of 39 passes for 357 yards, led Cincinnati to a 24-17 halftime lead with touchdown passes of 26 and 51 yards to Rodney Holman. Moseley's 39-yard field goal in the third quarter narrowed the gap to 24-20. Rogers's 34-yard scoring run midway through the final period proved decisive as Washington's defense shut out the Bengals in the second half. The Redskins' Art Monk set single-game club records with 13 receptions for 230 yards and earned NFC offensive player of the week honors.

Cincinnati	21	3	0	0	— 24
Washington	7	10	3	7	— 27

Wash — Rogers 1 run (Moseley kick)
Cin — Brown 8 pass from Brooks (Breech kick)
Cin — Holman 26 pass from Esiason (Breech kick)
Cin — Holman 51 pass from Esiason (Breech kick)
Cin — FG Breech 38
Wash — Monk 4 pass from Schroeder (Moseley kick)
Wash — FG Moseley 42
Wash — FG Moseley 39
Wash — Rogers 34 run (Moseley kick)

Green Bay 26, Detroit 23—At Pontiac Silverdome, attendance 49,379. Al Del Greco's career-high fourth field goal, a 27-yarder with one second remaining, lifted the Packers over the Lions. Green Bay rebounded from a 17-6 deficit to take a 23-17 lead on Gary Ellerson's 37-yard touchdown run, Del Greco's 25-yard field goal, and Mike Douglass's 80-yard interception return for a touchdown. Detroit responded with a Joe Ferguson to Leonard Thompson 30-yard scoring strike to tie the score 23-23. Del Greco's winning kick capped a seven-play, 71-yard drive.

Green Bay	0	6	7	13	— 26
Detroit	14	3	0	6	— 23

Det — Moore 1 run (Murray kick)
Det — Moore 1 run (Murray kick)
GB — FG Del Greco 38
GB — FG Del Greco 29
Det — FG Murray 19
GB — Ellerson 37 run (Del Greco kick)
GB — FG Del Greco 25
GB — Douglass 80 interception return (Del Greco kick)
Det — Thompson 30 pass from Ferguson (kick failed)
GB — FG Del Greco 27

Cleveland 28, Houston 21—At Cleveland Stadium, attendance 50,793. Bernie Kosar passed for three touchdowns and ran for another to help the Browns defeat the Oilers and take over sole possession of first place in the AFC Central. Kosar ran two yards for his first NFL touchdown and passed two yards to Ozzie Newsome for another score to give Cleveland a 14-7 halftime lead. Herman Fontenot's 81-yard return of the second-half kickoff set up Kosar's eight-yard scoring pass to Fred Banks. Kosar's five-yard touchdown pass to Kevin Mack, which gave the Browns a commanding 28-7 third-quarter edge, was set up by Al Gross's 22-yard interception return. Newsome had four catches for 85 yards to become the fourteenth player in NFL history to catch 500 passes.

Houston	0	7	0	14	— 21
Cleveland	7	7	14	0	— 28

Clev — Kosar 2 run (Bahr kick)
Clev — Newsome 2 pass from Kosar (Bahr kick)
Hou — Rozier 3 run (Zendejas kick)
Clev — F. Banks 8 pass from Kosar (Bahr kick)
Clev — Mack 5 pass from Kosar (Bahr kick)
Hou — Woolfolk 15 pass from Moon (Zendejas kick)
Hou — Smith 16 pass from Moon (Zendejas kick)

Indianapolis 31, Tampa Bay 23—At Tampa Stadium, attendance 25,577. Randy McMillan rushed for 108 yards on 13 carries and George Wonsley added a pair of touchdown runs to help the Colts snap a 10-game losing streak on the road. Wonsley scored on runs of seven and three yards and Raul Allegre kicked a 33-yard field goal to keep Indianapolis even with the Buccaneers 17-17 at the half. Following a Tampa Bay touchdown, Mike Pagel and Albert Bentley scored on runs of 3 and 26 yards, respectively, to secure the Colts' win.

Indianapolis	7	10	0	14	— 31
Tampa Bay	7	10	0	6	— 23

Ind — Wonsley 7 run (Allegre kick)
TB — Wilder 9 run (Igwebuike kick)
TB — FG Igwebuike 48
Ind — FG Allegre 33
Ind — Wonsley 3 run (Allegre kick)
TB — House 44 pass from Young (Igwebuike kick)
TB — Young 1 run (kick failed)
Ind — Pagel 3 run (Allegre kick)
Ind — Bentley 26 run (Allegre kick)

Atlanta 14, Minnesota 13—At Atlanta-Fulton County Stadium, attendance 14,167. Dave Archer passed for one touchdown and Joe Washington ran for another as the Falcons squeaked past the Vikings. Archer's 34-yard scoring pass to Charlie Brown and Washington's one-yard touchdown dive 2:27 before halftime were all the points Atlanta needed. The Falcons registered five turnovers (three fumble recoveries and two interceptions) and defensive end Rick Bryan had 2½ sacks. A missed extra point by Minnesota's Jan Stenerud proved to be the difference.

Minnesota	0	7	0	6	— 13
Atlanta	0	14	0	0	— 14

Atl — Brown 34 pass from Archer (Luckhurst kick)
Atl — Washington 1 run (Luckhurst kick)
Minn — Nelson 6 run (Stenerud kick)
Minn — Carter 49 pass from Kramer (kick failed)

Dallas 28, New York Giants 21—At Texas Stadium, attendance 62,310. Jim Jeffcoat and Mike Renfro scored touchdowns 46 seconds apart to help the Cowboys clinch their first division title since 1981. Dallas trailed New York 14-7, when Jeffcoat returned a deflected Phil Simms pass 65 yards for a touchdown. Danny White then completed a 12-yard scoring pass to Renfro to give the Cowboys a 21-14 halftime lead. Timmy Newsome's one-yard scoring run with 4:06 left proved decisive as the Giants rallied for a touchdown in the closing minutes. Victor Scott's interception deep in Dallas territory ended New York's final scoring threat. Jeffcoat had two of Dallas's five sacks to earn NFC defensive player of the week honors.

N.Y. Giants	0	14	0	7	— 21
Dallas	7	14	0	7	— 28

Dall — Renfro 58 pass from Hogeboom (Septien kick)
NYG — B. Johnson 7 pass from Simms (Schubert kick)
NYG — Galbreath 10 pass from Simms (Schubert kick)
Dall — Jeffcoat 65 interception return (Septien kick)
Dall — Renfro 12 pass from D. White (Septien kick)
Dall — Newsome 1 run (Septien kick)
NYG — Morris 1 run (Schubert kick)

San Diego 20, Philadelphia 14—At San Diego Jack Murphy Stadium, attendance 45,569. Mark Herrmann came off the bench to throw one touchdown and Bob Thomas added a pair of field goals as the Chargers downed the Eagles. Trailing 14-10 in the third quarter, Herrmann completed a 23-yard touchdown pass to Charlie Joiner to give San Diego a 17-14 lead. Thomas opened and closed the Chargers' scoring with field goals of 45 and 46 yards. Cornerback Danny Walters led the defense with two interceptions.

Philadelphia	7	0	7	0	— 14
San Diego	0	3	14	3	— 20

Phil — Spagnola 3 pass from Jaworski (McFadden kick)
SD — FG Thomas 45
SD — Spencer 6 run (Thomas kick)
Phil — Little fumble recovery in end zone (McFadden kick)
SD — Joiner 23 pass from Herrmann (Thomas kick)
SD — FG Thomas 46

Los Angeles Rams 46, St. Louis 14—At Anaheim Stadium, attendance 52,052. Eric Dickerson rushed for 124 yards on 20 carries and Dieter Brock threw four touchdown passes to help the Rams defeat the Cardinals and clinch their first NFC West title since 1979. Dickerson scored on runs of one and two yards and Brock connected on scoring passes to Ron Brown (13 yards), Tony Hunter (47), and Henry Ellard (43) as Los Angeles scored 36 straight points to take a 36-7 halftime lead. Brock, who directed the Rams' 425-yard offensive attack, completed a three-yard scoring pass to Hunter in the third quarter. Tim Fox intercepted two passes and Gary Jeter had two sacks to pace Los Angeles's defense, which yielded St. Louis only 213 total yards.

St. Louis	7	0	7	0	— 14
L.A. Rams	13	23	7	3	— 46

StL — Mitchell 1 run (Bojovic kick)
Rams — Dickerson 1 run (kick failed)
Rams — Brown 13 pass from Brock (Lansford kick)
Rams — Hunter 47 pass from Brock (Lansford kick)
Rams — Dickerson 2 run (Lansford kick)
Rams — Safety, Lomax tackled in end zone
Rams — Ellard 43 pass from Brock (Lansford kick)
Rams — Hunter 3 pass from Brock (Lansford kick)
StL — Marsh 12 pass from Lomax (Bojovic kick)
Rams — FG Lansford 46

San Francisco 31, New Orleans 19—At Louisiana Superdome, attendance 46,065. Joe Montana completed 25 of 38 passes for 354 yards and three touchdowns to lead the 49ers past the Saints 31-19. San Francisco led 17-16 after three quarters on Ray Wersching's 24-yard field goal and a pair of Montana scoring passes to Dwight Clark (26 yards) and Mike Wilson (52). New Orleans went ahead 19-16 on Morten Andersen's 41-yard field goal, but the 49ers recaptured the lead on Montana's 17-yard scoring pass to Russ Francis. Roger Craig added a 15-yard touchdown run and totalled 170 combined yards from scrimmage (88 rushing and 82 receiving) as the 49ers outgained the Saints 500 total yards to 289.

San Francisco	0	7	10	14	—	31
New Orleans	0	9	7	3	—	19

SF —Clark 26 pass from Montana (Wersching kick)
NO —FG Andersen 46
NO —Warren 42 blocked field goal return (kick failed)
SF —Wilson 52 pass from Montana (Wersching kick)
NO —Goodlow 76 pass from Hebert (Andersen kick)
SF —FG Wersching 24
NO —FG Andersen 41
SF —Francis 17 pass from Montana (Wersching kick)
SF —Craig 15 run (Wersching kick)

Los Angeles Raiders 13, Seattle 3—At Memorial Coliseum, attendance 77,425. Marcus Allen rushed for over 100 yards for the eighth straight week as the Raiders defeated the Seahawks to clinch the AFC West title. Los Angeles was led by Chris Bahr, who kicked field goals of 22 and 27 yards, and Allen, who gained 109 yards on 27 carries, including a seven-yard touchdown run with 6:09 left. The Raiders shut down the Seahawks' attack, limiting Seattle to 51 yards rushing while registering four takeaways and four sacks.

Seattle	3	0	0	0	—	3
L.A. Raiders	0	6	0	7	—	13

Sea —FG Johnson 37
Raiders —FG Bahr 22
Raiders —FG Bahr 27
Raiders —Allen 7 run (Bahr kick)

MONDAY, DECEMBER 16

Miami 30, New England 27—At Orange Bowl, attendance 69,489. Fuad Reveiz's 47-yard field goal with 4:27 left lifted the Dolphins over the Patriots and into sole possession of first place in the AFC East. Reveiz's 49-yard field goal and Ron Davenport's one-yard touchdown run extended Miami's 17-7 halftime lead to 27-13 with 11:08 remaining. New England tied the score 27-27 on Mosi Tatupu's one-yard run and Cedric Jones's 15-yard fumble recovery return of the subsequent kickoff just 15 seconds later. Glenn Blackwood intercepted two passes to halt Patriots scoring drives, his second at the Dolphins' 11-yard line with 58 seconds remaining.

New England	7	0	3	17	—	27
Miami	7	10	3	10	—	30

Mia —Rose 6 pass from Marino (Reveiz kick)
NE —Fryar 10 pass from Eason (Franklin kick)
Mia —FG Reveiz 44
Mia —Davenport 1 run (Reveiz kick)
NE —FG Franklin 22
Mia —FG Reveiz 49
NE —FG Franklin 49
Mia —Davenport 1 run (Reveiz kick)
NE —Tatupu 1 run (Franklin kick)
NE —C. Jones 15 fumbled kickoff return (Franklin kick)
Mia —FG Reveiz 47

SIXTEENTH WEEK SUMMARIES

STANDINGS

American Football Conference

Eastern Division	W	L	T	Pct.	Pts.	OP
Miami*	12	4	0	.750	428	320
N.Y. Jets*	11	5	0	.688	393	264
New England*	11	5	0	.688	362	290
Indianapolis	5	11	0	.313	320	386
Buffalo	2	14	0	.125	200	381
Central Division						
Cleveland*	8	8	0	.500	287	294
Cincinnati	7	9	0	.438	441	437
Pittsburgh	7	9	0	.438	379	355
Houston	5	11	0	.313	284	412
Western Division						
L.A. Raiders*	12	4	0	.750	354	308
Denver	11	5	0	.688	380	329
Seattle	8	8	0	.500	349	303
San Diego	8	8	0	.500	467	435
Kansas City	6	10	0	.375	317	360

National Football Conference

Eastern Division	W	L	T	Pct.	Pts.	OP
Dallas*	10	6	0	.625	357	333
N.Y. Giants*	10	6	0	.625	399	283
Washington	10	6	0	.625	297	312
Philadelphia	7	9	0	.438	286	310
St. Louis	5	11	0	.313	278	414
Central Division						
Chicago*	15	1	0	.938	456	198
Green Bay	8	8	0	.500	337	355
Minnesota	7	9	0	.438	346	359
Detroit	7	9	0	.438	307	366
Tampa Bay	2	14	0	.125	294	448
Western Division						
L.A. Rams*	11	5	0	.688	340	277
San Francisco*	10	6	0	.625	411	263
New Orleans	5	11	0	.313	294	401
Atlanta	4	12	0	.250	282	452

*denotes playoff team

FRIDAY, DECEMBER 20

Denver 27, Seattle 24—At Kingdome, attendance 56,283. John Elway completed 24 of 42 passes for 432 yards and a touchdown to rally the Broncos over the Seahawks. Trailing 17-10 after three quarters, Denver erupted for 17 points in the final period on one-yard touchdown runs by Gerald Willhite and Steve Sewell and Rich Karlis's 43-yard field goal. Elway opened Denver's scoring with a 17-yard touchdown pass to Steve Watson. The Broncos' victory kept them in playoff contention.

Denver	0	10	0	17	—	27
Seattle	7	10	0	7	—	24

Sea —Turner 41 pass from Krieg (Johnson kick)
Sea —FG Johnson 29
Sea —Taylor 15 blocked punt return (Johnson kick)
Den —Watson 17 pass from Elway (Karlis kick)
Den —FG Karlis 25
Den —Willhite 1 run (Karlis kick)
Sea —Warner 1 run (Johnson kick)
Den —Sewell 1 run (Karlis kick)
Den —FG Karlis 43

SATURDAY, DECEMBER 21

New York Giants 28, Pittsburgh 10—At Giants Stadium, attendance 66,785. Joe Morris gained 202 yards on 36 carries to set a club single-season record as the Giants downed the Steelers to clinch a Wild Card playoff berth. Morris's rushing output increased his season total to 1,336 yards to better Ron Johnson's club mark of 1,182 set in 1972. New York built a commanding 28-3 halftime lead on Morris's touchdown runs of 9, 1, and 65 yards and Phil Simms's 23-yard scoring pass to Bobby Johnson. The win assured the Giants of their second-straight playoff appearance for the first time since the 1962-63 seasons.

Pittsburgh	0	3	7	0	—	10
N.Y. Giants	7	21	0	0	—	28

NYG —Morris 9 run (Schubert kick)
Pitt —FG Anderson 26
NYG —Morris 65 run (Schubert kick)
NYG —Morris 1 run (Schubert kick)
NYG —Johnson 23 pass from Simms (Schubert kick)
Pitt —Stallworth 34 pass from Campbell (Anderson kick)

Washington 27, St. Louis 16—At Busch Memorial Stadium, attendance 28,090. George Rogers equaled his career-high by rushing for 206 yards on 34 carries as the Redskins defeated the Cardinals to remain in the hunt for a playoff berth. Washington built a 13-9 halftime lead on Mark Moseley field goals of 48 and 30 yards and Jay Schroeder's 27-yard touchdown pass to Gary Clark. Rogers and Keith Griffin added one-yard scoring runs in the second half to complete the Redskins' scoring. Clark finished with eight catches for 118 yards.

Washington	0	13	7	7	—	27
St. Louis	9	0	0	7	—	16

StL —FG Bojovic 42
StL —Green 8 pass from Lomax (kick blocked)
Wash —FG Moseley 48
Wash —Clark 27 pass from Schroeder (Moseley kick)
Wash —FG Moseley 30
Wash —Rogers 1 run (Moseley kick)
Wash —Griffin 1 run (Moseley kick)
StL —Duncan 2 pass from Lomax (Bojovic kick)

SUNDAY, DECEMBER 22

Atlanta 16, New Orleans 10—At Louisiana Superdome, attendance 37,717. Gerald Riggs carried 39 times for 158 yards and a touchdown to lead the Falcons past the Saints. Mick Luckhurst kicked field goals of 48 and 31 yards and Riggs scored on a two-yard run to give Atlanta a 13-0 halftime advantage. Luckhurst added a 22-yard field goal in the fourth quarter to clinch the win. New Orleans rallied for 10 points in the final period but still came up short. The Falcons controlled the ball for 41:15 and totaled 432 yards.

Atlanta	3	10	0	3	—	16
New Orleans	0	0	0	10	—	10

Atl —FG Luckhurst 48
Atl —Riggs 2 run (Luckhurst kick)
Atl —FG Luckhurst 31
Atl —FG Luckhurst 22
NO —Martin 9 pass from Hebert (Andersen kick)
NO —FG Andersen 28

Miami 28, Buffalo 0—At Orange Bowl, attendance 64,811. The Dolphins rushed for a season-high 179 yards and capitalized on six Bills' turnovers en route to their third straight AFC Eastern Division title. Dan Marino threw touchdown passes of 19 and 5 yards to Bruce Hardy to give Miami a 14-0 halftime advantage. Hardy's second scoring catch was set up by Jackie Shipp's interception. Bill Barnett's fumble recovery led to Tony Nathan's one-yard touchdown run. Ron Davenport raced 13 yards for a score to finish Miami's scoring.

Buffalo	0	0	0	0	—	0
Miami	7	7	0	14	—	28

Mia —Hardy 19 pass from Marino (Reveiz kick)
Mia —Hardy 5 pass from Marino (Reveiz kick)
Mia —Nathan 1 run (Reveiz kick)
Mia —Davenport 13 run (Reveiz kick)

Chicago 37, Detroit 17—At Pontiac Silverdome, attendance 74,042. The Bears rolled over the Lions to equal the NFL record for most wins in a season (15 to equal the 1984 San Francisco 49ers record). Kicker Kevin Butler had three field goals (25, 24, and 21 yards) and four extra points to set an NFL record for most points scored by a rookie. Butler totaled 144 points for the season, surpassing Gale Sayers's 1965 mark of 132. Dennis Gentry returned the second-half kickoff 94 yards for a touchdown to extend Chicago's lead to 13-3. Jim McMahon ran 14 yards for one score and passed 11 yards to Ken Margerum for another to add to the Bears' lead. Chicago had seven takeaways (three interceptions, four fumble recoveries), including Ron Rivera's five-yard fumble recovery return for a touchdown.

Chicago	3	3	10	21	—	37
Detroit	3	0	7	7	—	17

Chi —FG Butler 25
Det —FG Murray 42
Chi —FG Butler 24
Chi —Gentry 94 kickoff return (Butler kick)
Chi —FG Butler 21
Det —Lewis 2 pass from Hipple (Murray kick)
Chi —McMahon 14 run (Butler kick)
Chi —Rivera 5 fumble recovery return (Butler kick)
Det —Jones 2 run (Murray kick)
Chi —Margerum 11 pass from McMahon (Butler kick)

New England 34, Cincinnati 23—At Sullivan Stadium, attendance 57,953. Craig James ran for a career-high 142 yards on 25 carries to lead the Patriots to their first playoff berth since 1982. New England built a 20-6 halftime lead on two Tony Franklin field goals from 25 and 30 yards, Tony Collins's nine-yard touchdown run, and Tony Eason's 50-yard scoring pass to Stanley Morgan. James and Robert Weathers added touchdown runs of 11 and 42 yards, respectively, in the fourth quarter. New England ground out a season-high 281 rushing yards. Morgan caught four passes for 121 yards.

Cincinnati	3	3	7	10	—	23
New England	10	10	0	14	—	34

NE —FG Franklin 25
Cin —FG Breech 42
NE —Morgan 50 pass from Eason (Franklin kick)
Cin —FG Breech 22
NE —Collins 9 run (Franklin kick)
NE —FG Franklin 30
Cin —Brown 33 pass from Esiason (Breech kick)
Cin —FG Breech 30
NE —C. James 11 run (Franklin kick)
Cin —Collinsworth 8 pass from Esiason (Breech kick)
NE —Weathers 42 run (Franklin kick)

New York Jets 37, Cleveland 10—At Giants Stadium, attendance 59,073. Johnny Hector ran for two touchdowns and Pat Leahy kicked three field goals (46, 35, and 32 yards) as the Jets earned a playoff berth by downing the Browns. Hector scored on runs of one and five yards. Ken O'Brien completed 21 of 34 passes for 251 yards, including a 39-yard scoring pass to Kurt Sohn. Mickey Shuler caught six passes for 83 yards to total 76 for the season, breaking George Sauer's club-record 75 in 1967. Cleveland's Earnest Byner gained 101 yards on 15 carries to raise his season total to 1,002. Byner and Kevin Mack (1,104) became the first pair of teammates to go over the 1,000-yard mark in the same season since Pittsburgh's Franco Harris (1,128) and Rocky Bleier (1,036) performed the feat in 1976.

Cleveland	7	3	0	0	—	10
N.Y. Jets	10	7	10	10	—	37

NYJ —FG Leahy 46
Clev —Brennan 37 punt return (Bahr kick)
NYJ —Sohn 39 pass from O'Brien (Leahy kick)
Clev —FG Bahr 32
NYJ —Hector 5 run (Leahy kick)
NYJ —Hector 1 run (Leahy kick)
NYJ —FG Leahy 35
NYJ —FG Leahy 32
NYJ —Paige 1 run (Leahy kick)

San Francisco 31, Dallas 16—At Candlestick Park, attendance 60,114. Joe Montana completed 24 of 34 passes for 322 yards and two touchdowns to help the 49ers past the Cowboys and into the playoffs as a Wild Card. Montana opened and closed San Francisco's scoring with completions of 49 and 24 yards to Dwight Clark. Touchdown runs by Roger Craig (four yards) and wide receiver Jerry Rice (15) gave the 49ers a 24-16 third-quarter edge. Craig rushed for 72 yards and added 50 receiving to become the first player in NFL history to gain over 1,000 yards both rushing and receiving. Craig finished the season with 1,050 rushing yards on 214 carries and 1,015 receiving on an NFL-high 92 receptions.

Dallas	7	9	0	0	—	16
San Francisco	0	10	14	7	—	31

Dall —Cosbie 1 pass from Hogeboom (Septien kick)
Dall —FG Septien 29
Dall —FG Septien 48
SF —Clark 49 pass from Montana (Wersching kick)
Dall —FG Septien 41
SF —FG Wersching 39
SF —Craig 4 run (Wersching kick)
SF —Rice 15 run (Wersching kick)
SF —Clark 24 pass from Montana (Wersching kick)

Green Bay 20, Tampa Bay 17—At Tampa Stadium, attendance 33,992. Jessie Clark's six-yard touchdown run midway through the fourth quarter lifted the Packers over the Buccaneers. Al Del Greco's 40-yard field goal with 2:44 left in the third period broke a 10-10 tie to give Green Bay a 13-10 lead. Following a Tampa Bay touchdown, reserve quarterback Randy Wright directed the Packers 73 yards in 13 plays to set up Clark's game-winning score. The victory gave Green Bay its third consecutive 8-8 season.

Green Bay	7	3	3	7	— 20
Tampa Bay	3	7	0	7	— 17

TB —FG Igwebuike 33
GB —Epps 30 run (Del Greco kick)
TB —Wilder 1 run (Igwebuike kick)
GB —FG Del Greco 24
GB —FG Del Greco 40
TB —Giles 3 pass from Young (Igwebuike kick)
GB —Clark 6 run (Del Greco kick)

Indianapolis 34, Houston 16—At Hoosier Dome, attendance 55,818. Mike Pagel passed for three touchdowns to lead the Colts to a 34-16 win over Houston. Indianapolis built a 20-9 halftime lead on Pagel scoring strikes of 14 and 20 yards to Pat Beach, and Randy McMillan's 16-yard touchdown run. Albert Bentley's 24-yard run and Pagel's 22-yard completion to Oliver Williams finished the Colts' scoring. Houston's Warren Moon completed 22 of 40 passes for 364 yards, including touchdowns of 40 and 14 yards to Drew Hill, who had nine receptions for 210 yards.

Houston	0	9	0	7	— 16
Indianapolis	7	13	7	7	— 34

Ind —Beach 14 pass from Pagel (Allegre kick)
Ind —McMillan 16 run (kick blocked)
Hou —Hill 40 pass from Moon (kick blocked)
Ind —Beach 20 pass from Pagel (Allegre kick)
Hou —FG Zendejas 45
Ind —Bentley 24 run (Allegre kick)
Hou —Hill 14 pass from Moon (Zendejas kick)
Ind —O. Williams 22 pass from Pagel (Allegre kick)

Philadelphia 37, Minnesota 35—At Metrodome, attendance 49,722. Ron Jaworski passed for two touchdowns and Earnest Jackson ran for two more as the Eagles defeated the Vikings. Philadelphia built a 24-14 halftime advantage on Jaworski's scoring passes to Mike Quick (10 and 21 yards), Jackson's two-yard run, and Paul McFadden's 26-yard field goal. Minnesota responded with 21 points to take a 35-31 third-quarter lead, but McFadden kicked a pair of fourth-period field goals from 43 and 35 yards to seal the win for the Eagles.

Philadelphia	7	17	7	6	— 37
Minnesota	7	7	21	0	— 35

Phil —Quick 10 pass from Jaworski (McFadden kick)
Minn —Anderson 4 run (Stenerud kick)
Phil —Quick 21 pass from Jaworski (McFadden kick)
Phil —E. Jackson 2 run (McFadden kick)
Phil —FG McFadden 26
Minn —Brown 2 pass from Kramer (Stenerud kick)
Minn —Nelson 25 pass from Kramer (Stenerud kick)
Phil —E. Jackson 5 run (McFadden kick)
Minn —Nelson 8 run (Stenerud kick)
Minn —Brown 1 run (Stenerud kick)
Phil —FG McFadden 43
Phil —FG McFadden 35

Kansas City 38, San Diego 34—At Arrowhead Stadium, attendance 18,178. Stephone Paige caught eight passes for an NFL-record 309 yards and two touchdowns as the Chiefs held on to down the Chargers. Paige's effort bettered the record of Cleveland's Jim Benton (303 yards) set in 1945. Kansas City built a commanding 35-6 halftime lead on Todd Blackledge's 56-yard scoring pass to Paige and a pair of Bill Kenney touchdown passes to Paige (84 yards) and Jonathan Hayes (6). Herman Heard and Mike Pruitt also contributed to the Chiefs' first-half explosion, scoring on runs of seven and one yards, respectively.

San Diego	3	3	7	21	— 34
Kansas City	7	28	3	0	— 38

KC —Paige 56 pass from Blackledge (Lowery kick)
SD —FG Thomas 24
KC —Heard 7 run (Lowery kick)
KC —Pruitt 1 run (Lowery kick)
KC —Paige 84 pass from Kenney (Lowery kick)
KC —Hayes 6 pass from Kenney (Lowery kick)
SD —FG Thomas 26
SD —Chandler 5 pass from Herrmann (Thomas kick)
KC —FG Lowery 34
SD —Spencer 2 run (Thomas kick)
SD —James 8 pass from Herrmann (Thomas kick)
SD —Johnson 20 pass from Herrmann (Thomas kick)

MONDAY, DECEMBER 23

Los Angeles Raiders 16, Los Angeles Rams 6—At Anaheim Stadium, attendance 66,676. Marcus Allen ran for 123 yards on 24 carries in his NFL-record-tying ninth straight 100-yard rushing game to help the Raiders defeat the Rams. Marc Wilson provided the game's lone touchdown on a 21-yard pass to Dokie Williams. Chris Bahr added field goals of 27, 51, and 29 yards to complete the Raiders' scoring. Allen tied Walter Payton's record for consecutive 100-yard rushing games and surpassed Eric Dickerson's NFL-record 2,244 yards from scrimmage set in 1984. Allen caught eight passes for 25 yards to give him 2,314 yards from scrimmage for the season.

L.A. Raiders	0	6	0	10	— 16
L.A. Rams	0	3	3	0	— 6

Raiders —FG Bahr 27
Rams —FG Lansford 52
Raiders —FG Bahr 51
Rams —FG Lansford 40
Raiders —FG Bahr 29
Raiders —Williams 21 pass from Wilson (Bahr kick)

SEVENTEENTH WEEK SUMMARIES

SATURDAY, DECEMBER 28, 1985
AFC FIRST-ROUND PLAYOFF GAME

New England 26, New York Jets 14—At Giants Stadium, attendance 75,945. The Patriots capitalized on four Jets' turnovers to spark a 26-14 win for their first postseason victory since 1963. New York led 7-3 before New England scored 20 unanswered points, 17 following Jets' miscues. Safety Fred Marion's 26-yard interception return set up quarterback Tony Eason's 36-yard touchdown pass to wide receiver Stanley Morgan to give the Patriots a 13-7 halftime lead. New England took control of the game by scoring 10 points in a 15-second span of the third quarter. Following Tony Franklin's 20-yard field goal, Johnny Rembert returned Johnny Hector's fumble on the ensuing kickoff 15 yards for a score to give the Patriots a 23-7 lead. Franklin added a 26-yard field goal in the fourth quarter to tie the NFL postseason record of four field goals in a single game held by six others. Franklin's record-tying field goal was set up by defensive end Garin Veris, who intercepted a Pat Ryan pass. Veris also had three sacks. Eason completed 12 of 16 passes for 179 yards and one touchdown.

New England	3	10	10	3	— 26
N.Y. Jets	0	7	7	0	— 14

NE —FG Franklin 33
NYJ —Hector 11 pass from O'Brien (Leahy kick)
NE —FG Franklin 41
NE —Morgan 36 pass from Eason (Franklin kick)
NE —FG Franklin 20
NE —Rembert 15 fumble recovery return (Franklin kick)
NYJ —Shuler 12 pass from Ryan (Leahy kick)
NE —FG Franklin 26

SUNDAY, DECEMBER 29, 1985
NFC FIRST-ROUND PLAYOFF GAME

New York Giants 17, San Francisco 3—At Giants Stadium, attendance 75,131. An opportunistic New York Giants team ousted defending Super Bowl XIX champion San Francisco 17-3. The Giants won the game behind a balanced offense, which gained 174 yards rushing and 181 passing, and a defense that continually pressured 49ers quarterback Joe Montana, sacking him four times. Eric Schubert kicked a 47-yard field goal on New York's first possession. Giants rookie tight end Mark Bavaro's 18-yard touchdown catch was set up by safety Terry Kinard's interception that he returned to San Francisco's 38-yard line. Ray Wersching's 21-yard field goal with 22 seconds left in the first half completed a 49ers' 16-play, 85-yard drive. New York finished the scoring on its first possession of the third period when quarterback Phil Simms threw to tight end Don Hasselbeck for a three-yard touchdown. Simms completed 15 of 31 passes for 181 yards with two touchdowns and one interception. Running back Joe Morris paced all rushers with 28 carries for 141 yards. Montana connected on 26 of 47 passes for 296 yards with one interception.

San Francisco	0	3	0	0	— 3
N.Y. Giants	3	7	7	0	— 17

NYG —FG Schubert 47
NYG —Bavaro 18 pass from Simms (Schubert kick)
SF —FG Wersching 21
NYG —Hasselbeck 3 pass from Simms (Schubert kick)

EIGHTEENTH WEEK SUMMARIES

SATURDAY, JANUARY 4, 1986
AFC DIVISIONAL PLAYOFF

Miami 24, Cleveland 21—At Orange Bowl, attendance 74,667. AFC Eastern Division champion Miami rebounded from a 21-3 third-quarter deficit to defeat AFC Central champion Cleveland 24-21. The Dolphins earned their third trip to the AFC Championship Game in the past four years. Miami scored on its first possession on Fuad Reveiz's 51-yard field goal, but Cleveland responded by scoring 21 unanswered points. Earnest Byner, who rushed for 161 yards on 16 carries, scored on runs of 21 and 66 yards to give Cleveland a 21-3 lead 3:38 into the third quarter. The Dolphins rallied by scoring two touchdowns later in the third period. Quarterback Dan Marino and wide receiver Nat Moore combined on a six-yard touchdown pass to cap a 74-yard, 13-play drive, and running back Ron Davenport scored on a 31-yard run on Miami's next possession to cut Cleveland's lead to 21-17. Davenport's one-yard plunge with 1:57 remaining proved to be the game-winning score. Marino completed 25 of 45 passes for 238 yards and had one touchdown and one interception. Tony Nathan caught 10 passes for 101 yards.

Cleveland	7	7	7	0	— 21
Miami	3	0	14	7	— 24

Mia —FG Reveiz 51
Clev —Newsome 16 pass from Kosar (Bahr kick)
Clev —Byner 21 run (Bahr kick)
Clev —Byner 66 run (Bahr kick)
Mia —Moore 6 pass from Marino (Reveiz kick)
Mia —Davenport 31 run (Reveiz kick)
Mia —Davenport 1 run (Reveiz kick)

SATURDAY, JANUARY 4, 1986
NFC DIVISIONAL PLAYOFF

Los Angeles Rams 20, Dallas 0—At Anaheim Stadium, attendance 66,581. The NFC Western Division champion Los Angeles Rams combined a record-breaking effort by running back Eric Dickerson and a stingy defense to defeat NFC East champion Dallas 20-0. Dickerson rushed for a postseason game-record 248 yards on 34 carries, including touchdown runs of 55 and 40 yards. Los Angeles's defense had five sacks, including three by defensive end Gary Jeter, and limited the Cowboys to 243 total yards. The Rams held a 3-0 halftime lead on Mike Lansford's 33-yard field goal. Los Angeles took command early in the third quarter with a 10-point outburst on Dickerson's first touchdown run and Lansford's 34-yard field goal. Rams' quarterback Dieter Brock was 6 of 22 for 50 yards with one interception. The win advanced Los Angeles to its first NFC title game since 1979, when it defeated Tampa Bay 9-0.

Dallas	0	0	0	0	— 0
L.A. Rams	3	0	10	7	— 20

Rams —FG Lansford 33
Rams —Dickerson 55 run (Lansford kick)
Rams —FG Lansford 34
Rams —Dickerson 40 run (Lansford kick)

SUNDAY, JANUARY 5, 1986
AFC DIVISIONAL PLAYOFF

New England 27, Los Angeles Raiders 20—At Memorial Coliseum, attendance 87,163. AFC Wild Card representative New England advanced to its first AFC Championship Game by defeating the AFC Western Division champion Los Angeles Raiders. The Patriots, who led the AFC with 47 takeaways during the regular season, capitalized on three interceptions and three fumble recoveries to score 20 points. Reserve safety Jim Bowman's fumble recovery set up quarterback Tony Eason's 13-yard scoring pass to tight end Lin Dawson for a 7-0 New England lead. Following Tony Franklin's 32-yard field goal, which was set up by a Fred Marion fumble recovery, Bowman recovered the ensuing kickoff in the end zone for what proved to be the winning score with 57 seconds left in the third quarter. Craig James rushed for a Patriots' playoff-record 104 yards on 23 carries.

New England	7	10	10	0	— 27
L.A. Raiders	3	17	0	0	— 20

NE —Dawson 13 pass from Eason (Franklin kick)
Raiders —FG Bahr 29
Raiders —Hester 16 pass from Wilson (Bahr kick)
Raiders —Allen 11 run (Bahr kick)
NE —C. James 2 run (Franklin kick)
NE —FG Franklin 45
Raiders —FG Bahr 32
NE —FG Franklin 32
NE —Bowman fumble recovery in end zone (Franklin kick)

SUNDAY, JANUARY 5, 1986
NFC DIVISIONAL PLAYOFF

Chicago 21, New York Giants 0—At Soldier Field, attendance 65,670. Once-defeated NFC Central Division champion Chicago shut out the NFC Wild Card representative New York Giants 21-0. The temperature was 14 degrees at kickoff. Shaun Gayle's five-yard punt return for a touchdown was the only score of the first half. In the second half, Bears quarterback Jim McMahon and wide receiver Dennis McKinnon connected on touchdowns of 23 and 20 yards, while the defense, led by defensive end Richard Dent's 3½ sacks, stymied the Giants' offense. McMahon completed 11 of 21 passes for 216 yards and two touchdowns. Running back Walter Payton rushed 27 times for 93 yards.

N.Y. Giants	0	0	0	0	— 0
Chicago	7	0	14	0	— 21

Chi —Gayle 5 punt return (Butler kick)
Chi —McKinnon 23 pass from McMahon (Butler kick)
Chi —McKinnon 20 pass from McMahon (Butler kick)

NINETEENTH WEEK SUMMARIES

SUNDAY, JANUARY 12, 1986
AFC CHAMPIONSHIP GAME

New England 31, Miami 14—At Orange Bowl, attendance 75,662. The AFC Wild Card Patriots defeated the AFC Eastern Division champion Dolphins 31-14 to become the third Wild Card team ever to qualify for the Super Bowl. It was New England's first victory at Miami in 19 games since 1966. The Patriots converted four of their six takeaways (four fumble recoveries and two interceptions) into 24 points to hand Miami its first-ever AFC Championship Game loss. New England defensive end Garin Veris recovered Tony Nathan's fumble on the Dolphins' first play from scrimmage, which set up Tony Franklin's 23-yard field goal. Miami quarterback Dan Marino then directed an 80-yard, 11-play touchdown drive for a 7-3 lead, but New England quarterback Tony Eason found running back Tony Collins on a four-yard scoring pass to give the Patriots the lead for good 10-7. Eason threw only 12 passes and completed 10 for 71 yards, including touchdowns to Derrick Ramsey (one yard) and Robert Weathers (two). New England rushed an AFC Championship Game-record 59 times for 255 yards and dominated the Dolphins in time of possession 39:51 to 20:09. Craig James gained 105 yards on 22 carries to lead the Patriots. With New England leading 24-14 in the fourth quarter, Julius Adams recovered a Miami fumble to set up Mosi Tatupu's one-yard scoring run with 7:34 remaining to seal the Patriots' win. Raymond Clayborn and Fred Marion each intercepted passes, and Lester Williams and Greg Hawthorne each recovered fumbles. The victory made the Patriots the last of the original eight AFL teams to win an AFL or AFC conference title.

New England	3	14	7	7 —	31
Miami	0	7	0	7 —	14

NE —FG Franklin 23
Mia —Johnson 10 pass from Marino (Reveiz kick)
NE —Collins 4 pass from Eason (Franklin kick)
NE —D. Ramsey 1 pass from Eason (Franklin kick)
NE —Weathers 2 pass from Eason (Franklin kick)
Mia —Nathan 10 pass from Marino (Reveiz kick)
NE —Tatupu 1 run (Franklin kick)

SUNDAY, JANUARY 12, 1986
NFC CHAMPIONSHIP GAME
Chicago 24, Los Angeles Rams 0—At Soldier Field, attendance 66,030. NFC Central Division champion Chicago extended its overall season record to 17-1 by registering a playoff-record second consecutive shutout in winning the NFC title. The Bears defeated NFC Western Division champion Los Angeles Rams 24-0 to follow a 21-0 blanking of the New York Giants the previous week. Weather conditions at kickoff were 39 degrees with wind gusts up to 28 miles per hour and a cloudy sky. Toward the end of the game, temperatures had dropped to the high 20s and snow flurries fell. Chicago broke on top on its first possession of the game via a five-play, 66-yard drive capped by quarterback Jim McMahon's 16-yard scramble around left end for a touchdown. Following a Rams possession, Chicago marched to Los Angeles's 16-yard line and Kevin Butler kicked a 34-yard field goal. The Bears held a 10-0 halftime lead, plus an advantage in total yards (152 to 68) and first downs (9 to 3). On Chicago's second possession of the third quarter, the Bears drove 52 yards in nine plays, concluded by a 22-yard touchdown catch by wide receiver Willie Gault. Chicago finished its scoring late in the fourth quarter when defensive end Richard Dent forced Rams quarterback Dieter Brock to fumble and linebacker Wilber Marshall recovered and ran 52 yards for a touchdown.

L.A. Rams	0	0	0	0 —	0
Chicago	10	0	7	7 —	24

Chi —McMahon 16 run (Butler kick)
Chi —FG Butler 34
Chi —Gault 22 pass from McMahon (Butler kick)
Chi —Marshall 52 fumble recovery return (Butler kick)

TWENTIETH WEEK SUMMARY

SUNDAY, JANUARY 26, 1986
SUPER BOWL XX
NEW ORLEANS, LOUISIANA
Chicago 46, New England 10—Louisiana Superdome, attendance 73,818. The NFC champion Chicago Bears, seeking their first NFL title since 1963, scored a Super Bowl-record 46 points in downing AFC champion New England 46-10 in Super Bowl XX. The previous record for most points in a Super Bowl was 38, shared by San Francisco in XIX and the Los Angeles Raiders in XVIII. The Bears' league-leading defense tied the Super Bowl record for sacks (seven) and limited the Patriots to a record-low seven yards rushing. New England took the quickest lead in Super Bowl history when Tony Franklin kicked a 36-yard field goal with 1:19 elapsed in the first period. The score came about because of Larry McGrew's fumble recovery at Chicago's 19-yard line. However, the Bears rebounded for a 23-3 first-half lead, while building a yardage advantage of 236 total yards to New England's minus 19. Running back Matt Suhey rushed eight times for 37 yards, including an 11-yard touchdown run, and caught one pass for 24 yards in the first half. After the Patriots' first drive of the second half ended with a punt to the Bears' 4-yard line, Chicago marched 96 yards in nine plays with quarterback Jim McMahon's one-yard scoring run capping the drive. McMahon became the first quarterback in Super Bowl history to rush for a pair of touchdowns. The Bears completed their scoring via a 28-yard interception return by reserve cornerback Reggie Phillips, a one-yard run by defensive tackle/fullback William Perry, and a safety when defensive end Henry Waechter tackled New England quarterback Steve Grogan in the end zone. Bears' defensive end Richard Dent became the fourth defender to be named the game's most valuable player after contributing 1½ sacks. The Bears' victory margin of 36 points was the largest in Super Bowl history, bettering the previous mark of 29 by the Los Angeles Raiders when they topped Washington 38-9 in Super Bowl XVIII. McMahon completed 12 of 20 passes for 256 yards before leaving the game in the fourth period with a wrist injury. The NFL's all-time leading rusher, Bears running back Walter Payton, carried 22 times for 61 yards. Wide receiver Willie Gault caught four passes for 129 yards, the fourth-most receiving yards in a Super Bowl. Chicago coach Mike Ditka became the second man (Tom Flores of the Raiders is the other) who played in a Super Bowl and coached a team to a victory in the game.

Chicago	13	10	21	2 —	46
New England	3	0	0	7 —	10

NE —FG Franklin 36
Chi —FG Butler 28
Chi —FG Butler 24
Chi —Suhey 11 run (Butler kick)
Chi —McMahon 2 run (Butler kick)
Chi —FG Butler 24
Chi —McMahon 1 run (Butler kick)
Chi —Phillips 28 interception return (Butler kick)
Chi —Perry 1 run (Butler kick)
NE —Fryar 8 pass from Grogan (Franklin kick)
Chi —Safety, Waechter tackled Grogan in end zone

TWENTY-FIRST WEEK SUMMARY

FEBRUARY 2, 1986
AFC-NFC PRO BOWL
HONOLULU, HAWAII
NFC 28, AFC 24—At Aloha Stadium, attendance 50,101. New York Giants quarterback Phil Simms brought the NFC back from a 24-7 halftime deficit to a 28-24 win over the AFC. Simms, who completed 15 of 27 passes for 212 yards and three touchdowns, was named the most valuable player of the game. The AFC had taken its first-half lead behind a two-yard run by Los Angeles Raiders running back Marcus Allen, who also threw a 51-yard scoring pass to San Diego wide receiver Wes Chandler, an 11-yard touchdown catch by Pittsburgh wide receiver Louis Lipps, and a 34-yard field goal by Steelers' kicker Gary Anderson. Minnesota's Joey Browner accounted for the NFC's only score before halftime with a 48-yard interception return. After intermission, the NFC blanked the AFC while scoring three touchdowns via a 15-yard catch by Washington wide receiver Art Monk, a two-yard reception by Dallas tight end Doug Cosbie, and a 15-yard catch by Tampa Bay tight end Jimmie Giles with 2:47 remaining in the game. The victory gave the NFC a 10-6 Pro Bowl record against the AFC.

NFC	0	7	7	14 —	28
AFC	7	17	0	0 —	24

AFC —Allen 2 run (Anderson kick)
NFC —Browner 48 interception return (Andersen kick)
AFC —Chandler 51 pass from Allen (Anderson kick)
AFC —FG Anderson 34
AFC —Lipps 11 pass from O'Brien (Anderson kick)
NFC —Monk 15 pass from Simms (Andersen kick)
NFC —Cosbie 2 pass from Simms (Andersen kick)
NFC —Giles 15 pass from Simms (Andersen kick)

1985 PFWA ALL-PRO TEAM

Selected by Professional Football Writers Association

OFFENSE

Steve Largent, Seattle .... Wide Receiver
Louis Lipps, Pittsburgh .... Wide Receiver
Todd Christensen, Los Angeles Raiders .... Tight End
Jim Covert, Chicago .... Tackle
Anthony Muñoz, Cincinnati .... Tackle
Russ Grimm, Washington .... Guard
John Hannah, New England .... Guard
Dwight Stephenson, Miami .... Center
Dan Marino, Miami .... Quarterback
Walter Payton, Chicago .... Running Back
Marcus Allen, Los Angeles Raiders .... Running Back
Gary Anderson, Pittsburgh .... Kicker
Ron Brown, Los Angeles Rams .... Kick Returner

DEFENSE

Howie Long, Los Angeles Raiders .... Defensive End
Richard Dent, Chicago .... Defensive End
Joe Klecko, New York Jets .... Nose Tackle
Andre Tippett, New England .... Outside Linebacker
Lawrence Taylor, New York Giants .... Outside Linebacker
Mike Singletary, Chicago .... Inside Linebacker
Karl Mecklenburg, Denver .... Inside Linebacker
Mike Haynes, Los Angeles Raiders .... Cornerback
Everson Walls, Dallas .... Cornerback
Wes Hopkins, Philadelphia .... Safety
Kenny Easley, Seattle .... Safety
Dale Hatcher, Los Angeles Rams .... Punter

1985 NEA ALL-NFL TEAM

Selected by Newspaper Enterprise Association

OFFENSE

Louis Lipps, Pittsburgh .... Wide Receiver
Mike Quick, Philadelphia .... Wide Receiver
Todd Christensen, Los Angeles Raiders .... Tight End
Anthony Muñoz, Cincinnati .... Tackle
Jim Covert, Chicago .... Tackle
Russ Grimm, Washington .... Guard
Randy Cross, San Francisco .... Guard
Dwight Stephenson, Miami .... Center
Dan Fouts, San Diego .... Quarterback
Walter Payton, Chicago .... Running Back
Marcus Allen, Los Angeles Raiders .... Running Back
Nick Lowery, Kansas City .... Kicker

DEFENSE

Mark Gastineau, New York Jets .... Defensive End
Howie Long, Los Angeles Raiders .... Defensive End
Randy White, Dallas .... Nose Tackle
Mike Singletary, Chicago .... Inside Linebacker
Karl Mecklenburg, Denver .... Inside Linebacker
Lawrence Taylor, New York Giants .... Outside Linebacker
Andre Tippett, New England .... Outside Linebacker
Mike Haynes, Los Angeles Raiders .... Cornerback
Eric Wright, San Francisco .... Cornerback
Kenny Easley, Seattle .... Safety
Wes Hopkins, Philadelphia .... Safety
Rohn Stark, Indianapolis .... Punter

1985 ASSOCIATED PRESS ALL-PRO TEAM

OFFENSE

Steve Largent, Seattle .... Wide Receiver
Mike Quick, Philadelphia .... Wide Receiver
Todd Christensen, Los Angeles Raiders .... Tight End
Jim Covert, Chicago .... Tackle
Anthony Muñoz, Cincinnati .... Tackle
Russ Grimm, Washington .... Guard
John Hannah, New England .... Guard
Dwight Stephenson, Miami .... Center
Dan Marino, Miami .... Quarterback
Walter Payton, Chicago .... Running Back
Marcus Allen, Los Angeles Raiders .... Running Back
Nick Lowery, Kansas City .... Kicker
Ron Brown, Los Angeles Rams .... Kick Returner

DEFENSE

Howie Long, Los Angeles Raiders .... Defensive End
Richard Dent, Chicago .... Defensive End
Randy White, Dallas .... Defensive Tackle
Steve McMichael, Chicago .... Defensive Tackle
Joe Klecko, New York Jets .... Nose Tackle
Andre Tippett, New England .... Outside Linebacker
Lawrence Taylor, New York Giants .... Outside Linebacker
Mike Singletary, Chicago .... Inside Linebacker
Karl Mecklenburg, Denver .... Inside Linebacker
Mike Haynes, Los Angeles Raiders .... Cornerback
Eric Wright, San Francisco .... Cornerback
Wes Hopkins, Philadelphia .... Safety
Kenny Easley, Seattle .... Safety
Dale Hatcher, Los Angeles Rams .... Punter

1985 ALL-NFL TEAM

Selected by Associated Press, Newspaper Enterprise Association, and Professional Football Writers Association

OFFENSE

Steve Largent, Seattle (AP, PFWA) .... Wide Receiver
Louis Lipps, Pittsbugh (NEA, PFWA) .... Wide Receiver
Mike Quick, Philadelphia (AP, NEA) .... Wide Receiver
Todd Christensen, Los Angeles Raiders (AP, NEA, PFWA) .... Tight End
Jim Covert, Chicago (AP, NEA, PFWA) .... Tackle
Anthony Muñoz, Cincinnati (AP, NEA, PFWA) .... Tackle
Russ Grimm, Washington (AP, NEA, PFWA) .... Guard
John Hannah, New England (AP, PFWA) .... Guard
Randy Cross, San Francisco (NEA) .... Guard
Dwight Stephenson, Miami (AP, NEA, PFWA) .... Center
Dan Marino, Miami (AP, PFWA) .... Quarterback
Dan Fouts, San Diego (NEA) .... Quarterback
Marcus Allen, Los Angeles Raiders (AP, NEA, PFWA) .... Running Back
Walter Payton, Chicago (AP, NEA, PFWA) .... Running Back
Nick Lowery, Kansas City (AP, NEA) .... Kicker
Gary Anderson, Pittsburgh (PFWA) .... Kicker
Ron Brown, Los Angeles Rams (AP, PFWA) .... Kick Returner

DEFENSE

Howie Long, Los Angeles Raiders (AP, NEA, PFWA) .... Defensive End
Richard Dent, Chicago (AP, PFWA) .... Defensive End
Mark Gastineau, New York Jets (NEA) .... Defensive End
Randy White, Dallas (AP, NEA) .... Defensive Tackle
Steve McMichael, Chicago (AP) .... Defensive Tackle
Joe Klecko, New York Jets (AP, PFWA) .... Nose Tackle
Karl Mecklenburg, Denver (AP, NEA, PFWA) .... Inside Linebacker
Mike Singletary, Chicago (AP, NEA, PFWA) .... Inside Linebacker
Lawrence Taylor, New York Giants (AP, NEA, PFWA) .... Outside Linebacker
Andre Tippett, New England (AP, NEA, PFWA) .... Outside Linebacker
Mike Haynes, Los Angeles Raiders (AP, NEA, PFWA) .... Cornerback
Eric Wright, San Francisco (AP, NEA) .... Cornerback
Everson Walls, Dallas (PFWA) .... Cornerback
Kenny Easley, Seattle (AP, NEA, PFWA) .... Safety
Wes Hopkins, Philadelphia (AP, NEA, PFWA) .... Safety
Dale Hatcher, Los Angeles Rams (AP, PFWA) .... Punter
Rohn Stark, Indianapolis (NEA) .... Punter

1985 UPI ALL-AFC TEAM

Selected by United Press International

OFFENSE

Steve Largent, Seattle .... Wide Receiver
Louis Lipps, Pittsburgh .... Wide Receiver
Todd Christensen, Los Angeles Raiders .... Tight End
Anthony Muñoz, Cincinnati .... Tackle
Chris Hinton, Indianapolis .... Tackle
John Hannah, New England .... Guard
Roy Foster, Miami .... Guard
Dwight Stephenson, Miami .... Center
Dan Marino, Miami .... Quarterback
Marcus Allen, Los Angeles Raiders .... Running Back
Freeman McNeil, New York Jets .... Running Back
Gary Anderson, Pittsburgh .... Kicker

DEFENSE

Howie Long, Los Angeles Raiders .... Defensive End
Rulon Jones, Denver .... Defensive End
Joe Klecko, New York Jets .... Nose Tackle
Andre Tippett, New England .... Outside Linebacker
Chip Banks, Cleveland .... Outside Linebacker
Karl Mecklenburg, Denver .... Inside Linebacker
Lance Mehl, New York Jets .... Inside Linebacker
Mike Haynes, Los Angeles Raiders .... Cornerback
Louis Wright, Denver .... Cornerback
Kenny Easley, Seattle .... Safety
Deron Cherry, Kansas City .... Safety
Rohn Stark, Indianapolis .... Punter

1985 UPI ALL-NFC TEAM

Selected by United Press International

OFFENSE

Mike Quick, Philadelphia .... Wide Receiver
Art Monk, Washington .... Wide Receiver
Doug Cosbie, Dallas .... Tight End
Jim Covert, Chicago .... Tackle
Keith Dorney, Detroit .... Tackle
Russ Grimm, Washington .... Guard
Dennis Harrah, Los Angeles Rams .... Guard
Jay Hilgenberg, Chicago .... Center
Joe Montana, San Francisco .... Quarterback
Walter Payton, Chicago .... Running Back
Gerald Riggs, Atlanta .... Running Back
Morten Andersen, New Orleans .... Kicker

DEFENSE

Richard Dent, Chicago .... Defensive End
Leonard Marshall, New York Giants .... Defensive End
Randy White, Dallas .... Defensive Tackle
Otis Wilson, Chicago .... Outside Linebacker
Lawrence Taylor, New York Giants .... Outside Linebacker
Mike Singletary, Chicago .... Inside Linebacker
E.J. Junior, St. Louis .... Inside Linebacker
Everson Walls, Dallas .... Cornerback
Eric Wright, San Francisco .... Cornerback
Wes Hopkins, Philadelphia .... Safety
Michael Downs, Dallas .... Safety
Dale Hatcher, Los Angeles Rams .... Punter

1985 PFWA ALL-ROOKIE TEAM

Selected by Professional Football Writers Association

OFFENSE

Eddie Brown, Cincinnati .... Wide Receiver
Jerry Rice, San Francisco .... Wide Receiver
Mark Bavaro, New York Giants .... Tight End
Lomas Brown, Detroit .... Tackle
Jim Lachey, San Diego .... Tackle
Bill Fralic, Atlanta .... Guard
Tom Thayer, Chicago .... Guard
Bart Oates, New York Giants .... Center
Dieter Brock, Los Angeles Rams .... Quarterback
Kevin Mack, Cleveland .... Running Back
Gary Anderson, San Diego .... Running Back
Kevin Butler, Chicago .... Kicker

DEFENSE

Ray Childress, Houston .... Defensive End
Garin Veris, New England .... Defensive End
Tim Newton, Minnesota .... Nose Tackle
Duane Bickett, Indianapolis .... Outside Linebacker
Chris Doleman, Minnesota .... Outside Linebacker
Jack Del Rio, New Orleans .... Inside Linebacker
Brian Noble, Green Bay .... Inside Linebacker
John Hendy, San Diego .... Cornerback
Derrick Burroughs, Buffalo .... Cornerback
Raphel Cherry, Washington .... Safety
Lonnie Young, St. Louis .... Safety
Dale Hatcher, Los Angeles Rams .... Punter

1985 Professional Football Awards

	NFL	AFC	NFC
Professional Football Writers Association			
Most Valuable Player	Marcus Allen		
Rookie of the Year	Eddie Brown		
Coach of the Year		Raymond Berry	Mike Ditka
Associated Press			
Most Valuable Player	Marcus Allen		
Offensive Player of the Year	Marcus Allen		
Defensive Player of the Year	Mike Singletary		
Rookie of the Year—Offense	Eddie Brown		
Rookie of the Year—Defense	Duane Bickett		
Coach of the Year	Mike Ditka		
United Press International			
Offensive Player of the Year		Marcus Allen	Walter Payton
Defensive Player of the Year		Andre Tippett	Mike Singletary
Coach of the Year		Raymond Berry	Mike Ditka
Newspaper Enterprise Association			
Jim Thorpe Memorial Trophy—MVP	Walter Payton		
Rookie of the Year	Eddie Brown		
George Halas Trophy—Defensive Player of the Year	Andre Tippett Howie Long		
The Sporting News			
Player of the Year	Marcus Allen		
Rookie of the Year	Eddie Brown		
Coach of the Year	Mike Ditka		
Football News			
Coach of the Year		Raymond Berry	Mike Ditka
Player of the Year		Marcus Allen	Walter Payton
Super Bowl XX Most Valuable Player			
(Selected by Sport Magazine)	Richard Dent		
AFC-NFC Pro Bowl			
Player of the Game (Dan McGuire Award)	Phil Simms		
Maxwell Club			
Player of the Year (Bert Bell Trophy)	Walter Payton		
College and Pro Football Newsweekly			
Coach of the Year	Raymond Berry		
Football Digest			
Player of the Year	Marcus Allen		
Coach of the Year	Mike Ditka		

AFC-NFC Players-of-the-Week

	AFC Offense	AFC Defense	NFC Offense	NFC Defense
Week 1	Mark Malone, Pitt.	Steve Brown, Hou.	Jim McMahon, Chi.	Rufus Bess, Minn.
Week 2	Dave Krieg, Sea. Daryl Turner, Sea.	Gary Spani, KC	Roger Craig, SF	Mike Singletary, Chi.
Week 3	Lionel James, SD	Lance Mehl, NYJ	David Wilson, NO	Wes Hopkins, Phil.
Week 4	Dan Marino, Mia.	Deron Cherry, KC	Dieter Brock, Rams	Demetrious Johnson, Det.
Week 5	Kevin Mack, Clev.	Vann McElroy, Raiders	Joe Montana, SF	Jim Collins, Rams
Week 6	Freeman McNeil, NYJ	James Griffin, Cin.	Tony Dorsett, Dall.	LeRoy Irvin, Rams
Week 7	Greg Bell, Buff.	Andre Tippett, NE	Ron Jaworski, Phil.	Lawrence Taylor, NYG
Week 8	Wayne Capers, Ind.	Eugene Daniel, Ind.	Eric Hipple, Det.	Curtis Jordan, Wash.
Week 9	Dan Fouts, SD	Terry Taylor, Sea.	Walter Payton, Chi.	Leonard Smith, St.L.
Week 10	Lionel James, SD	Fred Marion, NE	Jimmie Giles, TB	Jim Jeffcoat, Dall.
Week 11	Ken O'Brien, NYJ	Louis Wright, Den.	Gerald Riggs, Atl.	Otis Wilson, Chi.
Week 12	Marcus Allen, Raiders	Bo Eason, Hou.	Ron Brown, Rams	George Martin, NYG
Week 13	Boomer Esiason, Cin.	Karl Mecklenburg, Den.	Danny White, Dall.	Alphonso Carreker, GB
Week 14	Dan Marino, Mia.	Tim Krumrie, Cin.	Jerry Rice, SF	Lonnie Young, St.L.
Week 15	Bernie Kosar, Clev.	Glenn Blackwood, Mia.	Art Monk, Wash.	Jim Jeffcoat, Dall.
Week 16	Stephone Paige, KC	Mark Gastineau, NYJ	George Rogers, Wash.	Dwight Hicks, SF

1985 Paid Attendance Breakdown

	Games	Attendance	Average
AFC Preseason	12	579,009	48,251
NFC Preseason	12	485,496	40,458
AFC-NFC Preseason, Interconference	33	1,640,958	49,726
NFL Preseason Total	**57**	**2,705,463**	**47,464**
AFC Regular Season	86	5,175,663	60,182
NFC Regular Season	86	5,051,291	58,736
AFC-NFC Regular Season, Interconference	52	3,118,093	59,963
NFL Regular Season Total	**224**	**13,345,047**	**59,567**
AFC First-Round Playoff	1		
(New England-New York Jets)		75,945	
AFC Divisional Playoffs	2		
(New England-Los Angeles Raiders)		87,163	
(Cleveland-Miami)		74,667	
AFC Championship Game	1		
(New England-Miami)		75,662	
NFC First-Round Playoff	1		
(San Francisco-New York Giants)		75,131	
NFC Divisional Playoffs	2		
(Dallas-Los Angeles Rams)		66,581	
(New York Giants-Chicago)		65,670	
NFC Championship Game	1		
(Los Angeles Rams-Chicago)		66,030	
Super Bowl XX at New Orleans, Louisiana	1		
(Chicago-New England)		73,818	
AFC-NFC Pro Bowl at Honolulu, Hawaii	1	50,101	
NFL Postseason Total	**10**	**710,768**	**71,077**
NFL All Games	**291**	**16,761,278**	**57,599**

Ten Best Rushing Performances, 1985

	Attempts	Yards	TD
1. George Rogers Washington vs. St. Louis, December 21	34	206	1
2. Joe Morris N.Y. Giants vs. Pittsburgh, December 21	36	202	3
3. Gerald Riggs Atlanta vs. Kansas City, December 8	26	197	1
4. Freeman McNeil N.Y. Jets vs. Buffalo, September 15	18	192	2
Walter Payton Chicago vs. Green Bay, November 3	28	192	1
6. Stump Mitchell St. Louis vs. Philadelphia, November 17	22	179	2
7. Marcus Allen L.A. Raiders vs. Denver, November 24	24	173	1
Freeman McNeil N.Y. Jets vs. Miami, October 14	28	173	0
9. George Wonsley Indianapolis vs. Detroit, September 22	27	170	0
10. Curt Warner Seattle vs. San Diego, September 15	28	169	2

100-Yard Rushing Performances, 1985

First Week

James Wilder, Tampa Bay	166 yards vs. Chicago
Gerald Riggs, Atlanta	131 yards vs. Detroit
Wendell Tyler, San Francisco	125 yards vs. Minnesota
Walter Payton, Chicago	120 yards vs. Tampa Bay
Larry Kinnebrew, Cincinnati	101 yards vs. Seattle

Second Week

Freeman McNeil, N.Y. Jets	192 yards vs. Buffalo
Curt Warner, Seattle	169 yards vs. San Diego
Charles White, L.A. Rams	144 yards vs. Philadelphia
James Wilder, Tampa Bay	113 yards vs. Minnesota
Roger Craig, San Francisco	107 yards vs. Atlanta

Third Week

George Wonsley, Indianapolis	170 yards vs. Detroit
Eric Dickerson, L.A. Rams	150 yards vs. Seattle
Lionel James, San Diego	127 yards vs. Cincinnati
James Wilder, Tampa Bay	114 yards vs. New Orleans

Fourth Week

Tony Dorsett, Dallas	159 yards vs. Houston
James Brooks, Cincinnati	133 yards vs. Pittsburgh
Kevin Mack, Cleveland	130 yards vs. San Diego
Freeman McNeil, N.Y. Jets	115 yards vs. Indianapolis
Jessie Clark, Green Bay	112 yards vs. St. Louis
Wayne Wilson, New Orleans	108 yards vs. San Francisco
Ottis Anderson, St. Louis	104 yards vs. Green Bay
James Wilder, Tampa Bay	104 yards vs. Detroit
Sammy Winder, Denver	103 yards vs. Miami

Fifth Week

Marcus Allen, L.A. Raiders	126 yards vs. Kansas City
Kevin Mack, Cleveland	115 yards vs. New England
Randy McMillan, Indianapolis	112 yards vs. Buffalo
George Rogers, Washington	104 yards vs. St. Louis
John Riggins, Washington	103 yards vs. St. Louis
Albert Bentley, Indianapolis	100 yards vs. Buffalo

Sixth Week

Freeman McNeil, N.Y. Jets	173 yards vs. Miami
Gerald Riggs, Atlanta	139 yards vs. Seattle
Walter Payton, Chicago	132 yards vs. San Francisco
John Riggins, Washington	114 yards vs. Detroit
Tony Dorsett, Dallas	113 yards vs. Pittsburgh
Marcus Allen, L.A. Raiders	107 yards vs. New Orleans
Earnest Jackson, Philadelphia	103 yards vs. St. Louis

Seventh Week

Curt Warner, Seattle	136 yards vs. Denver
James Jones, Detroit	116 yards vs. San Francisco
Walter Payton, Chicago	112 yards vs. Green Bay
Wendell Tyler, San Francisco	107 yards vs. Detroit
Tony Dorsett, Dallas	100 yards vs. Philadelphia

Eighth Week

Freeman McNeil, N.Y. Jets	151 yards vs. Seattle
Stump Mitchell, St. Louis	148 yards vs. Houston
Gerald Riggs, Atlanta	127 yards vs. Dallas
Randy McMillan, Indianapolis	126 yards vs. Green Bay
Walter Payton, Chicago	118 yards vs. Minnesota
James Jones, Detroit	114 yards vs. Miami
John Riggins, Washington	112 yards vs. Cleveland
Marcus Allen, L.A. Raiders	111 yards vs. San Diego
Joe Morris, N.Y. Giants	104 yards vs. New Orleans

Ninth Week

Walter Payton, Chicago	192 yards vs. Green Bay
Keith Griffin, Washington	164 yards vs. Atlanta
Freeman McNeil, N.Y. Jets	149 yards vs. Indianapolis
Joe Morris, N.Y. Giants	132 yards vs. Tampa Bay
Larry Kinnebrew, Cincinnati	128 yards vs. Buffalo
Gerald Riggs, Atlanta	127 yards vs. Washington
George Rogers, Washington	124 yards vs. Atlanta
Darrin Nelson, Minnesota	122 yards vs. Detroit
Craig James, New England	119 yards vs. Miami
Gary Anderson, San Diego	116 yards vs. Denver
Eric Dickerson, L.A. Rams	108 yards vs. New Orleans
Marcus Allen, L.A. Raiders	101 yards vs. Seattle
Butch Woolfolk, Houston	101 yards vs. Kansas City

Tenth Week

Darrin Nelson, Minnesota	146 yards vs. Green Bay
Gerald Riggs, Atlanta	129 yards vs. Philadelphia
James Wilder, Tampa Bay	120 yards vs. St. Louis
Marcus Allen, L.A. Raiders	119 yards vs. San Diego
Roger Craig, San Francisco	117 yards vs. Denver
Eddie Lee Ivery, Green Bay	111 yards vs. Minnesota
Freeman McNeil, N.Y. Jets	107 yards vs. Miami
Walter Payton, Chicago	107 yards vs. Detroit
Matt Suhey, Chicago	102 yards vs. Detroit
Eric Dickerson, L.A. Rams	101 yards vs. N.Y. Giants

Eleventh Week

Stump Mitchell, St. Louis	179 yards vs. Philadelphia
Earnest Jackson, Philadelphia	162 yards vs. St. Louis
Marcus Allen, L.A. Raiders	135 yards vs. Cincinnati
Walter Payton, Chicago	132 yards vs. Dallas
Frank Pollard, Pittsburgh	123 yards vs. Houston
Gerald Riggs, Atlanta	123 yards vs. L.A. Rams
Joe Morris, N.Y. Giants	118 yards vs. Washington
Wendell Tyler, San Francisco	111 yards vs. Kansas City
Earnest Byner, Cleveland	109 yards vs. Buffalo
Walter Abercrombie, Pittsburgh	107 yards vs. Houston
Curt Warner, Seattle	105 yards vs. New England

Twelfth Week

Marcus Allen, L.A. Raiders	173 yards vs. Denver
Earl Campbell, New Orleans	160 yards vs. Minnesota
Eric Dickerson, L.A. Rams	150 yards vs. Green Bay
Kevin Mack, Cleveland	117 yards vs. Cincinnati
George Adams, N.Y. Giants	113 yards vs. St. Louis
Gerald Riggs, Atlanta	110 yards vs. Chicago
Craig James, New England	108 yards vs. N.Y. Jets
Walter Payton, Chicago	102 yards vs. Atlanta

Thirteenth Week

Marcus Allen, L.A. Raiders	156 yards vs. Atlanta
Joe Morris, N.Y. Giants	131 yards vs. Cleveland
Walter Payton, Chicago	121 yards vs. Miami
Johnny Hector, N.Y. Jets	114 yards vs. Detroit
Eddie Lee Ivery, Green Bay	109 yards vs. Tampa Bay

Fourteenth Week

Gerald Riggs, Atlanta	197 yards vs. Kansas City
Stump Mitchell, St. Louis	158 yards vs. New Orleans
George Rogers, Washington	150 yards vs. Philadelphia
Marcus Allen, L.A. Raiders	135 yards vs. Denver
Joe Morris, N.Y. Giants	129 yards vs. Houston
Craig James, New England	115 yards vs. Detroit
Walter Payton, Chicago	111 yards vs. Indianapolis
James Brooks, Cincinnati	109 yards vs. Dallas
Mike Pruitt, Kansas City	102 yards vs. Atlanta

Fifteenth Week

Eric Dickerson, L.A. Rams	124 yards vs. St. Louis
Greg Bell, Buffalo	123 yards vs. Pittsburgh
Marcus Allen, L.A. Raiders	109 yards vs. Seattle
Randy McMillan, Indianapolis	108 yards vs. Tampa Bay
James Jones, Detroit	104 yards vs. Green Bay

Sixteenth Week

George Rogers, Washington	206 yards vs. St. Louis
Joe Morris, N.Y. Giants	202 yards vs. Pittsburgh
Gerald Riggs, Atlanta	158 yards vs. New Orleans
Craig James, New England	142 yards vs. Cincinnati
Stump Mitchell, St. Louis	129 yards vs. Washington
Marcus Allen, L.A. Raiders	123 yards vs. L.A. Rams
Earnest Jackson, Philadelphia	106 yards vs. Minnesota
Earnest Byner, Cleveland	101 yards vs. N.Y. Jets

Times 100 or More
Allen 11; Payton 10; Riggs 9; McNeil, Morris 6; Dickerson, Wilder 5; C. James, Mitchell, Rogers 4; Dorsett, Jackson, Jones, Mack, McMillan, Riggins, Tyler, Warner 3; Brooks, Byner, Craig, Ivery, Kinnebrew, Nelson 2.

Ten Best Passing Yardage Performances, 1985

	Att.	Comp.	Yards	TD
1. Phil Simms N.Y. Giants vs. Cincinnati, October 13	62	40	513	1
2. Dan Fouts San Diego vs. Seattle, September 15	43	29	440	4
3. Dan Fouts San Diego vs. L.A. Raiders, November 10	41	26	436	4
Tommy Kramer Minnesota vs. Chicago, September 19	55	28	436	3
5. John Elway Denver vs. Seattle, December 20	42	24	432	1
Phil Simms N.Y. Giants vs. Dallas, October 6	36	18	432	3
7. Joe Montana San Francisco vs. Atlanta, October 6	57	37	429	5
8. Dave Krieg Seattle vs. Atlanta, October 13	51	33	405	4
9. Bill Kenney Kansas City vs. New Orleans, September 8	34	22	397	3
10. Ron Jaworski Philadelphia vs. San Fran., November 3	48	24	394	1

300-Yard Passing Performances, 1985

First Week

Bill Kenney, Kansas City	397 yards vs. New Orleans
Vince Ferragamo, Buffalo	377 yards vs. San Diego

Second Week

Dan Fouts, San Diego	440 yards vs. Seattle
John Elway, Denver	353 yards vs. New Orleans
Dan Marino, Miami	329 yards vs. Indianapolis
Dave Krieg, Seattle	307 yards vs. San Diego
Jim Plunkett, L.A. Raiders	303 yards vs. Kansas City

Third Week

Tommy Kramer, Minnesota	436 yards vs. Chicago
Dan Fouts, San Diego	344 yards vs. Cincinnati
Boomer Esiason, Cincinnati	320 yards vs. San Diego

Fourth Week

Dan Marino, Miami	390 yards vs. Denver
Mark Malone, Pittsburgh	374 yards vs. Cincinnati

Fifth Week

Phil Simms, N.Y. Giants	432 yards vs. Dallas
Joe Montana, San Francisco	429 yards vs. Atlanta
Steve DeBerg, Tampa Bay	346 yards vs. Chicago
Mark Herrmann, San Diego	344 yards vs. Seattle
Danny White, Dallas	342 yards vs. N.Y. Giants
Tony Eason, New England	304 yards vs. Cleveland

Sixth Week

Phil Simms, N.Y. Giants	513 yards vs. Cincinnati
Dave Krieg, Seattle	405 yards vs. Atlanta
Mark Herrmann, San Diego	320 yards vs. Kansas City
Bill Kenney, Kansas City	304 yards vs. San Diego

Seventh Week

Boomer Esiason, Cincinnati	381 yards vs. Houston
Ron Jaworski, Philadelphia	380 yards vs. Dallas
Steve DeBerg, Tampa Bay	365 yards vs. Miami
Tommy Kramer, Minnesota	311 yards vs. San Diego
Dan Marino, Miami	302 yards vs. Tampa Bay
Dave Wilson, New Orleans	300 yards vs. Atlanta

Eighth Week

Danny White, Dallas	362 yards vs. Atlanta
Dieter Brock, L.A. Rams	344 yards vs. San Francisco
Dan Fouts, San Diego	315 yards vs. L.A. Raiders
Joe Montana, San Francisco	306 yards vs. L.A. Rams

Ninth Week

Ron Jaworski, Philadelphia	394 yards vs. San Francisco
Dan Fouts, San Diego	302 yards vs. Denver

Tenth Week

Dan Fouts, San Diego	436 yards vs. L.A. Raiders
Ken O'Brien, N.Y. Jets	393 yards vs. Miami
Dan Marino, Miami	362 yards vs. N.Y. Jets

Eleventh Week

Ken O'Brien, N.Y. Jets	367 yards vs. Tampa Bay
Dan Marino, Miami	330 yards vs. Indianapolis
Lynn Dickey, Green Bay	302 yards vs. New Orleans

Twelfth Week

Dan Fouts, San Diego	343 yards vs. Houston
Ken O'Brien, N.Y. Jets	311 yards vs. New England

Thirteenth Week

Jay Schroeder, Washington	348 yards vs. San Francisco
Boomer Esiason, Cincinnati	320 yards vs. Houston
Ron Jaworski, Philadelphia	320 yards vs. Minnesota
Neil Lomax, St. Louis	319 yards vs. Dallas

Fourteenth Week

Dan Fouts, San Diego	372 yards vs. Pittsburgh
Ken O'Brien, N.Y. Jets	370 yards vs. Buffalo
Bruce Mathison, Buffalo	357 yards vs. N.Y. Jets
Dan Marino, Miami	345 yards vs. Green Bay
Warren Moon, Houston	330 yards vs. N.Y. Giants
Joe Montana, San Francisco	328 yards vs. L.A. Rams
Tommy Kramer, Minnesota	309 yards vs. Tampa Bay

Fifteenth Week

Boomer Esiason, Cincinnati	357 yards vs. Washington
Joe Montana, San Francisco	354 yards vs. New Orleans
Warren Moon, Houston	339 yards vs. Cleveland
Ron Jaworski, Philadelphia	334 yards vs. San Diego
Phil Simms, N.Y. Giants	329 yards vs. Dallas
Tommy Kramer, Minnesota	315 yards vs. Atlanta
John Elway, Denver	301 yards vs. Kansas City

Sixteenth Week

John Elway, Denver	432 yards vs. Seattle
Gary Hogeboom, Dallas	389 yards vs. San Francisco
Warren Moon, Houston	364 yards vs. Indianapolis
Mark Herrmann, San Diego	362 yards vs. Kansas City
Joe Montana, San Francisco	322 yards vs. Dallas
Tommy Kramer, Minnesota	321 yards vs. Philadelphia

Times 300 or more

Fouts 7; Marino 6; Kramer, Montana 5; Esiason, Jaworski, O'Brien 4; Elway, Herrmann, Moon, Simms 3; DeBerg, Kenney, Krieg, White 2.

Ten Best Receiving Yardage Performances, 1985

		Yards	No.	TD
1.	Stephone Paige Kansas City vs. San Diego, December 22	309	8	2
2.	Wes Chandler San Diego vs. Seattle, September 15	243	13	1
3.	Jerry Rice San Francisco vs. L.A. Rams, December 9	241	10	1
4.	Art Monk Washington vs. Cincinnati, December 15	230	13	1
5.	Mark Duper Miami vs. N.Y. Jets, November 10	217	8	2
6.	Drew Hill Houston vs. Indianapolis, December 22	210	9	2
7.	Gary Clark Washington vs. N.Y. Giants, October 20	193	11	0
8.	Tony Hill Dallas vs. Detroit, September 15	181	11	2
9.	Mark Bavaro N.Y. Giants vs. Cincinnati, October 13	176	12	0
10.	Carlos Carson Kansas City vs. New Orleans, September 8	173	8	2

100-Yard Receiving Performances, 1985

(Number in parentheses is receptions.)

First Week

Carlos Carson, Kansas City	173 yards (8) vs. New Orleans
Louis Lipps, Pittsburgh	154 yards (9) vs. Indianapolis
Jerry Butler, Buffalo	140 yards (4) vs. San Diego
Dokie Williams, L.A. Raiders	131 yards (5) vs. N.Y. Jets
Butch Woolfolk, Houston	120 yards (3) vs. Miami
Cris Collinsworth, Cincinnati	101 yards (4) vs. Seattle

Second Week

Wes Chandler, San Diego	243 yards (13) vs. Seattle
Tony Hill, Dallas	181 yards (11) vs. Detroit
Doug Cosbie, Dallas	159 yards (11) vs. Detroit
Daryl Turner, Seattle	121 yards (7) vs. San Diego
Carlos Carson, Kansas City	118 yards (5) vs. L.A. Raiders
Todd Christensen, L.A. Raiders	116 yards (11) vs. Kansas City
Eddie Brown, Cincinnati	106 yards (5) vs. St. Louis
Mark Clayton, Miami	106 yards (8) vs. Indianapolis
Lionel Manuel, N.Y. Giants	105 yards (5) vs. Green Bay

Third Week

Cris Collinsworth, Cincinnati	161 yards (10) vs. San Diego
Willie Gault, Chicago	146 yards (6) vs. Minnesota
Dennis McKinnon, Chicago	133 yards (4) vs. Minnesota
Lionel James, San Diego	118 yards (5) vs. Cincinnati
Billy Johnson, Atlanta	110 yards (7) vs. Denver
Anthony Carter, Minnesota	102 yards (4) vs. Chicago

Fourth Week

John Stallworth, Pittsburgh	151 yards (11) vs. Cincinnati
Henry Ellard, L.A. Rams	123 yards (5) vs. Atlanta
Tony Nathan, Miami	120 yards (10) vs. Denver
Ray Butler, Indianapolis	113 yards (4) vs. N.Y. Jets
Kurt Sohn, N.Y. Jets	112 yards (8) vs. Indianapolis
Nat Moore, Miami	109 yards (5) vs. Denver
Louis Lipps, Pittsburgh	100 yards (5) vs. Cincinnati

Fifth Week

Roger Craig, San Francisco	167 yards (12) vs. Atlanta
James Lofton, Green Bay	151 yards (10) vs. Detroit
Wes Chandler, San Diego	150 yards (9) vs. Seattle
Mike Renfro, Dallas	141 yards (10) vs. N.Y. Giants
Stanley Morgan, New England	140 yards (6) vs. Cleveland
Lionel Manuel, N.Y. Giants	129 yards (6) vs. Dallas
John Spagnola, Philadelphia	124 yards (12) vs. New Orleans
Butch Woolfolk, Houston	124 yards (8) vs. Denver
Emery Moorehead, Chicago	114 yards (8) vs. Tampa Bay
Jeff Chadwick, Detroit	112 yards (7) vs. Green Bay
Jimmie Giles, Tampa Bay	112 yards (7) vs. Chicago
Brian Brennan, Cleveland	104 yards (7) vs. New England
Bobby Johnson, N.Y. Giants	104 yards (5) vs. Dallas
Tony Hill, Dallas	100 yards (8) vs. N.Y. Giants
Kevin House, Tampa Bay	100 yards (6) vs. Chicago

Sixth Week

Mark Bavaro, N.Y. Giants	176 yards (12) vs. Cincinnati
Clarence Weathers, Cleveland	146 yards (3) vs. Houston
Irving Fryar, New England	132 yards (6) vs. Buffalo
Herman Hunter, Philadelphia	120 yards (6) vs. St. Louis
Charlie Joiner, San Diego	118 yards (6) vs. Kansas City
Lionel Manuel, N.Y. Giants	111 yards (8) vs. Cincinnati
Steve Largent, Seattle	103 yards (8) vs. Atlanta

Seventh Week

Gary Clark, Washington	193 yards (11) vs. N.Y. Giants
Billy Johnson, Atlanta	153 yards (11) vs. New Orleans
Wesley Walker, N.Y. Jets	140 yards (6) vs. New England
Kenny Jackson, Philadelphia	134 yards (6) vs. Dallas
Eddie Brown, Cincinnati	124 yards (7) vs. Houston
Jimmie Giles, Tampa Bay	116 yards (7) vs. Miami
Hoby Brenner, New Orleans	111 yards (6) vs. Atlanta
Kevin House, Tampa Bay	111 yards (4) vs. Miami
James Lofton, Green Bay	103 yards (7) vs. Chicago

Eighth Week

Tony Hill, Dallas	161 yards (10) vs. Atlanta
Todd Christensen, L.A. Raiders	134 yards (7) vs. San Diego
Leonard Thompson, Detroit	133 yards (6) vs. Miami
Roger Craig, San Francisco	132 yards (6) vs. L.A. Rams
Drew Hill, Houston	132 yards (6) vs. St. Louis
Henry Ellard, L.A. Rams	120 yards (9) vs. San Francisco
Mike Quick, Philadelphia	117 yards (8) vs. Buffalo
Matt Bouza, Indianapolis	109 yards (6) vs. Green Bay
Tony Collins, New England	109 yards (6) vs. Tampa Bay
Wayne Capers, Indianapolis	104 yards (5) vs. Green Bay

Ninth Week

Mike Quick, Philadelphia	146 yards (6) vs. San Francisco
Mark Clayton, Miami	122 yards (7) vs. New England
Tony Hunter, L.A. Rams	113 yards (6) vs. New Orleans
Pat Tilley, St. Louis	113 yards (6) vs. Dallas
Art Monk, Washington	106 yards (6) vs. Atlanta

Tenth Week

Mark Duper, Miami	217 yards (8) vs. N.Y. Jets
Lionel James, San Diego	168 yards (11) vs. L.A. Raiders
Al Toon, N.Y. Jets	156 yards (10) vs. Miami
Mike Quick, Philadelphia	145 yards (3) vs. Atlanta
Tony Hill, Dallas	136 yards (7) vs. Washington
Cris Collinsworth, Cincinnati	135 yards (8) vs. Cleveland
Jimmie Giles, Tampa Bay	134 yards (6) vs. St. Louis
John Stallworth, Pittsburgh	126 yards (7) vs. Kansas City
Stanley Morgan, New England	120 yards (7) vs. Indianapolis
Phillip Epps, Green Bay	118 yards (6) vs. Minnesota
Todd Christensen, L.A. Raiders	112 yards (7) vs. San Diego
Steve Largent, Seattle	110 yards (5) vs. New Orleans
Art Monk, Washington	103 yards (5) vs. Dallas

Eleventh Week

Steve Largent, Seattle	138 yards (8) vs. New England
Al Toon, N.Y. Jets	133 yards (6) vs. Tampa Bay
Art Monk, Washington	130 yards (7) vs. N.Y. Giants
Anthony Carter, Minnesota	102 yards (6) vs. Detroit

Twelfth Week

Wesley Walker, N.Y. Jets	168 yards (6) vs. New England
Louis Lipps, Pittsburgh	121 yards (5) vs. Washington
Kellen Winslow, San Diego	107 yards (7) vs. Houston

Thirteenth Week

Art Monk, Washington	150 yards (8) vs. San Francisco
Billy Johnson, Atlanta	136 yards (6) vs. L.A. Raiders
Butch Woolfolk, Houston	130 yards (9) vs. Cincinnati
Drew Hill, Houston	129 yards (7) vs. Cincinnati
Mike Quick, Philadelphia	127 yards (8) vs. Minnesota
Anthony Carter, Minnesota	124 yards (5) vs. Philadelphia
Calvin Sweeney, Pittsburgh	119 yards (8) vs. Denver
Gary Clark, Washington	116 yards (10) vs. San Francisco
Leonard Thompson, Detroit	115 yards (7) vs. N.Y. Jets
Pat Tilley, St. Louis	115 yards (6) vs. Dallas
Doug Cosbie, Dallas	111 yards (5) vs. St. Louis
Todd Christensen, L.A. Raiders	109 yards (7) vs. Atlanta
Mark Duper, Miami	107 yards (5) vs. Chicago
James Lofton, Green Bay	106 yards (6) vs. Tampa Bay
Andre Reed, Buffalo	103 yards (6) vs. San Diego
Steve Largent, Seattle	101 yards (7) vs. Kansas City

Fourteenth Week

Jerry Rice, San Francisco	241 yards (10) vs. L.A. Rams
Wes Chandler, San Diego	154 yards (5) vs. Pittsburgh
Wesley Walker, N.Y. Jets	129 yards (4) vs. Buffalo
Chris Burkett, Buffalo	127 yards (5) vs. N.Y. Jets
Cris Collinsworth, Cincinnati	123 yards (7) vs. Dallas
Tim Smith, Houston	120 yards (7) vs. N.Y. Giants
Charlie Joiner, San Diego	110 yards (6) vs. Pittsburgh
Art Monk, Washington	109 yards (7) vs. Philadelphia
Mike Jones, Minnesota	104 yards (4) vs. Tampa Bay
Drew Hill, Houston	103 yards (6) vs. N.Y. Giants

Fifteenth Week

Art Monk, Washington	230 yards (13) vs. Cincinnati
Anthony Carter, Minnesota	144 yards (7) vs. Atlanta
Eugene Goodlow, New Orleans	135 yards (5) vs. San Francisco
Kevin House, Tampa Bay	131 yards (4) vs. Indianapolis
Phil McConkey, N.Y. Giants	128 yards (6) vs. Dallas
Tim Smith, Houston	125 yards (7) vs. Cleveland
Wes Chandler, San Diego	124 yards (5) vs. Philadelphia
Mike Renfro, Dallas	123 yards (4) vs. N.Y. Giants
Vance Johnson, Denver	116 yards (6) vs. Kansas City
Louis Lipps, Pittsburgh	116 yards (4) vs. Buffalo
Carl Bland, Detroit	109 yards (7) vs. Green Bay

Sixteenth Week

Stephone Paige, Kansas City	309 yards (8) vs. San Diego
Drew Hill, Houston	210 yards (9) vs. Indianapolis
Mike Renfro, Dallas	164 yards (9) vs. San Francisco
Anthony Carter, Minnesota	132 yards (6) vs. Philadelphia
Eddie Brown, Cincinnati	129 yards (5) vs. New England
Pete Mandley, Detroit	127 yards (5) vs. Chicago
Carl Powe, Dallas	127 yards (7) vs. San Francisco
Stanley Morgan, New England	121 yards (4) vs. Cincinnati
Gary Clark, Washington	118 yards (8) vs. St. Louis
Jerry Rice, San Francisco	111 yards (7) vs. Dallas
Leonard Thompson, Detroit	101 yards (9) vs. Chicago

Times 100 or More

Monk 6; Carter 5; Chandler, Christensen, Collinsworth, D. Hill, T. Hill, Largent, Lipps, Quick 4; E. Brown, Clark, Giles, House, B. Johnson, Lofton, Manuel, Morgan, Renfro, L. Thompson, Walker, Woolfolk 3; Carson, Clayton, Cosbie, Craig, Duper, Ellard, James, Joiner, Rice, T. Smith, Stallworth, Tilley, Toon 2.

AMERICAN FOOTBALL CONFERENCE OFFENSE

	Buff.	Cin.	Clev.	Den.	Hou.	Ind.	K.C.	Raid.	Mia.	N.E.	N.Y.J.	Pitt.	S.D.	Sea.
First Downs	256	344	271	339	270	282	258	304	361	294	344	315	380	299
Rushing	86	125	119	113	96	131	79	111	116	126	121	125	92	96
Passing	151	191	128	192	149	130	158	167	218	153	201	165	259	179
Penalty	19	28	24	34	25	21	21	26	27	15	22	25	29	24
Rushes	412	503	533	497	428	485	428	532	444	565	564	541	440	462
Net Yds. Gained	1611	2183	2285	1851	1570	2439	1486	2262	1729	2331	2312	2177	1665	1644
Avg. Gain	3.9	4.3	4.3	3.7	3.7	5.0	3.5	4.3	3.9	4.1	4.1	4.0	3.8	3.6
Avg. Yds. per Game	100.7	136.4	142.8	115.7	98.1	152.4	92.9	141.4	108.1	145.7	144.5	136.1	104.1	102.8
Passes Attempted	517	518	414	617	512	468	511	506	576	457	497	512	632	575
Completed	263	302	222	329	277	235	267	269	343	255	303	254	386	304
% Completed	50.9	58.3	53.6	53.3	54.1	50.2	52.3	53.2	59.5	55.8	61.0	49.6	61.1	52.9
Total Yds. Gained	3331	4082	2885	3952	3523	2811	3726	3481	4278	3483	3983	3397	5175	3820
Times Sacked	42	41	36	38	58	35	43	43	19	39	62	33	39	53
Yds. Lost	347	365	249	307	441	244	335	335	164	315	399	224	305	457
Net Yds. Gained	2984	3717	2636	3645	3082	2567	3391	3146	4114	3168	3584	3173	4870	3363
Avg. Yds. per Game	186.5	232.3	164.8	227.8	192.6	160.4	211.9	196.6	257.1	198.0	224.0	198.3	304.4	210.2
Net Yds. per Pass Play	5.34	6.65	5.86	5.56	5.41	5.10	6.12	5.73	6.91	6.39	6.41	5.82	7.26	5.36
Yds. Gained per Comp.	12.67	13.52	13.00	12.01	12.72	11.96	13.96	12.94	12.47	13.66	13.15	13.37	13.41	12.57
Combined Net Yds. Gained	4595	5900	4921	5496	4652	5006	4877	5408	5843	5499	5896	5350	6535	5007
% Total Yds. Rushing	35.1	37.0	46.4	33.7	33.7	48.7	30.5	41.8	29.6	42.4	39.2	40.7	25.5	32.8
% Total Yds. Passing	64.9	63.0	53.6	66.3	66.3	51.3	69.5	58.2	70.4	57.6	60.8	59.3	74.5	67.2
Avg. Yds. per Game	287.2	368.8	307.6	343.5	290.8	312.9	304.8	338.0	365.2	343.7	368.5	334.4	408.4	312.9
Ball Control Plays	971	1062	983	1152	998	988	982	1081	1039	1061	1123	1086	1111	1090
Avg. Yds. per Play	4.7	5.6	5.0	4.8	4.7	5.1	5.0	5.0	5.6	5.2	5.3	4.9	5.9	4.6
Avg. Time of Poss.	28:21	31:18	28:53	31:19	28:07	28:49	28:06	30:26	30:17	31:07	31:11	30:52	29:21	30:13
Third Down Efficiency	32.7	39.4	36.6	40.3	33.9	37.7	33.8	38.0	45.6	36.6	41.8	38.6	41.3	39.3
Had Intercepted	31	13	13	23	22	20	23	24	21	22	8	27	30	23
Yds. Opp. Returned	418	199	217	332	267	232	251	365	100	243	101	409	268	389
Ret. by Opp. for TD	4	0	1	2	1	0	0	1	0	2	1	5	0	1

	Buff.	Cin.	Clev.	Den.	Hou.	Ind.	K.C.	Raid.	Mia.	N.E.	N.Y.J.	Pitt.	S.D.	Sea.
Punts	92	63	81	94	84	80	95	89	59	92	74	79	68	91
Yds. Punted	3818	2563	3261	3764	3490	3584	3827	3627	2576	3953	2978	3088	2881	3667
Avg. Yds. per Punt	41.5	40.7	40.3	40.0	41.5	44.8	40.3	40.8	43.7	43.0	40.2	39.1	42.4	40.3
Punt Returns	38	32	47	46	30	42	43	71	39	42	39	49	25	53
Yds. Returned	293	268	371	429	250	449	381	785	319	530	386	483	213	483
Avg. Yds. per Return	7.7	8.4	7.9	9.3	8.3	10.7	8.9	11.1	8.2	12.6	9.9	9.9	8.5	9.1
Returned for TD	0	0	1	0	0	1	0	0	0	2	0	2	0	0
Kickoff Returns	68	67	53	52	67	67	59	54	52	57	53	65	71	58
Yds. Returned	1334	1385	1217	1203	1515	1403	1117	1132	1177	1119	1043	1337	1494	1166
Avg. Yds. per Return	19.6	20.7	23.0	23.1	22.6	20.9	18.9	21.0	22.6	19.6	19.7	20.6	21.0	20.1
Returned for TD	0	0	0	0	0	0	0	0	0	0	0	0	1	0
Penalties	132	110	99	85	127	87	87	116	77	114	119	85	100	102
Yds. Penalized	965	795	753	677	1150	678	666	962	637	842	907	665	937	827
Fumbles	36	35	40	24	41	27	22	27	31	37	35	31	44	34
Lost	21	16	23	8	15	14	11	14	20	20	21	9	19	18
Out of Bounds	1	3	0	2	3	2	1	0	1	4	3	1	6	3
Own Rec. for TD	0	0	0	0	0	0	0	1	0	0	0	0	0	0
Opp. Rec. by	15	19	9	12	20	17	14	13	18	24	20	14	16	20
Opp. Rec. for TD	1	0	0	0	0	1	1	0	1	3	1	0	0	1
Total Points Scored	200	441	287	380	284	320	317	354	428	362	393	379	467	349
Total TDs	23	53	35	45	32	39	35	42	52	41	45	40	60	44
TDs Rushing	13	20	16	20	13	22	10	18	19	15	18	14	20	9
TDs Passing	9	31	17	23	18	15	23	20	31	20	25	23	37	28
TDs on Ret. and Rec.	1	2	2	2	1	2	2	4	2	6	2	3	3	7
Extra Points	23	49	35	41	29	36	35	40	50	40	43	40	53	41
Safeties	0	1	0	0	0	1	0	1	0	2	1	0	0	1
Field Goals Made	13	24	14	23	21	16	24	20	22	24	26	33	18	14
Field Goals Attempted	17	33	18	38	27	26	27	32	27	30	34	42	28	25
% Successful	76.5	72.7	77.8	60.5	77.8	61.5	88.9	62.5	81.5	80.0	76.5	78.6	64.3	56.0

AMERICAN FOOTBALL CONFERENCE DEFENSE

	Buff.	Cin.	Clev.	Den.	Hou.	Ind.	K.C.	Raid.	Mia.	N.E.	N.Y.J.	Pitt.	S.D.	Sea.
First Downs	320	337	297	290	356	330	336	273	314	284	276	273	364	290
Rushing	142	118	106	103	150	124	129	73	135	92	85	105	122	90
Passing	159	194	172	168	158	192	184	166	160	168	154	144	218	179
Penalty	19	25	19	19	48	14	23	34	19	24	37	24	24	21
Rushes	569	461	497	475	588	539	513	461	509	466	433	470	470	473
Net Yds. Gained	2462	1999	1851	1973	2814	2145	2169	1605	2256	1655	1516	1876	1972	1837
Avg. Gain	4.3	4.3	3.7	4.2	4.8	4.0	4.2	3.5	4.4	3.6	3.5	4.0	4.2	3.9
Avg. Yds. per Game	153.9	124.9	115.7	123.3	175.9	134.1	135.6	100.3	141.0	103.4	94.8	117.3	123.3	114.8
Passes Attempted	477	518	509	547	462	504	576	511	487	525	507	484	595	496
Completed	265	297	289	277	260	275	332	251	257	262	267	287	357	273
% Completed	55.6	57.3	56.8	50.6	56.3	54.6	57.6	49.1	52.8	49.9	52.7	59.3	60.0	55.0
Total Yds. Gained	3301	3998	3460	3584	3654	3721	3752	3486	3789	3393	3626	3088	4597	3787
Times Sacked	25	40	44	47	41	36	37	65	38	51	49	36	40	61
Yds. Lost	223	334	353	378	313	267	263	488	278	334	370	305	304	464
Net Yds. Gained	3078	3664	3107	3206	3341	3454	3489	2998	3511	3059	3256	2783	4293	3323
Avg. Yds. per Game	192.4	229.0	194.2	200.4	208.8	215.9	218.1	187.4	219.4	191.2	203.5	173.9	268.3	207.7
Net Yds. per Pass Play	6.13	6.57	5.62	5.40	6.64	6.40	5.69	5.20	6.69	5.31	5.86	5.35	6.76	5.97
Yds. Gained per Comp.	12.46	13.46	11.97	12.94	14.05	13.53	11.30	13.89	14.74	12.95	13.58	10.76	12.88	13.87
Combined Net Yds. Gained	5540	5663	4958	5179	6155	5599	5658	4603	5767	4714	4772	4659	6265	5160
% Total Yds. Rushing	44.4	35.3	37.3	38.1	45.7	38.3	38.3	34.9	39.1	35.1	31.8	40.3	31.5	35.6
% Total Yds. Passing	55.6	64.7	62.7	61.9	54.3	61.7	61.7	65.1	60.9	64.9	68.2	59.7	68.5	64.4
Avg. Yds. per Game	346.3	353.9	309.9	323.7	384.7	349.9	353.6	287.7	360.4	294.6	298.3	291.2	391.6	322.5
Ball Control Plays	1071	1019	1050	1069	1091	1079	1126	1037	1034	1042	989	990	1105	1030
Avg. Yds. per Play	5.2	5.6	4.7	4.8	5.6	5.2	5.0	4.4	5.6	4.5	4.8	4.7	5.7	5.0
Third Down Efficiency	44.2	43.1	36.4	31.9	39.4	44.8	41.4	33.2	40.7	32.6	32.7	34.0	42.6	33.0
Intercepted by	20	19	18	24	15	16	27	17	23	23	22	20	26	24
Yds. Returned by	225	283	254	290	144	75	298	235	265	427	127	211	461	272
Returned for TD	0	2	1	1	0	0	1	3	1	1	1	1	2	3
Punts	81	60	91	94	68	72	75	104	73	97	88	86	70	97
Yds. Punted	3284	2477	3842	3868	2677	2982	3088	4356	2972	3933	3679	3515	2717	4081
Avg. Yds. per Punt	40.5	41.3	42.2	41.1	39.4	41.4	41.2	41.9	40.7	40.5	41.8	40.9	38.8	42.1
Punt Returns	49	42	36	38	45	43	48	26	27	56	36	43	36	47
Yds. Returned	438	554	304	325	345	572	530	159	371	598	319	380	274	374
Avg. Yds. per Return	8.9	13.2	8.4	8.6	7.7	13.3	11.0	6.1	13.7	10.7	8.9	8.8	7.6	8.0
Returned for TD	1	1	0	0	0	1	1	0	1	0	1	0	0	0
Kickoff Returns	41	81	51	64	39	59	69	59	63	76	58	65	68	47
Yds. Returned	798	1734	884	1346	970	1189	1626	1165	1370	1434	1135	1566	1363	918
Avg. Yds. per Return	19.5	21.4	17.3	21.0	24.9	20.2	23.6	19.7	21.7	18.9	19.6	24.1	20.0	19.5
Returned for TD	0	0	0	1	0	0	0	0	0	0	0	0	0	0
Penalties	107	84	102	91	121	90	89	109	112	83	113	89	86	106
Yds. Penalized	870	731	773	953	908	699	777	856	854	699	868	679	703	840
Fumbles	36	34	28	22	35	32	25	27	36	36	42	34	37	39
Lost	15	19	9	12	20	17	14	13	18	24	20	14	16	20
Out of Bounds	4	3	1	3	2	0	2	1	4	2	5	2	3	2
Own Rec. for TD	0	0	0	0	0	0	0	0	0	1	0	0	1	0
Opp. Rec. by	21	16	23	8	15	14	11	14	20	20	21	9	19	18
Opp. Rec. for TD	1	0	1	0	0	0	0	3	1	0	1	1	0	0
Total Points Scored	381	437	294	329	412	386	360	308	320	290	264	355	435	303
Total TDs	50	51	34	36	51	45	41	34	38	32	30	43	55	35
TDs Rushing	20	23	14	10	21	20	18	7	15	15	10	19	25	12
TDs Passing	24	26	18	22	29	24	22	22	21	14	17	18	28	22
TDs on Ret. and Rec.	6	2	2	4	1	1	1	5	2	3	3	6	2	1
Extra Points	45	51	33	35	49	41	39	32	35	30	30	40	51	31
Safeties	0	1	0	0	0	0	0	0	0	1	0	0	0	1
Field Goals Made	12	26	19	26	19	25	25	24	19	22	18	19	18	20
Field Goals Attempted	15	34	29	33	34	31	30	35	28	25	25	25	30	28
% Successful	80.0	76.5	65.5	78.8	55.9	80.6	83.3	68.6	67.9	88.0	72.0	76.0	60.0	71.4

NATIONAL FOOTBALL CONFERENCE OFFENSE

	Atl.	Chi.	Dall.	Det.	G.B.	Rams	Minn.	N.O.	N.Y.G.	Phil.	St.L.	S.F.	T.B.	Wash.
First Downs	296	343	336	259	318	258	317	250	356	292	301	340	291	319
Rushing	149	176	95	89	114	115	95	83	138	82	108	137	95	147
Passing	132	145	208	150	172	131	189	148	192	188	171	179	162	157
Penalty	15	22	33	20	32	12	33	19	26	22	22	24	34	15
Rushes	560	610	462	452	470	503	406	431	581	428	417	477	434	571
Net Yds. Gained	2466	2761	1741	1538	2208	2057	1516	1683	2451	1630	1974	2232	1644	2523
Avg. Gain	4.4	4.5	3.8	3.4	4.7	4.1	3.7	3.9	4.2	3.8	4.7	4.7	3.8	4.4
Avg. Yds. per Game	154.1	172.6	108.8	96.1	138.0	128.6	94.8	105.2	153.2	101.9	123.4	139.5	102.8	157.7
Passes Attempted	462	432	587	462	513	403	576	508	497	567	534	550	508	512
Completed	254	237	344	254	267	234	311	260	275	290	296	331	269	280
% Completed	55.0	54.9	58.6	55.0	52.0	58.1	54.0	51.2	55.3	51.1	55.4	60.2	53.0	54.7
Total Yds. Gained	3025	3303	4236	3316	3552	2872	3931	3257	3829	4036	3581	3987	3423	3243
Times Sacked	69	43	44	53	50	57	45	58	52	55	65	42	40	52
Yds. Lost	531	227	375	378	389	409	296	461	396	450	469	299	301	428
Net Yds. Gained	2494	3076	3861	2938	3163	2463	3635	2796	3433	3586	3112	3688	3122	2815
Avg. Yds. per Game	155.9	192.3	241.3	183.6	197.7	153.9	227.2	174.8	214.6	224.1	194.5	230.5	195.1	175.9
Net Yds. per Pass Play	4.70	6.48	6.12	5.70	5.62	5.35	5.85	4.94	6.25	5.77	5.20	6.23	5.70	4.99
Yds. Gained per Comp.	11.91	13.94	12.31	13.06	13.30	12.27	12.64	12.53	13.92	13.92	12.10	12.05	12.72	11.58
Combined Net Yds. Gained	4960	5837	5602	4476	5371	4520	5151	4479	5884	5216	5086	5920	4766	5338
% Total Yds. Rushing	49.7	47.3	31.1	34.4	41.1	45.5	29.4	37.6	41.7	31.3	38.8	37.7	34.5	47.3
% Total Yds. Passing	50.3	52.7	68.9	65.6	58.9	54.5	70.6	62.4	58.3	68.8	61.2	62.3	65.5	52.7
Avg. Yds. per Game	310.0	364.8	350.1	279.8	335.7	282.5	321.9	279.9	367.8	326.0	317.9	370.0	297.9	333.6
Ball Control Plays	1091	1085	1093	967	1033	963	1027	997	1130	1050	1016	1069	982	1135
Avg. Yds. per Play	4.5	5.4	5.1	4.6	5.2	4.7	5.0	4.5	5.2	5.0	5.0	5.5	4.9	4.7
Avg. Time of Poss.	33:11	34:33	30:34	27:30	28:59	29:51	28:07	28:33	31:49	29:13	29:22	28:45	27:55	33:17
Third Down Efficiency	36.4	38.5	42.3	38.4	33.0	33.7	39.3	29.9	41.3	35.5	32.7	38.8	32.5	43.3
Had Intercepted	20	16	25	21	27	14	29	23	20	28	18	14	26	21
Yds. Opp. Returned	172	99	319	247	326	138	311	251	285	474	245	80	368	215
Ret. by Opp. for TD	0	1	2	1	1	1	2	1	4	2	1	1	4	2
Punts	89	69	83	73	82	88	67	89	81	91	87	87	79	73
Yds. Punted	3757	2870	3439	3054	3262	3761	2867	3763	3472	3777	3545	3422	3233	2973
Avg. Yds. per Punt	42.2	41.6	41.4	41.8	39.8	42.7	42.8	42.3	42.9	41.5	40.7	39.3	40.9	40.7
Punt Returns	31	54	40	38	38	38	25	30	53	45	40	38	25	47
Yds. Returned	223	503	237	403	370	501	250	215	442	393	393	258	229	508
Avg. Yds. per Return	7.2	9.3	5.9	10.6	9.7	13.2	10.0	7.2	8.3	8.7	9.8	6.8	9.2	10.8
Returned for TD	0	0	0	1	0	1	0	0	0	0	0	0	0	0
Kickoff Returns	72	43	62	68	67	56	68	71	50	56	78	58	80	60
Yds. Returned	1406	1089	1210	1494	1318	1394	1576	1547	866	1160	1421	1269	1622	1349
Avg. Yds. per Return	19.5	25.3	19.5	22.0	19.7	24.9	23.2	21.8	17.3	20.7	18.2	21.9	20.3	22.5
Returned for TD	1	2	0	0	0	3	0	0	0	0	0	1	0	0
Penalties	126	104	100	104	101	97	88	96	80	98	101	105	103	74
Yds. Penalized	1149	912	759	741	798	730	690	805	781	736	816	868	751	596
Fumbles	23	24	29	36	39	35	27	23	36	25	38	29	37	27
Lost	10	15	16	20	18	21	18	13	18	12	16	20	22	19
Out of Bounds	3	2	1	3	1	1	0	0	2	1	5	1	6	1
Own Rec. for TD	0	0	0	0	0	0	0	0	0	1	0	0	0	0
Opp. Rec. by	12	20	15	18	25	16	22	16	13	14	14	17	22	11
Opp. Rec. for TD	1	1	0	0	1	0	1	2	0	0	0	3	0	0
Total Points Scored	282	456	357	307	337	340	346	294	399	286	278	411	294	297
Total TDs	30	51	43	33	40	39	43	29	48	30	34	53	33	33
TDs Rushing	14	27	11	13	16	15	19	4	24	8	14	20	11	20
TDs Passing	13	17	27	19	21	16	22	20	22	19	19	28	22	13
TDs on Ret. and Rec.	3	7	5	1	3	8	2	5	2	3	1	5	0	0
Extra Points	30	51	42	31	38	38	41	27	45	29	33	52	30	31
Safeties	0	3	0	0	1	1	1	0	0	1	1	1	0	1
Field Goals Made	24	31	19	26	19	22	15	31	22	25	13	13	22	22
Field Goals Attempted	31	37	28	31	26	29	26	35	33	30	28	21	32	35
% Successful	77.4	83.8	67.9	83.9	73.1	75.9	57.7	88.6	66.7	83.3	46.4	61.9	68.8	62.9

NATIONAL FOOTBALL CONFERENCE DEFENSE

	Atl.	Chi.	Dall.	Det.	G.B.	Rams	Minn.	N.O.	N.Y.G.	Phil.	St.L.	S.F.	T.B.	Wash.
First Downs	329	236	312	359	310	281	324	335	258	307	314	293	351	244
Rushing	112	74	98	179	111	104	139	125	77	122	115	89	146	94
Passing	181	141	193	156	178	155	163	188	163	160	169	183	185	134
Penalty	36	21	21	24	21	22	22	22	18	25	30	21	20	16
Rushes	437	359	465	560	494	444	542	508	419	526	552	435	547	424
Net Yds. Gained	2052	1319	1853	2685	2047	1586	2223	2162	1482	2205	2378	1683	2430	1734
Avg. Gain	4.7	3.7	4.0	4.8	4.1	3.6	4.1	4.3	3.5	4.2	4.3	3.9	4.4	4.1
Avg. Yds. per Game	128.3	82.4	115.8	167.8	127.9	99.1	138.9	135.1	92.6	137.8	148.6	105.2	151.9	108.4
Passes Attempted	535	522	549	478	509	548	490	529	535	478	461	621	505	465
Completed	289	249	279	283	295	296	280	306	278	251	253	346	318	239
% Completed	54.0	47.7	50.8	59.2	58.0	54.0	57.1	57.8	52.0	52.5	54.9	55.7	63.0	51.4
Total Yds. Gained	4129	3299	4214	3242	3509	3483	3464	3975	3377	3289	3257	3965	3955	3124
Times Sacked	42	64	62	45	48	56	33	46	68	53	32	60	35	52
Yds. Lost	331	483	459	336	383	421	223	322	539	359	254	457	277	378
Net Yds. Gained	3798	2816	3755	2906	3126	3062	3241	3653	2838	2930	3003	3508	3678	2746
Avg. Yds. per Game	237.4	176.0	234.7	181.6	195.4	191.4	202.6	228.3	177.4	183.1	187.7	219.3	229.9	171.6
Net Yds. per Pass Play	6.58	4.81	6.15	5.56	5.61	5.07	6.20	6.35	4.71	5.52	6.09	5.15	6.81	5.31
Yds. Gained per Comp.	14.29	13.25	15.10	11.46	11.89	11.77	12.37	12.99	12.15	13.10	12.87	11.46	12.44	13.07
Combined Net Yds. Gained	5850	4135	5608	5591	5173	4648	5464	5815	4320	5135	5381	5191	6108	4480
% Total Yds. Rushing	35.1	31.9	33.0	48.0	39.6	34.1	40.7	37.2	34.3	42.9	44.2	32.4	39.8	38.7
% Total Yds. Passing	64.9	68.1	67.0	52.0	60.4	65.9	59.3	62.8	65.7	57.1	55.8	67.6	60.2	61.3
Avg. Yds. per Game	365.6	258.4	350.5	349.4	323.3	290.5	341.5	363.4	270.0	320.9	336.3	324.4	381.8	280.0
Ball Control Plays	1014	945	1076	1083	1051	1048	1065	1083	1022	1057	1045	1116	1087	941
Avg. Yds. per Play	5.8	4.4	5.2	5.2	4.9	4.4	5.1	5.4	4.2	4.9	5.1	4.7	5.6	4.8
Third Down Efficiency	46.1	29.6	38.2	34.2	37.6	36.4	43.5	42.1	28.9	38.9	38.8	32.7	41.6	34.6
Intercepted by	22	34	33	18	15	29	22	21	24	18	13	18	18	23
Yds. Returned by	247	512	263	136	262	359	283	312	339	125	240	310	146	220
Returned for TD	1	4	4	0	2	4	1	2	2	2	1	1	0	0
Punts	69	90	78	64	77	89	65	81	107	92	75	92	59	85
Yds. Punted	2899	3639	3218	2572	3290	3738	2694	3417	4363	3918	3069	3644	2617	3723
Avg. Yds. per Punt	42.0	40.4	41.3	40.2	42.7	42.0	41.4	42.2	40.8	42.6	40.9	39.6	44.4	43.8
Punt Returns	52	23	44	44	46	43	36	45	29	41	51	33	47	32
Yds. Returned	417	203	286	420	411	297	328	397	247	462	456	294	519	285
Avg. Yds. per Return	8.0	8.8	6.5	9.5	8.9	6.9	9.1	8.8	8.5	11.3	8.9	8.9	11.0	8.9
Returned for TD	0	0	0	0	0	0	0	0	0	1	0	1	0	0
Kickoff Returns	62	78	68	60	71	66	68	43	79	65	56	72	51	53
Yds. Returned	1135	1827	1310	1313	1570	1253	1491	968	1697	1293	1150	1485	1187	1186
Avg. Yds. per Return	18.3	23.4	19.3	21.9	22.1	19.0	21.9	22.5	21.5	19.9	20.5	20.6	23.3	22.4
Returned for TD	0	0	0	1	2	0	0	1	0	0	0	1	0	2
Penalties	97	118	108	105	102	72	123	108	106	99	88	106	114	89
Yds. Penalized	738	944	990	729	797	529	1000	837	821	834	742	778	945	699
Fumbles	18	30	24	35	44	30	37	24	36	27	28	31	37	28
Lost	12	20	15	18	25	17	22	16	13	14	14	17	22	11
Out of Bounds	0	2	1	2	4	1	3	0	3	1	1	1	3	1
Own Rec. for TD	0	0	0	0	0	0	0	0	0	0	0	0	0	0
Opp. Rec. by	10	15	16	20	18	21	18	13	18	12	16	20	21	19
Opp. Rec. for TD	1	0	0	3	1	1	1	1	0	1	0	0	0	1
Total Points Scored	452	198	333	366	355	277	359	401	283	310	414	263	448	312
Total TDs	57	23	40	40	43	30	39	48	33	39	47	26	50	35
TDs Rushing	24	6	18	19	17	9	16	19	9	17	11	10	28	11
TDs Passing	32	16	20	16	22	19	20	26	20	18	34	11	18	19
TDs on Ret. and Rec.	1	1	2	5	4	2	3	3	4	4	2	5	4	5
Extra Points	55	22	37	40	41	28	38	48	31	37	46	24	50	34
Safeties	2	1	1	1	4	0	0	1	0	0	1	1	1	1
Field Goals Made	17	12	18	28	16	23	29	21	18	13	28	27	32	22
Field Goals Attempted	23	19	27	36	31	29	37	28	21	29	38	35	43	28
% Successful	73.9	63.2	66.7	77.8	51.6	79.3	78.4	75.0	85.7	44.8	73.7	77.1	74.4	78.6

AFC, NFC, AND NFL SUMMARY

	AFC Offense Total	AFC Offense Average	AFC Defense Total	AFC Defense Average	NFC Offense Total	NFC Offense Average	NFC Defense Total	NFC Defense Average	NFL Total	NFL Average
First Downs	4317	308.4	4340	310.0	4276	305.4	4253	303.8	8593	306.9
Rushing	1536	109.7	1574	112.4	1623	115.9	1585	113.2	3159	112.8
Passing	2441	174.4	2416	172.6	2324	166.0	2349	167.8	4765	170.2
Penalty	340	24.3	350	25.0	329	23.5	319	22.8	669	23.9
Rushes	6834	488.1	6924	494.6	6802	485.9	6712	479.4	13,636	487.0
Net Yds. Gained	27,545	1967.5	28,130	2009.3	28,424	2030.3	27,839	1988.5	55,969	1998.9
Avg. Gain	—	4.0	—	4.1	—	4.2	—	4.1	—	4.1
Avg. Yds. per Game	—	123.0	—	125.6	—	126.9	—	124.3	—	124.9
Passes Attempted	7312	522.3	7198	514.1	7111	507.9	7225	516.1	14,423	515.1
Completed	4009	286.4	3949	282.1	3902	278.7	3962	283.0	7911	282.5
% Completed	—	54.8	—	54.9	—	54.9	—	54.8	—	54.8
Total Yds. Gained	51,927	3709.1	51,236	3659.7	49,591	3542.2	50,282	3591.6	101,518	3625.6
Times Sacked	581	41.5	610	43.6	725	51.8	696	49.7	1306	46.6
Yds. Lost	4487	320.5	4674	333.9	5409	386.4	5222	373.0	9896	353.4
Net Yds. Gained	47,440	3388.6	46,562	3325.9	44,182	3155.9	45,060	3218.6	91,622	3272.2
Avg. Yds. per Game	—	211.8	—	207.9	—	197.2	—	201.2	—	204.5
Net Yds. per Pass Play	—	6.01	—	5.98	—	5.64	—	5.69	—	5.83
Yds. Gained per Comp.	—	12.95	—	12.97	—	12.71	—	12.69	—	12.83
Combined Net Yds. Gained	74,985	5356.1	74,692	5335.1	72,606	5186.1	72,899	5207.1	147,591	5271.1
% Total Yds. Rushing	—	36.7	—	37.7	—	39.1	—	38.2	—	37.9
% Total Yds. Passing	—	63.3	—	62.3	—	60.9	—	61.8	—	62.1
Avg. Yds. per Game	—	334.8	—	333.4	—	324.1	—	325.4	—	329.4
Ball Control Plays	14,727	1051.9	14,732	1052.3	14,638	1045.6	14,633	1045.2	29,365	1048.8
Avg. Yds. per Play	—	5.1	—	5.1	—	5.0	—	5.0	—	5.0
Third Down Efficiency	—	38.2	—	37.8	—	37.0	—	37.4	—	37.6
Interceptions	300	21.4	294	21.0	302	21.6	308	22.0	602	21.5
Yds. Returned	3791	270.8	3567	254.8	3530	252.1	3754	268.1	7321	261.5
Returned for TD	18	1.3	17	1.2	23	1.6	24	1.7	41	1.5
Punts	1141	81.5	1156	82.6	1138	81.3	1123	80.2	2279	81.4
Yds. Punted	47,077	3362.6	47,471	3390.8	47,195	3371.1	46,801	3342.9	94,272	3366.9
Avg. Yds. per Punt	—	41.3	—	41.1	—	41.5	—	41.7	—	41.4
Punt Returns	596	42.6	572	40.9	542	38.7	566	40.4	1138	40.6
Yds. Returned	5640	402.9	5543	395.9	4925	351.8	5022	358.7	10,565	377.3
Avg. Yds. per Return	—	9.5	—	9.7	—	9.1	—	8.9	—	9.3
Returned for TD	6	0.4	6	0.4	2	0.1	2	0.1	8	0.3
Kickoff Returns	843	60.2	840	60.0	889	63.5	892	63.7	1732	61.9
Yds. Returned	17,642	1260.1	17,498	1249.9	18,721	1337.2	18,865	1347.5	36,363	1298.7
Avg. Yds. per Return	—	20.9	—	20.8	—	21.1	—	21.1	—	21.0
Returned for TD	1	0.1	1	0.1	7	0.5	7	0.5	8	0.3
Penalties	1440	102.9	1382	98.7	1377	98.4	1435	102.5	2817	100.6
Yds. Penalized	11,461	818.6	11,210	800.7	11,132	795.1	11,383	813.1	22,593	806.9
Fumbles	464	33.1	463	33.1	428	30.6	429	30.6	892	31.9
Lost	229	16.4	231	16.5	238	17.0	236	16.9	467	16.7
Out of Bounds	30	2.1	34	2.4	27	1.9	23	1.6	57	2.0
Own Rec. for TD	1	0.1	2	0.1	1	0.1	0	0.0	2	0.1
Opp. Rec.	231	16.5	229	16.4	235	16.8	237	16.9	466	16.6
Opp. Rec. for TD	9	0.6	8	0.6	9	0.6	10	0.7	18	0.6
Total Points Scored	4961	354.4	4874	348.1	4684	334.6	4771	340.8	9645	344.5
Total TDs	586	41.9	575	41.1	539	38.5	550	39.3	1125	40.2
TDs Rushing	227	16.2	229	16.4	216	15.4	214	15.3	443	15.8
TDs Passing	320	22.9	307	21.9	278	19.9	291	20.8	598	21.4
TDs on Ret. and Rec.	39	2.8	39	2.8	45	3.2	45	3.2	84	3.0
Extra Points	555	39.6	542	38.7	518	37.0	531	37.9	1073	38.3
Safeties	7	0.5	3	0.2	10	0.7	14	1.0	17	0.6
Field Goals Made	292	20.9	292	20.9	304	21.7	304	21.7	596	21.3
Field Goals Attempted	404	28.9	402	28.7	422	30.1	424	30.3	826	29.5
% Successful	—	72.3	—	72.6	—	72.0	—	71.7	—	72.2

CLUB LEADERS

	Offense	Defense
First Downs	S.D. 380	Chi. 236
Rushing	Chi. 176	Raiders 73
Passing	S.D. 259	Wash. 134
Penalty	Den. & T.B. 34	Ind. 14
Rushes	Chi. 610	Chi. 359
Net Yds. Gained	Chi. 2761	Chi. 1319
Avg. Gain	Ind. 5.0	Raiders 3.5
Passes Attempted	S.D. 632	St. L. 461
Completed	S.D. 386	Wash. 239
% Completed	S.D. 61.1	Chi. 47.7
Total Yds. Gained	S.D. 5175	Pitt. 3088
Times Sacked	Mia. 19	Giants 68
Yds. Lost	Mia. 164	Giants 539
Net Yds. Gained	S.D. 4870	Wash. 2746
Net Yds. per Pass Play	S.D. 7.26	Giants 4.71
Yds. Gained per Comp.	K.C. 13.96	Pitt. 10.76
Combined Net Yds. Gained	S.D. 6535	Chi. 4135
% Total Yds. Rushing	Atl. 49.7	S.D. 31.5
% Total Yds. Passing	S.D. 74.5	Det. 52.0
Ball Control Plays	Den. 1152	Wash. 941
Avg. Yds. per Play	S.D. 5.9	Giants 4.2
Avg. Time of Poss.	Chi. 34:33	—
Third Down Efficiency	Mia. 45.6	Giants 28.9
Interceptions	—	Chi. 34
Yds. Returned	—	Chi. 512
Returned for TD	—	Chi., Dall., & Rams 4
Punts	K.C. 95	—
Yds. Punted	N.E. 3953	—
Avg. Yds. per Punt	Ind. 44.8	—
Punt Returns	Raiders 71	Chi. 23
Yds. Returned	Raiders 785	Raiders 159
Avg. Yds. per Return	Rams 13.2	Raiders 6.1
Returned for TD	N.E. & Pitt. 2	—
Kickoff Returns	T.B. 80	Hou. 39
Yds. Returned	T.B. 1622	Buff. 798
Avg. Yds. per Return	Chi. 25.3	Clev. 17.3
Returned for TD	Rams 3	—
Total Points Scored	S.D. 467	Chi. 198
Total TDs	S.D. 60	Chi. 23
TDs Rushing	Chi. 27	Chi. 6
TDs Passing	S.D. 37	S.F. 11
TDs on Ret. and Rec.	Rams 8	Six with 1
Extra Points	S.D. 53	Chi. 22
Safeties	Chi. 3	—
Field Goals Made	Pitt. 33	Buff. & Chi. 12
Field Goals Attempted	Pitt. 42	Buff. 15
% Successful	K.C. 88.9	G.B. 51.6

NATIONAL FOOTBALL LEAGUE CLUB RANKINGS BY YARDS

	Offense			Defense		
Team	**Total**	**Rush**	**Pass**	**Total**	**Rush**	**Pass**
Atlanta	20	3	27	25	17	27
Buffalo	25	24	21	17	26	11
Chicago	7	*1	20	*1	*1	3
Cincinnati	3	12	4	22	15	24
Cleveland	21	8	25	9	10	12
Dallas	8	17	3	20	11	26
Denver	10	16	6	13	14	14
Detroit	28	26	22	18	27	5
Green Bay	12	11	15	12	16	13
Houston	24	25	19	27	28	18
Indianapolis	19	5	26	19	18	19
Kansas City	22	28	11	21	20	20
Los Angeles Raiders	11	9	16	4	5	7
Los Angeles Rams	26	14	28	5	4	10
Miami	6	18	2	23	23	22
Minnesota	16	27	7	16	22	15
New England	9	6	14	7	6	9
New Orleans	27	19	24	24	19	23
New York Giants	5	4	10	2	2	4
New York Jets	4	7	9	8	3	16
Philadelphia	15	23	8	10	21	6
Pittsburgh	13	13	13	6	12	2
St. Louis	17	15	18	15	24	8
San Diego	*1	20	*1	28	13	28
San Francisco	2	10	5	14	7	21
Seattle	18	21t	12	11	9	17
Tampa Bay	23	21t	17	26	25	25
Washington	14	2	23	3	8	*1

t—Tie for position

**—League leader*

1985 TEAM & INDIVIDUAL STATISTICS

SCORING

POINTS

Kickers

NFC: 144—Kevin Butler, Chicago
AFC: 139—Gary Anderson, Pittsburgh

Non-kickers

NFC: 126—Joe Morris, New York Giants
AFC: 90—Louis Lipps, Pittsburgh

TOUCHDOWNS

NFC: 21—Joe Morris, New York Giants
AFC: 15—Louis Lipps, Pittsburgh

EXTRA POINTS

NFC: 52—Ray Wersching, San Francisco
AFC: 51—Bob Thomas, San Diego

FIELD GOALS

AFC: 42—Gary Anderson, Pittsburgh
NFC: 37—Kevin Butler, Chicago

MOST POINTS, GAME

AFC: 24—Daryl Turner, Seattle vs. San Diego, September 15 (4 TD)
NFC: 24—Jimmie Giles, Tampa Bay vs. Miami, October 20 (4 TD)

TEAM LEADERS

AFC: BUFFALO: 62, Scott Norwood; CINCINNATI: 120, Jim Breech; CLEVELAND: 77, Matt Bahr; DENVER: 110, Rich Karlis; HOUSTON: 92, Tony Zendejas; INDIANAPOLIS: 84, Raul Allegre; KANSAS CITY: 107, Nick Lowery; LOS ANGELES RAIDERS: 100, Chris Bahr; MIAMI: 116, Fuad Reveiz; NEW ENGLAND: 112, Tony Franklin; NEW YORK JETS: 121, Pat Leahy; PITTSBURGH: 139, Gary Anderson; SAN DIEGO: 105, Bob Thomas; SEATTLE: 82, Norm Johnson.

NFC: ATLANTA: 101, Mick Luckhurst; CHICAGO: 144, Kevin Butler; DALLAS: 99, Rafael Septien; DETROIT: 109, Ed Murray; GREEN BAY: 95, Al Del Greco; LOS ANGELES RAMS: 104, Mike Lansford; MINNESOTA: 86, Jan Stenerud; NEW ORLEANS: 120, Morten Andersen; NEW YORK GIANTS: 126, Joe Morris; PHILADELPHIA: 104, Paul McFadden; ST. LOUIS: 60, Stump Mitchell; SAN FRANCISCO: 91, Ray Wersching; TAMPA BAY: 96, Donald Igwebuike; WASHINGTON: 97, Mark Moseley.

TEAM CHAMPIONS

AFC: 467—San Diego
NFC: 456—Chicago

AFC SCORING—TEAM

	TD	TDR	TDP	TD Misc.	PAT	PAT Att.	FG	FG Att.	SAF	TP
San Diego	60	20	37	3	53	59	18	28	0	467
Cincinnati	53	20	31	2	49	53	24	33	1	441
Miami	52	19	31	2	50	52	22	27	0	428
N.Y. Jets	45	18	25	2	43	45	26	34	1	393
Denver	45	20	23	2	41	44	23	38	0	380
Pittsburgh	40	14	23	3	40	40	33	42	0	379
New England	41	15	20	6	40	41	24	30	2	362
L.A. Raiders	42	18	20	4	40	42	20	32	1	354
Seattle	44	9	28	7	41	44	14	25	1	349
Indianapolis	39	22	15	2	36	39	16	26	1	320
Kansas City	35	10	23	2	35	35	24	27	0	317
Cleveland	35	16	17	2	35	35	14	18	0	287
Houston	32	13	18	1	29	32	21	27	0	284
Buffalo	23	13	9	1	23	23	13	17	0	200
AFC Total	586	227	320	39	555	584	292	404	7	4961
AFC Average	41.9	16.2	22.9	2.8	39.6	41.7	20.9	28.9	0.5	354.4

NFC SCORING—TEAM

	TD	TDR	TDP	TD Misc.	PAT	PAT Att.	FG	FG Att.	SAF	TP
Chicago	51	27	17	7	51	51	31	37	3	456
San Francisco	53	20	28	5	52	53	13	21	1	411
N.Y. Giants	48	24	22	2	45	47	22	33	0	399
Dallas	43	11	27	5	42	43	19	28	0	357
Minnesota	43	19	22	2	41	43	15	26	1	346
L.A. Rams	39	15	16	8	38	39	22	29	1	340
Green Bay	40	16	21	3	38	40	19	26	1	337
Detroit	33	13	19	1	31	33	26	31	0	307
Washington	33	20	13	0	31	33	22	35	1	297
New Orleans	29	4	20	5	27	29	31	35	0	294
Tampa Bay	33	11	22	0	30	33	22	32	0	294
Philadelphia	30	8	19	3	29	29	25	30	1	286
Atlanta	30	14	13	3	30	30	24	31	0	282
St. Louis	34	14	19	1	33	34	13	28	1	278
NFC Total	539	216	278	45	518	537	304	422	10	4684
NFC Average	38.5	15.4	19.9	3.2	37.0	38.4	21.7	30.1	0.7	334.6
League Total	1125	443	598	84	1073	1121	596	826	17	9645
League Avg.	40.2	15.8	21.4	3.0	38.3	40.0	21.3	29.5	0.6	344.5

NFL TOP 10 SCORERS—TOUCHDOWNS

	TD	TDR	TDP	TD Misc.	TP
Morris, Joe, N.Y. Giants	21	21	0	0	126
Craig, Roger, San Francisco	15	9	6	0	90
Lipps, Louis, Pittsburgh	15	1	12	2	90
Allen, Marcus, L.A. Raiders	14	11	3	0	84
Davenport, Ron, Miami	13	11	2	0	78
Turner, Daryl, Seattle	13	0	13	0	78
Brooks, James, Cincinnati	12	7	5	0	72
Dickerson, Eric, L.A. Rams	12	12	0	0	72
Payton, Walter, Chicago	11	9	2	0	66
Quick, Mike, Philadelphia	11	0	11	0	66

NFL TOP 10 SCORERS—KICKING

	PAT	PAT Att.	FG	FG Att.	TP
Butler, Kevin, Chicago	51	51	31	37	144
Anderson, Gary, Pittsburgh	40	40	33	42	139
Leahy, Pat, N.Y. Jets	43	45	26	34	121
Andersen, Morten, New Orleans	27	29	31	35	120
Breech, Jim, Cincinnati	48	50	24	33	120
Reveiz, Fuad, Miami	50	52	22	27	116
Franklin, Tony, New England	40	41	24	30	112
Karlis, Rich, Denver	41	44	23	38	110
Murray, Ed, Detroit	31	33	26	31	109
Lowery, Nick, Kansas City	35	35	24	27	107

AFC SCORING—INDIVIDUAL

KICKERS	PAT	PAT Att.	FG	FG Att.	TP
Anderson, Gary, Pittsburgh	40	40	33	42	139
Leahy, Pat, N.Y. Jets	43	45	26	34	121
Breech, Jim, Cincinnati	48	50	24	33	120
Reveiz, Fuad, Miami	50	52	22	27	116
Franklin, Tony, New England	40	41	24	30	112
Karlis, Rich, Denver	41	44	23	38	110
Lowery, Nick, Kansas City	35	35	24	27	107
Thomas, Bob, San Diego	51	55	18	28	105
Bahr, Chris, L.A. Raiders	40	42	20	32	100
Zendejas, Tony, Houston	29	31	21	27	92
Allegre, Raul, Indianapolis	36	39	16	26	84
Johnson, Norm, Seattle	40	41	14	25	82
Bahr, Matt, Cleveland	35	35	14	18	77
Norwood, Scott, Buffalo	23	23	13	17	62
Benirschke, Rolf, San Diego	2	2	0	0	2

NON-KICKERS	TD	TDR	TDP	TD Misc.	TP
Lipps, Louis, Pittsburgh	15	1	12	2	90
Allen, Marcus, L.A. Raiders	14	11	3	0	84
Davenport, Ron, Miami	13	11	2	0	78
Turner, Daryl, Seattle	13	0	13	0	78
Brooks, James, Cincinnati	12	7	5	0	72
Byner, Earnest, Cleveland	10	8	2	0	60
Chandler, Wes, San Diego	10	0	10	0	60
Fryar, Irving, New England	10	1	7	2	60
Kinnebrew, Larry, Cincinnati	10	9	1	0	60
Mack, Kevin, Cleveland	10	7	3	0	60
Paige, Stephone, Kansas City	10	0	10	0	60
Paige, Tony, N.Y. Jets	10	8	2	0	60
Spencer, Tim, San Diego	10	10	0	0	60
Abercrombie, Walter, Pittsburgh	9	7	2	0	54
Bell, Greg, Buffalo	9	8	1	0	54
Hill, Drew, Houston	9	0	9	0	54
Warner, Curt, Seattle	9	8	1	0	54
Brown, Eddie, Cincinnati	8	0	8	0	48
James, Lionel, San Diego	8	2	6	0	48
Rozier, Mike, Houston	8	8	0	0	48
Winder, Sammy, Denver	8	8	0	0	48
Anderson, Gary, San Diego	7	4	2	1	42
Holman, Rodney, Cincinnati	7	0	7	0	42
James, Craig, New England	7	5	2	0	42
Joiner, Charlie, San Diego	7	0	7	0	42
Lang, Gene, Denver	7	5	2	0	42
McMillan, Randy, Indianapolis	7	7	0	0	42
Moore, Nat, Miami	7	0	7	0	42
Shuler, Mickey, N.Y. Jets	7	0	7	0	42
Largent, Steve, Seattle	6	0	6	0	#37
Beach, Pat, Indianapolis	6	0	6	0	36
Christensen, Todd, L.A. Raiders	6	0	6	0	36
Heard, Herman, Kansas City	6	4	2	0	36
Hector, Johnny, N.Y. Jets	6	6	0	0	36
Nathan, Tony, Miami	6	5	1	0	36
Sievers, Eric, San Diego	6	0	6	0	36
Wonsley, George, Indianapolis	6	6	0	0	36

	TD	TDR	TDP	TD Misc.	TP
Walker, Wesley, N.Y. Jets	5	0	5	0	*32
Capers, Wayne, Indianapolis	5	1	4	0	30
Collins, Tony, New England	5	3	2	0	30
Collinsworth, Cris, Cincinnati	5	0	5	0	30
Hester, Jessie, L.A. Raiders	5	1	4	0	30
McNeil, Freeman, N.Y. Jets	5	3	2	0	30
Morgan, Stanley, New England	5	0	5	0	30
Newsome, Ozzie, Cleveland	5	0	5	0	30
Reed, Andre, Buffalo	5	1	4	0	30
Sewell, Steve, Denver	5	4	1	0	30
Stallworth, John, Pittsburgh	5	0	5	0	30
Watson, Steve, Denver	5	0	5	0	30
Williams, Dokie, L.A. Raiders	5	0	5	0	30
Woolfolk, Butch, Houston	5	1	4	0	30
Carson, Carlos, Kansas City	4	0	4	0	24
Clayton, Mark, Miami	4	0	4	0	24
Hardy, Bruce, Miami	4	0	4	0	24
Hawkins, Frank, L.A. Raiders	4	4	0	0	24
Horton, Ethan, Kansas City	4	3	1	0	24
Jennings, Stanford, Cincinnati	4	1	3	0	24
Rose, Joe, Miami	4	0	4	0	24
Sampson, Clinton, Denver	4	0	4	0	24
Sohn, Kurt, N.Y. Jets	4	0	4	0	24
Willhite, Gerald, Denver	4	3	1	0	24
Duper, Mark, Miami	3	0	3	0	18
Erenberg, Rich, Pittsburgh	3	0	3	0	18
Hampton, Lorenzo, Miami	3	3	0	0	18
Holohan, Pete, San Diego	3	0	3	0	18
Johnson, Butch, Denver	3	0	3	0	18
Johnson, Dan, Miami	3	0	3	0	18
Johnson, Vance, Denver	3	0	3	0	18
Jones, Cedric, New England	3	0	2	1	18
Kay, Clarence, Denver	3	0	3	0	18
McGee, Buford, San Diego	3	3	0	0	18
Moriarty, Larry, Houston	3	3	0	0	18
Pollard, Frank, Pittsburgh	3	3	0	0	18
Toon, Al, N.Y. Jets	3	0	3	0	18
Walker, Byron, Seattle	3	0	2	1	18
Weathers, Clarence, Cleveland	3	0	3	0	18
Alexander, Charles, Cincinnati	2	2	0	0	12
Banks, Fred, Cleveland	2	0	2	0	12
Bendross, Jesse, San Diego	2	0	2	0	12
Bentley, Albert, Indianapolis	2	2	0	0	12
Bouza, Matt, Indianapolis	2	0	2	0	12
Butler, Jerry, Buffalo	2	0	2	0	12
Butler, Raymond, Indianapolis	2	0	2	0	12
Gill, Owen, Indianapolis	2	2	0	0	12
Green, Jacob, Seattle	2	0	0	2	12
Grogan, Steve, New England	2	2	0	0	12
Hancock, Anthony, Kansas City	2	0	2	0	12
Klever, Rocky, N.Y. Jets	2	0	2	0	12
Pagel, Mike, Indianapolis	2	2	0	0	12
Pruitt, Mike, Kansas City	2	2	0	0	12
Ross, Dan, Seattle	2	0	2	0	12
Smith, Jeff, Kansas City	2	0	2	0	12
Smith, Tim, Houston	2	0	2	0	12
Tatupu, Mosi, New England	2	2	0	0	12
Taylor, Terry, Seattle	2	0	0	2	12
Wilson, Marc, L.A. Raiders	2	2	0	0	12
Woodley, David, Pittsburgh	2	2	0	0	12
Young, Charle, Seattle	2	0	2	0	12
Alzado, Lyle, L.A. Raiders	1	0	0	1	*8
Kreider, Steve, Cincinnati	1	0	1	0	#7
Adams, Curtis, San Diego	1	1	0	0	6
Akiu, Mike, Houston	1	0	0	1	6
Arnold, Walt, Kansas City	1	0	1	0	6
Baldwin, Tom, N.Y. Jets	1	0	0	1	6
Bennett, Woody, Miami	1	0	1	0	6
Bligen, Dennis, N.Y. Jets	1	1	0	0	6
Brennan, Brian, Cleveland	1	0	0	1	6
Brown, Dave, Seattle	1	0	0	1	6
Brudzinski, Bob, Miami	1	0	0	1	6
Cherry, Deron, Kansas City	1	0	0	1	6
Clayborn, Ray, New England	1	0	0	1	6
Cribbs, Joe, Buffalo	1	1	0	0	6
Dale, Jeffery, San Diego	1	0	0	1	6
Dressel, Chris, Houston	1	0	1	0	6
Eason, Tony, New England	1	1	0	0	6
Edwards, Stan, Houston	1	1	0	0	6
Esiason, Boomer, Cincinnati	1	1	0	0	6
Ferragamo, Vince, Buffalo	1	1	0	0	6
Glenn, Kerry, N.Y. Jets	1	0	0	1	6
Greene, Danny, Seattle	1	0	1	0	6
Griffin, James, Cincinnati	1	0	0	1	6
Gross, Al, Cleveland	1	0	0	1	6
Harden, Mike, Denver	1	0	0	1	6
Harris, M.L., Cincinnati	1	0	1	0	6
Hawthorne, Greg, New England	1	0	1	0	6
Hayes, Jonathan, Kansas City	1	0	1	0	6
Hayes, Lester, L.A. Raiders	1	0	0	1	6
Heflin, Vince, Miami	1	0	1	0	6
Hendy, John, San Diego	1	0	0	1	6
Holt, Harry, Cleveland	1	0	1	0	6
Jackson, Robert, Cincinnati	1	0	0	1	6
Jensen, Jim, Miami	1	0	1	0	6
Johnson, Trumaine, San Diego	1	0	1	0	6
Judson, William, Miami	1	0	0	1	6
Junkin, Trey, L.A. Raiders	1	0	1	0	6
Kenney, Bill, Kansas City	1	1	0	0	6
Kofler, Matt, Indianapolis	1	1	0	0	6
Kosar, Bernie, Cleveland	1	1	0	0	6
Krieg, Dave, Seattle	1	1	0	0	6
Lewis, Albert, Kansas City	1	0	0	1	6
Malone, Mark, Pittsburgh	1	1	0	0	6
Martin, Robbie, Indianapolis	1	0	0	1	6
Mathison, Bruce, Buffalo	1	1	0	0	6
McCloskey, Mike, Houston	1	0	1	0	6
Merriman, Sam, Seattle	1	0	0	1	6
Merriweather, Mike, Pittsburgh	1	0	0	1	6
Metzelaars, Pete, Buffalo	1	0	1	0	6
Middleton, Frank, Indianapolis	1	1	0	0	6
Moore, Booker, Buffalo	1	1	0	0	6
Ramsey, Derrick, New England	1	0	1	0	6
Ramson, Eason, Buffalo	1	0	1	0	6
Rembert, Johnny, New England	1	0	0	1	6
Seale, Sam, L.A. Raiders	1	0	0	1	6
Skansi, Paul, Seattle	1	0	1	0	6
Smith, Jim, L.A. Raiders	1	0	1	0	6
Thompson, Weegie, Pittsburgh	1	0	1	0	6
Tippett, Andre, New England	1	0	0	1	6
Toran, Stacey, L.A. Raiders	1	0	0	1	6
Weathers, Robert, New England	1	1	0	0	6
Williams, Jamie, Houston	1	0	1	0	6
Williams, Oliver, Indianapolis	1	0	1	0	6
Wilson, Don, Buffalo	1	0	0	1	6
Wright, James, Denver	1	0	1	0	6
Wright, Louis, Denver	1	0	0	1	6
Young, Anthony, Indianapolis	1	0	0	1	6
Young, Glen, Cleveland	1	0	1	0	6
Blackmon, Don, New England	0	0	0	0	**4
Browner, Ross, Cincinnati	0	0	0	0	*2
Randle, Tate, Indianapolis	0	0	0	0	*2

***indicates two safeties scored*
**indicates safety (also team safety for Seattle)*
#indicates extra point scored.

NFC SCORING—INDIVIDUAL

KICKERS	PAT	PAT Att.	FG	FG Att.	TP
Butler, Kevin, Chicago	51	51	31	37	144
Andersen, Morten, New Orleans	27	29	31	35	120
Murray, Ed, Detroit	31	33	26	31	109
Lansford, Mike, L.A. Rams	38	39	22	29	104
McFadden, Paul, Philadelphia	29	29	25	30	104
Luckhurst, Mick, Atlanta	29	29	24	31	101
Septien, Rafael, Dallas	42	43	19	28	99
Moseley, Mark, Washington	31	33	22	34	97
Igwebuike, Donald, Tampa Bay	30	32	22	32	96
Del Greco, Al, Green Bay	38	40	19	26	95
Wersching, Ray, San Francisco	52	53	13	21	91
Stenerud, Jan, Minnesota	41	43	15	26	86
Schubert, Eric, N.Y. Giants	26	27	10	13	56
Atkinson, Jess, NYG-StL.	17	18	10	18	t-53
O'Donoghue, Neil, St. Louis	19	19	10	18	49
Bojovic, Novo, St. Louis	11	12	3	7	20
Haji-Sheikh, Ali, N.Y. Giants	5	5	2	5	11

t indicates touchdown scored

NON-KICKERS	TD	TDR	TDP	TD Misc.	TP
Morris, Joe, N.Y. Giants	21	21	0	0	126
Craig, Roger, San Francisco	15	9	6	0	90
Dickerson, Eric, L.A. Rams	12	12	0	0	72
Payton, Walter, Chicago	11	9	2	0	66
Quick, Mike, Philadelphia	11	0	11	0	66
Brown, Ted, Minnesota	10	7	3	0	60
Clark, Dwight, San Francisco	10	0	10	0	60
Dorsett, Tony, Dallas	10	7	3	0	60
Mitchell, Stump, St. Louis	10	7	3	0	60
Riggs, Gerald, Atlanta	10	10	0	0	60
Wilder, James, Tampa Bay	10	10	0	0	60
Jones, James, Detroit	9	6	3	0	54
Carter, Anthony, Minnesota	8	0	8	0	48
Giles, Jimmie, Tampa Bay	8	0	8	0	48
Johnson, Bobby, N.Y. Giants	8	0	8	0	48
Renfro, Mike, Dallas	8	0	8	0	48
Riggins, John, Washington	8	8	0	0	48
Tyler, Wendell, San Francisco	8	6	2	0	48

	TD	TDR	TDP	TD Misc.	TP
Clark, Jessie, Green Bay	7	5	2	0	42
Hill, Tony, Dallas	7	0	7	0	42
McKinnon, Dennis, Chicago	7	0	7	0	42
Rogers, George, Washington	7	7	0	0	42
Brown, Ron, L.A. Rams	6	0	3	3	36
Coffman, Paul, Green Bay	6	0	6	0	36
Cosbie, Doug, Dallas	6	0	6	0	36
Ellard, Henry, L.A. Rams	6	0	5	1	36
Jackson, Earnest, Philadelphia	6	5	1	0	36
Nelson, Darrin, Minnesota	6	5	1	0	36
Tilley, Pat, St. Louis	6	0	6	0	36
Anderson, Alfred, Minnesota	5	4	1	0	30
Clark, Gary, Washington	5	0	5	0	30
Ellis, Gerry, Green Bay	5	5	0	0	30
Fuller, Steve, Chicago	5	5	0	0	30
Green, Roy, St. Louis	5	0	5	0	30
House, Kevin, Tampa Bay	5	0	5	0	30
Johnson, Billy, Atlanta	5	0	5	0	30
Manuel, Lionel, N.Y. Giants	5	0	5	0	30
Moore, Alvin, Detroit	5	4	1	0	30
Spagnola, John, Philadelphia	5	0	5	0	30
Thompson, Leonard, Detroit	5	0	5	0	30
Adams, George, N.Y. Giants	4	2	2	0	24
Anderson, Ottis, St. Louis	4	4	0	0	24
Bavaro, Mark, N.Y. Giants	4	0	4	0	24
Didier, Clint, Washington	4	0	4	0	24
Epps, Phillip, Green Bay	4	1	3	0	24
Ferrell, Earl, St. Louis	4	2	2	0	24
Hunter, Tony, L.A. Rams	4	0	4	0	24
Ivery, Eddie Lee, Green Bay	4	2	2	0	24
Jones, Mike, Minnesota	4	0	4	0	24
Lofton, James, Green Bay	4	0	4	0	24
Martin, Eric, New Orleans	4	0	4	0	24
McMahon, Jim, Chicago	4	3	1	0	24
Nichols, Mark, Detroit	4	0	4	0	24
Rice, Allen, Minnesota	4	3	1	0	24
Rice, Jerry, San Francisco	4	1	3	0	24
Thomas, Calvin, Chicago	4	4	0	0	24
Brenner, Hoby, New Orleans	3	0	3	0	18
Carter, Gerald, Tampa Bay	3	0	3	0	18
Chadwick, Jeff, Detroit	3	0	3	0	18
Duckworth, Bobby, L.A. Rams	3	0	3	0	18
Francis, Russ, San Francisco	3	0	3	0	18
Gentry, Dennis, Chicago	3	2	0	1	18
Goodlow, Eugene, New Orleans	3	0	3	0	18
Griffin, Keith, Washington	3	3	0	0	18
Lewis, David, Detroit	3	0	3	0	18
Lewis, Leo, Minnesota	3	0	3	0	18
Magee, Calvin, Tampa Bay	3	0	3	0	18
Montana, Joe, San Francisco	3	3	0	0	18
Newsome, Tim, Dallas	3	2	1	0	18
Perry, William, Chicago	3	2	1	0	18
White, Charles, L.A. Rams	3	3	0	0	18
Wilson, Wayne, New Orleans	3	1	2	0	18
Allen, Anthony, Atlanta	2	0	2	0	12
Archer, David, Atlanta	2	2	0	0	12
Bell, Jerry, Tampa Bay	2	0	2	0	12
Brown, Charlie, Atlanta	2	0	2	0	12
Cox, Arthur, Atlanta	2	0	2	0	12
Dennard, Preston, Green Bay	2	0	2	0	12
Ellerson, Gary, Green Bay	2	2	0	0	12
Gajan, Hokie, New Orleans	2	2	0	0	12
Gault, Willie, Chicago	2	0	1	1	12
Groth, Jeff, New Orleans	2	0	2	0	12
Hardy, Larry, New Orleans	2	0	2	0	12
Hipple, Eric, Detroit	2	2	0	0	12
Hunter, Herman, Philadelphia	2	1	1	0	12
Jaworski, Ron, Philadelphia	2	2	0	0	12
Margerum, Ken, Chicago	2	0	2	0	12
Monk, Art, Washington	2	0	2	0	12
Suhey, Matt, Chicago	2	1	1	0	12
Theismann, Joe, Washington	2	2	0	0	12
Tice, John, New Orleans	2	0	2	0	12
Warren, Frank, New Orleans	2	0	0	2	12
Washington, Joe, Atlanta	2	1	1	0	12
White, Danny, Dallas	2	1	1	0	12
Wilson, Mike, San Francisco	2	0	2	0	12
Wilson, Otis, Chicago	1	0	0	1	*8
Armstrong, Adger, Tampa Bay	1	0	1	0	6
Austin, Cliff, Atlanta	1	0	0	1	6
Browner, Joey, Minnesota	1	0	0	1	6
Campbell, Earl, New Orleans	1	1	0	0	6
Cornwell, Fred, Dallas	1	0	1	0	6
Del Rio, Jack, New Orleans	1	0	0	1	6
Dent, Richard, Chicago	1	0	0	1	6
Dickey, Lynn, Green Bay	1	1	0	0	6
Douglass, Mike, Green Bay	1	0	0	1	6
Duncan, Clyde, St. Louis	1	0	1	0	6
Edwards, Herman, Philadelphia	1	0	0	1	6
Ekern, Carl, L.A. Rams	1	0	0	1	6
Ferguson, Joe, Detroit	1	1	0	0	6
Frank, John, San Francisco	1	0	1	0	6
Frazier, Leslie, Chicago	1	0	0	1	6
Galbreath, Tony, N.Y. Giants	1	0	1	0	6
Gann, Mike, Atlanta	1	0	0	1	6
Green, Gary, L.A. Rams	1	0	0	1	6
Harrington, Perry, St. Louis	1	1	0	0	6
Hasselbeck, Don, N.Y. Giants	1	0	1	0	6
Hebert, Bobby, New Orleans	1	0	1	0	6
Hill, David, L.A. Rams	1	0	1	0	6
Hoage, Terry, New Orleans	1	0	0	1	6
Hogeboom, Gary, Dallas	1	1	0	0	6
Holly, Bob, Atlanta	1	1	0	0	6
Hopkins, Wes, Philadelphia	1	0	0	1	6
Irvin, LeRoy, L.A. Rams	1	0	0	1	6
Jackson, Kenny, Philadelphia	1	0	1	0	6
Jeffcoat, Jim, Dallas	1	0	0	1	6
Johnson, Johnnie, L.A. Rams	1	0	0	1	6
Lewis, Tim, Green Bay	1	0	0	1	6
Little, David, Philadelphia	1	0	0	1	6
Lockhart, Eugene, Dallas	1	0	0	1	6
Mandley, Pete, Detroit	1	0	0	1	6
Marsh, Doug, St. Louis	1	0	1	0	6
Martin, George, N.Y. Giants	1	0	0	1	6
Matthews, Allama, Atlanta	1	0	1	0	6
McColl, Milt, San Francisco	1	0	0	1	6
McConkey, Phil, N.Y. Giants	1	0	1	0	6
McIntyre, Guy, San Francisco	1	0	0	1	6
Merkens, Guido, New Orleans	1	0	1	0	6
Monroe, Carl, San Francisco	1	0	0	1	6
Moore, Blake, Green Bay	1	0	1	0	6
Moorehead, Emery, Chicago	1	0	1	0	6
Muhammad, Calvin, Washington	1	0	1	0	6
Mularkey, Mike, Minnesota	1	0	1	0	6
Murphy, Mark, Green Bay	1	0	0	1	6
Patterson, Elvis, N.Y. Giants	1	0	0	1	6
Penn, Jesse, Dallas	1	0	0	1	6
Poe, Johnnie, New Orleans	1	0	0	1	6
Rade, John, Atlanta	1	0	0	1	6
Richardson, Mike, Chicago	1	0	0	1	6
Ring, Bill, San Francisco	1	1	0	0	6
Rivera, Ron, Chicago	1	0	0	1	6
Sanders, Thomas, Chicago	1	1	0	0	6
Scott, Victor, Dallas	1	0	0	1	6
Smith, J.T., St. Louis	1	0	1	0	6
Solomon, Freddie, San Francisco	1	0	1	0	6
Teal, Willie, Minnesota	1	0	0	1	6
Thurman, Dennis, Dallas	1	0	0	1	6
Turner, Keena, San Francisco	1	0	0	1	6
Warren, Don, Washington	1	0	1	0	6
Washington, Lionel, St. Louis	1	0	0	1	6
West, Ed, Green Bay	1	0	1	0	6
Williamson, Carlton, San Francisco	1	0	0	1	6
Wrightman, Tim, Chicago	1	0	1	0	6
Young, Steve, Tampa Bay	1	1	0	0	6
Brown, Robert, Green Bay	0	0	0	0	*2
Doss, Reggie, L.A. Rams	0	0	0	0	*2
Elshire, Neil, Minnesota	0	0	0	0	*2
Harty, John, San Francisco	0	0	0	0	*2
McMichael, Steve, Chicago	0	0	0	0	*2
Waechter, Henry, Chicago	0	0	0	0	*2
Bryan, Rick, Atlanta	0	0	0	0	#1

**indicates safety scored (also team safeties for Philadelphia, St. Louis, and Washington)*
#indicates extra point scored

FIELD GOALS

BEST PERCENTAGE
AFC: .889—Nick Lowery, Kansas City
NFC: .886—Morten Andersen, New Orleans
MADE
AFC: 33—Gary Anderson, Pittsburgh
NFC: 31—Morten Andersen, New Orleans
31—Kevin Butler, Chicago
ATTEMPTS
AFC: 42—Gary Anderson, Pittsburgh
NFC: 37—Kevin Butler, Chicago
LONGEST
AFC: 58—Nick Lowery, Kansas City vs. Los Angeles Raiders, September 12
NFC: 55—Morten Andersen, New Orleans vs. Denver, September 15
AVERAGE YARDS MADE
AFC: 38.3—Nick Lowery, Kansas City
NFC: 38.1—Morten Andersen, New Orleans

AFC FIELD GOALS—TEAM

	Made	Att.	Pct.	Long
Kansas City	24	27	.889	58
Miami	22	27	.815	49
New England	24	30	.800	50
Pittsburgh	33	42	.786	52
Cleveland	14	18	.778	45
Houston	21	27	.778	52
Buffalo	13	17	.765	49
New York Jets	26	34	.765	55
Cincinnati	24	33	.727	53
San Diego	18	28	.643	46
Los Angeles Raiders	20	32	.625	51
Indianapolis	16	26	.615	41
Denver	23	38	.605	48
Seattle	14	25	.560	51
AFC Totals	292	404	—	58
AFC Average	20.9	28.9	.723	—

NFC FIELD GOALS—TEAM

	Made	Att.	Pct.	Long
New Orleans	31	35	.886	55
Detroit	26	31	.839	51
Chicago	31	37	.838	46
Philadelphia	25	30	.833	52
Atlanta	24	31	.774	52
Los Angeles Rams	22	29	.759	52
Green Bay	19	26	.731	46
Tampa Bay	22	32	.688	53
Dallas	19	28	.679	53
New York Giants	22	33	.667	52
Washington	22	35	.629	48
San Francisco	13	21	.619	45
Minnesota	15	26	.577	49
St. Louis	13	28	.464	49
NFC Totals	304	422	—	55
NFC Average	21.7	30.1	.720	—
League Totals	596	826	—	58
League Average	21.3	29.5	.722	—

AFC FIELD GOALS—INDIVIDUAL

	1-19	20-29	30-39	40-49	50 & Over	Totals	Avg. Yds. Att.	Avg. Yds. Made	Avg. Yds. Miss	Long
Lowery, Nick	0-0	4-4	10-11	7-7	3-5	24-27	39.1	38.3	45.7	58
Kansas City	—	1.000	.909	1.000	.600	.889				
Reveiz, Fuad	0-0	8-9	5-6	9-9	0-3	22-27	36.1	34.6	42.8	49
Miami	—	.889	.833	1.000	.000	.815				
Franklin, Tony	1-1	7-9	9-9	5-9	2-2	24-30	34.9	34.2	37.5	50
New England	1.000	.778	1.000	.556	1.000	.800				
Anderson, Gary	1-1	12-13	14-15	5-9	1-4	33-42	35.1	32.8	43.4	52
Pittsburgh	1.000	.923	.933	.556	.250	.786				
Bahr, Matt	1-1	2-2	8-9	3-5	0-1	14-18	35.6	33.2	44.0	45
Cleveland	1.000	1.000	.875	.600	.000	.778				
Zendejas, Tony	0-0	6-7	8-11	4-6	3-3	21-27	36.7	37.0	35.8	52
Houston	—	.857	.727	.667	1.000	.778				
Leahy, Pat	2-2	11-11	6-8	4-8	3-5	26-34	35.1	32.1	44.9	55
N.Y. Jets	1.000	1.000	.750	.500	.600	.765				
Norwood, Scott	0-0	7-8	2-4	4-5	0-0	13-17	33.8	33.2	36.0	49
Buffalo	—	.875	.500	.800	—	.765				
Breech, Jim	0-0	7-8	12-13	4-6	1-6	24-33	37.5	34.2	46.3	53
Cincinnati	—	.875	.923	.667	.167	.727				
Thomas, Bob	1-1	8-8	6-10	3-7	0-2	18-28	34.1	30.6	40.5	46
San Diego	1.000	1.000	.600	.429	.000	.643				
Bahr, Chris	0-0	9-9	7-10	3-12	1-1	20-32	36.1	32.0	43.1	51
L.A. Raiders	—	1.000	.700	.250	1.000	.625				
Allegre, Raul	0-0	9-11	5-6	2-6	0-3	16-26	34.9	30.2	42.5	41
Indianapolis	—	.818	.833	.333	.000	.615				
Karlis, Rich	2-2	7-9	6-11	8-11	0-5	23-38	36.8	33.1	42.3	48
Denver	1.000	.778	.545	.727	.000	.605				
Johnson, Norm	0-0	5-5	7-9	1-8	1-3	14-25	38.9	33.6	45.7	51
Seattle	—	1.000	.778	.125	.333	.560				
AFC Totals	8-8	102-113	105-132	62-108	15-43	292-404	36.1	33.6	42.5	58
	1.000	.903	.795	.574	.349	.723				
League Totals	17-18	193-221	218-274	138-233	30-80	596-826	36.2	34.0	41.8	58
	.944	.873	.796	.592	.375	.722				

NFC FIELD GOALS — INDIVIDUAL

	1-19	20-29	30-39	40-49	50 & Over	Totals	Avg. Yds. Att.	Avg. Yds. Made	Avg. Yds. Miss	Long
Andersen, Morten	0-0	4-5	13-14	11-12	3-4	31-35	38.4	38.1	40.5	55
New Orleans	—	.800	.929	.917	.750	.886				
Murray, Ed	2-2	5-8	11-11	6-7	2-3	26-31	35.3	35.2	35.8	51
Detroit	1.000	.625	1.000	.857	.667	.839				
Butler, Kevin	2-2	13-13	13-14	3-6	0-2	31-37	32.6	29.8	46.8	46
Chicago	1.000	1.000	.929	.500	.000	.838				
McFadden, Paul	0-0	6-6	11-11	6-8	2-5	25-30	37.9	35.8	48.6	52
Philadelphia	—	1.000	1.000	.750	.400	.833				
Luckhurst, Mick	0-0	7-9	8-10	8-11	1-1	24-31	36.9	36.8	37.3	52
Atlanta	—	.778	.800	.727	1.000	.774				
Lansford, Mike	0-0	5-5	9-12	6-8	2-4	22-29	36.8	35.8	40.0	52
L.A. Rams	—	1.000	.750	.750	.500	.759				
Del Greco, Al	0-0	10-12	4-4	5-9	0-1	19-26	34.0	32.3	38.9	46
Green Bay	—	.833	1.000	.556	.000	.731				
Igwebuike, Donald	1-1	5-5	8-10	5-10	3-6	22-32	39.9	36.4	47.6	53
Tampa Bay	1.000	1.000	.800	.500	.500	.688				
Septien, Rafael	1-1	5-5	8-11	4-9	1-2	19-28	37.4	34.9	42.7	53
Dallas	1.000	1.000	.727	.444	.500	.679				
Moseley, Mark	0-0	7-8	8-13	7-12	0-1	22-34	36.2	34.5	39.4	48
Washington	—	.875	.615	.583	.000	.647				
Wersching, Ray	0-0	5-7	5-8	3-5	0-1	13-21	34.1	32.6	36.5	45
San Francisco	—	.714	.625	.600	.000	.619				
Stenerud, Jan	1-2	10-11	3-7	1-5	0-1	15-26	32.2	27.6	38.5	49
Minnesota	.500	.909	.429	.200	.000	.577				
Atkinson, Jess	1-1	2-3	3-4	4-9	0-1	10-18	38.8	35.8	42.6	49
N.Y. Giants-St. Louis	1.000	.667	.750	.444	.000	.556				
O'Donoghue, Neil	1-1	3-5	4-6	2-4	0-2	10-18	35.3	31.7	39.8	49
St. Louis	1.000	.600	.667	.500	.000	.556				
Non-Qualifiers (Fewer than 16 attempts)										
Schubert, Eric	0-0	3-5	4-5	3-3	0-0	10-13	32.5	33.4	29.7	41
N.Y. Giants	—	.600	.800	1.000	—	.769				
Bojovic, Novo	0-0	0-0	1-2	2-3	0-2	3-7	44.0	40.0	47.0	42
St. Louis	—	—	.500	.667	.000	.429				
Haji-Sheikh, Ali	0-0	1-1	0-0	0-3	1-1	2-5	43.2	37.5	47.0	52
N.Y. Giants	—	1.000	—	.000	1.000	.400				
Cox, Steve	0-0	0-0	0-0	0-1	0-0	0-1	48.0	—	48.0	—
Washington	—	—	—	.000	—	.000				
NFC Totals	9-10	91-108	113-142	76-125	15-37	304-422	36.3	34.4	41.1	55
	.900	.843	.796	.608	.405	.720				
League Totals	17-18	193-221	218-274	138-233	30-80	596-826	36.2	34.0	41.8	58
	.944	.873	.796	.592	.375	.722				

RUSHING

INDIVIDUAL CHAMPIONS

AFC: 1,759—Marcus Allen, Los Angeles Raiders
NFC: 1,719—Gerald Riggs, Atlanta

ATTEMPTS

NFC: 397—Gerald Riggs, Atlanta
AFC: 380—Marcus Allen, Los Angeles Raiders

MOST ATTEMPTS, GAME

NFC: 41—Gerald Riggs, Atlanta vs. Los Angeles Rams, November 17 (123 yards)
AFC: 31—Marcus Allen, Los Angeles Raiders vs. Cincinnati, November 17 (135 yards)

YARDS PER ATTEMPT

NFC: 5.5—Stump Mitchell, St. Louis
AFC: 5.2—George Wonsley, Indianapolis

MOST YARDS, GAME

NFC: 206—George Rogers, Washington vs. St. Louis, December 21, (34 attempts)
AFC: 192—Freeman McNeil, New York Jets vs. Buffalo, September 15 (18 attempts)

LONGEST

NFC: 80 yards—Jessie Clark, Green Bay vs. St. Louis, September 29
AFC: 77 yards—Greg Bell, Buffalo vs. Pittsburgh, December 15 (TD)

TOUCHDOWNS

NFC: 21—Joe Morris, New York Giants
AFC: 11—Marcus Allen, Los Angeles Raiders
11—Ron Davenport, Miami

TEAM LEADERS

AFC: BUFFALO: 883, Greg Bell; CINCINNATI: 929, James Brooks; CLEVELAND: 1104, Kevin Mack; DENVER: 714, Sammy Winder; HOUSTON: 462, Mike Rozier; INDIANAPOLIS: 858, Randy McMillan; KANSAS CITY: 595, Herman Heard; LOS ANGELES RAIDERS: 1759, Marcus Allen; MIAMI: 667, Tony Nathan; NEW ENGLAND: 1227, Craig James; NEW YORK JETS: 1331, Freeman McNeil; PITTSBURGH: 991, Frank Pollard; SAN DIEGO: 516, Lionel James; SEATTLE: 1094, Curt Warner.
NFC: ATLANTA: 1719, Gerald Riggs; CHICAGO: 1551, Walter Payton; DALLAS: 1307, Tony Dorsett; DETROIT: 886, James Jones; GREEN BAY: 636, Eddie Lee Ivery; LOS ANGELES RAMS: 1234, Eric Dickerson; MINNESOTA: 893, Darrin Nelson; NEW ORLEANS: 645, Wayne Wilson; NEW YORK GIANTS: 1336, Joe Morris; PHILADELPHIA: 1028, Earnest Jackson; ST. LOUIS: 1006, Stump Mitchell; SAN FRANCISCO: 1050, Roger Craig; TAMPA BAY: 1300, James Wilder; WASHINGTON: 1093, George Rogers.

TEAM CHAMPIONS

NFC: 2,761—Chicago
AFC: 2,439—Indianapolis

AFC RUSHING—TEAM

	Att.	Yards	Avg.	Long	TD
Indianapolis	485	2439	5.0	67	22
New England	565	2331	4.1	65t	15
New York Jets	564	2312	4.1	69	18
Cleveland	533	2285	4.3	61	16
Los Angeles Raiders	532	2262	4.3	61t	18
Cincinnati	503	2183	4.3	39	20
Pittsburgh	541	2177	4.0	56	14
Denver	497	1851	3.7	42	20
Miami	444	1729	3.9	33	19
San Diego	440	1665	3.8	56t	20
Seattle	462	1644	3.6	38	9
Buffalo	412	1611	3.9	77t	13
Houston	428	1570	3.7	43	13
Kansas City	428	1486	3.5	54	10
AFC Total	6834	27,545	—	77t	227
AFC Average	488.1	1967.5	4.0	—	16.2

NFC RUSHING—TEAM

	Att.	Yards	Avg.	Long	TD
Chicago	610	2761	4.5	40t	27
Washington	571	2523	4.4	66t	20
Atlanta	560	2466	4.4	50	14
New York Giants	581	2451	4.2	65t	24
San Francisco	477	2232	4.7	62t	20
Green Bay	470	2208	4.7	80	16
Los Angeles Rams	503	2057	4.1	43	15
St. Louis	417	1974	4.7	64	14
Dallas	462	1741	3.8	60t	11
New Orleans	431	1683	3.9	45	4
Tampa Bay	434	1644	3.8	28	11
Philadelphia	428	1630	3.8	74t	8
Detroit	452	1538	3.4	29	13
Minnesota	406	1516	3.7	37	19
NFC Total	6802	28,424	—	80	216
NFC Average	485.9	2030.3	4.2	—	15.4
League Total	13,636	55,969	—	80	443
League Average	487.0	1998.9	4.1	—	15.8

NFL TOP 10 RUSHERS

	Att.	Yards	Avg.	Long	TD
Allen, Marcus, L.A. Raiders	380	1759	4.6	61t	11
Riggs, Gerald, Atlanta	397	1719	4.3	50	10
Payton, Walter, Chicago	324	1551	4.8	40t	9
Morris, Joe, N.Y.Giants	294	1336	4.5	65t	21
McNeil, Freeman, N.Y. Jets	294	1331	4.5	69	3
Dorsett, Tony, Dallas	305	1307	4.3	60t	7
Wilder, James, Tampa Bay	365	1300	3.6	28	10
Dickerson, Eric, L.A. Rams	292	1234	4.2	43	12
James, Craig, New England	263	1227	4.7	65t	5
Mack, Kevin, Cleveland	222	1104	5.0	61	7

AFC RUSHING—INDIVIDUAL

	Att.	Yards	Avg.	Long	TD
Allen, Marcus, L.A. Raiders	380	1759	4.6	61t	11
McNeil, Freeman, N.Y. Jets	294	1331	4.5	69	3
James, Craig, New England	263	1227	4.7	65t	5
Mack, Kevin, Cleveland	222	1104	5.0	61	7
Warner, Curt, Seattle	291	1094	3.8	38	8
Byner, Earnest, Cleveland	244	1002	4.1	36	8
Pollard, Frank, Pittsburgh	233	991	4.3	56	3
Brooks, James, Cincinnati	192	929	4.8	39	7
Bell, Greg, Buffalo	223	883	4.0	77t	8
McMillan, Randy, Indianapolis	190	858	4.5	38	7
Abercrombie, Walter, Pittsburgh	227	851	3.7	32t	7
Wonsley, George, Indianapolis	138	716	5.2	36	6
Kinnebrew, Larry, Cincinnati	170	714	4.2	29	9
Winder, Sammy, Denver	199	714	3.6	42	8
Nathan, Tony, Miami	143	667	4.7	22	5
Collins, Tony, New England	163	657	4.0	28	3
Heard, Herman, Kansas City	164	595	3.6	33	4
Hector, Johnny, N.Y. Jets	145	572	3.9	22	6
James, Lionel, San Diego	105	516	4.9	56t	2
Spencer, Tim, San Diego	124	478	3.9	24	10
Rozier, Mike, Houston	133	462	3.5	30	8
Anderson, Gary, San Diego	116	429	3.7	27	4
Cribbs, Joe, Buffalo	122	399	3.3	16	1
Woolfolk, Butch, Houston	103	392	3.8	43	1
Pruitt, Mike, Buffalo-Kansas City	112	390	3.5	54	2
Moriarty, Larry, Houston	106	381	3.6	18	3
Davenport, Ron, Miami	98	370	3.8	33	11
Hampton, Lorenzo, Miami	105	369	3.5	15	3
Lang, Gene, Denver	84	318	3.8	26	5
Bentley, Albert, Indianapolis	54	288	5.3	26t	2
Sewell, Steve, Denver	81	275	3.4	16	4
Hawkins, Frank, L.A. Raiders	84	269	3.2	21t	4
Gill, Owen, Indianapolis	45	262	5.8	67	2
Bennett, Woody, Miami	54	256	4.7	17	0
Elway, John, Denver	51	253	5.0	22	0
Willhite, Gerald, Denver	66	237	3.6	14	3
Morris, Randall, Seattle	55	236	4.3	21	0
Mathison, Bruce, Buffalo	27	231	8.6	22	1
McGee, Buford, San Diego	42	181	4.3	44	3
Weathers, Robert, New England	41	174	4.2	42t	1
Pagel, Mike, Indianapolis	25	160	6.4	29	2
Paige, Tony, N.Y. Jets	55	158	2.9	30	8
Alexander, Charles, Cincinnati	44	156	3.5	18	2
Tatupu, Mosi, New England	47	152	3.2	11	2
Horton, Ethan, Kansas City	48	146	3.0	19t	3
Moon, Warren, Houston	39	130	3.3	17	0
Brown, Eddie, Cincinnati	14	129	9.2	35	0
Hughes, David, Seattle	40	128	3.2	9	0
Danielson, Gary, Cleveland	25	126	5.0	28	0
Krieg, Dave, Seattle	35	121	3.5	17	1
Smith, Jeff, Kansas City	30	118	3.9	27	0
Bligen, Dennis, N.Y. Jets	22	107	4.9	28t	1
Wilson, Marc, L.A. Raiders	24	98	4.1	17	2
Blackledge, Todd, Kansas City	17	97	5.7	25	0
Edwards, Stan, Houston	25	96	3.8	19	1
Luck, Oliver, Houston	15	95	6.3	17	0
Jennings, Stanford, Cincinnati	31	92	3.0	19	1
King, Bruce, Kansas City	28	83	3.0	9	0
Malone, Mark, Pittsburgh	15	80	5.3	25	1
Esiason, Boomer, Cincinnati	33	79	2.4	20	1
Carter, Joe, Miami	14	76	5.4	19	0
Woodley, David, Pittsburgh	17	71	4.2	13	2
Eason, Tony, New England	22	70	3.2	23	1
Erenberg, Rich, Pittsburgh	17	67	3.9	12	0
King, Kenny, L.A. Raiders	16	67	4.2	19	0
O'Brien, Ken, N.Y. Jets	25	58	2.3	22	0
Spencer, Todd, Pittsburgh	13	56	4.3	11	0
Adams, Curtis, San Diego	16	49	3.1	14	1
Johnson, Bill, Cincinnati	8	44	5.5	15	0
Barber, Marion, N.Y. Jets	9	41	4.6	10	0
Dickey, Curtis, Ind.-Clev.	11	40	3.6	11	0
Schonert, Turk, Cincinnati	8	39	4.9	17	0
Steels, Anthony, S.D.-Buff.	10	38	3.8	22	0
Johnson, Vance, Denver	10	36	3.6	14	0
Jensen, Derrick, L.A. Raiders	16	35	2.2	8	0
Middleton, Frank, Indianapolis	13	35	2.7	13	1
Kofler, Matt, Indianapolis	4	33	8.3	23	1
Allen, Greg, Cleveland	8	32	4.0	8	0
Lane, Eric, Seattle	14	32	2.3	12	0
Grogan, Steve, New England	20	29	1.5	12	2
Campbell, Scott, Pittsburgh	9	28	3.1	14	0
Fryar, Irving, New England	7	27	3.9	13	1
Carson, Carlos, Kansas City	3	25	8.3	13	0
Martin, Robbie, Indianapolis	1	23	23.0	23	0
Minter, Cedric, N.Y. Jets	8	23	2.9	11	0
Moore, Booker, Buffalo	15	23	1.5	4	1
Lacy, Ken, Kansas City	6	21	3.5	6	0
Jones, E.J., Kansas City	12	19	1.6	7	0
Parros, Rick, Seattle	8	19	2.4	6	0
Capers, Wayne, Indianapolis	3	18	6.0	20t	1
Weathers, Clarence, Cleveland	1	18	18.0	18	0
Morse, Steve, Pittsburgh	8	17	2.1	9	0
Lipps, Louis, Pittsburgh	2	16	8.0	15t	1
Tasker, Steve, Houston	2	16	8.0	13	0
Ferragamo, Vince, Buffalo	8	15	1.9	5	1
Paige, Stephone, Kansas City	1	15	15.0	15	0
Hester, Jessie, L.A. Raiders	1	13	13.0	13t	1
Schlichter, Art, Indianapolis	2	13	6.5	9	0
Plunkett, Jim, L.A. Raiders	5	12	2.4	7	0
Poole, Nathan, Denver	4	12	3.0	6	0
Sohn, Kurt, N.Y. Jets	1	12	12.0	12	0
Hutchison, Anthony, Buffalo	2	11	5.5	7	0
Moore, Nat, Miami	1	11	11.0	11	0
Clayton, Mark, Miami	1	10	10.0	10	0
Humphery, Bobby, N.Y. Jets	1	10	10.0	10	0
Chandler, Wes, San Diego	1	9	9.0	9	0
Davis, Johnny, Cleveland	4	9	2.3	5	0
Hilger, Rusty, L.A. Raiders	3	8	2.7	4	0
Kubiak, Gary, Denver	1	6	6.0	6	0
Franklin, Byron, Seattle	1	5	5.0	5	0
Hardy, Andre, Seattle	5	5	1.0	4	0
Toon, Al, N.Y. Jets	1	5	5.0	5	0
Gilbert, Gale, Seattle	7	4	0.6	8	0
Collinsworth, Cris, Cincinnati	1	3	3.0	3	0
Moroski, Mike, Houston	2	2	1.0	2	0
Williams, Eugene, Seattle	1	2	2.0	2	0
Kenney, Bill, Kansas City	14	1	0.1	5	1
Strachan, Steve, L.A. Raiders	2	1	0.5	1	0
Anderson, Ken, Cincinnati	1	0	0.0	0	0
Baab, Mike, Cleveland	1	0	0.0	0	0
Doornink, Dan, Seattle	4	0	0.0	3	0
Guy, Ray, L.A. Raiders	1	0	0.0	0	0
Johnson, Lee, Houston	1	0	0.0	0	0
Mojsiejenko, Ralf, San Diego	1	0	0.0	0	0
Morgan, Stanley, New England	1	0	0.0	0	0
Norman, Chris, Denver	1	0	0.0	0	0
Smith, Bruce, Buffalo	1	0	0.0	0	0
Butler, Raymond, Indianapolis	1	−1	−1.0	−1	0
Fouts, Dan, San Diego	11	−1	−0.1	7	0
Reed, Andre, Buffalo	3	−1	−0.3	14t	1
Finzer, David, Seattle	1	−2	−2.0	−2	0
McInally, Pat, Cincinnati	1	−2	−2.0	−2	0
Drewrey, Willie, Houston	2	−4	−2.0	5	0
Franklin, Tony, New England	1	−5	−5.0	−5	0
Ryan, Pat, N.Y. Jets	3	−5	−1.7	−1	0
Strock, Don, Miami	2	−6	−3.0	−3	0
Herrmann, Mark, San Diego	18	−8	−0.4	11	0
Kosar, Bernie, Cleveland	26	−12	−0.5	10	1
Marino, Dan, Miami	26	−24	−0.9	6	0

t indicates touchdown
Leader based on most yards gained.

NFC RUSHING—INDIVIDUAL

	Att.	Yards	Avg.	Long	TD
Riggs, Gerald, Atlanta	397	1719	4.3	50	10
Payton, Walter, Chicago	324	1551	4.8	40t	9
Morris, Joe, N.Y. Giants	294	1336	4.5	65t	21
Dorsett, Tony, Dallas	305	1307	4.3	60t	7
Wilder, James, Tampa Bay	365	1300	3.6	28	10
Dickerson, Eric, L.A. Rams	292	1234	4.2	43	12
Rogers, George, Washington	231	1093	4.7	35	7
Craig, Roger, San Francisco	214	1050	4.9	62t	9
Jackson, Earnest, Philadelphia	282	1028	3.6	59	5
Mitchell, Stump, St. Louis	183	1006	5.5	64	7
Nelson, Darrin, Minnesota	200	893	4.5	37	5
Jones, James, Detroit	244	886	3.6	29	6
Tyler, Wendell, San Francisco	171	867	5.1	30	6
Riggins, John, Washington	176	677	3.8	51	8
Wilson, Wayne, New Orleans	168	645	3.8	41t	1
Campbell, Earl, New Orleans	158	643	4.1	45	1

	Att.	Yards	Avg.	Long	TD
Ivery, Eddie Lee, Green Bay	132	636	4.8	34	2
Clark, Jessie, Green Bay	147	633	4.3	80	5
Ellis, Gerry, Green Bay	104	571	5.5	39t	5
Adams, George, N.Y. Giants	128	498	3.9	39	2
Anderson, Ottis, St. Louis	117	479	4.1	38	4
Griffin, Keith, Washington	102	473	4.6	66t	3
Suhey, Matt, Chicago	115	471	4.1	17	1
Redden, Barry, L.A. Rams	87	380	4.4	41	0
Archer, David, Atlanta	70	347	5.0	29t	2
Brown, Ted, Minnesota	93	336	3.6	30	7
White, Charles, L.A. Rams	70	310	4.4	32	3
McMahon, Jim, Chicago	47	252	5.4	19	3
Newsome, Tim, Dallas	88	252	2.9	15	2
Gajan, Hokie, New Orleans	50	251	5.0	26	2
Montgomery, Wilbert, Detroit	75	251	3.3	22	0
Young, Steve, Tampa Bay	40	233	5.8	20	1
Moore, Alvin, Detroit	80	221	2.8	18	4
Haddix, Michael, Philadelphia	67	213	3.2	12	0
Washington, Joe, Atlanta	52	210	4.0	14	1
Ferrell, Earl, St. Louis	46	208	4.5	30	2
Cunningham, Randall, Phil.	29	205	7.1	37	0
Ellerson, Gary, Green Bay	32	205	6.4	37t	2
Carpenter, Rob, N.Y. Giants	60	201	3.4	46	0
Galbreath, Tony, N.Y. Giants	29	187	6.4	18	0
Gentry, Dennis, Chicago	30	160	5.3	21	2
Montana, Joe, San Francisco	42	153	3.6	16	3
Simms, Phil, N.Y. Giants	37	132	3.6	28	0
Lomax, Neil, St. Louis	32	125	3.9	23	0
Thomas, Calvin, Chicago	31	125	4.0	17	4
Anderson, Alfred, Minnesota	50	121	2.4	10	4
Hunter, Herman, Philadelphia	27	121	4.5	74t	1
Theismann, Joe, Washington	25	115	4.6	25	2
Austin, Cliff, Atlanta	20	110	5.5	17	0
Rice, Allen, Minnesota	31	104	3.4	15	3
Sanders, Thomas, Chicago	25	104	4.2	28	1
Epps, Phillip, Green Bay	5	103	20.6	34	1
Harmon, Derrick, San Francisco	28	92	3.3	17	0
Hipple, Eric, Detroit	32	89	2.8	26	2
Fuller, Steve, Chicago	24	77	3.2	13	5
Carthon, Maurice, N.Y. Giants	27	70	2.6	12	0
Anthony, Tyrone, New Orleans	17	65	3.8	13	0
Wolfley, Ron, St. Louis	24	64	2.7	11	0
Kramer, Tommy, Minnesota	27	54	2.0	11	0
Springs, Ron, Tampa Bay	16	54	3.4	11	0
Monk, Art, Washington	7	51	7.3	16	0
Hogeboom, Gary, Dallas	8	48	6.0	15	1
Pridemore, Tom, Atlanta	1	48	48.0	48	0
Cain, Lynn, L.A. Rams	11	46	4.2	9	0
Kane, Rick, Detroit	11	44	4.0	7	0
White, Danny, Dallas	22	44	2.0	21	1
Harrington, Perry, St. Louis	7	42	6.0	22	1
Wattelet, Frank, New Orleans	2	42	21.0	23	0
Huckleby, Harlan, Green Bay	8	41	5.1	15	0
Williams, John, Dallas	13	40	3.1	9	0
Jenkins, Ken, Washington	2	39	19.5	37	0
Brock, Dieter, L.A. Rams	20	38	1.9	13	0
Holly, Bob, Atlanta	3	36	12.0	20t	1
Smith, J. T., St. Louis	3	36	12.0	30	0
Jaworski, Ron, Philadelphia	17	35	2.1	31	2
Lavette, Robert, Dallas	13	34	2.6	10	0
Guman, Mike, L.A. Rams	11	32	2.9	6	0
Schroeder, Jay, Washington	17	30	1.8	14	0
DeBerg, Steve, Tampa Bay	9	28	3.1	13	0
Hebert, Bobby, New Orleans	12	26	2.2	8	0
Rice, Jerry, San Francisco	6	26	4.3	15t	1
Fowler, Todd, Dallas	7	25	3.6	6	0
Ring, Bill, San Francisco	8	23	2.9	9t	1
Gault, Willie, Chicago	5	18	3.6	11	0
Meade, Mike, Detroit	3	18	6.0	9	0
Williams, Byron, N.Y. Giants	2	18	9.0	17	0
Walker, Rick, Washington	3	16	5.3	9	0
Nichols, Mark, Detroit	1	15	15.0	15	0
Atkinson, Jess, N.Y. Giants	1	14	14.0	14t	1
Lofton, James, Green Bay	4	14	3.5	21	0
Brown, Ron, L.A. Rams	2	13	6.5	9	0
Carter, Gerald, Tampa Bay	1	13	13.0	13	0
Everett, Major, Philadelphia	4	13	3.3	8	0
Cooper, Earl, San Francisco	2	12	6.0	14	0
Ferguson, Joe, Detroit	4	12	3.0	15	1
Horan, Mike, Philadelphia	1	12	12.0	12	0
Clark, Gary, Washington	2	10	5.0	7	0
Risher, Alan, Tampa Bay	1	10	10.0	10	0
Bartkowski, Steve, Atlanta	5	9	1.8	5	0
Zorn, Jim, Green Bay	10	9	0.9	8	0
Brunner, Scott, St. Louis	3	8	2.7	8	0
Ellard, Henry, L.A. Rams	3	8	2.7	16	0
Wonsley, Otis, Washington	4	8	2.0	5	0
Wright, Randy, Green Bay	8	8	1.0	8	0
Perry, William, Chicago	5	7	1.4	2	2
Wilson, Dave, New Orleans	18	7	0.4	17	0
Armstrong, Adger, Tampa Bay	2	6	3.0	8	0
Green, Darrell, Washington	1	6	6.0	6	0
Jones, Mike, Minnesota	2	6	3.0	6	0
Cavanaugh, Matt, San Francisco	4	5	1.3	13	0
Warren, Don, Washington	1	5	5.0	5	0
Fowler, Bobby, New Orleans	2	4	2.0	3	0
Love, Randy, St. Louis	1	4	4.0	4	0
Solomon, Freddie, San Francisco	2	4	2.0	6	0
Goodlow, Eugene, New Orleans	1	3	3.0	3	0
Oliver, Hubert, Philadelphia	1	3	3.0	3	0
Tomczak, Mike, Chicago	2	3	1.5	3	0
Whisenhunt, Ken, Atlanta	1	3	3.0	3	0
Green, Roy, St. Louis	1	2	2.0	2	0
Jones, A. J., Detroit	1	2	2.0	2	0
Lewis, Leo, Minnesota	1	2	2.0	2	0
Rouson, Lee, N.Y. Giants	1	1	1.0	1	0
Black, Mike, Detroit	1	0	0.0	0	0
Coleman, Greg, Minnesota	2	0	0.0	0	0
Jones, James, Dallas	1	0	0.0	0	0
Kemp, Jeff, L.A. Rams	5	0	0.0	3	0
McKinnon, Dennis, Chicago	1	0	0.0	0	0
Prather, Guy, Green Bay	1	0	0.0	0	0
West, Ed, Green Bay	1	0	0.0	0	0
Banks, Gordon, Dallas	1	−1	−1.0	−1	0
Martin, Eric, New Orleans	2	−1	−0.5	11	0
Merkens, Guido, New Orleans	1	−2	−2.0	−2	0
Pelluer, Steve, Dallas	3	−2	−0.7	1	0
Bailey, Stacey, Atlanta	1	−3	−3.0	−3	0
Dils, Steve, L.A. Rams	2	−4	−2.0	−2	0
Donnelly, Rick, Atlanta	2	−5	−2.5	0	0
Hill, Tony, Dallas	1	−6	−6.0	−6	0
Rutledge, Jeff, N.Y. Giants	2	−6	−3.0	−2	0
Margerum, Ken, Chicago	1	−7	−7.0	−7	0
Johnson, Billy, Atlanta	8	−8	−1.0	6	0
Dickey, Lynn, Green Bay	18	−12	−0.7	3	1

t indicates touchdown
Leader based on most yards gained.

PASSING

INDIVIDUAL CHAMPIONS (RATING POINTS)
AFC: 96.2—Ken O'Brien, New York Jets
NFC: 91.3—Joe Montana, San Francisco
ATTEMPTS
AFC: 605—John Elway, Denver
NFC: 506—Tommy Kramer, Minnesota
COMPLETIONS
AFC: 336—Dan Marino, Miami
NFC: 303—Joe Montana, San Francisco
COMPLETION PERCENTAGE
NFC: 61.3—Joe Montana, San Francisco
AFC: 60.9—Ken O'Brien, New York Jets
YARDS
AFC: 4,137—Dan Marino, Miami
NFC: 3,829—Phil Simms, New York Giants
MOST YARDS, GAME
NFC: 513—Phil Simms, New York Giants vs. Cincinnati, October 13 (62 attempts, 40 completions)
AFC: 440—Dan Fouts, San Diego vs. Seattle, September 15 (43 attempts, 29 completions)
YARDS PER ATTEMPT
AFC: 8.46—Dan Fouts, San Diego
NFC: 7.74—Phil Simms, New York Giants
TOUCHDOWN PASSES
AFC: 30—Dan Marino, Miami
NFC: 27—Joe Montana, San Francisco
MOST TOUCHDOWNS, GAME
AFC: 5—Mark Malone, Pittsburgh vs. Indianapolis, September 8
5—Dave Krieg, Seattle vs. San Diego, September 15
5—Ken O'Brien, New York Jets vs. Tampa Bay, November 17
5—Dan Marino, Miami vs. Green Bay, December 8
NFC: 5—Joe Montana, San Francisco vs. Atlanta, October 6
LONGEST
NFC: 99 yards—Ron Jaworski (to Mike Quick), Philadelphia vs. Atlanta, November 10 (TD)
AFC: 96 yards—Ken O'Brien (to Wesley Walker), N.Y. Jets vs. Buffalo, December 8 (TD)
LOWEST PERCENTAGE INTERCEPTED
AFC: 1.6—Ken O'Brien, New York Jets
NFC: 2.5—Neil Lomax, St. Louis
TEAM CHAMPIONS
AFC: 4,870—San Diego
NFC: 3,861—Dallas

AFC PASSING—TEAM

	Att.	Comp.	Pct. Comp.	Gross Yards	Tkd.	Yards Lost	Net Yards	TD	Pct. TD	Long	Had Int.	Pct. Int.	Avg. Yds. Att.	Avg. Yds. Comp.
San Diego	632	386	61.1	5175	39	305	4870	37	5.9	75t	30	4.7	8.19	13.41
Miami	576	343	59.5	4278	19	164	4114	31	5.4	73	21	3.6	7.43	12.47
Cincinnati	518	302	58.3	4082	41	365	3717	31	6.0	71	13	2.5	7.88	13.52
Denver	617	329	53.3	3952	38	307	3645	23	3.7	65t	23	3.7	6.41	12.01
New York Jets	497	303	61.0	3983	62	399	3584	25	5.0	96t	8	1.6	8.01	13.15
Kansas City	511	267	52.3	3726	43	335	3391	23	4.5	84t	23	4.5	7.29	13.96
Seattle	575	304	52.9	3820	53	457	3363	28	4.9	54	23	4.0	6.64	12.57
Pittsburgh	512	254	49.6	3397	33	224	3173	23	4.5	69	27	5.3	6.63	13.37
New England	457	255	55.8	3483	39	315	3168	20	4.4	90t	22	4.8	7.62	13.66
Los Angeles Raiders	506	269	53.2	3481	43	335	3146	20	4.0	59	24	4.7	6.88	12.94
Houston	512	277	54.1	3523	58	441	3082	18	3.5	80t	22	4.3	6.88	12.72
Buffalo	517	263	50.9	3331	42	347	2984	9	1.7	60t	31	6.0	6.44	12.67
Cleveland	414	222	53.6	2885	36	249	2636	17	4.1	72t	13	3.1	6.97	13.00
Indianapolis	468	235	50.2	2811	35	244	2567	15	3.2	80t	20	4.3	6.01	11.96
AFC Total	7312	4009	—	51,927	581	4487	47,440	320	—	96t	300	—	—	—
AFC Average	522.3	286.4	54.8	3709.1	41.5	320.5	3388.6	22.9	4.4	—	21.4	4.1	7.10	12.95

NFC PASSING—TEAM

	Att.	Comp.	Pct. Comp.	Gross Yards	Tkd.	Yards Lost	Net Yards	TD	Pct. TD	Long	Had Int.	Pct. Int.	Avg. Yds. Att.	Avg. Yds. Comp.
Dallas	587	344	58.6	4236	44	375	3861	27	4.6	58t	25	4.3	7.22	12.31
San Francisco	550	331	60.2	3987	42	299	3688	28	5.1	73	14	2.5	7.25	12.05
Minnesota	576	311	54.0	3931	45	296	3635	22	3.8	57t	29	5.0	6.82	12.64
Philadelphia	567	290	51.1	4036	55	450	3586	19	3.4	99t	28	4.9	7.12	13.92
New York Giants	497	275	55.3	3829	52	396	3433	22	4.4	70t	20	4.0	7.70	13.92
Green Bay	513	267	52.0	3552	50	389	3163	21	4.1	63	27	5.3	6.92	13.30
Tampa Bay	508	269	53.0	3423	40	301	3122	22	4.3	59	26	5.1	6.74	12.72
St. Louis	534	296	55.4	3581	65	469	3112	19	3.6	47	18	3.4	6.71	12.10
Chicago	432	237	54.9	3303	43	227	3076	17	3.9	70t	16	3.7	7.65	13.94
Detroit	462	254	55.0	3316	53	378	2938	19	4.1	56	21	4.5	7.18	13.06
Washington	512	280	54.7	3243	52	428	2815	13	2.5	55	21	4.1	6.33	11.58
New Orleans	508	260	51.2	3257	58	461	2796	20	3.9	76t	23	4.5	6.41	12.53
Atlanta	462	254	55.0	3025	69	531	2494	13	2.8	62t	20	4.3	6.55	11.91
Los Angeles Rams	403	234	58.1	2872	57	409	2463	16	4.0	64t	14	3.5	7.13	12.27
NFC Total	7111	3902	—	49,591	725	5409	44,182	278	—	99t	302	—	—	—
NFC Average	507.9	278.7	54.9	3542.2	51.8	386.4	3155.9	19.9	3.9	—	21.6	4.2	6.97	12.71
League Total	14,423	7911	—	101,518	1306	9896	91,622	598	—	99t	602	—	—	—
League Average	515.1	282.5	54.8	3625.6	46.6	353.4	3272.2	21.4	4.1	—	21.5	4.2	7.04	12.83

Leader based on net yards.

NFL TOP 10 INDIVIDUAL QUALIFIERS

	Att.	Comp.	Pct. Comp.	Yards	Avg. Gain	TD	Pct. TD	Long	Int.	Pct. Int.	Rating Points
O'Brien, Ken, New York Jets	488	297	60.9	3888	7.97	25	5.1	96t	8	1.6	96.2
Esiason, Boomer, Cincinnati	431	251	58.2	3443	7.99	27	6.3	68t	12	2.8	93.2
Montana, Joe, San Francisco	494	303	61.3	3653	7.39	27	5.5	73	13	2.6	91.3
Fouts, Dan, San Diego	430	254	59.1	3638	8.46	27	6.3	75t	20	4.7	88.1
Marino, Dan, Miami	567	336	59.3	4137	7.30	30	5.3	73	21	3.7	84.1
Kenney, Bill, Kansas City	338	181	53.6	2536	7.50	17	5.0	84t	9	2.7	83.6
McMahon, Jim, Chicago	313	178	56.9	2392	7.64	15	4.8	70t	11	3.5	82.6
Brock, Dieter, Los Angeles Rams	365	218	59.7	2658	7.28	16	4.4	64t	13	3.6	82.0
White, Danny, Dallas	450	267	59.3	3157	7.02	21	4.7	56t	17	3.8	80.6
Lomax, Neil, St. Louis	471	265	56.3	3214	6.82	18	3.8	47	12	2.5	79.5

AFC PASSING—INDIVIDUAL QUALIFIERS

	Att.	Comp.	Pct. Comp.	Yards	Avg. Gain	TD	Pct. TD	Long	Int.	Pct. Int.	Rating Points
O'Brien, Ken, New York Jets	488	297	60.9	3888	7.97	25	5.1	96t	8	1.6	96.2
Esiason, Boomer, Cincinnati	431	251	58.2	3443	7.99	27	6.3	68t	12	2.8	93.2
Fouts, Dan, San Diego	430	254	59.1	3638	8.46	27	6.3	75t	20	4.7	88.1
Marino, Dan, Miami	567	336	59.3	4137	7.30	30	5.3	73	21	3.7	84.1
Kenney, Bill, Kansas City	338	181	53.6	2536	7.50	17	5.0	84t	9	2.7	83.6
Krieg, Dave, Seattle	532	285	53.6	3602	6.77	27	5.1	54	20	3.8	76.2
Malone, Mark, Pittsburgh	233	117	50.2	1428	6.13	13	5.6	45t	7	3.0	75.5
Elway, John, Denver	605	327	54.0	3891	6.43	22	3.6	65t	23	3.8	70.2
Kosar, Bernie, Cleveland	248	124	50.0	1578	6.36	8	3.2	68t	7	2.8	69.3
Moon, Warren, Houston	377	200	53.1	2709	7.19	15	4.0	80t	19	5.0	68.5
Eason, Tony, New England	299	168	56.2	2156	7.21	11	3.7	90t	17	5.7	67.5
Pagel, Mike, Indianapolis	393	199	50.6	2414	6.14	14	3.6	80t	15	3.8	65.8
Wilson, Marc, L.A. Raiders	388	193	49.7	2608	6.72	16	4.1	59	21	5.4	62.7
Mathison, Bruce, Buffalo	228	113	49.6	1635	7.17	4	1.8	60t	14	6.1	53.5
Ferragamo, Vince, Buffalo	287	149	51.9	1677	5.84	5	1.7	48	17	5.9	50.8

Non-Qualifiers	Att.	Comp.	Pct. Comp.	Yards	Avg. Gain	TD	Pct. TD	Long	Int.	Pct. Int.	Rating Points
Schonert, Turk, Cincinnati	51	33	64.7	460	9.02	1	2.0	71	0	0.0	100.1
Plunkett, Jim, Los Angeles Raiders	103	71	68.9	803	7.80	3	2.9	41t	3	2.9	89.6
Anderson, Ken, Cincinnati	32	16	50.0	170	5.31	2	6.3	44t	0	0.0	86.7
Danielson, Gary, Cleveland	163	97	59.5	1274	7.82	8	4.9	72t	6	3.7	85.3
Herrmann, Mark, San Diego	201	132	65.7	1537	7.65	10	5.0	59	10	5.0	84.5
Grogan, Steve, New England	156	85	54.5	1311	8.40	7	4.5	56	5	3.2	84.1
Moroski, Mike, Houston	34	20	58.8	249	7.32	1	2.9	46	1	2.9	79.2
Luck, Oliver, Houston	100	56	56.0	572	5.72	2	2.0	46t	2	2.0	70.9
Hilger, Rusty, Los Angeles Raiders	13	4	30.8	54	4.15	1	7.7	29	0	0.0	70.7
Woodley, David, Pittsburgh	183	94	51.4	1357	7.42	6	3.3	69	14	7.7	54.8
Campbell, Scott, Pittsburgh	96	43	44.8	612	6.38	4	4.2	51	6	6.3	53.8
Gilbert, Gale, Seattle	40	19	47.5	218	5.45	1	2.5	37t	2	5.0	51.9
Blackledge, Todd, Kansas City	172	86	50.0	1190	6.92	6	3.5	70t	14	8.1	50.3
Kofler, Matt, Indianapolis	48	23	47.9	284	5.92	1	2.1	33t	3	6.3	47.6
Schlichter, Art, Indianapolis	25	12	48.0	107	4.28	0	0.0	16	2	8.0	26.6
Fewer than 10 attempts											
Allen, Marcus, Los Angeles Raiders	2	1	50.0	16	8.00	0	0.0	16	0	0.0	77.1
Anderson, Gary, San Diego	0	0	—	0	—	0	—	0	0	—	0.0
Bell, Greg, Buffalo	1	0	0.0	0	0.00	0	0.0	0	0	0.0	39.6
Bentley, Albert, Indianapolis	1	1	100.0	6	6.00	0	0.0	6	0	0.0	91.7
Brennan, Brian, Cleveland	1	1	100.0	33	33.00	1	100.0	33t	0	0.0	158.3
Brooks, James, Cincinnati	1	1	100.0	8	8.00	1	100.0	8t	0	0.0	139.6
Brown, Eddie, Cincinnati	0	0	—	0	—	0	—	0	0	—	0.0
Clayton, Mark, Miami	0	0	—	0	—	0	—	0	0	—	0.0
Collinsworth, Cris, Cincinnati	1	0	0.0	0	0.00	0	0.0	0	1	100.0	0.0
Finzer, David, Seattle	1	0	0.0	0	0.00	0	0.0	0	1	100.0	0.0
Fontenot, Herman, Cleveland	1	0	0.0	0	0.00	0	0.0	0	0	0.0	39.6
Gossett, Jeff, Cleveland	1	0	0.0	0	0.00	0	0.0	0	0	0.0	39.6
Holohan, Pete, San Diego	1	0	0.0	0	0.00	0	0.0	0	0	0.0	39.6
Horton, Ethan, Kansas City	1	0	0.0	0	0.00	0	0.0	0	0	0.0	39.6
James, Craig, New England	2	2	100.0	16	8.00	2	100.0	11t	0	0.0	139.6
Johnson, Vance, Denver	1	0	0.0	0	0.00	0	0.0	0	0	0.0	39.6
Kidd, John, Buffalo	0	0	—	0	—	0	—	0	0	—	0.0
Kreider, Steve, Cincinnati	1	1	100.0	1	1.00	0	0.0	1	0	0.0	79.2
Kubiak, Gary, Denver	5	2	40.0	61	12.20	1	20.0	54t	0	0.0	125.8
Largent, Steve, Seattle	1	0	0.0	0	0.00	0	0.0	0	0	0.0	39.6
McInally, Pat, Cincinnati	1	0	0.0	0	0.00	0	0.0	0	0	0.0	39.6
Morris, Randall, Seattle	1	0	0.0	0	0.00	0	0.0	0	0	0.0	39.6
Norman, Chris, Denver	1	0	0.0	0	0.00	0	0.0	0	0	0.0	39.6
Reich, Frank, Buffalo	1	1	100.0	19	19.00	0	0.0	19	0	0.0	118.8
Ryan, Pat, New York Jets	9	6	66.7	95	10.56	0	0.0	50	0	0.0	101.6
Sewell, Steve, Denver	1	0	0.0	0	0.00	0	0.0	0	0	0.0	39.6
Stark, Rohn, Indianapolis	1	0	0.0	0	0.00	0	0.0	0	0	0.0	39.6
Strock, Don, Miami	9	7	77.8	141	15.67	1	11.1	67t	0	0.0	155.8
Willhite, Gerald, Denver	3	0	0.0	0	0.00	0	0.0	0	0	0.0	39.6
Winder, Sammy, Denver	1	0	0.0	0	0.00	0	0.0	0	0	0.0	39.6
Zendejas, Tony, Houston	1	1	100.0	−7	−7.00	0	0.0	−7	0	0.0	79.2

t indicates touchdown.
Leader based on rating points, minimum 224 attempts.

NFC PASSING—INDIVIDUAL QUALIFIERS

	Att.	Comp.	Pct. Comp.	Yards	Avg. Gain	TD	Pct. TD	Long	Int.	Pct. Int.	Rating Points
Montana, Joe, San Francisco	494	303	61.3	3653	7.39	27	5.5	73	13	2.6	91.3
McMahon, Jim, Chicago	313	178	56.9	2392	7.64	15	4.8	70t	11	3.5	82.6
Brock, Dieter, Los Angeles Rams	365	218	59.7	2658	7.28	16	4.4	64t	13	3.6	82.0
White, Danny, Dallas	450	267	59.3	3157	7.02	21	4.7	56t	17	3.8	80.6
Lomax, Neil, St. Louis	471	265	56.3	3214	6.82	18	3.8	47	12	2.5	79.5
Simms, Phil, New York Giants	495	275	55.6	3829	7.74	22	4.4	70t	20	4.0	78.6
Hipple, Eric, Detroit	406	223	54.9	2952	7.27	17	4.2	56	18	4.4	73.6
DeBerg, Steve, Tampa Bay	370	197	53.2	2488	6.72	19	5.1	57	18	4.9	71.3
Dickey, Lynn, Green Bay	314	172	54.8	2206	7.03	15	4.8	63	17	5.4	70.4
Jaworski, Ron, Philadelphia	484	255	52.7	3450	7.13	17	3.5	99t	20	4.1	70.2
Kramer, Tommy, Minnesota	506	277	54.7	3522	6.96	19	3.8	57t	26	5.1	67.8
Wilson, Dave, New Orleans	293	145	49.5	1843	6.29	11	3.8	50	15	5.1	60.7
Theismann, Joe, Washington	301	167	55.5	1774	5.89	8	2.7	55	16	5.3	59.6
Archer, David, Atlanta	312	161	51.6	1992	6.38	7	2.2	62t	17	5.4	56.5

Non-Qualifiers	Att.	Comp.	Pct. Comp.	Yards	Avg. Gain	TD	Pct. TD	Long	Int.	Pct. Int.	Rating Points
Bartkowski, Steve, Atlanta	111	69	62.2	738	6.65	5	4.5	62t	1	0.9	92.8
Hebert, Bobby, New Orleans	181	97	53.6	1208	6.67	5	2.8	76t	4	2.2	74.6
Schroeder, Jay, Washington	209	112	53.6	1458	6.98	5	2.4	53	5	2.4	73.8
Holly, Bob, Atlanta	39	24	61.5	295	7.56	1	2.6	44	2	5.1	72.1
Wilson, Wade, Minnesota	60	33	55.0	404	6.73	3	5.0	42t	3	5.0	71.8
Hogeboom, Gary, Dallas	126	70	55.6	978	7.76	5	4.0	58t	7	5.6	70.8
Cavanaugh, Matt, San Francisco	54	28	51.9	334	6.19	1	1.9	41	1	1.9	69.5
Ferguson, Joe, Detroit	54	31	57.4	364	6.74	2	3.7	38	3	5.6	67.2
Wright, Randy, Green Bay	74	39	52.7	552	7.46	2	2.7	38	4	5.4	63.6
Todd, Richard, New Orleans	32	16	50.0	191	5.97	3	9.4	56t	4	12.5	60.3
Zorn, Jim, Green Bay	123	56	45.5	794	6.46	4	3.3	56t	6	4.9	57.4
Fuller, Steve, Chicago	107	53	49.5	777	7.26	1	0.9	69	5	4.7	57.3
Young, Steve, Tampa Bay	138	72	52.2	935	6.78	3	2.2	59	8	5.8	56.9
Kemp, Jeff, Los Angeles Rams	38	16	42.1	214	5.63	0	0.0	35	1	2.6	49.7
Bono, Steve, Minnesota	10	1	10.0	5	0.50	0	0.0	5	0	0.0	39.6
Brunner, Scott, St. Louis	60	30	50.0	336	5.60	1	1.7	40t	6	10.0	33.1
Cunningham, Randall, Philadelphia	81	34	42.0	548	6.77	1	1.2	69	8	9.9	29.8

	Att.	Comp.	Pct. Comp.	Yards	Avg. Gain	TD	Pct. TD	Long	Int.	Pct. Int.	Rating Points
Fewer than 10 attempts											
Adams, George, New York Giants	1	0	0.0	0	0.00	0	0.0	0	0	0.0	39.6
Birdsong, Carl, St. Louis	1	0	0.0	0	0.00	0	0.0	0	0	0.0	39.6
Buford, Maury, Chicago	1	1	100.0	5	5.00	0	0.0	5	0	0.0	87.5
Cox, Steve, Washington	1	1	100.0	11	11.00	0	0.0	11	0	0.0	112.5
Ellis, Gerry, Green Bay	1	0	0.0	0	0.00	0	0.0	0	0	0.0	39.6
Hansen, Brian, New Orleans	1	1	100.0	8	8.00	0	0.0	8	0	0.0	100.0
Harmon, Derrick, San Francisco	1	0	0.0	0	0.00	0	0.0	0	0	0.0	39.6
Hill, Tony, Dallas	1	1	100.0	42	42.00	0	0.0	42	0	0.0	118.8
Hunter, Herman, Philadelphia	2	1	50.0	38	19.00	1	50.0	38t	0	0.0	135.4
Ivery, Eddie Lee, Green Bay	1	0	0.0	0	0.00	0	0.0	0	0	0.0	39.6
Jones, James, Dallas	2	1	50.0	12	6.00	1	50.0	12t	1	50.0	68.8
Jones, James, Detroit	1	0	0.0	0	0.00	0	0.0	0	0	0.0	39.6
Landeta, Sean, New York Giants	1	0	0.0	0	0.00	0	0.0	0	0	0.0	39.6
Merkens, Guido, New Orleans	1	1	100.0	7	7.00	1	100.0	7t	0	0.0	135.4
Mitchell, Stump, St. Louis	2	1	50.0	31	15.50	0	0.0	31	0	0.0	95.8
Moore, Alvin, Detroit	1	0	0.0	0	0.00	0	0.0	0	0	0.0	39.6
Payton, Walter, Chicago	5	3	60.0	96	19.20	1	20.0	50	0	0.0	143.8
Pelluer, Steve, Dallas	8	5	62.5	47	5.88	0	0.0	28	0	0.0	78.6
Riggins, John, Washington	1	0	0.0	0	0.00	0	0.0	0	0	0.0	39.6
Solomon, Freddie, San Francisco	1	0	0.0	0	0.00	0	0.0	0	0	0.0	39.6
Tomczak, Mike, Chicago	6	2	33.3	33	5.50	0	0.0	24	0	0.0	52.8

t indicates touchdown.
Leader based on rating points, minimum 224 attempts.

PASS RECEIVING

INDIVIDUAL CHAMPIONS
NFC: 92—Roger Craig, San Francisco
AFC: 86—Lionel James, San Diego

MOST RECEPTIONS, GAME
AFC: 13—Greg Bell, Buffalo vs. San Diego, September 8 (80 yards)
13—Wes Chandler, San Diego vs. Seattle, September 15 (243 yards)
NFC: 13—James Wilder, Tampa Bay vs. Minnesota, September 15 (71 yards)
13—Art Monk, Washington vs. Cincinnati, December 15 (230 yards)

YARDS
AFC: 1,287—Steve Largent, Seattle
NFC: 1,247—Mike Quick, Philadelphia

MOST YARDS, GAME
AFC: 309—Stephone Paige, Kansas City vs. San Diego, December 22 (8 receptions)
NFC: 241—Jerry Rice, San Francisco vs. Los Angeles Rams, December 9 (10 receptions)

YARDS PER RECEPTION
AFC: 21.9—Stephone Paige, Kansas City
NFC: 21.3—Willie Gault, Chicago

LONGEST
NFC: 99 yards—Mike Quick (from Ron Jaworski), Philadelphia vs. Atlanta, November 10 (TD)
AFC: 96 yards—Wesley Walker (from Ken O'Brien), New York Jets vs. Buffalo, December 8 (TD)

TOUCHDOWNS
AFC: 13—Daryl Turner, Seattle
NFC: 11—Mike Quick, Philadelphia

TEAM LEADERS
AFC: BUFFALO: 58, Greg Bell; CINCINNATI: 65, Cris Collinsworth; CLEVELAND: 62, Ozzie Newsome; DENVER: 61, Steve Watson; HOUSTON: 80, Butch Woolfolk; INDIANAPOLIS: 36, Pat Beach; KANSAS CITY: 47, Carlos Carson; LOS ANGELES RAIDERS: 82, Todd Christensen; MIAMI: 72, Tony Nathan; NEW ENGLAND: 52, Tony Collins; NEW YORK JETS: 76, Mickey Shuler; PITTSBURGH: 75, John Stallworth; SAN DIEGO: 86, Lionel James; SEATTLE: 79, Steve Largent.
NFC: ATLANTA: 62, Billy Johnson; CHICAGO: 49, Walter Payton; DALLAS: 74, Tony Hill; DETROIT: 51, Leonard Thompson; GREEN BAY: 69, James Lofton; LOS ANGELES RAMS: 54, Henry Ellard; MINNESOTA: 68, Steve Jordan; NEW ORLEANS: 42, Hoby Brenner; NEW YORK GIANTS: 49, Lionel Manuel; PHILADELPHIA: 73, Mike Quick; ST. LOUIS: 50, Roy Green; SAN FRANCISCO: 92, Roger Craig; TAMPA BAY: 53, James Wilder; WASHINGTON: 91, Art Monk.

NFL TOP 10 PASS RECEIVERS

	No.	Yards	Avg.	Long	TD
Craig, Roger, San Francisco	92	1016	11.0	73	6
Monk, Art, Washington	91	1226	13.5	53	2
James, Lionel, San Diego	86	1027	11.9	67t	6
Christensen, Todd, L.A. Raiders	82	987	12.0	48	6
Woolfolk, Butch, Houston	80	814	10.2	80t	4
Largent, Steve, Seattle	79	1287	16.3	43	6
Shuler, Mickey, N.Y. Jets	76	879	11.6	35	7
Stallworth, John, Pittsburgh	75	937	12.5	41	5
Hill, Tony, Dallas	74	1113	15.0	53t	7
Quick, Mike, Philadelphia	73	1247	17.1	99t	11

NFL TOP 10 PASS RECEIVERS BY YARDS

	Yards	No.	Avg.	Long	TD
Largent, Steve, Seattle	1287	79	16.3	43	6
Quick, Mike, Philadelphia	1247	73	17.1	99t	11
Monk, Art, Washington	1226	91	13.5	53	2
Chandler, Wes, San Diego	1199	67	17.9	75t	10
Hill, Drew, Houston	1169	64	18.3	57t	9
Lofton, James, Green Bay	1153	69	16.7	56t	4
Lipps, Louis, Pittsburgh	1134	59	19.2	51	12
Collinsworth, Cris, Cincinnati	1125	65	17.3	71	5
Hill, Tony, Dallas	1113	74	15.0	53t	7
James, Lionel, San Diego	1027	86	11.9	67t	6

AFC PASS RECEIVING—INDIVIDUAL

	No.	Yards	Avg.	Long	TD
James, Lionel, San Diego	86	1027	11.9	67t	6
Christensen, Todd, L.A. Raiders	82	987	12.0	48	6
Woolfolk, Butch, Houston	80	814	10.2	80t	4
Largent, Steve, Seattle	79	1287	16.3	43	6
Shuler, Mickey, N.Y. Jets	76	879	11.6	35	7
Stallworth, John, Pittsburgh	75	937	12.5	41	5
Nathan, Tony, Miami	72	651	9.0	73	1
Clayton, Mark, Miami	70	996	14.2	45	4
Chandler, Wes, San Diego	67	1199	17.9	75t	10
Allen, Marcus, L.A. Raiders	67	555	8.3	44	3
Collinsworth, Cris, Cincinnati	65	1125	17.3	71	5
Hill, Drew, Houston	64	1169	18.3	57t	9
Newsome, Ozzie, Cleveland	62	711	11.5	38	5
Watson, Steve, Denver	61	915	15.0	60	5
Lipps, Louis, Pittsburgh	59	1134	19.2	51	12
Joiner, Charlie, San Diego	59	932	15.8	39t	7
Bell, Greg, Buffalo	58	576	9.9	49	1
Brooks, James, Cincinnati	55	576	10.5	57t	5
Brown, Eddie, Cincinnati	53	942	17.8	68t	8
Collins, Tony, New England	52	549	10.6	49	2
Johnson, Vance, Denver	51	721	14.1	63t	3
Moore, Nat, Miami	51	701	13.7	69t	7
Williams, Dokie, L.A. Raiders	48	925	19.3	55	5
Reed, Andre, Buffalo	48	637	13.3	32	4
Carson, Carlos, Kansas City	47	843	17.9	37t	4
Warner, Curt, Seattle	47	307	6.5	27t	1
Toon, Al, N.Y. Jets	46	662	14.4	78t	3
Smith, Tim, Houston	46	660	14.3	33	2
Byner, Earnest, Cleveland	45	460	10.2	31	2
Paige, Stephone, Kansas City	43	943	21.9	84t	10
Holohan, Pete, San Diego	42	458	10.9	23	3
Butler, Jerry, Buffalo	41	770	18.8	60t	2
Sievers, Eric, San Diego	41	438	10.7	30t	6
Morgan, Stanley, New England	39	760	19.5	50t	5
Fryar, Irving, New England	39	670	17.2	56	7
Sohn, Kurt, N.Y. Jets	39	534	13.7	39t	4
Williams, Jamie, Houston	39	444	11.4	29	1
Hardy, Bruce, Miami	39	409	10.5	31	4
Holman, Rodney, Cincinnati	38	479	12.6	64t	7
McNeil, Freeman, N.Y. Jets	38	427	11.2	25	2
Ramson, Eason, Buffalo	37	369	10.0	43	1
Beach, Pat, Indianapolis	36	376	10.4	30	6
Duper, Mark, Miami	35	650	18.6	67t	3
Anderson, Gary, San Diego	35	422	12.1	52t	2
Willhite, Gerald, Denver	35	297	8.5	21	1
Walker, Wesley, N.Y. Jets	34	725	21.3	96t	5
Turner, Daryl, Seattle	34	670	19.7	54	13

	No.	Yards	Avg.	Long	TD
Erenberg, Rich, Pittsburgh	33	326	9.9	35	3
Hester, Jessie, L.A. Raiders	32	665	20.8	59	4
Brennan, Brian, Cleveland	32	487	15.2	57	0
Heard, Herman, Kansas City	31	257	8.3	27	2
Winder, Sammy, Denver	31	197	6.4	24	0
Wonsley, George, Indianapolis	30	257	8.6	26	0
Kay, Clarence, Denver	29	339	11.7	27	3
Mack, Kevin, Cleveland	29	297	10.2	43	3
Young, Charle, Seattle	28	351	12.5	32t	2
Arnold, Walt, Kansas City	28	339	12.1	38	1
Ramsey, Derrick, New England	28	285	10.2	26	1
Wright, James, Denver	28	246	8.8	30	1
Horton, Ethan, Kansas City	28	185	6.6	22	1
Bouza, Matt, Indianapolis	27	381	14.1	40	2
James, Craig, New England	27	360	13.3	90t	2
Hawkins, Frank, L.A. Raiders	27	174	6.4	20	0
Sampson, Clinton, Denver	26	432	16.6	46	4
Marshall, Henry, Kansas City	25	446	17.8	50	0
Capers, Wayne, Indianapolis	25	438	17.5	80t	4
Winslow, Kellen, San Diego	25	318	12.7	26	0
Boyer, Mark, Indianapolis	25	274	11.0	33	0
Pollard, Frank, Pittsburgh	24	250	10.4	20	0
Sewell, Steve, Denver	24	224	9.3	54t	1
Abercrombie, Walter, Pittsburgh	24	209	8.7	27	2
Lang, Gene, Denver	23	180	7.8	24	2
Kinnebrew, Larry, Cincinnati	22	187	8.5	29t	1
McMillan, Randy, Indianapolis	22	115	5.2	17	0
Burkett, Chris, Buffalo	21	371	17.7	38	0
Skansi, Paul, Seattle	21	269	12.8	32	1
Jones, Cedric, New England	21	237	11.3	29t	2
Johnson, Butch, Denver	19	380	20.0	65t	3
Butler, Raymond, Indianapolis	19	345	18.2	72t	2
Rose, Joe, Miami	19	306	16.1	42	4
Walker, Byron, Seattle	19	285	15.0	28t	2
Hughes, David, Seattle	19	184	9.7	26	0
Smith, Jeff, Kansas City	18	157	8.7	45t	2
Cribbs, Joe, Buffalo	18	142	7.9	23	0
Paige, Tony, N.Y. Jets	18	120	6.7	19	2
Hector, Johnny, N.Y. Jets	17	164	9.6	28	0
Dawson, Lin, New England	17	148	8.7	26	0
Moriarty, Larry, Houston	17	112	6.6	16	0
Weathers, Clarence, Cleveland	16	449	28.1	72t	3
Starring, Stephen, New England	16	235	14.7	40	0
Sweeney, Calvin, Pittsburgh	16	234	14.6	69	0
Ross, Dan, Cincinnati-Seattle	16	135	8.4	20	2
Hancock, Anthony, Kansas City	15	286	19.1	48	2
Lane, Eric, Seattle	15	153	10.2	20	0
Alexander, Charles, Cincinnati	15	110	7.3	19	0
Martin, Mike, Cincinnati	14	187	13.4	28	0
Klever, Rocky, N.Y. Jets	14	183	13.1	23	2
Johnson, Dan, Miami	13	192	14.8	61t	3
Davenport, Ron, Miami	13	74	5.7	17t	2
Richardson, Eric, Buffalo	12	201	16.8	27	0
Townsell, JoJo, N.Y. Jets	12	187	15.6	36	0
Jennings, Stanford, Cincinnati	12	101	8.4	24	3
Metzelaars, Pete, Buffalo	12	80	6.7	13	1
Bendross, Jesse, San Diego	11	156	14.2	54t	2
Spencer, Tim, San Diego	11	135	12.3	43	0
Bentley, Albert, Indianapolis	11	85	7.7	16	0
Kreider, Steve, Cincinnati	10	184	18.4	56	1
Adams, Willis, Cleveland	10	132	13.2	22	0
Martin, Robbie, Indianapolis	10	128	12.8	22	0
Harris, M.L., Cincinnati	10	123	12.3	22t	1
Franklin, Byron, Seattle	10	119	11.9	28	0
Bennett, Woody, Miami	10	101	10.1	27t	1
Holt, Harry, Cleveland	10	95	9.5	23	1
Williams, Oliver, Indianapolis	9	175	19.4	30	1
Williams, Derwin, New England	9	163	18.1	30	0
Rozier, Mike, Houston	9	96	10.7	52	0
Thompson, Weegie, Pittsburgh	8	138	17.3	42	1
Hampton, Lorenzo, Miami	8	56	7.0	15	0
Doornink, Dan, Seattle	8	52	6.5	19	0
Edwards, Stan, Houston	7	71	10.1	31	0
King, Bruce, Kansas City	7	45	6.4	8	0
Moore, Booker, Buffalo	7	44	6.3	9	0
Pruitt, Mike, Kansas City	7	43	6.1	9	0
Heflin, Vince, Miami	6	98	16.3	46t	1
Gothard, Preston, Pittsburgh	6	83	13.8	24	0
Holston, Michael, Houston-K.C.	6	76	12.7	25	0
Cunningham, Bennie, Pittsburgh	6	61	10.2	17	0
Morris, Randall, Seattle	6	14	2.3	6	0
Young, Glen, Cleveland	5	111	22.2	45t	1
Moffett, Tim, L.A. Raiders	5	90	18.0	34	0
Sherwin, Tim, Indianapolis	5	64	12.8	29	0
Banks, Fred, Cleveland	5	62	12.4	17t	2
Scott, Willie, Kansas City	5	61	12.2	21	0
Middleton, Frank, Indianapolis	5	54	10.8	34	0
Gill, Owen, Indianapolis	5	52	10.4	20	0
Bligen, Dennis, N.Y. Jets	5	43	8.6	14	0
Hayes, Jonathan, Kansas City	5	39	7.8	12	1
Johnson, Trumaine, San Diego	4	51	12.8	20t	1
McCloskey, Mike, Houston	4	29	7.3	24t	1
Brookins, Mitchell, Buffalo	3	71	23.7	46	0
King, Kenny, L.A. Raiders	3	49	16.3	37	0
Barber, Marion, N.Y. Jets	3	46	15.3	22	0
Hawthorne, Greg, New England	3	42	14.0	28t	1
Jones, E.J., Kansas City	3	31	10.3	15	0
Dickey, Curtis, Indianapolis	3	30	10.0	11	0
Jefferson, John, Cleveland	3	30	10.0	17	0
Smith, Jim, L.A. Raiders	3	28	9.3	14	1
Spencer, Todd, Pittsburgh	3	25	8.3	13	0
Harris, Duriel, Miami	3	24	8.0	11	0
Dressel, Chris, Houston	3	17	5.7	12	1
McGee, Buford, San Diego	3	15	5.0	7	0
Hardy, Andre, Seattle	3	7	2.3	3	0
Barber, Mike, L.A. Rams-Denver	2	37	18.5	29	0
Akiu, Mike, Houston	2	32	16.0	24	0
Henry, Bernard, Indianapolis	2	31	15.5	16	0
Norris, Ulysses, Buffalo	2	30	15.0	18	0
Drewrey, Willie, Houston	2	28	14.0	19	0
Tucker, Travis, Cleveland	2	20	10.0	10	0
Fontenot, Herman, Cleveland	2	19	9.5	17	0
Tasker, Steve, Houston	2	19	9.5	14	0
Weathers, Robert, New England	2	18	9.0	13	0
Tatupu, Mosi, New England	2	16	8.0	15	0
Tice, Mike, Seattle	2	13	6.5	7	0
Greene, Danny, Seattle	2	10	5.0	7	1
Steels, Anthony, Buffalo	2	9	4.5	6	0
Junkin, Trey, L.A. Raiders	2	8	4.0	5	1
Carter, Joe, Miami	2	7	3.5	4	0
Parros, Rick, Seattle	1	27	27.0	27	0
Teal, Jimmy, Buffalo	1	24	24.0	24	0
Cooper, Mark, Denver	1	13	13.0	13	0
Minter, Cedric, N.Y. Jets	1	13	13.0	13	0
Adams, Curtis, San Diego	1	12	12.0	12	0
Faulkner, Chris, San Diego	1	12	12.0	12	0
Langhorne, Reggie, Cleveland	1	12	12.0	12	0
Vigorito, Tom, Miami	1	9	9.0	9	0
Walls, Herkie, Houston	1	7	7.0	7	0
Williams, Van, Buffalo	1	7	7.0	7	0
Pagel, Mike, Indianapolis	1	6	6.0	6	0
Blados, Brian, Cincinnati	1	4	4.0	4	0
Jensen, Jim, Miami	1	4	4.0	4t	1
Munoz, Anthony, Cincinnati	1	1	1.0	1	0

t indicates a touchdown
Leader based on most passes caught.

AFC TOP 25 PASS RECEIVERS BY YARDS

	Yards	No.	Avg.	Long	TD
Largent, Steve, Seattle	1287	79	16.3	43	6
Chandler, Wes, San Diego	1199	67	17.9	75t	10
Hill, Drew, Houston	1169	64	18.3	57t	9
Lipps, Louis, Pittsburgh	1134	59	19.2	51	12
Collinsworth, Cris, Cincinnati	1125	65	17.3	71	5
James, Lionel, San Diego	1027	86	11.9	67t	6
Clayton, Mark, Miami	996	70	14.2	45	4
Christensen, Todd, L.A. Raiders	987	82	12.0	48	6
Paige, Stephone, Kansas City	943	43	21.9	84t	10
Brown, Eddie, Cincinnati	942	53	17.8	68t	8
Stallworth, John, Pittsburgh	937	75	12.5	41	5
Joiner, Charlie, San Diego	932	59	15.8	39t	7
Williams, Dokie, L.A. Raiders	925	48	19.3	55	5
Watson, Steve, Denver	915	61	15.0	60	5
Shuler, Mickey, N.Y. Jets	879	76	11.6	35	7
Carson, Carlos, Kansas City	843	47	17.9	37t	4
Woolfolk, Butch, Houston	814	80	10.2	80t	4
Butler, Jerry, Buffalo	770	41	18.8	60t	2
Morgan, Stanley, New England	760	39	19.5	50t	5
Walker, Wesley, N.Y. Jets	725	34	21.3	96t	5
Johnson, Vance, Denver	721	51	14.1	63t	3
Newsome, Ozzie, Cleveland	711	62	11.5	38	5
Moore, Nat, Miami	701	51	13.7	69t	7
Fryar, Irving, New England	670	39	17.2	56	7
Turner, Daryl, Seattle	670	34	19.7	54	13

NFC PASS RECEIVING — INDIVIDUAL

	No.	Yards	Avg.	Long	TD
Craig, Roger, San Francisco	92	1016	11.0	73	6
Monk, Art, Washington	91	1226	13.5	53	2
Hill, Tony, Dallas	74	1113	15.0	53t	7
Quick, Mike, Philadelphia	73	1247	17.1	99t	11
Clark, Gary, Washington	72	926	12.9	55	5
Lofton, James, Green Bay	69	1153	16.7	56t	4
Jordan, Steve, Minnesota	68	795	11.7	32	0
Cosbie, Doug, Dallas	64	793	12.4	42	6
Spagnola, John, Philadelphia	64	772	12.1	35	5

	No.	Yards	Avg.	Long	TD
Johnson, Billy, Atlanta	62	830	13.4	62t	5
Renfro, Mike, Dallas	60	955	15.9	58t	8
Ellard, Henry, L.A. Rams	54	811	15.0	64t	5
Clark, Dwight, San Francisco	54	705	13.1	49t	10
Wilder, James, Tampa Bay	53	341	6.4	20	0
Thompson, Leonard, Detroit	51	736	14.4	48	5
Green, Roy, St. Louis	50	693	13.9	47	5
Hunter, Tony, L.A. Rams	50	562	11.2	47t	4
Rice, Jerry, San Francisco	49	927	18.9	66t	3
Manuel, Lionel, N.Y. Giants	49	859	17.5	51t	5
Tilley, Pat, St. Louis	49	726	14.8	46t	6
Coffman, Paul, Green Bay	49	666	13.6	32	6
Payton, Walter, Chicago	49	483	9.9	65	2
Mitchell, Stump, St. Louis	47	502	10.7	46	3
Jones, Mike, Minnesota	46	641	13.9	44t	4
Dorsett, Tony, Dallas	46	449	9.8	56t	3
Newsome, Tim, Dallas	46	361	7.8	24	1
Jones, James, Detroit	45	334	7.4	36	3
House, Kevin, Tampa Bay	44	803	18.3	59	5
Epps, Phillip, Green Bay	44	683	15.5	63	3
Francis, Russ, San Francisco	44	478	10.9	25	3
Carter, Anthony, Minnesota	43	821	19.1	57t	8
Giles, Jimmie, Tampa Bay	43	673	15.7	44	8
Smith, J.T., St. Louis	43	581	13.5	34	1
Bell, Jerry, Tampa Bay	43	496	11.5	27	2
Haddix, Michael, Philadelphia	43	330	7.7	17	0
Nelson, Darrin, Minnesota	43	301	7.0	25t	1
Brenner, Hoby, New Orleans	42	652	15.5	30	3
Didier, Clint, Washington	41	433	10.6	29	4
Jackson, Kenny, Philadelphia	40	692	17.3	54	1
Carter, Gerald, Tampa Bay	40	557	13.9	40	3
Wilson, Wayne, New Orleans	38	228	6.0	21	2
Bavaro, Mark, N.Y. Giants	37	511	13.8	32	4
Marsh, Doug, St. Louis	37	355	9.6	23	1
Washington, Joe, Atlanta	37	328	8.9	34	1
Griffin, Keith, Washington	37	285	7.7	28	0
Nichols, Mark, Detroit	36	592	16.4	43	4
Martin, Eric, New Orleans	35	522	14.9	50	4
Moorehead, Emery, Chicago	35	481	13.7	25	1
Gault, Willie, Chicago	33	704	21.3	70t	1
Johnson, Bobby, N.Y. Giants	33	533	16.2	42	8
Cox, Arthur, Atlanta	33	454	13.8	62t	2
Suhey, Matt, Chicago	33	295	8.9	35	1
Riggs, Gerald, Atlanta	33	267	8.1	44	0
Goodlow, Eugene, New Orleans	32	603	18.8	76t	3
McKinnon, Dennis, Chicago	31	555	17.9	48	7
Adams, George, N.Y. Giants	31	389	12.5	70t	2
Bailey, Stacey, Atlanta	30	364	12.1	31	0
Galbreath, Tony, N.Y. Giants	30	327	10.9	49	1
Brown, Ted, Minnesota	30	291	9.7	54t	3
Lewis, Leo, Minnesota	29	442	15.2	43t	3
Hill, David, L.A. Rams	29	271	9.3	37	1
Hunter, Herman, Philadelphia	28	405	14.5	43	1
Lewis, David, Detroit	28	354	12.6	40	3
Ivery, Eddie Lee, Green Bay	28	270	9.6	24	2
Anthony, Tyrone, New Orleans	28	185	6.6	36	0
Magee, Calvin, Tampa Bay	26	288	11.1	35	3
Chadwick, Jeff, Detroit	25	478	19.1	56	3
Duckworth, Bobby, L.A. Rams	25	422	16.9	42	3
McConkey, Phil, N.Y. Giants	25	404	16.2	48	1
Ferrell, Earl, St. Louis	25	277	11.1	30	2
Solomon, Freddie, San Francisco	25	259	10.4	39	1
Brown, Charlie, Atlanta	24	412	17.2	48	2
Wrightman, Tim, Chicago	24	407	17.0	49	1
Tice, John, New Orleans	24	266	11.1	39t	2
Clark, Jessie, Green Bay	24	252	10.5	55t	2
Ellis, Gerry, Green Bay	24	206	8.6	35	0
Jones, James, Dallas	24	179	7.5	35	0
Anderson, Ottis, St. Louis	23	225	9.8	43	0
Morris, Joe, N.Y. Giants	22	212	9.6	17	0
Carpenter, Rob, N.Y. Giants	20	162	8.1	23	0
Tyler, Wendell, San Francisco	20	154	7.7	16	2
Dickerson, Eric, L.A. Rams	20	126	6.3	33	0
Moore, Alvin, Detroit	19	154	8.1	14	1
Mandley, Pete, Detroit	18	316	17.6	37	0
Margerum, Ken, Chicago	17	190	11.2	20	2
Anderson, Alfred, Minnesota	16	175	10.9	54t	1
Redden, Barry, L.A. Rams	16	162	10.1	32	0
Williams, Byron, N.Y. Giants	15	280	18.7	45	0
Groth, Jeff, New Orleans	15	238	15.9	56t	2
Hardy, Larry, New Orleans	15	208	13.9	31	2
Warren, Don, Washington	15	163	10.9	19	1
Powe, Karl, Dallas	14	237	16.9	34	0
Brown, Ron, L.A. Rams	14	215	15.4	43t	3
Allen, Anthony, Atlanta	14	207	14.8	37t	2
Young, Mike, L.A. Rams	14	157	11.2	23	0
Harmon, Derrick, San Francisco	14	123	8.8	42	0
Mularkey, Mike, Minnesota	13	196	15.1	51t	1
Dennard, Preston, Green Bay	13	182	14.0	34	2
Bell, Theo, Tampa Bay	12	189	15.8	24	0
Bland, Carl, Detroit	12	157	13.1	24	0
Johnson, Ron, Philadelphia	11	186	16.9	37	0
Wilson, Mike, San Francisco	10	165	16.5	52t	2
Jackson, Earnest, Philadelphia	10	126	12.6	25	1
Monroe, Carl, San Francisco	10	51	5.1	9	0
Benson, Cliff, Atlanta	10	37	3.7	6	0
LaFleur, Greg, St. Louis	9	119	13.2	24	0
Muhammad, Calvin, Washington	9	116	12.9	32	1
Rice, Allen, Minnesota	9	61	6.8	13	1
West, Ed, Green Bay	8	95	11.9	30	1
Gajan, Hokie, New Orleans	8	87	10.9	22	0
Carthon, Maurice, N.Y. Giants	8	81	10.1	22	0
White, Sammy, Minnesota	8	76	9.5	15	0
Garrity, Gregg, Philadelphia	7	142	20.3	34	0
Little, David, Philadelphia	7	82	11.7	28	0
Scott, Lindsay, New Orleans	7	61	8.7	15	0
Matthews, Allama, Atlanta	7	57	8.1	15	1
Montgomery, Wilbert, Detroit	7	55	7.9	28	0
Frank, John, San Francisco	7	50	7.1	14	1
Campbell, Earl, New Orleans	6	88	14.7	39	0
Cornwell, Fred, Dallas	6	77	12.8	32	1
Riggins, John, Washington	6	18	3.0	8	0
Rhymes, Buster, Minnesota	5	124	24.8	36	0
McDonald, James, Det.-L.A. Rams	5	81	16.2	35	0
Gentry, Dennis, Chicago	5	77	15.4	30	0
Hasselbeck, Don, N.Y. Giants	5	71	14.2	30	1
Kane, Rick, Detroit	5	56	11.2	18	0
Thomas, Calvin, Chicago	5	45	9.0	15	0
Fowler, Bobby, New Orleans	5	43	8.6	11	0
Huckleby, Harlan, Green Bay	5	27	5.4	8	0
Cain, Lynn, L.A. Rams	5	24	4.8	13	0
Fowler, Todd, Dallas	5	24	4.8	10	0
Cooper, Earl, San Francisco	4	45	11.3	20	0
Duncan, Clyde, St. Louis	4	39	9.8	14	1
Rogers, George, Washington	4	29	7.3	23	0
Everett, Major, Philadelphia	4	25	6.3	11	0
Merkens, Guido, New Orleans	3	61	20.3	39t	1
Whisenhunt, Ken, Atlanta	3	48	16.0	29	0
Springs, Ron, Tampa Bay	3	44	14.7	22	0
Barnwell, Malcolm, Washington	3	28	9.3	13	0
Gonzalez, Leon, Dallas	3	28	9.3	13	0
Witte, Mark, Tampa Bay	3	28	9.3	13	0
Guman, Mike, L.A. Rams	3	23	7.7	11	0
Gray, Earnest, St. Louis	3	22	7.3	12	0
Rubick, Rob, Detroit	2	33	16.5	18	0
Baker, Keith, Philadelphia	2	25	12.5	20	0
Meade, Mike, Detroit	2	21	10.5	14	0
Wolfley, Ron, St. Louis	2	18	9.0	17	0
Ellerson, Gary, Green Bay	2	15	7.5	11	0
Ring, Bill, San Francisco	2	14	7.0	8	0
Armstrong, Adger, Tampa Bay	2	4	2.0	3	1
Love, Randy, St. Louis	2	4	2.0	3	0
Maness, James, Chicago	1	34	34.0	34	0
Austin, Cliff, Atlanta	1	21	21.0	21	0
Mack, Cedric, St. Louis	1	16	16.0	16	0
McMahon, Jim, Chicago	1	13	13.0	13t	1
White, Charles, L.A. Rams	1	12	12.0	12	0
White, Danny, Dallas	1	12	12.0	12t	1
Cherry, Raphel, Washington	1	11	11.0	11	0
Sanders, Thomas, Chicago	1	9	9.0	9	0
Carroll, Jay, Minnesota	1	8	8.0	8	0
Haynes, James, New Orleans	1	8	8.0	8	0
Lavette, Robert, Dallas	1	8	8.0	8	0
Walker, Rick, Washington	1	8	8.0	8	0
Hebert, Bobby, New Orleans	1	7	7.0	7t	1
McCall, Reese, Detroit	1	7	7.0	7	0
Anderson, Brad, Chicago	1	6	6.0	6	0
Novacek, Jay, St. Louis	1	4	4.0	4	0
Oliver, Hubert, Philadelphia	1	4	4.0	4	0
Perry, William, Chicago	1	4	4.0	4t	1
Moore, Blake, Green Bay	1	3	3.0	3t	1

t indicates touchdown
Leader based on most passes caught.

NFC TOP 25 PASS RECEIVERS BY YARDS

	Yards	No.	Avg.	Long	TD
Quick, Mike, Philadelphia	1247	73	17.1	99t	11
Monk, Art, Washington	1226	91	13.5	53	2
Lofton, James, Green Bay	1153	69	16.7	56t	4
Hill, Tony, Dallas	1113	74	15.0	53t	7
Craig, Roger, San Francisco	1016	92	11.0	73	6
Renfro, Mike, Dallas	955	60	15.9	58t	8
Rice, Jerry, San Francisco	927	49	18.9	66t	3
Clark, Gary, Washington	926	72	12.9	55	5
Manuel, Lionel, N.Y. Giants	859	49	17.5	51t	5
Johnson, Billy, Atlanta	830	62	13.4	62t	5

	Yards	No.	Avg.	Long	TD
Carter, Anthony, Minnesota	821	43	19.1	57t	8
Ellard, Henry, L.A. Rams	811	54	15.0	64t	5
House, Kevin, Tampa Bay	803	44	18.3	59	5
Jordan, Steve, Minnesota	795	68	11.7	32	0
Cosbie, Doug, Dallas	793	64	12.4	42	6
Spagnola, John, Philadelphia	772	64	12.1	35	5
Thompson, Leonard, Detroit	736	51	14.4	48	5
Tilley, Pat, St. Louis	726	49	14.8	46t	6
Clark, Dwight, San Francisco	705	54	13.1	49t	10
Gault, Willie, Chicago	704	33	21.3	70t	1
Green, Roy, St. Louis	693	50	13.9	47	5
Jackson, Kenny, Philadelphia	692	40	17.3	54	1
Epps, Phillip, Green Bay	683	44	15.5	63	3
Giles, Jimmie, Tampa Bay	673	43	15.7	44	8
Coffman, Paul, Green Bay	666	49	13.6	32	6

INTERCEPTIONS

INDIVIDUAL CHAMPIONS
NFC: 9—Everson Walls, Dallas
AFC: 8—Albert Lewis, Kansas City
8—Eugene Daniel, Indianapolis

MOST INTERCEPTIONS, GAME
AFC: 4—Deron Cherry, Kansas City vs. Seattle, September 29 (24 yards)
NFC: 3—Dave Waymer, New Orleans vs. Philadelphia, October 6 (28 yards)

YARDAGE
AFC: 189—Fred Marion, New England
NFC: 174—Mike Richardson, Chicago

LONGEST
NFC: 90 yards—Mike Richardson, Chicago vs. Washington, September 29
AFC: 83 yards—Fred Marion, New England vs. Seattle, November 17

TOUCHDOWNS
AFC: 1—By 17 players
NFC: 1—By 24 players

TEAM LEADERS
AFC: BUFFALO: 7, Charles Romes; CINCINNATI: 7, James Griffin; CLEVELAND: 5, Al Gross; DENVER: 5, Mike Harden & Louis Wright; HOUSTON: 5, Steve Brown; INDIANAPOLIS: 8, Eugene Daniel; KANSAS CITY: 8, Albert Lewis; LOS ANGELES RAIDERS: 4, Lester Hayes & Mike Haynes; MIAMI: 6, Glenn Blackwood; NEW ENGLAND: 7, Fred Marion; NEW YORK JETS: 4, Kerry Glenn & Bobby Jackson; PITTSBURGH: 5, Dwayne Woodruff; SAN DIEGO: 5, Danny Walters; SEATTLE: 7, John Harris.
NFC: ATLANTA: 5, Bobby Butler; CHICAGO: 6, Leslie Frazier; DALLAS: 9, Everson Walls; DETROIT: 5, Bobby Watkins; GREEN BAY: 4, Tim Lewis; LOS ANGELES RAMS: 6, Gary Green & LeRoy Irvin; MINNESOTA: 5, John Turner; NEW ORLEANS: 6, Dave Waymer; NEW YORK GIANTS: 6, Elvis Patterson; PHILADELPHIA: 6, Wes Hopkins; ST. LOUIS: 5, E.J. Junior; SAN FRANCISCO: 6, Ronnie Lott; TAMPA BAY: 7, Jeremiah Castille; WASHINGTON: 5, Vernon Dean & Curtis Jordan.

TEAM CHAMPIONS
NFC: 34—Chicago
AFC: 27—Kansas City

AFC INTERCEPTIONS—TEAM

	No.	Yards	Avg.	Long	TD
Kansas City	27	298	11.0	47t	1
San Diego	26	461	17.7	75t	2
Denver	24	290	12.1	42t	1
Seattle	24	272	11.3	75t	3
New England	23	427	18.6	83	1
Miami	23	265	11.5	61t	1
New York Jets	22	127	5.8	24	1
Buffalo	20	225	11.3	41	0
Pittsburgh	20	211	10.6	35t	1
Cincinnati	19	283	14.9	57t	2
Cleveland	18	254	14.1	40	1
Los Angeles Raiders	17	235	13.8	76t	3
Indianapolis	16	75	4.7	29	0
Houston	15	144	9.6	55	0
AFC Total	294	3567	—	83	17
AFC Average	21.0	254.8	12.1	—	1.2

NFC INTERCEPTIONS—TEAM

	No.	Yards	Avg.	Long	TD
Chicago	34	512	15.1	90	4
Dallas	33	263	8.0	65t	4
Los Angeles Rams	29	359	12.4	46	4
New York Giants	24	339	14.1	56t	2
Washington	23	220	9.6	36	0
Minnesota	22	283	12.9	63	1
Atlanta	22	247	11.2	47	1
New Orleans	21	312	14.9	53	2
San Francisco	18	310	17.2	82	1
Tampa Bay	18	146	8.1	25	0
Detroit	18	136	7.6	22	0
Philadelphia	18	125	6.9	26	2
Green Bay	15	262	17.5	80t	2
St. Louis	13	240	18.5	67	1
NFC Total	308	3754	—	90	24
NFC Average	22.0	268.1	12.2	—	1.7
League Total	602	7321	—	90	41
League Average	21.5	261.5	12.2	—	1.5

NFL TOP 10 INTERCEPTORS

	No.	Yards	Avg.	Long	TD
Walls, Everson, Dallas	9	31	3.4	19	0
Lewis, Albert, Kansas City	8	59	7.4	16	0
Daniel, Eugene, Indianapolis	8	53	6.6	29	0
Marion, Fred, New England	7	189	27.0	83	0
Griffin, James, Cincinnati	7	116	16.6	33	1
Cherry, Deron, Kansas City	7	87	12.4	47t	1
Romes, Charles, Buffalo	7	56	8.0	21	0
Castille, Jeremiah, Tampa Bay	7	49	7.0	20	0
Harris, John, Seattle	7	20	2.9	17	0
11 players tied	6				

AFC INTERCEPTIONS—INDIVIDUAL

	No.	Yards	Avg.	Long	TD
Lewis, Albert, Kansas City	8	59	7.4	16	0
Daniel, Eugene, Indianapolis	8	53	6.6	29	0
Marion, Fred, New England	7	189	27.0	83	0
Griffin, James, Cincinnati	7	116	16.6	33	1
Cherry, Deron, Kansas City	7	87	12.4	47t	1
Romes, Charles, Buffalo	7	56	8.0	21	0
Harris, John, Seattle	7	20	2.9	17	0
Jackson, Robert, Cincinnati	6	100	16.7	57t	1
Clayborn, Ray, New England	6	80	13.3	38	1
Brown, Dave, Seattle	6	58	9.7	28t	1
Blackwood, Glenn, Miami	6	36	6.0	17	0
Gross, Al, Cleveland	5	109	21.8	37t	1
Harden, Mike, Denver	5	100	20.0	42t	1
Woodruff, Dwayne, Pittsburgh	5	80	16.0	33	0
Walters, Danny, San Diego	5	71	14.2	30	0
Wright, Louis, Denver	5	44	8.8	24	0
Brown, Steve, Houston	5	41	8.2	22	0
Hendy, John, San Diego	4	139	34.8	75t	1
Judson, William, Miami	4	88	22.0	61t	1
Taylor, Terry, Seattle	4	75	18.8	75t	1
James, Roland, New England	4	51	12.8	39	0
Williams, Eric, Pittsburgh	4	47	11.8	29	0
Shell, Donnie, Pittsburgh	4	40	10.0	26	0
Hayes, Lester, L.A. Raiders	4	27	6.8	27t	1
Glenn, Kerry, N.Y. Jets	4	15	3.8	15t	1
Lankford, Paul, Miami	4	10	2.5	6	0
Haynes, Mike, L.A. Raiders	4	8	2.0	8	0
Jackson, Bobby, N.Y. Jets	4	8	2.0	8	0
Lippett, Ronnie, New England	3	93	31.0	58	0
Dixon, Hanford, Cleveland	3	65	21.7	37	0
Eason, Bo, Houston	3	55	18.3	55	0
Foley, Steve, Denver	3	47	15.7	29	0
Ross, Kevin, Kansas City	3	47	15.7	27	0
Smith, Dennis, Denver	3	46	15.3	39	0
Hill, Greg, Kansas City	3	37	12.3	37	0
Mehl, Lance, N.Y. Jets	3	33	11.0	18	0
Bostic, Keith, Houston	3	28	9.3	26	0
Cocroft, Sherman, Kansas City	3	27	9.0	27	0
Mullen, Davlin, N.Y. Jets	3	14	4.7	14	0
Clifton, Kyle, N.Y. Jets	3	10	3.3	10	0
Wilson, Steve, Denver	3	8	2.7	8	0
Lowe, Woodrow, San Diego	3	6	2.0	4	0
Dale, Jeffery, San Diego	2	83	41.5	47t	1
Bellinger, Rodney, Buffalo	2	64	32.0	41	0
Robinson, Eugene, Seattle	2	47	23.5	47	0
Braziel, Larry, Cleveland	2	40	20.0	40	0
Brown, Bud, Miami	2	40	20.0	26	0
Bradley, Carlos, San Diego	2	36	18.0	18	0
Merriweather, Mike, Pittsburgh	2	36	18.0	35t	1
Butler, Keith, Seattle	2	31	15.5	31	0
Davis, Wayne, San Diego	2	29	14.5	28	0
Breeden, Louis, Cincinnati	2	24	12.0	30	0
McElroy, Vann, L.A. Raiders	2	23	11.5	23	0
Wilson, Don, Buffalo	2	23	11.5	23	0
Easley, Ken, Seattle	2	22	11.0	16	0
Green, Mike, San Diego	2	17	8.5	12	0
Hill, Rod, Buffalo	2	17	8.5	17	0
Davis, Preston, Indianapolis	2	14	7.0	14	0
Hamilton, Harry, N.Y. Jets	2	14	7.0	14	0
Wright, Felix, Cleveland	2	11	5.5	10	0

	No.	Yards	Avg.	Long	TD
Bayless, Martin, Buffalo	2	10	5.0	10	0
Miano, Rich, N.Y. Jets	2	9	4.5	6	0
King, Linden, San Diego	2	8	4.0	5	0
Burroughs, Derrick, Buffalo	2	7	3.5	7	0
Kush, Rod, Houston	2	6	3.0	6	0
Lilly, Tony, Denver	2	4	2.0	4	0
Swain, John, Pittsburgh	2	4	2.0	4	0
Horton, Ray, Cincinnati	2	3	1.5	3	0
Little, David, Pittsburgh	2	0	0.0	3	0
Toran, Stacey, L.A. Raiders	1	76	76.0	76t	1
Brophy, Jay, Miami	1	41	41.0	41	0
Haslett, Jim, Buffalo	1	40	40.0	40	0
Turner, Jim, Cincinnati	1	40	40.0	40	0
Seale, Sam, L.A. Raiders	1	38	38.0	38t	1
McPherson, Miles, San Diego	1	30	30.0	30	0
Green, Hugh, Miami	1	28	28.0	28	0
Byrd, Gill, San Diego	1	25	25.0	25	0
Lynn, Johnny, N.Y. Jets	1	24	24.0	24	0
McKinney, Odis, L.A. Raiders	1	22	22.0	22	0
Van Pelt, Brad, L.A. Raiders	1	22	22.0	22	0
Radecic, Scott, Kansas City	1	21	21.0	21	0
Hunter, Daniel, Denver	1	20	20.0	20	0
Robinson, Mark, Kansas City	1	20	20.0	20	0
Green, Jacob, Seattle	1	19	19.0.	19t	1
Woodard, Ken, Denver	1	18	18.0	18	0
Williams, Lee, San Diego	1	17	17.0	17	0
Martin, Rod, L.A. Raiders	1	16	16.0	16	0
Blackmon, Don, New England	1	14	14.0	14	0
Riley, Avon, Houston	1	14	14.0	14	0
Weathers, Curtis, Cleveland	1	9	9.0	9	0
Frazier, Guy, Buffalo	1	8	8.0	8	0
Rockins, Chris, Cleveland	1	8	8.0	8	0
Cooks, Johnie, Indianapolis	1	7	7.0	7	0
Shipp, Jackie, Miami	1	7	7.0	7	0
Brudzinski, Bob, Miami	1	6	6.0	6	0
Johnson, Eddie, Cleveland	1	6	6.0	6	0
Brown, Mark, Miami	1	5	5.0	5	0
Cole, Robin, Pittsburgh	1	4	4.0	4	0
Moyer, Alex, Miami	1	4	4.0	4	0
Minnifield, Frank, Cleveland	1	3	3.0	3	0
Robbins, Randy, Denver	1	3	3.0	3	0
Rogers, Don, Cleveland	1	3	3.0	3	0
Squirek, Jack, L.A. Raiders	1	3	3.0	3	0
Anderson, Don, Indianapolis	1	1	1.0	1	0
Barnes, Jeff, L.A. Raiders	1	0	0.0	0	0
Bickett, Duane, Indianapolis	1	0	0.0	0	0
Blackwood, Lyle, Miami	1	0	0.0	0	0
Burruss, Lloyd, Kansas City	1	0	0.0	0	0
Cousineau, Tom, Cleveland	1	0	0.0	0	0
Johnson, Lawrence, Buffalo	1	0	0.0	0	0
Kemp, Bobby, Cincinnati	1	0	0.0	0	0
Krauss, Barry, Indianapolis	1	0	0.0	0	0
McGrew, Larry, New England	1	0	0.0	0	0
McSwain, Rod, New England	1	0	0.0	0	0
Randle, Tate, Indianapolis	1	0	0.0	0	0
Smith, Billy Ray, San Diego	1	0	0.0	0	0
Stensrud, Mike, Houston	1	0	0.0	0	0
Young, Anthony, Indianapolis	1	0	0.0	0	0

t indicates touchdown
Leader based on most interceptions.

NFC INTERCEPTIONS—INDIVIDUAL

	No.	Yards	Avg.	Long	TD
Walls, Everson, Dallas	9	31	3.4	19	0
Castille, Jeremiah, Tampa Bay	7	49	7.0	20	0
Frazier, Leslie, Chicago	6	119	19.8	33	1
Patterson, Elvis, N.Y. Giants	6	88	14.7	29t	1
Green, Gary, L.A. Rams	6	84	14.0	41t	1
Irvin, LeRoy, L.A. Rams	6	83	13.8	34t	1
Lott, Ronnie, San Francisco	6	68	11.3	25	0
Waymer, Dave, New Orleans	6	49	8.2	28	0
Hopkins, Wes, Philadelphia	6	36	6.0	24t	1
Junior, E.J., St. Louis	5	109	21.8	53	0
Kinard, Terry, N.Y. Giants	5	100	20.0	31	0
Johnson, Johnnie, L.A. Rams	5	96	19.2	46	1
Jordan, Curtis, Washington	5	88	17.6	36	0
Turner, John, Minnesota	5	62	12.4	25	0
Duerson, Dave, Chicago	5	53	10.6	20	0
Fencik, Gary, Chicago	5	43	8.6	22	0
Thurman, Dennis, Dallas	5	21	4.2	21t	1
Greenwood, David, Tampa Bay	5	15	3.0	7	0
Watkins, Bobby, Detroit	5	15	3.0	8	0
Dean, Vernon, Washington	5	8	1.6	8	0
Butler, Bobby, Atlanta	5	−4	−0.8	0	0
Richardson, Mike, Chicago	4	174	43.5	90	1
Hoage, Terry, New Orleans	4	79	19.8	52t	1
Case, Scott, Atlanta	4	78	19.5	47	0
Hicks, Dwight, San Francisco	4	68	17.0	25	0
Fellows, Ron, Dallas	4	52	13.0	29	0
Ellis, Ray, Philadelphia	4	32	8.0	18	0
Marshall, Wilber, Chicago	4	23	5.8	14	0
Bates, Bill, Dallas	4	15	3.8	8	0
Lewis, Tim, Green Bay	4	4	1.0	4	0
Williamson, Carlton, San Francisco	3	137	45.7	82	1
Lee, Carl, Minnesota	3	68	22.7	35	0
Poe, Johnnie, New Orleans	3	63	21.0	40t	1
Johnson, Demetrious, Detroit	3	39	13.0	19	0
Wilson, Otis, Chicago	3	35	11.7	23t	1
Cason, Wendell, Atlanta	3	30	10.0	22	0
Taylor, Ken, Chicago	3	28	9.3	18	0
Graham, William, Detroit	3	22	7.3	22	0
Newsome, Vince, L.A. Rams	3	20	6.7	20	0
Clinkscale, Dextor, Dallas	3	16	5.3	11	0
Downs, Michael, Dallas	3	11	3.7	11	0
Kaufman, Mel, Washington	3	10	3.3	10	0
Edwards, Herman, Philadelphia	3	8	2.7	3t	1
Teal, Willie, Minnesota	3	6	2.0	6	0
Young, Lonnie, St. Louis	3	0	0.0	0	0
Douglass, Mike, Green Bay	2	126	63.0	80t	1
Smith, Leonard, St. Louis	2	73	36.5	67	0
Newton, Tim, Minnesota	2	63	31.5	63	0
Ekern, Carl, L.A. Rams	2	55	27.5	33t	1
Murphy, Mark, Green Bay	2	50	25.0	50t	1
Scott, Randy, Green Bay	2	50	25.0	30	0
Pridemore, Tom, Atlanta	2	45	22.5	36	0
Rade, John, Atlanta	2	42	21.0	38t	1
Milot, Rich, Washington	2	33	16.5	22	0
Hill, Ken, N.Y. Giants	2	30	15.0	30	0
Cherry, Raphel, Washington	2	29	14.5	22	0
Williams, Perry, N.Y. Giants	2	28	14.0	28	0
Bess, Rufus, Minnesota	2	27	13.5	27	0
Greene, Tiger, Atlanta	2	27	13.5	27	0
Scott, Victor, Dallas	2	26	13.0	26t	1
Tullis, Willie, New Orleans	2	22	11.0	22	0
Peters, Tony, Washington	2	21	10.5	12	0
Studwell, Scott, Minnesota	2	20	10.0	13	0
Browner, Joey, Minnesota	2	17	8.5	15t	1
McNorton, Bruce, Detroit	2	14	7.0	10	0
Cooper, Evan, Philadelphia	2	13	6.5	13	0
Del Rio, Jack, New Orleans	2	13	6.5	11	0
Dent, Richard, Chicago	2	10	5.0	9	1
Mack, Cedric, St. Louis	2	10	5.0	10	0
Collins, Jim, L.A. Rams	2	8	4.0	4	0
Fox, Tim, L.A. Rams	2	8	4.0	8	0
Welch, Herb, N.Y. Giants	2	8	4.0	8	0
Headen, Andy, N.Y. Giants	2	7	3.5	7	0
Cromwell, Nolan, L.A. Rams	2	5	2.5	5	0
Anderson, John, Green Bay	2	2	1.0	2	0
Green, Darrell, Washington	2	0	0.0	0	0
Wattelet, Frank, New Orleans	2	0	0.0	0	0
Jeffcoat, Jim, Dallas	1	65	65.0	65t	1
Martin, George, N.Y. Giants	1	56	56.0	56t	1
Kovach, Jim, New Orleans	1	53	53.0	53	0
Washington, Lionel, St. Louis	1	48	48.0	48t	1
Shell, Todd, San Francisco	1	33	33.0	33	0
Kraynak, Rich, Philadelphia	1	26	26.0	26	0
Browner, Keith, Tampa Bay	1	25	25.0	25	0
Redd, Glen, New Orleans	1	25	25.0	25	0
Lee, Mark, Green Bay	1	23	23.0	23	0
Singletary, Mike, Chicago	1	23	23.0	23	0
Davis, Jeff, Tampa Bay	1	22	22.0	22	0
Olkewicz, Neal, Washington	1	21	21.0	21	0
Frye, David, Atlanta	1	20	20.0	20	0
Harrell, James, Detroit	1	20	20.0	20	0
Sully, Ivory, Tampa Bay	1	20	20.0	20	0
Lockhart, Eugene, Dallas	1	19	19.0	19t	1
Bunz, Dan, Detroit	1	17	17.0	17	0
Mullaney, Mark, Minnesota	1	15	15.0	15	0
Johnson, Cecil, Tampa Bay	1	12	12.0	12	0
Reasons, Gary, N.Y. Giants	1	10	10.0	10	0
Reichenbach, Mike, Philadelphia	1	10	10.0	10	0
Wilburn, Barry, Washington	1	10	10.0	10	0
Currier, Bill, N.Y. Giants	1	9	9.0	9	0
Britt, James, Atlanta	1	8	8.0	8	0
Flynn, Tom, Green Bay	1	7	7.0	7	0
Gay, William, Detroit	1	7	7.0	7	0
Hegman, Mike, Dallas	1	7	7.0	7	0
Doleman, Chris, Minnesota	1	5	5.0	5	0
Fuller, Jeff, San Francisco	1	4	4.0	4	0
Rivera, Ron, Chicago	1	4	4.0	4	0
Frizzell, William, Detroit	1	3	3.0	3	0
Holt, John, Tampa Bay	1	3	3.0	3	0
Marshall, Leonard, N.Y. Giants	1	3	3.0	3	0
Pitts, Mike, Atlanta	1	1	1.0	1	0
Cade, Mossy, Green Bay	1	0	0.0	0	0
Curry, Buddy, Atlanta	1	0	0.0	0	0
Holt, Issiac, Minnesota	1	0	0.0	0	0

	No.	Yards	Avg.	Long	TD
McLemore, Dana, San Francisco	1	0	0.0	0	0
Randle, Ervin, Tampa Bay	1	0	0.0	0	0
Walter, Mike, San Francisco	1	0	0.0	0	0
Watts, Ted, N.Y. Giants	1	0	0.0	0	0
Wilcher, Mike, L.A. Rams	1	0	0.0	0	0
Wright, Eric, San Francisco	1	0	0.0	0	0
Young, Roynell, Philadelphia	1	0	0.0	0	0
Barnes, Roosevelt, Detroit	1	−1	−1.0	−1	0
Winston, Dennis, New Orleans	0	8	—	8	0

t indicates touchdown
Leader based on most interceptions.

PUNTING

INDIVIDUAL CHAMPIONS
AFC: 45.9 — Rohn Stark, Indianapolis
NFC: 43.6 — Rick Donnelly, Atlanta
NET AVERAGE
NFC: 38.0 — Dale Hatcher, Los Angeles Rams
AFC: 36.3 — Ray Guy, Los Angeles Raiders
LONGEST
AFC: 75 yards — Rich Camarillo, New England vs. Chicago, September 15
NFC: 75 yards — Mike Horan, Philadelphia vs. Atlanta, November 10
MOST PUNTS
AFC: 93 — Jim Arnold, Kansas City
NFC: 91 — Mike Horan, Philadelphia
MOST PUNTS, GAME
NFC: 11—Mike Horan, Philadelphia vs. New York Giants, September 8
AFC: 11—Rich Camarillo, New England vs. Chicago, September 15
11—Chris Norman, Denver vs. Seattle, October 20
11—Jim Arnold, Kansas City vs. San Francisco, November 17
TEAM CHAMPIONS
AFC: 44.8 — Indianapolis
NFC: 42.9 — New York Giants

AFC PUNTING — TEAM

	Total Punts	Gross Yards	Long	Gross Avg.	TB	Blk.	Opp. Ret.	Ret. Yards	In 20	Net Avg.
Indianapolis	80	3584	68	44.8	14	2	43	572	12	34.2
Miami	59	2576	63	43.7	8	0	27	371	19	34.7
New England	92	3953	75	43.0	13	0	56	598	16	33.6
San Diego	68	2881	67	42.4	9	0	36	274	15	35.7
Houston	84	3490	65	41.5	8	0	45	345	23	35.5
Buffalo	92	3818	67	41.5	4	0	49	438	33	35.9
Los Angeles Raiders	89	3627	68	40.8	12	0	26	159	32	36.3
Cincinnati	63	2563	64	40.7	7	1	42	554	10	29.7
Seattle	91	3667	61	40.3	11	0	47	374	15	33.8
Kansas City	95	3827	62	40.3	11	2	48	530	15	32.4
Cleveland	81	3261	64	40.3	8	0	36	304	18	34.5
New York Jets	74	2978	66	40.2	8	0	36	319	23	33.8
Denver	94	3764	61	40.0	12	2	38	325	16	34.0
Pittsburgh	79	3088	59	39.1	7	1	43	380	17	32.5
AFC Total	1141	47077	75	—	132	8	572	5543	264	—
AFC Average	81.5	3362.6	—	41.3	9.4	0.6	40.9	395.9	18.9	34.1

NFC PUNTING — TEAM

	Total Punts	Gross Yards	Long	Gross Avg.	TB	Blk.	Opp. Ret.	Ret. Yards	In 20	Net Avg.
New York Giants	81	3472	68	42.9	14	0	29	247	20	36.4
Minnesota	67	2867	62	42.8	4	0	36	328	12	36.7
Los Angeles Rams	88	3761	67	42.7	6	1	43	297	32	38.0
New Orleans	89	3763	58	42.3	6	0	45	397	14	36.5
Atlanta	89	3757	68	42.2	7	0	52	417	20	36.0
Detroit	73	3054	60	41.8	5	0	44	420	17	34.7
Chicago	69	2870	69	41.6	14	1	23	203	18	34.6
Philadelphia	91	3777	75	41.5	10	0	41	462	20	34.2
Dallas	83	3439	57	41.4	11	1	44	286	20	35.3
Tampa Bay	79	3233	61	40.9	6	2	47	519	12	32.8
St. Louis	87	3545	67	40.7	8	2	51	456	20	33.7
Washington	73	2973	57	40.7	16	0	32	285	18	32.4
Green Bay	82	3262	66	39.8	8	0	46	411	10	32.8
San Francisco	87	3422	57	39.3	9	1	33	294	30	33.9
NFC Total	1138	47195	75	—	124	8	566	5022	263	—
NFC Average	81.3	3371.1	—	41.5	8.9	0.6	40.4	358.7	18.8	34.9
League Total	2279	94272	75	—	256	16	1138	10565	527	—
League Average	81.4	3366.9	—	41.4	9.1	0.6	40.6	377.3	18.8	34.5

NFL TOP 10 PUNTERS

	Net Punts	Gross Yards	Long	Gross Avg.	Total Punts	TB	Blk.	Opp. Ret.	Ret. Yards	In 20	Net Avg.
Stark, Rohn, Indianapolis	78	3584	68	45.9	80	14	2	43	572	12	34.2
Roby, Reggie, Miami	59	2576	63	43.7	59	8	0	27	371	19	34.7
Donnelly, Rick, Atlanta	59	2574	68	43.6	59	5	0	33	260	18	37.5
Hatcher, Dale, Los Angeles Rams	87	3761	67	43.2	88	6	1	43	297	32	38.0
Camarillo, Rich, New England	92	3953	75	43.0	92	13	0	56	598	16	33.6
Landeta, Sean, New York Giants	81	3472	68	42.9	81	14	0	29	247	20	36.4
Coleman, Greg, Minnesota	67	2867	62	42.8	67	4	0	36	328	12	36.7
Mojsiejenko, Ralf, San Diego	68	2881	67	42.4	68	9	0	36	274	15	35.7
Hansen, Brian, New Orleans	89	3763	58	42.3	89	6	0	45	397	14	36.5
McInally, Pat, Cincinnati	57	2410	64	42.3	58	7	1	41	535	8	29.9

AFC PUNTING — INDIVIDUAL

	Net Punts	Gross Yards	Long	Gross Avg.	Total Punts	TB	Blk.	Opp. Ret.	Ret. Yards	In 20	Net Avg.
Stark, Rohn, Indianapolis	78	3584	68	45.9	80	14	2	43	572	12	34.2
Roby, Reggie, Miami	59	2576	63	43.7	59	8	0	27	371	19	34.7
Camarillo, Rich, New England	92	3953	75	43.0	92	13	0	56	598	16	33.6
Mojsiejenko, Ralf, San Diego	68	2881	67	42.4	68	9	0	36	274	15	35.7
McInally, Pat, Cincinnati	57	2410	64	42.3	58	7	1	41	535	8	29.9
Johnson, Lee, Houston	83	3464	65	41.7	83	8	0	45	345	22	35.7
Kidd, John, Buffalo	92	3818	67	41.5	92	4	0	49	438	33	35.9
Arnold, Jim, Kansas City	93	3827	62	41.2	95	11	2	48	530	15	32.4
Norman, Chris, Denver	92	3764	61	40.9	94	12	2	38	325	16	34.0
Guy, Ray, Los Angeles Raiders	89	3627	68	40.8	89	12	0	26	159	32	36.3
Finzer, David, Seattle	68	2766	61	40.7	68	6	0	38	295	12	34.6
Gossett, Jeff, Cleveland	81	3261	64	40.3	81	8	0	36	304	18	34.5
Jennings, Dave, New York Jets	74	2978	66	40.2	74	8	0	36	319	23	33.8
Newsome, Harry, Pittsburgh	78	3088	59	39.6	79	7	1	43	380	17	32.5
Non-Qualifiers											
Colquitt, Jimmy, Seattle	12	481	55	40.1	12	2	0	3	30	3	34.3
West, Jeff, Seattle	11	420	52	38.2	11	3	0	6	49	0	28.3
Breech, Jim, Cincinnati	5	153	43	30.6	5	0	0	1	19	2	26.8
Smith, Tim, Houston	1	26	26	26.0	1	0	0	0	0	1	26.0

Leader based on gross average, minimum 40 punts.

NFC PUNTING — INDIVIDUAL

	Net Punts	Gross Yards	Long	Gross Avg.	Total Punts	TB	Blk.	Opp. Ret.	Ret. Yards	In 20	Net Avg.
Donnelly, Rick, Atlanta	59	2574	68	43.6	59	5	0	33	260	18	37.5
Hatcher, Dale, Los Angeles Rams	87	3761	67	43.2	88	6	1	43	297	32	38.0
Landeta, Sean, New York Giants	81	3472	68	42.9	81	14	0	29	247	20	36.4
Coleman, Greg, Minnesota	67	2867	62	42.8	67	4	0	36	328	12	36.7
Hansen, Brian, New Orleans	89	3763	58	42.3	89	6	0	45	397	14	36.5
Buford, Maury, Chicago	68	2870	69	42.2	69	14	1	23	203	18	34.6
Garcia, Frank, Tampa Bay	77	3233	61	42.0	79	6	2	47	519	12	32.8
Saxon, Mike, Dallas	81	3396	57	41.9	82	10	1	44	286	20	35.5
Black, Mike, Detroit	73	3054	60	41.8	73	5	0	44	420	17	34.7
Cox, Steve, Washington	52	2175	57	41.8	52	13	0	22	228	14	32.4
Birdsong, Carl, St. Louis	85	3545	67	41.7	87	8	2	51	456	20	33.7
Horan, Mike, Philadelphia	91	3777	75	41.5	91	10	0	41	462	20	34.2
Runager, Max, San Francisco	86	3422	57	39.8	87	9	1	33	294	30	33.9
Prokop, Joe, Green Bay	56	2210	66	39.5	56	6	0	30	265	9	32.6
Non-Qualifiers											
Giacomarro, Ralph, Atlanta	29	1157	52	39.9	29	2	0	19	157	1	33.1
Bracken, Don, Green Bay	26	1052	54	40.5	26	2	0	16	146	1	33.3
Hayes, Jeff, Washington	16	665	55	41.6	16	2	0	9	47	4	36.1
Schroeder, Jay, Washington	4	132	44	33.0	4	1	0	1	10	0	25.5
Luckhurst, Mick, Atlanta	1	26	26	26.0	1	0	0	0	0	1	26.0
Theismann, Joe, Washington	1	1	1	1.0	1	0	0	0	0	0	1.0
White, Danny, Dallas	1	43	43	43.0	1	1	0	0	0	0	23.0

Leader based on gross average, minimum 40 punts.

PUNT RETURNS

INDIVIDUAL CHAMPIONS (AVERAGE)

AFC: 14.1—Irving Fryar, New England
NFC: 13.5—Henry Ellard, Los Angeles Rams

YARDAGE

AFC: 692—Fulton Walker, Los Angeles Raiders
NFC: 501—Henry Ellard, Los Angeles Rams

LONGEST

AFC: 85 yards—Irving Fryar, New England vs. Buffalo, September 22 (TD)
NFC: 80 yards—Henry Ellard, Los Angeles Rams vs. Philadelphia, September 15 (TD)

MOST RETURNS

AFC: 62—Fulton Walker, Los Angeles Raiders
NFC: 53—Phil McConkey, New York Giants

MOST RETURNS, GAME

NFC: 7—Phil McConkey, New York Giants, vs. Philadelphia, September 8 (103 yards)
7—Evan Cooper, Philadelphia vs. Minnesota, December 1 (56 yards)
AFC: 7—Fulton Walker, Los Angeles Raiders vs. New England, September 29 (111 yards)
7—Fulton Walker, Los Angeles Raiders vs. Atlanta, December 1 (89 yards)
7—Fulton Walker, Los Angeles Raiders vs. Los Angeles Rams, December 23 (64 yards)

FAIR CATCHES

NFC: 18—Phil McConkey, New York Giants
AFC: 15—Irving Fryar, New England

MOST YARDS, GAME

AFC: 133—Irving Fryar, New England vs. Buffalo, September 22 (6 returns)
NFC: 103—Phil McConkey, New York Giants vs. Philadelphia, September 8 (7 returns)

TOUCHDOWNS

AFC: 2—Irving Fryar, New England
2—Louis Lipps, Pittsburgh
NFC: 1—Henry Ellard, Los Angeles Rams
1—Pete Mandley, Detroit

TEAM CHAMPIONS

NFC: 13.2—Los Angeles Rams
AFC: 12.6—New England

AFC PUNT RETURNS—TEAM

	No.	FC	Yards	Avg.	Long	TD
New England	42	16	530	12.6	85t	2
Los Angeles Raiders	71	8	785	11.1	32	0
Indianapolis	42	9	449	10.7	70t	1
New York Jets	39	14	386	9.9	46	0
Pittsburgh	49	4	483	9.9	71t	2
Denver	46	11	429	9.3	38	0
Seattle	53	11	483	9.1	32	0
Kansas City	43	7	381	8.9	57	0
San Diego	25	11	213	8.5	24	0
Cincinnati	32	8	268	8.4	26	0
Houston	30	11	250	8.3	23	0
Miami	39	14	319	8.2	21	0
Cleveland	47	8	371	7.9	37t	1
Buffalo	38	6	293	7.7	30	0
AFC Total	596	138	5640	—	85t	6
AFC Average	42.6	9.9	402.9	9.5	—	0.4

NFC PUNT RETURNS—TEAM

	No.	FC	Yards	Avg.	Long	TD
Los Angeles Rams	38	16	501	13.2	80t	1
Washington	47	11	508	10.8	37	0
Detroit	38	5	403	10.6	63t	1
Minnesota	25	8	250	10.0	41	0
St. Louis	40	12	393	9.8	31	0
Green Bay	38	10	370	9.7	46	0
Chicago	54	10	503	9.3	47	0
Tampa Bay	25	9	229	9.2	29	0
Philadelphia	45	10	393	8.7	56	0
New York Giants	53	18	442	8.3	37	0
Atlanta	31	8	223	7.2	23	0
New Orleans	30	18	215	7.2	17	0
San Francisco	38	14	258	6.8	22	0
Dallas	40	14	237	5.9	28	0
NFC Total	542	163	4925	—	80t	2
NFC Average	38.7	11.6	351.8	9.1	—	0.1
League Total	1138	301	10565	—	85t	8
League Average	40.6	10.8	377.3	9.3	—	0.3

NFL TOP 10 PUNT RETURNERS

	No.	FC	Yards	Avg.	Long	TD
Fryar, Irving, New England	37	15	520	14.1	85t	2
Ellard, Henry, L.A. Rams	37	9	501	13.5	80t	1
Lipps, Louis, Pittsburgh	36	2	437	12.1	71t	2
Walker, Fulton, L.A. Raiders	62	6	692	11.2	32	0
Martin, Robbie, Indianapolis	40	7	443	11.1	70t	1
Smith, J. T., St. Louis	26	10	283	10.9	31	0
Mandley, Pete, Detroit	38	5	403	10.6	63t	1
Jenkins, Ken, Washington	26	9	272	10.5	28	0
Skansi, Paul, Seattle	31	7	312	10.1	32	0
Drewrey, Willie, Houston	24	10	215	9.0	23	0

AFC PUNT RETURNS—INDIVIDUAL

	No.	FC	Yards	Avg.	Long	TD
Fryar, Irving, New England	37	15	520	14.1	85t	2
Lipps, Louis, Pittsburgh	36	2	437	12.1	71t	2
Walker, Fulton, L.A. Raiders	62	6	692	11.2	32	0
Martin, Robbie, Indianapolis	40	7	443	11.1	70t	1
Skansi, Paul, Seattle	31	7	312	10.1	32	0
Drewrey, Willie, Houston	24	10	215	9.0	23	0
Vigorito, Tom, Miami	22	5	197	9.0	21	0
Lane, Garcia, Kansas City	43	7	381	8.9	57	0
Johnson, Vance, Denver	30	6	260	8.7	38	0
James, Lionel, San Diego	25	8	213	8.5	24	0
Martin, Mike, Cincinnati	32	8	268	8.4	26	0
Weathers, Clarence, Cleveland	28	4	218	7.8	16	0
Non-Qualifiers						
Brennan, Brian, Cleveland	19	4	153	8.1	37t	1
Willhite, Gerald, Denver	16	5	169	10.6	18	0
Wilson, Don, Buffalo	16	5	161	10.1	30	0
Sohn, Kurt, N.Y. Jets	16	5	149	9.3	46	0
Hill, Rod, Buffalo	16	1	120	7.5	25	0
Springs, Kirk, N.Y. Jets	14	4	147	10.5	40	0
Woods, Rick, Pittsburgh	13	2	46	3.5	10	0
Greene, Danny, Seattle	11	3	60	5.5	13	0
Easley, Ken, Seattle	8	0	87	10.9	25	0
Montgomery, Cleotha, L.A. Raiders	8	2	84	10.5	32	0
Kozlowski, Mike, Miami	7	2	65	9.3	17	0
Townsell, JoJo, N.Y. Jets	6	1	65	10.8	22	0
Donaldson, Jeff, Houston	6	1	35	5.8	13	0

	No.	FC	Yards	Avg.	Long	TD
Lockett, Frank, Miami	5	0	23	4.6	8	0
Reed, Andre, Buffalo	5	0	12	2.4	5	0
Harris, John, Seattle	3	1	24	8.0	12	0
Blackwood, Glenn, Miami	3	3	20	6.7	18	0
Minter, Cedric, N.Y. Jets	2	4	25	12.5	20	0
Clayton, Mark, Miami	2	0	14	7.0	11	0
James, Roland, New England	2	0	13	6.5	13	0
Starring, Stephen, New England	2	0	0	0.0	0	0
Haynes, Mike, L.A. Raiders	1	0	9	9.0	9	0
Daniel, Eugene, Indianapolis	1	1	6	6.0	6	0
Humphery, Bobby, N.Y. Jets	1	0	0	0.0	0	0
Lowry, Orlando, Indianapolis	1	0	0	0.0	0	0
Wilson, Eric, Buffalo	1	0	0	0.0	0	0
Bowman, Jim, New England	1	0	−3	−3.0	−3	0
Blackwood, Lyle, Miami	0	4	0	—	0	0
Marion, Fred, New England	0	1	0	—	0	0
McPherson, Miles, San Diego	0	2	0	—	0	0
Steels, Anthony, San Diego	0	1	0	—	0	0
Young, Anthony, Indianapolis	0	1	0	—	0	0

t indicates touchdown
Leader based on average return, minimum 20 returns.

NFC PUNT RETURNS—INDIVIDUAL

	No.	FC	Yards	Avg.	Long	TD
Ellard, Henry, L.A. Rams	37	9	501	13.5	80t	1
Smith, J.T., St. Louis	26	10	283	10.9	31	0
Mandley, Pete, Detroit	38	5	403	10.6	63t	1
Jenkins, Ken, Washington	26	9	272	10.5	28	0
Cooper, Evan, Philadelphia	43	10	364	8.5	56	0
McConkey, Phil, N.Y. Giants	53	18	442	8.3	37	0
Taylor, Ken, Chicago	25	8	198	7.9	21	0
Bates, Bill, Dallas	22	6	152	6.9	21	0
McLemore, Dana, San Francisco	38	14	258	6.8	22	0
Allen, Anthony, Atlanta	21	8	141	6.7	23	0
Non-Qualifiers						
Ortego, Keith, Chicago	17	2	158	9.3	23	0
Tullis, Willie, New Orleans	17	6	141	8.3	17	0
Green, Darrell, Washington	16	0	214	13.4	37	0
Nelson, Darrin, Minnesota	16	3	133	8.3	21	0
Epps, Phillip, Green Bay	15	3	146	9.7	46	0
Gonzalez, Leon, Dallas	15	5	58	3.9	13	0
Stanley, Walter, Green Bay	14	3	179	12.8	27	0
Prior, Mike, Tampa Bay	13	7	105	8.1	19	0
Bright, Leon, Tampa Bay	12	2	124	10.3	29	0
Mitchell, Stump, St. Louis	11	2	97	8.8	21	0
Johnson, Billy, Atlanta	10	0	82	8.2	18	0
Carter, Anthony, Minnesota	9	5	117	13.0	41	0
Martin, Eric, New Orleans	8	10	53	6.6	13	0
Flynn, Tom, Green Bay	7	4	41	5.9	13	0
Duerson, Dave, Chicago	6	0	47	7.8	11	0
McKinnon, Dennis, Chicago	4	0	44	11.0	17	0
Cherry, Raphel, Washington	4	1	22	5.5	9	0
Roaches, Carl, New Orleans	4	2	21	5.3	10	0
Banks, Gordon, Dallas	3	3	27	9.0	28	0
Nelson, Lee, St. Louis	2	0	14	7.0	8	0
Maness, James, Chicago	2	0	9	4.5	5	0
Waters, Andre, Philadelphia	1	0	23	23.0	23	0
Hunter, Herman, Philadelphia	1	0	6	6.0	6	0
Murphy, Mark, Green Bay	1	0	4	4.0	4	0
Dean, Vernon, Washington	1	0	0	0.0	0	0
Groth, Jeff, New Orleans	1	0	0	0.0	0	0
Hayes, Gary, Green Bay	1	0	0	0.0	0	0
White, Charles, L.A. Rams	1	0	0	0.0	0	0
Tilley, Pat, St. Louis	1	0	−1	−1.0	−1	0
Gentry, Dennis, Chicago	0	0	47	—	47	0
Clark, Gary, Washington	0	1	0	—	0	0
Johnson, Johnnie, L.A. Rams	0	7	0	—	0	0

t indicates touchdown
Leader based on average return, minimum 20 returns.

KICKOFF RETURNS

INDIVIDUAL CHAMPIONS (AVERAGE)
NFC: 32.8—Ron Brown, Los Angeles Rams
AFC: 25.7—Glen Young, Cleveland
YARDAGE
NFC: 1,345—Buster Rhymes, Minnesota
AFC: 1,104—Mike Martin, Cincinnati
MOST YARDS, GAME
NFC: 184—Ron Brown, Los Angeles Rams vs. Green Bay, November 24 (2 returns)
AFC: 157—Glen Young, Cleveland vs. New York Giants, December 1 (5 returns)
MOST RETURNS
NFC: 53—Buster Rhymes, Minnesota
AFC: 48—Mike Martin, Cincinnati
48—Stephen Starring, New England
MOST RETURNS, GAME
NFC: 8—Gary Ellerson, Green Bay vs. St. Louis, September 29 (164 yards)
AFC: 7—Lionel James, San Diego vs. Kansas City, December 22 (141 yards)
LONGEST
NFC: 99 yards—Willie Gault, Chicago vs. Washington, September 29 (TD)
AFC: 98 yards —Gary Anderson, San Diego vs. Denver, November 17 (TD)
TOUCHDOWNS
NFC: 3—Ron Brown, Los Angeles Rams
AFC: 1—Gary Anderson, San Diego
TEAM CHAMPIONS
NFC: 25.3—Chicago
AFC: 23.1—Denver

AFC KICKOFF RETURNS—TEAM

	No.	Yards	Avg.	Long	TD
Denver	52	1203	23.1	39	0
Cleveland	53	1217	23.0	81	0
Miami	52	1177	22.6	46	0
Houston	67	1515	22.6	52	0
San Diego	71	1494	21.0	98t	1
Los Angeles Raiders	54	1132	21.0	57	0
Indianapolis	67	1403	20.9	48	0
Cincinnati	67	1385	20.7	45	0
Pittsburgh	65	1337	20.6	40	0
Seattle	58	1166	20.1	58	0
New York Jets	53	1043	19.7	58	0
New England	57	1119	19.6	53	0
Buffalo	68	1334	19.6	39	0
Kansas City	59	1117	18.9	40	0
AFC Total	843	17642	—	98t	1
AFC Average	60.2	1260.1	20.9	—	0.1

NFC KICKOFF RETURNS—TEAM

	No.	Yards	Avg.	Long	TD
Chicago	43	1089	25.3	99t	2
Los Angeles Rams	56	1394	24.9	98t	3
Minnesota	68	1576	23.2	88	0
Washington	60	1349	22.5	95	0
Detroit	68	1494	22.0	54	0
San Francisco	58	1269	21.9	95t	1
New Orleans	71	1547	21.8	69	0
Philadelphia	56	1160	20.7	51	0
Tampa Bay	80	1622	20.3	58	0
Green Bay	67	1318	19.7	48	0
Atlanta	72	1406	19.5	94t	1
Dallas	62	1210	19.5	34	0
St. Louis	78	1421	18.2	35	0
New York Giants	50	866	17.3	43	0
NFC Total	889	18721	—	99t	7
NFC Average	63.5	1337.2	21.1	—	0.5
League Total	1732	36363	—	99t	8
League Average	61.9	1298.7	21.0	—	0.3

NFL TOP 10 KICKOFF RETURNERS

	No.	Yards	Avg.	Long	TD
Brown, Ron, L.A. Rams	28	918	32.8	98t	3
Gault, Willie, Chicago	22	577	26.2	99t	1
Young, Glen, Cleveland	35	898	25.7	63	0
Monroe, Carl, San Francisco	28	717	25.6	95t	1
Rhymes, Buster, Minnesota	53	1345	25.4	88	0
Bentley, Albert, Indianapolis	27	674	25.0	48	0
Jenkins, Ken, Washington	41	1018	24.8	95	0
Drewrey, Willie, Houston	26	642	24.7	50	0
Johnson, Vance, Denver	30	740	24.7	39	0
Martin, Mike, Cincinnati	48	1104	23.0	45	0

AFC KICKOFF RETURNS—INDIVIDUAL

	No.	Yards	Avg.	Long	TD
Young, Glen, Cleveland	35	898	25.7	63	0
Bentley, Albert, Indianapolis	27	674	25.0	48	0
Drewrey, Willie, Houston	26	642	24.7	50	0
Johnson, Vance, Denver	30	740	24.7	39	0
Martin, Mike, Cincinnati	48	1104	23.0	45	0
Spencer, Todd, Pittsburgh	27	617	22.9	40	0
Hampton, Lorenzo, Miami	45	1020	22.7	46	0
Walker, Fulton, L.A. Raiders	21	467	22.2	57	0
James, Lionel, San Diego	36	779	21.6	46	0
Wilson, Don, Buffalo	22	465	21.1	37	0
Starring, Stephen, New England	48	1012	21.1	53	0

	No.	Yards	Avg.	Long	TD
Erenberg, Rich, Pittsburgh	21	441	21.0	35	0
Seale, Sam, L.A. Raiders	23	482	21.0	36	0
Morris, Randall, Seattle	31	636	20.5	58	0
Martin, Robbie, Indianapolis	32	638	19.9	36	0
Smith, Jeff, Kansas City	33	654	19.8	39	0
Steels, Anthony, SD-Buff.	30	561	18.7	54	0
Non-Qualifiers					
Skansi, Paul, Seattle	19	358	18.8	35	0
Tasker, Steve, Houston	17	447	26.3	52	0
Humphery, Bobby, N.Y. Jets	17	363	21.4	56	0
Lang, Gene, Denver	17	361	21.2	33	0
Anderson, Gary, San Diego	13	302	23.2	98t	1
Lane, Garcia, Kansas City	13	269	20.7	37	0
Lipps, Louis, Pittsburgh	13	237	18.2	26	0
Jennings, Stanford, Cincinnati	13	218	16.8	26	0
Hutchison, Anthony, Buffalo	12	239	19.9	36	0
Walls, Herkie, Houston	12	234	19.5	42	0
Hector, Johnny, N.Y. Jets	11	274	24.9	47	0
Springs, Kirk, N.Y. Jets	10	227	22.7	58	0
Fontenot, Herman, Cleveland	8	215	26.9	81	0
Montgomery, Cleotha, L.A. Raiders	7	150	21.4	30	0
McGee, Buford, San Diego	7	135	19.3	33	0
Brookins, Mitchell, Buffalo	6	152	25.3	39	0
Hancock, Anthony, Kansas City	6	125	20.8	40	0
Greene, Danny, Seattle	5	144	28.8	52	0
Donaldson, Jeff, Houston	5	93	18.6	22	0
Glenn, Kerry, N.Y. Jets	5	71	14.2	20	0
Carter, Joe, Miami	4	82	20.5	25	0
Richardson, Eric, Buffalo	3	69	23.0	31	0
Langhorne, Reggie, Cleveland	3	46	15.3	19	0
Williams, Oliver, Indianapolis	3	44	14.7	21	0
Elder, Donnie, N.Y. Jets	3	42	14.0	25	0
Fryar, Irving, New England	3	39	13.0	24	0
Brooks, James, Cincinnati	3	38	12.7	15	0
Jones, Cedric, New England	3	37	12.3	20	0
Washington, Sam, Pittsburgh	3	34	11.3	14	0
Moore, Booker, Buffalo	3	31	10.3	15	0
Sohn, Kurt, N.Y. Jets	3	7	2.3	4	0
Adams, Curtis, San Diego	2	50	25.0	26	0
Brown, Steve, Houston	2	45	22.5	28	0
Townsell, JoJo, N.Y. Jets	2	42	21.0	23	0
Willhite, Gerald, Denver	2	40	20.0	20	0
Paige, Stephone, Kansas City	2	36	18.0	23	0
Hunter, Daniel, Denver	2	33	16.5	18	0
Blackwood, Lyle, Miami	2	32	16.0	17	0
Williams, Jamie, Houston	2	21	10.5	12	0
Green, Boyce, Cleveland	2	20	10.0	13	0
Young, Anthony, Indianapolis	2	15	7.5	17	0
Arnold, Walt, Kansas City	2	9	4.5	9	0
Puzzuoli, Dave, Cleveland	2	8	4.0	8	0
Sewell, Steve, Denver	1	29	29.0	29	0
Hill, Drew, Houston	1	22	22.0	22	0
Middleton, Frank, Indianapolis	1	20	20.0	20	0
Teal, Jimmy, Buffalo	1	20	20.0	20	0
Williams, Van, Buffalo	1	20	20.0	20	0
Williams, Dokie, L.A. Raiders	1	19	19.0	19	0
Zander, Carl, Cincinnati	1	19	19.0	19	0
Weathers, Robert, New England	1	18	18.0	18	0
Tice, Mike, Seattle	1	17	17.0	17	0
Weathers, Clarence, Cleveland	1	17	17.0	17	0
Hawkins, Frank, L.A. Raiders	1	14	14.0	14	0
Minter, Cedric, N.Y. Jets	1	14	14.0	14	0
Hawthorne, Greg, New England	1	13	13.0	13	0
King, Bruce, Kansas City	1	13	13.0	13	0
Hardy, Bruce, Miami	1	11	11.0	11	0
Shorthose, George, Kansas City	1	11	11.0	11	0
Robinson, Eugene, Seattle	1	10	10.0	10	0
Nicolas, Scott, Cleveland	1	9	9.0	9	0
Tuggle, Anthony, Pittsburgh	1	8	8.0	8	0
Brown, Eddie, Cincinnati	1	6	6.0	6	0
Gill, Owen, Indianapolis	1	6	6.0	6	0
Lee, Keith, Indianapolis	1	6	6.0	6	0
Lyday, Allen, Houston	1	6	6.0	6	0
Briehl, Tom, Houston	1	5	5.0	5	0
Allen, Greg, Cleveland	1	4	4.0	4	0
Klever, Rocky, N.Y. Jets	1	3	3.0	3	0
Sievers, Eric, San Diego	1	3	3.0	3	0
Bendross, Jesse, San Diego	1	2	2.0	2	0
Lane, Eric, Seattle	1	1	1.0	1	0
Griffin, James, Cincinnati	1	0	0.0	0	0
Hayes, Jonathan, Kansas City	1	0	0.0	0	0
Hayes, Lester, L.A. Raiders	1	0	0.0	0	0
Holohan, Pete, San Diego	1	0	0.0	0	0
James, Craig, New England	1	0	0.0	0	0
Kozlowski, Mike, Miami	0	32	—	32	0

t indicates touchdown
Leader based on average return, minimum 20 returns.

NFC KICKOFF RETURNS—INDIVIDUAL

	No.	Yards	Avg.	Long	TD
Brown, Ron, L.A. Rams	28	918	32.8	98t	3
Gault, Willie, Chicago	22	577	26.2	99t	1
Monroe, Carl, San Francisco	28	717	25.6	95t	1
Rhymes, Buster, Minnesota	53	1345	25.4	88	0
Jenkins, Ken, Washington	41	1018	24.8	95	0
Hall, Alvin, Detroit	39	886	22.7	54	0
Freeman, Phil, Tampa Bay	48	1085	22.6	58	0
Hunter, Herman, Philadelphia	48	1047	21.8	51	0
Austin, Cliff, Atlanta	39	838	21.5	94t	1
Anthony, Tyrone, New Orleans	23	476	20.7	52	0
Tullis, Willie, New Orleans	23	470	20.4	62	0
Harmon, Derrick, San Francisco	23	467	20.3	37	0
Lavette, Robert, Dallas	34	682	20.1	34	0
Duncan, Clyde, St. Louis	28	550	19.6	34	0
Ellerson, Gary, Green Bay	29	521	18.0	32	0
Non-Qualifiers					
Mitchell, Stump, St. Louis	19	345	18.2	35	0
Gentry, Dennis, Chicago	18	466	25.9	94t	1
White, Charles, L.A. Rams	17	300	17.6	32	0
Martin, Eric, New Orleans	15	384	25.6	69	0
Adams, George, N.Y. Giants	14	241	17.2	29	0
Wagoner, Danny, Atlanta	13	262	20.2	34	0
Ellis, Gerry, Green Bay	13	247	19.0	40	0
Wolfley, Ron, St. Louis	13	234	18.0	28	0
Moore, Alvin, Detroit	13	230	17.7	24	0
Epps, Phillip, Green Bay	12	279	23.3	48	0
McConkey, Phil, N.Y. Giants	12	234	19.5	43	0
Bright, Leon, Tampa Bay	11	213	19.4	47	0
Hill, Ken, N.Y. Giants	11	186	16.9	27	0
Jones, A.J., Detroit	10	226	22.6	30	0
Prior, Mike, Tampa Bay	10	131	13.1	27	0
Stanley, Walter, Green Bay	9	212	23.6	36	0
Duckett, Kenny, Dallas	9	173	19.2	25	0
Jones, James, Dallas	9	161	17.9	26	0
Allen, Anthony, Atlanta	8	140	17.5	26	0
Griffin, Keith, Washington	7	142	20.3	35	0
Galbreath, Tony, N.Y. Giants	7	120	17.1	37	0
Mandley, Pete, Detroit	6	152	25.3	35	0
Morton, Michael, Washington	6	131	21.8	27	0
Williams, John, Dallas	6	129	21.5	30	0
Cain, Lynn, L.A. Rams	6	115	19.2	28	0
Springs, Ron, Tampa Bay	5	112	22.4	34	0
Smith, Leonard, St. Louis	5	68	13.6	26	0
Stamps, Sylvester, Atlanta	4	89	22.3	32	0
Fowler, Bobby, New Orleans	4	78	19.5	23	0
Harrington, Perry, St. Louis	4	77	19.3	35	0
McLemore, Dana, San Francisco	4	76	19.0	26	0
Roaches, Carl, New Orleans	4	76	19.0	23	0
Waters, Andre, Philadelphia	4	74	18.5	23	0
Rice, Allen, Minnesota	4	70	17.5	27	0
Turner, Maurice, Minnesota	4	61	15.3	18	0
Verser, David, Tampa Bay	4	61	15.3	18	0
Smith, J.T., St. Louis	4	59	14.8	33	0
Whisenhunt, Ken, Atlanta	4	33	8.3	14	0
Nelson, Darrin, Minnesota	3	51	17.0	26	0
Nelson, Lee, St. Louis	3	49	16.3	26	0
Fowler, Todd, Dallas	3	48	16.0	20	0
Cooper, Evan, Philadelphia	3	32	10.7	13	0
Rouson, Lee, N.Y. Giants	2	35	17.5	26	0
Bess, Rufus, Minnesota	2	33	16.5	22	0
Guman, Mike, L.A. Rams	2	30	15.0	17	0
Wonsley, Otis, Washington	2	26	13.0	19	0
Morris, Joe, N.Y. Giants	2	25	12.5	18	0
Magee, Calvin, Tampa Bay	2	20	10.0	15	0
Rackley, David, New Orleans	1	63	63.0	63	0
Hasselbeck, Don, N.Y. Giants	1	21	21.0	21	0
Flynn, Tom, Green Bay	1	20	20.0	20	0
Johnson, Kenny, Atlanta	1	20	20.0	20	0
Novacek, Jay, St. Louis	1	20	20.0	20	0
Mumford, Tony, St. Louis	1	19	19.0	19	0
Slaton, Tony, L.A. Rams	1	18	18.0	18	0
Taylor, Ken, Chicago	1	18	18.0	18	0
Powe, Karl, Dallas	1	17	17.0	17	0
McKinnon, Dennis, Chicago	1	16	16.0	16	0
Anderson, John, Green Bay	1	14	14.0	14	0
Hamel, Dean, Washington	1	14	14.0	14	0
Stills, Ken, Green Bay	1	14	14.0	14	0
Tyrrell, Tim, Atlanta	1	13	13.0	13	0
Jones, Daryll, Green Bay	1	11	11.0	11	0
Matthews, Allama, Atlanta	1	11	11.0	11	0
Miller, Shawn, L.A. Rams	1	10	10.0	10	0
Sanders, Thomas, Chicago	1	10	10.0	10	0
Cherry, Raphel, Washington	1	9	9.0	9	0
Keating, Chris, Washington	1	9	9.0	9	0
Brown, Ted, Minnesota	1	7	7.0	7	0
Foules, Elbert, Philadelphia	1	7	7.0	7	0
Rice, Jerry, San Francisco	1	6	6.0	6	0

	No.	Yards	Avg.	Long	TD
Salley, Jerome, N.Y. Giants	1	4	4.0	4	0
Cromwell, Nolan, L.A. Rams	1	3	3.0	3	0
Lott, Ronnie, San Francisco	1	2	2.0	2	0
Frank, John, San Francisco	1	1	1.0	1	0
Browner, Joey, Minnesota	1	0	0.0	0	0
Jones, Anthony, Washington	1	0	0.0	0	0
Merkens, Guido, New Orleans	1	0	0.0	0	0
Washington, Ronnie, Atlanta	1	0	0.0	0	0
Mularkey, Mike, Minnesota	0	9	—	9	0
Marshall, Wilber, Chicago	0	2	—	2	0

t indicates touchdown
Leader based on average return, minimum 20 returns.

AFC FUMBLES — TEAM

	Fum.	Own Rec.	Fum. *O.B.	TD	Opp. Rec.	Yds.	TD	Tot. Rec.
Kansas City	22	10	1	0	14	−18	1	24
Denver	24	14	2	0	12	−22	0	26
Indianapolis	27	11	2	0	17	81	1	28
L.A. Raiders	27	13	0	1	13	−26	0	26
Miami	31	10	1	0	18	12	1	28
Pittsburgh	31	21	1	0	14	14	0	35
Seattle	34	13	3	0	20	98	1	33
Cincinnati	35	16	3	0	19	64	0	35
N.Y. Jets	35	11	3	0	20	60	1	31
Buffalo	36	14	1	0	15	54	1	29
New England	37	13	4	0	24	34	3	37
Cleveland	40	17	0	0	9	−17	0	26
Houston	41	23	3	0	20	10	0	43
San Diego	44	19	6	0	16	4	0	35
AFC Totals	464	205	30	1	231	348	9	436
AFC Average	33.1	14.6	2.1	0.1	16.5	24.9	0.6	31.1

NFC FUMBLES — TEAM

	Fum.	Own Rec.	Fum. *O.B.	TD	Opp. Rec.	Yds.	TD	Tot. Rec.
Atlanta	23	10	3	0	12	49	1	22
New Orleans	23	10	0	0	16	39	2	26
Chicago	24	7	2	0	20	66	1	27
Philadelphia	25	12	1	1	14	37	0	26
Minnesota	27	9	0	0	22	73	1	31
Washington	27	7	1	0	11	−3	0	18
Dallas	29	12	1	0	15	15	0	27
San Francisco	29	8	1	0	17	93	3	25
L.A. Rams	35	13	1	0	16	19	0	29
Detroit	36	13	3	0	18	17	0	31
N.Y. Giants	36	16	2	0	13	6	0	29
Tampa Bay	37	9	6	0	22	12	0	31
St. Louis	38	17	5	0	14	−1	0	31
Green Bay	39	20	1	0	25	12	1	45
NFC Totals	428	163	27	1	235	434	9	398
NFC Average	30.6	11.6	1.9	0.1	16.8	31.0	0.6	28.4
League Totals	892	368	57	2	466	782	18	834
League Average	31.9	13.1	2.0	0.1	16.6	27.9	0.6	29.8

**indicates fumbled out of bounds.*
Total yards include all fumble yardage (aborted plays, own & opp. recoveries). Fumbled through the end zone, ball awarded to opponents: Tampa Bay (awarded to Los Angeles Rams).

AFC FUMBLES — INDIVIDUAL

	Fum.	Own Rec.	Opp. Rec.	Yds.	Tot. Rec.
Abercrombie, Walter, Pittsburgh	5	1	0	0	1
Abraham, Robert, Houston	0	0	4	0	4
Adams, Julius, New England	0	0	2	12	2
Adams, Willis, Cleveland	0	1	0	4	1
Ahrens, Dave, Indianapolis	0	0	1	0	1
Alexander, Charles, Cincinnati	0	1	0	0	1
Allen, Greg, Cleveland	1	0	0	0	0
Allen, Marcus, L.A. Raiders	3	2	0	-6	2
Allen, Patrick, Houston	0	1	1	0	2
Alzado, Lyle, L.A. Raiders	0	1	0	0	1
Anderson, Don, Indianapolis	1	0	0	0	0
Anderson, Gary, San Diego	5	3	0	0	3
Anderson, Ken, Cincinnati	1	0	0	0	0
Baab, Mike, Cleveland	1	0	0	-2	0
Baldwin, Tom, N.Y. Jets	0	0	1	9	1
Barnes, Jeff, L.A. Raiders	0	0	4	14	4
Barnett, Bill, Miami	0	0	1	0	1
Bayless, Martin, Buffalo	0	1	0	0	1
Beach, Pat, Indianapolis	3	0	1	5	1
Bell, Greg, Buffalo	8	2	0	0	2
Bell, Mike, Kansas City	0	0	1	0	1
Bellinger, Rodney, Buffalo	0	0	1	0	1
Bentley, Albert, Indianapolis	1	1	0	0	1
Bickett, Duane, Indianapolis	0	0	2	0	2
Blackledge, Todd, Kansas City	3	1	0	0	1
Blackmon, Don, New England	0	0	2	0	2
Blackwood, Glenn, Miami	0	0	1	0	1
Bligen, Dennis, N.Y. Jets	1	0	0	0	0
Bostic, Keith, Houston	0	0	1	0	1
Boyer, Mark, Indianapolis	0	1	0	0	1
Braziel, Larry, Cleveland	0	0	1	0	1
Brennan, Brian, Cleveland	3	0	0	0	0
Brooks, James, Cincinnati	7	1	0	0	1
Brophy, Jay, Miami	0	0	1	0	1
Brown, Bud, Miami	0	0	5	6	5
Brown, Dave, Seattle	0	0	1	0	1
Brown, Eddie, Cincinnati	2	1	0	0	1
Brown, Mark, Miami	0	0	2	0	2
Brown, Steve, Houston	1	0	1	0	1
Browner, Ross, Cincinnati	0	0	2	0	2
Brudzinski, Bob, Miami	0	0	2	7	2
Bryan, Bill, Denver	0	1	0	0	1
Bryant, Jeff, Seattle	0	0	4	0	4
Bush, Blair, Seattle	0	1	0	0	1
Bush, Frank, Houston	0	0	3	3	3
Busick, Steve, Denver	0	0	1	0	1
Butler, Keith, Seattle	0	0	3	0	3
Byner, Earnest, Cleveland	5	4	0	0	4
Byrd, Gill, San Diego	0	0	1	0	1
Byrd, Richard, Houston	0	0	1	0	1
Camp, Reggie, Cleveland	0	0	1	0	1
Campbell, Scott, Pittsburgh	3	3	0	0	3
Capers, Wayne, Indianapolis	1	0	0	0	0
Carr, Gregg, Pittsburgh	0	1	1	0	2
Carter, Joe, Miami	2	0	1	0	1
Carter, Rubin, Denver	0	0	1	6	1
Catano, Mark, Pittsburgh	0	0	1	17	1
Chandler, Wes, San Diego	1	0	0	0	0
Chavous, Barney, Denver	0	0	1	0	1
Childress, Ray, Houston	0	0	1	0	1
Christensen, Todd, L.A. Raiders	0	1	0	0	1
Claphan, Sam, San Diego	0	1	0	0	1
Clark, Steve, Miami	0	0	1	0	1
Clayton, Mark, Miami	2	1	0	0	1
Clifton, Kyle, N.Y. Jets	0	0	2	0	2
Cocroft, Sherman, Kansas City	0	0	2	0	2
Cole, Robin, Pittsburgh	0	0	3	0	3
Collins, Tony, New England	6	2	0	0	2
Collinsworth, Cris, Cincinnati	1	0	0	0	0
Cousineau, Tom, Cleveland	0	0	1	0	1
Crable, Bob, N.Y. Jets	0	0	1	0	1
Cribbs, Joe, Buffalo	5	1	0	0	1
Daniel, Eugene, Indianapolis	1	1	2	25	3
Daniels, Calvin, Kansas City	0	0	2	0	2
Danielson, Gary, Cleveland	5	1	0	-17	1
Davenport, Ron, Miami	2	0	0	0	0
Davis, Mike, L.A. Raiders	0	0	1	0	1
Davis, Preston, Indianapolis	0	0	2	0	2
Davis, Wayne, San Diego	0	0	1	0	1
Dawson, Lin, New England	1	1	0	0	1
Donaldson, Jeff, Houston	1	0	2	0	2
Donaldson, Ray, Indianapolis	0	1	0	0	1
Dressel, Chris, Houston	0	0	1	0	1
Drewrey, Willie, Houston	2	0	0	0	0
Dunn, Gary, Pittsburgh	0	0	3	0	3
Duper, Mark, Miami	1	1	0	3	1
Easley, Ken, Seattle	2	1	0	0	1
Eason, Bo, Houston	1	0	0	0	0
Eason, Tony, New England	4	1	0	-19	1
Edwards, Eddie, Cincinnati	0	0	2	0	2
Edwards, Randy, Seattle	0	0	1	0	1
Ehin, Chuck, San Diego	0	0	1	0	1
Elder, Donnie, N.Y. Jets	1	0	0	0	0
Elway, John, Denver	7	2	0	-35	2
Erenberg, Rich, Pittsburgh	1	0	0	-12	0
Esiason, Boomer, Cincinnati	9	4	0	-5	4
Faulkner, Chris, San Diego	0	1	0	0	1
Ferguson, Keith, San Diego	0	0	1	0	1
Ferragamo, Vince, Buffalo	1	0	0	0	0
Fields, Joe, N.Y. Jets	0	1	0	0	1
Fontenot, Herman, Cleveland	1	0	0	0	0
Fouts, Dan, San Diego	13	6	0	-11	6
Fryar, Irving, New England	4	0	0	0	0
Gaines, Greg, Seattle	0	0	2	7	2
Gary, Keith, Pittsburgh	0	0	1	0	1
Gastineau, Mark, N.Y. Jets	0	0	3	0	3
Giesler, Jon, Miami	0	1	0	0	1
Gilbert, Gale, Seattle	1	1	0	−5	1
Gill, Owen, Indianapolis	1	0	0	0	0
Glenn, Kerry, N.Y. Jets	0	0	2	31	2
Gothard, Preston, Pittsburgh	0	0	1	0	1
Grant, Will, Buffalo	0	1	0	0	1
Green, Hugh, Miami	0	0	1	0	1
Green, Jacob, Seattle	0	0	2	79	2

	Fum.	Own Rec.	Opp. Rec.	Yds.	Tot. Rec.
Green, Mike, San Diego	0	0	2	0	2
Greene, Danny, Seattle	1	0	0	0	0
Griffin, James, Cincinnati	0	0	1	29	1
Grimsley, John, Houston	0	0	1	5	1
Grogan, Steve, New England	6	1	0	−10	1
Gross, Al, Cleveland	0	0	2	2	2
Guilbeau, Rusty, N.Y. Jets	0	0	1	0	1
Guy, Ray, L.A. Raiders	1	0	0	−28	0
Hairston, Carl, Cleveland	0	0	1	0	1
Hamilton, Harry, N.Y. Jets	0	0	1	0	1
Hampton, Lorenzo, Miami	3	1	0	0	1
Hancock, Anthony, Kansas City	1	0	0	0	0
Hannah, Charley, L.A. Raiders	0	1	0	0	1
Harden, Mike, Denver	0	1	1	5	2
Hardy, Andre, Seattle	1	1	0	0	1
Hardy, Bruce, Miami	1	0	0	0	0
Harris, Duriel, Miami	1	0	0	0	0
Harris, John, Seattle	0	0	2	0	2
Haslett, Jim, Buffalo	1	1	2	0	3
Hayes, Lester, L.A. Raiders	0	0	1	0	1
Heard, Herman, Kansas City	4	1	0	0	1
Hector, Johnny, N.Y. Jets	2	1	0	0	1
Hendy, John, San Diego	0	0	1	0	1
Herrmann, Mark, San Diego	8	2	0	−26	2
Hester, Jessie, L.A. Raiders	0	1	0	0	1
Hilger, Rusty, L.A. Raiders	1	1	0	0	1
Hill, Rod, Buffalo	1	0	0	0	0
Holloway, Brian, New England	0	2	0	0	2
Holman, Rodney, Cincinnati	1	1	0	0	1
Holohan, Pete, San Diego	1	0	0	0	0
Holt, Harry, Cleveland	1	0	0	0	0
Horton, Ethan, Kansas City	2	0	0	0	0
Horton, Ray, Cincinnati	1	1	1	0	2
Hughes, David, Seattle	2	1	0	0	1
Humphery, Bobby, N.Y. Jets	2	1	0	0	1
Ilkin, Tunch, Pittsburgh	0	1	0	0	1
Jackson, Charles, N.Y. Jets	0	0	1	0	1
Jackson, Robert, Cincinnati	0	0	1	0	1
James, Craig, New England	8	4	0	−7	4
James, Lionel, San Diego	9	1	0	0	1
James, Roland, New England	1	0	0	0	0
Jennings, Stanford, Cincinnati	1	0	1	0	1
Johnson, Lee, Houston	2	1	0	7	1
Johnson, Richard, Houston	0	1	0	0	1
Johnson, Vance, Denver	5	2	0	0	2
Joiner, Charlie, San Diego	1	0	0	0	0
Jolly, Ken, Kansas City	0	0	1	0	1
Jones, Cedric, New England	0	0	1	15	1
Jones, Rulon, Denver	0	0	3	0	3
Jones, Sean, L.A. Raiders	0	0	1	0	1
Kay, Clarence, Denver	1	1	0	0	1
Kenney, Bill, Kansas City	6	5	0	−18	5
King, Bruce, Kansas City	0	0	1	0	1
King, Emanuel, Cincinnati	0	0	1	0	1
King, Kenny, L.A. Raiders	1	0	0	0	0
Kinnebrew, Larry, Cincinnati	4	1	0	0	1
Klecko, Joe, N.Y. Jets	0	0	1	0	1
Klever, Rocky, N.Y. Jets	0	0	1	0	1
Kosar, Bernie, Cleveland	14	2	0	−25	2
Krauss, Barry, Indianapolis	0	0	2	0	2
Krieg, Dave, Seattle	11	3	0	−2	3
Krumrie, Tim, Cincinnati	0	0	2	0	2
Lacy, Ken, Kansas City	1	0	0	0	0
Lane, Eric, Seattle	0	1	1	0	2
Lane, Garcia, Kansas City	3	1	0	0	1
Lang, Gene, Denver	3	1	0	0	1
Langhorne, Reggie, Cleveland	1	1	0	0	1
Lewis, Albert, Kansas City	0	0	1	0	1
Lilja, George, Cleveland	0	1	0	0	1
Lilly, Tony, Denver	0	0	1	0	1
Lipps, Louis, Pittsburgh	5	4	0	3	4
Little, David, Pittsburgh	0	1	1	11	2
Luck, Oliver, Houston	9	3	0	0	3
Lutz, Dave, Kansas City	0	1	0	0	1
Lyday, Allen, Houston	1	0	1	0	1
Lyles, Lester, N.Y. Jets	0	0	1	13	1
Lynn, Johnny, N.Y. Jets	0	0	1	7	1
Maas, Bill, Kansas City	0	0	1	0	1
Mack, Kevin, Cleveland	4	3	0	0	3
Maidlow, Steve, Buffalo	0	0	1	0	1
Malone, Mark, Pittsburgh	3	3	0	−5	3
Marino, Dan, Miami	9	2	0	−4	2
Marion, Fred, New England	0	0	3	9	3
Marshall, Henry, Kansas City	1	0	0	0	0
Martin, Mike, Cincinnati	4	0	0	0	0
Martin, Robbie, Indianapolis	5	0	0	0	0
Martin, Rod, L.A. Raiders	1	0	3	3	3
Marve, Eugene, Buffalo	0	0	1	0	1

	Fum.	Own Rec.	Opp. Rec.	Yds.	Tot. Rec.
Mathison, Bruce, Buffalo	8	2	0	−9	2
Matthews, Bruce, Houston	0	2	1	0	3
Matthews, Clay, Cleveland	0	0	1	15	1
McCloskey, Mike, Houston	0	1	0	0	1
McElroy, Vann, L.A. Raiders	0	0	1	0	1
McGee, Buford, San Diego	4	2	0	0	2
McGrew, Larry, New England	0	0	2	0	2
McKenzie, Reggie, L.A. Raiders	0	0	1	0	1
McKinney, Odis, L.A. Raiders	0	1	0	0	1
McNeil, Freeman, N.Y. Jets	9	0	0	0	0
McPherson, Miles, San Diego	0	1	0	0	1
Mecklenburg, Karl, Denver	0	0	1	0	1
Mehl, Lance, N.Y. Jets	1	0	0	0	0
Merriweather, Mike, Pittsburgh	1	0	0	0	0
Metzelaars, Pete, Buffalo	0	1	0	2	1
Minnifield, Frank, Cleveland	0	0	1	6	1
Moffett, Tim, L.A. Raiders	1	0	0	0	0
Mojsiejenko, Ralf, San Diego	1	0	0	−13	0
Monger, Matt, N.Y. Jets	0	0	2	0	2
Moon, Warren, Houston	12	5	0	−8	5
Moore, Booker, Buffalo	1	0	0	0	0
Morgan, Stanley, New England	1	0	0	0	0
Moriarty, Larry, Houston	2	0	0	0	0
Morris, Randall, Seattle	4	0	0	0	0
Morse, Steve, Pittsburgh	0	1	0	0	1
Moyer, Alex, Miami	0	0	1	0	1
Munchak, Mike, Houston	0	2	0	3	2
Nathan, Tony, Miami	7	1	0	0	1
Nelson, Steve, New England	0	0	3	0	3
Newsome, Ozzie, Cleveland	0	1	0	0	1
Nicolas, Scott, Cleveland	0	0	1	0	1
Norman, Chris, Denver	1	1	0	0	1
Norris, Ulysses, Buffalo	1	0	0	0	0
O'Brien, Ken, N.Y. Jets	14	4	0	0	4
Odom, Clifton, Indianapolis	0	0	2	0	2
Osby, Vince, San Diego	0	0	1	46	1
Pagel, Mike, Indianapolis	6	2	0	0	2
Paige, Tony, N.Y. Jets	1	1	0	0	1
Parros, Rick, Seattle	1	0	0	0	0
Plunkett, Jim, L.A. Raiders	6	1	0	−5	1
Pollard, Frank, Pittsburgh	2	1	0	0	1
Pratt, Bob, Seattle	0	1	0	0	1
Radecic, Scott, Kansas City	0	0	1	0	1
Ramsey, Derrick, New England	1	0	0	0	0
Ramson, Eason, Buffalo	1	0	0	0	0
Randle, Tate, Indianapolis	0	0	2	14	2
Reed, Andre, Buffalo	2	2	0	0	2
Rembert, Johnny, New England	0	0	3	9	3
Riley, Avon, Houston	0	0	1	0	1
Rimington, Dave, Cincinnati	0	3	0	0	3
Robinson, Fred, San Diego	0	0	1	0	1
Robinson, Mark, Kansas City	0	0	1	0	1
Robinson, Shelton, Seattle	0	0	1	6	1
Romes, Charles, Buffalo	0	0	1	0	1
Ross, Dan, Cincinnati	1	1	0	0	1
Ross, Kevin, Kansas City	0	0	1	0	1
Rozier, Mike, Houston	3	3	0	0	3
Ryan, Jim, Denver	0	0	1	0	1
Sanford, Lucius, Buffalo	0	0	1	0	1
Schlichter, Art, Indianapolis	1	1	0	0	1
Scholtz, Bruce, Seattle	0	0	1	0	1
Schonert, Turk, Cincinnati	3	2	0	−2	2
Schuh, Jeff, Cincinnati	0	0	1	0	1
Sewell, Steve, Denver	1	1	0	0	1
Shell, Donnie, Pittsburgh	0	0	2	0	2
Sherwin, Tim, Indianapolis	1	0	0	0	0
Shipp, Jackie, Miami	0	0	2	0	2
Shuler, Mickey, N.Y. Jets	1	1	0	0	1
Simpkins, Ron, Cincinnati	0	0	1	4	1
Sims, Kenneth, New England	0	0	2	0	2
Skansi, Paul, Seattle	1	1	0	0	1
Smerlas, Fred, Buffalo	0	0	1	0	1
Smith, Billy Ray, San Diego	0	0	3	0	3
Smith, Bruce, Buffalo	0	0	4	0	4
Smith, Don, Buffalo	0	0	2	0	2
Smith, Jeff, Kansas City	1	1	0	0	1
Smith, Tim, Houston	1	1	0	0	1
Spencer, Tim, San Diego	1	0	0	0	0
Spencer, Todd, Pittsburgh	3	1	0	0	1
Springs, Kirk, N.Y. Jets	1	1	1	0	2
Stark, Rohn, Indianapolis	0	1	0	0	1
Starring, Stephen, New England	4	1	0	0	1
Steels, Anthony, San Diego-Buffalo	2	2	0	0	2
Stensrud, Mike, Houston	0	0	1	0	1
Still, Art, Kansas City	0	0	2	0	2
Studdard, Dave, Denver	0	2	0	0	2

	Fum.	Own Rec.	Opp. Rec.	Yds.	Tot. Rec.
Sweeney, Calvin, Pittsburgh	0	0	1	0	1
Tatupu, Mosi, New England	1	1	0	0	1
Thompson, Donnell, Indianapolis	0	0	1	9	1
Tippett, Andre, New England	0	0	4	25	4
Toews, Jeff, Miami	0	1	0	0	1
Townsell, JoJo, N.Y. Jets	1	1	0	0	1
Townsend, Andre, Denver	0	0	1	0	1
Townsend, Greg, L.A. Raiders	0	0	1	0	1
Traynowicz, Mark, Buffalo	0	1	0	0	1
Umphrey, Rich, San Diego	0	0	1	6	1
Veris, Garin, New England	0	0	2	0	2
Vigorito, Tom, Miami	3	2	0	0	2
Vogler, Tim, Buffalo	0	1	0	0	1
Walker, Byron, Seattle	1	0	1	0	1
Walker, Fulton, L.A. Raiders	5	2	0	0	2
Walker, Wesley, N.Y. Jets	1	0	1	0	1
Walters, Danny, San Diego	0	0	1	0	1
Warner, Curt, Seattle	8	2	0	0	2
Washington, Sam, Cincinnati	0	0	1	0	1
Weathers, Clarence, Cleveland	3	1	0	0	1
Webster, Mike, Pittsburgh	0	1	0	0	1
Willhite, Gerald, Denver	2	0	0	0	0
Williams, Jamie, Houston	1	0	0	0	0
Williams, Lee, San Diego	0	0	1	2	1
Williams, Oliver, Indianapolis	2	1	0	0	1
Williams, Reggie, Cincinnati	0	0	4	4	4
Wilson, Don, Buffalo	5	0	1	61	1
Wilson, Earl, San Diego	0	0	1	0	1
Wilson, Eric, Buffalo	0	1	0	0	1
Wilson, Marc, L.A. Raiders	8	2	0	−4	2
Wilson, Steve, Denver	0	0	1	2	1
Winder, Sammy, Denver	4	1	0	0	1
Wolfley, Craig, Pittsburgh	0	1	0	0	1
Wonsley, George, Indianapolis	4	0	0	0	0
Woodley, David, Pittsburgh	8	2	0	0	2
Woolfolk, Butch, Houston	5	2	0	0	2
Wright, Felix, Cleveland	0	2	0	0	2
Wright, James, Denver	0	1	0	0	1
Young, Anthony, Indianapolis	0	2	2	28	4
Young, Charle, Seattle	1	0	0	0	0
Young, Fredd, Seattle	0	0	1	13	1
Young, Glen, Cleveland	1	0	0	0	0
Zander, Carl, Cincinnati	0	0	1	34	1
Zendejas, Tony, Houston	0	1	0	0	1

Yards includes aborted plays, own recoveries, and opponent recoveries.

Touchdowns: Lyle Alzado, L.A. Raiders; Tom Baldwin, N.Y. Jets; Bob Brudzinski, Miami; Jacob Green, Seattle; Cedric Jones, New England; Albert Lewis, Kansas City; Johnny Rembert, New England; Andre Tippett, New England; Don Wilson, Buffalo; and Anthony Young, Indianapolis.

Includes both offensive and defensive recoveries for touchdowns.

NFC FUMBLES—INDIVIDUAL

	Fum.	Own Rec.	Opp. Rec.	Yds.	Tot. Rec.
Adams, George, N.Y. Giants	7	2	0	0	2
Allen, Anthony, Atlanta	0	1	0	0	1
Allen, Kevin, Philadelphia	0	1	0	0	1
Anderson, John, Green Bay	0	0	1	0	1
Anderson, Ottis, St. Louis	3	1	0	0	1
Archer, David, Atlanta	9	2	0	0	2
Armstrong, Adger, Tampa Bay	0	1	0	0	1
Baack, Steve, Detroit	0	0	1	0	1
Bailey, Stacey, Atlanta	1	0	0	0	0
Baker, Al, St. Louis	0	0	1	0	1
Banks, Carl, N.Y. Giants	0	0	1	0	1
Bartkowski, Steve, Atlanta	3	1	0	−8	1
Bell, Jerry, Tampa Bay	2	0	0	0	0
Benish, Dan, Atlanta	0	0	1	0	1
Benson, Thomas, Atlanta	0	2	0	0	2
Bess, Rufus, Minnesota	0	0	2	0	2
Birdsong, Carl, St. Louis	0	1	0	0	1
Black, Mike, Detroit	1	0	0	−7	0
Blair, Matt, Minnesota	0	0	1	0	1
Board, Dwaine, San Francisco	0	0	1	0	1
Bostic, Jeff, Washington	0	1	0	0	1
Brady, Ed, L.A. Rams	0	0	1	0	1
Brenner, Hoby, New Orleans	1	0	0	0	0
Bright, Leon, Tampa Bay	4	0	0	0	0
Brock, Dieter, L.A. Rams	6	1	0	−7	1
Brock, Stan, New Orleans	0	1	0	0	1
Brown, Greg, Philadelphia	0	0	2	0	2
Brown, Robert, Green Bay	0	0	4	0	4
Brown, Ron, L.A. Rams	2	0	0	0	0
Brown, Ted, Minnesota	1	0	1	0	1
Browner, Joey, Minnesota	1	0	3	5	3
Browner, Keith, Tampa Bay	1	0	1	0	1
Brunner, Scott, St. Louis	3	0	0	0	0
Bryan, Rick, Atlanta	0	0	0	4	0
Burt, Jim, N.Y. Giants	0	0	2	0	2
Butz, Dave, Washington	0	0	1	0	1
Cade, Mossy, Green Bay	0	0	1	0	1
Campbell, Earl, New Orleans	4	0	0	0	0
Cannon, John, Tampa Bay	0	0	3	0	3
Cannon, Mark, Green Bay	0	2	0	0	2
Carroll, Jay, Minnesota	0	0	1	0	1
Carter, Anthony, Minnesota	1	0	1	0	1
Carter, Gerald, Tampa Bay	1	0	0	0	0
Carthon, Maurice, N.Y. Giants	1	0	0	0	0
Case, Scott, Atlanta	0	0	1	13	1
Cason, Wendell, Atlanta	0	0	2	2	2
Castille, Jeremiah, Tampa Bay	1	1	1	0	2
Clark, Bruce, New Orleans	0	0	1	4	1
Clark, Jessie, Green Bay	4	2	0	0	2
Clarke, Ken, Philadelphia	0	0	2	0	2
Clinkscale, Dextor, Dallas	0	0	2	0	2
Coffman, Paul, Green Bay	1	0	0	0	0
Coleman, Greg, Minnesota	1	1	0	0	1
Collins, Jim, L.A. Rams	0	0	1	0	1
Cooper, Evan, Philadelphia	1	1	0	0	1
Cosbie, Doug, Dallas	2	0	0	0	0
Courson, Steve, Tampa Bay	0	1	0	2	1
Craig, Roger, San Francisco	5	0	0	0	0
Cromwell, Nolan, L.A. Rams	0	0	4	12	4
Croudip, David, Atlanta	0	0	1	0	1
Cunningham, Randall, Philadelphia	3	0	0	0	0
Davis, Jeff, Tampa Bay	0	0	2	0	2
Dawson, Doug, St. Louis	0	1	0	0	1
Dean, Fred, San Francisco	0	0	1	0	1
Dean, Vernon, Washington	0	0	1	0	1
DeBerg, Steve, Tampa Bay	3	0	0	0	0
Del Rio, Jack, New Orleans	0	0	5	22	5
Dennard, Mark, Philadelphia	1	0	0	−19	0
Dennard, Preston, Green Bay	1	0	0	0	0
Dent, Richard, Chicago	0	0	2	0	2
Dickerson, Eric, L.A. Rams	10	3	0	0	3
Dickey, Lynn, Green Bay	8	5	0	−18	5
Doleman, Chris, Minnesota	0	0	3	0	3
Donnelly, Rick, Atlanta	0	1	0	0	1
Dorsett, Tony, Dallas	7	3	0	0	3
Dorsey, John, Green Bay	0	0	2	0	2
Doss, Reggie, L.A. Rams	0	0	2	0	2
Douglass, Mike, Green Bay	1	0	2	0	2
Downs, Michael, Dallas	0	0	3	0	3
Duckett, Kenny, Dallas	1	1	0	0	1
Duda, Mark, St. Louis	0	0	1	0	1
Duerson, Dave, Chicago	1	0	1	0	1
Duncan, Clyde, St. Louis	3	1	0	0	1
Dutton, John, Dallas	0	0	1	0	1
Edwards, Herman, Philadelphia	0	0	1	4	1
Ellard, Henry, L.A. Rams	5	5	0	0	5
Ellerson, Gary, Green Bay	3	2	1	0	3
Elliott, Tony, New Orleans	0	0	2	0	2
Ellis, Gerry, Green Bay	2	1	0	0	1
Ellis, Ray, Philadelphia	0	0	3	8	3
Ellison, Riki, San Francisco	0	0	2	7	2
Epps, Phillip, Green Bay	1	0	0	0	0
Everett, Major, Philadelphia	2	2	0	0	2
Fencik, Gary, Chicago	0	1	0	0	1
Ferguson, Joe, Detroit	1	0	0	0	0
Ferrell, Earl, St. Louis	2	1	0	0	1
Flowers, Larry, N.Y. Giants	0	1	0	0	1
Flynn, Tom, Green Bay	0	0	1	0	1
Foules, Elbert, Philadelphia	0	1	0	0	1
Fowlkes, Dennis, Minnesota	0	0	1	0	1
Francis, Russ, San Francisco	2	0	0	0	0
Freeman, Phil, Tampa Bay	1	0	0	0	0
Frye, David, Atlanta	0	0	1	13	1
Fuller, Steve, Chicago	3	1	0	−15	1
Gajan, Hokie, New Orleans	3	0	0	0	0
Galbreath, Tony, N.Y. Giants	2	0	0	0	0
Galloway, David, St. Louis	0	0	1	0	1
Gann, Mike, Atlanta	0	0	1	42	1
Gay, William, Detroit	0	0	6	3	6
Gayle, Shaun, Chicago	0	0	1	0	1
Giles, Jimmie, Tampa Bay	3	0	0	0	0
Gonzalez, Leon, Dallas	1	0	0	0	0
Graham, William, Detroit	0	0	1	0	1
Green, Curtis, Detroit	0	0	1	0	1
Green, Darrell, Washington	2	0	1	0	1
Green, Roy, St. Louis	2	0	0	0	0
Greenwood, David, Tampa Bay	2	0	1	9	1
Greer, Curtis, St. Louis	0	0	1	0	1
Griffin, Jeff, St. Louis	0	0	1	0	1
Griffin, Keith, Washington	1	0	0	0	0
Haddix, Michael, Philadelphia	2	0	0	0	0
Hall, Alvin, Detroit	2	2	0	0	2

	Fum.	Own Rec.	Opp. Rec.	Yds.	Tot. Rec.
Hallstrom, Ron, Green Bay	0	1	0	0	1
Hampton, Dan, Chicago	0	0	3	0	3
Harmon, Derrick, San Francisco	2	1	0	0	1
Harrington, Perry, St. Louis	1	0	0	0	0
Hartenstine, Mike, Chicago	0	0	1	0	1
Hayes, Gary, Green Bay	1	1	2	0	3
Haynes, James, New Orleans	0	0	2	0	2
Hebert, Bobby, New Orleans	1	1	0	0	1
Hegman, Mike, Dallas	0	0	1	0	1
Hicks, Dwight, San Francisco	1	0	2	19	2
Hilgenberg, Jay, Chicago	0	1	0	0	1
Hilgenberg, Joel, New Orleans	0	1	0	0	1
Hill, David, L.A. Rams	2	0	0	0	0
Hill, Ken, N.Y. Giants	1	1	1	0	2
Hill, Tony, Dallas	2	0	0	0	0
Hipple, Eric, Detroit	13	3	0	−3	3
Hoage, Terry, New Orleans	0	1	1	0	2
Holly, Bob, Atlanta	1	0	0	0	0
Holmes, Ron, Tampa Bay	0	0	2	0	2
Holt, John, Tampa Bay	0	0	2	0	2
Hopkins, Wes, Philadelphia	1	0	2	42	2
House, Kevin, Tampa Bay	0	0	1	0	1
Huffman, Dave, Minnesota	1	0	0	−26	0
Hunt, Byron, N.Y. Giants	0	0	1	0	1
Hunter, Herman, Philadelphia	4	2	0	0	2
Hunter, Tony, L.A. Rams	3	1	0	0	1
Ivery, Eddie Lee, Green Bay	1	0	1	0	1
Jackson, Earnest, Philadelphia	3	0	0	0	0
James, June, Detroit	0	0	1	0	1
Jaworski, Ron, Philadelphia	5	2	0	0	2
Jeffcoat, Jim, Dallas	0	0	2	0	2
Jenkins, Ken, Washington	1	1	0	0	1
Jerue, Mark, L.A. Rams	0	0	1	0	1
Jeter, Gary, L.A. Rams	0	0	1	0	1
Johnson, Billy, Atlanta	4	0	0	0	0
Johnson, Bobby, St. Louis	0	0	1	0	1
Johnson, Cecil, Tampa Bay	0	0	1	0	1
Johnson, Demetrious, Detroit	1	1	4	24	5
Johnson, Dennis, Minnesota	0	0	1	0	1
Johnson, Ezra, Green Bay	0	0	2	0	2
Johnson, Johnnie, L.A. Rams	0	0	1	0	1
Jones, David, Detroit	0	1	0	0	1
Jones, James, Detroit	7	1	0	0	1
Jordan, Curtis, Washington	0	0	2	0	2
Jordan, Steve, Minnesota	2	0	0	0	0
Kane, Rick, Detroit	1	0	0	0	0
Kaufman, Mel, Washington	0	0	2	0	2
Kemp, Jeff, L.A. Rams	2	0	0	0	0
Kiewel, Jeff, Atlanta	0	2	0	0	2
Kinard, Terry, N.Y. Giants	0	0	1	0	1
Koch, Greg, Green Bay	0	1	0	0	1
Korte, Steve, New Orleans	1	0	0	−18	0
Kramer, Tommy, Minnesota	9	0	0	−16	0
Lafary, Dave, New Orleans	0	1	0	0	1
Leonard, Jim, San Francisco	1	0	0	−15	0
Lewis, David, Detroit	1	0	0	0	0
Lewis, Leo, Minnesota	1	1	0	0	1
Lewis, Tim, Green Bay	0	0	1	6	1
Lindstrom, Chris, Tampa Bay	0	0	1	0	1
Little, David, Philadelphia	0	1	0	0	1
Lockhart, Eugene, Dallas	0	0	4	17	4
Lofton, James, Green Bay	3	0	0	0	0
Logan, Dave, Tampa Bay	0	0	1	2	1
Lomax, Neil, St. Louis	10	4	0	−1	4
Lott, Ronnie, San Francisco	0	0	2	0	2
Mack, Cedric, St. Louis	0	1	1	0	2
Magee, Calvin, Tampa Bay	1	0	0	0	0
Mandley, Pete, Detroit	3	2	0	0	2
Mann, Charles, Washington	0	0	1	0	1
Manuel, Lionel, N.Y. Giants	1	0	0	0	0
Margerum, Ken, Chicago	1	0	0	0	0
Marshall, Wilber, Chicago	0	0	1	8	1
Martin, Charles, Green Bay	0	0	1	0	1
Martin, Doug, Minnesota	0	0	2	29	2
Martin, Eric, New Orleans	1	0	0	0	0
Martin, George, N.Y. Giants	0	0	1	0	1
Maxie, Brett, New Orleans	0	0	1	0	1
May, Mark, Washington	0	1	0	0	1
McColl, Milt, San Francisco	0	0	1	28	1
McConkey, Phil, N.Y. Giants	1	1	1	0	2
McGriff, Curtis, N.Y. Giants	0	0	1	3	1
McIntyre, Guy, San Francisco	0	0	1	0	1
McKinnon, Dennis, Chicago	1	0	0	0	0
McLemore, Dana, San Francisco	5	2	0	0	2
McMahon, Jim, Chicago	4	0	0	0	0
McMichael, Steve, Chicago	0	0	1	0	1
Millard, Keith, Minnesota	0	0	1	0	1
Mitchell, Stump, St. Louis	6	2	0	0	2

	Fum.	Own Rec.	Opp. Rec.	Yds.	Tot. Rec.
Monk, Art, Washington	2	0	0	0	0
Montana, Joe, San Francisco	5	3	0	−11	3
Montgomery, Wilbert, Detroit	0	1	0	0	1
Moore, Alvin, Detroit	5	1	0	0	1
Moore, Blake, Green Bay	1	0	0	0	0
Morgan, Karl, Tampa Bay	0	0	2	0	2
Morris, Joe, N.Y. Giants	6	2	0	0	2
Mott, Steven, Detroit	0	1	0	0	1
Mullaney, Mark, Minnesota	0	0	2	0	2
Mumford, Tony, St. Louis	1	0	0	0	0
Murphy, Mark, Green Bay	0	0	1	0	1
Nelson, Darrin, Minnesota	7	2	0	16	2
Nelson, Karl, N.Y. Giants	0	1	0	0	1
Nelson, Lee, St. Louis	1	0	0	0	0
Newsome, Tim, Dallas	2	0	0	0	0
Newsome, Vince, L.A. Rams	0	0	1	0	1
Newton, Tim, Minnesota	1	1	0	0	1
Nichols, Mark, Detroit	1	0	0	0	0
Noga, Falaniko, St. Louis	0	1	1	0	2
Nunn, Freddie Joe, St. Louis	0	0	2	0	2
Oates, Bart, N.Y. Giants	0	2	0	0	2
Olkewicz, Neal, Washington	0	0	1	0	1
Owens, Mel, L.A. Rams	0	0	2	14	2
Pankey, Irv, L.A. Rams	0	0	1	0	1
Patterson, Elvis, N.Y. Giants	0	0	1	0	1
Payton, Walter, Chicago	6	1	0	0	1
Pelluer, Scott, New Orleans	0	0	1	0	1
Penn, Jesse, Dallas	0	0	1	0	1
Perrin, Benny, St. Louis	0	0	1	0	1
Perry, William, Chicago	0	0	2	66	2
Petersen, Kurt, Dallas	0	1	0	0	1
Phillips, Reggie, Chicago	0	0	1	0	1
Pitts, Mike, Atlanta	1	0	1	6	1
Poe, Johnnie, New Orleans	1	0	1	0	1
Powe, Karl, Dallas	1	0	0	0	0
Prather, Guy, Green Bay	1	0	0	0	0
Prior, Mike, Tampa Bay	4	3	0	0	3
Quick, Mike, Philadelphia	1	1	0	0	1
Rafferty, Tom, Dallas	0	2	0	0	2
Randle, Ervin, Tampa Bay	0	1	1	0	2
Redd, Glen, New Orleans	0	1	1	0	2
Redden, Barry, L.A. Rams	1	0	0	0	0
Reeves, Ken, Philadelphia	0	0	1	0	1
Renfro, Mike, Dallas	3	1	0	0	1
Rhymes, Buster, Minnesota	2	2	0	0	2
Rice, Allen, Minnesota	0	0	1	0	1
Rice, Jerry, San Francisco	1	0	0	0	0
Richardson, Mike, Chicago	1	0	1	4	1
Riggins, John, Washington	3	0	0	0	0
Ring, Bill, San Francisco	0	0	1	0	1
Rivera, Ron, Chicago	0	0	1	5	1
Roaches, Carl, New Orleans	1	0	0	0	0
Robbins, Tootie, St. Louis	0	1	0	0	1
Rogers, George, Washington	9	2	0	0	2
Rouse, Curtis, Minnesota	0	1	0	0	1
Rutledge, Jeff, N.Y. Giants	1	0	0	0	0
Sanders, Eric, Atlanta	1	0	0	−23	0
Sanders, Thomas, Chicago	1	0	0	0	0
Schroeder, Jay, Washington	5	1	0	−3	1
Scott, Carlos, St. Louis	1	0	0	0	0
Scott, Randy, Green Bay	0	0	5	31	5
Scott, Victor, Dallas	1	0	0	0	0
Shell, Todd, San Francisco	0	0	1	0	1
Simms, Phil, N.Y. Giants	16	5	0	−22	5
Singletary, Mike, Chicago	0	0	3	11	3
Slater, Jackie, L.A. Rams	0	1	0	0	1
Slaton, Tony, L.A. Rams	0	1	0	0	1
Smith, Doug, L.A. Rams	0	1	0	0	1
Smith, J.T., St. Louis	3	0	0	0	0
Smith, Lance, St. Louis	0	1	0	0	1
Smith, Leonard, St. Louis	1	2	1	0	3
Smith, Wayne, St. Louis	0	0	1	0	1
Solomon, Freddie, San Francisco	1	0	0	0	0
Spagnola, John, Philadelphia	1	0	0	0	0
Stanley, Walter, Green Bay	2	0	0	0	0
Stover, Jeff, San Francisco	0	0	1	0	1
Stuckey, Jim, San Francisco	0	0	1	0	1
Suhey, Matt, Chicago	2	1	0	0	1
Sully, Ivory, Tampa Bay	0	0	1	0	1
Swilley, Dennis, Minnesota	0	1	0	0	1
Taylor, Johnny, Atlanta	0	0	1	0	1
Taylor, Ken, Chicago	3	1	0	0	1
Taylor, Lawrence, N.Y. Giants	0	0	2	25	2
Teal, Willie, Minnesota	0	0	2	65	2
Theismann, Joe, Washington	4	0	0	0	0
Tice, John, New Orleans	0	1	0	0	1
Tomczak, Mike, Chicago	1	1	0	−13	1
Tullis, Willie, New Orleans	1	0	0	0	0

	Fum.	Own Rec.	Opp. Rec.	Yds.	Tot. Rec.
Turner, Keena, San Francisco	0	0	2	65	2
Tyler, Wendell, San Francisco	6	2	0	0	2
Tyrrell, Tim, Atlanta	1	0	0	0	0
Uecker, Keith, Green Bay	0	1	0	0	1
Vann, Norwood, L.A. Rams	0	0	1	0	1
Verser, David, Tampa Bay	1	0	0	0	0
Wagoner, Danny, Atlanta	0	0	1	0	1
Walls, Everson, Dallas	0	0	1	4	1
Warren, Don, Washington	0	1	0	0	1
Warren, Frank, New Orleans	0	0	1	50	1
Washington, Chris, Tampa Bay	0	0	1	0	1
Washington, Joe, Atlanta	1	1	0	0	1
Washington, Ronnie, Atlanta	1	0	1	0	1
Waters, Andre, Philadelphia	1	0	1	0	1
Watkins, Bobby, Detroit	0	0	2	0	2
Wattelet, Frank, New Orleans	0	1	0	4	1
Waymer, Dave, New Orleans	1	0	0	0	0
Wersching, Ray, San Francisco	0	0	1	0	1
West, Ed, Green Bay	1	0	0	0	0
Whisenhunt, Ken, Atlanta	0	0	1	0	1
White, Charles, L.A. Rams	3	0	0	0	0
White, Danny, Dallas	6	2	0	−6	2
White, Reggie, Philadelphia	0	0	2	0	2
Wilburn, Barry, Washington	0	0	1	0	1
Wilder, James, Tampa Bay	9	1	0	0	1
Williams, Byron, N.Y. Giants	0	1	0	0	1
Williams, Eric, Detroit	0	0	1	0	1
Williams, Greg, Washington	0	0	1	0	1
Williams, Jimmy, Detroit	0	0	1	0	1
Williams, John, Dallas	3	2	0	0	2
Williams, Perry, N.Y. Giants	0	0	1	0	1
Wilson, Brenard, Philadelphia	0	1	0	2	1
Wilson, Dave, New Orleans	6	1	0	−23	1
Wilson, Otis, Chicago	0	0	2	0	2
Wilson, Wayne, New Orleans	2	1	0	0	1
Witte, Mark, Tampa Bay	0	0	1	0	1
Wolfley, Ron, St. Louis	1	0	0	0	0
Wright, Randy, Green Bay	5	2	0	−6	2
Young, Lonnie, St. Louis	0	0	1	0	1
Young, Mike, L.A. Rams	1	0	0	0	0
Young, Steve, Tampa Bay	4	1	0	−1	1
Zorn, Jim, Green Bay	3	2	0	−1	2

Yards includes aborted plays, own recoveries, and opp. recoveries.
Touchdowns: Jack Del Rio, New Orleans; Mike Gann, Atlanta; Tim Lewis, Green Bay; David Little, Philadelphia; Milt McColl, San Francisco; Guy McIntyre, San Francisco; Ron Rivera, Chicago; Willie Teal, Minnesota; Keena Turner, San Francisco; and Frank Warren, New Orleans.
Includes both offensive and defensive recoveries for touchdowns.

SACKS

INDIVIDUAL CHAMPIONS
NFC: 17.0—Richard Dent, Chicago
AFC: 16.5—Andre Tippett, New England
TEAM CHAMPIONS
NFC: 68—New York Giants
AFC: 65—Los Angeles Raiders

AFC SACKS—TEAM

	Sacks	Yards
Los Angeles Raiders	65	488
Seattle	61	464
New England	51	334
New York Jets	49	370
Denver	47	378
Cleveland	44	353
Houston	41	313
Cincinnati	40	334
San Diego	40	304
Miami	38	278
Kansas City	37	263
Indianapolis	36	267
Pittsburgh	36	305
Buffalo	25	223
AFC Total	610	4674
AFC Average	43.6	333.9

NFC SACKS—TEAM

	Sacks	Yards
New York Giants	68	539
Chicago	64	483
Dallas	62	459
San Francisco	60	457
Los Angeles Rams	56	421
Philadelphia	53	359
Washington	52	378
Green Bay	48	383
New Orleans	46	322
Detroit	45	336
Atlanta	42	331
Tampa Bay	35	277
Minnesota	33	223
St. Louis	32	254
NFC Total	696	5222
NFC Average	49.7	373.0
League Total	1306	9896
League Average	46.6	353.4

NFL TOP 10 INDIVIDUAL LEADERS IN SACKS

	Total		Total
Dent, Richard, Chicago	17.0	Green, Jacob, Seattle	13.5
Tippett, Andre, New England	16.5	Brown, Greg, Philadelphia	13.0
Marshall, Leonard, N.Y. Giants	15.5	Jones, Ed, Dallas	13.0
Manley, Dexter, Washington	15.0	Mecklenburg, Karl, Denver	13.0
Mann, Charles, Washington	14.5	Taylor, Lawrence, N.Y. Giants	13.0
Gastineau, Mark, N.Y. Jets	13.5	White, Reggie, Philadelphia	13.0

AFC SACKS—INDIVIDUAL

Tippett, Andre, New England	16.5	Bush, Frank, Houston	3.0
Gastineau, Mark, N.Y. Jets	13.5	Catano, Mark, Pittsburgh	3.0
Green, Jacob, Seattle	13.5	Cole, Robin, Pittsburgh	3.0
Mecklenburg, Karl, Denver	13.0	Gary, Keith, Pittsburgh	3.0
Pickel, Bill, L.A. Raiders	12.5	Golic, Bob, Cleveland	3.0
Banks, Chip, Cleveland	11.0	Lyles, Lester, N.Y. Jets	3.0
Edwards, Randy, Seattle	10.5	McNanie, Sean, Buffalo	3.0
Jones, Rulon, Denver	10.0	Radecic, Scott, Kansas City	3.0
Long, Howie, L.A. Raiders	10.0	Simpson, Keith, Seattle	3.0
Townsend, Greg, L.A. Raiders	10.0	Smith, Byron, Indianapolis	3.0
Veris, Garin, New England	10.0	Smith, Don, Buffalo	3.0
Browner, Ross, Cincinnati	9.0	Weathers, Curtis, Cleveland	3.0
Nash, Joe, Seattle	9.0	Wilson, Earl, San Diego	3.0
Williams, Lee, San Diego	9.0	Woodard, Ken, Denver	3.0
Bryant, Jeff, Seattle	8.5	Young, Fredd, Seattle	3.0
Camp, Reggie, Cleveland	8.5	Bokamper, Kim, Miami	2.5
Edwards, Eddie, Cincinnati	8.5	Bowser, Charles, Miami	2.5
Jones, Sean, L.A. Raiders	8.5	Daniels, Calvin, Kansas City	2.5
Blackmon, Don, New England	8.0	Dunn, Gary, Pittsburgh	2.5
Bennett, Barry, N.Y. Jets	7.5	Eason, Bo, Houston	2.5
Green, Hugh, Tampa Bay-Miami	7.5	Scholtz, Bruce, Seattle	2.5
Klecko, Joe, N.Y. Jets	7.5	Barnes, Jeff, L.A. Raiders	2.0
Charles, Mike, Miami	7.0	Bradley, Carlos, San Diego	2.0
Hairston, Carl, Cleveland	7.0	Burruss, Lloyd, Kansas City	2.0
Maas, Bill, Kansas City	7.0	Easley, Ken, Seattle	2.0
Martin, Rod, L.A. Raiders	7.0	Gaines, Greg, Seattle	2.0
Robinson, Fred, San Diego	7.0	Garnett, Scott, San Fran.-S.D.	2.0
Lyons, Marty, N.Y. Jets	6.5	Glasgow, Nesby, Indianapolis	2.0
Smith, Bruce, Buffalo	6.5	Goodman, John, Pittsburgh	2.0
Bell, Mike, Kansas City	6.0	Guilbeau, Rusty, N.Y. Jets	2.0
Bickett, Duane, Indianapolis	6.0	Jackson, Michael, Seattle	2.0
Chavous, Barney, Denver	6.0	King, Emanuel, Cincinnati	2.0
King, Linden, San Diego	6.0	Koch, Pete, Kansas City	2.0
Matthews, Clay, Cleveland	6.0	Kragen, Greg, Denver	2.0
Baker, Jesse, Houston	5.5	Nelson, Steve, New England	2.0
Betters, Doug, Miami	5.5	Odom, Clifton, Indianapolis	2.0
Lowe, Woodrow, San Diego	5.5	Perryman, Jim, Buffalo	2.0
Mehl, Lance, N.Y. Jets	5.5	Riley, Avon, Houston	2.0
Moore, Mack, Miami	5.5	Robinson, Mark, Kansas City	2.0
Sims, Kenneth, New England	5.5	Sanford, Lucius, Buffalo	2.0
Willis, Keith, Pittsburgh	5.5	Sims, Darryl, Pittsburgh	2.0
Adams, Julius, New England	5.0	Smith, Billy Ray, San Diego	2.0
Bostic, Keith, Houston	5.0	Smith, Doug, Houston	2.0
Cooks, Johnie, Indianapolis	5.0	Sochia, Brian, Houston	2.0
Hinkle, Bryan, Pittsburgh	5.0	Talley, Darryl, Buffalo	2.0
Kush, Rod, Houston	5.0	Williams, Toby, New England	2.0
Scott, Chris, Indianapolis	5.0	Willis, Mitch, L.A. Raiders	2.0
Stensrud, Mike, Houston	5.0	Zander, Carl, Cincinnati	2.0
Thompson, Donnell, Indianapolis	5.0	Cousineau, Tom, Cleveland	1.5
Townsend, Andre, Denver	5.0	Ehin, Chuck, San Diego	1.5
Van Pelt, Brad, L.A. Raiders	5.0	Johnson, Lawrence, Buffalo	1.5
Jackson, Terry, Seattle	4.0	Lewis, Albert, Kansas City	1.5
Merriweather, Mike, Pittsburgh	4.0	Lindstrom, Dave, Kansas City	1.5
Schuh, Jeff, Cincinnati	4.0	Meads, Johnny, Houston	1.5
Smith, Dennis, Denver	4.0	Williams, Ben, Buffalo	1.5
Still, Art, Kansas City	4.0	Abraham, Robert, Houston	1.0
Virkus, Scott, Indianapolis	4.0	Baldwin, Keith, Cleveland	1.0
Childress, Ray, Houston	3.5	Boyarsky, Jerry, Cincinnati	1.0
Krumrie, Tim, Cincinnati	3.5	Breeden, Louis, Cincinnati	1.0
Simpkins, Ron, Cincinnati	3.5	Brophy, Jay, Miami	1.0
Williams, Reggie, Cincinnati	3.5	Broughton, Willie, Indianapolis	1.0
Alzado, Lyle, L.A. Raiders	3.0	Brown, Mark, Miami	1.0
Brudzinski, Bob, Miami	3.0	Brown, Steve, Houston	1.0

Byrd, Richard, Houston	1.0
Carr, Gregg, Pittsburgh	1.0
Carter, Rubin, Denver	1.0
Carter, Russell, N.Y. Jets	1.0
Clancy, Sam, Cleveland	1.0
Crable, Bob, N.Y. Jets	1.0
Davis, Mike, L.A. Raiders	1.0
Davis, Wayne, San Diego	1.0
Donaldson, Jeff, Houston	1.0
Fletcher, Simon, Denver	1.0
Frazier, Guy, Buffalo	1.0
Green, Mike, San Diego	1.0
Griffin, James, Cincinnati	1.0
Hamilton, Harry, N.Y. Jets	1.0
Hamm, Bob, Kansas City	1.0
Harden, Mike, Denver	1.0
Haslett, Jim, Buffalo	1.0
Haynes, Mike, L.A. Raiders	1.0
Kemp, Bobby, Cincinnati	1.0
Krauss, Barry, Indianapolis	1.0
Lankford, Paul, Miami	1.0
Lee, Keith, Indianapolis	1.0
Little, David, Pittsburgh	1.0
Little, George, Miami	1.0
McGrew, Larry, New England	1.0
McKenzie, Reggie, L.A. Raiders	1.0
Millen, Matt, L.A. Raiders	1.0
Moyer, Paul, Seattle	1.0
Nelson, Edmund, Pittsburgh	1.0
Nicolas, Scott, Cleveland	1.0
Paine, Jeff, Kansas City	1.0
Ryan, Jim, Denver	1.0
Shiver, Sanders, Miami	1.0
Sowell, Robert, Miami	1.0
Spani, Gary, Kansas City	1.0
Toran, Stacey, L.A. Raiders	1.0
White, Brad, Indianapolis	1.0
Williams, Lester, New England	1.0
Woods, Rick, Pittsburgh	1.0
Blanton, Jerry, Kansas City	0.5
Holle, Eric, Kansas City	0.5
Johnson, Eddie, Cleveland	0.5
Lane, Garcia, Kansas City	0.5
Rockins, Chris, Cleveland	0.5
Smerlas, Fred, Buffalo	0.5
Springs, Kirk, N.Y. Jets	0.5

NFC SACKS—INDIVIDUAL

Dent, Richard, Chicago	17.0
Marshall, Leonard, N.Y. Giants	15.5
Manley, Dexter, Washington	15.0
Mann, Charles, Washington	14.5
Brown, Greg, Philadelphia	13.0
Jones, Ed, Dallas	13.0
Taylor, Lawrence, N.Y. Giants	13.0
White, Reggie, Philadelphia	13.0
Wilcher, Mike, L.A. Rams	12.5
Jeffcoat, Jim, Dallas	12.0
Board, Dwaine, San Francisco	11.5
Jackson, Rickey, New Orleans	11.0
Jeter, Gary, L.A. Rams	11.0
Millard, Keith, Minnesota	11.0
White, Randy, Dallas	10.5
Wilson, Otis, Chicago	10.5
Martin, George, N.Y. Giants	10.0
Stover, Jeff, San Francisco	10.0
Johnson, Ezra, Green Bay	9.5
Carreker, Alphonso, Green Bay	9.0
Owens, Mel, L.A. Rams	9.0
Clark, Bruce, New Orleans	8.5
McMichael, Steve, Chicago	8.0
Bryan, Rick, Atlanta	7.5
Gay, William, Detroit	7.5
Sally, Jerome, N.Y. Giants	7.5
Williams, Jimmy, Detroit	7.5
Carter, Michael, San Francisco	7.0
Clarke, Ken, Philadelphia	7.0
Green, Curtis, Detroit	7.0
Greer, Curtis, St. Louis	7.0
Pitts, Mike, Atlanta	7.0
Reed, Doug, L.A. Rams	7.0
Geathers, James, New Orleans	6.5
Hampton, Dan, Chicago	6.5
Logan, Dave, Tampa Bay	6.5
Anderson, John, Green Bay	6.0
Hamel, Dean, Washington	6.0
Marshall, Wilber, Chicago	6.0
Turner, Keena, San Francisco	6.0
Williams, Eric, Detroit	6.0
Duda, Mark, St. Louis	5.5
Headen, Andy, N.Y. Giants	5.5
Hegman, Mike, Dallas	5.5
Strauthers, Thomas, Philadelphia	5.5
Warren, Frank, New Orleans	5.5
Butz, Dave, Washington	5.0
Cobb, Garry, Philadelphia	5.0
Elshire, Neil, Minnesota	5.0
Miller, Shawn, L.A. Rams	5.0
Paul, Whitney, New Orleans	5.0
Perry, William, Chicago	5.0
Rade, John, Atlanta	5.0
Cannon, John, Tampa Bay	4.5
Gann, Mike, Atlanta	4.5
Holmes, Ron, Tampa Bay	4.5
Baker, Al, St. Louis	4.0
Burt, Jim, N.Y. Giants	4.0
Dutton, John, Dallas	4.0
Frye, David, Atlanta	4.0
Johnson, Gary, San Francisco	4.0
Kaufman, Mel, Washington	4.0
King, Angelo, Detroit	4.0
Martin, Doug, Minnesota	4.0
Morgan, Karl, Tampa Bay	4.0
Murphy, Mark, Green Bay	4.0
Shell, Todd, San Francisco	4.0
Benish, Dan, Atlanta	3.5
Galloway, David, St. Louis	3.5
Lockhart, Eugene, Dallas	3.5
Martin, Chris, Minnesota	3.5
Richardson, Al, Atlanta	3.5
Banks, Carl, N.Y. Giants	3.0
Brown, Robert, Green Bay	3.0
Dean, Fred, San Francisco	3.0
Greenwood, David, Tampa Bay	3.0
Harrison, Dennis, L.A. Rams	3.0
Johnson, Demetrious, Detroit	3.0
Martin, Charles, Green Bay	3.0
Merrill, Casey, N.Y. Giants	3.0
Milot, Rich, Washington	3.0
Noble, Brian, Green Bay	3.0
Nunn, Freddie Joe, St. Louis	3.0
Scott, Randy, Green Bay	3.0
Scott, Victor, Dallas	3.0
Singletary, Mike, Chicago	3.0
Smith, Leonard, St. Louis	3.0
Tuiasosopo, Manu, San Fran.	3.0
Walter, Mike, San Francisco	3.0
Davis, Jeff, Tampa Bay	2.5
Doss, Reggie, L.A. Rams	2.5
English, Doug, Detroit	2.5
Ferguson, Keith, S.D.-Detroit	2.5
Waechter, Henry, Chicago	2.5
Wilks, Jim, New Orleans	2.5
Baack, Steve, Detroit	2.0
Brooks, Kevin, Dallas	2.0
Butler, Mike, Green Bay	2.0
Clinkscale, Dextor, Dallas	2.0
Collins, Jim, L.A. Rams	2.0
Duerson, Dave, Chicago	2.0
Ellis, Ray, Philadelphia	2.0
Fowlkes, Dennis, Minnesota	2.0
Fuller, Jeff, San Francisco	2.0
Haynes, James, New Orleans	2.0
Hopkins, Wes, Philadelphia	2.0
Humphrey, Donnie, Green Bay	2.0
Junior, E.J., St. Louis	2.0
Keys, Tyrone, Chicago	2.0
Mays, Stafford, St. Louis	2.0
Mullaney, Mark, Minnesota	2.0
Newton, Tim, Minnesota	2.0
Pillers, Lawrence, Atlanta	2.0
Prather, Guy, Green Bay	2.0
Smerek, Don, Dallas	2.0
Stuckey, Jim, San Francisco	2.0
Washington, Chris, Tampa Bay	2.0
Wilkes, Reggie, Philadelphia	2.0
Williams, Perry, N.Y. Giants	2.0
Benson, Thomas, Atlanta	1.5
Browner, Keith, Tampa Bay	1.5
Darby, Byron, Philadelphia	1.5
Douglass, Mike, Green Bay	1.5
Grant, Darryl, Washington	1.5
Hunt, Byron, N.Y. Giants	1.5
Lott, Ronnie, San Francisco	1.5
Rohrer, Jeff, Dallas	1.5
Bates, Bill, Dallas	1.0
Beasley, Tom, Washington	1.0
Bess, Rufus, Minnesota	1.0
Blair, Matt, Minnesota	1.0
Browner, Joey, Minnesota	1.0
Carson, Harry, N.Y. Giants	1.0
Case, Scott, Atlanta	1.0
Cofer, Mike, Detroit	1.0
Coleman, Monte, Washington	1.0
Cooper, Evan, Philadelphia	1.0
Creswell, Smiley, Philadelphia	1.0
Cromwell, Nolan, L.A. Rams	1.0
Curry, Craig, Tampa Bay	1.0
DeJurnett, Charles, L.A. Rams	1.0
Elliott, Tony, New Orleans	1.0
Ellison, Riki, San Francisco	1.0
Fielder, Don, Tampa Bay	1.0
Graham, William, Detroit	1.0
Green, Gary, L.A. Rams	1.0
Grooms, Elois, St. Louis	1.0
Hall, Alvin, Detroit	1.0
Hamilton, Steve, Washington	1.0
Hartenstine, Mike, Chicago	1.0
Hicks, Dwight, San Francisco	1.0
Hoage, Terry, New Orleans	1.0
Johnson, Cecil, Tampa Bay	1.0
Kinard, Terry, N.Y. Giants	1.0
Kovach, Jim, New Orleans	1.0
Newsome, Vince, L.A. Rams	1.0
Noga, Falaniko, St. Louis	1.0
Provence, Andrew, Atlanta	1.0
Randle, Ervin, Tampa Bay	1.0
Redd, Glen, New Orleans	1.0
Taylor, Johnny, Atlanta	1.0
Thurman, Dennis, Dallas	1.0
Wattelet, Frank, New Orleans	1.0
Doleman, Chris, Minnesota	0.5
Downs, Michael, Dallas	0.5
Patterson, Elvis, N.Y. Giants	0.5
Ponder, David, Dallas	0.5
Reasons, Gary, N.Y. Giants	0.5
Rivera, Ron, Chicago	0.5
Washington, Ronnie, Atlanta	0.5

INSIDE THE NUMBERS

NFL Home/Road Records, Past Five Seasons
Most Points in a Game by Each NFL Team
Teams That Have Scored Sixty Points in a Game
Youngest/Oldest Starters in NFL in 1985
Opening Day Records, 1933–85
Team's Records Trailing at Halftime/After Three Quarters
Walter Payton's Rushing vs. Each Opponent
Tony Dorsett's Rushing vs. Each Opponent
Earl Campbell's Rushing vs. Each Opponent
Eric Dickerson's Rushing vs. Each Opponent
Records in Out-of-Division Games, 1978–85
1985 Score by Quarters
December Team Records, 1977–85
Retired Uniform Numbers
Active Players, Not Drafted, Eight Years Experience
Active Players, Not Drafted, Who Played in One Pro Bowl
Longest Held Individual Records

NFL Home/Road Records, Past 5 Seasons

AFC

BUFFALO

	Total	Home	Road	Playoffs
1981	10-6	7-1	3-5	1-1*
1982	4-5	4-1	0-4	None
1983	8-8	3-5	5-3	None
1984	2-14	2-6	0-8	None
1985	2-14	2-6	0-8	None

*Lost divisional playoff game.

CINCINNATI

	Total	Home	Road	Playoffs
1981	12-4	6-2	6-2	2-1*
1982	7-2	4-0	3-2	0-1**
1983	7-9	4-4	3-5	None
1984	8-8	5-3	3-5	None
1985	7-9	5-3	2-6	None

*Lost Super Bowl XVI
**Lost first-round game

CLEVELAND

	Total	Home	Road	Playoffs
1981	5-11	3-5	2-6	None
1982	4-5	2-2	2-3	0-1*
1983	9-7	6-2	3-5	None
1984	5-11	2-6	3-5	None
1985	8-8	5-3	3-5	0-1**

*Lost first-round game
**Lost divisional playoff game

DENVER

	Total	Home	Road	Playoffs
1981	10-6	8-0	2-6	None
1982	2-7	1-4	1-3	None
1983	9-7	6-2	3-5	0-1*
1984	13-3	7-1	6-2	0-1**
1985	11-5	6-2	5-3	None

*Lost first-round game
**Lost divisional playoff game

HOUSTON

	Total	Home	Road	Playoffs
1981	7-9	5-3	2-6	None
1982	1-8	1-4	0-4	None
1983	2-14	2-6	0-8	None
1984	3-13	2-6	1-7	None
1985	5-11	4-4	1-7	None

INDIANAPOLIS/BALTIMORE (1981-83)

	Total	Home	Road	Playoffs
1981	2-14	1-7	1-7	None
1982	0-8-1	0-3-1	0-5	None
1983	7-9	3-5	4-4	None
1984	4-12	2-6	2-6	None
1985	5-11	4-4	1-7	None

KANSAS CITY

	Total	Home	Road	Playoffs
1981	9-7	5-3	4-4	None
1982	3-6	2-2	1-4	None
1983	6-10	5-3	1-7	None
1984	8-8	5-3	3-5	None
1985	6-10	5-3	1-7	None

LOS ANGELES RAIDERS/OAKLAND (1981)

	Total	Home	Road	Playoffs
1981	7-9	4-4	3-5	None
1982	8-1	4-0	4-1	1-1*
1983	12-4	6-2	6-2	3-0**
1984	11-5	6-2	5-3	0-1***
1985	12-4	7-1	5-3	0-1#

*Lost second-round game
**Won Super Bowl XVIII
***Lost first-round game
Lost divisional playoff game

MIAMI

	Total	Home	Road	Playoffs
1981	11-4-1	6-1-1	5-3	0-1*
1982	7-2	4-0	3-2	3-1**
1983	12-4	7-1	5-3	0-1***
1984	14-2	7-1	7-1	2-1#
1985	12-4	8-0	4-4	1-1##

* Lost divisional playoff game
** Lost Super Bowl XVII
*** Lost divisional playoff game
#Lost Super Bowl XIX
##Lost AFC Championship Game

NEW ENGLAND

	Total	Home	Road	Playoffs
1981	2-14	2-6	0-8	None
1982	5-4	3-1	2-3	0-1*
1983	8-8	5-3	3-5	None
1984	9-7	5-3	4-4	None
1985	11-5	7-1	4-4	3-1**

*Lost first-round game
**Lost Super Bowl XX

NEW YORK JETS

	Total	Home	Road	Playoffs
1981	10-5-1	6-2	4-3-1	0-1*
1982	6-3	3-1	3-2	2-1**
1983	7-9	2-6	5-3	None
1984	7-9	3-5	4-4	None
1985	11-5	7-1	4-4	0-1***

*Lost first-round game
**Lost AFC Championship Game
***Lost first-round game

PITTSBURGH

	Total	Home	Road	Playoffs
1981	8-8	5-3	3-5	None
1982	6-3	4-0	2-3	0-1*
1983	10-6	4-4	6-2	0-1**
1984	9-7	6-2	3-5	1-1***
1985	7-9	5-3	2-6	None

*Lost first-round game
**Lost first-round game
***Lost AFC Championship Game

SAN DIEGO

	Total	Home	Road	Playoffs
1981	10-6	5-3	5-3	1-1*
1982	6-3	3-1	3-2	1-1**
1983	6-10	4-4	2-6	None
1984	7-9	4-4	3-5	None
1985	8-8	6-2	2-6	None

*Lost AFC Championship Game
**Lost second-round game

SEATTLE

	Total	Home	Road	Playoffs
1981	6-10	5-3	1-7	None
1982	4-5	3-2	1-3	None
1983	9-7	5-3	4-4	2-1*
1984	12-4	7-1	5-3	1-1**
1985	8-8	5-3	3-5	None

*Lost AFC Championship Game
**Lost divisional playoff game

NFC

ATLANTA

	Total	Home	Road	Playoffs
1981	7-9	4-4	3-5	None
1982	5-4	2-3	3-1	0-1*
1983	7-9	4-4	3-5	None
1984	4-12	2-6	2-6	None
1985	4-12	3-5	1-7	None

*Lost first-round game

CHICAGO

	Total	Home	Road	Playoffs
1981	6-10	4-4	2-6	None
1982	3-6	2-2	1-4	None
1983	8-8	5-3	3-5	None
1984	10-6	6-2	4-4	1-1*
1985	15-1	8-0	7-1	3-0**

*Lost NFC Championship Game
**Won Super Bowl XX

DALLAS

	Total	Home	Road	Playoffs
1981	12-4	8-0	4-4	1-1*
1982	6-3	3-2	3-1	2-1**
1983	12-4	6-2	6-2	0-1***
1984	9-7	5-3	4-4	None
1985	10-6	7-1	3-5	0-1#

*Lost NFC Championship Game
**Lost NFC Championship Game
***Lost first-round game
Lost divisional playoff game

DETROIT

	Total	Home	Road	Playoffs
1981	8-8	7-1	1-7	None
1982	4-5	2-3	2-2	0-1*
1983	9-7	6-2	3-5	0-1**
1984	4-11-1	2-5-1	2-6	None
1985	7-9	6-2	1-7	None

*Lost first-round game
**Lost divisional playoff game

GREEN BAY

	Total	Home	Road	Playoffs
1981	8-8	4-4	4-4	None
1982	5-3-1	3-1	2-2-1	1-1*
1983	8-8	5-3	3-5	None
1984	8-8	5-3	3-5	None
1985	8-8	5-3	3-5	None

*Lost second-round game

LOS ANGELES RAMS

	Total	Home	Road	Playoffs
1981	6-10	4-4	2-6	None
1982	2-7	1-4	1-3	None
1983	9-7	5-3	4-4	1-1*
1984	10-6	5-3	5-3	0-1**
1985	11-5	6-2	5-3	1-1***

*Lost divisional playoff game
**Lost first-round game
***Lost NFC Championship Game

MINNESOTA

	Total	Home	Road	Playoffs
1981	7-9	5-3	2-6	None
1982	5-4	4-1	1-3	1-1*
1983	8-8	3-5	5-3	None
1984	3-13	2-6	1-7	None
1985	7-9	4-4	3-5	None

*Lost second-round game

NEW ORLEANS

	Total	Home	Road	Playoffs
1981	4-12	2-6	2-6	None
1982	4-5	2-3	2-2	None
1983	8-8	5-3	3-5	None
1984	7-9	3-5	4-4	None
1985	5-11	3-5	2-6	None

NEW YORK GIANTS

	Total	Home	Road	Playoffs
1981	9-7	4-4	5-3	1-1*
1982	4-5	2-3	2-2	None
1983	3-12-1	1-7	2-5-1	None
1984	9-7	6-2	3-5	1-1**
1985	10-6	6-2	4-4	1-1***

*Lost divisional playoff game
**Lost divisional playoff game
***Lost divisional playoff game

PHILADELPHIA

	Total	Home	Road	Playoffs
1981	10-6	6-2	4-4	0-1*
1982	3-6	1-4	2-2	None
1983	5-11	1-7	4-4	None
1984	6-9-1	5-3	1-6-1	None
1985	7-9	4-4	3-5	None

*Lost first-round game

ST. LOUIS

	Total	Home	Road	Playoffs
1981	7-9	5-3	2-6	None
1982	5-4	1-3	4-1	0-1*
1983	8-7-1	4-3-1	4-4	None
1984	9-7	5-3	4-4	None
1985	5-11	4-4	1-7	None

*Lost first-round game

SAN FRANCISCO

	Total	Home	Road	Playoffs
1981	13-3	7-1	6-2	3-0*
1982	3-6	0-5	3-1	None
1983	10-6	4-4	6-2	1-1**
1984	15-1	7-1	8-0	3-0***
1985	10-6	5-3	5-3	0-1#

*Won Super Bowl XVI
**Lost NFC Championship Game
***Won Super Bowl XIX
Lost first-round game

TAMPA BAY

	Total	Home	Road	Playoffs
1981	9-7	6-2	3-5	0-1*
1982	5-4	4-1	1-3	0-1**
1983	2-14	1-7	1-7	None
1984	6-10	6-2	0-8	None
1985	2-14	2-6	0-8	None

*Lost divisional playoff game
**Lost first-round game

WASHINGTON

	Total	Home	Road	Playoffs
1981	8-8	5-3	3-5	None
1982	8-1	3-1	5-0	4-0*
1983	14-2	7-1	7-1	2-1**
1984	11-5	7-1	4-4	0-1***
1985	10-6	5-3	5-3	None

*Won Super Bowl XVII
**Lost Super Bowl XVIII
***Lost divisional playoff game

Records for Each Current NFL Team for Most Points in a Game (Regular Season Only)

Note: When the record has been achieved more than once, only the most recent game is shown; summaries are listed in order of record-setting teams' point totals. Bold face indicates team holding record.

November 27, 1966, at Washington
New York Giants......... 0 14 14 13 — 41
Washington............. 13 21 14 24 — 72
TDs: Wash—A. D. Whitfield 3, Brig Owens 2, Charley Taylor 2, Rickie Harris, Joe Don Looney, Bobby Mitchell; NYG—Allen Jacobs, Homer Jones, Dan Lewis, Joe Morrison, Aaron Thomas, Gary Wood. TD Passes: Wash—Sonny Jurgensen 3; NYG—Gary Wood 2, Tom Kennedy. FG: Wash—Charlie Gogolak.

October 22, 1950, at Los Angeles
Baltimore .... 13 0 7 7 — 27
Los Angeles............ 21 14 14 21 — 70
TDs: LA—Bob Boyd 2, Vitamin Smith 2, Tom Fears, Elroy Hirsch, Dick Hoerner, Ralph Pasquariello, Dan Towler, Bob Waterfield; Balt—Chet Mutryn 2, Adrian Burk, Billy Stone. TD Passes: LA—Norm Van Brocklin 2, Bob Waterfield 2, Glenn Davis; Balt—Adrian Burk 3.

November 13, 1949, at New York
Chicago Cardinals ...... 7 31 14 13 — 65
New York Bulldogs....... 7 0 6 7 — 20
TDs: Chi—Red Cochran 2, Pat Harder 2, Bill Dewell, Mel Kutner, Bob Ravensburg, Vic Schwall, Charlie Trippi; NY—Joe Golding, Frank Muehlheuser, Johnny Rauch. TD Passes: Chi—Paul Christman 3, Jim Hardy 3; NY—Bobby Layne. FG: Chi—Pat Harder.

November 6, 1934, at Philadelphia
Cincinnati Reds.......... 0 0 0 0 — 0
Philadelphia............ 26 6 12 20 — 64
TDs: Phil—Joe Carter 3, Swede Hanson 3, Marvin Ellstrom, Roger Kirkman, Ed Matesic, Ed Storm. TD Passes: Phil—Ed Matesic 2, Albert Weiner 2, Marvin Elstrom.

November 30, 1952, at Pittsburgh
New York Giants......... 0 0 7 0 — 7
Pittsburgh.............. 14 14 7 28 — 63
TDs: Pitt—Lynn Chandnois 2, Dick Hensley 2, Jack Butler, George Hays, Ray Mathews, Ed Modzelewski, Elbie Nickel; NYG—Bill Stribling. TD Passes: Pitt—Jim Finks 4, Gary Kerkorian; NYG—Tom Landry.

November 7, 1954, at Cleveland
Washington .... 0 3 0 0 — 3
Cleveland............... 13 14 21 14 — 62
TDs: Clev—Darrell Brewster 2, Mo Bassett, Ken Gorgal, Otto Graham, Dub Jones, Dante Lavelli, Curley Morrison. TD Passes: Clev—George Ratterman 3, Otto Graham. FGs: Clev—Lou Groza 2; Wash—Vic Janowicz.

November 26, 1972, at New York
Philadelphia............. 3 7 0 0 — 10
New York Giants........ 14 24 10 14 — 62
TDs: NYG—Don Herrmann 2, Ron Johnson 2, Bob Tucker 2, Randy Johnson; Phil—Harold Jackson. TD Passes: NYG—Norm Snead 3, Randy Johnson 2; Phil—John Reaves. FGs: NYG—Pete Gogolak 2; Phil—Tom Dempsey.

September 16, 1973, at New Orleans
Atlanta................. 0 24 21 17 — 62
New Orleans............ 0 0 7 0 — 7
TDs: Atl—Ken Burrow 2, Eddie Ray 2, Wes Chesson, Tom Hayes, Art Malone, Joe Profit; NO—Bill Butler. TD Passes: Atl—Dick Shiner 3, Bob Lee; NO—Archie Manning. FGs: Atl—Nick Mike-Mayer.

November 17, 1985, at New York
Tampa Bay.............. 14 7 7 0 — 28
New York Jets.......... 17 24 14 7 — 62
TDs: NYJ—Mickey Shuler 3, Johnny Hector 2, Tony Paige, Al Toon, Wesley Walker; TB—James Wilder 2, Kevin House, Calvin Magee. TD Passes: NYJ—Ken O'Brien 5; TB—Steve DeBerg 2. FGs: NYJ—Pat Leahy 2.

December 17, 1972, at Houston
Cincinnati.............. 3 13 17 28 — 61
Houston .... 3 7 0 7 — 17
TDs: Cin—Doug Dressler 3, Lemar Parrish 2, Ken Anderson, Neal Craig; Hou—Ken Burrough, Fred Willis. TD Passes: Cin—Ken Anderson; Hou—Kent Nix 2. FGs: Cin—Horst Muhlmann 4; Hou—Skip Butler.

December 7, 1980, at Chicago
Green Bay .... 0 7 0 0 — 7
Chicago................ 0 28 13 20 — 61
TDs: Chi—Walter Payton 3, Brian Baschnagel, Robin Earl, Roland Harper, Willie McClendon, Len Walterscheid, Rickey Watts; GB—James Lofton. TD Passes: Chi—Vince Evans 3; GB—Lynn Dickey.

September 7, 1963, at Denver
Kansas City............ 14 14 21 10 — 59
Denver .... 0 7 0 0 — 7
TDs: KC—Chris Burford 2, Frank Jackson 2, Dave Grayson, Abner Haynes, Sherrill Headrick, Curtis McClinton; Den—Lionel Taylor. TD Passes: KC—Len Dawson 4, Curtis McClinton; Den—Mickey Slaughter. FG: KC—Tommy Brooker.

October 12, 1980, at Dallas
San Francisco........... 0 7 0 7 — 14
Dallas.................. 14 24 14 7 — 59
TDs: Dall—Drew Pearson 3, Ron Springs 2, Tony Dorsett, Billy Joe DuPree, Robert Newhouse; SF—Dwight Clark 2. TD Passes: Dall—Danny White 4; SF—Steve DeBerg 2. FG: Dall—Rafael Septien.

December 22, 1963, at San Diego
Denver .... 7 10 3 0 — 20
San Diego.............. 10 16 10 22 — 58
TDs: SD—Paul Lowe 2, Chuck Allen, Bobby Jackson, Dave Kocourek, Keith Lincoln, Jacque MacKinnon; Den—Billy Joe, Donnie Stone. TD Passes: SD—John Hadl, Tobin Rote; Den—Don Breaux. FGs: SD—George Blair 3; Den—Gene Mingo 2.

September 18, 1966, at Buffalo
Miami.................. 3 7 0 14 — 24
Buffalo................ 21 27 3 7 — 58
TDs: Buff—Bobby Burnett 2, Butch Byrd 2, Jack Spikes 2, Bobby Crockett, Jack Kemp; Mia—Dave Kocourek, Bo Roberson, John Roderick. TD Passes: Buff—Jack Kemp, Daryle Lamonica; Mia—George Wilson 3. FGs: Buff—Booth Lusteg; Mia—Gene Mingo.

December 12, 1976, at Baltimore
Buffalo................. 3 3 7 7 — 20
Baltimore Colts......... 7 13 28 10 — 58
TDs: Balt—Roger Carr, Raymond Chester, Glenn Doughty, Roosevelt Leaks, Derrel Luce, Lydell Mitchell, Howard Stevens; Buff—Bob Chandler, O.J. Simpson. TD Passes: Balt—Bert Jones 3; Buff—Gary Marangi. FGs: Balt—Toni Linhart 3; Buff—George Jakowenko 2.

October 7, 1945, at Milwaukee
Detroit................. 0 7 7 7 — 21
Green Bay............. 0 41 9 7 — 57
TDs: GB—Don Hutson 4, Charley Brock, Irv Comp, Ted Fritsch, Clyde Goodnight; Det—Chuck Fenenbock, John Greene, Bob Westfall. TD Passes: GB—Tex McKay 4, Lou Brock, Irv Comp; Det—Dave Ryan.

October 14, 1962, at Houston
New York Titans......... 3 7 7 0 — 17
Houston................ 14 21 14 7 — 56
TDs: Hou—Bill Groman, 2, Bob McLeod 2, Dave Smith 2, Willard Dewveall, Charley Hennigan; NY—Dick Christy, Ed Cooke. TD Passes: Hou—George Blanda 6, Jacky Lee. FGs: NY—Bill Shockley.

October 30, 1977, at Seattle
Buffalo.................. 3 0 7 7 — 17
Seattle................. 14 28 7 7 — 56
TDs: Sea—Steve Largent 2, Duke Fergerson, Al Hunter, David Sims, Sherman Smith, Don Testerman, Jim Zorn; Buff—Joe Ferguson, John Kimbrough. TD Passes: Sea—Jim Zorn 4; Buff—Joe Ferguson. FG: Buff—Carson Long.

September 9, 1979, at New England
New York Jets........... 3 0 0 0 — 3
New England........... 14 21 7 14 — 56
TDs: NE—Harold Jackson 3, Stanley Morgan 2, Allan Clark, Andy Johnson, Don Westbrook. TD Passes: NE—Steve Grogan 5, Tom Owen. FG: NYJ—Pat Leahy.

November 24, 1977, at St. Louis
Miami................. 14 14 20 7 — 55
St. Louis............... 7 0 0 7 — 14
TDs: Mia—Nat Moore 3, Gary Davis, Duriel Harris, Leroy Harris, Benny Malone, Andre Tillman; StL—Ike Harris, Terry Metcalf. TD Passes: Mia—Bob Griese 6; StL—Jim Hart.

October 18, 1970, at Minnesota
Dallas .... 3 3 0 7 — 13
Minnesota............. 14 20 17 3 — 54
TDs: Minn—Clint Jones 2, Ed Sharockman 2, John Beasley, Dave Osborn; Dall—Calvin Hill. TD Pass: Minn—Gary Cuozzo. FGs: Minn—Fred Cox 4; Dall—Mike Clark 2.

October 26, 1952, at Green Bay
Detroit................ 14 14 14 10 — 52
Green Bay .... 7 3 7 0 — 17
TDs: Det—Jug Girard 2, Bob Hoernschemeyer 2, Jack Christiansen, Jim Smith, Bill Swiacki; GB—Billy Howton, Jim Keane. TD Passes: Det—Bobby Layne 3; GB—Babe Parilli, Tobin Rote. FGs: Det—Pat Harder; GB—Bill Reichardt.

December 22, 1963, at Oakland
Houston .... 14 21 14 0 — 49
Oakland Raiders........ 7 28 7 10 — 52
TDs: Oak—Art Powell 4, Clem Daniels, Claude Gibson, Ken Herock; Hou—Willard Dewveall 2, Dave Smith 2, Charley Hennigan, Bob McLeod, Charley Tolar. TD Passes: Oak—Tom Flores 6; Hou—George Blanda 5. FG: Oak—Mike Mercer.

September 19, 1965, at San Francisco
Chicago................. 3 0 0 21 — 24
San Francisco.......... 0 24 21 7 — 52
TDs: SF—Bernie Casey 2, John David Crow, Charlie Krueger, Gary Lewis, Dave Parks, Ken Willard; Chi—Charlie Bivins 2, Andy Livingston. TD Passes: SF—John Brodie 4; Chi—Rudy Bukich 2. FGs: SF—Tommy Davis; Chi—Roger LeClerc.

November 21, 1976, at Seattle
New Orleans............ 3 17 28 3 — 51
Seattle.................. 6 0 7 14 — 27
TDs: NO—Bobby Douglass 2, Tony Galbreath, Chuck Muncie, Tom Myers, Elex Price; Sea—Sherman Smith 2, Steve Largent, Jim Zorn. TD Pass: Sea—Bill Munson. FGs: NO—Rich Szaro 3.

October 6, 1963, at Denver
San Diego .... 13 7 0 14 — 34
Denver................ 3 14 9 24 — 50
TDs: Den—Lionel Taylor 2, Goose Gonsoulin, Gene Prebola, Donnie Stone; SD—Keith Lincoln 2, Lance Alworth, Paul Lowe, Jacque MacKinnon. TD Passes: Den—John McCormick 3; SD—Tobin Rote 3, John Hadl 2. FGs: Den—Gene Mingo 5.

December 16, 1984, at Tampa Bay
New York Jets........... 0 7 0 14 — 21
Tampa Bay............. 10 7 3 21 — 41
TDs: TB—Jerry Bell 2, James Wilder 2, Jay Carroll; NYJ—Glenn Dennison, Johnny Hector, Tony Paige. TD Passes: TB—Steve DeBerg 3; NYJ—Ken O'Brien 2. FGs: TB—Obed Ariri.

NFL Games In Which a Team Has Scored 60 or More Points

(Home team in capitals)

Regular Season

WASHINGTON 72, New York Giants 41	November 27, 1966
LOS ANGELES RAMS 70, Baltimore 27	October 22, 1950
Chicago Cardinals 65, NEW YORK BULLDOGS 20	November 13, 1949
LOS ANGELES RAMS 65, Detroit 24	October 29, 1950
PHILADELPHIA 64, Cincinnati 0	November 6, 1934
CHICAGO CARDINALS 63, New York Giants 35	October 17, 1948
PITTSBURGH 62, New York Giants 7	November 30, 1952
CLEVELAND 62, New York Giants 14	December 6, 1953
CLEVELAND 62, Washington 3	November 7, 1954
NEW YORK GIANTS 62, Philadelphia 10	November 26, 1972
Atlanta 62, NEW ORLEANS 7	September 16, 1973
NEW YORK JETS 62, Tampa Bay 28	November 17, 1985
CHICAGO 61, San Francisco 20	December 12, 1965
Cincinnati 61, HOUSTON 17	December 17, 1972
CHICAGO 61, Green Bay 7	December 7, 1980
CHICAGO CARDINALS 60, Rochester 0	October 7, 1923

Postseason

Chicago Bears 73, WASHINGTON 0	December 8, 1940

Youngest and Oldest Regular Starters in NFL in 1985

Minimum, 8 Games Started

Five Youngest Regular Starters

	Birthdate	Games Started	Position
Andre Reed, Buff.	1/29/64	15	WR
Bernie Kosar, Clev.	11/25/63	10	QB
Mike Gann, Atl.	10/10/63	16	DE
Anthony Young, Ind.	10/8/63	12	S
Ron Holmes, T.B.	8/26/63	14	DE

Five Oldest Regular Starters

	Birthdate	Games Started	Position
Jeff Van Note, Atl.	2/7/46	16	C
Ed White, S.D.	4/4/47	16	G
Charlie Joiner, S.D.	10/14/47	14	WR
Julius Adams, N.E.	4/26/48	12	DE
Lyle Alzado, Raiders	4/3/49	11	DE

Oldest and Youngest Regular Starters By Position

Minimum, 8 Games Started

	Youngest	Oldest
Quarterback	11/25/63 Bernie Kosar, Clev.	9/9/49 Joe Theismann, Wash.
Running back	10/14/62 Tony Paige, Jets	8/ 4/49 John Riggins, Wash.
Wide receiver	1/29/64 Andre Reed, Buff.	10/14/47 Charlie Joiner, S.D.
Tight end	4/28/63 Mark Bavaro, Giants	2/ 5/51 Charle Young, Sea.
Center	6/14/62 Mark Cannon, G.B.	2/ 7/46 Jeff Van Note, Atl.
Guard	8/ 8/62 Jim Sweeney, Jets	4/ 4/47 Ed White, S.D.
Tackle	6/ 4/63 Jim Lachey, S.D.	4/ 2/51 Matt Herkenhoff, K.C.
Def. end	10/10/63 Mike Gann, Atl.	4/28/48 Julius Adams, N.E.
Def. tackle	3/23/63 Tim Newton, Minn.	6/23/50 Dave Butz, Wash.
Linebacker	4/ 4/63 Jack Del Rio, N.O.	4/ 5/51 Brad Van Pelt, Raiders
Cornerback	1/22/63 Wendell Cason, Atl.	1/16/53 Dave Brown, Sea.
Safety	10/ 8/63 Anthony Young, Ind.	8/26/52 Donnie Shell, Pitt.

Records of Teams on Opening Day, 1933-85

AFC	W	L	T	Pct.	Longest W Strk.	Longest L Strk.	Current Streak
Chargers	17	9	0	.654	6	4	W-2
Colts	20	13	0	.606	8	3	L-2
Broncos	15	10	1	.600	3	4	L-1
Browns	21	15	0	.583	5	3	L-3
Raiders	15	11	0	.577	5	5	W-4
Steelers	25	22	4	.532	4	3	W-1
Dolphins	10	9	1	.526	4	3	L-1
Bengals	9	9	0	.500	4	4	L-3
Oilers	13	13	0	.500	4	3	W-1
Chiefs	13	13	0	.500	4	4	W-3
Jets	11	15	0	.423	3	5	L-1
Patriots	11	15	0	.423	2	3	W-2
Bills	9	17	0	.346	3	5	L-3
Seahawks	2	8	0	.200	2	8	W-2

NFC	W	L	T	Pct.	Longest W Strk.	Longest L Strk.	Current Streak
Cowboys	21	4	1	.840	17	2	W-3
Vikings	15	9	1	.625	4	2	W-1
Falcons	12	8	0	.600	5	3	L-1
Giants	29	20	4	.592	3	3	W-2
Packers	28	22	3	.560	5	6	L-1
Lions	28	23	2	.549	7	4	W-1
Rams	26	22	0	.542	5	6	W-1
Bears	28	24	1	.538	7	6	W-2
Redskins	24	25	4	.490	6	5	L-3
Cardinals	23	28	1	.451	6	6	W-1
49ers	15	20	1	.429	4	3	L-1
Eagles	20	31	1	.392	5	9	L-2
Buccaneers	3	7	0	.300	3	4	L-4
Saints	3	16	0	.158	1	6	L-2

Note: All tied games occurred prior to 1972, when calculation of ties as half-win, half-loss in percentages was begun.

Trailing at Halftime

	1981–85	1985 ONLY
Home Teams	112-286-2 (.283)	27-53 (.338)
Road Teams	92-439-1 (.174)	19-111 (.146)
All Teams	204-725-3 (.220)	46-164 (.219)

Trailing After 3 Quarters

	1981–85	1985 ONLY
Home Teams	89-326-1 (.215)	16-59 (.213)
Road Teams	72-473-2 (.133)	15-123 (.109)
All Teams	161-799-3 (.169)	31-182 (.146)

The records of all NFL teams for 1985 in each category of games:

	Status at Halftime			Status After 3 Quarters		
AFC	Leading	Tied	Trailing	Leading	Tied	Trailing
Buffalo	2-5	0-0	0-9	2-2	0-0	0-12
Cincinnati	6-1	0-0	1-8	6-2	0-2	1-5
Cleveland	5-1	1-0	2-7	6-0	0-0	2-8
Denver	9-3	0-0	2-2	8-1	0-1	3-3
Houston	3-1	0-0	2-10	2-0	0-1	3-10
Indianapolis	4-0	1-2	0-9	4-0	1-0	0-11
Kansas City	5-0	0-2	1-8	6-1	0-0	0-9
L.A. Raiders	8-2	0-0	4-2	9-1	3-0	0-3
Miami	9-2	2-0	1-2	11-2	1-0	0-2
New England	8-1	0-0	3-4	8-1	1-0	2-4
N.Y. Jets	10-0	0-0	1-5	10-0	0-1	1-4
Pittsburgh	5-1	0-0	2-8	6-1	0-1	1-7
San Diego	5-4	1-1	2-3	5-3	1-0	2-5
Seattle	6-2	0-1	2-5	7-3	0-0	1-5
NFC	**Leading**	**Tied**	**Trailing**	**Leading**	**Tied**	**Trailing**
Atlanta	4-3	0-0	0-9	4-1	0-0	0-11
Chicago	11-0	1-0	3-1	14-0	0-0	1-1
Dallas	10-3	0-0	0-3	8-1	1-0	1-5
Detroit	6-2	0-0	1-7	7-2	0-0	0-7
Green Bay	4-0	2-0	2-8	5-1	1-0	2-7
L.A. Rams	7-1	1-0	3-4	9-0	0-1	2-4
Minnesota	4-2	0-1	3-6	4-2	1-1	2-6
New Orleans	5-1	0-0	0-10	5-0	0-0	0-11
N.Y. Giants	6-0	2-1	2-5	10-3	0-0	0-3
Philadelphia	3-3	2-1	2-5	3-2	1-0	3-7
St. Louis	4-1	0-2	1-8	5-1	0-1	0-9
San Francisco	7-2	0-0	3-4	10-1	0-1	0-4
Tampa Bay	1-5	0-2	1-7	1-0	0-1	1-13
Washington	7-0	1-1	2-5	7-0	0-0	3-6

Walter Payton's Career Rushing vs. Each Opponent

Opponent	Games	Rushes	Yards	Yards Per Rush	Yards Per Game	TD
Atlanta	6	119	434	3.6	72.3	3
Buffalo	1	39	155	4.0	155.0	1
Cincinnati	1	18	78	4.3	78.0	0
Cleveland	1	11	30	2.7	30.0	0
Dallas	5	124	641	5.2	128.2	2
Denver	5	98	538	5.5	107.6	2
Detroit	22	443	1750	4.0	79.5	10
Green Bay	20	479	2271	4.7	113.6	17
Houston	2	36	139	3.9	69.5	0
Indianapolis	3	37	115	3.1	38.3	1
Kansas City	2	54	262	4.9	131.0	3
L.A. Rams	8	137	585	4.3	73.1	3
L.A. Raiders	4	97	359	3.7	89.8	5
Miami	3	45	190	4.2	63.3	1
Minnesota	21	439	2104	4.8	100.2	14
New England	3	39	151	3.9	50.3	0
New Orleans	6	130	792	6.1	132.0	6
N.Y. Giants	1	15	47	3.1	47.0	0
N.Y. Jets	2	48	106	2.2	53.0	0
Philadelphia	4	91	387	4.3	96.8	0
Pittsburgh	1	12	60	5.0	60.0	0
St. Louis	6	130	525	4.0	87.5	6
San Diego	3	76	249	3.3	83.0	2
San Francisco	7	162	774	4.8	110.6	8
Seattle	4	83	448	5.4	112.0	1
Tampa Bay	16	346	1358	3.9	84.9	10
Washington	5	63	312	5.0	62.4	3
Totals	162	3371	14860	4.4	91.7	98

Indianapolis totals include two games vs. Baltimore
L.A. Raiders totals include three games vs. Oakland

Tony Dorsett's Career Rushing vs. Each Opponent

Opponent	Games	Rushes	Yards	Yards Per Rush	Yards Per Game	TD
Atlanta	1	16	90	5.6	90.0	1
Buffalo	2	45	187	4.2	93.5	0
Chicago	4	69	275	4.0	68.8	0
Cincinnati	2	37	183	4.9	91.5	0
Cleveland	3	49	247	5.0	82.3	2
Denver	2	34	112	3.3	56.0	0
Detroit	3	40	165	4.1	55.0	0
Green Bay	3	65	270	4.2	90.0	4
Houston	3	53	278	5.2	92.7	1
Indianapolis	3	69	426	6.2	142.0	0
Kansas City	1	18	108	6.0	108.0	2
L.A. Rams	5	109	458	4.2	91.6	3
L.A. Raiders	2	45	162	3.6	81.0	1
Miami	3	53	229	4.3	76.3	0
Minnesota	5	78	488	6.3	97.6	4
New England	3	53	260	4.9	86.7	1
New Orleans	4	88	461	5.2	115.3	4
N.Y. Giants	16	297	1241	4.2	77.6	7
N.Y. Jets	1	29	121	4.2	121.0	1
Philadelphia	17	308	1274	4.1	74.9	10
Pittsburgh	4	68	289	4.3	72.3	2
St. Louis	16	281	1427	5.1	89.2	11
San Diego	1	17	58	3.4	53.0	0
San Francisco	6	101	323	3.2	53.8	2
Seattle	2	50	224	4.5	112.0	4
Tampa Bay	4	69	292	4.2	73.0	0
Washington	16	300	1184	3.9	74.0	6
Totals	132	2441	10832	4.4	82.1	66

Indianapolis totals include two games vs. Baltimore
L.A. Raiders totals include one game vs. Oakland

Earl Campbell's Career Rushing vs. Each Opponent

Opponent	Games	Rushes	Yards	Yards Per Rush	Yards Per Game	TD
Atlanta	5	59	341	5.8	68.2	2
Buffalo	2	49	247	5.0	123.5	1
Chicago	1	31	206	6.6	206.0	0
Cincinnati	13	263	1264	4.8	97.2	6
Cleveland	10	191	725	3.8	72.5	7
Dallas	3	52	274	5.3	91.3	2
Denver	3	69	299	4.3	99.7	3
Detroit	1	28	107	3.8	107.0	0
Green Bay	4	74	330	4.5	82.5	5
Indianapolis	4	71	297	4.2	74.3	7
Kansas City	6	131	616	4.7	102.7	4
L.A. Rams	5	70	328	4.7	65.6	0
L.A. Raiders	5	121	408	3.4	81.6	2
Miami	4	107	535	5.0	133.8	5
Minnesota	3	93	493	5.3	164.3	3
New England	4	97	327	3.4	81.8	4
New Orleans	3	65	201	3.1	67.0	4
N.Y. Giants	3	40	130	3.3	43.3	0
N.Y. Jets	3	42	185	4.4	61.7	2
Philadelphia	3	34	160	4.7	53.3	1
Pittsburgh	12	206	683	3.3	56.9	6
St. Louis	2	24	88	3.7	44.0	1
San Diego	2	21	85	4.0	42.5	0
San Francisco	5	56	174	3.1	34.8	2
Seattle	5	90	401	4.5	80.2	3
Tampa Bay	3	71	337	4.7	112.3	2
Washington	1	32	166	5.2	166.0	2
Totals	115	2187	9407	4.3	81.8	74

Indianapolis totals include three games vs. Baltimore
L.A. Raiders totals include three games vs. Oakland

Eric Dickerson's Career Rushing vs. Each Opponent

Opponent	Games	Rushes	Yards	Yards Per Rush	Yards Per Game	TD
Atlanta	6	111	529	4.8	88.2	8
Buffalo	1	32	125	3.9	125.0	1
Chicago	2	62	276	4.5	138.0	4
Cincinnati	1	22	89	4.0	89.0	1
Cleveland	1	27	102	3.8	102.0	0
Dallas	1	21	138	6.6	138.0	1
Detroit	1	30	199	6.6	199.0	3
Green Bay	3	76	357	4.7	119.0	2
Houston	1	27	215	8.0	215.0	2
Indianapolis	1	19	80	4.2	80.0	0
Kansas City	1	26	68	2.6	68.0	1
L.A. Raiders	1	25	98	3.9	98.0	0
Miami	1	14	101	7.2	101.0	1
Minnesota	1	25	55	2.2	55.0	1
New England	1	27	94	3.5	94.0	0
New Orleans	5	110	600	5.5	120.0	5
N.Y. Giants	3	77	312	4.1	104.0	1
N.Y. Jets	1	28	192	6.9	192.0	2
Philadelphia	1	28	103	3.7	103.0	0
Pittsburgh	1	23	49	2.1	49.0	0
St. Louis	2	41	332	8.1	166.0	2
San Francisco	6	114	580	5.1	96.7	2
Seattle	1	31	150	4.8	150.0	3
Tampa Bay	2	53	266	5.0	133.0	4
Washington	1	12	37	3.1	37.0	0
Totals	46	1061	5147	4.9	111.9	44

Indianapolis totals reflect one game vs. Baltimore

Records of NFL Divisions in Out-of-Division Games 1978–85

The NFL's current schedule format went into effect in 1978. These charts indicate the annual records for each division's teams in games against teams from other divisions:

NFC East

	W	L	T	Pct.	Pos.
1978	21	19	0	.525	2T
1979	23	17	0	.575	3
1980	19	21	0	.475	4
1981	26	14	0	.650	1
1982	13	6	0	.684	1
1983	23	17	0	.575	1
1984	24	15	1	.613	2
1985	22	18	0	.550	2
Totals	171	127	1	.574	2

NFC Central

	W	L	T	Pct.	Pos.
1978	16	24	0	.400	6
1979	14	26	0	.350	5
1980	16	24	0	.400	6
1981	18	22	0	.450	4
1982	12	12	1	.500	3T
1983	15	25	0	.375	6
1984	11	28	1	.288	6
1985	19	21	0	.475	4
Totals	121	182	2	.400	6

NFC West

	W	L	T	Pct.	Pos.
1978	14	18	0	.438	5
1979	9	23	0	.281	6
1980	14	18	0	.438	5
1981	14	18	0	.438	5
1982	7	15	0	.318	6
1983	22	18	0	.550	2T
1984	24	16	0	.600	3
1985	18	22	0	.450	5
Totals	122	148	0	.452	5

AFC East

	W	L	T	Pct.	Pos.
1978	20	20	0	.500	4
1979	19	21	0	.475	4
1980	20	20	0	.500	3
1981	16	24	0	.400	6
1982	10	10	1	.500	3T
1983	22	18	0	.550	2T
1984	16	24	0	.400	4
1985	21	19	0	.475	3
Totals	144	156	1	.480	4

AFC Central

	W	L	T	Pct.	Pos.
1978	20	12	0	.625	1
1979	20	12	0	.625	2
1980	21	11	0	.656	1
1981	16	16	0	.500	3
1982	10	10	0	.500	3T
1983	16	24	0	.400	5
1984	13	27	0	.325	5
1985	15	25	0	.375	6
Totals	131	137	0	.489	3

AFC West

	W	L	T	Pct.	Pos.
1978	21	19	0	.525	2T
1979	27	13	0	.675	1
1980	22	18	0	.550	2
1981	22	18	0	.550	2
1982	12	11	0	.522	2
1983	22	18	0	.550	2T
1984	31	9	0	.775	1
1985	25	15	0	.625	1
Totals	182	121	0	.601	1

Composite Standings for Eight Seasons

	W	L	T	Pct.
AFC West	182	121	0	.601
NFC East	171	127	1	.574
AFC Central	131	137	0	.489
AFC East	144	156	1	.480
NFC West	122	148	0	.452
NFC Central	121	182	2	.400

1985 NFL Score by Quarters

AFC Offense	1	2	3	4	OT	PTS
San Diego	86	134	96	145	6	467
Cincinnati	115	106	119	101	0	441
Miami	88	136	95	109	0	428
N.Y. Jets	70	128	111	81	3	393
Denver	82	142	39	108	9	380
Pittsburgh	58	134	83	104	0	379
New England	54	115	44	149	0	362
L.A. Raiders	79	93	76	100	6	354
Seattle	43	116	90	100	0	349
Indianapolis	65	98	52	105	0	320
Kansas City	77	111	66	63	0	317
Cleveland	44	68	78	97	0	287
Houston	24	90	63	107	0	284
Buffalo	58	63	41	38	0	200

NFC Offense	1	2	3	4	OT	PTS
Chicago	67	144	123	122	0	456
San Francisco	69	111	102	129	0	411
N.Y. Giants	62	118	118	95	6	399
Dallas	55	122	78	102	0	357
Minnesota	44	91	83	128	0	346
L.A. Rams	54	102	82	102	0	340
Green Bay	50	82	89	116	0	337
Detroit	76	95	79	57	0	307
Washington	81	105	44	67	0	297
New Orleans	46	77	43	128	0	294
Tampa Bay	71	109	31	80	3	294
Philadelphia	60	72	56	92	6	286
Atlanta	68	90	33	91	0	282
St. Louis	67	73	48	87	3	278

AFC Defense	1	2	3	4	OT	PTS
N.Y. Jets	50	91	59	64	0	264
New England	75	64	56	92	3	290
Cleveland	75	81	50	85	3	294
Seattle	47	78	63	112	3	303
L.A. Raiders	73	93	67	69	6	308
Miami	44	96	78	102	0	320
Denver	48	89	102	84	6	329
Pittsburgh	72	129	53	101	0	355
Kansas City	39	135	65	121	0	360
Buffalo	51	144	78	108	0	381
Indianapolis	81	145	64	96	0	386
Houston	126	94	112	80	0	412
San Diego	82	124	114	109	6	435
Cincinnati	61	131	107	138	0	437

NFC Defense	1	2	3	4	OT	PTS
Chicago	50	77	34	37	0	198
San Francisco	53	65	47	98	0	263
L.A. Rams	47	99	53	78	0	277
N.Y. Giants	75	85	34	89	0	283
Philadelphia	69	67	76	92	6	310
Washington	59	107	78	68	0	312
Dallas	66	73	98	96	0	333
Green Bay	68	109	66	112	0	355
Minnesota	81	92	96	90	0	359
Detroit	68	96	85	114	3	366
New Orleans	55	142	51	153	0	401
St. Louis	78	122	77	137	0	414
Tampa Bay	75	144	110	119	0	448
Atlanta	45	153	89	159	6	452

NFL TOTALS	1	2	3	4	OT	PTS
	1813	2925	2062	2803	42	9645

Team Leaders

Offense	**Most Scored**	**Fewest Scored**
First Quarter	115, Cincinnati	24, Houston
Second Quarter	144, Chicago	63, Buffalo
Third Quarter	123, Chicago	31, Tampa Bay
Fourth Quarter	149, New England	38, Buffalo

Defense	**Most Allowed**	**Fewest Allowed**
First Quarter	126, Houston	39, Kansas City
Second Quarter	153, Atlanta	64, New England
Third Quarter	114, San Diego	34, Chicago 34, N.Y. Giants
Fourth Quarter	159, Atlanta	37, Chicago

December Records Since 1977

AFC	1977	1978	1979	1980	1981	1982	1983	1984	1985	Total	Pct.
Miami	2-1	3-0	1-1	2-1	3-0	3-1	3-0	2-1	4-0	23- 5	.821
L.A. Raiders	2-1	1-2	2-1	3-1	1-2	4-0	2-1	2-1	4-0	21- 9	.700
Cincinnati	2-1	3-0	1-2	2-1	2-1	3-1	2-1	3-0	2-2	20- 9	.690
San Diego	1-2	3-0	2-1	2-1	2-1	4-0	1-2	1-2	3-1	19-10	.655
N.Y. Jets	1-2	1-2	3-0	1-2	2-1	3-1	1-2	1-2	2-1	15-13	.536
Denver	2-1	2-1	1-2	1-3	2-1	1-3	2-1	2-1	3-1	16-14	.533
New England	2-1	1-2	1-1	2-1	0-3	2-2	2-1	1-2	3-1	14-14	.500
Pittsburgh	2-1	3-0	2-1	1-2	0-3	2-2	1-2	2-1	1-3	14-15	.483
Seattle	2-1	2-1	2-1	0-3	2-1	1-3	2-1	1-2	2-2	14-15	.483
Kansas City	0-3	1-2	2-1	2-1	1-2	1-3	1-2	3-0	2-2	13-16	.448
Houston	2-1	1-2	1-2	3-0	2-1	0-4	1-2	1-2	0-4	11-18	.379
Cleveland	0-3	1-2	1-2	2-1	0-3	2-2	1-2	1-2	2-2	10-19	.345
Buffalo	1-2	1-2	0-3	2-1	2-1	1-3	1-2	1-2	0-4	9-20	.310
Indianapolis	1-2	0-3	1-2	0-3	1-2	0-3-1	1-2	0-3	2-2	6-22-1	.224

NFC	1977	1978	1979	1980	1981	1982	1983	1984	1985	Total	Pct.
Washington	3-0	0-3	2-1	3-0	3-0	3-1	3-0	2-0	3-1	22- 6	.786
Chicago	3-0	2-1	3-0	2-1	3-0	2-2	2-1	1-2	3-1	21- 8	.724
Dallas	3-0	3-0	3-0	2-1	2-1	3-1	1-2	1-2	1-2	19- 9	.679
San Francisco	0-3	1-2	1-2	1-2	3-0	2-2	3-0	3-0	3-1	17-12	.586
Green Bay	2-1	1-2	1-2	0-3	2-1	2-1-1	2-1	3-0	3-1	16-12-1	.569
St. Louis	0-3	2-1	2-1	1-2	1-2	3-1	3-0	2-1	1-2	15-13	.536
L.A. Rams	2-1	2-1	2-1	2-1	1-2	0-4	1-2	2-1	2-2	14-15	.483
Atlanta	1-2	1-2	2-1	2-1	0-3	3-1	1-2	1-2	2-2	13-16	.448
Philadelphia	2-1	1-2	2-1	1-2	1-2	2-2	1-2	1-2	1-3	12-17	.414
Minnesota	2-1	1-2	1-2	2-1	0-3	2-2	1-2	0-2	2-2	11-17	.393
N.Y. Giants	1-2	1-2	0-3	1-2	3-0	2-2	0-3	1-2	2-2	11-18	.379
Tampa Bay	2-1	0-3	1-2	0-3	2-1	3-1	0-3	2-1	0-4	10-19	.345
Detroit	1-2	2-1	0-3	2-1	1-2	1-3	2-1	0-3	0-3	9-19	.321
New Orleans	0-3	2-1	1-2	1-2	0-3	0-4	1-2	1-2	1-3	7-22	.241

L.A. Raiders totals include Oakland, 1977–1981
Indianapolis totals include Baltimore, 1977–1983

Retired Uniform Numbers in NFL

AFC

Buffalo:	None	
Cincinnati:	Bob Johnson	54
Cleveland:	Otto Graham	14
	Jim Brown	32
	Ernie Davis	45
	Don Fleming	46
	Lou Groza	76
Denver:	Frank Tripucka	18
	Floyd Little	44
Houston:	Jim Norton	43
	Elvin Bethea	65
Indianapolis:	Johnny Unitas	19
	Buddy Young	22
	Lenny Moore	24
	Art Donovan	70
	Jim Parker	77
	Raymond Berry	82
	Gino Marchetti	89
Kansas City:	Len Dawson	16
	Abner Haynes	28
	Stone Johnson	33
	Mack Lee Hill	36
	Bobby Bell	78
Los Angeles Raiders:	None	
Miami:	Bob Griese	12
New England:	Gino Cappelletti	20
	Jim Hunt	79
	Bob Dee	89
New York Jets:	Joe Namath	12
Pittsburgh:	None	
San Diego:	None	
Seattle:	"Fans/the twelfth man"	12

NFC

Atlanta:	Tommy Nobis	60
Chicago:	Bronko Nagurski	3
	George McAfee	5
	Willie Galimore	28
	Brian Piccolo	41
	Sid Luckman	42
	Bill Hewitt	56
	Bill George	61
	Bulldog Turner	66
	Red Grange	77
Dallas:	None	
Detroit:	Dutch Clark	7
	Bobby Layne	22
	Doak Walker	37
	Joe Schmidt	56
	Chuck Hughes	85
	Charlie Sanders	88
Green Bay:	Tony Canadeo	3
	Don Hutson	14
	Bart Starr	15
	Ray Nitschke	66
Los Angeles Rams:	Bob Waterfield	7
	Elroy (Crazylegs) Hirsch	40
Minnesota:	Fran Tarkenton	10
New Orleans:	Doug Atkins	81
	Jim Taylor	31
New York Giants:	Ray Flaherty	1
	Mel Hein	7
	Y. A. Tittle	14
	Al Blozis	32
	Joe Morrison	40
	Charlie Conerly	42
	Ken Strong	50
Philadelphia:	Steve Van Buren	15
	Tom Brookshier	40
	Pete Retzlaff	44
	Chuck Bednarik	60
	Al Wistert	70
St. Louis:	Larry Wilson	8
	Stan Mauldin	77
	J. V. Cain	88
	Marshall Goldberg	99
San Francisco:	John Brodie	12
	Joe Perry	34
	Jimmy Johnson	37
	Hugh McElhenny	39
	Charlie Krueger	70
	Leo Nomellini	73
Tampa Bay:	None	
Washington:	Sammy Baugh	33

NFL Players Active in 1985 Who Were Not Drafted by an NFL Team But Have Played at Least 8 Years in NFL

	Yrs.	Pos.	Games	Starts
Ken Clarke, Philadelphia	8	NT	16	16
Paul Coffman, Green Bay	8	TE	16	16
Gary Danielson, Cleveland	9	QB	8	6
Preston Dennard, Green Bay	8	WR	16	0
Herman Edwards, Philadelphia	9	CB	16	16
Glenn Hyde, Denver	8	C-G	11	0
Robert Jackson, Cleveland	11	G	15	1
Dave Jennings, New York Jets	12	P	16	0
Cecil Johnson, Tampa Bay	9	LB	16	2
Pat Leahy, New York Jets	12	K	16	0
Guido Merkens, New Orleans	8	WR	16	0
Donnie Shell, Pittsburgh	12	S	16	16
Doug Smith, Los Angeles Rams	8	C	13	13
J. T. Smith, St. Louis	8	WR	14	5
Ray Wersching, San Francisco	13	K	16	0
Jim Zorn, Green Bay	10	QB	13	5

NFL Players Active in 1985 Who Were Not Drafted by an NFL Team But Have Played in at Least 1 AFC-NFC Pro Bowl

	Yrs.	Pos.	Pro Bowls
Bill Bates, Dallas	3	S	1
Carl Birdsong, St. Louis	5	P	1
Jeff Bostic, Washington	6	C	1
Rich Camarillo, New England	5	P	1
Deron Cherry, Kansas City	5	S	3
Paul Coffman, Green Bay	8	TE	3
Jay Hilgenberg, Chicago	5	C	1
Joe Jacoby, Washington	5	T	3
Dave Jennings, New York Jets	12	P	4
Norm Johnson, Seattle	4	K	1
Dave Krieg, Seattle	6	QB	1
Nick Lowery, Kansas City	6	K	1
Joe Nash, Seattle	4	NT	1
Donnie Shell, Pittsburgh	12	S	5
Doug Smith, Los Angeles Rams	8	C	1
J. T. Smith, St. Louis	8	WR	1
Everson Walls, Dallas	5	CB	4
Steve Watson, Denver	7	WR	1

Oldest Individual Single-Season or Single-Game Records in NFL Record & Fact Book

Regular Season Records That Have Not Been Surpassed or Tied

Most Points, Game—40, Ernie Nevers, Chi. Cardinals vs. Chi. Bears, Nov. 28, 1929 (6-td, 4-pat)

Most Touchdowns Rushing, Game—6, Ernie Nevers, Chi. Cardinals vs. Chi. Bears, Nov. 28, 1929

Highest Average Gain, Rushing, Season (Qualifiers)—9.94, Beattie Feathers, Chi. Bears, 1934 (101-1,004)

Highest Punting Average, Season (Qualifiers)—51.40, Sammy Baugh, Washington, 1940 (35-1,799)

Highest Punting Average, Game (minimum: 4 punts)—61.75, Bob Cifers, Detroit vs. Chi. Bears, Nov. 24, 1946 (4-247)

Highest Average Gain, Pass Receptions, Season (minimum: 24 receptions)—32.58, Don Currivan, Boston, 1947 (24-782)

Highest Average Gain, Passing, Game (minimum: 20 passes)—18.58, Sammy Baugh, Washington vs. Boston, Oct. 31, 1948 (24-446)

Most Touchdowns, Fumble Recoveries, Game—2, Fred (Dippy) Evans, Chi. Bears vs. Washington, Nov. 28, 1948

Most Yards Gained, Intercepted Passes, Rookie, Season—301, Don Doll, Detroit, 1949

Most Passes Had Intercepted, Game—8, Jim Hardy, Chi. Cardinals vs. Philadelphia, Sept. 24, 1950

Highest Average Gain, Rushing, Game (minimum: 10 attempts)—17.09, Marion Motley, Cleveland vs. Pittsburgh, Oct. 29, 1950 (11-188)

Most Yards Gained, Kickoff Returns, Game—294, Wally Triplett, Detroit vs. Los Angeles, Oct. 29, 1950

Highest Kickoff Return Average, Game (minimum: 3 returns)—73.50, Wally Triplett, Detroit vs. Los Angeles, Oct. 29, 1950 (4-294)

Most Pass Receptions, Game—18, Tom Fears, Los Angeles vs. Green Bay, Dec. 3, 1950

Highest Punt Return Average, Season (Qualifiers)—23.00, Herb Rich, Baltimore, 1950 (12-276)

Highest Punt Return Average, Rookie, Season (Qualifiers)—23.00, Herb Rich, Baltimore, 1950 (12-276)

Most Yards Passing, Game—554, Norm Van Brocklin, Los Angeles vs. N.Y. Yanks, Sept. 28, 1951

Most Touchdowns, Punt Returns, Rookie, Season—4, Jack Christiansen, Detroit, 1951

Most Interceptions By, Season—14, Dick (Night Train) Lane, Los Angeles, 1952

Most Interceptions By, Rookie, Season—14, Dick (Night Train) Lane, Los Angeles, 1952

Highest Average Gain, Passing, Season (Qualifiers)—11.17, Tommy O'Connell, Cleveland, 1957 (110-1,229)

Most Points, Season—176, Paul Hornung, Green Bay, 1960 (15-td, 41-pat, 15-fg)

Highest Pass Rating, Season—110.4, Milt Plum, Cleveland, 1960

Most Yards Gained, Pass Receptions, Season—1,473, Bill Groman, Houston, 1960

HISTORY

Pro Football Hall of Fame
Chronology
Past NFL Standings
All-Time Team vs. Team Results
Super Bowl Game Summaries
Playoff Game Summaries
AFC-NFC Pro Bowl Game Summaries
AFC-NFC Interconference Games
Monday Night Results
History of Overtime Games
Number-One Draft Choices
NFL Paid Attendance
NFL's 10 Biggest Attendance Weekends
NFL's 10 Highest Scoring Weekends
Top 10 Televised Sports Events of All Time
Ten Most Watched Programs in TV History
Chicago All-Star Game
NFL Playoff Bowl

PRO FOOTBALL HALL OF FAME

The Professional Football Hall of Fame is located in Canton, Ohio, site of the organizational meeting on September 17, 1920, from which the National Football League evolved. The NFL recognized Canton as the Hall of Fame site on April 27, 1961. Canton area individuals, foundations, and companies donated almost $400,000 in cash and services to provide funds for the construction of the original two-building complex, which was dedicated on September 7, 1963. The original Hall of Fame complex was almost doubled in size with the completion of a $620,000 expansion project that was dedicated on May 10, 1971. A second expansion project was completed on November 20, 1978. It features three exhibition areas and a theater twice the size of the original one.

The Hall represents the sport of pro football in many ways—through three large and colorful exhibition galleries, in the twin enshrinement halls, with numerous fan-participation electronic devices, a research library, and an NFL gift shop.

In recent years, the Pro Football Hall of Fame has become an extremely popular tourist attraction. At the end of 1985, a total of 3,864,887 fans had visited the Pro Football Hall of Fame.

New members of the Pro Football Hall of Fame are elected annually by a 29-member National Board of Selectors, made up of media representatives from every league city and the president of the Pro Football Writers Association. Between three and six new members are elected each year. An affirmative vote of approximately 80 percent is needed for election.

Any fan may nominate any eligible player or contributor simply by writing to the Pro Football Hall of Fame. Players must be retired five years to be eligible, while a coach need only to be retired with no time limit specified. Contributors (administrators, owners, *et al.*) may be elected while they are still active.

The charter class of 17 enshrinees was elected in 1963 and the honor roll now stands at 133 with the election of a five-man class in 1986. That class consists of Paul Hornung, Ken Houston, Willie Lanier, Fran Tarkenton, and Doak Walker.

Roster of Members

HERB ADDERLEY
Defensive back. 6-1, 200. Born in Philadelphia, Pennsylvania, June 8, 1939. Michigan State. Inducted in 1980. 1961-69 Green Bay Packers, 1970-72 Dallas Cowboys.

LANCE ALWORTH
Wide receiver. 6-0, 184. Born in Houston, Texas, August 3, 1940. Arkansas. Inducted in 1978. 1962-70 San Diego Chargers, 1971-72 Dallas Cowboys.

DOUG ATKINS
Defensive end. 6-8, 275. Born in Humboldt, Tennessee, May 8, 1930. Tennessee. Inducted in 1982. 1953-54 Cleveland Browns, 1955-66 Chicago Bears, 1967-69 New Orleans Saints.

MORRIS (RED) BADGRO
End. 6-0, 190. Born in Orilla, Washington, December 1, 1902. Southern California. Inducted in 1981. 1927 New York Yankees, 1930-35 New York Giants, 1936 Brooklyn Dodgers.

CLIFF BATTLES
Halfback. 6-1, 201. Born in Akron, Ohio, May 1, 1910. Died April 27, 1981. West Virginia Wesleyan. Inducted in 1968. 1932 Boston Braves, 1933-36 Boston Redskins, 1937 Washington Redskins.

SAMMY BAUGH
Quarterback. 6-2, 180. Born in Temple, Texas, March 17, 1914. Texas Christian. Inducted in 1963. 1937-52 Washington Redskins.

CHUCK BEDNARIK
Center-linebacker. 6-3, 230. Born in Bethlehem, Pennsylvania, May 1, 1925. Pennsylvania. Inducted in 1967. 1949-62 Philadelphia Eagles.

BERT BELL
Commissioner. Team owner. Born in Philadelphia, Pennsylvania, February 25, 1895. Died October 11, 1959. Pennsylvania. Inducted in 1963. 1933-1940 Philadelphia Eagles, 1941-42 Pittsburgh Steelers, 1943 Phil-Pitt, 1944-46 Pittsburgh Steelers. Commissioner, 1946-59.

BOBBY BELL
Linebacker. 6-4, 225. Born in Shelby, North Carolina, June 17, 1940. Minnesota. Inducted in 1983. 1963-74 Kansas City Chiefs.

RAYMOND BERRY
End. 6-2, 187. Born in Corpus Christi, Texas, February 27, 1933. Southern Methodist. Inducted in 1973. 1955-67 Baltimore Colts.

CHARLES W. BIDWILL, SR.
Team owner. Born in Chicago, Illinois, September 16, 1895. Died April 19, 1947. Loyola of Chicago. Inducted in 1967. 1933-43 Chicago Cardinals, 1944 Card-Pitt, 1945-47 Chicago Cardinals.

GEORGE BLANDA
Quarterback-kicker. 6-2, 215. Born in Youngwood, Pennsylvania, September 17, 1927. Kentucky. Inducted in 1981. 1949-58 Chicago Bears, 1950 Baltimore Colts, 1960-66 Houston Oilers, 1967-75 Oakland Raiders.

JIM BROWN
Fullback. 6-2, 232. Born in St. Simons, Georgia, February 17, 1936. Syracuse. Inducted in 1971. 1957-65 Cleveland Browns.

PAUL BROWN
Coach. Born in Norwalk, Ohio, September 7, 1908. Miami, Ohio. Inducted in 1967. 1946-49 Cleveland Browns (AAFC), 1950-62 Cleveland Browns, 1968-75 Cincinnati Bengals.

ROOSEVELT BROWN
Offensive tackle. 6-3, 255. Born in Charlottesville, Virginia, October 20, 1932. Morgan State. Inducted in 1975. 1953-65 New York Giants.

WILLIE BROWN
Defensive back. 6-1, 210. Born in Yazoo City, Mississippi, December 2, 1940. Grambling. Inducted in 1984. 1963-66 Denver Broncos, 1967-78 Oakland Raiders.

DICK BUTKUS
Linebacker. 6-3, 245. Born in Chicago, Illinois, December 9, 1942. Illinois. Inducted in 1979. 1965-73 Chicago Bears.

TONY CANADEO
Halfback. 5-11, 195. Born in Chicago, Illinois, May 5, 1919. Gonzaga. Inducted in 1974. 1941-44, 1946-52 Green Bay Packers.

JOE CARR
NFL president. Born in Columbus, Ohio, October 22, 1880. Died May 20, 1939. Did not attend college. Inducted in 1963. President, 1921-39 National Football League.

GUY CHAMBERLIN
End. Coach. 6-2, 210. Born in Blue Springs, Nebraska, January 16, 1894. Died April 4, 1967. Nebraska. Inducted in 1965. 1920 Decatur Staleys, 1921 Chicago Staleys, player-coach 1922-23 Canton Bulldogs, 1924 Cleveland Bulldogs, 1925-26 Frankford Yellow Jackets, 1927 Chicago Cardinals.

JACK CHRISTIANSEN
Defensive back. 6-1, 185. Born in Sublette, Kansas, December 20, 1928. Colorado State. Inducted in 1970. 1951-58 Detroit Lions.

EARL (DUTCH) CLARK
Quarterback. 6-0, 185. Born in Fowler, Colorado, October 11, 1906. Died August 5, 1978. Colorado College. Inducted in 1963. 1931-32 Portsmouth Spartans, 1934-38 Detroit Lions.

GEORGE CONNOR
Tackle-linebacker. 6-3, 240. Born in Chicago, Illinois, January 1, 1925. Holy Cross, Notre Dame. Inducted in 1975. 1948-55 Chicago Bears.

JIMMY CONZELMAN
Quarterback. Coach. Team owner. 6-0, 180. Born in St. Louis, Missouri, March 6, 1898. Died July 31, 1970. Washington, Missouri. Inducted in 1964. 1920 Decatur Staleys, 1921-22 Rock Island, Ill., Independents, 1923-24 Milwaukee Badgers; owner-coach, 1925-26 Detroit Panthers; player-coach 1927-29, coach 1930 Providence Steamroller; coach, 1940-42 Chicago Cardinals, 1946-48 Chicago Cardinals.

WILLIE DAVIS
Defensive end. 6-3, 245. Born in Lisbon, Louisiana, July 24, 1934. Grambling. Inducted in 1981. 1958-59 Cleveland Browns, 1960-69 Green Bay Packers.

ART DONOVAN
Defensive tackle. 6-3, 265. Born in Bronx, New York, June 5, 1925. Boston College. Inducted in 1968. 1950 Baltimore Colts, 1951 New York Yanks, 1952 Dallas Texans, 1953-61 Baltimore Colts.

JOHN (PADDY) DRISCOLL
Quarterback. 5-11, 160. Born in Evanston, Illinois, January 11, 1896. Died June 29, 1968. Northwestern. Inducted in 1965. 1920 Decatur Staleys, 1920-25 Chicago Cardinals, 1926-29 Chicago Bears. Head coach, 1956-57 Chicago Bears.

BILL DUDLEY
Halfback. 5-10, 176. Born in Bluefield, Virginia, December 24, 1921. Virginia. Inducted in 1966. 1942 Pittsburgh Steelers, 1945-46 Pittsburgh Steelers, 1947-49 Detroit Lions, 1950-51, 1953 Washington Redskins.

GLEN (TURK) EDWARDS
Tackle. 6-2, 260. Born in Mold, Washington, September 28, 1907. Died January 10, 1973. Washington State. Inducted in 1969. 1932 Boston Braves, 1933-36 Boston Redskins, 1937-40 Washington Redskins.

WEEB EWBANK
Coach. Born in Richmond, Indiana, May 6, 1907. Miami, Ohio. Inducted in 1978. 1954-62 Baltimore Colts, 1963-73 New York Jets.

TOM FEARS
End. 6-2, 215. Born in Los Angeles, California, December 3, 1923. Santa Clara, UCLA. Inducted in 1970. 1948-56 Los Angeles Rams.

RAY FLAHERTY
End. Coach. Born in Spokane, Washington, September 1, 1904. Gonzaga. Inducted in 1976. 1926 Los Angeles Wildcats (AFL), 1927-28 New York Yankees, 1928-29, 1931-35 New York Giants. Coach, 1936 Boston Redskins, 1937-42 Washington Redskins, 1946-48 New York Yankees (AAFC), 1949 Chicago Hornets (AAFC).

LEN FORD
End. 6-5, 260. Born in Washington, D.C., February 18, 1926. Died March 14, 1972. Michigan. Inducted in 1976. 1948-49 Los Angeles Dons (AAFC), 1950-57 Cleveland Browns, 1958 Green Bay Packers.

DAN FORTMANN
Guard. 6-0, 207. Born in Pearl River, New York, April 11, 1916. Colgate. Inducted in 1965. 1936-43 Chicago Bears.

FRANK GATSKI
Center. 6-3, 240. Born in Farmington, West Virginia, March 13, 1922. Marshall, Auburn. Inducted in 1985. 1946-49 Cleveland Browns (AAFC), 1950-56 Cleveland Browns, 1957 Detroit Lions.

BILL GEORGE
Linebacker. 6-2, 230. Born in Waynesburg, Pennsylvania, October 27, 1930. Wake Forest. Inducted in 1974. 1952-65 Chicago Bears, 1966 Los Angeles Rams.

FRANK GIFFORD
Halfback. 6-1, 195. Born in Santa Monica, California, August 16, 1930. Southern California. Inducted in 1977. 1952-60, 1962-64 New York Giants.

SID GILLMAN
Coach. Born in Minneapolis, Minnesota, October 26, 1911. Ohio State. Inducted in 1983. 1955-59 Los Angeles Rams, 1960 Los Angeles Chargers, 1961-69 San Diego Chargers, 1973-74 Houston Oilers.

ed in 1964. 1932-41 Green Bay Packers.

OTTO GRAHAM
Quarterback. 6-1, 195. Born in Waukegan, Illinois, December 6, 1921. Northwestern. Inducted in 1965. 1946-49 Cleveland Browns (AAFC), 1950-55 Cleveland Browns.

HAROLD (RED) GRANGE
Halfback. 6-0, 185. Born in Forksville, Pennsylvania, June 13, 1903. Illinois. Inducted in 1963. 1925 Chicago Bears, 1926 New York Yankees (AFL), 1927 New York Yankees, 1929-34 Chicago Bears.

FORREST GREGG
Tackle. 6-4, 250. Born in Sulphur Springs, Texas, October 18, 1933. Southern Methodist. Inducted in 1977. 1956, 1958-70 Green Bay Packers, 1971 Dallas Cowboys.

LOU GROZA
Tackle-kicker. 6-3, 250. Born in Martin's Ferry, Ohio, January 25, 1924. Ohio State. Inducted in 1974. 1946-49 Cleveland Browns (AAFC), 1950-59, 1961-67 Cleveland Browns.

JOE GUYON
Halfback. 6-1, 180. Born in Mahnomen, Minnesota, November 26, 1892. Died November 27, 1971. Carlisle, Georgia Tech. Inducted in 1966. 1920 Canton Bulldogs, 1921 Cleveland Indians, 1922-23 Oorang Indians, 1924 Rock Island, Ill., Independents, 1924-25 Kansas City Cowboys, 1927 New York Giants.

GEORGE HALAS
End. Coach. Team owner. Born in Chicago, Illinois, February 2, 1895. Died October 31, 1983. Illinois. Inducted in 1963. 1920 Decatur Staleys, 1921 Chicago Staleys, 1922-29 Chicago Bears; coach, 1933-42, 1946-55, 1958-67 Chicago Bears.

ED HEALEY
Tackle. 6-3, 220. Born in Indian Orchard, Massachusetts, December 28, 1894. Died December 9, 1978. Dartmouth. Inducted in 1964. 1920-22 Rock Island, Ill., Independents, 1922-27 Chicago Bears.

MEL HEIN
Center. 6-2, 225. Born in Redding, California, August 22, 1909. Washington State. Inducted in 1963. 1931-45 New York Giants.

WILBUR (PETE) HENRY
Tackle. 6-0, 250. Born in Mansfield, Ohio, October 31, 1897. Died February 7, 1952. Washington & Jefferson. Inducted in 1963. 1920-23 Canton Bulldogs, 1925-26 Canton Bulldogs, 1927 New York Giants, 1927-28 Pottsville Maroons.

ARNIE HERBER
Quarterback. 6-1, 200. Born in Green Bay, Wisconsin, April 2, 1910. Died October 14, 1969. Wisconsin, Regis College. Inducted in 1966. 1930-40 Green Bay Packers, 1944-45 New York Giants.

BILL HEWITT
End. 5-11, 191. Born in Bay City, Michigan, October 8, 1909. Died January 14, 1947. Michigan. Inducted in 1971. 1932-36 Chicago Bears, 1937-39 Philadelphia Eagles, 1943 Phil-Pitt.

CLARKE HINKLE
Fullback. 5-11, 201. Born in Toronto, Ohio, April 10, 1912. Bucknell. Inducted in 1964. 1932-41 Green Bay Packers.

ELROY (CRAZYLEGS) HIRSCH
Halfback-end. 6-2, 190. Born in Wausau, Wisconsin, June 17, 1923. Wisconsin, Michigan. Inducted in 1968. 1946-48 Chicago Rockets (AAFC), 1949-57 Los Angeles Rams.

PAUL HORNUNG
Halfback. 6-2, 220. Born in Louisville, Kentucky, December 23, 1935. Notre Dame. Inducted in 1986. 1957-62, 1964-66 Green Bay Packers.

KEN HOUSTON
Safety. 6-3, 198. Born in Lufkin, Texas, November 12, 1944. Prairie View A&M. Inducted in 1986. 1967-72 Houston Oilers, 1973-80 Washington Redskins.

CAL HUBBARD
Tackle. 6-5, 250. Born in Keytesville, Missouri, October 11, 1900. Died October 17, 1977. Centenary, Geneva. Inducted in 1963. 1927-28 New York Giants, 1929-33, 1935 Green Bay Packers, 1936 New York Giants, 1936 Pittsburgh Pirates.

SAM HUFF
Linebacker. 6-1, 230. Born in Morgantown, West Virginia, October 4, 1934. West Virginia. Inducted in 1982. 1956-63 New York Giants, 1964-67, 1969 Washington Redskins.

LAMAR HUNT
Team owner. Born in El Dorado, Arkansas, August 2, 1932. Southern Methodist. Inducted in 1972. 1960-62 Dallas Texans, 1963-86 Kansas City Chiefs.

DON HUTSON
End. 6-1, 180. Born in Pine Bluff, Arkansas, January 31, 1913. Alabama. Inducted in 1963. 1935-45 Green Bay Packers.

DAVID (DEACON) JONES
Defensive end. 6-5, 250. Born in Eatonville, Florida, December 9, 1938. South Carolina State. Inducted 1980. 1961-71 Los Angeles Rams, 1972-73 San Diego Chargers, 1974 Washington Redskins.

SONNY JURGENSEN
Quarterback. 6-0, 203. Born in Wilmington, North Carolina, August 23, 1934. Duke. Inducted in 1983. 1957-63 Philadelphia Eagles, 1964-74 Washington Redskins.

WALT KIESLING
Guard. Coach. 6-2, 245. Born in St. Paul, Minnesota, March 27, 1903. Died March 2, 1962. St. Thomas (Minnesota). Inducted in 1966. 1926-27 Duluth Eskimos, 1928 Pottsville Maroons, 1929-33 Chicago Cardinals, 1934 Chicago Bears, 1935-36 Green Bay Packers, 1937-38 Pittsburgh Pirates; coach, 1939-42 Pittsburgh Steelers; co-coach, 1943 Phil-Pitt, 1944 Card-Pitt; coach, 1954-56 Pittsburgh Steelers.

FRANK (BRUISER) KINARD
Tackle. 6-1, 210. Born in Pelahatchie, Mississippi, October 23, 1914. Mississippi. Inducted in 1971. 1938-44 Brooklyn Dodgers-Tigers, 1946-47 New York Yankees (AAFC).

EARL (CURLY) LAMBEAU
Coach. Born in Green Bay, Wisconsin, April 9, 1898. Died June 1, 1965. Notre Dame. Inducted in 1963. 1919-49 Green Bay Packers, 1950-51 Chicago Cardinals, 1952-53 Washington Redskins.

DICK (NIGHT TRAIN) LANE
Defensive back. 6-2, 210. Born in Austin, Texas, April 16, 1928. Scottsbluff Junior College. Inducted in 1974. 1952-53 Los Angeles Rams, 1954-59 Chicago Cardinals, 1960-65 Detroit Lions.

WILLIE LANIER
Linebacker. 6-1, 245. Born in Clover, Virginia, August 8, 1945. Morgan State. Inducted in 1986. 1967-77 Kansas City Chiefs.

YALE LARY
Defensive back-punter. 5-11, 189. Born in Fort Worth, Texas, November 24, 1930. Texas A&M. Inducted in 1979. 1952-53, 1956-64 Detroit Lions.

DANTE LAVELLI
End. 6-0, 199. Born in Hudson, Ohio, February 23, 1923. Ohio State. Inducted in 1975. 1946-49 Cleveland Browns (AAFC), 1950-56 Cleveland Browns.

BOBBY LAYNE
Quarterback. 6-2, 190. Born in Santa Anna, Texas, December 19, 1926. Texas. Inducted in 1967. 1948 Chicago Bears, 1949 New York Bulldogs, 1950-58 Detroit Lions, 1958-62 Pittsburgh Steelers.

ALPHONSE (TUFFY) LEEMANS
Fullback. 6-0, 200. Born in Superior, Wisconsin, November 12, 1912. Died January 19, 1979. George Washington. Inducted in 1978. 1936-43 New York Giants.

BOB LILLY
Defensive tackle. 6-5, 260. Born in Olney, Texas, July 24, 1939. Texas Christian. Inducted in 1980. 1961-74 Dallas Cowboys.

VINCE LOMBARDI
Coach. Born in Brooklyn, New York, June 11, 1913. Died September 3, 1970. Fordham. Inducted in 1971. 1959-67 Green Bay Packers, 1969 Washington Redskins.

SID LUCKMAN
Quarterback. 6-0, 195. Born in Brooklyn, New York, November 21, 1916. Columbia. Inducted in 1965. 1939-50 Chicago Bears.

ROY (LINK) LYMAN
Tackle. 6-2, 252. Born in Table Rock, Nebraska, November 30, 1898. Died December 28, 1972. Nebraska. Inducted in 1964. 1922-23, 1925 Canton Bulldogs, 1924 Cleveland Bulldogs, 1925 Frankford Yellow Jackets, 1926-28, 1930-31, 1933-34 Chicago Bears.

TIM MARA
Team owner. Born in New York, New York, July 29, 1887. Died February 17, 1959. Did not attend college. Inducted in 1963. 1925-59 New York Giants.

GINO MARCHETTI
Defensive end. 6-4, 245. Born in Antioch, California, January 2, 1927. San Francisco. Inducted in 1972. 1952 Dallas Texans, 1953-64, 1966 Baltimore Colts.

GEORGE PRESTON MARSHALL
Team owner. Born in Grafton, West Virginia, October 11, 1897. Died August 9, 1969. Randolph-Macon. Inducted in 1963. 1932 Boston Braves, 1933-36 Boston Redskins, 1937-69 Washington Redskins.

OLLIE MATSON
Halfback. 6-2, 220. Born in Trinity, Texas, May 1, 1930. San Francisco. Inducted in 1972. 1952, 1954-58 Chicago Cardinals, 1959-62 Los Angeles Rams, 1963 Detroit Lions, 1964-66 Philadelphia Eagles.

GEORGE McAFEE
Halfback. 6-0, 177. Born in Ironton, Ohio, March 13, 1918. Duke. Inducted in 1966. 1940-41, 1945-50 Chicago Bears.

MIKE McCORMACK
Offensive tackle. 6-4, 248. Born in Chicago, Illinois, June 21, 1930. Kansas. Inducted in 1984. 1951 New York Yanks, 1954-62 Cleveland Browns.

HUGH McELHENNY
Halfback. 6-1, 198. Born in Los Angeles, California, December 31, 1928. Washington. Inducted in 1970. 1952-60 San Francisco 49ers, 1961-62 Minnesota Vikings, 1963 New York Giants, 1964 Detroit Lions.

JOHNNY BLOOD (McNALLY)
Halfback. 6-0, 185. Born in New Richmond, Wisconsin, November 27, 1903. Died November 28, 1985. St. John's (Minnesota). Inducted in 1963. 1925-26 Milwaukee Badgers, 1926-27 Duluth Eskimos, 1928 Pottsville Maroons, 1929-33 Green Bay Packers, 1934 Pittsburgh Pirates, 1935-36 Green Bay Packers; player-coach, 1937-39 Pittsburgh Pirates.

MIKE MICHALSKE
Guard. 6-0, 209. Born in Cleveland, Ohio, April 24, 1903. Penn State. Inducted in 1964. 1926 New York Yankees (AFL), 1927-28 New York Yankees, 1929-35, 1937 Green Bay Packers.

WAYNE MILLNER
End. 6-0, 191. Born in Roxbury, Massachusetts, January 31, 1913. Died November 19, 1976. Notre Dame. Inducted in 1968. 1936 Boston Redskins, 1937-41, 1945 Washington Redskins.

BOBBY MITCHELL
Running back-wide receiver. 6-0, 195. Born in Hot Springs, Arkansas, June 6, 1935. Illinois. Inducted in 1983. 1958-61 Cleveland Browns, 1962-68 Washington Redskins.

RON MIX
Tackle. 6-4, 250. Born in Los Angeles, California, March 10, 1938. Southern California. Inducted in 1979. 1960 Los Angeles Chargers, 1961-69 San Diego Chargers, 1971 Oakland Raiders.

LENNY MOORE
Back. 6-1, 198. Born in Reading, Pennsylvania, November 25, 1933. Penn State. Inducted in 1975. 1956-67 Baltimore Colts.

MARION MOTLEY
Fullback. 6-1, 238. Born in Leesburg, Georgia, June 5, 1920. South Carolina State, Nevada. Inducted in 1968. 1946-49 Cleveland Browns (AAFC),

1950-53 Cleveland Browns, 1955 Pittsburgh Steelers.

GEORGE MUSSO
Guard-tackle. 6-2, 270. Born in Collinsville, Illinois. April 8, 1910. Millikin. Inducted in 1982. 1933-44 Chicago Bears.

BRONKO NAGURSKI
Fullback. 6-2, 225. Born in Rainy River, Ontario, Canada, November 3, 1908. Minnesota. Inducted in 1963. 1930-37, 1943 Chicago Bears.

JOE NAMATH
Quarterback. 6-2, 200. Born in Beaver Falls, Pennsylvania, May 31, 1943. Alabama. Inducted in 1985. 1965-76 New York Jets, 1977 Los Angeles Rams.

EARLE (GREASY) NEALE
Coach. Born in Parkersburg, West Virginia, November 5, 1891. Died November 2, 1973. West Virginia Wesleyan. Inducted in 1969. 1941-42, 1944-50 Philadelphia Eagles; co-coach, Phil-Pitt 1943.

ERNIE NEVERS
Fullback. 6-1, 205. Born in Willow River, Minnesota, June 11, 1903. Died May 3, 1976. Stanford. Inducted in 1963. 1926-27 Duluth Eskimos, 1929-31 Chicago Cardinals.

RAY NITSCHKE
Linebacker. 6-3, 235. Born in Elmwood Park, Illinois, December 29, 1936. Illinois. Inducted in 1978. 1958-72 Green Bay Packers.

LEO NOMELLINI
Defensive tackle. 6-3, 264. Born in Lucca, Italy, June 19, 1924. Minnesota. Inducted in 1969. 1950-63 San Francisco 49ers.

MERLIN OLSEN
Defensive tackle. 6-5, 270. Born in Logan, Utah, September 14, 1940. Utah State. Inducted in 1982. 1962-76 Los Angeles Rams.

JIM OTTO
Center. 6-2, 255. Born in Wausau, Wisconsin, January 5, 1938. Miami. Inducted in 1980. 1960-74 Oakland Raiders.

STEVE OWEN
Tackle. Coach. 6-0, 235. Born in Cleo Springs, Oklahoma, April 21, 1898. Died May 17, 1964. Phillips. Inducted in 1966. 1924-25 Kansas City Cowboys, 1926-30 New York Giants; coach, 1931-53 New York Giants.

CLARENCE (ACE) PARKER
Quarterback. 5-11, 168. Born in Portsmouth, Virginia, May 17, 1912. Duke. Inducted in 1972. 1937-41 Brooklyn Dodgers, 1945 Boston Yanks, 1946 New York Yankees (AAFC).

JIM PARKER
Guard-tackle. 6-3, 273. Born in Macon, Georgia, April 3, 1934. Ohio State. Inducted in 1973. 1957-67 Baltimore Colts.

JOE PERRY
Fullback. 6-0, 200. Born in Stevens, Arkansas, January 27, 1927. Compton Junior College. Inducted in 1969. 1948-49 San Francisco 49ers (AAFC), 1950-60, 1963 San Francisco 49ers, 1961-62 Baltimore Colts.

PETE PIHOS
End. 6-1, 210. Born in Orlando, Florida, October 22, 1923. Indiana. Inducted in 1970. 1947-55 Philadelphia Eagles.

HUGH (SHORTY) RAY
Supervisor of officials 1938-56. Born in Highland Park, Illinois, September 21, 1884. Died September 16, 1956. Illinois. Inducted in 1966.

DAN REEVES
Team owner. Born in New York, New York, June 30, 1912. Died April 15, 1971. Georgetown. Inducted in 1967. 1941-45 Cleveland Rams, 1946-71 Los Angeles Rams.

JIM RINGO
Center. 6-1, 235. Born in Orange, New Jersey, November 21, 1932. Syracuse. Inducted in 1981. 1953-63 Green Bay Packers, 1964-67 Philadelphia Eagles.

ANDY ROBUSTELLI
Defensive end. 6-0, 230. Born in Stamford, Connecticut, December 6, 1925. Arnold College. Inducted in 1971. 1951-55 Los Angeles Rams, 1956-64 New York Giants.

ART ROONEY
Team owner. Born in Coulterville, Pennsylvania, January 27, 1901. Georgetown, Duquesne. Inducted in 1964. 1933-40 Pittsburgh Pirates, 1941-42, 1949-86 Pittsburgh Steelers, 1943 Phil-Pitt, 1944 Card-Pitt.

PETE ROZELLE
Commissioner. Born in South Gate, California, March 1, 1926. San Francisco. Inducted in 1985. Commissioner 1960-86.

GALE SAYERS
Running back. 6-0, 200. Born in Wichita, Kansas, May 30, 1943. Kansas. Inducted in 1977. 1965-71 Chicago Bears.

JOE SCHMIDT
Linebacker. 6-0, 222. Born in Pittsburgh, Pennsylvania, January 19, 1932. Pittsburgh. Inducted in 1973. 1953-65 Detroit Lions.

O.J. SIMPSON
Running back. 6-1, 212. Born in San Francisco, California, July 9, 1947. Southern California. Inducted in 1985. 1969-77 Buffalo Bills, 1978-79 San Francisco 49ers.

BART STARR
Quarterback. 6-1, 200. Born in Montgomery, Alabama, January 9, 1934. Alabama. Inducted in 1977. 1956-71 Green Bay Packers; coach, 1975-83 Green Bay Packers.

ROGER STAUBACH
Quarterback. 6-3, 202. Born in Cincinnati, Ohio, February 5, 1942. Navy. Inducted in 1985. 1969-79 Dallas Cowboys.

ERNIE STAUTNER
Defensive tackle. 6-2, 235. Born in Cham, Bavaria, Germany, April 20, 1925. Boston College. Inducted in 1969. 1950-63 Pittsburgh Steelers.

KEN STRONG
Halfback. 5-11, 210. Born in New Haven, Connecticut, August 6, 1906. Died October 5, 1979. New York University. Inducted in 1967. 1929-32 Staten Island Stapletons, 1936-37 New York Yanks (AFL), 1933-35, 1939, 1944-47 New York Giants.

JOE STYDAHAR
Tackle. 6-4, 230. Born in Kaylor, Pennsylvania, March 3, 1912. Died March 23, 1977. West Virginia. Inducted in 1967. 1936-42, 1945-46 Chicago Bears.

FRAN TARKENTON
Quarterback. 6-0, 185. Born in Richmond, Virginia, February 3, 1940. Georgia. Inducted in 1986. 1961-66, 1972-78 Minnesota Vikings, 1967-71 New York Giants.

CHARLEY TAYLOR
Wide receiver-running back. 6-3, 210. Born in Grand Prairie, Texas, September 28, 1941. Arizona State. Inducted in 1984. 1964-75, 1977 Washington Redskins.

JIM TAYLOR
Fullback. 6-0, 216. Born in Baton Rouge, Louisiana, September 20, 1935. Louisiana State. Inducted in 1976. 1958-66 Green Bay Packers, 1967 New Orleans Saints.

JIM THORPE
Halfback. 6-1, 190. Born in Prague, Oklahoma, May 28, 1888. Died March 28, 1953. Carlisle. Inducted in 1963. 1920 Canton Bulldogs, 1921 Cleveland Indians, 1922-23 Oorang Indians, 1923 Toledo Maroons, 1924 Rock Island, Ill., Independents, 1925 New York Giants, 1926 Canton Bulldogs, 1928 Chicago Cardinals.

Y.A. TITTLE
Quarterback. 6-0, 200. Born in Marshall, Texas, October 24, 1926. Louisiana State. Inducted in 1971. 1948-49 Baltimore Colts (AAFC), 1950 Baltimore Colts, 1951-60 San Francisco 49ers, 1961-64 New York Giants.

GEORGE TRAFTON
Center. 6-2, 235. Born in Chicago, Illinois, December 6, 1896. Died September 5, 1971. Notre Dame. Inducted in 1964. 1920 Decatur Staleys, 1921 Chicago Staleys, 1922-32 Chicago Bears.

CHARLEY TRIPPI
Halfback. 6-0, 185. Born in Pittston, Pennsylvania, December 14, 1922. Georgia. Inducted in 1968. 1947-55 Chicago Cardinals.

EMLEN TUNNELL
Safety. 6-1, 200. Born in Bryn Mawr, Pennsylvania, March 29, 1925. Died July 23, 1975. Toledo, Iowa. Inducted in 1967. 1948-58 New York Giants, 1959-61 Green Bay Packers.

CLYDE (BULLDOG) TURNER
Center. 6-2, 235. Born in Sweetwater, Texas, November 10, 1919. Hardin-Simmons. Inducted in 1966. 1940-52 Chicago Bears.

JOHNNY UNITAS
Quarterback. 6-1, 195. Born in Pittsburgh, Pennsylvania, May 7, 1933. Louisville. Inducted in 1979. 1956-72 Baltimore Colts, 1973 San Diego Chargers.

NORM VAN BROCKLIN
Quarterback. 6-1, 190. Born in Eagle Butte, South Dakota, March 15, 1926. Died May 1, 1983. Oregon. Inducted in 1971. 1949-57 Los Angeles Rams, 1958-60 Philadelphia Eagles.

STEVE VAN BUREN
Halfback. 6-1, 200. Born in La Ceiba, Honduras, December 28, 1920. Louisiana State. Inducted in 1965. 1944-51 Philadelphia Eagles.

DOAK WALKER
Halfback. 5-10, 172. Born in Dallas, Texas, January 1, 1927. Southern Methodist. Inducted in 1986. 1950-55 Detroit Lions.

PAUL WARFIELD
Wide receiver. 6-0, 188. Born in Warren, Ohio, November 28, 1942. Ohio State. Inducted in 1983. 1964-69, 1976-77 Cleveland Browns, 1970-74 Miami Dolphins, 1975 Memphis Grizzlies (WFL).

BOB WATERFIELD
Quarterback. 6-2, 200. Born in Elmira, New York, July 26, 1920. Died April 25, 1983. UCLA. Inducted in 1965. 1945 Cleveland Rams, 1946-52 Los Angeles Rams.

ARNIE WEINMEISTER
Defensive tackle. 6-4, 235. Born in Rhein, Saskatchewan, Canada, March 23, 1923. Washington. Inducted in 1984. 1948-49 New York Yankees (AAFC), 1950-53 New York Giants.

BILL WILLIS
Guard. 6-2, 215. Born in Columbus, Ohio, October 5, 1921. Ohio State. Inducted in 1977. 1946-49 Cleveland Browns (AAFC), 1950-53 Cleveland Browns.

LARRY WILSON
Defensive back. 6-0, 190. Born in Rigby, Idaho, March 24, 1938. Utah. Inducted in 1978. 1960-72 St. Louis Cardinals.

ALEX WOJCIECHOWICZ
Center. 6-0, 235. Born in South River, New Jersey, August 12, 1915. Fordham. Inducted in 1968. 1938-46 Detroit Lions, 1946-50 Philadelphia Eagles.

A CHRONOLOGY OF PROFESSIONAL FOOTBALL

1892 Rutgers and Princeton had played a college soccer football game, the first ever, in 1869. Rugby had gained favor over soccer, however, and from it rugby football, then football, had evolved among American colleges. It was also played by athletic clubs. Intensive competition existed between two Pittsburgh clubs, Allegheny Athletic Association and Pittsburgh Athletic Club. William (Pudge) Heffelfinger, former star at Yale, brought in by AAA, paid $500 to play in game against PAC, becoming first person known to have been paid openly to play football, Nov. 12. AAA won 4-0 when Heffelfinger picked up PAC fumble and ran for touchdown, which then counted four points.

1898 Morgan AC founded on Chicago's South Side, later became Chicago Normals, Racine (a Chicago street) Cardinals, Chicago Cardinals, and St. Louis Cardinals, oldest continuing operation in pro football.

1899 Duquesne Country and Athletic Club, or Pittsburgh Duquesnes, included large payroll signing players returning from Spanish-American War, sought help from Pittsburgh sportsman William C. Temple. He bought football team from athletic club, became first known individual club owner.

1901 Temple and Barney Dreyfuss of baseball Pirates formed new team and urged cross-state rivalry with Philadelphia.

1902 Philadelphia Athletics, managed by Connie Mack, and Nationals or Phillies formed football teams. Athletics won first night football game, 39-0 over Kanaweola AC at Elmira, N.Y., Nov. 21.

Athletics claimed pro championship after winning two, losing one against Phillies and going 1-1-1 against Pittsburgh Pros. Pitcher Rube Waddell played for Athletics, pitcher Christy Matthewson was fullback for Pittsburgh in one game.

"World Series," actually four-team tournament, played among Athletics, New York Knickerbockers, Watertown, N.Y., Red and Blacks, and Syracuse AC, was played in Madison Square Garden. Philadelphia and Syracuse played first indoor football game before 3,000, Dec. 28. Syracuse, with Pop Warner at guard, won game 6-0, went on to win tournament.

1903 Franklin (Pa.) AC won second and last "World Series" of pro football over Philadelphia, Watertown, and Orange, N.J., AC.

Pro football declined in Pittsburgh area. Some PAC players hired by Massillon, Ohio, Tigers, making Massillon first openly professional team in Ohio. Emphasis shifted there from Pennsylvania.

1904 Ohio had at least eight pro teams. Attempt failed to form league to end cutthroat bidding for players, write rules for all.

1905 Canton Bulldogs turned professional.

1906 Archrivals Massillon and Canton played twice, Massillon won both. Because of betting scandal, Canton manager Blondy Wallace left in disgrace, interest in pro football in two cities declined.

1913 Jim Thorpe, former football star for Carlisle Indian School and hero of 1912 Olympics, played season for Pine Village Pros in Indiana.

1915 Canton revived name "Bulldogs" and signed Thorpe for $250 a game.

1916 With Thorpe starring, Canton won 10 straight, most by lopsided scores, was acclaimed pro football champion of world.

1919 George Calhoun, Curly Lambeau organized Green Bay Packers. Indian Packing Company provided equipment, name "Packers." They had 10-1 record against other company teams.

1920 Pro football was in state of confusion, teams were loosely organized, players moved freely among teams, there was no system for recruiting players. A league in which all followed the same rules was needed. Meeting was held among interested teams in August, second meeting was held in Canton and American Professional Football Association, forerunner of National Football League, formed Sept. 17. Teams were from four states — Akron Pros, Canton Bulldogs, Cleveland Indians, Dayton Triangles from Ohio; Hammond Pros, Muncie Flyers from Indiana; Racine (Chicago) Cardinals, Rock Island Independents, Decatur Staleys, represented by George Halas, from Illinois; Rochester, N.Y., Jeffersons.

Capitalizing on his fame, Thorpe was chosen league president, Stan Cofall of Cleveland vice president. Membership fee of $100 arrived at to give aura of respectability. No team ever paid it. Buffalo All-Americans, Chicago Tigers, Columbus, Ohio, Panhandles, and Detroit Tigers joined league later in year. League operated sporadically, teams played as many non-members as members, either no standings kept or have since been lost. Akron, Buffalo, Canton all claimed championship, hastily arranged series of games, one of them between Buffalo and Canton at Polo Grounds, New York City, failed to settle issue of championship.

First recorded player deal sale of Bob Nash, tackle and end for Akron, to Buffalo for $300, five percent of gate receipts.

1921 APFA reorganized at Akron, Joe Carr of Panhandles named president, Apr. 30. Carl Storck of Dayton named secretary-treasurer. Carr established league headquarters at Columbus. Carr's first order was to declare Akron 1920 league champions.

Chicago Tigers, beaten by Racine Cardinals in 1920 game for "rights" to Chicago, dropped out, so did Hammond.

J.E. Clair of Acme Packing Company granted franchise for Green Bay Packers, Aug. 27. Cincinnati Celts also joined league.

Thorpe moved from Canton to Cleveland Indians.

A. E. Staley turned Decatur Staleys over to George Halas, who moved them to Cubs Park in Chicago, promising to keep the name "Staleys" one more year.

Chicago Staleys claimed league championship with 10-1-1 record. Buffalo, 9-1-2, claimed Chicago included nonleague games in record, but Carr ruled for Staleys.

1922 Packers disciplined for using college players under assumed names, Clair turned franchise back to league, Jan. 28. Curly Lambeau promised to obey rules, used $50 of own money to buy back franchise, June 24. Bad weather, low attendance plagued Packers, merchants raised $2,500, public non-profit corporation set up to operate team with Lambeau as manager, coach.

APFA changed name to National Football League, June 24. Staleys became Chicago Bears.

Thorpe, other Indian players formed Oorang Indians in Marion, Ohio, sponsored by Oorang dog kennels.

1923 Oorang folded with 1-10 record, Thorpe moved to Toledo Maroons. Player-coach Halas of Chicago recovered fumble by Thorpe in game against Oorang, ran 98 yards for touchdown.

1924 Frankford Yellowjackets of Philadelphia awarded franchise, that city entered league for first time. League champion Canton moved to Cleveland to play before larger crowds to meet rising payroll.

1925 Tim Mara and Billy Gibson awarded franchise for New York City for $500. Detroit Panthers, coached by Jimmy Conzelman, Pottsville, Pa., Maroons, Providence, R.I., Steam Roller also entered league. New team in Canton took name "Bulldogs."

University of Illinois season ended and Red Grange signed contract to play for Chicago Bears immediately, Nov. 22. Crowd of 38,000 watched Grange and Bears in traditional Thanksgiving game against Cardinals. Barnstorming tour began in which Bears played seven games in 11 days in St. Louis, Philadelphia, New York, then cities in South and West. Crowd of 70,000 watched game against Giants at Polo Grounds, helping assure future of NFL franchise in New York.

Carr repeatedly warned Pottsville Maroons of "dire consequences" if exhibition game with Notre Dame All-Stars was played in Frankford's "protected territory." Pottsville played anyway, its franchise was cancelled and any claim to NFL championship it thought it had won was voided. Chicago Cardinals, with best record, were the 1925 champions.

1926 Grange's manager, C.C. Pyle, asked Bears for five-figure salary for Grange, one-third ownership of team. Bears refused, lost Grange. Pyle leased Yankee Stadium in New York City, petitioned for NFL franchise, was refused, started first American Football League. It lasted one season, included Grange's New York Yankees, eight other teams. AFL champion Philadelphia Quakers played postseason game against NFL New York Giants, lost 31-0.

Halas pushed through rule prohibiting any team from signing player whose college class had not graduated, Feb. 6.

NFL membership swelled to 22, frustrating AFL growth. Paddy Driscoll of Cardinals moved to rival Bears. Ole Haugsrud, operator of Duluth, Minn., Eskimos, gained NFL franchise, signed Ernie Nevers of Stanford, giving NFL gate attraction to rival Grange. Thirteen-member Eskimos, "Iron Men of the North," played 28 exhibition or league games, 26 on road.

1927 AFL folded, NFL shrank to 12 teams. Akron, Canton, Columbus left NFL. New York Yankees and Grange joined NFL. Grange suffered knee injury. New York Giants won first NFL championship, scoring five consecutive shutouts at one point.

1928 Grange left football, appeared in movie and on vaudeville circuit. Duluth disbanded, Nevers quit pro football, played baseball, was assistant coach at Stanford.

1929 Chris O'Brien sold Chicago Cardinals to David Jones, July 27. NFL added fourth official, field judge, July 28. Cardinals became first pro team to go to out-of-town training camp, Coldwater, Mich., Aug. 21. Dayton played final season, last of original Ohio teams to leave league.

Grange, Nevers returned to NFL. Nevers scored 40 points for Cardinals against Bears, Nov. 28, six touchdowns rushing, four extra points. Grange returned to Bears.

Packers signed back Johnny Blood (McNally), tackle Cal Hubbard, guard Mike Michalske, and won first NFL championship.

1930 Portsmouth, Ohio, Spartans joined NFL. Defunct Dayton franchise bought by John Dwyer, became Brooklyn Dodgers. Bears, Cardinals played exhibition for unemployment relief funds, indoors at Chicago Stadium, layer of dirt covering arena floor. New York Giants, "Notre Dame All-Stars" coached by Knute Rockne, played charity exhibition before 55,000 at Polo Grounds.

Halas retired as player, resigned as coach of Bears in favor of Ralph Jones.

Packers won second straight NFL championship.

1931 Pro football shrank to 10 teams. Carr fined Bears, Packers, Portsmouth $1,000 each for using players whose college classes had not graduated, July 11.

Playing career of Al Nesser, last of six brothers to play in NFL, ended when Cleveland Indians disbanded.

Green Bay won third straight NFL championship.

1932 George P. Marshall, Vincent Bendix, Jay O'Brien, M. Dorland Doyle awarded franchise for Boston, July 9. Named team "Braves" after baseball team using same park.

NFL membership dropped to eight, lowest in history. First playoff in NFL history arranged between Bears and Spartans. Moved indoors to Chicago Stadium because of blizzard conditions in city. Arena allowed only 80-yard field that came right to walls. For safety, goal posts moved from end to goal lines, inbounds lines or hashmarks drawn 10 yards from sidelines for ball to be put in play. Bears won 9-0, Dec. 18, scoring touchdown disputed by Spartans who claimed Bronko Nagurski threw jump pass to Red Grange from point less than five yards behind the line of scrimmage, violating existing passing rule.

1933 NFL made significant changes in rules of football first time. Innovations of 1932 indoor playoffs — inbounds lines or hashmarks 10 yards from sidelines, goal posts on goal lines — became rules. Also, the forward pass legalized anywhere behind line of scrimmage, Feb. 25.

Following resolution by George P. Marshall, NFL divided into two five-team divisions, winners to meet in annual championship playoff, July 8.

Franchise was awarded to Art Rooney and A. McCool for Pittsburgh, July 8; team was named "Pirates." Inactive Frankford franchise declared forfeited, Philadelphia franchise awarded to Bert Bell, Lud Wray, July 9; named team "Eagles." Boston changed name to "Redskins." George Halas bought out Ed (Dutch) Sternaman, became sole owner of Chicago Bears, reinstated himself as head coach. David Jones sold Cardinals to Charles W. Bidwill, Cincinnati Reds joined league.

Eastern Division champion New York Giants met Western Division champion Bears at Wrigley Field in first NFL championship game, Dec. 17. Bears won 23-21.

1934 Bears played scoreless tie against collegians in first Chicago All-Star Game before 79,432 at Soldier Field, Aug. 31.

G.A. (Dick) Richards purchased Portsmouth Spartans, moved them to Detroit, June 30; they took name "Lions." Cincinnati Reds franchise moved during season, became St. Louis Gunners.

Player waiver rule adopted, Dec. 10.

Grange retired from football.

1935 Bell of Philadelphia proposed, NFL adopted annual draft of college players, to begin in 1936, with team finishing last in standings having first choice each round of draft, May 19.

Cincinnati Reds-St. Louis Gunners franchise died.

Inbounds lines or hashmarks moved nearer center of field, 15 yards from sidelines.

1936 No franchise shifts for first time since formation of NFL and for first time all teams played same number of games.

Last place previous year, Philadelphia Eagles made Jay Berwanger, University of Chicago back, first choice in first NFL draft, Feb. 8. Eagles later traded negotiation rights to him to Bears. He never played pro football.

Rival league was formed, became second to call itself American Football League. It included six teams, Boston Shamrocks won championship.

1937 Cleveland returned to NFL. Homer Marshman was granted a franchise, Feb. 12; he named new team "Rams." Marshall moved Redskins to Washington, Feb. 13.

Los Angeles Bulldogs had 8-0 record in American Football League; six-team league folded.

1938 Fifteen-yard penalty adopted for roughing passer.

Hugh (Shorty) Ray became technical advisor on rules and officiating to NFL. Marshall, Los Angeles newspaper officials established Pro Bowl game between NFL champion, team of all-stars.

1939 New York Giants defeated Pro All-Stars 13-10 in first Pro Bowl game at Wrigley Field, Los Angeles, Jan. 15.

Carr, NFL president since 1921, died in Columbus, May 20. Carl Storck named successor, May 25.

National Broadcasting Company camera beamed Brooklyn Dodgers-Philadelphia Eagles game from Ebbets Field back to studios of network, handful of sets then in New York City, first NFL game to be televised.

1940 Clipping penalty reduced from 25 to 15 yards, all distance penalties enforced from spot on field of play limited to half distance to goal, Apr. 12.

Pittsburgh changed nickname from Pirates to Steelers.

Rival league formed, became third to call itself American Football League. It included six teams, Columbus, Ohio, Bullies won championship.

Art Rooney sold Pittsburgh to Alexis Thompson, Dec. 9, and later purchased part-interest in Philadelphia.

Bears, playing T-formation with man-in-motion, defeated Washington 73-0 in NFL championship, Dec. 8. It was first championship carried on network radio, broadcast by Red Barber to 120 stations of Mutual Broadcasting System, which paid $2,500 for rights.

1941 Elmer Layden, head coach, athletic director at Notre Dame, named first commissioner of NFL, March 1. Moved league headquarters to Chicago. Carl Storck resigned as president-secretary, Apr. 5.

Co-owners Bell, Rooney of Eagles transferred ownership to Alexis Thompson in exchange for Pittsburgh franchise. Homer Marshman, associates sold Cleveland Rams to Daniel F. Reeves, Fred Levy, June 1.

Playoffs were provided for in case of ties in division races. Sudden death overtime provided for in case playoff was tied after four quarters.

Columbus won championship of five-team American Football League; it folded.

Bears defeated Green Bay 33-14 in first divisional playoff in NFL history, winning Western Division championship, Dec. 14.

1942 Players departing for service in World War II reduced rosters of NFL teams. Halas left Bears for armed forces, was replaced by co-coaches Hunk Anderson, Luke Johnsos.

1943 Cleveland Rams, with co-owners Lt. Daniel F. Reeves, Maj. Fred Levy, Jr., in service, granted permission to suspend operations for one season, April. 6. Levy transferred his stock in team to Reeves, Apr. 16.

NFL adopted free substitution, Apr. 7. Abbreviated wartime rosters, however, prevented its effects from taking place immediately. Also made helmets mandatory and approved 10-game schedule.

Philadelphia, Pittsburgh granted permission to merge, became Phil-Pitt, June 19. They divided home games between two cities, Greasy Neale, Walt Kiesling were co-coaches. Merger automatically dissolved last day of season, Dec. 5.

Ted Collins granted franchise for Boston to become active in 1944.

1944 Collins, who had wanted franchise in Yankee Stadium in New York, named new team in Boston "Yanks." Cleveland resumed operations. Brooklyn Dodgers changed name to "Tigers."

Cardinals, Pittsburgh requested by league to merge for one year under name, Card-Pitt, Apr. 21. Merger automatically dissolved last day of season, Dec. 3.

Coaching from bench legalized, Apr. 20.

1945 Inbounds lines or hashmarks moved nearer center of field, 20 yards from sidelines. Players required to wear long stockings, Apr. 9.

Boston Yanks, Brooklyn Tigers merged as "Yanks," Apr. 10.

Halas rejoined Bears after service with U.S. Navy in Pacific. Returned to head coaching.

After Japanese surrender ending World War II, count showed NFL service roster, limited to men who played in league games, totaled 638, 21 of whom had died.

1946 Layden resigned as commissioner, replaced by Bell, co-owner of Pittsburgh Steelers, Jan. 11. Bell moved league headquarters from Chicago to Philadelphia suburb of Bala Cynwyd.

Free substitution withdrawn, substitutions limited to no more than three men at time. Forward passes made automatically incomplete upon striking goal posts, Jan. 11.

NFL champion Cleveland given permission to transfer to Los Angeles, Jan. 12. NFL became coast-to-coast league first time.

Rival league, All-America Football Conference, formed. Four of its eight teams were in same population centers as NFL teams — Brooklyn Dodgers, New York Yankees, Chicago Rockets, Los Angeles Dons. Cleveland Browns won AAFC championship.

Backs Frank Filchock and Merle Hapes of the Giants questioned about attempt by New York man to fix championship game vs. Chicago; Commissioner Bell suspended Hapes, permitted Filchock to play. He played well but Chicago won 24-14.

1947 Bell's contract as commissioner was renewed for five years, Jan. 1; same day NFL Constitution amended imposing major penalty for anyone not reporting offer of bribe, attempt to fix game, or any other infraction of rules having to do with gambling.

NFL added fifth official, back judge. Sudden death readopted for championship games, Jan. 24.

"Bonus" draft choice made for first time; one team each year would get special bonus choice before first round began.

Halfback Fred Gehrke of Los Angeles Rams painted horns on Rams' helmets, first helmet emblems in pro football.

AAFC again had eight teams, Cleveland Browns won second championship.

1948 Plastic head protectors prohibited. Flexible artificial tee permitted at kickoff. Officials besides referee equipped with whistles, not horns, Jan. 14.

Fred Mandel sold Lions to syndicate headed by D. Lyle Fife, Jan. 15.

Cleveland Browns won third straight championhip of eight-team AAFC.

1949 Thompson sold NFL champion Philadelphia Eagles to syndicate headed by James P. Clark, Jan. 15.

Commissioner Bell, vice president and treasurer Dennis Shea, given 10-year contracts, Jan. 20.

Free substitution adopted for one year, Jan. 20.

Boston Yanks became New York Bulldogs, shared Polo Grounds with Giants.

Cleveland won fourth straight championship of AAFC, reduced to seven teams. Bell announced merger agreement Dec. 9 in which three AAFC teams — Cleveland, San Francisco 49ers, Baltimore Colts — would enter NFL in 1950.

1950 Free substitution restored, way opened for two-platoon era, specialization in pro football, Jan. 23.

Name "National Football League" returned after about three months as "National-American Football League." American, National conferences replaced Eastern, Western divisions, Mar. 3.

New York Bulldogs became "Yanks," divided players of former AAFC Yankees with Giants. Special allocation draft held in which 13 teams drafted remaining AAFC players, with special consideration for Baltimore, 15 choices compared to 10 for other teams.

Los Angeles Rams became first NFL team to contract to have all its games televised. Arrangement covered both home and away games, sponsor agreed to make up difference in home game income if lower than year before (cost sponsor $307,000). Washington also arranged to televise games, other teams made deals to put selected games on television.

For first time in history deadlocks occurred, playoffs were necessary in both conferences (divisions). Cleveland defeated Giants in American, Los Angeles defeated Bears in National. In one of the most exciting championship games, Cleveland defeated Los Angeles 30-28, Dec. 24.

1951 Pro Bowl game, dormant since 1942, revived under new format matching all-stars of each conference at Los Angeles Memorial Coliseum. American Conference defeated National 28-27, Jan. 14.

Abraham Watner returned Baltimore Colts franchise to league, was voted $50,000 for Colts' players, Jan. 18.

Rule passed that no tackle, guard, or center eligible for forward pass, Jan. 18.

DuMont Network paid $75,000 for rights to championship game, televised coast-to-coast for first time, Los Angeles defeated Cleveland 24-17, Dec. 23.

1952 Ted Collins sold New York Yanks' franchise to NFL, Jan. 19. New franchise awarded to Dallas Texans, first NFL team in Texas, Jan. 24. Yanks had been, in order, Boston Yanks, New York Bulldogs, New York Yanks. Texans, won 1, lost 11, folded, last NFL team to become extinct.

Pittsburgh Steelers abandoned single wing for T formation, last pro team to do so.

Los Angeles reversed television policy, aired only road games.

1953 Baltimore re-entered NFL. League awarded holdings of defunct Dallas franchise to group headed by Carroll Rosenbloom that formed team with name "Colts," same as former franchise, Jan. 23.

Names of American, National Conferences changed to Eastern, Western Conferences, Jan. 24.

Thorpe died, Mar. 28.

Arthur McBride sold Cleveland to syndicate headed by Dave R. Jones, June 10.

NFL policy of blacking out television of home games upheld by Judge Allan K. Grim of U.S. District Court in Philadelphia, Nov. 12.

1954 Bell given new 12-year contract.

1955 Sudden death overtime rule used for first time, on experimental basis in preseason game between Los Angeles, New York at Portland, Ore., Aug. 28. Los Angeles won 23-17 three minutes into overtime.

Runners could advance ball, even by crawling along ground, until stopped, sometimes leading to rough play. As result, rules changed so ball declared dead immediately if player touched ground with any part of body except hands or feet while in grasp of opponent.

Quarterback Otto Graham played last game for Cleveland, 38-14 victory over Los Angeles for NFL championship.

NBC replaced DuMont as network for title game, paying rights fee of $100,000.

1956 Halas retired as coach of Bears, replaced by Paddy Driscoll. Giants moved from Polo Grounds to Yankee Stadium.

Grabbing opponent's facemask made illegal, with exception of ball carrier's. "Loudspeaker coaching" from sidelines prohibited. Brown ball with white stripes replaced white with black stripes for night games. Language of "dead ball rule" improved, stipulating ball dead when runner contacted by defensive player and touched ground with any part of body except hands and feet.

CBS became first to broadcast some NFL regular season games to selected television markets across nation.

Hugh (Shorty) Ray, former NFL rules advisor and rules author, died.

1957 Pete Rozelle named general manager of Los Angeles. Anthony J. Morabito, founder, co-owner of 49ers died of heart attack during game against Bears, Oct. 28. Then NFL-record crowd, 102,368, saw 49ers-Rams game at Los Angeles Memorial Coliseum, Nov. 10. Detroit Lions came from 20 points down for playoff victory over 49ers 31-27, Dec. 22.

1958 "Bonus" draft choice eliminated, Jan. 29.

Halas reinstated himself as Bears coach for third time; others were in 1933, 1946.

Jim Brown of Cleveland gained NFL-record 1,527 yards rushing.

Baltimore, coached by Weeb Ewbank, defeated New York 23-17 in first sudden death NFL championship game, Alan Ameche scoring for Colts after 8 minutes, 15 seconds of overtime, Dec. 28.

1959 Tim Mara, co-founder of Giants, died, Feb. 17.

Lamar Hunt announced intentions to form second pro football league. Hunt representing Dallas, others representing Denver, Houston, Los Angeles, Minneapolis-St. Paul, New York City. Held first meeting of league at Chicago, Aug. 14. Made plans to begin play in 1960. Eight days later at second meeting announced name of organization would be "American Football League." Buffalo became seventh AFL team, Oct. 28, Boston eighth, Nov. 22. First AFL draft held, Nov. 22. Joe Foss named AFL commissioner, Nov. 30. Second draft held, Dec. 2.

NFL commissioner Bell died of heart attack suffered at Franklin Field, Philadelphia, during last two minutes of game between Eagles-Pittsburgh, Oct. 11. Treasurer Austin Gunsel named President in office of commissioner until January, 1960, annual meeting, Oct. 14.

1960 Pete Rozelle elected NFL commissioner on twenty-third ballot, succeeding Bell, Jan. 26.

Hunt, founder of AFL, elected president for 1960, Jan. 26. Oakland became eighth AFL team, Jan. 30. Eastern, Western divisions set up, Jan. 30. Five-year contact signed with American Broadcasting Company for network televising of selected games, June 9.

AFL adopted two-point option on points after touchdown, one point if successful kick, two for successful run or pass across goal line from 2-yard line, Jan. 28.

NFL awarded Dallas 1960 franchise, Minnesota 1961 franchise, expanding to 14 teams, Jan. 28. They took nicknames "Cowboys," "Vikings."

"No-tampering" verbal pact, relative to players' contracts, agreed to between NFL, AFL, Feb. 9.

Chicago Cardinals transferred to St. Louis, Mar. 13.

Boston Patriots defeated Bills 28-7 at Buffalo in first AFL preseason game before 16,000, July 30. Denver Broncos defeated Patriots 13-10 at Boston in first AFL regular season game before 21,597, Sept. 9.

1961 Houston Oilers defeated Los Angeles Chargers 24-16 for first AFL championship before 32,183 at Houston, Jan. 1.

Detroit defeated Cleveland 17-16 in first Playoff Bowl, or Bert Bell Benefit Bowl, between second-place teams in each conference in Miami, Jan. 7.

End Willard Dewveall of Bears played out his option, joined Houston of AFL, first player to deliberately move from one league to other, Jan. 14.

Ed McGah, Wayne Valley, Robert Osborne bought out their partners in ownership of Oakland Raiders, Jan. 17. Chargers transferred to San Diego, Feb. 10. Dave R. Jones sold Cleveland to group headed by Arthur B. Modell, Mar. 22. Howsam brothers sold Denver to group headed by Calvin Kunz, Gerry Phipps, May 26.

NBC awarded two-year contract for radio and television rights to NFL championship game for $615,000 annually, $300,000 of which was to go directly into NFL Player Benefit Plan, Apr. 5.

Canton, where league that became NFL had been formed in 1920, chosen site of Pro Football Hall of Fame, Apr. 27.

Bill legalizing single network television contracts by professional sports leagues introduced in Congress by Rep. Emanuel Celler passed House, Senate, signed into law by President John F. Kennedy, Sept. 30.

Green Bay won first NFL championship since 1944, defeating New York 37-0, Dec. 31.

1962 West defeated East 47-27 in first AFL All-Star Game before 20,973 in San Diego, Jan. 7.

NFL prohibited grabbing any player's facemask, Jan. 9.

Commissioners Rozelle of NFL, Foss of AFL given new five-year contracts, Jan. 8, 9.

NFL entered into single network agreement with CBS for telecasting all regular season games for $4,650,000 annually, Jan. 10.

Judge Roszel Thompson of U.S. District Court, Baltimore, ruled against AFL in antitrust suit against NFL, May 21. AFL had charged monopoly, conspiracy in areas of expansion, television, player signings. Case lasted two and a half years, trial lasted two months.

McGah, Valley acquired controlling interest in Oakland, May 24. AFL assumed financial responsibility for New York Titans, Nov. 8. Dan Reeves purchased partners' stock in Los Angeles Rams, becoming majority owner, Dec. 27.

Dallas defeated Oilers 20-17 for AFL championship at Houston after 17 minutes, 54 seconds of sudden death overtime on 25-yard field goal by Tommy Brooker, Dec. 23. Game lasted record 77 minutes, 54 seconds.

Judge Edward Weinfeld of U.S. District Court, New York City, upheld legality of NFL's television blackout within 75-mile radius of home games, denied injunction sought by persons who had demanded championship between Giants, Green Bay be televised in New York City area, Dec. 28.

1963 AFL's guarantee for visiting teams during regular season increased from $20,000 to $30,000, Jan. 10.

Hunt's Dallas Texans transferred to Kansas City, becoming "Chiefs," Feb. 8. New York Titans sold to five-member syndicate headed by David (Sonny) Werblin, name changed to "Jets," Mar. 28.

Commissioner Rozelle suspended indefinitely Paul Hornung, Green Bay halfback, Alex Karras, Detroit defensive tackle, for placing bets on their own teams and on other games; also fined five other Detroit players $2,000 each for betting on one game in which they did not participate, and the Detroit Lions Football Co. $2,000 on each of two counts for failure to report promptly information and for lack of sideline supervision.

AFL allowed New York, Oakland to select players from other franchises in hopes of giving league more competitive balance, May 11.

NBC awarded exclusive network broadcasting rights for 1963 AFL championship game for $926,000, May 23.

U.S. Fourth Circuit Court of Appeals reaffirmed lower court's finding for NFL in $10-million suit brought by AFL, ending three and a half years of litigation, Nov. 21.

Boston defeated Buffalo 26-8 in first divisional playoff in AFL history before 33,044 in Buffalo, Dec. 28.

Chicago defeated New York 14-10 for NFL championship, record sixth and last title for Halas in his thirty-sixth season as Bears' coach, Dec. 29.

1964 William Clay Ford, their president since 1961, purchased Detroit, Jan. 10. Group representing late James P. Clark sold Philadelphia to group headed by Jerry Wolman, Jan. 21. Carroll Rosenbloom, majority owner since 1953, acquired complete ownership of Baltimore, Jan. 23.

CBS submitted winning bid of $14.1 million per year for NFL regular season television rights for 1964, 1965, Jan. 24. CBS acquired rights to 1964, 1965 NFL championship games for $1.8 million per game, Apr. 17. AFL signed five-year, $36-million television contract with NBC to begin with 1965 season, assuring each team approximately $900,000 a year from television rights, Jan. 29.

Paul Hornung of Green Bay, Alex Karras of Detroit reinstated by Rozelle, Mar. 16.

Paul Brown departed Cleveland after 17 years as their head coach, Blanton Collier replaced him.

AFL commissioner Foss given new three-year contract commencing in 1965, May 22.

New York defeated Denver 30-6 before then AFL-record crowd of 46,665 in first game at Shea Stadium, Sept. 12.

Pete Gogolak of Cornell signed contract with Buffalo, becoming first soccer-style kicker in pro football.

1965 NFL teams pledged not to sign college seniors until completion of all their games, including bowl games, empowered commissioner to discipline clubs up to as much as loss of entire draft list for violation of pledge, Feb. 15.

NFL added sixth official, line judge, Feb. 19. Color of officials' penalty flags changed from white to bright gold, Apr. 5.

Atlanta awarded NFL franchise for 1966, with Rankin Smith as owner, June 30. Miami awarded AFL franchise for 1966, with Joe Robbie, Danny Thomas as owners, Aug. 16.

Green Bay defeated Baltimore 13-10 in sudden death Western Conference playoff game, Don Chandler kicking 25-yard field goal for Packers after 13 minutes, 39 seconds of overtime, Dec. 26.

CBS acquired rights to NFL regular season games in 1966, 1967, plus option for 1968, for $18.8 million per year, Dec. 29.

1966 AFL-NFL war reached its peak, leagues spent combined total of $7 million to sign 1966 draft choices. NFL signed 75 percent of its 232 draftees, AFL 46 percent of its 181. Of 111 common draft choices, 79 joined NFL, 28 joined AFL, four went unsigned.

Rights to NFL 1966, 1967 championship games sold to CBS for $2 million per game, Feb. 14.

Joe Foss resigned as AFL commissioner, Apr. 7. Al Davis, head coach, general manager of Oakland Raiders, named to replace him, Apr. 8.

Goal posts offset from goal line, colored bright gold, with uprights 20 feet above crossbar made standard in NFL, May 16.

Merger announced; NFL, AFL entered into agreement to form combined league of 24 teams, expanding to 26 in 1968, June 8. Rozelle named commissioner. Leagues agreed to play separate schedules until 1970, but would meet, starting in 1967, in world championship game (Super Bowl) and play each other in preseason games.

Davis rejoined Oakland Raiders, Milt Woodard named president of AFL, July 25.

Barron Hilton sold San Diego to group headed by Eugene Klein, Sam Schulman, Aug. 25.

Congress approved merger, passing special legislation exempting agreement itself from antitrust action, Oct. 21.

New Orleans awarded NFL franchise to begin play in 1967, Nov. 1.

NFL realigned for 1967-69 seasons into Capitol, Century divisions in Eastern Conference, Central, Coastal divisions in Western Conference, Dec. 2. New Orleans, New York agreed to switch divisions in 1968, return to 1967 alignment in 1969.

Rights to Super Bowl for four years sold to CBS and NBC for $9.5 million, Dec. 13.

1967 Green Bay Packers of NFL defeated Kansas City of AFL 35-10 at Los Angeles in first Super Bowl, Jan. 15. Winning share for Packers was $15,000 each, losing share for Chiefs $7,500 each.

"Sling-shot" goal post, six-foot-wide border around field made standard in NFL, Feb. 22.

Baltimore made Bubba Smith, Michigan State defensive lineman, first choice in first combined AFL-NFL draft, Mar. 14.

AFL awarded franchise to Cincinnati, to begin play in 1968, with Paul Brown as part-owner, general manager, head coach, May 24.

Arthur B. Modell, president of the Cleveland Browns, elected president of the NFL, May 28.

AFL team defeated NFL team for first time, Denver beat Detroit 13-7 in preseason game, Aug. 5.

Green Bay defeated Dallas 21-17 for NFL championship on last-minute one-yard quarterback sneak by Bart Starr in 13-below temperature at Green Bay, Dec. 31.

George Halas retired fourth and last time as head coach of Chicago Bears at age 73.

1968 Green Bay defeated Oakland 33-14 in Super Bowl II at Miami, game had first $3-million gate in pro football history, Jan. 14.

Lombardi resigned as head coach of Packers, remained as general manager.

Sonny Werblin sold his shares in New York Jets to partners Don Lillis, Leon Hess, Townsend Martin, Phil Iselin; Lillis assumed presidency of Jets, May 21. Lillis died, July 23. Iselin appointed president, Aug. 6.

"Heidi" became a part of the nation's vocabulary when last 1:05 of key Jets-Raiders game was cut off the air to permit children's special to begin on time. Raiders scored two touchdowns in last 42 seconds to win 43-32, Nov. 17.

Ewbank became first coach to win titles in both NFL, AFL, his Jets defeated Oakland 27-23 for AFL championship, Dec. 29.

1969 AFL established format of interdivisional playoffs with winner in one division playing runner-up in other, for 1969 only, Jan. 11.

AFL team won Super Bowl for first time; Jets defeated Baltimore 16-7 at Miami, Jan. 12.

Lombardi became part-owner, executive vice president, head coach of Washington Redskins.

NFL and AFL scrapped preseason experiment "Pressure Point" run or pass one-point conversion tried in 1969, Mar. 20.

Wolman sold Philadelphia Eagles to Leonard Tose, May 1.

Baltimore, Cleveland, Pittsburgh agreed to join AFL teams to form 13-team American Football Conference, remaining NFL teams to form National Football Conference in NFL in 1970, May 17. AFC teams voted to realign in Eastern, Central, Western divisions.

Monday night football set for 1970; ABC acquired rights to televise 13 NFL regular season Monday night games in 1970, 1971, 1972.

George P. Marshall, president emeritus of Redskins, died at 72, Aug. 9.

1970 Kansas City defeated Minnesota 23-7 in Super Bowl IV at New Orleans, Jan. 11. Gross receipts of approximately $3.8 million largest ever for one-day team sports event, television audience largest ever for one-day sports event.

NFC realigned into Eastern, Central, Western divisions, Jan. 16.

CBS acquired rights to televise all NFC games, except Monday night games, in 1970-73, including divisional playoffs and NFC championship, also rights to Super Bowl in 1972, 1974, AFC-NFC Pro Bowl in 1971, 1973, Jan. 26.

NBC acquired rights to televise all AFC games, except Monday night games, in 1970-73, including divisional playoffs and AFC championship, also rights to Super Bowl in 1971, 1973, AFC-NFC Pro Bowl in 1972, 1974, Jan. 26.

Art Modell resigned as president of NFL, Mar. 12. Milt Woodard resigned as president of AFL, Mar. 13. Lamar Hunt elected president of AFC, George S. Halas, Sr., elected president of NFC, Mar. 19.

Merged league adopted rules changes putting names on backs of players' jerseys, making Wilson brand official football of league, making point after touchdown worth one point, making scoreboard clock official timing device of game, Mar. 18.

Players Negotiating Committee, NFL Players Association announced four-year agreement guaranteeing approximately $4,535,000 annually to player pension, insurance benefits, Aug. 3. Owners also agreed to contribute $250,000 annually to improve or implement such items as disability payments, widows' benefits, maternity benefits, dental benefits. Agreement also provided for increased preseason game and per diem payments averaging approximately $2,600,000 annually.

Lombardi, part-owner, executive vice president, head coach of Redskins, died at 57, Sept. 3.

Tom Dempsey of New Orleans Saints kicked game-winning NFL-record 63-yard field goal against Detroit Lions, Nov. 8.

1971 Baltimore defeated Dallas 16-13 on Jim O'Brien's 32-yard field goal with five seconds to go in Super Bowl V at Miami, Jan. 17. NBC telecast was viewed in estimated 23,980,000 homes, largest audience ever for one-day sports event.

NFC defeated AFC 27-6 in first AFC-NFC Pro Bowl at Los Angeles, Jan. 24.

Boston Patriots changed name to New England Patriots, Mar. 25.

Rules change adopted making sole criteria for determining intentional grounding whether passer was making deliberate attempt to prevent loss of yardage, Mar. 25.

Reeves, president, general manager of Rams, died at 58, Apr. 15.

Miami defeated Kansas City 27-24 in sudden death in AFC divisional playoff game, Garo Yepremian kicking 37-yard field goal for Dolphins after 22 minutes, 40 seconds of overtime, game lasting 82 minutes, 40 seconds in all, longest in history, Dec. 25.

1972 Dallas defeated Miami 24-3 in Super Bowl VI at Miami, Jan. 16. CBS telecast was viewed in estimated 27,450,000 homes, top-rated one-day telecast ever.

Inbounds lines or hashmarks moved nearer center of field, 23 yards, 1 foot, 9 inches from sidelines, Mar. 23. Exception made to the rule allowing team in possession on its own 15-yard line or within would put ball in play at spot 20 yards from nearest sideline so it could punt without direct conflict with goal post, May 24.

Method of determining won-lost percentage in standings changed, May 24. Tie games, previously not counted in standings, made equal to half-game won and half-game lost.

Hunt, Halas, reelected presidents of AFC, NFC, May 25.

Robert Irsay purchased Los Angeles, tranferred ownership to Carroll Rosenbloom in exchange for Baltimore, July 13.

William V. Bidwill purchased stock of brother Charles (Stormy) Bidwill, became sole owner, president of St. Louis Cardinals, Sept. 2.

National District Attorneys Association endorsed position of professional leagues in opposing proposed legalization of gambling in professional team sports, Sept. 28.

Franco Harris's "Immaculate Reception" gave Steelers first postseason win in franchise's 40-year history, 13-7 over the Raiders, Dec. 23.

1973 Rozelle announced all Super Bowl VII tickets sold, game would be telecast in Los Angeles, site of game, on experimental basis, Jan. 3.

Miami defeated Washington 14-7 in Super Bowl VII at Los Angeles, completing undefeated 17-0 record for 1972 season, Jan. 14. NBC telecast viewed by approximately 75,000,000 people. Although all 90,182 tickets had been sold and temperature reached 84 degrees on clear, sunny day, 8,476 ticket buyers did not attend game that was first ever televised locally.

AFC defeated NFC 33-28 in Pro Bowl in Dallas, first time since 1951 game played outside Los Angeles, Jan. 21.

Jersey numbering system adopted, 1-19 for quarterbacks, specialists; 20-49, running, defensive backs; 50-59, centers, linebackers; 60-79, defensive linemen, interior offensive linemen except centers; 80-89, wide receivers, tight ends, Apr. 5. Players who had been in NFL in 1972 could continue to use old numbers.

Dan Rooney of Pittsburgh appointed chairman of Expansion Committee, Apr. 6.

NFL Charities non-profit organization created to derive income from monies generated by licensing of NFL trademarks and names, June 26; would support education, charitable activities, supply economic support to persons formerly associated with professional football no longer able to support themselves.

Congress adopted for three years experimental legislation requiring any NFL game that had been declared a sellout 72 hours prior to kickoff to be made available for local telecast, Sept. 14. Legislation provided for annual review to be made by Federal Communications Commission.

1974 Miami defeated Minnesota 24-7 in Super Bowl VIII at Houston, second straight Super Bowl championship for Miami, Jan. 13. CBS telecast viewed by approximately 75 million people.

Rival league formed; World Football League held organizational meeting, Jan. 14.

Rozelle given 10-year contract effective January 1, 1973, Feb. 27.

Tampa awarded franchise to begin play in 1976, Apr. 24. NFL announced one more franchise would be awarded to become operative in 1976.

Sweeping rules changes adopted as recommended by Competition Committee to add action, tempo to game: sudden death for preseason, regular season games, limited to one 15-minute overtime; goal posts moved from goal line to end lines; kickoffs to be made from 35- not 40-yard line; after missed field goals ball to be returned to line of scrimmage or 20-yard line, whichever is farthest from goal line; restrictions placed on members of punting team to open up return possibilities; roll-blocking, cutting of wide receivers eliminated; extent of downfield contact defender can have with eligible receivers restricted; penalty for offensive holding, illegal use of hands, tripping reduced from 15 yards to 10 yards when occurs within three yards of line of scrimmage; wide receivers blocking back toward ball within three yards of line of scrimmage prevented from blocking below the waist, Apr. 25.

Toronto Northmen of World Football League signed Larry Csonka, Jim Kiick, Paul Warfield of Miami, Mar. 31.

Seattle awarded NFL franchise to begin play in 1976, June 4. Lloyd W. Nordstrom, president of Seattle Seahawks, Hugh F. Culverhouse, president of Tampa Bay Buccaneers, sign franchise agreement, Dec. 5.

Birmingham Americans defeated Florida Blazers 22-21 in WFL World Bowl, winning championship of the 12-team league, Dec.5.

1975 Pittsburgh defeated Minnesota 16-6 in Super Bowl IX at New Orleans, Steelers' first championship since entering NFL in 1933. NBC telecast was viewed by approximately 78 million people.

Rules changed making incomplete pass into end zone on fourth down with line of scrimmage inside 20 returned to line of scrimmage instead of 20; double shift on or inside opponent's 20 permitted provided it has been shown three times in game instead of three times in quarter; penalty for ineligible receiver downfield reduced from 15 to 10 yards; goal post uprights raised to 30 feet above crossbar, Mar. 19. Also voted to equip referees with wireless microphones in preseason experiment. Test results positive; microphone adopted for all preseason, regular season and post-season games.

Divisional winners with highest won-lost percentage made home teams for playoffs, surviving winners with highest percentage made home teams for championship games, June 26.

World Football League folded, Oct. 22.

Roger Staubach and Drew Pearson combine on 50-yard "Hail Mary" pass with 24 seconds left to give Cowboys a 17-14 divisional playoff win over the Vikings, Dec. 28.

1976 Pittsburgh defeated Dallas 21-17 in Super Bowl X in Miami; Steelers joined Green Bay, Miami as two-time winners of Super Bowl, CBS telecast viewed by estimated 80 million people, largest television audience in history.

Lloyd Nordstrom, president of Seattle, died at 66, Jan. 20. His brother Elmer succeeded him as majority representative of the team.

Super Bowl XII awarded to New Orleans. Owners adopted use of two, 30-second clocks for all games, visible to both players and fans to note the official time between the ready-for-play-signal and snap of the ball, Mar. 16.

Proposal to add 18-inch wind directional ribbons to the top of each upright approved, Mar. 18.

Veteran player allocation held to stock Seattle, Tampa Bay franchises with 39 players each, Mar. 30-31. College draft held, with Seattle, Tampa Bay getting eight extra choices each, Apr. 8-9.

Steelers defeated College All-Stars 24-0 in storm-shortened final Chicago All-Star Game, July 23. St. Louis defeated San Diego 20-10 in preseason game before 38,000 in Korakuen Stadium, Tokyo, in first NFL game outside North America, Aug. 16.

1977 Oakland defeated Minnesota 32-14 before record crowd of 100,421 in Super Bowl XI at Pasadena, Jan. 9. Paid attendance was pro-record 103,438. NBC telecast was viewed by 81.9 million people, largest ever to view sports event. Victory was fifth straight for AFC in Super Bowl.

Players Association, NFL Management Council ratified collective bargaining agreement extending until July 15, 1982, covering five football seasons while continuing pension plan — including years 1974, 1975, and 1976 — with contributions totaling more than $55 million. Total cost of agreement estimated at $107 million. Agreement called for college draft at least through 1986, contained no-strike, no-suit clause, established 43-man active player limit, reducing pension vesting to four years, provided for increases in minimum salaries, preseason and postseason pay, improved insurance, medical, dental benefits, modified previous practices in player movement and control. Reaffirmed NFL commissioner's disciplinary authority. Additionally, agreement called for NFL member clubs to make payments totaling $16 million the next 10 years to settle various legal disputes, Feb. 25.

NFL regular season paid attendance was record 11,070,543.

San Francisco 49ers sold to Edward J. DeBartolo, Jr., Mar. 28.

Sixteen-game regular season, four-game preseason adopted to begin in 1978, Mar. 29. Second wild card team adopted for playoffs beginning in 1978, wild card teams to play each other with winners advancing to round of eight postseason series along with six division winners.

Defender permitted to contact eligible receiver either in three-yard zone at or beyond line of scrimmage or once beyond that zone, but not both, Mar. 31. Wide receivers prohibited from clipping anywhere, even in legal clipping zone. Penalty of loss of coin toss option in addition to 15-yard penalty provided if team does not arrive on field for warmup at least 15 minutes prior to scheduled kickoff.

Seattle Seahawks permanently aligned in AFC Western Division, Tampa Bay in NFC Central Division, Mar. 31.

NFL decided to experiment with seventh official in selected preseason games, Apr. 1.

Owners awarded Super Bowl XIII, to be played January 21, 1979, to Miami to be played in the Orange Bowl, and Super Bowl XIV, to be played January 20, 1980, to Pasadena, to be played in the Rose Bowl, June 14.

Rules changes made it illegal to strike an opponent above shoulders (head slap) during initial charge of a defensive lineman; made it illegal for an offensive lineman to thrust his hands to an opponent's neck, face, or head; made it illegal for a back who lines up inside the tight end to break to the outside and then cut back inside to deliver a block below the waist of an opponent. Also, if a punting team commits a foul before its opponent takes possession and the receiving team subsequently commits a foul, the penalties offset each other and the down is replayed, June 14-15.

Commissioner Rozelle confirmed that agreements were negotiated with the three television networks — ABC, CBS, and NBC — to televise all NFL regular season and postseason games, plus selected preseason games, for four years beginning with the 1978 season. ABC was awarded rights to 16 Monday night, four prime time (with possible expansion to six during the last three years of the contract), the AFC-NFC Pro Bowl, and the AFC-NFC Hall of Fame games. CBS received rights to all NFC regular season and postseason games (except those in the ABC package) and Super Bowls XIV (1980) and XVI (1982). NBC received rights to all AFC regular season and postseason games (except those in the ABC package) and Super Bowls XIII (1979) and XV (1981). Industry sources considered it the largest single television package ever negotiated, October.

Chicago's Walter Payton set a single-game rushing record with 275 yards (40 carries) against Minnesota, Nov. 20.

Cincinnati defeated Kansas City 27-7 at Arrowhead Stadium in the NFL's 5,000th game in recorded history, Dec. 4.

1978 Dallas defeated Denver 27-10 in Super Bowl XII, held indoors for the first time, at the Louisiana Superdome in New Orleans, Jan. 15. CBS telecast viewed by 102,010,000 people, meaning the game was watched by more viewers than any other show of any kind in the history of televison. Dallas's win was first NFC victory in last six Super Bowls.

According to Harris Sports Survey, 70 percent of the nation's sports fans said they follow football, compared to 54 percent who follow baseball. As far as fans' favorite sport, football increased its lead as the country's favorite to 26 to 16 percent over baseball, Jan. 19.

NFL regular season paid attendance was 11,018,632. In addition, during five years of TV blackout legislation, percent of capacity in NFL attendance had declined from record level of 95.5 percent in 1973 to 87.8 percent in 1977. NFL had over 1.5 million unsold seats in 1977, compared to fewer than one-half million in 1973.

Added seventh official, side judge, Mar. 14.

Study on the use of instant replay as an officiating aid to be made during seven nationally televised preseason games in 1978, Mar. 16.

Rules changes adopted permitting defender to maintain contact on receivers within a five-yard zone beyond scrimmage line, but restricted contact on receivers beyond that point; further clarified the pass blocking rule interpretation to permit extended arms and open hands, Mar. 17.

The NFL played for the first time in Mexico City with the Saints defeating the Eagles, 14-7, in a preseason game before a sellout crowd, Aug. 5.

1979 Pittsburgh defeated Dallas 35-31 in Super Bowl XIII to become the first team ever to win three Super Bowls, Jan. 21. Super Bowl XIII was the top-ranked TV sporting event of all time, according to figures compiled by A.C. Nielsen Co. The NBC telecast was viewed in 35,090,000 homes, which bettered the previous record of Super Bowl XII with 34,410,000.

Bolstered by the expansion of the regular season schedule from 14 to 16 weeks, the NFL paid attendance exceeded 12 million (12,771,800) for the first time. The per-game average of 57,017 was the third highest in league history and best since 1973.

Owners awarded three future Super Bowl sites: Super Bowl XV to the Louisiana Superdome in New Orleans to be played on January 25, 1981, Super Bowl XVI to the Pontiac Silverdome in Pontiac, Mich., to be played on January 24, 1982, and Super Bowl XVII to Pasadena's Rose Bowl to be played on January 30, 1983, Mar. 13.

Rule changes emphasized additional player safety: officials instructed to blow play dead as soon as quarterback is in grasp of a defender; prohibited players on the receiving team from blocking below the waist during kickoffs, punts, and field goal attempts; prohibited wearing of torn or altered equipment and exposed pads that may be hazardous; extended the zone in which there can be no crackback blocks from three yards on either side of the line of scrimmage to five yards in order to provide a greater measure of protection; permitted free activation of three players from the injured reserve list after the final cutdown to 45 players, Mar. 16.

Commissioner Pete Rozelle announced that the 1980 AFC-NFC Pro Bowl Game would be played at Aloha Stadium in Honolulu, Hawaii. This would mark the first time in the 30-year history of the Pro Bowl that the game would be played in a non-NFL city.

Carroll D. Rosenbloom, president of the Rams, died at 72, April 2.

1980 Nielsen figures showed that the CBS telecast of Super Bowl XIV between Pittsburgh and Los Angeles was the most watched sports event of all time. It was viewed in 35,330,000 homes.

Rules changes adopted placed greater restrictions on contact in the area of the head, neck, and face. Under the heading of "Personal Foul," players have been prohibited from directly striking, swinging, or clubbing on the head, neck, or face. Starting in 1980, a penalty may be called for such contact to the head, neck, or face whether or not the initial contact is made below the neck area.

The NFL entered into an agreement with the National Athletic Injury/Illness Reporting System (NAIRS) to proceed with developing a program to study injuries.

CBS, with a record bid of $12 million, won the national radio rights to 26 National Football League regular season games and all 10 postseason games for the 1980 through 1983 seasons.

NFL regular season attendance of nearly 13.4 million set a record for the second year in a row; 1979's total was 13.2 million. Average paid attendance for the 224-game 1980 regular season was 59,787, highest in the league's 61-year history. The previous high was 58,961 for 182 games in 1973. NFL games in 1980 were played before 92.4 percent of total stadium capacity.

Television ratings in 1980 were the second-best in NFL history, trailing only the combined ratings of the 1976 season.

1981 The Oakland Raiders became the first wild card team to win the Super Bowl by defeating Philadelphia 27-10 at the Louisiana Superdome in New Orleans, Jan. 25. The Raiders finished second to San Diego in the AFC Western Division. In the playoffs they beat Houston at Oakland and Cleveland and San Diego on the road to advance to the Super Bowl.

The 1980 season concluded with a record Aloha Stadium crowd viewing the NFC's win over the AFC in the annual AFC-NFC Pro Bowl game in Honolulu, Feb. 1. It was the second straight sellout of the game in Honolulu.

NFL paid attendance reached record levels for the second year in a row. The 1980 figure of 13.4 million was 1.5 percent above last year's record 13.2 million. NFL games in 1980 were played before 92.4 percent of total stadium capacity.

Television ratings in 1980 were the second best in history, exceeded only in 1976. All three networks posted gains. NBC's 15.0 rating was its best ever. CBS and ABC had their best rating seasons since 1977 with 15.3 and 20.8 ratings respectively. CBS Radio reported a record average audience of seven million for Monday night and special games.

Industrialist Edgar F. Kaiser, Jr., purchased the Denver Broncos from Gerald and Allan Phipps, Feb. 26.

Adopted rules changes outlawed stickum, clarified interpretation crediting player with pass reception as long as he controlled ball when his second foot clearly landed on the ground inbounds, Mar. 18.

Owners adopted Disaster Plan for re-stocking team should club be involved in fatal accident, Mar. 20.

Report by National Athletic Injury/Illness Reporting System (NAIRS) revealed the following: highest occurrence of injuries to the knee, hip/leg, ankle/foot; sprains represent the most frequent type of injury; average team has about the same injury rate on both natural and artificial surfaces, June 2.

Owners awarded Super Bowl XVIII to Tampa to be played in Tampa Stadium on January 22, 1984, June 3.

A CBS-N.Y. Times poll showed 48 percent of sports fans prefer football to 31 percent for baseball.

NFL teams hosted 167 representatives from 44 predominantly black colleges during training camp for a total of 289 days.

1982 The 1981 NFL regular season paid attendance of 13,606,990 for an average of 60,745 was the highest in the league's 62-year history. It also was the first time the season average exceeded 60,000. NFL games in 1981 were played before 93.8 percent of total stadium capacity.

ABC and CBS set all-time rating highs. ABC finished with a 21.7 rating, up four percent over the 20.8 recorded in 1980 and up two percent from its previous high of 21.2 in 1977. CBS jumped 14 percent to 17.5 from 15.3 in 1980. The former CBS record was 17.3 in 1976. NBC was down seven percent to 13.9 from 15.0 in 1980.

NFL signed a five-year contract with the three TV networks (ABC, CBS, NBC) to televise all NFL regular and postseason games starting with the 1982 season.

The San Francisco-Cincinnati Super Bowl XVI game on January 24 achieved the highest rating of any televised sports event. The game was watched by a record 110,230,000 viewers in this country for a rating of 49.1. CBS Radio reported 14 million listeners for the game.

Owners awarded 1983, 1984 and 1985 Pro Bowls to Honolulu's Aloha Stadium. Clarified unnecessary roughness rule to make it illegal for any player to use crown or top of his helmet against a passer, receiver in act of catching a pass, or runner in the grasp of a tackler, Mar. 25.

Raiders defeated Green Bay 24-3 in first game in Los Angeles, Aug. 29.

The 1982 season was reduced from a 16-game schedule to 9 as the result of the 57-day players' strike. The strike was called at 12:00 midnight on Monday, Sept. 20 following the Green Bay at N.Y. Giants game. Play resumed the weekend of Nov. 21-22 following ratification of the agreement by NFL owners, Nov. 17 in New York.

The Collective Bargaining Agreement, which expires after the 1986 season, set a salary minimum for each year of experience for players; doubled postseason playoff shares; and set up a severance pay schedule to aid career transition, the first of its kind in professional sports.

Miami defeated Minnesota 22-14 at the Orange Bowl in the NFL's 6,000th regular season game in recorded history, Dec. 5.

Super Bowl XIX, to be played Jan. 20, 1985, awarded to Stanford University Stadium, Palo Alto, Calif., with San Francisco as host city, and Super Bowl XX, to be played on Jan. 26, 1986, to the Louisiana Superdome in New Orleans, Dec. 14.

1983 Because of the shortened season, the league adopted for the 1982 playoffs a format of 16 teams competing in a Super Bowl Tournament. NFC number-one seed Washington eventually defeated AFC number-two seed Miami, 27-17, in Super Bowl XVII at the Rose Bowl to mark only the second time the NFC had won consecutive Super Bowls.

Despite the players' strike, the average paid attendance in 1982 was 58,472, the fifth-highest in league history, compared to 1981's record average of 60,745.

Super Bowl XVII was the second-highest rated live television program of all time and gave the NFL a sweep of the top 10 live programs in TV history. Super Bowl XVII was viewed in over 40 million homes, the largest total ever for a live telecast.

Rule changes permitted any player on the field to call a team time out; stipulated that there is no pass interference if there is incidental contact while moving to the ball that does not materially affect the route of a receiver or defender to the ball; and provided for automatic disqualification of a player who uses a helmet he is not wearing as a weapon Mar. 22.

Followed change adopted after 1982 players' strike by approving 49-man roster limit for 1983, Aug. 16.

1984 The Los Angeles Raiders-Washington Redskins Super Bowl XVIII game on Jan. 22 achieved a 46.4 television rating to become the eleventh-highest-rated TV program of all time and fifth-highest Super Bowl.

An 11-man group headed by H.R. Bright purchased the Dallas Cowboys from Clint Murchison, Jr., March 20. Club President Tex Schramm was designated as managing general partner.

Businessman Patrick Bowlen purchased a majority interest in the Denver Broncos from Edgar Kaiser, March 21.

Colts relocated to Indianapolis, Mar. 28.

At their May 23-25 meetings in Washington, D.C., owners awarded Super Bowl XXI to the Los Angeles area to be played at the Rose Bowl in Pasadena and Super Bowl XXII to San Diego to be played in San Diego Jack Murphy Stadium.

Real estate developer Alex G. Spanos purchased a majority interest in the San Diego Chargers from Eugene V. Klein, Aug. 28.

Houston defeated Pittsburgh 23-20 to mark the 100th overtime game in regular season play since the rule was adopted in 1974, Dec. 2.

National Football League paid attendance exceeded 13 million for the fifth consecutive complete season when 13,398,112 attended NFL games for an average of 59,813, the second-highest in league history. Teams averaged 42.4 points per game, the second-highest total since the 1970 merger.

According to a CBS Sports/New York Times survey, 53 percent of the nation's sports fans said they most enjoy watching football, compared to 18 percent for baseball, Dec. 2-4.

1985 Super Bowl XIX, in which San Francisco defeated Miami 38-16, was viewed on television by more people than any other live event in history. President Ronald Reagan, who took his second oath of office before tossing the coin for Super Bowl XIX, was one of 115,936,000 viewers who watched a portion of the Jan. 20 game. The game drew a 46.4 rating and a 63 percent share. In addition, six million viewed the game live in the United Kingdom and close to that figure in Italy. Super Bowl XIX had a direct economic impact of $113.5 million on the San Francisco Bay Area.

NBC Radio and the NFL entered into a two-year agreement granting NBC the radio rights to a 37-game package in each of the next two NFL seasons, Mar. 6. The package included 27 regular season games and 10 postseason games.

Super Bowl XXIII was awarded to the Miami area to be played at the proposed Dolphins Stadium and Super Bowl XXIV to be played at the Louisiana Superdome in New Orleans, it was announced at the NFL annual meeting in Phoenix, Mar. 10-15.

Norman Braman, in partnership with Edward Leibowitz, bought the Philadelphia Eagles from Leonard Tose, Apr. 29.

Bruce Smith, Virginia Tech defensive lineman, selected by Buffalo, was the first player chosen in the fiftieth NFL draft, Apr. 30.

The group headed by Tom Benson, Jr., was conditionally approved to purchase the New Orleans Saints from John W. Mecom, Jr., May 9. Benson and Mecom announced final sale, June 3.

NFL announced that a voice amplification experiment, designed to combat excessive sound levels in noisy stadiums, would be tested with equipment furnished by the Telex Corporation during the preseason, May 22.

Owners adopted resolution calling for a series of overseas preseason games, beginning in 1986, with one game to be played in England/Europe, and/or one game in Japan each year. Game would be fifth preseason game for involved clubs and all arrangements and selection of clubs will be under the control of the Commissioner, May 23.

Conversion to coaching tape from film approved. Commissioner authorized to extend commitment to Honolulu's Aloha Stadium for AFC-NFC Pro Bowl for 1988, 1989, and 1990, Oct. 15.

NFL sets single weekend paid attendance record when 902,657 tickets were sold for the weekend of Oct. 27-28.

A December Louis Harris poll revealed that pro football remained the sport most followed by Americans. Fifty-nine percent of those surveyed noted pro football, compared with 54 percent who follow baseball.

The Chicago-Miami Monday night game on Dec. 2 produced the highest rating, 29.6, and share, 46.0, of any prime-time game in NFL history. It was viewed in over 25 million homes.

1986 The NFC Chicago Bears captured their first NFL title since 1963 by defeating AFC Wild Card entrant New England Patriots, 46-10 in Super Bowl XX, played in the Louisiana Superdome on Jan. 26. The game was also crowned the champion of television by drawing an audience of 127 million, the largest in television history, replacing the final episode of M*A*S*H, according to A.C. Nielsen figures. Of the six shows in TV history to attract audiences of over 100 million, five are Super Bowls.

In addition to drawing a 48.3 rating and 70 percent share in the United States, Super Bowl XX was televised in 59 foreign countries and beamed via satellite to the QE II. An estimated 300 million Chinese viewed a tape delay of the game in March. NBC Radio figures indicated an audience of 10 million for the game.

Super Bowl XX injected over $100 million into the local New Orleans economy and fans spent $250 per day and a record $17.69 per person on game day.

The NFL showed a ratings increase on all three major networks for the 1985 season, gaining four percent on NBC, 10 on CBS, and 16 on ABC.

Paid attendance exceeded 13 million for the sixth consecutive season when the per-game average was 59,567, the fourth-highest in history. NFL teams played before 88.45 percent of stadium capacity in 1985.

Owners adopted limited use of instant replay as an officiating aid, prohibited players from wearing or otherwise displaying equipment, apparel, or other items which carry commercial names, names of organizations, or personal messages of any type, Mar. 11.

Commissioner Rozelle announced that the series of international preseason games would begin on Sunday, Aug. 3, 1986, when the Super Bowl XX Champion Chicago Bears play the Dallas Cowboys at Wembley Stadium in London in the first American Bowl, Mar. 12.

New England Patriots president William H. Sullivan announced the sale of a minority interest in the team with a three-year option to buy the club, plus other real estate interests, to a group of six Philadelphia businessmen headed by John Charlton, Apr. 11.

NFL COMMISSIONERS AND PRESIDENTS

1920 .... Jim Thorpe, President
1921-39 .... Joe Carr, President
1939-41 ..... Carl Storck, President
1941-46 .... Elmer Layden, Commissioner
1946-59 ... Bert Bell, Commissioner
1960–present .... Pete Rozelle, Commissioner

PAST STANDINGS

1985

AMERICAN CONFERENCE

EASTERN DIVISION

	W	L	T	Pct.	Pts.	OP
Miami	12	4	0	.750	428	320
N.Y. Jets*	11	5	0	.688	393	264
New England*	11	5	0	.688	362	290
Indianapolis	5	11	0	.313	320	386
Buffalo	2	14	0	.125	200	381

CENTRAL DIVISION

	W	L	T	Pct.	Pts.	OP
Cleveland	8	8	0	.500	287	294
Cincinnati	7	9	0	.438	441	437
Pittsburgh	7	9	0	.438	379	355
Houston	5	11	0	.313	284	412

WESTERN DIVISION

	W	L	T	Pct.	Pts.	OP
L.A. Raiders	12	4	0	.750	354	308
Denver	11	5	0	.688	380	329
Seattle	8	8	0	.500	349	303
San Diego	8	8	0	.500	467	435
Kansas City	6	10	0	.375	317	360

NATIONAL CONFERENCE

EASTERN DIVISION

	W	L	T	Pct.	Pts.	OP
Dallas	10	6	0	.625	357	333
N.Y. Giants*	10	6	0	.625	399	283
Washington	10	6	0	.625	297	312
Philadelphia	7	9	0	.438	286	310
St. Louis	5	11	0	.313	278	414

CENTRAL DIVISION

	W	L	T	Pct.	Pts.	OP
Chicago	15	1	0	.938	456	198
Green Bay	8	8	0	.500	337	355
Minnesota	7	9	0	.438	346	359
Detroit	7	9	0	.438	307	366
Tampa Bay	2	14	0	.125	294	448

WESTERN DIVISION

	W	L	T	Pct.	Pts.	OP
L.A. Rams	11	5	0	.688	340	277
San Francisco*	10	6	0	.625	411	263
New Orleans	5	11	0	.313	294	401
Atlanta	4	12	0	.250	282	452

*Wild Card qualifiers for playoffs

New York Jets gained first AFC Wild Card position on better conference record (9-3) over New England (8-4) and Denver (8-4). New England gained second AFC Wild Card position based on better record vs. common opponents (4-2) than Denver (3-3). Dallas won NFC Eastern Division title based on better record (3-1) vs. New York Giants (1-3) and Washington (1-3). New York Giants gained first NFC Wild Card position based on better conference record (8-4) over San Francisco (7-5) and Washington (6-6). San Francisco gained second NFC Wild Card position based on head-to-head victory over Washington.

First round playoff: New England 26, NEW YORK JETS 14
Divisional playoffs: MIAMI 24, Cleveland 21;
New England 27, LOS ANGELES RAIDERS 20
AFC championship: New England 31, MIAMI 14
First round playoff: NEW YORK GIANTS 17, San Francisco 3
Divisional playoffs: LOS ANGELES RAMS 20, Dallas 0;
CHICAGO 21, New York Giants 0
NFC championship: CHICAGO 24, Los Angeles Rams 0
Super Bowl XX: Chicago (NFC) 46, New England (AFC) 10, at Louisiana Superdome, New Orleans, La.

In the Past Standings section, home teams in playoff games are indicated by capital letters.

1984

AMERICAN CONFERENCE

EASTERN DIVISION

	W	L	T	Pct.	Pts.	OP
Miami	14	2	0	.875	513	298
New England	9	7	0	.563	362	352
N.Y. Jets	7	9	0	.438	332	364
Indianapolis	4	12	0	.250	239	414
Buffalo	2	14	0	.125	250	454

CENTRAL DIVISION

	W	L	T	Pct.	Pts.	OP
Pittsburgh	9	7	0	.563	387	310
Cincinnati	8	8	0	.500	339	339
Cleveland	5	11	0	.313	250	297
Houston	3	13	0	.188	240	437

WESTERN DIVISION

	W	L	T	Pct.	Pts.	OP
Denver	13	3	0	.813	353	241
Seattle*	12	4	0	.750	418	282
L.A. Raiders*	11	5	0	.688	368	278
Kansas City	8	8	0	.500	314	324
San Diego	7	9	0	.438	394	413

NATIONAL CONFERENCE

EASTERN DIVISION

	W	L	T	Pct.	Pts.	OP
Washington	11	5	0	.688	426	310
N.Y. Giants*	9	7	0	.563	299	301
St. Louis	9	7	0	.563	423	345
Dallas	9	7	0	.563	308	308
Philadelphia	6	9	1	.406	278	320

CENTRAL DIVISION

	W	L	T	Pct.	Pts.	OP
Chicago	10	6	0	.625	325	248
Green Bay	8	8	0	.500	390	309
Tampa Bay	6	10	0	.375	335	380
Detroit	4	11	1	.281	283	408
Minnesota	3	13	0	.188	276	484

WESTERN DIVISION

	W	L	T	Pct.	Pts.	OP
San Francisco	15	1	0	.938	475	227
L.A. Rams*	10	6	0	.625	346	316
New Orleans	7	9	0	.438	298	361
Atlanta	4	12	0	.250	281	382

*Wild Card qualifiers for playoffs

New York Giants clinched Wild Card berth based on 3-1 record vs. St. Louis's 2-2 and Dallas's 1-3. St. Louis finished ahead of Dallas based on better division record (5-3 to 3-5).

First round playoff: SEATTLE 13, Los Angeles Raiders 7
Divisional playoffs: MIAMI 31, Seattle 10; Pittsburgh 24, DENVER 17
AFC championship: MIAMI 45, Pittsburgh 28
First round playoff: New York Giants 16, LOS ANGELES RAMS 13
Divisional playoffs: SAN FRANCISCO 21, New York Giants 10;
Chicago 23, WASHINGTON 19
NFC championship: SAN FRANCISCO 23, Chicago 0
Super Bowl XIX: San Francisco (NFC) 38, Miami (AFC) 16, at Stanford Stadium, Stanford, Calif.

1983

AMERICAN CONFERENCE

EASTERN DIVISION

	W	L	T	Pct.	Pts.	OP
Miami	12	4	0	.750	389	250
New England	8	8	0	.500	274	289
Buffalo	8	8	0	.500	283	351
Baltimore	7	9	0	.438	264	354
N.Y. Jets	7	9	0	.438	313	331

CENTRAL DIVISION

	W	L	T	Pct.	Pts.	OP
Pittsburgh	10	6	0	.625	355	303
Cleveland	9	7	0	.563	356	342
Cincinnati	7	9	0	.438	346	302
Houston	2	14	0	.125	288	460

WESTERN DIVISION

	W	L	T	Pct.	Pts.	OP
L.A. Raiders	12	4	0	.750	442	338
Seattle*	9	7	0	.563	403	397
Denver*	9	7	0	.563	302	327
San Diego	6	10	0	.375	358	462
Kansas City	6	10	0	.375	386	367

NATIONAL CONFERENCE

EASTERN DIVISION

	W	L	T	Pct.	Pts.	OP
Washington	14	2	0	.875	541	332
Dallas*	12	4	0	.750	479	360
St. Louis	8	7	1	.531	374	428
Philadelphia	5	11	0	.313	233	322
N.Y. Giants	3	12	1	.219	267	347

CENTRAL DIVISION

	W	L	T	Pct.	Pts.	OP
Detroit	9	7	0	.563	347	286
Green Bay	8	8	0	.500	429	439
Chicago	8	8	0	.500	311	301
Minnesota	8	8	0	.500	316	348
Tampa Bay	2	14	0	.125	241	380

WESTERN DIVISION

	W	L	T	Pct.	Pts.	OP
San Francisco	10	6	0	.625	432	293
L.A. Rams*	9	7	0	.563	361	344
New Orleans	8	8	0	.500	319	337
Atlanta	7	9	0	.438	370	389

*Wild Card qualifiers for playoffs

Seattle and Denver gained Wild Card berths over Cleveland because of their victories over the Browns.

First round playoff: SEATTLE 31, Denver 7
Divisional playoffs: Seattle 27, MIAMI 20, LOS ANGELES RAIDERS 38, Pittsburgh 10
AFC championship: LOS ANGELES RAIDERS 30, Seattle 14
First round playoff: Los Angeles Rams 24, DALLAS 17
Divisional playoffs: SAN FRANCISCO 24, Detroit 23, WASHINGTON 51, L.A. Rams 7
NFC championship: WASHINGTON 24, San Francisco 21
Super Bowl XVIII: Los Angeles Raiders (AFC) 38, Washington (NFC) 9, at Tampa Stadium, Tampa, Fla.

1982

AMERICAN CONFERENCE

	W	L	T	Pct.	Pts.	OP
L.A. Raiders	8	1	0	.889	260	200
Miami	7	2	0	.778	198	131
Cincinnati	7	2	0	.778	232	177
Pittsburgh	6	3	0	.667	204	146
San Diego	6	3	0	.667	288	221
N.Y. Jets	6	3	0	.667	245	166
New England	5	4	0	.556	143	157
Cleveland	4	5	0	.444	140	182
Buffalo	4	5	0	.444	150	154
Seattle	4	5	0	.444	127	147
Kansas City	3	6	0	.333	176	184
Denver	2	7	0	.222	148	226
Houston	1	8	0	.111	136	245
Baltimore	0	8	1	.056	113	236

NATIONAL CONFERENCE

	W	L	T	Pct.	Pts.	OP
Washington	8	1	0	.889	190	128
Dallas	6	3	0	.667	226	145
Green Bay	5	3	1	.611	226	169
Minnesota	5	4	0	.556	187	198
Atlanta	5	4	0	.556	183	199
St. Louis	5	4	0	.556	135	170
Tampa Bay	5	4	0	.556	158	178
Detroit	4	5	0	.444	181	176
New Orleans	4	5	0	.444	129	160
N.Y. Giants	4	5	0	.444	164	160
San Francisco	3	6	0	.333	209	206
Chicago	3	6	0	.333	141	174
Philadelphia	3	6	0	.333	191	195
L.A. Rams	2	7	0	.222	200	250

As the result of a 57-day players' strike, the 1982 NFL regular season schedule was reduced from 16 weeks to 9. At the conclusion of the regular season, the NFL conducted a 16-team postseason Super Bowl Tournament. Eight teams from each conference were seeded 1-8 based on their records during the season.

Miami finished ahead of Cincinnati based on better conference record (6-1 to 6-2). Pittsburgh won common games tie-breaker with San Diego (3-1 to 2-1) after New York Jets were eliminated from three-way tie based on conference record (Pittsburgh and San Diego 5-3 vs. Jets 2-3). Cleveland finished ahead of Buffalo and Seattle based on better conference record (4-3 to 3-3 to 3-5). Minnesota (4-1), Atlanta (4-3), St. Louis (5-4), Tampa Bay (3-3) seeds were determined by best won-lost record in conference games. Detroit finished ahead of New Orleans and the New York Giants based on better conference record (4-4 to 3-5 to 3-5).

First round playoff: MIAMI 28, New England 13
LOS ANGELES RAIDERS 27, Cleveland 10
New York Jets 44, CINCINNATI 17
San Diego 31, PITTSBURGH 28
Second round playoff: New York Jets 17, LOS ANGELES RAIDERS 14
MIAMI 34, San Diego 13
AFC championship: MIAMI 14, New York Jets 0
First round playoff: WASHINGTON 31, Detroit 7
GREEN BAY 41, St. Louis 16
MINNESOTA 30, Atlanta 24
DALLAS 30, Tampa Bay 17
Second round playoff: WASHINGTON 21, Minnesota 7
DALLAS 37, Green Bay 26
NFC championship: WASHINGTON 31, Dallas 17
Super Bowl XVII: Washington (NFC) 27, Miami (AFC) 17, at Rose Bowl, Pasadena, Calif.

1981

AMERICAN CONFERENCE

EASTERN DIVISION

	W	L	T	Pct.	Pts.	OP
Miami	11	4	1	.719	345	275
N.Y. Jets*	10	5	1	.656	355	287
Buffalo*	10	6	0	.625	311	276
Baltimore	2	14	0	.125	259	533
New England	2	14	0	.125	322	370

CENTRAL DIVISION

	W	L	T	Pct.	Pts.	OP
Cincinnati	12	4	0	.750	421	304
Pittsburgh	8	8	0	.500	356	297
Houston	7	9	0	.438	281	355
Cleveland	5	11	0	.313	276	375

WESTERN DIVISION

	W	L	T	Pct.	Pts.	OP
San Diego	10	6	0	.625	478	390
Denver	10	6	0	.625	321	289
Kansas City	9	7	0	.563	343	290
Oakland	7	9	0	.438	273	343
Seattle	6	10	0	.375	322	388

NATIONAL CONFERENCE

EASTERN DIVISION

	W	L	T	Pct.	Pts.	OP
Dallas	12	4	0	.750	367	277
Philadelphia*	10	6	0	.625	368	221
N.Y. Giants*	9	7	0	.563	295	257
Washington	8	8	0	.500	347	349
St. Louis	7	9	0	.438	315	408

CENTRAL DIVISION

	W	L	T	Pct.	Pts.	OP
Tampa Bay	9	7	0	.563	315	268
Detroit	8	8	0	.500	397	322
Green Bay	8	8	0	.500	324	361
Minnesota	7	9	0	.438	325	369
Chicago	6	10	0	.375	253	324

WESTERN DIVISION

	W	L	T	Pct.	Pts.	OP
San Francisco	13	3	0	.813	357	250
Atlanta	7	9	0	.438	426	355
Los Angeles	6	10	0	.375	303	351
New Orleans	4	12	0	.250	207	378

**Wild Card qualifiers for playoffs*

San Diego won AFC Western title over Denver on the basis of a better division record (6-2 to 5-3). Buffalo won a Wild Card playoff berth over Denver as the result of a 9-7 victory in head-to-head competition.

First round playoff: Buffalo 31, NEW YORK JETS 27
Divisional playoffs: San Diego 41, MIAMI 38, sudden death overtime; CINCINNATI 28, Buffalo 21
AFC championship: CINCINNATI 27, San Diego 7
First round playoff: New York Giants 27, PHILADELPHIA 21
Divisional playoffs: DALLAS 38, Tampa Bay 0, SAN FRANCISCO 38, New York Giants 24
NFC championship: SAN FRANCISCO 28, Dallas 27
Super Bowl XVI: San Francisco (NFC) 26, Cincinnati (AFC) 21, at Silverdome, Pontiac, Mich.

1980

AMERICAN CONFERENCE

EASTERN DIVISION

	W	L	T	Pct.	Pts.	OP
Buffalo	11	5	0	.688	320	260
New England	10	6	0	.625	441	325
Miami	8	8	0	.500	266	305
Baltimore	7	9	0	.438	355	387
N.Y. Jets	4	12	0	.250	302	395

CENTRAL DIVISION

	W	L	T	Pct.	Pts.	OP
Cleveland	11	5	0	.688	357	310
Houston*	11	5	0	.688	295	251
Pittsburgh	9	7	0	.563	352	313
Cincinnati	6	10	0	.375	244	312

WESTERN DIVISION

	W	L	T	Pct.	Pts.	OP
San Diego	11	5	0	.688	418	327
Oakland*	11	5	0	.688	364	306
Kansas City	8	8	0	.500	319	336
Denver	8	8	0	.500	310	323
Seattle	4	12	0	.250	291	408

NATIONAL CONFERENCE

EASTERN DIVISION

	W	L	T	Pct.	Pts.	OP
Philadelphia	12	4	0	.750	384	222
Dallas*	12	4	0	.750	454	311
Washington	6	10	0	.375	261	293
St. Louis	5	11	0	.313	299	350
N.Y. Giants	4	12	0	.250	249	425

CENTRAL DIVISION

	W	L	T	Pct.	Pts.	OP
Minnesota	9	7	0	.563	317	308
Detroit	9	7	0	.563	334	272
Chicago	7	9	0	.438	304	264
Tampa Bay	5	10	1	.344	271	341
Green Bay	5	10	1	.344	231	371

WESTERN DIVISION

	W	L	T	Pct.	Pts.	OP
Atlanta	12	4	0	.750	405	272
Los Angeles*	11	5	0	.688	424	289
San Francisco	6	10	0	.375	320	415
New Orleans	1	15	0	.063	291	487

**Wild Card qualifiers for playoffs*

Philadelphia won division title over Dallas on the basis of best net points in division games (plus 84 net points to plus 50). Minnesota won division title because of a better conference record than Detroit (8-4 to 9-5). Cleveland won division title because of a better conference record than Houston (8-4 to 7-5). San Diego won division title over Oakland on the basis of best net points in division games (plus 60 net points to plus 37).

First round playoff: OAKLAND 27, Houston 7
Divisional playoffs: SAN DIEGO 20, Buffalo 14; Oakland 14, CLEVELAND 12
AFC championship: Oakland 34, SAN DIEGO 27
First round playoff: DALLAS 34, Los Angeles 13
Divisional playoffs: PHILADELPHIA 31, Minnesota 16; Dallas 30, ATLANTA 27
NFC championship: PHILADELPHIA 20, Dallas 7
Super Bowl XV: Oakland (AFC) 27, Philadelphia (NFC) 10, at Louisiana Superdome, New Orleans, La.

1979

AMERICAN CONFERENCE

EASTERN DIVISION

	W	L	T	Pct.	Pts.	OP
Miami	10	6	0	.625	341	257
New England	9	7	0	.563	411	326
N.Y. Jets	8	8	0	.500	337	383
Buffalo	7	9	0	.438	268	279
Baltimore	5	11	0	.313	271	351

CENTRAL DIVISION

	W	L	T	Pct.	Pts.	OP
Pittsburgh	12	4	0	.750	416	262
Houston*	11	5	0	.688	362	331
Cleveland	9	7	0	.563	359	352
Cincinnati	4	12	0	.250	337	421

WESTERN DIVISION

	W	L	T	Pct.	Pts.	OP
San Diego	12	4	0	.750	411	246
Denver*	10	6	0	.625	289	262
Seattle	9	7	0	.563	378	372
Oakland	9	7	0	.563	365	337
Kansas City	7	9	0	.438	238	262

NATIONAL CONFERENCE

EASTERN DIVISION

	W	L	T	Pct.	Pts.	OP
Dallas	11	5	0	.688	371	313
Philadelphia*	11	5	0	.688	339	282
Washington	10	6	0	.625	348	295
N.Y. Giants	6	10	0	.375	237	323
St. Louis	5	11	0	.313	307	358

CENTRAL DIVISION

	W	L	T	Pct.	Pts.	OP
Tampa Bay	10	6	0	.625	273	237
Chicago*	10	6	0	.625	306	249
Minnesota	7	9	0	.438	259	337
Green Bay	5	11	0	.313	246	316
Detroit	2	14	0	.125	219	365

WESTERN DIVISION

	W	L	T	Pct.	Pts.	OP
Los Angeles	9	7	0	.563	323	309
New Orleans	8	8	0	.500	370	360
Atlanta	6	10	0	.375	300	388
San Francisco	2	14	0	.125	308	416

**Wild Card qualifiers for playoffs*

Dallas won division title because of a better conference record than Philadelphia (10-2 to 9-3). Tampa Bay won division title because of a better division record than Chicago (6-2 to 5-3). Chicago won a Wild Card berth over Washington on the basis of best net points in all games (plus 57 net points to plus 53).

First round playoff: HOUSTON 13, Denver 7
Divisional playoffs: Houston 17, SAN DIEGO 14; PITTSBURGH 34, Miami 14
AFC championship: PITTSBURGH 27, Houston 13
First round playoff: PHILADELPHIA 27, Chicago 17
Divisional playoffs: TAMPA BAY 24, Philadelphia 17; Los Angeles 21, DALLAS 19
NFC championship: Los Angeles 9, TAMPA BAY 0
Super Bowl XIV: Pittsburgh (AFC) 31, Los Angeles (NFC) 19, at Rose Bowl, Pasadena, Calif.

1978

AMERICAN CONFERENCE

EASTERN DIVISION

	W	L	T	Pct.	Pts.	OP
New England	11	5	0	.688	358	286
Miami*	11	5	0	.688	372	254
N.Y. Jets	8	8	0	.500	359	364
Buffalo	5	11	0	.313	302	354
Baltimore	5	11	0	.313	239	421

CENTRAL DIVISION

	W	L	T	Pct.	Pts.	OP
Pittsburgh	14	2	0	.875	356	195
Houston*	10	6	0	.625	283	298
Cleveland	8	8	0	.500	334	356
Cincinnati	4	12	0	.250	252	284

WESTERN DIVISION

	W	L	T	Pct.	Pts.	OP
Denver	10	6	0	.625	282	198
Oakland	9	7	0	.563	311	283
Seattle	9	7	0	.563	345	358
San Diego	9	7	0	.563	355	309
Kansas City	4	12	0	.250	243	327

NATIONAL CONFERENCE

EASTERN DIVISION

	W	L	T	Pct.	Pts.	OP
Dallas	12	4	0	.750	384	208
Philadelphia*	9	7	0	.563	270	250
Washington	8	8	0	.500	273	283
St. Louis	6	10	0	.375	248	296
N.Y. Giants	6	10	0	.375	264	298

CENTRAL DIVISION

	W	L	T	Pct.	Pts.	OP
Minnesota	8	7	1	.531	294	306
Green Bay	8	7	1	.531	249	269
Detroit	7	9	0	.438	290	300
Chicago	7	9	0	.438	253	274
Tampa Bay	5	11	0	.313	241	259

WESTERN DIVISION

	W	L	T	Pct.	Pts.	OP
Los Angeles	12	4	0	.750	316	245
Atlanta*	9	7	0	.563	240	290
New Orleans	7	9	0	.438	281	298
San Francisco	2	14	0	.125	219	350

**Wild Card qualifiers for playoffs*

New England won division title on the basis of a better division record than Miami (6-2 to 5-3). Minnesota won division title because of a better head-to-head record against Green Bay (1-0-1).

First round playoff: Houston 17, MIAMI 9

Divisional playoffs: Houston 31, NEW ENGLAND 14; PITTSBURGH 33, Denver 10

AFC championship: PITTSBURGH 34, Houston 5

First round playoff: ATLANTA 14, Philadelphia 13

Divisional playoffs: DALLAS 27, Atlanta 20; LOS ANGELES 34, Minnesota 10

NFC championship: Dallas 28, LOS ANGELES 0

Super Bowl XIII: Pittsburgh (AFC) 35, Dallas (NFC) 31, at Orange Bowl, Miami, Fla.

1977

AMERICAN CONFERENCE

EASTERN DIVISION

	W	L	T	Pct.	Pts.	OP
Baltimore	10	4	0	.714	295	221
Miami	10	4	0	.714	313	197
New England	9	5	0	.643	278	217
N.Y. Jets	3	11	0	.214	191	300
Buffalo	3	11	0	.214	160	313

CENTRAL DIVISION

	W	L	T	Pct.	Pts.	OP
Pittsburgh	9	5	0	.643	283	243
Houston	8	6	0	.571	299	230
Cincinnati	8	6	0	.571	238	235
Cleveland	6	8	0	.429	269	267

WESTERN DIVISION

	W	L	T	Pct.	Pts.	OP
Denver	12	2	0	.857	274	148
Oakland*	11	3	0	.786	351	230
San Diego	7	7	0	.500	222	205
Seattle	5	9	0	.357	282	373
Kansas City	2	12	0	.143	225	349

NATIONAL CONFERENCE

EASTERN DIVISION

	W	L	T	Pct.	Pts.	OP
Dallas	12	2	0	.857	345	212
Washington	9	5	0	.643	196	189
St. Louis	7	7	0	.500	272	287
Philadelphia	5	9	0	.357	220	207
N.Y. Giants	5	9	0	.357	181	265

CENTRAL DIVISION

	W	L	T	Pct.	Pts.	OP
Minnesota	9	5	0	.643	231	227
Chicago*	9	5	0	.643	255	253
Detroit	6	8	0	.429	183	252
Green Bay	4	10	0	.286	134	219
Tampa Bay	2	12	0	.143	103	223

WESTERN DIVISION

	W	L	T	Pct.	Pts.	OP
Los Angeles	10	4	0	.714	302	146
Atlanta	7	7	0	.500	179	129
San Francisco	5	9	0	.357	220	260
New Orleans	3	11	0	.214	232	336

**Wild Card qualifier for playoffs*

Baltimore won division title on the basis of a better conference record than Miami (9-3 to 8-4). Chicago won a wild card berth over Washington on the basis of best net points in conference games (plus 48 net points to plus 4).

Divisional playoffs: DENVER 34, Pittsburgh 21; Oakland 37, BALTIMORE 31, sudden death overtime

AFC championship: DENVER 20, Oakland 17

Divisional playoffs: DALLAS 37, Chicago 7, Minnesota 14, LOS ANGELES 7

NFC championship: DALLAS 23, Minnesota 6

Super Bowl XII: Dallas (NFC) 27, Denver (AFC) 10, at Louisiana Superdome, New Orleans, La.

1976

AMERICAN CONFERENCE

EASTERN DIVISION

	W	L	T	Pct.	Pts.	OP
Baltimore	11	3	0	.786	417	246
New England*	11	3	0	.786	376	236
Miami	6	8	0	.429	263	264
N.Y. Jets	3	11	0	.214	169	383
Buffalo	2	12	0	.143	245	363

CENTRAL DIVISION

	W	L	T	Pct.	Pts.	OP
Pittsburgh	10	4	0	.714	342	138
Cincinnati	10	4	0	.714	335	210
Cleveland	9	5	0	.643	267	287
Houston	5	9	0	.357	222	273

WESTERN DIVISION

	W	L	T	Pct.	Pts.	OP
Oakland	13	1	0	.929	350	237
Denver	9	5	0	.643	315	206
San Diego	6	8	0	.429	248	285
Kansas City	5	9	0	.357	290	376
Tampa Bay	0	14	0	.000	125	412

NATIONAL CONFERENCE

EASTERN DIVISION

	W	L	T	Pct.	Pts.	OP
Dallas	11	3	0	.786	296	194
Washington*	10	4	0	.714	291	217
St. Louis	10	4	0	.714	309	267
Philadelphia	4	10	0	.286	165	286
N.Y. Giants	3	11	0	.214	170	250

CENTRAL DIVISION

	W	L	T	Pct.	Pts.	OP
Minnesota	11	2	1	.821	305	176
Chicago	7	7	0	.500	253	216
Detroit	6	8	0	.429	262	220
Green Bay	5	9	0	.357	218	299

WESTERN DIVISION

	W	L	T	Pct.	Pts.	OP
Los Angeles	10	3	1	.750	351	190
San Francisco	8	6	0	.571	270	190
Atlanta	4	10	0	.286	172	312
New Orleans	4	10	0	.286	253	346
Seattle	2	12	0	.143	229	429

**Wild Card qualifier for playoffs*

Baltimore won division title on the basis of a better division record than New England (7-1 to 6-2). Pittsburgh won division title because of a two-game sweep over Cincinnati. Washington won wild card berth over St. Louis because of a two-game sweep over Cardinals.

Divisional playoffs: OAKLAND 24, New England 21; Pittsburgh 40, BALTIMORE 14

AFC championship: OAKLAND 24, Pittsburgh 7

Divisional playoffs: MINNESOTA 35, Washington 20; Los Angeles 14, DALLAS 12

NFC championship: MINNESOTA 24, Los Angeles 13

Super Bowl XI: Oakland (AFC) 32, Minnesota (NFC) 14, at Rose Bowl, Pasadena, Calif.

1975

AMERICAN CONFERENCE

EASTERN DIVISION

	W	L	T	Pct.	Pts.	OP
Baltimore	10	4	0	.714	395	269
Miami	10	4	0	.714	357	222
Buffalo	8	6	0	.571	420	355
New England	3	11	0	.214	258	358
N.Y. Jets	3	11	0	.214	258	433

CENTRAL DIVISION

	W	L	T	Pct.	Pts.	OP
Pittsburgh	12	2	0	.857	373	162
Cincinnati*	11	3	0	.786	340	246
Houston	10	4	0	.714	293	226
Cleveland	3	11	0	.214	218	372

WESTERN DIVISION

	W	L	T	Pct.	Pts.	OP
Oakland	11	3	0	.786	375	255
Denver	6	8	0	.429	254	307
Kansas City	5	9	0	.357	282	341
San Diego	2	12	0	.143	189	345

NATIONAL CONFERENCE

EASTERN DIVISION

	W	L	T	Pct.	Pts.	OP
St. Louis	11	3	0	.786	356	276
Dallas*	10	4	0	.714	350	268
Washington	8	6	0	.571	325	276
N.Y. Giants	5	9	0	.357	216	306
Philadelphia	4	10	0	.286	225	302

CENTRAL DIVISION

	W	L	T	Pct.	Pts.	OP
Minnesota	12	2	0	.857	377	180
Detroit	7	7	0	.500	245	262
Chicago	4	10	0	.286	191	379
Green Bay	4	10	0	.286	226	285

WESTERN DIVISION

	W	L	T	Pct.	Pts.	OP
Los Angeles	12	2	0	.857	312	135
San Francisco	5	9	0	.357	255	286
Atlanta	4	10	0	.286	240	289
New Orleans	2	12	0	.143	165	360

**Wild Card qualifier for playoffs*

Baltimore won division title on the basis of a two-game sweep over Miami.

Divisional playoffs: PITTSBURGH 28, Baltimore 10; OAKLAND 31, Cincinnati 28

AFC championship: PITTSBURGH 16, Oakland 10

Divisional playoffs: LOS ANGELES 35, St. Louis 23; Dallas 17, MINNESOTA 14

NFC championship: Dallas 37, LOS ANGELES 7

Super Bowl X: Pittsburgh (AFC) 21, Dallas (NFC) 17, at Orange Bowl, Miami, Fla.

1974

AMERICAN CONFERENCE

EASTERN DIVISION

	W	L	T	Pct.	Pts.	OP
Miami	11	3	0	.786	327	216
Buffalo*	9	5	0	.643	264	244
New England	7	7	0	.500	348	289
N.Y. Jets	7	7	0	.500	279	300
Baltimore	2	12	0	.143	190	329

CENTRAL DIVISION

	W	L	T	Pct.	Pts.	OP
Pittsburgh	10	3	1	.750	305	189
Cincinnati	7	7	0	.500	283	259
Houston	7	7	0	.500	236	282
Cleveland	4	10	0	.286	251	344

WESTERN DIVISION

	W	L	T	Pct.	Pts.	OP
Oakland	12	2	0	.857	355	228
Denver	7	6	1	.536	302	294
Kansas City	5	9	0	.357	233	293
San Diego	5	9	0	.357	212	285

NATIONAL CONFERENCE

EASTERN DIVISION

	W	L	T	Pct.	Pts.	OP
St. Louis	10	4	0	.714	285	218
Washington*	10	4	0	.714	320	196
Dallas	8	6	0	.571	297	235
Philadelphia	7	7	0	.500	242	217
N.Y. Giants	2	12	0	.143	195	299

CENTRAL DIVISION

	W	L	T	Pct.	Pts.	OP
Minnesota	10	4	0	.714	310	195
Detroit	7	7	0	.500	256	270
Green Bay	6	8	0	.429	210	206
Chicago	4	10	0	.286	152	279

WESTERN DIVISION

	W	L	T	Pct.	Pts.	OP
Los Angeles	10	4	0	.714	263	181
San Francisco	6	8	0	.429	226	236
New Orleans	5	9	0	.357	166	263
Atlanta	3	11	0	.214	111	271

**Wild Card qualifier for playoffs*

St. Louis won division title because of a two-game sweep over Washington.

Divisional playoffs: OAKLAND 28, Miami 26; PITTSBURGH 32, Buffalo 14

AFC championship: Pittsburgh 24, OAKLAND 13

Divisional playoffs: MINNESOTA 30, St. Louis 14; LOS ANGELES 19, Washington 10

NFC championship: MINNESOTA 14, Los Angeles 10

Super Bowl IX: Pittsburgh (AFC) 16, Minnesota (NFC) 6, at Tulane Stadium, New Orleans, La.

1973

AMERICAN CONFERENCE

EASTERN DIVISION

	W	L	T	Pct.	Pts.	OP
Miami	12	2	0	.857	343	150
Buffalo	9	5	0	.643	259	230
New England	5	9	0	.357	258	300
Baltimore	4	10	0	.286	226	341
N.Y. Jets	4	10	0	.286	240	306

CENTRAL DIVISION

	W	L	T	Pct.	Pts.	OP
Cincinnati	10	4	0	.714	286	231
Pittsburgh*	10	4	0	.714	347	210
Cleveland	7	5	2	.571	234	255
Houston	1	13	0	.071	199	447

WESTERN DIVISION

	W	L	T	Pct.	Pts.	OP
Oakland	9	4	1	.679	292	175
Denver	7	5	2	.571	354	296
Kansas City	7	5	2	.571	231	192
San Diego	2	11	1	.179	188	386

NATIONAL CONFERENCE

EASTERN DIVISION

	W	L	T	Pct.	Pts.	OP
Dallas	10	4	0	.714	382	203
Washington*	10	4	0	.714	325	198
Philadelphia	5	8	1	.393	310	393
St. Louis	4	9	1	.321	286	365
N.Y. Giants	2	11	1	.179	226	362

CENTRAL DIVISION

	W	L	T	Pct.	Pts.	OP
Minnesota	12	2	0	.857	296	168
Detroit	6	7	1	.464	271	247
Green Bay	5	7	2	.429	202	259
Chicago	3	11	0	.214	195	334

WESTERN DIVISION

	W	L	T	Pct.	Pts.	OP
Los Angeles	12	2	0	.857	388	178
Atlanta	9	5	0	.643	318	224
New Orleans	5	9	0	.357	163	312
San Francisco	5	9	0	.357	262	319

**Wild Card qualifier for playoffs*

Cincinnati won division title on the basis of a better conference record than Pittsburgh (8-3 to 7-4). Dallas won division title on the basis of a better point differential vs. Washington (net 13 points).

Divisional playoffs: OAKLAND 33, Pittsburgh 14; MIAMI 34, Cincinnati 16

AFC championship: MIAMI 27, Oakland 10

Divisional playoffs: MINNESOTA 27, Washington 20; DALLAS 27, Los Angeles 16

NFC championship: Minnesota 27, DALLAS 10

Super Bowl VIII: Miami (AFC) 24, Minnesota (NFC) 7, at Rice Stadium, Houston, Tex.

1972

AMERICAN CONFERENCE

EASTERN DIVISION

	W	L	T	Pct.	Pts.	OP
Miami	14	0	0	1.000	385	171
N.Y. Jets	7	7	0	.500	367	324
Baltimore	5	9	0	.357	235	252
Buffalo	4	9	1	.321	257	377
New England	3	11	0	.214	192	446

CENTRAL DIVISION

	W	L	T	Pct.	Pts.	OP
Pittsburgh	11	3	0	.786	343	175
Cleveland*	10	4	0	.714	268	249
Cincinnati	8	6	0	.571	299	229
Houston	1	13	0	.071	164	380

WESTERN DIVISION

	W	L	T	Pct.	Pts.	OP
Oakland	10	3	1	.750	365	248
Kansas City	8	6	0	.571	287	254
Denver	5	9	0	.357	325	350
San Diego	4	9	1	.321	264	344

NATIONAL CONFERENCE

EASTERN DIVISION

	W	L	T	Pct.	Pts.	OP
Washington	11	3	0	.786	336	218
Dallas*	10	4	0	.714	319	240
N.Y. Giants	8	6	0	.571	331	247
St. Louis	4	9	1	.321	193	303
Philadelphia	2	11	1	.179	145	352

CENTRAL DIVISION

	W	L	T	Pct.	Pts.	OP
Green Bay	10	4	0	.714	304	226
Detroit	8	5	1	.607	339	290
Minnesota	7	7	0	.500	301	252
Chicago	4	9	1	.321	225	275

WESTERN DIVISION

	W	L	T	Pct.	Pts.	OP
San Francisco	8	5	1	.607	353	249
Atlanta	7	7	0	.500	269	274
Los Angeles	6	7	1	.464	291	286
New Orleans	2	11	1	.179	215	361

**Wild Card qualifier for playoffs*

Divisional playoffs: PITTSBURGH 13, Oakland 7; MIAMI 20, Cleveland 14
AFC championship: Miami 21, PITTSBURGH 17
Divisional playoffs: Dallas 30, SAN FRANCISCO 28; WASHINGTON 16, Green Bay 3
NFC championship: WASHINGTON 26, Dallas 3
Super Bowl VII: Miami (AFC) 14, Washington (NFC) 7, at Memorial Coliseum, Los Angeles, Calif.

1971

AMERICAN CONFERENCE

EASTERN DIVISION

	W	L	T	Pct.	Pts.	OP
Miami	10	3	1	.769	315	174
Baltimore*	10	4	0	.714	313	140
New England	6	8	0	.429	238	325
N.Y. Jets	6	8	0	.429	212	299
Buffalo	1	13	0	.071	184	394

CENTRAL DIVISION

	W	L	T	Pct.	Pts.	OP
Cleveland	9	5	0	.643	285	273
Pittsburgh	6	8	0	.429	246	292
Houston	4	9	1	.308	251	330
Cincinnati	4	10	0	.286	284	265

WESTERN DIVISION

	W	L	T	Pct.	Pts.	OP
Kansas City	10	3	1	.769	302	208
Oakland	8	4	2	.667	344	278
San Diego	6	8	0	.429	311	341
Denver	4	9	1	.308	203	275

NATIONAL CONFERENCE

EASTERN DIVISION

	W	L	T	Pct.	Pts.	OP
Dallas	11	3	0	.786	406	222
Washington*	9	4	1	.692	276	190
Philadelphia	6	7	1	.462	221	302
St. Louis	4	9	1	.308	231	279
N.Y. Giants	4	10	0	.286	228	362

CENTRAL DIVISION

	W	L	T	Pct.	Pts.	OP
Minnesota	11	3	0	.786	245	139
Detroit	7	6	1	.538	341	286
Chicago	6	8	0	.429	185	276
Green Bay	4	8	2	.333	274	298

WESTERN DIVISION

	W	L	T	Pct.	Pts.	OP
San Francisco	9	5	0	.643	300	216
Los Angeles	8	5	1	.615	313	260
Atlanta	7	6	1	.538	274	277
New Orleans	4	8	2	.333	266	347

**Wild Card qualifier for playoffs*

Divisional playoffs: Miami 27, KANSAS CITY 24, sudden death overtime; Baltimore 20, CLEVELAND 3
AFC championship: MIAMI 21, Baltimore 0
Divisional playoffs: Dallas 20, MINNESOTA 12; SAN FRANCISCO 24, Washington 20
NFC championship: DALLAS 14, San Francisco 3
Super Bowl VI: Dallas (NFC) 24, Miami (AFC) 3, at Tulane Stadium, New Orleans, La.

1970

AMERICAN CONFERENCE

EASTERN DIVISION

	W	L	T	Pct.	Pts.	OP
Baltimore	11	2	1	.846	321	234
Miami*	10	4	0	.714	297	228
N.Y. Jets	4	10	0	.286	255	286
Buffalo	3	10	1	.231	204	337
Boston Patriots	2	12	0	.143	149	361

CENTRAL DIVISION

	W	L	T	Pct.	Pts.	OP
Cincinnati	8	6	0	.571	312	255
Cleveland	7	7	0	.500	286	265
Pittsburgh	5	9	0	.357	210	272
Houston	3	10	1	.231	217	352

WESTERN DIVISION

	W	L	T	Pct.	Pts.	OP
Oakland	8	4	2	.667	300	293
Kansas City	7	5	2	.583	272	244
San Diego	5	6	3	.455	282	278
Denver	5	8	1	.385	253	264

NATIONAL CONFERENCE

EASTERN DIVISION

	W	L	T	Pct.	Pts.	OP
Dallas	10	4	0	.714	299	221
N.Y. Giants	9	5	0	.643	301	270
St. Louis	8	5	1	.615	325	228
Washington	6	8	0	.429	297	314
Philadelphia	3	10	1	.231	241	332

CENTRAL DIVISION

	W	L	T	Pct.	Pts.	OP
Minnesota	12	2	0	.857	335	143
Detroit*	10	4	0	.714	347	202
Chicago	6	8	0	.429	256	261
Green Bay	6	8	0	.429	196	293

WESTERN DIVISION

	W	L	T	Pct.	Pts.	OP
San Francisco	10	3	1	.769	352	267
Los Angeles	9	4	1	.692	325	202
Atlanta	4	8	2	.333	206	261
New Orleans	2	11	1	.154	172	347

**Wild Card qualifier for playoffs*

Divisional playoffs: BALTIMORE 17, Cincinnati 0; OAKLAND 21, Miami 14
AFC championship: BALTIMORE 27, Oakland 17
Divisional playoffs: DALLAS 5, Detroit 0; San Francisco 17, MINNESOTA 14
NFC championship: Dallas 17, SAN FRANCISCO 10
Super Bowl V: Baltimore (AFC) 16, Dallas (NFC) 13, at Orange Bowl, Miami, Fla.

1969 NFL

EASTERN CONFERENCE

Capitol Division

	W	L	T	Pct.	Pts.	OP
Dallas	11	2	1	.846	369	223
Washington	7	5	2	.583	307	319
New Orleans	5	9	0	.357	311	393
Philadelphia	4	9	1	.308	279	377

Century Division

	W	L	T	Pct.	Pts.	OP
Cleveland	10	3	1	.769	351	300
N.Y. Giants	6	8	0	.429	264	298
St. Louis	4	9	1	.308	314	389
Pittsburgh	1	13	0	.071	218	404

WESTERN CONFERENCE

Coastal Division

	W	L	T	Pct.	Pts.	OP
Los Angeles	11	3	0	.786	320	243
Baltimore	8	5	1	.615	279	268
Atlanta	6	8	0	.429	276	268
San Francisco	4	8	2	.333	277	319

Central Division

	W	L	T	Pct.	Pts.	OP
Minnesota	12	2	0	.857	379	133
Detroit	9	4	1	.692	259	188
Green Bay	8	6	0	.571	269	221
Chicago	1	13	0	.071	210	339

Conference championships: Cleveland 38, DALLAS 14; MINNESOTA 23, Los Angeles 20
NFL championship: MINNESOTA 27, Cleveland 7
Super Bowl IV: Kansas City (AFL) 23, Minnesota (NFL) 7, at Tulane Stadium, New Orleans, La.

1969 AFL

EASTERN DIVISION

	W	L	T	Pct.	Pts.	OP
N.Y. Jets	10	4	0	.714	353	269
Houston	6	6	2	.500	278	279
Boston Patriots	4	10	0	.286	266	316
Buffalo	4	10	0	.286	230	359
Miami	3	10	1	.231	233	332

WESTERN DIVISION

	W	L	T	Pct.	Pts.	OP
Oakland	12	1	1	.923	377	242
Kansas City	11	3	0	.786	359	177
San Diego	8	6	0	.571	288	276
Denver	5	8	1	.385	297	344
Cincinnati	4	9	1	.308	280	367

Divisional Playoffs: Kansas City 13, N.Y. JETS 6; OAKLAND 56, Houston 7
AFL championship: Kansas City 17, OAKLAND 7

1968 NFL

EASTERN CONFERENCE

Capitol Division

	W	L	T	Pct.	Pts.	OP
Dallas	12	2	0	.857	431	186
N.Y. Giants	7	7	0	.500	294	325
Washington	5	9	0	.357	249	358
Philadelphia	2	12	0	.143	202	351

Century Division

	W	L	T	Pct.	Pts.	OP
Cleveland	10	4	0	.714	394	273
St. Louis	9	4	1	.692	325	289
New Orleans	4	9	1	.308	246	327
Pittsburgh	2	11	1	.154	244	397

WESTERN CONFERENCE

Coastal Division

	W	L	T	Pct.	Pts.	OP
Baltimore	13	1	0	.929	402	144
Los Angeles	10	3	1	.769	312	200
San Francisco	7	6	1	.538	303	310
Atlanta	2	12	0	.143	170	389

Central Division

	W	L	T	Pct.	Pts.	OP
Minnesota	8	6	0	.571	282	242
Chicago	7	7	0	.500	250	333
Green Bay	6	7	1	.462	281	227
Detroit	4	8	2	.333	207	241

Conference championships: CLEVELAND 31, Dallas 20; BALTIMORE 24, Minnesota 14
NFL championship: Baltimore 34, CLEVELAND 0
Super Bowl III: N.Y. Jets (AFL) 16, Baltimore (NFL) 7, at Orange Bowl, Miami, Fla.

1968 AFL

EASTERN DIVISION

	W	L	T	Pct.	Pts.	OP
N.Y. Jets	11	3	0	.786	419	280
Houston	7	7	0	.500	303	248
Miami	5	8	1	.385	276	355
Boston Patriots	4	10	0	.286	229	406
Buffalo	1	12	1	.077	199	367

WESTERN DIVISION

	W	L	T	Pct.	Pts.	OP
Oakland	12	2	0	.857	453	233
Kansas City	12	2	0	.857	371	170
San Diego	9	5	0	.643	382	310
Denver	5	9	0	.357	255	404
Cincinnati	3	11	0	.214	215	329

Western Division playoff: OAKLAND 41, Kansas City 6
AFL championship: N.Y. JETS 27, Oakland 23

1967 NFL

EASTERN CONFERENCE

Capitol Division

	W	L	T	Pct.	Pts.	OP
Dallas	9	5	0	.643	342	268
Philadelphia	6	7	1	.462	351	409
Washington	5	6	3	.455	347	353
New Orleans	3	11	0	.214	233	379

Century Division

	W	L	T	Pct.	Pts.	OP
Cleveland	9	5	0	.643	334	297
N.Y. Giants	7	7	0	.500	369	379
St. Louis	6	7	1	.462	333	356
Pittsburgh	4	9	1	.308	281	320

WESTERN CONFERENCE

Coastal Division

	W	L	T	Pct.	Pts.	OP
Los Angeles	11	1	2	.917	398	196
Baltimore	11	1	2	.917	394	198
San Francisco	7	7	0	.500	273	337
Atlanta	1	12	1	.077	175	422

Central Division

	W	L	T	Pct.	Pts.	OP
Green Bay	9	4	1	.692	332	209
Chicago	7	6	1	.538	239	218
Detroit	5	7	2	.417	260	259
Minnesota	3	8	3	.273	233	294

Los Angeles won division title on the basis of advantage in points (58-34) in two games vs. Baltimore.

Conference championships: DALLAS 52, Cleveland 14; GREEN BAY 28, Los Angeles 7
NFL championship: GREEN BAY 21, Dallas 17
Super Bowl II: Green Bay (NFL) 33, Oakland (AFL) 14, at Orange Bowl, Miami, Fla.

1967 AFL

EASTERN DIVISION

	W	L	T	Pct.	Pts.	OP
Houston	9	4	1	.692	258	199
N.Y. Jets	8	5	1	.615	371	329
Buffalo	4	10	0	.286	237	285
Miami	4	10	0	.286	219	407
Boston Patriots	3	10	1	.231	280	389

WESTERN DIVISION

	W	L	T	Pct.	Pts.	OP
Oakland	13	1	0	.929	468	233
Kansas City	9	5	0	.643	408	254
San Diego	8	5	1	.615	360	352
Denver	3	11	0	.214	256	409

AFL championship: OAKLAND 40, Houston 7

1966 NFL

EASTERN CONFERENCE	W	L	T	Pct.	Pts.	OP
Dallas	10	3	1	.769	445	239
Cleveland	9	5	0	.643	403	259
Philadelphia	9	5	0	.643	326	340
St. Louis	8	5	1	.615	264	265
Washington	7	7	0	.500	351	355
Pittsburgh	5	8	1	.385	316	347
Atlanta	3	11	0	.214	204	437
N.Y. Giants	1	12	1	.077	263	501

WESTERN CONFERENCE	W	L	T	Pct.	Pts.	OP
Green Bay	12	2	0	.857	335	163
Baltimore	9	5	0	.643	314	226
Los Angeles	8	6	0	.571	289	212
San Francisco	6	6	2	.500	320	325
Chicago	5	7	2	.417	234	272
Detroit	4	9	1	.308	206	317
Minnesota	4	9	1	.308	292	304

NFL championship: Green Bay 34, DALLAS 27

Super Bowl I: Green Bay (NFL) 35, Kansas City (AFL) 10, at Memorial Coliseum, Los Angeles, Calif.

1966 AFL

EASTERN DIVISION	W	L	T	Pct.	Pts.	OP
Buffalo	9	4	1	.692	358	255
Boston Patriots	8	4	2	.677	315	283
N.Y. Jets	6	6	2	.500	322	312
Houston	3	11	0	.214	335	396
Miami	3	11	0	.214	213	362

WESTERN DIVISION	W	L	T	Pct.	Pts.	OP
Kansas City	11	2	1	.846	448	276
Oakland	8	5	1	.615	315	288
San Diego	7	6	1	.538	335	284
Denver	4	10	0	.286	196	381

AFL championship: Kansas City 31, BUFFALO 7

1965 NFL

EASTERN CONFERENCE	W	L	T	Pct.	Pts.	OP
Cleveland	11	3	0	.786	363	325
Dallas	7	7	0	.500	325	280
N.Y. Giants	7	7	0	.500	270	338
Washington	6	8	0	.429	257	301
Philadelphia	5	9	0	.357	363	359
St. Louis	5	9	0	.357	296	309
Pittsburgh	2	12	0	.143	202	397

WESTERN CONFERENCE	W	L	T	Pct.	Pts.	OP
Green Bay	10	3	1	.769	316	224
Baltimore	10	3	1	.769	389	284
Chicago	9	5	0	.643	409	275
San Francisco	7	6	1	.538	421	402
Minnesota	7	7	0	.500	383	403
Detroit	6	7	1	.462	257	295
Los Angeles	4	10	0	.286	269	328

Western Conference playoff: GREEN BAY 13, Baltimore 10, sudden death overtime

NFL championship: GREEN BAY 23, Cleveland 12

1965 AFL

EASTERN DIVISION	W	L	T	Pct.	Pts.	OP
Buffalo	10	3	1	.769	313	226
N.Y. Jets	5	8	1	.385	285	303
Boston Patriots	4	8	2	.333	244	302
Houston	4	10	0	.286	298	429

WESTERN DIVISION	W	L	T	Pct.	Pts.	OP
San Diego	9	2	3	.818	340	227
Oakland	8	5	1	.615	298	239
Kansas City	7	5	2	.583	322	285
Denver	4	10	0	.286	303	392

AFL championship: Buffalo 23, SAN DIEGO 0

1964 NFL

EASTERN CONFERENCE	W	L	T	Pct.	Pts.	OP
Cleveland	10	3	1	.769	415	293
St. Louis	9	3	2	.750	357	331
Philadelphia	6	8	0	.429	312	313
Washington	6	8	0	.429	307	305
Dallas	5	8	1	.385	250	289
Pittsburgh	5	9	0	.357	253	315
N.Y. Giants	2	10	2	.167	241	399

WESTERN CONFERENCE	W	L	T	Pct.	Pts.	OP
Baltimore	12	2	0	.857	428	225
Green Bay	8	5	1	.615	342	245
Minnesota	8	5	1	.615	355	296
Detroit	7	5	2	.583	280	260
Los Angeles	5	7	2	.417	283	339
Chicago	5	9	0	.357	260	379
San Francisco	4	10	0	.286	236	330

NFL championship: CLEVELAND 27, Baltimore 0

1964 AFL

EASTERN DIVISION	W	L	T	Pct.	Pts.	OP
Buffalo	12	2	0	.857	400	242
Boston Patriots	10	3	1	.769	365	297
N.Y. Jets	5	8	1	.385	278	315
Houston	4	10	0	.286	310	355

WESTERN DIVISION	W	L	T	Pct.	Pts.	OP
San Diego	8	5	1	.615	341	300
Kansas City	7	7	0	.500	366	306
Oakland	5	7	2	.417	303	350
Denver	2	11	1	.154	240	438

AFL championship: BUFFALO 20, San Diego 7

1963 NFL

EASTERN CONFERENCE	W	L	T	Pct.	Pts.	OP
N.Y. Giants	11	3	0	.786	448	280
Cleveland	10	4	0	.714	343	262
St. Louis	9	5	0	.643	341	283
Pittsburgh	7	4	3	.636	321	295
Dallas	4	10	0	.286	305	378
Washington	3	11	0	.214	279	398
Philadelphia	2	10	2	.167	242	381

WESTERN CONFERENCE	W	L	T	Pct.	Pts.	OP
Chicago	11	1	2	.917	301	144
Green Bay	11	2	1	.846	369	206
Baltimore	8	6	0	.571	316	285
Detroit	5	8	1	.385	326	265
Minnesota	5	8	1	.385	309	390
Los Angeles	5	9	0	.357	210	350
San Francisco	2	12	0	.143	198	391

NFL championship: CHICAGO 14, N.Y. Giants 10

1963 AFL

EASTERN DIVISION	W	L	T	Pct.	Pts.	OP
Boston Patriots	7	6	1	.538	327	257
Buffalo	7	6	1	.538	304	291
Houston	6	8	0	.429	302	372
N.Y. Jets	5	8	1	.385	249	399

WESTERN DIVISION	W	L	T	Pct.	Pts.	OP
San Diego	11	3	0	.786	399	255
Oakland	10	4	0	.714	363	282
Kansas City	5	7	2	.417	347	263
Denver	2	11	1	.154	301	473

Eastern Division playoff: Boston 26, BUFFALO 8

AFL championship: SAN DIEGO 51, Boston 10

1962 NFL

EASTERN CONFERENCE	W	L	T	Pct.	Pts.	OP
N.Y. Giants	12	2	0	.857	398	283
Pittsburgh	9	5	0	.643	312	363
Cleveland	7	6	1	.538	291	257
Washington	5	7	2	.417	305	376
Dallas Cowboys	5	8	1	.385	398	402
St. Louis	4	9	1	.308	287	361
Philadelphia	3	10	1	.231	282	356

WESTERN CONFERENCE	W	L	T	Pct.	Pts.	OP
Green Bay	13	1	0	.929	415	148
Detroit	11	3	0	.786	315	177
Chicago	9	5	0	.643	321	287
Baltimore	7	7	0	.500	293	288
San Francisco	6	8	0	.429	282	331
Minnesota	2	11	1	.154	254	410
Los Angeles	1	12	1	.077	220	334

NFL championship: Green Bay 16, N.Y. GIANTS 7

1962 AFL

EASTERN DIVISION	W	L	T	Pct.	Pts.	OP
Houston	11	3	0	.786	387	270
Boston Patriots	9	4	1	.692	346	295
Buffalo	7	6	1	.538	309	272
N.Y. Titans	5	9	0	.357	278	423

WESTERN DIVISION	W	L	T	Pct.	Pts.	OP
Dallas Texans	11	3	0	.786	389	233
Denver	7	7	0	.500	353	334
San Diego	4	10	0	.286	314	392
Oakland	1	13	0	.071	213	370

AFL championship: Dallas Texans 20, HOUSTON 17, sudden death overtime

1961 NFL

EASTERN CONFERENCE	W	L	T	Pct.	Pts.	OP
N.Y. Giants	10	3	1	.769	368	220
Philadelphia	10	4	0	.714	361	297
Cleveland	8	5	1	.615	319	270
St. Louis	7	7	0	.500	279	267
Pittsburgh	6	8	0	.429	295	287
Dallas Cowboys	4	9	1	.308	236	380
Washington	1	12	1	.077	174	392

WESTERN CONFERENCE	W	L	T	Pct.	Pts.	OP
Green Bay	11	3	0	.786	391	223
Detroit	8	5	1	.615	270	258
Baltimore	8	6	0	.571	302	307
Chicago Bears	8	6	0	.571	326	302
San Francisco	7	6	1	.538	346	272
Los Angeles	4	10	0	.286	263	333
Minnesota	3	11	0	.214	285	407

NFL championship: GREEN BAY 37, N.Y. Giants 0

1961 AFL

EASTERN DIVISION	W	L	T	Pct.	Pts.	OP
Houston	10	3	1	.769	513	242
Boston Patriots	9	4	1	.692	413	313
N.Y. Titans	7	7	0	.500	301	390
Buffalo	6	8	0	.429	294	342

WESTERN DIVISION	W	L	T	Pct.	Pts.	OP
San Diego	12	2	0	.857	396	219
Dallas Texans	6	8	0	.429	334	343
Denver	3	11	0	.214	251	432
Oakland	2	12	0	.143	237	458

AFL championship: Houston 10, SAN DIEGO 3

1960 NFL

EASTERN CONFERENCE	W	L	T	Pct.	Pts.	OP
Philadelphia	10	2	0	.833	321	246
Cleveland	8	3	1	.727	362	217
N.Y. Giants	6	4	2	.600	271	261
St. Louis	6	5	1	.545	288	230
Pittsburgh	5	6	1	.455	240	275
Washington	1	9	2	.100	178	309

WESTERN CONFERENCE	W	L	T	Pct.	Pts.	OP
Green Bay	8	4	0	.667	332	209
Detroit	7	5	0	.583	239	212
San Francisco	7	5	0	.583	208	205
Baltimore	6	6	0	.500	288	234
Chicago	5	6	1	.455	194	299
L.A. Rams	4	7	1	.364	265	297
Dallas Cowboys	0	11	1	.000	177	369

NFL championship: PHILADELPHIA 17, Green Bay 13

1960 AFL

EASTERN CONFERENCE	W	L	T	Pct.	Pts.	OP
Houston	10	4	0	.714	379	285
N.Y. Titans	7	7	0	.500	382	399
Buffalo	5	8	1	.385	296	303
Boston	5	9	0	.357	286	349

WESTERN CONFERENCE	W	L	T	Pct.	Pts.	OP
L.A. Chargers	10	4	0	.714	373	336
Dallas Texans	8	6	0	.571	362	253
Oakland	6	8	0	.429	319	388
Denver	4	9	1	.308	309	393

AFL championship: HOUSTON 24, L.A. Chargers 16

1959

EASTERN CONFERENCE	W	L	T	Pct.	Pts.	OP
N.Y. Giants	10	2	0	.833	284	170
Cleveland	7	5	0	.583	270	214
Philadelphia	7	5	0	.583	268	278
Pittsburgh	6	5	1	.545	257	216
Washington	3	9	0	.250	185	350
Chi. Cardinals	2	10	0	.167	234	324

WESTERN CONFERENCE	W	L	T	Pct.	Pts.	OP
Baltimore	9	3	0	.750	374	251
Chi. Bears	8	4	0	.667	252	196
Green Bay	7	5	0	.583	248	246
San Francisco	7	5	0	.583	255	237
Detroit	3	8	1	.273	203	275
Los Angeles	2	10	0	.167	242	315

NFL championship: BALTIMORE 31, N.Y. Giants 16

1958

EASTERN CONFERENCE	W	L	T	Pct.	Pts.	OP
N.Y. Giants	9	3	0	.750	246	183
Cleveland	9	3	0	.750	302	217
Pittsburgh	7	4	1	.636	261	230
Washington	4	7	1	.364	214	268
Chi. Cardinals	2	9	1	.182	261	356
Philadelphia	2	9	1	.182	235	306

WESTERN CONFERENCE	W	L	T	Pct.	Pts.	OP
Baltimore	9	3	0	.750	381	203
Chi. Bears	8	4	0	.667	298	230
Los Angeles	8	4	0	.667	344	278
San Francisco	6	6	0	.500	257	324
Detroit	4	7	1	.364	261	276
Green Bay	1	10	1	.091	193	382

Eastern Conference playoff: N.Y. GIANTS 10, Cleveland 0

NFL championship: Baltimore 23, N.Y. GIANTS 17, sudden death overtime

1957

EASTERN CONFERENCE	W	L	T	Pct.	Pts.	OP
Cleveland	9	2	1	.818	269	172
N.Y. Giants	7	5	0	.583	254	211
Pittsburgh	6	6	0	.500	161	178
Washington	5	6	1	.455	251	230
Philadelphia	4	8	0	.333	173	230
Chi. Cardinals	3	9	0	.250	200	299

WESTERN CONFERENCE	W	L	T	Pct.	Pts.	OP
Detroit	8	4	0	.667	251	231
San Francisco	8	4	0	.667	260	264
Baltimore	7	5	0	.583	303	235
Los Angeles	6	6	0	.500	307	278
Chi. Bears	5	7	0	.417	203	211
Green Bay	3	9	0	.250	218	311

Western Conference playoff: Detroit 31, SAN FRANCISCO 27

NFL championship: DETROIT 59, Cleveland 14

1956

EASTERN CONFERENCE

	W	L	T	Pct.	Pts.	OP
N.Y. Giants	8	3	1	.727	264	197
Chi. Cardinals	7	5	0	.583	240	182
Washington	6	6	0	.500	183	225
Cleveland	5	7	0	.417	167	177
Pittsburgh	5	7	0	.417	217	250
Philadelphia	3	8	1	.273	143	215

WESTERN CONFERENCE

	W	L	T	Pct.	Pts.	OP
Chi. Bears	9	2	1	.818	363	246
Detroit	9	3	0	.750	300	188
San Francisco	5	6	1	.455	233	284
Baltimore	5	7	0	.417	270	322
Green Bay	4	8	0	.333	264	342
Los Angeles	4	8	0	.333	291	307

NFL championship: N.Y. GIANTS 47, Chi. Bears 7

1955

EASTERN CONFERENCE

	W	L	T	Pct.	Pts.	OP
Cleveland	9	2	1	.818	349	218
Washington	8	4	0	.667	246	222
N.Y. Giants	6	5	1	.545	267	223
Chi. Cardinals	4	7	1	.364	224	252
Philadelphia	4	7	1	.364	248	231
Pittsburgh	4	8	0	.333	195	285

WESTERN CONFERENCE

	W	L	T	Pct.	Pts.	OP
Los Angeles	8	3	1	.727	260	231
Chi. Bears	8	4	0	.667	294	251
Green Bay	6	6	0	.500	258	276
Baltimore	5	6	1	.455	214	239
San Francisco	4	8	0	.333	216	298
Detroit	3	9	0	.250	230	275

NFL championship: Cleveland 38, LOS ANGELES 14

1954

EASTERN CONFERENCE

	W	L	T	Pct.	Pts.	OP
Cleveland	9	3	0	.750	336	162
Philadelphia	7	4	1	.636	284	230
N.Y. Giants	7	5	0	.583	293	184
Pittsburgh	5	7	0	.417	219	263
Washington	3	9	0	.250	207	432
Chi. Cardinals	2	10	0	.167	183	347

WESTERN CONFERENCE

	W	L	T	Pct.	Pts.	OP
Detroit	9	2	1	.818	337	189
Chi. Bears	8	4	0	.667	301	279
San Francisco	7	4	1	.636	313	251
Los Angeles	6	5	1	.545	314	285
Green Bay	4	8	0	.333	234	251
Baltimore	3	9	0	.250	131	279

NFL championship: CLEVELAND 56, Detroit 10

1953

EASTERN CONFERENCE

	W	L	T	Pct.	Pts.	OP
Cleveland	11	1	0	.917	348	162
Philadelphia	7	4	1	.636	352	215
Washington	6	5	1	.545	208	215
Pittsburgh	6	6	0	.500	211	263
N.Y. Giants	3	9	0	.250	179	277
Chi. Cardinals	1	10	1	.091	190	337

WESTERN CONFERENCE

	W	L	T	Pct.	Pts.	OP
Detroit	10	2	0	.833	271	205
San Francisco	9	3	0	.750	372	237
Los Angeles	8	3	1	.727	366	236
Chi. Bears	3	8	1	.273	218	262
Baltimore	3	9	0	.250	182	350
Green Bay	2	9	1	.182	200	338

NFL championship: DETROIT 17, Cleveland 16

1952

AMERICAN CONFERENCE

	W	L	T	Pct.	Pts.	OP
Cleveland	8	4	0	.667	310	213
N.Y. Giants	7	5	0	.583	234	231
Philadelphia	7	5	0	.583	252	271
Pittsburgh	5	7	0	.417	300	273
Chi. Cardinals	4	8	0	.333	172	221
Washington	4	8	0	.333	240	287

NATIONAL CONFERENCE

	W	L	T	Pct.	Pts.	OP
Detroit	9	3	0	.750	344	192
Los Angeles	9	3	0	.750	349	234
San Francisco	7	5	0	.583	285	221
Green Bay	6	6	0	.500	295	312
Chi. Bears	5	7	0	.417	245	326
Dallas Texans	1	11	0	.083	182	427

National Conference playoff: DETROIT 31, Los Angeles 21
NFL championship: Detroit 17, CLEVELAND 7

1951

AMERICAN CONFERENCE

	W	L	T	Pct.	Pts.	OP
Cleveland	11	1	0	.917	331	152
N.Y. Giants	9	2	1	.818	254	161
Washington	5	7	0	.417	183	296
Pittsburgh	4	7	1	.364	183	235
Philadelphia	4	8	0	.333	234	264
Chi. Cardinals	3	9	0	.250	210	287

NATIONAL CONFERENCE

	W	L	T	Pct.	Pts.	OP
Los Angeles	8	4	0	.667	392	261
Detroit	7	4	1	.636	336	259
San Francisco	7	4	1	.636	255	205
Chi. Bears	7	5	0	.583	286	282
Green Bay	3	9	0	.250	254	375
N.Y. Yanks	1	9	2	.100	241	382

NFL championship: LOS ANGELES 24, Cleveland 17

1950

AMERICAN CONFERENCE

	W	L	T	Pct.	Pts.	OP
Cleveland	10	2	0	.833	310	144
N.Y. Giants	10	2	0	.833	268	150
Philadelphia	6	6	0	.500	254	141
Pittsburgh	6	6	0	.500	180	195
Chi. Cardinals	5	7	0	.417	233	287
Washington	3	9	0	.250	232	326

NATIONAL CONFERENCE

	W	L	T	Pct.	Pts.	OP
Los Angeles	9	3	0	.750	466	309
Chi. Bears	9	3	0	.750	279	207
N.Y. Yanks	7	5	0	.583	366	367
Detroit	6	6	0	.500	321	285
Green Bay	3	9	0	.250	244	406
San Francisco	3	9	0	.250	213	300
Baltimore	1	11	0	.083	213	462

American Conference playoff: CLEVELAND 8, N.Y. Giants 3
National Conference playoff: LOS ANGELES 24, Chi. Bears 14
NFL championship: CLEVELAND 30, Los Angeles 28

1949

EASTERN DIVISION

	W	L	T	Pct.	Pts.	OP
Philadelphia	11	1	0	.917	364	134
Pittsburgh	6	5	1	.545	224	214
N.Y. Giants	6	6	0	.500	287	298
Washington	4	7	1	.364	268	339
N.Y. Bulldogs	1	10	1	.091	153	365

WESTERN DIVISION

	W	L	T	Pct.	Pts.	OP
Los Angeles	8	2	2	.800	360	239
Chi. Bears	9	3	0	.750	332	218
Chi. Cardinals	6	5	1	.545	360	301
Detroit	4	8	0	.333	237	259
Green Bay	2	10	0	.167	114	329

NFL championship: Philadelphia 14, LOS ANGELES 0

1948

EASTERN DIVISION

	W	L	T	Pct.	Pts.	OP
Philadelphia	9	2	1	.818	376	156
Washington	7	5	0	.583	291	287
N.Y. Giants	4	8	0	.333	297	388
Pittsburgh	4	8	0	.333	200	243
Boston	3	9	0	.250	174	372

WESTERN DIVISION

	W	L	T	Pct.	Pts.	OP
Chi. Cardinals	11	1	0	.917	395	226
Chi. Bears	10	2	0	.833	375	151
Los Angeles	6	5	1	.545	327	269
Green Bay	3	9	0	.250	154	290
Detroit	2	10	0	.167	200	407

NFL championship: PHILADELPHIA 7, Chi. Cardinals 0

1947

EASTERN DIVISION

	W	L	T	Pct.	Pts.	OP
Philadelphia	8	4	0	.667	308	242
Pittsburgh	8	4	0	.667	240	259
Boston	4	7	1	.364	168	256
Washington	4	8	0	.333	295	367
N.Y. Giants	2	8	2	.200	190	309

WESTERN DIVISION

	W	L	T	Pct.	Pts.	OP
Chi. Cardinals	9	3	0	.750	306	231
Chi. Bears	8	4	0	.667	363	241
Green Bay	6	5	1	.545	274	210
Los Angeles	6	6	0	.500	259	214
Detroit	3	9	0	.250	231	305

Eastern Division playoff: Philadelphia 21, PITTSBURGH 0
NFL championship: CHI. CARDINALS 28, Philadelphia 21

1946

EASTERN DIVISION

	W	L	T	Pct.	Pts.	OP
N.Y. Giants	7	3	1	.700	236	162
Philadelphia	6	5	0	.545	231	220
Washington	5	5	1	.500	171	191
Pittsburgh	5	5	1	.500	136	117
Boston	2	8	1	.200	189	273

WESTERN DIVISION

	W	L	T	Pct.	Pts.	OP
Chi. Bears	8	2	1	.800	289	193
Los Angeles	6	4	1	.600	277	257
Green Bay	6	5	0	.545	148	158
Chi. Cardinals	6	5	0	.545	260	198
Detroit	1	10	0	.091	142	310

NFL championship: Chi. Bears 24, N.Y. GIANTS 14

1945

EASTERN DIVISION

	W	L	T	Pct.	Pts.	OP
Washington	8	2	0	.800	209	121
Philadelphia	7	3	0	.700	272	133
N.Y. Giants	3	6	1	.333	179	198
Boston	3	6	1	.333	123	211
Pittsburgh	2	8	0	.200	79	220

WESTERN DIVISION

	W	L	T	Pct.	Pts.	OP
Cleveland	9	1	0	.900	244	136
Detroit	7	3	0	.700	195	194
Green Bay	6	4	0	.600	258	173
Chi. Bears	3	7	0	.300	192	235
Chi. Cardinals	1	9	0	.100	98	228

NFL championship: CLEVELAND 15, Washington 14

1944

EASTERN DIVISION

	W	L	T	Pct.	Pts.	OP
N.Y. Giants	8	1	1	.889	206	75
Philadelphia	7	1	2	.875	267	131
Washington	6	3	1	.667	169	180
Boston	2	8	0	.200	82	233
Brooklyn	0	10	0	.000	69	166

WESTERN DIVISION

	W	L	T	Pct.	Pts.	OP
Green Bay	8	2	0	.800	238	141
Chi. Bears	6	3	1	.667	258	172
Detroit	6	3	1	.667	216	151
Cleveland	4	6	0	.400	188	224
Card-Pitt	0	10	0	.000	108	328

NFL championship: Green Bay 14, N.Y. GIANTS 7

1943

EASTERN DIVISION

	W	L	T	Pct.	Pts.	OP
Washington	6	3	1	.667	229	137
N.Y. Giants	6	3	1	.667	197	170
Phil-Pitt	5	4	1	.556	225	230
Brooklyn	2	8	0	.200	65	234

WESTERN DIVISION

	W	L	T	Pct.	Pts.	OP
Chi. Bears	8	1	1	.889	303	157
Green Bay	7	2	1	.778	264	172
Detroit	3	6	1	.333	178	218
Chi. Cardinals	0	10	0	.000	95	238

Eastern Division playoff: Washington 28, N.Y. GIANTS 0
NFL championship: CHI. BEARS 41, Washington 21

1942

EASTERN DIVISION

	W	L	T	Pct.	Pts.	OP
Washington	10	1	0	.909	227	102
Pittsburgh	7	4	0	.636	167	119
N.Y. Giants	5	5	1	.500	155	139
Brooklyn	3	8	0	.273	100	168
Philadelphia	2	9	0	.182	134	239

WESTERN DIVISION

	W	L	T	Pct.	Pts.	OP
Chi. Bears	11	0	0	1.000	376	84
Green Bay	8	2	1	.800	300	215
Cleveland	5	6	0	.455	150	207
Chi. Cardinals	3	8	0	.273	98	209
Detroit	0	11	0	.000	38	263

NFL championship: WASHINGTON 14, Chi. Bears 6

1941

EASTERN DIVISION

	W	L	T	Pct.	Pts.	OP
N.Y. Giants	8	3	0	.727	238	114
Brooklyn	7	4	0	.636	158	127
Washington	6	5	0	.545	176	174
Philadelphia	2	8	1	.200	119	218
Pittsburgh	1	9	1	.100	103	276

WESTERN DIVISION

	W	L	T	Pct.	Pts.	OP
Chi. Bears	10	1	0	.909	396	147
Green Bay	10	1	0	.909	258	120
Detroit	4	6	1	.400	121	195
Chi. Cardinals	3	7	1	.300	127	197
Cleveland	2	9	0	.182	116	244

Western Division playoff: CHI. BEARS 33, Green Bay 14
NFL championship: CHI. BEARS 37, N.Y. Giants 9

1940

EASTERN DIVISION

	W	L	T	Pct.	Pts.	OP
Washington	9	2	0	.818	245	142
Brooklyn	8	3	0	.727	186	120
N.Y. Giants	6	4	1	.600	131	133
Pittsburgh	2	7	2	.222	60	178
Philadelphia	1	10	0	.091	111	211

WESTERN DIVISION

	W	L	T	Pct.	Pts.	OP
Chi. Bears	8	3	0	.727	238	152
Green Bay	6	4	1	.600	238	155
Detroit	5	5	1	.500	138	153
Cleveland	4	6	1	.400	171	191
Chi. Cardinals	2	7	2	.222	139	222

NFL championship: Chi. Bears 73, WASHINGTON 0

1939

EASTERN DIVISION

	W	L	T	Pct.	Pts.	OP
N.Y. Giants	9	1	1	.900	168	85
Washington	8	2	1	.800	242	94
Brooklyn	4	6	1	.400	108	219
Philadelphia	1	9	1	.100	105	200
Pittsburgh	1	9	1	.100	114	216

WESTERN DIVISION

	W	L	T	Pct.	Pts.	OP
Green Bay	9	2	0	.818	233	153
Chi. Bears	8	3	0	.727	298	157
Detroit	6	5	0	.545	145	150
Cleveland	5	5	1	.500	195	164
Chi. Cardinals	1	10	0	.091	84	254

NFL championship: GREEN BAY 27, N.Y. Giants 0

1938

EASTERN DIVISION

	W	L	T	Pct.	Pts.	OP
N.Y. Giants	8	2	1	.800	194	79
Washington	6	3	2	.667	148	154
Brooklyn	4	4	3	.500	131	161
Philadelphia	5	6	0	.455	154	164
Pittsburgh	2	9	0	.182	79	169

WESTERN DIVISION

	W	L	T	Pct.	Pts.	OP
Green Bay	8	3	0	.727	223	118
Detroit	7	4	0	.636	119	108
Chi. Bears	6	5	0	.545	194	148
Cleveland	4	7	0	.364	131	215
Chi. Cardinals	2	9	0	.182	111	168

NFL championship: N.Y. GIANTS 23, Green Bay 17

1937

EASTERN DIVISION

	W	L	T	Pct.	Pts.	OP
Washington	8	3	0	.727	195	120
N.Y. Giants	6	3	2	.667	128	109
Pittsburgh	4	7	0	.364	122	145
Brooklyn	3	7	1	.300	82	174
Philadelphia	2	8	1	.200	86	177

WESTERN DIVISION

	W	L	T	Pct.	Pts.	OP
Chi. Bears	9	1	1	.900	201	100
Green Bay	7	4	0	.636	220	122
Detroit	7	4	0	.636	180	105
Chi. Cardinals	5	5	1	.500	135	165
Cleveland	1	10	0	.091	75	207

NFL championship: Washington 28, CHI. BEARS 21

1936

EASTERN DIVISION

	W	L	T	Pct.	Pts.	OP
Boston	7	5	0	.583	149	110
Pittsburgh	6	6	0	.500	98	187
N.Y. Giants	5	6	1	.455	115	163
Brooklyn	3	8	1	.273	92	161
Philadelphia	1	11	0	.083	51	206

WESTERN DIVISION

	W	L	T	Pct.	Pts.	OP
Green Bay	10	1	1	.909	248	118
Chi. Bears	9	3	0	.750	222	94
Detroit	8	4	0	.667	235	102
Chi. Cardinals	3	8	1	.273	74	143

NFL championship: Green Bay 21, Boston 6, at Polo Grounds, N.Y.

1935

EASTERN DIVISION

	W	L	T	Pct.	Pts.	OP
N. Y. Giants	9	3	0	.750	180	96
Brooklyn	5	6	1	.455	90	141
Pittsburgh	4	8	0	.333	100	209
Boston	2	8	1	.200	65	123
Philadelphia	2	9	0	.182	60	179

WESTERN DIVISION

	W	L	T	Pct.	Pts.	OP
Detroit	7	3	2	.700	191	111
Green Bay	8	4	0	.667	181	96
Chi. Bears	6	4	2	.600	192	106
Chi. Cardinals	6	4	2	.600	99	97

NFL championship: DETROIT 26, N.Y. Giants 7
One game between Boston and Philadelphia was canceled.

1934

EASTERN DIVISION

	W	L	T	Pct.	Pts.	OP
N.Y. Giants	8	5	0	.615	147	107
Boston	6	6	0	.500	107	94
Brooklyn	4	7	0	.364	61	153
Philadelphia	4	7	0	.364	127	85
Pittsburgh	2	10	0	.167	51	206

WESTERN DIVISION

	W	L	T	Pct.	Pts.	OP
Chi. Bears	13	0	0	1.000	286	86
Detroit	10	3	0	.769	238	59
Green Bay	7	6	0	.538	156	112
Chi. Cardinals	5	6	0	.455	80	84
St. Louis	1	2	0	.333	27	61
Cincinnati	0	8	0	.000	10	243

NFL championship: N.Y. GIANTS 30, Chi. Bears 13

1933

EASTERN DIVISION

	W	L	T	Pct.	Pts.	OP
N.Y. Giants	11	3	0	.786	244	101
Brooklyn	5	4	1	.556	93	54
Boston	5	5	2	.500	103	97
Philadelphia	3	5	1	.375	77	158
Pittsburgh	3	6	2	.333	67	208

WESTERN DIVISION

	W	L	T	Pct.	Pts.	OP
Chi. Bears	10	2	1	.833	133	82
Portsmouth	6	5	0	.545	128	87
Green Bay	5	7	1	.417	170	107
Cincinnati	3	6	1	.333	38	110
Chi. Cardinals	1	9	1	.100	52	101

NFL championship: CHI. BEARS 23, N.Y. Giants 21

1932

	W	L	T	Pct.
Chicago Bears	7	1	6	.875
Green Bay Packers	10	3	1	.769
Portsmouth, O., Spartans	6	2	4	.750
Boston Braves	4	4	2	.500
New York Giants	4	6	2	.400
Brooklyn Dodgers	3	9	0	.250
Chicago Cardinals	2	6	2	.250
Stapleton Stapes	2	7	3	.222

1931

	W	L	T	Pct.
Green Bay Packers	12	2	0	.857
Portsmouth, O., Spartans	11	3	0	.786
Chicago Bears	8	5	0	.615
Chicago Cardinals	5	4	0	.556
New York Giants	7	6	1	.538
Providence Steam Roller	4	4	3	.500
Stapleton Stapes	4	6	1	.400
Cleveland Indians	2	8	0	.200
Brooklyn Dodgers	2	12	0	.143
Frankford Yellow Jackets	1	6	1	.143

1930

	W	L	T	Pct.
Green Bay Packers	10	3	1	.769
New York Giants	13	4	0	.765
Chicago Bears	9	4	1	.692
Brooklyn Dodgers	7	4	1	.636
Providence Steam Roller	6	4	1	.600
Stapleton Stapes	5	5	2	.500
Chicago Cardinals	5	6	2	.455
Portsmouth, O., Spartans	5	6	3	.455
Frankford Yellow Jackets	4	13	1	.222
Minneapolis Red Jackets	1	7	1	.125
Newark Tornadoes	1	10	1	.091

1929

	W	L	T	Pct.
Green Bay Packers	12	0	1	1.000
New York Giants	13	1	1	.929
Frankford Yellowjackets	9	4	5	.692
Chicago Cardinals	6	6	1	.500
Boston Bulldogs	4	4	0	.500
Orange, N.J., Tornadoes	3	4	4	.429
Stapleton Stapes	3	4	3	.429
Providence Steamroller	4	6	2	.400
Chicago Bears	4	9	2	.308
Buffalo Bisons	1	7	1	.125
Minneapolis Red Jackets	1	9	0	.100
Dayton Triangles	0	6	0	.000

1928

	W	L	T	Pct.
Providence Steamroller	8	1	2	.889
Frankford Yellowjackets	11	3	2	.786
Detroit Wolverines	7	2	1	.778
Green Bay Packers	6	4	3	.600
Chicago Bears	7	5	1	.583
New York Giants	4	7	2	.364
New York Yankees	4	8	1	.333
Pottsville, Pa., Maroons	2	8	0	.200
Chicago Cardinals	1	5	0	.167
Dayton Triangles	0	7	0	.000

1927

	W	L	T	Pct.
New York Giants	11	1	1	.917
Green Bay Packers	7	2	1	.778
Chicago Bears	9	3	2	.750
Cleveland Bulldogs	8	4	1	.667
Providence Steam Roller	8	5	1	.615
New York Yankees	7	8	1	.467
Frankford Yellow Jackets	6	9	3	.400
Pottsville, Pa., Maroons	5	8	0	.385
Chicago Cardinals	3	7	1	.300
Dayton Triangles	1	6	1	.143
Duluth Eskimos	1	8	0	.111
Buffalo Bisons	0	5	0	.000

1926

	W	L	T	Pct.
Frankford Yellow Jackets	14	1	1	.933
Chicago Bears	12	1	3	.923
Pottsville, Pa., Maroons	10	2	1	.833
Kansas City Cowboys	8	3	1	.727
Green Bay Packers	7	3	3	.700
Los Angeles Buccaneers	6	3	1	.667
New York Giants	8	4	1	.667
Duluth Eskimos	6	5	3	.545
Buffalo Rangers	4	4	2	.500
Chicago Cardinals	5	6	1	.455
Providence Steam Roller	5	7	0	.417
Detroit Panthers	4	6	2	.400
Hartford Blues	3	7	0	.300
Brooklyn Lions	3	8	0	.273
Milwaukee Badgers	2	7	0	.222
Akron Pros	1	4	3	.200
Dayton Triangles	1	4	1	.200
Racine, Wis., Tornadoes	1	4	0	.200
Columbus Tigers	1	6	0	.143
Canton, Ohio, Bulldogs	1	9	3	.100
Hammond, Ind., Pros	0	4	0	.000
Louisville Colonels	0	4	0	.000

1925

	W	L	T	Pct.
Chicago Cardinals	11	2	1	.846
Pottsville, Pa., Maroons	10	2	0	.833
Detroit Panthers	8	2	2	.800
New York Giants	8	4	0	.667
Akron Pros	4	2	2	.667
Frankford Yellow Jackets	13	7	0	.650
Chicago Bears	9	5	3	.643
Rock Island Independents	5	3	3	.625
Green Bay Packers	8	5	0	.615
Providence Steam Roller	6	5	1	.545
Canton, Ohio, Bulldogs	4	4	0	.500
Cleveland Bulldogs	5	8	1	.385
Kansas City Cowboys	2	5	1	.286
Hammond, Ind., Pros	1	4	0	.250
Buffalo Bisons	1	6	2	.143
Duluth Kelleys	0	3	0	.000
Rochester Jeffersons	0	6	1	.000
Milwaukee Badgers	0	6	0	.000
Dayton Triangles	0	7	1	.000
Columbus Tigers	0	9	0	.000

1924

	W	L	T	Pct.
Cleveland Bulldogs	7	1	1	.875
Chicago Bears	6	1	4	.857
Frankford Yellowjackets	11	2	1	.846
Duluth Kelleys	5	1	0	.833
Rock Island Independents	6	2	2	.750
Green Bay Packers	8	4	0	.667
Buffalo Bisons	6	4	0	.600
Racine, Wis., Legion	4	3	3	.571
Chicago Cardinals	5	4	1	.556
Columbus Tigers	4	4	0	.500
Hammond, Ind., Pros	2	2	1	.500
Milwaukee Badgers	5	8	0	.385
Dayton Triangles	2	7	0	.222
Kansas City Cowboys	2	7	0	.222
Akron, Ohio, Indians	1	6	0	.143
Kenosha, Wis., Maroons	0	5	1	.000
Minneapolis Marines	0	6	0	.000
Rochester Jeffersons	0	7	0	.000

1923

	W	L	T	Pct.
Canton, Ohio, Bulldogs	11	0	1	1.000
Chicago Bears	9	2	1	.818
Green Bay Packers	7	2	1	.778
Milwaukee Badgers	7	2	3	.778
Cleveland Indians	3	1	3	.750
Chicago Cardinals	8	4	0	.667
Duluth Kelleys	4	3	0	.571
Buffalo All-Americans	5	4	3	.556
Columbus Tigers	5	4	1	.556
Racine, Wis., Legion	4	4	2	.500
Toledo Maroons	2	3	2	.400
Rock Island Independents	2	3	3	.400
Minneapolis Marines	2	5	2	.286
St. Louis All-Stars	1	4	2	.200
Hammond, Ind., Pros	1	5	1	.167
Dayton Triangles	1	6	1	.143
Akron, Ohio, Indians	1	6	0	.143
Oorang Indians	1	10	0	.091
Rochester Jeffersons	0	2	0	.000
Louisville Brecks	0	3	0	.000

1922

	W	L	T	Pct.
Canton, Ohio, Bulldogs	10	0	2	1.000
Chicago Bears	9	3	0	.750
Chicago Cardinals	8	3	0	.727
Toledo Maroons	5	2	2	.714
Rock Island Independents	4	2	1	.667
Dayton Triangles	4	3	1	.571
Green Bay Packers	4	3	3	.571
Racine, Wis., Legion	5	4	1	.556
Akron, Ohio, Pros	3	4	2	.429
Buffalo All-Americans	3	4	1	.429
Milwaukee Badgers	2	4	3	.333
Oorang Indians	2	6	0	.250
Minneapolis Marines	1	3	0	.250
Evansville Crimson Giants	0	2	0	.000
Louisville Brecks	0	3	0	.000
Rochester Jeffersons	0	3	1	.000
Hammond, Ind., Pros	0	4	1	.000
Columbus Panhandles	0	7	0	.000

1921

	W	L	T	Pct.
Chicago Staleys	10	1	1	.909
Buffalo All-Americans	9	1	2	.900
Akron, Ohio, Pros	7	2	1	.778
Green Bay Packers	6	2	2	.750
Canton, Ohio, Bulldogs	4	3	3	.571
Dayton Triangles	4	3	1	.571
Rock Island Independents	5	4	1	.556
Chicago Cardinals	2	3	2	.400
Cleveland Indians	2	6	0	.250
Rochester Jeffersons	2	6	0	.250
Detroit Heralds	1	7	1	.125
Columbus Panhandles	0	6	0	.000
Cincinnati Celts	0	8	0	.000

ATLANTA vs. BUFFALO
Series tied, 2-2
1973—Bills, 17-6 (A)
1977—Bills, 3-0 (B)
1980—Falcons, 30-14 (B)
1983—Falcons, 31-14 (A)
(Points—Falcons 67, Bills 48)
ATLANTA vs. CHICAGO
Falcons lead series, 9-5
1966—Bears, 23-6 (C)
1967—Bears, 23-14 (A)
1968—Falcons, 16-13 (C)
1969—Falcons, 48-31 (A)
1970—Bears, 23-14 (A)
1972—Falcons, 37-21 (C)
1973—Falcons, 46-6 (A)
1974—Falcons, 13-10 (A)
1976—Falcons, 10-0 (C)
1977—Falcons, 16-10 (C)
1978—Bears, 13-7 (C)
1980—Falcons, 28-17 (A)
1983—Falcons, 20-17 (C)
1985—Bears, 36-0 (C)
(Points—Falcons 275, Bears 243)
ATLANTA vs. CINCINNATI
Bengals lead series, 4-1
1971—Falcons, 9-6 (C)
1975—Bengals, 21-14 (A)
1978—Bengals, 37-7 (C)
1981—Bengals, 30-28 (A)
1984—Bengals, 35-14 (C)
(Points—Bengals 129, Falcons 72)
ATLANTA vs. CLEVELAND
Browns lead series, 6-1
1966—Browns, 49-17 (A)
1968—Browns, 30-7 (C)
1971—Falcons, 31-14 (C)
1976—Browns, 20-17 (A)
1978—Browns, 24-16 (A)
1981—Browns, 28-17 (C)
1984—Browns, 23-7 (A)
(Points—Browns 188, Falcons 112)
ATLANTA vs. DALLAS
Cowboys lead series, 8-1
1966—Cowboys, 47-14 (A)
1967—Cowboys, 37-7 (D)
1969—Cowboys, 24-17 (A)
1970—Cowboys, 13-0 (D)
1974—Cowboys, 24-0 (A)
1976—Falcons, 17-10 (A)
1978—*Cowboys, 27-20 (D)
1980—*Cowboys, 30-27 (A)
1985—Cowboys, 24-10 (D)
(Points—Cowboys 236, Falcons 112)
**NFC Divisional Playoff*
ATLANTA vs. DENVER
Series tied, 3-3
1970—Broncos, 24-10 (D)
1972—Falcons, 23-20 (A)
1975—Falcons, 35-21 (A)
1979—Broncos, 20-17 (A) OT
1982—Falcons, 34-27 (D)
1985—Broncos, 44-28 (A)
(Points—Broncos 156, Falcons 147)
ATLANTA vs. DETROIT
Lions lead series, 12-4
1966—Lions, 28-10 (D)
1967—Lions, 24-3 (D)
1968—Lions, 24-7 (A)
1969—Lions, 27-21 (D)
1971—Lions, 41-38 (D)
1972—Lions, 26-23 (A)
1973—Lions, 31-6 (D)
1975—Lions, 17-14 (A)
1976—Lions, 24-10 (D)
1977—Falcons, 17-6 (A)
1978—Falcons, 14-0 (A)
1979—Lions, 24-23 (D)
1980—Falcons, 43-28 (A)
1983—Falcons, 30-14 (D)
1984—Lions, 27-24 (A) OT
1985—Lions, 28-27 (A)
(Points—Lions 369, Falcons 310)
ATLANTA vs. GREEN BAY
Packers lead series, 8-6
1966—Packers, 56-3 (Mil)
1967—Packers, 23-0 (Mil)
1968—Packers, 38-7 (A)
1969—Packers, 28-10 (GB)
1970—Packers, 27-24 (GB)
1971—Falcons, 28-21 (A)
1972—Falcons, 10-9 (Mil)
1974—Falcons, 10-3 (A)
1975—Packers, 22-13 (GB)
1976—Packers, 24-20 (A)
1979—Falcons, 25-7 (A)
1981—Falcons, 31-17 (GB)
1982—Packers, 38-7 (A)
1983—Falcons, 47-41 (A) OT
(Points—Packers 354, Falcons 235)

ATLANTA vs. HOUSTON
Falcons lead series, 4-1
1972—Falcons, 20-10 (A)
1976—Oilers, 20-14 (H)
1978—Falcons, 20-14 (A)
1981—Falcons, 31-27 (H)
1984—Falcons, 42-10 (A)
(Points—Falcons 127, Oilers 81)
ATLANTA vs. *INDIANAPOLIS
Colts lead series, 8-0
1966—Colts, 19-7 (A)
1967—Colts, 38-31 (B)
Colts, 49-7 (A)
1968—Colts, 28-20 (A)
Colts, 44-0 (B)
1969—Colts, 21-14 (A)
Colts, 13-6 (B)
1974—Colts, 17-7 (A)
(Points—Colts 229, Falcons 92)
**Franchise in Baltimore prior to 1984*
ATLANTA vs. KANSAS CITY
Chiefs lead series, 2-0
1972—Chiefs, 17-14 (A)
1985—Chiefs, 38-10 (KC)
(Points—Chiefs 55, Falcons 24)
ATLANTA vs. *L.A. RAIDERS
Raiders lead series, 4-1
1971—Falcons, 24-13 (A)
1975—Raiders, 37-34 (O) OT
1979—Raiders, 50-19 (O)
1982—Raiders, 38-14 (A)
1985—Raiders, 34-24 (A)
(Points—Raiders 172, Falcons 115)
**Franchise in Oakland prior to 1982*
ATLANTA vs. L.A. RAMS
Rams lead series, 28-8-2
1966—Rams, 19-14 (A)
1967—Rams, 31-3 (A)
Rams, 20-3 (LA)
1968—Rams, 27-14 (LA)
Rams, 17-10 (A)
1969—Rams, 17-7 (LA)
Rams, 38-6 (A)
1970—Tie, 10-10 (LA)
Rams, 17-7 (A)
1971—Tie, 20-20 (LA)
Rams, 24-16 (A)
1972—Falcons, 31-3 (A)
Rams, 20-7 (LA)
1973—Rams, 31-0 (LA)
Falcons, 15-13 (A)
1974—Rams, 21-0 (LA)
Rams, 30-7 (A)
1975—Rams, 22-7 (LA)
Rams, 16-7 (A)
1976—Rams, 30-14 (A)
Rams, 59-0 (LA)
1977—Falcons, 17-6 (A)
Rams, 23-7 (LA)
1978—Rams, 10-0 (LA)
Falcons, 15-7 (A)
1979—Rams, 20-14 (LA)
Rams, 34-13 (A)
1980—Falcons, 13-10 (A)
Rams, 20-17 (LA) OT
1981—Rams, 37-35 (A)
Rams, 21-16 (LA)
1982—Falcons, 34-17 (A)
1983—Rams, 27-21 (LA)
Rams, 36-13 (A)
1984—Falcons, 30-28 (LA)
Rams, 24-10 (A)
1985—Rams, 17-6 (LA)
Falcons, 30-14 (A)
(Points—Rams 836, Falcons 489)
ATLANTA vs. MIAMI
Dolphins lead series, 4-0
1970—Dolphins, 20-7 (A)
1974—Dolphins, 42-7 (M)
1980—Dolphins, 20-17 (A)
1983—Dolphins, 31-24 (M)
(Points—Dolphins 113, Falcons 55)
ATLANTA vs. MINNESOTA
Vikings lead series, 9-6
1966—Falcons, 20-13 (M)
1967—Falcons, 21-20 (A)
1968—Vikings, 47-7 (M)
1969—Falcons, 10-3 (A)
1970—Vikings, 37-7 (A)
1971—Vikings, 24-7 (M)
1973—Falcons, 20-14 (A)
1974—Vikings, 23-10 (M)
1975—Vikings, 38-0 (M)
1977—Vikings, 14-7 (A)
1980—Vikings, 24-23 (M)
1981—Falcons, 31-30 (A)
1982—*Vikings, 30-24 (M)
1984—Vikings, 27-20 (M)
1985—Falcons, 14-13 (A)
(Points—Vikings 357, Falcons 221)

**NFC First Round Playoff*
ATLANTA vs. NEW ENGLAND
Series tied, 2-2
1972—Patriots, 21-20 (NE)
1977—Patriots, 16-10 (A)
1980—Falcons, 37-21 (NE)
1983—Falcons, 24-13 (A)
(Points—Falcons 91, Patriots 71)
ATLANTA vs. NEW ORLEANS
Falcons lead series, 23-11
1967—Saints, 27-24 (NO)
1969—Falcons, 45-17 (A)
1970—Falcons, 14-3 (NO)
Falcons, 32-14 (A)
1971—Falcons, 28-6 (A)
Falcons, 24-20 (NO)
1972—Falcons, 21-14 (NO)
Falcons, 36-20 (A)
1973—Falcons, 62-7 (NO)
Falcons, 14-10 (A)
1974—Saints, 14-13 (NO)
Saints, 13-3 (A)
1975—Falcons, 14-7 (A)
Saints, 23-7 (NO)
1976—Saints, 30-0 (NO)
Falcons, 23-20 (A)
1977—Saints, 21-20 (NO)
Falcons, 35-7 (A)
1978—Falcons, 20-17 (NO)
Falcons, 20-17 (A)
1979—Falcons, 40-34 (NO) OT
Saints, 37-6 (A)
1980—Falcons, 41-14 (NO)
Falcons, 31-13 (A)
1981—Falcons, 27-0 (A)
Falcons, 41-10 (NO)
1982—Falcons, 35-0 (A)
Saints, 35-6 (NO)
1983—Saints, 19-17 (A)
Saints, 27-10 (NO)
1984—Falcons, 36-28 (NO)
Saints, 17-13 (A)
1985—Falcons, 31-24 (A)
Falcons, 16-10 (NO)
(Points—Falcons 805, Saints 575)
ATLANTA vs. N.Y. GIANTS
Falcons lead series, 6-5
1966—Falcons, 27-16 (NY)
1968—Falcons, 24-21 (A)
1971—Giants, 21-17 (A)
1974—Falcons, 14-7 (New Haven)
1977—Falcons, 17-3 (A)
1978—Falcons, 23-20 (A)
1979—Giants, 24-3 (NY)
1981—Giants, 27-24 (A) OT
1982—Falcons, 16-14 (NY)
1983—Giants, 16-13 (A) OT
1984—Giants, 19-7 (A)
(Points—Giants 188, Falcons 185)
ATLANTA vs. N.Y. JETS
Falcons lead series, 2-1
1973—Falcons, 28-20 (NY)
1980—Jets, 14-7 (A)
1983—Falcons, 27-21 (NY)
(Points—Falcons 62, Jets 55)
ATLANTA vs. PHILADELPHIA
Series tied, 6-6-1
1966—Eagles, 23-10 (P)
1967—Eagles, 38-7 (A)
1969—Falcons, 27-3 (P)
1970—Tie, 13-13 (P)
1973—Falcons, 44-27 (P)
1976—Eagles, 14-13 (A)
1978—*Falcons, 14-13 (A)
1979—Falcons, 14-10 (P)
1980—Falcons, 20-17 (P)
1981—Eagles, 16-13 (P)
1983—Eagles, 28-24 (A)
1984—Falcons, 26-10 (A)
1985—Eagles, 23-17 (P) OT
(Points—Falcons 242, Eagles 235)
**NFC First Round Playoff*
ATLANTA vs. PITTSBURGH
Steelers lead series, 6-1
1966—Steelers, 57-33 (A)
1968—Steelers, 41-21 (A)
1970—Falcons, 27-16 (A)
1974—Steelers, 24-17 (P)
1978—Steelers, 31-7 (P)
1981—Steelers, 34-20 (A)
1984—Steelers, 35-10 (P)
(Points—Steelers 238, Falcons 135)
ATLANTA vs. ST. LOUIS
Cardinals lead series, 6-3
1966—Falcons, 16-10 (A)
1968—Cardinals, 17-12 (StL)
1971—Cardinals, 26-9 (A)
1973—Cardinals, 32-10 (A)
1975—Cardinals, 23-20 (StL)
1978—Cardinals, 42-21 (StL)

1980—Falcons, 33-27 (StL) OT
1981—Falcons, 41-20 (A)
1982—Cardinals, 23-20 (A)
(Points—Cardinals 220, Falcons 182)
ATLANTA vs. SAN DIEGO
Falcons lead series, 2-0
1973—Falcons, 41-0 (SD)
1979—Falcons, 28-26 (SD)
(Points—Falcons 69, Chargers 26)
ATLANTA vs. SAN FRANCISCO
49ers lead series, 21-17
1966—49ers, 44-7 (A)
1967—49ers, 38-7 (SF)
49ers, 34-28 (A)
1968—49ers, 28-13 (SF)
49ers, 14-12 (A)
1969—Falcons, 24-12 (A)
Falcons, 21-7 (SF)
1970—Falcons, 21-20 (A)
49ers, 24-20 (SF)
1971—Falcons, 20-17 (A)
49ers, 24-3 (SF)
1972—49ers, 49-14 (A)
49ers, 20-0 (SF)
1973—49ers, 13-9 (A)
Falcons, 17-3 (SF)
1974—49ers, 16-10 (A)
49ers, 27-0 (SF)
1975—Falcons, 17-3 (SF)
Falcons, 31-9 (A)
1976—49ers, 15-0 (SF)
Falcons, 21-16 (A)
1977—Falcons, 7-0 (SF)
49ers, 10-3 (A)
1978—Falcons, 20-17 (SF)
Falcons, 21-10 (A)
1979—49ers, 20-15 (SF)
Falcons, 31-21 (A)
1980—Falcons, 20-17 (SF)
Falcons, 35-10 (A)
1981—Falcons, 34-17 (A)
49ers, 17-14 (SF)
1982—Falcons, 17-7 (SF)
1983—49ers, 24-20 (SF)
Falcons, 28-24 (A)
1984—49ers, 14-5 (SF)
49ers, 35-17 (A)
1985—49ers, 35-16 (SF)
49ers, 38-17 (A)
(Points—49ers 749, Falcons 615)
ATLANTA vs. SEATTLE
Seahawks lead series, 3-0
1976—Seahawks, 30-13 (S)
1979—Seahawks, 31-28 (A)
1985—Seahawks, 30-26 (S)
(Points—Seahawks 91, Falcons 67)
ATLANTA vs. TAMPA BAY
Buccaneers lead series, 3-2
1977—Falcons, 17-0 (TB)
1978—Buccaneers, 14-9 (TB)
1979—Falcons, 17-14 (A)
1981—Buccaneers, 24-23 (TB)
1984—Buccaneers, 23-6 (TB)
(Points—Buccaneers 75, Falcons 72)
ATLANTA vs. WASHINGTON
Redskins lead series, 9-2-1
1966—Redskins, 33-20 (W)
1967—Tie, 20-20 (A)
1969—Redskins, 27-20 (W)
1972—Redskins, 24-13 (W)
1975—Redskins, 30-27 (A)
1977—Redskins, 10-6 (W)
1978—Falcons, 20-17 (A)
1979—Redskins, 16-7 (A)
1980—Falcons, 10-6 (A)
1983—Redskins, 37-21 (W)
1984—Redskins, 27-14 (W)
1985—Redskins, 44-10 (A)
(Points—Redskins 291, Falcons 188)

BUFFALO vs. ATLANTA
Series tied, 2-2;
See Atlanta vs. Buffalo
BUFFALO vs. CHICAGO
Bears lead series, 2-1
1970—Bears, 31-13 (C)
1974—Bills, 16-6 (B)
1979—Bears, 7-0 (B)
(Points—Bears 44, Bills 29)
BUFFALO vs. CINCINNATI
Bengals lead series, 8-5
1968—Bengals, 34-23 (C)
1969—Bills, 16-13 (B)
1970—Bengals, 43-14 (B)
1973—Bengals, 16-13 (B)
1975—Bengals, 33-24 (C)
1978—Bills, 5-0 (B)
1979—Bills, 51-24 (B)
1980—Bills, 14-0 (C)
1981—Bengals, 27-24 (C) OT

*Bengals, 28-21 (C)
1983—Bills, 10-6 (C)
1984—Bengals, 52-21 (C)
1985—Bengals, 23-17 (B)
(Points—Bengals 299, Bills 253)
AFC Divisional Playoff

BUFFALO vs. CLEVELAND
Browns lead series, 5-2
1972—Browns, 27-10 (C)
1974—Bills, 15-10 (C)
1977—Browns, 27-16 (B)
1978—Browns, 41-20 (C)
1981—Bills, 22-13 (B)
1984—Browns, 13-10 (B)
1985—Browns, 17-7 (C)
(Points—Browns 148, Bills 100)

BUFFALO vs. DALLAS
Cowboys lead series, 3-1
1971—Cowboys, 49-37 (B)
1976—Cowboys, 17-10 (D)
1981—Cowboys, 27-14 (D)
1984—Bills, 14-3 (B)
(Points—Cowboys 96, Bills 75)

BUFFALO vs. DENVER
Bills lead series, 13-9-1
1960—Broncos, 27-21 (B)
Tie, 38-38 (D)
1961—Broncos, 22-10 (B)
Bills, 23-10 (D)
1962—Broncos, 23-20 (B)
Bills, 45-38 (D)
1963—Bills, 30-28 (D)
Bills, 27-17 (B)
1964—Bills, 30-13 (B)
Bills, 30-19 (D)
1965—Bills, 30-15 (D)
Bills, 31-13 (B)
1966—Bills, 38-21 (B)
1967—Bills, 17-16 (D)
Broncos, 21-20 (B)
1968—Broncos, 34-32 (D)
1969—Bills, 41-28 (B)
1970—Broncos, 25-10 (B)
1975—Bills, 38-14 (B)
1977—Broncos, 26-6 (D)
1979—Broncos, 19-16 (B)
1981—Bills, 9-7 (B)
1984—Broncos, 37-7 (B)
(Points—Bills 569, Broncos 511)

BUFFALO vs. DETROIT
Series tied, 1-1-1
1972—Tie, 21-21 (B)
1976—Lions, 27-14 (D)
1979—Bills, 20-17 (D)
(Points—Lions 65, Bills 55)

BUFFALO vs. GREEN BAY
Bills lead series, 2-1
1974—Bills, 27-7 (GB)
1979—Bills, 19-12 (B)
1982—Packers, 33-21 (Mil)
(Points—Bills 67, Packers 52)

BUFFALO vs. HOUSTON
Oilers lead series, 17-9
1960—Bills, 25-24 (B)
Oilers, 31-23 (H)
1961—Bills, 22-12 (H)
Oilers, 28-16 (B)
1962—Oilers, 28-23 (B)
Oilers, 17-14 (H)
1963—Oilers, 31-20 (B)
Oilers, 28-14 (H)
1964—Bills, 48-17 (H)
Bills, 24-10 (B)
1965—Oilers, 19-17 (B)
Bills, 29-18 (H)
1966—Bills, 27-20 (B)
Bills, 42-20 (H)
1967—Oilers, 20-3 (B)
Oilers, 10-3 (H)
1968—Oilers, 30-7 (B)
Oilers, 35-6 (H)
1969—Oilers, 17-3 (B)
Oilers, 28-14 (H)
1971—Oilers, 20-14 (B)
1974—Oilers, 21-9 (B)
1976—Oilers, 13-3 (B)
1978—Oilers, 17-10 (H)
1983—Bills, 30-13 (B)
1985—Bills, 20-0 (B)
(Points—Oilers 527, Bills 466)

BUFFALO vs. *INDIANAPOLIS
Series tied, 15-15-1
1970—Tie, 17-17 (Balt)
Colts, 20-14 (Buff)
1971—Colts, 43-0 (Buff)
Colts, 24-0 (Balt)
1972—Colts, 17-0 (Buff)
Colts, 35-7 (Balt)
1973—Bills, 31-13 (Buff)
Bills, 24-17 (Balt)
1974—Bills, 27-14 (Balt)
Bills, 6-0 (Buff)
1975—Bills, 38-31 (Balt)
Colts, 42-35 (Buff)
1976—Colts, 31-13 (Buff)
Colts, 58-20 (Balt)
1977—Colts, 17-14 (Balt)
Colts, 31-13 (Buff)
1978—Bills, 24-17 (Buff)
Bills, 21-14 (Balt)
1979—Bills, 31-13 (Balt)
Colts, 14-13 (Buff)
1980—Colts, 17-12 (Buff)
Colts, 28-24 (Balt)
1981—Bills, 35-3 (Balt)
Bills, 23-17 (Buff)
1982—Bills, 20-0 (Buff)
1983—Bills, 28-23 (Buff)
Bills, 30-7 (Balt)
1984—Colts, 31-17 (I)
Bills, 21-15 (Buff)
1985—Colts, 49-17 (I)
Bills, 21-9 (Buff)
(Points—Colts 667, Bills 596)
Franchise in Baltimore prior to 1984

BUFFALO vs. *KANSAS CITY
Bills lead series, 14-11-1
1960—Texans, 45-28 (B)
Texans, 24-7 (D)
1961—Bills, 27-24 (B)
Bills, 30-20 (D)
1962—Texans, 41-21 (D)
Bills, 23-14 (B)
1963—Tie, 27-27 (B)
Bills, 35-26 (KC)
1964—Bills, 34-17 (B)
Bills, 35-22 (KC)
1965—Bills, 23-7 (KC)
Bills, 34-25 (B)
1966—Chiefs, 42-20 (B)
Bills, 29-14 (KC)
**Chiefs, 31-7 (B)
1967—Chiefs, 23-13 (KC)
1968—Chiefs, 18-7 (B)
1969—Chiefs, 29-7 (B)
Chiefs, 22-19 (KC)
1971—Chiefs, 22-9 (KC)
1973—Bills, 23-14 (B)
1976—Bills, 50-17 (B)
1978—Bills, 28-13 (B)
Chiefs, 14-10 (KC)
1982—Bills, 14-9 (B)
1983—Bills, 14-9 (KC)
(Points—Chiefs 574, Bills 569)
Franchise in Dallas prior to 1963 and known as Texans
***AFL Championship*

BUFFALO vs. *L.A. RAIDERS
Raiders lead series, 12-11
1960—Bills, 38-9 (B)
Raiders, 20-7 (O)
1961—Raiders, 31-22 (B)
Bills, 26-21 (O)
1962—Bills, 14-6 (B)
Bills, 10-6 (O)
1963—Raiders, 35-17 (O)
Bills, 12-0 (B)
1964—Bills, 23-20 (B)
Raiders, 16-13 (O)
1965—Bills, 17-12 (B)
Bills, 17-14 (O)
1966—Bills, 31-10 (O)
1967—Raiders, 24-20 (B)
Raiders, 28-21 (O)
1968—Raiders, 48-6 (B)
Raiders, 13-10 (O)
1969—Raiders, 50-21 (O)
1972—Raiders, 28-16 (O)
1974—Bills, 21-20 (B)
1977—Raiders, 34-13 (O)
1980—Bills, 24-7 (B)
1983—Raiders, 27-24 (B)
(Points—Raiders 479, Bills 423)
Franchise in Oakland prior to 1982

BUFFALO vs. L.A. RAMS
Rams lead series, 3-1
1970—Rams, 19-0 (B)
1974—Rams, 19-14 (LA)
1980—Bills, 10-7 (B) OT
1983—Rams, 41-17 (LA)
(Points—Rams 86, Bills 41)

BUFFALO vs. MIAMI
Dolphins lead series, 32-7-1
1966—Bills, 58-24 (B)
Bills, 29-0 (M)
1967—Bills, 35-13 (B)
Dolphins, 17-14 (M)
1968—Tie, 14-14 (M)
Dolphins, 21-17 (B)
1969—Dolphins, 24-6 (M)
Bills, 28-3 (B)
1970—Dolphins, 33-14 (B)
Dolphins, 45-7 (M)
1971—Dolphins, 29-14 (B)
Dolphins, 34-0 (M)
1972—Dolphins, 24-23 (M)
Dolphins, 30-16 (B)
1973—Dolphins, 27-6 (M)
Dolphins, 17-0 (B)
1974—Dolphins, 24-16 (B)
Dolphins, 35-28 (M)
1975—Dolphins, 35-30 (B)
Dolphins, 31-21 (M)
1976—Dolphins, 30-21 (B)
Dolphins, 45-27 (M)
1977—Dolphins, 13-0 (B)
Dolphins, 31-14 (M)
1978—Dolphins, 31-24 (M)
Dolphins, 25-24 (B)
1979—Dolphins, 9-7 (B)
Dolphins, 17-7 (M)
1980—Bills, 17-7 (B)
Dolphins, 17-14 (M)
1981—Bills, 31-21 (B)
Dolphins, 16-6 (M)
1982—Dolphins, 9-7 (B)
Dolphins, 27-10 (M)
1983—Dolphins, 12-0 (B)
Bills, 38-35 (M) OT
1984—Dolphins, 21-17 (B)
Dolphins, 38-7 (M)
1985—Dolphins, 23-14 (B)
Dolphins, 28-0 (M)
(Points—Dolphins 935, Bills 661)

BUFFALO vs. MINNESOTA
Vikings lead series, 4-1
1971—Vikings, 19-0 (M)
1975—Vikings, 35-13 (B)
1979—Vikings, 10-3 (M)
1982—Bills, 23-22 (B)
1985—Vikings, 27-20 (B)
(Points—Vikings 113, Bills 59)

BUFFALO vs. *NEW ENGLAND
Patriots lead series, 28-23-1
1960—Bills, 13-0 (Bos)
Bills, 38-14 (Buff)
1961—Patriots, 23-21 (Buff)
Patriots, 52-21 (Bos)
1962—Tie, 28-28 (Buff)
Patriots, 21-10 (Bos)
1963—Bills, 28-21 (Buff)
Patriots, 17-7 (Bos)
**Patriots, 26-8 (Buff)
1964—Patriots, 36-28 (Buff)
Bills, 24-14 (Bos)
1965—Bills, 24-7 (Buff)
Bills, 23-7 (Bos)
1966—Patriots, 20-10 (Buff)
Patriots, 14-3 (Bos)
1967—Patriots, 23-0 (Buff)
Bills, 44-16 (Bos)
1968—Patriots, 16-7 (Buff)
Patriots, 23-6 (Bos)
1969—Bills, 23-16 (Buff)
Patriots, 35-21 (Bos)
1970—Bills, 45-10 (Bos)
Patriots, 14-10 (Buff)
1971—Patriots, 38-33 (NE)
Bills, 27-20 (Buff)
1972—Bills, 38-14 (Buff)
Bills, 27-24 (NE)
1973—Bills, 31-13 (NE)
Bills, 37-13 (Buff)
1974—Bills, 30-28 (Buff)
Bills, 29-28 (NE)
1975—Bills, 45-31 (Buff)
Bills, 34-14 (NE)
1976—Patriots, 26-22 (Buff)
Patriots, 20-10 (NE)
1977—Bills, 24-14 (NE)
Patriots, 20-7 (Buff)
1978—Patriots, 14-10 (Buff)
Patriots, 26-24 (NE)
1979—Patriots, 26-6 (Buff)
Bills, 16-13 (NE) OT
1980—Bills, 31-13 (Buff)
Patriots, 24-2 (NE)
1981—Bills, 20-17 (Buff)
Bills, 19-10 (NE)
1982—Patriots, 30-19 (NE)
1983—Patriots, 31-0 (Buff)
Patriots, 21-7 (NE)
1984—Patriots, 21-17 (Buff)
Patriots, 38-10 (NE)
1985—Patriots, 17-14 (Buff)
Patriots, 14-3 (NE)
(Points—Patriots 1,071, Bills 1,034)
Franchise in Boston prior to 1971
***Division Playoff*

BUFFALO vs. NEW ORLEANS
Bills lead series, 2-1
1973—Saints, 13-0 (NO)
1980—Bills, 35-26 (NO)
1983—Bills, 27-21 (B)
(Points—Bills 62, Saints 60)

BUFFALO vs. N.Y. GIANTS
Giants lead series, 2-1
1970—Giants, 20-6 (NY)
1975—Giants, 17-14 (B)
1978—Bills, 41-17 (B)
(Points—Bills 61, Giants 54)

BUFFALO vs. *N.Y. JETS
Bills lead series, 26-25
1960—Titans, 27-3 (NY)
Titans, 17-13 (B)
1961—Bills, 41-31 (B)
Titans, 21-14 (NY)
1962—Titans, 17-6 (B)
Bills, 20-3 (NY)
1963—Bills, 45-14 (B)
Bills, 19-10 (NY)
1964—Bills, 34-24 (B)
Bills, 20-7 (NY)
1965—Bills, 33-21 (B)
Jets, 14-12 (NY)
1966—Bills, 33-23 (NY)
Bills, 14-3 (B)
1967—Bills, 20-17 (B)
Jets, 20-10 (NY)
1968—Bills, 37-35 (B)
Jets, 25-21 (NY)
1969—Jets, 33-19 (B)
Jets, 16-6 (NY)
1970—Bills, 34-31 (B)
Bills, 10-6 (NY)
1971—Jets, 28-17 (NY)
Jets, 20-7 (B)
1972—Jets, 41-24 (B)
Jets, 41-3 (NY)
1973—Bills, 9-7 (B)
Bills, 34-14 (NY)
1974—Bills, 16-12 (B)
Jets, 20-10 (NY)
1975—Bills, 42-14 (B)
Bills, 24-23 (NY)
1976—Jets, 17-14 (NY)
Jets, 19-14 (B)
1977—Jets, 24-19 (B)
Bills, 14-10 (NY)
1978—Jets, 21-20 (B)
Jets, 45-14 (NY)
1979—Bills, 46-31 (B)
Bills, 14-12 (NY)
1980—Bills, 20-10 (B)
Bills, 31-24 (NY)
1981—Bills, 31-0 (B)
Jets, 33-14 (NY)
**Bills, 31-27 (NY)
1983—Jets, 34-10 (B)
Bills, 24-17 (NY)
1984—Jets, 28-26 (B)
Jets, 21-17 (NY)
1985—Jets, 42-3 (NY)
Jets, 27-7 (B)
(Points—Jets 1,077, Bills 1,019)
Jets known as Titans prior to 1963
***AFC First Round Playoff*

BUFFALO vs. PHILADELPHIA
Eagles lead series, 3-1
1973—Bills, 27-26 (B)
1981—Eagles, 20-14 (B)
1984—Eagles, 27-17 (B)
1985—Eagles, 21-17 (P)
(Points—Eagles 94, Bills 75)

BUFFALO vs. PITTSBURGH
Steelers lead series, 6-3
1970—Steelers, 23-10 (P)
1972—Steelers, 38-21 (B)
1974—*Steelers, 32-14 (P)
1975—Bills, 30-21 (P)
1978—Steelers, 28-17 (B)
1979—Steelers, 28-0 (P)
1980—Bills, 28-13 (B)
1982—Bills, 13-0 (B)
1985—Steelers, 30-24 (P)
(Points—Steelers 213, Bills 157)
AFC Divisional Playoff

BUFFALO vs. ST. LOUIS
Cardinals lead series, 3-1
1971—Cardinals, 28-23 (B)
1975—Bills, 32-14 (StL)
1981—Cardinals, 24-0 (StL)
1984—Cardinals, 37-7 (StL)
(Points—Cardinals 103, Bills 62)

BUFFALO vs. *SAN DIEGO
Chargers lead series, 17-9-2
1960—Chargers, 24-10 (B)
Bills, 32-3 (LA)
1961—Chargers, 19-11 (B)
Chargers, 28-10 (SD)
1962—Bills, 35-10 (B)
Bills, 40-20 (SD)
1963—Chargers, 14-10 (SD)
Chargers, 23-13 (B)
1964—Bills, 30-3 (B)
Bills, 27-24 (SD)
**Bills, 20-7 (B)
1965—Chargers, 34-3 (B)
Tie, 20-20 (SD)
**Bills, 23-0 (SD)
1966—Chargers, 27-7 (SD)
Tie, 17-17 (B)

1967—Chargers, 37-17 (B)
1968—Chargers, 21-6 (B)
1969—Chargers, 45-6 (SD)
1971—Chargers, 20-3 (SD)
1973—Chargers, 34-7 (SD)
1976—Chargers, 34-13 (B)
1979—Chargers, 27-19 (SD)
1980—Bills, 26-24 (SD)
***Chargers, 20-14 (SD)
1981—Bills, 28-27 (SD)
1985—Chargers, 14-9 (B)
Chargers, 40-7 (SD)
(Points—Chargers 616, Bills 463)
Franchise in Los Angeles prior to 1961
**AFL Championship*
***AFC Divisional Playoff*

BUFFALO vs. SAN FRANCISCO
Bills lead series, 2-1
1972—Bills, 27-20 (B)
1980—Bills, 18-13 (SF)
1983—49ers, 23-10 (B)
(Points—49ers 56, Bills 55)

BUFFALO vs. SEATTLE
Seahawks lead series, 2-0
1977—Seahawks, 56-17 (S)
1984—Seahawks, 31-28 (S)
(Points—Seahawks 87, Bills 45)

BUFFALO vs. TAMPA BAY
Buccaneers lead series, 2-1
1976—Bills, 14-9 (TB)
1978—Buccaneers, 31-10 (TB)
1982—Buccaneers, 24-23 (TB)
(Points—Buccaneers 64, Bills 47)

BUFFALO vs. WASHINGTON
Series tied 2-2
1972—Bills, 24-17 (W)
1977—Redskins, 10-0 (B)
1981—Bills, 21-14 (B)
1984—Redskins, 41-14 (W)
(Points—Redskins 82, Bills 59)

CHICAGO vs. ATLANTA
Falcons lead series, 9-5;
See Atlanta vs. Chicago

CHICAGO vs. BUFFALO
Bears lead series, 2-1;
See Buffalo vs. Chicago

CHICAGO vs. CINCINNATI
Bengals lead series, 2-0;
1972—Bengals, 13-3 (Chi)
1980—Bengals, 17-14 (Chi) OT
(Points—Bengals 30, Bears 17)

CHICAGO vs. CLEVELAND
Browns lead series, 6-2
1951—Browns, 42-21 (Cle)
1954—Browns, 39-10 (Chi)
1960—Browns, 42-0 (Cle)
1961—Bears, 17-14 (Chi)
1967—Browns, 24-0 (Cle)
1969—Browns, 28-24 (Chi)
1972—Bears, 17-0 (Cle)
1980—Browns, 27-21 (Cle)
(Points—Browns 216, Bears 110)

CHICAGO vs. DALLAS
Cowboys lead series, 8-4
1960—Bears, 17-7 (C)
1962—Bears, 34-33 (D)
1964—Cowboys, 24-10 (C)
1968—Cowboys, 34-3 (C)
1971—Bears, 23-19 (C)
1973—Cowboys, 20-17 (C)
1976—Cowboys, 31-21 (D)
1977—*Cowboys, 37-7 (D)
1979—Cowboys, 24-20 (D)
1981—Cowboys, 10-9 (D)
1984—Cowboys, 23-14 (C)
1985—Bears, 44-0 (D)
(Points—Cowboys 262, Bears 219)
NFC Divisional Playoff

CHICAGO vs. DENVER
Bears lead series, 4-3
1971—Broncos, 6-3 (D)
1973—Bears, 33-14 (D)
1976—Broncos, 28-14 (C)
1978—Broncos, 16-7 (D)
1981—Bears, 35-24 (C)
1983—Bears, 31-14 (C)
1984—Bears, 27-0 (C)
(Points—Bears 150, Broncos 102)

CHICAGO vs. *DETROIT
Bears lead series, 64-44-5
1930—Spartans, 7-6 (P)
Bears, 14-6 (C)
1931—Bears, 9-6 (C)
Spartans, 3-0 (P)
1932—Tie, 13-13 (C)
Tie, 7-7 (P)
**Bears, 9-0 (C)
1933—Bears, 17-14 (C)
Bears, 17-7 (P)
1934—Bears, 19-16 (D)
Bears, 10-7 (C)
1935—Tie, 20-20 (C)
Lions, 14-2 (D)
1936—Bears, 12-10 (C)
Lions, 13-7 (D)
1937—Bears, 28-20 (C)
Bears, 13-0 (D)
1938—Lions, 13-7 (C)
Lions, 14-7 (D)
1939—Lions, 10-0 (C)
Bears, 23-13 (D)
1940—Bears, 7-0 (C)
Lions, 17-14 (D)
1941—Bears, 49-0 (C)
Bears, 24-7 (D)
1942—Bears, 16-0 (C)
Bears, 42-0 (D)
1943—Bears, 27-21 (D)
Bears, 35-14 (C)
1944—Tie, 21-21 (C)
Lions, 41-21 (D)
1945—Lions, 16-10 (D)
Lions, 35-28 (C)
1946—Bears, 42-6 (C)
Bears, 45-24 (D)
1947—Bears, 33-24 (C)
Bears, 34-14 (D)
1948—Bears, 28-0 (C)
Bears, 42-14 (D)
1949—Bears, 27-24 (C)
Bears, 28-7 (D)
1950—Bears, 35-21 (D)
Bears, 6-3 (C)
1951—Bears, 28-23 (D)
Lions, 41-28 (C)
1952—Bears, 24-23 (C)
Lions, 45-21 (D)
1953—Lions, 20-16 (C)
Lions, 13-7 (D)
1954—Lions, 48-23 (D)
Bears, 28-24 (C)
1955—Bears, 24-14 (D)
Bears, 21-20 (C)
1956—Lions, 42-10 (D)
Bears, 38-21 (C)
1957—Bears, 27-7 (D)
Lions, 21-13 (C)
1958—Bears, 20-7 (D)
Bears, 21-16 (C)
1959—Bears, 24-14 (D)
Bears, 25-14 (C)
1960—Bears, 28-7 (C)
Lions, 36-0 (D)
1961—Bears, 31-17 (D)
Lions, 16-15 (C)
1962—Lions, 11-3 (D)
Bears, 3-0 (C)
1963—Bears, 37-21 (D)
Bears, 24-14 (C)
1964—Lions, 10-0 (C)
Bears, 27-24 (D)
1965—Bears, 38-10 (C)
Bears, 17-10 (D)
1966—Lions, 14-3 (D)
Tie, 10-10 (C)
1967—Bears, 14-3 (C)
Bears, 27-13 (D)
1968—Lions, 42-0 (D)
Lions, 28-10 (C)
1969—Lions, 13-7 (D)
Lions, 20-3 (C)
1970—Lions, 28-14 (D)
Lions, 16-10 (C)
1971—Bears, 28-23 (D)
Lions, 28-3 (C)
1972—Lions, 38-24 (C)
Lions, 14-0 (D)
1973—Lions, 30-7 (C)
Lions, 40-7 (D)
1974—Bears, 17-9 (C)
Lions, 34-17 (D)
1975—Lions, 27-7 (D)
Bears, 25-21 (C)
1976—Bears, 10-3 (C)
Lions, 14-10 (D)
1977—Bears, 30-20 (C)
Bears, 31-14 (D)
1978—Bears, 19-0 (D)
Lions, 21-17 (C)
1979—Bears, 35-7 (C)
Lions, 20-0 (D)
1980—Bears, 24-7 (C)
Bears, 23-17 (D) OT
1981—Lions, 48-17 (D)
Lions, 23-7 (C)
1982—Lions, 17-10 (D)
Bears, 20-17 (C)
1983—Lions, 31-17 (D)
Lions, 38-17 (C)
1984—Bears, 16-14 (C)
Bears, 30-13 (D)
1985—Bears, 24-3 (C)
Bears, 37-17 (D)
(Points—Bears 2,102, Lions 1,906)
Franchise in Portsmouth prior to 1934 and known as the Spartans
**Championship*

***CHICAGO vs. GREEN BAY**
Bears lead series, 70-55-6
1921—Staleys, 20-0 (C)
1923—Bears, 3-0 (GB)
1924—Bears, 3-0 (C)
1925—Packers, 14-10 (GB)
Bears, 21-0 (C)
1926—Tie, 6-6 (GB)
Bears, 19-13 (C)
Tie, 3-3 (C)
1927—Bears, 7-6 (GB)
Bears, 14-6 (C)
1928—Tie, 12-12 (GB)
Packers, 16-6 (C)
Packers, 6-0 (C)
1929—Packers, 23-0 (GB)
Packers, 14-0 (C)
Packers, 25-0 (C)
1930—Packers, 7-0 (GB)
Packers, 13-12 (C)
Bears, 21-0 (C)
1931—Packers, 7-0 (GB)
Packers, 6-2 (C)
Bears, 7-6 (C)
1932—Tie, 0-0 (GB)
Packers, 2-0 (C)
Bears, 9-0 (C)
1933—Bears, 14-7 (GB)
Bears, 10-7 (C)
Bears, 7-6 (C)
1934—Bears, 24-10 (GB)
Bears, 27-14 (C)
1935—Packers, 7-0 (GB)
Packers, 17-14 (C)
1936—Bears, 30-3 (GB)
Packers, 21-10 (C)
1937—Bears, 14-2 (GB)
Packers, 24-14 (C)
1938—Bears, 2-0 (GB)
Packers, 24-17 (C)
1939—Packers, 21-16 (GB)
Bears, 30-27 (C)
1940—Bears, 41-10 (GB)
Bears, 14-7 (C)
1941—Bears, 25-17 (GB)
Packers, 16-14 (C)
**Bears, 33-14 (C)
1942—Bears, 44-28 (GB)
Bears, 38-7 (C)
1943—Tie, 21-21 (GB)
Bears, 21-7 (C)
1944—Packers, 42-28 (GB)
Bears, 21-0 (C)
1945—Packers, 31-21 (GB)
Bears, 28-24 (C)
1946—Bears, 30-7 (GB)
Bears, 10-7 (C)
1947—Packers, 29-20 (GB)
Bears, 20-17 (C)
1948—Bears, 45-7 (GB)
Bears, 7-6 (C)
1949—Bears, 17-0 (GB)
Bears, 24-3 (C)
1950—Packers, 31-21 (GB)
Bears, 28-14 (C)
1951—Bears, 31-20 (GB)
Bears, 24-13 (C)
1952—Bears, 24-14 (GB)
Packers, 41-28 (C)
1953—Bears, 17-13 (GB)
Tie, 21-21 (C)
1954—Bears, 10-3 (GB)
Bears, 28-23 (C)
1955—Packers, 24-3 (GB)
Bears, 52-31 (C)
1956—Bears, 37-21 (GB)
Bears, 38-14 (C)
1957—Packers, 21-17 (GB)
Bears, 21-14 (C)
1958—Bears, 34-20 (GB)
Bears, 24-10 (C)
1959—Packers, 9-6 (GB)
Bears, 28-17 (C)
1960—Bears, 17-14 (GB)
Packers, 41-13 (C)
1961—Packers, 24-0 (GB)
Packers, 31-28 (C)
1962—Packers, 49-0 (GB)
Packers, 38-7 (C)
1963—Bears, 10-3 (GB)
Bears, 26-7 (C)
1964—Packers, 23-12 (GB)
Packers, 17-3 (C)
1965—Packers, 23-14 (GB)
Bears, 31-10 (C)
1966—Packers, 17-0 (C)
Packers, 13-6 (GB)
1967—Packers, 13-10 (GB)
Packers, 17-13 (C)
1968—Bears, 13-10 (GB)
Packers, 28-27 (C)
1969—Packers, 17-0 (GB)
Packers, 21-3 (C)
1970—Packers, 20-19 (GB)
Bears, 35-17 (C)
1971—Packers, 17-14 (C)
Packers, 31-10 (GB)
1972—Packers, 20-17 (GB)
Packers, 23-17 (C)
1973—Bears, 31-17 (GB)
Packers, 21-0 (C)
1974—Bears, 10-9 (C)
Packers, 20-3 (Mil)
1975—Bears, 27-14 (C)
Packers, 28-7 (GB)
1976—Bears, 24-13 (C)
Bears, 16-10 (GB)
1977—Bears, 26-0 (GB)
Bears, 21-10 (C)
1978—Packers, 24-14 (GB)
Bears, 14-0 (C)
1979—Bears, 6-3 (C)
Bears, 15-14 (GB)
1980—Packers, 12-6 (GB) OT
Bears, 61-7 (C)
1981—Packers, 16-9 (C)
Packers, 21-17 (GB)
1983—Packers, 31-28 (GB)
Bears, 23-21 (C)
1984—Bears, 9-7 (GB)
Packers, 20-14 (C)
1985—Bears, 23-7 (C)
Bears, 16-10 (GB)
(Points—Bears 2,183, Packers 1,928)
Bears known as Staleys prior to 1922
**Division Playoff*

CHICAGO vs. HOUSTON
Oilers lead series, 2-1
1973—Bears, 35-14 (C)
1977—Oilers, 47-0 (H)
1980—Oilers, 10-6 (C)
(Points—Oilers 71, Bears 41)

CHICAGO vs. *INDIANAPOLIS
Colts lead series, 21-14
1953—Colts, 13-9 (B)
Colts, 16-14 (C)
1954—Bears, 28-9 (C)
Bears, 28-13 (B)
1955—Colts, 23-17 (B)
Bears, 38-10 (C)
1956—Colts, 28-21 (B)
Bears, 58-27 (C)
1957—Colts, 21-10 (B)
Colts, 29-14 (C)
1958—Colts, 51-38 (B)
Colts, 17-0 (C)
1959—Bears, 26-21 (B)
Colts, 21-7 (C)
1960—Colts, 42-7 (B)
Colts, 24-20 (C)
1961—Bears, 24-10 (C)
Bears, 21-20 (B)
1962—Bears, 35-15 (C)
Bears, 57-0 (B)
1963—Bears, 10-3 (C)
Bears, 17-7 (B)
1964—Colts, 52-0 (B)
Colts, 40-24 (C)
1965—Colts, 26-21 (C)
Bears, 13-0 (B)
1966—Bears. 27-17 (C)
Colts, 21-16 (B)
1967—Colts, 24-3 (C)
1968—Colts, 28-7 (B)
1969—Colts, 24-21 (C)
1970—Colts, 21-20 (B)
1975—Colts, 35-7 (C)
1983—Colts, 22-19 (B) OT
1985—Bears, 17-10 (C)
(Points—Colts 740, Bears 694)
Franchise in Baltimore prior to 1984

CHICAGO vs. KANSAS CITY
Bears lead series, 2-1
1973—Chiefs, 19-7 (KC)
1977—Bears, 28-27 (C)
1981—Bears, 16-13 (KC) OT
(Points—Chiefs 59, Bears 51)

CHICAGO vs. *L.A. RAIDERS
Raiders lead series, 3-2
1972—Raiders, 28-21 (O)
1976—Raiders, 28-27 (C)
1978—Raiders, 25-19 (C) OT
1981—Bears, 23-6 (O)
1984—Bears, 17-6 (C)
(Points—Bears 107, Raiders 93)
Franchise in Oakland prior to 1982

CHICAGO vs. *L.A. RAMS
Bears lead series, 43-27-3
1937—Bears, 20-2 (Clev)
Bears, 15-7 (C)
1938—Rams, 14-7 (C)
Rams, 23-21 (Clev)
1939—Bears, 30-21 (Clev)
Bears, 35-21 (C)
1940—Bears, 21-14 (Clev)
Bears, 47-25 (C)
1941—Bears, 48-21 (Clev)

Bears, 31-13 (C)
1942—Bears, 21-7 (Clev)
Bears, 47-0 (C)
1944—Rams, 19-7 (Clev)
Bears, 28-21 (C)
1945—Rams, 17-0 (Clev)
Rams, 41-21 (C)
1946—Tie, 28-28 (C)
Bears, 27-21 (LA)
1947—Bears, 41-21 (LA)
Rams, 17-14 (C)
1948—Bears, 42-21 (C)
Bears, 21-6 (LA)
1949—Rams, 31-16 (C)
Rams, 27-24 (LA)
1950—Bears, 24-20 (LA)
Bears, 24-14 (C)
**Rams, 24-14 (LA)
1951—Rams, 42-17 (C)
1952—Rams, 31-7 (LA)
Rams, 40-24 (C)
1953—Rams, 38-24 (LA)
Bears, 24-21 (C)
1954—Rams, 42-38 (LA)
Bears, 24-13 (C)
1955—Bears, 31-20 (LA)
Bears, 24-3 (C)
1956—Bears, 35-24 (LA)
Bears, 30-21 (C)
1957—Bears, 34-26 (C)
Bears, 16-10 (LA)
1958—Bears, 31-10 (C)
Rams, 41-35 (LA)
1959—Rams, 28-21 (C)
Bears, 26-21 (LA)
1960—Bears, 34-27 (C)
Tie, 24-24 (LA)
1961—Bears, 21-17 (LA)
Bears, 28-24 (C)
1962—Bears, 27-23 (LA)
Bears, 30-14 (C)
1963—Bears, 52-14 (LA)
Bears, 6-0 (C)
1964—Bears, 38-17 (C)
Bears, 34-24 (LA)
1965—Rams, 30-28 (LA)
Bears, 31-6 (C)
1966—Rams, 31-17 (LA)
Bears, 17-10 (C)
1967—Rams, 28-17 (C)
1968—Bears, 17-16 (LA)
1969—Rams, 9-7 (C)
1971—Rams, 17-3 (LA)
1972—Tie, 13-13 (C)
1973—Rams, 26-0 (C)
1975—Rams, 38-10 (LA)
1976—Rams, 20-12 (LA)
1977—Bears, 24-23 (C)
1979—Bears, 27-23 (C)
1981—Rams, 24-7 (C)
1982—Bears, 34-26 (LA)
1983—Rams, 21-14 (LA)
1984—Rams, 29-13 (LA)
1985—***Bears, 24-0 (C)
(Points—Bears 1,724, Rams 1,501)
**Franchise in Cleveland prior to 1946*
***Conference Playoff*
****NFC Championship*

CHICAGO vs. MIAMI
Dolphins lead series, 4-0
1971—Dolphins, 34-3 (M)
1975—Dolphins, 46-13 (C)
1979—Dolphins, 31-16 (M)
1985—Dolphins, 38-24 (M)
(Points—Dolphins 149, Bears 56)

CHICAGO vs. MINNESOTA
Vikings lead series, 25-22-2
1961—Vikings, 37-13 (M)
Bears, 52-35 (C)
1962—Bears, 13-0 (M)
Bears, 31-30 (C)
1963—Bears, 28-7 (M)
Tie, 17-17 (C)
1964—Bears, 34-28 (M)
Vikings, 41-14 (C)
1965—Bears, 45-37 (M)
Vikings, 24-17 (C)
1966—Bears, 13-10 (M)
Bears, 41-28 (C)
1967—Bears, 17-7 (M)
Tie, 10-10 (C)
1968—Bears, 27-17 (M)
Bears, 26-24 (C)
1969—Vikings, 31-0 (C)
Vikings, 31-14 (M)
1970—Vikings, 24-0 (C)
Vikings, 16-13 (M)
1971—Bears, 20-17 (M)
Vikings, 27-10 (C)
1972—Bears, 13-10 (C)
Vikings, 23-10 (M)
1973—Vikings, 22-13 (C)
Vikings, 31-13 (M)
1974—Vikings, 11-7 (M)
Vikings, 17-0 (C)
1975—Vikings, 28-3 (M)
Vikings, 13-9 (C)
1976—Vikings, 20-19 (M)
Bears, 14-13 (C)
1977—Vikings, 22-16 (M) OT
Bears, 10-7 (C)
1978—Vikings, 24-20 (C)
Vikings, 17-14 (M)
1979—Bears, 26-7 (C)
Vikings, 30-27 (M)
1980—Vikings, 34-14 (C)
Vikings, 13-7 (M)
1981—Vikings, 24-21 (M)
Bears, 10-9 (C)
1982—Vikings, 35-7 (M)
1983—Vikings, 23-14 (C)
Bears, 19-13 (M)
1984—Bears, 16-7 (C)
Bears, 34-3 (M)
1985—Bears, 33-24 (M)
Bears, 27-9 (C)
(Points—Vikings 987, Bears 871)

CHICAGO vs. NEW ENGLAND
Bears lead series, 3-2
1973—Patriots, 13-10 (C)
1979—Patriots, 27-7 (C)
1982—Bears, 26-13 (C)
1985—Bears, 20-7 (C)
*Bears, 46-10 (New Orleans)
(Points—Bears 109, Patriots 70)
**Super Bowl XX*

CHICAGO vs. NEW ORLEANS
Bears lead series, 7-4
1968—Bears, 23-17 (NO)
1970—Bears, 24-3 (NO)
1971—Bears, 35-14 (C)
1973—Saints, 21-16 (NO)
1974—Bears, 24-10 (C)
1975—Bears, 42-17 (NO)
1977—Saints, 42-24 (C)
1980—Bears, 22-3 (C)
1982—Saints, 10-0 (C)
1983—Saints, 34-31 (NO) OT
1984—Bears, 20-7 (C)
(Points—Bears 261, Saints 178)

CHICAGO vs. N.Y. GIANTS
Bears lead series, 27-16-2
1925—Bears, 19-7 (NY)
Giants, 9-0 (C)
1926—Bears, 7-0 (C)
1927—Giants, 13-7 (NY)
1928—Bears, 13-0 (C)
1929—Giants, 26-14 (C)
Giants, 34-0 (NY)
Giants, 14-9 (C)
1930—Giants, 12-0 (C)
Bears, 12-0 (NY)
1931—Bears, 6-0 (C)
Bears, 12-6 (NY)
Giants, 25-6 (C)
1932—Bears, 28-8 (NY)
Bears, 6-0 (C)
1933—Bears, 14-10 (C)
Giants, 3-0 (NY)
*Bears, 23-21 (C)
1934—Bears, 27-7 (C)
Bears, 10-9 (NY)
*Giants, 30-13 (NY)
1935—Bears, 20-3 (NY)
Giants, 3-0 (C)
1936—Bears, 25-7 (NY)
1937—Tie, 3-3 (NY)
1939—Giants, 16-13 (NY)
1940—Bears, 37-21 (NY)
1941—*Bears, 37-9 (C)
1942—Bears, 26-7 (NY)
1943—Bears, 56-7 (NY)
1946—Giants, 14-0 (NY)
*Bears, 24-14 (NY)
1948—Bears, 35-14 (C)
1949—Giants, 35-28 (NY)
1956—Tie, 17-17 (NY)
*Giants, 47-7 (NY)
1962—Giants, 26-24 (C)
1963—*Bears, 14-10 (C)
1965—Bears, 35-14 (NY)
1967—Bears, 34-7 (C)
1969—Giants, 28-24 (NY)
1970—Bears, 24-16 (NY)
1974—Bears, 16-13 (C)
1977—Bears, 12-9 (NY) OT
1985—**Bears, 21-0 (C)
(Points—Bears 758, Giants 574)
**NFL Championship*
***NFC Divisional Playoff*

CHICAGO vs. N.Y. JETS
Bears lead series, 2-1
1974—Jets, 23-21 (C)
1979—Bears, 23-13 (C)
1985—Bears, 19-6 (NY)
(Points—Bears 63, Jets 42)

CHICAGO vs. PHILADELPHIA
Bears lead series, 19-4-1
1933—Tie, 3-3 (P)
1935—Bears, 39-0 (P)
1936—Bears, 17-0 (P)
Bears, 28-7 (P)
1938—Bears, 28-6 (P)
1939—Bears, 27-14 (C)
1941—Bears, 49-14 (P)
1942—Bears, 45-14 (C)
1944—Bears, 28-7 (P)
1946—Bears, 21-14 (C)
1947—Bears, 40-7 (C)
1948—Eagles, 12-7 (P)
1949—Bears, 38-21 (C)
1955—Bears, 17-10 (C)
1961—Eagles, 16-14 (P)
1963—Bears, 16-7 (C)
1968—Bears, 29-16 (P)
1970—Bears, 20-16 (C)
1972—Bears, 21-12 (P)
1975—Bears, 15-13 (C)
1979—*Eagles, 27-17 (P)
1980—Eagles, 17-14 (P)
1983—Bears, 7-6 (P)
Bears, 17-14 (C)
(Points—Bears 557, Eagles 273)
**NFC First Round Playoff*

CHICAGO vs. *PITTSBURGH
Bears lead series, 13-4-1
1934—Bears, 28-0 (P)
1935—Bears, 23-7 (P)
1936—Bears, 27-9 (P)
Bears, 26-6 (C)
1937—Bears, 7-0 (P)
1939—Bears, 32-0 (P)
1941—Bears, 34-7 (C)
1945—Bears, 28-7 (P)
1947—Bears, 49-7 (C)
1949—Bears, 30-21 (C)
1958—Steelers, 24-10 (P)
1959—Bears, 27-21 (C)
1963—Tie, 17-17 (P)
1967—Steelers, 41-13 (P)
1969—Bears, 38-7 (C)
1971—Bears, 17-15 (C)
1975—Steelers, 34-3 (P)
1980—Steelers, 38-3 (P)
(Points—Bears 412, Steelers 261)
**Steelers known as Pirates prior to 1941*

***CHICAGO vs. **ST. LOUIS**
Bears lead series, 50-25-6
(NP denotes Normal Park;
Wr denotes Wrigley Field;
Co denotes Comiskey Park;
So denotes Soldier Field;
all Chicago)
1920—Cardinals, 7-6 (NP)
Staleys, 10-0 (Wr)
1921—Tie, 0-0 (Wr)
1922—Cardinals, 6-0 (Co)
Cardinals, 9-0 (Co)
1923—Bears, 3-0 (Wr)
1924—Bears, 6-0 (Wr)
Bears, 21-0 (Co)
1925—Cardinals, 9-0 (Co)
Tie, 0-0 (Wr)
1926—Bears, 16-0 (Wr)
Bears, 10-0 (So)
Tie, 0-0 (Wr)
1927—Bears, 9-0 (NP)
Cardinals, 3-0 (Wr)
1928—Bears, 15-0 (NP)
Bears, 34-0 (Wr)
1929—Tie, 0-0 (Wr)
Cardinals, 40-6 (Co)
1930—Bears, 32-6 (Co)
Bears, 6-0 (Wr)
1931—Bears, 26-13 (Wr)
Bears, 18-7 (Wr)
1932—Tie, 0-0 (Wr)
Bears, 34-0 (Wr)
1933—Bears, 12-9 (Wr)
Bears, 22-6 (Wr)
1934—Bears, 20-0 (Wr)
Bears, 17-6 (Wr)
1935—Tie, 7-7 (Wr)
Bears, 13-0 (Wr)
1936—Bears, 7-3 (Wr)
Cardinals, 14-7 (Wr)
1937—Bears, 16-7 (Wr)
Bears, 42-28 (Wr)
1938—Bears, 16-13 (So)
Bears, 34-28 (Wr)
1939—Bears, 44-7 (Wr)
Bears, 48-7 (Co)
1940—Cardinals, 21-7 (Co)
Bears, 31-23 (Wr)
1941—Bears, 53-7 (Wr)
Bears, 34-24 (Co)
1942—Bears, 41-14 (Wr)
Bears, 21-7 (Co)
1943—Bears, 20-0 (Wr)
Bears, 35-24 (Co)
1945—Cardinals, 16-7 (Wr)
Bears, 28-20 (Co)
1946—Bears, 34-17 (Co)
Cardinals, 35-28 (Wr)
1947—Cardinals, 31-7 (Co)
Cardinals, 30-21 (Wr)
1948—Bears, 28-17 (Co)
Cardinals, 24-21 (Wr)
1949—Bears, 17-7 (Co)
Bears, 52-21 (Wr)
1950—Bears, 27-6 (Wr)
Cardinals, 20-10 (Co)
1951—Cardinals, 28-14 (Co)
Cardinals, 24-14 (Wr)
1952—Cardinals, 21-10 (Co)
Bears, 10-7 (Wr)
1953—Cardinals, 24-17 (Wr)
1954—Bears, 29-7 (Co)
1955—Cardinals, 53-14 (Co)
1956—Bears, 10-3 (Wr)
1957—Bears, 14-6 (Co)
1958—Bears, 30-14 (Wr)
1959—Bears, 31-7 (So)
1965—Bears, 34-13 (Wr)
1966—Cardinals, 24-17 (StL)
1967—Bears, 30-3 (Wr)
1969—Cardinals, 20-17 (StL)
1972—Bears, 27-10 (StL)
1975—Cardinals, 34-20 (So)
1977—Cardinals, 16-13 (StL)
1978—Bears, 17-10 (So)
1979—Bears, 42-6 (So)
1982—Cardinals, 10-7 (So)
1984—Cardinals, 38-21 (StL)
(Points—Bears 1,517, Cardinals 977)
**Franchise in Decatur prior to 1921; Bears known as Staleys prior to 1922*
***Franchise in Chicago prior to 1960*

CHICAGO vs. SAN DIEGO
Chargers lead series, 4-1
1970—Chargers, 20-7 (C)
1974—Chargers, 28-21 (SD)
1978—Chargers, 40-7 (SD)
1981—Bears, 20-17 (C) OT
1984—Chargers, 20-7 (SD)
(Points—Chargers 125, Bears 62)

CHICAGO vs. SAN FRANCISCO
Bears lead series, 24-23-1
1950—Bears, 32-20 (SF)
Bears, 17-0 (C)
1951—Bears, 13-7 (C)
1952—49ers, 40-16 (C)
Bears, 20-17 (SF)
1953—49ers, 35-28 (C)
49ers, 24-14 (SF)
1954—49ers, 31-24 (C)
Bears, 31-27 (SF)
1955—49ers, 20-19 (C)
Bears, 34-23 (SF)
1956—Bears, 31-7 (C)
Bears, 38-21 (SF)
1957—49ers, 21-17 (C)
49ers, 21-17 (SF)
1958—Bears, 28-6 (C)
Bears, 27-14 (SF)
1959—49ers, 20-17 (SF)
Bears, 14-3 (C)
1960—Bears, 27-10 (C)
49ers, 25-7 (SF)
1961—Bears, 31-0 (C)
49ers, 41-31 (SF)
1962—Bears, 30-14 (SF)
49ers, 34-27 (C)
1963—49ers, 20-14 (SF)
Bears, 27-7 (C)
1964—49ers, 31-21 (SF)
Bears, 23-21 (C)
1965—49ers, 52-24 (SF)
Bears, 61-20 (C)
1966—Tie, 30-30 (C)
49ers, 41-14 (SF)
1967—Bears, 28-14 (SF)
1968—Bears, 27-19 (C)
1969—49ers, 42-21 (SF)
1970—49ers, 37-16 (C)
1971—49ers, 13-0 (SF)
1972—49ers, 34-21 (C)
1974—49ers, 34-0 (C)
1975—49ers, 31-3 (SF)
1976—Bears, 19-12 (SF)
1978—Bears, 16-13 (SF)
1979—Bears, 28-27 (SF)
1981—49ers, 28-17 (SF)
1983—Bears, 13-3 (C)
1984—*49ers, 23-0 (SF)
1985—Bears, 26-10 (SF)
(Points—49ers 1,043, Bears 1,039)
**NFC Championship*

CHICAGO vs. SEATTLE
Seahawks lead series, 3-1
1976—Bears, 34-7 (S)
1978—Seahawks, 31-29 (C)

1982—Seahawks, 20-14 (S)
1984—Seahawks, 38-9 (S)
(Points—Seahawks 96, Bears 86)
CHICAGO vs. TAMPA BAY
Bears lead series, 12-4
1977—Bears, 10-0 (TB)
1978—Buccaneers, 33-19 (TB)
Bears, 14-3 (C)
1979—Buccaneers, 17-13 (C)
Bears, 14-0 (TB)
1980—Bears, 23-0 (C)
Bears, 14-13 (TB)
1981—Bears, 28-17 (C)
Buccaneers, 20-10 (TB)
1982—Buccaneers, 26-23 (TB) OT
1983—Bears, 17-10 (C)
Bears, 27-0 (TB)
1984—Bears, 34-14 (C)
Bears, 44-9 (TB)
1985—Bears, 38-28 (C)
Bears, 27-19 (TB)
(Points—Bears 355, Buccaneers 209)
CHICAGO vs. *WASHINGTON
Bears lead series, 20-11-1
1932—Tie, 7-7 (B)
1933—Bears, 7-0 (C)
Redskins, 10-0 (B)
1934—Bears, 21-0 (B)
1935—Bears, 30-14 (B)
1936—Bears, 26-0 (B)
1937—**Redskins, 28-21 (C)
1938—Bears, 31-7 (C)
1940—Redskins, 7-3 (W)
**Bears, 73-0 (W)
1941—Bears, 35-21 (C)
1942—**Redskins, 14-6 (W)
1943—Redskins, 21-7 (W)
**Bears, 41-21 (C)
1945—Redskins, 28-21 (W)
1946—Bears, 24-20 (C)
1947—Bears, 56-20 (W)
1948—Bears, 48-13 (C)
1949—Bears, 31-21 (W)
1951—Bears, 27-0 (W)
1953—Bears, 27-24 (W)
1957—Redskins, 14-3 (C)
1964—Redskins, 27-20 (W)
1968—Redskins, 38-28 (C)
1971—Bears, 16-15 (C)
1974—Redskins, 42-0 (W)
1976—Bears, 33-7 (C)
1978—Bears, 14-10 (W)
1980—Bears, 35-21 (C)
1981—Redskins, 24-7 (C)
1984—***Bears, 23-19 (W)
1985—Bears, 45-10 (C)
(Points—Bears 766, Redskins 503)
**Franchise in Boston prior to 1937 and known as Braves prior to 1933*
***NFL Championship*
****NFC Divisional Playoff*

CINCINNATI vs. ATLANTA
Bengals lead series, 4-1;
See Atlanta vs. Cincinnati
CINCINNATI vs. BUFFALO
Bengals lead series, 8-5;
See Buffalo vs. Cincinnati
CINCINNATI vs. CHICAGO
Bengals lead series, 2-0;
See Chicago vs. Cincinnati
CINCINNATI vs. CLEVELAND
Bengals lead series, 16-15
1970—Browns, 30-27 (Cle)
Bengals, 14-10 (Cin)
1971—Browns, 27-24 (Cin)
Browns, 31-27 (Cle)
1972—Browns, 27-6 (Cle)
Browns, 27-24 (Cin)
1973—Browns, 17-10 (Cle)
Bengals, 34-17 (Cin)
1974—Bengals, 33-7 (Cin)
Bengals, 34-24 (Cle)
1975—Bengals, 24-17 (Cin)
Browns, 35-23 (Cle)
1976—Bengals, 45-24 (Cle)
Bengals, 21-6 (Cin)
1977—Browns, 13-3 (Cin)
Bengals, 10-7 (Cle)
1978—Browns, 13-10 (Cle) OT
Bengals, 48-16 (Cin)
1979—Browns, 28-27 (Cle)
Bengals, 16-12 (Cin)
1980—Browns, 31-7 (Cle)
Browns, 27-24 (Cin)
1981—Browns, 20-17 (Cin)
Bengals, 41-21 (Cle)
1982—Bengals, 23-10 (Cin)
1983—Browns, 17-7 (Clev)
Bengals, 28-21 (Cin)
1984—Bengals, 12-9 (Cin)
Bengals, 20-17 (Clev) OT
1985—Bengals, 27-10 (Cin)
Browns, 24-6 (Clev)
(Points—Bengals 672, Browns 595)
CINCINNATI vs. DALLAS
Cowboys lead series, 2-1
1973—Cowboys, 38-10 (D)
1979—Cowboys, 38-13 (D)
1985—Bengals, 50-24 (C)
(Points—Cowboys 100, Bengals 73)
CINCINNATI vs. DENVER
Broncos lead series, 8-6
1968—Bengals, 24-10 (C)
Broncos, 10-7 (D)
1969—Broncos, 30-23 (C)
Broncos, 27-16 (D)
1971—Bengals, 24-10 (D)
1972—Bengals, 21-10 (C)
1973—Broncos, 28-10 (D)
1975—Bengals, 17-16 (D)
1976—Bengals, 17-7 (C)
1977—Broncos, 24-13 (C)
1979—Broncos, 10-0 (D)
1981—Bengals, 38-21 (C)
1983—Broncos, 24-17 (D)
1984—Broncos, 20-17 (D)
(Points—Broncos 247, Bengals 244)
CINCINNATI vs. DETROIT
Lions lead series, 2-1
1970—Lions, 38-3 (D)
1974—Lions, 23-19 (C)
1983—Bengals, 17-9 (C)
(Points—Lions 70, Bengals 39)
CINCINNATI vs. GREEN BAY
Bengals lead series, 3-2
1971—Packers, 20-17 (GB)
1976—Bengals, 28-7 (C)
1977—Bengals, 17-7 (Mil)
1980—Packers, 14-9 (GB)
1983—Bengals, 34-14 (C)
(Points—Bengals 105, Packers 62)
CINCINNATI vs. HOUSTON
Bengals lead series, 20-13-1
1968—Oilers, 27-17 (C)
1969—Tie, 31-31 (H)
1970—Oilers, 20-13 (C)
Bengals, 30-20 (H)
1971—Oilers, 10-6 (H)
Bengals, 28-13 (C)
1972—Bengals, 30-7 (C)
Bengals, 61-17 (H)
1973—Bengals, 24-10 (C)
Bengals, 27-24 (H)
1974—Oilers, 34-21 (C)
Oilers, 20-3 (H)
1975—Bengals, 21-19 (H)
Bengals, 23-19 (C)
1976—Bengals, 27-7 (H)
Bengals, 31-27 (C)
1977—Bengals, 13-10 (C) OT
Oilers, 21-16 (H)
1978—Bengals, 28-13 (C)
Oilers, 17-10 (H)
1979—Oilers, 30-27 (C) OT
Oilers, 42-21 (H)
1980—Oilers, 13-10 (C)
Oilers, 23-3 (H)
1981—Oilers, 17-10 (H)
Bengals, 34-21 (C)
1982—Bengals, 27-6 (C)
Bengals, 35-27 (H)
1983—Bengals, 55-14 (H)
Bengals, 38-10 (C)
1984—Bengals, 13-3 (C)
Bengals, 31-13 (H)
1985—Oilers, 44-27 (H)
Bengals, 45-27 (C)
(Points—Bengals 836, Oilers 656)
CINCINNATI vs.*INDIANAPOLIS
Colts lead series, 5-4
1970—**Colts, 17-0 (B)
1972—Colts, 20-19 (C)
1974—Bengals, 24-14 (B)
1976—Colts, 28-27 (B)
1979—Colts, 38-28 (B)
1980—Bengals, 34-33 (C)
1981—Bengals, 41-19 (B)
1982—Bengals, 20-17 (B)
1983—Colts, 34-31 (C)
(Points—Bengals 224, Colts 220)
**Franchise in Baltimore prior to 1984*
***AFC Divisional Playoff*
CINCINNATI vs. KANSAS CITY
Chiefs lead series, 8-7
1968—Chiefs, 13-3 (KC)
Chiefs, 16-9 (C)
1969—Bengals, 24-19 (C)
Chiefs, 42-22 (KC)
1970—Chiefs, 27-19 (C)
1972—Bengals, 23-16 (KC)
1973—Bengals, 14-6 (C)
1974—Bengals, 33-6 (C)
1976—Bengals, 27-24 (KC)
1977—Bengals, 27-7 (KC)
1978—Chiefs, 24-23 (C)
1979—Chiefs, 10-7 (C)
1980—Bengals, 20-6 (KC)
1983—Chiefs, 20-15 (KC)
1984—Chiefs, 27-22 (C)
(Points—Bengals 288, Chiefs 263)
CINCINNATI vs. *L.A. RAIDERS
Raiders lead series, 12-4
1968—Raiders, 31-10 (O)
Raiders, 34-0 (C)
1969—Bengals, 31-17 (C)
Raiders, 37-17 (O)
1970—Bengals, 31-21 (C)
1971—Raiders, 31-27 (O)
1972—Raiders, 20-14 (C)
1974—Raiders, 30-27 (O)
1975—Bengals, 14-10 (C)
**Raiders, 31-28 (O)
1976—Raiders, 35-20 (O)
1978—Raiders, 34-21 (C)
1980—Raiders, 28-17 (O)
1982—Bengals, 31-17 (C)
1983—Raiders, 20-10 (C)
1985—Raiders, 13-6 (LA)
(Points—Raiders 409, Bengals 304)
**Franchise in Oakland prior to 1982*
***AFC Divisional Playoff*
CINCINNATI vs. L.A. RAMS
Bengals lead series, 3-2
1972—Rams, 15-12 (LA)
1976—Bengals, 20-12 (C)
1978—Bengals, 20-19 (LA)
1981—Bengals, 24-10 (C)
1984—Rams, 24-14 (C)
(Points—Bengals 90, Rams 80)
CINCINNATI vs. MIAMI
Dolphins lead series, 7-3
1968—Dolphins, 24-22 (C)
Bengals, 38-21 (M)
1969—Bengals, 27-21 (C)
1971—Dolphins, 23-13 (C)
1973—*Dolphins, 34-16 (M)
1974—Dolphins, 24-3 (M)
1977—Bengals, 23-17 (C)
1978—Dolphins, 21-0 (M)
1980—Dolphins, 17-16 (M)
1983—Dolphins, 38-14 (M)
(Points—Dolphins 240, Bengals 172)
**AFC Divisional Playoff*
CINCINNATI vs. MINNESOTA
Series tied, 2-2
1973—Bengals, 27-0 (C)
1977—Vikings, 42-10 (M)
1980—Bengals, 14-0 (C)
1983—Vikings, 20-14 (M)
(Points—Bengals 65, Vikings 62)
CINCINNATI vs. *NEW ENGLAND
Patriots lead series, 6-3
1968—Patriots, 33-14 (B)
1969—Patriots, 25-14 (C)
1970—Bengals, 45-7 (C)
1972—Bengals, 31-7 (NE)
1975—Bengals, 27-10 (C)
1978—Patriots, 10-3 (C)
1979—Patriots, 20-14 (C)
1984—Patriots, 20-14 (NE)
1985—Patriots,.34-23 (NE)
(Points—Bengals 185, Patriots 166)
**Franchise in Boston prior to 1971*
CINCINNATI vs. NEW ORLEANS
Bengals lead series 3-2
1970—Bengals, 26-6 (C)
1975—Bengals, 21-0 (NO)
1978—Saints, 20-18 (C)
1981—Saints, 17-7 (NO)
1984—Bengals, 24-21 (NO)
(Points—Bengals 96, Saints 64)
CINCINNATI vs. N.Y. GIANTS
Bengals lead series, 3-0
1972—Bengals, 13-10 (C)
1977—Bengals, 30-13 (C)
1985—Bengals, 35-30 (C)
(Points—Bengals 78, Giants 53)
CINCINNATI vs. N.Y. JETS
Jets lead series, 7-3
1968—Jets, 27-14 (NY)
1969—Jets, 21-7 (C)
Jets, 40-7 (NY)
1971—Jets, 35-21 (NY)
1973—Bengals, 20-14 (C)
1976—Bengals, 42-3 (NY)
1981—Bengals, 31-30 (NY)
1982—*Jets, 44-17 (C)
1984—Jets, 43-23 (NY)
1985—Jets, 29-20 (C)
(Points—Jets 286, Bengals 202)
**AFC First Round Playoff*
CINCINNATI vs. PHILADELPHIA
Bengals lead series, 4-0
1971—Bengals, 37-14 (C)
1975—Bengals, 31-0 (P)
1979—Bengals, 37-13 (C)
1982—Bengals, 18-14 (P)
(Points—Bengals 123, Eagles 41)
CINCINNATI vs. PITTSBURGH
Steelers lead series, 17-14
1970—Steelers, 21-10 (P)
Bengals, 34-7 (C)
1971—Steelers, 21-10 (P)
Steelers, 21-13 (C)
1972—Bengals, 15-10 (C)
Steelers, 40-17 (P)
1973—Bengals, 19-7 (C)
Steelers, 20-13 (P)
1974—Bengals, 17-10 (C)
Steelers, 27-3 (P)
1975—Steelers, 30-24 (C)
Steelers, 35-14 (P)
1976—Steelers, 23-6 (P)
Steelers, 7-3 (C)
1977—Steelers, 20-14 (P)
Bengals, 17-10 (C)
1978—Steelers, 28-3 (C)
Steelers, 7-6 (P)
1979—Bengals, 34-10 (C)
Steelers, 37-17 (P)
1980—Bengals, 30-28 (C)
Bengals, 17-16 (P)
1981—Bengals, 34-7 (C)
Bengals, 17-10 (P)
1982—Steelers, 26-20 (P) OT
1983—Steelers, 24-14 (C)
Bengals, 23-10 (P)
1984—Steelers, 38-17 (P)
Bengals, 22-20 (C)
1985—Bengals, 37-24 (P)
Bengals, 26-21 (C)
(Points—Steelers 615, Bengals 546)
CINCINNATI vs. ST. LOUIS
Bengals lead series, 2-1
1973—Bengals, 42-24 (C)
1979—Bengals, 34-28 (C)
1985—Cardinals, 41-27 (StL)
(Points—Bengals 103, Cardinals 93)
CINCINNATI vs. SAN DIEGO
Chargers lead series, 10-7
1968—Chargers, 29-13 (SD)
Chargers, 31-10 (C)
1969—Bengals, 34-20 (C)
Chargers, 21-14 (SD)
1970—Bengals, 17-14 (SD)
1971—Bengals, 31-0 (C)
1973—Bengals, 20-13 (SD)
1974—Chargers, 20-17 (C)
1975—Bengals, 47-17 (C)
1977—Chargers, 24-3 (SD)
1978—Chargers, 22-13 (SD)
1979—Chargers, 26-24 (C)
1980—Chargers, 31-14 (C)
1981—Bengals, 40-17 (SD)
*Bengals, 27-7 (C)
1982—Chargers, 50-34 (SD)
1985—Chargers, 44-41 (C)
(Points—Bengals 399, Chargers 386)
**AFC Championship*
CINCINNATI vs. SAN FRANCISCO
49ers lead series, 4-1
1974—Bengals, 21-3 (SF)
1978—49ers, 28-12 (SF)
1981—49ers, 21-3 (C)
*49ers, 26-21 (Detroit)
1984—49ers, 23-17 (SF)
(Points—49ers 101, Bengals 74)
**Super Bowl XVI*
CINCINNATI vs. SEATTLE
Bengals lead series, 3-2
1977—Bengals, 42-20 (C)
1981—Bengals, 27-21 (C)
1982—Bengals, 24-10 (C)
1984—Seahawks, 26-6 (C)
1985—Seahawks, 28-24 (C)
(Points—Bengals 123, Seahawks 105)
CINCINNATI vs. TAMPA BAY
Bengals lead series, 2-1
1976—Bengals, 21-0 (C)
1980—Buccaneers, 17-12 (C)
1983—Bengals, 23-17 (TB)
(Points—Bengals 56, Buccaneers 34)
CINCINNATI vs. WASHINGTON
Redskins lead series, 3-1
1970—Redskins, 20-0 (W)
1974—Bengals, 28-17 (C)
1979—Redskins, 28-14 (W)
1985—Redskins, 27-24 (W)
(Points—Redskins 92, Bengals 66)

CLEVELAND vs. ATLANTA
Browns lead series, 6-1;
See Atlanta vs. Cleveland
CLEVELAND vs. BUFFALO
Browns lead series, 5-2;
See Buffalo vs. Cleveland
CLEVELAND vs. CHICAGO
Browns lead series, 6-2;
See Chicago vs. Cleveland
CLEVELAND vs. CINCINNATI
Bengals lead series, 16-15;
See Cincinnati vs. Cleveland

CLEVELAND vs. DALLAS
Browns lead series, 15-9
1960—Browns, 48-7 (D)
1961—Browns, 25-7 (C)
Browns, 38-17 (D)
1962—Browns, 19-10 (C)
Cowboys, 45-21 (D)
1963—Browns, 41-24 (D)
Browns, 27-17 (C)
1964—Browns, 27-6 (C)
Browns, 20-16 (D)
1965—Browns, 23-17 (C)
Browns, 24-17 (D)
1966—Browns, 30-21 (C)
Cowboys, 26-14 (D)
1967—Cowboys, 21-14 (C)
*Cowboys, 52-14 (D)
1968—Cowboys, 28-7 (C)
*Browns, 31-20 (C)
1969—Browns, 42-10 (C)
*Browns, 38-14 (D)
1970—Cowboys, 6-2 (C)
1974—Cowboys, 41-17 (D)
1979—Browns, 26-7 (C)
1982—Cowboys, 31-14 (D)
1985—Cowboys, 20-7 (D)
(Points—Browns 569, Cowboys 480)
Conference Championship
CLEVELAND vs. DENVER
Broncos lead series, 8-3
1970—Browns, 27-13 (D)
1971—Broncos, 27-0 (C)
1972—Browns, 27-20 (D)
1974—Browns, 23-21 (C)
1975—Broncos, 16-15 (D)
1976—Broncos, 44-13 (D)
1978—Broncos, 19-7 (C)
1980—Broncos, 19-16 (C)
1981—Broncos, 23-20 (D) OT
1983—Broncos, 27-6 (D)
1984—Broncos, 24-14 (C)
(Points—Broncos 253, Browns 168)
CLEVELAND vs. DETROIT
Lions lead series, 12-3
1952—Lions, 17-6 (D)
*Lions, 17-7 (C)
1953—*Lions, 17-16 (D)
1954—Lions, 14-10 (C)
*Browns, 56-10 (C)
1957—Lions, 20-7 (D)
*Lions, 59-14 (D)
1958—Lions, 30-10 (C)
1963—Lions, 38-10 (D)
1964—Browns, 37-21 (C)
1967—Lions, 31-14 (D)
1969—Lions, 28-21 (C)
1970—Lions, 41-24 (C)
1975—Lions, 21-10 (D)
1983—Browns, 31-26 (D)
(Points—Lions 390, Browns 273)
NFL Championship
CLEVELAND vs. GREEN BAY
Packers lead series, 7-5
1953—Browns, 27-0 (Mil)
1955—Browns, 41-10 (C)
1956—Browns, 24-7 (Mil)
1961—Packers, 49-17 (C)
1964—Packers, 28-21 (Mil)
1965—*Packers, 23-12 (GB)
1966—Packers, 21-20 (C)
1967—Packers, 55-7 (Mil)
1969—Browns, 20-7 (C)
1972—Packers, 26-10 (C)
1980—Browns, 26-21 (C)
1983—Packers, 35-21 (Mil)
(Points—Packers 282, Browns 246)
NFL Championship
CLEVELAND vs. HOUSTON
Browns lead series, 20-11
1970—Browns, 28-14 (C)
Browns, 21-10 (H)
1971—Browns, 31-0 (C)
Browns, 37-24 (H)
1972—Browns, 23-17 (H)
Browns, 20-0 (C)
1973—Browns, 42-13 (C)
Browns, 23-13 (H)
1974—Browns, 20-7 (C)
Oilers, 28-24 (H)
1975—Oilers, 40-10 (C)
Oilers, 21-10 (H)
1976—Browns, 21-7 (H)
Browns, 13-10 (C)
1977—Browns, 24-23 (H)
Oilers, 19-15 (C)
1978—Oilers, 16-13 (C)
Oilers, 14-10 (H)
1979—Oilers, 31-10 (H)
Browns, 14-7 (C)
1980—Oilers, 16-7 (C)
Browns, 17-14 (H)
1981—Oilers, 9-3 (C)
Oilers, 17-13 (H)
1982—Browns, 20-14 (H)
1983—Browns, 25-19 (C) OT
Oilers, 34-27 (H)
1984—Browns, 27-10 (C)
Browns, 27-20 (H)
1985—Browns, 21-6 (H)
Browns, 28-21 (C)
(Points—Browns 624, Oilers 494)
CLEVELAND vs. *INDIANAPOLIS
Browns lead series, 10-5
1956—Colts, 21-7 (C)
1959—Browns, 38-31 (B)
1962—Colts, 36-14 (C)
1964—**Browns, 27-0 (C)
1968—Browns, 30-20 (B)
**Colts, 34-0 (C)
1971—Browns, 14-13 (B)
***Colts, 20-3 (C)
1973—Browns, 24-14 (C)
1975—Colts, 21-7 (B)
1978—Browns, 45-24 (B)
1979—Browns, 13-10 (C)
1980—Browns, 28-27 (B)
1981—Browns, 42-28 (C)
1983—Browns, 41-23 (C)
(Points—Browns 333, Colts 322)
Franchise in Baltimore prior to 1984
***NFL Championship*
****AFC Divisional Playoff*
CLEVELAND vs. KANSAS CITY
Chiefs lead series, 5-4-1
1971—Chiefs, 13-7 (KC)
1972—Chiefs, 31-7 (C)
1973—Tie, 20-20 (KC)
1975—Browns, 40-14 (C)
1976—Chiefs, 39-14 (KC)
1977—Browns, 44-7 (C)
1978—Chiefs, 17-3 (KC)
1979—Browns, 27-24 (KC)
1980—Browns, 20-13 (C)
1984—Chiefs, 10-6 (KC)
(Points—Browns 188, Chiefs 188)
CLEVELAND vs. *L.A.RAIDERS
Raiders lead series, 9-1
1970—Raiders, 23-20 (O)
1971—Raiders, 34-20 (C)
1973—Browns, 7-3 (O)
1974—Raiders, 40-24 (C)
1975—Raiders, 38-17 (O)
1977—Raiders, 26-10 (C)
1979—Raiders, 19-14 (O)
1980—**Raiders, 14-12 (C)
1982—***Raiders, 27-10 (LA)
1985—Raiders, 21-20 (C)
(Points—Raiders 245, Browns 154)
Franchise in Oakland prior to 1982
***AFC Divisional Playoff*
****AFC First Round Playoff*
CLEVELAND vs. L.A. RAMS
Browns lead series, 8-7
1950—*Browns, 30-28 (C)
1951—Browns, 38-23 (LA)
*Rams, 24-17 (LA)
1952—Browns, 37-7 (C)
1955—*Browns, 38-14 (LA)
1957—Browns, 45-31 (C)
1958—Browns, 30-27 (LA)
1963—Browns, 20-6 (C)
1965—Rams, 42-7 (LA)
1968—Rams, 24-6 (C)
1973—Rams, 30-17 (LA)
1977—Rams, 9-0 (C)
1978—Browns, 30-19 (C)
1981—Rams, 27-16 (LA)
1984—Rams, 20-17 (LA)
(Points—Browns 348, Rams 331)
NFL Championship
CLEVELAND vs. MIAMI
Series tied, 3-3
1970—Browns, 28-0 (M)
1972—*Dolphins, 20-14 (M)
1973—Dolphins, 17-9 (C)
1976—Browns, 17-13 (C)
1979—Browns, 30-24 (C) OT
1985—*Dolphins, 24-21 (M)
(Points—Browns 119, Dolphins 98)
AFC Divisional Playoff
CLEVELAND vs. MINNESOTA
Vikings lead series, 7-1
1965—Vikings, 27-17 (C)
1967—Browns, 14-10 (C)
1969—Vikings, 51-3 (M)
*Vikings, 27-7 (M)
1973—Vikings, 26-3 (M)
1975—Vikings, 42-10 (C)
1980—Vikings, 28-23 (M)
1983—Vikings, 27-21 (C)
(Points—Vikings 238, Browns 98)
NFL Championship
CLEVELAND vs. NEW ENGLAND
Browns lead series, 6-2
1971—Browns, 27-7 (C)
1974—Browns, 21-14 (NE)
1977—Browns, 30-27 (C) OT
1980—Patriots, 34-17 (NE)
1982—Browns, 10-7 (C)
1983—Browns, 30-0 (NE)
1984—Patriots, 17-16 (C)
1985—Browns, 24-20 (C)
(Points—Browns 175, Patriots 126)
CLEVELAND vs. NEW ORLEANS
Browns lead series, 8-1
1967—Browns, 42-7 (NO)
1968—Browns, 24-10 (NO)
Browns, 35-17 (C)
1969—Browns, 27-17 (NO)
1971—Browns, 21-17 (NO)
1975—Browns, 17-16 (C)
1978—Browns, 24-16 (NO)
1981—Browns, 20-17 (C)
1984—Saints 16-14 (C)
(Points—Browns 224, Saints 133)
CLEVELAND vs. N.Y. GIANTS
Browns lead series, 26-16-2
1950—Giants, 6-0 (C)
Giants, 17-13 (NY)
*Browns, 8-3 (C)
1951—Browns, 14-13 (C)
Browns, 10-0 (NY)
1952—Giants, 17-9 (C)
Giants, 37-34 (NY)
1953—Browns, 7-0 (NY)
Browns, 62-14 (C)
1954—Browns, 24-14 (C)
Browns, 16-7 (NY)
1955—Browns, 24-14 (C)
Tie, 35-35 (NY)
1956—Giants, 21-9 (C)
Browns, 24-7 (NY)
1957—Browns, 6-3 (C)
Browns, 34-28 (NY)
1958—Giants, 21-17 (C)
Giants, 13-10 (NY)
*Giants, 10-0 (NY)
1959—Giants, 10-6 (C)
Giants, 48-7 (NY)
1960—Giants, 17-13 (C)
Browns, 48-34 (NY)
1961—Giants, 37-21 (C)
Tie, 7-7 (NY)
1962—Browns, 17-7 (C)
Giants, 17-13 (NY)
1963—Browns, 35-24 (NY)
Giants, 33-6 (C)
1964—Browns, 42-20 (C)
Browns, 52-20 (NY)
1965—Browns, 38-14 (NY)
Browns, 34-21 (C)
1966—Browns, 28-7 (NY)
Browns, 49-40 (C)
1967—Giants, 38-34 (NY)
Browns, 24-14 (C)
1968—Browns, 45-10 (C)
1969—Browns, 28-17 (C)
Giants, 27-14 (NY)
1973—Browns, 12-10 (C)
1977—Browns, 21-7 (NY)
1985—Browns, 35-33 (NY)
(Points—Browns 985, Giants 792)
Conference Playoff
CLEVELAND vs. N.Y. JETS
Browns lead series, 7-3
1970—Browns, 31-21 (C)
1972—Browns, 26-10 (NY)
1976—Browns, 38-17 (C)
1978—Browns, 37-34 (C) OT
1979—Browns, 25-22 (NY) OT
1980—Browns, 17-14 (C)
1981—Jets, 14-13 (C)
1983—Browns, 10-7 (C)
1984—Jets, 24-20 (C)
1985—Jets, 37-10 (NY)
(Points—Browns 227, Jets 200)
CLEVELAND vs. PHILADELPHIA
Browns lead series, 29-11-1
1950—Browns, 35-10 (P)
Browns, 13-7 (C)
1951—Browns, 20-17 (C)
Browns, 24-9 (NY)
1952—Browns, 49-7 (P)
Eagles, 28-20 (C)
1953—Browns, 37-13 (C)
Eagles, 42-27 (P)
1954—Eagles, 28-10 (P)
Browns, 6-0 (C)
1955—Browns, 21-17 (C)
Eagles, 33-17 (P)
1956—Browns, 16-0 (P)
Browns, 17-14 (C)
1957—Browns, 24-7 (C)
Eagles, 17-7 (P)
1958—Browns, 28-14 (C)
Browns, 21-14 (P)
1959—Browns, 28-7 (C)
Browns, 28-21 (P)
1960—Browns, 41-24 (P)
Eagles, 31-29 (C)
1961—Eagles, 27-20 (P)
Browns, 45-24 (C)
1962—Eagles, 35-7 (P)
Tie, 14-14 (C)
1963—Browns, 37-7 (C)
Browns, 23-17 (P)
1964—Browns, 28-20 (P)
Browns, 38-24 (C)
1965—Browns, 35-17 (P)
Browns, 38-34 (C)
1966—Browns, 27-7 (C)
Eagles, 33-21 (P)
1967—Eagles, 28-24 (P)
1968—Browns, 47-13 (C)
1969—Browns, 27-20 (P)
1972—Browns, 27-17 (P)
1976—Browns, 24-3 (C)
1979—Browns, 24-19 (P)
1982—Eagles, 24-21 (C)
(Points—Browns 1,045, Eagles 743)
CLEVELAND vs. PITTSBURGH
Browns lead series, 41-31
1950—Browns, 30-17 (P)
Browns, 45-7 (C)
1951—Browns, 17-0 (C)
Browns, 28-0 (P)
1952—Browns, 21-20 (P)
Browns, 29-28 (C)
1953—Browns, 34-16 (C)
Browns, 20-16 (P)
1954—Steelers, 55-27 (P)
Browns, 42-7 (C)
1955—Browns, 41-14 (C)
Browns, 30-7 (P)
1956—Browns, 14-10 (P)
Steelers, 24-16 (C)
1957—Browns, 23-12 (P)
Browns, 24-0 (C)
1958—Browns, 45-12 (P)
Browns, 27-10 (C)
1959—Steelers, 17-7 (P)
Steelers, 21-20 (C)
1960—Browns, 28-20 (C)
Steelers, 14-10 (P)
1961—Browns, 30-28 (P)
Steelers, 17-13 (C)
1962—Browns, 41-14 (P)
Browns, 35-14 (C)
1963—Browns, 35-23 (C)
Steelers, 9-7 (P)
1964—Steelers, 23-7 (C)
Browns, 30-17 (P)
1965—Browns, 24-19 (C)
Browns, 42-21 (P)
1966—Browns, 41-10 (C)
Steelers, 16-6 (P)
1967—Browns, 21-10 (C)
Browns, 34-14 (P)
1968—Browns, 31-24 (C)
Browns, 45-24 (P)
1969—Browns, 42-31 (C)
Browns, 24-3 (P)
1970—Browns, 15-7 (C)
Steelers, 28-9 (P)
1971—Browns, 27-17 (C)
Steelers, 26-9 (P)
1972—Browns, 26-24 (C)
Steelers, 30-0 (P)
1973—Steelers, 33-6 (P)
Browns, 21-16 (C)
1974—Steelers, 20-16 (P)
Steelers, 26-16 (C)
1975—Steelers, 42-6 (C)
Steelers, 31-17 (P)
1976—Steelers, 31-14 (P)
Browns, 18-16 (C)
1977—Steelers, 28-14 (C)
Steelers, 35-31 (P)
1978—Steelers, 15-9 (P) OT
Steelers, 34-14 (C)
1979—Steelers, 51-35 (C)
Steelers, 33-30 (P) OT
1980—Browns, 27-26 (C)
Steelers, 16-13 (P)
1981—Steelers, 13-7 (P)
Steelers, 32-10 (C)
1982—Browns, 10-9 (C)
Steelers, 37-21 (P)
1983—Steelers, 44-17 (P)
Browns, 30-17 (C)
1984—Browns, 20-10 (C)
Steelers, 23-20 (P)
1985—Browns, 17-7 (C)
Steelers, 10-9 (P)
(Points—Browns 1,620, Steelers 1,431)
CLEVELAND vs. *ST. LOUIS
Browns lead series, 30-10-3
1950—Browns, 34-24 (Cle)
Browns, 10-7 (Chi)
1951—Browns, 34-17 (Chi)
Browns, 49-28 (Cle)
1952—Browns, 28-13 (Cle)

Browns, 10-0 (Chi)
1953—Browns, 27-7 (Chi)
Browns, 27-16 (Cle)
1954—Browns, 31-7 (Cle)
Browns, 35-3 (Chi)
1955—Browns, 26-20 (Chi)
Browns, 35-24 (Cle)
1956—Cardinals, 9-7 (Chi)
Cardinals, 24-7 (Cle)
1957—Browns, 17-7 (Chi)
Browns, 31-0 (Cle)
1958—Browns, 35-28 (Cle)
Browns, 38-24 (Chi)
1959—Browns, 34-7 (Chi)
Browns, 17-7 (Cle)
1960—Browns, 28-27 (Cle)
Tie, 17-17 (StL)
1961—Browns, 20-17 (Cle)
Browns, 21-10 (StL)
1962—Browns, 34-7 (StL)
Browns, 38-14 (Cle)
1963—Cardinals, 20-14 (Cle)
Browns, 24-10 (StL)
1964—Tie, 33-33 (Cle)
Cardinals, 28-19 (StL)
1965—Cardinals, 49-13 (Cle)
Browns, 27-24 (StL)
1966—Cardinals, 34-28 (Cle)
Browns, 38-10 (StL)
1967—Browns, 20-16 (Cle)
Browns, 20-16 (StL)
1968—Cardinals, 27-21 (Cle)
Cardinals, 27-16 (StL)
1969—Tie, 21-21 (Cle)
Browns, 27-21 (StL)
1974—Cardinals, 29-7 (StL)
1979—Browns, 38-20 (StL)
1985—Cardinals, 27-24 (Cle) OT
(Points—Browns 1,080, Cardinals 776)
Franchise in Chicago prior to 1960

CLEVELAND vs. SAN DIEGO
Chargers lead series, 5-4-1
1970—Chargers, 27-10 (C)
1972—Browns, 21-17 (SD)
1973—Tie, 16-16 (C)
1974—Chargers, 36-35 (SD)
1976—Browns, 21-17 (C)
1977—Chargers, 37-14 (SD)
1981—Chargers, 44-14 (C)
1982—Chargers, 30-13 (C)
1983—Browns, 30-24 (SD) OT
1985—Browns, 21-7 (SD)
(Points—Chargers 255, Browns 195)

CLEVELAND vs. SAN FRANCISCO
Browns lead series, 8-4
1950—Browns, 34-14 (C)
1951—49ers, 24-10 (SF)
1953—Browns, 23-21 (C)
1955—Browns, 38-3 (SF)
1959—49ers, 21-20 (C)
1962—Browns, 13-10 (SF)
1968—Browns, 33-21 (SF)
1970—49ers, 34-31 (SF)
1974—Browns, 7-0 (C)
1978—Browns, 24-7 (C)
1981—Browns, 15-12 (SF)
1984—49ers, 41-7 (C)
(Points—Browns 255, 49ers 208)

CLEVELAND vs. SEATTLE
Seahawks lead series, 7-2
1977—Seahawks, 20-19 (S)
1978—Seahawks, 47-24 (S)
1979—Seahawks, 29-24 (C)
1980—Browns, 27-3 (S)
1981—Seahawks, 42-21 (S)
1982—Browns, 21-7 (S)
1983—Seahawks, 24-9 (C)
1984—Seahawks, 33-0 (S)
1985—Seahawks, 31-13 (S)
(Points—Seahawks 236, Browns 158)

CLEVELAND vs. TAMPA BAY
Browns lead series, 3-0
1976—Browns, 24-7 (TB)
1980—Browns, 34-27 (TB)
1983—Browns, 20-0 (C)
(Points—Browns 78, Buccaneers 34)

CLEVELAND vs. WASHINGTON
Browns lead series, 31-8-1
1950—Browns, 20-14 (C)
Browns, 45-21 (W)
1951—Browns, 45-0 (C)
1952—Browns, 19-15 (C)
Browns, 48-24 (W)
1953—Browns, 30-14 (W)
Browns, 27-3 (C)
1954—Browns, 62-3 (C)
Browns, 34-14 (W)
1955—Redskins, 27-17 (C)
Browns, 24-14 (W)
1956—Redskins, 20-9 (W)
Redskins, 20-17 (C)
1957—Browns, 21-17 (C)
Tie, 30-30 (W)
1958—Browns, 20-10 (W)
Browns, 21-14 (C)
1959—Browns, 34-7 (C)
Browns, 31-17 (W)
1960—Browns, 31-10 (W)
Browns, 27-16 (C)
1961—Browns, 31-7 (C)
Browns, 17-6 (W)
1962—Redskins, 17-16 (C)
Redskins, 17-9 (W)
1963—Browns, 37-14 (C)
Browns, 27-20 (W)
1964—Browns, 27-13 (W)
Browns, 34-24 (C)
1965—Browns, 17-7 (W)
Browns, 24-16 (C)
1966—Browns, 38-14 (W)
Browns, 14-3 (C)
1967—Browns, 42-37 (C)
1968—Browns, 24-21 (W)
1969—Browns, 27-23 (C)
1971—Browns, 20-13 (W)
1975—Redskins, 23-7 (C)
1979—Redskins, 13-9 (C)
1985—Redskins, 14-7 (C)
(Points—Browns 1,039, Redskins 612)

DALLAS vs. ATLANTA
Cowboys lead series, 8-1;
See Atlanta vs. Dallas

DALLAS vs. BUFFALO
Cowboys lead series, 3-1;
See Buffalo vs. Dallas

DALLAS vs. CHICAGO
Cowboys lead series, 8-4;
See Chicago vs. Dallas

DALLAS vs. CINCINNATI
Cowboys lead series, 2-1;
See Cincinnati vs. Dallas

DALLAS vs. CLEVELAND
Browns lead series, 15-9;
See Cleveland vs. Dallas

DALLAS vs. DENVER
Cowboys lead series, 3-1
1973—Cowboys, 22-10 (Den)
1977—Cowboys, 14-6 (Dal)
*Cowboys, 27-10 (New Orleans)
1980—Broncos, 41-20 (Den)
(Points—Cowboys 83, Broncos 67)
**Super Bowl XII*

DALLAS vs. DETROIT
Cowboys lead series, 6-3
1960—Lions, 23-14 (Det)
1963—Cowboys, 17-14 (Dal)
1968—Cowboys, 59-13 (Dal)
1970—*Cowboys, 5-0 (Dal)
1972—Cowboys, 28-24 (Dal)
1975—Cowboys, 36-10 (Det)
1977—Cowboys, 37-0 (Dal)
1981—Lions, 27-24 (Det)
1985—Lions, 26-21 (Det)
(Points—Cowboys 241, Lions 137)
**NFC Divisional Playoff*

DALLAS vs. GREEN BAY
Packers lead series, 8-5
1960—Packers, 41-7 (GB)
1964—Packers, 45-21 (D)
1965—Packers, 13-3 (Mil)
1966—*Packers, 34-27 (D)
1967—*Packers, 21-17 (GB)
1968—Packers, 28-17 (D)
1970—Cowboys, 16-3 (D)
1972—Packers, 16-13 (Mil)
1975—Packers, 19-17 (D)
1978—Cowboys, 42-14 (Mil)
1980—Cowboys, 28-7 (Mil)
1982—**Cowboys, 37-26 (D)
1984—Cowboys, 20-6 (D)
(Points—Packers 273, Cowboys 265)
**NFL Championship*
***NFC Second Round Playoff*

DALLAS vs. HOUSTON
Cowboys lead series, 4-1
1970—Cowboys, 52-10 (D)
1974—Cowboys, 10-0 (H)
1979—Oilers, 30-24 (D)
1982—Cowboys, 37-7 (H)
1985—Cowboys, 17-10 (H)
(Points—Cowboys 140, Oilers 57)

DALLAS vs. *INDIANAPOLIS
Cowboys lead series, 6-3
1960—Colts, 45-7 (D)
1967—Colts, 23-17 (B)
1969—Cowboys, 27-10 (D)
1970—**Colts, 16-13 (Miami)
1972—Cowboys, 21-0 (B)
1976—Cowboys, 30-27 (D)
1978—Cowboys, 38-0 (D)
1981—Cowboys, 37-13 (B)
1984—Cowboys, 22-3 (D)
(Points—Cowboys 212, Colts 137)
**Franchise in Baltimore prior to 1984*
***Super Bowl V*

DALLAS vs. KANSAS CITY
Cowboys lead series, 2-1
1970—Cowboys, 27-16 (KC)
1975—Chiefs, 34-31 (D)
1983—Cowboys, 41-21 (D)
(Points—Cowboys 99, Chiefs 71)

DALLAS vs. *L.A. RAIDERS
Raiders lead series, 2-1
1974—Raiders, 27-23 (O)
1980—Cowboys, 19-13 (O)
1983—Raiders, 40-38 (D)
(Points—Raiders 80, Cowboys 80)
**Franchise in Oakland prior to 1982*

DALLAS vs. L.A. RAMS
Series tied, 10-10
1960—Rams, 38-13 (D)
1962—Cowboys, 27-17 (LA)
1967—Rams, 35-13 (D)
1969—Rams, 24-23 (LA)
1971—Cowboys, 28-21 (D)
1973—Rams, 37-31 (LA)
*Cowboys, 27-16 (D)
1975—Cowboys, 18-7 (D)
**Cowboys, 37-7 (LA)
1976—*Rams, 14-12 (D)
1978—Rams, 27-14 (LA)
**Cowboys, 28-0 (LA)
1979—Cowboys, 30-6 (D)
*Rams, 21-19 (D)
1980—Rams, 38-14 (LA)
***Cowboys, 34-13 (D)
1981—Cowboys, 29-17 (D)
1983—***Rams, 24-17 (D)
1984—Cowboys, 20-13 (LA)
1985—*Rams, 20-0 (LA)
(Points—Cowboys 434, Rams 395)
**NFC Divisional Playoff*
***NFC Championship*
****NFC First Round Playoff*

DALLAS vs. MIAMI
Dolphins lead series, 3-2
1971—*Cowboys, 24-3 (New Orleans)
1973—Dolphins, 14-7 (D)
1978—Dolphins, 23-16 (M)
1981—Cowboys, 28-27 (D)
1984—Dolphins, 28-21 (M)
(Points—Cowboys 96, Dolphins 95)
**Super Bowl VI*

DALLAS vs. MINNESOTA
Cowboys lead series, 10-5
1961—Cowboys, 21-7 (D)
Cowboys, 28-0 (M)
1966—Cowboys, 28-17 (D)
1968—Cowboys, 20-7 (M)
1970—Vikings, 54-13 (M)
1971—*Cowboys, 20-12 (M)
1973—**Vikings, 27-10 (D)
1974—Vikings, 23-21 (D)
1975—*Cowboys, 17-14 (M)
1977—Cowboys, 16-10 (M) OT
**Cowboys, 23-6 (D)
1978—Vikings, 21-10 (D)
1979—Cowboys, 36-20 (M)
1982—Vikings, 31-27 (M)
1983—Cowboys, 37-24 (M)
(Points—Cowboys 327, Vikings 273)
**NFC Divisional Playoff*
***NFC Championship*

DALLAS vs. NEW ENGLAND
Cowboys lead series, 5-0
1971—Cowboys, 44-21 (D)
1975—Cowboys, 34-31 (NE)
1978—Cowboys, 17-10 (D)
1981—Cowboys, 35-21 (NE)
1984—Cowboys, 20-17 (D)
(Points—Cowboys 150, Patriots 100)

DALLAS vs. NEW ORLEANS
Cowboys lead series, 11-1
1967—Cowboys, 14-10 (D)
Cowboys, 27-10 (NO)
1968—Cowboys, 17-3 (NO)
1969—Cowboys, 21-17 (NO)
Cowboys, 33-17 (D)
1971—Saints, 24-14 (NO)
1973—Cowboys, 40-3 (D)
1976—Cowboys, 24-6 (NO)
1978—Cowboys, 27-7 (D)
1982—Cowboys, 21-7 (D)
1983—Cowboys, 21-20 (D)
1984—Cowboys, 30-27 (D) OT
(Points—Cowboys 289, Saints 151)

DALLAS vs. N.Y. GIANTS
Cowboys lead series, 32-13-2
1960—Tie, 31-31 (NY)
1961—Giants, 31-10 (D)
Cowboys, 17-16 (NY)
1962—Giants, 41-10 (D)
Giants, 41-31 (NY)
1963—Giants, 37-21 (NY)
Giants, 34-27 (D)
1964—Tie, 13-13 (D)
Cowboys, 31-21 (NY)
1965—Cowboys, 31-2 (D)
Cowboys, 38-20 (NY)
1966—Cowboys, 52-7 (D)
Cowboys, 17-7 (NY)
1967—Cowboys, 38-24 (D)
1968—Giants, 27-21 (D)
Cowboys, 28-10 (NY)
1969—Cowboys, 25-3 (D)
1970—Cowboys, 28-10 (D)
Giants, 23-20 (NY)
1971—Cowboys, 20-13 (D)
Cowboys, 42-14 (NY)
1972—Cowboys, 23-14 (NY)
Giants, 23-3 (D)
1973—Cowboys, 45-28 (D)
Cowboys, 23-10 (New Haven)
1974—Giants, 14-6 (D)
Cowboys, 21-7 (New Haven)
1975—Cowboys, 13-7 (NY)
Cowboys, 14-3 (D)
1976—Cowboys, 24-14 (NY)
Cowboys, 9-3 (D)
1977—Cowboys, 41-21 (D)
Cowboys, 24-10 (NY)
1978—Cowboys, 34-24 (NY)
Cowboys, 24-3 (D)
1979—Cowboys, 16-14 (NY)
Cowboys, 28-7 (D)
1980—Cowboys, 24-3 (D)
Giants, 38-35 (NY)
1981—Cowboys, 18-10 (D)
Giants, 13-10 (NY) OT
1983—Cowboys, 28-13 (D)
Cowboys, 38-20 (NY)
1984—Giants, 28-7 (NY)
Giants, 19-7 (D)
1985—Cowboys, 30-29 (NY)
Cowboys, 28-21 (D)
(Points—Cowboys 1,124, Giants 821)

DALLAS vs. N.Y. JETS
Cowboys lead series, 3-0
1971—Cowboys, 52-10 (D)
1975—Cowboys, 31-21 (NY)
1978—Cowboys, 30-7 (NY)
(Points—Cowboys 113, Jets 38)

DALLAS vs. PHILADELPHIA
Cowboys lead series, 34-17
1960—Eagles, 27-25 (D)
1961—Eagles, 43-7 (D)
Eagles, 35-13 (P)
1962—Cowboys, 41-19 (D)
Eagles, 28-14 (P)
1963—Eagles, 24-21 (P)
Cowboys, 27-20 (D)
1964—Eagles, 17-14 (D)
Eagles, 24-14 (P)
1965—Eagles, 35-24 (D)
Cowboys, 21-19 (P)
1966—Cowboys, 56-7 (D)
Eagles, 24-23 (P)
1967—Eagles, 21-14 (P)
Cowboys, 38-17 (D)
1968—Cowboys, 45-13 (P)
Cowboys, 34-14 (D)
1969—Cowboys, 38-7 (P)
Cowboys, 49-14 (D)
1970—Cowboys, 17-7 (P)
Cowboys, 21-17 (D)
1971—Cowboys, 42-7 (P)
Cowboys, 20-7 (D)
1972—Cowboys, 28-6 (D)
Cowboys, 28-7 (P)
1973—Eagles, 30-16 (P)
Cowboys, 31-10 (D)
1974—Eagles, 13-10 (P)
Cowboys, 31-24 (D)
1975—Cowboys, 20-17 (P)
Cowboys, 27-17 (D)
1976—Cowboys, 27-7 (D)
Cowboys, 26-7 (P)
1977—Cowboys, 16-10 (P)
Cowboys, 24-14 (D)
1978—Cowboys, 14-7 (D)
Cowboys, 31-13 (P)
1979—Eagles, 31-21 (D)
Cowboys, 24-17 (P)
1980—Eagles, 17-10 (P)
Cowboys, 35-27 (D)
*Eagles, 20-7 (P)
1981—Cowboys, 17-14 (P)
Cowboys, 21-10 (D)
1982—Eagles, 24-20 (D)
1983—Cowboys, 37-7 (D)
Cowboys, 27-20 (P)
1984—Cowboys, 23-17 (D)
Cowboys, 26-10 (P)
1985—Eagles, 16-14 (P)
Cowboys, 34-17 (D)
(Points—Cowboys 1,263, Eagles 875)
**NFC Championship*

DALLAS vs. PITTSBURGH
Steelers lead series, 12-11
1960—Steelers, 35-28 (D)
1961—Cowboys, 27-24 (D)

Steelers, 37-7 (P)
1962—Steelers, 30-28 (D)
Cowboys, 42-27 (P)
1963—Steelers, 27-21 (P)
Steelers, 24-19 (D)
1964—Steelers, 23-17 (P)
Cowboys, 17-14 (D)
1965—Steelers, 22-13 (P)
Cowboys, 24-17 (D)
1966—Cowboys, 52-21 (D)
Cowboys, 20-7 (P)
1967—Cowboys, 24-21 (P)
1968—Cowboys, 28-7 (D)
1969—Cowboys, 10-7 (P)
1972—Cowboys, 17-13 (D)
1975—*Steelers, 21-17 (Miami)
1977—Steelers, 28-13 (P)
1978—**Steelers, 35-31 (Miami)
1979—Steelers, 14-3 (P)
1982—Steelers, 36-28 (D)
1985—Cowboys, 27-13 (D)
(Points—Cowboys 513, Steelers 503)
Super Bowl X
***Super Bowl XIII*

DALLAS vs. ST. LOUIS
Cowboys lead series, 29-17-1
1960—Cardinals, 12-10 (StL)
1961—Cardinals, 31-17 (D)
Cardinals, 31-13 (StL)
1962—Cardinals, 28-24 (D)
Cardinals, 52-20 (StL)
1963—Cardinals, 34-7 (D)
Cowboys, 28-24 (StL)
1964—Cardinals, 16-6 (D)
Cowboys, 31-13 (StL)
1965—Cardinals, 20-13 (StL)
Cowboys, 27-13 (D)
1966—Tie, 10-10 (StL)
Cowboys, 31-17 (D)
1967—Cowboys, 46-21 (D)
1968—Cowboys, 27-10 (StL)
1969—Cowboys, 24-3 (D)
1970—Cardinals, 20-7 (StL)
Cardinals, 38-0 (D)
1971—Cowboys, 16-13 (StL)
Cowboys, 31-12 (D)
1972—Cowboys, 33-24 (D)
Cowboys, 27-6 (StL)
1973—Cowboys, 45-10 (D)
Cowboys, 30-3 (StL)
1974—Cardinals, 31-28 (StL)
Cowboys, 17-14 (D)
1975—Cowboys, 37-31 (D) OT
Cardinals, 31-17 (StL)
1976—Cardinals, 21-17 (StL)
Cowboys, 19-14 (D)
1977—Cowboys, 30-24 (StL)
Cardinals, 24-17 (D)
1978—Cowboys, 21-12 (D)
Cowboys, 24-21 (StL) OT
1979—Cowboys, 22-21 (StL)
Cowboys, 22-13 (D)
1980—Cowboys, 27-24 (StL)
Cowboys, 31-21 (D)
1981—Cowboys, 30-17 (D)
Cardinals, 20-17 (StL)
1982—Cowboys, 24-7 (StL)
1983—Cowboys, 34-17 (StL)
Cowboys, 35-17 (D)
1984—Cardinals, 31-20 (D)
Cowboys, 24-17 (StL)
1985—Cardinals, 21-10 (StL)
Cowboys, 35-17 (D)
(Points—Cowboys 1,081, Cardinals 927)

DALLAS vs. SAN DIEGO
Cowboys lead series, 2-1
1972—Cowboys, 34-28 (SD)
1980—Cowboys, 42-31 (D)
1983—Chargers, 24-23 (SD)
(Points—Cowboys 99, Chargers 83)

DALLAS vs. SAN FRANCISCO
Series tied, 8-8-1
1960—49ers, 26-14 (D)
1963—49ers, 31-24 (SF)
1965—Cowboys, 39-31 (D)
1967—49ers, 24-16 (SF)
1969—Tie, 24-24 (D)
1970—*Cowboys, 17-10 (SF)
1971—*Cowboys, 14-3 (D)
1972—49ers, 31-10 (D)
**Cowboys, 30-28 (SF)
1974—Cowboys, 20-14 (D)
1977—Cowboys, 42-35 (SF)
1979—Cowboys, 21-13 (SF)
1980—Cowboys, 59-14 (D)
1981—49ers, 42-14 (SF)
*49ers, 28-27 (SF)
1983—49ers, 42-17 (SF)
1985—49ers, 31-16 (SF)
(Points—49ers 430, Cowboys 404)
NFC Championship
***NFC Divisional Playoff*

DALLAS vs. SEATTLE
Cowboys lead series, 3-0
1976—Cowboys, 28-13 (S)
1980—Cowboys, 51-7 (D)
1983—Cowboys, 35-10 (S)
(Points—Cowboys 114, Seahawks 30)

DALLAS vs. TAMPA BAY
Cowboys lead series, 6-0
1977—Cowboys, 23-7 (D)
1980—Cowboys, 28-17 (D)
1981—*Cowboys, 38-0 (D)
1982—Cowboys, 14-9 (D)
**Cowboys, 30-17 (D)
1983—Cowboys, 27-24 (D) OT
(Points—Cowboys 160, Buccaneers 74)
NFC Divisional Playoff
***NFC First Round Playoff*

DALLAS vs. WASHINGTON
Cowboys lead series, 30-20-2
1960—Redskins, 26-14 (W)
1961—Tie, 28-28 (D)
Redskins, 34-24 (W)
1962—Tie, 35-35 (D)
Cowboys, 38-10 (W)
1963—Redskins, 21-17 (W)
Cowboys, 35-20 (D)
1964—Cowboys, 24-18 (D)
Redskins, 28-16 (W)
1965—Cowboys, 27-7 (D)
Redskins, 34-31 (W)
1966—Cowboys, 31-30 (W)
Redskins, 34-31 (D)
1967—Cowboys, 17-14 (W)
Redskins, 27-20 (D)
1968—Cowboys, 44-24 (W)
Cowboys, 29-20 (D)
1969—Cowboys, 41-28 (W)
Cowboys, 20-10 (D)
1970—Cowboys, 45-21 (W)
Cowboys, 34-0 (D)
1971—Redskins, 20-16 (D)
Cowboys, 13-0 (W)
1972—Redskins, 24-20 (W)
Cowboys, 34-24 (D)
*Redskins, 26-3 (W)
1973—Redskins, 14-7 (W)
Cowboys, 27-7 (D)
1974—Redskins, 28-21 (W)
Cowboys, 24-23 (D)
1975—Redskins, 30-24 (W) OT
Cowboys, 31-10 (D)
1976—Cowboys, 20-7 (W)
Redskins, 27-14 (D)
1977—Cowboys, 34-16 (D)
Cowboys, 14-7 (W)
1978—Redskins, 9-5 (W)
Cowboys, 37-10 (D)
1979—Redskins, 34-20 (W)
Cowboys, 35-34 (D)
1980—Cowboys, 17-3 (W)
Cowboys, 14-10 (D)
1981—Cowboys, 26-10 (W)
Cowboys, 24-10 (D)
1982—Cowboys, 24-10 (W)
*Redskins, 31-17 (W)
1983—Cowboys, 31-30 (W)
Redskins, 31-10 (D)
1984—Redskins, 34-14 (W)
Redskins, 30-28 (D)
1985—Cowboys, 44-14 (D)
Cowboys, 13-7 (W)
(Points—Cowboys 1,262, Redskins 1,039)
NFC Championship

DENVER vs. ATLANTA
Series tied, 3-3;
See Atlanta vs. Denver

DENVER vs. BUFFALO
Bills lead series, 13-9-1;
See Buffalo vs. Denver

DENVER vs. CHICAGO
Bears lead series, 4-3;
See Chicago vs. Denver

DENVER vs. CINCINNATI
Broncos lead series, 8-6;
See Cincinnati vs. Denver

DENVER vs. CLEVELAND
Broncos lead series, 8-3;
See Cleveland vs. Denver

DENVER vs. DALLAS
Cowboys lead series, 3-1;
See Dallas vs. Denver

DENVER vs. DETROIT
Broncos lead series, 3-2
1971—Lions, 24-20 (Den)
1974—Broncos, 31-27 (Det)
1978—Lions, 17-14 (Det)
1981—Broncos, 27-21 (Den)
1984—Broncos, 28-7 (Det)
(Points—Broncos 120, Lions 96)

DENVER vs. GREEN BAY
Broncos lead series, 3-1
1971—Packers, 34-13 (Mil)
1975—Broncos, 23-13 (D)
1978—Broncos, 16-3 (D)
1984—Broncos, 17-14 (D)
(Points—Broncos 69, Packers 64)

DENVER vs. HOUSTON
Oilers lead series, 18-10-1
1960—Oilers, 45-25 (D)
Oilers, 20-10 (H)
1961—Oilers, 55-14 (D)
Oilers, 45-14 (H)
1962—Broncos, 20-10 (D)
Oilers, 34-17 (H)
1963—Oilers, 20-14 (H)
Oilers, 33-24 (D)
1964—Oilers, 38-17 (D)
Oilers, 34-15 (H)
1965—Broncos, 28-17 (D)
Broncos, 31-21 (H)
1966—Oilers, 45-7 (H)
Broncos, 40-38 (D)
1967—Oilers, 10-6 (H)
Oilers, 20-18 (D)
1968—Oilers, 38-17 (H)
1969—Oilers, 24-21 (H)
Tie, 20-20 (D)
1970—Oilers, 31-21 (H)
1972—Broncos, 30-17 (D)
1973—Broncos, 48-20 (H)
1974—Broncos, 37-14 (D)
1976—Oilers, 17-3 (H)
1977—Broncos, 24-14 (H)
1979—*Oilers, 13-7 (H)
1980—Oilers, 20-16 (D)
1983—Broncos, 26-14 (H)
1985—Broncos, 31-20 (D)
(Points—Oilers 747, Broncos 601)
AFC First Round Playoff

DENVER vs. *INDIANAPOLIS
Broncos lead series, 6-1
1974—Broncos, 17-6 (B)
1977—Broncos, 27-13 (D)
1978—Colts, 7-6 (B)
1981—Broncos, 28-10 (D)
1983—Broncos, 17-10 (B)
Broncos, 21-19 (D)
1985—Broncos, 15-10 (I)
(Points—Broncos 131, Colts 75)
Franchise in Baltimore prior to 1984

DENVER vs. *KANSAS CITY
Chiefs lead series, 33-18
1960—Texans, 17-14 (D)
Texans, 34-7 (Da)
1961—Texans, 19-12 (D)
Texans, 49-21 (Da)
1962—Texans, 24-3 (D)
Texans, 17-10 (Da)
1963—Chiefs, 59-7 (D)
Chiefs, 52-21 (KC)
1964—Broncos, 33-27 (D)
Chiefs, 49-39 (KC)
1965—Chiefs, 31-23 (D)
Chiefs, 45-35 (KC)
1966—Chiefs, 37-10 (KC)
Chiefs, 56-10 (D)
1967—Chiefs, 52-9 (KC)
Chiefs, 38-24 (D)
1968—Chiefs, 34-2 (KC)
Chiefs, 30-7 (D)
1969—Chiefs, 26-13 (D)
Chiefs, 31-17 (KC)
1970—Broncos, 26-13 (D)
Chiefs, 16-0 (KC)
1971—Chiefs, 16-3 (D)
Chiefs, 28-10 (KC)
1972—Chiefs, 45-24 (D)
Chiefs, 24-21 (KC)
1973—Chiefs, 16-14 (KC)
Broncos, 14-10 (D)
1974—Broncos, 17-14 (KC)
Chiefs, 42-34 (D)
1975—Broncos, 37-33 (D)
Chiefs, 26-13 (KC)
1976—Broncos, 35-26 (KC)
Broncos, 17-16 (D)
1977—Broncos, 23-7 (D)
Broncos, 14-7 (KC)
1978—Broncos, 23-17 (KC) OT
Broncos, 24-3 (D)
1979—Broncos, 24-10 (KC)
Broncos, 20-3 (D)
1980—Chiefs, 23-17 (D)
Chiefs, 31-14 (KC)
1981—Chiefs, 28-14 (KC)
Broncos, 16-13 (D)
1982—Chiefs, 37-16 (D)
1983—Broncos, 27-24 (D)
Chiefs, 48-17 (KC)
1984—Broncos, 21-0 (D)
Chiefs, 16-13 (KC)
1985—Broncos, 30-10 (KC)
Broncos, 14-13 (D)
(Points—Chiefs 1,342, Broncos 909)
Franchise in Dallas prior to 1963 and known as Texans

DENVER vs. *L.A. RAIDERS
Raiders lead series, 36-14-2
1960—Broncos, 31-14 (D)
Raiders, 48-10 (O)
1961—Raiders, 33-19 (O)
Broncos, 27-24 (D)
1962—Broncos, 44-7 (D)
Broncos, 23-6 (O)
1963—Raiders, 26-10 (D)
Raiders, 35-31 (O)
1964—Raiders, 40-7 (O)
Tie, 20-20 (D)
1965—Raiders, 28-20 (D)
Raiders, 24-13 (O)
1966—Raiders, 17-3 (D)
Raiders, 28-10 (O)
1967—Raiders, 51-0 (O)
Raiders, 21-17 (D)
1968—Raiders, 43-7 (D)
Raiders, 33-27 (O)
1969—Raiders, 24-14 (D)
Raiders, 41-10 (O)
1970—Raiders, 35-23 (O)
Raiders, 24-19 (D)
1971—Raiders, 27-16 (D)
Raiders, 21-13 (O)
1972—Broncos, 30-23 (O)
Raiders, 37-20 (D)
1973—Tie, 23-23 (D)
Raiders, 21-17 (O)
1974—Raiders, 28-17 (D)
Broncos, 20-17 (O)
1975—Raiders, 42-17 (D)
Raiders, 17-10 (O)
1976—Raiders, 17-10 (D)
Raiders, 19-6 (O)
1977—Broncos, 30-7 (O)
Raiders, 24-14 (D)
**Broncos, 20-17 (D)
1978—Broncos, 14-6 (D)
Broncos, 21-6 (O)
1979—Raiders, 27-3 (O)
Raiders, 14-10 (D)
1980—Raiders, 9-3 (O)
Raiders, 24-21 (D)
1981—Broncos, 9-7 (D)
Broncos, 17-0 (O)
1982—Raiders, 27-10 (LA)
1983—Raiders, 22-7 (D)
Raiders, 22-20 (LA)
1984—Broncos, 16-13 (D)
Broncos, 22-19 (LA) OT
1985—Raiders, 31-28 (LA) OT
Raiders, 17-14 (D) OT
(Points—Raiders 1,206, Broncos 863)
Franchise in Oakland prior to 1982
***AFC Championship*

DENVER vs. L.A. RAMS
Rams lead series, 3-2
1972—Broncos, 16-10 (LA)
1974—Rams, 17-10 (D)
1979—Rams, 13-9 (D)
1982—Broncos, 27-24 (LA)
1985—Rams, 20-16 (LA)
(Points—Rams 84, Broncos 78)

DENVER vs. MIAMI
Dolphins lead series, 5-2-1
1966—Dolphins, 24-7 (M)
Broncos, 17-7 (D)
1967—Dolphins, 35-21 (M)
1968—Broncos, 21-14 (D)
1969—Dolphins, 27-24 (M)
1971—Tie, 10-10 (D)
1975—Dolphins, 14-13 (M)
1985—Dolphins, 30-26 (D)
(Points—Dolphins 161, Broncos 139)

DENVER vs. MINNESOTA
Series tied, 2-2
1972—Vikings, 23-20 (D)
1978—Vikings, 12-9 (M) OT
1981—Broncos, 19-17 (D)
1984—Broncos, 42-21 (D)
(Points—Broncos 90, Vikings 73)

DENVER vs. *NEW ENGLAND
Patriots lead series, 12-11
1960—Broncos, 13-10 (B)
Broncos, 31-24 (D)
1961—Patriots, 45-17 (B)
Patriots, 28-24 (D)
1962—Patriots, 41-16 (B)
Patriots, 33-29 (D)
1963—Broncos, 14-10 (D)
Patriots, 40-21 (B)
1964—Patriots, 39-10 (D)
Patriots, 12-7 (B)
1965—Broncos, 27-10 (B)
Patriots, 28-20 (D)
1966—Patriots, 24-10 (D)
Broncos, 17-10 (B)
1967—Broncos, 26-21 (D)
1968—Patriots, 20-17 (D)
Broncos, 35-14 (B)
1969—Broncos, 35-7 (D)

1972—Broncos, 45-21 (D)
1976—Patriots, 38-14 (NE)
1979—Broncos, 45-10 (D)
1980—Patriots, 23-14 (NE)
1984—Broncos, 26-19 (D)
(Points—Patriots 527, Broncos 513)
Franchise in Boston prior to 1971

DENVER vs. NEW ORLEANS
Broncos lead series, 4-0
1970—Broncos, 31-6 (NO)
1974—Broncos, 33-17 (D)
1979—Broncos, 10-3 (D)
1985—Broncos, 34-23 (D)
(Points—Broncos 108, Saints 49)

DENVER vs. N. Y. GIANTS
Broncos lead series, 2-1
1972—Giants, 29-17 (NY)
1976—Broncos, 14-13 (D)
1980—Broncos, 14-9 (NY)
(Points—Giants 51, Broncos 45)

DENVER vs. *N. Y. JETS
Series tied, 10-10-1
1960—Titans, 28-24 (NY)
Titans, 30-27 (D)
1961—Titans, 35-28 (NY)
Broncos, 27-10 (D)
1962—Broncos, 32-10 (NY)
Titans, 46-45 (D)
1963—Tie, 35-35 (NY)
Jets, 14-9 (D)
1964—Jets, 30-6 (NY)
Broncos, 20-16 (D)
1965—Broncos, 16-13 (D)
Jets, 45-10 (NY)
1966—Jets, 16-7 (D)
1967—Jets, 38-24 (D)
Broncos, 33-24 (NY)
1968—Broncos, 21-13 (NY)
1969—Broncos, 21-19 (D)
1973—Broncos, 40-28 (NY)
1976—Broncos, 46-3 (D)
1978—Jets, 31-28 (D)
1980—Broncos, 31-24 (D)
(Points—Broncos 530, Jets 508)
Jets known as Titans prior to 1963

DENVER vs. PHILADELPHIA
Eagles lead series, 3-1
1971—Eagles, 17-16 (P)
1975—Broncos, 25-10 (D)
1980—Eagles, 27-6 (P)
1983—Eagles, 13-10 (D)
(Points—Eagles 67, Broncos 57)

DENVER vs. PITTSBURGH
Broncos lead series, 7-5-1
1970—Broncos, 16-13 (D)
1971—Broncos, 22-10 (P)
1973—Broncos, 23-13 (P)
1974—Tie, 35-35 (D) OT
1975—Steelers, 20-9 (P)
1977—Broncos, 21-7 (D)
*Broncos, 34-21 (D)
1978—Steelers, 21-17 (D)
*Steelers, 33-10 (P)
1979—Steelers, 42-7 (P)
1983—Broncos, 14-10 (P)
1984—*Steelers, 24-17 (D)
1985—Broncos, 31-23 (P)
(Points—Steelers 272, Broncos 256)
AFC Divisional Playoff

DENVER vs. ST. LOUIS
Broncos lead series, 1-0-1
1973—Tie, 17-17 (StL)
1977—Broncos, 7-0 (D)
(Points—Broncos 24, Cardinals 17)

DENVER vs. *SAN DIEGO
Chargers lead series, 27-24-1
1960—Chargers, 23-19 (D)
Chargers, 41-33 (LA)
1961—Chargers, 37-0 (SD)
Chargers, 19-16 (D)
1962—Broncos, 30-21 (D)
Broncos, 23-20 (SD)
1963—Broncos, 50-34 (D)
Chargers, 58-20 (SD)
1964—Chargers, 42-14 (SD)
Chargers, 31-20 (D)
1965—Chargers, 34-31 (SD)
Chargers, 33-21 (D)
1966—Chargers, 24-17 (SD)
Broncos, 20-17 (D)
1967—Chargers, 38-21 (D)
Chargers, 24-20 (SD)
1968—Chargers, 55-24 (SD)
Chargers, 47-23 (D)
1969—Broncos, 13-0 (D)
Chargers, 45-24 (SD)
1970—Chargers, 24-21 (SD)
Tie, 17-17 (D)
1971—Broncos, 20-16 (D)
Chargers, 45-17 (SD)
1972—Chargers, 37-14 (SD)
Broncos, 38-13 (D)
1973—Broncos, 30-19 (D)
Broncos, 42-28 (SD)
1974—Broncos, 27-7 (D)
Chargers, 17-0 (SD)
1975—Broncos, 27-17 (SD)
Broncos, 13-10 (D) OT
1976—Broncos, 26-0 (D)
Broncos, 17-0 (SD)
1977—Broncos, 17-14 (SD)
Broncos, 17-9 (D)
1978—Broncos, 27-14 (D)
Chargers, 23-0 (SD)
1979—Broncos, 7-0 (D)
Chargers, 17-7 (SD)
1980—Chargers, 30-13 (D)
Broncos, 20-13 (SD)
1981—Broncos, 42-24 (D)
Chargers, 34-17 (SD)
1982—Chargers, 23-3 (D)
Chargers, 30-20 (SD)
1983—Broncos, 14-6 (D)
Chargers, 31-7 (SD)
1984—Broncos, 16-13 (SD)
Broncos, 16-13 (D)
1985—Chargers, 30-10 (SD)
Broncos, 30-24 (D) OT
(Points—Chargers 1,241, Broncos 1,031)
Franchise in Los Angeles prior to 1961

DENVER vs. SAN FRANCISCO
Broncos lead series, 3-2
1970—49ers, 19-14 (SF)
1973—49ers, 36-34 (D)
1979—Broncos, 38-28 (SF)
1982—Broncos, 24-21 (D)
1985—Broncos, 17-16 (D)
(Points—Broncos 127, 49ers 120)

DENVER vs. SEATTLE
Broncos lead series, 11-7
1977—Broncos, 24-13 (S)
1978—Broncos, 28-7 (D)
Broncos, 20-17 (S) OT
1979—Broncos, 37-34 (D)
Seahawks, 28-23 (S)
1980—Broncos, 36-20 (D)
Broncos, 25-17 (S)
1981—Seahawks, 13-10 (S)
Broncos, 23-13 (D)
1982—Seahawks, 17-10 (D)
Seahawks, 13-11 (S)
1983—Seahawks, 27-19 (S)
Broncos, 38-27 (D)
*Seahawks, 31-7 (S)
1984—Seahawks, 27-24 (D)
Broncos, 31-14 (S)
1985—Broncos, 13-10 (D) OT
Broncos, 27-24 (S)
(Points—Broncos 406, Seahawks 352)
AFC First Round Playoff

DENVER vs. TAMPA BAY
Broncos lead series, 2-0
1976—Broncos, 48-13 (D)
1981—Broncos, 24-7 (TB)
(Points—Broncos 72, Buccaneers 20)

DENVER vs. WASHINGTON
Redskins lead series, 2-1
1970—Redskins, 19-3 (D)
1974—Redskins, 30-3 (W)
1980—Broncos, 20-17 (D)
(Points—Redskins 66, Broncos 26)

DETROIT vs. ATLANTA
Lions lead series, 12-4;
See Atlanta vs. Detroit

DETROIT vs. BUFFALO
Series tied, 1-1-1;
See Buffalo vs. Detroit

DETROIT vs. CHICAGO
Bears lead series, 64-44-5;
See Chicago vs. Detroit

DETROIT vs. CINCINNATI
Lions lead series, 2-1;
See Cincinnati vs. Detroit

DETROIT vs. CLEVELAND
Lions lead series, 12-3;
See Cleveland vs. Detroit

DETROIT vs. DALLAS
Cowboys lead series, 6-3;
See Dallas vs. Detroit

DETROIT vs. DENVER
Broncos lead series, 3-2;
See Denver vs. Detroit

***DETROIT vs. GREEN BAY**
Packers lead series, 57-47-7
1930—Packers, 47-13 (GB)
Tie, 6-6 (P)
1932—Packers, 15-10 (GB)
Spartans, 19-0 (P)
1933—Packers, 17-0 (GB)
Spartans, 7-0 (P)
1934—Lions, 3-0 (GB)
Packers, 3-0 (D)
1935—Packers, 13-9 (GB)
Packers, 31-7 (GB)
Lions, 20-10 (D)
1936—Packers, 20-18 (GB)
Packers, 26-17 (D)
1937—Packers, 26-6 (GB)
Packers, 14-13 (D)
1938—Lions, 17-7 (GB)
Packers, 28-7 (D)
1939—Packers, 26-7 (GB)
Packers, 12-7 (D)
1940—Lions, 23-14 (GB)
Packers, 50-7 (D)
1941—Packers, 23-0 (GB)
Packers, 24-7 (D)
1942—Packers, 38-7 (Mil)
Packers, 28-7 (D)
1943—Packers, 35-14 (GB)
Packers, 27-6 (D)
1944—Packers, 27-6 (GB)
Packers, 14-0 (D)
1945—Packers, 57-21 (Mil)
Lions, 14-3 (D)
1946—Packers, 10-7 (Mil)
Packers, 9-0 (D)
1947—Packers, 34-17 (GB)
Packers, 35-14 (D)
1948—Packers, 33-21 (GB)
Lions, 24-20 (D)
1949—Packers, 16-14 (GB)
Lions, 21-7 (D)
1950—Lions, 45-7 (GB)
Lions, 24-21 (D)
1951—Lions, 24-17 (GB)
Lions, 52-35 (D)
1952—Lions, 52-17 (GB)
Lions, 48-24 (D)
1953—Lions, 14-7 (GB)
Lions, 34-15 (D)
1954—Lions, 21-17 (GB)
Lions, 28-24 (D)
1955—Packers, 20-17 (GB)
Lions, 24-10 (D)
1956—Lions, 20-16 (GB)
Packers, 24-20 (D)
1957—Lions, 24-14 (GB)
Lions, 18-6 (D)
1958—Tie, 13-13 (GB)
Lions, 24-14 (D)
1959—Packers, 28-10 (GB)
Packers, 24-17 (D)
1960—Packers, 28-9 (GB)
Lions, 23-10 (D)
1961—Lions, 17-13 (Mil)
Packers, 17-9 (D)
1962—Packers, 9-7 (GB)
Lions, 26-14 (D)
1963—Packers, 31-10 (Mil)
Tie, 13-13 (D)
1964—Packers, 14-10 (D)
Packers, 30-7 (GB)
1965—Packers, 31-21 (D)
Lions, 12-7 (GB)
1966—Packers, 23-14 (GB)
Packers, 31-7 (D)
1967—Tie, 17-17 (GB)
Packers, 27-17 (D)
1968—Lions, 23-17 (GB)
Tie, 14-14 (D)
1969—Packers, 28-17 (D)
Lions, 16-10 (GB)
1970—Lions, 40-0 (GB)
Lions, 20-0 (D)
1971—Lions, 31-28 (D)
Tie, 14-14 (Mil)
1972—Packers, 24-23 (D)
Packers, 33-7 (GB)
1973—Tie, 13-13 (GB)
Lions, 34-0 (D)
1974—Packers, 21-19 (Mil)
Lions, 19-17 (D)
1975—Lions, 30-16 (Mil)
Lions, 13-10 (D)
1976—Packers, 24-14 (GB)
Lions, 27-6 (D)
1977—Lions, 10-6 (D)
Packers, 10-9 (GB)
1978—Packers, 13-7 (D)
Packers, 35-14 (Mil)
1979—Packers, 24-16 (Mil)
Packers, 18-13 (D)
1980—Lions, 29-7 (Mil)
Lions, 24-3 (D)
1981—Lions, 31-27 (D)
Packers, 31-17 (GB)
1982—Lions, 30-10 (GB)
Lions, 27-24 (D)
1983—Lions, 38-14 (D)
Lions, 23-20 (Mil) OT
1984—Packers, 41-9 (GB)
Lions, 31-28 (D)
1985—Packers, 43-10 (GB)
Packers, 26-23 (D)
(Points—Packers 2,128, Lions 1,899)
Franchise in Portsmouth prior to 1934 and known as the Spartans

DETROIT vs. HOUSTON
Oilers lead series, 2-1
1971—Lions, 31-7 (H)
1975—Oilers, 24-8 (H)
1983—Oilers, 27-17 (H)
(Points—Oilers 58, Lions 56)

DETROIT vs. *INDIANAPOLIS
Colts lead series, 17-16-2
1953—Lions, 27-17 (B)
Lions, 17-7 (D)
1954—Lions, 35-0 (D)
Lions, 27-3 (B)
1955—Colts, 28-13 (B)
Lions, 24-14 (D)
1956—Lions, 31-14 (B)
Lions, 27-3 (D)
1957—Colts, 34-14 (B)
Lions, 31-27 (D)
1958—Colts, 28-15 (B)
Colts, 40-14 (D)
1959—Colts, 21-9 (B)
Colts, 31-24 (D)
1960—Lions, 30-17 (D)
Lions, 20-15 (B)
1961—Lions, 16-15 (B)
Colts, 17-14 (D)
1962—Lions, 29-20 (B)
Lions, 21-14 (D)
1963—Colts, 25-21 (D)
Colts, 24-21 (B)
1964—Colts, 34-0 (D)
Lions, 31-14 (B)
1965—Colts, 31-7 (B)
Tie, 24-24 (D)
1966—Colts, 45-14 (B)
Lions, 20-14 (D)
1967—Colts, 41-7 (B)
1968—Colts, 27-10 (D)
1969—Tie, 17-17 (B)
1973—Colts, 29-27 (D)
1977—Lions, 13-10 (B)
1980—Colts, 10-9 (D)
1985—Colts, 14-6 (I)
(Points—Colts 724, Lions 665)
Franchise in Baltimore prior to 1984

DETROIT vs. KANSAS CITY
Series tied, 2-2
1971—Lions, 32-21 (D)
1975—Chiefs, 24-21 (KC) OT
1980—Chiefs, 20-17 (KC)
1981—Lions, 27-10 (D)
(Points—Lions 97, Chiefs 75)

DETROIT vs. *L.A. RAIDERS
Raiders lead series, 3-2
1970—Lions, 28-14 (D)
1974—Raiders, 35-13 (O)
1978—Raiders, 29-17 (O)
1981—Lions, 16-0 (D)
1984—Raiders, 24-3 (D)
(Points—Raiders 102, Lions 77)
Franchise in Oakland prior to 1982

DETROIT vs. *L.A. RAMS
Rams lead series, 36-34-1
1937—Lions, 28-0 (C)
Lions, 27-7 (D)
1938—Rams, 21-17 (C)
Lions, 6-0 (D)
1939—Lions, 15-7 (D)
Rams, 14-3 (C)
1940—Lions, 6-0 (D)
Rams, 24-0 (C)
1941—Lions, 17-7 (D)
Lions, 14-0 (C)
1942—Rams, 14-0 (D)
Rams, 27-7 (C)
1944—Rams, 20-17 (D)
Lions, 26-14 (C)
1945—Rams, 28-21 (D)
1946—Rams, 35-14 (LA)
Rams, 41-20 (D)
1947—Rams, 27-13 (D)
Rams, 28-17 (LA)
1948—Rams, 44-7 (LA)
Rams, 34-27 (D)
1949—Rams, 27-24 (LA)
Rams, 21-10 (D)
1950—Rams, 30-28 (D)
Rams, 65-24 (LA)
1951—Rams, 27-21 (D)
Lions, 24-22 (LA)
1952—Lions, 17-14 (LA)
Lions, 24-16 (D)
**Lions, 31-21 (D)
1953—Rams, 31-19 (D)
Rams, 37-24 (LA)
1954—Lions, 21-3 (D)
Lions, 27-24 (LA)
1955—Rams, 17-10 (D)
Rams, 24-13 (LA)
1956—Lions, 24-21 (D)
Lions, 16-7 (LA)
1957—Lions, 10-7 (D)
Rams, 35-17 (LA)

1958—Rams, 42-28 (D)
Lions, 41-24 (LA)
1959—Lions, 17-7 (LA)
Lions, 23-17 (D)
1960—Rams, 48-35 (LA)
Lions, 12-10 (D)
1961—Lions, 14-13 (D)
Lions, 28-10 (LA)
1962—Lions, 13-10 (D)
Lions, 12-3 (LA)
1963—Lions, 23-2 (LA)
Rams, 28-21 (D)
1964—Tie, 17-17 (LA)
Lions, 37-17 (D)
1965—Lions, 20-0 (D)
Lions, 31-7 (LA)
1966—Rams, 14-7 (D)
Rams, 23-3 (LA)
1967—Rams, 31-7 (D)
1968—Rams, 10-7 (LA)
1969—Lions, 28-0 (D)
1970—Lions, 28-23 (LA)
1971—Rams, 21-13 (D)
1972—Lions, 34-17 (LA)
1974—Rams, 16-13 (LA)
1975—Rams, 20-0 (D)
1976—Rams, 20-17 (D)
1980—Lions, 41-20 (LA)
1981—Rams, 20-13 (LA)
1982—Lions, 19-14 (LA)
1983—Rams, 21-10 (LA)
(Points—Rams 1,366, Lions 1,298)
Franchise in Cleveland prior to 1946
***Conference Playoff*

DETROIT vs. MIAMI
Dolphins lead series, 2-1
1973—Dolphins, 34-7 (M)
1979—Dolphins, 28-10 (D)
1985—Lions, 31-21 (D)
(Points—Dolphins 83, Lions 48)

DETROIT vs. MINNESOTA
Vikings lead series, 30-17-2
1961—Lions, 37-10 (M)
Lions, 13-7 (D)
1962—Lions, 17-6 (M)
Lions, 37-23 (D)
1963—Lions, 28-10 (D)
Vikings, 34-31 (M)
1964—Lions, 24-20 (M)
Tie, 23-23 (D)
1965—Lions, 31-29 (M)
Vikings, 29-7 (D)
1966—Lions, 32-31 (M)
Vikings, 28-16 (D)
1967—Tie, 10-10 (M)
Lions, 14-3 (D)
1968—Vikings, 24-10 (M)
Vikings, 13-6 (D)
1969—Vikings, 24-10 (M)
Vikings, 27-0 (D)
1970—Vikings, 30-17 (D)
Vikings, 24-20 (M)
1971—Vikings, 16-13 (D)
Vikings, 29-10 (M)
1972—Vikings, 34-10 (D)
Vikings, 16-14 (M)
1973—Vikings, 23-9 (D)
Vikings, 28-7 (M)
1974—Vikings, 7-6 (D)
Lions, 20-16 (M)
1975—Vikings, 25-19 (M)
Lions, 17-10 (D)
1976—Vikings, 10-9 (D)
Vikings, 31-23 (M)
1977—Vikings, 14-7 (M)
Vikings, 30-21 (D)
1978—Vikings, 17-7 (M)
Lions, 45-14 (D)
1979—Vikings, 13-10 (D)
Vikings, 14-7 (M)
1980—Lions, 27-7 (D)
Vikings, 34-0 (M)
1981—Vikings, 26-24 (M)
Lions, 45-7 (D)
1982—Vikings, 34-31 (D)
1983—Vikings, 20-17 (M)
Lions, 13-2 (D)
1984—Vikings, 29-28 (D)
Lions, 16-14 (M)
1985—Vikings, 16-13 (M)
Lions, 41-21 (D)
(Points—Vikings 962, Lions 892)

DETROIT vs. NEW ENGLAND
Series tied, 2-2
1971—Lions, 34-7 (NE)
1976—Lions, 30-10 (D)
1979—Patriots, 24-17 (NE)
1985—Patriots, 23-6 (NE)
(Points—Lions 87, Patriots 64)

DETROIT vs. NEW ORLEANS
Series tied, 4-4-1
1968—Tie, 20-20 (D)
1970—Saints, 19-17 (NO)
1972—Lions, 27-14 (D)
1973—Saints, 20-13 (NO)
1974—Lions, 19-14 (D)
1976—Saints, 17-16 (NO)
1977—Lions, 23-19 (D)
1979—Saints, 17-7 (NO)
1980—Lions, 24-13 (D)
(Points—Lions 166, Saints 153)

***DETROIT vs. N.Y. GIANTS**
Lions lead series, 18-11-1
1930—Giants, 19-6 (P)
1931—Spartans, 14-6 (P)
Giants, 14-0 (NY)
1932—Spartans, 7-0 (P)
Spartans, 6-0 (NY)
1933—Spartans, 17-7 (P)
Giants, 13-10 (NY)
1934—Lions, 9-0 (D)
1935—**Lions, 26-7 (D)
1936—Giants, 14-7 (NY)
Lions, 38-0 (D)
1937—Lions, 17-0 (NY)
1939—Lions, 18-14 (D)
1941—Giants, 20-13 (NY)
1943—Tie, 0-0 (D)
1945—Giants, 35-14 (NY)
1947—Lions, 35-7 (D)
1949—Lions, 45-21 (NY)
1953—Lions, 27-16 (NY)
1955—Giants, 24-19 (D)
1958—Giants, 19-17 (D)
1962—Giants, 17-14 (NY)
1964—Lions, 26-3 (D)
1967—Lions, 30-7 (NY)
1969—Lions, 24-0 (D)
1972—Lions, 30-16 (D)
1974—Lions, 20-19 (D)
1976—Giants, 24-10 (NY)
1982—Giants, 13-6 (D)
1983—Lions, 15-9 (D)
(Points—Lions 520, Giants 344)
**Franchise in Portsmouth prior to 1934 and known as the Spartans*
***NFL Championship*

DETROIT vs. N.Y. JETS
Series tied, 2-2
1972—Lions, 37-20 (D)
1979—Jets, 31-10 (NY)
1982—Jets, 28-13 (D)
1985—Lions, 31-20 (D)
(Points—Jets 99, Lions 91)

***DETROIT vs. PHILADELPHIA**
Lions lead series, 11-9-2
1933—Spartans, 25-0 (P)
1934—Lions, 10-0 (P)
1935—Lions, 35-0 (D)
1936—Lions, 23-0 (P)
1938—Eagles, 21-7 (D)
1940—Lions, 21-0 (P)
1941—Lions, 21-17 (D)
1945—Lions, 28-24 (D)
1948—Eagles, 45-21 (P)
1949—Eagles, 22-14 (D)
1951—Lions, 28-10 (P)
1954—Tie, 13-13 (D)
1957—Lions, 27-16 (P)
1960—Eagles, 28-10 (P)
1961—Eagles, 27-24 (D)
1965—Lions, 35-28 (P)
1968—Eagles, 12-0 (D)
1971—Eagles, 23-20 (D)
1974—Eagles, 28-17 (P)
1977—Lions, 17-13 (D)
1979—Eagles, 44-7 (P)
1984—Tie, 23-23 (D) OT
(Points—Lions 426, Eagles 394)
**Franchise in Portsmouth prior to 1934 and known as the Spartans*

DETROIT vs. *PITTSBURGH
Lions lead series, 13-8-1
1934—Lions, 40-7 (D)
1936—Lions, 28-3 (D)
1937—Lions, 7-3 (D)
1938—Lions, 16-7 (D)
1940—Pirates, 10-7 (D)
1942—Steelers, 35-7 (D)
1946—Lions, 17-7 (D)
1947—Steelers, 17-10 (P)
1948—Lions, 17-14 (D)
1949—Steelers, 14-7 (P)
1950—Lions, 10-7 (D)
1952—Lions, 31-6 (P)
1953—Lions, 38-21 (D)
1955—Lions, 31-28 (P)
1956—Lions, 45-7 (D)
1959—Tie, 10-10 (P)
1962—Lions, 45-7 (D)
1966—Steelers, 17-3 (P)
1967—Steelers, 24-14 (D)
1969—Steelers, 16-13 (P)
1973—Steelers, 24-10 (P)
1983—Lions, 45-3 (D)
(Points—Lions 451, Steelers 287)
**Steelers known as Pirates prior to 1941*

***DETROIT vs. **ST. LOUIS**
Lions lead series, 25-15-5
1930—Tie, 0-0 (P)
Cardinals, 23-0 (C)
1931—Cardinals, 20-19 (C)
1932—Tie, 7-7 (P)
1933—Spartans, 7-6 (P)
1934—Lions, 6-0 (D)
Lions, 17-13 (C)
1935—Tie, 10-10 (D)
Lions, 7-6 (C)
1936—Lions, 39-0 (D)
Lions, 14-7 (C)
1937—Lions, 16-7 (C)
Lions, 16-7 (D)
1938—Lions, 10-0 (D)
Lions, 7-3 (C)
1939—Lions, 21-3 (D)
Lions, 17-3 (C)
1940—Tie, 0-0 (Buffalo)
Lions, 43-14 (C)
1941—Tie, 14-14 (C)
Lions, 21-3 (D)
1942—Cardinals, 13-0 (C)
Cardinals, 7-0 (D)
1943—Lions, 35-17 (D)
Lions, 7-0 (C)
1945—Lions, 10-0 (C)
Lions, 26-0 (D)
1946—Cardinals, 34-14 (C)
Cardinals, 36-14 (D)
1947—Cardinals, 45-21 (C)
Cardinals, 17-7 (D)
1948—Cardinals, 56-20 (C)
Cardinals, 28-14 (D)
1949—Lions, 24-7 (C)
Cardinals, 42-19 (D)
1959—Lions, 45-21 (D)
1961—Lions, 45-14 (StL)
1967—Cardinals, 38-28 (StL)
1969—Lions, 20-0 (D)
1970—Lions, 16-3 (D)
1973—Lions, 20-16 (StL)
1975—Cardinals, 24-13 (D)
1978—Cardinals, 21-14 (StL)
1980—Lions, 20-7 (D)
Cardinals, 24-23 (StL)
(Points—Lions 746, Cardinals 626)
**Franchise in Portsmouth prior to 1934 and known as the Spartans*
***Franchise in Chicago prior to 1960*

DETROIT vs. SAN DIEGO
Lions lead series, 3-2
1972—Lions, 34-20 (D)
1977—Lions, 20-0 (D)
1978—Lions, 31-14 (D)
1981—Chargers, 28-23 (SD)
1984—Chargers, 27-24 (SD)
(Points—Lions 132, Chargers 89)

DETROIT vs. SAN FRANCISCO
Lions lead series, 26-23-1
1950—Lions, 24-7 (D)
49ers, 28-27 (SF)
1951—49ers, 20-10 (D)
49ers, 21-17 (SF)
1952—49ers, 17-3 (SF)
49ers, 28-0 (D)
1953—Lions, 24-21 (D)
Lions, 14-10 (SF)
1954—49ers, 37-31 (SF)
Lions, 48-7 (D)
1955—49ers, 27-24 (D)
49ers, 38-21 (SF)
1956—Lions, 20-17 (D)
Lions, 17-13 (SF)
1957—49ers, 35-31 (SF)
Lions, 31-10 (D)
*Lions, 31-27 (SF)
1958—49ers, 24-21 (SF)
Lions, 35-21 (D)
1959—49ers, 34-13 (D)
49ers, 33-7 (SF)
1960—49ers, 14-10 (D)
Lions, 24-0 (SF)
1961—49ers, 49-0 (D)
Tie, 20-20 (SF)
1962—Lions, 45-24 (D)
Lions, 38-24 (SF)
1963—Lions, 26-3 (D)
Lions, 45-7 (SF)
1964—Lions, 26-17 (SF)
Lions, 24-7 (D)
1965—49ers, 27-21 (D)
49ers, 17-14 (SF)
1966—49ers, 27-24 (SF)
49ers, 41-14 (D)
1967—Lions, 45-3 (SF)
1968—49ers, 14-7 (D)
1969—Lions, 26-14 (SF)
1970—Lions, 28-7 (D)
1971—49ers, 31-27 (SF)
1973—Lions, 30-20 (D)
1974—Lions, 17-13 (D)
1975—Lions, 28-17 (SF)
1977—49ers, 28-7 (SF)
1978—Lions, 33-14 (D)
1980—Lions, 17-13 (D)
1981—Lions, 24-17 (D)
1983—**49ers, 24-23 (SF)
1984—49ers, 30-27 (D)
1985—Lions, 23-21 (D)
(Points—Lions 1,142, 49ers 1,018)
**Conference Playoff*
***NFC Divisional Playoff*

DETROIT vs. SEATTLE
Seahawks lead series, 2-1
1976—Lions, 41-14 (S)
1978—Seahawks, 28-16 (S)
1984—Seahawks, 38-17 (S)
(Points—Seahawks 80, Lions 74)

DETROIT vs. TAMPA BAY
Lions lead series, 9-7
1977—Lions, 16-7 (D)
1978—Lions, 15-7 (TB)
Lions, 34-23 (D)
1979—Buccaneers, 31-16 (TB)
Buccaneers, 16-14 (D)
1980—Lions, 24-10 (TB)
Lions, 27-14 (D)
1981—Buccaneers, 28-10 (TB)
Buccaneers, 20-17 (D)
1982—Buccaneers, 23-21 (TB)
1983—Lions, 11-0 (TB)
Lions, 23-20 (D)
1984—Buccaneers, 21-17 (TB)
Lions, 13-7 (D) OT
1985—Lions, 30-9 (D)
Buccaneers, 19-16 (TB) OT
(Points—Lions 304, Buccaneers 255)

***DETROIT vs. **WASHINGTON**
Redskins lead series, 19-8
1932—Spartans, 10-0 (P)
1933—Spartans, 13-0 (B)
1934—Lions, 24-0 (D)
1935—Lions, 17-7 (B)
Lions, 14-0 (D)
1938—Redskins, 7-5 (D)
1939—Redskins, 31-7 (W)
1940—Redskins, 20-14 (D)
1942—Redskins, 15-3 (D)
1943—Redskins, 42-20 (W)
1946—Redskins, 17-16 (W)
1947—Lions, 38-21 (D)
1948—Redskins, 46-21 (W)
1951—Lions, 35-17 (D)
1956—Redskins, 18-17 (W)
1965—Lions, 14-10 (D)
1968—Redskins, 14-3 (W)
1970—Redskins, 31-10 (W)
1973—Redskins, 20-0 (D)
1976—Redskins, 20-7 (W)
1978—Redskins, 21-19 (D)
1979—Redskins, 27-24 (D)
1981—Redskins, 33-31 (W)
1982—***Redskins, 31-7 (W)
1983—Redskins, 38-17 (W)
1984—Redskins, 28-14 (W)
1985—Redskins, 24-3 (W)
(Points—Redskins 538, Lions 403)
**Franchise in Portsmouth prior to 1934 and known as the Spartans.*
***Franchise in Boston prior to 1937*
****NFC First Round Playoff*

GREEN BAY vs. ATLANTA
Packers lead series, 8-6;
See Atlanta vs. Green Bay

GREEN BAY vs. BUFFALO
Bills lead series, 2-1;
See Buffalo vs. Green Bay

GREEN BAY vs. CHICAGO
Bears lead series, 70-55-6;
See Chicago vs. Green Bay

GREEN BAY vs. CINCINNATI
Bengals lead series, 3-2;
See Cincinnati vs. Green Bay

GREEN BAY vs. CLEVELAND
Packers lead series, 7-5;
See Cleveland vs. Green Bay

GREEN BAY vs. DALLAS
Packers lead series, 8-5;
See Dallas vs. Green Bay

GREEN BAY vs. DENVER
Broncos lead series, 3-1;
See Denver vs. Green Bay

GREEN BAY vs. DETROIT
Packers lead series, 57-47-7;
See Detroit vs. Green Bay

GREEN BAY vs. HOUSTON
Series tied, 2-2
1972—Packers, 23-10 (H)
1977—Oilers, 16-10 (GB)
1980—Oilers, 22-3 (GB)
1983—Packers, 41-38 (H) OT

GREEN BAY vs. *INDIANAPOLIS
Packers lead series, 18-17-1

1953—Packers, 37-14 (GB)
Packers, 35-24 (B)
1954—Packers, 7-6 (B)
Packers, 24-13 (Mil)
1955—Colts, 24-20 (Mil)
Colts, 14-10 (B)
1956—Packers, 38-33 (Mil)
Colts, 28-21 (B)
1957—Colts, 45-17 (Mil)
Packers, 24-21 (B)
1958—Colts, 24-17 (Mil)
Colts, 56-0 (B)
1959—Colts, 38-21 (B)
Colts, 28-24 (Mil)
1960—Packers, 35-21 (GB)
Colts, 38-24 (B)
1961—Packers, 45-7 (GB)
Colts, 45-21 (B)
1962—Packers, 17-6 (B)
Packers, 17-13 (GB)
1963—Packers, 31-20 (GB)
Packers, 34-20 (B)
1964—Colts, 21-20 (GB)
Colts, 24-21 (B)
1965—Packers, 20-17 (Mil)
Packers, 42-27 (B)
**Packers, 13-10 (GB) OT
1966—Packers, 24-3 (Mil)
Packers, 14-10 (B)
1967—Colts, 13-10 (B)
1968—Colts, 16-3 (GB)
1969—Colts, 14-6 (B)
1970—Colts, 13-10 (Mil)
1974—Packers, 20-13 (B)
1982—Tie, 20-20 (B) OT
1985—Colts, 37-10 (I)
(Points—Colts 776, Packers 752)
Franchise in Baltimore prior to 1984
**Conference Playoff*

GREEN BAY vs. KANSAS CITY
Series tied, 1-1-1
1966—*Packers, 35-10 (Los Angeles)
1973—Tie, 10-10 (Mil)
1977—Chiefs, 20-10 (KC)
(Points—Packers 55, Chiefs 40)
Super Bowl I

GREEN BAY vs. *L.A. RAIDERS
Raiders lead series, 4-1
1967—**Packers, 33-14 (Miami)
1972—Raiders, 20-14 (GB)
1976—Raiders, 18-14 (O)
1978—Raiders, 28-3 (GB)
1984—Raiders, 28-7 (LA)
(Points—Raiders 108, Packers 71)
Franchise in Oakland prior to 1982
**Super Bowl II*

GREEN BAY vs. *L.A. RAMS
Rams lead series, 39-34-2
1937—Packers, 35-10 (C)
Packers, 35-7 (GB)
1938—Packers, 26-17 (GB)
Packers, 28-7 (C)
1939—Rams, 27-24 (GB)
Packers, 7-6 (C)
1940—Packers, 31-14 (GB)
Tie, 13-13 (C)
1941—Packers, 24-7 (Mil)
Packers, 17-14 (C)
1942—Packers, 45-28 (GB)
Packers, 30-12 (C)
1944—Packers, 30-21 (GB)
Packers, 42-7 (C)
1945—Rams, 27-14 (GB)
Rams, 20-7 (C)
1946—Rams, 21-17 (Mil)
Rams, 38-17 (LA)
1947—Packers, 17-14 (Mil)
Packers, 30-10 (LA)
1948—Packers, 16-0 (GB)
Rams, 24-10 (LA)
1949—Rams, 48-7 (GB)
Rams, 35-7 (LA)
1950—Rams, 45-14 (Mil)
Rams, 51-14 (LA)
1951—Rams, 28-0 (Mil)
Rams, 42-14 (LA)
1952—Rams, 30-28 (Mil)
Rams, 45-27 (LA)
1953—Rams, 38-20 (Mil)
Rams, 33-17 (LA)
1954—Packers, 35-17 (Mil)
Rams, 35-27 (LA)
1955—Packers, 30-28 (Mil)
Rams, 31-17 (LA)
1956—Packers, 42-17 (Mil)
Rams, 49-21 (LA)
1957—Rams, 31-27 (Mil)
Rams, 42-17 (LA)
1958—Rams, 20-7 (GB)
Rams, 34-20 (LA)
1959—Rams, 45-6 (Mil)
Packers, 38-20 (LA)
1960—Rams, 33-31 (Mil)
Packers, 35-2 (LA)
1961—Packers, 35-17 (GB)
Packers, 24-17 (LA)
1962—Packers, 41-10 (Mil)
Packers, 20-17 (LA)
1963—Packers, 42-10 (GB)
Packers, 31-14 (LA)
1964—Rams, 27-17 (Mil)
Tie, 24-24 (LA)
1965—Packers, 6-3 (Mil)
Rams, 21-10 (LA)
1966—Packers, 24-13 (GB)
Packers, 27-23 (LA)
1967—Rams, 27-24 (LA)
**Packers, 28-7 (Mil)
1968—Rams, 16-14 (Mil)
1969—Rams, 34-21 (LA)
1970—Rams, 31-21 (GB)
1971—Rams, 30-13 (LA)
1973—Rams, 24-7 (LA)
1974—Packers, 17-6 (Mil)
1975—Rams, 22-5 (LA)
1977—Rams, 24-6 (Mil)
1978—Rams, 31-14 (LA)
1980—Rams, 51-21 (LA)
1981—Rams, 35-23 (LA)
1982—Packers, 35-23 (Mil)
1983—Packers, 27-24 (Mil)
1984—Packers, 31-6 (Mil)
1985—Rams, 34-17 (LA)
(Points—Rams 1,783, Packers 1,641)
Franchise in Cleveland prior to 1946
**Conference Championship*

GREEN BAY vs. MIAMI
Dolphins lead series, 4-0
1971—Dolphins, 27-6 (Mia)
1975—Dolphins, 31-7 (GB)
1979—Dolphins, 27-7 (Mia)
1985—Dolphins, 34-24 (GB)
(Points—Dolphins 119, Packers 44)

GREEN BAY vs. MINNESOTA
Series tied, 24-24-1
1961—Packers, 33-7 (Minn)
Packers, 28-10 (Mil)
1962—Packers, 34-7 (GB)
Packers, 48-21 (Minn)
1963—Packers, 37-28 (Minn)
Packers, 28-7 (GB)
1964—Vikings, 24-23 (GB)
Packers, 42-13 (Minn)
1965—Packers, 38-13 (Minn)
Packers, 24-19 (GB)
1966—Vikings, 20-17 (GB)
Packers, 28-16 (Minn)
1967—Vikings, 10-7 (Mil)
Packers, 30-27 (Minn)
1968—Vikings, 26-13 (Mil)
Vikings, 14-10 (Minn)
1969—Vikings, 19-7 (Minn)
Vikings, 9-7 (Mil)
1970—Packers, 13-10 (Mil)
Vikings, 10-3 (Minn)
1971—Vikings, 24-13 (GB)
Vikings, 3-0 (Minn)
1972—Vikings, 27-13 (GB)
Packers, 23-7 (Minn)
1973—Vikings, 11-3 (Minn)
Vikings, 31-7 (GB)
1974—Vikings, 32-17 (GB)
Packers, 19-7 (Minn)
1975—Vikings, 28-17 (GB)
Vikings, 24-3 (Minn)
1976—Vikings, 17-10 (Mil)
Vikings, 20-9 (Minn)
1977—Vikings, 19-7 (Minn)
Vikings, 13-6 (GB)
1978—Vikings, 21-7 (Minn)
Tie, 10-10 (GB) OT
1979—Vikings, 27-21 (Minn) OT
Packers, 19-7 (Mil)
1980—Packers, 16-3 (GB)
Packers, 25-13 (Minn)
1981—Vikings, 30-13 (Mil)
Packers, 35-23 (Minn)
1982—Packers, 26-7 (Mil)
1983—Vikings, 20-17 (GB) OT
Packers, 29-21 (Minn)
1984—Packers, 45-17 (Mil)
Packers, 38-14 (Minn)
1985—Packers, 20-17 (Mil)
Packers, 27-17 (Minn)
(Points—Packers 965, Vikings 820)

GREEN BAY vs. NEW ENGLAND
Patriots lead series, 2-1
1973—Patriots, 33-24 (NE)
1979—Packers, 27-14 (GB)
1985—Patriots, 26-20 (NE)
(Points—Patriots 73, Packers 71)

GREEN BAY vs. NEW ORLEANS
Packers lead series, 10-2
1968—Packers, 29-7 (Mil)
1971—Saints, 29-21 (Mil)
1972—Packers, 30-20 (NO)
1973—Packers, 30-10 (Mil)
1975—Saints, 20-19 (NO)
1976—Packers, 32-27 (Mil)
1977—Packers, 24-20 (NO)
1978—Packers, 28-17 (Mil)
1979—Packers, 28-19 (Mil)
1981—Packers, 35-7 (NO)
1984—Packers, 23-13 (NO)
1985—Packers, 38-14 (Mil)
(Points—Packers 337, Saints 203)

GREEN BAY vs. N.Y. GIANTS
Packers lead series, 25-18-2
1928—Giants, 6-0 (GB)
Packers, 7-0 (NY)
1929—Packers, 20-6 (NY)
1930—Packers, 14-7 (GB)
Giants, 13-6 (NY)
1931—Packers, 27-7 (GB)
Packers, 14-10 (NY)
1932—Packers, 13-0 (GB)
Giants, 6-0 (NY)
1933—Giants, 10-7 (Mil)
Giants, 17-6 (NY)
1934—Packers, 20-6 (Mil)
Giants, 17-3 (NY)
1935—Packers, 16-7 (GB)
1936—Packers, 26-14 (NY)
1937—Giants, 10-0 (NY)
1938—Giants, 15-3 (NY)
*Giants, 23-17 (NY)
1939—*Packers, 27-0 (Mil)
1940—Giants, 7-3 (NY)
1942—Tie, 21-21 (NY)
1943—Packers, 35-21 (NY)
1944—Giants, 24-0 (NY)
*Packers, 14-7 (NY)
1945—Packers, 23-14 (NY)
1947—Tie, 24-24 (NY)
1948—Giants, 49-3 (Mil)
1949—Giants, 30-10 (GB)
1952—Packers, 17-3 (NY)
1957—Giants, 31-17 (GB)
1959—Giants, 20-3 (NY)
1961—Packers, 20-17 (Mil)
*Packers, 37-0 (GB)
1962—*Packers, 16-7 (NY)
1967—Packers, 48-21 (NY)
1969—Packers, 20-10 (Mil)
1971—Giants, 42-40 (GB)
1973—Packers, 16-14 (New Haven)
1975—Packers, 40-14 (Mil)
1980—Giants, 27-21 (NY)
1981—Packers, 27-14 (NY)
Packers, 26-24 (Mil)
1982—Packers, 27-19 (NY)
1983—Giants, 27-3 (NY)
1985—Packers, 23-20 (GB)
(Points—Packers 760, Giants 681)
NFL Championship

GREEN BAY vs. N.Y. JETS
Jets lead series, 4-1
1973—Packers, 23-7 (Mil)
1979—Jets, 27-22 (GB)
1981—Jets, 28-3 (NY)
1982—Jets, 15-13 (NY)
1985—Jets, 24-3 (Mil)
(Points—Jets 101, Packers 64)

GREEN BAY vs. PHILADELPHIA
Packers lead series, 17-5
1933—Packers, 35-9 (GB)
Packers, 10-0 (P)
1934—Packers, 19-6 (GB)
1935—Packers, 13-6 (P)
1937—Packers, 37-7 (Mil)
1939—Packers, 23-16 (P)
1940—Packers, 27-20 (GB)
1942—Packers, 7-0 (P)
1946—Packers, 19-7 (P)
1947—Eagles, 28-14 (P)
1951—Packers, 37-24 (GB)
1952—Packers, 12-10 (Mil)
1954—Packers, 37-14 (P)
1958—Packers, 38-35 (GB)
1960—*Eagles, 17-13 (P)
1962—Packers, 49-0 (P)
1968—Packers, 30-13 (GB)
1970—Packers, 30-17 (Mil)
1974—Eagles, 36-14 (P)
1976—Packers, 28-13 (GB)
1978—Eagles, 10-3 (P)
1979—Eagles, 21-10 (GB)
(Points—Packers 505, Eagles 309)
NFL Championship

GREEN BAY vs. *PITTSBURGH
Packers lead series, 16-10
1933—Packers, 47-0 (GB)
1935—Packers, 27-0 (GB)
Packers, 34-14 (P)
1936—Packers, 42-10 (Mil)
1938—Packers, 20-0 (GB)
1940—Packers, 24-3 (Mil)
1941—Packers, 54-7 (P)
1942—Packers, 24-21 (Mil)
1946—Packers, 17-7 (GB)
1947—Steelers, 18-17 (Mil)
1948—Steelers, 38-7 (P)
1949—Steelers, 30-7 (Mil)
1951—Packers, 35-33 (Mil)
Steelers, 28-7 (P)
1953—Steelers, 31-14 (P)
1954—Steelers, 21-20 (GB)
1957—Packers, 27-10 (P)
1960—Packers, 19-13 (P)
1963—Packers, 33-14 (Mil)
1965—Packers, 41-9 (P)
1967—Steelers, 24-17 (GB)
1969—Packers, 38-34 (P)
1970—Packers, 20-12 (P)
1975—Steelers, 16-13 (Mil)
1980—Steelers, 22-20 (P)
1983—Steelers, 25-21 (GB)
(Points—Packers 645, Steelers 440)
Steelers known as Pirates prior to 1941

GREEN BAY vs. *ST. LOUIS
Packers lead series, 38-21-4
1921—Tie, 3-3 (C)
1922—Cardinals, 16-3 (C)
1924—Cardinals, 3-0 (C)
1925—Cardinals, 9-6 (C)
1926—Cardinals, 13-7 (GB)
Packers, 3-0 (C)
1927—Packers, 13-0 (GB)
Tie, 6-6 (C)
1928—Packers, 20-0 (GB)
1929—Packers, 9-2 (GB)
Packers, 7-6 (C)
Packers, 12-0 (C)
1930—Packers, 14-0 (GB)
Cardinals, 13-6 (C)
1931—Packers, 26-7 (GB)
Cardinals, 21-13 (C)
1932—Packers, 15-7 (GB)
Packers, 19-9 (C)
1933—Packers, 14-6 (C)
1934—Packers, 15-0 (GB)
Cardinals, 9-0 (Mil)
Cardinals, 6-0 (C)
1935—Cardinals, 7-6 (GB)
Cardinals, 3-0 (Mil)
Cardinals, 9-7 (C)
1936—Packers, 10-7 (GB)
Packers, 24-0 (Mil)
Tie, 0-0 (C)
1937—Cardinals, 14-7 (GB)
Packers, 34-13 (Mil)
1938—Packers, 28-7 (Mil)
Packers, 24-22 (Buffalo)
1939—Packers, 14-10 (GB)
Packers, 27-20 (Mil)
1940—Packers, 31-6 (Mil)
Packers, 28-7 (C)
1941—Packers, 14-13 (Mil)
Packers, 17-9 (GB)
1942—Packers, 17-13 (C)
Packers, 55-24 (GB)
1943—Packers, 28-7 (C)
Packers, 35-14 (Mil)
1945—Packers, 33-14 (GB)
1946—Packers, 19-7 (C)
Cardinals, 24-6 (GB)
1947—Cardinals, 14-10 (GB)
Cardinals, 21-20 (C)
1948—Cardinals, 17-7 (Mil)
Cardinals, 42-7 (C)
1949—Cardinals, 39-17 (Mil)
Cardinals, 41-21 (C)
1955—Packers, 31-14 (GB)
1956—Packers, 24-21 (C)
1962—Packers, 17-0 (Mil)
1963—Packers, 30-7 (StL)
1967—Packers, 31-23 (StL)
1969—Packers, 45-28 (GB)
1971—Tie, 16-16 (StL)
1973—Packers, 25-21 (GB)
1976—Cardinals, 29-0 (StL)
1982—**Packers, 41-16 (GB)
1984—Packers, 24-23 (GB)
1985—Cardinals, 43-28 (StL)
(Points—Packers 1,069, Cardinals 801)
Franchise in Chicago prior to 1960
**NFC First Round Playoff*

GREEN BAY vs. SAN DIEGO
Packers lead series, 3-1
1970—Packers, 22-20 (SD)
1974—Packers, 34-0 (GB)
1978—Packers, 24-3 (SD)
1984—Chargers, 34-28 (GB)
(Points—Packers 108, Chargers 57)

GREEN BAY vs. SAN FRANCISCO
49ers lead series, 22-20-1
1950—Packers, 25-21 (GB)
49ers, 30-14 (SF)
1951—49ers, 31-19 (SF)
1952—49ers, 24-14 (SF)
1953—49ers, 37-7 (Mil)
49ers, 48-14 (SF)

1954—49ers, 23-17 (Mil)
49ers, 35-0 (SF)
1955—Packers, 27-21 (Mil)
Packers, 28-7 (SF)
1956—49ers, 17-16 (GB)
49ers, 38-20 (SF)
1957—49ers, 24-14 (Mil)
49ers, 27-20 (SF)
1958—49ers, 33-12 (Mil)
49ers, 48-21 (SF)
1959—Packers, 21-20 (GB)
Packers, 36-14 (SF)
1960—Packers, 41-14 (Mil)
Packers, 13-0 (SF)
1961—Packers, 30-10 (GB)
49ers, 22-21 (SF)
1962—Packers, 31-13 (Mil)
Packers, 31-21 (SF)
1963—Packers, 28-10 (Mil)
Packers, 21-17 (SF)
1964—Packers, 24-14 (Mil)
49ers, 24-14 (SF)
1965—Packers, 27-10 (GB)
Tie, 24-24 (SF)
1966—49ers, 21-20 (SF)
Packers, 20-7 (Mil)
1967—Packers, 13-0 (GB)
1968—49ers, 27-20 (SF)
1969—Packers, 14-7 (Mil)
1970—49ers, 26-10 (SF)
1972—Packers, 34-24 (Mil)
1973—49ers, 20-6 (SF)
1974—49ers, 7-6 (SF)
1976—49ers, 26-14 (GB)
1977—Packers, 16-14 (Mil)
1980—Packers, 23-16 (Mil)
1981—49ers, 13-3 (Mil)
(Points—49ers 885, Packers 829)

GREEN BAY vs. SEATTLE
Packers lead series, 3-1
1976—Packers, 27-20 (Mil)
1978—Packers, 45-28 (Mil)
1981—Packers, 34-24 (GB)
1984—Seahawks, 30-24 (Mil)
(Points—Packers 130, Seahawks 102)

GREEN BAY vs. TAMPA BAY
Packers lead series, 8-6-1
1977—Packers, 13-0 (TB)
1978—Packers, 9-7 (GB)
Packers, 17-7 (TB)
1979—Buccaneers, 21-10 (GB)
Buccaneers, 21-3 (TB)
1980—Tie, 14-14 (TB) OT
Buccaneers, 20-17 (Mil)
1981—Buccaneers, 21-10 (GB)
Buccaneers, 37-3 (TB)
1983—Packers, 55-14 (GB)
Packers, 12-9 (TB) OT
1984—Buccaneers, 30-27 (TB) OT
Packers, 27-14 (GB)
1985—Packers, 21-0 (GB)
Packers, 20-17 (TB)
(Points—Packers 258, Buccaneers 232)

GREEN BAY vs. *WASHINGTON
Packers lead series, 14-11-1
1932—Packers, 21-0 (B)
1933—Tie, 7-7 (GB)
Redskins, 20-7 (B)
1934—Packers, 10-0 (B)
1936—Packers, 31-2 (GB)
Packers, 7-3 (B)
**Packers, 21-6 (New York)
1937—Redskins, 14-6 (W)
1939—Packers, 24-14 (Mil)
1941—Packers, 22-17 (W)
1943—Redskins, 33-7 (Mil)
1946—Packers, 20-7 (W)
1947—Packers, 27-10 (Mil)
1948—Redskins, 23-7 (Mil)
1949—Redskins, 30-0 (W)
1950—Packers, 35-21 (Mil)
1952—Packers, 35-20 (Mil)
1958—Redskins, 37-21 (W)
1959—Packers, 21-0 (GB)
1968—Packers, 27-7 (W)
1972—Redskins, 21-16 (W)
***Redskins, 16-3 (W)
1974—Redskins, 17-6 (GB)
1977—Redskins, 10-9 (W)
1979—Redskins, 38-21 (W)
1983—Packers, 48-47 (GB)
(Points—Packers 459, Redskins 420)
Franchise in Boston prior to 1937 and known as Braves prior to 1933
***NFL Championship*
****NFC Divisional Playoff*

HOUSTON vs. ATLANTA
Falcons lead series, 4-1;
See Atlanta vs. Houston

HOUSTON vs. BUFFALO
Oilers lead series, 17-9;
See Buffalo vs. Houston

HOUSTON vs. CHICAGO
Oilers lead series, 2-1;
See Chicago vs. Houston

HOUSTON vs. CINCINNATI
Bengals lead series, 20-13-1;
See Cincinnati vs. Houston

HOUSTON vs. CLEVELAND
Browns lead series, 20-11;
See Cleveland vs. Houston

HOUSTON vs. DALLAS
Cowboys lead series, 4-1;
See Dallas vs. Houston

HOUSTON vs. DENVER
Oilers lead series, 18-10-1;
See Denver vs. Houston

HOUSTON vs. DETROIT
Oilers lead series, 2-1;
See Detroit vs. Houston

HOUSTON vs. GREEN BAY
Series tied, 2-2;
See Green Bay vs. Houston

HOUSTON vs. *INDIANAPOLIS
Colts lead series, 5-3
1970—Colts, 24-20 (H)
1973—Oilers, 31-27 (B)
1976—Colts, 38-14 (B)
1979—Oilers, 28-16 (B)
1980—Oilers, 21-16 (H)
1983—Colts, 20-10 (B)
1984—Colts, 35-21 (H)
1985—Colts, 34-16 (I)
(Points—Colts 210, Oilers 161)
Franchise in Baltimore prior to 1984

HOUSTON vs. *KANSAS CITY
Chiefs lead series, 20-12
1960—Oilers, 20-10 (H)
Texans, 24-0 (D)
1961—Texans, 26-21 (D)
Oilers, 38-7 (H)
1962—Texans, 31-7 (H)
Oilers, 14-6 (D)
**Texans, 20-17 (H) OT
1963—Chiefs, 28-7 (KC)
Oilers, 28-7 (H)
1964—Chiefs, 28-7 (KC)
Chiefs, 28-19 (H)
1965—Chiefs, 52-21 (KC)
Oilers, 38-36 (H)
1966—Chiefs, 48-23 (KC)
1967—Chiefs, 25-20 (H)
Oilers, 24-19 (KC)
1968—Chiefs, 26-21 (H)
Chiefs, 24-10 (KC)
1969—Chiefs, 24-0 (KC)
1970—Chiefs, 24-9 (KC)
1971—Chiefs, 20-16 (H)
1973—Chiefs, 38-14 (KC)
1974—Chiefs, 17-7 (H)
1975—Oilers, 17-13 (KC)
1977—Oilers, 34-20 (H)
1978—Oilers, 20-17 (KC)
1979—Oilers, 20-6 (H)
1980—Chiefs, 21-20 (KC)
1981—Chiefs, 23-10 (KC)
1983—Chiefs, 13-10 (H) OT
1984—Oilers, 17-16 (KC)
1985—Oilers, 23-20 (H)
(Points—Chiefs 717, Oilers 552)
Franchise in Dallas prior to 1963 and known as Texans
***AFL Championship*

HOUSTON vs. *L.A. RAIDERS
Raiders lead series, 21-10
1960—Oilers, 37-22 (O)
Raiders, 14-13 (H)
1961—Oilers, 55-0 (H)
Oilers, 47-16 (O)
1962—Oilers, 28-20 (O)
Oilers, 32-17 (H)
1963—Raiders, 24-13 (H)
Raiders, 52-49 (O)
1964—Oilers, 42-28 (H)
Raiders, 20-10 (O)
1965—Raiders, 21-17 (O)
Raiders, 33-21 (H)
1966—Oilers, 31-0 (H)
Raiders, 38-23 (O)
1967—Raiders, 19-7 (H)
**Raiders, 40-7 (O)
1968—Raiders, 24-15 (H)
1969—Raiders, 21-17 (O)
***Raiders, 56-7 (O)
1971—Raiders, 41-21 (O)
1972—Raiders, 34-0 (H)
1973—Raiders, 17-6 (H)
1975—Oilers, 27-26 (O)
1976—Raiders, 14-13 (H)
1977—Raiders, 34-29 (O)
1978—Raiders, 21-17 (O)
1979—Oilers, 31-17 (H)
1980—****Raiders, 27-7 (O)
1981—Oilers, 17-16 (H)
1983—Raiders, 20-6 (LA)
1984—Raiders, 24-14 (H)
(Points—Raiders 756, Oilers 659)
Franchise in Oakland prior to 1982
***AFL Championship*
****Inter-Divisional Playoff*
*****AFC First Round Playoff*

HOUSTON vs. L.A. RAMS
Rams lead series, 3-1
1973—Rams, 31-26 (H)
1978—Rams, 10-6 (H)
1981—Oilers, 27-20 (LA)
1984—Rams, 27-16 (LA)
(Points—Rams 88, Oilers 75)

HOUSTON vs. MIAMI
Oilers lead series, 10-9
1966—Dolphins, 20-13 (H)
Dolphins, 29-28 (M)
1967—Oilers, 17-14 (H)
Oilers, 41-10 (M)
1968—Oilers, 24-10 (M)
Dolphins, 24-7 (H)
1969—Oilers, 22-10 (H)
Oilers, 32-7 (M)
1970—Dolphins, 20-10 (H)
1972—Dolphins, 34-13 (M)
1975—Oilers, 20-19 (H)
1977—Dolphins, 27-7 (M)
1978—Oilers, 35-30 (H)
*Oilers, 17-9 (M)
1979—Oilers, 9-6 (M)
1981—Dolphins, 16-10 (H)
1983—Dolphins, 24-17 (H)
1984—Dolphins, 28-10 (M)
1985—Oilers, 26-23 (H)
(Points—Dolphins 360, Oilers 358)
AFC First Round Playoff

HOUSTON vs. MINNESOTA
Vikings lead series, 2-1
1974—Vikings, 51-10 (M)
1980—Oilers, 20-16 (H)
1983—Vikings, 34-14 (M)
(Points—Vikings 101, Oilers 44)

HOUSTON vs. *NEW ENGLAND
Patriots lead series 14-13-1
1960—Oilers, 24-10 (B)
Oilers, 37-21 (H)
1961—Tie, 31-31 (B)
Oilers, 27-15 (H)
1962—Patriots, 34-21 (B)
Oilers, 21-17 (H)
1963—Patriots, 45-3 (B)
Patriots, 46-28 (H)
1964—Patriots, 25-24 (B)
Patriots, 34-17 (H)
1965—Oilers, 31-10 (H)
Patriots, 42-14 (B)
1966—Patriots, 27-21 (B)
Patriots, 38-14 (H)
1967—Patriots, 18-7 (B)
Oilers, 27-6 (H)
1968—Oilers, 16-0 (B)
Oilers, 45-17 (H)
1969—Patriots, 24-0 (B)
Oilers, 27-23 (H)
1971—Patriots, 28-20 (NE)
1973—Patriots, 32-0 (H)
1975—Oilers, 7-0 (NE)
1978—Oilers, 26-23 (NE)
**Oilers, 31-14 (NE)
1980—Oilers, 38-34 (H)
1981—Patriots, 38-10 (NE)
1982—Patriots, 29-21 (NE)
(Points—Patriots 681, Oilers 588)
Franchise in Boston prior to 1971
***AFC Divisional Playoff*

HOUSTON vs. NEW ORLEANS
Series tied, 2-2-1
1971—Tie, 13-13 (H)
1976—Oilers, 31-26 (NO)
1978—Oilers, 17-12 (NO)
1981—Saints, 27-24 (H)
1984—Saints, 27-10 (H)
(Points—Saints 105, Oilers 95)

HOUSTON vs. N.Y. GIANTS
Giants lead series, 3-0
1973—Giants, 34-14 (NY)
1982—Giants, 17-14 (NY)
1985—Giants, 35-14 (H)
(Points—Giants 86, Oilers 42)

HOUSTON vs. *N.Y. JETS
Oilers lead series, 15-10-1
1960—Oilers, 27-21 (H)
Oilers, 42-28 (NY)
1961—Oilers, 49-13 (H)
Oilers, 48-21 (NY)
1962—Oilers, 56-17 (H)
Oilers, 44-10 (NY)
1963—Jets, 24-17 (NY)
Oilers, 31-27 (H)
1964—Jets, 24-21 (NY)
Oilers, 33-17 (H)
1965—Oilers, 27-21 (H)
Jets, 41-14 (NY)
1966—Jets, 52-13 (NY)
Oilers, 24-0 (H)
1967—Tie, 28-28 (NY)
1968—Jets, 20-14 (H)
Jets, 26-7 (NY)
1969—Jets, 26-17 (NY)
Jets, 34-26 (H)
1972—Oilers, 26-20 (H)
1974—Oilers, 27-22 (NY)
1977—Oilers, 20-0 (H)
1979—Oilers, 27-24 (H) OT
1980—Jets, 31-28 (NY) OT
1981—Jets, 33-17 (NY)
1984—Oilers, 31-20 (H)
(Points—Oilers 714, Jets 600)
Jets known as Titans prior to 1963

HOUSTON vs. PHILADELPHIA
Eagles lead series, 3-0
1972—Eagles, 18-17 (H)
1979—Eagles, 26-20 (H)
1982—Eagles, 35-14 (P)
(Points—Eagles 79, Oilers 51)

HOUSTON vs. PITTSBURGH
Steelers lead series, 24-9
1970—Oilers, 19-7 (P)
Steelers, 7-3 (H)
1971—Steelers, 23-16 (P)
Oilers, 29-3 (H)
1972—Steelers, 24-7 (P)
Steelers, 9-3 (H)
1973—Steelers, 36-7 (H)
Steelers, 33-7 (P)
1974—Steelers, 13-7 (H)
Oilers, 13-10 (P)
1975—Steelers, 24-17 (P)
Steelers, 32-9 (H)
1976—Steelers, 32-16 (P)
Steelers, 21-0 (H)
1977—Oilers, 27-10 (H)
Steelers, 27-10 (P)
1978—Oilers, 24-17 (P)
Steelers, 13-3 (H)
*Steelers, 34-5 (P)
1979—Steelers, 38-7 (P)
Oilers, 20-17 (H)
*Steelers, 27-13 (P)
1980—Steelers, 31-17 (P)
Oilers, 6-0 (H)
1981—Steelers, 26-13 (P)
Oilers, 21-20 (H)
1982—Steelers, 24-10 (H)
1983—Steelers, 40-28 (H)
Steelers, 17-10 (P)
1984—Steelers, 35-7 (P)
Oilers, 23-20 (H) OT
1985—Steelers, 20-0 (P)
Steelers, 30-7 (H)
(Points—Steelers 720, Oilers 404)
AFC Championship

HOUSTON vs. ST. LOUIS
Cardinals lead series, 3-1
1970—Cardinals, 44-0 (StL)
1974—Cardinals, 31-27 (H)
1979—Cardinals, 24-17 (H)
1985—Oilers, 20-10 (StL)
(Points—Cardinals 109, Oilers 64)

HOUSTON vs. *SAN DIEGO
Chargers lead series, 16-12-1
1960—Oilers, 38-28 (H)
Chargers, 24-21 (LA)
**Oilers, 24-16 (H)
1961—Chargers, 34-24 (SD)
Oilers, 33-13 (H)
**Oilers, 10-3 (SD)
1962—Oilers, 42-17 (SD)
Oilers, 33-27 (H)
1963—Chargers, 27-0 (SD)
Chargers 20-14 (H)
1964—Chargers, 27-21 (SD)
Chargers, 20-17 (H)
1965—Chargers, 31-14 (SD)
Chargers, 37-26 (H)
1966—Chargers, 28-22 (H)
1967—Chargers, 13-3 (SD)
Oilers, 24-17 (H)
1968—Chargers, 30-14 (SD)
1969—Chargers, 21-17 (H)
1970—Tie, 31-31 (SD)
1971—Oilers, 49-33 (H)
1972—Chargers, 34-20 (SD)
1974—Oilers, 21-14 (H)
1975—Oilers, 33-17 (H)
1976—Chargers, 30-27 (SD)
1978—Chargers, 45-24 (H)
1979—***Oilers, 17-14 (SD)
1984—Chargers, 31-14 (SD)
1985—Oilers, 37-35 (H)
(Points—Chargers 717, Oilers 670)
Franchise in Los Angeles prior to 1961
***AFL Championship*
****AFC Divisional Playoff*

HOUSTON vs. SAN FRANCISCO
49ers lead series, 3-2
1970—49ers, 30-20 (H)

1975—Oilers, 27-13 (SF)
1978—Oilers, 20-19 (H)
1981—49ers, 28-6 (SF)
1984—49ers, 34-21 (H)
(Points—49ers 124, Oilers 94)
HOUSTON vs. SEATTLE
Oilers lead series, 3-2
1977—Oilers, 22-10 (S)
1979—Seahawks, 34-14 (S)
1980—Seahawks, 26-7 (H)
1981—Oilers, 35-17 (H)
1982—Oilers, 23-21 (H)
(Points—Seahawks 108, Oilers 101)
HOUSTON vs. TAMPA BAY
Oilers lead series, 2-1
1976—Oilers, 20-0 (H)
1980—Oilers, 20-14 (H)
1983—Buccaneers, 33-24 (TB)
(Points—Oilers 64, Buccaneers 47)
HOUSTON vs. WASHINGTON
Series tied, 2-2
1971—Redskins, 22-13 (W)
1975—Oilers, 13-10 (H)
1979—Oilers, 29-27 (W)
1985—Redskins, 16-13 (W)
(Points—Redskins 75, Oilers 68)

INDIANAPOLIS vs. ATLANTA
Colts lead series, 8-0;
See Atlanta vs. Indianapolis
INDIANAPOLIS vs. BUFFALO
Series tied, 15-15-1;
See Buffalo vs. Indianapolis
INDIANAPOLIS vs. CHICAGO
Colts lead series, 21-14;
See Chicago vs. Indianapolis
INDIANAPOLIS vs. CINCINNATI
Colts lead series, 5-4;
See Cincinnati vs. Indianapolis
INDIANAPOLIS vs. CLEVELAND
Browns lead series, 10-5;
See Cleveland vs. Indianapolis
INDIANAPOLIS vs. DALLAS
Cowboys lead series, 6-3;
See Dallas vs. Indianapolis
INDIANAPOLIS vs. DENVER
Broncos lead series, 6-1;
See Denver vs. Indianapolis
INDIANAPOLIS vs. DETROIT
Colts lead series, 17-16-2;
See Detroit vs. Indianapolis
INDIANAPOLIS vs. GREEN BAY
Packers lead series, 18-17-1;
See Green Bay vs. Indianapolis
INDIANAPOLIS vs. HOUSTON
Colts lead series, 5-3;
See Houston vs. Indianapolis
***INDIANAPOLIS vs. KANSAS CITY**
Chiefs lead series, 6-3
1970—Chiefs, 44-24 (B)
1972—Chiefs, 24-10 (KC)
1975—Colts, 28-14 (B)
1977—Colts, 17-6 (KC)
1979—Chiefs, 14-0 (KC)
Chiefs, 10-7 (B)
1980—Colts, 31-24 (KC)
Chiefs, 38-28 (B)
1985—Chiefs, 20-7 (KC)
(Points—Chiefs 194, Colts 152)
**Franchise in Baltimore prior to 1984*
***INDIANAPOLIS vs **L.A. RAIDERS**
Raiders lead series, 4-2
1970—***Colts, 27-17 (B)
1971—Colts, 37-14 (O)
1973—Raiders, 34-21 (B)
1975—Raiders, 31-20 (B)
1977—****Raiders, 37-31 (B) OT
1984—Raiders, 21-7 (LA)
(Points—Raiders 154, Colts 143)
**Franchise in Baltimore prior to 1984*
***Franchise in Oakland prior to 1982*
****AFC Championship*
*****AFC Divisional Playoff*
***INDIANAPOLIS vs. L.A. RAMS**
Colts lead series, 20-14-2
1953—Rams, 21-13 (B)
Rams, 45-2 (LA)
1954—Rams, 48-0 (B)
Colts, 22-21 (LA)
1955—Tie, 17-17 (B)
Rams, 20-14 (LA)
1956—Colts, 56-21 (B)
Rams, 31-7 (LA)
1957—Colts, 31-14 (B)
Rams, 37-21 (LA)
1958—Colts, 34-7 (B)
Rams, 30-28 (LA)
1959—Colts, 35-21 (B)
Colts, 45-26 (LA)
1960—Colts, 31-17 (B)
Rams, 10-3 (LA)
1961—Colts, 27-24 (B)
Rams, 34-17 (LA)
1962—Colts, 30-27 (B)
Colts, 14-2 (LA)
1963—Rams, 17-16 (LA)
Colts, 19-16 (B)
1964—Colts, 35-20 (B)
Colts, 24-7 (LA)
1965—Colts, 35-20 (B)
Colts, 20-17 (LA)
1966—Colts, 17-3 (LA)
Rams, 23-7 (B)
1967—Tie, 24-24 (B)
Rams, 34-10 (LA)
1968—Colts, 27-10 (B)
Colts, 28-24 (LA)
1969—Rams, 27-20 (B)
Colts, 13-7 (LA)
1971—Colts, 24-17 (B)
1975—Rams, 24-13 (LA)
(Points—Colts 779, Rams 763)
**Franchise in Baltimore prior to 1984*
***INDIANAPOLIS vs. MIAMI**
Dolphins lead series, 24-9
1970—Colts, 35-0 (B)
Dolphins, 34-17 (M)
1971—Dolphins, 17-14 (M)
Colts, 14-3 (B)
**Dolphins, 21-0 (M)
1972—Dolphins, 23-0 (B)
Dolphins, 16-0 (M)
1973—Dolphins, 44-0 (M)
Colts, 16-3 (B)
1974—Dolphins, 17-7 (M)
Dolphins, 17-16 (B)
1975—Colts, 33-17 (M)
Colts, 10-7 (B) OT
1976—Colts, 28-14 (B)
Colts, 17-16 (M)
1977—Colts, 45-28 (B)
Dolphins, 17-6 (M)
1978—Dolphins, 42-0 (B)
Dolphins, 26-8 (M)
1979—Dolphins, 19-0 (M)
Dolphins, 28-24 (B)
1980—Colts, 30-17 (M)
Dolphins, 24-14 (B)
1981—Dolphins, 31-28 (B)
Dolphins, 27-10 (M)
1982—Dolphins, 24-20 (M)
Dolphins, 34-7 (B)
1983—Dolphins, 21-7 (B)
Dolphins, 37-0 (M)
1984—Dolphins, 44-7 (M)
Dolphins, 35-17 (I)
1985—Dolphins, 30-13 (M)
Dolphins, 34-20 (I)
(Points—Dolphins 767, Colts 463)
**Franchise in Baltimore prior to 1984*
***AFC Championship*
***INDIANAPOLIS vs. MINNESOTA**
Colts lead series, 12-5-1
1961—Colts, 34-33 (B)
Vikings, 28-20 (M)
1962—Colts, 34-7 (M)
Colts, 42-17 (B)
1963—Colts, 37-34 (M)
Colts, 41-10 (B)
1964—Vikings, 34-24 (M)
Colts, 17-14 (B)
1965—Colts, 35-16 (B)
Colts, 41-21 (M)
1966—Colts, 38-23 (M)
Colts, 20-17 (B)
1967—Tie, 20-20 (M)
1968—Colts, 21-9 (B)
**Colts, 24-14 (B)
1969—Vikings, 52-14 (M)
1971—Vikings, 10-3 (M)
1982—Vikings, 13-10 (M)
(Points—Colts 475, Vikings 372)
**Franchise in Baltimore prior to 1984*
**Conference Championship*
***INDIANAPOLIS vs. **NEW ENGLAND**
Patriots lead series, 16-15
1970—Colts, 14-6 (Bos)
Colts, 27-3 (Balt)
1971—Colts, 23-3 (NE)
Patriots, 21-17 (Balt)
1972—Colts, 24-17 (NE)
Colts, 31-0 (Balt)
1973—Patriots, 24-16 (NE)
Colts, 18-13 (Balt)
1974—Patriots, 42-3 (NE)
Patriots, 27-17 (Balt)
1975—Patriots, 21-10 (NE)
Colts, 34-21 (Balt)
1976—Colts, 27-13 (NE)
Patriots, 21-14 (Balt)
1977—Patriots, 17-3 (NE)
Colts, 30-24 (Balt)
1978—Colts, 34-27 (NE)
Patriots, 35-14 (Balt)
1979—Colts, 31-26 (Balt)
Patriots, 50-21 (NE)
1980—Patriots, 37-21 (Balt)
Patriots, 47-21 (NE)
1981—Colts, 29-28 (NE)
Colts, 23-21 (Balt)
1982—Patriots, 24-13 (Balt)
1983—Colts, 29-23 (NE) OT
Colts, 12-7 (B)
1984—Patriots, 50-17 (I)
Patriots, 16-10 (NE)
1985—Patriots, 34-15 (NE)
Patriots, 38-31 (I)
(Points—Patriots 736, Colts 629)
**Franchise in Baltimore prior to 1984*
***Franchise in Boston prior to 1971*
***INDIANAPOLIS vs. NEW ORLEANS**
Colts lead series, 3-0
1967—Colts, 30-10 (B)
1969—Colts, 30-10 (NO)
1973—Colts, 14-10 (B)
(Points—Colts 74, Saints 30)
**Franchise in Baltimore prior to 1984*
***INDIANAPOLIS vs. N.Y. GIANTS**
Colts lead series, 7-3
1954—Colts, 20-14 (B)
1955—Giants, 17-7 (NY)
1958—Giants, 24-21 (NY)
**Colts, 23-17 (NY) OT
1959—**Colts, 31-16 (B)
1963—Giants, 37-28 (B)
1968—Colts, 26-0 (NY)
1971—Colts, 31-7 (NY)
1975—Colts, 21-0 (NY)
1979—Colts, 31-7 (NY)
(Points—Colts 239, Giants 139)
**Franchise in Baltimore prior to 1984*
***NFL Championship*
***INDIANAPOLIS vs. N.Y. JETS**
Series tied, 16-16
1968—**Jets 16-7 (Miami)
1970—Colts, 29-22 (NY)
Colts, 35-20 (B)
1971—Colts, 22-0 (B)
Colts, 14-13 (NY)
1972—Jets, 44-34 (B)
Jets, 24-20 (NY)
1973—Jets, 34-10 (B)
Jets, 20-17 (NY)
1974—Colts, 35-20 (NY)
Jets, 45-38 (B)
1975—Colts, 45-28 (NY)
Colts, 52-19 (B)
1976—Colts, 20-0 (NY)
Colts, 33-16 (B)
1977—Colts, 20-12 (NY)
Colts, 33-12 (B)
1978—Jets, 33-10 (B)
Jets, 24-16 (NY)
1979—Colts, 10-8 (B)
Jets, 30-17 (NY)
1980—Colts, 17-14 (NY)
Colts, 35-21 (B)
1981—Jets, 41-14 (B)
Jets, 25-0 (NY)
1982—Jets, 37-0 (NY)
1983—Colts, 17-14 (NY)
Jets, 10-6 (B)
1984—Jets, 23-14 (I)
Colts, 9-5 (NY)
1985—Jets, 25-20 (NY)
Jets, 35-17 (I)
(Points—Jets 690, Colts 666)
**Franchise in Baltimore prior to 1984*
***Super Bowl III*
***INDIANAPOLIS vs. PHILADELPHIA**
Series tied, 5-5
1953—Eagles, 45-14 (P)
1965—Colts, 34-24 (B)
1967—Colts, 38-6 (P)
1969—Colts, 24-20 (B)
1970—Colts, 29-10 (B)
1974—Eagles, 30-10 (P)
1978—Eagles, 17-14 (B)
1981—Eagles, 38-13 (P)
1983—Colts, 22-21 (P)
1984—Eagles, 16-7 (P)
(Points—Eagles 227, Colts 205)
**Franchise in Baltimore prior to 1984*
***INDIANAPOLIS vs. PITTSBURGH**
Steelers lead series, 9-4
1957—Steelers, 19-13 (B)
1968—Colts, 41-7 (P)
1971—Colts, 34-21 (B)
1974—Steelers, 30-0 (B)
1975—**Steelers, 28-10 (P)
1976—**Steelers, 40-14 (B)
1977—Colts, 31-21 (B)
1978—Steelers, 35-13 (P)
1979—Steelers, 17-13 (P)
1980—Steelers, 20-17 (B)
1983—Steelers, 24-13 (B)
1984—Colts, 17-16 (I)
1985—Steelers, 45-3 (P)
(Points—Steelers 323, Colts 219)
**Franchise in Baltimore prior to 1984*
***AFC Divisional Playoff*
***INDIANAPOLIS vs. ST. LOUIS**
Cardinals lead series 5-4
1961—Colts, 16-0 (B)
1964—Colts, 47-27 (B)
1968—Colts, 27-0 (B)
1972—Cardinals, 10-3 (B)
1976—Cardinals, 24-17 (StL)
1978—Colts, 30-17 (StL)
1980—Cardinals, 17-10 (B)
1981—Cardinals, 35-24 (B)
1984—Cardinals, 34-33 (I)
(Points—Colts 207, Cardinals 164)
**Franchise in Baltimore prior to 1984*
***INDIANAPOLIS vs. SAN DIEGO**
Chargers lead series, 4-2
1970—Colts, 16-14 (SD)
1972—Chargers, 23-20 (B)
1976—Colts, 37-21 (SD)
1981—Chargers, 43-14 (B)
1982—Chargers, 44-26 (SD)
1984—Chargers, 38-10 (I)
(Points—Chargers 183, Colts 123)
**Franchise in Baltimore prior to 1984*
***INDIANAPOLIS vs. SAN FRANCISCO**
Colts lead series, 21-14
1953—49ers, 38-21 (B)
49ers, 45-14 (SF)
1954—Colts, 17-13 (B)
49ers, 10-7 (SF)
1955—Colts, 26-14 (B)
49ers, 35-24 (SF)
1956—49ers, 20-17 (B)
49ers, 30-17 (SF)
1957—Colts, 27-21 (B)
49ers, 17-13 (SF)
1958—Colts, 35-27 (B)
49ers, 21-12 (SF)
1959—Colts, 45-14 (B)
Colts, 34-14 (SF)
1960—49ers, 30-22 (B)
49ers, 34-10 (SF)
1961—Colts, 20-17 (B)
Colts, 27-24 (SF)
1962—49ers, 21-13 (B)
Colts, 22-3 (SF)
1963—Colts, 20-14 (SF)
Colts, 20-3 (B)
1964—Colts, 37-7 (B)
Colts, 14-3 (SF)
1965—Colts, 27-24 (B)
Colts, 34-28 (SF)
1966—Colts, 36-14 (B)
Colts, 30-14 (SF)
1967—Colts, 41-7 (B)
Colts, 26-9 (SF)
1968—Colts, 27-10 (B)
Colts, 42-14 (SF)
1969—49ers, 24-21 (B)
49ers, 20-17 (SF)
1972—49ers, 24-21 (SF)
(Points—Colts 836, 49ers 663)
**Franchise in Baltimore prior to 1984*
***INDIANAPOLIS vs. SEATTLE**
Colts lead series, 2-0
1977—Colts, 29-14 (S)
1978—Colts, 17-14 (S)
(Points—Colts 46, Seahawks 28)
**Franchise in Baltimore prior to 1984*
***INDIANAPOLIS vs. TAMPA BAY**
Colts lead series, 2-1
1976—Colts, 42-17 (B)
1979—Buccaneers, 29-26 (B) OT
1985—Colts, 31-23 (TB)
(Points—Colts 99, Buccaneers 69)
**Franchise in Baltimore prior to 1984*
***INDIANAPOLIS vs. WASHINGTON**
Colts lead series, 15-6
1953—Colts, 27-17 (B)
1954—Redskins, 24-21 (W)
1955—Redskins, 14-13 (B)
1956—Colts, 19-17 (B)
1957—Colts, 21-17 (W)
1958—Colts, 35-10 (B)
1959—Redskins, 27-24 (W)
1960—Colts, 20-0 (B)
1961—Colts, 27-6 (W)
1962—Colts, 34-21 (B)
1963—Colts, 36-20 (W)
1964—Colts, 45-17 (B)
1965—Colts, 38-7 (W)
1966—Colts, 37-10 (B)
1967—Colts, 17-13 (W)
1969—Colts, 41-17 (B)
1973—Redskins, 22-14 (W)
1977—Colts, 10-3 (B)
1978—Colts, 21-17 (B)
1981—Redskins, 38-14 (W)
1984—Redskins, 35-7 (I)
(Points—Colts 521, Redskins 352)
**Franchise in Baltimore prior to 1984*

KANSAS CITY vs. ATLANTA
Chiefs lead series, 2-0;
See Atlanta vs. Kansas City
KANSAS CITY vs. BUFFALO
Bills lead series, 14-11-1;
See Buffalo vs. Kansas City
KANSAS CITY vs. CHICAGO
Bears lead series, 2-1;
See Chicago vs. Kansas City
KANSAS CITY vs. CINCINNATI
Chiefs lead series, 8-7;
See Cincinnati vs. Kansas City
KANSAS CITY vs. CLEVELAND
Chiefs lead series, 5-4-1;
See Cleveland vs. Kansas City
KANSAS CITY vs. DALLAS
Cowboys lead series, 2-1;
See Dallas vs. Kansas City
KANSAS CITY vs. DENVER
Chiefs lead series, 33-18;
See Denver vs. Kansas City
KANSAS CITY vs. DETROIT
Series tied, 2-2;
See Detroit vs. Kansas City
KANSAS CITY vs. GREEN BAY
Series tied, 1-1-1;
See Green Bay vs. Kansas City
KANSAS CITY vs. HOUSTON
Chiefs lead series, 20-12;
See Houston vs. Kansas City
KANSAS CITY vs. INDIANAPOLIS
Chiefs lead series, 6-3;
See Indianapolis vs. Kansas City
***KANSAS CITY vs. **L.A. RAIDERS**
Raiders lead series, 30-21-2
1960—Texans, 34-16 (O)
Raiders, 20-19 (D)
1961—Texans, 42-35 (O)
Texans, 43-11 (D)
1962—Texans, 26-16 (O)
Texans, 35-7 (D)
1963—Raiders, 10-7 (O)
Raiders, 22-7 (KC)
1964—Chiefs, 21-9 (O)
Chiefs, 42-7 (KC)
1965—Raiders, 37-10 (O)
Chiefs, 14-7 (KC)
1966—Chiefs, 32-10 (O)
Raiders, 34-13 (KC)
1967—Raiders, 23-21 (O)
Raiders, 44-22 (KC)
1968—Chiefs, 24-10 (KC)
Raiders, 38-21 (O)
***Raiders, 41-6 (O)
1969—Raiders, 27-24 (KC)
Raiders, 10-6 (O)
****Chiefs, 17-7 (O)
1970—Tie, 17-17 (KC)
Raiders, 20-6 (O)
1971—Tie, 20-20 (O)
Chiefs, 16-14 (KC)
1972—Chiefs, 27-14 (KC)
Raiders, 26-3 (O)
1973—Chiefs, 16-3 (KC)
Raiders, 37-7 (O)
1974—Raiders, 27-7 (O)
Raiders, 7-6 (KC)
1975—Chiefs, 42-10 (KC)
Raiders, 28-20 (O)
1976—Raiders, 24-21 (KC)
Raiders, 21-10 (O)
1977—Raiders, 37-28 (KC)
Raiders, 21-20 (O)
1978—Raiders, 28-6 (O)
Raiders, 20-10 (KC)
1979—Chiefs, 35-7 (KC)
Chiefs, 24-21 (O)
1980—Raiders, 27-14 (KC)
Chiefs, 31-17 (O)
1981—Chiefs, 27-0 (KC)
Chiefs, 28-17 (O)
1982—Raiders, 21-16 (KC)
1983—Raiders, 21-20 (LA)
Raiders, 28-20 (KC)
1984—Raiders, 22-20 (KC)
Raiders, 17-7 (LA)
1985—Chiefs, 36-20 (KC)
Raiders, 19-10 (LA)
(Points—Chiefs 1,056, Raiders 1,052)
**Franchise in Dallas prior to 1963 and known as Texans*
***Franchise in Oakland prior to 1982*
****Division Playoff*
*****AFL Championship*
KANSAS CITY vs. L.A. RAMS
Rams lead series, 3-0
1973—Rams, 23-13 (KC)
1982—Rams, 20-14 (LA)
1985—Rams, 16-0 (KC)
(Points—Rams 59, Chiefs 27)
KANSAS CITY vs. MIAMI
Chiefs lead series, 7-6
1966—Chiefs, 34-16 (KC)
Chiefs, 19-18 (M)
1967—Chiefs, 24-0 (M)
Chiefs, 41-0 (KC)
1968—Chiefs, 48-3 (M)
1969—Chiefs, 17-10 (KC)
1971—*Dolphins, 27-24 (KC) OT
1972—Dolphins, 20-10 (KC)
1974—Dolphins, 9-3 (M)
1976—Chiefs, 20-17 (M) OT
1981—Dolphins, 17-7 (KC)
1983—Dolphins, 14-6 (M)
1985—Dolphins, 31-0 (M)
(Points—Chiefs 253, Dolphins 182)
**AFC Divisional Playoff*
KANSAS CITY vs. MINNESOTA
Series tied, 2-2
1969—*Chiefs, 23-7 (New Orleans)
1970—Vikings, 27-10 (M)
1974—Vikings, 35-15 (KC)
1981—Chiefs, 10-6 (M)
(Points—Vikings 75, Chiefs 58)
**Super Bowl IV*
***KANSAS CITY vs. **NEW ENGLAND**
Chiefs lead series, 11-7-3
1960—Patriots, 42-14 (B)
Texans, 34-0 (D)
1961—Patriots, 18-17 (D)
Patriots, 28-21 (B)
1962—Texans, 42-28 (D)
Texans, 27-7 (B)
1963—Tie, 24-24 (B)
Chiefs, 35-3 (KC)
1964—Patriots, 24-7 (B)
Patriots, 31-24 (KC)
1965—Chiefs, 27-17 (KC)
Tie, 10-10 (B)
1966—Chiefs, 43-24 (B)
Tie, 27-27 (KC)
1967—Chiefs, 33-10 (B)
1968—Chiefs, 31-17 (KC)
1969—Chiefs, 31-0 (B)
1970—Chiefs, 23-10 (KC)
1973—Chiefs, 10-7 (NE)
1977—Patriots, 21-17 (NE)
1981—Patriots, 33-17 (NE)
(Points—Chiefs 514, Patriots 381)
**Franchise located in Dallas prior to 1963 and known as Texans*
***Franchise in Boston prior to 1971*
KANSAS CITY vs. NEW ORLEANS
Series tied, 2-2
1972—Chiefs, 20-17 (NO)
1976—Saints, 27-17 (KC)
1982—Saints, 27-17 (NO)
1985—Chiefs, 47-27 (NO)
(Points—Chiefs 101, Saints 98)
KANSAS CITY vs. N.Y. GIANTS
Giants lead series, 4-1
1974—Giants, 33-27 (KC)
1978—Giants, 26-10 (NY)
1979—Giants, 21-17 (KC)
1983—Chiefs, 38-17 (KC)
1984—Giants, 28-27 (NY)
(Points—Giants 125, Chiefs 119)
***KANSAS CITY vs. **N.Y. JETS**
Chiefs lead series, 13-11
1960—Titans, 37-35 (D)
Titans, 41-35 (NY)
1961—Titans, 28-7 (NY)
Texans, 35-24 (D)
1962—Texans, 20-17 (D)
Texans, 52-31 (NY)
1963—Jets, 17-0 (NY)
Chiefs, 48-0 (KC)
1964—Jets, 27-14 (NY)
Chiefs, 24-7 (KC)
1965—Chiefs, 14-10 (NY)
Jets, 13-10 (KC)
1966—Chiefs, 32-24 (NY)
1967—Chiefs, 42-18 (KC)
Chiefs, 21-7 (NY)
1968—Jets, 20-19 (KC)
1969—Chiefs, 34-16 (NY)
***Chiefs, 13-6 (NY)
1971—Jets, 13-10 (NY)
1974—Chiefs, 24-16 (KC)
1975—Jets, 30-24 (KC)
1982—Chiefs, 37-13 (KC)
1984—Jets, 17-16 (KC)
Jets, 28-7 (NY)
(Points—Chiefs 573, Jets 460)
**Franchise in Dallas prior to 1963 and known as Texans*
***Jets known as Titans prior to 1963*
****Inter-Divisional Playoff*
KANSAS CITY vs. PHILADELPHIA
Eagles lead series, 1-0
1972—Eagles, 21-20 (KC)
KANSAS CITY vs. PITTSBURGH
Steelers lead series, 9-4
1970—Chiefs, 31-14 (P)
1971—Chiefs, 38-16 (KC)
1972—Steelers, 16-7 (P)
1974—Steelers, 34-24 (KC)
1975—Steelers, 28-3 (P)
1976—Steelers, 45-0 (KC)
1978—Steelers, 27-24 (P)
1979—Steelers, 30-3 (KC)
1980—Steelers, 21-16 (P)
1981—Chiefs, 37-33 (P)
1982—Steelers, 35-14 (P)
1984—Chiefs, 37-27 (P)
1985—Steelers, 36-28 (KC)
(Points—Steelers 362, Chiefs 262)
KANSAS CITY vs. ST. LOUIS
Chiefs lead series, 3-0-1
1970—Tie, 6-6 (KC)
1974—Chiefs, 17-13 (StL)
1980—Chiefs, 21-13 (StL)
1983—Chiefs, 38-14 (KC)
(Points—Chiefs 82, Cardinals 46)
***KANSAS CITY vs. **SAN DIEGO**
Chargers lead series, 26-24-1
1960—Chargers, 21-20 (LA)
Texans, 17-0 (D)
1961—Chargers, 26-10 (D)
Chargers, 24-14 (SD)
1962—Chargers, 32-28 (SD)
Texans, 26-17 (D)
1963—Chargers, 24-10 (SD)
Chargers, 38-17 (KC)
1964—Chargers, 28-14 (KC)
Chiefs, 49-6 (SD)
1965—Tie, 10-10 (SD)
Chiefs, 31-7 (KC)
1966—Chiefs, 24-14 (KC)
Chiefs, 27-17 (SD)
1967—Chargers, 45-31 (SD)
Chargers, 17-16 (KC)
1968—Chiefs, 27-20 (KC)
Chiefs, 40-3 (SD)
1969—Chiefs, 27-9 (SD)
Chiefs, 27-3 (KC)
1970—Chiefs, 26-14 (KC)
Chargers, 31-13 (SD)
1971—Chargers, 21-14 (SD)
Chiefs, 31-10 (KC)
1972—Chiefs, 26-14 (SD)
Chargers, 27-17 (KC)
1973—Chiefs, 19-0 (SD)
Chiefs, 33-6 (KC)
1974—Chiefs, 24-14 (SD)
Chargers, 14-7 (KC)
1975—Chiefs, 12-10 (SD)
Chargers, 28-20 (KC)
1976—Chargers, 30-16 (KC)
Chiefs, 23-20 (SD)
1977—Chargers, 23-7 (KC)
Chiefs, 21-16 (SD)
1978—Chargers, 29-23 (SD) OT
Chiefs, 23-0 (KC)
1979—Chargers, 20-14 (KC)
Chargers, 28-7 (SD)
1980—Chargers, 24-7 (KC)
Chargers, 20-7 (SD)
1981—Chargers, 42-31 (KC)
Chargers, 22-20 (SD)
1982—Chiefs, 19-12 (KC)
1983—Chargers, 17-14 (KC)
Chargers, 41-38 (SD)
1984—Chiefs, 31-13 (KC)
Chiefs, 42-21 (SD)
1985—Chargers, 31-20 (SD)
Chiefs, 38-34 (KC)
(Points—Chiefs 1,108, Chargers 993)
**Franchise in Dallas prior to 1963 and known as Texans*
***Franchise in Los Angeles prior to 1961*
KANSAS CITY vs. SAN FRANCISCO
49ers lead series, 3-1
1971—Chiefs, 26-17 (SF)
1975—49ers, 20-3 (KC)
1982—49ers, 26-13 (KC)
1985—49ers, 31-3 (SF)
(Points—49ers 94, Chiefs 45)
KANSAS CITY vs. SEATTLE
Chiefs lead series, 8-7
1977—Seahawks, 34-31 (KC)
1978—Seahawks, 13-10 (KC)
Seahawks, 23-19 (S)
1979—Chiefs, 24-6 (S)
Chiefs, 37-21 (KC)
1980—Seahawks, 17-16 (KC)
Chiefs, 31-30 (S)
1981—Chiefs, 20-14 (S)
Chiefs, 40-13 (KC)
1983—Chiefs, 17-13 (KC)
Seahawks, 51-48 (S) OT
1984—Seahawks, 45-0 (S)
Chiefs, 34-7 (KC)
1985—Chiefs, 28-7 (KC)
Seahawks, 24-6 (S)
(Points—Chiefs 361, Seahawks 318)
KANSAS CITY vs. TAMPA BAY
Chiefs lead series, 3-2
1976—Chiefs, 28-19 (TB)
1978—Buccaneers, 30-13 (KC)
1979—Buccaneers, 3-0 (TB)
1981—Chiefs, 19-10 (KC)
1984—Chiefs, 24-20 (KC)
(Points—Chiefs 84, Buccaneers 82)
KANSAS CITY vs. WASHINGTON
Chiefs lead series, 2-1
1971—Chiefs, 27-20 (KC)
1976—Chiefs, 33-30 (W)
1983—Redskins, 27-12 (W)
(Points—Redskins 77, Chiefs 72)

L.A. RAIDERS vs. ATLANTA
Raiders lead series, 4-1;
See Atlanta vs. L.A. Raiders
L.A. RAIDERS vs. BUFFALO
Raiders lead series, 12-11;
See Buffalo vs. L.A. Raiders
L.A. RAIDERS vs. CHICAGO
Raiders lead series, 3-2;
See Chicago vs. L.A. Raiders
L.A. RAIDERS vs. CINCINNATI
Raiders lead series, 12-4;
See Cincinnati vs. L.A. Raiders
L.A. RAIDERS vs. CLEVELAND
Raiders lead series, 9-1;
See Cleveland vs. L.A. Raiders
L.A. RAIDERS vs. DALLAS
Raiders lead series, 2-1;
See Dallas vs. L.A. Raiders
L.A. RAIDERS vs. DENVER
Raiders lead series, 36-14-2;
See Denver vs. L.A. Raiders
L.A. RAIDERS vs. DETROIT
Raiders lead series, 3-2;
See Detroit vs. L.A. Raiders
L.A. RAIDERS vs. GREEN BAY
Raiders lead series, 4-1;
See Green Bay vs. L.A. Raiders
L.A. RAIDERS vs. HOUSTON
Raiders lead series, 21-10;
See Houston vs. L.A. Raiders
L.A. RAIDERS vs. INDIANAPOLIS
Raiders lead series, 4-2;
See Indianapolis vs. L.A. Raiders
L.A. RAIDERS vs. KANSAS CITY
Raiders lead series, 30-21-2;
See Kansas City vs. L.A. Raiders
***L.A. RAIDERS vs. L.A. RAMS**
Raiders lead series, 4-1
1972—Raiders, 45-17 (O)
1977—Rams, 20-14 (LA)
1979—Raiders, 24-17 (LA)
1982—Raiders, 37-31 (LA Raiders)
1985—Raiders, 16-6 (LA Rams)
(Points—Raiders 136, Rams 91)
**Franchise in Oakland prior to 1982*
***L.A. RAIDERS vs. MIAMI**
Raiders lead series, 14-3-1
1966—Raiders, 23-14 (M)
Raiders, 21-10 (O)
1967—Raiders, 31-17 (O)
1968—Raiders, 47-21 (M)
1969—Raiders, 20-17 (O)
Tie, 20-20 (M)
1970—Dolphins, 20-13 (M)
**Raiders, 21-14 (O)
1973—Raiders, 12-7 (O)
***Dolphins, 27-10 (M)
1974—**Raiders, 28-26 (O)
1975—Raiders, 31-21 (M)
1978—Dolphins, 23-6 (M)
1979—Raiders, 13-3 (O)
1980—Raiders, 16-10 (O)
1981—Raiders, 33-17 (M)
1983—Raiders, 27-14 (LA)
1984—Raiders, 45-34 (M)
(Points—Raiders 417, Dolphins 315)
**Franchise in Oakland prior to 1982*
***AFC Divisional Playoff*
****AFC Championship*
***L.A. RAIDERS vs. MINNESOTA**
Raiders lead series, 5-1
1973—Vikings, 24-16 (M)
1976—**Raiders, 32-14 (Pasadena)
1977—Raiders, 35-13 (O)
1978—Raiders, 27-20 (O)
1981—Raiders, 36-10 (M)
1984—Raiders, 23-20 (LA)
(Points—Raiders 169, Vikings 101)
**Franchise in Oakland prior to 1982*
***Super Bowl XI*
***L.A. RAIDERS vs. **NEW ENGLAND**
Series tied, 12-12-1
1960—Raiders, 27-14 (O)
Patriots, 34-28 (B)
1961—Patriots, 20-17 (B)
Patriots, 35-21 (O)
1962—Patriots, 26-16 (B)
Raiders, 20-0 (O)
1963—Patriots, 20-14 (O)
Patriots, 20-14 (B)
1964—Patriots, 17-14 (O)
Tie, 43-43 (B)

1965—Raiders, 24-10 (B)
Raiders, 30-21 (O)
1966—Patriots, 24-21 (B)
1967—Raiders, 35-7 (O)
Raiders, 48-14 (B)
1968—Raiders, 41-10 (O)
1969—Raiders, 38-23 (B)
1971—Patriots, 20-6 (NE)
1974—Raiders, 41-26 (O)
1976—Patriots, 48-17 (NE)
***Raiders, 24-21 (O)
1978—Patriots, 21-14 (O)
1981—Raiders, 27-17 (O)
1985—Raiders, 35-20 (NE)
***Patriots, 27-20 (LA)
(Points—Raiders 635, Patriots 538)
Franchise in Oakland prior to 1982
***Franchise in Boston prior to 1971*
****AFC Divisional Playoff*

***L.A. RAIDERS vs. NEW ORLEANS**
Raiders lead series, 3-0-1
1971—Tie, 21-21 (NO)
1975—Raiders, 48-10 (O)
1979—Raiders, 42-35 (NO)
1985—Raiders, 23-13 (LA)
(Points—Raiders 134, Saints 79)
Franchise in Oakland prior to 1982

***L.A. RAIDERS vs. N.Y. GIANTS**
Raiders lead series, 3-0
1973—Raiders, 42-0 (O)
1980—Raiders, 33-17 (NY)
1983—Raiders, 27-12 (LA)
(Points—Raiders 102, Giants 29)
Franchise in Oakland prior to 1982

***L.A. RAIDERS vs. **N.Y. JETS**
Raiders lead series, 12-11-2
1960—Raiders, 28-27 (NY)
Titans, 31-28 (O)
1961—Titans, 14-6 (O)
Titans, 23-12 (NY)
1962—Titans, 28-17 (O)
Titans, 31-21 (NY)
1963—Jets, 10-7 (NY)
Raiders, 49-26 (O)
1964—Jets, 35-13 (NY)
Raiders, 35-26 (O)
1965—Tie, 24-24 (NY)
Raiders, 24-14 (O)
1966—Raiders, 24-21 (NY)
Tie, 28-28 (O)
1967—Jets, 27-14 (NY)
Raiders, 38-29 (O)
1968—Raiders, 43-32 (O)
***Jets, 27-23 (NY)
1969—Raiders, 27-14 (NY)
1970—Raiders, 14-13 (NY)
1972—Raiders, 24-16 (O)
1977—Raiders, 28-27 (NY)
1979—Jets, 28-19 (NY)
1982—****Jets, 17-14 (LA)
1985—Raiders, 31-0 (LA)
(Points—Raiders 591, Jets 568)
Franchise in Oakland prior to 1982
***Jets known as Titans prior to 1963*
****AFL Championship*
*****AFC Second Round Playoff*

***L.A. RAIDERS vs. PHILADELPHIA**
Raiders lead series, 3-1
1971—Raiders, 34-10 (O)
1976—Raiders, 26-7 (P)
1980—Eagles, 10-7 (P)
**Raiders, 27-10 (NO)
(Points—Raiders 94, Eagles 37)
Franchise in Oakland prior to 1982
***Super Bowl XV*

***L.A. RAIDERS vs. PITTSBURGH**
Raiders lead series, 9-6
1970—Raiders, 31-14 (O)
1972—Steelers, 34-28 (P)
**Steelers, 13-7 (P)
1973—Steelers, 17-9 (O)
**Raiders, 33-14 (O)
1974—Raiders, 17-0 (P)
***Steelers, 24-13 (O)
1975—***Steelers, 16-10 (P)
1976—Raiders, 31-28 (O)
***Raiders, 24-7 (O)
1977—Raiders, 16-7 (P)
1980—Raiders, 45-34 (P)
1981—Raiders, 30-27 (O)
1983—**Raiders, 38-10 (LA)
1984—Steelers, 13-7 (LA)
(Points—Raiders 339, Steelers 258)
Franchise in Oakland prior to 1982
***AFC Divisional Playoff*
****AFC Championship*

***L.A. RAIDERS vs. ST. LOUIS**
Series tied, 1-1
1973—Raiders, 17-10 (StL)
1983—Cardinals, 34-24 (LA)
(Points—Cardinals 44, Raiders 41)
Franchise in Oakland prior to 1982

***L.A. RAIDERS vs. **SAN DIEGO**
Raiders lead series, 33-18-2
1960—Chargers, 52-28 (LA)
Chargers, 41-17 (O)
1961—Chargers, 44-0 (SD)
Chargers, 41-10 (O)
1962—Chargers, 42-33 (O)
Chargers, 31-21 (SD)
1963—Raiders, 34-33 (SD)
Raiders, 41-27 (O)
1964—Chargers, 31-17 (O)
Raiders, 21-20 (SD)
1965—Chargers, 17-6 (O)
Chargers, 24-14 (SD)
1966—Chargers, 29-20 (O)
Raiders, 41-19 (SD)
1967—Raiders, 51-10 (O)
Raiders, 41-21 (SD)
1968—Chargers, 23-14 (O)
Raiders, 34-27 (SD)
1969—Raiders, 24-12 (SD)
Raiders, 21-16 (O)
1970—Tie, 27-27 (SD)
Raiders, 20-17 (O)
1971—Raiders, 34-0 (SD)
Raiders, 34-33 (O)
1972—Tie, 17-17 (O)
Raiders, 21-19 (SD)
1973—Raiders, 27-17 (SD)
Raiders, 31-3 (O)
1974—Raiders, 14-10 (SD)
Raiders, 17-10 (O)
1975—Raiders, 6-0 (SD)
Raiders, 25-0 (O)
1976—Raiders, 27-17 (SD)
Raiders, 24-0 (O)
1977—Raiders, 24-0 (O)
Chargers, 12-7 (SD)
1978—Raiders, 21-20 (SD)
Chargers, 27-23 (O)
1979—Chargers, 30-10 (SD)
Raiders, 45-22 (O)
1980—Chargers, 30-24 (SD) OT
Raiders, 38-24 (O)
***Raiders, 34-27 (SD)
1981—Chargers, 55-21 (O)
Chargers, 23-10 (SD)
1982—Raiders, 28-24 (LA)
Raiders, 41-34 (SD)
1983—Raiders, 42-10 (SD)
Raiders, 30-14 (LA)
1984—Raiders, 33-30 (LA)
Raiders, 44-37 (SD)
1985—Raiders, 34-21 (LA)
Chargers, 40-34 (SD) OT
(Points—Raiders 1,355, Chargers 1,210)
Franchise in Oakland prior to 1982
***Franchise in Los Angeles prior to 1961*
****AFC Championship*

***L.A. RAIDERS vs. SAN FRANCISCO**
Raiders lead series, 3-2
1970—49ers, 38-7 (O)
1974—Raiders, 35-24 (SF)
1979—Raiders, 23-10 (O)
1982—Raiders, 23-17 (SF)
1985—49ers, 34-10 (LA)
(Points—49ers 123, Raiders 98)
Franchise in Oakland prior to 1982

***L.A. RAIDERS vs. SEATTLE**
Series tied, 9-9
1977—Raiders, 44-7 (O)
1978—Seahawks, 27-7 (S)
Seahawks, 17-16 (O)
1979—Seahawks, 27-10 (S)
Seahawks, 29-24 (O)
1980—Raiders, 33-14 (O)
Raiders, 19-17 (S)
1981—Raiders, 20-10 (O)
Raiders, 32-31 (S)
1982—Raiders, 28-23 (LA)
1983—Seahawks, 38-36 (S)
Seahawks, 34-21 (LA)
**Raiders, 30-14 (LA)
1984—Raiders, 28-14 (LA)
Seahawks, 17-14 (S)
***Seahawks, 13-7 (S)
1985—Seahawks, 33-3 (S)
Raiders, 13-3 (LA)
(Points—Raiders 385, Seahawks 368)
Franchise in Oakland prior to 1982
***AFC Championship*
****AFC First Round Playoff*

***L.A. RAIDERS vs. TAMPA BAY**
Raiders lead series, 2-0
1976—Raiders, 49-16 (O)
1981—Raiders, 18-16 (O)
(Points—Raiders 67, Buccaneers 32)
Franchise in Oakland prior to 1982

***L.A. RAIDERS vs. WASHINGTON**
Raiders lead series, 4-1
1970—Raiders, 34-20 (O)
1975—Raiders, 26-23 (W) OT
1980—Raiders, 24-21 (O)
1983—Redskins, 37-35 (W)
**Raiders, 38-9 (Tampa)
(Points—Raiders 157, Redskins 110)
Franchise in Oakland prior to 1982
***Super Bowl XVIII*

L.A. RAMS vs. ATLANTA
Rams lead series, 28-8-2;
See Atlanta vs. L.A. Rams

L.A. RAMS vs. BUFFALO
Rams lead series, 3-1;
See Buffalo vs. L.A. Rams

L.A. RAMS vs. CHICAGO
Bears lead series, 43-27-3;
See Chicago vs. L.A. Rams

L.A. RAMS vs. CINCINNATI
Bengals lead series, 3-2;
See Cincinnati vs. L.A. Rams

L.A. RAMS vs. CLEVELAND
Browns lead series, 8-7;
See Cleveland vs. L.A. Rams

L.A. RAMS vs. DALLAS
Series tied, 10-10;
See Dallas vs. L.A. Rams

L.A. RAMS vs. DENVER
Rams lead series, 3-2;
See Denver vs. L.A. Rams

L.A. RAMS vs. DETROIT
Rams lead series, 36-34-1;
See Detroit vs. L.A. Rams

L.A. RAMS vs. GREEN BAY
Rams lead series, 39-34-2;
See Green Bay vs. L.A. Rams

L.A. RAMS vs. HOUSTON
Rams lead series, 3-1;
See Houston vs. L.A. Rams

L.A. RAMS vs. INDIANAPOLIS
Colts lead series, 20-14-2;
See Indianapolis vs. L.A. Rams

L.A. RAMS vs. KANSAS CITY
Rams lead series, 3-0;
See Kansas City vs. L.A. Rams

L.A. RAMS VS. L.A. RAIDERS
Raiders lead series, 4-1;
See L.A. Raiders vs. L.A. Rams

L.A. RAMS vs. MIAMI
Dolphins lead series, 3-1
1971—Dolphins, 20-14 (LA)
1976—Rams, 31-28 (M)
1980—Dolphins, 35-14 (LA)
1983—Dolphins, 30-14 (M)
(Points—Dolphins 113, Rams 73)

L.A. RAMS vs. MINNESOTA
Vikings lead series, 15-12-2
1961—Rams, 31-17 (LA)
Vikings, 42-21 (M)
1962—Vikings, 38-14 (LA)
Tie, 24-24 (M)
1963—Rams, 27-24 (LA)
Vikings, 21-13 (M)
1964—Rams, 22-13 (LA)
Vikings, 34-13 (M)
1965—Vikings, 38-35 (LA)
Vikings, 24-13 (M)
1966—Vikings, 35-7 (M)
Rams, 21-6 (LA)
1967—Rams, 39-3 (LA)
1968—Rams, 31-3 (M)
1969—Vikings, 20-13 (LA)
*Vikings, 23-20 (M)
1970—Vikings, 13-3 (M)
1972—Vikings, 45-41 (LA)
1973—Vikings, 10-9 (M)
1974—Rams, 20-17 (LA)
**Vikings, 14-10 (M)
1976—Tie, 10-10 (M) OT
**Vikings, 24-13 (M)
1977—Rams, 35-3 (LA)
***Vikings, 14-7 (LA)
1978—Rams, 34-17 (M)
***Rams, 34-10 (LA)
1979—Rams, 27-21 (LA) OT
1985—Rams, 13-10 (LA)
(Points—Rams 600, Vikings 573)
Conference Championship
***NFC Championship*
****NFC Divisional Playoff*

L.A. RAMS vs. NEW ENGLAND
Patriots lead series, 2-1
1974—Patriots, 20-14 (NE)
1980—Rams, 17-14 (NE)
1983—Patriots, 21-7 (LA)
(Points—Patriots 55, Rams 38)

L.A. RAMS vs. NEW ORLEANS
Rams lead series, 23-9
1967—Rams 27-13 (NO)
1969—Rams, 36-17 (LA)
1970—Rams, 30-17 (NO)
Rams, 34-16 (LA)
1971—Saints, 24-20 (NO)
Rams, 45-28 (LA)
1972—Rams, 34-14 (LA)
Saints, 19-16 (NO)
1973—Rams, 29-7 (LA)
Rams, 24-13 (NO)
1974—Rams, 24-0 (LA)
Saints, 20-7 (NO)
1975—Rams, 38-14 (LA)
Rams, 14-7 (NO)
1976—Rams, 16-10 (NO)
Rams, 33-14 (LA)
1977—Rams, 14-7 (LA)
Saints, 27-26 (NO)
1978—Rams, 26-20 (NO)
Saints, 10-3 (LA)
1979—Rams, 35-17 (NO)
Saints, 29-14 (LA)
1980—Rams, 45-31 (LA)
Rams, 27-7 (NO)
1981—Saints, 23-17 (NO)
Saints, 21-13 (LA)
1983—Rams, 30-27 (LA)
Rams, 26-24 (NO)
1984—Rams, 28-10 (NO)
Rams, 34-21 (LA)
1985—Rams, 28-10 (LA)
Saints, 29-3 (NO)
(Points—Rams 796, Saints 546)

***L.A. RAMS vs. N.Y. GIANTS**
Rams lead series, 16-8
1938—Giants, 28-0 (NY)
1940—Rams, 13-0 (NY)
1941—Giants, 49-14 (NY)
1945—Rams, 21-17 (NY)
1946—Rams, 31-21 (NY)
1947—Rams, 34-10 (LA)
1948—Rams, 52-37 (NY)
1953—Rams, 21-7 (LA)
1954—Rams, 17-16 (NY)
1959—Giants, 23-21 (LA)
1961—Giants, 24-14 (NY)
1966—Rams, 55-14 (LA)
1968—Rams, 24-21 (LA)
1970—Rams, 31-3 (NY)
1973—Rams, 40-6 (LA)
1976—Rams, 24-10 (LA)
1978—Rams, 20-17 (NY)
1979—Giants, 20-14 (LA)
1980—Rams, 28-7 (NY)
1981—Giants, 10-7 (NY)
1983—Rams, 16-6 (NY)
1984—Rams, 33-12 (LA)
**Giants, 16-13 (LA)
1985—Giants, 24-19 (NY)
(Points—Rams 562, Giants 398)
Franchise in Cleveland prior to 1946
***NFC First Round Playoff*

L.A. RAMS vs. N.Y. JETS
Series tied, 2-2
1970—Jets, 31-20 (LA)
1974—Rams, 20-13 (NY)
1980—Rams, 38-13 (LA)
1983—Jets, 27-24 (NY) OT
(Points—Rams 102, Jets 84)

***L.A. RAMS vs. PHILADELPHIA**
Rams lead series, 15-9-1
1937—Rams, 21-3 (P)
1939—Rams, 35-13 (Colorado Springs)
1940—Rams, 21-13 (C)
1942—Rams, 24-14 (Akron)
1944—Eagles, 26-13 (P)
1945—Eagles, 28-14 (P)
1946—Eagles, 25-14 (LA)
1947—Eagles, 14-7 (P)
1948—Tie, 28-28 (LA)
1949—Eagles, 38-14 (P)
**Eagles, 14-0 (LA)
1950—Eagles, 56-20 (P)
1955—Rams, 23-21 (P)
1956—Rams, 27-7 (LA)
1957—Rams, 17-13 (LA)
1959—Eagles, 23-20 (P)
1964—Rams, 20-10 (LA)
1967—Rams, 33-17 (LA)
1969—Rams, 23-17 (P)
1972—Rams, 34-3 (P)
1975—Rams, 42-3 (P)
1977—Rams, 20-0 (LA)
1978—Rams, 16-14 (P)
1983—Eagles, 13-9 (P)
1985—Rams, 17-6 (P)
(Points—Rams 512, Eagles 419)
Franchise in Cleveland prior to 1946
***NFL Championship*

***L.A. RAMS vs. **PITTSBURGH**
Rams lead series, 12-4-2
1938—Rams, 13-7 (New Orleans)
1939—Tie, 14-14 (C)
1941—Rams, 17-14 (Akron)
1947—Rams, 48-7 (P)
1948—Rams, 31-14 (LA)
1949—Tie, 7-7 (P)
1952—Rams, 28-14 (LA)
1955—Rams, 27-26 (LA)
1956—Steelers, 30-13 (P)
1961—Rams, 24-14 (LA)
1964—Rams, 26-14 (P)

1968—Rams, 45-10 (LA)
1971—Rams, 23-14 (P)
1975—Rams, 10-3 (LA)
1978—Rams, 10-7 (LA)
1979—***Steelers, 31-19 (Pasadena)
1981—Steelers, 24-0 (P)
1984—Steelers, 24-14 (P)
(Points—Rams 369, Steelers 274)
**Franchise in Cleveland prior to 1946*
***Steelers known as Pirates prior to 1941*
****Super Bowl XIV*

***L.A. RAMS vs. **ST. LOUIS**
Rams lead series, 20-15-2
1937—Cardinals, 6-0 (Clev)
Cardinals, 13-7 (Chi)
1938—Cardinals, 7-6 (Clev)
Cardinals, 31-17 (Chi)
1939—Rams, 24-0 (Chi)
Rams, 14-0 (Clev)
1940—Rams, 26-14 (Clev)
Cardinals, 17-7 (Chi)
1941—Rams, 10-6 (Clev)
Cardinals, 7-0 (Chi)
1942—Cardinals, 7-0 (Chi)
Rams, 7-3 (Clev)
1945—Rams, 21-0 (Clev)
Rams, 35-21 (Chi)
1946—Cardinals, 34-10 (Chi)
Rams, 17-14 (LA)
1947—Rams, 27-7 (LA)
Cardinals, 17-10 (Chi)
1948—Cardinals, 27-22 (LA)
Cardinals, 27-24 (Chi)
1949—Tie, 28-28 (Chi)
Cardinals, 31-27 (LA)
1951—Rams, 45-21 (LA)
1953—Tie, 24-24 (Chi)
1954—Rams, 28-17 (LA)
1958—Rams, 20-14 (Chi)
1960—Cardinals, 43-21 (LA)
1965—Rams, 27-3 (StL)
1968—Rams, 24-13 (StL)
1970—Rams, 34-13 (LA)
1972—Cardinals, 24-14 (StL)
1975—***Rams, 35-23 (LA)
1976—Cardinals, 30-28 (LA)
1979—Rams, 21-0 (LA)
1980—Rams, 21-13 (StL)
1984—Rams, 16-13 (StL)
1985—Rams, 46-14 (LA)
(Points—Rams 743, Cardinals 582)
**Franchise in Cleveland prior to 1946*
***Franchise in Chicago prior to 1960*
****NFC Divisional Playoff*

L.A. RAMS vs. SAN DIEGO
Rams lead series, 2-1
1970—Rams, 37-10 (LA)
1975—Rams, 13-10 (SD) OT
1979—Chargers, 40-16 (LA)
(Points—Rams 66, Chargers 60)

L.A. RAMS vs. SAN FRANCISCO
Rams lead series, 44-26-2
1950—Rams, 35-14 (SF)
Rams, 28-21 (LA)
1951—49ers, 44-17 (SF)
Rams, 23-16 (LA)
1952—Rams, 35-9 (LA)
Rams, 34-21 (SF)
1953—49ers, 31-30 (SF)
49ers, 31-27 (LA)
1954—Tie, 24-24 (LA)
Rams, 42-34 (SF)
1955—Rams, 23-14 (SF)
Rams, 27-14 (LA)
1956—49ers, 33-30 (SF)
Rams, 30-6 (LA)
1957—49ers, 23-20 (SF)
Rams, 37-24 (LA)
1958—Rams, 33-3 (SF)
Rams, 56-7 (LA)
1959—49ers, 34-0 (SF)
49ers, 24-16 (LA)
1960—49ers, 13-9 (SF)
49ers, 23-7 (LA)
1961—49ers, 35-0 (SF)
Rams, 17-7 (LA)
1962—Rams, 28-14 (SF)
49ers, 24-17 (LA)
1963—Rams, 28-21 (LA)
Rams, 21-17 (SF)
1964—Rams, 42-14 (LA)
49ers, 28-7 (SF)
1965—49ers, 45-21 (LA)
49ers, 30-27 (SF)
1966—Rams, 34-3 (LA)
49ers, 21-13 (SF)
1967—49ers, 27-24 (LA)
Rams, 17-7 (SF)
1968—Rams, 24-10 (LA)
Tie, 20-20 (SF)
1969—Rams, 27-21 (SF)
Rams, 41-30 (LA)
1970—49ers, 20-6 (LA)
Rams, 30-13 (SF)
1971—Rams, 20-13 (SF)
Rams, 17-6 (LA)
1972—Rams, 31-7 (LA)
Rams, 26-16 (SF)
1973—Rams, 40-20 (SF)
Rams, 31-13 (LA)
1974—Rams, 37-14 (LA)
Rams, 15-13 (SF)
1975—Rams, 23-14 (SF)
49ers, 24-23 (LA)
1976—49ers, 16-0 (LA)
Rams, 23-3 (SF)
1977—Rams, 34-14 (LA)
Rams, 23-10 (SF)
1978—Rams, 27-10 (LA)
Rams, 31-28 (SF)
1979—Rams, 27-24 (LA)
Rams, 26-20 (SF)
1980—Rams, 48-26 (LA)
Rams, 31-17 (SF)
1981—49ers, 20-17 (SF)
49ers, 33-31 (LA)
1982—49ers, 30-24 (LA)
Rams, 21-20 (SF)
1983—Rams, 10-7 (SF)
49ers, 45-35 (LA)
1984—49ers, 33-0 (LA)
49ers, 19-16 (SF)
1985—49ers, 28-14 (LA)
Rams, 27-20 (SF)
(Points—Rams 1,755, 49ers 1,433)

L.A. RAMS vs. SEATTLE
Rams lead series, 3-0
1976—Rams, 45-6 (LA)
1979—Rams, 24-0 (S)
1985—Rams, 35-24 (S)
(Points—Rams 104, Seahawks 30)

L.A. RAMS vs. TAMPA BAY
Rams lead series, 5-2
1977—Rams, 31-0 (LA)
1978—Rams, 26-23 (LA)
1979—Buccaneers, 21-6 (TB)
*Rams, 9-0 (TB)
1980—Buccaneers, 10-9 (TB)
1984—Rams, 34-33 (TB)
1985—Rams, 31-27 (TB)
(Points—Rams 146, Buccaneers 114)
**NFC Championship*

***L.A. RAMS vs. WASHINGTON**
Redskins lead series, 14-5-1
1937—Redskins, 16-7 (C)
1938—Redskins, 37-13 (W)
1941—Redskins, 17-13 (W)
1942—Redskins, 33-14 (W)
1944—Redskins, 14-10 (W)
1945—**Rams, 15-14 (C)
1948—Rams, 41-13 (W)
1949—Rams, 53-27 (LA)
1951—Redskins, 31-21 (W)
1962—Redskins, 20-14 (W)
1963—Redskins, 37-14 (LA)
1967—Tie, 28-28 (LA)
1969—Rams, 24-13 (W)
1971—Redskins, 38-24 (LA)
1974—Redskins, 23-17 (LA)
***Rams, 19-10 (LA)
1977—Redskins, 17-14 (W)
1981—Redskins, 30-7 (LA)
1983—Redskins, 42-20 (LA)
***Redskins, 51-7 (W)
(Points—Redskins 511, Rams 375)
**Franchise in Cleveland prior to 1946*
***NFL Championship*
****NFC Divisional Playoff*

MIAMI vs. ATLANTA
Dolphins lead series, 4-0;
See Atlanta vs. Miami

MIAMI vs. BUFFALO
Dolphins lead series, 32-7-1;
See Buffalo vs. Miami

MIAMI vs. CHICAGO
Dolphins lead series, 4-0;
See Chicago vs. Miami

MIAMI vs. CINCINNATI
Dolphins lead series, 7-3;
See Cincinnati vs. Miami

MIAMI vs. CLEVELAND
Series tied, 3-3;
See Cleveland vs. Miami

MIAMI vs. DALLAS
Dolphins lead series, 3-2;
See Dallas vs. Miami

MIAMI vs. DENVER
Dolphins lead series, 5-2-1;
See Denver vs. Miami

MIAMI vs. DETROIT
Dolphins lead series, 2-1;
See Detroit vs. Miami

MIAMI vs. GREEN BAY
Dolphins lead series, 4-0;
See Green Bay vs. Miami

MIAMI vs. HOUSTON
Oilers lead series, 10-9;
See Houston vs. Miami

MIAMI vs. INDIANAPOLIS
Dolphins lead series, 24-9;
See Indianapolis vs. Miami

MIAMI vs. KANSAS CITY
Chiefs lead series, 7-6;
See Kansas City vs. Miami

MIAMI vs. L.A. RAIDERS
Raiders lead series, 14-3-1;
See L.A. Raiders vs. Miami

MIAMI vs. L.A. RAMS
Dolphins lead series, 3-1;
See L.A. Rams vs. Miami

MIAMI vs. MINNESOTA
Dolphins lead series, 4-1
1972—Dolphins, 16-14 (Minn)
1973—*Dolphins, 24-7 (Houston)
1976—Vikings, 29-7 (Mia)
1979—Dolphins, 27-12 (Minn)
1982—Dolphins, 22-14 (Mia)
(Points—Dolphins 96, Vikings 76)
**Super Bowl VIII*

MIAMI vs. *NEW ENGLAND
Dolphins lead series, 25-15
1966—Patriots, 20-14 (M)
1967—Patriots, 41-10 (B)
Dolphins, 41-32 (M)
1968—Dolphins, 34-10 (B)
Dolphins, 38-7 (M)
1969—Dolphins, 17-16 (B)
Patriots, 38-23 (Tampa)
1970—Patriots, 27-14 (B)
Dolphins, 37-20 (M)
1971—Dolphins, 41-3 (M)
Patriots, 34-13 (NE)
1972—Dolphins, 52-0 (M)
Dolphins, 37-21 (NE)
1973—Dolphins, 44-23 (M)
Dolphins, 30-14 (NE)
1974—Patriots, 34-24 (NE)
Dolphins, 34-27 (M)
1975—Dolphins, 22-14 (NE)
Dolphins, 20-7 (M)
1976—Patriots, 30-14 (NE)
Dolphins, 10-3 (M)
1977—Dolphins, 17-5 (M)
Patriots, 14-10 (NE)
1978—Patriots, 33-24 (NE)
Dolphins, 23-3 (M)
1979—Patriots, 28-13 (NE)
Dolphins, 39-24 (M)
1980—Patriots, 34-0 (NE)
Dolphins, 16-13 (M) OT
1981—Dolphins, 30-27 (NE) OT
Dolphins, 24-14 (M)
1982—Patriots, 3-0 (NE)
**Dolphins, 28-13 (M)
1983—Dolphins, 34-24 (M)
Patriots, 17-6 (NE)
1984—Dolphins, 28-7 (M)
Dolphins, 44-24 (NE)
1985—Patriots, 17-13 (NE)
Dolphins, 30-27 (M)
***Patriots, 31-14 (M)
(Points—Dolphins 962, Patriots 779)
**Franchise in Boston prior to 1971*
***AFC First Round Playoff*
****AFC Championship*

MIAMI vs. NEW ORLEANS
Dolphins lead series, 3-1
1970—Dolphins, 21-10 (M)
1974—Dolphins, 21-0 (NO)
1980—Dolphins, 21-16 (M)
1983—Saints, 17-7 (NO)
(Points—Dolphins 70, Saints 43)

MIAMI vs. N.Y. GIANTS
Dolphins lead series, 1-0
1972—Dolphins, 23-13 (NY)

MIAMI vs. N.Y. JETS
Dolphins lead series, 22-18-1
1966—Jets, 19-14 (M)
Jets, 30-13 (NY)
1967—Jets, 29-7 (NY)
Jets, 33-14 (M)
1968—Jets, 35-17 (NY)
Jets, 31-7 (M)
1969—Jets, 34-31 (NY)
Jets, 27-9 (M)
1970—Dolphins, 20-6 (NY)
Dolphins, 16-10 (M)
1971—Jets, 14-10 (M)
Dolphins, 30-14 (NY)
1972—Dolphins, 27-17 (NY)
Dolphins, 28-24 (M)
1973—Dolphins, 31-3 (M)
Dolphins, 24-14 (NY)
1974—Dolphins, 21-17 (M)
Jets, 17-14 (NY)
1975—Dolphins, 43-0 (NY)
Dolphins, 27-7 (M)
1976—Dolphins, 16-0 (M)
Dolphins, 27-7 (NY)
1977—Dolphins, 21-17 (M)
Dolphins, 14-10 (NY)
1978—Jets, 33-20 (NY)
Jets, 24-13 (M)
1979—Jets, 33-27 (NY)
Jets, 27-24 (M)
1980—Jets, 17-14 (NY)
Jets, 24-17 (M)
1981—Tie, 28-28 (M) OT
Jets, 16-15 (NY)
1982—Dolphins, 45-28 (NY)
Dolphins, 20-19 (M)
*Dolphins, 14-0 (M)
1983—Dolphins, 32-14 (NY)
Dolphins, 34-14 (M)
1984—Dolphins, 31-17 (NY)
Dolphins, 28-17 (M)
1985—Jets, 23-7 (NY)
Dolphins, 21-17 (M)
(Points—Dolphins 871, Jets 766)
**AFC Championship*

MIAMI vs. PHILADELPHIA
Dolphins lead series, 3-2
1970—Eagles, 24-17 (P)
1975—Dolphins, 24-16 (M)
1978—Eagles, 17-3 (P)
1981—Dolphins, 13-10 (M)
1984—Dolphins, 24-23 (M)
(Points—Eagles 90, Dolphins 81)

MIAMI vs. PITTSBURGH
Dolphins lead series, 7-3
1971—Dolphins, 24-21 (M)
1972—*Dolphins, 21-17 (P)
1973—Dolphins, 30-26 (M)
1976—Steelers, 14-3 (P)
1979—**Steelers, 34-14 (P)
1980—Steelers, 23-10 (P)
1981—Dolphins, 30-10 (M)
1984—Dolphins, 31-7 (P)
*Dolphins, 45-28 (M)
1985—Dolphins, 24-20 (M)
(Points—Dolphins 232, Steelers 200)
**AFC Championship*
***AFC Divisional Playoff*

MIAMI vs. ST. LOUIS
Dolphins lead series, 5-0
1972—Dolphins, 31-10 (M)
1977—Dolphins, 55-14 (StL)
1978—Dolphins, 24-10 (M)
1981—Dolphins, 20-7 (StL)
1984—Dolphins, 36-28 (StL)
(Points—Dolphins 166, Cardinals 69)

MIAMI vs. SAN DIEGO
Chargers lead series, 8-5
1966—Chargers, 44-10 (SD)
1967—Chargers, 24-0 (SD)
Dolphins, 41-24 (M)
1968—Chargers, 34-28 (SD)
1969—Chargers, 21-14 (M)
1972—Dolphins, 24-10 (M)
1974—Dolphins, 28-21 (SD)
1977—Chargers, 14-13 (M)
1978—Dolphins, 28-21 (SD)
1980—Chargers, 27-24 (M) OT
1981—*Chargers, 41-38 (M) OT
1982—**Dolphins, 34-13 (M)
1984—Chargers, 34-28 (SD) OT
(Points—Chargers 328, Dolphins 310)
**AFC Divisional Playoff*
***AFC Second Round Playoff*

MIAMI vs. SAN FRANCISCO
Dolphins lead series, 4-1
1973—Dolphins, 21-13 (M)
1977—Dolphins, 19-15 (SF)
1980—Dolphins, 17-13 (M)
1983—Dolphins, 20-17 (SF)
1984—*49ers, 38-16 (Stanford)
(Points—49ers 96, Dolphins 93)
**Super Bowl XIX*

MIAMI vs. SEATTLE
Dolphins lead series, 3-1
1977—Dolphins, 31-13 (M)
1979—Dolphins, 19-10 (M)
1983—*Seahawks, 27-20 (M)
1984—*Dolphins, 31-10 (M)
(Points—Dolphins 101, Seahawks 60)
**AFC Divisional Playoff*

MIAMI vs. TAMPA BAY
Dolphins lead series, 2-1
1976—Dolphins, 23-20 (TB)
1982—Buccaneers, 23-17 (TB)
1985—Dolphins, 41-38 (M)
(Points—Dolphins 81, Buccaneers 81)

MIAMI vs. WASHINGTON
Dolphins lead series, 4-2
1972—*Dolphins, 14-7 (Los Angeles)
1974—Redskins, 20-17 (W)
1978—Dolphins, 16-0 (W)
1981—Dolphins, 13-10 (M)
1982—**Redskins, 27-17 (Pasadena)
1984—Dolphins, 35-17 (W)
(Points—Dolphins 112, Redskins 81)
**Super Bowl VII*
***Super Bowl XVII*

MINNESOTA vs. ATLANTA
Vikings lead series, 9-6;
See Atlanta vs. Minnesota
MINNESOTA vs. BUFFALO
Vikings lead series, 4-1;
See Buffalo vs. Minnesota
MINNESOTA vs. CHICAGO
Vikings lead series, 25-22-2;
See Chicago vs. Minnesota
MINNESOTA vs. CINCINNATI
Series tied, 2-2;
See Cincinnati vs. Minnesota
MINNESOTA vs. CLEVELAND
Vikings lead series, 7-1;
See Cleveland vs. Minnesota
MINNESOTA vs. DALLAS
Cowboys lead series, 10-5;
See Dallas vs. Minnesota
MINNESOTA vs. DENVER
Series tied, 2-2;
See Denver vs. Minnesota
MINNESOTA vs. DETROIT
Vikings lead series, 30-17-2;
See Detroit vs. Minnesota
MINNESOTA vs. GREEN BAY
Series tied, 24-24-1;
See Green Bay vs. Minnesota
MINNESOTA vs. HOUSTON
Vikings lead series, 2-1;
See Houston vs. Minnesota
MINNESOTA vs. INDIANAPOLIS
Colts lead series, 12-5-1;
See Indianapolis vs. Minnesota
MINNESOTA vs. KANSAS CITY
Series tied, 2-2;
See Kansas City vs. Minnesota
MINNESOTA vs. L.A. RAIDERS
Raiders lead series, 5-1;
See L.A. Raiders vs. Minnesota
MINNESOTA vs. L.A. RAMS
Vikings lead series, 15-12-2;
See L.A. Rams vs. Minnesota
MINNESOTA vs. MIAMI
Dolphins lead series, 4-1;
See Miami vs. Minnesota
MINNESOTA vs. *NEW ENGLAND
Patriots lead series, 2-1
1970—Vikings, 35-14 (B)
1974—Patriots, 17-14 (M)
1979—Patriots, 27-23 (NE)
(Points—Vikings 72, Patriots 58)
Franchise in Boston prior to 1971
MINNESOTA vs. NEW ORLEANS
Vikings lead series, 8-4
1968—Saints, 20-17 (NO)
1970—Vikings, 26-0 (M)
1971—Vikings, 23-10 (NO)
1972—Vikings, 37-6 (M)
1974—Vikings, 29-9 (M)
1975—Vikings, 20-7 (NO)
1976—Vikings, 40-9 (NO)
1978—Saints, 31-24 (NO)
1980—Vikings, 23-20 (NO)
1981—Vikings, 20-10 (M)
1983—Saints, 17-16 (NO)
1985—Saints, 30-23 (M)
(Points—Vikings 298, Saints 169)
MINNESOTA vs. N.Y. GIANTS
Vikings lead series, 6-1
1964—Vikings, 30-21 (NY)
1965—Vikings, 40-14 (M)
1967—Vikings, 27-24 (M)
1969—Giants, 24-23 (NY)
1971—Vikings, 17-10 (NY)
1973—Vikings, 31-7 (New Haven)
1976—Vikings, 24-7 (M)
(Points—Vikings 192, Giants 107)
MINNESOTA vs. N.Y. JETS
Jets lead series, 3-1
1970—Jets, 20-10 (NY)
1975—Vikings, 29-21 (M)
1979—Jets, 14-7 (NY)
1982—Jets 42-14 (M)
(Points—Jets 97, Vikings 60)
MINNESOTA vs. PHILADELPHIA
Vikings lead series, 9-4
1962—Vikings, 31-21 (M)
1963—Vikings, 34-13 (P)
1968—Vikings, 24-17 (P)
1971—Vikings, 13-0 (P)
1973—Vikings, 28-21 (M)
1976—Vikings, 31-12 (P)
1978—Vikings, 28-27 (M)
1980—Eagles, 42-7 (M)
*Eagles, 31-16 (P)
1981—Vikings, 35-23 (M)
1984—Eagles, 19-17 (P)
1985—Vikings, 28-23 (P)
Eagles, 37-35 (M)
(Points—Vikings 327, Eagles 286)
NFC Divisional Playoff
MINNESOTA vs. PITTSBURGH
Vikings lead series, 5-4
1962—Steelers, 39-31 (P)
1964—Vikings, 30-10 (M)
1967—Vikings, 41-27 (P)
1969—Vikings, 52-14 (M)
1972—Steelers, 23-10 (P)
1974—*Steelers, 16-6 (New Orleans)
1976—Vikings, 17-6 (M)
1980—Steelers, 23-17 (M)
1983—Vikings, 17-14 (P)
(Points—Vikings 221, Steelers 172)
Super Bowl IX
MINNESOTA vs. ST. LOUIS
Cardinals lead series, 7-3
1963—Cardinals, 56-14 (M)
1967—Cardinals, 34-24 (M)
1969—Vikings, 27-10 (StL)
1972—Cardinals, 19-17 (M)
1974—Vikings, 28-24 (StL)
*Vikings, 30-14 (M)
1977—Cardinals, 27-7 (M)
1979—Cardinals, 37-7 (StL)
1981—Cardinals, 30-17 (StL)
1983—Cardinals, 41-31 (StL)
(Points—Cardinals 292, Vikings 202)
NFC Divisional Playoff
MINNESOTA vs. SAN DIEGO
Series tied, 3-3
1971—Chargers, 30-14 (SD)
1975—Vikings, 28-13 (M)
1978—Chargers, 13-7 (M)
1981—Vikings, 33-31 (SD)
1984—Chargers, 42-13 (M)
1985—Vikings, 21-17 (M)
(Points—Chargers 146, Vikings 116)
MINNESOTA vs. SAN FRANCISCO
Vikings lead series, 13-12-1
1961—49ers, 38-24 (M)
49ers, 38-28 (SF)
1962—49ers, 21-7 (SF)
49ers, 35-12 (M)
1963—Vikings, 24-20 (SF)
Vikings, 45-14 (M)
1964—Vikings, 27-22 (SF)
Vikings, 24-7 (M)
1965—Vikings, 42-41 (SF)
49ers, 45-24 (M)
1966—Tie, 20-20 (SF)
Vikings, 28-3 (SF)
1967—49ers, 27-21 (M)
1968—Vikings, 30-20 (SF)
1969—Vikings, 10-7 (M)
1970—*49ers, 17-14 (M)
1971—49ers, 13-9 (M)
1972—49ers, 20-17 (SF)
1973—Vikings, 17-13 (SF)
1975—Vikings, 27-17 (M)
1976—49ers, 20-16 (SF)
1977—Vikings, 28-27 (M)
1979—Vikings, 28-22 (M)
1983—49ers, 48-17 (M)
1984—49ers, 51-7 (SF)
1985—Vikings, 28-21 (M)
(Points—49ers 627, Vikings 574)
NFC Divisional Playoff
MINNESOTA vs. SEATTLE
Seahawks lead series, 2-1
1976—Vikings, 27-21 (M)
1978—Seahawks, 29-28 (S)
1984—Seahawks, 20-12 (M)
(Points—Seahawks 70, Vikings 67)
MINNESOTA vs. TAMPA BAY
Vikings lead series, 11-5
1977—Vikings, 9-3 (TB)
1978—Buccaneers, 16-10 (M)
Vikings, 24-7 (TB)
1979—Buccaneers, 12-10 (M)
Vikings, 23-22 (TB)
1980—Vikings, 38-30 (M)
Vikings, 21-10 (TB)
1981—Buccaneers, 21-13 (TB)
Vikings, 25-10 (M)
1982—Vikings, 17-10 (M)
1983—Vikings, 19-16 (TB) OT
Buccaneers, 17-12 (M)
1984—Buccaneers, 35-31 (TB)
Vikings, 27-24 (M)
1985—Vikings, 31-16 (TB)
Vikings, 26-7 (M)
(Points—Vikings 336, Buccaneers 256)
MINNESOTA vs. WASHINGTON
Vikings lead series, 5-4
1968—Vikings, 27-14 (M)
1970—Vikings, 19-10 (W)
1972—Redskins, 24-21 (M)
1973—*Vikings, 27-20 (M)
1975—Redskins, 31-30 (W)
1976—*Vikings 35-20 (M)
1980—Vikings, 39-14 (W)
1982—**Redskins, 21-7 (W)
1984—Redskins, 31-17 (M)
(Points—Vikings 222, Redskins 185)
NFC Divisional Playoff
***NFC Second Round Playoff*

NEW ENGLAND vs. ATLANTA
Series tied, 2-2;
See Atlanta vs. New England
NEW ENGLAND vs. BUFFALO
Patriots lead series, 28-23-1;
See Buffalo vs. New England
NEW ENGLAND vs. CHICAGO
Bears lead series, 3-2;
See Chicago vs. New England
NEW ENGLAND vs. CINCINNATI
Patriots lead series, 6-3;
See Cincinnati vs. New England
NEW ENGLAND vs. CLEVELAND
Browns lead series, 6-2;
See Cleveland vs. New England
NEW ENGLAND vs. DALLAS
Cowboys lead series, 5-0;
See Dallas vs. New England
NEW ENGLAND vs. DENVER
Patriots lead series, 12-11;
See Denver vs. New England
NEW ENGLAND vs. DETROIT
Series tied, 2-2;
See Detroit vs. New England
NEW ENGLAND vs. GREEN BAY
Patriots lead series, 2-1;
See Green Bay vs. New England
NEW ENGLAND vs. HOUSTON
Patriots lead series, 14-13-1;
See Houston vs. New England
NEW ENGLAND vs. INDIANAPOLIS
Patriots lead series, 16-15;
See Indianapolis vs. New England
NEW ENGLAND vs. KANSAS CITY
Chiefs lead series, 11-7-3;
See Kansas City vs. New England
NEW ENGLAND vs. L.A. RAIDERS
Series tied, 12-12-1;
See L.A. Raiders vs. New England
NEW ENGLAND vs. L.A. RAMS
Patriots lead series, 2-1;
See L.A. Rams vs. New England
NEW ENGLAND vs. MIAMI
Dolphins lead series, 25-15;
See Miami vs. New England
NEW ENGLAND vs. MINNESOTA
Patriots lead series, 2-1;
See Minnesota vs. New England
NEW ENGLAND vs. NEW ORLEANS
Patriots lead series, 4-0
1972—Patriots, 17-10 (NO)
1976—Patriots, 27-6 (NE)
1980—Patriots, 38-27 (NO)
1983—Patriots, 7-0 (NE)
(Points—Patriots 89, Saints 43)
***NEW ENGLAND vs. N.Y. GIANTS**
Series tied, 1-1
1970—Giants, 16-0 (B)
1974—Patriots, 28-20 (New Haven)
(Points—Giants 36, Patriots 28)
Franchise in Boston prior to 1971
***NEW ENGLAND vs. **N.Y. JETS**
Jets lead series, 29-22-1
1960—Patriots, 28-24 (NY)
Patriots, 38-21 (B)
1961—Titans, 21-20 (B)
Titans, 37-30 (NY)
1962—Patriots, 43-14 (NY)
Patriots, 24-17 (B)
1963—Patriots, 38-14 (B)
Jets, 31-24 (NY)
1964—Patriots, 26-10 (B)
Jets, 35-14 (NY)
1965—Jets, 30-20 (B)
Patriots, 27-23 (NY)
1966—Tie, 24-24 (B)
Jets, 38-28 (NY)
1967—Jets, 30-23 (NY)
Jets, 29-24 (B)
1968—Jets, 47-31 (Birmingham)
Jets, 48-14 (NY)
1969—Jets, 23-14 (B)
Jets, 23-17 (NY)
1970—Jets, 31-21 (B)
Jets, 17-3 (NY)
1971—Patriots, 20-0 (NE)
Jets, 13-6 (NY)
1972—Jets, 41-13 (NE)
Jets, 34-10 (NY)
1973—Jets, 9-7 (NE)
Jets, 33-13 (NY)
1974—Patriots, 24-0 (NY)
Jets, 21-16 (NE)
1975—Jets, 36-7 (NY)
Jets, 30-28 (NE)
1976—Patriots, 41-7 (NE)
Patriots, 38-24 (NY)
1977—Jets, 30-27 (NY)
Patriots, 24-13 (NE)
1978—Patriots, 55-21 (NE)
Patriots, 19-17 (NY)
1979—Patriots, 56-3 (NE)
Jets, 27-26 (NY)
1980—Patriots, 21-11 (NY)
Patriots, 34-21 (NE)
1981—Jets, 28-24 (NY)
Jets, 17-6 (NE)
1982—Jets, 31-7 (NE)
1983—Patriots, 23-13 (NE)
Jets, 26-3 (NY)
1984—Patriots, 28-21 (NY)
Patriots, 30-20 (NE)
1985—Patriots, 20-13 (NE)
Jets, 16-13 (NY) OT
***Patriots, 26-14 (NY)
(Points—Patriots 1,196, Jets 1,177)
Franchise in Boston prior to 1971
***Jets known as Titans prior to 1963*
****AFC First Round Playoff*
NEW ENGLAND vs. PHILADELPHIA
Eagles lead series, 3-2
1973—Eagles, 24-23 (P)
1977—Patriots, 14-6 (NE)
1978—Patriots, 24-14 (NE)
1981—Eagles, 13-3 (P)
1984—Eagles, 27-17 (P)
(Points—Eagles 84, Patriots 81)
NEW ENGLAND vs. PITTSBURGH
Steelers lead series, 5-2
1972—Steelers, 33-3 (P)
1974—Steelers, 21-17 (NE)
1976—Patriots, 30-27 (P)
1979—Steelers, 16-13 (NE) OT
1981—Steelers, 27-21 (P) OT
1982—Steelers, 37-14 (P)
1983—Patriots, 28-23 (P)
(Points—Steelers 184, Patriots 126)
***NEW ENGLAND vs. ST. LOUIS**
Cardinals lead series, 4-1
1970—Cardinals, 31-0 (StL)
1975—Cardinals, 24-17 (StL)
1978—Patriots, 16-6 (StL)
1981—Cardinals, 27-20 (NE)
1984—Cardinals, 33-10 (NE)
(Points—Cardinals 121, Patriots 63)
Franchise in Boston prior to 1971
***NEW ENGLAND vs. **SAN DIEGO**
Patriots lead series, 13-12-2
1960—Patriots, 35-0 (LA)
Chargers, 45-16 (B)
1961—Chargers, 38-27 (B)
Patriots, 41-0 (SD)
1962—Patriots, 24-20 (B)
Patriots, 20-14 (SD)
1963—Chargers, 17-13 (SD)
Chargers, 7-6 (B)
***Chargers, 51-10 (SD)
1964—Patriots, 33-28 (SD)
Chargers, 26-17 (B)
1965—Tie, 10-10 (B)
Patriots, 22-6 (SD)
1966—Chargers, 24-0 (SD)
Patriots, 35-17 (B)
1967—Chargers, 28-14 (SD)
Tie, 31-31 (SD)
1968—Chargers, 27-17 (B)
1969—Chargers, 13-10 (B)
Chargers, 28-18 (SD)
1970—Chargers, 16-14 (B)
1973—Patriots, 30-14 (NE)
1975—Patriots, 33-19 (SD)
1977—Patriots, 24-20 (SD)
1978—Patriots, 28-23 (NE)
1979—Patriots, 27-21 (NE)
1983—Patriots, 37-21 (NE)
(Points—Patriots 592, Chargers 564)
Franchise in Boston prior to 1971
***Franchise in Los Angeles prior to 1961*
****AFL Championship*
NEW ENGLAND vs. SAN FRANCISCO
49ers lead series, 3-1
1971—49ers, 27-10 (SF)
1975—Patriots, 24-16 (NE)
1980—49ers, 21-17 (SF)
1983—49ers, 33-13 (NE)
(Points—49ers 97, Patriots 64)
NEW ENGLAND vs. SEATTLE
Patriots lead series, 5-1
1977—Patriots, 31-0 (NE)
1980—Patriots, 37-31 (S)
1982—Patriots, 16-0 (S)
1983—Seahawks, 24-6 (S)
1984—Patriots, 38-23 (NE)
1985—Patriots, 20-13 (S)
(Points—Patriots 148, Seahawks 91)
NEW ENGLAND vs. TAMPA BAY
Patriots lead series, 2-0
1976—Patriots, 31-14 (TB)
1985—Patriots, 32-14 (TB)
(Points—Patriots 63, Buccaneers 28)
NEW ENGLAND vs. WASHINGTON
Redskins lead series, 3-1
1972—Patriots, 24-23 (NE)
1978—Redskins, 16-14 (NE)
1981—Redskins, 24-22 (W)

1984—Redskins, 26-10 (NE)
(Points—Redskins 89, Patriots 70)

NEW ORLEANS vs. ATLANTA
Falcons lead series, 23-11;
See Atlanta vs. New Orleans
NEW ORLEANS vs. BUFFALO
Bills lead series, 2-1;
See Buffalo vs. New Orleans
NEW ORLEANS vs. CHICAGO
Bears lead series, 7-4;
See Chicago vs. New Orleans
NEW ORLEANS vs. CINCINNATI
Bengals lead series, 3-2;
See Cincinnati vs. New Orleans
NEW ORLEANS vs. CLEVELAND
Browns lead series, 8-1;
See Cleveland vs. New Orleans
NEW ORLEANS vs. DALLAS
Cowboys lead series, 11-1;
See Dallas vs. New Orleans
NEW ORLEANS vs. DENVER
Broncos lead series, 4-0;
See Denver vs. New Orleans
NEW ORLEANS vs. DETROIT
Series tied, 4-4-1;
See Detroit vs. New Orleans
NEW ORLEANS vs. GREEN BAY
Packers lead series, 10-2;
See Green Bay vs. New Orleans
NEW ORLEANS vs. HOUSTON
Series tied, 2-2-1;
See Houston vs. New Orleans
NEW ORLEANS vs. INDIANAPOLIS
Colts lead series, 3-0;
See Indianapolis vs. New Orleans
NEW ORLEANS vs. KANSAS CITY
Series tied, 2-2;
See Kansas City vs. New Orleans
NEW ORLEANS vs. L.A. RAIDERS
Raiders lead series, 3-0-1;
See L.A. Raiders vs. New Orleans
NEW ORLEANS vs. L.A. RAMS
Rams lead series, 23-9;
See L.A. Rams vs. New Orleans
NEW ORLEANS vs. MIAMI
Dolphins lead series, 3-1;
See Miami vs. New Orleans
NEW ORLEANS vs. MINNESOTA
Vikings lead series, 8-4;
See Minnesota vs. New Orleans
NEW ORLEANS vs. NEW ENGLAND
Patriots lead series, 4-0;
See New England vs. New Orleans
NEW ORLEANS vs. N.Y. GIANTS
Giants lead series, 6-5
1967—Giants, 27-21 (NY)
1968—Giants, 38-21 (NY)
1969—Saints, 25-24 (NY)
1970—Saints, 14-10 (NO)
1972—Giants, 45-21 (NY)
1975—Giants, 28-14 (NY)
1978—Saints, 28-17 (NO)
1979—Saints, 24-14 (NO)
1981—Giants, 20-7 (NY)
1984—Saints, 10-3 (NY)
1985—Giants, 21-13 (NO)
(Points—Giants 247, Saints 198)
NEW ORLEANS vs. N.Y. JETS
Jets lead series, 3-1
1972—Jets, 18-17 (NY)
1977—Jets, 16-13 (NO)
1980—Saints, 21-20 (NY)
1983—Jets, 31-28 (NO)
(Points—Jets 85, Saints 79)
NEW ORLEANS vs. PHILADELPHIA
Eagles lead series, 8-6
1967—Saints, 31-24 (NO)
Eagles, 48-21 (P)
1968—Eagles, 29-17 (P)
1969—Eagles, 13-10 (P)
Saints, 26-17 (NO)
1972—Saints, 21-3 (NO)
1974—Saints, 14-10 (NO)
1977—Eagles, 28-7 (P)
1978—Eagles, 24-17 (NO)
1979—Eagles, 26-14 (NO)
1980—Eagles, 34-21 (NO)
1981—Eagles, 31-14 (NO)
1983—Saints, 20-17 (P) OT
1985—Saints, 23-21 (NO)
(Points—Eagles 325, Saints 256)
NEW ORLEANS vs. PITTSBURGH
Series tied 4-4
1967—Steelers, 14-10 (NO)
1968—Saints, 16-12 (P)
Saints, 24-14 (NO)
1969—Saints, 27-24 (NO)
1974—Steelers, 28-7 (NO)
1978—Steelers, 20-14 (P)
1981—Steelers, 20-6 (NO)
1984—Saints, 27-24 (NO)
(Points—Steelers 156, Saints 131)
NEW ORLEANS vs. ST. LOUIS
Cardinals lead series, 9-4
1967—Cardinals, 31-20 (StL)
1968—Cardinals, 21-20 (NO)
Cardinals, 31-17 (StL)
1969—Saints, 51-42 (StL)
1970—Cardinals, 24-17 (StL)
1974—Saints, 14-0 (NO)
1977—Cardinals, 49-31 (StL)
1980—Cardinals, 40-7 (NO)
1981—Cardinals, 30-3 (StL)
1982—Cardinals, 21-7 (NO)
1983—Saints, 28-17 (NO)
1984—Saints, 34-24 (NO)
1985—Cardinals, 28-16 (StL)
(Points—Cardinals 358, Saints 265)
NEW ORLEANS vs. SAN DIEGO
Chargers lead series, 3-0
1973—Chargers, 17-14 (SD)
1977—Chargers, 14-0 (NO)
1979—Chargers, 35-0 (NO)
(Points—Chargers 66, Saints 14)
NEW ORLEANS vs. SAN FRANCISCO
49ers lead series, 22-9-2
1967—49ers, 27-13 (SF)
1969—Saints, 43-38 (NO)
1970—Tie, 20-20 (SF)
49ers, 38-27 (NO)
1971—49ers, 38-20 (NO)
Saints, 26-20 (SF)
1972—49ers, 37-2 (NO)
Tie, 20-20 (SF)
1973—49ers, 40-0 (SF)
Saints, 16-10 (NO)
1974—49ers, 17-13 (NO)
49ers, 35-21 (SF)
1975—49ers, 35-21 (SF)
49ers, 16-6 (NO)
1976—49ers, 33-3 (SF)
49ers, 27-7 (NO)
1977—49ers, 10-7 (NO) OT
49ers, 20-17 (SF)
1978—Saints, 14-7 (SF)
Saints, 24-13 (NO)
1979—Saints, 30-21 (SF)
Saints, 31-20 (NO)
1980—49ers, 26-23 (NO)
49ers, 38-35 (SF) OT
1981—49ers, 21-14 (SF)
49ers, 21-17 (NO)
1982—Saints, 23-20 (SF)
1983—49ers, 32-13 (NO)
49ers, 27-0 (SF)
1984—49ers, 30-20 (SF)
49ers, 35-3 (NO)
1985—Saints, 20-17 (SF)
49ers, 31-19 (NO)
(Points—49ers 840, Saints 568)
NEW ORLEANS vs. SEATTLE
Seahawks lead series, 2-1
1976—Saints, 51-27 (S)
1979—Seahawks, 38-24 (S)
1985—Seahawks, 27-3 (NO)
(Points—Seahawks, 92, Saints 78)
NEW ORLEANS vs. TAMPA BAY
Saints lead series, 5-3
1977—Buccaneers, 33-14 (NO)
1978—Saints, 17-10 (TB)
1979—Saints, 42-14 (TB)
1981—Buccaneers, 31-14 (NO)
1982—Buccaneers, 13-10 (NO)
1983—Saints, 24-21 (TB)
1984—Saints, 17-13 (NO)
1985—Saints, 20-13 (NO)
(Points—Saints 158, Buccaneers 148)
NEW ORLEANS vs. WASHINGTON
Redskins lead series, 7-4
1967—Redskins, 30-10 (NO)
Saints, 30-14 (W)
1968—Saints, 37-17 (NO)
1969—Redskins, 26-20 (NO)
Redskins, 17-14 (W)
1971—Redskins, 24-14 (W)
1973—Saints, 19-3 (NO)
1975—Redskins, 41-3 (W)
1979—Saints, 14-10 (W)
1980—Redskins, 22-14 (W)
1982—Redskins, 27-10 (NO)
(Points—Redskins 231, Saints 185)

N.Y. GIANTS vs. ATLANTA
Falcons lead series, 6-5;
See Atlanta vs. N.Y. Giants
N.Y. GIANTS vs. BUFFALO
Giants lead series, 2-1;
See Buffalo vs. N.Y. Giants
N.Y. GIANTS vs. CHICAGO
Bears lead series, 27-16-2;
See Chicago vs. N.Y. Giants
N.Y. GIANTS vs. CINCINNATI
Bengals lead series, 3-0;
See Cincinnati vs. N.Y. Giants
N.Y. GIANTS vs. CLEVELAND
Browns lead series, 26-16-2;
See Cleveland vs. N.Y. Giants
N.Y. GIANTS vs. DALLAS
Cowboys lead series, 32-13-2;
See Dallas vs. N.Y. Giants
N.Y. GIANTS vs. DENVER
Broncos lead series, 2-1;
See Denver vs. N.Y. Giants
N.Y. GIANTS vs. DETROIT
Lions lead series, 18-11-1;
See Detroit vs. N.Y. Giants
N.Y. GIANTS vs. GREEN BAY
Packers lead series, 25-18-2;
See Green Bay vs. N.Y. Giants
N.Y. GIANTS vs. HOUSTON
Giants lead series, 3-0;
See Houston vs. N.Y. Giants
N.Y. GIANTS vs. INDIANAPOLIS
Colts lead series, 7-3;
See Indianapolis vs. N.Y. Giants
N.Y. GIANTS vs. KANSAS CITY
Giants lead series, 4-1;
See Kansas City vs. N.Y. Giants
N.Y. GIANTS vs. L.A. RAIDERS
Raiders lead series, 3-0;
See L.A. Raiders vs. N.Y. Giants
N.Y. GIANTS vs. L.A. RAMS
Rams lead series, 16-8;
See L.A. Rams vs. N.Y. Giants
N.Y. GIANTS vs. MIAMI
Dolphins lead series, 1-0;
See Miami vs. N.Y. Giants
N.Y. GIANTS vs. MINNESOTA
Vikings lead series, 6-1;
See Minnesota vs. N.Y. Giants
N.Y. GIANTS vs. NEW ENGLAND
Series tied, 1-1;
See New England vs. N.Y. Giants
N.Y. GIANTS vs. NEW ORLEANS
Giants lead series, 6-5;
See New Orleans vs. N.Y. Giants
N.Y. GIANTS vs. N.Y. JETS
Series tied, 2-2
1970—Giants, 22-10 (NYJ)
1974—Jets, 26-20 (New Haven) OT
1981—Jets, 26-7 (NYG)
1984—Giants, 20-10 (NYJ)
(Points—Jets 72, Giants 69)
N.Y. GIANTS vs. PHILADELPHIA
Giants lead series, 56-45-2
1933—Giants, 56-0 (NY)
Giants, 20-14 (P)
1934—Giants, 17-0 (NY)
Eagles, 6-0 (P)
1935—Giants, 10-0 (NY)
Giants, 21-14 (P)
1936—Eagles, 10-7 (P)
Giants, 21-17 (NY)
1937—Giants, 16-7 (P)
Giants, 21-0 (NY)
1938—Eagles, 14-10 (P)
Giants, 17-7 (NY)
1939—Giants, 13-3 (P)
Giants, 27-10 (NY)
1940—Giants, 20-14 (P)
Giants, 17-7 (NY)
1941—Giants, 24-0 (P)
Giants, 16-0 (NY)
1942—Giants, 35-17 (NY)
Giants, 14-0 (P)
1944—Eagles, 24-17 (NY)
Tie, 21-21 (P)
1945—Eagles, 38-17 (P)
Giants, 28-21 (NY)
1946—Eagles, 24-14 (P)
Giants, 45-17 (NY)
1947—Eagles, 23-0 (P)
Eagles, 41-24 (NY)
1948—Eagles, 45-0 (P)
Eagles, 35-14 (NY)
1949—Eagles, 24-3 (NY)
Eagles, 17-3 (P)
1950—Giants, 7-3 (NY)
Giants, 9-7 (P)
1951—Giants, 26-24 (NY)
Giants, 23-7 (P)
1952—Giants, 31-7 (P)
Eagles, 14-10 (NY)
1953—Eagles, 30-7 (P)
Giants, 37-28 (NY)
1954—Giants, 27-14 (NY)
Eagles, 29-14 (P)
1955—Eagles, 27-17 (P)
Giants, 31-7 (NY)
1956—Giants, 20-3 (NY)
Giants, 21-7 (P)
1957—Giants, 24-20 (P)
Giants, 13-0 (NY)
1958—Eagles, 27-24 (P)
Giants, 24-10 (NY)
1959—Eagles, 49-21 (P)
Giants, 24-7 (NY)
1960—Eagles, 17-10 (NY)
Eagles, 31-23 (P)
1961—Giants, 38-21 (NY)
Giants, 28-24 (P)
1962—Giants, 29-13 (P)
Giants, 19-14 (NY)
1963—Giants, 37-14 (P)
Giants, 42-14 (NY)
1964—Eagles, 38-7 (P)
Eagles, 23-17 (NY)
1965—Giants, 16-14 (P)
Giants, 35-27 (NY)
1966—Eagles, 35-17 (P)
Eagles, 31-3 (NY)
1967—Giants, 44-7 (NY)
1968—Giants, 34-25 (P)
Giants, 7-6 (NY)
1969—Eagles, 23-20 (NY)
1970—Giants, 30-23 (NY)
Eagles, 23-20 (P)
1971—Eagles, 23-7 (P)
Eagles, 41-28 (NY)
1972—Giants, 27-12 (P)
Giants, 62-10 (NY)
1973—Tie, 23-23 (NY)
Eagles, 20-16 (P)
1974—Eagles, 35-7 (P)
Eagles, 20-7 (New Haven)
1975—Giants, 23-14 (P)
Eagles, 13-10 (NY)
1976—Eagles, 20-7 (P)
Eagles, 10-0 (NY)
1977—Eagles, 28-10 (NY)
Eagles, 17-14 (P)
1978—Eagles, 19-17 (NY)
Eagles, 20-3 (P)
1979—Eagles, 23-17 (P)
Eagles, 17-13 (NY)
1980—Eagles, 35-3 (P)
Eagles, 31-16 (NY)
1981—Eagles, 24-10 (NY)
Giants, 20-10 (P)
*Giants, 27-21 (P)
1982—Giants, 23-7 (NY)
Giants, 26-24 (P)
1983—Eagles, 17-13 (NY)
Giants, 23-0 (P)
1984—Giants, 28-27 (NY)
Eagles, 24-10 (P)
1985—Giants, 21-0 (NY)
Giants, 16-10 (P) OT
(Points—Giants 1,981, Eagles 1,808)
NFC First Round Playoff
N.Y. GIANTS vs. *PITTSBURGH
Giants lead series, 41-26-3
1933—Giants, 23-2 (P)
Giants, 27-3 (NY)
1934—Giants, 14-12 (P)
Giants, 17-7 (NY)
1935—Giants, 42-7 (P)
Giants, 13-0 (NY)
1936—Pirates, 10-7 (P)
1937—Giants, 10-7 (P)
Giants, 17-0 (NY)
1938—Giants, 27-14 (P)
Pirates, 13-10 (NY)
1939—Giants, 14-7 (P)
Giants, 23-7 (NY)
1940—Tie, 10-10 (P)
Giants, 12-0 (NY)
1941—Giants, 37-10 (P)
Giants, 28-7 (NY)
1942—Steelers, 13-10 (P)
Steelers, 17-9 (NY)
1945—Giants, 34-6 (P)
Steelers, 21-7 (NY)
1946—Giants, 17-14 (P)
Giants, 7-0 (NY)
1947—Steelers, 38-21 (NY)
Steelers, 24-7 (P)
1948—Giants, 34-27 (NY)
Steelers, 38-28 (P)
1949—Steelers, 28-7 (P)
Steelers, 21-17 (NY)
1950—Giants, 18-7 (P)
Steelers, 17-6 (NY)
1951—Tie, 13-13 (P)
Giants, 14-0 (NY)
1952—Steelers, 63-7 (P)
1953—Steelers, 24-14 (P)
Steelers, 14-10 (NY)
1954—Giants, 30-6 (P)
Giants, 24-3 (NY)
1955—Steelers, 30-23 (P)
Steelers, 19-17 (NY)
1956—Giants, 38-10 (NY)
Giants, 17-14 (P)
1957—Giants, 35-0 (NY)
Steelers, 21-10 (P)
1958—Giants, 17-6 (NY)
Steelers, 31-10 (P)
1959—Giants, 21-16 (P)
Steelers, 14-9 (NY)
1960—Giants, 19-17 (P)

Giants, 27-24 (NY)
1961—Giants, 17-14 (P)
Giants, 42-21 (NY)
1962—Giants, 31-27 (P)
Steelers, 20-17 (NY)
1963—Steelers, 31-0 (P)
Giants, 33-17 (NY)
1964—Steelers, 27-24 (P)
Steelers, 44-17 (NY)
1965—Giants, 23-13 (P)
Giants, 35-10 (NY)
1966—Tie, 34-34 (P)
Steelers, 47-28 (NY)
1967—Giants, 27-24 (P)
Giants, 28-20 (NY)
1968—Giants, 34-20 (P)
1969—Giants, 10-7 (NY)
Giants, 21-17 (P)
1971—Steelers, 17-13 (P)
1976—Steelers, 27-0 (NY)
1985—Giants, 28-10 (NY)
(Points—Giants 1,370, Steelers 1,159)
Steelers known as Pirates prior to 1941

N.Y. GIANTS vs. *ST. LOUIS
Giants lead series, 53-31-2
1926—Giants, 20-0 (NY)
1927—Giants, 28-7 (NY)
1929—Giants, 24-21 (NY)
1930—Giants, 25-12 (NY)
Giants, 13-7 (C)
1935—Cardinals, 14-13 (NY)
1936—Giants, 14-6 (NY)
1938—Giants, 6-0 (NY)
1939—Giants, 17-7 (NY)
1941—Cardinals, 10-7 (NY)
1942—Giants, 21-7 (NY)
1943—Giants, 24-13 (NY)
1946—Giants, 28-24 (NY)
1947—Giants, 35-31 (NY)
1948—Cardinals, 63-35 (NY)
1949—Giants, 41-38 (C)
1950—Cardinals, 17-3 (C)
Giants, 51-21 (NY)
1951—Giants, 28-17 (NY)
Giants, 10-0 (C)
1952—Cardinals, 24-23 (NY)
Giants, 28-6 (C)
1953—Giants, 21-7 (NY)
Giants, 23-20 (C)
1954—Giants, 41-10 (C)
Giants, 31-17 (NY)
1955—Cardinals, 28-17 (C)
Giants, 10-0 (NY)
1956—Cardinals, 35-27 (C)
Giants, 23-10 (NY)
1957—Giants, 27-14 (NY)
Giants, 28-21 (C)
1958—Giants, 37-7 (Buffalo)
Cardinals, 23-6 (NY)
1959—Giants, 9-3 (NY)
Giants, 30-20 (Minn)
1960—Giants, 35-14 (StL)
Cardinals, 20-13 (NY)
1961—Cardinals, 21-10 (NY)
Giants, 24-9 (StL)
1962—Giants, 31-14 (StL)
Giants, 31-28 (NY)
1963—Giants, 38-21 (StL)
Cardinals, 24-17 (NY)
1964—Giants, 34-17 (NY)
Tie, 10-10 (StL)
1965—Giants, 14-10 (NY)
Giants, 28-15 (StL)
1966—Cardinals, 24-19 (StL)
Cardinals, 20-17 (NY)
1967—Giants, 37-20 (StL)
Giants, 37-14 (NY)
1968—Cardinals, 28-21 (NY)
1969—Cardinals, 42-17 (StL)
Giants, 49-6 (NY)
1970—Giants, 35-17 (NY)
Giants, 34-17 (StL)
1971—Giants, 21-20 (StL)
Cardinals, 24-7 (NY)
1972—Giants, 27-21 (NY)
Giants, 13-7 (StL)
1973—Cardinals, 35-27 (StL)
Giants, 24-13 (New Haven)
1974—Cardinals, 23-21 (New Haven)
Cardinals, 26-14 (StL)
1975—Cardinals, 26-14 (StL)
Cardinals, 20-13 (NY)
1976—Cardinals, 27-21 (StL)
Cardinals, 17-14 (NY)
1977—Cardinals, 28-0 (StL)
Giants, 27-7 (NY)
1978—Cardinals, 20-10 (StL)
Giants, 17-0 (NY)
1979—Cardinals, 27-14 (NY)
Cardinals, 29-20 (StL)
1980—Giants, 41-35 (StL)
Cardinals, 23-7 (NY)
1981—Giants, 34-14 (NY)
Giants, 20-10 (StL)
1982—Cardinals, 24-21 (StL)
1983—Tie, 20-20 (StL) OT
Cardinals, 10-6 (NY)
1984—Giants, 16-10 (NY)
Cardinals, 31-21 (StL)
1985—Giants, 27-17 (NY)
Giants, 34-3 (StL)
(Points—Giants 1,926, Cardinals 1,518)
Franchise in Chicago prior to 1960

N.Y. GIANTS vs. SAN DIEGO
Series tied, 2-2
1971—Giants, 35-17 (NY)
1975—Giants, 35-24 (NY)
1980—Chargers, 44-7 (SD)
1983—Chargers, 41-34 (NY)
(Points—Chargers 126, Giants 111)

N.Y. GIANTS vs. SAN FRANCISCO
Giants lead series, 10-7
1952—Giants, 23-14 (NY)
1956—Giants, 38-21 (SF)
1957—49ers, 27-17 (NY)
1960—Giants, 21-19 (SF)
1963—Giants, 48-14 (NY)
1968—49ers, 26-10 (NY)
1972—Giants, 23-17 (SF)
1975—Giants, 26-23 (SF)
1977—Giants, 20-17 (NY)
1978—Giants, 27-10 (NY)
1979—Giants, 32-16 (NY)
1980—49ers, 12-0 (SF)
1981—49ers, 17-10 (SF)
*49ers, 38-24 (SF)
1984—49ers, 31-10 (NY)
*49ers, 21-10 (SF)
1985—**Giants, 17-3 (NY)
(Points—Giants 356, 49ers 326)
*NFC Divisional Playoff
**NFC First Round Playoff*

N.Y. GIANTS vs. SEATTLE
Giants lead series, 3-1
1976—Giants, 28-16 (NY)
1980—Giants, 27-21 (S)
1981—Giants, 32-0 (S)
1983—Seahawks, 17-12 (NY)
(Points—Giants 99, Seahawks 54)

N.Y. GIANTS vs. TAMPA BAY
Giants lead series, 6-3
1977—Giants, 10-0 (TB)
1978—Giants, 19-13 (TB)
Giants, 17-14 (NY)
1979—Giants, 17-14 (NY)
Buccaneers, 31-3 (TB)
1980—Buccaneers, 30-13 (TB)
1984—Giants, 17-14 (NY)
Buccaneers, 20-17 (TB)
1985—Giants, 22-20 (NY)
(Points—Buccaneers 156, Giants 135)

N.Y. GIANTS vs. *WASHINGTON
Giants lead series, 58-46-3
1932—Braves, 14-6 (B)
Tie, 0-0 (NY)
1933—Redskins, 21-20 (B)
Giants, 7-0 (NY)
1934—Giants, 16-13 (B)
Giants, 3-0 (NY)
1935—Giants, 20-12 (B)
Giants, 17-6 (NY)
1936—Giants, 7-0 (B)
Redskins, 14-0 (NY)
1937—Redskins, 13-3 (W)
Redskins, 49-14 (NY)
1938—Giants, 10-7 (W)
Giants, 36-0 (NY)
1939—Tie, 0-0 (W)
Giants, 9-7 (NY)
1940—Redskins, 21-7 (W)
Giants, 21-7 (NY)
1941—Giants, 17-10 (W)
Giants, 20-13 (NY)
1942—Giants, 14-7 (W)
Redskins, 14-7 (NY)
1943—Giants, 14-10 (NY)
Giants, 31-7 (W)
**Redskins, 28-0 (NY)
1944—Giants, 16-13 (NY)
Giants, 31-0 (W)
1945—Redskins, 24-14 (NY)
Redskins, 17-0 (W)
1946—Redskins, 24-14 (W)
Giants, 31-0 (NY)
1947—Redskins, 28-20 (W)
Giants, 35-10 (NY)
1948—Redskins, 41-10 (W)
Redskins, 28-21 (NY)
1949—Giants, 45-35 (W)
Giants, 23-7 (NY)
1950—Giants, 21-17 (W)
Giants, 24-21 (NY)
1951—Giants, 35-14 (W)
Giants, 28-14 (NY)
1952—Giants, 14-10 (W)
Redskins, 27-17 (NY)
1953—Redskins, 13-9 (W)
Redskins, 24-21 (NY)
1954—Giants, 51-21 (W)
Giants, 24-7 (NY)
1955—Giants, 35-7 (NY)
Giants, 27-20 (W)
1956—Redskins, 33-7 (W)
Giants, 28-14 (NY)
1957—Giants, 24-20 (W)
Redskins, 31-14 (NY)
1958—Giants, 21-14 (W)
Giants, 30-0 (NY)
1959—Giants, 45-14 (NY)
Giants, 24-10 (W)
1960—Tie, 24-24 (NY)
Giants, 17-3 (W)
1961—Giants, 24-21 (W)
Giants, 53-0 (NY)
1962—Giants, 49-34 (NY)
Giants, 42-24 (NY)
1963—Giants, 24-14 (W)
Giants, 44-14 (NY)
1964—Giants, 13-10 (NY)
Redskins, 36-21 (W)
1965—Redskins, 23-7 (NY)
Giants, 27-10 (W)
1966—Giants, 13-10 (NY)
Redskins, 72-41 (W)
1967—Redskins, 38-34 (W)
1968—Giants, 48-21 (NY)
Giants, 13-10 (W)
1969—Redskins, 20-14 (W)
1970—Giants, 35-33 (NY)
Giants, 27-24 (W)
1971—Redskins, 30-3 (NY)
Redskins, 23-7 (W)
1972—Redskins, 23-16 (NY)
Redskins, 27-13 (W)
1973—Redskins, 21-3 (New Haven)
Redskins, 27-24 (W)
1974—Redskins, 13-10 (New Haven)
Redskins, 24-3 (W)
1975—Redskins, 49-13 (W)
Redskins, 21-13 (NY)
1976—Redskins, 19-17 (W)
Giants, 12-9 (NY)
1977—Giants, 20-17 (NY)
Giants, 17-6 (W)
1978—Giants, 17-6 (NY)
Redskins, 16-13 (W) OT
1979—Redskins, 27-0 (W)
Giants, 14-6 (NY)
1980—Redskins, 23-21 (NY)
Redskins, 16-13 (W)
1981—Giants, 17-7 (W)
Redskins, 30-27 (NY) OT
1982—Redskins, 27-17 (NY)
Redskins, 15-14 (W)
1983—Redskins, 33-17 (NY)
Redskins, 31-22 (W)
1984—Redskins, 30-14 (W)
Giants, 37-13 (NY)
1985—Giants, 17-3 (NY)
Redskins, 23-21 (W)
(Points—Giants 2,080, Redskins 1,887)
*Franchise in Boston prior to 1937 and known as Braves prior to 1933
**Division Playoff*

N.Y. JETS vs. ATLANTA
Falcons lead series, 2-1;
See Atlanta vs. N.Y. Jets

N.Y. JETS vs. BUFFALO
Bills lead series, 26-25;
See Buffalo vs. N.Y. Jets

N.Y. JETS vs. CHICAGO
Bears lead series, 2-1;
See Chicago vs. N.Y. Jets

N.Y. JETS vs. CINCINNATI
Jets lead series, 7-3;
See Cincinnati vs. N.Y. Jets

N.Y. JETS vs. CLEVELAND
Browns lead series, 7-3;
See Cleveland vs. N.Y. Jets

N.Y. JETS vs. DALLAS
Cowboys lead series, 3-0;
See Dallas vs. N.Y. Jets

N.Y. JETS vs. DENVER
Series tied, 10-10-1;
See Denver vs. N.Y. Jets

N.Y. JETS vs. DETROIT
Series tied, 2-2;
See Detroit vs. N.Y. Jets

N.Y. JETS vs. GREEN BAY
Jets lead series, 4-1;
See Green Bay vs. N.Y. Jets

N.Y. JETS vs. HOUSTON
Oilers lead series, 15-10-1;
See Houston vs. N.Y. Jets

N.Y. JETS vs. INDIANAPOLIS
Series tied, 16-16;
See Indianapolis vs. N.Y. Jets

N.Y. JETS vs. KANSAS CITY
Chiefs lead series, 13-11;
See Kansas City vs. N.Y. Jets

N.Y. JETS vs. L.A. RAIDERS
Raiders lead series, 12-11-2;
See L.A. Raiders vs. N.Y. Jets

N.Y. JETS vs. L.A. RAMS
Series tied, 2-2;
See L.A. Rams vs. N.Y. Jets

N.Y. JETS vs. MIAMI
Dolphins lead series, 22-18-1;
See Miami vs. N.Y. Jets

N.Y. JETS vs. MINNESOTA
Jets lead series, 3-1;
See Minnesota vs. N.Y. Jets

N.Y. JETS vs. NEW ENGLAND
Jets lead series, 29-22-1;
See New England vs. N.Y. Jets

N.Y. JETS vs. NEW ORLEANS
Jets lead series, 3-1;
See New Orleans vs. N.Y. Jets

N.Y. JETS vs. N.Y. GIANTS
Series tied, 2-2;
See N.Y. Giants vs. N.Y. Jets

N.Y. JETS vs. PHILADELPHIA
Eagles lead series, 3-0
1973—Eagles, 24-23 (P)
1977—Eagles, 27-0 (P)
1978—Eagles, 17-9 (P)
(Points—Eagles 68, Jets 32)

N.Y. JETS vs. PITTSBURGH
Steelers lead series, 8-0
1970—Steelers, 21-17 (P)
1973—Steelers, 26-14 (P)
1975—Steelers, 20-7 (NY)
1977—Steelers, 23-20 (NY)
1978—Steelers, 28-17 (NY)
1981—Steelers, 38-10 (P)
1983—Steelers, 34-7 (NY)
1984—Steelers, 23-17 (NY)
(Points—Steelers 213, Jets 109)

N.Y. JETS vs. ST. LOUIS
Cardinals lead series, 2-1
1971—Cardinals, 17-10 (StL)
1975—Cardinals 37-6 (NY)
1978—Jets, 23-10 (NY)
(Points—Cardinals 64, Jets 39)

***N.Y. JETS vs. **SAN DIEGO**
Chargers lead series, 14-7-1
1960—Chargers, 21-7 (NY)
Chargers, 50-43 (LA)
1961—Chargers, 25-10 (NY)
Chargers, 48-13 (SD)
1962—Chargers, 40-14 (SD)
Titans, 23-3 (NY)
1963—Chargers, 24-20 (SD)
Chargers, 53-7 (NY)
1964—Tie, 17-17 (NY)
Chargers, 38-3 (SD)
1965—Chargers, 34-9 (NY)
Chargers, 38-7 (SD)
1966—Jets, 17-16 (NY)
Chargers, 42-27 (SD)
1967—Jets, 42-31 (SD)
1968—Jets, 23-20 (NY)
Jets, 37-15 (SD)
1969—Chargers, 34-27 (SD)
1971—Chargers, 49-21 (SD)
1974—Jets, 27-14 (NY)
1975—Chargers, 24-16 (SD)
1983—Jets, 41-29 (SD)
(Points—Chargers 665, Jets 451)
*Jets known as Titans prior to 1963
**Franchise in Los Angeles prior to 1961*

N.Y. JETS vs. SAN FRANCISCO
49ers lead series, 3-1
1971—49ers, 24-21 (NY)
1976—49ers, 17-6 (SF)
1980—49ers, 37-27 (NY)
1983—Jets, 27-13 (SF)
(Points—49ers 91, Jets 81)

N.Y. JETS vs. SEATTLE
Seahawks lead series, 7-1
1977—Seahawks, 17-0 (NY)
1978—Seahawks, 24-17 (NY)
1979—Seahawks, 30-7 (S)
1980—Seahawks, 27-17 (NY)
1981—Seahawks, 19-3 (NY)
Seahawks, 27-23 (S)
1983—Seahawks, 17-10 (NY)
1985—Jets, 17-14 (NY)
(Points—Seahawks 175, Jets 94)

N.Y. JETS vs. TAMPA BAY
Jets lead series, 3-1
1976—Jets, 34-0 (NY)
1982—Jets, 32-17 (NY)
1984—Buccaneers, 41-21 (TB)
1985—Jets, 62-28 (NY)
(Points—Jets 149, Buccaneers 86)

N.Y. JETS vs. WASHINGTON
Redskins lead series, 3-0
1972—Redskins, 35-17 (NY)
1976—Redskins, 37-16 (NY)
1978—Redskins, 23-3 (W)
(Points—Redskins 95, Jets 36)

PHILADELPHIA vs. ATLANTA
Series tied, 6-6-1;
See Atlanta vs. Philadelphia
PHILADELPHIA vs. BUFFALO
Eagles lead series, 3-1;
See Buffalo vs. Philadelphia
PHILADELPHIA vs. CHICAGO
Bears lead series, 19-4-1;
See Chicago vs. Philadelphia
PHILADELPHIA vs. CINCINNATI
Bengals lead series, 4-0;
See Cincinnati vs. Philadelphia
PHILADELPHIA vs. CLEVELAND
Browns lead series, 29-11-1;
See Cleveland vs. Philadelphia
PHILADELPHIA vs. DALLAS
Cowboys lead series, 34-17;
See Dallas vs. Philadelphia
PHILADELPHIA vs. DENVER
Eagles lead series, 3-1;
See Denver vs. Philadelphia
PHILADELPHIA vs. DETROIT
Lions lead series, 11-9-2;
See Detroit vs. Philadelphia
PHILADELPHIA vs. GREEN BAY
Packers lead series, 17-5;
See Green Bay vs. Philadelphia
PHILADELPHIA vs. HOUSTON
Eagles lead series, 3-0;
See Houston vs. Philadelphia
PHILADELPHIA vs. INDIANAPOLIS
Series tied, 5-5;
See Indianapolis vs. Philadelphia
PHILADELPHIA vs. KANSAS CITY
Eagles lead series, 1-0;
See Kansas City vs. Philadelphia
PHILADELPHIA vs. L.A. RAIDERS
Raiders lead series, 3-1;
See L.A. Raiders vs. Philadelphia
PHILADELPHIA vs. L.A. RAMS
Rams lead series, 15-9-1;
See L.A. Rams vs. Philadelphia
PHILADELPHIA vs. MIAMI
Dolphins lead series, 3-2;
See Miami vs. Philadelphia
PHILADELPHIA vs. MINNESOTA
Vikings lead series, 9-4;
See Minnesota vs. Philadelphia
PHILADELPHIA vs. NEW ENGLAND
Eagles lead series, 3-2;
See New England vs. Philadelphia
PHILADELPHIA vs. NEW ORLEANS
Eagles lead series, 8-6;
See New Orleans vs. Philadelphia
PHILADELPHIA vs. N.Y. GIANTS
Giants lead series, 56-45-2;
See N.Y. Giants vs. Philadelphia
PHILADELPHIA vs. N.Y. JETS
Eagles lead series, 3-0;
See N.Y. Jets vs. Philadelphia
PHILADELPHIA vs. *PITTSBURGH
Eagles lead series, 42-25-3
1933—Eagles, 25-6 (Phila)
1934—Eagles, 17-0 (Pitt)
Pirates, 9-7 (Phila)
1935—Pirates, 17-7 (Phila)
Eagles, 17-6 (Pitt)
1936—Pirates, 17-0 (Pitt)
Pirates, 6-0 (Johnstown, Pa.)
1937—Pirates, 27-14 (Pitt)
Pirates, 16-7 (Pitt)
1938—Eagles, 27-7 (Buffalo)
Eagles, 14-7 (Charleston, W. Va.)
1939—Eagles, 17-14 (Phila)
Pirates, 24-12 (Pitt)
1940—Pirates, 7-3 (Pitt)
Eagles, 7-0 (Phila)
1941—Eagles, 10-7 (Pitt)
Tie, 7-7 (Phila)
1942—Eagles, 24-14 (Pitt)
Steelers, 14-0 (Phila)
1945—Eagles, 45-3 (Pitt)
Eagles, 30-6 (Phila)
1946—Steelers, 10-7 (Pitt)
Eagles, 10-7 (Phila)
1947—Steelers, 35-24 (Pitt)
Eagles, 21-0 (Phila)
**Eagles, 21-0 (Pitt)
1948—Eagles, 34-7 (Pitt)
Eagles, 17-0 (Phila)
1949—Eagles, 38-7 (Pitt)
Eagles, 34-17 (Phila)
1950—Eagles, 17-10 (Pitt)
Steelers, 9-7 (Phila)
1951—Eagles, 34-13 (Pitt)
Steelers, 17-13 (Phila)
1952—Eagles, 31-25 (Pitt)
Eagles, 26-21 (Phila)
1953—Eagles, 23-17 (Phila)
Eagles, 35-7 (Pitt)
1954—Eagles, 24-22 (Phila)
Steelers, 17-7 (Pitt)
1955—Steelers, 13-7 (Pitt)
Eagles, 24-0 (Phila)
1956—Eagles, 35-21 (Pitt)
Eagles, 14-7 (Phila)
1957—Steelers, 6-0 (Pitt)
Eagles, 7-6 (Phila)
1958—Steelers, 24-3 (Pitt)
Steelers, 31-24 (Phila)
1959—Eagles, 28-24 (Phila)
Steelers, 31-0 (Pitt)
1960—Eagles, 34-7 (Phila)
Steelers, 27-21 (Pitt)
1961—Eagles, 21-16 (Phila)
Eagles, 35-24 (Pitt)
1962—Steelers, 13-7 (Pitt)
Steelers, 26-17 (Phila)
1963—Tie, 21-21 (Phila)
Tie, 20-20 (Pitt)
1964—Eagles, 21-7 (Phila)
Eagles, 34-10 (Pitt)
1965—Steelers, 20-14 (Phila)
Eagles, 47-13 (Pitt)
1966—Eagles, 31-14 (Pitt)
Eagles, 27-23 (Phila)
1967—Eagles, 34-24 (Phila)
1968—Steelers, 6-3 (Pitt)
1969—Eagles, 41-27 (Phila)
1970—Eagles, 30-20 (Phila)
1974—Steelers, 27-0 (Pitt)
1979—Eagles, 17-14 (Phila)
(Points—Eagles 1,330, Steelers 967)
**Steelers known as Pirates prior to 1941*
***Division Playoff*
PHILADELPHIA vs. *ST. LOUIS
Cardinals lead series, 40-34-4
1935—Cardinals, 12-3 (C)
1936—Cardinals, 13-0 (C)
1937—Tie, 6-6 (P)
1938—Eagles, 7-0 (Erie, Pa.)
1941—Eagles, 21-14 (P)
1945—Eagles, 21-6 (P)
1947—Cardinals, 45-21 (P)
**Cardinals, 28-21 (C)
1948—Cardinals, 21-14 (C)
**Eagles, 7-0 (P)
1949—Eagles, 28-3 (P)
1950—Eagles, 45-7 (C)
Cardinals, 14-10 (P)
1951—Eagles, 17-14 (C)
1952—Eagles, 10-7 (P)
Cardinals, 28-22 (C)
1953—Eagles, 56-17 (C)
Eagles, 38-0 (P)
1954—Eagles, 35-16 (C)
Eagles, 30-14 (P)
1955—Tie, 24-24 (C)
Eagles, 27-3 (P)
1956—Cardinals, 20-6 (P)
Cardinals, 28-17 (C)
1957—Eagles, 38-21 (C)
Cardinals, 31-27 (P)
1958—Tie, 21-21 (C)
Eagles, 49-21 (P)
1959—Eagles, 28-24 (Minn)
Eagles, 27-17 (P)
1960—Eagles, 31-27 (P)
Eagles, 20-6 (StL)
1961—Cardinals, 30-27 (P)
Eagles, 20-7 (StL)
1962—Cardinals, 27-21 (P)
Cardinals, 45-35 (StL)
1963—Cardinals, 28-24 (P)
Cardinals, 38-14 (StL)
1964—Cardinals, 38-13 (P)
Cardinals, 36-34 (StL)
1965—Eagles, 34-27 (P)
Eagles, 28-24 (StL)
1966—Cardinals, 16-13 (StL)
Cardinals, 41-10 (P)
1967—Cardinals, 48-14 (StL)
1968—Cardinals, 45-17 (P)
1969—Eagles, 34-30 (StL)
1970—Cardinals, 35-20 (P)
Cardinals, 23-14 (StL)
1971—Eagles, 37-20 (StL)
Eagles, 19-7 (P)
1972—Tie, 6-6 (P)
Cardinals, 24-23 (StL)
1973—Cardinals, 34-23 (P)
Eagles, 27-24 (StL)
1974—Cardinals, 7-3 (StL)
Cardinals, 13-3 (P)
1975—Cardinals, 31-20 (StL)
Cardinals, 24-23 (P)
1976—Cardinals, 33-14 (StL)
Cardinals, 17-14 (P)
1977—Cardinals, 21-17 (P)
Cardinals, 21-16 (StL)
1978—Cardinals, 16-10 (P)
Eagles, 14-10 (StL)
1979—Eagles, 24-20 (StL)
Eagles, 16-13 (P)
1980—Cardinals, 24-14 (StL)
Eagles, 17-3 (P)
1981—Eagles, 52-10 (StL)
Eagles, 38-0 (P)
1982—Cardinals, 23-20 (P)
1983—Cardinals, 14-11 (P)
Cardinals, 31-7 (StL)
1984—Cardinals, 34-14 (P)
Cardinals, 17-16 (StL)
1985—Eagles, 30-7 (P)
Eagles, 24-14 (StL)
(Points—Eagles 1,651, Cardinals 1,564)
**Franchise in Chicago prior to 1960*
***NFL Championship*
PHILADELPHIA vs. SAN DIEGO
Chargers lead series, 2-1
1974—Eagles, 13-7 (SD)
1980—Chargers, 22-21 (SD)
1985—Chargers, 20-14 (SD)
(Points—Chargers 49, Eagles 48)
PHILADELPHIA vs. SAN FRANCISCO
49ers lead series, 10-4-1
1951—Eagles, 21-14 (P)
1953—49ers, 31-21 (SF)
1956—Tie, 10-10 (P)
1958—49ers, 30-24 (P)
1959—49ers, 24-14 (SF)
1964—49ers, 28-24 (P)
1966—Eagles, 35-34 (SF)
1967—49ers, 28-27 (P)
1969—49ers, 14-13 (SF)
1971—49ers, 31-3 (P)
1973—49ers, 38-28 (SF)
1975—Eagles, 27-17 (P)
1983—Eagles, 22-17 (SF)
1984—49ers, 21-9 (P)
1985—49ers, 24-13 (SF)
(Points—49ers 361, Eagles 291)
PHILADELPHIA vs. SEATTLE
Eagles lead series, 2-0
1976—Eagles, 27-10 (P)
1980—Eagles, 27-20 (S)
(Points—Eagles 54, Seahawks 30)
PHILADELPHIA vs. TAMPA BAY
Eagles lead series, 2-1
1977—Eagles, 13-3 (P)
1979—*Buccaneers, 24-17 (TB)
1981—Eagles, 20-10 (P)
(Points—Eagles 50, Buccaneers 37)
**NFC Divisional Playoff*
PHILADELPHIA vs. *WASHINGTON
Redskins lead series, 57-39-5
1934—Redskins, 6-0 (B)
Redskins, 14-7 (P)
1935—Eagles, 7-6 (B)
1936—Redskins, 26-3 (P)
Redskins, 17-7 (B)
1937—Eagles, 14-0 (W)
Redskins, 10-7 (P)
1938—Redskins, 26-23 (P)
Redskins, 20-14 (W)
1939—Redskins, 7-0 (P)
Redskins, 7-6 (W)
1940—Redskins, 34-17 (P)
Redskins, 13-6 (W)
1941—Redskins, 21-17 (P)
Redskins, 20-14 (W)
1942—Redskins, 14-10 (P)
Redskins, 30-27 (W)
1944—Tie, 31-31 (P)
Eagles, 37-7 (W)
1945—Redskins, 24-14 (W)
Eagles, 16-0 (P)
1946—Eagles, 28-24 (W)
Redskins, 27-10 (P)
1947—Eagles, 45-42 (P)
Eagles, 38-14 (W)
1948—Eagles, 45-0 (W)
Eagles, 42-21 (P)
1949—Eagles, 49-14 (P)
Eagles, 44-21 (W)
1950—Eagles, 35-3 (P)
Eagles, 33-0 (W)
1951—Redskins, 27-23 (P)
Eagles, 35-21 (W)
1952—Eagles, 38-20 (P)
Redskins, 27-21 (W)
1953—Tie, 21-21 (P)
Redskins, 10-0 (W)
1954—Eagles, 49-21 (W)
Eagles, 41-33 (P)
1955—Redskins, 31-30 (P)
Redskins, 34-21 (W)
1956—Eagles, 13-9 (P)
Redskins, 19-17 (W)
1957—Eagles, 21-12 (P)
Redskins, 42-7 (W)
1958—Redskins, 24-14 (P)
Redskins, 20-0 (W)
1959—Eagles, 30-23 (P)
Eagles, 34-14 (W)
1960—Eagles, 19-13 (P)
Eagles, 38-28 (W)
1961—Eagles, 14-7 (P)
Eagles, 27-24 (W)
1962—Redskins, 27-21 (P)
Eagles, 37-14 (W)
1963—Eagles, 37-24 (W)
Redskins, 13-10 (P)
1964—Redskins, 35-20 (W)
Redskins, 21-10 (P)
1965—Redskins, 23-21 (W)
Eagles, 21-14 (P)
1966—Redskins, 27-13 (P)
Eagles, 37-28 (W)
1967—Eagles, 35-24 (P)
Tie, 35-35 (W)
1968—Redskins, 17-14 (W)
Redskins, 16-10 (P)
1969—Tie, 28-28 (W)
Redskins, 34-29 (P)
1970—Redskins, 33-21 (P)
Redskins, 24-6 (W)
1971—Tie, 7-7 (W)
Redskins, 20-13 (P)
1972—Redskins, 14-0 (W)
Redskins, 23-7 (P)
1973—Redskins, 28-7 (P)
Redskins, 38-20 (W)
1974—Redskins, 27-20 (P)
Redskins, 26-7 (W)
1975—Eagles, 26-10 (P)
Eagles, 26-3 (W)
1976—Redskins, 20-17 (P) OT
Redskins, 24-0 (W)
1977—Redskins, 23-17 (W)
Redskins, 17-14 (P)
1978—Redskins, 35-30 (W)
Eagles, 17-10 (P)
1979—Eagles, 28-17 (P)
Redskins, 17-7 (W)
1980—Eagles, 24-14 (P)
Eagles, 24-0 (W)
1981—Eagles, 36-13 (P)
Redskins, 15-13 (W)
1982—Redskins, 37-34 (P) OT
Redskins, 13-9 (W)
1983—Redskins, 23-13 (P)
Redskins, 28-24 (W)
1984—Redskins, 20-0 (W)
Eagles, 16-10 (P)
1985—Eagles, 19-6 (W)
Redskins, 17-12 (P)
(Points—Eagles 2,051, Redskins 1,971)
**Franchise in Boston prior to 1937*

PITTSBURGH vs. ATLANTA
Steelers lead series, 6-1;
See Atlanta vs. Pittsburgh
PITTSBURGH vs. BUFFALO
Steelers lead series, 6-3;
See Buffalo vs. Pittsburgh
PITTSBURGH vs. CHICAGO
Bears lead series, 13-4-1;
See Chicago vs. Pittsburgh
PITTSBURGH vs. CINCINNATI
Steelers lead series, 17-14;
See Cincinnati vs. Pittsburgh
PITTSBURGH vs. CLEVELAND
Browns lead series, 41-31;
See Cleveland vs. Pittsburgh
PITTSBURGH vs. DALLAS
Steelers lead series, 12-11;
See Dallas vs. Pittsburgh
PITTSBURGH vs. DENVER
Broncos lead series, 7-5-1;
See Denver vs. Pittsburgh
PITTSBURGH vs. DETROIT
Lions lead series, 13-8-1;
See Detroit vs. Pittsburgh
PITTSBURGH vs. GREEN BAY
Packers lead series, 16-10;
See Green Bay vs. Pittsburgh
PITTSBURGH vs. HOUSTON
Steelers lead series, 24-9;
See Houston vs. Pittsburgh
PITTSBURGH vs. INDIANAPOLIS
Steelers lead series, 9-4;
See Indianapolis vs. Pittsburgh
PITTSBURGH vs. KANSAS CITY
Steelers lead series, 9-4;
See Kansas City vs. Pittsburgh
PITTSBURGH vs. L.A. RAIDERS
Raiders lead series, 9-6;
See L.A. Raiders vs. Pittsburgh
PITTSBURGH vs. L.A. RAMS
Rams lead series, 12-4-2;
See L.A. Rams vs. Pittsburgh
PITTSBURGH vs. MIAMI
Dolphins lead series, 7-3;
See Miami vs. Pittsburgh
PITTSBURGH vs. MINNESOTA
Vikings lead series, 5-4;
See Minnesota vs. Pittsburgh
PITTSBURGH vs. NEW ENGLAND
Steelers lead series, 5-2;

See New England vs. Pittsburgh
PITTSBURGH vs. NEW ORLEANS
Series tied, 4-4;
See New Orleans vs. Pittsburgh
PITTSBURGH vs. N.Y. GIANTS
Giants lead series, 41-26-3;
See N.Y. Giants vs. Pittsburgh
PITTSBURGH vs. N.Y. JETS
Steelers lead series, 8-0;
See N.Y. Jets vs. Pittsburgh
PITTSBURGH vs. PHILADELPHIA
Eagles lead series, 42-25-3;
See Philadelphia vs. Pittsburgh
***PITTSBURGH vs. **ST. LOUIS**
Steelers lead series, 29-20-3
1933—Pirates, 14-13 (C)
1935—Pirates, 17-13 (P)
1936—Cardinals, 14-6 (C)
1937—Cardinals, 13-7 (P)
1939—Cardinals, 10-0 (P)
1940—Tie, 7-7 (P)
1942—Steelers, 19-3 (P)
1945—Steelers, 23-0 (P)
1946—Steelers, 14-7 (P)
1948—Cardinals, 24-7 (P)
1950—Steelers, 28-17 (C)
Steelers, 28-7 (P)
1951—Steelers, 28-14 (C)
1952—Steelers, 34-28 (C)
Steelers, 17-14 (P)
1953—Steelers, 31-28 (P)
Steelers, 21-17 (C)
1954—Cardinals, 17-14 (C)
Steelers, 20-17 (P)
1955—Steelers, 14-7 (P)
Cardinals, 27-13 (C)
1956—Steelers, 14-7 (P)
Cardinals, 38-27 (C)
1957—Steelers, 29-20 (P)
Steelers, 27-2 (C)
1958—Steelers, 27-20 (C)
Steelers, 38-21 (P)
1959—Cardinals, 45-24 (C)
Steelers, 35-20 (P)
1960—Steelers, 27-14 (P)
Cardinals, 38-7 (StL)
1961—Steelers, 30-27 (P)
Cardinals, 20-0 (StL)
1962—Steelers, 26-17 (StL)
Steelers, 19-7 (P)
1963—Steelers, 23-10 (P)
Cardinals, 24-23 (StL)
1964—Cardinals, 34-30 (StL)
Cardinals, 21-20 (P)
1965—Cardinals, 20-7 (P)
Cardinals, 21-17 (P)
1966—Steelers, 30-9 (P)
Cardinals, 6-3 (StL)
1967—Cardinals, 28-14 (P)
Tie, 14-14 (StL)
1968—Tie, 28-28 (StL)
Cardinals, 20-10 (P)
1969—Cardinals, 27-14 (P)
Cardinals, 47-10 (StL)
1972—Steelers, 25-19 (StL)
1979—Steelers, 24-21 (StL)
1985—Steelers, 23-10 (P)
(Points—Steelers 1,007, Cardinals 952)
**Steelers known as Pirates prior to 1941*
***Franchise in Chicago prior to 1960*
PITTSBURGH vs. SAN DIEGO
Steelers lead series, 8-4
1971—Steelers, 21-17 (P)
1972—Steelers, 24-2 (SD)
1973—Steelers, 38-21 (P)
1975—Steelers, 37-0 (SD)
1976—Steelers, 23-0 (P)
1977—Steelers, 10-9 (SD)
1979—Chargers, 35-7 (SD)
1980—Chargers, 26-17 (SD)
1982—*Chargers, 31-28 (P)
1983—Steelers, 26-3 (P)
1984—Steelers, 52-24 (P)
1985—Chargers, 54-44 (SD)
(Points—Steelers 327, Chargers 222)
**AFC First Round Playoff*
PITTSBURGH vs. SAN FRANCISCO
Series tied, 6-6
1951—49ers, 28-24 (P)
1952—Steelers, 24-7 (SF)
1954—49ers, 31-3 (SF)
1958—49ers, 23-20 (SF)
1961—Steelers, 20-10 (P)
1965—49ers, 27-17 (SF)
1968—49ers, 45-28 (P)
1973—Steelers, 37-14 (SF)
1977—Steelers, 27-0 (P)
1978—Steelers, 24-7 (SF)
1981—49ers, 17-14 (P)
1984—Steelers, 20-17 (SF)
(Points—Steelers 258, 49ers 226)
PITTSBURGH vs. SEATTLE
Steelers lead series, 3-2
1977—Steelers, 30-20 (P)
1978—Steelers, 21-10 (P)
1981—Seahawks, 24-21 (S)
1982—Seahawks, 16-0 (S)
1983—Steelers, 27-21 (S)
(Points—Steelers 99, Seahawks 91)
PITTSBURGH vs. TAMPA BAY
Steelers lead series, 3-0
1976—Steelers, 42-0 (P)
1980—Steelers, 24-21 (TB)
1983—Steelers, 17-12 (P)
(Points—Steelers 83, Buccaneers 33)
***PITTSBURGH vs. **WASHINGTON**
Redskins lead series, 40-27-3
1933—Redskins, 21-6 (P)
Pirates, 16-14 (B)
1934—Redskins, 7-0 (P)
Redskins, 39-0 (B)
1935—Pirates, 6-0 (P)
Redskins, 13-3 (B)
1936—Pirates, 10-0 (P)
Redskins, 30-0 (B)
1937—Redskins, 34-20 (W)
Pirates, 21-13 (P)
1938—Redskins, 7-0 (P)
Redskins, 15-0 (W)
1939—Redskins, 44-14 (W)
Redskins, 21-14 (P)
1940—Redskins, 40-10 (P)
Redskins, 37-10 (W)
1941—Redskins, 24-20 (P)
Redskins, 23-3 (W)
1942—Redskins, 28-14 (W)
Redskins, 14-0 (P)
1945—Redskins, 14-0 (P)
Redskins, 24-0 (W)
1946—Tie, 14-14 (W)
Steelers, 14-7 (P)
1947—Redskins, 27-26 (W)
Steelers, 21-14 (P)
1948—Redskins, 17-14 (W)
Steelers, 10-7 (P)
1949—Redskins, 27-14 (P)
Redskins, 27-14 (W)
1950—Steelers, 26-7 (W)
Redskins, 24-7 (P)
1951—Redskins, 22-7 (P)
Steelers, 20-10 (W)
1952—Redskins, 28-24 (P)
Steelers, 24-23 (W)
1953—Redskins, 17-9 (P)
Steelers, 14-13 (W)
1954—Steelers, 37-7 (P)
Redskins, 17-14 (W)
1955—Redskins, 23-14 (P)
Redskins, 28-17 (W)
1956—Steelers, 30-13 (P)
Steelers, 23-0 (W)
1957—Steelers, 28-7 (P)
Redskins, 10-3 (W)
1958—Steelers, 24-16 (P)
Tie, 14-14 (W)
1959—Redskins, 23-17 (P)
Steelers, 27-6 (W)
1960—Tie, 27-27 (W)
Steelers, 22-10 (P)
1961—Steelers, 20-0 (P)
Steelers, 30-14 (P)
1962—Steelers, 23-21 (P)
Steelers, 27-24 (W)
1963—Steelers, 38-27 (P)
Steelers, 34-28 (W)
1964—Redskins, 30-0 (P)
Steelers, 14-7 (W)
1965—Redskins, 31-3 (P)
Redskins, 35-14 (W)
1966—Redskins, 33-27 (P)
Redskins, 24-10 (W)
1967—Redskins, 15-10 (P)
1968—Redskins, 16-13 (W)
1969—Redskins, 14-7 (P)
1973—Steelers, 21-16 (P)
1979—Steelers, 38-7 (P)
1985—Redskins, 30-23 (P)
(Points—Redskins 1,319, Steelers 1,074)
**Steelers known as Pirates prior to 1941*
***Franchise in Boston prior to 1937*

ST. LOUIS vs. ATLANTA
Cardinals lead series, 6-3;
See Atlanta vs. St. Louis
ST. LOUIS vs. BUFFALO
Cardinals lead series, 3-1;
See Buffalo vs. St. Louis
ST. LOUIS vs. CHICAGO
Bears lead series, 50-25-6;
See Chicago vs. St. Louis
ST. LOUIS vs. CINCINNATI
Bengals lead series, 2-1;
See Cincinnati vs. St. Louis
ST. LOUIS vs. CLEVELAND
Browns lead series, 30-10-3;
See Cleveland vs. St. Louis
ST. LOUIS vs. DALLAS
Cowboys lead series, 29-17-1;
See Dallas vs. St. Louis
ST. LOUIS vs. DENVER
Broncos lead series, 1-0-1;
See Denver vs. St. Louis
ST. LOUIS vs. DETROIT
Lions lead series, 25-15-5;
See Detroit vs. St. Louis
ST. LOUIS vs. GREEN BAY
Packers lead series, 38-21-4;
See Green Bay vs. St. Louis
ST. LOUIS vs. HOUSTON
Cardinals lead series, 3-1;
See Houston vs. St. Louis
ST. LOUIS vs. INDIANAPOLIS
Cardinals lead series, 5-4;
See Indianapolis vs. St. Louis
ST. LOUIS vs. KANSAS CITY
Chiefs lead series, 3-0-1;
See Kansas City vs. St. Louis
ST. LOUIS vs. L.A. RAIDERS
Series tied, 1-1;
See L.A. Raiders vs. St. Louis
ST. LOUIS vs. L.A. RAMS
Rams lead series, 20-15-2;
See L.A. Rams vs. St. Louis
ST. LOUIS vs. MIAMI
Dolphins lead series, 5-0;
See Miami vs. St. Louis
ST. LOUIS vs. MINNESOTA
Cardinals lead series, 7-3;
See Minnesota vs. St. Louis
ST. LOUIS vs. NEW ENGLAND
Cardinals lead series, 4-1;
See New England vs. St. Louis
ST. LOUIS vs. NEW ORLEANS
Cardinals lead series, 9-4;
See New Orleans vs. St. Louis
ST. LOUIS vs. N.Y. GIANTS
Giants lead series, 53-31-2;
See N.Y. Giants vs. St. Louis
ST. LOUIS vs. N.Y. JETS
Cardinals lead series, 2-1;
See N.Y. Jets vs. St. Louis
ST. LOUIS vs. PHILADELPHIA
Cardinals lead series, 40-34-4;
See Philadelphia vs. St. Louis
ST. LOUIS vs. PITTSBURGH
Steelers lead series, 29-20-3;
See Pittsburgh vs. St. Louis
ST. LOUIS vs. SAN DIEGO
Chargers lead series, 2-1;
1971—Chargers, 20-17 (SD)
1976—Chargers, 43-24 (SD)
1983—Cardinals, 44-14 (StL)
(Points—Cardinals 85, Chargers 77)
***ST. LOUIS vs. SAN FRANCISCO**
Cardinals lead series, 7-6
1951—Cardinals, 27-21 (SF)
1957—Cardinals, 20-10 (SF)
1962—49ers, 24-17 (StL)
1964—Cardinals, 23-13 (SF)
1968—49ers, 35-17 (SF)
1971—49ers, 26-14 (StL)
1974—Cardinals, 34-9 (SF)
1976—Cardinals, 23-20 (StL) OT
1978—Cardinals, 16-10 (SF)
1979—Cardinals, 13-10 (StL)
1980—49ers, 24-21 (SF) OT
1982—49ers, 31-20 (StL)
1983—49ers, 42-27 (StL)
(Points—49ers 275, Cardinals 272)
**Team in Chicago prior to 1960*
ST. LOUIS vs. SEATTLE
Cardinals lead series, 2-0
1976—Cardinals, 30-24 (S)
1983—Cardinals, 33-28 (StL)
(Points—Cardinals 63, Seahawks 52)
ST. LOUIS vs. TAMPA BAY
Buccaneers lead series, 3-1
1977—Buccaneers, 17-7 (TB)
1981—Buccaneers, 20-10 (TB)
1983—Cardinals, 34-27 (TB)
1985—Buccaneers, 16-0 (TB)
(Points—Buccaneers 80, Cardinals 51)
***ST. LOUIS vs. **WASHINGTON**
Redskins lead series, 49-32-2
1932—Cardinals, 9-0 (B)
Braves, 8-6 (C)
1933—Redskins, 10-0 (C)
Tie, 0-0 (B)
1934—Redskins, 9-0 (B)
1935—Cardinals, 6-0 (B)
1936—Redskins, 13-10 (B)
1937—Cardinals, 21-14 (W)
1939—Redskins, 28-7 (W)
1940—Redskins, 28-21 (W)
1942—Redskins, 28-0 (W)
1943—Redskins, 13-7 (W)
1945—Redskins, 24-21 (W)
1947—Redskins, 45-21 (W)
1949—Cardinals, 38-7 (C)
1950—Cardinals, 38-28 (W)
1951—Redskins, 7-3 (C)
Redskins, 20-17 (W)
1952—Redskins, 23-7 (C)
Cardinals, 17-6 (W)
1953—Redskins, 24-13 (C)
Redskins, 28-17 (W)
1954—Cardinals, 38-16 (C)
Redskins, 37-20 (W)
1955—Cardinals, 24-10 (W)
Redskins, 31-0 (C)
1956—Cardinals, 31-3 (W)
Redskins, 17-14 (C)
1957—Redskins, 37-14 (C)
Cardinals, 44-14 (W)
1958—Cardinals, 37-10 (C)
Redskins, 45-31 (W)
1959—Cardinals, 49-21 (C)
Redskins, 23-14 (W)
1960—Cardinals, 44-7 (StL)
Cardinals, 26-14 (W)
1961—Cardinals, 24-0 (W)
Cardinals, 38-24 (StL)
1962—Redskins, 24-14 (W)
Tie, 17-17 (StL)
1963—Cardinals, 21-7 (W)
Cardinals, 24-20 (StL)
1964—Cardinals, 23-17 (W)
Cardinals, 38-24 (StL)
1965—Cardinals, 37-16 (W)
Redskins, 24-20 (StL)
1966—Cardinals, 23-7 (StL)
Redskins, 26-20 (W)
1967—Cardinals, 27-21 (W)
1968—Cardinals, 41-14 (StL)
1969—Redskins, 33-17 (W)
1970—Cardinals, 27-17 (StL)
Redskins, 28-27 (W)
1971—Redskins, 24-17 (StL)
Redskins, 20-0 (W)
1972—Redskins, 24-10 (W)
Redskins, 33-3 (StL)
1973—Cardinals, 34-27 (StL)
Redskins, 31-13 (W)
1974—Cardinals, 17-10 (W)
Cardinals, 23-20 (StL)
1975—Redskins, 27-17 (W)
Cardinals, 20-17 (StL) OT
1976—Redskins, 20-10 (W)
Redskins, 16-10 (StL)
1977—Redskins, 24-14 (W)
Redskins, 26-20 (StL)
1978—Redskins, 28-10 (StL)
Cardinals, 27-17 (W)
1979—Redskins, 17-7 (StL)
Redskins, 30-28 (W)
1980—Redskins, 23-0 (W)
Redskins, 31-7 (StL)
1981—Cardinals, 40-30 (StL)
Redskins, 42-21 (W)
1982—Redskins, 12-7 (StL)
Redskins, 28-0 (W)
1983—Redskins, 38-14 (StL)
Redskins, 45-7 (W)
1984—Cardinals, 26-24 (StL)
Redskins, 29-27 (W)
1985—Redskins, 27-10 (W)
Redskins, 27-16 (StL)
(Points—Redskins 1,734, Cardinals 1,558)
**Team in Chicago prior to 1960*
***Team in Boston prior to 1937 and known as Braves prior to 1933*

SAN DIEGO vs. ATLANTA
Falcons lead series, 2-0;
See Atlanta vs. San Diego
SAN DIEGO vs. BUFFALO
Chargers lead series, 17-9-2;
See Buffalo vs. San Diego
SAN DIEGO vs. CHICAGO
Chargers lead series, 4-1;
See Chicago vs. San Diego
SAN DIEGO vs. CINCINNATI
Chargers lead series, 10-7;
See Cincinnati vs. San Diego
SAN DIEGO vs. CLEVELAND
Chargers lead series, 5-4-1;
See Cleveland vs. San Diego
SAN DIEGO vs. DALLAS
Cowboys lead series, 2-1;
See Dallas vs. San Diego
SAN DIEGO vs. DENVER
Chargers lead series, 27-24-1;
See Denver vs. San Diego
SAN DIEGO vs. DETROIT
Lions lead series, 3-2;
See Detroit vs. San Diego
SAN DIEGO vs. GREEN BAY
Packers lead series, 3-1;
See Green Bay vs. San Diego
SAN DIEGO vs. HOUSTON
Chargers lead series, 16-12-1;
See Houston vs. San Diego

SAN DIEGO vs. INDIANAPOLIS
Chargers lead series, 4-2;
See Indianapolis vs. San Diego
SAN DIEGO vs. KANSAS CITY
Chargers lead series, 26-24-1;
See Kansas City vs. San Diego
SAN DIEGO vs. L.A. RAIDERS
Raiders lead series, 33-18-2;
See L.A. Raiders vs. San Diego
SAN DIEGO vs. L.A. RAMS
Rams lead series, 2-1;
See L.A. Rams vs. San Diego
SAN DIEGO vs. MIAMI
Chargers lead series, 8-5;
See Miami vs. San Diego
SAN DIEGO vs. MINNESOTA
Series tied, 3-3;
See Minnesota vs. San Diego
SAN DIEGO vs. NEW ENGLAND
Patriots lead series, 13-12-2;
See New England vs. San Diego
SAN DIEGO vs. NEW ORLEANS
Chargers lead series, 3-0;
See New Orleans vs. San Diego
SAN DIEGO vs. N.Y. GIANTS
Series tied, 2-2;
See N.Y. Giants vs. San Diego
SAN DIEGO vs. N.Y. JETS
Chargers lead series, 14-7-1;
See N.Y. Jets vs. San Diego
SAN DIEGO vs. PHILADELPHIA
Chargers lead series, 2-1;
See Philadelphia vs. San Diego
SAN DIEGO vs. PITTSBURGH
Steelers lead series, 8-4;
See Pittsburgh vs. San Diego
SAN DIEGO vs. ST. LOUIS
Chargers lead series, 2-1;
See St. Louis vs. San Diego
SAN DIEGO vs. SAN FRANCISCO
Chargers lead series, 3-1
1972—49ers, 34-3 (SF)
1976—Chargers, 13-7 (SD) OT
1979—Chargers, 31-9 (SD)
1982—Chargers, 41-37 (SF)
(Points—Chargers, 88, 49ers 87)
SAN DIEGO vs. SEATTLE
Chargers lead series, 9-6
1977—Chargers, 30-28 (S)
1978—Chargers, 24-20 (S)
Chargers, 37-10 (SD)
1979—Chargers, 33-16 (S)
Chargers, 20-10 (SD)
1980—Chargers, 34-13 (S)
Chargers, 21-14 (SD)
1981—Chargers, 24-10 (SD)
Seahawks, 44-23 (S)
1983—Seahawks, 34-31 (S)
Chargers, 28-21 (SD)
1984—Seahawks, 31-17 (S)
Seahawks, 24-0 (SD)
1985—Seahawks, 49-35 (SD)
Seahawks, 26-21 (S)
(Points—Chargers 378, Seahawks 350)
SAN DIEGO vs. TAMPA BAY
Chargers lead series, 2-0
1976—Chargers, 23-0 (TB)
1981—Chargers, 24-23 (TB)
(Points—Chargers 47, Buccaneers 23)
SAN DIEGO vs. WASHINGTON
Redskins lead series, 3-0
1973—Redskins, 38-0 (W)
1980—Redskins, 40-17 (W)
1983—Redskins, 27-24 (SD)
(Points—Redskins 105, Chargers 41)

SAN FRANCISCO vs. ATLANTA
49ers lead series, 21-17;
See Atlanta vs. San Francisco
SAN FRANCISCO vs. BUFFALO
Bills lead series, 2-1;
See Buffalo vs. San Francisco
SAN FRANCISCO vs. CHICAGO
Bears lead series, 24-23-1;
See Chicago vs. San Francisco
SAN FRANCISCO vs. CINCINNATI
49ers lead series, 4-1;
See Cincinnati vs. San Francisco
SAN FRANCISCO vs. CLEVELAND
Browns lead series, 8-4;
See Cleveland vs. San Francisco
SAN FRANCISCO vs. DALLAS
Series tied, 8-8-1;
See Dallas vs. San Francisco
SAN FRANCISCO vs. DENVER
Broncos lead series, 3-2;
See Denver vs. San Francisco
SAN FRANCISCO vs. DETROIT
Lions lead series, 26-23-1;
See Detroit vs. San Francisco
SAN FRANCISCO vs. GREEN BAY
49ers lead series, 22-20-1;
See Green Bay vs. San Francisco
SAN FRANCISCO vs. HOUSTON
49ers lead series, 3-2;
See Houston vs. San Francisco
SAN FRANCISCO vs. INDIANAPOLIS
Colts lead series, 21-14;
See Indianapolis vs. San Francisco
SAN FRANCISCO vs. KANSAS CITY
49ers lead series, 3-1;
See Kansas City vs. San Francisco
SAN FRANCISCO vs. L.A RAIDERS
Raiders lead series, 3-2;
See L.A. Raiders vs. San Francisco
SAN FRANCISCO vs. L.A. RAMS
Rams lead series, 44-26-2;
See L.A. Rams vs. San Francisco
SAN FRANCISCO vs. MIAMI
Dolphins lead series, 4-1;
See Miami vs. San Francisco
SAN FRANCISCO vs. MINNESOTA
Vikings lead series, 13-12-1;
See Minnesota vs. San Francisco
SAN FRANCISCO vs. NEW ENGLAND
49ers lead series, 3-1;
See New England vs. San Francisco
SAN FRANCISCO vs. NEW ORLEANS
49ers lead series, 22-9-2;
See New Orleans vs. San Francisco
SAN FRANCISCO vs. N.Y. GIANTS
Giants lead series, 10-7;
See N.Y. Giants vs. San Francisco
SAN FRANCISCO vs. N.Y. JETS
49ers lead series, 3-1;
See N.Y. Jets vs. San Francisco
SAN FRANCISCO vs. PHILADELPHIA
49ers lead series, 10-4-1;
See Philadelphia vs. San Francisco
SAN FRANCISCO vs. PITTSBURGH
Series tied, 6-6;
See Pittsburgh vs. San Francisco
SAN FRANCISCO vs. ST. LOUIS
Cardinals lead series, 7-6;
See St. Louis vs. San Francisco
SAN FRANCISCO vs. SAN DIEGO
Chargers lead series, 3-1;
See San Diego vs. San Francisco
SAN FRANCISCO vs. SEATTLE
49ers lead series, 2-1
1976—49ers, 37-21 (S)
1979—Seahawks, 35-24 (SF)
1985—49ers, 19-6 (SF)
(Points—49ers 80, Seahawks 62)
SAN FRANCISCO vs. TAMPA BAY
49ers lead series, 5-1
1977—49ers, 20-10 (SF)
1978—49ers, 6-3 (SF)
1979—49ers, 23-7 (SF)
1980—Buccaneers, 24-23 (SF)
1983—49ers, 35-21 (SF)
1984—49ers, 24-17 (SF)
(Points—49ers 131, Buccaneers 82)
SAN FRANCISCO vs. WASHINGTON
49ers lead series, 8-6-1
1952—49ers, 23-17 (W)
1954—49ers, 41-7 (SF)
1955—Redskins, 7-0 (W)
1961—49ers, 35-3 (SF)
1967—Redskins, 31-28 (W)
1969—Tie, 17-17 (SF)
1970—49ers, 26-17 (SF)
1971—*49ers, 24-20 (SF)
1973—Redskins, 33-9 (W)
1976—Redskins, 24-21 (SF)
1978—Redskins, 38-20 (W)
1981—49ers, 30-17 (W)
1983—**Redskins, 24-21 (W)
1984—49ers, 37-31 (SF)
1985—49ers, 35-8 (W)
(Points—49ers 367, Redskins 294)
**NFC Divisional Playoff*
***NFC Championship*

SEATTLE vs. ATLANTA
Seahawks lead series, 3-0;
See Atlanta vs. Seattle
SEATTLE vs. BUFFALO
Seahawks lead series, 2-0;
See Buffalo vs. Seattle
SEATTLE vs. CHICAGO
Seahawks lead series, 3-1;
See Chicago vs. Seattle
SEATTLE vs. CINCINNATI
Bengals lead series, 3-2;
See Cincinnati vs. Seattle
SEATTLE vs. CLEVELAND
Seahawks lead series, 7-2;
See Cleveland vs. Seattle
SEATTLE vs. DALLAS
Cowboys lead series, 3-0;
See Dallas vs. Seattle
SEATTLE vs. DENVER
Broncos lead series, 11-7;
See Denver vs. Seattle
SEATTLE vs. DETROIT
Seahawks lead series, 2-1;
See Detroit vs. Seattle
SEATTLE vs. GREEN BAY
Packers lead series, 3-1;
See Green Bay vs. Seattle
SEATTLE vs. HOUSTON
Oilers lead series, 3-2;
See Houston vs. Seattle
SEATTLE vs. INDIANAPOLIS
Colts lead series, 2-0;
See Indianapolis vs. Seattle
SEATTLE vs. KANSAS CITY
Chiefs lead series, 8-7;
See Kansas City vs. Seattle
SEATTLE vs. L.A. RAIDERS
Series tied, 9-9;
See L.A. Raiders vs. Seattle
SEATTLE vs. L.A. RAMS
Rams lead series, 3-0;
See L.A. Rams vs. Seattle
SEATTLE vs. MIAMI
Dolphins lead series, 3-1;
See Miami vs. Seattle
SEATTLE vs. MINNESOTA
Seahawks lead series, 2-1;
See Minnesota vs. Seattle
SEATTLE vs. NEW ENGLAND
Patriots lead series, 5-1;
See New England vs. Seattle
SEATTLE vs. NEW ORLEANS
Seahawks lead series, 2-1;
See New Orleans vs. Seattle
SEATTLE vs. N.Y. GIANTS
Giants lead series, 3-1;
See N.Y. Giants vs. Seattle
SEATTLE vs. N.Y. JETS
Seahawks lead series, 7-1;
See N.Y. Jets vs. Seattle
SEATTLE vs. PHILADELPHIA
Eagles lead series, 2-0;
See Philadelphia vs. Seattle
SEATTLE vs. PITTSBURGH
Steelers lead series, 3-2;
See Pittsburgh vs. Seattle
SEATTLE vs. ST. LOUIS
Cardinals lead series, 2-0;
See St. Louis vs. Seattle
SEATTLE vs. SAN DIEGO
Chargers lead series, 9-6;
See San Diego vs. Seattle
SEATTLE vs. SAN FRANCISCO
49ers lead series, 2-1;
See San Francisco vs. Seattle
SEATTLE vs. TAMPA BAY
Seahawks lead series, 2-0
1976—Seahawks, 13-10 (TB)
1977—Seahawks, 30-23 (S)
(Points—Seahawks 43, Buccaneers 33)
SEATTLE vs. WASHINGTON
Redskins lead series, 2-1
1976—Redskins, 31-7 (W)
1980—Seahawks, 14-0 (W)
1983—Redskins, 27-17 (S)
(Points—Redskins 58, Seahawks 38)

TAMPA BAY vs. ATLANTA
Buccaneers lead series, 3-2;
See Atlanta vs. Tampa Bay
TAMPA BAY vs. BUFFALO
Buccaneers lead series, 2-1;
See Buffalo vs. Tampa Bay
TAMPA BAY vs. CHICAGO
Bears lead series, 12-4;
See Chicago vs. Tampa Bay
TAMPA BAY vs. CINCINNATI
Bengals lead series, 2-1;
See Cincinnati vs. Tampa Bay
TAMPA BAY vs. CLEVELAND
Browns lead series, 3-0;
See Cleveland vs. Tampa Bay
TAMPA BAY vs. DALLAS
Cowboys lead series, 6-0;
See Dallas vs. Tampa Bay
TAMPA BAY vs. DENVER
Broncos lead series, 2-0;
See Denver vs. Tampa Bay
TAMPA BAY vs. DETROIT
Lions lead series, 9-7;
See Detroit vs. Tampa Bay
TAMPA BAY vs. GREEN BAY
Packers lead series, 8-6-1;
See Green Bay vs. Tampa Bay
TAMPA BAY vs. HOUSTON
Oilers lead series, 2-1;
See Houston vs. Tampa Bay
TAMPA BAY vs. INDIANAPOLIS
Colts lead series, 2-1;
See Indianapolis vs. Tampa Bay
TAMPA BAY vs. KANSAS CITY
Chiefs lead series, 3-2;
See Kansas City vs. Tampa Bay
TAMPA BAY vs. L.A RAIDERS
Raiders lead series, 2-0;
See L.A. Raiders vs. Tampa Bay
TAMPA BAY vs. L.A. RAMS
Rams lead series, 5-2;
See L.A. Rams vs. Tampa Bay
TAMPA BAY vs. MIAMI
Dolphins lead series, 2-1;
See Miami vs. Tampa Bay
TAMPA BAY vs. MINNESOTA
Vikings lead series, 11-5;
See Minnesota vs. Tampa Bay
TAMPA BAY vs. NEW ENGLAND
Patriots lead series, 2-0;
See New England vs. Tampa Bay
TAMPA BAY vs. NEW ORLEANS
Saints lead series, 5-3;
See New Orleans vs. Tampa Bay
TAMPA BAY vs. N.Y. GIANTS
Giants lead series, 6-3;
See N.Y. Giants vs. Tampa Bay
TAMPA BAY vs. N.Y. JETS
Jets lead series, 3-1;
See N.Y. Jets vs. Tampa Bay
TAMPA BAY vs. PHILADELPHIA
Eagles lead series, 2-1;
See Philadelphia vs. Tampa Bay
TAMPA BAY vs. PITTSBURGH
Steelers lead series, 3-0;
See Pittsburgh vs. Tampa Bay
TAMPA BAY vs. ST. LOUIS
Buccaneers lead series, 3-1;
See St. Louis vs. Tampa Bay
TAMPA BAY vs. SAN DIEGO
Chargers lead series, 2-0;
See San Diego vs. Tampa Bay
TAMPA BAY vs. SAN FRANCISCO
49ers lead series, 5-1;
See San Francisco vs. Tampa Bay
TAMPA BAY vs. SEATTLE
Seahawks lead series, 2-0;
See Seattle vs. Tampa Bay
TAMPA BAY vs. WASHINGTON
Redskins lead series, 2-0
1977—Redskins, 10-0 (TB)
1982—Redskins, 21-13 (TB)
(Points—Redskins 31, Buccaneers 13)

WASHINGTON vs. ATLANTA
Redskins lead series, 9-2-1;
See Atlanta vs. Washington
WASHINGTON vs. BUFFALO
Series tied 2-2;
See Buffalo vs. Washington
WASHINGTON vs. CHICAGO
Bears lead series, 20-11-1;
See Chicago vs. Washington
WASHINGTON vs. CINCINNATI
Redskins lead series, 3-1;
See Cincinnati vs. Washington
WASHINGTON vs. CLEVELAND
Browns lead series, 31-8-1;
See Cleveland vs. Washington
WASHINGTON vs. DALLAS
Cowboys lead series, 30-20-2;
See Dallas vs. Washington
WASHINGTON vs. DENVER
Redskins lead series, 2-1;
See Denver vs. Washington
WASHINGTON vs. DETROIT
Redskins lead series, 19-8;
See Detroit vs. Washington
WASHINGTON vs. GREEN BAY
Packers lead series, 14-11-1;
See Green Bay vs. Washington
WASHINGTON vs. HOUSTON
Series tied, 2-2;
See Houston vs. Washington
WASHINGTON vs. INDIANAPOLIS
Colts lead series, 15-6;
See Indianapolis vs. Washington
WASHINGTON vs. KANSAS CITY
Chiefs lead series, 2-1;
See Kansas City vs. Washington
WASHINGTON vs. L.A. RAIDERS
Raiders lead series, 4-1;
See L.A. Raiders vs. Washington
WASHINGTON vs. L.A. RAMS
Redskins lead series, 14-5-1;
See L.A. Rams vs. Washington
WASHINGTON vs. MIAMI
Dolphins lead series, 4-2;
See Miami vs. Washington
WASHINGTON vs. MINNESOTA
Vikings lead series, 5-4;
See Minnesota vs. Washington
WASHINGTON vs. NEW ENGLAND
Redskins lead series, 3-1;
See New England vs. Washington
WASHINGTON vs. NEW ORLEANS
Redskins lead series, 7-4;
See New Orleans vs. Washington

WASHINGTON vs. N.Y. GIANTS
Giants lead series, 58-46-3;
See N.Y. Giants vs. Washington
WASHINGTON vs. N.Y. JETS
Redskins lead series, 3-0;
See N.Y. Jets vs. Washington
WASHINGTON vs. PHILADELPHIA
Redskins lead series, 57-39-5;
See Philadelphia vs. Washington
WASHINGTON vs. PITTSBURGH
Redskins lead series, 40-27-3;
See Pittsburgh vs. Washington
WASHINGTON vs. ST. LOUIS
Redskins lead series, 49-32-2;
See St. Louis vs. Washington
WASHINGTON vs. SAN DIEGO
Redskins lead series, 3-0;
See San Diego vs. Washington
WASHINGTON vs. SAN FRANCISCO
49ers lead series, 8-6-1;
See San Francisco vs. Washington
WASHINGTON vs. SEATTLE
Redskins lead series, 2-1;
See Seattle vs. Washington
WASHINGTON vs. TAMPA BAY
Redskins lead series, 2-0;
See Tampa Bay vs. Washington

SUPER BOWL SUMMARIES

RESULTS

Game	Date	Winner	Loser	Site	Attendance
XX	1-26-86	Chicago (NFC) 46	New England (AFC) 10	New Orleans	73,818
XIX	1-20-85	San Francisco (NFC) 38	Miami (AFC) 16	Stanford	84,059
XVIII	1-22-84	L.A. Raiders (AFC) 38	Washington (NFC) 9	Tampa	72,920
XVII	1-30-83	Washington (NFC) 27	Miami (AFC) 17	Pasadena	103,667
XVI	1-24-82	San Francisco (NFC) 26	Cincinnati (AFC) 21	Pontiac	81,270
XV	1-25-81	Oakland (AFC) 27	Philadelphia (NFC) 10	New Orleans	76,135
XIV	1-20-80	Pittsburgh (AFC) 31	Los Angeles (NFC) 19	Pasadena	103,985
XIII	1-21-79	Pittsburgh (AFC) 35	Dallas (NFC) 31	Miami	79,484
XII	1-15-78	Dallas (NFC) 27	Denver (AFC) 10	New Orleans	75,583
XI	1- 9-77	Oakland (AFC) 32	Minnesota (NFC) 14	Pasadena	103,438
X	1-18-76	Pittsburgh (AFC) 21	Dallas (NFC) 17	Miami	80,187
IX	1-12-75	Pittsburgh (AFC) 16	Minnesota (NFC) 6	New Orleans	80,997
VIII	1-13-74	Miami (AFC) 24	Minnesota (NFC) 7	Houston	71,882
VII	1-14-73	Miami (AFC) 14	Washington (NFC) 7	Los Angeles	90,182
VI	1-16-72	Dallas (NFC) 24	Miami (AFC) 3	New Orleans	81,023
V	1-17-71	Baltimore (AFC) 16	Dallas (NFC) 13	Miami	79,204
IV	1-11-70	Kansas City (AFL) 23	Minnesota (NFL) 7	New Orleans	80,562
III	1-12-69	N.Y. Jets (AFL) 16	Baltimore (NFL) 7	Miami	75,389
II	1-14-68	Green Bay (NFL) 33	Oakland (AFL) 14	Miami	75,546
I	1-15-67	Green Bay (NFL) 35	Kansas City (AFL) 10	Los Angeles	61,946

SUPER BOWL COMPOSITE STANDINGS

	W	L	Pct	Pts.	OP
Pittsburgh Steelers	4	0	1.000	103	73
Green Bay Packers	2	0	1.000	68	24
San Francisco 49ers	2	0	1.000	64	37
Chicago Bears	1	0	1.000	46	10
New York Jets	1	0	1.000	16	7
Oakland/L.A. Raiders	3	1	.750	111	66
Baltimore Colts	1	1	.500	23	29
Kansas City Chiefs	1	1	.500	33	42
Dallas Cowboys	2	3	.400	112	85
Miami Dolphins	2	3	.400	74	103
Washington Redskins	1	2	.333	43	69
Cincinnati Bengals	0	1	.000	21	26
Denver Broncos	0	1	.000	10	27
Los Angeles Rams	0	1	.000	19	31
New England Patriots	0	1	.000	10	46
Philadelphia Eagles	0	1	.000	10	27
Minnesota Vikings	0	4	.000	34	95

PAST SUPER BOWL MOST VALUABLE PLAYERS

(Selected by Sport Magazine)

Super Bowl I — Bart Starr, Green Bay
Super Bowl II — Bart Starr, Green Bay
Super Bowl III — Joe Namath, New York Jets
Super Bowl IV — Len Dawson, Kansas City
Super Bowl V — Chuck Howley, Dallas
Super Bowl VI — Roger Staubach, Dallas
Super Bowl VII — Jake Scott, Miami
Super Bowl VIII — Larry Csonka, Miami
Super Bowl IX — Franco Harris, Pittsburgh
Super Bowl X — Lynn Swann, Pittsburgh
Super Bowl XI — Fred Biletnikoff, Oakland
Super Bowl XII — Randy White and Harvey Martin, Dallas
Super Bowl XIII — Terry Bradshaw, Pittsburgh
Super Bowl XIV — Terry Bradshaw, Pittsburgh
Super Bowl XV — Jim Plunkett, Oakland
Super Bowl XVI — Joe Montana, San Francisco
Super Bowl XVII — John Riggins, Washington
Super Bowl XVIII — Marcus Allen, Los Angeles Raiders
Super Bowl XIX — Joe Montana, San Francisco
Super Bowl XX — Richard Dent, Chicago

SUPER BOWL XX

Louisiana Superdome, New Orleans, Louisiana — January 26, 1986
Attendance: 73,818

Chicago 46, New England 10—The NFC champion Chicago Bears, seeking their first NFL title since 1963, scored a Super Bowl-record 46 points in downing AFC champion New England 46-10 in Super Bowl XX. The previous record for most points in a Super Bowl was 38, shared by San Francisco in XIX and the Los Angeles Raiders in XVIII. The Bears' league-leading defense tied the Super Bowl record for sacks (7) and limited the Patriots to a record-low seven yards rushing. New England took the quickest lead in Super Bowl history when Tony Franklin kicked a 36-yard field goal with 1:19 elapsed in the first period. The score came about because of Larry McGrew's fumble recovery at the Chicago 19-yard line. However, the Bears rebounded for a 23-3 first half lead, while building a yardage advantage of 236 total yards to New England's minus 19. Running back Matt Suhey rushed eight times for 37 yards, including an 11-yard touchdown run, and caught one pass for 24 yards in the first half. After the Patriots first drive of the second half ended with a punt to the Bears' 4-yard line, Chicago marched 96 yards in nine plays with quarterback Jim McMahon's one-yard scoring run capping the drive. McMahon became the first quarterback in Super Bowl history to rush for a pair of touchdowns. The Bears completed their scoring via a 28-yard interception return by reserve cornerback Reggie Phillips, a one-yard run by defensive tackle/fullback William Perry, and a safety when defensive end Henry Waechter tackled Patriots quarterback Steve Grogan in the end zone. Bears defensive end Richard Dent became the fourth defender to be named the game's most valuable player after contributing 1½ sacks. The Bears' victory margin of 36 points was the largest in Super Bowl history, bettering the previous mark of 29 by the Los Angeles Raiders when they topped Washington 38-9 in Game XVIII. McMahon completed 12 of 20 passes for 256 yards before leaving the game in the fourth period with a wrist injury. The NFL's all-time leading rusher, Bears running back Walter Payton, carried 22 times for 61 yards. Wide receiver Willie Gault caught four passes for 129 yards, the fourth-most receiving yards in a Super Bowl. Chicago coach Mike Ditka became the second man (Tom Flores of Raiders is other) who played in a Super Bowl and coached a team to a victory in the game.

Chicago (46)	**Offense**	**New England (10)**
Willie Gault	WR	Stanley Morgan
Jim Covert	LT	Brian Holloway
Mark Bortz	LG	John Hannah
Jay Hilgenberg	C	Pete Brock
Tom Thayer	RG	Ron Wooten
Keith Van Horne	RT	Steve Moore
Emery Moorehead	TE	Lin Dawson
Dennis McKinnon	WR	Stephen Starring
Jim McMahon	QB	Tony Eason
Walter Payton	RB	Anthony Collins
Matt Suhey	RB	Craig James
	Defense	
Dan Hampton	LE	Garin Veris
Steve McMichael	LT-NT	Lester Williams
William Perry	RT-RE	Julius Adams
Richard Dent	RE-LOLB	Andre Tippett
Otis Wilson	LLB-LILB	Steve Nelson
Mike Singletary	MLB-RILB	Larry McGrew
Wilber Marshall	RLB-ROLB	Don Blackmon
Mike Richardson	LCB	Ronnie Lippett
Leslie Frazier	RCB	Raymond Clayborn
Dave Duerson	SS	Roland James
Gary Fencik	FS	Fred Marion

SUBSTITUTIONS

Chicago—Offense: K—Kevin Butler. P—Maury Buford. QB—Steve Fuller, Mike Tomczak. RB—Dennis Gentry, Thomas Sanders, Calvin Thomas. TE—Tim Wrightman. WR—Ken Margerum, Keith Ortego. C—Tom Andrews. G—Stefan Humphries. T—Andy Frederick. Defense: E—Mike Hartenstine, Tyrone Keys. T—Henry Waechter. LB—Brian Cabral, Jim Morrissey, Ron Rivera, Cliff Thrift. CB—Reggie Phillips, Ken Taylor. S—Shaun Gayle.
New England—Offense: K—Tony Franklin. P—Rich Camarillo. QB—Steve Grogan. RB—Greg Hawthorne, Mosi Tatupu, Robert Weathers. TE—Derrick Ramsey. WR—Irving Fryar, Cedric Jones. C—Guy Morriss. G—Paul Fairchild. T—Art Plunkett. Defense: E—Smiley Creswell, Ben Thomas. NT—Dennis Owens. LB—Brian Ingram, Johnny Rembert, Ed Reynolds, Ed Williams. CB—Ernest Gibson, Rod McSwain. S—Jim Bowman. DNP: QB—Tom Ramsey.

OFFICIALS

Referee—Red Cashion. Umpire—Ron Botchan. Head Linesman—Bama Glass. Line Judge—Dale Williams. Back Judge—Al Jury. Side Judge—Bob Rice. Field Judge—Jack Vaughan.

SCORING

Chicago (NFC)	13	10	21	2	— 46
New England (AFC)	3	0	0	7	— 10

NE —FG Franklin 36
Chi—FG Butler 28
Chi—FG Butler 24
Chi—Suhey 11 run (Butler kick)
Chi—McMahon 2 run (Butler kick)
Chi—FG Butler 24
Chi—McMahon 1 run (Butler kick)
Chi—Phillips 28 interception return (Butler kick)
Chi—Perry 1 run (Butler kick)
NE —Fryar 8 pass from Grogan (Franklin kick)
Chi—Safety, Waechter tackled Grogan in end zone

TEAM STATISTICS

	Chicago	New England
Total First Downs	23	12
First Downs Rushing	13	1
First Downs Passing	9	10
First Downs Penalty	1	1
Total Net Yardage	408	123
Total Offensive Plays	76	54
Average Gain per Offensive Play	5.4	2.3

Rushes	49	11
Yards Gained Rushing (net)	167	7
Average Yards per Rush	3.4	0.6
Passes Attempted	24	36
Passes Completed	12	17
Had Intercepted	0	2
Times Tackled Attempting to Pass	3	7
Yards Lost Attempting to Pass	15	61
Yards Gained Passing (net)	241	116
Punts	4	6
Average Distance	43.3	43.8
Punt Returns	2	2
Punt Return Yardage	20	22
Kickoff Returns	4	7
Kickoff Return Yardage	49	153
Interception Return Yardage	75	0
Total Return Yardage	144	175
Fumbles	3	4
Own Fumbles Recovered	1	0
Opponent Fumbles Recovered	4	2
Penalties	7	5
Yards Penalized	40	35
Total Points Scored	46	10
Touchdowns	5	1
Touchdowns Rushing	4	0
Touchdowns Passing	0	1
Touchdowns Returns	1	0
Extra Points	5	1
Field Goals	3	1
Field Goals Attempted	3	1
Safeties	1	0
Third Down Efficiency	7/14	1/10
Fourth Down Efficiency	0/1	1/1
Time of Possession	39:15	20:45

INDIVIDUAL STATISTICS

RUSHING

Chicago	**Att.**	**Yds.**	**LG**	**TD**
Payton	22	61	7	0
Suhey	11	52	11t	1
Gentry	3	15	8	0
Sanders	4	15	10	0
McMahon	5	14	7	2
Thomas	2	8	7	0
Fuller	1	1	1	0
Perry	1	1	1t	1
New England	**Att.**	**Yds.**	**LG**	**TD**
Collins	3	4	3	0
Grogan	1	3	3	0
Weathers	1	3	3	0
C. James	5	1	3	0
Hawthorne	1	−4	−4	0

PASSING

Chicago	**Att.**	**Comp.**	**Yds.**	**TD**	**Int.**
McMahon	20	12	256	0	0
Fuller	4	0	0	0	0
New Eng.	**Att.**	**Comp.**	**Yds.**	**TD**	**Int.**
Grogan	30	17	177	1	2
Eason	6	0	0	0	0

RECEIVING

Chicago	**No.**	**Yds.**	**LG**	**TD**
Gault	4	129	60	0
Gentry	2	41	27	0
Margerum	2	36	29	0
Moorehead	2	22	14	0
Suhey	1	24	24	0
Thomas	1	4	4	0
New England	**No.**	**Yds.**	**LG**	**TD**
Morgan	7	70	19	0
Starring	2	39	24	0
Fryar	2	24	16	1
Collins	2	19	11	0
Ramsey	2	16	11	0
C. James	1	6	6	0
Weathers	1	3	3	0

INTERCEPTIONS

Chicago	**No.**	**Yds.**	**LG**	**TD**
Morrissey	1	47	47	0
Phillips	1	28	28t	1
New England	**No.**	**Yds.**	**LG**	**TD**
None				

PUNTING

Chicago	**No.**	**Avg.**	**LG**	**Blk.**
Buford	4	43.3	52	0
New England	**No.**	**Avg.**	**LG**	**Blk.**
Camarillo	6	43.8	62	0

PUNT RETURNS

Chicago	**No.**	**FC**	**Yds.**	**LG**	**TD**
Ortego	2	1	20	12	0
New England	**No.**	**FC**	**Yds.**	**LG**	**TD**
Fryar	2	0	22	12	0

KICKOFF RETURNS

Chicago	**No.**	**Yds.**	**LG**	**TD**
Gault	4	49	18	0
New England	**No.**	**Yds.**	**LG**	**TD**
Starring	7	153	36	0

SUPER BOWL XIX

Stanford Stadium, Stanford, California — January 20, 1985
Attendance: 84,059

SAN FRANCISCO 38, MIAMI 16—The San Francisco 49ers captured their second Super Bowl title with a dominating offense and a defense that tamed Miami's explosive passing attack. The Dolphins held a 10-7 lead at the end of the first period, which represented the most points scored by two teams in an opening quarter of a Super Bowl. However, the 49ers used excellent field position in the second period to build a 28-16 halftime lead. Running back Roger Craig set a Super Bowl record by scoring three touchdowns on pass receptions of 8 and 16 yards and a run of 2 yards. San Francisco's Joe Montana was voted the game's most valuable player. He joined Green Bay's Bart Starr and Pittsburgh's Terry Bradshaw as the only two-time Super Bowl most valuable players. Montana completed 24 of 35 passes for a Super Bowl-record 331 yards and three touchdowns, and rushed five times for 59 yards, including a six-yard touchdown. Craig had 58 yards on 15 carries and caught seven passes for 77 yards. Wendell Tyler rushed 13 times for 65 yards and had four catches for 70 yards. Dwight Clark had six receptions for 77 yards, while Russ Francis had five for 60. San Francisco's 537 total net yards bettered the previous Super Bowl record of 429 yards by Oakland in Super Bowl XI. The 49ers also held a time of possession advantage over the Dolphins of 37:11 to 22:49.

Miami (AFC)	10	6	0	0	— 16
San Francisco (NFC)	7	21	10	0	— 38

Mia —FG von Schamann 37
SF —Monroe 33 pass from Montana (Wersching kick)
Mia —D. Johnson 2 pass from Marino (von Schamann kick)
SF —Craig 8 pass from Montana (Wersching kick)
SF —Montana 6 run (Wersching kick)
SF —Craig 2 run (Wersching kick)
Mia —FG von Schamann 31
Mia —FG von Schamann 30
SF —FG Wersching 27
SF —Craig 16 pass from Montana (Wersching kick)

SUPER BOWL XVIII

Tampa Stadium, Tampa, Florida — January 22, 1984
Attendance: 72,920

LOS ANGELES RAIDERS 38, WASHINGTON 9—The Los Angeles Raiders dominated the Washington Redskins from the beginning in Super Bowl XVIII and achieved the most lopsided victory in Super Bowl history, surpassing Green Bay's 35-10 win over Kansas City in Super Bowl I. The Raiders took a 7-0 lead 4:52 into the game when Derrick Jensen blocked a Jeff Hayes punt and recovered it in the end zone for a touchdown. With 9:14 remaining in the first half, Raiders quarterback Jim Plunkett threw a 12-yard touchdown pass to wide receiver Cliff Branch to complete a three-play, 65-yard drive. Washington cut the Raiders' lead to 14-3 on a 24-yard field goal by Mark Moseley. With seven seconds left in the first half, Raiders linebacker Jack Squirek intercepted a Joe Theismann pass at the Redskins' 5-yard line and ran it in for a touchdown to give Los Angeles a 21-3 halftime lead. In the third period, running back Marcus Allen, who rushed for a Super Bowl record 191 yards on 20 carries, increased the Raiders' lead to 35-3 on touchdown runs of 5 and 74 yards, the latter erasing the previous Super Bowl record of 58 yards set by Baltimore's Tom Matte in Game III. Allen was named the game's most valuable player. The victory over Washington raised Raiders coach Tom Flores' playoff record to 8-1, including a 27-10 win against Philadelphia in Super Bowl XV. The 38 points scored by the Raiders was the highest total by a Super Bowl team. The previous high was 35 points by Green Bay in Game I.

Washington (NFC)	0	3	6	0	— 9
L.A. Raiders (AFC)	7	14	14	3	— 38

Raiders—Jensen recovered blocked punt in end zone (Bahr kick)
Raiders—Branch 12 pass from Plunkett (Bahr kick)
Wash —FG Moseley 24
Raiders—Squirek 5 interception return (Bahr kick)
Wash —Riggins 1 run (kick blocked)
Raiders—Allen 5 run (Bahr kick)
Raiders—Allen 74 run (Bahr kick)
Raiders—FG Bahr 21

SUPER BOWL XVII

Rose Bowl, Pasadena, California — January 30, 1983
Attendance: 103,667

WASHINGTON 27, MIAMI 17—Fullback John Riggins's Super Bowl record 166 yards on 38 carries sparked Washington to a 27-17 victory over AFC champion Miami. It was Riggins's fourth straight 100-yard rushing game during the playoffs, also a record. The win marked Washington's first NFL title since 1942, and was only the second time in Super Bowl history NFC teams scored consecutive victories (Green Bay did it in Super Bowls I and II and San Francisco won Super Bowl XVI). The Redskins, under second-year head coach Joe Gibbs, used a balanced offense that accounted for 400 total yards (a Super Bowl record 276 yards rushing and 124 passing), second in Super Bowl history to 429 yards by Oakland in Super Bowl XI. The Dolphins built a 17-10 halftime lead on a 76-yard touchdown pass from quarterback David Woodley to wide receiver Jimmy Cefalo 6:49 into the first period, a 20-yard field goal by Uwe von Schamann with 6:00 left in the half, and a Super Bowl record 98-yard kickoff return by Fulton Walker with 1:38 remaining. Washington had tied the score at 10-10 with 1:51 left on a four-yard touchdown pass from Joe Theismann to wide receiver Alvin Garrett. Mark Moseley started the Redskins' scoring with a 31-yard field goal late in the first period, and added a 20-yarder midway through the third period to cut the Dolphins' lead to 17-13. Riggins, who was voted the game's most valuable player, gave Washington its first lead of the game with 10:01 left when he ran 43 yards off left tackle for a touchdown on a fourth-and-one situation. Wide receiver Charlie Brown caught a six-yard scoring pass from Theismann with 1:55 left to complete the scoring. The Dolphins managed only 176 yards (142 in first half). Theismann completed 15 of 23 passes for 143 yards, two touchdowns, and had two interceptions. For Miami, Woodley was 4 of 14 for 97 yards, with one touchdown, and one interception. Don Strock was 0 for 3 in relief.

Miami (AFC)	7	10	0	0	— 17
Washington (NFC)	0	10	3	14	— 27

Mia —Cefalo 76 pass from Woodley (von Schamann kick)
Wash—FG Moseley 31
Mia —FG von Schamann 20
Wash—Garrett 4 pass from Theismann (Moseley kick)
Mia —Walker 98 kickoff return (von Schamann kick)
Wash—FG Moseley 20
Wash—Riggins 43 run (Moseley kick)
Wash—Brown 6 pass from Theismann (Moseley kick)

SUPER BOWL XVI

Pontiac Silverdome, Pontiac, Michigan — January 24, 1982
Attendance: 81,270

SAN FRANCISCO 26, CINCINNATI 21—Ray Wersching's Super Bowl record-tying four field goals and Joe Montana's controlled passing helped lift the San Francisco 49ers to their first NFL championship with a 26-21 victory over Cincinnati. The 49ers built a game-record 20-0 halftime lead via Montana's one-yard touchdown run, which capped an 11-play, 68-yard drive; fullback Earl Cooper's 11-yard scoring pass from Montana, which climaxed a Super Bowl record 92-yard drive on 12 plays; and Wersching's 22- and 26-yard field goals. The Bengals rebounded in the second half, closing the gap to 20-14 on quarterback Ken Anderson's five-yard run and Dan Ross's four-yard reception from Anderson, who established Super Bowl passing records for completions (25) and completion percentage (73.5 percent on 25 of 34). Wersching added early fourth-period field goals of 40 and 23 yards to increase the 49ers' lead to 26-14. The Bengals managed to score on an Anderson-to-Ross three-yard pass with only 16 seconds remaining. Ross set a Super Bowl record with 11 receptions for 104 yards. Montana, the game's most valuable player, completed 14 of 22 passes for 157 yards. Cincinnati compiled 356 yards to San Francisco's 275, which marked the first time in Super Bowl history that the team that gained the most yards from scrimmage lost the game.

San Francisco (NFC)	7	13	0	6	— 26
Cincinnati (AFC)	0	0	7	14	— 21

SF —Montana 1 run (Wersching kick)
SF —Cooper 11 pass from Montana (Wersching kick)
SF —FG Wersching 22
SF —FG Wersching 26
Cin—Anderson 5 run (Breech kick)
Cin—Ross 4 pass from Anderson (Breech kick)
SF —FG Wersching 40
SF —FG Wersching 23
Cin—Ross 3 pass from Anderson (Breech kick)

SUPER BOWL XV

Louisiana Superdome, New Orleans, Louisiana — January 25, 1981
Attendance: 76,135

OAKLAND 27, PHILADELPHIA 10—Jim Plunkett threw three touchdown passes, including an 80-yarder to Kenny King, as the Raiders became the first wild card team to win the Super Bowl. Plunkett's touchdown bomb to King—the longest play in Super Bowl history—gave Oakland a decisive 14-0 lead with nine seconds left in the first period. Linebacker Rod Martin had set up Oakland's first touchdown, a two-yard reception by Cliff Branch, with a 16-yard interception return to the Eagles' 32 yard line. The Eagles never recovered from that early deficit, managing only a Tony Franklin field goal (30 yards) and an eight-yard touchdown pass from Ron Jaworski to Keith Krepfle the rest of the game. Plunkett, who became a starter in the sixth game of the season, completed 13 of 21 for 261 yards and was named the game's most valuable player. Oakland won 9 of 11 games with Plunkett starting, but that was good enough only for second place in the AFC West, although they tied division winner San Diego with an 11-5 record. The Raiders, who had previously won Super Bowl XI over Minnesota, had to win three playoff games to get to the championship game. Oakland defeated Houston 27-7 at home followed by road victories over Cleveland, 14-12 and San Diego, 34-27. Oakland's Mark van Eeghen was the game's leading rusher with 80 yards on 19 carries. Philadelphia's Wilbert Montgomery led all receivers with six receptions for 91 yards. Branch had five for 67 and Harold Carmichael of Philadelphia five for 83. Martin finished the game with three interceptions, a Super Bowl record.

Oakland (AFC)	14	0	10	3	— 27
Philadelphia (NFC)	0	3	0	7	— 10

Oak—Branch 2 pass from Plunkett (Bahr kick)
Oak—King 80 pass from Plunkett (Bahr kick)
Phil —FG Franklin 30
Oak—Branch 29 pass from Plunkett (Bahr kick)
Oak—FG Bahr 46
Phil —Krepfle 8 pass from Jaworski (Franklin kick)
Oak—FG Bahr 35

SUPER BOWL XIV

Rose Bowl, Pasadena, California — January 20, 1980
Attendance: 103,985

PITTSBURGH 31, LOS ANGELES 19—Terry Bradshaw completed 14 of 21 passes for 309 yards and set two passing records as the Steelers became the first team to win four Super Bowls. Despite three interceptions by the Rams, Bradshaw kept his poise and brought the Steelers from behind twice in the second half. Trailing 13-10 at halftime, Pittsburgh went ahead 17-13 when Bradshaw hit Lynn Swann with a 47-yard touchdown pass after 2:48 of the third quarter. On the Rams' next possession Vince Ferragamo, who completed 15 of 25 passes for 212 yards, responded with a 50-yard pass to Billy Waddy that moved Los Angeles from its own 26 to the Steelers' 24. On the following play, Lawrence McCutcheon connected with Ron Smith on a halfback option pass that gave the Rams a 19-17 lead. On Pittsburgh's initial possession of the final period, Bradshaw lofted a 73-yard scoring pass to John Stallworth to put the Steelers in front to stay, 24-19. Franco Harris scored on a one-yard run later in the quarter to seal the verdict. A 45-yard pass from Bradshaw to Stallworth was the key play in the drive to Harris's score. Bradshaw, the game's most valuable player for the second straight year, set career Super Bowl records for most touchdown passes (nine) and most passing yards (932). Larry Anderson gave the Steelers excellent field position throughout the game with five kickoff returns for a record 162 yards.

Los Angeles (NFC)	7	6	6	0	— 19
Pittsburgh (AFC)	3	7	7	14	— 31

Pitt—FG Bahr 41
LA —Bryant 1 run (Corral kick)
Pitt—Harris 1 run (Bahr kick)
LA —FG Corral 31
LA —FG Corral 45
Pitt—Swann 47 pass from Bradshaw (Bahr kick)
LA —Smith 24 pass from McCutcheon (kick failed)
Pitt—Stallworth 73 pass from Bradshaw (Bahr kick)
Pitt—Harris 1 run (Bahr kick)

SUPER BOWL XIII

Orange Bowl, Miami, Florida — January 21, 1979
Attendance: 79,484

PITTSBURGH 35, DALLAS 31—Terry Bradshaw threw a record four touchdown passes to lead the Steelers to victory. The Steelers became the first team to win three Super Bowls, mostly because of Bradshaw's accurate arm. Bradshaw, voted the game's most valuable player, completed 17 of 30 passes for 318 yards, a personal high. Three of those passes went for touchdowns—two to John Stallworth and the third, with 26 seconds remaining in the second period, to Rocky Bleier. The Cowboys scored twice before intermission on Roger Staubach's 39-yard pass to Tony Hill and a 37-yard run by linebacker Mike Hegman, who stole the ball from Bradshaw. The Steelers broke open the contest with two touchdowns in a span of 19 seconds midway through the final period. Franco Harris rambled 22 yards up the middle to give the Steelers a 28-17 lead with 7:10 left. Pittsburgh got the ball right back when Randy White fumbled the kickoff and Dennis Winston recovered for the Steelers. On first down, Bradshaw hit Lynn Swann with an 18-yard scoring pass to boost the Steelers' lead to 35-17 with 6:51 to play. The Cowboys refused to let the Steelers run away with the contest. Staubach connected with Billy Joe DuPree on a seven-yard scoring pass with 2:23 left. Then the Cowboys recovered an onside kick and Staubach took them in for another score, passing four yards to Butch Johnson with 22 seconds remaining. Bleier recovered another onside kick with 17 seconds left to seal the victory for the Steelers.

Pittsburgh (AFC)	7	14	0	14	— 35
Dallas (NFC)	7	7	3	14	— 31

Pitt —Stallworth 28 pass from Bradshaw (Gerela kick)
Dall—Hill 39 pass from Staubach (Septien kick)
Dall—Hegman 37 fumble recovery return (Septien kick)
Pitt —Stallworth 75 pass from Bradshaw (Gerela kick)
Pitt —Bleier 7 pass from Bradshaw (Gerela kick)
Dall—FG Septien 27
Pitt —Harris 22 run (Gerela kick)
Pitt —Swann 18 pass from Bradshaw (Gerela kick)
Dall—DuPree 7 pass from Staubach (Septien kick)
Dall—B. Johnson 4 pass from Staubach (Septien kick)

SUPER BOWL XII

Louisiana Superdome, New Orleans, Louisiana — January 15, 1978
Attendance: 75,583

DALLAS 27, DENVER 10—The Cowboys evened their Super Bowl record at 2-2 by defeating Denver before a sellout crowd of 75,583, plus 102,010,000 television viewers, the largest audience ever to watch a sporting event. Dallas converted two interceptions into 10 points and Efren Herrera added a 35-yard field goal for a 13-0 halftime advantage. In the third period Craig Morton engineered a drive to the Cowboys' 30 and Jim Turner's 47-yard field goal made the score 13-3. After an exchange of punts, Butch Johnson made a spectacular diving catch in the end zone to complete a 45-yard pass from Roger Staubach and put the Cowboys ahead 20-3. Following Rick Upchurch's 67-yard kickoff return, Norris Weese guided the Broncos to a touchdown to cut the Dallas lead to 20-10. Dallas clinched the victory when running back Robert Newhouse threw a 29-yard touchdown pass to Golden Richards with 7:04 remaining in the game. It was the first pass thrown by Newhouse since 1975. Harvey Martin and Randy White, who were named co-most valuable players, led the Cowboys' defense, which recovered four fumbles and intercepted four passes.

Dallas (NFC)	10	3	7	7	— 27
Denver (AFC)	0	0	10	0	— 10

Dall—Dorsett 3 run (Herrera kick)
Dall—FG Herrera 35
Dall—FG Herrera 43
Den—FG Turner 47
Dall—Johnson 45 pass from Staubach (Herrera kick)
Den—Lytle 1 run (Turner kick)
Dall—Richards 29 pass from Newhouse (Herrera kick)

SUPER BOWL XI

Rose Bowl, Pasadena, California — January 9, 1977
Attendance: 103,438

OAKLAND 32, MINNESOTA 14—The Raiders won their first NFL championship before a record Super Bowl crowd plus 81 million television viewers, the largest audience ever to watch a sporting event. The Raiders gained a record-breaking 429 yards, including running back Clarence Davis's 137 yards rushing. Wide receiver Fred Biletnikoff made four key receptions, which earned him the game's most valuable player trophy. Oakland scored on three successive possessions in the second quarter to build a 16-0 halftime lead. Errol Mann's 24-yard field goal opened the scoring, then the AFC champions put together drives of 64 and 35 yards, scoring on a one-yard pass from Ken Stabler to Dave Casper and a one-yard run by Pete Banaszak. The Raiders increased their lead to 19-0 on a 40-yard field goal in the third quarter, but Minnesota responded with a 12-play, 58-yard drive late in the period, with Fran Tarkenton passing eight yards to wide receiver Sammy White to cut the deficit to 19-7. Two fourth-quarter interceptions clinched the title for the Raiders. One set up Banaszak's second touchdown run, the other resulted in cornerback Willie Brown's Super Bowl record 75-yard interception return.

Oakland (AFC)	0	16	3	13	— 32
Minnesota (NFC)	0	0	7	7	— 14

Oak —FG Mann 24
Oak —Casper 1 pass from Stabler (Mann kick)
Oak —Banaszak 1 run (kick failed)
Oak —FG Mann 40
Minn—S. White 8 pass from Tarkenton (Cox kick)
Oak —Banaszak 2 run (Mann kick)
Oak —Brown 75 interception return (kick failed)
Minn—Voigt 13 pass from Lee (Cox kick)

SUPER BOWL X

Orange Bowl, Miami, Florida — January 18, 1976
Attendance: 80,187

PITTSBURGH 21, DALLAS 17—The Steelers won the Super Bowl for the second year in a row on Terry Bradshaw's 64-yard touchdown pass to Lynn Swann and an aggressive defense that snuffed out a late rally by the Cowboys with an end-zone interception on the final play of the game. In the fourth quarter, Pittsburgh ran on fourth down and gave up the ball on the Cowboys' 39 with 1:22 to play. Roger Staubach ran and passed for two first downs but his last desperation pass was picked off by Glen Edwards. Dallas's scoring was the result of two touchdown passes by Staubach, one to Drew Pearson for 29 yards and the other to Percy Howard for 34 yards. Toni Fritsch had a 36-yard field goal. The Steelers scored on two touchdown passes by Bradshaw, one to Randy Grossman for seven yards and the long bomb to Swann. Roy Gerela had 36- and 18-yard field goals. Reggie Harrison blocked a punt through the end zone for a safety. Swann set a Super Bowl record by gaining 161 yards on his four receptions.

Dallas (NFC)	7	3	0	7	— 17
Pittsburgh (AFC)	7	0	0	14	— 21

Dall—D. Pearson 29 pass from Staubach (Fritsch kick)
Pitt —Grossman 7 pass from Bradshaw (Gerela kick)
Dall—FG Fritsch 36
Pitt —Safety, Harrison blocked Hoopes's punt through end zone
Pitt —FG Gerela 36
Pitt —FG Gerela 18
Pitt —Swann 64 pass from Bradshaw (kick failed)
Dall—P. Howard 34 pass from Staubach (Fritsch kick)

SUPER BOWL IX

Tulane Stadium, New Orleans, Louisiana — January 12, 1975
Attendance: 80,997

PITTSBURGH 16, MINNESOTA 6—AFC champion Pittsburgh, in its initial Super Bowl appearance, and NFC champion Minnesota, making a third bid for its first Super Bowl title, struggled through a first half in which the only score was produced by the Steelers' defense when Dwight White downed Vikings' quarterback Fran Tarkenton in the end zone for a safety 7:49 into the second period. The Steelers forced another break and took advantage on the second half kickoff when Minnesota's Bill Brown fumbled and Marv Kellum recovered for Pittsburgh on the Vikings' 30. After Rocky Bleier failed to gain on first down, Franco Harris carried three consecutive times for 24 yards, a loss of 3, and a 12-yard touchdown and a 9-0 lead. Though its offense was completely stymied by Pittsburgh's defense, Minnesota managed to move into a threatening position after 4:27 of the final period when Matt Blair blocked Bobby Walden's punt and Terry Brown recovered the ball in the end zone for a touchdown. Fred Cox's kick failed and the Steelers led 9-6. Pittsburgh wasted no time putting the victory away. The Steelers took the ensuing kickoff and marched 66 yards in 11 plays, climaxed by Terry Bradshaw's four-yard scoring pass to Larry Brown with 3:31 left. Pittsburgh's defense permitted Minnesota only 119 yards total offense, including a Super Bowl low of 17 yards rushing. The Steelers, meanwhile, gained 333 yards, including Harris's record 158 yards on 34 carries.

Pittsburgh (AFC)	0	2	7	7	— 16
Minnesota (NFC)	0	0	0	6	— 6

Pitt —Safety, White downed Tarkenton in end zone
Pitt —Harris 12 run (Gerela kick)
Minn—T. Brown recovered blocked punt in end zone (kick failed)
Pitt —L. Brown 4 pass from Bradshaw (Gerela kick)

SUPER BOWL VIII

Rice Stadium, Houston, Texas — January 13, 1974
Attendance: 71,882

MIAMI 24, MINNESOTA 7—The defending NFL champion Dolphins, representing the AFC for the third straight year, scored the first two times they had possession on marches of 62 and 56 yards in the first period while the Miami defense limited the Vikings to only seven plays. Larry Csonka climaxed the initial 10-play drive with a five-yard touchdown bolt through right guard after 5:27 had elapsed. Four plays later, Miami began another 10-play scoring drive, which ended with Jim Kiick bursting one yard through the middle for another touchdown after 13:38 of the period. Garo Yepremian added a 28-yard field goal midway in the second period for a 17-0 Miami lead. Minnesota then drove from its 20 to a second-and-two situation on the Miami 7 yard line with 1:18 left in the half. But on two plays, Miami limited Oscar Reed to one yard. On fourth-and-one from the 6, Reed went over right tackle, but Dolphins middle linebacker Nick Buoniconti jarred the ball loose and Jake Scott recovered for Miami to halt the Minnesota threat. The Vikings were unable to muster enough offense in the second half to threaten the Dolphins. Csonka rushed 33 times for a Super Bowl record 145 yards. Bob Griese of Miami completed six of seven passes for 73 yards.

Minnesota (NFC)	0	0	0	7	— 7
Miami (AFC)	14	3	7	0	— 24

Mia —Csonka 5 run (Yepremian kick)
Mia —Kiick 1 run (Yepremian kick)
Mia —FG Yepremian 28
Mia —Csonka 2 run (Yepremian kick)
Minn—Tarkenton 4 run (Cox kick)

SUPER BOWL VII

Memorial Coliseum, Los Angeles, California — January 14, 1973
Attendance: 90,182

MIAMI 14, WASHINGTON 7—The Dolphins played virtually perfect football in the first half as their defense permitted the Redskins to cross midfield only once and their offense turned good field position into two touchdowns. On its third possession, Miami opened its first scoring drive from the Dolphins' 37 yard line. An 18-yard pass from Bob Griese to Paul Warfield preceded by three plays Griese's 28-yard touchdown pass to Howard Twilley. After Washington moved from its 17 to the Miami 48 with two minutes remaining in the first half, Dolphins linebacker Nick Buoniconti intercepted a Billy Kilmer pass at the Miami 41 and returned it to the Washington 27. Jim Kiick ran for three yards, Larry Csonka for three, Griese passed to Jim Mandich for 19, and Kiick gained one to the 1 yard line. With 18 seconds left until intermission, Kiick scored from the 1. Washington's only touchdown came with 7:07 left in the game and resulted from a misplayed field goal attempt and fumble by Garo Yepremian, with the Redskins' Mike Bass picking the ball out of the air and running 49 yards for the score.

Miami (AFC)	7	7	0	0	— 14
Washington (NFC)	0	0	0	7	— 7

Mia —Twilley 28 pass from Griese (Yepremian kick)
Mia —Kiick 1 run (Yepremian kick)
Wash—Bass 49 fumble recovery return (Knight kick)

SUPER BOWL VI

Tulane Stadium, New Orleans, Louisiana — January 16, 1972
Attendance: 81,023

DALLAS 24, MIAMI 3—The Cowboys rushed for a record 252 yards and their defense limited the Dolphins to a low of 185 yards while not permitting a touchdown for the first time in Super Bowl history. Dallas converted Chuck Howley's recovery of Larry Csonka's first fumble of the season into a 3-0 advantage and led at halftime 10-3. After Dallas received the second half kickoff, Duane Thomas led a 71-yard march in eight plays for a 17-3 margin. Howley intercepted Bob Griese's pass at the 50 and returned it to the Miami 9 early in the fourth period, and three plays later Roger Staubach passed seven yards to Mike Ditka for the final touchdown. Thomas rushed for 95 yards and Walt Garrison gained 74. Staubach, voted the game's most valuable player, completed 12 of 19 passes for 119 yards and two touchdowns.

Dallas (NFC)	3	7	7	7	— 24
Miami (AFC)	0	3	0	0	— 3

Dall—FG Clark 9
Dall—Alworth 7 pass from Staubach (Clark kick)
Mia—FG Yepremian 31
Dall—D. Thomas 3 run (Clark kick)
Dall—Ditka 7 pass from Staubach (Clark kick)

SUPER BOWL V

Orange Bowl, Miami, Florida — January 17, 1971
Attendance: 79,204

BALTIMORE 16, DALLAS 13—A 32-yard field goal by first-year kicker Jim O'Brien brought the Baltimore Colts a victory over the Dallas Cowboys in the final five seconds of Super Bowl V. The game between the champions of the AFC and NFC was played on artificial turf for the first time. Dallas led 13-6 at the half but interceptions by Rick Volk and Mike Curtis set up a Baltimore touchdown and O'Brien's decisive kick in the fourth period. Earl Morrall relieved an injured Johnny Unitas late in the first half, although Unitas completed the Colts' only scoring pass. It caromed off receiver Eddie Hinton's finger tips, off Dallas defensive back Mel Renfro, and finally settled into the grasp of John Mackey, who went 45 yards to score on a 75-yard play.

Baltimore (AFC)	0	6	0	10	— 16
Dallas (NFC)	3	10	0	0	— 13

Dall—FG Clark 14
Dall—FG Clark 30
Balt—Mackey 75 pass from Unitas (kick blocked)
Dall—Thomas 7 pass from Morton (Clark kick)
Balt—Nowatzke 2 run (O'Brien kick)
Balt—FG O'Brien 32

SUPER BOWL IV

Tulane Stadium, New Orleans, Louisiana — January 11, 1970
Attendance: 80,562

KANSAS CITY 23, MINNESOTA 7—The AFL squared the Super Bowl at two games apiece with the NFL, building a 16-0 halftime lead behind Len Dawson's superb quarterbacking and a powerful defense. Dawson, the fourth consecutive quarterback to be chosen the Super Bowl's top player, called an almost flawless game, completing 12 of 17 passes and hitting Otis Taylor on a 46-yard play for the final Chiefs touchdown. The Kansas City defense limited Minnesota's strong rushing game to 67 yards and had three interceptions and two fumble recoveries. The crowd of 80,562 set a Super Bowl record, as did the gross receipts of $3,817,872.69.

Minnesota (NFL)	0	0	7	0 — 7
Kansas City (AFL)	3	13	7	0 — 23

KC —FG Stenerud 48
KC —FG Stenerud 32
KC —FG Stenerud 25
KC —Garrett 5 run (Stenerud kick)
Minn—Osborn 4 run (Cox kick)
KC —Taylor 46 pass from Dawson (Stenerud kick)

SUPER BOWL III

Orange Bowl, Miami, Florida January 12, 1969
Attendance: 75,389

NEW YORK JETS 16, BALTIMORE 7—Jets quarterback Joe Namath "guaranteed" victory on the Thursday before the game, then went out and led the AFL to its first Super Bowl victory over a Baltimore team that had lost only once in 16 games all season. Namath, chosen the outstanding player, completed 17 of 28 passes for 206 yards and directed a steady attack that dominated the NFL champions after the Jets' defense had intercepted Colts quarterback Earl Morrall three times in the first half. The Jets had 337 total yards, including 121 yards rushing by Matt Snell. Johnny Unitas, who had missed most of the season with a sore elbow, came off the bench and led Baltimore to its only touchdown late in the fourth quarter after New York led 16-0.

New York Jets (AFL)	0	7	6	3 — 16
Baltimore (NFL)	0	0	0	7 — 7

NYJ—Snell 4 run (Turner kick)
NYJ—FG Turner 32
NYJ—FG Turner 30
NYJ—FG Turner 9
Balt—Hill 1 run (Michaels kick)

SUPER BOWL II

Orange Bowl, Miami, Florida January 14, 1968
Attendance: 75,546

GREEN BAY 33, OAKLAND 14—Green Bay, after winning its third consecutive NFL championship, won the Super Bowl title for the second straight year 33-14 over the AFL champion Raiders in a game that drew the first $3 million dollar gate in football history. Bart Starr again was chosen the game's most valuable player as he completed 13 of 24 passes for 202 yards and one touchdown and directed a Packers attack that was in control all the way after building a 16-7 halftime lead. Don Chandler kicked four field goals and all-pro cornerback Herb Adderley capped the Green Bay scoring with a 60-yard run with an interception. The game marked the last for Vince Lombardi as Packers coach, ending nine years at Green Bay in which he won six Western Conference championships, five NFL championships, and two Super Bowls.

Green Bay (NFL)	3	13	10	7 — 33
Oakland (AFL)	0	7	0	7 — 14

GB —FG Chandler 39
GB —FG Chandler 20
GB —Dowler 62 pass from Starr (Chandler kick)
Oak—Miller 23 pass from Lamonica (Blanda kick)
GB —FG Chandler 43
GB —Anderson 2 run (Chandler kick)
GB —FG Chandler 31
GB —Adderley 60 interception return (Chandler kick)
Oak—Miller 23 pass from Lamonica (Blanda kick)

SUPER BOWL I

Memorial Coliseum, Los Angeles, California January 15, 1967
Attendance: 61,946

GREEN BAY 35, KANSAS CITY 10—The Green Bay Packers opened the Super Bowl series by defeating Kansas City's American Football League champions 35-10 behind the passing of Bart Starr, the receiving of Max McGee, and a key interception by all-pro safety Willie Wood. Green Bay broke open the game with three second-half touchdowns, the first of which was set up by Wood's 40-yard return of an interception to the Chiefs' 5 yard line. McGee, filling in for ailing Boyd Dowler after having caught only three passes all season, caught seven from Starr for 138 yards and two touchdowns. Elijah Pitts ran for two other scores. The Chiefs' 10 points came in the second quarter, the only touchdown on a seven-yard pass from Len Dawson to Curtis McClinton. Starr completed 16 of 23 passes for 250 yards and two touchdowns and was chosen the most valuable player. The Packers collected $15,000 per man and the Chiefs $7,500—the largest single-game shares in the history of team sports.

Kansas City (AFL)	0	10	0	0 — 10
Green Bay (NFL)	7	7	14	7 — 35

GB—McGee 37 pass from Starr (Chandler kick)
KC—McClinton 7 pass from Dawson (Mercer kick)
GB—Taylor 14 run (Chandler kick)
KC—FG Mercer 31
GB—Pitts 5 run (Chandler kick)
GB—McGee 13 pass from Starr (Chandler kick)
GB—Pitts 1 run (Chandler kick)

AFC Championship Game

Includes AFL Championship Games (1960-69)

RESULTS

Season	Date	Winner (Share)	Loser (Share)	Score	Site	Attendance
1985	Jan. 12	New England ($18,000)	Miami ($18,000)	31-14	Miami	75,662
1984	Jan. 6	Miami ($18,000)	Pittsburgh ($18,000)	45-28	Miami	76,029
1983	Jan. 8	L.A. Raiders ($18,000)	Seattle ($18,000)	30-14	Los Angeles	91,445
1982	Jan. 23	Miami ($18,000)	N.Y. Jets ($18,000)	14-0	Miami	67,396
1981	Jan. 10	Cincinnati ($9,000)	San Diego ($9,000)	27-7	Cincinnati	46,302
1980	Jan. 11	Oakland ($9,000)	San Diego ($9,000)	34-27	San Diego	52,675
1979	Jan. 6	Pittsburgh ($9,000)	Houston ($9,000)	27-13	Pittsburgh	50,475
1978	Jan. 7	Pittsburgh ($9,000)	Houston ($9,000)	34-5	Pittsburgh	50,725
1977	Jan. 1	Denver ($9,000)	Oakland ($9,000)	20-17	Denver	75,044
1976	Dec. 26	Oakland ($8,500)	Pittsburgh ($5,500)	24-7	Oakland	53,821
1975	Jan. 4	Pittsburgh ($8,500)	Oakland ($5,500)	16-10	Pittsburgh	50,609
1974	Dec. 29	Pittsburgh ($8,500)	Oakland ($5,500)	24-13	Oakland	53,800
1973	Dec. 30	Miami ($8,500)	Oakland ($5,500)	27-10	Miami	79,325
1972	Dec. 31	Miami ($8,500)	Pittsburgh ($5,500)	21-17	Pittsburgh	50,845
1971	Jan. 2	Miami ($8,500)	Baltimore ($5,500)	21-0	Miami	76,622
1970	Jan. 3	Baltimore ($8,500)	Oakland ($5,500)	27-17	Baltimore	54,799
1969	Jan. 4	Kansas City ($7,755)	Oakland ($6,252)	17-7	Oakland	53,564
1968	Dec. 29	N.Y. Jets ($7,007)	Oakland ($5,349)	27-23	New York	62,627
1967	Dec. 31	Oakland ($6,321)	Houston ($4,996)	40-7	Oakland	53,330
1966	Jan. 1	Kansas City ($5,309)	Buffalo ($3,799)	31-7	Buffalo	42,080
1965	Dec. 26	Buffalo ($5,189)	San Diego ($3,447)	23-0	San Diego	30,361
1964	Dec. 26	Buffalo ($2,668)	San Diego ($1,738)	20-7	Buffalo	40,242
1963	Jan. 5	San Diego ($2,498)	Boston ($1,596)	51-10	San Diego	30,127
1962	Dec. 23	Dallas ($2,206)	Houston ($1,471)	20-17*	Houston	37,981
1961	Dec. 24	Houston ($1,792)	San Diego ($1,111)	10-3	San Diego	29,556
1960	Jan. 1	Houston ($1,025)	Los Angeles ($718)	24-16	Houston	32,183

Sudden death overtime.

AFC CHAMPIONSHIP GAME COMPOSITE STANDINGS

	W	L	Pct.	Pts.	OP
Kansas City Chiefs*	3	0	1.000	68	31
Cincinnati Bengals	1	0	1.000	27	7
Denver Broncos	1	0	1.000	20	17
Miami Dolphins	5	1	.833	142	86
Buffalo Bills	2	1	.667	50	38
Pittsburgh Steelers	4	3	.571	153	131
Baltimore Colts	1	1	.500	27	38
New England Patriots**	1	1	.500	41	65
New York Jets	1	1	.500	27	37
Oakland/L.A. Raiders	4	7	.364	225	213
Houston Oilers	2	4	.333	76	140
San Diego Chargers***	1	6	.143	111	148
Seattle Seahawks	0	1	.000	14	30

*One game played when franchise was in Dallas (Texans). (Won 20-17)
**One game played when franchise was in Boston. (Lost 51-10)
***One game played when franchise was in Los Angeles. (Lost 24-16)

1985 AMERICAN FOOTBALL CONFERENCE CHAMPIONSHIP GAME

Orange Bowl, Miami, Florida — January 12, 1986

Attendance: 75,662

NEW ENGLAND 31, MIAMI 14—The AFC Wild Card Patriots defeated the AFC Eastern Division champion Dolphins 31-14 to become the third Wild Card team ever to qualify for the Super Bowl. It was New England's first victory at Miami in 19 games since 1966. New England converted four of its six takeaways (four fumble recoveries and two interceptions) into 24 points to hand Miami its first-ever AFC Championship Game loss. New England defensive end Garin Veris recovered Tony Nathan's fumble on the Dolphins' first play from scrimmage to set up Tony Franklin's 23-yard field goal. Miami quarterback Dan Marino then directed an 80-yard, 11-play touchdown drive for a 7-3 lead, but New England quarterback Tony Eason found running back Tony Collins on a four-yard scoring pass to give the Patriots the lead for good 10-7. Eason threw only 12 passes and completed 10 for 71 yards, including touchdowns to Derrick Ramsey (one yard) and Robert Weathers (two). New England rushed an AFC Championship Game-record 59 times for 255 yards and dominated Miami in time of possession, 39:51 to 20:09. Craig James gained 105 yards on 22 carries to lead the Patriots. With New England leading 24-14 in the fourth quarter, Julius Adams recovered a Miami fumble to set up Mosi Tatupu's one-yard scoring run with 7:34 remaining to seal the Patriots' win. Raymond Clayborn and Fred Marion each intercepted passes and Lester Williams and Greg Hawthorne each recovered fumbles. The victory made the Patriots the last of the original eight AFL teams to win an AFL or AFC Conference title.

New England (31)	Offense	Miami (14)
Stanley Morgan	WR	Mark Duper
Brian Holloway	LT	Jon Giesler
John Hannah	LG	Roy Foster
Pete Brock	C	Dwight Stephenson
Ron Wooten	RG	Steve Clark
Steve Moore	RT	Ronnie Lee
Lin Dawson	TE	Bruce Hardy
Stephen Starring	WR	Mark Clayton
Tony Eason	QB	Dan Marino
Tony Collins	RB	Tony Nathan
Craig James	RB-WR	Nat Moore
	Defense	
Garin Veris	LE	Doug Betters
Lester Williams	NT	Mike Charles
Julius Adams	RE	Kim Bokamper
Andre Tippett	LOLB	Bob Brudzinski
Steve Nelson	LILB	Jay Brophy
Larry McGrew	RILB	Jackie Shipp
Don Blackmon	ROLB	Hugh Green
Ronnie Lippett	LCB	Paul Lankford
Raymond Clayborn	RCB	William Judson
Roland James	SS	Glenn Blackwood
Fred Marion	FS	Bud Brown

SUBSTITUTIONS

New England—Offense: K—Tony Franklin. P—Rich Camarillo. RB—Greg Hawthorne, Mosi Tatupu, Robert Weathers. TE—Derrick Ramsey. WR—Cedric Jones. C—Guy Morriss. G—Paul Fairchild. T—Art Plunkett. Defense: E—Smiley Creswell, Ben Thomas. NT—Dennis Owens. LB—Brian Ingram, Johnny Rembert, Ed Reynolds, Ed Williams. CB—Ernest Gibson, Rod McSwain. S—Jim Bowman. DNP: QB—Steve Grogan, Tom Ramsey. WR—Irving Fryar.
Miami—Offense: K—Fuad Reveiz. P—Reggie Roby. QB—Don Strock. RB—Woody Bennett, Joe Carter, Ron Davenport, Lorenzo Hampton, Tommy Vigorito. TE—Dan Johnson, Joe Rose. WR—Jim Jensen. G—Larry Lee. T—Jeff Dellenbach, Cleveland Green. Defense: E—Mack Moore. NT—George Little. LB—Mark Brown, Alex Moyer, Robin Sendlein. CB—Don McNeal, Mike Smith. S—Lyle Blackwood, Mike Kozlowski. DNP: none.

OFFICIALS

Referee—Gene Barth. Umpire—Gordon Wells. Head Linesman—Sid Semon. Line Judge—Jack Johnson. Back Judge—Ben Tompkins. Side Judge—Nathan Jones. Field Judge—Don Hakes.

SCORING

New England	3	14	7	7 — 31
Miami	0	7	0	7 — 14

NE —FG Franklin 23
Mia—Johnson 10 pass from Marino (Reveiz kick)
NE —Collins 4 pass from Eason (Franklin kick)
NE —D. Ramsey 1 pass from Eason (Franklin kick)
NE —Weathers 2 pass from Eason (Franklin kick)
Mia—Nathan 10 pass from Marino (Reveiz kick)
NE —Tatupu 1 run (Franklin kick)

TEAM STATISTICS

	New England	Miami
Total First Downs	21	18
First Downs Rushing	15	3
First Downs Passing	6	15
First Downs Penalty	0	0
Total Net Yardage	326	302
Total Offensive Plays	71	62
Average Gain per Offensive Play	4.6	4.9
Rushes	59	13
Yards Gained Rushing (net)	255	68
Average Yards per Rush	4.3	5.2
Passes Attempted	12	48
Passes Completed	10	20
Had Intercepted	0	2
Times Tackled Attempting to Pass	0	1
Yards Lost Attempting to Pass	0	14
Yards Gained Passing (net)	71	234
Punts	5	4
Average Distance	40.2	41.3
Punt Returns	2	1
Punt Return Yardage	2	8
Kickoff Returns	3	6
Kickoff Return Yardage	67	91
Interception Return Yardage	21	0
Total Return Yardage	90	99
Fumbles	2	5
Own Fumbles Recovered	0	1
Opponent Fumbles Recovered	4	2
Penalties	2	4
Yards Penalized	15	35
Total Points Scored	31	14
Touchdowns	4	2
Touchdowns Rushing	1	0
Touchdowns Passing	3	2
Touchdown Returns	0	0
Extra Points	4	2
Field Goals	1	0
Field Goals Attempted	2	1
Third Down Efficiency	7/16	3/10
Fourth Down Efficiency	2/2	0/2
Time of Possession	39:51	20:09

INDIVIDUAL STATISTICS

RUSHING

New England	Att.	Yds.	LG	TD
C. James	22	105	13	0
Weathers	16	87	45	0
Collins	12	61	14	0
Tatupu	6	9	2	1
Eason	3	−7	−2	0
Miami	**Att.**	**Yds.**	**LG**	**TD**
Carter	6	56	19	0
Davenport	3	6	3	0
Nathan	2	4	2	0
Bennett	1	2	2	0
Marino	1	0	0	0

PASSING

New Eng.	Att.	Comp.	Yds.	TD	Int.
Eason	12	10	71	3	0
Miami	**Att.**	**Comp.**	**Yds.**	**TD**	**Int.**
Marino	48	20	248	2	2

RECEIVING

New England	No.	Yds.	LG	TD
D. Ramsey	3	18	15	1
Collins	3	15	9	1
Morgan	2	30	18	0
Tatupu	1	6	6	0
Weathers	1	2	2t	1
Miami	**No.**	**Yds.**	**LG**	**TD**
Nathan	5	57	20	1
Hardy	3	52	29	0
Duper	3	45	18	0
Clayton	3	41	16	0
Davenport	3	23	9	0
Johnson	1	10	10t	1
Moore	1	10	10	0
Rose	1	10	10	0

INTERCEPTIONS

New England	No.	Yds.	LG	TD
Marion	1	21	21	0
Clayborn	1	0	0	0
Miami	**No.**	**Yds.**	**LG**	**TD**
None				

PUNTING

New England	No.	Avg.	LG	Blk.
Camarillo	5	40.2	49	0
Miami	**No.**	**Avg.**	**LG**	**Blk.**
Roby	4	41.3	49	0

PUNT RETURNS

New England	No.	FC	Yds.	LG	TD
R. James	2	2	2	2	0
Miami	**No.**	**FC**	**Yds.**	**LG**	**TD**
Vigorito	1	1	8	8	0

KICKOFF RETURNS

New England	No.	Yds.	LG	TD
Starring	3	67	37	0
Miami	**No.**	**Yds.**	**LG**	**TD**
Hampton	6	91	23	0

NFC Championship Game

Includes NFL Championship Games (1933-69)

RESULTS

Season	Date	Winner (Share)	Loser (Share)	Score	Site	Attendance
1985	Jan. 12	Chicago ($18,000)	L.A. Rams ($18,000)	24-0	Chicago	66,030
1984	Jan. 6	San Francisco ($18,000)	Chicago ($18,000)	23-0	San Francisco	61,336
1983	Jan. 8	Washington ($18,000)	San Francisco ($18,000)	24-21	Washington	55,363
1982	Jan. 22	Washington ($18,000)	Dallas ($18,000)	31-17	Washington	55,045
1981	Jan. 10	San Francisco ($9,000)	Dallas ($9,000)	28-27	San Francisco	60,525
1980	Jan. 11	Philadelphia ($9,000)	Dallas ($9,000)	20-7	Philadelphia	71,522
1979	Jan. 6	Los Angeles ($9,000)	Tampa Bay ($9,000)	9-0	Tampa Bay	72,033
1978	Jan. 7	Dallas ($9,000)	Los Angeles ($9,000)	28-0	Los Angeles	71,086
1977	Jan. 1	Dallas ($9,000)	Minnesota ($9,000)	23-6	Dallas	64,293
1976	Dec. 26	Minnesota ($8,500)	Los Angeles ($5,500)	24-13	Minnesota	48,379
1975	Jan. 4	Dallas ($8,500)	Los Angeles ($5,500)	37-7	Los Angeles	88,919
1974	Dec. 29	Minnesota ($8,500)	Los Angeles ($5,500)	14-10	Minnesota	48,444
1973	Dec. 30	Minnesota ($8,500)	Dallas ($5,500)	27-10	Dallas	64,422
1972	Dec. 31	Washington ($8,500)	Dallas ($5,500)	26-3	Washington	53,129
1971	Jan. 2	Dallas ($8,500)	San Francisco ($5,500)	14-3	Dallas	63,409
1970	Jan. 3	Dallas ($8,500)	San Francisco ($5,500)	17-10	San Francisco	59,364
1969	Jan. 4	Minnesota ($7,930)	Cleveland ($5,118)	27-7	Minnesota	46,503
1968	Dec. 29	Baltimore ($9,306)	Cleveland ($5,963)	34-0	Cleveland	78,410
1967	Dec. 31	Green Bay ($7,950)	Dallas ($5,299)	21-17	Green Bay	50,861
1966	Jan. 1	Green Bay ($9,813)	Dallas ($6,527)	34-27	Dallas	74,152
1965	Jan. 2	Green Bay ($7,819)	Cleveland ($5,288)	23-12	Green Bay	50,777
1964	Dec. 27	Cleveland ($8,052)	Baltimore ($5,571)	27-0	Cleveland	79,544
1963	Dec. 29	Chicago ($5,899)	New York ($4,218)	14-10	Chicago	45,801
1962	Dec. 30	Green Bay ($5,888)	New York ($4,166)	16-7	New York	64,892
1961	Dec. 31	Green Bay ($5,195)	New York ($3,339)	37-0	Green Bay	39,029
1960	Dec. 26	Philadelphia ($5,116)	Green Bay ($3,105)	17-13	Philadelphia	67,325
1959	Dec. 27	Baltimore ($4,674)	New York ($3,083)	31-16	Baltimore	57,545
1958	Dec. 28	Baltimore ($4,718)	New York ($3,111)	23-17*	New York	64,185
1957	Dec. 29	Detroit ($4,295)	Cleveland ($2,750)	59-14	Detroit	55,263
1956	Dec. 30	New York ($3,779)	Chi. Bears ($2,485)	47-7	New York	56,836
1955	Dec. 26	Cleveland ($3,508)	Los Angeles ($2,316)	38-14	Los Angeles	85,693
1954	Dec. 26	Cleveland ($2,478)	Detroit ($1,585)	56-10	Cleveland	43,827
1953	Dec. 27	Detroit ($2,424)	Cleveland ($1,654)	17-16	Detroit	54,577
1952	Dec. 28	Detroit ($2,274)	Cleveland ($1,712)	17-7	Cleveland	50,934
1951	Dec. 23	Los Angeles ($2,108)	Cleveland ($1,483)	24-17	Los Angeles	57,522
1950	Dec. 24	Cleveland ($1,113)	Los Angeles ($686)	30-28	Cleveland	29,751
1949	Dec. 18	Philadelphia ($1,094)	Los Angeles ($739)	14-0	Los Angeles	27,980
1948	Dec. 19	Philadelphia ($1,540)	Chi. Cardinals ($874)	7-0	Philadelphia	36,309
1947	Dec. 28	Chi. Cardinals ($1,132)	Philadelphia ($754)	28-21	Chicago	30,759

1946	Dec. 15	Chi. Bears ($1,975)	New York ($1,295)	24-14	New York	58,346
1945	Dec. 16	Cleveland ($1,469)	Washington ($902)	15-14	Cleveland	32,178
1944	Dec. 17	Green Bay ($1,449)	New York ($814)	14-7	New York	46,016
1943	Dec. 26	Chi. Bears ($1,146)	Washington ($765)	41-21	Chicago	34,320
1942	Dec. 13	Washington ($965)	Chi. Bears ($637)	14-6	Washington	36,006
1941	Dec. 21	Chi. Bears ($430)	New York ($288)	37-9	Chicago	13,341
1940	Dec. 8	Chi. Bears ($873)	Washington ($606)	73-0	Washington	36,034
1939	Dec. 10	Green Bay ($703.97)	New York ($455.57)	27-0	Milwaukee	32,279
1938	Dec. 11	New York ($504.45)	Green Bay ($368.81)	23-17	New York	48,120
1937	Dec. 12	Washington ($225.90)	Chi. Bears ($127.78)	28-21	Chicago	15,870
1936	Dec. 13	Green Bay ($250)	Boston ($180)	21-6	New York	29,545
1935	Dec. 15	Detroit ($313.35)	New York ($200.20)	26-7	Detroit	15,000
1934	Dec. 9	New York ($621)	Chi. Bears ($414.02)	30-13	New York	35,059
1933	Dec. 17	Chi. Bears ($210.34)	New York ($140.22)	23-21	Chicago	26,000

**Sudden death overtime.*

NFC CHAMPIONSHIP GAME COMPOSITE STANDINGS

	W	L	Pct.	Pts.	OP
Green Bay Packers	8	2	.800	223	116
Detroit Lions	4	1	.800	129	100
Minnesota Vikings	4	1	.800	98	63
Philadelphia Eagles	4	1	.800	79	48
Baltimore Colts	3	1	.750	88	60
Chicago Bears	7	5	.583	283	217
Washington Redskins*	5	4	.556	164	218
St. Louis Cardinals**	1	1	.500	28	28
Dallas Cowboys	5	7	.417	227	213
San Francisco 49ers	2	3	.400	85	82
Cleveland Browns	4	7	.364	224	253
Los Angeles Rams***	3	8	.273	120	240
New York Giants	3	11	.214	208	309
Tampa Bay Buccaneers	0	1	.000	0	9

**One game played when franchise was in Boston. (Lost 21-6)*
***Both games played when franchise was in Chicago. (Won 28-21, lost 7-0)*
****One game played when franchise was in Cleveland. (Won 15-14)*

1985 NATIONAL FOOTBALL CONFERENCE CHAMPIONSHIP GAME

Soldier Field, Chicago, Illinois — January 12, 1986
Attendance: 66,030

CHICAGO 24, LOS ANGELES RAMS 0—NFC Central Division champion Chicago extended its overall season record to 17-1 by registering a playoff record second consecutive shutout in winning the NFC title. The Bears defeated the NFC Western Division champion Los Angeles Rams 24-0 to follow a 21-0 blanking of the New York Giants the previous week. Weather conditions at kick-off were 39 degrees with wind gusts up to 28 miles per hour and a cloudy sky. Toward the end of the game, temperatures had dropped to the high 20s and snow flurries fell. Chicago broke on top on its first possession of the game via a five-play, 66-yard drive capped by quarterback Jim McMahon's 16-yard scramble around left end for a touchdown. Following a Rams possession, Chicago marched to the Los Angeles 16-yard line and Kevin Butler kicked a 34-yard field goal. The Bears held a 10-0 halftime lead, plus an advantage in total yards (152 to 68) and first downs (9 to 3). On Chicago's second possession of the third quarter, the Bears drove 52 yards in nine plays, concluded by a 22-yard touchdown catch by wide receiver Willie Gault. Chicago finished its scoring late in the fourth quarter when defensive end Richard Dent forced Rams quarterback Dieter Brock to fumble and linebacker Wilber Marshall recovered and ran 52 yards for the touchdown.

L.A. Rams (0)	Offense	Chicago (24)
Henry Ellard	WR	Willie Gault
Irv Pankey	LT	Jim Covert
Kent Hill	LG	Mark Bortz
Tony Slaton	C	Jay Hilgenberg
Dennis Harrah	RG	Tom Thayer
Jackie Slater	RT	Keith Van Horne
David Hill	TE	Emery Moorehead
Ron Brown	WR	Dennis McKinnon
Dieter Brock	QB	Jim McMahon
Barry Redden	RB	Matt Suhey
Eric Dickerson	RB	Walter Payton
	Defense	
Doug Reed	LE	Dan Hampton
Charles DeJurnett	NT-LT	Steve McMichael
Reggie Doss	RE-RT	William Perry
Mel Owens	LOLB-RE	Richard Dent
Carl Ekern	LILB-LLB	Otis Wilson
Jim Collins	RILB-MLB	Mike Singletary
Mike Wilcher	ROLB-RLB	Wilber Marshall
Gary Green	LCB	Mike Richardson
LeRoy Irvin	RCB	Leslie Frazier
Nolan Cromwell	SS	Dave Duerson
Johnnie Johnson	FS	Gary Fencik

SUBSTITUTIONS

Rams—Offense: K—Mike Lansford. P—Dale Hatcher. RB—Mike Guman, Charles White. WR—Bobby Duckworth, Mike Young. TE—Tony Hunter. T—Bill Bain. Defense: E—Dennis Harrison, Gary Jeter. NT—Greg Meisner, Shawn Miller. LB—Ed Brady, Kevin Greene, Mark Jerue, Jim Laughlin, Norwood Vann. CB—Jerry Gray. S—Tim Fox, Vince Newsome. DNP: QB—Steve Dils, Jeff Kemp. G—Russ Bolinger.

Chicago—Offense: K—Kevin Butler. P—Maury Buford. QB—Steve Fuller. RB—Dennis Gentry, Thomas Sanders, Calvin Thomas. TE—Tim Wrightman. WR—Ken Margerum, Keith Ortego. C—Tom Andrews. G—Stefan Humphries. T—Andy Frederick. Defense: E—Mike Hartenstine, Tyrone Keys. T—Henry Waechter. LB—Brian Cabral, Jim Morrissey, Ron Rivera, Cliff Thrift. CB—Shaun Gayle, Reggie Phillips, Ken Taylor. DNP: QB—Mike Tomczak.

OFFICIALS

Referee: Jim Tunney. Umpire—Al Conway. Head Linesman—Burl Toler. Line Judge—Dick McKenzie. Back Judge—Dick Hantak. Side Judge—Bill Quinby. Field Judge—Bob Lewis.

SCORING

L.A. Rams	0	0	0	0	— 0
Chicago	10	0	7	7	— 24

Chi —McMahon 16 run (Butler kick)
Chi —FG Butler 34
Chi —Gault 22 pass from McMahon (Butler kick)
Chi —Marshall 52 fumble recovery return (Butler kick)

TEAM STATISTICS

	L.A. Rams	Chicago
Total First Downs	9	13
First Downs Rushing	5	5
First Downs Passing	3	8
First Downs Penalty	1	0
Total Net Yardage	130	232
Total Offensive Plays	60	61
Average Gain per Offensive Play	2.2	3.8
Rushes	26	33
Yards Gained Rushing (net)	86	91
Average Yards per Rush	3.3	2.8
Passes Attempted	31	25
Passes Completed	10	16
Had Intercepted	1	0
Times Tackled Attempting to Pass	3	3
Yards Lost Attempting to Pass	22	23
Yards Gained Passing (net)	44	141
Punts	11	10
Average Distance	39.2	36.3
Punt Returns	4	5
Punt Return Yardage	16	21
Kickoff Returns	4	1
Kickoff Return Yardage	76	22
Interception Return Yardage	0	−3
Total Return Yardage	92	40
Fumbles	4	3
Own Fumbles Recovered	2	2
Opponent Fumbles Recovered	1	2
Penalties	4	6
Yards Penalized	25	48
Total Points Scored	0	24
Touchdowns	0	3
Touchdowns Rushing	0	1
Touchdowns Passing	0	1
Touchdown Returns	0	1
Extra Points	0	3
Field Goals	0	1
Field Goals Attempted	0	1
Third Down Efficiency	2/14	4/16
Fourth Down Efficiency	0/0	1/1
Time of Possession	25:33	34:27

INDIVIDUAL STATISTICS

RUSHING

L.A. Rams	Att.	Yds.	LG	TD
Dickerson	17	46	9	0
Redden	9	40	12	0
Chicago	**Att.**	**Yds.**	**LG**	**TD**
Payton	18	32	8	0
McMahon	4	28	16t	1
Suhey	6	23	9	0
Gentry	2	9	7	0
Thomas	3	−1	1	0

PASSING

L.A. Rams	Att.	Comp.	Yds.	TD	Int.
Brock	31	10	66	0	1
Chicago	**Att.**	**Comp.**	**Yds.**	**TD**	**Int.**
McMahon	25	16	164	1	0

RECEIVING

L.A. Rams	No.	Yds.	LG	TD
Hunter	3	29	15	0
Dickerson	3	10	7	0
Brown	2	14	11	0
Duckworth	1	8	8	0
Ellard	1	5	5	0
Chicago	**No.**	**Yds.**	**LG**	**TD**
Payton	7	48	19	0
Gault	4	56	22t	1
Moorehead	2	28	20	0
McKinnon	1	17	17	0
Wrightman	1	8	8	0
Suhey	1	7	7	0

INTERCEPTIONS

L.A. Rams	No.	Yds.	LG	TD
None				
Chicago	**No.**	**Yds.**	**LG**	**TD**
Frazier	1	−3	−3	0

PUNTING

L.A. Rams	No.	Avg.	LG	Blk.
Hatcher	11	39.2	51	0
Chicago	**No.**	**Avg.**	**LG**	**Blk.**
Buford	10	36.3	55	0

PUNT RETURNS

L.A. Rams	No.	FC	Yds.	LG	TD
Johnson	2	1	6	3	0
Ellard	1	0	6	6	0
Irvin	1	0	4	4	0
Chicago	**No.**	**FC**	**Yds.**	**LG**	**TD**
Ortego	4	0	21	8	0
Phillips	1	0	0	0	0
Duerson	0	1	0	0	0

KICKOFF RETURNS

L.A. Rams	No.	Yds.	LG	TD
Brown	3	63	45	0
Redden	1	13	13	0
Chicago	**No.**	**Yds.**	**LG**	**TD**
Gentry	1	22	22	0

AFC Divisional Playoffs

Includes Second-Round Playoff Games (1982), AFL Inter-Divisional Playoff Games (1969), and special playoff games to break ties for AFL Division Championships (1963, 1968)

RESULTS

Season	Date	Winner	Loser	Site	Attendance
1985	Jan. 5	New England 27	L.A. Raiders 20	Los Angeles	87,163
	Jan. 4	Miami 24	Cleveland 21	Miami	74,667
1984	Dec. 30	Pittsburgh 24	Denver 17	Denver	74,981
	Dec. 29	Miami 31	Seattle 10	Miami	73,469
1983	Jan. 1	L.A. Raiders 38	Pittsburgh 10	Los Angeles	90,380
	Dec. 31	Seattle 27	Miami 20	Miami	74,136
1982	Jan. 16	Miami 34	San Diego 13	Miami	71,383
	Jan. 15	N.Y. Jets 17	L.A. Raiders 14	Los Angeles	90,038
1981	Jan. 3	Cincinnati 28	Buffalo 21	Cincinnati	55,420
	Jan. 2	*San Diego 41	Miami 38	Miami	73,735
1980	Jan. 4	Oakland 14	Cleveland 12	Cleveland	78,245
	Jan. 3	San Diego 20	Buffalo 14	San Diego	52,253
1979	Dec. 30	Pittsburgh 34	Miami 14	Pittsburgh	50,214
	Dec. 29	Houston 17	San Diego 14	San Diego	51,192
1978	Dec. 31	Houston 31	New England 14	New England	60,735
	Dec. 30	Pittsburgh 33	Denver 10	Pittsburgh	50,230
1977	Dec. 24	*Oakland 37	Baltimore 31	Baltimore	59,925
	Dec. 24	Denver 34	Pittsburgh 21	Denver	75,059
1976	Dec. 19	Pittsburgh 40	Baltimore 14	Baltimore	59,296
	Dec. 18	Oakland 24	New England 21	Oakland	53,050
1975	Dec. 28	Oakland 31	Cincinnati 28	Oakland	53,030
	Dec. 27	Pittsburgh 28	Baltimore 10	Pittsburgh	49,557
1974	Dec. 22	Pittsburgh 32	Buffalo 14	Pittsburgh	49,841
	Dec. 21	Oakland 28	Miami 26	Oakland	53,023
1973	Dec. 23	Miami 34	Cincinnati 16	Miami	78,928
	Dec. 22	Oakland 33	Pittsburgh 14	Oakland	52,646
1972	Dec. 24	Miami 20	Cleveland 14	Miami	78,916
	Dec. 23	Pittsburgh 13	Oakland 7	Pittsburgh	50,327
1971	Dec. 26	Baltimore 20	Cleveland 3	Cleveland	70,734
	Dec. 25	*Miami 27	Kansas City 24	Kansas City	45,822
1970	Dec. 27	Oakland 21	Miami 14	Oakland	52,594
	Dec. 26	Baltimore 17	Cincinnati 0	Baltimore	49,694
1969	Dec. 21	Oakland 56	Houston 7	Oakland	53,539
	Dec. 20	Kansas City 13	N.Y. Jets 6	New York	62,977
1968	Dec. 22	Oakland 41	Kansas City 6	Oakland	53,605
1963	Dec. 28	Boston 26	Buffalo 8	Buffalo	33,044

Sudden death overtime.

1985 AFC DIVISIONAL PLAYOFFS

Orange Bowl, Miami, Florida — January 4, 1986

Attendance: 74,667

MIAMI 24, CLEVELAND 21—Miami rebounded from a 21-3 third-quarter deficit to defeat Cleveland 24-21. Miami scored on its first possession on Fuad Reveiz's 51-yard field goal, but Cleveland responded by scoring 21 unanswered points. Earnest Byner, who rushed for 161 yards on 16 carries, scored on runs of 21 and 66 yards to give Cleveland a 21-3 lead 3:38 into the third quarter. The Dolphins rallied by scoring two touchdowns later in the third period. Quarterback Dan Marino and wide receiver Nat Moore combined on a six-yard touchdown pass and running back Ron Davenport scored on a 31-yard run to cut Cleveland's lead to 21-17. Davenport's one-yard plunge with 1:57 remaining proved to be the game-winning score.

Cleveland	7	7	7	0	— 21
Miami	3	0	14	7	— 24

Mia —FG Reveiz 51
Clev—Newsome 16 pass from Kosar (Bahr kick)
Clev—Byner 21 run (Bahr kick)
Clev—Byner 66 (Bahr kick)
Mia —Moore 6 pass from Marino (Reveiz kick)
Mia —Davenport 31 run (Reveiz kick)
Mia —Davenport 1 run (Reveiz kick)

Memorial Coliseum, Los Angeles, California — January 5, 1986

Attendance: 87,163

NEW ENGLAND 27, LOS ANGELES RAIDERS 20—New England advanced to its first AFC Championship Game by defeating the AFC Western champion Los Angeles Raiders. The Patriots capitalized on three interceptions and three fumble recoveries to score 20 points. Reserve safety Jim Bowman's fumble recovery set up quarterback Tony Eason's 13-yard scoring pass to tight end Lin Dawson for a 7-0 Patriots lead. Following Tony Franklin's 32-yard field goal, which was set up by a Fred Marion fumble recovery, Bowman recovered the ensuing kickoff in the end zone for what proved to be the game-winning score.

New England	7	10	10	0	— 27
L.A. Raiders	3	17	0	0	— 20

NE —Dawson 13 pass from Eason (Franklin kick)
Raiders —FG Bahr 29
Raiders —Hester 16 pass from Wilson (Bahr kick)
Raiders —Allen 11 run (Bahr kick)
NE —C. James 2 run (Franklin kick)
NE —FG Franklin 45
Raiders —FG Bahr 32
NE —FG Franklin 32
NE —Bowman fumble recovery in end zone (Franklin kick)

NFC Divisional Playoffs

Includes Second-Round Playoff Games (1982), NFL Conference Championship Games (1967-69), and special playoff games to break ties for NFL Division or Conference Championships (1941, 1943, 1947, 1950, 1952, 1957, 1958, 1965)

RESULTS

Season	Date	Winner	Loser	Site	Attendance
1985	Jan. 5	Chicago 21	N.Y. Giants 0	Chicago	65,670
	Jan. 4	L.A. Rams 20	Dallas 0	Anaheim	66,581
1984	Dec. 30	Chicago 23	Washington 19	Washington	55,431
	Dec. 29	San Francisco 21	N.Y. Giants 10	San Francisco	60,303
1983	Jan.1	Washington 51	L.A. Rams 7	Washington	54,440
	Dec. 31	San Francisco 24	Detroit 23	San Francisco	59,979
1982	Jan. 16	Dallas 37	Green Bay 26	Dallas	63,972
	Jan. 15	Washington 21	Minnesota 7	Washington	54,593
1981	Jan. 3	San Francisco 38	N.Y. Giants 24	San Francisco	58,360
	Jan. 2	Dallas 38	Tampa Bay 0	Dallas	64,848
1980	Jan. 4	Dallas 30	Atlanta 27	Atlanta	59,793
	Jan. 3	Philadelphia 31	Minnesota 16	Philadelphia	70,178
1979	Dec. 30	Los Angeles 21	Dallas 19	Dallas	64,792
	Dec. 29	Tampa Bay 24	Philadelphia 17	Tampa Bay	71,402
1978	Dec. 31	Los Angeles 34	Minnesota 10	Los Angeles	70,436
	Dec. 30	Dallas 27	Atlanta 20	Dallas	63,406
1977	Dec. 26	Dallas 37	Chicago 7	Dallas	63,260
	Dec. 26	Minnesota 14	Los Angeles 7	Los Angeles	70,203
1976	Dec. 19	Los Angeles 14	Dallas 12	Dallas	63,283
	Dec. 18	Minnesota 35	Washington 20	Minnesota	47,466
1975	Dec. 28	Dallas 17	Minnesota 14	Minnesota	48,050
	Dec. 27	Los Angeles 35	St. Louis 23	Los Angeles	73,459
1974	Dec. 22	Los Angeles 19	Washington 10	Los Angeles	77,925
	Dec. 21	Minnesota 30	St. Louis 14	Minnesota	48,150
1973	Dec. 23	Dallas 27	Los Angeles 16	Dallas	63,272
	Dec. 22	Minnesota 27	Washington 20	Minnesota	48,040
1972	Dec. 24	Washington 16	Green Bay 3	Washington	52,321
	Dec. 23	Dallas 30	San Francisco 28	San Francisco	59,746
1971	Dec. 26	San Francisco 24	Washington 20	San Francisco	45,327
	Dec. 25	Dallas 20	Minnesota 12	Minnesota	47,307
1970	Dec. 27	San Francisco 17	Minnesota 14	Minnesota	45,103
	Dec. 26	Dallas 5	Detroit 0	Dallas	69,613
1969	Dec. 28	Cleveland 38	Dallas 14	Dallas	69,321
	Dec. 27	Minnesota 23	Los Angeles 20	Minnesota	47,900
1968	Dec. 22	Baltimore 24	Minnesota 14	Baltimore	60,238
	Dec. 21	Cleveland 31	Dallas 20	Cleveland	81,497
1967	Dec. 24	Dallas 52	Cleveland 14	Dallas	70,786
	Dec. 23	Green Bay 28	Los Angeles 7	Milwaukee	49,861
1965	Dec. 26	*Green Bay 13	Baltimore 10	Green Bay	50,484
1958	Dec. 21	N.Y. Giants 10	Cleveland 0	New York	61,274
1957	Dec. 22	Detroit 31	San Francisco 27	San Francisco	60,118
1952	Dec. 21	Detroit 31	Los Angeles 21	Detroit	47,645
1950	Dec. 17	Los Angeles 24	Chi. Bears 14	Los Angeles	83,501
	Dec. 17	Cleveland 8	N.Y. Giants 3	Cleveland	33,054
1947	Dec. 21	Philadelphia 21	Pittsburgh 0	Pittsburgh	35,729
1943	Dec. 19	Washington 28	N.Y. Giants 0	New York	42,800
1941	Dec. 14	Chi. Bears 33	Green Bay 14	Chicago	43,425

**Sudden death overtime.*

1985 NFC DIVISIONAL PLAYOFFS

Anaheim Stadium, Anaheim, California — January 4, 1986

Attendance: 66,581

LOS ANGELES RAMS 20, DALLAS 0—The NFC Western Division champion Los Angeles Rams combined a stingy defense and a record-breaking effort by running back Eric Dickerson to defeat NFC East champion Dallas 20-0. Dickerson rushed for a playoff-record 248 yards on 34 carries, including touchdown runs of 55 and 40 yards. The Rams' defense had five sacks, including three by defensive end Gary Jeter, and limited the Cowboys to 243 total yards. The Rams held a 3-0 halftime lead on Mike Lansford's 33-yard field goal. Los Angeles took command early in the third quarter with a 10-point outburst on Dickerson's first touchdown run and Lansford's 34-yard field goal. Los Angeles quarterback Dieter Brock was 6 of 22 for 50 yards with one interception. The win advanced the Rams to their first NFC title game since 1979 when they defeated Tampa Bay 9-0.

Dallas	0	0	0	0	— 0
L.A. Rams	3	0	10	7	— 20

Rams—FG Lansford 33
Rams—Dickerson 55 run (Lansford kick)
Rams—FG Lansford 34
Rams—Dickerson 40 run (Lansford kick)

Soldier Field, Chicago, Illinois — January 5, 1986

Attendance: 65,670

CHICAGO 21, NEW YORK GIANTS 0—Once-defeated NFC Central Division champion Chicago shut out the NFC Wild Card survivor New York Giants 21-0. The temperature was 14 degrees at kickoff. Shaun Gayle's five-yard punt return for a touchdown was the only score of the first half. In the second half, Bears quarterback Jim McMahon and wide receiver Dennis McKinnon connected on touchdowns of 23 and 20 yards, while the defense, led by defensive end Richard Dent's 3½ sacks, stymied the Giants' offense. McMahon completed 11 of 21 for 216 yards and two touchdowns. Running back Walter Payton rushed 27 times for 93 yards.

N.Y. Giants	0	0	0	0	— 0
Chicago	7	0	14	0	— 21

Chi– Gayle 5 punt return (Butler kick)
Chi– McKinnon 23 pass from McMahon (Butler kick)
Chi– McKinnon 20 pass from McMahon (Butler kick)

AFC First-Round Playoff Games

RESULTS

Season	Date	Winner	Loser	Site	Attendance
1985	Dec. 28	New England 26	N.Y. Jets 14	East Rutherford	75,945
1984	Dec. 22	Seattle 13	L.A. Raiders 7	Seattle	62,049
1983	Dec. 24	Seattle 31	Denver 7	Seattle	64,275
1982	Jan. 9	N.Y. Jets 44	Cincinnati 17	Cincinnati	57,560
	Jan. 9	San Diego 31	Pittsburgh 28	Pittsburgh	53,546
	Jan. 8	L.A. Raiders 27	Cleveland 10	Los Angeles	56,555
	Jan. 8	Miami 28	New England 13	Miami	68,842
1981	Dec. 27	Buffalo 31	N.Y. Jets 27	New York	57,050
1980	Dec. 28	Oakland 27	Houston 7	Oakland	53,333
1979	Dec. 23	Houston 13	Denver 7	Houston	48,776
1978	Dec. 24	Houston 17	Miami 9	Miami	72,445

1985 AFC FIRST-ROUND PLAYOFF GAME

Giants Stadium, East Rutherford, New Jersey — December 28, 1985

Attendance: 75,945

NEW ENGLAND 26, NEW YORK JETS 14—The Patriots capitalized on four Jets turnovers to spark a 26-14 win for their first postseason victory since 1963. New York led 7-3 before New England scored 20 unanswered points, 17 following Jets' miscues. Safety Fred Marion's 26-yard interception return set up quarterback Tony Eason's 36-yard touchdown pass to wide receiver Stanley Morgan to give the Patriots a 13-7 halftime lead. New England took control of the game by scoring 10 points in a 15-second span of the third quarter. Following Tony Franklin's 20-yard field goal, Johnny Rembert returned Johnny Hector's fumble on the ensuing kickoff 15 yards for a score to give the Patriots a 23-7 lead. Franklin added a 26-yard field goal in the fourth quarter to tie the NFL postseason record of four field goals in a single game held by six others. Franklin's record-tying field goal was set up by defensive end Garin Veris, who intercepted a Pat Ryan pass. Veris also had three sacks. Eason completed 12 of 16 passes for 179 yards and one touchdown.

New England	3	10	10	3	— 26
N.Y. Jets	0	7	7	0	— 14

NE —FG Franklin 33
NYJ—Hector 11 pass from O'Brien (Leahy kick)
NE —FG Franklin 41
NE —Morgan 36 pass from Eason (Franklin kick)
NE —FG Franklin 20
NE —Rembert 15 fumble recovery return (Franklin kick)
NYJ—Shuler 12 pass from Ryan (Leahy kick)
NE —FG Franklin 26

NFC First-Round Playoff Games

RESULTS

Season	Date	Winner	Loser	Site	Attendance
1985	Dec. 29	N.Y. Giants 17	San Francisco 3	East Rutherford	75,131
1984	Dec. 23	N.Y. Giants 16	L.A. Rams 13	Anaheim	67,037
1983	Dec. 26	L.A. Rams 24	Dallas 17	Dallas	62,118
1982	Jan. 9	Dallas 30	Tampa Bay 17	Dallas	65,042
	Jan. 9	Minnesota 30	Atlanta 24	Minnesota	60,560
	Jan. 8	Green Bay 41	St. Louis 16	Green Bay	54,282
	Jan. 8	Washington 31	Detroit 7	Washington	55,045
1981	Dec. 27	N.Y. Giants 27	Philadelphia 21	Philadelphia	71,611
1980	Dec. 28	Dallas 34	Los Angeles 13	Dallas	63,052
1979	Dec. 23	Philadelphia 27	Chicago 17	Philadelphia	69,397
1978	Dec. 24	Atlanta 14	Philadelphia 13	Atlanta	59,403

Giants Stadium, East Rutherford, New Jersey — December 29, 1985

Attendance: 75,131

NEW YORK GIANTS 17, SAN FRANCISCO 3—An opportunistic New York Giants team ousted defending Super Bowl XIX champion San Francisco 17-3. The Giants won the game behind a balanced offense, which gained 174 yards rushing and 181 passing, and a defense that continually pressured 49ers quarterback Joe Montana, sacking him four times. Eric Schubert kicked a 47-yard field goal on New York's first possession. New York rookie tight end Mark Bavaro's 18-yard touchdown catch was set up by safety Terry Kinard's interception that he returned to San Francisco's 38-yard line. Ray Wersching's 21-yard field goal with 22 seconds left in the first half completed a 49ers 16-play, 85-yard drive. New York finished the scoring on its first possession of the third period when quarterback Phil Simms threw to tight end Don Hasselbeck for a 3-yard touchdown. Simms completed 15 of 31 passes for 181 yards with two touchdowns and one interception. Running back Joe Morris paced all rushers with 28 carries for 141 yards. Montana connected on 26 of 47 passes for 296 yards with one interception.

San Francisco	0	3	0	0	— 3
N.Y. Giants	3	7	7	0	— 17

NYG—FG Schubert 47
NYG—Bavaro 18 pass from Simms (Schubert kick)
SF —FG Wersching 21
NYG—Hasselbeck 3 pass from Simms (Schubert kick)

AFC-NFC PRO BOWL SUMMARIES

NFC leads series, 10-6

RESULTS

Year	Date	Winner	Loser	Site	Attendance
1986	Feb. 2	NFC 28	AFC 24	Honolulu	50,101
1985	Jan. 27	AFC 22	NFC 14	Honolulu	50,385
1984	Jan. 29	NFC 45	AFC 3	Honolulu	50,445
1983	Feb. 6	NFC 20	AFC 19	Honolulu	49,883
1982	Jan. 31	AFC 16	NFC 13	Honolulu	50,402
1981	Feb. 1	NFC 21	AFC 7	Honolulu	50,360
1980	Jan. 27	NFC 37	AFC 27	Honolulu	49,800
1979	Jan. 29	NFC 13	AFC 7	Los Angeles	46,281
1978	Jan. 23	NFC 14	AFC 13	Tampa	51,337
1977	Jan. 17	AFC 24	NFC 14	Seattle	64,752
1976	Jan. 26	NFC 23	AFC 20	New Orleans	30,546
1975	Jan. 20	NFC 17	AFC 10	Miami	26,484
1974	Jan. 20	AFC 15	NFC 13	Kansas City	66,918
1973	Jan. 21	AFC 33	NFC 28	Irving	37,091
1972	Jan. 23	AFC 26	NFC 13	Los Angeles	53,647
1971	Jan. 24	NFC 27	AFC 6	Los Angeles	48,222

1986 AFC-NFC PRO BOWL

Aloha Stadium, Honolulu, Hawaii — February 2, 1986

Attendance: 50,101

NFC 28, AFC 24—New York Giants quarterback Phil Simms brought the NFC back from a 24-7 halftime deficit to a 28-24 win over the AFC. Simms, who completed 15 of 27 passes for 212 yards and three touchdowns, was named the most valuable player of the game. The AFC had taken its first-half lead behind a two-yard run by Los Angeles Raiders running back Marcus Allen, who also threw a 51-yard scoring pass to San Diego wide receiver Wes Chandler, an 11-yard touchdown catch by Pittsburgh wide receiver Louis Lipps, and a 34-yard field goal by Steelers kicker Gary Anderson. Minnesota's Joey Browner accounted for the NFC's only score before halftime with a 48-yard touchdown interception return. After intermission, the NFC blanked the AFC while scoring three touchdowns via a 15-yard catch by Washington wide receiver Art Monk, a 2-yard reception by Dallas tight end Doug Cosbie, and a 15-yard catch by Tampa Bay tight end Jimmie Giles with 2:47 remaining in the game. The victory gave the NFC a 10-6 Pro Bowl record vs. the AFC.

NFC (28)	Offense	AFC (24)
Mike Quick (Philadelphia)	WR	Wes Chandler (San Diego)
Jim Covert (Chicago)	LT	Anthony Munoz (Cincinnati)
Kent Hill (L.A. Rams)	LG	John Hannah (New England)
Jay Hilgenberg (Chicago)	C	Dwight Stephenson (Miami)
Russ Grimm (Washington)	RG	Mike Munchak (Houston)
Jackie Slater (L.A. Rams)	RT	Brian Holloway (New England)
Doug Cosbie (Dallas)	TE	Ozzie Newsome (Cleveland)
Art Monk (Washington)	WR	Steve Largent (Seattle)
Phil Simms (N.Y. Giants)	QB	Dan Fouts (San Diego)
Walter Payton (Chicago)	RB	Marcus Allen (L.A. Raiders)
Roger Craig (San Francisco)	RB	Craig James (New England)
	Defense	
Leonard Marshall (N.Y. Giants)	LE	Mark Gastineau (N.Y. Jets)
Randy White (Dallas)	NT	Joe Klecko (N.Y. Jets)
Richard Dent (Chicago)	RE	Howie Long (L.A. Raiders)
Rickey Jackson (New Orleans)	LOLB	Mike Merriweather (Pittsburgh)
Mike Singletary (Chicago)	LILB	Steve Nelson (New England)
Harry Carson (N.Y. Giants)	RILB	Karl Mecklenburg (Denver)
Lawrence Taylor (N.Y. Giants)	ROLB	Andre Tippett (New England)
Everson Walls (Dallas)	LCB	Louis Wright (Denver)
LeRoy Irvin (L.A. Rams)	RCB	Mike Haynes (L.A. Raiders)
Carlton Williamson (San Francisco)	SS	Kenny Easley (Seattle)
Wes Hopkins (Philadelphia)	FS	Deron Cherry (Kansas City)

SUBSTITUTIONS

NFC—Offense: K—Morten Andersen (New Orleans). P—Dale Hatcher (L.A. Rams). QB—Jim McMahon (Chicago). RB—Joe Morris (N.Y. Giants), Gerald Riggs (Atlanta). TE—Jimmie Giles (Tampa Bay). WR—Tony Hill (Dallas), James Lofton (Green Bay). KR—Ron Brown (L.A. Rams). C—Fred Quillan (San Francisco). G—Dennis Harrah (L.A. Rams). T—Joe Jacoby (Washington). Defense: DE—Dan Hampton (Chicago). NT—Michael Carter (San Francisco). LB—Jim Collins (L.A. Rams), E.J. Junior (St. Louis), Otis Wilson (Chicago). CB—Gary Green (L.A. Rams). S—Dave Duerson (Chicago). ST—Joey Browner (Minnesota).

AFC—Offense: K—Gary Anderson (Pittsburgh). P—Rohn Stark (Indianapolis). QB—Ken O'Brien (N.Y. Jets). RB—Kevin Mack (Cleveland), Freeman McNeil (N.Y. Jets). TE—Todd Christensen (L.A. Raiders). WR—Mark Clayton (Miami), Louis Lipps (Pittsburgh). KR—Irving Fryar (New England). C—Mike Webster (Pittsburgh). G—Roy Foster (Miami). T—Chris Hinton (Indianapolis). Defense: DE—Rulon Jones (Denver). NT—Bob Golic (Cleveland). LB—Clay Matthews (Cleveland), Lance Mehl (N.Y. Jets). CB—Raymond Clayborn (New England). S— Fred Marion (New England), Dennis Smith (Denver). ST—Fredd Young (Seattle).

HEAD COACHES

NFC—John Robinson (L.A. Rams)
AFC—Don Shula (Miami)

OFFICIALS

Referee—Bob McElwee. Umpire—Art Demmas. Head Linesman—Earnie Frantz. Line Judge—Howard Roe. Back Judge—Don Wedge. Side Judge—Dave Parry. Field Judge—Ron Spitler.

SCORING

NFC	0	7	7	14	— 28
AFC	7	17	0	0	— 24

AFC—Allen 2 run (Anderson kick)
NFC—Browner 48 interception return (Andersen kick)
AFC—Chandler 51 pass from Allen (Anderson kick)
AFC—FG Anderson 34
AFC—Lipps 11 pass from O'Brien (Anderson kick)
NFC—Monk 15 pass from Simms (Andersen kick)
NFC—Cosbie 2 pass from Simms (Andersen kick)
NFC—Giles 15 pass from Simms (Andersen kick)

TEAM STATISTICS

	NFC	AFC
Total First Downs	18	24
First Downs Rushing	5	5
First Downs Passing	13	18
First Downs Penalty	0	1
Total Net Yardage	272	382
Total Offensive Plays	69	76
Average Gain per Offensive Play	3.9	5.0
Rushes	30	30
Yards Gained Rushing (net)	88	93
Average Yards per Rush	2.9	3.1
Passes Attempted	34	43
Passes Completed	16	25
Had Intercepted	1	4
Times Tackled Attempting to Pass	5	3
Yards Lost Attempting to Pass	35	22
Yards Gained Passing (net)	184	289
Punts	5	5
Average Distance	45.2	46.2
Punt Returns	3	2
Punt Return Yardage	43	3
Kickoff Returns	5	5
Kickoff Return Yardage	108	105
Interception Return Yardage	78	12
Total Return Yardage	229	120
Fumbles	4	1
Own Fumbles Recovered	3	0
Opponents Fumbles Recovered	1	1
Penalties	2	3
Yards Penalized	17	15
Total Points Scored	28	24
Touchdowns	4	3
Touchdowns Rushing	0	1
Touchdowns Passing	3	2
Touchdowns Returns	1	0
Extra Points	4	3
Field Goals	0	1
Field Goals Attempted	1	1
Third Down Efficiency	4/14	9/16
Fourth Down Efficiency	0/1	0/0
Time of Possession	29:07	30:53

INDIVIDUAL STATISTICS

RUSHING

NFC	Att.	Yds.	LG	TD
Morris	8	34	11	0
Craig	8	25	7	0
Riggs	6	17	6	0
Payton	3	14	7	0
McMahon	2	6	6	0
Simms	3	−8	−2	0
AFC	**Att.**	**Yds.**	**LG**	**TD**
Allen	16	58	9	1
McNeil	10	30	8	0
James	1	5	5	0
Mack	1	3	3	0
O'Brien	2	−3	0	0

PASSING

NFC	Att.	Comp.	Yds.	TD	Int.
Simms	27	15	212	3	0
McMahon	6	1	7	0	1
Payton	1	0	0	0	0
AFC	**Att.**	**Comp.**	**Yds.**	**TD**	**Int.**
Fouts	27	16	173	0	3
O'Brien	15	8	87	1	1
Allen	1	1	51	1	0

RECEIVING

NFC	No.	Yds.	LG	TD
Monk	4	61	17	1
Cosbie	4	55	23	1
Giles	3	40	16	1
Lofton	2	35	19	0
Craig	2	21	19	0
Riggs	1	7	7	0
AFC	**No.**	**Yds.**	**LG**	**TD**
Largent	8	82	21	0
Chandler	4	114	51t	1
Clayton	4	46	15	0
Allen	3	13	5	0
Lipps	2	22	11t	1

Christensen	1	13	13	0
Newsome	1	8	8	0
James	1	7	7	0
McNeil	1	6	6	0

INTERCEPTIONS

NFC	**No.**	**Yds.**	**LG**	**TD**
Irvin	2	30	30	0
Browner	1	48	48t	1
Singletary	1	0	0	0
AFC	**No.**	**Yds.**	**LG**	**TD**
Wright	1	12	12	0

PUNTING

NFC	**No.**	**Avg.**	**LG**	**Bk.**
Hatcher	5	45.2	55	0
AFC	**No.**	**Avg.**	**LG**	**Bk.**
Stark	5	46.2	57	0

PUNT RETURNS

NFC	**No.**	**FC**	**Yds.**	**LG**	**TD**
Irvin	3	1	43	16	0
AFC	**No.**	**FC**	**Yds.**	**LG**	**TD**
Fryar	2	1	3	2	0
Marion	0	1	0	0	0

KICKOFF RETURNS

NFC	**No.**	**Yds.**	**LG**	**TD**
Brown	4	93	28	0
Morris	1	15	15	0
AFC	**No.**	**Yds.**	**LG**	**TD**
Cherry	2	39	20	0
Fryar	2	39	20	0
Smith	1	27	27	0

1985 AFC-NFC PRO BOWL

Aloha Stadium, Honolulu, Hawaii January 27, 1985
Attendance: 50,385

AFC 22, NFC 14—Defensive end Art Still of the Kansas City Chiefs recovered a fumble and returned it 83 yards for a touchdown to clinch the AFC's victory over the NFC. Still's touchdown came in the fourth period with the AFC trailing 14-12 and was one of several outstanding defensive plays in a Pro Bowl dominated by two record-breaking defenses. Both teams combined for a Pro Bowl-record 17 sacks, including four by New York Jets defensive end Mark Gastineau, who was named the game's outstanding player. The AFC's first score came on a safety when Gastineau tackled running back Eric Dickerson of the Los Angeles Rams in the end zone. The AFC's second score, a six-yard pass from Miami's Dan Marino to Los Angeles Raiders running back Marcus Allen, was set up by a partial block of a punt by Seahawks linebacker Fredd Young. The NFC leads the series 9-6, since it started in 1971.

AFC	0	9	0	13	— 22
NFC	0	0	7	7	— 14

AFC—Safety, Gastineau tackled Dickerson in end zone
AFC—Allen 6 pass from Marino (Johnson kick)
NFC—Lofton 13 pass from Montana (Stenerud kick)
NFC—Payton 1 run (Stenerud kick)
AFC—FG Johnson 33
AFC—Still 83 fumble recovery return (Johnson kick)
AFC—FG Johnson 22

1984 AFC-NFC PRO BOWL

Aloha Stadium, Honolulu, Hawaii January 29, 1984
Attendance: 50,445

NFC 45, AFC 3—The NFC won its sixth Pro Bowl in the last seven seasons, 45-3 over the AFC. The NFC was led by the passing of most valuable player Joe Theismann of Washington, who completed 21 of 27 passes for 242 yards and three touchdowns. Theismann set Pro Bowl records for completions and touchdown passes. The NFC established Pro Bowl marks for most points scored and fewest points allowed. Running back William Andrews of Atlanta had six carries for 43 yards and caught four passes for 49 yards, including scoring receptions of 16 and 2 yards. Los Angeles Rams rookie Eric Dickerson gained 46 yards on 11 carries, including a 14-yard touchdown run, and had 45 yards on five catches. Rams safety Nolan Cromwell had a 44-yard interception return for a touchdown early in the third period to give the NFC a commanding 24-3 lead. Green Bay wide receiver James Lofton caught an eight-yard touchdown pass, while tight end teammate Paul Coffman had a six-yard scoring catch.

NFC	3	14	14	14	— 45
AFC	0	3	0	0	— 3

NFC—FG Haji-Sheikh 23
NFC—Andrews 16 pass from Theismann (Haji-Sheikh kick)
NFC—Andrews 2 pass from Montana (Haji-Sheikh kick)
AFC—FG Anderson 43
NFC—Cromwell 44 interception return (Haji-Sheikh kick)
NFC—Lofton 8 pass from Theismann (Haji-Sheikh kick)
NFC—Coffman 6 pass from Theismann (Haji-Sheikh kick)
NFC—Dickerson 14 run (Haji-Sheikh kick)

1983 AFC-NFC PRO BOWL

Aloha Stadium, Honolulu, Hawaii Sunday, February 6, 1983
Attendance: 49,883

NFC 20, AFC 19—Danny White threw an 11-yard touchdown pass to John Jefferson with 35 seconds remaining to give the NFC a 20-19 victory over the AFC. White, who completed 14 of 26 passes for 162 yards, kept the winning 65-yard drive alive with a 14-yard completion to Jefferson on a fourth-and-seven play at the AFC 25. The AFC was ahead 12-10 at halftime and increased the lead to 19-10 in the third period, when Marcus Allen scored on a one-yard run. Dan Fouts, who attempted 30 passes, set Pro Bowl records for most completions (17) and yards (274). John Stallworth was the AFC's leading receiver with seven catches for 67 yards. William Andrews topped the NFC with five receptions for 48 yards. Fouts and Jefferson were voted co-winners of the player of the game award.

AFC	9	3	7	0	— 19
NFC	0	10	0	10	— 20

AFC—Walker 34 pass from Fouts (Benirschke kick)
AFC—Safety, Still tackled Theismann in end zone
NFC—Andrews 3 run (Moseley kick)
NFC—FG Moseley 35
AFC—FG Benirschke 29
AFC—Allen 1 run (Benirschke kick)
NFC—FG Moseley 41
NFC—Jefferson 11 pass from D. White (Moseley kick)

1982 AFC-NFC PRO BOWL

Aloha Stadium, Honolulu, Hawaii Sunday, January 31, 1982
Attendance: 50,402

AFC 16, NFC 13—Nick Lowery kicked a 23-yard field goal with three seconds remaining to give the AFC a 16-13 victory over the NFC. Lowery's kick climaxed a 69-yard drive directed by quarterback Dan Fouts. The NFC gained a 13-13 tie with 2:43 to go when Tony Dorsett ran four yards for a touchdown. In the drive to the game-winning field goal, Fouts completed three passes, including a 23-yarder to San Diego teammate Kellen Winslow that put the ball on the NFC's 5 yard line. Two plays later, Lowery kicked the field goal. Winslow, who caught six passes for 86 yards, was named co-player of the game along with NFC defensive end Lee Roy Selmon.

NFC	0	6	0	7	— 13
AFC	0	0	13	3	— 16

NFC—Giles 4 pass from Montana (kick blocked)
AFC—Muncie 2 run (kick failed)
AFC—Campbell 1 run (Lowery kick)
NFC—Dorsett 4 run (Septien kick)
AFC—FG Lowery 23

1981 AFC-NFC PRO BOWL

Aloha Stadium, Honolulu, Hawaii February 1, 1981
Attendance: 50,360

NFC 21, AFC 7—Ed Murray kicked four field goals and Steve Bartkowski fired a 55-yard scoring pass to Alfred Jenkins to lead the NFC to its fourth straight victory over the AFC and a 7-4 edge in the series. Murray was named the game's most valuable player and missed tying Garo Yepremian's Pro Bowl record of five goals when a 37-yard attempt hit the crossbar with 22 seconds remaining. The AFC's only score came on a nine-yard pass from Brian Sipe to Stanley Morgan in the second period. Bartkowski completed 9 of 21 passes for 173 yards, while Sipe connected on 10 of 15 for 142 yards. Ottis Anderson led all rushers with 70 yards on 10 carries. Earl Campbell, the NFL's leading rusher in 1980, was limited to 24 yards on eight attempts.

AFC	0	7	0	0	— 7
NFC	3	6	0	12	— 21

NFC—FG Murray 31
AFC—Morgan 9 pass from Sipe (J. Smith kick)
NFC—FG Murray 31
NFC—FG Murray 34
NFC—Jenkins 55 pass from Bartkowski (Murray kick)
NFC—FG Murray 36
NFC—Safety (Team)

1980 AFC-NFC PRO BOWL

Aloha Stadium, Honolulu, Hawaii January 27, 1980
Attendance: 49,800

NFC 37, AFC 27—Running back Chuck Muncie ran for two touchdowns and threw a 25-yard option pass for another score to give the NFC its third consecutive victory over the AFC. Muncie, who was selected the game's most valuable player, snapped a 3-3 tie on a one-yard touchdown run at 1:41 of the second quarter, then scored on an 11-yard run in the fourth quarter for the NFC's final touchdown. Two scoring records were set in the game—37 points by the NFC, eclipsing the 33 by the AFC in 1973, and the 64 points by both teams, surpassing the 61 scored in 1973.

NFC	3	20	7	7	— 37
AFC	3	7	10	7	— 27

NFC—FG Moseley 37
AFC—FG Fritsch 19
NFC—Muncie 1 run (Moseley kick)
AFC—Pruitt 1 pass from Bradshaw (Fritsch kick)
NFC—D. Hill 13 pass from Manning (kick failed)
NFC—T. Hill 25 pass from Muncie (Moseley kick)
NFC—Henry 86 punt return (Moseley kick)
AFC—Campbell 2 run (Fritsch kick)
AFC—FG Fritsch 29
NFC—Muncie 11 run (Moseley kick)
AFC—Campbell 1 run (Fritsch kick)

1979 AFC-NFC PRO BOWL

Memorial Coliseum, Los Angeles, California — January 29, 1979

Attendance: 46,281

NFC 13, AFC 7—Roger Staubach completed 9 of 15 passes for 125 yards, including the winning touchdown on a 19-yard strike to Dallas Cowboys teammate Tony Hill in the third period. The winning drive began at the AFC's 45 yard line after a shanked punt. Staubach hit Ahmad Rashad with passes of 15 and 17 yards to set up Hill's decisive catch. The victory gave the NFC a 5-4 advantage in Pro Bowl games. Rashad, who accounted for 89 yards on five receptions, was named the player of the game. The AFC led 7-6 at halftime on Bob Griese's eight-yard scoring toss to Steve Largent late in the second quarter. Largent finished the game with five receptions for 75 yards. The NFC scored first as Archie Manning marched his team 70 yards in 11 plays, capped by Wilbert Montgomery's two-yard touchdown run. The AFC's Earl Campbell was the game's leading rusher with 66 yards on 12 carries.

AFC	0	7	0	0	— 7
NFC	0	6	7	0	— 13

NFC—Montgomery 2 run (kick failed)
AFC—Largent 8 pass from Griese (Yepremian kick)
NFC—T. Hill 19 pass from Staubach (Corral kick)

1978 AFC-NFC PRO BOWL

Tampa Stadium, Tampa, Florida — January 23, 1978

Attendance: 51,337

NFC 14, AFC 13—Walter Payton, the NFL's leading rusher in 1977, sparked a second-half comeback to give the NFC a 14-13 win and tie the series between the two conferences at four victories each. Payton, who was the game's most valuable player, gained 77 yards on 13 carries and scored the tying touchdown on a one-yard burst with 7:37 left in the game. Efren Herrera kicked the winning extra point. The AFC dominated the first half of the game, taking a 13-0 lead on field goals of 21 and 39 yards by Toni Linhart and a 10-yard touchdown pass from Ken Stabler to Oakland teammate Cliff Branch. On the NFC's first possession of the second half, Pat Haden put together the first touchdown drive after Eddie Brown returned Ray Guy's punt to the AFC 46 yard line. Haden connected on all four of his passes on that drive, finally hitting Terry Metcalf with a four-yard scoring toss. The NFC continued to rally and, with Jim Hart at quarterback, moved 63 yards in 12 plays for the go-ahead score. During the winning drive, Hart completed five of six passes for 38 yards and Payton picked up 20 more on the ground.

AFC	3	10	0	0	— 13
NFC	0	0	7	7	— 14

AFC—FG Linhart 21
AFC—Branch 10 pass from Stabler (Linhart kick)
AFC—FG Linhart 39
NFC—Metcalf 4 pass from Haden (Herrera kick)
NFC—Payton 1 run (Herrera kick)

1977 AFC-NFC PRO BOWL

Kingdome, Seattle, Washington — January 17, 1977

Attendance: 64,752

AFC 24, NFC 14—O. J. Simpson's three-yard touchdown burst at 7:03 of the first quarter gave the AFC a lead it would not surrender, the victory breaking a two-game NFC win streak and giving the American Conference stars a 4-3 series lead. The AFC took a 17-7 lead midway through the second period on the first of two Ken Anderson touchdown passes, a 12-yarder to Charlie Joiner. But the NFC mounted a 73-yard drive capped by Lawrence McCutcheon's one-yard touchdown plunge to pull within three of the AFC, 17-14, at the half. Following a scoreless third quarter, player of the game Mel Blount thwarted a possible NFC score when he intercepted Jim Hart's pass in the end zone. Less than three minutes later, Blount again picked off a Hart pass, returning it 16 yards to the NFC 27. That set up Anderson's 27-yard touchdown strike to Cliff Branch for the final score.

NFC	0	14	0	0	— 14
AFC	10	7	0	7	— 24

AFC—Simpson 3 run (Linhart kick)
AFC—FG Linhart 31
NFC—Thomas 15 run (Bakken kick)
AFC—Joiner 12 pass from Anderson (Linhart kick)
NFC—McCutcheon 1 run (Bakken kick)
AFC—Branch 27 pass from Anderson (Linhart kick)

1976 AFC-NFC PRO BOWL

Superdome, New Orleans, Louisiana — January 26, 1976

Attendance: 30,546

NFC 23, AFC 20—Mike Boryla, a late substitute who did not enter the game until 5:39 remained, lifted the National Football Conference to a 23-20 victory over the American Football Conference with two touchdown passes in the final minutes. It was the second straight NFC win, squaring the series at 3-3. Until Boryla started firing the ball the AFC was in control, leading 13-0 at the half. Boryla entered the game after Billy Johnson had raced 90 yards with a punt to make the score 20-9 in favor of the AFC. He floated a 14-yard pass to Terry Metcalf and later fired an eight-yarder to Mel Gray for the winner.

AFC	0	13	0	7	— 20
NFC	0	0	9	14	— 23

AFC—FG Stenerud 20
AFC—FG Stenerud 35
AFC—Burrough 64 pass from Pastorini (Stenerud kick)
NFC—FG Bakken 42
NFC—Foreman 4 pass from Hart (kick blocked)
AFC—Johnson 90 punt return (Stenerud kick)
NFC—Metcalf 14 pass from Boryla (Bakken kick)
NFC—Gray 8 pass from Boryla (Bakken kick)

1975 AFC-NFC PRO BOWL

Orange Bowl, Miami, Florida — January 20, 1975

Attendance: 26,484

NFC 17, AFC 10—Los Angeles quarterback James Harris, who took over the NFC offense after Jim Hart of St. Louis suffered a laceration above his right eye in the second period, threw a pair of touchdown passes early in the fourth period to pace the NFC to its second victory in the five-game Pro Bowl series. The NFC win snapped a three-game AFC victory string. Harris, who was named the player of the game, connected with St. Louis's Mel Gray for an eight-yard touchdown 2:03 into the final period. One minute and 24 seconds later, following a recovery by Washington's Ken Houston of a fumble by Franco Harris of Pittsburgh, Harris tossed another eight-yard scoring pass to Washington's Charley Taylor for the decisive points.

NFC	0	3	0	14	— 17
AFC	0	0	10	0	— 10

NFC—FG Marcol 33
AFC—Warfield 32 pass from Griese (Gerela kick)
AFC—FG Gerela 33
NFC—Gray 8 pass from J. Harris (Marcol kick)
NFC—Taylor 8 pass from J. Harris (Marcol kick)

1974 AFC-NFC PRO BOWL

Arrowhead Stadium, Kansas City, Missouri — January 20, 1974

Attendance: 66,918

AFC 15, NFC 13—Miami's Garo Yepremian kicked his fifth consecutive field goal without a miss from the 42 yard line with 21 seconds remaining to give the AFC its third straight victory since the NFC won the inaugural game following the 1970 season. The field goal by Yepremian, who was voted the game's outstanding player, offset a 21-yard field goal by Atlanta's Nick Mike-Mayer that had given the NFC a 13-12 advantage with 1:41 remaining. The only touchdown in the game was scored by the NFC on a 14-yard pass from Roman Gabriel to Lawrence McCutcheon.

NFC	0	10	0	3	— 13
AFC	3	3	3	6	— 15

AFC—FG Yepremian 16
NFC—FG Mike-Mayer 27
NFC—McCutcheon 14 pass from Gabriel (Mike-Mayer kick)
AFC—FG Yepremian 37
AFC—FG Yepremian 27
AFC—FG Yepremian 41
NFC—FG Mike-Mayer 21
AFC—FG Yepremian 42

1973 AFC-NFC PRO BOWL

Texas Stadium, Irving, Texas — January 21, 1973

Attendance: 37,091

AFC 33, NFC 28—Paced by the rushing and receiving of player of the game O.J. Simpson, the AFC erased a 14-0 first period deficit and built a commanding 33-14 lead midway through the fourth period before the NFC managed two touchdowns in the final minute of play. Simpson rushed for 112 yards and caught three passes for 58 more to gain unanimous recognition in the balloting for player of the game. John Brockington scored three touchdowns for the NFC.

AFC	0	10	10	13	— 33
NFC	14	0	0	14	— 28

NFC—Brockington 1 run (Marcol kick)
NFC—Brockington 3 pass from Kilmer (Marcol kick)
AFC—Simpson 7 run (Gerela kick)
AFC—FG Gerela 18
AFC—FG Gerela 22
AFC—Hubbard 11 run (Gerela kick)
AFC—O. Taylor 5 pass from Lamonica (kick failed)
AFC—Bell 12 interception return (Gerela kick)
NFC—Brockington 1 run (Marcol kick)
NFC—Kwalick 12 pass from Snead (Marcol kick)

1972 AFC-NFC PRO BOWL

Memorial Coliseum, Los Angeles, California — January 23, 1972

Attendance: 53,647

AFC 26, NFC 13—Four field goals by Jan Stenerud of Kansas City, including a 6-6 tie-breaker from 48 yards, helped lift the AFC from a 6-0 deficit to a 19-6 advantage early in the fourth period. The AFC defense picked off three interceptions. Stenerud was selected as the outstanding offensive player and his Kansas City teammate, linebacker Willie Lanier, was the game's outstanding defensive player.

AFC	0	3	13	10	— 26
NFC	0	6	0	7	— 13

NFC—Grim 50 pass from Landry (kick failed)
AFC—FG Stenerud 25
AFC—FG Stenerud 23
AFC—FG Stenerud 48
AFC—Morin 5 pass from Dawson (Stenerud kick)
AFC—FG Stenerud 42
NFC—V. Washington 2 run (Knight kick)
AFC—F. Little 6 run (Stenerud kick)

1971 AFC-NFC PRO BOWL

Memorial Coliseum, Los Angeles, California — January 24, 1971

Attendance: 48,222

NFC 27, AFC 6—Mel Renfro of Dallas broke open the first meeting between the American Football Conference and National Football Conference all-pro teams as he returned a pair of punts 82 and 56 yards for touchdowns in the final period to provide the NFC with a 27-6 victory over the AFC. Renfro was voted the game's outstanding back and linebacker Fred Carr of Green Bay the outstanding lineman.

AFC	0	3	3	0	— 6
NFC	0	3	10	14	— 27

AFC—FG Stenerud 37
NFC—FG Cox 13
NFC—Osborn 23 pass from Brodie (Cox kick)
NFC—FG Cox 35
AFC—FG Stenerud 16
NFC—Renfro 82 punt return (Cox kick)
NFC—Renfro 56 punt return (Cox kick)

Regular Season Interconference Records, 1970-1985

American Football Conference

Eastern Division	W	L	T	Pct.
Miami	43	9	0	.827
New England	23	28	0	.451
Indianapolis	20	25	1	.446
New York Jets	22	28	0	.440
Buffalo	18	30	1	.378
Central Division				
Pittsburgh	34	17	0	.667
Cincinnati	31	21	0	.596
Cleveland	26	27	0	.491
Houston	18	34	1	.349
Western Division				
Los Angeles Raiders	40	13	1	.750
Seattle	16	12	0	.571
Denver	30	25	1	.545
San Diego	25	24	0	.510
Kansas City	19	24	2	.444

National Football Conference

Eastern Division	W	L	T	Pct.
Dallas	38	15	0	.717
Washington	29	21	0	.580
Philadelphia	28	21	0	.571
St. Louis	23	23	2	.500
New York Giants	18	25	0	.419
Central Division				
Minnesota	27	26	0	.509
Detroit	22	27	1	.450
Chicago	19	32	0	.373
Green Bay	17	33	2	.346
Tampa Bay	9	17	0	.346
Western Division				
Los Angeles Rams	31	23	0	.574
San Francisco	26	29	0	.473
Atlanta	19	34	0	.358
New Orleans	11	39	2	.231

Interconference Victories, 1970-1985

Regular Season

	AFC	NFC	Tie
1970	12	27	1
1971	15	23	2
1972	20	19	1
1973	19	19	2
1974	23	17	0
1975	23	17	0
1976	16	12	0
1977	19	9	0
1978	31	21	0
1979	36	16	0
1980	33	19	0
1981	24	28	0
1982	15	14	1
1983	26	26	0
1984	26	26	0
1985	27	25	0
Total	365	318	7

Preseason

	AFC	NFC	Tie
1970	21	28	1
1971	28	28	3
1972	27	25	4
1973	23	35	2
1974	35	25	0
1975	30	26	1
1976	30	31	0
1977	38	25	0
1978	20	19	0
1979	25	18	0
1980	22	20	1
1981	18	19	0
1982	25	16	0
1983	15	24	0
1984	16	19	0
1985	10	22	1
Total	383	380	13

AFC VS. NFC (REGULAR SEASON), 1970-1985

	1970	1971	1972	1973	1974	1975	1976	1977	1978	1979	1980	1981	1982	1983	1984	1985	Totals
Miami	2-1	3-0	3-0	3-0	2-1	3-0	0-2	2-0	3-1	4-0	4-0	3-1	1-1	3-1	4-0	3-1	43-9
L.A. Raiders	1-2	1-1-1	3-0	2-1	3-0	3-0	3-0	1-1	4-0	4-0	2-2	2-2	3-0	2-2	3-1	3-1	40-13-1
Pittsburgh	0-3	1-2	2-1	3-0	3-0	2-1	1-1	2-0	3-1	3-1	4-0	3-1	1-0	2-2	3-1	1-3	34-17
Cincinnati	1-2	1-2	2-1	2-1	2-1	3-0	2-0	2-1	2-2	2-2	2-2	2-2	1-0	3-1	2-2	2-2	31-21
Denver	2-2	1-3	1-3	0-3-1	2-2	2-1	2-0	1-1	2-2	3-1	3-1	3-1	2-1	0-2	3-1	3-1	30-25-1
Cleveland	0-3	2-1	1-2	1-2	1-2	1-3	2-0	1-1	4-0	3-1	3-1	3-1	0-2	2-2	1-3	1-3	26-27
San Diego	1-2	2-1	0-3	1-2	1-2	0-3	2-0	1-1	2-2	3-1	2-2	2-2	1-0	2-2	4-0	1-1	25-24
New England	0-3	0-3	3-0	2-1	3-0	1-2	1-1	2-0	2-2	3-1	1-3	0-4	0-1	2-2	0-4	3-1	23-28
N.Y. Jets	2-1	0-3	1-2	0-3	2-1	0-3	0-2	1-1	1-3	3-1	1-3	2-0	4-0	3-1	0-2	2-2	22-28
Indianapolis	3-0	2-1	0-3	2-1	1-2	2-1	0-2	1-1	2-2	1-1	1-1	0-4	0-1-1	2-0	0-4	3-1	20-25-1
Kansas City	0-2-1	2-1	2-1	1-1-1	1-2	2-1	1-1	1-1	0-2	0-2	2-0	2-2	0-3	2-2	1-1	2-2	19-24-2
Buffalo	0-3	0-3	2-0-1	2-1	2-1	1-2	0-2	1-1	1-1	2-2	3-1	1-3	1-2	1-3	1-3	0-2	18-30-1
Houston	0-3	0-2-1	0-3	0-3	0-3	3-0	2-0	2-0	2-2	2-2	4-0	1-3	0-3	1-3	0-4	1-3	18-34-1
Seattle								1-0	3-1	3-1	1-3	0-2	1-0	1-3	4-0	2-2	16-12
Tampa Bay							0-1										0-1
TOTALS	12-27-1	15-23-2	20-19-1	19-19-2	23-17	23-17	16-12	19-9	31-21	36-16	33-19	24-28	15-14-1	26-26	26-26	27-25	365-318-7

NFC VS. AFC (REGULAR SEASON), 1970-1985

	1970	1971	1972	1973	1974	1975	1976	1977	1978	1979	1980	1981	1982	1983	1984	1985	Totals
Dallas	3-0	3-0	3-0	2-1	2-1	2-1	2-0	1-1	3-1	1-3	3-1	4-0	2-1	2-2	2-2	3-1	38-15
L.A. Rams	2-1	1-2	1-2	3-0	3-1	3-0	1-1	2-0	2-2	2-2	2-2	1-3	1-2	1-3	3-1	3-1	31-23
Washington	2-1	1-2	1-2	2-1	2-1	1-2	1-1	1-1	2-2	2-2	1-3	2-2		4-0	3-1	4-0	29-21
Philadelphia	2-1	1-2	2-1	2-1	2-1	0-3	0-2	1-1	3-1	2-2	3-1	3-1	2-1	1-1	3-1	1-1	28-21
Minnesota	2-1	2-1	1-2	2-1	2-1	4-0	2-0	1-1	1-3	1-3	1-3	1-3	1-3	4-0	0-4	2-0	27-26
San Francisco	4-0	2-1	2-1	1-2	0-3	1-2	1-1	0-2	1-3	0-4	2-2	3-1	1-3	2-2	3-1	3-1	26-29
St. Louis	2-0-1	2-1	1-2	0-2-1	2-1	2-1	1-1	0-2	0-4	1-3	1-1	3-1		3-1	3-1	2-2	23-23-2
Detroit	3-0	4-0	2-0-1	0-3	1-2	1-2	2-0	2-0	2-2	0-4	0-2	2-2	0-1	1-3	0-4	2-2	22-27-1
Chicago	1-2	1-2	1-2	2-2	0-3	0-3	0-2	1-1	0-4	2-2	0-4	4-0	1-1	1-1	2-2	3-1	19-32
Atlanta	1-2	3-0	2-2	2-1	0-3	1-2	0-2	0-2	1-3	1-3	2-2	1-3	1-1	3-1	1-3	0-4	19-34
N.Y. Giants	3-0	1-2	1-2	1-2	1-2	2-1	0-2	0-2	1-1	1-1	1-3	1-1	1-0	0-4	2-0	2-2	18-25
Green Bay	2-1	2-1	2-1	1-1-1	2-1	0-3	0-2	0-3	2-2	1-3	1-3	1-1	1-1-1	2-2	0-4	0-4	17-33-2
New Orleans	0-3	0-1-2	0-3	1-2	0-3	0-3	1-2	0-2	1-3	0-4	1-3	2-2	1-0	1-3	3-1	0-4	11-39-2
Tampa Bay								0-1	2-0	2-0	1-3	0-4	2-1	1-3	1-1	0-4	9-17
Seattle							1-0										1-0
TOTALS	27-12-1	23-15-2	19-20-1	19-19-2	17-23	17-23	12-16	9-19	21-31	16-36	19-33	28-24	14-15-1	26-26	26-26	25-27	318-365-7

1985 Interconference Games

(Home Team in capital letters)

AFC 27, NFC 25

AFC Victories

Kansas City 47, NEW ORLEANS 27
NEW ENGLAND 26, Green Bay 20
DENVER 34, New Orleans 23
Denver 44, ATLANTA 28
INDIANAPOLIS 14, Detroit 6
N.Y. Jets 24, GREEN BAY 3
CINCINNATI 35, N.Y. Giants 30
L.A. RAIDERS 23, New Orleans 13
SEATTLE 30, Atlanta 26
PITTSBURGH 23, St. Louis 10
MIAMI 41, Tampa Bay 38
Houston 20, ST. LOUIS 10
INDIANAPOLIS 37, Green Bay 10
New England 32, TAMPA BAY 14
Seattle 27, NEW ORLEANS 3
DENVER 17, San Francisco 16
N.Y. JETS 62, Tampa Bay 28
Cleveland 35, N.Y. GIANTS 33
L.A. Raiders 34, ATLANTA 24
MIAMI 38, Chicago 24
CINCINNATI 50, Dallas 24
KANSAS CITY 38, Atlanta 10
Miami 34, GREEN BAY 24
NEW ENGLAND 23, Detroit 6
Indianapolis 31, TAMPA BAY 23
SAN DIEGO 20, Philadelphia 14
L.A. Raiders 16, L.A. RAMS 6

NFC Victories

L.A. RAMS 20, Denver 16
St. Louis 27, CLEVELAND 24
CHICAGO 20, New England 7
ST. LOUIS 41, Cincinnati 27
WASHINGTON 16, Houston 13
DALLAS 20, Cleveland 7
San Francisco 34, L.A. RAIDERS 10
L.A. Rams 35, SEATTLE 24
Dallas 17, HOUSTON 10
Minnesota 27, BUFFALO 20
DALLAS 27, Pittsburgh 13
L.A. Rams 16, KANSAS CITY 10
MINNESOTA 21, San Diego 17
DETROIT 31, Miami 21
PHILADELPHIA 21, Buffalo 17
Washington 14, CLEVELAND 7
SAN FRANCISCO 31, Kansas City 3
Washington 30, PITTSBURGH 23
SAN FRANCISCO 19, Seattle 6
DETROIT 31, N.Y. Jets 20
CHICAGO 17, Indianapolis 10
N.Y. Giants 35, HOUSTON 14
Chicago 19, N.Y. JETS 6
WASHINGTON 27, Cincinnati 24
N.Y. GIANTS 28, Pittsburgh 10

Monday Night Football, 1970–1985

(Home Team in capitals, games listed in chronological order.)

1985
DALLAS 44, Washington 14
CLEVELAND 17, Pittsburgh 7
Los Angeles Rams 35, SEATTLE 24
Cincinnati 37, PITTSBURGH 24
WASHINGTON 27, St. Louis 10
NEW YORK JETS 23, Miami 7
CHICAGO 23, Green Bay 7
LOS ANGELES RAIDERS 34, San Diego 21
ST. LOUIS 21, Dallas 10
DENVER 17, San Francisco 16
WASHINGTON 23, New York Giants 21
SAN FRANCISCO 19, Seattle 6
MIAMI 38, Chicago 24
Los Angeles Rams 27, SAN FRANCISCO 20
MIAMI 30, New England 27
L.A. Raiders 16, L.A. RAMS 6

1984
Dallas 20, LOS ANGELES RAMS 13
SAN FRANCISCO 37, Washington 31
Miami 21, BUFFALO 17
LOS ANGELES RAIDERS 33, San Diego 30
PITTSBURGH 38, Cincinnati 17
San Francisco 31, NEW YORK GIANTS 10
DENVER 17, Green Bay 14
Los Angeles Rams 24, ATLANTA 10
Seattle 24, SAN DIEGO 0
WASHINGTON 27, Atlanta 14
SEATTLE 17, Los Angeles Raiders 14
NEW ORLEANS 27, Pittsburgh 24
MIAMI 28, New York Jets 17
SAN DIEGO 20, Chicago 7
Los Angeles Raiders 24, DETROIT 3
MIAMI 28, Dallas 21

1983
Dallas 31, WASHINGTON 30
San Diego 17, KANSAS CITY 14
LOS ANGELES RAIDERS 27, Miami 14
NEW YORK GIANTS 27, Green Bay 3
New York Jets 34, BUFFALO 10
Pittsburgh 24, CINCINNATI 14
GREEN BAY 48, Washington 47
ST. LOUIS 20, New York Giants 20 (OT)
Washington 27, SAN DIEGO 24
DETROIT 15, New York Giants 9
Los Angeles Rams 36, ATLANTA 13
New York Jets 31, NEW ORLEANS 28
MIAMI 38, Cincinnati 14
DETROIT 13, Minnesota 2
Green Bay 12, TAMPA BAY 9 (OT)
SAN FRANCISCO 42, Dallas 17

1982
Pittsburgh 36, DALLAS 28
Green Bay 27, NEW YORK GIANTS 19
LOS ANGELES RAIDERS 28, San Diego 24
TAMPA BAY 23, Miami 17
New York Jets 28, DETROIT 13
Dallas 37, HOUSTON 7
SAN DIEGO 50, Cincinnati 34
MIAMI 27, Buffalo 10
MINNESOTA 31, Dallas 27

1981
San Diego 44, CLEVELAND 14
Oakland 36, MINNESOTA 10
Dallas 35, NEW ENGLAND 21
Los Angeles 24, CHICAGO 7
PHILADELPHIA 16, Atlanta 13
BUFFALO 31, Miami 21
DETROIT 48, Chicago 17
PITTSBURGH 26, Houston 13
DENVER 19, Minnesota 17
DALLAS 27, Buffalo 14
SEATTLE 44, San Diego 23
ATLANTA 31, Minnesota 30
MIAMI 13, Philadelphia 10
OAKLAND 30, Pittsburgh 27
LOS ANGELES 21, Atlanta 16
SAN DIEGO 23, Oakland 10

1980
Dallas 17, WASHINGTON 3
Houston 16, CLEVELAND 7
PHILADELPHIA 35, New York Giants 3
NEW ENGLAND 23, Denver 14
CHICAGO 23, Tampa Bay 0
DENVER 20, Washington 17
Oakland 45, PITTSBURGH 34
NEW YORK JETS 17, Miami 14
CLEVELAND 27, Chicago 21
HOUSTON 38, New England 34
Oakland 19, SEATTLE 17
Los Angeles 27, NEW ORLEANS 7
OAKLAND 9, Denver 3
MIAMI 16, New England 13 (OT)
LOS ANGELES 38, Dallas 14
SAN DIEGO 26, Pittsburgh 17

1979
Pittsburgh 16, NEW ENGLAND 13 (OT)
Atlanta 14, PHILADELPHIA 10
WASHINGTON 27, New York Giants 0
CLEVELAND 26, Dallas 7
GREEN BAY 27, New England 14
OAKLAND 13, Miami 3
NEW YORK JETS 14, Minnesota 7
PITTSBURGH 42, Denver 7
Seattle 31, ATLANTA 28
Houston 9, MIAMI 6
Philadelphia 31, DALLAS 21
LOS ANGELES 20, Atlanta 14
SEATTLE 30, New York Jets 7
Oakland 42, NEW ORLEANS 35
HOUSTON 20, Pittsburgh 17
SAN DIEGO 17, Denver 7

1978
DALLAS 38, Baltimore 0
MINNESOTA 12, Denver 9 (OT)
Baltimore 34, NEW ENGLAND 27
Minnesota 24, CHICAGO 20
WASHINGTON 9, Dallas 5
MIAMI 21, Cincinnati 0
DENVER 16, Chicago 7
Houston 24, PITTSBURGH 17
ATLANTA 15, Los Angeles 7
BALTIMORE 21, Washington 17
Oakland 34, CINCINNATI 21
HOUSTON 35, Miami 30
Pittsburgh 24, SAN FRANCISCO 7
SAN DIEGO 40, Chicago 7
Cincinnati 20, LOS ANGELES 19
MIAMI 23, New England 3

1977
PITTSBURGH 27, San Francisco 0
CLEVELAND 30, New England 27 (OT)
Oakland 37, KANSAS CITY 28
CHICAGO 24, Los Angeles 23
PITTSBURGH 20, Cincinnati 14
LOS ANGELES 35, Minnesota 3
ST. LOUIS 28, New York Giants 0
BALTIMORE 10, Washington 3
St. Louis 24, DALLAS 17
WASHINGTON 10, Green Bay 9
OAKLAND 34, Buffalo 13
MIAMI 16, Baltimore 6
Dallas 42, SAN FRANCISCO 35

1976
Miami 30, BUFFALO 21
Oakland 24, KANSAS CITY 21
Washington 20, PHILADELPHIA 17 (OT)
MINNESOTA 17, Pittsburgh 6
San Francisco 16, LOS ANGELES 0
NEW ENGLAND 41, New York Jets 7
WASHINGTON 20, St. Louis 10
BALTIMORE 38, Houston 14
CINCINNATI 20, Los Angeles 12
DALLAS 17, Buffalo 10
Baltimore 17, MIAMI 16
SAN FRANCISCO 20, Minnesota 16
OAKLAND 35, Cincinnati 20

1975
Oakland 31, MIAMI 21
DENVER 23, Green Bay 13
Dallas 36, DETROIT 10
WASHINGTON 27, St. Louis 17
New York Giants 17, BUFFALO 14
Minnesota 13, CHICAGO 9
Los Angeles 42, PHILADELPHIA 3
Kansas City 34, DALLAS 31
CINCINNATI 33, Buffalo 24
Pittsburgh 32, HOUSTON 9
MIAMI 20, New England 7
OAKLAND 17, Denver 10
SAN DIEGO 24, New York Jets 16

1974
BUFFALO 21, Oakland 20
PHILADELPHIA 13, Dallas 10
WASHINGTON 30, Denver 3
MIAMI 21, New York Jets 17
DETROIT 17, San Francisco 13
CHICAGO 10, Green Bay 9
PITTSBURGH 24, Atlanta 17
Los Angeles 15, SAN FRANCISCO 13
Minnesota 28, ST. LOUIS 24
Kansas City 42, DENVER 34
Pittsburgh 28, NEW ORLEANS 7
MIAMI 24, Cincinnati 3
Washington 23, LOS ANGELES 17

1973
GREEN BAY 23, New York Jets 7
DALLAS 40, New Orleans 3
DETROIT 31, Atlanta 6
WASHINGTON 14, Dallas 7
Miami 17, CLEVELAND 9
DENVER 23, Oakland 23
BUFFALO 23, Kansas City 14
PITTSBURGH 21, Washington 16
KANSAS CITY 19, Chicago 7
ATLANTA 20, Minnesota 14
SAN FRANCISCO 20, Green Bay 6
MIAMI 30, Pittsburgh 26
LOS ANGELES 40, New York Giants 6

1972
Washington 24, MINNESOTA 21
Kansas City 20, NEW ORLEANS 17
New York Giants 27, PHILADELPHIA 12
Oakland 34, HOUSTON 0
Green Bay 24, DETROIT 23
CHICAGO 13, Minnesota 10
DALLAS 28, Detroit 24
Baltimore 24, NEW ENGLAND 17
Cleveland 21, SAN DIEGO 17
WASHINGTON 24, Atlanta 13
MIAMI 31, St. Louis 10
Los Angeles 26, SAN FRANCISCO 16
OAKLAND 24, New York Jets 16

1971
Minnesota 16, DETROIT 13
ST. LOUIS 17, New York Jets 10
Oakland 34, CLEVELAND 20
DALLAS 20, New York Giants 13
KANSAS CITY 38, Pittsburgh 16
MINNESOTA 10, Baltimore 3
GREEN BAY 14, Detroit 14
BALTIMORE 24, Los Angeles 17
SAN DIEGO 20, St. Louis 17
ATLANTA 28, Green Bay 21
MIAMI 34, Chicago 3
Kansas City 26, SAN FRANCISCO 17
Washington 38, LOS ANGELES 24

1970
CLEVELAND 31, New York Jets 21
Kansas City 44, BALTIMORE 24
DETROIT 28, Chicago 14
Green Bay 22, SAN DIEGO 20
OAKLAND 34, Washington 20
MINNESOTA 13, Los Angeles 3
PITTSBURGH 21, Cincinnati 10
Baltimore 13, GREEN BAY 10
St. Louis 38, DALLAS 0
PHILADELPHIA 23, New York Giants 20
Miami 20, ATLANTA 7
Cleveland 21, HOUSTON 10
Detroit 28, LOS ANGELES 23

Monday Night Won-Loss Records, 1970-1985

	Total	1985	1984	1983	1982	1981	1980	1979	1978	1977	1976	1975	1974	1973	1972	1971	1970
Buffalo	3-9		0-1	0-1	0-1	1-1				0-1	0-2	0-2	1-0	1-0			
Cincinnati	4-10	1-0	0-1	0-2	0-1				1-2	0-1	1-1	1-0	0-1				0-1
Cleveland	7-4	1-0				0-1	1-1	1-0		1-0				0-1	1-0	0-1	2-0
Denver	6-8-1	1-0	1-0			1-0	1-2	0-2	1-1			1-1	0-2	0-0-1			
Houston	6-6				0-1	0-1	2-0	2-0	2-0		0-1	0-1			0-1		0-1
Indianapolis	8-4								2-1	1-1	2-0				1-0	1-1	1-1
Kansas City	7-4			0-1						0-1	0-1	1-0	1-0	1-1	1-0	2-0	1-0
L.A. Raiders	24-3-1	2-0	2-1	1-0	1-0	2-1	3-0	2-0	1-0	2-0	2-0	2-0	0-1	0-0-1	2-0	1-0	1-0
Miami	21-10	2-1	3-0	1-1	1-1	1-1	1-1	0-2	2-1	1-0	1-1	1-1	2-0	2-0	1-0	1-0	1-0
New England	2-11	0-1				0-1	1-2	0-2	0-2	0-1	1-0	0-1			0-1		
New York Jets	6-9	1-0	0-1	2-0	1-0		1-0	1-1			0-1	0-1	0-1	0-1	0-1	0-1	0-1
Pittsburgh	14-11	0-2	1-1	1-0	1-0	1-1	0-2	2-1	1-1	2-0	0-1	1-0	2-0	1-1		0-1	1-0
San Diego	10-8	0-1	1-2	1-1	1-1	2-1	1-0	1-0	1-0			1-0			0-1	1-0	0-1
Seattle	5-3	0-2	2-0			1-0	0-1	2-0									
Atlanta	5-11		0-2	0-1		1-2		1-2	1-0				0-1	1-1	0-1	1-0	0-1
Chicago	5-12	1-1	0-1			0-2	1-1		0-3	1-0		0-1	1-0	0-1	1-0	0-1	0-1
Dallas	14-14	1-1	1-1	1-1	1-2	2-0	1-1	0-2	1-1	1-1	1-0	1-1	0-1	1-1	1-0	1-0	0-1
Detroit	7-6-1		0-1	2-0	0-1	1-0						0-1	1-0	1-0	0-2	0-1-1	2-0
Green Bay	7-9-1	0-1	0-1	2-1	1-0			1-0		0-1		0-1	0-1	1-1	1-0	0-1-1	1-1
L.A. Rams	14-12	2-1	1-1	1-0		2-0	2-0	1-0	0-2	1-1	0-2	1-0	1-1	1-0	1-0	0-2	0-2
Minnesota	9-10			0-1	1-0	0-3		0-1	2-0	0-1	1-1	1-0	1-0	0-1	0-2	2-0	1-0
New Orleans	1-6		1-0	0-1			0-1	0-1					0-1	0-1	0-1		
New York Giants	3-10-1	0-1	0-1	1-1-1	0-1		0-1	0-1		0-1		1-0		0-1	1-0	0-1	0-1
Philadelphia	5-5					1-1	1-0	1-1			0-1	0-1	1-0		0-1		1-0
St. Louis	5-6-1	1-1		0-0-1						2-0	0-1	0-1	0-1		0-1	1-1	1-0
San Francisco	7-9	1-2	2-0	1-0					0-1	0-2	2-0		0-2	1-0	0-1	0-1	
Tampa Bay	1-2			0-1	1-0		0-1										
Washington	16-10	2-1	1-1	1-2			0-2	1-0	1-1	1-1	2-0	1-0	2-0	1-1	2-0	1-0	0-1

Monday Night Syndrome

1985

Of the 15 winning teams:	9 won the next week 6 lost the next week 0 tied the next week	Of the 30 NFL teams:	20 won the next week 10 lost the next week 0 tied the next week
Of the 15 losing teams:	11 won the next week 4 lost the next week 0 tied the next week		

1970-85

Of the 214 winning teams:	118 won the next week 93 lost the next week 3 tied the next week	Of the 434 NFL teams:	237 won the next week 193 lost the next week 4 tied the next week
Of the 214 losing teams:	114 won the next week 99 lost the next week 1 tied the next week		
Of the 6 tying teams:	5 won the next week 1 lost the next week 0 tied the next week		

Thursday-Sunday Night Football, 1978-1985

(Home Team in capitals, games listed in chronological order.)

1985
KANSAS CITY 36, L.A. Raiders 20 (Thur.)
Chicago 33, MINNESOTA 24 (Thur.)
Dallas 30, N.Y. GIANTS 29 (Sun.)
SAN DIEGO 54, Pittsburgh 44 (Sun.)
Denver 27, SEATTLE 24 (Fri.)

1984
Pittsburgh 23, NEW YORK JETS 17 (Thur.)
Denver 24, CLEVELAND 14 (Sun.)
DALLAS 30, New Orleans 27 (Sun.)
Washington 31, MINNESOTA 17 (Thur.)
SAN FRANCISCO 19, L.A. Rams 16 (Fri.)

1983
San Francisco 48, MINNESOTA 17 (Thur.)
CLEVELAND 17, Cincinnati 7 (Thur.)
L.A. Raiders 40, DALLAS 38 (Sun.)
L.A. Raiders 42, SAN DIEGO 10 (Thur.)
MIAMI 34, N.Y. Jets 14 (Fri.)

1982
BUFFALO 23, Minnesota 22 (Thur.)
SAN FRANCISCO 30, L.A. Rams 24 (Thur.)
ATLANTA 17, San Francisco 7 (Sun.)

1981
MIAMI 30, Pittsburgh 10 (Thur.)
Philadelphia 20, BUFFALO 14 (Thur.)
DALLAS 29, Los Angeles 17 (Sun.)
HOUSTON 17, Cleveland 13 (Thur.)

1980
TAMPA BAY 10, Los Angeles 9 (Thur.)
DALLAS 42, San Diego 31 (Sun.)
San Diego 27, MIAMI 24 (OT) (Thur.)
HOUSTON 6, Pittsburgh 0 (Thur.)

1979
Los Angeles 13, DENVER 9 (Thur.)
DALLAS 30, Los Angeles 6 (Sun.)
OAKLAND 45, San Diego 22 (Thur.)
MIAMI 39, New England 24 (Thur.)

1978
New England 21, OAKLAND 14 (Sun.)
Minnesota 21, DALLAS 10 (Thur.)
LOS ANGELES 10, Pittsburgh 7 (Sun.)
Denver 21, OAKLAND 6 (Sun.)

1977
Minnesota 30, DETROIT 21 (Sat.)

1976
Los Angeles 20, DETROIT 17 (Sat.)

1975
LOS ANGELES 10, Pittsburgh 3 (Sat.)

1974
OAKLAND 27, Dallas 23 (Sat.)

History of Overtime Games

Preseason

Aug. 28, 1955	Los Angeles 23, New York Giants 17, at Portland, Oregon
Aug. 24, 1962	Denver 27, Dallas Texans 24, at Fort Worth, Texas
Aug. 10, 1974	San Diego 20, New York Jets 14, at San Diego
Aug. 17, 1974	Pittsburgh 33, Philadelphia 30, at Philadelphia
Aug. 17, 1974	Dallas 19, Houston 13, at Dallas
Aug. 17, 1974	Cincinnati 13, Atlanta 7, at Atlanta
Sept. 6, 1974	Buffalo 23, New York Giants 17, at Buffalo
Aug. 9, 1975	Baltimore 23, Denver 20, at Denver
Aug. 30, 1975	New England 20, Green Bay 17, at Milwaukee
Sept. 13, 1975	Minnesota 14, San Diego 14, at San Diego
Aug. 1, 1976	New England 13, New York Giants 7, at New England
Aug. 2, 1976	Kansas City 9, Houston 3, at Kansas City
Aug. 20, 1976	New Orleans 26, Baltimore 20, at Baltimore
Sept. 4, 1976	Dallas 26, Houston 20, at Dallas
Aug. 13, 1977	Seattle 23, Dallas 17, at Seattle
Aug. 28, 1977	New England 13, Pittsburgh 10, at New England
Aug. 28, 1977	New York Giants 24, Buffalo 21, at East Rutherford, N.J.
Aug. 2, 1979	Seattle 12, Minnesota 9, at Minnesota
Aug. 4, 1979	Los Angeles 20, Oakland 14, at Los Angeles
Aug. 24, 1979	Denver 20, New England 17, at Denver
Aug. 23, 1980	Tampa Bay 20, Cincinnati 14, at Tampa Bay
Aug. 5, 1981	San Francisco 27, Seattle 24, at Seattle
Aug. 29, 1981	New Orleans 20, Detroit 17, at New Orleans
Aug. 28, 1982	Miami 17, Kansas City 17, at Kansas City
Sept. 3, 1982	Miami 16, New York Giants 13, at Miami
Aug. 6, 1983	L.A. Raiders 26, San Francisco 23, at Los Angeles
Aug. 6, 1983	Atlanta 13, Washington 10, at Atlanta
Aug. 13, 1983	St. Louis 27, Chicago 24, at St. Louis
Aug. 18, 1983	New York Jets 20, Cincinnati 17, at Cincinnati
Aug. 27, 1983	Chicago 20, Kansas City 17, at Chicago
Aug. 11, 1984	Pittsburgh 20, Philadelphia 17, at Pittsburgh
Aug. 9, 1985	Buffalo 10, Detroit 10 at Pontiac, Mich.
Aug. 10, 1985	Minnesota 16, Miami 13 at Miami
Aug. 17, 1985	Dallas 27, San Diego 24 at San Diego
Aug. 24, 1985	New York Giants 34, New York Jets 31, at East Rutherford, N.J.

Regular Season

Sept. 22, 1974—Pittsburgh 35, Denver 35, at Denver; Steelers win toss. Gilliam's pass intercepted and returned by Rowser to Denver's 42. Turner misses 41-yard field goal. Walden punts and Greer returns to Broncos' 39. Van Heusen punts and Edwards returns to Steelers' 16. Game ends with Steelers on own 26.

Nov. 10, 1974—New York Jets 26, New York Giants 20, at New Haven, Conn.; Giants win toss. Gogolak misses 42-yard field goal. Namath passes to Boozer for five yards and touchdown at 6:53.

Sept. 28, 1975—Dallas 37, St. Louis 31, at Dallas; Cardinals win toss. Hart's pass intercepted and returned by Jordan to Cardinals' 37. Staubach passes to DuPree for three yards and touchdown at 7:53.

Oct. 12, 1975—Los Angeles 13, San Diego 10, at San Diego; Chargers win toss. Partee punts to Rams' 14. Dempsey kicks 22-yard field goal at 9:27.

Nov. 2, 1975—Washington 30, Dallas 24, at Washington; Cowboys win toss. Staubach's pass intercepted and returned by Houston to Cowboys' 35. Kilmer runs one yard for touchdown at 6:34.

Nov. 16, 1975—St. Louis 20, Washington 17, at St. Louis; Cardinals win toss. Bakken kicks 37-yard field goal at 7:00.

Nov. 23, 1975—Kansas City 24, Detroit 21, at Kansas City; Lions win toss. Chiefs take over on downs at own 38. Stenerud kicks 26-yard field goal at 6:44.

Nov. 23, 1975—Oakland 26, Washington 23, at Washington; Redskins win toss. Bragg punts to Raiders' 42. Blanda kicks 27-yard field goal at 7:13.

Nov. 30, 1975—Denver 13, San Diego 10, at Denver; Broncos win toss. Turner kicks 25-yard field goal at 4:13.

Nov. 30, 1975—Oakland 37, Atlanta 34, at Oakland; Falcons win toss. James punts to Raiders' 16. Guy punts and Herron returns to Falcons' 41. Nick Mike-Mayer misses 45-yard field goal. Guy punts into Falcons' end zone. James punts to Raiders' 39. Blanda kicks 36-yard field goal at 15:00.

Dec. 14, 1975—Baltimore 10, Miami 7, at Baltimore; Dolphins win toss. Seiple punts to Colts' 4. Linhart kicks 31-yard field goal at 12:44.

Sept. 19, 1976—Minnesota 10, Los Angeles 10, at Minnesota; Vikings win toss. Tarkenton's pass intercepted by Monte Jackson and returned to Minnesota 16. Allen blocks Dempsey's 30-yard field goal attempt, ball rolls into end zone for touchback. Clabo punts and Scribner returns to Rams' 20. Rusty Jackson punts to Vikings' 35. Tarkenton's pass intercepted by Kay at Rams' 1, no return. Game ends with Rams on own 3.

***Sept. 27, 1976—Washington 20, Philadelphia 17,** at Philadelphia; Eagles win toss. Jones punts and E. Brown loses one yard on return to Redskins' 40. Bragg punts 51 yards into end zone for touchback. Jones punts and E. Brown returns to Redskins' 42. Bragg punts and Marshall returns to Eagles' 41. Boryla's pass intercepted by Dusek at Redskins' 37, no return. Bragg punts and Bradley returns. Philadelphia holding penalty moves ball back to Eagles' 8. Boryla pass intercepted by E. Brown and returned to Eagles' 22. Moseley kicks 29-yard field goal at 12:49.

Oct. 17, 1976—Kansas City 20, Miami 17, at Miami; Chiefs win toss. Wilson punts into end zone for touchback. Bulaich fumbles into Kansas City end zone, Collier recovers for touchback. Stenerud kicks 34-yard field goal at 14:48.

Oct. 31, 1976—St. Louis 23, San Francisco 20, at St. Louis; Cardinals win toss. Joyce punts and Leonard fumbles on return, Jones recovers at 49ers' 43. Bakken kicks 21-yard field goal at 6:42.

Dec. 5, 1976—San Diego 13, San Francisco 7, at San Diego; Chargers win toss. Morris runs 13 yards for touchdown at 5:12.

Sept. 18, 1977—Dallas 16, Minnesota 10, at Minnesota; Vikings win toss. Dallas starts on Vikings' 47 after a punt early in the overtime period. Staubach scores seven plays later on a four-yard run at 6:14.

***Sept. 26, 1977—Cleveland 30, New England 27,** at Cleveland; Browns win toss. Sipe throws a 22-yard pass to Logan at Patriots' 19. Cockroft kicks 35-yard field goal at 4:45.

Oct. 16, 1977—Minnesota 22, Chicago 16, at Minnesota; Bears win toss. Parsons punts 53 yards to Vikings' 18. Minnesota drives to Bears' 11. On a first-and-10, Vikings fake a field goal and holder Krause hits Voigt with a touchdown pass at 6:45.

Oct. 30, 1977—Cincinnati 13, Houston 10, at Cincinnati; Bengals win toss. Bahr kicks a 22-yard field goal at 5:51.

Nov. 13, 1977—San Francisco 10, New Orleans 7, at New Orleans; Saints win toss. Saints fail to move ball and Blanchard punts to 49ers' 41. Wersching kicks a 33-yard field goal at 6:33.

Dec. 18, 1977—Chicago 12, New York Giants 9, at East Rutherford, N.J.; Giants win toss. The ball changes hands eight times before Thomas kicks a 28-yard field goal at 14:51.

Sept. 10, 1978—Cleveland 13, Cincinnati 10, at Cleveland; Browns win toss. Collins returns kickoff 41 yards to Browns' 47. Cockroft kicks 27-yard field goal at 4:30.

***Sept. 11, 1978—Minnesota 12, Denver 9,** at Minnesota; Vikings win toss. Danmeier kicks 44-yard field goal at 2:56.

Sept. 24, 1978—Pittsburgh 15, Cleveland 9, at Pittsburgh; Steelers win toss. Cunningham scores on a 37-yard "gadget" pass from Bradshaw at 3:43. Steelers start winning drive on their 21.

Sept. 24, 1978—Denver 23, Kansas City 17, at Kansas City; Broncos win toss. Dilts punts to Kansas City. Chiefs advance to Broncos' 40 where Reed fails to make first down on fourth-and-one situation. Broncos march downfield. Preston scores two-yard touchdown at 10:28.

Oct. 1, 1978—Oakland 25, Chicago 19, at Chicago; Bears win toss. Both teams punt on first possession. On Chicago's second offensive series, Colzie intercepts Avellini's pass and returns it to Bears' 3. Three plays later, Whittington runs two yards for a touchdown at 5:19.

Oct. 15, 1978—Dallas 24, St. Louis 21, at St. Louis; Cowboys win toss. Dallas drives from its 23 into field goal range. Septien kicks 27-yard field goal at 3:28.

Oct. 29, 1978—Denver 20, Seattle 17, at Seattle; Broncos win toss. Ball changes hands four times before Turner kicks 18-yard field goal at 12:59.

Nov. 12, 1978—San Diego 29, Kansas City 23, at San Diego; Chiefs win toss. Fouts hits Jefferson for decisive 14-yard touchdown pass on the last play (15:00) of overtime period.

Nov. 12, 1978—Washington 16, New York Giants 13, at Washington; Redskins win toss. Moseley kicks winning 45-yard field goal at 8:32 after missing first down field goal attempt of 35 yards at 4:50.

Nov. 26, 1978—Green Bay 10, Minnesota 10, at Green Bay; Packers win toss. Both teams have possession of the ball four times.

Dec. 9, 1978—Cleveland 37, New York Jets 34, at Cleveland; Browns win toss. Cockroft kicks 22-yard field goal at 3:07.

Sept. 2, 1979—Atlanta 40, New Orleans 34, at New Orleans; Falcons win toss. Bartkowski's pass intercepted by Myers and returned to Falcons' 46. Erxleben punts to Falcons' 4. James punts to Chandler on Saints' 43. Erxleben punts and Ryckman returns to Falcons' 28. James punts and Chandler returns to Saints' 36. Erxleben retrieves punt snap on Saints' 1 and attempts pass. Mayberry intercepts and returns six yards for touchdown at 8:22.

Sept. 2, 1979—Cleveland 25, New York Jets 22, at New York; Jets win toss. Leahy's 43-yard field goal attempt goes wide right at 4:41. Evans's punt blocked by Dykes is recovered by Newton. Ramsey punts into end zone for touchback. Evans punts and Harper returns to Jets' 24. Robinson's pass intercepted by Davis and returned 33 yards to Jets' 31. Cockroft kicks 27-yard field goal at 14:45.

***Sept. 3, 1979—Pittsburgh 16, New England 13,** at Foxboro; Patriots win toss. Hare punts to Swann at Steelers' 31. Bahr kicks 41-yard field goal at 5:10.

Sept. 9, 1979—Tampa Bay 29, Baltimore 26, at Baltimore; Colts win toss. Landry fumbles, recovered by Kollar at Colts' 14. O'Donoghue kicks 31-yard, first-down field goal at 1:41.

Sept. 16, 1979—Denver 20, Atlanta 17, at Atlanta; Broncos win toss. Broncos march 65 yards to Falcons' 7. Turner kicks 24-yard field goal at 6:15.

Sept. 23, 1979—Houston 30, Cincinnati 27, at Cincinnati; Oilers win toss. Parsley punts and Lusby returns to Bengals' 33. Bahr's 32-yard field goal attempt is wide right at 8:05. Parsley's punt downed on Bengals' 5. McInally punts and Ellender returns to Bengals' 42. Fritsch's third down, 29-yard field goal attempt hits left upright and bounces through at 14:28.

Sept. 23, 1979—Minnesota 27, Green Bay 21, at Minnesota; Vikings win toss. Kramer throws 50-yard touchdown pass to Rashad at 3:18.

Oct. 28, 1979—Houston 27, New York Jets 24, at Houston; Oilers win toss. Oilers march 58 yards to Jets' 18. Fritsch kicks 35-yard field goal at 5:10.

Nov. 18, 1979—Cleveland 30, Miami 24, at Cleveland; Browns win toss. Sipe passes 39 yards to Rucker for touchdown at 1:59.

Nov. 25, 1979—Pittsburgh 33, Cleveland 30, at Pittsburgh; Browns win toss. Sipe's pass intercepted by Blount on Steelers' 4. Bradshaw pass intercepted by Bolton on Browns' 12. Evans punts and Bell returns to Steelers' 17. Bahr kicks 37-yard field goal at 14:51.

Nov. 25, 1979—Buffalo 16, New England 13, at Foxboro; Patriots win toss. Hare's punt downed on Bills' 38. Jackson punts and Morgan returns to Patriots' 20. Grogan's pass intercepted by Haslett and returned to Bills' 42. Ferguson's 51-yard pass to Butler sets up N. Mike-Mayer's 29-yard field goal at 9:15.

Dec. 2, 1979—Los Angeles 27, Minnesota 21, at Los Angeles; Rams win toss. Clark punts and Miller returns to Vikings' 25. Kramer's pass intercepted by Brown and returned to Rams' 40. Cromwell, holding for 22-yard field goal attempt, runs around left end untouched for winning score at 6:53.

Sept. 7, 1980—Green Bay 12, Chicago 6, at Green Bay; Bears win toss. Parsons punts and Nixon returns 16 yards. Five plays later, Marcol returns own blocked field goal attempt 24 yards for touchdown at 6:00.

*indicates Monday night game
#indicates Thursday night game

Sept. 14, 1980—San Diego 30, Oakland 24, at San Diego; Raiders win toss. Pastorini's first-down pass intercepted by Edwards. Millen intercepts Fouts' first-down pass and returns to San Diego 46. Bahr's 50-yard field goal attempt partially blocked by Williams and recovered on Chargers' 32. Eight plays later, Fouts throws 24-yard touchdown pass to Jefferson at 8:09.

Sept. 14, 1980—San Francisco 24, St. Louis 21, at San Francisco; Cardinals win toss. Swider punts and Robinson returns to 49ers' 32. San Francisco drives 52 yards to St. Louis 16, where Wersching kicks 33-yard field goal at 4:12.

Oct. 12, 1980—Green Bay 14, Tampa Bay 14, at Tampa Bay; Packers win toss. Teams trade punts twice. Lee returns second Tampa Bay punt to Green Bay 42. Dickey completes three passes to Buccaneers' 18, where Birney's 36-yard field goal attempt is wide right as time expires.

Nov. 9, 1980—Atlanta 33, St. Louis 27, at St. Louis; Falcons win toss. Strong runs 21 yards for touchdown at 4:20.

#**Nov. 20, 1980—San Diego 27, Miami 24,** at Miami; Chargers win toss. Partridge punts into end zone, Dolphins take over on their own 20. Woodley's pass for Nathan intercepted by Lowe and returned 28 yards to Dolphins' 12. Benirschke kicks 28-yard field goal at 7:14.

Nov. 23, 1980—New York Jets 31, Houston 28, at New York; Jets win toss. Leahy kicks 38-yard field goal at 3:58.

Nov. 27, 1980—Chicago 23, Detroit 17, at Detroit; Bears win toss. Williams returns kickoff 95 yards for touchdown at 0:21.

Dec. 7, 1980—Buffalo 10, Los Angeles 7, at Buffalo; Rams win toss. Corral punts and Hooks returns to Bills' 34. Ferguson's 30-yard pass to Lewis sets up N. Mike-Mayer's 30-yard field goal at 5:14.

Dec. 7, 1980—San Francisco 38, New Orleans 35, at San Francisco; Saints win toss. Erxleben's punt downed by Hardy on 49ers' 27. Wersching kicks 36-yard field goal at 7:40.

***Dec. 8, 1980—Miami 16, New England 13,** at Miami; Dolphins win toss. Von Schamann kicks 23-yard field goal at 3:20.

Dec. 14, 1980—Cincinnati 17, Chicago 14, at Chicago; Bengals win toss. Breech kicks 28-yard field goal at 4:23.

Dec. 21, 1980—Los Angeles 20, Atlanta 17, at Los Angeles; Rams win toss. Corral's punt downed at Rams' 37. James punts into end zone for touchback. Corral's punt downed on Falcons' 17. Bartkowski fumbles when hit by Harris, recovered by Delaney. Corral kicks 23-yard field goal on first play of possession at 7:00.

Sept. 27, 1981—Cincinnati 27, Buffalo 24, at Cincinnati; Bills win toss. Cater punts into end zone for touchback. Bengals drive to the Bills' 10 where Breech kicks 28-yard field goal at 9:33.

Sept. 27, 1981—Pittsburgh 27, New England 21, at Pittsburgh; Patriots win toss. Hubach punts and Smith returns five yards to midfield. Four plays later Bradshaw throws 24-yard touchdown pass to Swann at 3:19.

Oct. 4, 1981—Miami 28, New York Jets 28, at Miami; Jets win toss. Teams trade punts twice. Leahy's 48-yard field goal attempt is wide right as time expires.

Oct. 25, 1981—New York Giants 27, Atlanta 24, at Atlanta; Giants win toss. Jennings' punt goes out of bounds at New York 47. Bright returns Atlanta punt to Giants' 14. Woerner fair catches punt at own 28. Andrews fumbles on first play, recovered by Van Pelt. Danelo kicks 40-yard field goal four plays later at 9:20.

Oct. 25, 1981—Chicago 20, San Diego 17, at Chicago; Bears win toss. Teams trade punts. Bears' second punt returned by Brooks to Chargers' 33. Fouts pass intercepted by Fencik and returned 32 yards to San Diego 27. Roveto kicks 27-yard field goal seven plays later at 9:30.

Nov. 8, 1981—Chicago 16, Kansas City 13, at Kansas City; Bears win toss. Teams trade punts. Kansas City takes over on downs on its own 38. Fuller's fumble recovered by Harris on Chicago 36. Roveto's 37-yard field goal wide, but Chiefs penalized for leverage. Roveto's 22-yard field goal attempt three plays later is good at 13:07.

Nov. 8, 1981—Denver 23, Cleveland 20, at Denver; Browns win toss. D. Smith recovers Hill's fumble at Denver 48. Morton's 33-yard pass to Upchurch and six-yard run by Preston set up Steinfort's 30-yard field goal at 4:10.

Nov. 8, 1981—Miami 30, New England 27, at New England; Dolphins win toss. Orosz punts and Morgan returns six yards to New England 26. Grogan's pass intercepted by Brudzinski who returns 19 yards to Patriots' 26. Von Schamann kicks 30-yard field goal on first down at 7:09.

Nov. 15, 1981—Washington 30, New York Giants 27, at New York; Giants win toss. Nelms returns Giants' punt 26 yards to New York 47. Five plays later Moseley kicks 48-yard field goal at 3:44.

Dec. 20, 1981—New York Giants 13, Dallas 10, at New York; Cowboys win toss and kick off. Jennings punts to Dallas 40. Taylor recovers Dorsett's fumble on second down. Danelo's 33-yard field goal attempt hits right upright and bounces back. White's pass for Pearson intercepted by Hunt and returned seven yards to Dallas 24. Four plays later Danelo kicks 35-yard field goal at 6:19.

Sept. 12, 1982—Washington 37, Philadelphia 34, at Philadelphia; Redskins win toss. Theismann completes five passes for 63 yards to set up Moseley's 26-yard field goal at 4:47.

Sept. 19, 1982—Pittsburgh 26, Cincinnati 20, at Pittsburgh; Bengals win toss. Anderson's pass intended for Kreider intercepted by Woodruff and returned 30 yards to Cincinnati 2. Bradshaw completes two-yard touchdown pass to Stallworth on first down at 1:08.

Dec. 19, 1982—Baltimore 20, Green Bay 20, at Baltimore; Packers win toss. K. Anderson intercepts Dickey's first-down pass and returns to Packers' 42. Miller's 44-yard field goal attempt blocked by G. Lewis. Teams trade punts before Stenerud's 47-yard field goal attempt is wide right. Teams trade punts again before time expires in Colts possession.

Jan. 2, 1983—Tampa Bay 26, Chicago 23, at Tampa Bay; Bears win toss. Parsons punts to T. Bell at Buccaneers' 40. Capece kicks 33-yard field goal at 3:14.

Sept. 4, 1983—Baltimore 29, New England 23, at New England; Patriots win toss. Cooks runs 52 yards with fumble recovery three plays into overtime at 0:30.

Sept. 4, 1983—Green Bay 41, Houston 38, at Houston; Packers win toss. Stenerud kicks 42-yard field goal at 5:55.

Sept. 11, 1983—New York Giants 16, Atlanta 13, at Atlanta; Giants win toss. Dennis returns kickoff 54 yards to Atlanta 41. Haji-Sheikh kicks 30-yard field goal at 3:38.

Sept. 18, 1983—New Orleans 34, Chicago 31, at New Orleans; Bears win toss. Parsons punts and Groth returns five yards to New Orleans 34. Stabler pass intercepted by Schmidt at Chicago 47. Parsons punt downed by Gentry at New Orleans 2. Stabler gains 36 yards in four passes; Wilson 38 in six carries. Andersen kicks 41-yard field goal at 10:57.

Sept. 18, 1983—Minnesota 19, Tampa Bay 16, at Tampa; Vikings win toss. Coleman punts and Bell returns eight yards to Tampa Bay 47. Capece's 33-yard field goal attempt sails wide at 7:26. Dils and Young combine for 48-yard gain to Tampa Bay 27. Ricardo kicks 42-yard field goal at 9:27.

Sept. 25, 1983—Baltimore 22, Chicago 19, at Baltimore; Colts win toss. Allegre kicks 33-yard field goal nine plays later at 4:51.

Sept. 25, 1983—Cleveland 30, San Diego 24, at San Diego; Browns win toss. Walker returns kickoff 33 yards to Cleveland 37. Sipe completes 48-yard touchdown pass to Holt four plays later at 1:53.

Sept. 25, 1983—New York Jets 27, Los Angeles Rams 24, at New York; Jets win toss. Ramsey punts to Irvin who returns to 25 but penalty puts Rams on own 13. Holmes 30-yard interception return sets up Leahy's 26-yard field goal at 3:22.

Oct. 9, 1983—Buffalo 38, Miami 35, at Miami; Dolphins win toss. Von Schamann's 52-yard field goal attempt goes wide at 12:36. Cater punts to Clayton who loses 11 to own 13. Von Schamann's 43-yard field goal attempt sails wide at 5:15. Danelo kicks 36-yard field goal nine plays later at 13:58.

Oct. 9, 1983—Dallas 27, Tampa Bay 24, at Dallas; Cowboys win toss. Septien's 51-yard field goal attempt goes wide but Buccaneers penalized for roughing kicker. Septien kicks 42-yard field goal at 4:38.

Oct. 23, 1983—Kansas City 13, Houston 10, at Houston; Chiefs win toss. Lowery kicks 41-yard field goal 13 plays later at 7:41.

Oct. 23, 1983—Minnesota 20, Green Bay 17, at Green Bay; Packers win toss. Scribner's punt downed on Vikings' 42. Ricardo kicks 32-yard field goal eight plays later at 5:05.

***Oct. 24, 1983—New York Giants 20, St. Louis 20,** at St. Louis; Cardinals win toss. Teams trade punts before O'Donoghue's 44-yard field goal attempt is wide left. Jennings' punt returned by Bird to St. Louis 21. Lomax pass intercepted by Haynes who loses six yards to New York 33. Jennings' punt downed on St. Louis 17. O'Donoghue's 19-yard field goal attempt is wide right. Rutledge's pass intercepted by L. Washington who returns 25 yards to New York 25. O'Donoghue's 42-yard field goal attempt is wide right. Rutledge's pass intercepted by W. Smith at St. Louis 33 to end game.

Oct. 30, 1983—Cleveland 25, Houston 19, at Cleveland; Oilers win toss. Teams trade punts. Nielsen's pass intercepted by Whitwell who returns to Houston 20. Green runs 20 yards for touchdown on first down at 6:34.

Nov. 20, 1983—Detroit 23, Green Bay 20, at Milwaukee; Packers win toss. Scribner punts and Jenkins returns 14 yards to Green Bay 45. Murray's 33-yard field goal attempt is wide left at 9:32. Whitehurst's pass intercepted by Watkins and returned to Green Bay 27. Murray kicks 37-yard field goal four plays later at 8:30.

Nov. 27, 1983—Atlanta 47, Green Bay 41, at Atlanta; Packers win toss. K. Johnson returns interception 31 yards for touchdown at 2:13.

Nov. 27, 1983—Seattle 51, Kansas City 48, at Seattle; Seahawks win toss. Dixon's 47-yard kickoff return sets up N. Johnson's 42-yard field goal at 1:36.

Dec. 11, 1983—New Orleans 20, Philadelphia 17, at Philadelphia; Eagles win toss. Runager punts to Groth who fair catches on New Orleans 32. Stabler completes two passes for 36 yards to Goodlow to set up Andersen's 50-yard field goal at 5:30.

***Dec. 12, 1983—Green Bay 12, Tampa Bay 9,** at Tampa; Packers win toss. Stenerud kicks 23-yard field goal 11 plays later at 4:07.

Sept. 9, 1984—Detroit 27, Atlanta 24, at Atlanta; Lions win toss. Murray kicks 48-yard field goal nine plays later at 5:06.

Sept. 30, 1984—Tampa Bay 30, Green Bay 27, at Tampa; Packers win toss. Scribner punts 44 yards to Tampa Bay 2. Epps returns Garcia's punt three yards to Green Bay 27. Scribner's punt downed on Buccaneers' 33. Ariri kicks 46-yard field goal 11 plays later at 10:32.

Oct. 14, 1984—Detroit 13, Tampa Bay 7, at Detroit; Buccaneers win toss. Tampa Bay drives to Lions' 39 before Wilder fumbles. Five plays later Danielson hits Thompson with 37-yard touchdown pass at 4:34.

Oct. 21, 1984—Dallas 30, New Orleans 27, at Dallas; Cowboys win toss. Septien kicks 41-yard field goal eight plays later at 3:42.

Oct. 28, 1984—Denver 22, Los Angeles Raiders 19, at Los Angeles; Raiders win toss. Hawkins fumble recovered by Foley at Denver 7. Teams trade punts. Karlis' 42-yard field goal attempt is wide left. Teams trade punts. Wilson pass intercepted by R. Jackson at Los Angeles 45, returned 23 yards to Los Angeles 22. Karlis kicks 35-yard field goal two plays later at 15:00.

Nov. 4, 1984—Philadelphia 23, Detroit 23, at Detroit; Lions win toss. Lions drive to Eagles' 3 in eight plays. Murray's 21-yard field goal attempt hits right upright and bounces back. Jaworski's pass intercepted by Watkins at Detroit 5. Teams trade punts. Cooper returns Black's punt five yards to Eagles' 14. Time expires four plays later with Eagles on own 21.

Nov. 18, 1984—San Diego 34, Miami 28, at San Diego; Chargers win toss. McGee scores eight plays later on a 25-yard run at 3:17.

Dec. 2, 1984—Cincinnati 20, Cleveland 17, at Cleveland; Browns win toss. Simmons returns Cox's punt 30 yards to Cleveland 35. Breech kicks 35-yard field goal seven plays later at 4:34.

Dec. 2, 1984—Houston 23, Pittsburgh 20, at Houston; Oilers win toss. Cooper kicks 30-yard field goal 16 plays later at 5:53.

*indicates Monday night game
#indicates Thursday night game

Sept. 8, 1985—St. Louis 27, Cleveland 24, at Cleveland; Cardinals win toss. O'Donoghue kicks 35-yard field goal nine plays later at 5:27.

Sept. 29, 1985—New York Giants 16, Philadelphia 10, at Philadelphia; Eagles win toss. Jaworski's pass tipped by Quick and intercepted by Patterson who returns 29 yards for touchdown at 0:55.

Oct. 20, 1985—Denver 13, Seattle 10, at Denver; Seahawks win toss. Teams trade punts twice. Krieg's pass intercepted by Hunter and returned to Seahawks' 15. Karlis kicks 24-yard field goal four plays later at 9:19.

Nov. 10, 1985—Philadelphia 23, Atlanta 17, at Philadelphia; Falcons win toss. Donnelly's 62-yard punt goes out of bounds at Eagles' 1. Jaworski completes 99-yard touchdown pass to Quick two plays later at 1:49.

Nov. 10, 1985—San Diego 40, Los Angeles Raiders 34, at San Diego; Chargers win toss. James scores on 17-yard run seven plays later at 3:44.

Nov. 17, 1985—Denver 30, San Diego 24, at Denver; Chargers win toss. Thomas' 40-yard field goal attempt blocked by Smith and returned 60 yards by Wright for touchdown at 4:45.

Nov. 24, 1985—New York Jets 16, New England 13, at New York; Jets win toss. Teams trade punts twice. Patriots' second punt returned 46 yards by Sohn to Patriots' 15. Leahy kicks 32-yard field goal one play later at 10:05.

Nov. 24, 1985—Tampa Bay 19, Detroit 16, at Tampa; Lions win toss. Teams trade punts. Lions' punt downed on Buccaneers' 38. Igwebuike kicks 24-yard field goal 11 plays later at 12:31.

Nov. 24, 1985—Los Angeles Raiders 31, Denver 28, at Los Angeles; Raiders win toss. Bahr kicks 32-yard field goal six plays later at 2:42.

Dec. 8, 1985—Los Angeles Raiders 17, Denver 14, at Denver; Broncos win toss. Teams trade punts twice. Elway's fumble recovered by Townsend at Broncos' 8. Bahr kicks 26-yard field goal one play later at 4:55.

*indicates Monday night game
#indicates Thursday night game

Postseason

Dec. 28, 1958—Baltimore 23, New York Giants 17, at New York; Giants win toss. Maynard returns kickoff to Giants' 20. Chandler punts and Taseff returns one yard to Colts' 20. Colts win at 8:15 on a one-yard run by Ameche.

Dec. 23, 1962—Dallas Texans 20, Houston Oilers 17, at Houston; Texans win toss and kick off. Jancik returns kickoff to Oilers' 33. Norton punts and Jackson makes fair catch on Texans' 22. Wilson punts and Jancik makes fair catch on Oilers' 45. Robinson intercepts Blanda's pass and returns 13 yards to Oilers' 47. Wilson's punt rolls dead at Oilers' 12. Hull intercepts Blanda's pass and returns 23 yards to midfield. Texans win at 17:54 on a 25-yard field goal by Brooker.

Dec. 26, 1965—Green Bay 13, Baltimore 10, at Green Bay; Packers win toss. Moore returns kickoff to Packers' 22. Chandler punts and Haymond returns nine yards to Colts' 41. Gilburg punts and Wood makes fair catch at Packers' 21. Chandler punts and Haymond returns one yard to Colts' 41. Michaels misses 47-yard field goal. Packers win at 13:39 on 25-yard field goal by Chandler.

Dec. 25, 1971—Miami 27, Kansas City 24, at Kansas City; Chiefs win toss. Podolak, after a lateral from Buchanan, returns kickoff to Chiefs' 46. Stenerud's 42-yard field goal is blocked. Seiple punts and Podolak makes fair catch at Chiefs' 17. Wilson punts and Scott returns 18 yards to Dolphins' 39. Yepremian misses 62-yard field goal. Scott intercepts Dawson's pass and returns 13 yards to Dolphins' 46. Seiple punts and Podolak loses one yard to Chiefs' 15. Wilson punts and Scott makes fair catch on Dolphins' 30. Dolphins win at 22:40 on a 37-yard field goal by Yepremian.

Dec. 24, 1977—Oakland 37, Baltimore 31, at Baltimore; Colts win toss. Raiders start on own 42 following a punt late in the first overtime. Oakland works way into a threatening position on Stabler's 19-yard pass to Branch at Colts' 26. Four plays later, on the second play of the second overtime, Stabler hits Casper with a 10-yard touchdown pass at 15:43.

Jan. 2, 1982—San Diego 41, Miami 38, at Miami; Chargers win toss. San Diego drives from its 13 to Miami 8. On second-and-goal, Benirschke misses 27-yard field goal attempt wide left at 9:15. Miami has the ball twice and San Diego twice more before the Dolphins get their third possession. Miami drives from the San Diego 46 to Chargers' 17 and on fourth-and-two, von Schamann's 34-yard field goal attempt is blocked by San Diego's Winslow after 11:27. Fouts then completes four of five passes, including a 29-yarder to Joiner that puts the ball on Dolphins' 10. On first down, Benirschke kicks a 20-yard field goal at 13:52. San Diego's winning drive covered 74 yards in six plays.

Overtime Won-Lost Records, 1974–1985 (Regular Season)

	W	L	T
Atlanta	3	7	0
Buffalo	3	1	0
Chicago	4	7	0
Cincinnati	4	3	0
Cleveland	7	5	0
Dallas	5	2	0
Denver	8	3	1
Detroit	3	3	1
Green Bay	3	5	3
Houston	3	5	0
Indianapolis	3	1	1
Kansas City	3	4	0
Los Angeles Raiders	5	3	0
Los Angeles Rams	3	2	1
Miami	2	6	1
Minnesota	5	2	2
New England	0	8	0
New Orleans	2	4	0
New York Giants	4	4	1
New York Jets	4	3	1
Philadelphia	1	4	1
Pittsburgh	5	1	1
St. Louis	3	4	1
San Diego	6	5	0
San Francisco	3	2	0
Seattle	1	2	0
Tampa Bay	4	4	1
Washington	5	2	0

Overtime Games By Year (Regular Season)

1985-10	1979-12
1984- 9	1978-11
1983-19	1977- 6
1982- 4	1976- 5
1981-10	1975- 9
1980-13	1974- 2

Overtime Game Summary—1974-1985

There have been 110 overtime games in regular-season play since the rule was adopted in 1974. The breakdown follows:

75 times both teams had at least one possession (68%)

35 times the team which won the toss drove for winning score (26 FG, 9 TD) (32%)

52 times the team which won the toss won the game (47%)

50 times the team which lost the toss won the game (46%)

72 games were decided by a field goal (66%)

30 games were decided by a touchdown (27%)

8 games ended tied (7%). Last time: Philadelphia 23 at Detroit 23; 11/4/84

Shortest Overtime Games

0:21 (Chicago 23, Detroit 17; 11/27/80) Initial overtime kickoff return for a touchdown.

0:30 (Baltimore 29, New England 23; 9/4/83)

0:55 (New York Giants 16, Philadelphia 10; 9/29/85)

Longest Overtime Games (all postseason)

22:40 (Miami 27, Kansas City 24; 12/25/71)

17:54 (Dallas Texans 20, Houston 17; 12/13/67)

15:43 (Oakland 37, Baltimore 31; 12/24/77)

There have been six postseason overtime games dating back to 1958. In all cases, both teams had at least one possession. Last postseason overtime: San Diego 41, Miami 38; 1/2/82.

Number One-Draft Choices

Season	Team	Player	Position	College
1986	Tampa Bay	Bo Jackson	RB	Auburn
1985	Buffalo	Bruce Smith	DE	Virginia Tech
1984	New England	Irving Fryar	WR	Nebraska
1983	Baltimore	John Elway	QB	Stanford
1982	New England	Kenneth Sims	DT	Texas
1981	New Orleans	George Rogers	RB	South Carolina
1980	Detroit	Billy Sims	RB	Oklahoma
1979	Buffalo	Tom Cousineau	LB	Ohio State
1978	Houston	Earl Campbell	RB	Texas
1977	Tampa Bay	Ricky Bell	RB	Southern California
1976	Tampa Bay	Lee Roy Selmon	DE	Oklahoma
1975	Atlanta	Steve Bartkowski	QB	California
1974	Dallas	Ed Jones	DE	Tennessee State
1973	Houston	John Matuszak	DE	Tampa
1972	Buffalo	Walt Patulski	DE	Notre Dame
1971	New England	Jim Plunkett	QB	Stanford
1970	Pittsburgh	Terry Bradshaw	QB	Louisiana Tech
1969	Buffalo (AFL)	O.J. Simpson	RB	Southern California
1968	Minnesota	Ron Yary	T	Southern California
1967	Baltimore	Bubba Smith	DT	Michigan State
1966	Atlanta	Tommy Nobis	LB	Texas
	Miami (AFL)	Jim Grabowski	RB	Illinois
1965	New York Giants	Tucker Frederickson	RB	Auburn
	Houston (AFL)	Lawrence Elkins	E	Baylor
1964	San Francisco	Dave Parks	E	Texas Tech
	Boston (AFL)	Jack Concannon	QB	Boston College
1963	Los Angeles	Terry Baker	QB	Oregon State
	Kansas City (AFL)	Buck Buchanan	DT	Grambling
1962	Washington	Ernie Davis	RB	Syracuse
	Oakland (AFL)	Roman Gabriel	QB	North Carolina State
1961	Minnesota	Tommy Mason	RB	Tulane
	Buffalo (AFL)	Ken Rice	G	Auburn
1960	Los Angeles	Billy Cannon	RB	Louisiana State
	(AFL had no formal first pick)			
1959	Green Bay	Randy Duncan	QB	Iowa
1958	Chicago Cardinals	King Hill	QB	Rice
1957	Green Bay	Paul Hornung	HB	Notre Dame
1956	Pittsburgh	Gary Glick	DB	Colorado A&M
1955	Baltimore	George Shaw	QB	Oregon
1954	Cleveland	Bobby Garrett	QB	Stanford
1953	San Francisco	Harry Babcock	E	Georgia
1952	Los Angeles	Bill Wade	QB	Vanderbilt
1951	New York Giants	Kyle Rote	HB	Southern Methodist
1950	Detroit	Leon Hart	E	Notre Dame
1949	Philadelphia	Chuck Bednarik	C	Pennsylvania
1948	Washington	Harry Gilmer	QB	Alabama
1947	Chicago Bears	Bob Fenimore	HB	Oklahoma A&M
1946	Boston	Frank Dancewicz	QB	Notre Dame
1945	Chicago Cardinals	Charley Trippi	HB	Georgia
1944	Boston	Angelo Bertelli	QB	Notre Dame
1943	Detroit	Frank Sinkwich	HB	Georgia
1942	Pittsburgh	Bill Dudley	HB	Virginia
1941	Chicago Bears	Tom Harmon	HB	Michigan
1940	Chicago Cardinals	George Cafego	HB	Tennessee
1939	Chicago Cardinals	Ki Aldrich	C	Texas Christian
1938	Cleveland	Corbett Davis	FB	Indiana
1937	Philadelphia	Sam Francis	FB	Nebraska
1936	Philadelphia	Jay Berwanger	HB	Chicago

NFL Paid Attendance

Year	Regular Season	Average	Postseason	Super Bowl
1985	13,345,047 (224 games)	59,567	710,768 (10)	73,818
1984	13,398,112 (224 games)	59,813	665,194 (10)	84,059
1983	13,277,222 (224 games)	59,273	675,513 (10)	72,932
1982*	7,367,438 (126 games)	58,472	1,033,153 (16)	103,667
1981	13,606,990 (224 games)	60,745	637,763 (10)	81,270
1980	13,392,230 (224 games)	59,787	624,430 (10)	75,500
1979	13,182,039 (224 games)	58,848	630,326 (10)	103,985
1978	12,771,800 (224 games)	57,017	624,388 (10)	79,641
1977	11,018,632 (196 games)	56,218	534,925 (8)	75,804
1976	11,070,543 (196 games)	56,482	492,884 (8)	103,438
1975	10,213,193 (182 games)	56,116	475,919 (8)	80,187
1974	10,236,322 (182 games)	56,244	438,664 (8)	80,997
1973	10,730,933 (182 games)	58,961	525,433 (8)	71,882
1972	10,445,827 (182 games)	57,395	483,345 (8)	90,182
1971	10,076,035 (182 games)	55,363	483,891 (8)	81,023
1970	9,533,333 (182 games)	52,381	458,493 (8)	79,204
1969	6,096,127 (112 games) NFL	54,430	162,279 (3)	80,562
	2,843,373 (70 games) AFL	40,620	167,088 (3)	
1968	5,882,313 (112 games) NFL	52,521	215,902 (3)	75,377
	2,635,004 (70 games) AFL	37,643	114,438 (2)	
1967	5,938,924 (112 games) NFL	53,026	166,208 (3)	75,546
	2,295,697 (63 games) AFL	36,439	53,330 (1)	
1966	5,337,044 (105 games) NFL	50,829	74,152 (1)	61,946**
	2,160,369 (63 games) AFL	34,291	42,080 (1)	
1965	4,634,021 (98 games) NFL	47,286	100,304 (2)	
	1,782,384 (56 games) AFL	31,828	30,361 (1)	
1964	4,563,049 (98 games) NFL	46,562	79,544 (1)	
	1,447,875 (56 games) AFL	25,855	40,242 (1)	
1963	4,163,643 (98 games) NFL	42,486	45,801 (1)	
	1,208,697 (56 games) AFL	21,584	63,171 (2)	
1962	4,003,421 (98 games) NFL	40,851	64,892 (1)	
	1,147,302 (56 games) AFL	20,487	37,981 (1)	
1961	3,986,159 (98 games) NFL	40,675	39,029 (1)	
	1,002,657 (56 games) AFL	17,904	29,556 (1)	
1960	3,128,296 (78 games) NFL	40,106	67,325 (1)	
	926,156 (56 games) AFL	16,538	32,183 (1)	
1959	3,140,000 (72 games)	43,617	57,545 (1)	
1958	3,006,124 (72 games)	41,752	123,659 (2)	
1957	2,836,318 (72 games)	39,393	119,579 (2)	
1956	2,551,263 (72 games)	35,434	56,836 (1)	
1955	2,521,836 (72 games)	35,026	85,693 (1)	
1954	2,190,571 (72 games)	30,425	43,827 (1)	
1953	2,164,585 (72 games)	30,064	54,577 (1)	
1952	2,052,126 (72 games)	28,502	97,507 (2)	
1951	1,913,019 (72 games)	26,570	57,522 (1)	
1950	1,977,753 (78 games)	25,356	136,647 (3)	
1949	1,391,735 (60 games)	23,196	27,980 (1)	
1948	1,525,243 (60 games)	25,421	36,309 (1)	
1947	1,837,437 (60 games)	30,624	66,268 (2)	
1946	1,732,135 (55 games)	31,493	58,346 (1)	
1945	1,270,401 (50 games)	25,408	32,178 (1)	
1944	1,019,649 (50 games)	20,393	46,016 (1)	
1943	969,128 (40 games)	24,228	71,315 (2)	
1942	887,920 (55 games)	16,144	36,006 (1)	
1941	1,108,615 (55 games)	20,157	55,870 (2)	
1940	1,063,025 (55 games)	19,328	36,034 (1)	
1939	1,071,200 (55 games)	19,476	32,279 (1)	
1938	937,197 (55 games)	17,040	48,120 (1)	
1937	963,039 (55 games)	17,510	15,878 (1)	
1936	816,007 (54 games)	15,111	29,545 (1)	
1935	638,178 (53 games)	12,041	15,000 (1)	
1934	492,684 (60 games)	8,211	35,059 (1)	

*Players 57-day strike reduced 224-game schedule to 126 games.

**Only Super Bowl that did not sell out.

NFL's 10 Biggest Attendance Weekends

(Paid Count)

Weekend	Games	Attendance
October 27-28, 1985	14	902,657
October 12-13, 1980	14	898,223
September 23-24, 1984	14	894,402
November 11-12, 1979	14	890,972
September 16, 19-20, 1983	14	886,323
November 20, 23-24, 1980	14	885,601
September 12-13, 1982	14	882,042
November 15-16, 1981	14	881,486
September 5-6-7, 1981	14	881,439
September 12, 15-16, 1985	14	880,013

NFL's 10 Highest Scoring Weekends

Point Total	Date	Weekend
761	October 16-17, 1983	7th
732	November 9-10, 1980	10th
725	November 24, 27-28, 1983	13th
710	November 28, December 1-2, 1985	13th
696	October 2-3, 1983	5th
676	September 21-22, 1980	3rd
675	October 23-24, 1983	8th
667	November 22-23, 1981	12th
667	November 22, 25-26, 1984	13th
661	October 25-26, 1981	8th

Top 10 Televised Sports Events

Program	Date	Network	Rating	Share
Super Bowl XVI	1/24/82	CBS	49.1	73.0
Super Bowl XVII	1/30/83	NBC	48.6	69.0
Super Bowl XX	1/26/86	NBC	48.3	70.0
Super Bowl XII	1/15/78	CBS	47.2	67.0
Super Bowl XIII	1/21/79	NBC	47.1	74.0
Super Bowl XVIII	1/22/84	CBS	46.4	71.0
Super Bowl XIX	1/20/85	ABC	46.4	63.0
Super Bowl XIV	1/20/80	CBS	46.3	67.0
Super Bowl XI	1/9/77	NBC	44.4	73.0
Super Bowl XV	1/25/81	NBC	44.4	63.0

Ten Most Watched TV Programs & Estimated Total Number of Viewers

(Based on A.C. Nielsen Figures)

Program	Date	Network	*Total Viewers
Super Bowl XX	Jan. 26, 1986	NBC	127,000,000
M*A*S*H (Special)	Feb. 28, 1983	CBS	121,624,000
Super Bowl XIX	Jan. 20, 1985	ABC	115,936,000
Super Bowl XVI	Jan. 24, 1982	CBS	110,230,000
Super Bowl XVII	Jan. 30, 1983	NBC	109,040,000
Super Bowl XII	Jan. 15, 1978	CBS	102,010,000
Roots, Part 8	Jan. 30, 1977	ABC	98,706,000
Super Bowl XIV	Jan. 20, 1980	CBS	97,800,000
Super Bowl XIII	Jan. 21, 1979	NBC	96,640,000
Super Bowl XV	Jan. 25, 1981	NBC	94,120,000

*Watched some portion of the broadcast

Chicago All-Star Game

Pro teams won 31, lost 19, and tied 2. The game was discontinued after 1976.

Year	Date	Winner	Loser	Attendance
1976	July 23	Pittsburgh 24	All-Stars 0	52,895
1975	Aug. 1	Pittsburgh 21	All-Stars 14	54,103
1974		No game was played		
1973	July 27	Miami 14	All-Stars 3	54,103
1972	July 28	Dallas 20	All-Stars 7	54,162
1971	July 30	Baltimore 24	All-Stars 17	52,289
1970	July 31	Kansas City 24	All-Stars 3	69,940
1969	Aug. 1	N.Y. Jets 26	All-Stars 24	74,208
1968	Aug. 2	Green Bay 34	All-Stars 17	69,917
1967	Aug. 4	Green Bay 27	All-Stars 0	70,934
1966	Aug. 5	Green Bay 38	All-Stars 0	72,000
1965	Aug. 6	Cleveland 24	All-Stars 16	68,000
1964	Aug. 7	Chicago 28	All-Stars 17	65,000
1963	Aug. 2	All-Stars 20	Green Bay 17	65,000
1962	Aug. 3	Green Bay 42	All-Stars 20	65,000
1961	Aug. 4	Philadelphia 28	All-Stars 14	66,000
1960	Aug. 12	Baltimore 32	All-Stars 7	70,000
1959	Aug. 14	Baltimore 29	All-Stars 0	70,000
1958	Aug. 15	All-Stars 35	Detroit 19	70,000
1957	Aug. 9	N.Y. Giants 22	All-Stars 12	75,000
1956	Aug. 10	Cleveland 26	All-Stars 0	75,000
1955	Aug. 12	All-Stars 30	Cleveland 27	75,000
1954	Aug. 13	Detroit 31	All-Stars 6	93,470
1953	Aug. 14	Detroit 24	All-Stars 10	93,818
1952	Aug. 15	Los Angeles 10	All-Stars 7	88,316
1951	Aug. 17	Cleveland 33	All-Stars 0	92,180
1950	Aug. 11	All-Stars 17	Philadelphia 7	88,885
1949	Aug. 12	Philadelphia 38	All-Stars 0	93,780
1948	Aug. 20	Chi. Cardinals 28	All-Stars 0	101,220
1947	Aug. 22	All-Stars 16	Chi. Bears 0	105,840
1946	Aug. 23	All-Stars 16	Los Angeles 0	97,380
1945	Aug. 30	Green Bay 19	All-Stars 7	92,753
1944	Aug. 30	Chi. Bears 24	All-Stars 21	48,769
1943	Aug. 25	All-Stars 27	Washington 7	48,471
1942	Aug. 28	Chi. Bears 21	All-Stars 0	101,100
1941	Aug. 28	Chi. Bears 37	All-Stars 13	98,203
1940	Aug. 29	Green Bay 45	All-Stars 28	84,567
1939	Aug. 30	N.Y. Giants 9	All-Stars 0	81,456
1938	Aug. 31	All-Stars 28	Washington 16	74,250
1937	Sept. 1	All-Stars 6	Green Bay 0	84,560
1936	Sept. 3	All-Stars 7	Detroit 7 (tie)	76,000
1935	Aug. 29	Chi. Bears 5	All-Stars 0	77,450
1934	Aug. 31	Chi. Bears 0	All-Stars 0 (tie)	79,432

NFL Playoff Bowl

Western Conference won 8, Eastern Conference won 2. All games played at Miami's Orange Bowl.

1970	Los Angeles Rams 31, Dallas Cowboys 0
1969	Dallas Cowboys 17, Minnesota Vikings 13
1968	Los Angeles Rams 30, Cleveland Browns 6
1967	Baltimore Colts 20, Philadelphia Eagles 14
1966	Baltimore Colts 35, Dallas Cowboys 3
1965	St. Louis Cardinals 24, Green Bay Packers 17
1964	Green Bay Packers 40, Cleveland Browns 23
1963	Detroit Lions 17, Pittsburgh Steelers 10
1962	Detroit Lions 28, Philadelphia Eagles 10
1961	Detroit Lions 17, Cleveland Browns 16

RECORDS

All-Time Records
Outstanding Performers
Yearly Statistical Leaders
Super Bowl Records
Postseason Game Records
AFC-NFC Pro Bowl Game Records

ALL-TIME RECORDS

Compiled by Elias Sports Bureau

The following records reflect all available official information on the National Football League from its formation in 1920 to date. Also included are all applicable records from the American Football League, 1960-69. Rookie records are limited to those players who had never played in a professional game in the United States in any previous season.

INDIVIDUAL RECORDS

SERVICE

Most Seasons

26 George Blanda, Chi. Bears, 1949, 1950-58; Baltimore, 1950; Houston, 1960-66; Oakland, 1967-75
21 Earl Morrall, San Francisco, 1956; Pittsburgh, 1957-58; Detroit, 1958-64; N.Y. Giants, 1965-67; Baltimore, 1968-71; Miami, 1972-76
20 Jim Marshall, Cleveland, 1960; Minnesota, 1961-79

Most Seasons, One Club

19 Jim Marshall, Minnesota, 1961-79
18 Jim Hart, St. Louis, 1966-83
17 Lou Groza, Cleveland, 1950-59, 1961-67
Johnny Unitas, Baltimore, 1956-72
John Brodie, San Francisco, 1957-73
Jim Bakken, St. Louis, 1962-78
Mick Tingelhoff, Minnesota, 1962-78
Jeff Van Note, Atlanta, 1969-85

Most Games Played, Career

340 George Blanda, Chi. Bears, 1949, 1950-58; Baltimore, 1950; Houston, 1960-66; Oakland, 1967-75
282 Jim Marshall, Cleveland, 1960; Minnesota, 1961-79
263 Jan Stenerud, Kansas City, 1967-79; Green Bay, 1980-83; Minnesota, 1984-85

Most Consecutive Games Played, Career

282 Jim Marshall, Cleveland, 1960; Minnesota, 1961-79
240 Mick Tingelhoff, Minnesota, 1962-78
234 Jim Bakken, St. Louis, 1962-78

Most Seasons, Coach

40 George Halas, Chi. Bears, 1920-29, 1933-42, 1946-55, 1958-67
33 Earl (Curly) Lambeau, Green Bay, 1921-49; Chi. Cardinals, 1950-51; Washington, 1952-53
26 Tom Landry, Dallas, 1960-85

SCORING

Most Seasons Leading League

5 Don Hutson, Green Bay, 1940-44
Gino Cappelletti, Boston, 1961, 1963-66
3 Earl (Dutch) Clark, Portsmouth, 1932; Detroit, 1935-36
Pat Harder, Chi. Cardinals, 1947-49
Paul Hornung, Green Bay, 1959-61
2 Jack Manders, Chi. Bears, 1934, 1937
Gordy Soltau, San Francisco, 1952-53
Doak Walker, Detroit, 1950, 1955
Gene Mingo, Denver, 1960, 1962
Jim Turner, N.Y. Jets, 1968-69
Fred Cox, Minnesota, 1969-70
Chester Marcol, Green Bay, 1972, 1974
John Smith, New England, 1979-80

Most Consecutive Seasons Leading League

5 Don Hutson, Green Bay, 1940-44
4 Gino Cappelletti, Boston, 1963-66
3 Pat Harder, Chi. Cardinals, 1947-49
Paul Hornung, Green Bay, 1959-61

POINTS

Most Points, Career

2,002 George Blanda, Chi. Bears, 1949, 1950-58; Baltimore, 1950; Houston, 1960-66; Oakland, 1967-75 (9-td, 943-pat, 335-fg)
1,699 Jan Stenerud, Kansas City, 1967-79; Green Bay, 1980-83; Minnesota, 1984-85 (580-pat, 373-fg)
1,439 Jim Turner, N.Y. Jets, 1964-70; Denver, 1971-79 (1-td, 521-pat, 304-fg)

Most Points, Season

176 Paul Hornung, Green Bay, 1960 (15-td, 41-pat, 15-fg)
161 Mark Moseley, Washington, 1983 (62-pat, 33-fg)
155 Gino Cappelletti, Boston, 1964 (7-td, 38-pat, 25-fg)

Most Points, No Touchdowns, Season

161 Mark Moseley, Washington, 1983 (62-pat, 33-fg)
145 Jim Turner, N.Y. Jets, 1968 (43-pat, 34-fg)
144 Kevin Butler, Chicago, 1985 (51-pat, 31-fg)

Most Seasons, 100 or More Points

7 Jan Stenerud, Kansas City, 1967-71; Green Bay, 1981, 1983
6 Gino Cappelletti, Boston, 1961-66
George Blanda, Houston, 1960-61; Oakland, 1967-69, 1973
Bruce Gossett, Los Angeles, 1966-67, 1969; San Francisco, 1970-71, 1973
5 Lou Michaels, Pittsburgh, 1962; Baltimore, 1964-65, 1967-68

Most Points, Rookie, Season

144 Kevin Butler, Chicago, 1985 (51-pat, 31-fg)
132 Gale Sayers, Chicago, 1965 (22-td)
128 Doak Walker, Detroit, 1950 (11-td, 38-pat, 8-fg)
Cookie Gilchrist, Buffalo, 1962 (15-td, 14-pat, 8-fg)
Chester Marcol, Green Bay, 1972 (29-pat, 33-fg)

Most Points, Game

40 Ernie Nevers, Chi. Cardinals vs. Chi. Bears, Nov. 28, 1929 (6-td, 4-pat)
36 Dub Jones, Cleveland vs. Chi. Bears, Nov. 25, 1951 (6-td)
Gale Sayers, Chicago vs. San Francisco, Dec. 12, 1965 (6-td)
33 Paul Hornung, Green Bay vs. Baltimore, Oct. 8, 1961 (4-td, 6-pat, 1-fg)

Most Consecutive Games Scoring

151 Fred Cox, Minnesota, 1963-73
133 Garo Yepremian, Miami, 1970-78; New Orleans, 1979
128 Rafael Septien, Los Angeles, 1977; Dallas, 1978-85

TOUCHDOWNS

Most Seasons Leading League

8 Don Hutson, Green Bay, 1935-38, 1941-44
3 Jim Brown, Cleveland, 1958-59, 1963
Lance Alworth, San Diego, 1964-66
2 By many players

Most Consecutive Seasons Leading League

4 Don Hutson, Green Bay, 1935-38, 1941-44
3 Lance Alworth, San Diego, 1964-66
2 By many players

Most Touchdowns, Career

126 Jim Brown, Cleveland, 1957-65 (106-r, 20-p)
116 John Riggins, N.Y. Jets, 1971-75; Washington, 1976-79, 1981-85 (104-r, 12-p)
113 Lenny Moore, Baltimore, 1956-67 (63-r, 48-p, 2-ret)

Most Touchdowns, Season

24 John Riggins, Washington, 1983 (24-r)
23 O.J. Simpson, Buffalo, 1975 (16-r, 7-p)
22 Gale Sayers, Chicago, 1965 (14-r, 6-p, 2-ret)
Chuck Foreman, Minnesota, 1975 (13-r, 9-p)

Most Touchdowns, Rookie, Season

22 Gale Sayers, Chicago, 1965 (14-r, 6-p, 2-ret)
20 Eric Dickerson, L.A. Rams, 1983 (18-r, 2-p)
16 Billy Sims, Detroit, 1980 (13-r, 3-p)

Most Touchdowns, Game

6 Ernie Nevers, Chi. Cardinals vs. Chi. Bears, Nov. 28, 1929 (6-r)
Dub Jones, Cleveland vs. Chi. Bears, Nov. 25, 1951 (4-r, 2-p)
Gale Sayers, Chicago vs. San Francisco, Dec. 12, 1965 (4-r, 1-p, 1-ret)
5 Bob Shaw, Chi. Cardinals vs. Baltimore, Oct. 2, 1950 (5-p)
Jim Brown, Cleveland vs. Baltimore, Nov. 1, 1959 (5-r)
Abner Haynes, Dall. Texans vs. Oakland, Nov. 26, 1961 (4-r, 1-p)
Billy Cannon, Houston vs. N.Y. Titans, Dec. 10, 1961 (3-r, 2-p)
Cookie Gilchrist, Buffalo vs. N.Y. Jets, Dec. 8, 1963 (5-r)
Paul Hornung, Green Bay vs. Baltimore, Dec. 12, 1965 (3-r, 2-p)
Kellen Winslow, San Diego vs. Oakland, Nov. 22, 1981 (5-p)
4 By many players

Most Consecutive Games Scoring Touchdowns

18 Lenny Moore, Baltimore, 1963-65
14 O.J. Simpson, Buffalo, 1975
13 John Riggins, Washington, 1982-83

POINTS AFTER TOUCHDOWN

Most Seasons Leading League

8 George Blanda, Chi. Bears, 1956; Houston, 1961-62; Oakland, 1967-69, 1972, 1974
4 Bob Waterfield, Cleveland, 1945; Los Angeles, 1946, 1950, 1952
3 Earl (Dutch) Clark, Portsmouth, 1932; Detroit, 1935-36
Jack Manders, Chi. Bears, 1933-35
Don Hutson, Green Bay, 1941-42, 1945

Most Points After Touchdown Attempted, Career

959 George Blanda, Chi. Bears, 1949, 1950-58; Baltimore, 1950; Houston, 1960-66; Oakland, 1967-75
657 Lou Groza, Cleveland, 1950-59, 1961-67
601 Jan Stenerud, Kansas City, 1967-79; Green Bay, 1980-83; Minnesota, 1984-85

Most Points After Touchdown Attempted, Season

70 Uwe von Schamann, Miami, 1984
65 George Blanda, Houston, 1961
63 Mark Moseley, Washington, 1983

Most Points After Touchdown Attempted, Game

10 Charlie Gogolak, Washington vs. N.Y. Giants, Nov. 27, 1966
9 Pat Harder, Chi. Cardinals vs. N.Y. Giants, Oct. 17, 1948; vs. N.Y. Bulldogs, Nov. 13, 1949
Bob Waterfield, Los Angeles vs. Baltimore, Oct. 22, 1950
Bob Thomas, Chicago vs. Green Bay, Dec. 7, 1980
8 By many players

Most Points After Touchdown, Career

943 George Blanda, Chi. Bears, 1949, 1950-58; Baltimore, 1950; Houston, 1960-66; Oakland, 1967-75
641 Lou Groza, Cleveland, 1950-59, 1961-67
580 Jan Stenerud, Kansas City, 1967-79; Green Bay, 1980-83; Minnesota, 1984-85

Most Points After Touchdown, Season

66 Uwe von Schamann, Miami, 1984
64 George Blanda, Houston, 1961
62 Mark Moseley, Washington, 1983

Most Points After Touchdown, Game

9 Pat Harder, Chi. Cardinals vs. N.Y. Giants, Oct. 17, 1948
Bob Waterfield, Los Angeles vs. Baltimore, Oct. 22, 1950
Charlie Gogolak, Washington vs. N.Y. Giants, Nov. 27, 1966
8 By many players

Most Consecutive Points After Touchdown

234 Tommy Davis, San Francisco, 1959-65
221 Jim Turner, N.Y. Jets, 1967-70; Denver, 1971-74
201 George Blanda, Oakland, 1967-71

Highest Points After Touchdown Percentage, Career (200 points after touchdown)

99.43 Tommy Davis, San Francisco, 1959-69 (350-348)
99.07 Nick Lowery, New England, 1978; Kansas City, 1980-85 (214-212)
98.33 George Blanda, Chi. Bears, 1949, 1950-58; Baltimore, 1950; Houston, 1960-66; Oakland, 1967-75 (959-943)

Most Points After Touchdown, No Misses, Season

56 Danny Villanueva, Dallas, 1966
Ray Wersching, San Francisco, 1984
54 Mike Clark, Dallas, 1968
George Blanda, Oakland, 1968
53 Pat Harder, Chi. Cardinals, 1948

Most Points After Touchdown, No Misses, Game

9 Pat Harder, Chi. Cardinals vs. N.Y. Giants, Oct. 17, 1948
Bob Waterfield, Los Angeles vs. Baltimore, Oct. 22, 1950
8 By many players

FIELD GOALS

Most Seasons Leading League

5 Lou Groza, Cleveland, 1950, 1952-54, 1957
4 Jack Manders, Chi. Bears, 1933-34, 1936-37
Ward Cuff, N.Y. Giants, 1938-39, 1943; Green Bay, 1947
Mark Moseley, Washington, 1976-77, 1979, 1982
3 Bob Waterfield, Los Angeles, 1947, 1949, 1951
Gino Cappelletti, Boston, 1961, 1963-64
Fred Cox, Minnesota, 1965, 1969-70
Jan Stenerud, Kansas City, 1967, 1970, 1975

Most Consecutive Seasons Leading League

3 Lou Groza, Cleveland, 1952-54
2 By many players

Most Field Goals Attempted, Career

638 George Blanda, Chi. Bears, 1949, 1950-58; Baltimore, 1950; Houston, 1960-66; Oakland, 1967-75
558 Jan Stenerud, Kansas City, 1967-79; Green Bay, 1980-83; Minnesota, 1984-85
488 Jim Turner, N.Y. Jets, 1964-70; Denver, 1971-79

Most Field Goals Attempted, Season

49 Bruce Gossett, Los Angeles, 1966
Curt Knight, Washington, 1971
48 Chester Marcol, Green Bay, 1972
47 Jim Turner, N.Y. Jets, 1969
David Ray, Los Angeles, 1973
Mark Moseley, Washington, 1983

Most Field Goals Attempted, Game

9 Jim Bakken, St. Louis vs. Pittsburgh, Sept. 24, 1967
8 Lou Michaels, Pittsburgh vs. St. Louis, Dec. 2, 1962
Garo Yepremian, Detroit vs. Minnesota, Nov. 13, 1966
Jim Turner, N.Y. Jets vs. Buffalo, Nov. 3, 1968
7 By many players

Most Field Goals, Career

373 Jan Stenerud, Kansas City, 1967-79; Green Bay, 1980-83; Minnesota, 1984-85
335 George Blanda, Chi. Bears, 1949, 1950-58; Baltimore, 1950; Houston, 1960-66; Oakland, 1967-75
304 Jim Turner, N.Y. Jets, 1964-70; Denver, 1971-79

Most Field Goals, Season

35 Ali Haji-Sheikh, N.Y. Giants, 1983
34 Jim Turner, N.Y. Jets, 1968
33 Chester Marcol, Green Bay, 1972
Mark Moseley, Washington, 1983
Gary Anderson, Pittsburgh, 1985

Most Field Goals, Rookie, Season

35 Ali Haji-Sheikh, N.Y. Giants, 1983
33 Chester Marcol, Green Bay, 1972
31 Kevin Butler, Chicago, 1985

Most Field Goals, Game

7 Jim Bakken, St. Louis vs. Pittsburgh, Sept. 24, 1967
6 Gino Cappelletti, Boston vs. Denver, Oct. 4, 1964
Garo Yepremian, Detroit vs. Minnesota, Nov. 13, 1966
Jim Turner, N.Y. Jets vs. Buffalo, Nov. 3, 1968
Tom Dempsey, Philadelphia vs. Houston, Nov. 12, 1972
Bobby Howfield, N.Y. Jets vs. New Orleans, Dec. 3, 1972
Jim Bakken, St. Louis vs. Atlanta, Dec. 9, 1973
Joe Danelo, N.Y. Giants vs. Seattle, Oct. 18, 1981
Ray Wersching, San Francisco vs. New Orleans, Oct. 16, 1983
5 By many players

Most Field Goals, One Quarter

4 Garo Yepremian, Detroit vs. Minnesota, Nov. 13, 1966 (second quarter)
Curt Knight, Washington vs. N.Y. Giants, Nov. 15, 1970 (second quarter)
3 By many players

Most Consecutive Games Scoring Field Goals

31 Fred Cox, Minnesota, 1968-70
28 Jim Turner, N.Y. Jets, 1970; Denver, 1971-72
21 Bruce Gossett, San Francisco, 1970-72

Most Consecutive Field Goals

23 Mark Moseley, Washington, 1981-82
20 Garo Yepremian, Miami, 1978; New Orleans, 1979
18 Gary Anderson, Pittsburgh, 1985

Longest Field Goal

63 Tom Dempsey, New Orleans vs. Detroit, Nov. 8, 1970
60 Steve Cox, Cleveland vs. Cincinnati, Oct. 21, 1984
59 Tony Franklin, Philadelphia vs. Dallas, Nov. 12, 1979

Highest Field Goal Percentage, Career (100 field goals)

76.84 Nick Lowery, New England, 1978; Kansas City, 1980-85 (177-136)
74.86 Ed Murray, Detroit, 1980-85 (179-134)
71.04 Rolf Benirschke, San Diego, 1977-85 (183-130)

Highest Field Goal Percentage, Season (Qualifiers)

95.24 Mark Moseley, Washington, 1982 (21-20)
91.67 Jan Stenerud, Green Bay, 1981 (24-22)
88.89 Nick Lowery, Kansas City, 1985 (27-24)

Most Field Goals, No Misses, Game

6 Gino Cappelletti, Boston vs. Denver, Oct. 4, 1964
Joe Danelo, N.Y. Giants vs. Seattle, Oct. 18, 1981
Ray Wersching, San Francisco vs. New Orleans, Oct. 16, 1983
5 Roger LeClerc, Chicago vs. Detroit, Dec. 3, 1961
Lou Michaels, Baltimore vs. San Francisco, Sept. 25, 1966
Mac Percival, Chicago vs. Philadelphia, Oct. 20, 1968
Roy Gerela, Houston vs. Miami, Sept. 28, 1969
Jan Stenerud, Kansas City vs. Buffalo, Nov. 2, 1969; vs. Buffalo, Dec. 7, 1969; Minnesota vs. Detroit, Sept. 23, 1984
Horst Muhlmann, Cincinnati vs. Buffalo, Nov. 8, 1970; vs. Pittsburgh, Sept. 24, 1972
Bruce Gossett, San Francisco vs. Denver, Sept. 23, 1973
Nick Mike-Mayer, Atlanta vs. Los Angeles, Nov. 4, 1973
Curt Knight, Washington vs. Baltimore, Nov. 18, 1973
Tim Mazzetti, Atlanta vs. Los Angeles, Oct. 30, 1978
Ed Murray, Detroit vs. Green Bay, Sept. 14, 1980
Rich Karlis, Denver vs. Seattle, Nov. 20, 1983
Pat Leahy, N.Y. Jets vs. Cincinnati, Sept. 16, 1984
Nick Lowery, Kansas City vs. L.A. Raiders, Sept. 12, 1985
Eric Schubert, N.Y. Giants vs. Tampa Bay, Nov. 3, 1985
Gary Anderson, Pittsburgh vs. Kansas City, Nov. 10, 1985
Morten Andersen, New Orleans vs. L.A. Rams, Dec. 1, 1985

Most Field Goals, 50 or More Yards, Career

17 Jan Stenerud, Kansas City, 1967-79; Green Bay, 1980-83; Minnesota, 1984-85
12 Tom Dempsey, New Orleans, 1969-70; Philadelphia, 1971-74; Los Angeles, 1975-76; Houston, 1977; Buffalo, 1978-79
Mark Moseley, Philadelphia, 1970; Houston, 1971-72; Washington, 1974-85
Nick Lowery, New England, 1978; Kansas City, 1980-85
10 Joe Danelo, Green Bay, 1975; N.Y. Giants, 1976-82; Buffalo, 1983-84
Ed Murray, Detroit, 1980-85

Most Field Goals, 50 or More Yards, Season

5 Fred Steinfort, Denver, 1980
4 Horst Muhlmann, Cincinnati, 1970
Mark Moseley, Washington, 1977
Nick Lowery, Kansas City, 1980
Raul Allegre, Baltimore, 1983
3 By many players

Most Field Goals, 50 or More Yards, Game

2 Jim Martin, Detroit vs. Baltimore, Oct. 23, 1960
Tom Dempsey, New Orleans vs. Los Angeles, Dec. 6, 1970
Chris Bahr, Cincinnati vs. Houston, Sept. 23, 1979
Nick Lowery, Kansas City vs. Seattle, Sept. 14, 1980; vs. New Orleans, Sept. 8, 1985
Mark Moseley, Washington vs. New Orleans, Oct. 26, 1980
Fred Steinfort, Denver vs. Seattle, Dec. 21, 1980
Mick Luckhurst, Atlanta vs. Denver, Dec. 5, 1982; vs. L.A. Rams, Oct. 7, 1984
Morten Andersen, New Orleans vs. Philadelphia, Dec. 11, 1983
Paul McFadden, Philadelphia vs. Detroit, Nov. 4, 1984
Pat Leahy, N.Y. Jets vs. New England, Oct. 20, 1985
Tony Zendejas, Houston vs. San Diego, Nov. 24, 1985

SAFETIES

Most Safeties, Career

4 Ted Hendricks, Baltimore, 1969-73; Green Bay, 1974; Oakland, 1975-81; L.A. Raiders, 1982-83
Doug English, Detroit, 1975-79, 1981-85
3 Bill McPeak, Pittsburgh, 1949-57
Charlie Krueger, San Francisco, 1959-73
Ernie Stautner, Pittsburgh, 1950-63
Jim Katcavage, N.Y. Giants, 1956-68
Roger Brown, Detroit, 1960-66; Los Angeles, 1967-69
Bruce Maher, Detroit, 1960-67; N.Y. Giants, 1968-69
Ron McDole, St. Louis, 1961; Houston, 1962; Buffalo, 1963-70; Washington, 1971-78
Alan Page, Minnesota, 1967-78; Chicago, 1979-81
2 By many players

Most Safeties, Season

2 Tom Nash, Green Bay, 1932
Roger Brown, Detroit, 1962
Ron McDole, Buffalo, 1964
Alan Page, Minnesota, 1971
Fred Dryer, Los Angeles, 1973
Benny Barnes, Dallas, 1973
James Young, Houston, 1977
Tom Hannon, Minnesota, 1981
Doug English, Detroit, 1983
Don Blackmon, New England, 1985

Most Safeties, Game

2 Fred Dryer, Los Angeles vs. Green Bay, Oct. 21, 1973

RUSHING

Most Seasons Leading League

8 Jim Brown, Cleveland, 1957-61, 1963-65
4 Steve Van Buren, Philadelphia, 1945, 1947-49
O.J. Simpson, Buffalo, 1972-73, 1975-76
3 Earl Campbell, Houston, 1978-80

Most Consecutive Seasons Leading League

5 Jim Brown, Cleveland, 1957-61
3 Steve Van Buren, Philadelphia, 1947-49
Jim Brown, Cleveland, 1963-65
Earl Campbell, Houston, 1978-80
2 Bill Paschal, N.Y. Giants, 1943-44
Joe Perry, San Francisco, 1953-54
Jim Nance, Boston, 1966-67
Leroy Kelly, Cleveland, 1967-68
O.J. Simpson, Buffalo, 1972-73; 1975-76
Eric Dickerson, L.A. Rams, 1983-84

ATTEMPTS

Most Seasons Leading League

6 Jim Brown, Cleveland, 1958-59, 1961, 1963-65
4 Steve Van Buren, Philadelphia, 1947-50
Walter Payton, Chicago, 1976-79
3 Cookie Gilchrist, Buffalo, 1963-64; Denver, 1965
Jim Nance, Boston, 1966-67, 1969
O. J. Simpson, Buffalo, 1973-75

Most Consecutive Seasons Leading League

4 Steve Van Buren, Philadelphia, 1947-50
Walter Payton, Chicago, 1976-79
3 Jim Brown, Cleveland, 1963-65
Cookie Gilchrist, Buffalo, 1963-64; Denver, 1965
O.J. Simpson, Buffalo, 1973-75
2 By many players

Most Attempts, Career

3,371 Walter Payton, Chicago, 1975-85
2,949 Franco Harris, Pittsburgh, 1972-83; Seattle, 1984
2,916 John Riggins, N.Y. Jets, 1971-75; Washington, 1976-79, 1981-85

Most Attempts, Season

407 James Wilder, Tampa Bay, 1984
397 Gerald Riggs, Atlanta, 1985
390 Eric Dickerson, L.A. Rams, 1983

Most Attempts, Rookie, Season

390 Eric Dickerson, L.A. Rams, 1983
378 George Rogers, New Orleans, 1981
335 Curt Warner, Seattle, 1983

Most Attempts, Game
43 Butch Woolfolk, N.Y. Giants vs. Philadelphia, Nov. 20, 1983
James Wilder, Tampa Bay vs. Green Bay, Sept. 30, 1984 (OT)
42 James Wilder, Tampa Bay vs. Pittsburgh, Oct. 30, 1983
41 Franco Harris, Pittsburgh vs. Cincinnati, Oct. 17, 1976
Gerald Riggs, Atlanta vs. L.A. Rams, Nov. 17, 1985

YARDS GAINED
Most Yards Gained, Career
14,860 Walter Payton, Chicago, 1975-85
12,312 Jim Brown, Cleveland, 1957-65
12,120 Franco Harris, Pittsburgh, 1972-83; Seattle, 1984
Most Seasons, 1,000 or More Yards Rushing
9 Walter Payton, Chicago, 1976-81, 1983-85
8 Franco Harris, Pittsburgh, 1972, 1974-79, 1983
Tony Dorsett, Dallas, 1977-81, 1983-85
7 Jim Brown, Cleveland, 1958-61, 1963-65
Most Consecutive Seasons, 1,000 or More Yards Rushing
6 Franco Harris, Pittsburgh, 1974-79
Walter Payton, Chicago, 1976-81
5 Jim Taylor, Green Bay, 1960-64
O.J. Simpson, Buffalo, 1972-76
Tony Dorsett, Dallas, 1977-81
4 Jim Brown, Cleveland, 1958-61
Earl Campbell, Houston, 1978-81
Most Yards Gained, Season
2,105 Eric Dickerson, L.A. Rams, 1984
2,003 O.J. Simpson, Buffalo, 1973
1,934 Earl Campbell, Houston, 1980
Most Yards Gained, Rookie, Season
1,808 Eric Dickerson, L.A. Rams, 1983
1,674 George Rogers, New Orleans, 1981
1,605 Ottis Anderson, St. Louis, 1979
Most Yards Gained, Game
275 Walter Payton, Chicago vs. Minnesota, Nov. 20, 1977
273 O.J. Simpson, Buffalo vs. Detroit, Nov. 25, 1976
250 O.J. Simpson, Buffalo vs. New England, Sept. 16, 1973
Most Games, 200 or More Yards Rushing, Career
6 O.J. Simpson, Buffalo, 1969-77; San Francisco, 1978-79
4 Jim Brown, Cleveland, 1957-65
Earl Campbell, Houston, 1978-84; New Orleans, 1984-85
2 Walter Payton, Chicago, 1975-85
Eric Dickerson, L.A. Rams, 1983-85
George Rogers, New Orleans, 1981-84; Washington, 1985
Most Games, 200 or More Yards Rushing, Season
4 Earl Campbell, Houston, 1980
3 O.J. Simpson, Buffalo, 1973
2 Jim Brown, Cleveland, 1963
O.J. Simpson, Buffalo, 1976
Walter Payton, Chicago, 1977
Eric Dickerson, L.A. Rams, 1984
Most Consecutive Games, 200 or More Yards Rushing
2 O.J. Simpson, Buffalo, 1973, 1976
Earl Campbell, Houston, 1980
Most Games, 100 or More Yards Rushing, Career
73 Walter Payton, Chicago, 1975-85
58 Jim Brown, Cleveland, 1957-65
47 Franco Harris, Pittsburgh, 1972-83; Seattle, 1984
Most Games, 100 or More Yards Rushing, Season
12 Eric Dickerson, L.A. Rams, 1984
11 O.J. Simpson, Buffalo, 1973
Earl Campbell, Houston, 1979
Marcus Allen, L.A. Raiders, 1985
10 Walter Payton, Chicago, 1977, 1985
Earl Campbell, Houston, 1980
Most Consecutive Games, 100 or More Yards Rushing
9 Walter Payton, Chicago, 1985
Marcus Allen, L.A. Raiders, 1985 (current)
7 O.J. Simpson, Buffalo, 1972-73
Earl Campbell, Houston, 1979
6 Jim Brown, Cleveland, 1958
Franco Harris, Pittsburgh, 1972
Earl Campbell, Houston, 1980
Walter Payton, Chicago, 1984
Eric Dickerson, L.A. Rams, 1984
James Wilder, Tampa Bay, 1984-85
Longest Run From Scrimmage
99 Tony Dorsett, Dallas vs. Minnesota, Jan. 3, 1983 (TD)
97 Andy Uram, Green Bay vs. Chi. Cardinals, Oct. 8, 1939 (TD)
Bob Gage, Pittsburgh vs. Chi. Bears, Dec. 4, 1949 (TD)
96 Jim Spavital, Baltimore vs. Green Bay, Nov. 5, 1950 (TD)
Bob Hoernschemeyer, Detroit vs. N.Y. Yanks, Nov. 23, 1950 (TD)

AVERAGE GAIN
Highest Average Gain, Career (700 attempts)
5.22 Jim Brown, Cleveland, 1957-65 (2,359-12,312)
5.14 Eugene (Mercury) Morris, Miami, 1969-75; San Diego, 1976 (804-4,133)
5.00 Gale Sayers, Chicago, 1965-71 (991-4,956)
Highest Average Gain, Season (Qualifiers)
9.94 Beattie Feathers, Chi. Bears, 1934 (101-1,004)
6.87 Bobby Douglass, Chicago, 1972 (141-968)
6.78 Dan Towler, Los Angeles, 1951 (126-854)
Highest Average Gain, Game (10 attempts)
17.09 Marion Motley, Cleveland vs. Pittsburgh, Oct. 29, 1950 (11-188)
16.70 Bill Grimes, Green Bay vs. N.Y. Yanks, Oct. 8, 1950 (10-167)
16.57 Bobby Mitchell, Cleveland vs. Washington, Nov. 15, 1959 (14-232)

TOUCHDOWNS
Most Seasons Leading League
5 Jim Brown, Cleveland, 1957-59, 1963, 1965
4 Steve Van Buren, Philadelphia, 1945, 1947-49
3 Abner Haynes, Dall. Texans, 1960-62
Cookie Gilchrist, Buffalo, 1962-64
Paul Lowe, L.A. Chargers, 1960; San Diego, 1961, 1965
Leroy Kelly, Cleveland, 1966-68
Most Consecutive Seasons Leading League
3 Steve Van Buren, Philadelphia, 1947-49
Jim Brown, Cleveland, 1957-59
Abner Haynes, Dall. Texans, 1960-62
Cookie Gilchrist, Buffalo, 1962-64
Leroy Kelly, Cleveland, 1966-68
Most Touchdowns, Career
106 Jim Brown, Cleveland, 1957-65
104 John Riggins, N.Y. Jets, 1971-75; Washington, 1976-79, 1981-85
98 Walter Payton, Chicago, 1975-85
Most Touchdowns, Season
24 John Riggins, Washington, 1983
21 Joe Morris, N.Y. Giants, 1985
19 Jim Taylor, Green Bay, 1962
Earl Campbell, Houston, 1979
Chuck Muncie, San Diego, 1981
Most Touchdowns, Rookie, Season
18 Eric Dickerson, L.A. Rams, 1983
14 Gale Sayers, Chicago, 1965
13 Cookie Gilchrist, Buffalo, 1962
Earl Campbell, Houston, 1978
Billy Sims, Detroit, 1980
George Rogers, New Orleans, 1981
Curt Warner, Seattle, 1983
Most Touchdowns, Game
6 Ernie Nevers, Chi. Cardinals vs. Chi. Bears, Nov. 28, 1929
5 Jim Brown, Cleveland vs. Baltimore, Nov. 1, 1959
Cookie Gilchrist, Buffalo vs. N.Y. Jets, Dec. 8, 1963
4 By many players
Most Consecutive Games Rushing for Touchdowns
13 John Riggins, Washington, 1982-83
11 Lenny Moore, Baltimore, 1963-64
9 Leroy Kelly, Cleveland, 1968

PASSING

Most Seasons Leading League
6 Sammy Baugh, Washington, 1937, 1940, 1943, 1945, 1947, 1949
4 Len Dawson, Dall. Texans; 1962; Kansas City, 1964, 1966, 1968
Roger Staubach, Dallas, 1971, 1973, 1978-79
Ken Anderson, Cincinnati, 1974-75, 1981-82
3 Arnie Herber, Green Bay, 1932, 1934, 1936
Norm Van Brocklin, Los Angeles, 1950, 1952, 1954
Bart Starr, Green Bay, 1962, 1964, 1966
Most Consecutive Seasons Leading League
2 Cecil Isbell, Green Bay, 1941-42
Milt Plum, Cleveland, 1960-61
Ken Anderson, Cincinnati, 1974-75, 1981-82
Roger Staubach, Dallas, 1978-79

PASS RATING
Highest Pass Rating, Career (1,500 attempts)
92.4 Joe Montana, San Francisco, 1979-85
83.4 Roger Staubach, Dallas, 1969-79
82.6 Sonny Jurgensen, Philadelphia, 1957-63; Washington, 1964-74
Highest Pass Rating, Season (Qualifiers)
110.4 Milt Plum, Cleveland, 1960
109.9 Sammy Baugh, Washington, 1945
108.9 Dan Marino, Miami, 1984
Highest Pass Rating, Rookie, Season (Qualifiers)
96.0 Dan Marino, Miami, 1983
88.2 Greg Cook, Cincinnati, 1969
84.0 Charlie Conerly, N.Y. Giants, 1948

ATTEMPTS
Most Seasons Leading League
4 Sammy Baugh, Washington, 1937, 1943, 1947-48
Johnny Unitas, Baltimore, 1957, 1959-61
George Blanda, Chi. Bears, 1953; Houston, 1963-65
3 Arnie Herber, Green Bay, 1932, 1934, 1936
Sonny Jurgensen, Washington, 1966-67, 1969
2 By many players
Most Consecutive Seasons Leading League
3 Johnny Unitas, Baltimore, 1959-61
George Blanda, Houston, 1963-65
2 By many players
Most Passes Attempted, Career
6,467 Fran Tarkenton, Minnesota, 1961-66, 1972-78; N.Y. Giants, 1967-71
5,186 Johnny Unitas, Baltimore, 1956-72; San Diego, 1973
5,076 Jim Hart, St. Louis, 1966-83; Washington, 1984
Most Passes Attempted, Season
609 Dan Fouts, San Diego, 1981
605 John Elway, Denver, 1985
603 Bill Kenney, Kansas City, 1983
Most Passes Attempted, Rookie, Season
450 Warren Moon, Houston, 1984
439 Jim Zorn, Seattle, 1976
392 Butch Songin, Boston, 1960
Most Passes Attempted, Game
68 George Blanda, Houston vs. Buffalo, Nov. 1, 1964
62 Joe Namath, N.Y. Jets vs. Baltimore, Oct. 18, 1970
Steve Dils, Minnesota vs. Tampa Bay, Sept. 5, 1981
Phil Simms, N.Y. Giants vs. Cincinnati, Oct. 13, 1985
61 Tommy Kramer, Minnesota vs. Buffalo, Dec. 16, 1979

COMPLETIONS
Most Seasons Leading League
5 Sammy Baugh, Washington, 1937, 1943, 1945, 1947-48
4 George Blanda, Chi. Bears, 1953; Houston, 1963-65
Sonny Jurgensen, Philadelphia, 1961; Washington, 1966-67, 1969
3 Arnie Herber, Green Bay, 1932, 1934, 1936
Johnny Unitas, Baltimore, 1959-60, 1963

John Brodie, San Francisco, 1965, 1968, 1970
Fran Tarkenton, Minnesota, 1975-76, 1978

Most Consecutive Seasons Leading League
3 George Blanda, Houston, 1963-65
2 By many players

Most Passes Completed, Career
3,686 Fran Tarkenton, Minnesota, 1961-66, 1972-78; N.Y. Giants, 1967-71
2,839 Dan Fouts, San Diego, 1973-85
2,830 Johnny Unitas, Baltimore, 1956-72; San Diego, 1973

Most Passes Completed, Season
362 Dan Marino, Miami, 1984
360 Dan Fouts, San Diego, 1981
348 Dan Fouts, San Diego, 1980

Most Passes Completed, Rookie, Season
259 Warren Moon, Houston, 1984
218 Dieter Brock, L.A. Rams, 1985
208 Jim Zorn, Seattle, 1976

Most Passes Completed, Game
42 Richard Todd, N.Y. Jets vs. San Francisco, Sept. 21, 1980
40 Ken Anderson, Cincinnati vs. San Diego, Dec. 20, 1982
Phil Simms, N.Y. Giants vs. Cincinnati, Oct. 13, 1985
38 Tommy Kramer, Minnesota vs. Cleveland, Dec. 14, 1980
Tommy Kramer, Minnesota vs. Green Bay, Nov. 29, 1981
Joe Ferguson, Buffalo vs. Miami, Oct. 9, 1983 (OT)

Most Consecutive Passes Completed
20 Ken Anderson, Cincinnati vs. Houston, Jan. 2, 1983
18 Steve DeBerg, Denver vs. L.A. Rams (17), Dec. 12, 1982; vs. Kansas City (1), Dec. 19, 1982
Lynn Dickey, Green Bay vs. Houston, Sept. 4, 1983
Joe Montana, San Francisco vs. L.A. Rams (13), Oct. 28, 1984; vs. Cincinnati (5), Nov. 4, 1984
17 Bert Jones, Baltimore vs. N.Y. Jets, Dec. 15, 1974

COMPLETION PERCENTAGE

Most Seasons Leading League
8 Len Dawson, Dall. Texans, 1962; Kansas City, 1964-69, 1975
7 Sammy Baugh, Washington, 1940, 1942-43, 1945, 1947-49
4 Bart Starr, Green Bay, 1962, 1966, 1968-69

Most Consecutive Seasons Leading League
6 Len Dawson, Kansas City, 1964-69
3 Sammy Baugh, Washington, 1947-49
Otto Graham, Cleveland, 1953-55
Milt Plum, Cleveland, 1959-61
2 By many players

Highest Completion Percentage, Career (1,500 attempts)
63.28 Joe Montana, San Francisco, 1979-85 (2,571-1,627)
59.85 Ken Stabler, Oakland, 1970-79; Houston, 1980-81; New Orleans, 1982-84 (3,793-2,270)
59.42 Danny White, Dallas, 1976-85 (2,393-1,422)

Highest Completion Percentage, Season (Qualifiers)
70.55 Ken Anderson, Cincinnati, 1982 (309-218)
70.33 Sammy Baugh, Washington, 1945 (182-128)
67.29 Steve Bartkowski, Atlanta, 1984 (269-181)

Highest Completion Percentage, Rookie, Season (Qualifiers)
59.73 Dieter Brock, L.A. Rams, 1985 (365-218)
58.45 Dan Marino, Miami, 1983 (296-173)
57.56 Warren Moon, Houston, 1984 (450-259)

Highest Completion Percentage, Game (20 attempts)
90.91 Ken Anderson, Cincinnati vs. Pittsburgh, Nov. 10, 1974 (22-20)
90.48 Lynn Dickey, Green Bay vs. New Orleans, Dec. 13, 1981 (21-19)
87.50 Danny White, Dallas vs. Philadelphia, Nov. 6, 1983 (24-21)

YARDS GAINED

Most Seasons Leading League
5 Sonny Jurgensen, Philadelphia, 1961-62; Washington, 1966-67, 1969
4 Sammy Baugh, Washington, 1937, 1940, 1947-48
Johnny Unitas, Baltimore, 1957, 1959-60, 1963
Dan Fouts, San Diego, 1979-82
3 Arnie Herber, Green Bay, 1932, 1934, 1936
Sid Luckman, Chi. Bears, 1943, 1945-46
John Brodie, San Francisco, 1965, 1968, 1970
John Hadl, San Diego, 1965, 1968, 1971
Joe Namath, N.Y. Jets, 1966-67, 1972

Most Consecutive Seasons Leading League
4 Dan Fouts, San Diego, 1979-82
2 By many players

Most Yards Gained, Career
47,003 Fran Tarkenton, Minnesota, 1961-66, 1972-78; N.Y. Giants, 1967-71
40,239 Johnny Unitas, Baltimore, 1956-72; San Diego, 1973
37,492 Dan Fouts, San Diego, 1973-85

Most Seasons, 3,000 or More Yards Passing
5 Sonny Jurgensen, Philadelphia, 1961-62; Washington, 1966-67, 1969
Dan Fouts, San Diego, 1979-81, 1984-85
4 Brian Sipe, Cleveland, 1979-81, 1983
Ron Jaworski, Philadelphia, 1980-81, 1983, 1985
Tommy Kramer, Minnesota, 1979-81, 1985
Joe Montana, San Francisco, 1981, 1983-85
Danny White, Dallas, 1980-81, 1983, 1985
3 By many players

Most Yards Gained, Season
5,084 Dan Marino, Miami, 1984
4,802 Dan Fouts, San Diego, 1981
4,715 Dan Fouts, San Diego, 1980

Most Yards Gained, Rookie, Season
3,338 Warren Moon, Houston, 1984
2,658 Dieter Brock, L.A. Rams, 1985
2,571 Jim Zorn, Seattle, 1976

Most Yards Gained, Game
554 Norm Van Brocklin, Los Angeles vs. N.Y. Yanks, Sept. 28, 1951
513 Phil Simms, N.Y. Giants vs. Cincinnati, Oct. 13, 1985
509 Vince Ferragamo, L.A. Rams vs. Chicago, Dec. 26, 1982

Most Games, 400 or More Yards Passing, Career
6 Dan Fouts, San Diego, 1973-85
5 Sonny Jurgensen, Philadelphia, 1957-63; Washington, 1964-74
4 Dan Marino, Miami, 1983-85

Most Games, 400 or More Yards Passing, Season
4 Dan Marino, Miami, 1984
2 George Blanda, Houston, 1961
Sonny Jurgensen, Philadelphia, 1961
Joe Namath, N.Y. Jets, 1972
Dan Fouts, San Diego, 1982, 1985
Phil Simms, N.Y. Giants, 1985

Most Consecutive Games, 400 or More Yards Passing
2 Dan Fouts, San Diego, 1982
Dan Marino, Miami, 1984
Phil Simms, N.Y. Giants, 1985

Most Games, 300 or More Yards Passing, Career
47 Dan Fouts, San Diego, 1973-85
26 Johnny Unitas, Baltimore, 1956-72; San Diego, 1973
25 Sonny Jurgensen, Philadelphia, 1957-63; Washington, 1964-74

Most Games, 300 or More Yards Passing, Season
9 Dan Marino, Miami, 1984
8 Dan Fouts, San Diego, 1980
7 Dan Fouts, San Diego, 1981, 1985
Bill Kenney, Kansas City, 1983
Neil Lomax, St. Louis, 1984

Most Consecutive Games, 300 or More Yards Passing, Season
5 Joe Montana, San Francisco, 1982
4 Dan Fouts, San Diego, 1979
Bill Kenney, Kansas City, 1983
3 By many players

Longest Pass Completion (All TDs except as noted)
99 Frank Filchock (to Farkas), Washington vs. Pittsburgh, Oct. 15, 1939
George Izo (to Mitchell), Washington vs. Cleveland, Sept. 15, 1963
Karl Sweetan (to Studstill), Detroit vs. Baltimore, Oct. 16, 1966
Sonny Jurgensen (to Allen), Washington vs. Chicago, Sept. 15, 1968
Jim Plunkett (to Branch), L.A. Raiders vs. Washington, Oct. 2, 1983
Ron Jaworski (to Quick), Philadelphia vs. Atlanta, Nov. 10, 1985
98 Doug Russell (to Tinsley), Chi. Cardinals vs. Cleveland, Nov. 27, 1938
Ogden Compton (to Lane), Chi. Cardinals vs. Green Bay, Nov. 13, 1955
Bill Wade (to Farrington), Chicago Bears vs. Detroit, Oct. 8, 1961
Jacky Lee (to Dewveall), Houston vs. San Diego, Nov. 25, 1962
Earl Morrall (to Jones), N.Y. Giants vs. Pittsburgh, Sept. 11, 1966
Jim Hart (to Moore), St. Louis vs. Los Angeles, Dec. 10, 1972 (no TD)
97 Pat Coffee (to Tinsley), Chi. Cardinals vs. Chi. Bears, Dec. 5, 1937
Bobby Layne (to Box), Detroit vs. Green Bay, Nov. 26, 1953
George Shaw (to Tarr), Denver vs. Boston, Sept. 21, 1962

AVERAGE GAIN

Most Seasons Leading League
7 Sid Luckman, Chi. Bears, 1939-43, 1946-47
3 Arnie Herber, Green Bay, 1932, 1934, 1936
Norm Van Brocklin, Los Angeles, 1950, 1952, 1954
Len Dawson, Dall. Texans, 1962; Kansas City, 1966, 1968
Bart Starr, Green Bay, 1966-68

Most Consecutive Seasons Leading League
5 Sid Luckman, Chi. Bears, 1939-43
3 Bart Starr, Green Bay, 1966-68
2 Bernie Masterson, Chi. Bears, 1937-38
Sid Luckman, Chi. Bears, 1946-47
Johnny Unitas, Baltimore, 1964-65
Terry Bradshaw, Pittsburgh, 1977-78
Steve Grogan, New England, 1980-81

Highest Average Gain, Career (1,500 attempts)
8.63 Otto Graham, Cleveland, 1950-55 (1,565-13,499)
8.42 Sid Luckman, Chi. Bears, 1939-50 (1,744-14,686)
8.16 Norm Van Brocklin, Los Angeles, 1949-57; Philadelphia, 1958-60 (2,895-23,611)

Highest Average Gain, Season (Qualifiers)
11.17 Tommy O'Connell, Cleveland, 1957 (110-1,229)
10.86 Sid Luckman, Chi. Bears, 1943 (202-2,194)
10.55 Otto Graham, Cleveland, 1953 (258-2,722)

Highest Average Gain, Rookie, Season (Qualifiers)
9.411 Greg Cook, Cincinnati, 1969 (197-1,854)
9.409 Bob Waterfield, Cleveland, 1945 (171-1,609)
8.36 Zeke Bratkowski, Chi. Bears, 1954 (130-1,087)

Highest Average Gain, Game (20 attempts)
18.58 Sammy Baugh, Washington vs. Boston, Oct. 31, 1948 (24-446)
18.50 Johnny Unitas, Baltimore vs. Atlanta, Nov. 12, 1967 (20-370)
17.71 Joe Namath, N.Y. Jets vs. Baltimore, Sept. 24, 1972 (28-496)

TOUCHDOWNS

Most Seasons Leading League
4 Johnny Unitas, Baltimore, 1957-60
Len Dawson, Dall. Texans, 1962; Kansas City, 1963, 1965-66
3 Arnie Herber, Green Bay, 1932, 1934, 1936
Sid Luckman, Chi. Bears, 1943, 1945-46
Y.A. Tittle, San Francisco, 1955; N.Y. Giants, 1962-63
2 By many players

Most Consecutive Seasons Leading League
4 Johnny Unitas, Baltimore, 1957-60
2 By many players

Most Touchdown Passes, Career
342 Fran Tarkenton, Minnesota, 1961-66, 1972-78; N.Y. Giants, 1967-71
290 Johnny Unitas, Baltimore, 1956-72: San Diego, 1973
255 Sonny Jurgensen, Philadelphia, 1957-63; Washington, 1964-74

Most Touchdown Passes, Season
48 Dan Marino, Miami, 1984
36 George Blanda, Houston, 1961
Y.A. Tittle, N.Y. Giants, 1963
34 Daryle Lamonica, Oakland, 1969

Most Touchdown Passes, Rookie, Season
22 Charlie Conerly, N.Y. Giants, 1948
Butch Songin, Boston, 1960
20 Dan Marino, Miami, 1983
19 Jim Plunkett, New England, 1971

Most Touchdown Passes, Game
7 Sid Luckman, Chi. Bears vs. N.Y. Giants, Nov. 14, 1943
Adrian Burk, Philadelphia vs. Washington, Oct. 17, 1954
George Blanda, Houston vs. N.Y. Titans, Nov. 19, 1961
Y.A. Tittle, N.Y. Giants vs. Washington, Oct. 28, 1962
Joe Kapp, Minnesota vs. Baltimore, Sept. 28, 1969
6 By many players. Last time: Dan Fouts, San Diego vs. Oakland, Nov. 22, 1981
Most Games, Four or More Touchdown Passes, Career
17 Johnny Unitas, Baltimore, 1956-72; San Diego, 1973
13 George Blanda, Chi. Bears, 1949, 1950-58; Baltimore, 1950; Houston, 1960-66; Oakland, 1967-75
12 Sonny Jurgensen, Philadelphia, 1957-63; Washington, 1964-74
Fran Tarkenton, Minnesota, 1961-66, 1972-78; N.Y. Giants, 1967-71
Dan Fouts, San Diego, 1973-85
Most Games, Four or More Touchdown Passes, Season
6 Dan Marino, Miami, 1984
4 George Blanda, Houston, 1961
Vince Ferragamo, Los Angeles, 1980
3 By many players
Most Consecutive Games, Four or More Touchdown Passes
4 Dan Marino, Miami, 1984
2 By many players
Most Consecutive Games, Touchdown Passes
47 Johnny Unitas, Baltimore, 1956-60
28 Dave Krieg, Seattle, 1983-85
25 Daryle Lamonica, Oakland, 1968-70

HAD INTERCEPTED
Most Consecutive Passes Attempted, None Intercepted
294 Bart Starr, Green Bay, 1964-65
208 Milt Plum, Cleveland, 1959-60
206 Roman Gabriel, Los Angeles, 1968-69
Most Passes Had Intercepted, Career
277 George Blanda, Chi. Bears, 1949, 1950-58; Baltimore, 1950; Houston, 1960-66; Oakland, 1967-75
268 John Hadl, San Diego, 1962-72; Los Angeles, 1973-74; Green Bay, 1974-75; Houston, 1976-77
266 Fran Tarkenton, Minnesota, 1961-66, 1972-78; N.Y. Giants, 1967-71
Most Passes Had Intercepted, Season
42 George Blanda, Houston, 1962
34 Frank Tripucka, Denver, 1960
32 John Hadl, San Diego, 1968
Fran Tarkenton, Minnesota, 1978
Most Passes Had Intercepted, Game
8 Jim Hardy, Chi. Cardinals vs. Philadelphia, Sept. 24, 1950
7 Parker Hall, Cleveland vs. Green Bay, Nov. 8, 1942
Frank Sinkwich, Detroit vs. Green Bay, Oct. 24, 1943
Bob Waterfield, Los Angeles vs. Green Bay, Oct. 17, 1948
Zeke Bratkowski, Chicago vs. Baltimore, Oct. 2, 1960
Tommy Wade, Pittsburgh vs. Philadelphia, Dec. 12, 1965
Ken Stabler, Oakland vs. Denver, Oct. 16, 1977
6 By many players
Most Attempts, No Interceptions, Game
57 Joe Montana, San Francisco vs. Atlanta, Oct. 6, 1985
51 Scott Brunner, N.Y. Giants vs. St. Louis, Dec. 26, 1982
50 Dan Fouts, San Diego vs. Green Bay, Oct. 7, 1984

LOWEST PERCENTAGE, PASSES HAD INTERCEPTED
Most Seasons Leading League, Lowest Percentage, Passes Had Intercepted
5 Sammy Baugh, Washington, 1940, 1942, 1944-45, 1947
3 Charlie Conerly, N.Y. Giants, 1950, 1956, 1959
Bart Starr, Green Bay, 1962, 1964, 1966
Roger Staubach, Dallas, 1971, 1977, 1979
Ken Anderson, Cincinnati, 1972, 1981-82
2 By many players
Lowest Percentage, Passes Had Intercepted, Career (1,500 attempts)
2.61 Joe Montana, San Francisco, 1979-85 (2,571-67)
3.31 Roman Gabriel, Los Angeles, 1962-72; Philadelphia, 1973-77 (4,498-149)
3.52 Bill Kenney, Kansas City, 1980-85 (1,735-61)
Lowest Percentage, Passes Had Intercepted, Season (Qualifiers)
0.66 Joe Ferguson, Buffalo, 1976 (151-1)
1.16 Steve Bartkowski, Atlanta, 1983 (432-5)
1.20 Bart Starr, Green Bay, 1966 (251-3)
Lowest Percentage, Passes Had Intercepted, Rookie, Season (Qualifiers)
2.03 Dan Marino, Miami, 1983 (296-6)
2.10 Gary Wood, N.Y. Giants, 1964 (143-3)
2.82 Bernie Kosar, Cleveland, 1985 (248-7)

TIMES SACKED
Times Sacked has been compiled since 1963.
Most Times Sacked, Career
483 Fran Tarkenton, Minnesota, 1961-66, 1972-78; N.Y. Giants, 1967-71
405 Craig Morton, Dallas, 1965-74; N.Y. Giants, 1974-76; Denver, 1977-82
397 Ken Anderson, Cincinnati, 1971-85
Most Times Sacked, Season
62 Ken O'Brien, N.Y. Jets, 1985
61 Neil Lomax, St. Louis, 1985
59 Tony Eason, New England, 1984
Most Times Sacked, Game
12 Bert Jones, Baltimore vs. St. Louis, Oct. 26, 1980
Warren Moon, Houston vs. Dallas, Sept. 29, 1985
11 Charley Johnson, St. Louis vs. N.Y. Giants, Nov. 1, 1964
Bart Starr, Green Bay vs. Detroit, Nov. 7, 1965
Jack Kemp, Buffalo vs. Oakland, Oct. 15, 1967
Bob Berry, Atlanta vs. St. Louis, Nov. 24, 1968
Greg Landry, Detroit vs. Dallas, Oct. 6, 1975
Ron Jaworski, Philadelphia vs. St. Louis, Dec. 18, 1983
Paul McDonald, Cleveland vs. Kansas City, Sept. 30, 1984
Archie Manning, Minnesota vs. Chicago, Oct. 28, 1984
10 By many players

PASS RECEIVING

Most Seasons Leading League
8 Don Hutson, Green Bay, 1936-37, 1939, 1941-45
5 Lionel Taylor, Denver, 1960-63, 1965
3 Tom Fears, Los Angeles, 1948-50
Pete Pihos, Philadelphia, 1953-55
Billy Wilson, San Francisco, 1954, 1956-57
Raymond Berry, Baltimore, 1958-60
Lance Alworth, San Diego, 1966, 1968-69
Most Consecutive Seasons Leading League
5 Don Hutson, Green Bay, 1941-45
4 Lionel Taylor, Denver, 1960-63
3 Tom Fears, Los Angeles, 1948-50
Pete Pihos, Philadelphia, 1953-55
Raymond Berry, Baltimore, 1958-60
Most Pass Receptions, Career
716 Charlie Joiner, Houston, 1969-72; Cincinnati, 1972-75; San Diego, 1976-85
649 Charley Taylor, Washington, 1964-75, 1977
633 Don Maynard, N.Y. Giants, 1958; N.Y. Jets, 1960-72; St. Louis, 1973
Most Seasons, 50 or More Pass Receptions
8 Steve Largent, Seattle, 1976, 1978-81, 1983-85
7 Raymond Berry, Baltimore, 1958-62, 1965-66
Art Powell, N.Y. Titans, 1960-62; Oakland, 1963-66
Lance Alworth, San Diego, 1963-69
Charley Taylor, Washington, 1964, 1966-67, 1969, 1973-75
Charlie Joiner, San Diego, 1976, 1979-81, 1983-85
6 Lionel Taylor, Denver, 1960-65
Bobby Mitchell, Washington, 1962-67
Ahmad Rashad, Minnesota, 1976-81
Wes Chandler, New Orleans, 1979-80; New Orleans-San Diego, 1981; San Diego, 1983-85
Dwight Clark, San Francisco, 1980-85
James Lofton, Green Bay, 1979-81, 1983-85
Ozzie Newsome, Cleveland, 1979-81, 1983-85
Most Pass Receptions, Season
106 Art Monk, Washington, 1984
101 Charley Hennigan, Houston, 1964
100 Lionel Taylor, Denver, 1961
Most Pass Receptions, Rookie, Season
83 Earl Cooper, San Francisco, 1980
72 Bill Groman, Houston, 1960
67 Jack Clancy, Miami, 1967
Cris Collinsworth, Cincinnati, 1981
Most Pass Receptions, Game
18 Tom Fears, Los Angeles vs. Green Bay, Dec. 3, 1950
17 Clark Gaines, N.Y. Jets vs. San Francisco, Sept. 21, 1980
16 Sonny Randle, St. Louis vs. N.Y. Giants, Nov. 4, 1962
Most Consecutive Games, Pass Receptions
127 Harold Carmichael, Philadelphia, 1972-80
123 Steve Largent, Seattle, 1977-85 (current)
121 Mel Gray, St. Louis, 1973-82

YARDS GAINED
Most Seasons Leading League
7 Don Hutson, Green Bay, 1936, 1938-39, 1941-44
3 Raymond Berry, Baltimore, 1957, 1959-60
Lance Alworth, San Diego, 1965-66, 1968
2 By many players
Most Consecutive Seasons Leading League
4 Don Hutson, Green Bay, 1941-44
2 By many players
Most Yards Gained, Career
11,834 Don Maynard, N.Y. Giants, 1958; N.Y. Jets, 1960-72; St. Louis, 1973
11,706 Charlie Joiner, Houston, 1969-72; Cincinnati, 1972-75; San Diego, 1976-85
10,372 Harold Jackson, Los Angeles, 1968, 1973-77; Philadelphia, 1969-72; New England, 1978-81; Minnesota, 1982; Seattle, 1983
Most Seasons, 1,000 or More Yards, Pass Receiving
7 Lance Alworth, San Diego, 1963-69
Steve Largent, Seattle, 1978-81, 1983-85
5 Art Powell, N.Y. Titans, 1960, 1962; Oakland, 1963-64, 1966
Don Maynard, N.Y. Jets, 1960, 1962, 1965, 1967-68
James Lofton, Green Bay, 1980-81, 1983-85
4 Del Shofner, Los Angeles, 1958; N.Y. Giants, 1961-63
Lionel Taylor, Denver, 1960-61, 1963, 1965
Charlie Joiner, San Diego, 1976, 1979-81
Wes Chandler, New Orleans, 1979; New Orleans-San Diego, 1981; San Diego, 1982, 1985
Most Yards Gained, Season
1,746 Charley Hennigan, Houston, 1961
1,602 Lance Alworth, San Diego, 1965
1,555 Roy Green, St. Louis, 1984
Most Yards Gained, Rookie, Season
1,473 Bill Groman, Houston, 1960
1,231 Bill Howton, Green Bay, 1952
1,124 Harlon Hill, Chi. Bears, 1954
Most Yards Gained, Game
309 Stephone Paige, Kansas City vs. San Diego, Dec. 22, 1985
303 Jim Benton, Cleveland vs. Detroit, Nov. 22, 1945
302 Cloyce Box, Detroit vs. Baltimore, Dec. 3, 1950
Most Games, 200 or More Yards Pass Receiving, Career
5 Lance Alworth, San Diego, 1962-70; Dallas, 1971-72
4 Don Hutson, Green Bay, 1935-45
Charley Hennigan, Houston, 1960-66
3 Don Maynard, N.Y. Giants, 1958; N.Y. Jets, 1960-72; St. Louis, 1973
Wes Chandler, New Orleans, 1978-81; San Diego, 1981-85
Most Games, 200 or More Yards Pass Receiving, Season
3 Charley Hennigan, Houston, 1961
2 Don Hutson, Green Bay, 1942
Gene Roberts, N.Y. Giants, 1949
Lance Alworth, San Diego, 1963
Don Maynard, N.Y. Jets, 1968

Most Games, 100 or More Yards Pass Receiving, Career
50 Don Maynard, N.Y. Giants, 1958; N.Y. Jets, 1960-72; St. Louis, 1973
41 Lance Alworth, San Diego, 1962-70; Dallas, 1971-72
36 Steve Largent, Seattle, 1976-85
Most Games, 100 or More Yards Pass Receiving, Season
10 Charley Hennigan, Houston, 1961
9 Elroy (Crazylegs) Hirsch, Los Angeles, 1951
Bill Groman, Houston, 1960
Lance Alworth, San Diego, 1965
Don Maynard, N.Y. Jets, 1967
8 Charley Hennigan, Houston, 1964
Lance Alworth, San Diego, 1967
Most Consecutive Games, 100 or More Yards Pass Receiving
7 Charley Hennigan, Houston, 1961
Bill Groman, Houston, 1961
6 Raymond Berry, Baltimore, 1960
Pat Studstill, Detroit, 1966
5 Elroy (Crazylegs) Hirsch, Los Angeles, 1951
Bob Boyd, Los Angeles, 1954
Terry Barr, Detroit, 1963
Lance Alworth, San Diego, 1966
Longest Pass Reception (All TDs except as noted)
99 Andy Farkas (from Filchock), Washington vs. Pittsburgh, Oct. 15, 1939
Bobby Mitchell (from Izo), Washington vs. Cleveland, Sept. 15, 1963
Pat Studstill (from Sweetan), Detroit vs. Baltimore, Oct. 16, 1966
Gerry Allen (from Jurgensen), Washington vs. Chicago, Sept. 15, 1968
Cliff Branch (from Plunkett), L.A. Raiders vs. Washington, Oct. 2, 1983
Mike Quick (from Jaworski), Philadelphia vs. Atlanta, Nov. 10, 1985
98 Gaynell Tinsley (from Russell), Chi. Cardinals vs. Cleveland, Nov. 17, 1938
Dick (Night Train) Lane (from Compton), Chi. Cardinals vs. Green Bay, Nov. 13, 1955
John Farrington (from Wade), Chicago vs. Detroit, Oct. 8, 1961
Willard Dewveall (from Lee), Houston vs. San Diego, Nov. 25, 1962
Homer Jones (from Morrall), N.Y. Giants vs. Pittsburgh, Sept. 11, 1966
Bobby Moore (from Hart), St. Louis vs. Los Angeles, Dec. 10, 1972 (no TD)
97 Gaynell Tinsley (from Coffee), Chi. Cardinals vs. Chi. Bears, Dec. 5, 1937
Cloyce Box (from Layne), Detroit vs. Green Bay, Nov. 26, 1953
Jerry Tarr (from Shaw), Denver vs. Boston, Sept. 21, 1962

AVERAGE GAIN
Highest Average Gain, Career (200 receptions)
22.26 Homer Jones, N.Y. Giants, 1964-69; Cleveland, 1970 (224-4,986)
20.82 Buddy Dial, Pittsburgh, 1959-63; Dallas, 1964-66 (261-5,436)
20.52 Stanley Morgan, New England, 1977-85 (351-7,201)
Highest Average Gain, Season (24 receptions)
32.58 Don Currivan, Boston, 1947 (24-782)
31.44 Bucky Pope, Los Angeles, 1964 (25-786)
27.58 Jimmy Orr, Pittsburgh, 1958 (33-910)
Highest Average Gain, Game (3 receptions)
60.67 Bill Groman, Houston vs. Denver, Nov. 20, 1960 (3-182)
Homer Jones, N.Y. Giants vs. Washington, Dec. 12, 1965 (3-182)
60.33 Don Currivan, Boston vs. Washington, Nov. 30, 1947 (3-181)
59.67 Bobby Duckworth, San Diego vs. Chicago, Dec. 3, 1984 (3-179)

TOUCHDOWNS
Most Seasons Leading League
9 Don Hutson, Green Bay, 1935-38, 1940-44
3 Lance Alworth, San Diego, 1964-66
2 By many players
Most Consecutive Seasons Leading League
5 Don Hutson, Green Bay, 1940-44
4 Don Hutson, Green Bay, 1935-38
3 Lance Alworth, San Diego, 1964-66
Most Touchdowns, Career
99 Don Hutson, Green Bay, 1935-45
88 Don Maynard, N.Y. Giants, 1958; N.Y. Jets, 1960-72; St. Louis, 1973
85 Lance Alworth, San Diego, 1962-70; Dallas, 1971-72
Paul Warfield, Cleveland, 1964-69, 1976-77; Miami, 1970-74
Most Touchdowns, Season
18 Mark Clayton, Miami, 1984
17 Don Hutson, Green Bay, 1942
Elroy (Crazylegs) Hirsch, Los Angeles, 1951
Bill Groman, Houston, 1961
16 Art Powell, Oakland, 1963
Most Touchdowns, Rookie, Season
13 Bill Howton, Green Bay, 1952
John Jefferson, San Diego, 1979
12 Harlon Hill, Chi. Bears, 1954
Bill Groman, Houston, 1960
Mike Ditka, Chicago, 1961
Bob Hayes, Dallas, 1965
10 Bill Swiacki, N.Y. Giants, 1948
Bucky Pope, Los Angeles, 1964
Sammy White, Minnesota, 1976
Daryl Turner, Seattle, 1984
Most Touchdowns, Game
5 Bob Shaw, Chi. Cardinals vs. Baltimore, Oct. 2, 1950
Kellen Winslow, San Diego vs. Oakland, Nov. 22, 1981
4 By many players
Most Consecutive Games, Touchdowns
11 Elroy (Crazylegs) Hirsch, Los Angeles, 1950-51
Buddy Dial, Pittsburgh, 1959-60
9 Lance Alworth, San Diego, 1963
8 Bill Groman, Houston, 1961
Dave Parks, San Francisco, 1965

INTERCEPTIONS BY

Most Seasons Leading League
3 Everson Walls, Dallas, 1981-82, 1985
2 Dick (Night Train) Lane, Los Angeles, 1952; Chi. Cardinals, 1954
Jack Christiansen, Detroit, 1953, 1957
Milt Davis, Baltimore, 1957, 1959
Dick Lynch, N.Y. Giants, 1961, 1963
Johnny Robinson, Kansas City, 1966, 1970
Bill Bradley, Philadelphia, 1971-72
Emmitt Thomas, Kansas City, 1969, 1974
Most Interceptions By, Career
81 Paul Krause, Washington, 1964-67; Minnesota, 1968-79
79 Emlen Tunnell, N.Y. Giants, 1948-58; Green Bay, 1959-61
68 Dick (Night Train) Lane, Los Angeles, 1952-53; Chi. Cardinals, 1954-59; Detroit, 1960-65
Most Interceptions By, Season
14 Dick (Night Train) Lane, Los Angeles, 1952
13 Dan Sandifer, Washington, 1948
Orban (Spec) Sanders, N.Y. Yanks, 1950
Lester Hayes, Oakland, 1980
12 By nine players
Most Interceptions By, Rookie, Season
14 Dick (Night Train) Lane, Los Angeles, 1952
13 Dan Sandifer, Washington, 1948
12 Woodley Lewis, Los Angeles, 1950
Paul Krause, Washington, 1964
Most Interceptions By, Game
4 Sammy Baugh, Washington vs. Detroit, Nov. 14, 1943
Dan Sandifer, Washington vs. Boston, Oct. 31, 1948
Don Doll, Detroit vs. Chi. Cardinals, Oct. 23, 1949
Bob Nussbaumer, Chi. Cardinals vs. N.Y. Bulldogs, Nov. 13, 1949
Russ Craft, Philadelphia vs. Chi. Cardinals, Sept. 24, 1950
Bobby Dillon, Green Bay vs. Detroit, Nov. 26, 1953
Jack Butler, Pittsburgh vs. Washington, Dec. 13, 1953
Austin (Goose) Gonsoulin, Denver vs. Buffalo, Sept. 18, 1960
Jerry Norton, St. Louis vs. Washington, Nov. 20, 1960; vs. Pittsburgh, Nov. 26, 1961
Dave Baker, San Francisco vs. L.A. Rams, Dec. 4, 1960
Bobby Ply, Dall. Texans vs. San Diego, Dec. 16, 1962
Bobby Hunt, Kansas City vs. Houston, Oct. 4, 1964
Willie Brown, Denver vs. N.Y. Jets, Nov. 15, 1964
Dick Anderson, Miami vs. Pittsburgh, Dec. 3, 1973
Willie Buchanon, Green Bay vs. San Diego, Sept. 24, 1978
Deron Cherry, Kansas City vs. Seattle, Sept. 29, 1985
Most Consecutive Games, Passes Intercepted By
8 Tom Morrow, Oakland, 1962-63
7 Paul Krause, Washington, 1964
Larry Wilson, St. Louis, 1966
Ben Davis, Cleveland, 1968
6 Dick (Night Train) Lane, Chi. Cardinals, 1954-55
Will Sherman, Los Angeles, 1954-55
Jim Shofner, Cleveland, 1960
Paul Krause, Minnesota, 1968
Willie Williams, N.Y. Giants, 1968
Kermit Alexander, San Francisco, 1968-69
Mel Blount, Pittsburgh, 1975
Eric Harris, Kansas City, 1980
Lester Hayes, Oakland, 1980

YARDS GAINED
Most Seasons Leading League
2 Dick (Night Train) Lane, Los Angeles, 1952; Chi. Cardinals, 1954
Herb Adderley, Green Bay, 1965, 1969
Dick Anderson, Miami, 1968, 1970
Most Yards Gained, Career
1,282 Emlen Tunnell, N.Y. Giants, 1948-58; Green Bay, 1959-61
1,207 Dick (Night Train) Lane, Los Angeles, 1952-53; Chi. Cardinals, 1954-59; Detroit, 1960-65
1,185 Paul Krause, Washington, 1964-67; Minnesota, 1968-79
Most Yards Gained, Season
349 Charlie McNeil, San Diego, 1961
301 Don Doll, Detroit, 1949
298 Dick (Night Train) Lane, Los Angeles, 1952
Most Yards Gained, Rookie, Season
301 Don Doll, Detroit, 1949
298 Dick (Night Train) Lane, Los Angeles, 1952
275 Woodley Lewis, Los Angeles, 1950
Most Yards Gained, Game
177 Charlie McNeil, San Diego vs. Houston, Sept. 24, 1961
167 Dick Jauron, Detroit vs. Chicago, Nov. 18, 1973
151 Tom Myers, New Orleans vs. Minnesota, Sept. 3, 1978
Mike Haynes, L.A. Raiders vs. Miami, Dec. 2, 1984
Longest Return (All TDs)
102 Bob Smith, Detroit vs. Chi. Bears, Nov. 24, 1949
Erich Barnes, N.Y. Giants vs. Dall. Cowboys, Oct. 22, 1961
Gary Barbaro, Kansas City vs. Seattle, Dec. 11, 1977
Louis Breeden, Cincinnati vs. San Diego, Nov. 8, 1981
101 Richie Petitbon, Chicago vs Los Angeles, Dec. 9, 1962
Henry Carr, N.Y. Giants vs. Los Angeles, Nov. 13, 1966
Tony Greene, Buffalo vs. Kansas City, Oct. 3, 1976
Tom Pridemore, Atlanta vs. San Francisco, Sept. 20, 1981
100 Vern Huffman, Detroit vs. Brooklyn, Oct. 17, 1937
Mike Gaechter, Dall. Cowboys vs. Philadelphia, Oct. 14, 1962
Les (Speedy) Duncan, San Diego vs. Kansas City, Oct. 15, 1967
Tom Janik, Buffalo vs. N.Y. Jets, Sept. 29, 1968
Tim Collier, Kansas City vs. Oakland, Dec. 18, 1977

TOUCHDOWNS
Most Touchdowns, Career
9 Ken Houston, Houston, 1967-72; Washington, 1973-80
7 Herb Adderley, Green Bay, 1961-69; Dallas, 1970-72
Erich Barnes, Chi. Bears, 1958-60; N.Y. Giants, 1961-64; Cleveland, 1965-70
Lem Barney, Detroit, 1967-77
6 Tom Janik, Denver, 1963-64; Buffalo, 1965-68; Boston, 1969-70; New England, 1971
Miller Farr, Denver, 1965; San Diego, 1965-66; Houston, 1967-69; St. Louis, 1970-72; Detroit, 1973
Bobby Bell, Kansas City, 1963-74
Most Touchdowns, Season
4 Ken Houston, Houston, 1971

Jim Kearney, Kansas City, 1972
3 Dick Harris, San Diego, 1961
Dick Lynch, N.Y. Giants, 1963
Herb Adderley, Green Bay, 1965
Lem Barney, Detroit, 1967
Miller Farr, Houston, 1967
Monte Jackson, Los Angeles, 1976
Rod Perry, Los Angeles, 1978
Ronnie Lott, San Francisco, 1981
2 By many players

Most Touchdowns, Rookie, Season
3 Lem Barney, Detroit, 1967
Ronnie Lott, San Francisco, 1981
2 By many players

Most Touchdowns, Game
2 Bill Blackburn, Chi. Cardinals vs. Boston, Oct. 24, 1948
Dan Sandifer, Washington vs. Boston, Oct. 31, 1948
Bob Franklin, Cleveland vs. Chicago, Dec. 11, 1960
Bill Stacy, St. Louis vs. Dall. Cowboys, Nov. 5, 1961
Jerry Norton, St. Louis vs. Pittsburgh, Nov. 26, 1961
Miller Farr, Houston vs. Buffalo, Dec. 7, 1968
Ken Houston, Houston vs. San Diego, Dec. 19, 1971
Jim Kearney, Kansas City vs. Denver, Oct. 1, 1972
Lemar Parrish, Cincinnati vs. Houston, Dec. 17, 1972
Dick Anderson, Miami vs. Pittsburgh, Dec. 3, 1973
Prentice McCray, New England vs. N.Y. Jets, Nov. 21, 1976
Kenny Johnson, Atlanta vs. Green Bay, Nov. 27, 1983 (OT)
Mike Kozlowski, Miami vs. N.Y. Jets, Dec. 16, 1983
Dave Brown, Seattle vs. Kansas City, Nov. 4, 1984

PUNTING

Most Seasons Leading League
4 Sammy Baugh, Washington, 1940-43
Jerrel Wilson, Kansas City, 1965, 1968, 1972-73
3 Yale Lary, Detroit, 1959, 1961, 1963
Jim Fraser, Denver, 1962-64
Ray Guy, Oakland, 1974-75, 1977
2 By many players

Most Consecutive Seasons Leading League
4 Sammy Baugh, Washington, 1940-43
3 Jim Fraser, Denver, 1962-64
2 By many players

PUNTS

Most Punts, Career
1,083 John James, Atlanta, 1972-81; Detroit, 1982, Houston, 1982-84
1,072 Jerrel Wilson, Kansas City, 1963-77; New England, 1978
1,005 Dave Jennings, N.Y. Giants, 1974-84; N.Y. Jets, 1985

Most Punts, Season
114 Bob Parsons, Chicago, 1981
109 John James, Atlanta, 1978
106 David Beverly, Green Bay, 1978

Most Punts, Rookie, Season
96 Mike Connell, San Francisco, 1978
Chris Norman, Denver, 1984
93 Wilbur Summers, Detroit, 1977
Ken Clark, Los Angeles, 1979
Jim Arnold, Kansas City, 1983
92 Mike Horan, Philadelphia, 1984

Most Punts, Game
14 Dick Nesbitt, Chi. Cardinals vs. Chi. Bears, Nov. 30, 1933
Keith Molesworth, Chi. Bears vs. Green Bay, Dec. 10, 1933
Sammy Baugh, Washington vs. Philadelphia, Nov. 5, 1939
Carl Kinscherf, N.Y. Giants vs. Detroit, Nov. 7, 1943
George Taliaferro, N.Y. Yanks vs. Los Angeles, Sept. 28, 1951
12 Parker Hall, Cleveland vs. Green Bay, Nov. 26, 1939
Beryl Clark, Chi. Cardinals vs. Detroit, Sept. 15, 1940
Len Barnum, Philadelphia vs. Washington, Oct. 4, 1942
Horace Gillom, Cleveland vs. Philadelphia, Dec. 3, 1950
Adrian Burk, Philadelphia vs. Green Bay, Nov. 2, 1952; vs. N.Y. Giants, Dec. 12, 1954
Bob Scarpitto, Denver vs. Oakland, Sept. 10, 1967
Bill Van Heusen, Denver vs. Cincinnati, Oct. 6, 1968
Tom Blanchard, New Orleans vs. Minnesota, Nov. 16, 1975
Rusty Jackson, Los Angeles vs. San Francisco, Nov. 21, 1976
Wilbur Summers, Detroit vs. San Francisco, Oct. 23, 1977
John James, Atlanta vs. Washington, Dec. 10, 1978
Luke Prestridge, Denver vs. Buffalo, Oct. 25, 1981
Greg Coleman, Minnesota vs. Green Bay, Nov. 21, 1982
11 By many players

Longest Punt
98 Steve O'Neal, N.Y. Jets vs. Denver, Sept. 21, 1969
94 Joe Lintzenich, Chi. Bears vs. N.Y. Giants, Nov. 16, 1931
90 Don Chandler, Green Bay vs. San Francisco, Oct. 10, 1965

AVERAGE YARDAGE

Highest Average, Punting, Career (300 punts)
45.16 Rohn Stark, Baltimore, 1982-83; Indianapolis, 1984-85 (313-14,135)
45.10 Sammy Baugh, Washington, 1937-52 (338-15,245)
44.68 Tommy Davis, San Francisco, 1959-69 (511-22,833)

Highest Average, Punting, Season (Qualifiers)
51.40 Sammy Baugh, Washington, 1940 (35-1,799)
48.94 Yale Lary, Detroit, 1963 (35-1,713)
48.73 Sammy Baugh, Washington, 1941 (30-1,462)

Highest Average, Punting, Rookie, Season (Qualifiers)
46.40 Bobby Walden, Minnesota, 1964 (72-3,341)
46.22 Dave Lewis, Cincinnati, 1970 (79-3,651)
45.92 Frank Sinkwich, Detroit, 1943 (12-551)

Highest Average, Punting, Game (4 punts)
61.75 Bob Cifers, Detroit vs. Chi. Bears, Nov. 24, 1946 (4-247)
61.60 Roy McKay, Green Bay vs. Chi. Cardinals, Oct. 28, 1945 (5-308)
59.40 Sammy Baugh, Washington vs. Detroit, Oct. 27, 1940 (5-297)

PUNTS HAD BLOCKED

Most Consecutive Punts, None Blocked
623 Dave Jennings, N.Y. Giants, 1976-83
578 Bobby Walden, Minnesota, 1964-67; Pittsburgh, 1968-72
533 Bobby Joe Green, Pittsburgh, 1960-61; Chicago, 1962-68

Most Punts Had Blocked, Career
14 Herman Weaver, Detroit, 1970-76; Seattle, 1977-80
12 Jerrel Wilson, Kansas City, 1963-77; New England, 1978
Tom Blanchard, N.Y. Giants, 1971-73; New Orleans, 1974-78; Tampa Bay, 1979-81
11 David Lee, Baltimore, 1966-78

PUNT RETURNS

Most Seasons Leading League
3 Les (Speedy) Duncan, San Diego, 1965-66; Washington, 1971
Rick Upchurch, Denver, 1976, 1978, 1982
2 Dick Christy, N.Y. Titans, 1961-62
Claude Gibson, Oakland, 1963-64
Billy Johnson, Houston, 1975, 1977

PUNT RETURNS

Most Punt Returns, Career
258 Emlen Tunnell, N.Y. Giants, 1948-58; Green Bay, 1959-61
253 Alvin Haymond, Baltimore, 1964-67; Philadelphia, 1968; Los Angeles, 1969-71; Washington, 1972; Houston, 1973
252 Mike Fuller, San Diego, 1975-80; Cincinnati, 1981-82

Most Punt Returns, Season
70 Danny Reece, Tampa Bay, 1979
62 Fulton Walker, Miami-L.A. Raiders, 1985
58 J. T. Smith, Kansas City, 1979
Greg Pruitt, L.A. Raiders, 1983

Most Punt Returns, Rookie, Season
54 James Jones, Dallas, 1980
53 Louis Lipps, Pittsburgh, 1984
52 Leon Bright, N.Y. Giants, 1981
Robbie Martin, Detroit, 1981

Most Punt Returns, Game
11 Eddie Brown, Washington vs. Tampa Bay, Oct. 9, 1977
10 Theo Bell, Pittsburgh vs. Buffalo, Dec. 16, 1979
Mike Nelms, Washington vs. New Orleans, Dec. 26, 1982
9 Rodger Bird, Oakland vs. Denver, Sept. 10, 1967
Ralph McGill, San Francisco vs. Atlanta, Oct. 29, 1972
Ed Podolak, Kansas City vs. San Diego, Nov. 10, 1974
Anthony Leonard, San Francisco vs. New Orleans, Oct. 17, 1976
Butch Johnson, Dallas vs. Buffalo, Nov. 15, 1976
Larry Marshall, Philadelphia vs. Tampa Bay, Sept. 18, 1977
Nesby Glasgow, Baltimore vs. Kansas City, Sept. 2, 1979
Mike Nelms, Washington vs. St. Louis, Dec. 21, 1980
Leon Bright, N.Y. Giants vs. Philadelphia, Dec. 11, 1982
Pete Shaw, N.Y. Giants vs. Philadelphia, Nov. 20, 1983
Cleotha Montgomery, L.A. Raiders vs. Detroit, Dec. 10, 1984

FAIR CATCHES

Most Fair Catches, Season
24 Ken Graham, San Diego, 1969
22 Lem Barney, Detroit, 1976
21 Ed Podolak, Kansas City, 1970
Steve Schubert, Chicago, 1978
Stanley Morgan, New England, 1979

Most Fair Catches, Game
7 Lem Barney, Detroit vs. Chicago, Nov. 21, 1976
6 Jake Scott, Miami vs. Buffalo, Dec. 20, 1970
Greg Pruitt, L.A. Raiders vs. Seattle, Oct. 7, 1984
5 By many players

YARDS GAINED

Most Seasons Leading League
3 Alvin Haymond, Baltimore, 1965-66; Los Angeles, 1969
2 Bill Dudley, Pittsburgh, 1942, 1946
Emlen Tunnell, N.Y. Giants, 1951-52
Dick Christy, N.Y. Titans, 1961-62
Claude Gibson, Oakland, 1963-64
Rodger Bird, Oakland, 1966-67
J. T. Smith, Kansas City, 1979-80

Most Yards Gained, Career
3,036 Billy Johnson, Houston, 1974-80; Atlanta, 1982-85
3,008 Rick Upchurch, Denver, 1975-83
2,660 Mike Fuller, San Diego, 1975-80; Cincinnati, 1981-82

Most Yards Gained, Season
692 Fulton Walker, Miami-L.A. Raiders, 1985
666 Greg Pruitt, L.A. Raiders, 1983
656 Louis Lipps, Pittsburgh, 1984

Most Yards Gained, Rookie, Season
656 Louis Lipps, Pittsburgh, 1984
655 Neal Colzie, Oakland, 1975
608 Mike Haynes, New England, 1976

Most Yards Gained, Game
207 LeRoy Irvin, Los Angeles vs. Atlanta, Oct. 11, 1981
205 George Atkinson, Oakland vs. Buffalo, Sept. 15, 1968
184 Tom Watkins, Detroit vs. San Francisco, Oct. 6, 1963

Longest Punt Return (All TDs)
98 Gil LeFebvre, Cincinnati vs. Brooklyn, Dec. 3, 1933
Charlie West, Minnesota vs. Washington, Nov. 3, 1968
Dennis Morgan, Dallas vs. St. Louis, Oct. 13, 1974
97 Greg Pruitt, L.A. Raiders vs. Washington, Oct. 2, 1983
96 Bill Dudley, Washington vs. Pittsburgh, Dec. 3, 1950

AVERAGE YARDAGE

Highest Average, Career (75 returns)
13.51 Henry Ellard, L.A. Rams, 1983-85 (83-1,121)
12.78 George McAfee, Chi. Bears, 1940-41, 1945-50 (112-1,431)
12.75 Jack Christiansen, Detroit, 1951-58 (85-1,084)

Highest Average, Season (Qualifiers)
23.00 Herb Rich, Baltimore, 1950 (12-276)
21.47 Jack Christiansen, Detroit, 1952 (15-322)
21.28 Dick Christy, N.Y. Titans, 1961 (18-383)
Highest Average, Rookie, Season (Qualifiers)
23.00 Herb Rich, Baltimore, 1950 (12-276)
20.88 Jerry Davis, Chi. Cardinals, 1948 (16-334)
20.73 Frank Sinkwich, Detroit, 1943 (11-228)
Highest Average, Game (3 returns)
47.67 Chuck Latourette, St. Louis vs. New Orleans, Sept. 29, 1968 (3-143)
47.33 Johnny Roland, St. Louis vs. Philadelphia, Oct. 2, 1966 (3-142)
45.67 Dick Christy, N.Y. Titans vs. Denver, Sept. 24, 1961 (3-137)

TOUCHDOWNS
Most Touchdowns, Career
8 Jack Christiansen, Detroit, 1951-58
Rick Upchurch, Denver, 1975-83
6 Billy Johnson, Houston, 1974-80; Atlanta, 1982-85
5 Emlen Tunnell, N.Y. Giants, 1948-58; Green Bay, 1959-61
Most Touchdowns, Season
4 Jack Christiansen, Detroit, 1951
Rick Upchurch, Denver, 1976
3 Emlen Tunnell, N.Y. Giants, 1951
Billy Johnson, Houston, 1975
LeRoy Irvin, Los Angeles, 1981
2 By many players
Most Touchdowns, Rookie, Season
4 Jack Christiansen, Detroit, 1951
2 By five players
Most Touchdowns, Game
2 Jack Christiansen, Detroit vs. Los Angeles, Oct. 14, 1951; vs. Green Bay, Nov. 22, 1951
Dick Christy, N.Y. Titans vs. Denver, Sept. 24, 1961
Rick Upchurch, Denver vs. Cleveland, Sept. 26, 1976
LeRoy Irvin, Los Angeles vs. Atlanta, Oct. 11, 1981

KICKOFF RETURNS

Most Seasons Leading League
3 Abe Woodson, San Francisco, 1959, 1962-63
2 Lynn Chandnois, Pittsburgh, 1951-52
Bobby Jancik, Houston, 1962-63
Travis Williams, Green Bay, 1967; Los Angeles, 1971

KICKOFF RETURNS
Most Kickoff Returns, Career
275 Ron Smith, Chicago, 1965, 1970-72; Atlanta, 1966-67; Los Angeles, 1968-69; San Diego, 1973; Oakland, 1974
243 Bruce Harper, N.Y. Jets, 1977-84
193 Abe Woodson, San Francisco, 1958-64; St. Louis, 1965-66
Most Kickoff Returns, Season
60 Drew Hill, Los Angeles, 1981
55 Bruce Harper, N.Y. Jets, 1978, 1979
David Turner, Cincinnati, 1979
Stump Mitchell, St. Louis, 1981
53 Eddie Payton, Minnesota, 1980
Buster Rhymes, Minnesota, 1985
Most Kickoff Returns, Rookie, Season
55 Stump Mitchell, St. Louis, 1981
53 Buster Rhymes, Minnesota, 1985
50 Nesby Glasgow, Baltimore, 1979
Dino Hall, Cleveland, 1979
Most Kickoff Returns, Game
9 Noland Smith, Kansas City vs. Oakland, Nov. 23, 1967
Dino Hall, Cleveland vs. Pittsburgh, Oct. 7, 1979
8 George Taliaferro, N.Y. Yanks vs. N.Y. Giants, Dec. 3, 1950
Bobby Jancik, Houston vs. Boston, Dec. 8, 1963; vs. Oakland, Dec. 22, 1963
Mel Renfro, Dallas vs. Green Bay, Nov. 29, 1964
Willie Porter, Boston vs. N.Y. Jets, Sept. 22, 1968
Keith Moody, Buffalo vs. Seattle, Oct. 30, 1977
Brian Baschnagel, Chicago vs. Houston, Nov. 6, 1977
Bruce Harper, N.Y. Jets vs. New England, Oct. 29, 1978; vs. New England, Sept. 9, 1979
Dino Hall, Cleveland vs. Pittsburgh, Nov. 25, 1979
Terry Metcalf, Washington vs. St. Louis, Sept. 20, 1981
Harlan Huckleby, Green Bay vs. Washington, Oct. 17, 1983
Gary Ellerson, Green Bay vs. St. Louis, Sept. 29, 1985
7 By many players

YARDS GAINED
Most Seasons Leading League
3 Bruce Harper, N.Y. Jets, 1977-79
2 Marshall Goldberg, Chi. Cardinals, 1941-42
Woodley Lewis, Los Angeles, 1953-54
Al Carmichael, Green Bay, 1956-57
Timmy Brown, Philadelphia, 1961, 1963
Bobby Jancik, Houston, 1963, 1966
Ron Smith, Atlanta, 1966-67
Most Yards Gained, Career
6,922 Ron Smith, Chicago, 1965, 1970-72; Atlanta, 1966-67; Los Angeles, 1968-69; San Diego, 1973; Oakland, 1974
5,538 Abe Woodson, San Francisco, 1958-64; St. Louis, 1965-66
5,407 Bruce Harper, N.Y. Jets, 1977-84
Most Yards Gained, Season
1,345 Buster Rhymes, Minnesota, 1985
1,317 Bobby Jancik, Houston, 1963
1,314 Dave Hampton, Green Bay, 1971
Most Yards Gained, Rookie, Season
1,345 Buster Rhymes, Minnesota, 1985
1,292 Stump Mitchell, St. Louis, 1981
1,245 Odell Barry, Denver, 1964
Most Yards Gained, Game
294 Wally Triplett, Detroit vs. Los Angeles, Oct. 29, 1950
247 Timmy Brown, Philadelphia vs. Dallas Nov. 6, 1966
244 Noland Smith, Kansas City vs. San Diego, Oct. 15, 1967
Longest Kickoff Return (All TDs)
106 Al Carmichael, Green Bay vs. Chi. Bears, Oct. 7, 1956
Noland Smith, Kansas City vs. Denver, Dec. 17, 1967
Roy Green, St. Louis vs. Dallas, Oct. 21, 1979
105 Frank Seno, Chi. Cardinals vs. N.Y. Giants, Oct. 20, 1946
Ollie Matson, Chi. Cardinals vs. Washington, Oct. 14, 1956
Abe Woodson, San Francisco vs. Los Angeles, Nov. 8, 1959
Timmy Brown, Philadelphia vs. Cleveland, Sept. 17, 1961
Jon Arnett, Los Angeles vs. Detroit, Oct. 29, 1961
Eugene (Mercury) Morris, Miami vs. Cincinnati, Sept. 14, 1969
Travis Williams, Los Angeles vs. New Orleans, Dec. 5, 1971
104 By many players

AVERAGE YARDAGE
Highest Average, Career (75 returns)
30.56 Gale Sayers, Chicago, 1965-71 (91-2,781)
29.57 Lynn Chandnois, Pittsburgh, 1950-56 (92-2,720)
28.69 Abe Woodson, San Francisco, 1958-64; St. Louis, 1965-66 (193-5,538)
Highest Average, Season (Qualifiers)
41.06 Travis Williams, Green Bay, 1967 (18-739)
37.69 Gale Sayers, Chicago, 1967 (16-603)
35.50 Ollie Matson, Chi. Cardinals, 1958 (14-497)
Highest Average, Rookie, Season (Qualifiers)
41.06 Travis Williams, Green Bay, 1967 (18-739)
33.08 Tom Moore, Green Bay, 1960 (12-397)
32.88 Duriel Harris, Miami, 1976 (17-559)
Highest Average, Game (3 returns)
73.50 Wally Triplett, Detroit vs. Los Angeles, Oct. 29, 1950 (4-294)
67.33 Lenny Lyles, San Francisco vs. Baltimore, Dec. 18, 1960 (3-202)
65.33 Ken Hall, Houston vs. N.Y. Titans, Oct. 23, 1960 (3-196)

TOUCHDOWNS
Most Touchdowns, Career
6 Ollie Matson, Chi. Cardinals, 1952, 1954-58; L.A. Rams, 1959-62; Detroit, 1963; Philadelphia, 1964
Gale Sayers, Chicago, 1965-71
Travis Williams, Green Bay, 1967-70; Los Angeles, 1971
5 Bobby Mitchell, Cleveland, 1958-61; Washington, 1962-68
Abe Woodson, San Francisco, 1958-64; St. Louis, 1965-66
Timmy Brown, Green Bay, 1959; Philadelphia, 1960-67; Baltimore, 1968
4 Cecil Turner, Chicago, 1968-73
Most Touchdowns, Season
4 Travis Williams, Green Bay, 1967
Cecil Turner, Chicago, 1970
3 Verda (Vitamin T) Smith, Los Angeles, 1950
Abe Woodson, San Francisco, 1963
Gale Sayers, Chicago, 1967
Raymond Clayborn, New England, 1977
Ron Brown, L.A. Rams, 1985
2 By many players
Most Touchdowns, Rookie, Season
4 Travis Williams, Green Bay, 1967
3 Raymond Clayborn, New England, 1977
2 By six players
Most Touchdowns, Game
2 Timmy Brown, Philadelphia vs. Dallas, Nov. 6, 1966
Travis Williams, Green Bay vs. Cleveland, Nov. 12, 1967
Ron Brown, L.A. Rams vs. Green Bay, Nov. 24, 1985

COMBINED KICK RETURNS

Most Combined Kick Returns, Career
510 Ron Smith, Chicago, 1965, 1970-72; Atlanta, 1966-67; Los Angeles, 1968-69; San Diego, 1973; Oakland, 1974 (p-235, k-275)
426 Bruce Harper, N.Y. Jets, 1977-84 (p-183, k-243)
423 Alvin Haymond, Baltimore, 1964-67; Philadelphia, 1968; Los Angeles, 1969-71; Washington, 1972; Houston, 1973 (p-253, k-170)
Most Combined Kick Returns, Season
100 Larry Jones, Washington, 1975 (p-53, k-47)
97 Stump Mitchell, St. Louis, 1981 (p-42, k-55)
94 Nesby Glasgow, Baltimore, 1979 (p-44, k-50)
Most Combined Kick Returns, Game
13 Stump Mitchell, St. Louis vs. Atlanta, Oct. 18, 1981 (p-6, k-7)
12 Mel Renfro, Dallas vs. Green Bay, Nov. 29, 1964 (p-4, k-8)
Larry Jones, Washington vs. Dallas, Dec. 13, 1975 (p-6, k-6)
Eddie Brown, Washington vs. Tampa Bay, Oct. 9, 1977 (p-11, k-1)
Nesby Glasgow, Baltimore vs. Denver, Sept. 2, 1979 (p-9, k-3)
11 By many players

YARDS GAINED
Most Yards Returned, Career
8,710 Ron Smith, Chicago, 1965, 1970-72; Atlanta, 1966-67; Los Angeles, 1968-69; San Diego, 1973; Oakland, 1974 (p-1,788, k-6,922)
7,191 Bruce Harper, N.Y. Jets, 1977-84 (p-1,784, k-5,407)
6,740 Les (Speedy) Duncan, San Diego, 1964-70; Washington, 1971-74 (p-2,201, k-4,539)
Most Yards Returned, Season
1,737 Stump Mitchell, St. Louis, 1981 (p-445, k-1,292)
1,658 Bruce Harper, N.Y. Jets, 1978 (p-378, k-1,280)
1,591 Mike Nelms, Washington, 1981 (p-492, k-1,099)
Most Yards Returned, Game
294 Wally Triplett, Detroit vs. Los Angeles, Oct. 29, 1950 (k-294)
Woodley Lewis, Los Angeles vs. Detroit, Oct. 18, 1953 (p-120, k-174)
289 Eddie Payton, Detroit vs. Minnesota, Dec. 17, 1977 (p-105, k-184)
282 Les (Speedy) Duncan, San Diego vs. N.Y. Jets, Nov. 24, 1968 (p-102, k-180)

TOUCHDOWNS
Most Touchdowns, Career
9 Ollie Matson, Chi. Cardinals, 1952, 1954-58; Los Angeles, 1959-62; Detroit, 1963; Philadelphia, 1964-66 (p-3, k-6)
8 Jack Christiansen, Detroit, 1951-58 (p-8)
Bobby Mitchell, Cleveland, 1958-61; Washington, 1962-68 (p-3, k-5)
Gale Sayers, Chicago, 1965-71 (p-2, k-6)

Rick Upchurch, Denver, 1975-83 (p-8)
Billy Johnson, Houston, 1974-80; Atlanta, 1982-85 (p-6, k-2)
7 Abe Woodson, San Francisco, 1958-64; St. Louis, 1965-66 (p-2, k-5)

Most Touchdowns, Season
4 Jack Christiansen, Detroit, 1951 (p-4)
Emlen Tunnell, N.Y. Giants, 1951 (p-3, k-1)
Gale Sayers, Chicago, 1967 (p-1, k-3)
Travis Williams, Green Bay, 1967 (k-4)
Cecil Turner, Chicago, 1970 (k-4)
Billy Johnson, Houston, 1975 (p-3, k-1)
Rick Upchurch, Denver, 1976 (p-4)
3 Verda (Vitamin T) Smith, Los Angeles, 1950 (k-3)
Abe Woodson, San Francisco, 1963 (k-3)
Raymond Clayborn, New England, 1977 (k-3)
Billy Johnson, Houston, 1977 (p-2, k-1)
LeRoy Irvin, Los Angeles, 1981 (p-3)
Ron Brown, L.A. Rams, 1985 (k-3)
2 By many players

Most Touchdowns, Game
2 Jack Christiansen, Detroit vs. Los Angeles, Oct. 14, 1951 (p-2); vs. Green Bay, Nov. 22, 1951 (p-2)
Jim Patton, N.Y. Giants vs. Washington, Oct. 30, 1955 (p-1, k-1)
Bobby Mitchell, Cleveland vs. Philadelphia, Nov. 23, 1958 (p-1, k-1)
Dick Christy, N.Y. Titans vs. Denver, Sept. 24, 1961 (p-2)
Al Frazier, Denver vs. Boston, Dec. 3, 1961 (p-1, k-1)
Timmy Brown, Philadelphia vs. Dallas, Nov. 6, 1966 (k-2)
Travis Williams, Green Bay vs. Cleveland, Nov. 12, 1967 (k-2); vs. Pittsburgh, Nov. 2, 1969 (p-1, k-1)
Gale Sayers, Chicago vs. San Francisco, Dec. 3, 1967 (p-1, k-1)
Rick Upchurch, Denver vs. Cleveland, Sept. 26, 1976 (p-2)
Eddie Payton, Detroit vs. Minnesota, Dec. 17, 1977 (p-1, k-1)
LeRoy Irvin, Los Angeles vs. Atlanta, Oct. 11, 1981 (p-2)
Ron Brown, L.A. Rams vs. Green Bay, Nov. 24, 1985 (k-2)

FUMBLES

Most Fumbles, Career
105 Roman Gabriel, Los Angeles, 1962-72; Philadelphia, 1973-77
95 Johnny Unitas, Baltimore, 1956-72; San Diego, 1973
92 Dan Fouts, San Diego, 1973-85

Most Fumbles, Season
17 Dan Pastorini, Houston, 1973
Warren Moon, Houston, 1984
16 Don Meredith, Dallas, 1964
Joe Cribbs, Buffalo, 1980
Steve Fuller, Kansas City, 1980
Paul McDonald, Cleveland, 1984
Phil Simms, N.Y. Giants, 1985
15 Paul Christman, Chi. Cardinals, 1946
Sammy Baugh, Washington, 1947
Sam Etcheverry, St. Louis, 1961
Len Dawson, Kansas City, 1964
Terry Metcalf, St. Louis, 1976
Steve DeBerg, Tampa Bay, 1984

Most Fumbles, Game
7 Len Dawson, Kansas City vs. San Diego, Nov. 15, 1964
6 Sam Etcheverry, St. Louis vs. N.Y. Giants, Sept, 17, 1961
5 Paul Christman, Chi. Cardinals vs. Green Bay, Nov. 10, 1946
Charlie Conerly, N.Y. Giants vs. San Francisco, Dec. 1, 1957
Jack Kemp, Buffalo vs. Houston, Oct. 29, 1967
Roman Gabriel, Philadelphia vs. Oakland, Nov. 21, 1976

FUMBLES RECOVERED

Most Fumbles Recovered, Career, Own and Opponents'
43 Fran Tarkenton, Minnesota, 1961-66, 1972-78; N.Y. Giants, 1967-71 (43 own)
38 Jack Kemp, Pittsburgh, 1957; L.A. Chargers, 1960; San Diego, 1961-62; Buffalo, 1962-67, 1969 (38 own)
37 Roman Gabriel, Los Angeles, 1962-72; Philadelphia, 1973-77 (37 own)

Most Fumbles Recovered, Season, Own and Opponents'
9 Don Hultz, Minnesota, 1963 (9 opp)
8 Paul Christman, Chi. Cardinals, 1945 (8 own)
Joe Schmidt, Detroit, 1955 (8 opp)
Bill Butler, Minnesota, 1963 (8 own)
Kermit Alexander, San Francisco, 1965 (4 own, 4 opp)
Jack Lambert, Pittsburgh, 1976 (1 own, 7 opp)
Danny White, Dallas, 1981 (8 own)
7 By many players

Most Fumbles Recovered, Game, Own and Opponents'
4 Otto Graham, Cleveland vs. N.Y. Giants, Oct. 25, 1953 (4 own)
Sam Etcheverry, St. Louis vs. N.Y. Giants, Sept. 17, 1961 (4 own)
Roman Gabriel, Los Angeles vs. San Francisco, Oct. 12, 1969 (4 own)
Joe Ferguson, Buffalo vs. Miami, Sept. 18, 1977 (4 own)
3 By many players

OWN FUMBLES RECOVERED

Most Own Fumbles Recovered, Career
43 Fran Tarkenton, Minnesota, 1961-66, 1972-78; N.Y. Giants, 1967-71
38 Jack Kemp, Pittsburgh, 1957; L.A. Chargers, 1960; San Diego, 1961-62; Buffalo, 1962-67, 1969
37 Roman Gabriel, Los Angeles, 1962-72; Philadelphia, 1973-77

Most Own Fumbles Recovered, Season
8 Paul Christman, Chi. Cardinals, 1945
Bill Butler, Minnesota, 1963
Danny White, Dallas, 1981
7 Sammy Baugh, Washington, 1947
Tommy Thompson, Philadelphia, 1947
John Roach, St. Louis, 1960
Jack Larscheid, Oakland, 1960
Gary Huff, Chicago, 1974
Terry Metcalf, St. Louis, 1974
Joe Ferguson, Buffalo, 1977
Fran Tarkenton, Minnesota, 1978
Greg Pruitt, L.A. Raiders, 1983
Warren Moon, Houston, 1984
6 By many players

Most Own Fumbles Recovered, Game
4 Otto Graham, Cleveland vs. N.Y. Giants, Oct. 25, 1953
Sam Etcheverry, St. Louis vs. N.Y. Giants, Sept. 17, 1961
Roman Gabriel, Los Angeles vs. San Francisco, Oct. 12, 1969
Joe Ferguson, Buffalo vs. Miami, Sept. 18, 1977
3 By many players

OPPONENTS' FUMBLES RECOVERED

Most Opponents' Fumbles Recovered, Career
29 Jim Marshall, Cleveland, 1960; Minnesota, 1961-79
25 Dick Butkus, Chicago, 1965-73
23 Carl Eller, Minnesota, 1964-78; Seattle, 1979

Most Opponents' Fumbles Recovered, Season
9 Don Hultz, Minnesota, 1963
8 Joe Schmidt, Detroit, 1955
7 Alan Page, Minnesota, 1970
Jack Lambert, Pittsburgh, 1976

Most Opponents' Fumbles Recovered, Game
3 Corwin Clatt, Chi. Cardinals vs. Detroit, Nov. 6, 1949
Vic Sears, Philadelphia vs. Green Bay, Nov. 2, 1952
Ed Beatty, San Francisco vs. Los Angeles, Oct. 7, 1956
Ron Carroll, Houston vs. Cincinnati, Oct. 27, 1974
Maurice Spencer, New Orleans vs. Atlanta, Oct. 10, 1976
Steve Nelson, New England vs. Philadelphia, Oct. 8, 1978
Charles Jackson, Kansas City vs. Pittsburgh, Sept. 6, 1981
Willie Buchanon, San Diego vs. Denver, Sept. 27, 1981
Joey Browner, Minnesota vs. San Francisco, Sept. 8, 1985
2 By many players

YARDS RETURNING FUMBLES

Longest Fumble Run (All TDs)
104 Jack Tatum, Oakland vs. Green Bay, Sept. 24, 1972 (opp)
98 George Halas, Chi. Bears vs. Oorang Indians, Marion, Ohio, Nov. 4, 1923 (opp)
97 Chuck Howley, Dallas vs. Atlanta, Oct. 2, 1966 (opp)

TOUCHDOWNS

Most Touchdowns, Career (Total)
4 Bill Thompson, Denver, 1969-81
3 Ralph Heywood, Detroit, 1947-48; Boston, 1948; N.Y. Bulldogs, 1949
Leo Sugar, Chi. Cardinals, 1954-59; St. Louis, 1960; Philadelphia, 1961; Detroit, 1962
Bud McFadin, Los Angeles, 1952-56; Denver, 1960-63; Houston, 1964-65
Doug Cline, Houston, 1960-66; San Diego, 1966
Bob Lilly, Dall. Cowboys, 1961-74
Chris Hanburger, Washington, 1965-78
Lemar Parrish, Cincinnati, 1970-77; Washington, 1978-81; Buffalo, 1982
Paul Krause, Washington, 1964-67; Minnesota, 1968-79
Brad Dusek, Washington, 1974-81
David Logan, Tampa Bay, 1979-85
Thomas Howard, Kansas City, 1977-83; St. Louis, 1984-85
2 By many players

Most Touchdowns, Season (Total)
2 Harold McPhail, Boston, 1934
Harry Ebding, Detroit, 1937
John Morelli, Boston, 1944
Frank Maznicki, Boston, 1947
Fred (Dippy) Evans, Chi. Bears, 1948
Ralph Heywood, Boston, 1948
Art Tait, N.Y. Yanks, 1951
John Dwyer, Los Angeles, 1952
Leo Sugar, Chi. Cardinals, 1957
Doug Cline, Houston, 1961
Jim Bradshaw, Pittsburgh, 1964
Royce Berry, Cincinnati, 1970
Ahmad Rashad, Buffalo, 1974
Tim Gray, Kansas City, 1977
Charles Phillips, Oakland, 1978
Kenny Johnson, Atlanta, 1981
George Martin, N.Y. Giants, 1981
Del Rodgers, Green Bay, 1982
Mike Douglass, Green Bay, 1983
Shelton Robinson, Seattle, 1983

Most Touchdowns, Career (Own recovered)
2 Ken Kavanaugh, Chi. Bears, 1940-41, 1945-50
Mike Ditka, Chicago, 1961-66; Philadelphia, 1967-68; Dallas, 1969-72
Gail Cogdill, Detroit, 1960-68; Baltimore, 1968; Atlanta, 1969-70
Ahmad Rashad, St. Louis, 1972-73; Buffalo, 1974; Minnesota, 1976-82
Jim Mitchell, Atlanta, 1969-79
Drew Pearson, Dallas, 1973-83
Del Rodgers, Green Bay, 1982, 1984

Most Touchdowns, Season (Own recovered)
2 Ahmad Rashad, Buffalo, 1974
Del Rodgers, Green Bay, 1982
1 By many players

Most Touchdowns, Career (Opponents' recovered)
3 Leo Sugar, Chi. Cardinals, 1954-59; St. Louis, 1960; Philadelphia, 1961; Detroit, 1962
Doug Cline, Houston, 1960-66; San Diego, 1966
Bud McFadin, Los Angeles, 1952-56; Denver, 1960-63; Houston, 1964-65
Bob Lilly, Dall. Cowboys, 1961-74
Chris Hanburger, Washington, 1965-78
Paul Krause, Washington, 1964-67; Minnesota, 1968-79
Lemar Parrish, Cincinnati, 1970-77; Washington, 1978-81; Buffalo, 1982
Bill Thompson, Denver, 1969-81
Brad Dusek, Washington, 1974-81
David Logan, Tampa Bay, 1979-85
Thomas Howard, Kansas City, 1977-83; St. Louis, 1984-85
2 By many players

Most Touchdowns, Season (Opponents' recovered)
2 Harold McPhail, Boston, 1934
Harry Ebding, Detroit, 1937

John Morelli, Boston, 1944
Frank Maznicki, Boston, 1947
Fred (Dippy) Evans, Chi. Bears, 1948
Ralph Heywood, Boston, 1948
Art Tait, N.Y. Yanks, 1951
John Dwyer, Los Angeles, 1952
Leo Sugar, Chi. Cardinals, 1957
Doug Cline, Houston, 1961
Jim Bradshaw, Pittsburgh, 1964
Royce Berry, Cincinnati, 1970
Tim Gray, Kansas City, 1977
Charles Phillips, Oakland, 1978
Kenny Johnson, Atlanta, 1981
George Martin, N.Y. Giants, 1981
Mike Douglass, Green Bay, 1983
Shelton Robinson, Seattle, 1983

Most Touchdowns, Game (Opponents' recovered)
2 Fred (Dippy) Evans, Chi. Bears vs. Washington, Nov. 28, 1948

COMBINED NET YARDS GAINED

Rushing, receiving, interception returns, punt returns, kickoff returns, and fumble returns

Most Seasons Leading League
5 Jim Brown, Cleveland, 1958-61, 1964
3 Cliff Battles, Boston, 1932-33; Washington, 1937
Gale Sayers, Chicago, 1965-67
2 By many players

Most Consecutive Seasons Leading League
4 Jim Brown, Cleveland, 1958-61
3 Gale Sayers, Chicago, 1965-67
2 Cliff Battles, Boston, 1932-33
Charley Trippi, Chi. Cardinals, 1948-49
Timmy Brown, Philadelphia, 1962-63
Floyd Little, Denver, 1967-68
James Brooks, San Diego, 1981-82
Eric Dickerson, L.A. Rams, 1983-84

ATTEMPTS

Most Attempts, Career
3,831 Walter Payton, Chicago, 1975-85
3,281 Franco Harris, Pittsburgh, 1972-83; Seattle, 1984
3,174 John Riggins, N.Y. Jets, 1971-75; Washington, 1976-79, 1981-85

Most Attempts, Season
496 James Wilder, Tampa Bay, 1984
449 Marcus Allen, L.A. Raiders, 1985
442 Eric Dickerson, L.A. Rams, 1983

Most Attempts, Rookie, Season
442 Eric Dickerson, L.A. Rams, 1983
395 George Rogers, New Orleans, 1981
390 Joe Cribbs, Buffalo, 1980

Most Attempts, Game
48 James Wilder, Tampa Bay vs. Pittsburgh, Oct. 30, 1983
47 James Wilder, Tampa Bay vs. Green Bay, Sept. 30, 1984 (OT)
46 Gerald Riggs, Atlanta vs. L.A. Rams, Nov. 17, 1985

YARDS GAINED

Most Yards Gained, Career
19,338 Walter Payton, Chicago, 1975-85
15,459 Jim Brown, Cleveland, 1957-65
14,622 Franco Harris, Pittsburgh, 1972-83; Seattle, 1984

Most Yards Gained, Season
2,535 Lionel James, San Diego, 1985
2,462 Terry Metcalf, St. Louis, 1975
2,444 Mack Herron, New England, 1974

Most Yards Gained, Rookie, Season
2,272 Gale Sayers, Chicago, 1965
2,212 Eric Dickerson, L.A. Rams, 1983
2,100 Abner Haynes, Dall. Texans, 1960

Most Yards Gained, Game
373 Billy Cannon, Houston vs. N.Y. Titans, Dec. 10, 1961
345 Lionel James, San Diego vs. L.A. Raiders, Nov. 10, 1985 (OT)
341 Timmy Brown, Philadelphia vs. St. Louis, Dec. 16, 1962

SACKS

Sacks have been compiled since 1982.

Most Sacks, Career
60.5 Mark Gastineau, N.Y. Jets, 1982-85
46 Dexter Manley, Washington, 1982-85
45.5 Jacob Green, Seattle, 1982-85

Most Sacks, Season
22 Mark Gastineau, N.Y. Jets, 1984
19 Mark Gastineau, N.Y. Jets, 1983
18.5 Andre Tippett, New England, 1984

Most Sacks, Game
6 Fred Dean, San Francisco vs. New Orleans, Nov. 13, 1983
5.5 William Gay, Detroit vs. Tampa Bay, Sept. 4, 1983
5 Howie Long, L.A. Raiders vs. Washington, Oct. 2, 1983
Jim Jeffcoat, Dallas vs. Washington, Nov. 10, 1985

MISCELLANEOUS

Longest Return of Missed Field Goal (All TDs)
101 Al Nelson, Philadelphia vs. Dallas, Sept. 26, 1971
100 Al Nelson, Philadelphia vs. Cleveland, Dec. 11, 1966
Ken Ellis, Green Bay vs. N.Y. Giants, Sept. 19, 1971
99 Jerry Williams, Los Angeles vs. Green Bay, Dec. 16, 1951
Carl Taseff, Baltimore vs. Los Angeles, Dec. 12, 1959
Timmy Brown, Philadelphia vs. St. Louis, Sept. 16, 1962

TEAM RECORDS

CHAMPIONSHIPS

Most Seasons League Champion
11 Green Bay, 1929-31, 1936, 1939, 1944, 1961-62, 1965-67
9 Chi. Bears, 1921, 1932-33, 1940-41, 1943, 1946, 1963, 1985
4 N.Y. Giants, 1927, 1934, 1938, 1956
Detroit, 1935, 1952-53, 1957
Clev. Browns, 1950, 1954-55, 1964
Baltimore, 1958-59, 1968, 1970
Pittsburgh, 1974-75, 1978-79
Oakland/L.A. Raiders, 1967, 1976, 1980, 1983

Most Consecutive Seasons League Champion
3 Green Bay, 1929-31, 1965-67
2 Canton, 1922-23
Chi. Bears, 1932-33, 1940-41
Philadelphia, 1948-49
Detroit, 1952-53
Cleveland, 1954-55
Baltimore, 1958-59
Houston, 1960-61
Green Bay, 1961-62
Buffalo, 1964-65
Miami, 1972-73
Pittsburgh, 1974-75, 1978-79

Most Times Finishing First, Regular Season (Since 1933)
15 Clev./L.A. Rams, 1945, 1949-51, 1955, 1967, 1969, 1973-79, 1985
Clev. Browns, 1950-55, 1957, 1964-65, 1967-69, 1971, 1980, 1985
14 N.Y. Giants, 1933-35, 1938-39, 1941, 1944, 1946, 1956, 1958-59, 1961-63
13 Dall. Cowboys, 1966-71, 1973, 1976-79, 1981, 1985

Most Consecutive Times Finishing First, Regular Season (Since 1933)
7 Los Angeles, 1973-79
6 Cleveland, 1950-55
Dallas, 1966-71
Minnesota, 1973-78
Pittsburgh, 1974-79
5 Oakland, 1972-76

GAMES WON

Most Consecutive Games Won (Incl. postseason games)
18 Chi. Bears, 1933-34, 1941-42
Miami, 1972-73
17 Oakland, 1976-77
14 Washington, 1942-43

Most Consecutive Games Won (Regular season)
17 Chi. Bears, 1933-34
16 Chi. Bears, 1941-42
Miami, 1971-73; 1983-84
15 L.A. Chargers/San Diego, 1960-61

Most Consecutive Games Without Defeat (Incl. postseason games)
24 Canton, 1922-23 (won 21, tied 3)
23 Green Bay, 1928-30 (won 21, tied 2)
18 Chi. Bears, 1933-34 (won 18); 1941-42 (won 18)
Miami, 1972-73 (won 18)

Most Consecutive Games Without Defeat (Regular season)
24 Canton, 1922-23 (won 21, tied 3)
Chi. Bears, 1941-43 (won 23, tied 1)
23 Green Bay, 1928-30 (won 21, tied 2)
17 Chi. Bears, 1933-34 (won 17)

Most Games Won, One Season (Incl. postseason games)
18 San Francisco, 1984
Chicago, 1985
17 Miami, 1972
Pittsburgh, 1978
16 Oakland, 1976
San Francisco, 1981
Washington, 1983
Miami, 1984

Most Games Won, Season (Since 1932)
15 San Francisco, 1984
Chicago, 1985
14 Miami, 1972, 1984
Pittsburgh, 1978
Washington, 1983
13 Chi. Bears, 1934
Green Bay, 1962
Oakland, 1967, 1976
Baltimore, 1968
San Francisco, 1981
Denver, 1984

Most Consecutive Games Won, One Season (Incl. postseason games)
17 Miami, 1972
13 Chi. Bears, 1934
Oakland, 1976
12 Minnesota, 1969
San Francisco, 1984
Chicago, 1985

Most Consecutive Games Won, One Season
14 Miami, 1972
13 Chi. Bears, 1934
12 Minnesota, 1969
Chicago, 1985

Most Consecutive Games Won, Start of Season
14 Miami, 1972, entire season
13 Chi. Bears, 1934, entire season
12 Chicago, 1985

Most Consecutive Games Won, End of Season
14 Miami, 1972, entire season
13 Chi. Bears, 1934, entire season
11 Chi. Bears, 1942, entire season
Cleveland, 1951

Most Consecutive Games Without Defeat, One Season (Incl. postseason games)
17 Miami, 1972
13 Chi. Bears, 1926, 1934
Green Bay, 1929
Baltimore, 1967
Oakland, 1976
12 Canton, 1922, 1923

Minnesota, 1969
San Francisco, 1984
Chicago, 1985

Most Consecutive Games Without Defeat, One Season
14 Miami, 1972
13 Chi. Bears, 1926, 1934
Green Bay, 1929
Baltimore, 1967
12 Canton, 1922, 1923
Minnesota, 1969
Chicago, 1985

Most Consecutive Games Without Defeat, Start of Season
14 Miami, 1972, entire season
13 Chi. Bears, 1926, 1934, entire seasons
Green Bay, 1929, entire season
Baltimore, 1967
12 Canton, 1922, 1923, entire seasons
Chicago, 1985

Most Consecutive Games Without Defeat, End of Season
14 Miami, 1972, entire season
13 Green Bay, 1929, entire season
Chi. Bears, 1934, entire season
12 Canton, 1922, 1923, entire seasons

Most Consecutive Home Games Won
27 Miami, 1971-74
20 Green Bay, 1929-32
18 Oakland, 1968-70
Dallas, 1979-81

Most Consecutive Home Games Without Defeat
30 Green Bay, 1928-33 (won 27, tied 3)
27 Miami, 1971-74 (won 27)
18 Chi. Bears, 1932-35 (won 17, tied 1); 1941-44 (won 17, tied 1)
Oakland, 1968-70 (won 18)
Dallas, 1979-81 (won 18)

Most Consecutive Road Games Won
11 L.A. Chargers/San Diego, 1960-61
10 Chi. Bears, 1941-42
Dallas, 1968-69
9 Chi. Bears, 1933-34
Kansas City, 1966-67
Oakland, 1967-68, 1974-75, 1976-77
Pittsburgh, 1974-75
Washington, 1981-83
San Francisco, 1983-84

Most Consecutive Road Games Without Defeat
13 Chi. Bears, 1941-43 (won 12, tied 1)
12 Green Bay, 1928-30 (won 10, tied 2)
11 L.A. Chargers/San Diego, 1960-61 (won 11)
Los Angeles, 1966-68 (won 10, tied 1)

Most Shutout Games Won or Tied, Season (Since 1932)
7 Chi. Bears, 1932 (won 4, tied 3)
Green Bay, 1932 (won 6, tied 1)
Detroit, 1934 (won 7)
5 Chi. Cardinals, 1934 (won 5)
N.Y. Giants, 1944 (won 5)
Pittsburgh, 1976 (won 5)
4 By many teams

Most Consecutive Shutout Games Won or Tied (Since 1932)
7 Detroit, 1934 (won 7)
3 Chi. Bears, 1932 (tied 3)
Green Bay, 1932 (won 3)
New York, 1935 (won 3)
St. Louis, 1970 (won 3)
Pittsburgh, 1976 (won 3)
2 By many teams

GAMES LOST

Most Consecutive Games Lost
26 Tampa Bay, 1976-77
19 Chi. Cardinals, 1942-43, 1945
Oakland, 1961-62
18 Houston, 1972-73

Most Consecutive Games Without Victory
26 Tampa Bay, 1976-77 (lost 26)
23 Washington, 1960-61 (lost 20, tied 3)

Most Games Lost, Season (Since 1932)
15 New Orleans, 1980
14 Tampa Bay, 1976, 1983, 1985
San Francisco, 1978, 1979
Detroit, 1979
Baltimore, 1981
New England, 1981
Houston, 1983
Buffalo, 1984, 1985
13 Oakland, 1962
Chicago, 1969
Pittsburgh, 1969
Buffalo, 1971
Houston, 1972, 1973, 1984
Minnesota, 1984

Most Consecutive Games Lost, One Season
14 Tampa Bay, 1976
New Orleans, 1980
Baltimore, 1981
13 Oakland, 1962
12 Tampa Bay, 1977

Most Consecutive Games Lost, Start of Season
14 Tampa Bay, 1976, entire season
New Orleans, 1980
13 Oakland, 1962
12 Tampa Bay, 1977

Most Consecutive Games Lost, End of Season
14 Tampa Bay, 1976, entire season
13 Pittsburgh, 1969
11 Philadelphia, 1936
Detroit, 1942, entire season
Houston, 1972

Most Consecutive Games Without Victory, One Season
14 Tampa Bay, 1976, entire season
New Orleans, 1980
Baltimore, 1981
13 Washington, 1961
Oakland, 1962
12 Dall. Cowboys, 1960, entire season
Tampa Bay, 1977

Most Consecutive Games Without Victory, Start of Season
14 Tampa Bay, 1976, entire season
New Orleans, 1980
13 Washington, 1961
Oakland, 1962
12 Dall. Cowboys, 1960, entire season
Tampa Bay, 1977

Most Consecutive Games Without Victory, End of Season
14 Tampa Bay, 1976, entire season
13 Pittsburgh, 1969
12 Dall. Cowboys, 1960, entire season

Most Consecutive Home Games Lost
13 Houston, 1972-73
Tampa Bay, 1976-77
11 Oakland, 1961-62
Los Angeles, 1961-63
10 Pittsburgh, 1937-39, 1943-45
Washington, 1960-61
N.Y. Giants, 1973-75
New Orleans, 1979-80

Most Consecutive Home Games Without Victory
13 Houston, 1972-73 (lost 13)
Tampa Bay, 1976-77 (lost 13)
12 Philadelphia, 1936-38 (lost 11, tied 1)
11 Washington, 1960-61 (lost 10, tied 1)
Oakland, 1961-62 (lost 11)
Los Angeles, 1961-63 (lost 11)

Most Consecutive Road Games Lost
23 Houston, 1981-84
19 Tampa Bay, 1983-85 (current)
18 San Francisco, 1977-79

Most Consecutive Road Games Without Victory
23 Houston, 1981-84 (lost 23)
19 Tampa Bay, 1983-85 (lost 19; current)
18 Washington, 1959-62 (lost 15, tied 3)
New Orleans, 1971-74 (lost 17, tied 1)
San Francisco, 1977-79 (lost 18)

Most Shutout Games Lost or Tied, Season (Since 1932)
6 Cincinnati, 1934 (lost 6)
Pittsburgh, 1934 (lost 6)
Philadelphia, 1936 (lost 6)
Tampa Bay, 1977 (lost 6)
5 Boston, 1932 (lost 4, tied 1), 1933 (lost 4, tied 1)
N.Y. Giants, 1932 (lost 4, tied 1)
Cincinnati, 1933 (lost 4, tied 1)
Brooklyn, 1934 (lost 5), 1942 (lost 5)
Detroit, 1942 (lost 5)
Tampa Bay, 1976 (lost 5)
4 By many teams

Most Consecutive Shutout Games Lost or Tied (Since 1932)
6 Brooklyn, 1942-43 (lost 6)
4 Chi. Bears, 1932 (lost 1, tied 3)
Philadelphia, 1936 (lost 4)
3 Chi. Cardinals, 1934 (lost 3), 1938 (lost 3)
Brooklyn, 1935 (lost 3), 1937 (lost 3)
Oakland, 1981 (lost 3)

TIE GAMES

Most Tie Games, Season
6 Chi. Bears, 1932
5 Frankford, 1929
4 Chi. Bears, 1924
Orange, 1929
Portsmouth, 1929

Most Consecutive Tie Games
3 Chi. Bears, 1932
2 By many teams

SCORING

Most Seasons Leading League
9 Chi. Bears, 1934-35, 1939, 1941-43, 1946-47, 1956
6 Green Bay, 1932, 1936-38, 1961-62
L.A. Rams, 1950-52, 1957, 1967, 1973
5 Oakland, 1967-69, 1974, 1977
Dall. Cowboys, 1966, 1968, 1971, 1978, 1980
San Diego, 1963, 1965, 1981-82, 1985

Most Consecutive Seasons Leading League
3 Green Bay, 1936-38
Chi. Bears, 1941-43
Los Angeles, 1950-52
Oakland, 1967-69

POINTS

Most Points, Season
541 Washington, 1983
513 Houston, 1961
Miami, 1984
479 Dallas, 1983

Fewest Points, Season (Since 1932)
37 Cincinnati/St. Louis, 1934

38 Cincinnati, 1933
Detroit, 1942
51 Pittsburgh, 1934
Philadelphia, 1936

Most Points, Game
72 Washington vs. N.Y. Giants, Nov. 27, 1966
70 Los Angeles vs. Baltimore, Oct. 22, 1950
65 Chi. Cardinals vs. N.Y. Bulldogs, Nov. 13, 1949
Los Angeles vs. Detroit, Oct. 29, 1950

Most Points, Both Teams, Game
113 Washington (72) vs. N.Y. Giants (41), Nov. 27, 1966
101 Oakland (52) vs. Houston (49), Dec. 22, 1963
99 Seattle (51) vs. Kansas City (48), Nov. 27, 1983 (OT)

Fewest Points, Both Teams, Game
0 In many games. Last time: N.Y. Giants vs. Detroit, Nov. 7, 1943

Most Points, Shutout Victory, Game
64 Philadelphia vs. Cincinnati, Nov. 6, 1934
59 Los Angeles vs. Atlanta, Dec. 4, 1976
57 Chicago vs. Baltimore, Nov. 25, 1962

Fewest Points, Shutout Victory, Game
2 Green Bay vs. Chi. Bears, Oct. 16, 1932
Chi. Bears vs. Green Bay, Sept. 18, 1938

Most Points Overcome to Win Game
28 San Francisco vs. New Orleans, Dec. 7, 1980 (OT) (trailed 7-35, won 38-35)
24 Philadelphia vs. Washington, Oct. 27, 1946 (trailed 0-24, won 28-24)
Detroit vs. Baltimore, Oct. 20, 1957 (trailed 3-27, won 31-27)
Philadelphia vs. Chi. Cardinals, Oct. 25, 1959 (trailed 0-24, won 28-24)
Denver vs. Boston, Oct. 23, 1960 (trailed 0-24, won 31-24)
Miami vs. New England, Dec. 15, 1974 (trailed 0-24, won 34-27)
Minnesota vs. San Francisco, Dec. 4, 1977 (trailed 0-24, won 28-27)
Denver vs. Seattle, Sept. 23, 1979 (trailed 10-34, won 37-34)
Houston vs. Cincinnati, Sept. 23, 1979 (OT) (trailed 0-24, won 30-27)
L.A. Raiders vs. San Diego, Nov. 22, 1982 (trailed 0-24, won 28-24)

Most Points Overcome to Tie Game
31 Denver vs. Buffalo, Nov. 27, 1960 (trailed 7-38, tied 38-38)
28 Los Angeles vs. Philadelphia, Oct. 3, 1948 (trailed 0-28, tied 28-28)

Most Points, Each Half
1st: 49 Green Bay vs. Tampa Bay, Oct. 2, 1983
45 Green Bay vs. Cleveland, Nov. 12, 1967
2nd: 49 Chi. Bears vs. Philadelphia, Nov. 30, 1941
48 Chi. Cardinals vs. Baltimore, Oct. 2, 1950
N.Y. Giants vs. Baltimore, Nov. 19, 1950

Most Points, Both Teams, Each Half
1st: 70 Houston (35) vs. Oakland (35), Dec. 22, 1963
2nd: 65 Washington (38) vs. N.Y. Giants (27), Nov. 27, 1966

Most Points, One Quarter
41 Green Bay vs. Detroit, Oct. 7, 1945 (second quarter)
Los Angeles vs. Detroit, Oct. 29, 1950 (third quarter)
37 Los Angeles vs. Green Bay, Sept. 21, 1980 (second quarter)
35 Chi. Cardinals vs. Boston, Oct. 24, 1948 (third quarter)
Green Bay vs. Cleveland, Nov. 12, 1967 (first quarter); vs. Tampa Bay, Oct. 2, 1983 (second quarter)

Most Points, Both Teams, One Quarter
49 Oakland (28) vs. Houston (21), Dec. 22, 1963 (second quarter)
48 Green Bay (41) vs. Detroit (7), Oct. 7, 1945 (second quarter)
Los Angeles (41) vs. Detroit (7), Oct. 29, 1950 (third quarter)
47 St. Louis (27) vs. Philadelphia (20), Dec. 13, 1964 (second quarter)

Most Points, Each Quarter
1st: 35 Green Bay vs. Cleveland, Nov. 12, 1967
2nd: 41 Green Bay vs. Detroit, Oct. 7, 1945
3rd: 41 Los Angeles vs. Detroit, Oct. 29, 1950
4th: 31 Oakland vs. Denver, Dec. 17, 1960; vs. San Diego, Dec. 8, 1963
Atlanta vs. Green Bay, Sept. 13, 1981

Most Points, Both Teams, Each Quarter
1st: 42 Green Bay (35) vs. Cleveland (7), Nov. 12, 1967
2nd: 49 Oakland (28) vs. Houston (21), Dec. 22, 1963
3rd: 48 Los Angeles (41) vs. Detroit (7), Oct. 29, 1950
4th: 42 Chi. Cardinals (28) vs. Philadelphia (14), Dec. 7, 1947
Green Bay (28) vs. Chi. Bears (14), Nov. 6, 1955
N.Y. Jets (28) vs. Boston (14), Oct. 27, 1968
Pittsburgh (21) vs. Cleveland (21), Oct. 18, 1969

GAMES

Most Consecutive Games Scoring
274 Cleveland, 1950-71
218 Dallas, 1970-85
217 Oakland, 1966-81

TOUCHDOWNS

Most Seasons Leading League, Touchdowns
13 Chi. Bears, 1932, 1934-35, 1939, 1941-44, 1946-48, 1956, 1965
7 Dall. Cowboys, 1966, 1968, 1971, 1973, 1977-78, 1980
6 Oakland, 1967-69, 1972, 1974, 1977
San Diego, 1963, 1965, 1979, 1981-82, 1985

Most Consecutive Seasons Leading League, Touchdowns
4 Chi. Bears, 1941-44
Los Angeles, 1949-52
3 Chi. Bears, 1946-48
Baltimore, 1957-59
Oakland, 1967-69
2 By many teams

Most Touchdowns, Season
70 Miami, 1984
66 Houston, 1961
64 Los Angeles, 1950

Fewest Touchdowns, Season (Since 1932)
3 Cincinnati, 1933
4 Cincinnati/St. Louis, 1934
5 Detroit, 1942

Most Touchdowns, Game
10 Philadelphia vs. Cincinnati, Nov. 6, 1934
Los Angeles vs. Baltimore, Oct. 22, 1950
Washington vs. N.Y. Giants, Nov. 27, 1966
9 Chi. Cardinals vs. Rochester, Oct. 7, 1923; vs. N.Y. Giants, Oct. 17, 1948; vs. N.Y. Bulldogs, Nov. 13, 1949
Los Angeles vs. Detroit, Oct. 29, 1950
Pittsburgh vs. N.Y. Giants, Nov. 30, 1952
Chicago vs. San Francisco, Dec. 12, 1965; vs. Green Bay, Dec. 7, 1980
8 By many teams.

Most Touchdowns, Both Teams, Game
16 Washington (10) vs. N.Y. Giants (6), Nov. 27, 1966
14 Chi. Cardinals (9) vs. N.Y. Giants (5), Oct. 17, 1948
Los Angeles (10) vs. Baltimore (4), Oct. 22, 1950
Houston (7) vs. Oakland (7), Dec. 22, 1963
13 New Orleans (7) vs. St. Louis (6), Nov. 2, 1969
Kansas City (7) vs. Seattle (6), Nov. 27, 1983 (OT)
San Diego (8) vs. Pittsburgh (5), Dec. 8, 1985

Most Consecutive Games Scoring Touchdowns
166 Cleveland, 1957-69
97 Oakland, 1966-73
96 Kansas City, 1963-70

POINTS AFTER TOUCHDOWN

Most Points After Touchdown, Season
66 Miami, 1984
65 Houston, 1961
62 Washington, 1983

Fewest Points After Touchdown, Season
2 Chi. Cardinals, 1933
3 Cincinnati, 1933
Pittsburgh, 1934
4 Cincinnati/St. Louis, 1934

Most Points After Touchdown, Game
10 Los Angeles vs. Baltimore, Oct. 22, 1950
9 Chi. Cardinals vs. N.Y. Giants, Oct. 17, 1948
Pittsburgh vs. N.Y. Giants, Nov. 30, 1952
Washington vs. N.Y. Giants, Nov. 27, 1966
8 By many teams

Most Points After Touchdown, Both Teams, Game
14 Chi. Cardinals (9) vs. N.Y. Giants (5), Oct. 17, 1948
Houston (7) vs. Oakland (7), Dec. 22, 1963
Washington (9) vs. N.Y. Giants (5), Nov. 27, 1966
13 Los Angeles (10) vs. Baltimore (3), Oct. 22, 1950
12 In many games

FIELD GOALS

Most Seasons Leading League, Field Goals
11 Green Bay, 1935-36, 1940-43, 1946-47, 1955, 1972, 1974
7 Washington, 1945, 1956, 1971, 1976-77, 1979, 1982
N.Y. Giants, 1933, 1937, 1939, 1941, 1944, 1959, 1983
5 Portsmouth/Detroit, 1932-33, 1937-38, 1980

Most Consecutive Seasons Leading League, Field Goals
4 Green Bay, 1940-43
3 Cleveland, 1952-54
2 By many teams

Most Field Goals Attempted, Season
49 Los Angeles, 1966
Washington, 1971
48 Green Bay, 1972
47 N.Y. Jets, 1969
Los Angeles, 1973
Washington, 1983

Fewest Field Goals Attempted, Season (Since 1938)
0 Chi. Bears, 1944
2 Cleveland, 1939
Card-Pitt, 1944
Boston, 1946
Chi. Bears, 1947
3 Chi. Bears, 1945
Cleveland, 1945

Most Field Goals Attempted, Game
9 St. Louis vs. Pittsburgh, Sept. 24, 1967
8 Pittsburgh vs. St. Louis, Dec. 2, 1962
Detroit vs. Minnesota, Nov. 13, 1966
N.Y. Jets vs. Buffalo, Nov. 3, 1968
7 By many teams

Most Field Goals Attempted, Both Teams, Game
11 St. Louis (6) vs. Pittsburgh (5), Nov. 13, 1966
Washington (6) vs. Chicago (5), Nov. 14, 1971
Green Bay (6) vs. Detroit (5), Sept. 29, 1974
Washington (6) vs. N.Y. Giants (5), Nov. 14, 1976
10 Denver (5) vs. Boston (5), Nov. 11, 1962
Boston (7) vs. San Diego (3), Sept. 20, 1964
Buffalo (7) vs. Houston (3), Dec. 5, 1965
St. Louis (7) vs. Atlanta (3), Dec. 11, 1966
Boston (7) vs. Buffalo (3), Sept. 24, 1967
Detroit (7) vs. Minnesota (3), Sept. 20, 1971
Washington (7) vs. Houston (3), Oct. 10, 1971
Green Bay (5) vs. St. Louis (5), Dec. 5, 1971
Kansas City (7) vs. Buffalo (3), Dec. 19, 1971
Kansas City (5) vs. San Diego (5), Oct. 29, 1972
Minnesota (6) vs. Chicago (4), Sept. 23, 1973
Cleveland (7) vs. Denver (3), Oct. 19, 1975
Cleveland (5) vs. Denver (5), Oct. 5, 1980
9 In many games

Most Field Goals, Season
35 N.Y. Giants, 1983
34 N.Y. Jets, 1968
33 Green Bay, 1972
Washington, 1983
Pittsburgh, 1985

Fewest Field Goals, Season (Since 1932)
0 Boston, 1932, 1935
Chi. Cardinals, 1932, 1945
Green Bay, 1932, 1944
New York, 1932

Brooklyn, 1944
Card-Pitt, 1944
Chi. Bears, 1944, 1947
Boston, 1946
Baltimore, 1950
Dallas, 1952

Most Field Goals, Game
7 St. Louis vs. Pittsburgh, Sept. 24, 1967
6 Boston vs. Denver, Oct. 4, 1964
Detroit vs. Minnesota, Nov. 13, 1966
N.Y. Jets vs. Buffalo, Nov. 3, 1968; vs. New Orleans, Dec. 3, 1972
Philadelphia vs. Houston, Nov. 12, 1972
St. Louis vs. Atlanta, Dec. 9, 1973
N.Y. Giants vs. Seattle, Oct. 18, 1981
San Francisco vs. New Orleans, Oct. 16, 1983
5 By many teams

Most Field Goals, Both Teams, Game
8 Cleveland (4) vs. St. Louis (4), Sept. 20, 1964
Chicago (5) vs. Philadelphia (3), Oct. 20, 1968
Washington (5) vs. Chicago (3), Nov. 14, 1971
Kansas City (5) vs. Buffalo (3), Dec. 19, 1971
Detroit (4) vs. Green Bay (4), Sept. 29, 1974
Cleveland (5) vs. Denver (3), Oct. 19, 1975
New England (4) vs. San Diego (4), Nov. 9, 1975
San Francisco (6) vs. New Orleans (2), Oct. 16, 1983
7 In many games

Most Consecutive Games Scoring Field Goals
31 Minnesota, 1968-70
21 San Francisco, 1970-72
20 Los Angeles, 1970-71
Miami, 1970-72

SAFETIES

Most Safeties, Season
4 Detroit, 1962
3 Green Bay, 1932, 1975
Pittsburgh, 1947
N.Y. Yanks, 1950
Detroit, 1960
St. Louis, 1960
Buffalo, 1964
Minnesota, 1965, 1981
Cleveland, 1970
L.A. Rams, 1973, 1984
Houston, 1977
Dallas, 1981
Oakland, 1981
Chicago, 1985
2 By many teams

Most Safeties, Game
3 L.A. Rams vs. N.Y. Giants, Sept. 30, 1984
2 Cincinnati vs. Chi. Cardinals, Nov. 19, 1933
Detroit vs. Brooklyn, Dec. 1, 1935
N.Y. Giants vs. Pittsburgh, Sept. 17, 1950; vs. Washington, Nov. 5, 1961
Chicago vs. Pittsburgh, Nov. 9, 1969
Dallas vs. Philadelphia, Nov. 19, 1972
Los Angeles vs. Green Bay, Oct. 21, 1973
Oakland vs. San Diego, Oct. 26, 1975
Denver vs. Seattle, Jan. 2, 1983

Most Safeties, Both Teams, Game
3 L.A. Rams (3) vs. N.Y. Giants (0), Sept. 30, 1984
2 Chi. Bears (1) vs. San Francisco (1), Oct. 19, 1952
Cincinnati (1) vs. Los Angeles (1), Oct. 22, 1972
Atlanta (1) vs. Detroit (1), Oct. 5, 1980
(Also see previous record)

FIRST DOWNS

Most Seasons Leading League
9 Chi. Bears, 1935, 1939, 1941, 1943, 1945, 1947-49, 1955
7 San Diego, 1965, 1969, 1980-83, 1985
6 L.A. Rams, 1946, 1950-51, 1954, 1957, 1973

Most Consecutive Seasons Leading League
4 San Diego, 1980-83
3 Chi. Bears, 1947-49
2 By many teams

Most First Downs, Season
387 Miami, 1984
380 San Diego, 1985
379 San Diego, 1981

Fewest First Downs, Season
51 Cincinnati, 1933
64 Pittsburgh, 1935
67 Philadelphia, 1937

Most First Downs, Game
38 Los Angeles vs. N.Y. Giants, Nov. 13, 1966
37 Green Bay vs. Philadelphia, Nov. 11, 1962
36 Pittsburgh vs. Cleveland, Nov. 25, 1979 (OT)

Fewest First Downs, Game
0 N.Y. Giants vs. Green Bay, Oct. 1, 1933; vs. Washington, Sept. 27, 1942
Pittsburgh vs. Boston, Oct. 29, 1933
Philadelphia vs. Detroit, Sept. 20, 1935
Denver vs. Houston, Sept. 3, 1966

Most First Downs, Both Teams, Game
62 San Diego (32) vs. Seattle (30), Sept. 15, 1985
59 Miami (31) vs. Buffalo (28), Oct. 9, 1983 (OT)
Seattle (33) vs. Kansas City (26), Nov. 27, 1983 (OT)
58 Los Angeles (30) vs. Chi. Bears (28), Oct. 24, 1954
Denver (34) vs. Kansas City (24), Nov. 18, 1974
Atlanta (35) vs. New Orleans (23), Sept. 2, 1979 (OT)
Pittsburgh (36) vs. Cleveland (22), Nov. 25, 1979 (OT)
San Diego (34) vs. Miami (24), Nov. 18, 1984 (OT)
Cincinnati (32) vs. San Diego (26), Sept. 22, 1985

Fewest First Downs, Both Teams, Game
5 N.Y. Giants (0) vs. Green Bay (5), Oct. 1, 1933

Most First Downs, Rushing, Season
181 New England, 1978
177 Los Angeles, 1973
176 Chicago, 1985

Fewest First Downs, Rushing, Season
36 Cleveland, 1942
Boston, 1944
39 Brooklyn, 1943
40 Philadelphia, 1940
Detroit, 1945

Most First Downs, Rushing, Game
25 Philadelphia vs. Washington, Dec. 2, 1951
21 Cleveland vs. Philadelphia, Dec. 13, 1959
Los Angeles vs. New Orleans, Nov. 25, 1973
Pittsburgh vs. Kansas City, Nov. 7, 1976
New England vs. Denver, Nov. 28, 1976
Oakland vs. Green Bay, Sept. 17, 1978
20 By eight teams

Fewest First Downs, Rushing, Game
0 By many teams

Most First Downs, Passing, Season
259 San Diego, 1985
244 San Diego, 1980
243 Miami, 1984

Fewest First Downs, Passing, Season
18 Pittsburgh, 1941
23 Brooklyn, 1942
N.Y. Giants, 1944
24 N.Y. Giants, 1943

Most First Downs, Passing, Game
29 N.Y. Giants vs. Cincinnati, Oct. 13, 1985
27 San Diego vs. Seattle, Sept. 15, 1985
25 Denver vs. Kansas City, Nov. 18, 1974
N.Y Jets vs. San Francisco, Sept. 21, 1980

Fewest First Downs, Passing, Game
0 By many teams

Most First Downs, Penalty, Season
39 Seattle, 1978
38 Buffalo, 1983
Denver, 1983
37 Cleveland, 1981

Fewest First Downs, Penalty, Season
2 Brooklyn, 1940
4 Chi. Cardinals, 1940
N.Y. Giants, 1942, 1944
Washington, 1944
Cleveland, 1952
Kansas City, 1969
5 Brooklyn, 1939
Chi. Bears, 1939
Detroit, 1953
Los Angeles, 1953
Houston, 1982

Most First Downs, Penalty, Game
11 Denver vs. Houston, Oct. 6, 1985
9 Chi. Bears vs. Cleveland, Nov. 25, 1951
Baltimore vs. Pittsburgh, Oct. 30, 1977
8 Philadelphia vs. Detroit, Dec. 2, 1979
Cincinnati vs. N.Y. Jets, Oct. 6, 1985

Fewest First Downs, Penalty, Game
0 By many teams

NET YARDS GAINED RUSHING AND PASSING

Most Seasons Leading League
12 Chi. Bears, 1932, 1934-35, 1939, 1941-44, 1947, 1949, 1955-56
7 San Diego, 1963, 1965, 1980-83, 1985
6 L.A. Rams, 1946, 1950-51, 1954, 1957, 1973
Baltimore, 1958-60, 1964, 1967, 1976
Dall. Cowboys, 1966, 1968-69, 1971, 1974, 1977

Most Consecutive Seasons Leading League
4 Chi. Bears, 1941-44
San Diego, 1980-83
3 Baltimore, 1958-60
Houston, 1960-62
Oakland, 1968-70
2 By many teams

Most Yards Gained, Season
6,936 Miami, 1984
6,744 San Diego, 1981
6,535 San Diego, 1985

Fewest Yards Gained, Season
1,150 Cincinnati, 1933
1,443 Chi. Cardinals, 1934
1,486 Chi. Cardinals, 1933

Most Yards Gained, Game
735 Los Angeles vs. N.Y. Yanks, Sept. 28, 1951
683 Pittsburgh vs. Chi. Cardinals, Dec. 13, 1958
682 Chi. Bears vs. N.Y. Giants, Nov. 14, 1943

Fewest Yards Gained, Game
−7 Seattle vs. Los Angeles, Nov. 4, 1979
−5 Denver vs. Oakland, Sept. 10, 1967
14 Chi. Cardinals vs. Detroit, Sept. 15, 1940

Most Yards Gained, Both Teams, Game
1,133 Los Angeles (636) vs. N.Y. Yanks (497), Nov. 19, 1950
1,102 San Diego (661) vs. Cincinnati (441), Dec. 20, 1982
1,087 St. Louis (589) vs. Philadelphia (498), Dec. 16, 1962

Fewest Yards Gained, Both Teams, Game
30 Chi. Cardinals (14) vs. Detroit (16), Sept. 15, 1940

Most Consecutive Games, 400 or More Yards Gained
11 San Diego, 1982-83
6 Houston, 1961-62

San Diego, 1981
5 Chi. Bears, 1947, 1955
Los Angeles, 1950
Philadelphia, 1953
Oakland, 1968
New England, 1981

Most Consecutive Games, 300 or More Yards Gained
29 Los Angeles, 1949-51
26 Miami, 1983-85
20 Chi. Bears, 1948-50

RUSHING

Most Seasons Leading League
15 Chi. Bears, 1932, 1934-35, 1939-42, 1951, 1955-56, 1968, 1977, 1983-85
6 Cleveland, 1958-59, 1963, 1965-67
5 Buffalo, 1962, 1964, 1973, 1975, 1982

Most Consecutive Seasons Leading League
4 Chi. Bears, 1939-42
3 Detroit, 1936-38
San Francisco, 1952-54
Cleveland, 1965-67
Chicago, 1983-85
2 By many teams

Most Rushing Attempts, Season
681 Oakland, 1977
674 Chicago, 1984
671 New England, 1978

Fewest Rushing Attempts, Season
211 Philadelphia, 1982
219 San Francisco, 1982
225 Houston, 1982

Most Rushing Attempts, Game
72 Chi. Bears vs. Brooklyn, Oct. 20, 1935
70 Chi. Cardinals vs. Green Bay, Dec. 5, 1948
69 Chi. Cardinals vs. Green Bay, Dec. 6, 1936
Kansas City vs. Cincinnati, Sept. 3, 1978

Fewest Rushing Attempts, Game
6 Chi. Cardinals vs. Boston, Oct. 29, 1933
7 Oakland vs. Buffalo, Oct. 15, 1963
Houston vs. N.Y. Giants, Dec. 8, 1985
8 Denver vs. Oakland, Dec. 17, 1960
Buffalo vs. St. Louis, Sept. 9, 1984

Most Rushing Attempts, Both Teams, Game
108 Chi. Cardinals (70) vs. Green Bay (38), Dec. 5, 1948
105 Oakland (62) vs. Atlanta (43), Nov. 30, 1975 (OT)
103 Kansas City (53) vs. San Diego (50), Nov. 12, 1978 (OT)

Fewest Rushing Attempts, Both Teams, Game
36 Cincinnati (16) vs. Chi. Bears (20), Sept. 30, 1934
37 Atlanta (18) vs. San Francisco (19), Oct. 6, 1985
38 N.Y. Jets (13) vs. Buffalo (25), Nov. 8, 1964

YARDS GAINED

Most Yards Gained Rushing, Season
3,165 New England, 1978
3,088 Buffalo, 1973
2,986 Kansas City, 1978

Fewest Yards Gained Rushing, Season
298 Philadelphia, 1940
467 Detroit, 1946
471 Boston, 1944

Most Yards Gained Rushing, Game
426 Detroit vs. Pittsburgh, Nov. 4, 1934
423 N.Y. Giants vs. Baltimore, Nov. 19, 1950
420 Boston vs. N.Y. Giants, Oct. 8, 1933

Fewest Yards Gained Rushing, Game
−53 Detroit vs. Chi. Cardinals, Oct. 17, 1943
−36 Philadelphia vs. Chi. Bears, Nov. 19, 1939
−33 Phil-Pitt vs. Brooklyn, Oct. 2, 1943

Most Yards Gained Rushing, Both Teams, Game
595 Los Angeles (371) vs. N.Y. Yanks (224), Nov. 18, 1951
574 Chi. Bears (396) vs. Pittsburgh (178), Oct. 10, 1934
557 Chi. Bears (406) vs. Green Bay (151), Nov. 6, 1955

Fewest Yards Gained Rushing, Both Teams, Game
−15 Detroit (−53) vs. Chi. Cardinals (38), Oct. 17, 1943
4 Detroit (−10) vs. Chi. Cardinals (14), Sept. 15, 1940
63 Chi. Cardinals (−1) vs. N.Y. Giants (64), Oct. 18, 1953

AVERAGE GAIN

Highest Average Gain, Rushing, Season
5.74 Cleveland, 1963
5.65 San Francisco, 1954
5.56 San Diego, 1963

Lowest Average Gain, Rushing, Season
0.94 Philadelphia, 1940
1.45 Boston, 1944
1.55 Pittsburgh, 1935

TOUCHDOWNS

Most Touchdowns, Rushing, Season
36 Green Bay, 1962
33 Pittsburgh, 1976
30 Chi. Bears, 1941
New England, 1978
Washington, 1983

Fewest Touchdowns, Rushing, Season
1 Brooklyn, 1934
2 Chi. Cardinals, 1933
Cincinnati, 1933
Pittsburgh, 1934, 1940
Philadelphia, 1935, 1936, 1937, 1938, 1972
3 By many teams

Most Touchdowns, Rushing, Game
7 Los Angeles vs. Atlanta, Dec. 4, 1976
6 By many teams

Most Touchdowns, Rushing, Both Teams, Game
8 Los Angeles (6) vs. N.Y. Yanks (2), Nov. 18, 1951
Cleveland (6) vs. Los Angeles (2), Nov. 24, 1957
7 In many games

PASSING

ATTEMPTS

Most Passes Attempted, Season
709 Minnesota, 1981
662 San Diego, 1984
641 Kansas City, 1983

Fewest Passes Attempted, Season
102 Cincinnati, 1933
106 Boston, 1933
120 Detroit, 1937

Most Passes Attempted, Game
68 Houston vs. Buffalo, Nov 1, 1964
63 Minnesota vs. Tampa Bay, Sept. 5, 1981
62 N.Y. Jets vs. Denver, Dec. 3, 1967; vs. Baltimore, Oct. 18, 1970
Dallas vs. Detroit, Sept. 15, 1985
N.Y. Giants vs. Cincinnati, Oct. 13, 1985

Fewest Passes Attempted, Game
0 Green Bay vs. Portsmouth, Oct. 8, 1933; vs. Chi. Bears, Sept. 25, 1949
Detroit vs. Cleveland, Sept. 10, 1937
Pittsburgh vs. Brooklyn, Nov. 16, 1941; vs. Los Angeles, Nov. 13, 1949
Cleveland vs. Philadelphia, Dec. 3, 1950

Most Passes Attempted, Both Teams, Game
102 San Francisco (57) vs. Atlanta (45), Oct. 6, 1985
100 Tampa Bay (54) vs. Kansas City (46), Oct. 28, 1984
98 Minnesota (56) vs. Baltimore (42), Sept. 28, 1969

Fewest Passes Attempted, Both Teams, Game
4 Chi. Cardinals (1) vs. Detroit (3), Nov. 3, 1935
Detroit (0) vs. Cleveland (4), Sept. 10, 1937
6 Chi. Cardinals (2) vs. Detroit (4), Sept. 15, 1940
8 Brooklyn (2) vs. Philadelphia (6), Oct. 1, 1939

COMPLETIONS

Most Passes Completed, Season
401 San Diego, 1984
386 San Diego, 1985
382 Minnesota, 1981

Fewest Passes Completed, Season
25 Cincinnati, 1933
33 Boston, 1933
34 Chi. Cardinals, 1934
Detroit, 1934

Most Passes Completed, Game
42 N.Y. Jets vs. San Francisco, Sept. 21, 1980
40 Cincinnati vs. San Diego, Dec. 20, 1982
Dallas vs. Detroit, Sept. 15, 1985
N.Y. Giants vs. Cincinnati, Oct. 13, 1985
38 Minnesota vs. Cleveland, Dec. 14, 1980; vs. Green Bay, Nov. 29, 1981
Buffalo vs. Miami, Oct. 9, 1983 (OT)

Fewest Passes Completed, Game
0 By many teams. Last time: Buffalo vs. N.Y. Jets, Sept. 29, 1974

Most Passes Completed, Both Teams, Game
68 San Francisco (37) vs. Atlanta (31), Oct. 6, 1985
66 Cincinnati (40) vs. San Diego (26), Dec. 20, 1982
65 San Diego (33) vs. San Francisco (32), Dec. 11, 1982
San Diego (37) vs. Miami (28), Nov. 18, 1984 (OT)

Fewest Passes Completed, Both Teams, Game
1 Chi. Cardinals (0) vs. Philadelphia (1), Nov. 8, 1936
Detroit (0) vs. Cleveland (1), Sept. 10, 1937
Chi. Cardinals (0) vs. Detroit (1), Sept. 15, 1940
Brooklyn (0) vs. Pittsburgh (1), Nov. 29, 1942
2 Chi. Cardinals (0) vs. Detroit (2), Nov. 3, 1935
Buffalo (0) vs. N.Y. Jets (2), Sept. 29, 1974
3 Brooklyn (1) vs. Philadelphia (2), Oct. 1, 1939

YARDS GAINED

Most Seasons Leading League, Passing Yardage
10 San Diego, 1965, 1968, 1971, 1978-83, 1985
8 Chi. Bears, 1932, 1939, 1941, 1943, 1945, 1949, 1954, 1964
7 Washington, 1938, 1940, 1944, 1947-48, 1967, 1974

Most Consecutive Seasons Leading League, Passing Yardage
6 San Diego, 1978-83
4 Green Bay, 1934-37
2 By many teams

Most Yards Gained, Passing, Season
5,018 Miami, 1984
4,870 San Diego, 1985
4,739 San Diego, 1981

Fewest Yards Gained, Passing, Season
302 Chi. Cardinals, 1934
357 Cincinnati, 1933
459 Boston, 1934

Most Yards Gained, Passing, Game
554 Los Angeles vs. N.Y. Yanks, Sept. 28, 1951
530 Minnesota vs. Baltimore, Sept. 28, 1969
506 L.A. Rams vs. Chicago, Dec. 26, 1982

Fewest Yards Gained, Passing, Game
−53 Denver vs. Oakland, Sept. 10, 1967
−52 Cincinnati vs. Houston, Oct. 31, 1971
−39 Atlanta vs. San Francisco, Oct. 23, 1976

Most Yards Gained, Passing, Both Teams, Game
883 San Diego (486) vs. Cincinnati (397), Dec. 20, 1982
834 Philadelphia (419) vs. St. Louis (415), Dec. 16, 1962
822 N.Y. Jets (490) vs. Baltimore (332), Sept. 24, 1972

Fewest Yards Gained, Passing, Both Teams, Game
−11 Green Bay (−10) vs. Dallas (−1), Oct. 24, 1965
1 Chi. Cardinals (0) vs. Philadelphia (1), Nov. 8, 1936
7 Brooklyn (0) vs. Pittsburgh (7), Nov. 29, 1942

TIMES SACKED

Most Seasons Leading League, Fewest Times Sacked
5 Miami, 1973, 1982-85
4 San Diego, 1963-64, 1967-68
San Francisco, 1964-65, 1970-71
3 N.Y. Jets, 1965-66, 1968
Houston, 1961-62, 1978
St. Louis, 1974-76

Most Consecutive Seasons Leading League, Fewest Times Sacked
4 Miami, 1982-85
3 St. Louis, 1974-76
2 By many teams

Most Times Sacked, Season
70 Atlanta, 1968
69 Atlanta, 1985
68 Dallas, 1964

Fewest Times Sacked, Season
8 San Francisco, 1970
St. Louis, 1975
9 N.Y. Jets, 1966
10 N.Y. Giants, 1972

Most Times Sacked, Game
12 Pittsburgh vs. Dallas, Nov. 20, 1966
Baltimore vs. St. Louis, Oct. 26, 1980
Detroit vs. Chicago, Dec. 16, 1984
Houston vs. Dallas, Sept. 29, 1985
11 St. Louis vs. N.Y. Giants, Nov. 1, 1964
Los Angeles vs. Baltimore, Nov. 22, 1964
Denver vs. Buffalo, Dec. 13, 1964; vs. Oakland, Nov. 5, 1967
Green Bay vs. Detroit, Nov. 7, 1965
Buffalo vs. Oakland, Oct. 15, 1967
Atlanta vs. St. Louis, Nov. 24, 1968; vs. Cleveland, Nov. 18, 1984
Detroit vs. Dallas, Oct. 6, 1975
Philadelphia vs. St. Louis, Dec. 18, 1983
Cleveland vs. Kansas City, Sept. 30, 1984
Minnesota vs. Chicago, Oct. 28, 1984
10 By many teams

Most Times Sacked, Both Teams, Game
18 Green Bay (10) vs. San Diego (8), Sept. 24, 1978
17 Buffalo (10) vs. N.Y. Titans (7), Nov. 23, 1961
Pittsburgh (12) vs. Dallas (5), Nov. 20, 1966
Atlanta (9) vs. Philadelphia (8), Dec. 16, 1984
16 Los Angeles (11) vs. Baltimore (5), Nov. 22, 1964
Buffalo (11) vs. Oakland (5), Oct. 15, 1967

COMPLETION PERCENTAGE

Most Seasons Leading League, Completion Percentage
11 Washington, 1937, 1939-40, 1942-45, 1947-48, 1969-70
7 Green Bay, 1936, 1941, 1961-62, 1964, 1966, 1968
6 Cleveland, 1951, 1953-55, 1959-60
Dall. Texans/Kansas City, 1962, 1964, 1966-69
San Francisco, 1952, 1957-58, 1965, 1981, 1983

Most Consecutive Seasons Leading League, Completion Percentage
4 Washington, 1942-45
Kansas City, 1966-69
3 Cleveland, 1953-55
2 By many teams

Highest Completion Percentage, Season
70.6 Cincinnati, 1982 (310-219)
64.3 Oakland, 1976 (361-232)
64.2 San Francisco, 1983 (528-339)

Lowest Completion Percentage, Season
22.9 Philadelphia, 1936 (170-39)
24.5 Cincinnati, 1933 (102-25)
25.0 Pittsburgh, 1941 (168-42)

TOUCHDOWNS

Most Touchdowns, Passing, Season
49 Miami, 1984
48 Houston, 1961
39 N.Y. Giants, 1963

Fewest Touchdowns, Passing, Season
0 Cincinnati, 1933
Pittsburgh, 1945
1 Boston, 1932, 1933
Chi. Cardinals, 1934
Cincinnati/St. Louis, 1934
Detroit, 1942
2 Chi. Cardinals, 1932, 1935
Stapleton, 1932
Brooklyn, 1936
Pittsburgh, 1942

Most Touchdowns, Passing, Game
7 Chi. Bears vs. N.Y. Giants, Nov. 14, 1943
Philadelphia vs. Washington, Oct. 17, 1954
Houston vs. N.Y. Titans, Nov. 19, 1961; vs. N.Y. Titans, Oct. 14, 1962
N.Y. Giants vs. Washington, Oct. 28, 1962
Minnesota vs. Baltimore, Sept. 28, 1969
San Diego vs. Oakland, Nov. 22, 1981
6 By many teams.

Most Touchdowns, Passing, Both Teams, Game
12 New Orleans (6) vs. St. Louis (6), Nov. 2, 1969
11 N.Y. Giants (7) vs. Washington (4), Oct. 28, 1962
Oakland (6) vs. Houston (5), Dec. 22, 1963
9 In many games

PASSES HAD INTERCEPTED

Most Passes Had Intercepted, Season
48 Houston, 1962
45 Denver, 1961
41 Card-Pitt, 1944

Fewest Passes Had Intercepted, Season
5 Cleveland, 1960
Green Bay, 1966
6 Green Bay, 1964
St. Louis, 1982
7 Los Angeles, 1969

Most Passes Had Intercepted, Game
9 Detroit vs. Green Bay, Oct. 24, 1943
Pittsburgh vs. Philadelphia, Dec. 12, 1965
8 Green Bay vs. N.Y. Giants, Nov. 21, 1948
Chi. Cardinals vs. Philadelphia, Sept. 24, 1950
N.Y. Yanks vs. N.Y. Giants, Dec. 16, 1951
Denver vs. Houston, Dec. 2, 1962
Chi. Bears vs. Detroit, Sept. 22, 1968
Baltimore vs. N.Y. Jets, Sept. 23, 1973
7 By many teams. Last time: Detroit vs. Denver, Oct. 7, 1984

Most Passes Had Intercepted, Both Teams, Game
13 Denver (8) vs. Houston (5), Dec. 2, 1962
11 Philadelphia (7) vs. Boston (4), Nov. 3, 1935
Boston (6) vs. Pittsburgh (5), Dec. 1, 1935
Cleveland (7) vs. Green Bay (4), Oct. 30, 1938
Green Bay (7) vs. Detroit (4), Oct. 20, 1940
Detroit (7) vs. Chi. Bears (4), Nov. 22, 1942
Detroit (7) vs. Cleveland (4), Nov. 26, 1944
Chi. Cardinals (8) vs. Philadelphia (3), Sept. 24, 1950
Washington (7) vs. N.Y. Giants (4), Dec. 8, 1963
Pittsburgh (9) vs. Philadelphia (2), Dec 12, 1965
10 In many games

PUNTING

Most Seasons Leading League (Average Distance)
6 Washington, 1940-43, 1945, 1958
Denver, 1962-64, 1966-67, 1982
Kansas City, 1968, 1971-73, 1979, 1984
4 L.A. Rams, 1946, 1949, 1955-56
Baltimore/Indianapolis, 1966, 1969, 1983, 1985
3 Cleveland, 1950-52
San Francisco, 1957, 1962, 1965
Oakland, 1974, 1975, 1977
Cincinnati, 1970, 1978, 1981

Most Consecutive Seasons Leading League (Average Distance)
4 Washington, 1940-43
3 Cleveland, 1950-52
Denver, 1962-64
Kansas City, 1971-73

Most Punts, Season
114 Chicago, 1981
113 Boston, 1934
Brooklyn, 1934
112 Boston, 1935

Fewest Punts, Season
23 San Diego, 1982
31 Cincinnati, 1982
32 Chi. Bears, 1941

Most Punts, Game
17 Chi. Bears vs. Green Bay, Oct. 22, 1933
Cincinnati vs. Pittsburgh, Oct. 22, 1933
16 Cincinnati vs. Portsmouth, Sept. 17, 1933
Chi. Cardinals vs. Chi. Bears, Nov. 30, 1933; vs. Detroit, Sept. 15, 1940

Fewest Punts, Game
0 By many teams. Last time: Minnesota vs. Detroit, Nov. 3, 1985

Most Punts, Both Teams, Game
31 Chi. Bears (17) vs. Green Bay (14), Oct. 22, 1933
Cincinnati (17), vs. Pittsburgh (14), Oct. 22, 1933
29 Chi. Cardinals (15) vs. Cincinnati (14), Nov. 12, 1933
Chi. Cardinals (16) vs. Chi. Bears (13), Nov. 30, 1933
Chi. Cardinals (16) vs. Detroit (13), Sept. 15, 1940

Fewest Punts, Both Teams, Game
1 Dall. Cowboys (0) vs. Cleveland (1), Dec. 3, 1961
Chicago (0) vs. Detroit (1), Oct. 1, 1972
San Francisco (0) vs. N.Y. Giants (1), Oct. 15, 1972
Green Bay (0) vs. Buffalo (1), Dec. 5, 1982
2 In many games

AVERAGE YARDAGE

Highest Average Distance, Punting, Season
47.6 Detroit, 1961 (56-2,664)
47.0 Pittsburgh, 1961 (73-3,431)
46.9 Pittsburgh, 1953 (80-3,752)

Lowest Average Distance, Punting, Season
32.7 Card-Pitt, 1944 (60-1,964)
33.9 Detroit, 1969 (74-2,510)
34.4 Phil-Pitt, 1943 (62-2,132)

PUNT RETURNS

Most Seasons Leading League (Average Return)
8 Detroit, 1943-45, 1951-52, 1962, 1966, 1969
5 Chi. Cardinals, 1948-49, 1955-56, 1959
Cleveland, 1958, 1960, 1964-65, 1967
Green Bay, 1950, 1953-54, 1961, 1972
Dall. Texans/Kansas City, 1960, 1968, 1970, 1979-80
4 Denver, 1963, 1967, 1969, 1982

Most Consecutive Seasons Leading League (Average Return)
3 Detroit, 1943-45
2 By many teams

Most Punt Returns, Season
71 Pittsburgh, 1976
Tampa Bay, 1979
L.A. Raiders, 1985
67 Pittsburgh, 1974
Los Angeles, 1978
L.A. Raiders, 1984
65 San Francisco, 1976

Fewest Punt Returns, Season
12 Baltimore, 1981

San Diego, 1982
14 Los Angeles, 1961
Philadelphia, 1962
Baltimore, 1982
15 Houston, 1960
Washington, 1960
Oakland, 1961
N.Y. Giants, 1969
Philadelphia, 1973
Kansas City, 1982

Most Punt Returns, Game
12 Philadelphia vs. Cleveland, Dec. 3, 1950
11 Chi. Bears vs. Chi. Cardinals, Oct. 8, 1950
Washington vs. Tampa Bay, Oct. 9, 1977
10 Philadelphia vs. N.Y. Giants, Nov. 26, 1950
Philadelphia vs. Tampa Bay, Sept. 18, 1977
Pittsburgh vs. Buffalo, Dec. 16, 1979
Washington vs. New Orleans, Dec. 26, 1982

Most Punt Returns, Both Teams, Game
17 Philadelphia (12) vs. Cleveland (5), Dec. 3, 1950
16 N.Y. Giants (9) vs. Philadelphia (7), Dec. 12, 1954
Washington (11) vs. Tampa Bay (5), Oct. 9, 1977
15 Detroit (8) vs. Cleveland (7), Sept. 27, 1942
Los Angeles (8) vs. Baltimore (7), Nov. 27, 1966
Pittsburgh (8) vs. Houston (7), Dec. 1, 1974
Philadelphia (10) vs. Tampa Bay (5), Sept. 18, 1977
Baltimore (9) vs. Kansas City (6), Sept. 2, 1979
Washington (10) vs. New Orleans (5), Dec. 26, 1982

FAIR CATCHES

Most Fair Catches, Season
34 Baltimore, 1971
32 San Diego, 1969
30 St. Louis, 1967
Minnesota, 1971

Fewest Fair Catches, Season
0 San Diego, 1975
New England, 1976
Tampa Bay, 1976
Pittsburgh, 1977
Dallas, 1982
1 Cleveland, 1974
San Francisco, 1975
Kansas City, 1976
St. Louis, 1976, 1982
San Diego, 1976
L.A. Rams, 1982
Tampa Bay, 1982
2 By many teams

Most Fair Catches, Game
7 Minnesota vs. Dallas, Sept. 25, 1966
Detroit vs. Chicago, Nov. 21, 1976
6 By many teams

YARDS GAINED

Most Yards, Punt Returns, Season
785 L.A. Raiders, 1985
781 Chi. Bears, 1948
774 Pittsburgh, 1974

Fewest Yards, Punt Returns, Season
27 St. Louis, 1965
35 N.Y. Giants, 1965
37 New England, 1972

Most Yards, Punt Returns, Game
231 Detroit vs. San Francisco, Oct. 6, 1963
225 Oakland vs. Buffalo, Sept. 15, 1968
219 Los Angeles vs. Atlanta, Oct. 11, 1981

Most Yards, Punt Returns, Both Teams, Game
282 Los Angeles (219) vs. Atlanta (63), Oct. 11, 1981
245 Detroit (231) vs. San Francisco (14), Oct. 6, 1963
244 Oakland (225) vs. Buffalo (19), Sept. 15, 1968

AVERAGE YARDS RETURNING PUNTS

Highest Average, Punt Returns, Season
20.2 Chi. Bears, 1941 (27-546)
19.1 Chi. Cardinals, 1948 (35-669)
18.2 Chi. Cardinals, 1949 (30-546)

Lowest Average, Punt Returns, Season
1.2 St. Louis, 1965 (23-27)
1.5 N.Y. Giants, 1965 (24-35)
1.7 Washington, 1970 (27-45)

TOUCHDOWNS RETURNING PUNTS

Most Touchdowns, Punt Returns, Season
5 Chi. Cardinals, 1959
4 Chi. Cardinals, 1948
Detroit, 1951
N.Y. Giants, 1951
Denver, 1976
3 Washington, 1941
Detroit, 1952
Pittsburgh, 1952
Houston, 1975
Los Angeles, 1981

Most Touchdowns, Punt Returns, Game
2 Detroit vs. Los Angeles, Oct. 14, 1951; vs. Green Bay, Nov. 22, 1951
Chi. Cardinals vs. Pittsburgh, Nov. 1, 1959; vs. N.Y. Giants, Nov. 22, 1959
N.Y. Titans vs. Denver, Sept. 24, 1961
Denver vs. Cleveland, Sept. 26, 1976
Los Angeles vs. Atlanta, Oct. 11, 1981

Most Touchdowns, Punt Returns, Both Teams, Game
2 Philadelphia (1) vs. Washington (1), Nov. 9, 1952
Kansas City (1) vs. Buffalo (1), Sept. 11, 1966
Baltimore (1) vs. New England (1), Nov. 18, 1979
(Also see previous record)

KICKOFF RETURNS

Most Seasons Leading League (Average Return)
7 Washington, 1942, 1947, 1962-63, 1973-74, 1981
6 Chicago Bears, 1943, 1948, 1958, 1966, 1972, 1985
5 N.Y. Giants, 1944, 1946, 1949, 1951, 1953

Most Consecutive Seasons Leading League (Average Return)
3 Denver, 1965-67
2 By many teams

Most Kickoff Returns, Season
88 New Orleans, 1980
86 Minnesota, 1984
84 Baltimore, 1981

Fewest Kickoff Returns, Season
17 N.Y. Giants, 1944
20 N.Y. Giants, 1941, 1943
Chi. Bears, 1942
23 Washington, 1942

Most Kickoff Returns, Game
12 N.Y. Giants vs. Washington, Nov. 27, 1966
10 By many teams

Most Kickoff Returns, Both Teams, Game
19 N.Y. Giants (12) vs. Washington (7), Nov. 27, 1966
18 Houston (10) vs. Oakland (8), Dec. 22, 1963
17 Washington (9) vs. Green Bay (8), Oct. 17, 1983
San Diego (9) vs. Pittsburgh (8), Dec. 8, 1985

YARDS GAINED

Most Yards, Kickoff Returns, Season
1,973 New Orleans, 1980
1,824 Houston, 1963
1,801 Denver, 1963

Fewest Yards, Kickoff Returns, Season
282 N.Y. Giants, 1940
381 Green Bay, 1940
424 Chicago, 1963

Most Yards, Kickoff Returns, Game
362 Detroit vs. Los Angeles, Oct. 29, 1950
304 Chi. Bears vs. Green Bay, Nov. 9, 1952
295 Denver vs. Boston, Oct. 4, 1964

Most Yards, Kickoff Returns, Both Teams, Game
560 Detroit (362) vs. Los Angeles (198), Oct. 29, 1950
453 Washington (236) vs. Philadelphia (217), Sept. 28, 1947
447 N.Y. Giants (236) vs. Cleveland (211), Dec. 4, 1966

AVERAGE YARDAGE

Highest Average, Kickoff Returns, Season
29.4 Chicago, 1972 (52-1,528)
28.9 Pittsburgh, 1952 (39-1,128)
28.2 Washington, 1962 (61-1,720)

Lowest Average, Kickoff Returns, Season
16.3 Chicago, 1963 (26-424)
16.4 Chicago, 1983 (58-953)
16.5 San Diego, 1961 (51-642)

TOUCHDOWNS

Most Touchdowns, Kickoff Returns, Season
4 Green Bay, 1967
Chicago, 1970
3 L.A. Rams, 1950, 1985
Chi. Cardinals, 1954
San Francisco, 1963
Denver, 1966
Chicago, 1967
New England, 1977
2 By many teams

Most Touchdowns, Kickoff Returns, Game
2 Chi. Bears vs. Green Bay, Sept. 22, 1940; vs. Green Bay, Nov. 9, 1952
Philadelphia vs. Dallas, Nov. 6, 1966
Green Bay vs. Cleveland, Nov. 12, 1967
L.A. Rams vs. Green Bay, Nov. 24, 1985

Most Touchdowns, Kickoff Returns, Both Teams, Game
2 Washington (1) vs. Philadelphia (1), Nov. 1, 1942
Washington (1) vs. Philadelphia (1), Sept. 28, 1947
Los Angeles (1) vs. Detroit (1), Oct. 29, 1950
N.Y. Yanks (1) vs. N.Y. Giants (1), Nov. 4, 1951 (consecutive)
Baltimore (1) vs. Chi. Bears (1), Oct. 4, 1958
Buffalo (1) vs. Boston (1), Nov. 3, 1962
Pittsburgh (1) vs. Dallas (1), Oct. 30, 1966
St. Louis (1) vs. Washington (1), Sept. 23, 1973 (consecutive)
(Also see previous record)

FUMBLES

Most Fumbles, Season
56 Chi. Bears, 1938
San Francisco, 1978
54 Philadelphia, 1946
51 New England, 1973

Fewest Fumbles, Season
8 Cleveland, 1959
11 Green Bay, 1944
12 Brooklyn, 1934
Detroit, 1943
Cincinnati, 1982
Minnesota, 1982

Most Fumbles, Game
10 Phil-Pitt vs. New York, Oct. 9, 1943
Detroit vs. Minnesota, Nov. 12, 1967
Kansas City vs. Houston, Oct. 12, 1969
San Francisco vs. Detroit, Dec. 17, 1978

9 Philadelphia vs. Green Bay, Oct. 13, 1946
Kansas City vs. San Diego, Nov. 15, 1964
N.Y. Giants vs. Buffalo, Oct. 20, 1975
St. Louis vs. Washington, Oct. 25, 1976
San Diego vs. Green Bay, Sept. 24, 1978
Pittsburgh vs. Cincinnati, Oct. 14, 1979
Cleveland vs. Seattle, Dec. 20, 1981
8 By many teams. Last time: Tampa Bay vs. New York Jets, Dec. 12, 1982

Most Fumbles, Both Teams, Game
14 Chi. Bears (7) vs. Cleveland (7), Nov. 24, 1940
St. Louis (8) vs. N.Y. Giants (6), Sept. 17, 1961
Kansas City (10) vs. Houston (4), Oct. 12, 1969
13 Washington (8) vs. Pittsburgh (5), Nov. 14, 1937
Philadelphia (7) vs. Boston (6), Dec. 8, 1946
N.Y. Giants (7) vs. Washington (6), Nov. 5, 1950
Kansas City (9) vs. San Diego (4), Nov. 15, 1964
Buffalo (7) vs. Denver (6), Dec. 13, 1964
N.Y. Jets (7) vs. Houston (6), Sept. 12, 1965
Houston (8) vs. Pittsburgh (5), Dec. 9, 1973
St. Louis (9) vs. Washington (4), Oct. 25, 1976
Cleveland (9) vs. Seattle (4), Dec. 20, 1981
Green Bay (7) vs. Detroit (6), Oct. 6, 1985
12 In many games

FUMBLES LOST

Most Fumbles Lost, Season
36 Chi. Cardinals, 1959
31 Green Bay, 1952
29 Chi. Cardinals, 1946
Pittsburgh, 1950

Fewest Fumbles Lost, Season
3 Philadelphia, 1938
Minnesota, 1980
4 San Francisco, 1960
Kansas City, 1982
5 Chi. Cardinals, 1943
Detroit, 1943
N.Y. Giants, 1943
Cleveland, 1959
Minnesota, 1982

Most Fumbles Lost, Game
8 St. Louis vs. Washington, Oct. 25, 1976
7 Cincinnati vs. Buffalo, Nov. 30, 1969
Cleveland vs. Seattle, Dec. 20, 1981
6 By many teams. Last time: L.A. Rams vs. New England, Dec. 11, 1983

FUMBLES RECOVERED

Most Fumbles Recovered, Season, Own and Opponents'
58 Minnesota, 1963 (27 own, 31 opp)
51 Chi. Bears, 1938 (37 own, 14 opp)
San Francisco, 1978 (24 own, 27 opp)
47 Atlanta, 1978 (22 own, 25 opp)

Fewest Fumbles Recovered, Season, Own and Opponents'
9 San Francisco, 1982 (5 own, 4 opp)
11 Cincinnati, 1982 (5 own, 6 opp)
13 Baltimore, 1967 (5 own, 8 opp)
N.Y. Jets, 1967 (7 own, 6 opp)
Philadelphia, 1968 (6 own, 7 opp)
Miami, 1973 (5 own, 8 opp)
Chicago, 1982 (6 own, 7 opp)
Denver, 1982 (6 own, 7 opp)
Miami, 1982 (5 own, 8 opp)
N.Y. Giants, 1982 (7 own, 6 opp)

Most Fumbles Recovered, Game, Own and Opponents'
10 Denver vs. Buffalo, Dec. 13, 1964 (5 own, 5 opp)
Pittsburgh vs. Houston, Dec. 9, 1973 (5 own, 5 opp)
Washington vs. St. Louis, Oct. 25, 1976 (2 own, 8 opp)
9 St. Louis vs. N.Y. Giants, Sept. 17, 1961 (6 own, 3 opp)
Houston vs. Cincinnati, Oct. 27, 1974 (4 own, 5 opp)
Kansas City vs. Dallas, Nov. 10, 1975 (4 own, 5 opp)
Green Bay vs. Detroit, Oct. 6, 1985 (5 own, 4 opp)
8 By many teams

Most Own Fumbles Recovered, Season
37 Chi. Bears, 1938
27 Philadelphia, 1946
Minnesota, 1963
26 Washington, 1940
Pittsburgh, 1948

Fewest Own Fumbles Recovered, Season
2 Washington, 1958
3 Detroit, 1956
Cleveland, 1959
Houston, 1982
4 By many teams

Most Opponents' Fumbles Recovered, Season
31 Minnesota, 1963
29 Cleveland, 1951
28 Green Bay, 1946
Houston, 1977
Seattle, 1983

Fewest Opponents' Fumbles Recovered, Season
3 Los Angeles, 1974
4 Philadelphia, 1944
San Francisco, 1982
5 Baltimore, 1982

Most Opponents' Fumbles Recovered, Game
8 Washington vs. St. Louis, Oct. 25, 1976
7 Buffalo vs. Cincinnati, Nov. 30, 1969
Seattle vs. Cleveland, Dec. 20, 1981
6 By many teams. Last time: New England vs. L.A. Rams, Dec. 11, 1983

TOUCHDOWNS

Most Touchdowns, Fumbles Recovered, Season, Own and Opponents'
5 Chi. Bears, 1942 (1 own, 4 opp)
Los Angeles, 1952 (1 own, 4 opp)
San Francisco, 1965 (1 own, 4 opp)
Oakland, 1978 (2 own, 3 opp)
4 Chi. Bears, 1948 (1 own, 3 opp)
Boston, 1948 (4 opp)
Denver, 1979 (1 own, 3 opp), 1984 (4 opp)
Atlanta, 1981 (1 own, 3 opp)
3 By many teams

Most Touchdowns, Own Fumbles Recovered, Season
2 Chi. Bears, 1953
New England, 1973
Buffalo, 1974
Denver, 1975
Oakland, 1978
Green Bay, 1982
New Orleans, 1983

Most Touchdowns, Opponents' Fumbles Recovered, Season
4 Detroit, 1937
Chi. Bears, 1942
Boston, 1948
Los Angeles, 1952
San Francisco, 1965
Denver, 1984
3 By many teams

Most Touchdowns, Fumbles Recovered, Game, Own and Opponents'
2 Detroit vs. Cleveland, Nov. 7, 1937 (2 opp); vs. Green Bay, Sept. 17, 1950 (1 own, 1 opp); vs. Chi. Cardinals, Dec. 6, 1959 (1 own, 1 opp); vs. Minnesota, Dec. 9, 1962 (1 own, 1 opp)
Philadelphia vs. New York, Sept. 25, 1938 (2 opp); vs. St. Louis, Nov. 21, 1971 (1 own, 1 opp)
Chi. Bears vs. Washington, Nov. 28, 1948 (2 opp)
N.Y. Giants vs. Pittsburgh, Sept. 17, 1950 (2 opp); vs. Green Bay, Sept. 19, 1971 (2 opp)
Cleveland vs. Dall. Cowboys, Dec. 3, 1961 (2 opp); vs. N.Y. Giants, Oct. 25, 1964 (2 opp)
Green Bay vs. Dallas, Nov. 26, 1964 (2 opp)
San Francisco vs. Detroit, Nov. 14, 1965 (2 opp)
Oakland vs. Buffalo, Dec. 24, 1967 (2 opp)
Washington vs. San Diego, Sept. 16, 1973 (2 opp); vs. Minnesota, Nov. 29, 1984 (1 own, 1 opp)
New Orleans vs. San Francisco, Oct. 19, 1975 (2 opp)
Cincinnati vs. Pittsburgh, Oct. 14, 1979 (2 opp)
Atlanta vs. Detroit, Oct. 5, 1980 (2 opp)
Kansas City vs. Oakland, Oct. 5, 1980 (2 opp)
New England vs. Baltimore, Nov. 23, 1980 (2 opp)
Denver vs. Green Bay, Oct. 15, 1984 (2 opp)

Most Touchdowns, Own Fumbles Recovered, Game
1 By many teams

Most Touchdowns, Opponents' Fumbles Recovered, Game
2 Detroit vs. Cleveland, Nov. 7, 1937
Philadelphia vs. N.Y. Giants, Sept. 25, 1938
Chi. Bears vs. Washington, Nov. 28, 1948
N.Y. Giants vs. Pittsburgh, Sept. 17, 1950; vs. Green Bay, Sept. 19, 1971
Cleveland vs. Dall. Cowboys, Dec. 3, 1961; vs. N.Y. Giants, Oct. 25, 1964
Green Bay vs. Dallas, Nov. 26, 1964
San Francisco vs. Detroit, Nov. 14, 1965
Oakland vs. Buffalo, Dec. 24, 1967
Washington vs. San Diego, Sept. 16, 1973
New Orleans vs. San Francisco, Oct. 19, 1975
Cincinnati vs. Pittsburgh, Oct. 14, 1979
Atlanta vs. Detroit, Oct. 5, 1980
Kansas City vs. Oakland, Oct. 5, 1980
New England vs. Baltimore, Nov. 23, 1980
Denver vs. Green Bay, Oct. 15, 1984

TURNOVERS

(Number of times losing the ball on interceptions and fumbles.)

Most Turnovers, Season
63 San Francisco, 1978
58 Chi. Bears, 1947
Pittsburgh, 1950
N.Y. Giants, 1983
57 Green Bay, 1950
Houston, 1962, 1963
Pittsburgh, 1965

Fewest Turnovers, Season
12 Kansas City, 1982
14 N.Y. Giants, 1943
Cleveland, 1959
16 San Francisco, 1960
Cincinnati, 1982
St. Louis, 1982
Washington, 1982

Most Turnovers, Game
12 Detroit vs. Chi. Bears, Nov. 22, 1942
Chi. Cardinals vs. Philadelphia, Sept. 24, 1950
Pittsburgh vs. Philadelphia, Dec. 12, 1965
11 San Diego vs. Green Bay, Sept. 24, 1978
10 Washington vs. N.Y. Giants, Dec. 4, 1938; vs. N.Y. Giants, Dec. 8, 1963
Pittsburgh vs. Green Bay, Nov. 23, 1941
Detroit vs. Green Bay, Oct. 24, 1943; vs. Denver, Oct. 7, 1984
Chi. Cardinals vs. Green Bay, Nov. 10, 1946; vs. N.Y. Giants, Nov. 2, 1952
Minnesota vs. Detroit, Dec. 9, 1962
Houston vs. Oakland, Sept. 7, 1963
Chicago vs. Detroit, Sept. 22, 1968
St. Louis vs. Washington, Oct. 25, 1976
N.Y. Jets vs. New England, Nov. 21, 1976
San Francisco vs. Dallas, Oct. 12, 1980
Cleveland vs. Seattle, Dec. 20, 1981

Most Turnovers, Both Teams, Game
17 Detroit (12) vs. Chi. Bears (5), Nov. 22, 1942
Boston (9) vs. Philadelphia (8), Dec. 8, 1946
16 Chi. Cardinals (12) vs. Philadelphia (4), Sept. 24, 1950
Chi. Cardinals (8) vs. Chi. Bears (8), Dec. 7, 1958
Minnesota (10) vs. Detroit (6), Dec. 9, 1962
Houston (9) vs. Kansas City (7), Oct. 12, 1969
15 Philadelphia (8) vs. Chi. Cardinals (7), Oct. 3, 1954
Denver (9) vs. Houston (6), Dec. 2, 1962
Washington (10) vs. N.Y. Giants (5), Dec. 8, 1963
St. Louis (9) vs. Kansas City (6), Oct. 2, 1983

PENALTIES

Most Seasons Leading League, Fewest Penalties
10 Miami, 1968, 1976-84
9 Pittsburgh, 1946-47, 1950-52, 1954, 1963, 1965, 1968
5 Green Bay, 1955-56, 1966-67, 1974
Most Consecutive Seasons Leading League, Fewest Penalties
9 Miami, 1976-84
3 Pittsburgh, 1950-52
2 By many teams
Most Seasons Leading League, Most Penalties
16 Chi. Bears, 1941-44, 1946-49, 1951, 1959-61, 1963, 1965, 1968, 1976
7 Oakland/L.A. Raiders, 1963, 1966, 1968-69, 1975, 1982, 1984
6 L.A. Rams, 1950, 1952, 1962, 1969, 1978, 1980
Most Consecutive Seasons Leading League, Most Penalties
4 Chi. Bears, 1941-44, 1946-49
3 Chi. Cardinals, 1954-56
Chi. Bears, 1959-61
Fewest Penalties, Season
19 Detroit, 1937
21 Boston, 1935
24 Philadelphia, 1936
Most Penalties, Season
144 Buffalo, 1983
143 L.A. Raiders, 1984
138 Detroit, 1984
Fewest Penalties, Game
0 By many teams. Last time: New Orleans vs. Seattle, Nov. 10, 1985
Most Penalties, Game
22 Brooklyn vs. Green Bay, Sept. 17, 1944
Chi. Bears vs. Philadelphia, Nov. 26, 1944
21 Cleveland vs. Chi. Bears, Nov. 25, 1951
20 Tampa Bay vs. Seattle, Oct. 17, 1976
Fewest Penalties, Both Teams, Game
0 Brooklyn vs. Pittsburgh, Oct. 28, 1934
Brooklyn vs. Boston, Sept. 28, 1936
Cleveland vs. Chi. Bears, Oct. 9, 1938
Pittsburgh vs. Philadelphia, Nov. 10, 1940
Most Penalties, Both Teams, Game
37 Cleveland (21) vs. Chi. Bears (16), Nov. 25, 1951
35 Tampa Bay (20) vs. Seattle (15), Oct. 17, 1976
33 Brooklyn (22) vs. Green Bay (11), Sept. 17, 1944

YARDS PENALIZED

Most Seasons Leading League, Fewest Yards Penalized
11 Miami, 1967-68, 1973, 1977-84
8 Boston/Washington, 1935, 1953-54, 1956-58, 1970, 1985
7 Pittsburgh, 1946-47, 1950, 1952, 1962, 1965, 1968
Most Consecutive Seasons Leading League, Fewest Yards Penalized
8 Miami, 1977-84
3 Washington, 1956-58
Boston, 1964-66
2 By many teams
Most Seasons Leading League, Most Yards Penalized
15 Chi. Bears, 1935, 1937, 1939-44, 1946-47, 1949, 1951, 1961-62, 1968
7 Oakland/L.A. Raiders, 1963-64, 1968-69, 1975, 1982, 1984
6 Buffalo, 1962, 1967, 1970, 1972, 1981, 1983
Most Consecutive Seasons Leading League, Most Yards Penalized
6 Chi. Bears, 1939-44
3 Cleveland, 1976-78
2 By many teams
Fewest Yards Penalized, Season
139 Detroit, 1937
146 Philadelphia, 1937
159 Philadelphia, 1936
Most Yards Penalized, Season
1,274 Oakland, 1969
1,239 Baltimore, 1979
1,209 L.A. Raiders, 1984
Fewest Yards Penalized, Game
0 By many teams. Last time: New Orleans vs. Seattle, Nov. 10, 1985
Most Yards Penalized, Game
209 Cleveland vs. Chi. Bears, Nov. 25, 1951
190 Tampa Bay vs. Seattle, Oct. 17, 1976
189 Houston vs. Buffalo, Oct. 31, 1965
Fewest Yards Penalized, Both Teams, Game
0 Brooklyn vs. Pittsburgh, Oct. 28, 1934
Brooklyn vs. Boston, Sept. 28, 1936
Cleveland vs. Chi. Bears, Oct. 9, 1938
Pittsburgh vs. Philadelphia, Nov. 10, 1940
Most Yards Penalized, Both Teams, Game
374 Cleveland (209) vs. Chi. Bears (165), Nov. 25, 1951
310 Tampa Bay (190) vs. Seattle (120), Oct. 17, 1976
309 Green Bay (184) vs. Boston (125), Oct. 21, 1945

DEFENSE

SCORING

Most Seasons Leading League, Fewest Points Allowed
8 N.Y. Giants, 1935, 1938-39, 1941, 1944, 1958-59, 1961
7 Chi. Bears, 1932, 1936-37, 1942, 1948, 1963, 1985
6 Clev. Browns, 1951, 1953-57
Most Consecutive Seasons Leading League, Fewest Points Allowed
5 Cleveland, 1953-57
3 Buffalo, 1964-66
Minnesota, 1969-71
2 By many teams
Fewest Points Allowed, Season (Since 1932)
44 Chi. Bears, 1932
54 Brooklyn, 1933
59 Detroit, 1934
Most Points Allowed, Season
533 Baltimore, 1981
501 N.Y. Giants, 1966
487 New Orleans, 1980
Fewest Touchdowns Allowed, Season (Since 1932)
6 Chi. Bears, 1932
Brooklyn, 1933
7 Detroit, 1934
8 Green Bay, 1932
Most Touchdowns Allowed, Season
68 Baltimore, 1981
66 N.Y. Giants, 1966
63 Baltimore, 1950

FIRST DOWNS

Fewest First Downs Allowed Season
77 Detroit, 1935
79 Boston, 1935
82 Washington, 1937
Most First Downs Allowed, Season
406 Baltimore, 1981
371 Seattle, 1981
366 Green Bay, 1983
Fewest First Downs Allowed, Rushing, Season
35 Chi. Bears, 1942
40 Green Bay, 1939
41 Brooklyn, 1944
Most First Downs Allowed, Rushing, Season
179 Detroit, 1985
178 New Orleans, 1980
175 Seattle, 1981
Fewest First Downs Allowed, Passing, Season
33 Chi. Bears, 1943
34 Pittsburgh, 1941
Washington, 1943
35 Detroit, 1940
Philadelphia, 1940, 1944
Most First Downs Allowed, Passing, Season
218 San Diego, 1985
216 San Diego, 1981
214 Baltimore, 1981
Fewest First Downs Allowed, Penalty, Season
1 Boston, 1944
3 Philadelphia, 1940
Pittsburgh, 1945
Washington, 1957
4 Cleveland, 1940
Green Bay, 1943
N.Y. Giants, 1943
Most First Downs Allowed, Penalty, Season
48 Houston, 1985
43 L.A. Raiders, 1984
41 Detroit, 1979

NET YARDS ALLOWED RUSHING AND PASSING

Most Seasons Leading League, Fewest Yards Allowed
7 Chi. Bears, 1942-43, 1948, 1958, 1963, 1984-85
6 N.Y. Giants, 1938, 1940-41, 1951, 1956, 1959
5 Boston/Washington, 1935-37, 1939, 1946
Philadelphia, 1944-45, 1949, 1953, 1981
Most Consecutive Seasons Leading League, Fewest Yards Allowed
3 Boston/Washington, 1935-37
2 By many teams
Fewest Yards Allowed, Season
1,539 Chi. Cardinals, 1934
1,703 Chi. Bears, 1942
1,789 Brooklyn, 1933
Most Yards Allowed, Season
6,793 Baltimore, 1981
6,403 Green Bay, 1983
6,352 Minnesota, 1984

RUSHING

Most Seasons Leading League, Fewest Yards Allowed
8 Chi. Bears, 1937, 1939, 1942, 1946, 1949, 1963, 1984-85
7 Detroit, 1938, 1950, 1952, 1962, 1970, 1980-81
6 Dallas, 1966-69, 1972, 1978
Most Consecutive Seasons Leading League, Fewest Yards Allowed
4 Dallas, 1966-69
2 By many teams
Fewest Yards Allowed, Rushing, Season
519 Chi. Bears, 1942
558 Philadelphia, 1944
762 Pittsburgh, 1982
Most Yards Allowed, Rushing, Season
3,228 Buffalo, 1978
3,106 New Orleans, 1980
3,010 Baltimore, 1978
Fewest Touchdowns Allowed, Rushing, Season
2 Detroit, 1934
Dallas, 1968
Minnesota, 1971
3 By many teams

Most Touchdowns Allowed, Rushing, Season
36 Oakland, 1961
31 N.Y. Giants, 1980
30 Baltimore, 1981

PASSING

Most Seasons Leading League, Fewest Yards Allowed
8 Green Bay, 1947-48, 1962, 1964-68
7 Washington, 1939, 1942, 1945, 1952-53, 1980, 1985
6 Chi. Bears, 1938, 1943-44, 1958, 1960, 1963
Most Consecutive Seasons Leading League, Fewest Yards Allowed
5 Green Bay, 1964-68
2 By many teams
Fewest Yards Allowed, Passing, Season
545 Philadelphia, 1934
558 Portsmouth, 1933
585 Chi. Cardinals, 1934
Most Yards Allowed, Passing, Season
4,311 San Diego, 1981
4,293 San Diego, 1985
4,128 Baltimore, 1981
Fewest Touchdowns Allowed, Passing, Season
1 Portsmouth, 1932
Philadelphia, 1934
2 Brooklyn, 1933
Chi. Bears, 1934
3 Chi. Bears, 1932, 1936
Green Bay, 1932, 1934
N.Y. Giants, 1939, 1944
Most Touchdowns Allowed, Passing, Season
40 Denver, 1963
38 St. Louis, 1969
37 Washington, 1961
Baltimore, 1981

SACKS
Most Seasons Leading League
4 Boston/New England, 1961, 1963, 1977, 1979
Dallas, 1966, 1968-69, 1978
Oakland/L.A. Raiders, 1966-68, 1982
3 Dallas/Kansas City, 1960, 1965, 1969
San Francisco, 1967, 1972, 1976
2 Baltimore, 1964, 1975
San Diego, 1962, 1980
N.Y. Giants, 1963, 1985
Most Consecutive Seasons Leading League
3 Oakland, 1966-68
2 Dallas, 1968-69
Most Sacks, Season
72 Chicago, 1984
68 N.Y. Giants, 1985
67 Oakland, 1967
Fewest Sacks, Season
11 Baltimore, 1982
12 Buffalo, 1982
13 Baltimore, 1981
Most Sacks, Game
12 Dallas vs. Pittsburgh, Nov. 20, 1966; vs. Houston, Sept. 29, 1985
St. Louis vs. Baltimore, Oct. 26, 1980
Chicago vs. Detroit, Dec. 16, 1984
11 N.Y. Giants vs. St. Louis, Nov. 1, 1964
Baltimore vs. Los Angeles, Nov. 22, 1964
Buffalo vs. Denver, Dec. 13, 1964
Detroit vs. Green Bay, Nov. 7, 1965
Oakland vs. Buffalo, Oct. 15, 1967; vs. Denver, Nov. 5, 1967
St. Louis vs. Atlanta, Nov. 24, 1968; vs. Philadelphia, Dec. 18, 1983
Dallas vs. Detroit, Oct. 6, 1975
Kansas City vs. Cleveland, Sept. 30, 1984
Chicago vs. Minnesota, Oct. 28, 1984
Cleveland vs. Atlanta, Nov. 18, 1984
10 By many teams
Most Opponents Yards Lost Attempting to Pass, Season
666 Oakland, 1967
583 Chicago, 1984
573 San Francisco, 1976
Fewest Opponents Yards Lost Attempting to Pass, Season
75 Green Bay, 1956
77 N.Y. Bulldogs, 1949
78 Green Bay, 1958

INTERCEPTIONS BY

Most Seasons Leading League
9 N.Y. Giants, 1933, 1937-39, 1944, 1948, 1951, 1954, 1961
8 Green Bay, 1940, 1942-43, 1947, 1955, 1957, 1962, 1965
7 Chi. Bears, 1935-36, 1941-42, 1946, 1963, 1985
Most Consecutive Seasons Leading League
5 Kansas City, 1966-70
3 N.Y. Giants, 1937-39
2 By many teams
Most Passes Intercepted By, Season
49 San Diego, 1961
42 Green Bay, 1943
41 N.Y. Giants, 1951
Fewest Passes Intercepted By, Season
3 Houston, 1982
5 Baltimore, 1982
6 Houston, 1972
St. Louis, 1982
Most Passes Intercepted By, Game
9 Green Bay vs. Detroit, Oct. 24, 1943
Philadelphia vs. Pittsburgh, Dec. 12, 1965
8 N.Y. Giants vs. Green Bay, Nov. 21, 1948; vs. N.Y. Yanks, Dec. 16, 1951
Philadelphia vs. Chi. Cardinals, Sept. 24, 1950
Houston vs. Denver, Dec. 2, 1962
Detroit vs. Chicago, Sept. 22, 1968
N.Y. Jets vs. Baltimore, Sept. 23, 1973
7 By many teams. Last time: Denver vs. Detroit, Oct. 7, 1984
Most Consecutive Games, One or More Interceptions By
46 L.A. Chargers/San Diego, 1960-63
37 Detroit, 1960-63
36 Boston, 1944-47
Washington, 1962-65
Most Yards Returning Interceptions, Season
929 San Diego, 1961
712 Los Angeles, 1952
697 Seattle, 1984
Fewest Yards Returning Interceptions, Season
5 Los Angeles, 1959
42 Philadelphia, 1982
47 Houston, 1982
Most Yards Returning Interceptions, Game
325 Seattle vs. Kansas City, Nov. 4, 1984
314 Los Angeles vs. San Francisco, Oct. 18, 1964
245 Houston vs. N.Y. Jets, Oct. 15, 1967
Most Touchdowns, Returning Interceptions, Season
9 San Diego, 1961
7 Seattle, 1984
6 Cleveland, 1960
Green Bay, 1966
Detroit, 1967
Houston, 1967
Most Touchdowns Returning Interceptions, Game
4 Seattle vs. Kansas City, Nov. 4, 1984
3 Baltimore vs. Green Bay, Nov. 5, 1950
Cleveland vs. Chicago, Dec. 11, 1960
Philadelphia vs. Pittsburgh, Dec, 12, 1965
Baltimore vs. Pittsburgh, Sept. 29, 1968
Buffalo vs. N.Y. Jets, Sept. 29, 1968
Houston vs. San Diego, Dec. 19, 1971
Cincinnati vs. Houston, Dec. 17, 1972
Tampa Bay vs. New Orleans, Dec. 11, 1977
2 By many teams
Most Touchdowns Returning Interceptions, Both Teams, Game
4 Philadelphia (3) vs. Pittsburgh (1), Dec. 12, 1965
Seattle (4) vs. Kansas City (0), Nov. 4, 1984
3 Los Angeles (2) vs. Detroit (1), Nov. 1, 1953
Cleveland (2) vs. N.Y. Giants (1), Dec. 18, 1960
Pittsburgh (2) vs. Cincinnati (1), Oct. 10, 1983
(Also see previous record)

PUNT RETURNS

Fewest Opponents Punt Returns, Season
7 Washington, 1962
San Diego, 1982
10 Buffalo, 1982
11 Boston, 1962
Most Opponents Punt Returns, Season
71 Tampa Bay, 1976, 1977
69 N.Y. Giants, 1953
68 Cleveland, 1974
Fewest Yards Allowed, Punt Returns, Season
22 Green Bay, 1967
34 Washington, 1962
39 Cleveland, 1959
Washington, 1972
Most Yards Allowed, Punt Returns, Season
932 Green Bay, 1949
913 Boston, 1947
906 New Orleans, 1974
Lowest Average Allowed, Punt Returns, Season
1.20 Chi. Cardinals, 1954 (46-55)
1.22 Cleveland, 1959 (32-39)
1.55 Chi. Cardinals, 1953 (44-68)
Highest Average Allowed, Punt Returns, Season
18.6 Green Bay, 1949 (50-932)
18.0 Cleveland, 1977 (31-558)
17.9 Boston, 1960 (20-357)
Most Touchdowns Allowed, Punt Returns, Season
4 New York, 1959
3 Green Bay, 1949
Chi. Cardinals, 1951
Los Angeles, 1951
Washington, 1952
Dallas, 1952
Pittsburgh, 1959
N.Y. Jets, 1968
Cleveland, 1977
2 By many teams

KICKOFF RETURNS

Fewest Opponents Kickoff Returns, Season
10 Brooklyn, 1943
15 Detroit, 1942
Brooklyn, 1944
18 Cleveland, 1941
Boston, 1944
Most Opponents Kickoff Returns, Season
91 Washington, 1983
89 New England, 1980
88 San Diego, 1981
Fewest Yards Allowed, Kickoff Returns, Season
225 Brooklyn, 1943
293 Brooklyn, 1944
361 Seattle, 1982
Most Yards Allowed, Kickoff Returns, Season
2,045 Kansas City, 1966

1,827 Chicago, 1985
1,816 N.Y. Giants, 1963

Lowest Average Allowed, Kickoff Returns, Season
14.3 Cleveland, 1980 (71-1,018)
15.0 Seattle, 1982 (24-361)
15.8 Oakland, 1977 (63-997)

Highest Average Allowed, Kickoff Returns, Season
29.5 N.Y. Jets, 1972 (47-1,386)
29.4 Los Angeles, 1950 (48-1,411)
29.1 New England, 1971 (49-1,427)

Most Touchdowns Allowed, Kickoff Returns, Season
3 Minnesota, 1963, 1970
Dallas, 1966
Detroit, 1980
2 By many teams

FUMBLES

Fewest Opponents Fumbles, Season
11 Cleveland, 1956
Baltimore, 1982
13 Los Angeles, 1956
Chicago, 1960
Cleveland, 1963, 1965
Detroit, 1967
San Diego, 1969
14 Baltimore, 1970
Oakland, 1975
Buffalo, 1982
St. Louis, 1982
San Francisco, 1982

Most Opponents Fumbles, Season
50 Minnesota, 1963
San Francisco, 1978
48 N.Y. Giants, 1980
47 N.Y. Giants, 1977
Seattle, 1984

TURNOVERS

(Number of times losing the ball on interceptions and fumbles.)

Fewest Opponents Turnovers, Season
11 Baltimore, 1982
13 San Francisco, 1982
15 St. Louis, 1982

Most Opponents Turnovers, Season
66 San Diego, 1961
63 Seattle, 1984
61 Washington, 1983

Most Opponents Turnovers, Game
12 Chi. Bears vs. Detroit, Nov. 22, 1942
Philadelphia vs. Chi. Cardinals, Sept. 24, 1950; vs. Pittsburgh, Dec. 12, 1965
11 Green Bay vs. San Diego, Sept. 24, 1978
10 N.Y. Giants vs. Washington, Dec. 4, 1938; vs. Chi. Cardinals, Nov. 2, 1952; vs. Washington, Dec. 8, 1963
Green Bay vs. Pittsburgh, Nov. 23, 1941; vs. Detroit, Oct. 24, 1943; vs. Chi. Cardinals, Nov. 10, 1946
Detroit vs. Minnesota, Dec. 9, 1962; vs. Chicago, Sept. 22, 1968
Oakland vs. Houston, Sept. 7, 1963
Washington vs. St. Louis, Oct. 25, 1976
New England vs. N.Y. Jets, Nov. 21, 1976
Dallas vs. San Francisco, Oct. 12, 1980
Seattle vs. Cleveland, Dec. 20, 1981
Denver vs. Detroit, Oct. 7, 1984

OUTSTANDING PERFORMERS

1,000 YARDS RUSHING IN A SEASON

Year	Player, Team	Att.	Yards	Avg.	Long	TD
1985	Marcus Allen, L.A. Raiders[3]	390	1,759	4.6	61	11
	Gerald Riggs, Atlanta[2]	397	1,719	4.3	50	10
	Walter Payton, Chicago[9]	324	1,551	4.8	40	9
	Joe Morris, N.Y. Giants	294	1,336	4.5	65	21
	Freeman McNeil, N.Y. Jets[2]	294	1,331	4.5	69	3
	Tony Dorsett, Dallas[8]	305	1,307	4.3	60	7
	James Wilder, Tampa Bay[2]	365	1,300	3.6	28	10
	Eric Dickerson, L.A. Rams[3]	292	1,234	4.2	43	12
	Craig James, New England	263	1,227	4.7	65	5
	*Kevin Mack, Cleveland	222	1,104	5.0	61	7
	Curt Warner, Seattle[2]	291	1,094	3.8	38	8
	George Rogers, Washington[3]	231	1,093	4.7	35	7
	Roger Craig, San Francisco	214	1,050	4.9	62	9
	Earnest Jackson, Philadelphia[2]	282	1,028	3.6	59	5
	Stump Mitchell, St. Louis	183	1,006	5.5	64	7
	Earnest Byner, Cleveland	244	1,002	4.1	36	8
1984	Eric Dickerson, L.A. Rams[2]	379	2,105	5.6	66	14
	Walter Payton, Chicago[8]	381	1,684	4.4	72	11
	James Wilder, Tampa Bay	407	1,544	3.8	37	13
	Gerald Riggs, Atlanta	353	1,486	4.2	57	13
	Wendell Tyler, San Francisco[3]	246	1,262	5.1	40	7
	John Riggins, Washington[5]	327	1,239	3.8	24	14
	Tony Dorsett, Dallas[7]	302	1,189	3.9	31	6
	Earnest Jackson, San Diego	296	1,179	4.0	32	8
	Ottis Anderson, St. Louis[5]	289	1,174	4.1	24	6
	Marcus Allen, L.A. Raiders[2]	275	1,168	4.2	52	13
	Sammy Winder, Denver	296	1,153	3.9	24	4
	*Greg Bell, Buffalo	262	1,100	4.2	85	7
	Freeman McNeil, N.Y. Jets	229	1,070	4.7	53	5
1983	*Eric Dickerson, L.A. Rams	390	1,808	4.6	85	18
	William Andrews, Atlanta[4]	331	1,567	4.7	27	7
	*Curt Warner, Seattle	335	1,449	4.3	60	13
	Walter Payton, Chicago[7]	314	1,421	4.5	49	6
	John Riggins, Washington[4]	375	1,347	3.6	44	24
	Tony Dorsett, Dallas[6]	289	1,321	4.6	77	8
	Earl Campbell, Houston[5]	322	1,301	4.0	42	12
	Ottis Anderson, St. Louis[4]	296	1,270	4.3	43	5
	Mike Pruitt, Cleveland[4]	293	1,184	4.0	27	10
	George Rogers, New Orleans[2]	256	1,144	4.5	76	5
	Joe Cribbs, Buffalo[3]	263	1,131	4.3	45	3
	Curtis Dickey, Baltimore	254	1,122	4.4	56	4
	Tony Collins, New England	219	1,049	4.8	50	10
	Billy Sims, Detroit[3]	220	1,040	4.7	41	7
	Marcus Allen, L.A. Raiders	266	1,014	3.8	19	9
	Franco Harris, Pittsburgh[8]	279	1,007	3.6	19	5
1981	*George Rogers, New Orleans	378	1,674	4.4	79	13
	Tony Dorsett, Dallas[5]	342	1,646	4.8	75	4
	Billy Sims, Detroit[2]	296	1,437	4.9	51	13
	Wilbert Montgomery, Philadelphia[3]	286	1,402	4.9	41	8
	Ottis Anderson, St. Louis[3]	328	1,376	4.2	28	9
	Earl Campbell, Houston[4]	361	1,376	3.8	43	10
	William Andrews, Atlanta[3]	289	1,301	4.5	29	10
	Walter Payton, Chicago[6]	339	1,222	3.6	39	6
	Chuck Muncie, San Diego[2]	251	1,144	4.6	73	19
	*Joe Delaney, Kansas City	234	1,121	4.8	82	3
	Mike Pruitt, Cleveland[3]	247	1,103	4.5	21	7
	Joe Cribbs, Buffalo[2]	257	1,097	4.3	35	3
	Pete Johnson, Cincinnati	274	1,077	3.9	39	12
	Wendell Tyler, Los Angeles[2]	260	1,074	4.1	69	12
	Ted Brown, Minnesota	274	1,063	3.9	34	6
1980	Earl Campbell, Houston[3]	373	1,934	5.2	55	13
	Walter Payton, Chicago[5]	317	1,460	4.6	69	6
	Ottis Anderson, St. Louis[2]	301	1,352	4.5	52	9
	William Andrews, Atlanta[2]	265	1,308	4.9	33	4
	*Billy Sims, Detroit	313	1,303	4.2	52	13
	Tony Dorsett, Dallas[4]	278	1,185	4.3	56	11
	*Joe Cribbs, Buffalo	306	1,185	3.9	48	11
	Mike Pruitt, Cleveland[2]	249	1,034	4.2	56	6
1979	Earl Campbell, Houston[2]	368	1,697	4.6	61	19
	Walter Payton, Chicago[4]	369	1,610	4.4	43	14
	*Ottis Anderson, St. Louis	331	1,605	4.8	76	8
	Wilbert Montgomery, Philadelphia[2]	338	1,512	4.5	62	9
	Mike Pruitt, Cleveland	264	1,294	4.9	77	9
	Ricky Bell, Tampa Bay	283	1,263	4.5	49	7
	Chuck Muncie, New Orleans	238	1,198	5.0	69	11
	Franco Harris, Pittsburgh[7]	267	1,186	4.4	71	11
	John Riggins, Washington[3]	260	1,153	4.4	66	9
	Wendell Tyler, Los Angeles	218	1,109	5.1	63	9
	Tony Dorsett, Dallas[3]	250	1,107	4.4	41	6
	*William Andrews, Atlanta	239	1,023	4.3	23	3
1978	*Earl Campbell, Houston	302	1,450	4.8	81	13
	Walter Payton, Chicago[3]	333	1,395	4.2	76	11
	Tony Dorsett, Dallas[2]	290	1,325	4.6	63	7
	Delvin Williams, Miami[2]	272	1,258	4.6	58	8
	Wilbert Montgomery, Philadelphia	259	1,220	4.7	47	9
	Terdell Middleton, Green Bay	284	1,116	3.9	76	11
	Franco Harris, Pittsburgh[6]	310	1,082	3.5	37	8
	Mark van Eeghen, Oakland[3]	270	1,080	4.0	34	9
	*Terry Miller, Buffalo	238	1,060	4.5	60	7
	Tony Reed, Kansas City	206	1,053	5.1	62	5
	John Riggins, Washington[2]	248	1,014	4.1	31	5
1977	Walter Payton, Chicago[2]	339	1,852	5.5	73	14
	Mark van Eeghen, Oakland[2]	324	1,273	3.9	27	7
	Lawrence McCutcheon, Los Angeles[4]	294	1,238	4.2	48	7
	Franco Harris, Pittsburgh[5]	300	1,162	3.9	61	11
	Lydell Mitchell, Baltimore[3]	301	1,159	3.9	64	3
	Chuck Foreman, Minnesota[3]	270	1,112	4.1	51	6
	Greg Pruitt, Cleveland[3]	236	1,086	4.6	78	3
	Sam Cunningham, New England	270	1,015	3.8	31	4
	*Tony Dorsett, Dallas	208	1,007	4.8	84	12
1976	O.J. Simpson, Buffalo[5]	290	1,503	5.2	75	8
	Walter Payton, Chicago	311	1,390	4.5	60	13
	Delvin Williams, San Francisco	248	1,203	4.9	80	7
	Lydell Mitchell, Baltimore[2]	289	1,200	4.2	43	5
	Lawrence McCutcheon, Los Angeles[3]	291	1,168	4.0	40	9
	Chuck Foreman, Minnesota[2]	278	1,155	4.2	46	13
	Franco Harris, Pittsburgh[4]	289	1,128	3.9	30	14
	Mike Thomas, Washington	254	1,101	4.3	28	5
	Rocky Bleier, Pittsburgh	220	1,036	4.7	28	5
	Mark van Eeghen, Oakland	233	1,012	4.3	21	3
	Otis Armstrong, Denver[2]	247	1,008	4.1	31	5
	Greg Pruitt, Cleveland[2]	209	1,000	4.8	64	4
1975	O.J. Simpson, Buffalo[4]	329	1,817	5.5	88	16
	Franco Harris, Pittsburgh[3]	262	1,246	4.8	36	10
	Lydell Mitchell, Baltimore	289	1,193	4.1	70	11
	Jim Otis, St. Louis	269	1,076	4.0	30	5
	Chuck Foreman, Minnesota	280	1,070	3.8	31	13
	Greg Pruitt, Cleveland	217	1,067	4.9	50	8
	John Riggins, N.Y. Jets	238	1,005	4.2	42	8
	Dave Hampton, Atlanta	250	1,002	4.0	22	5
1974	Otis Armstrong, Denver	263	1,407	5.3	43	9
	*Don Woods, San Diego	227	1,162	5.1	56	7
	O.J. Simpson, Buffalo[3]	270	1,125	4.2	41	3
	Lawrence McCutcheon, Los Angeles[2]	236	1,109	4.7	23	3
	Franco Harris, Pittsburgh[2]	208	1,006	4.8	54	5
1973	O.J. Simpson, Buffalo[2]	332	2,003	6.0	80	12
	John Brockington, Green Bay[3]	265	1,144	4.3	53	3
	Calvin Hill, Dallas[2]	273	1,142	4.2	21	6
	Lawrence McCutcheon, Los Angeles	210	1,097	5.2	37	2
	Larry Csonka, Miami[3]	219	1,003	4.6	25	5
1972	O.J. Simpson, Buffalo	292	1,251	4.3	94	6
	Larry Brown, Washington[2]	285	1,216	4.3	38	8
	Ron Johnson, N.Y. Giants[2]	298	1,182	4.0	35	9
	Larry Csonka, Miami[2]	213	1,117	5.2	45	6
	Marv Hubbard, Oakland	219	1,100	5.0	39	4
	*Franco Harris, Pittsburgh	188	1,055	5.6	75	10
	Calvin Hill, Dallas	245	1,036	4.2	26	6
	Mike Garrett, San Diego[2]	272	1,031	3.8	41	6
	John Brockington, Green Bay[2]	274	1,027	3.7	30	8
	Eugene (Mercury) Morris, Miami	190	1,000	5.3	33	12
1971	Floyd Little, Denver	284	1,133	4.0	40	6
	*John Brockington, Green Bay	216	1,105	5.1	52	4
	Larry Csonka, Miami	195	1,051	5.4	28	7
	Steve Owens, Detroit	246	1,035	4.2	23	8
	Willie Ellison, Los Angeles	211	1,000	4.7	80	4
1970	Larry Brown, Washington	237	1,125	4.7	75	5
	Ron Johnson, N.Y. Giants	263	1,027	3.9	68	8
1969	Gale Sayers, Chicago[2]	236	1,032	4.4	28	8
1968	Leroy Kelly, Cleveland[3]	248	1,239	5.0	65	16
	*Paul Robinson, Cincinnati	238	1,023	4.3	87	8
1967	Jim Nance, Boston[2]	269	1,216	4.5	53	7
	Leroy Kelly, Cleveland[2]	235	1,205	5.1	42	11
	Hoyle Granger, Houston	236	1,194	5.1	67	6
	Mike Garrett, Kansas City	236	1,087	4.6	58	9
1966	Jim Nance, Boston	299	1,458	4.9	65	11
	Gale Sayers, Chicago	229	1,231	5.4	58	8
	Leroy Kelly, Cleveland	209	1,141	5.5	70	15
	Dick Bass, Los Angeles[2]	248	1,090	4.4	50	8
1965	Jim Brown, Cleveland[7]	289	1,544	5.3	67	17
	Paul Lowe, San Diego[2]	222	1,121	5.0	59	7
1964	Jim Brown, Cleveland[6]	280	1,446	5.2	71	7
	Jim Taylor, Green Bay[5]	235	1,169	5.0	84	12
	John Henry Johnson, Pittsburgh[2]	235	1,048	4.5	45	7
1963	Jim Brown, Cleveland[5]	291	1,863	6.4	80	12
	Clem Daniels, Oakland	215	1,099	5.1	74	3
	Jim Taylor, Green Bay[4]	248	1,018	4.1	40	9
	Paul Lowe, San Diego	177	1,010	5.7	66	8
1962	Jim Taylor, Green Bay[3]	272	1,474	5.4	51	19
	John Henry Johnson, Pittsburgh	251	1,141	4.5	40	7
	*Cookie Gilchrist, Buffalo	214	1,096	5.1	44	13
	Abner Haynes, Dall. Texans	221	1,049	4.7	71	13
	Dick Bass, Los Angeles	196	1,033	5.3	57	6
	Charlie Tolar, Houston	244	1,012	4.1	25	7
1961	Jim Brown, Cleveland[4]	305	1,408	4.6	38	8
	Jim Taylor, Green Bay[2]	243	1,307	5.4	53	15
1960	Jim Brown, Cleveland[3]	215	1,257	5.8	71	9
	Jim Taylor, Green Bay	230	1,101	4.8	32	11
	John David Crow, St. Louis	183	1,071	5.9	57	6
1959	Jim Brown, Cleveland[2]	290	1,329	4.6	70	14
	J. D. Smith, San Francisco	207	1,036	5.0	73	10
1958	Jim Brown, Cleveland	257	1,527	5.9	65	17
1956	Rick Casares, Chi. Bears	234	1,126	4.8	68	12
1954	Joe Perry, San Francisco[2]	173	1,049	6.1	58	8
1953	Joe Perry, San Francisco	192	1,018	5.3	51	10
1949	Steve Van Buren, Philadelphia[2]	263	1,146	4.4	41	11
	Tony Canadeo, Green Bay	208	1,052	5.1	54	4
1947	Steve Van Buren, Philadelphia	217	1,008	4.6	45	13
1934	*Beattie Feathers, Chi. Bears	101	1,004	9.9	82	8

**First year in the league.*

200 YARDS RUSHING IN A GAME

Date	Player, Team, Opponent	Att.	Yards	TD
Dec. 21, 1985	George Rogers, Washington vs. St. Louis	34	206	1
Dec. 21, 1985	Joe Morris, N.Y. Giants vs. Pittsburgh	36	202	3

Dec. 9, 1984	Eric Dickerson, L.A. Rams vs. Houston	27	215	2
Nov. 18, 1984	*Greg Bell, Buffalo vs. Dallas	27	206	1
Nov. 4, 1984	Eric Dickerson, L.A. Rams vs. St. Louis	21	208	0
Sept. 2, 1984	Gerald Riggs, Atlanta vs. New Orleans	35	202	2
Nov. 27, 1983	*Curt Warner, Seattle vs. Kansas City (OT)	32	207	3
Nov. 6, 1983	James Wilder, Tampa Bay vs. Minnesota	31	219	1
Sept. 18, 1983	Tony Collins, New England vs. N.Y. Jets	23	212	3
Sept. 4, 1983	George Rogers, New Orleans vs. St. Louis	24	206	2
Dec. 21, 1980	Earl Campbell, Houston vs. Minnesota	29	203	1
Nov. 16, 1980	Earl Campbell, Houston vs. Chicago	31	206	0
Oct. 26, 1980	Earl Campbell, Houston vs. Cincinnati	27	202	2
Oct. 19, 1980	Earl Campbell, Houston vs. Tampa Bay	33	203	0
Nov. 26, 1978	*Terry Miller, Buffalo vs. N.Y. Giants	21	208	2
Dec. 4, 1977	*Tony Dorsett, Dallas vs. Philadelphia	23	206	2
Nov. 20, 1977	Walter Payton, Chicago vs. Minnesota	40	275	1
Oct. 30, 1977	Walter Payton, Chicago vs. Green Bay	23	205	2
Dec. 5, 1976	O.J. Simpson, Buffalo vs. Miami	24	203	1
Nov. 25, 1976	O.J. Simpson, Buffalo vs. Detroit	29	273	2
Oct. 24, 1976	Chuck Foreman, Minnesota vs. Philadelphia	28	200	2
Dec. 14, 1975	Greg Pruitt, Cleveland vs. Kansas City	26	214	3
Sept. 28, 1975	O.J. Simpson, Buffalo vs. Pittsburgh	28	227	1
Dec. 16, 1973	O.J. Simpson, Buffalo vs. N.Y. Jets	34	200	1
Dec. 9, 1973	O.J. Simpson, Buffalo vs. New England	22	219	1
Sept. 16, 1973	O.J. Simpson, Buffalo vs. New England	29	250	2
Dec. 5, 1971	Willie Ellison, Los Angeles vs. New Orleans	26	247	1
Dec. 20, 1970	John (Frenchy) Fuqua, Pittsburgh vs. Philadelphia	20	218	2
Nov. 3, 1968	Gale Sayers, Chicago vs. Green Bay	24	205	0
Oct. 30, 1966	Jim Nance, Boston vs. Oakland	38	208	2
Oct. 10, 1964	John Henry Johnson, Pittsburgh vs. Cleveland	30	200	3
Dec. 8, 1963	Cookie Gilchrist, Buffalo vs. N.Y. Jets	36	243	5
Nov. 3, 1963	Jim Brown, Cleveland vs. Philadelphia	28	223	1
Oct. 20, 1963	Clem Daniels, Oakland vs. N.Y. Jets	27	200	2
Sept. 22, 1963	Jim Brown, Cleveland vs. Dallas	20	232	2
Dec. 10, 1961	Billy Cannon, Houston vs. N.Y. Titans	25	216	3
Nov. 19, 1961	Jim Brown, Cleveland vs. Philadelphia	34	237	4
Dec. 18, 1960	John David Crow, St. Louis vs. Pittsburgh	24	203	0
Nov. 15, 1959	Bobby Mitchell, Cleveland vs. Washington	14	232	3
Nov. 24, 1957	*Jim Brown, Cleveland vs. Los Angeles	31	237	4
Dec. 16, 1956	*Tom Wilson, Los Angeles vs. Green Bay	23	223	0
Nov. 22, 1953	Dan Towler, Los Angeles vs. Baltimore	14	205	1
Nov. 12, 1950	Gene Roberts, N.Y. Giants vs. Chi. Cardinals	26	218	2
Nov. 27, 1949	Steve Van Buren, Philadelphia vs. Pittsburgh	27	205	0
Oct. 8, 1933	Cliff Battles, Boston vs. N.Y. Giants	16	215	1

**First year in the league.*

Times 200 or More
43 times by 30 players . . . Simpson 6; Brown, Campbell 4; Dickerson, Payton, Rogers 2.

400 YARDS PASSING IN A GAME

Date	Player, Team, Opponent	Att.	Comp.	Yards	TD
Dec. 20, 1985	John Elway, Denver vs. Seattle	42	24	432	1
Nov. 10, 1985	Dan Fouts, San Diego vs. L.A. Raiders (OT)	41	26	436	4
Oct. 13, 1985	Phil Simms, N.Y. Giants vs. Cincinnati	62	40	513	1
Oct. 13, 1985	Dave Krieg, Seattle vs. Atlanta	51	33	405	4
Oct. 6, 1985	Phil Simms, N.Y. Giants vs. Dallas	36	18	432	3
Oct. 6, 1985	Joe Montana, San Francisco vs. Atlanta	57	37	429	5
Sept. 19, 1985	Tommy Kramer, Minnesota vs. Chicago	55	28	436	3
Sept. 15, 1985	Dan Fouts, San Diego vs. Seattle	43	29	440	4
Dec. 16, 1984	Neil Lomax, St. Louis vs. Washington	46	37	468	2
Dec. 9, 1984	Dan Marino, Miami vs. Indianapolis	41	29	404	4
Dec. 2, 1984	Dan Marino, Miami vs. L.A. Raiders	57	35	470	4
Nov. 25, 1984	Dave Krieg, Seattle vs. Denver	44	30	406	3
Nov. 4, 1984	Dan Marino, Miami vs. N.Y. Jets	42	23	422	2
Oct. 21, 1984	Dan Fouts, San Diego vs. L.A. Raiders	45	24	410	3
Sept. 30, 1984	Dan Marino, Miami vs. St. Louis	36	24	429	3
Sept. 2, 1984	Phil Simms, N.Y. Giants vs. Philadelphia	30	23	409	4
Dec. 11, 1983	Bill Kenney, Kansas City vs. San Diego	41	31	411	4
Nov. 20, 1983	Dave Krieg, Seattle vs. Denver	42	31	418	3
Oct. 9, 1983	Joe Ferguson, Buffalo vs. Miami (OT)	55	38	419	5
Oct. 2, 1983	Joe Theismann, Washington vs. L.A. Raiders	39	23	417	3
Sept. 25, 1983	Richard Todd, N.Y. Jets vs. L.A. Rams (OT)	50	37	446	2
Dec. 26, 1982	Vince Ferragamo, L.A. Rams vs. Chicago	46	30	509	3
Dec. 20, 1982	Dan Fouts, San Diego vs. Cincinnati	40	25	435	1
Dec. 20, 1982	Ken Anderson, Cincinnati vs. San Diego	56	40	416	2
Dec. 11, 1982	Dan Fouts, San Diego vs. San Francisco	48	33	444	5
Nov. 21, 1982	Joe Montana, San Francisco vs. St. Louis	39	26	408	3
Nov. 15, 1981	Steve Bartkowski, Atlanta vs. Pittsburgh	50	33	416	2
Oct. 25, 1981	Brian Sipe, Cleveland vs. Baltimore	41	30	444	4
Oct. 25, 1981	David Woodley, Miami vs. Dallas	37	21	408	3
Oct. 11, 1981	Tommy Kramer, Minnesota vs. San Diego	43	27	444	4
Dec. 14, 1980	Tommy Kramer, Minnesota vs. Cleveland	49	38	456	4
Nov. 16, 1980	Doug Williams, Tampa Bay vs. Minnesota	55	30	486	4
Oct. 19, 1980	Dan Fouts, San Diego vs. N.Y. Giants	41	26	444	3
Oct. 12, 1980	Lynn Dickey, Green Bay vs. Tampa Bay (OT)	51	35	418	1
Sept. 21, 1980	Richard Todd, N.Y. Jets vs. San Francisco	60	42	447	3
Oct. 3, 1976	James Harris, Los Angeles vs. Miami	29	17	436	2
Nov. 17, 1975	Ken Anderson, Cincinnati vs. Buffalo	46	30	447	2
Nov. 18, 1974	Charley Johnson, Denver vs. Kansas City	42	28	445	2
Dec. 11, 1972	Joe Namath, N.Y. Jets vs. Oakland	46	25	403	1
Sept. 24, 1972	Joe Namath, N.Y. Jets vs. Baltimore	28	15	496	6
Dec. 21, 1969	Don Horn, Green Bay vs. St. Louis	31	22	410	5
Sept. 28, 1969	Joe Kapp, Minnesota vs. Baltimore	43	28	449	7
Sept. 9, 1968	Pete Beathard, Houston vs. Kansas City	48	23	413	2
Nov. 26, 1967	Sonny Jurgensen, Washington vs. Cleveland	50	32	418	3
Oct. 1, 1967	Joe Namath, N.Y. Jets vs. Miami	39	23	415	3
Sept. 17, 1967	Johnny Unitas, Baltimore vs. Atlanta	32	22	401	2
Nov. 13, 1966	Don Meredith, Dallas vs. Washington	29	21	406	2
Nov. 28, 1965	Sonny Jurgensen, Washington vs. Dallas	43	26	411	3
Oct. 24, 1965	Fran Tarkenton, Minnesota vs. San Francisco	35	21	407	3
Nov. 1, 1964	Len Dawson, Kansas City vs. Denver	38	23	435	6
Oct. 25, 1964	Cotton Davidson, Oakland vs. Denver	36	23	427	5
Oct. 16, 1964	Babe Parilli, Boston vs. Oakland	47	25	422	4
Dec. 22, 1963	Tom Flores, Oakland vs. Houston	29	17	407	6
Nov. 17, 1963	Norm Snead, Washington vs. Pittsburgh	40	23	424	2
Nov. 10, 1963	Don Meredith, Dallas vs. San Francisco	48	30	460	3
Oct. 13, 1963	Charley Johnson, St. Louis vs. Pittsburgh	41	20	428	2
Dec. 16, 1962	Sonny Jurgensen, Philadelphia vs. St. Louis	34	15	419	5
Nov. 18, 1962	Bill Wade, Chicago vs. Dall. Cowboys	46	28	466	2
Oct. 28, 1962	Y.A. Tittle, N.Y. Giants vs. Washington	39	27	505	7
Sept. 15, 1962	Frank Tripucka, Denver vs. Buffalo	56	29	447	2
Dec. 17, 1961	Sonny Jurgensen, Philadelphia vs. Detroit	42	27	403	3
Nov. 19, 1961	George Blanda, Houston vs. N.Y. Titans	32	20	418	7
Oct. 29, 1961	George Blanda, Houston vs. Buffalo	32	18	464	4
Oct. 29, 1961	Sonny Jurgensen, Philadelphia vs. Washington	41	27	436	3
Oct. 13, 1961	Jacky Lee, Houston vs. Boston	41	27	457	2
Dec. 13, 1958	Bobby Layne, Pittsburgh vs. Chi. Cardinals	49	23	409	2
Nov. 8, 1953	Bobby Thomason, Philadelphia vs. N.Y. Giants	44	22	437	4
Oct. 4, 1952	Otto Graham, Cleveland vs. Pittsburgh	49	21	401	3
Sept. 28, 1951	Norm Van Brocklin, Los Angeles vs. N.Y. Yanks	41	27	554	5
Dec. 11, 1949	Johnny Lujack, Chi. Bears vs. Chi. Cardinals	39	24	468	6
Oct. 31, 1948	Sammy Baugh, Washington vs. Boston	24	17	446	4
Oct. 31, 1948	Jim Hardy, Los Angeles vs. Chi. Cardinals	53	28	406	3
Nov. 14, 1943	Sid Luckman, Chi. Bears vs. N.Y. Giants	32	21	433	7

Times 400 or More
73 times by 47 players . . . Fouts 6; Jurgensen 5; Marino 4; Kramer, Krieg, Namath, Simms 3; Anderson, Blanda, Johnson, Meredith, Todd 2.

1,000 YARDS PASS RECEIVING IN A SEASON

Year	Player, Team	No.	Yards	Avg.	Long	TD
1985	Steve Largent, Seattle[7]	79	1,287	16.3	43	6
	Mike Quick, Philadelphia[3]	73	1,247	17.1	99	11
	Art Monk, Washington[2]	91	1,226	13.5	53	2
	Wes Chandler, San Diego[4]	67	1,199	17.9	75	10
	Drew Hill, Houston	64	1,169	18.3	57	9
	James Lofton, Green Bay[5]	69	1,153	16.7	56	4
	Louis Lipps, Pittsburgh	59	1,134	19.2	51	12
	Cris Collinsworth, Cincinnati[3]	65	1,125	17.3	71	5
	Tony Hill, Dallas[3]	74	1,113	15.0	53	7
	Lionel James, San Diego	86	1,027	11.9	67	6
	Roger Craig, San Francisco	92	1,016	11.0	73	6
1984	Roy Green, St. Louis[2]	78	1,555	19.9	83	12
	John Stallworth, Pittsburgh[3]	80	1,395	17.4	51	11
	Mark Clayton, Miami	73	1,389	19.0	65	18
	Art Monk, Washington	106	1,372	12.9	72	7
	James Lofton, Green Bay[4]	62	1,361	22.0	79	7
	Mark Duper, Miami[2]	71	1,306	18.4	80	8
	Steve Watson, Denver[3]	69	1,170	17.0	73	7
	Steve Largent, Seattle[6]	74	1,164	15.7	65	12
	Tim Smith, Houston[2]	69	1,141	16.5	75	4
	Stacey Bailey, Atlanta	67	1,138	17.0	61	6
	Carlos Carson, Kansas City[2]	57	1,078	18.9	57	4
	Mike Quick, Philadelphia[2]	61	1,052	17.2	90	9
	Todd Christensen, L.A. Raiders[2]	80	1,007	12.6	38	7
	Kevin House, Tampa Bay[2]	76	1,005	13.2	55	5
	Ozzie Newsome, Cleveland[2]	89	1,001	11.2	52	5
1983	Mike Quick, Philadelphia	69	1,409	20.4	83	13
	Carlos Carson, Kansas City	80	1,351	16.9	50	7
	James Lofton, Green Bay[3]	58	1,300	22.4	74	8
	Todd Christensen, L.A. Raiders	92	1,247	13.6	45	12
	Roy Green, St. Louis	78	1,227	15.7	71	14
	Charlie Brown, Washington	78	1,225	15.7	75	8
	Tim Smith, Houston	83	1,176	14.2	47	6
	Kellen Winslow, San Diego[3]	88	1,172	13.3	46	8
	Earnest Gray, N.Y. Giants	78	1,139	14.6	62	5
	Steve Watson, Denver[2]	59	1,133	19.2	78	5
	Cris Collinsworth, Cincinnati[2]	66	1,130	17.1	63	5
	Steve Largent, Seattle[5]	72	1,074	14.9	46	11
	Mark Duper, Miami	51	1,003	19.7	85	10
1982	Wes Chandler, San Diego[3]	49	1,032	21.1	66	9
1981	Alfred Jenkins, Atlanta[2]	70	1,358	19.4	67	13
	James Lofton, Green Bay[2]	71	1,294	18.2	75	8
	Frank Lewis, Buffalo[2]	70	1,244	17.8	33	4
	Steve Watson, Denver	60	1,244	20.7	95	13
	Steve Largent, Seattle[4]	75	1,224	16.3	57	9
	Charlie Joiner, San Diego[4]	70	1,188	17.0	57	7
	Kevin House, Tampa Bay	56	1,176	21.0	84	9
	Wes Chandler, N.O.-San Diego[2]	69	1,142	16.6	51	6
	Dwight Clark, San Francisco	85	1,105	13.0	78	4
	John Stallworth, Pittsburgh[2]	63	1,098	17.4	55	5
	Kellen Winslow, San Diego[2]	88	1,075	12.2	67	10
	Pat Tilley, St. Louis	66	1,040	15.8	75	3
	Stanley Morgan, New England[2]	44	1,029	23.4	76	6
	Harold Carmichael, Philadelphia[3]	61	1,028	16.9	85	6
	Freddie Scott, Detroit	53	1,022	19.3	48	5
	*Cris Collinsworth, Cincinnati	67	1,009	15.1	74	8
	Joe Senser, Minnesota	79	1,004	12.7	53	8
	Ozzie Newsome, Cleveland	69	1,002	14.5	62	6
	Sammy White, Minnesota	66	1,001	15.2	53	3
1980	John Jefferson, San Diego[2]	82	1,340	16.3	58	13
	Kellen Winslow, San Diego	89	1,290	14.5	65	9
	James Lofton, Green Bay	71	1,226	17.3	47	4
	Charlie Joiner, San Diego[3]	71	1,132	15.9	51	4
	Ahmad Rashad, Minnesota[2]	69	1,095	15.9	76	5

	Steve Largent, Seattle[3]	66	1,064	16.1	67	6
	Tony Hill, Dallas[2]	60	1,055	17.6	58	8
	Alfred Jenkins, Atlanta	57	1,026	18.0	57	6
1979	Steve Largent, Seattle[2]	66	1,237	18.7	55	9
	John Stallworth, Pittsburgh	70	1,183	16.9	65	8
	Ahmad Rashad, Minnesota	80	1,156	14.5	52	9
	John Jefferson, San Diego[2]	61	1,090	17.9	65	10
	Frank Lewis, Buffalo	54	1,082	20.0	55	2
	Wes Chandler, New Orleans	65	1,069	16.4	85	6
	Tony Hill, Dallas	60	1,062	17.7	75	10
	Drew Pearson, Dallas[2]	55	1,026	18.7	56	8
	Wallace Francis, Atlanta	74	1,013	13.7	42	8
	Harold Jackson, New England[3]	45	1,013	22.5	59	7
	Charlie Joiner, San Diego[2]	72	1,008	14.0	39	4
	Stanley Morgan, New England	44	1,002	22.8	63	12
1978	Wesley Walker, N.Y. Jets	48	1,169	24.4	77	8
	Steve Largent, Seattle	71	1,168	16.5	57	8
	Harold Carmichael, Philadelphia[2]	55	1,072	19.5	56	8
	*John Jefferson, San Diego	56	1,001	17.9	46	13
1976	Roger Carr, Baltimore	43	1,112	25.9	79	11
	Cliff Branch, Oakland[2]	46	1,111	24.2	88	12
	Charlie Joiner, San Diego	50	1,056	21.1	81	7
1975	Ken Burrough, Houston	53	1,063	20.1	77	8
1974	Cliff Branch, Oakland	60	1,092	18.2	67	13
	Drew Pearson, Dallas	62	1,087	17.5	50	2
1973	Harold Carmichael, Philadelphia	67	1,116	16.7	73	9
1972	Harold Jackson, Philadelphia[2]	62	1,048	16.9	77	4
	John Gilliam, Minnesota	47	1,035	22.0	66	7
1971	Otis Taylor, Kansas City[2]	57	1,110	19.5	82	7
1970	Gene Washington, San Francisco	53	1,100	20.8	79	12
	Marlin Briscoe, Buffalo	57	1,036	18.2	48	8
	Dick Gordon, Chicago	71	1,026	14.5	69	13
	Gary Garrison, San Diego[2]	44	1,006	22.9	67	12
1969	Warren Wells, Oakland[2]	47	1,260	26.8	80	14
	Harold Jackson, Philadelphia	65	1,116	17.2	65	9
	Roy Jefferson, Pittsburgh[2]	67	1,079	16.1	63	9
	Dan Abramowicz, New Orleans	73	1,015	13.9	49	7
	Lance Alworth, San Diego[7]	64	1,003	15.7	76	4
1968	Lance Alworth, San Diego[6]	68	1,312	19.3	80	10
	Don Maynard, N.Y. Jets[5]	57	1,297	22.8	87	10
	George Sauer, N.Y. Jets[3]	66	1,141	17.3	43	3
	Warren Wells, Oakland	53	1,137	21.5	94	11
	Gary Garrison, San Diego	52	1,103	21.2	84	10
	Roy Jefferson, Pittsburgh	58	1,074	18.5	62	11
	Paul Warfield, Cleveland	50	1,067	21.3	65	12
	Homer Jones, N.Y. Giants[3]	45	1,057	23.5	84	7
	Fred Biletnikoff, Oakland	61	1,037	17.0	82	6
	Lance Rentzel, Dallas	54	1,009	18.7	65	6
1967	Don Maynard, N.Y. Jets[4]	71	1,434	20.2	75	10
	Ben Hawkins, Philadelphia	59	1,265	21.4	87	10
	Homer Jones, N.Y. Giants[2]	49	1,209	24.7	70	13
	Jackie Smith, St. Louis	56	1,205	21.5	76	9
	George Sauer, N.Y. Jets[2]	75	1,189	15.9	61	6
	Lance Alworth, San Diego[5]	52	1,010	19.4	71	9
1966	Lance Alworth, San Diego[4]	73	1,383	18.9	78	13
	Otis Taylor, Kansas City	58	1,297	22.4	89	8
	Pat Studstill, Detroit	67	1,266	18.9	99	5
	Bob Hayes, Dallas[2]	64	1,232	19.3	95	13
	Charlie Frazier, Houston	57	1,129	19.8	79	12
	Charley Taylor, Washington	72	1,119	15.5	86	12
	George Sauer, N.Y. Jets	63	1,081	17.2	77	5
	Homer Jones, N.Y. Giants	48	1,044	21.8	98	8
	Art Powell, Oakland[5]	53	1,026	19.4	46	11
1965	Lance Alworth, San Diego[3]	69	1,602	23.2	85	14
	Dave Parks, San Francisco	80	1,344	16.8	53	12
	Don Maynard, N.Y. Jets[3]	68	1,218	17.9	56	14
	Pete Retzlaff, Philadelphia	66	1,190	18.0	78	10
	Lionel Taylor, Denver[4]	85	1,131	13.3	63	6
	Tommy McDonald, Los Angeles[3]	67	1,036	15.5	51	9
	*Bob Hayes, Dallas	46	1,003	21.8	82	12
1964	Charley Hennigan, Houston[3]	101	1,546	15.3	53	8
	Art Powell, Oakland[4]	76	1,361	17.9	77	11
	Lance Alworth, San Diego[2]	61	1,235	20.2	82	13
	Johnny Morris, Chicago	93	1,200	12.9	63	10
	Elbert Dubenion, Buffalo	42	1,139	27.1	72	10
	Terry Barr, Detroit[2]	57	1,030	18.1	58	9
1963	Bobby Mitchell, Washington[2]	69	1,436	20.8	99	7
	Art Powell, Oakland[3]	73	1,304	17.9	85	16
	Buddy Dial, Pittsburgh[2]	60	1,295	21.6	83	9
	Lance Alworth, San Diego	61	1,205	19.8	85	11
	Del Shofner, N.Y. Giants[4]	64	1,181	18.5	70	9
	Lionel Taylor, Denver[3]	78	1,101	14.1	72	10
	Terry Barr, Detroit	66	1,086	16.5	75	13
	Charley Hennigan, Houston[2]	61	1,051	17.2	83	10
	Sonny Randle, St. Louis[2]	51	1,014	19.9	68	12
	Bake Turner, N.Y. Jets	71	1,009	14.2	53	6
1962	Bobby Mitchell, Washington	72	1,384	19.2	81	11
	Sonny Randle, St. Louis	63	1,158	18.4	86	7
	Tommy McDonald, Philadelphia[2]	58	1,146	19.8	60	10
	Del Shofner, N.Y. Giants[3]	53	1,133	21.4	69	12
	Art Powell, N.Y. Titans[2]	64	1,130	17.7	80	8
	Frank Clarke, Dall. Cowboys	47	1,043	22.2	66	14
	Don Maynard, N.Y. Titans[2]	56	1,041	18.6	86	8
1961	Charley Hennigan, Houston	82	1,746	21.3	80	12
	Lionel Taylor, Denver[2]	100	1,176	11.8	52	4
	Bill Groman, Houston[2]	50	1,175	23.5	80	17
	Tommy McDonald, Philadelphia	64	1,144	17.9	66	13
	Del Shofner, N.Y. Giants[2]	68	1,125	16.5	46	11
	Jim Phillips, Los Angeles	78	1,092	14.0	69	5
	*Mike Ditka, Chicago	56	1,076	19.2	76	12
	Dave Kocourek, San Diego	55	1,055	19.2	76	4
	Buddy Dial, Pittsburgh	53	1,047	19.8	88	12
	R.C. Owens, San Francisco	55	1,032	18.8	54	5
1960	*Bill Groman, Houston	72	1,473	20.5	92	12
	Raymond Berry, Baltimore	74	1,298	17.5	70	10
	Don Maynard, N.Y. Titans	72	1,265	17.6	65	6
	Lionel Taylor, Denver	92	1,235	13.4	80	12
	Art Powell, N.Y. Titans	69	1,167	16.9	76	14
1958	Del Shofner, Los Angeles	51	1,097	21.5	92	8
1956	Bill Howton, Green Bay[2]	55	1,188	21.6	66	12
	Harlon Hill, Chi. Bears[2]	47	1,128	24.0	79	11
1954	Bob Boyd, Los Angeles	53	1,212	22.9	80	6
	*Harlon Hill, Chi. Bears	45	1,124	25.0	76	12
1953	Pete Pihos, Philadelphia	63	1,049	16.7	59	10
1952	*Bill Howton, Green Bay	53	1,231	23.2	90	13
1951	Elroy (Crazylegs) Hirsch, Los Angeles	66	1,495	22.7	91	17
1950	Tom Fears, Los Angeles[2]	84	1,116	13.3	53	7
	Cloyce Box, Detroit	50	1,009	20.2	82	11
1949	Bob Mann, Detroit	66	1,014	15.4	64	4
	Tom Fears, Los Angeles	77	1,013	13.2	51	9
1945	Jim Benton, Cleveland	45	1,067	23.7	84	8
1942	Don Hutson, Green Bay	74	1,211	16.4	73	17

First year in the league.

250 YARDS PASS RECEIVING IN A GAME

Date	Player, Team, Opponent	No.	Yards	TD
Dec. 22, 1985	Stephone Paige, Kansas City vs. San Diego	8	309	2
Dec. 20, 1982	Wes Chandler, San Diego vs. Cincinnati	10	260	2
Sept. 23, 1979	*Jerry Butler, Buffalo vs. N.Y. Jets	10	255	4
Nov. 4, 1962	Sonny Randle, St. Louis vs. N.Y. Giants	16	256	1
Oct. 28, 1962	Del Shofner, N.Y. Giants vs. Washington	11	269	1
Oct. 13, 1961	Charley Hennigan, Houston vs. Boston	13	272	1
Oct. 21, 1956	Billy Howton, Green Bay vs. Los Angeles	7	257	2
Dec. 3, 1950	Cloyce Box, Detroit vs. Baltimore	12	302	4
Nov. 22, 1945	Jim Benton, Cleveland vs. Detroit	10	303	1

First year in the league.

2,000 COMBINED NET YARDS GAINED IN A SEASON

Year	Player, Team	Rushing Att.-Yds.	Pass Rec.	Punt Ret.	Kickoff Ret.	Fum. Runs	Total Yds.
1985	Lionel James, San Diego	105-516	86-1,027	25-213	36-779	1-0	253-2,535
	Marcus Allen, L.A. Raiders	380-1,759	67-555	0-0	0-0	2-(−6)	449-2,308
	Roger Craig, San Fran.	214-1,050	92-1,016	0-0	0-0	0-0	306-2,066
	Walter Payton, Chicago	324-1,551	49-483	0-0	0-0	1-0	374-2,034
1984	Eric Dickerson, L.A. Rams	379-2,105	21-139	0-0	0-0	4-15	404-2,259
	James Wilder, Tampa Bay	407-1,544	85-685	0-0	0-0	4-0	496-2,229
	Walter Payton, Chicago	381-1,684	45-368	0-0	0-0	1-0	427-2,052
1983	*Eric Dickerson, L.A. Rams	390-1,808	51-404	0-0	0-0	1-0	442-2,212
	William Andrews, Atlanta	331-1,567	59-609	0-0	0-0	2-0	392-2,176
	Walter Payton, Chicago	314-1,421	53-607	0-0	0-0	2-0	369-2,028
1981	*James Brooks, San Diego	109-525	46-329	22-290	40-949	2-0	219-2,093
	William Andrews, Atlanta	289-1,301	81-735	0-0	0-0	0-0	370-2,036
1980	Bruce Harper, N.Y. Jets	45-126	50-634	28-242	49-1,070	3-0	175-2,072
1979	Wilbert Montgomery, Phil.	338-1,512	41-494	0-0	1-6	2-0	382-2,012
1978	Bruce Harper, N.Y. Jets	58-303	13-196	30-378	55-1,280	1-0	157-2,157
1977	Walter Payton, Chicago	339-1,852	27-269	0-0	2-95	5-0	373-2,216
	Terry Metcalf, St. Louis	149-739	34-403	14-108	32-772	1-0	230-2,022
1975	Terry Metcalf, St. Louis	165-816	43-378	23-285	35-960	2-23	268-2,462
	O.J. Simpson, Buffalo	329-1,817	28-426	0-0	0-0	1-0	358-2,243
1974	Mack Herron, New England	231-824	38-474	35-517	28-629	3-0	335-2,444
	Otis Armstrong, Denver	263-1,407	38-405	0-0	16-386	1-0	318-2,198
	Terry Metcalf, St. Louis	152-718	50-377	26-340	20-623	7-0	255-2,058
1973	O.J. Simpson, Buffalo	332-2,003	6-70	0-0	0-0	0-0	338-2,073
1966	Gale Sayers, Chicago	229-1,231	34-447	6-44	23-718	3-0	295-2,440
	Leroy Kelly, Cleveland	209-1,141	32-366	13-104	19-403	0-0	273-2,014
1965	*Gale Sayers, Chicago	166-867	29-507	16-238	21-660	4-0	236-2,272
1963	Timmy Brown, Philadelphia	192-841	36-487	16-152	33-945	2-3	279-2,428
	Jim Brown, Cleveland	291-1,863	24-268	0-0	0-0	0-0	315-2,131
1962	Timmy Brown, Philadelphia	137-545	52-849	6-81	30-831	4-0	229-2,306
	Dick Christy, N.Y. Titans	114-535	62-538	15-250	38-824	2-0	231-2,147
1961	Billy Cannon, Houston	200-948	43-586	9-70	18-439	2-0	272-2,043
1960	*Abner Haynes, Dall. Texans	156-875	55-576	14-215	19-434	4-0	248-2,100

First year in the league.

300 COMBINED NET YARDS GAINED IN A GAME

Date	Player, Team, Opponent	No.	Yards	TD
Dec. 22, 1985	Stephone Paige, Kansas City vs. San Diego	8	309	2
Nov. 10, 1985	Lionel James, San Diego vs. L.A. Raiders (OT)	23	345	0
Sept. 22, 1985	Lionel James, San Diego vs. Cincinnati	20	316	2
Dec. 21, 1975	Walter Payton, Chicago vs. New Orleans	32	300	1
Nov. 23, 1975	Greg Pruitt, Cleveland vs. Cincinnati	28	304	2
Nov. 1, 1970	Eugene (Mercury) Morris, Miami vs. Baltimore	17	302	0
Oct. 4, 1970	O. J. Simpson, Buffalo vs. N.Y. Jets	26	303	2
Dec. 6, 1969	Jerry LeVias, Houston vs. N.Y. Jets	18	329	1
Nov. 2, 1969	Travis Williams, Green Bay vs. Pittsburgh	11	314	3
Dec. 18, 1966	Gale Sayers, Chicago vs. Minnesota	20	339	2
Dec. 12, 1965	Gale Sayers, Chicago vs. San Francisco	17	336	6
Nov. 17, 1963	Gary Ballman, Pittsburgh vs. Washington	12	320	2
Dec. 16, 1962	Timmy Brown, Philadelphia vs. St. Louis	19	341	2
Dec. 10, 1961	Billy Cannon, Houston vs. N.Y. Titans	32	373	5
Nov 19, 1961	Jim Brown, Cleveland vs. Philadelphia	38	313	4
Dec. 3, 1950	Cloyce Box, Detroit vs. Baltimore	13	302	4
Oct. 29, 1950	Wally Triplett, Detroit vs. Los Angeles	11	331	1
Nov. 22, 1945	Jim Benton, Cleveland vs. Detroit	10	303	1

TOP 10 SCORERS

Player	Years	TD	FG	PAT	TP
George Blanda	26	9	335	943	2,002
Jan Stenerud	19	0	373	580	1,699
Jim Turner	16	1	304	521	1,439
Jim Bakken	17	0	282	534	1,380
Fred Cox	15	0	282	519	1,365
Lou Groza	17	1	234	641	1,349
Mark Moseley	15	0	288	457	1,321
Gino Cappelletti	11	42	176	350	1,130
Don Cockroft	13	0	216	432	1,080
Garo Yepremian	14	0	210	444	1,074

Cappelletti's total includes four two-point conversions.

TOP 10 TOUCHDOWN SCORERS

Player	Years	Rush	Pass Rec.	Returns	Total TD
Jim Brown	9	106	20	0	126
John Riggins	14	104	12	0	116
Lenny Moore	12	63	48	2	113
Walter Payton	11	98	11	0	109
Don Hutson	11	3	99	3	105
Franco Harris	13	91	9	0	100
Jim Taylor	10	83	10	0	93
Bobby Mitchell	11	18	65	8	91
Leroy Kelly	10	74	13	3	90
Charley Taylor	13	11	79	0	90

TOP 10 RUSHERS

Player	Years	Att.	Yards	Avg.	Long	TD
Walter Payton	11	3,371	14,860	4.4	76	98
Jim Brown	9	2,359	12,312	5.2	80	106
Franco Harris	13	2,949	12,120	4.1	75	91
John Riggins	14	2,916	11,352	3.9	66	104
O.J. Simpson	11	2,404	11,236	4.7	94	61
Tony Dorsett	9	2,441	10,832	4.4	99	66
Earl Campbell	8	2,187	9,407	4.3	81	74
Jim Taylor	10	1,941	8,597	4.4	84	83
Joe Perry	14	1,737	8,378	4.8	78	53
Larry Csonka	11	1,891	8,081	4.3	54	64

TOP 10 PASSERS

Player	Years	Att.	Comp.	Pct. Comp.	Yards	TD	Pct. TD	Int.	Pct. Int.	Avg. Gain	Rating
Joe Montana	7	2,571	1,627	63.3	19,262	133	5.2	67	2.6	7.49	92.4
Roger Staubach	11	2,958	1,685	57.0	22,700	153	5.2	109	3.7	7.67	83.4
Sonny Jurgensen	18	4,262	2,433	57.1	32,224	255	6.0	189	4.4	7.56	82.6
Len Dawson	19	3,741	2,136	57.1	28,711	239	6.4	183	4.9	7.67	82.6
Neil Lomax	5	1,826	1,047	57.3	13,406	79	4.3	55	3.0	7.34	82.3
Danny White	10	2,393	1,422	59.4	17,911	130	5.4	107	4.5	7.48	82.3
Ken Anderson	15	4,452	2,643	59.4	32,667	196	4.4	158	3.5	7.34	82.0
Dan Fouts	13	4,810	2,839	59.0	37,492	228	4.7	205	4.3	7.79	81.8
Bart Starr	16	3,149	1,808	57.4	24,718	152	4.8	138	4.4	7.85	80.5
Fran Tarkenton	18	6,467	3,686	57.0	47,003	342	5.3	266	4.1	7.27	80.4

1,500 or more attempts. The passing ratings are based on performance standards established for completion percentage, interception percentage, touchdown percentage, and average gain. Passers are allocated points according to how their marks compare with those standards.

TOP 10 PASS RECEIVERS

Player	Years	No.	Yards	Avg.	Long	TD
Charlie Joiner	17	716	11,706	16.3	87	63
Charley Taylor	13	649	9,110	14.0	88	79
Don Maynard	15	633	11,834	18.7	87	88
Raymond Berry	13	631	9,275	14.7	70	68
Steve Largent	10	624	10,059	16.1	74	78
Harold Carmichael	14	590	8,985	15.2	85	79
Fred Biletnikoff	14	589	8,974	15.2	82	76
Harold Jackson	16	579	10,372	17.9	79	76
Lionel Taylor	10	567	7,195	12.7	80	45
Lance Alworth	11	542	10,266	18.9	85	85

TOP 10 INTERCEPTORS

Player	Years	No.	Yards	Avg.	Long	TD
Paul Krause	16	81	1,185	14.6	81	3
Emlen Tunnell	14	79	1,282	16.2	55	4
Dick (Night Train) Lane	14	68	1,207	17.8	80	5
Ken Riley	15	65	596	9.2	66	5
Dick LeBeau	13	62	762	12.3	70	3
Emmitt Thomas	13	58	937	16.2	73	5
Bobby Boyd	9	57	994	17.4	74	4
Johnny Robinson	12	57	741	13.0	57	1
Mel Blount	14	57	736	12.9	52	2
Lem Barney	11	56	1,077	19.2	71	7
Pat Fischer	17	56	941	16.8	69	4

TOP 10 PUNTERS

Player	Years	No.	Yards	Avg.	Long	Blk.
Rohn Stark	4	313	14,135	45.2	72	2
Sammy Baugh	16	338	15,245	45.1	85	9
Tommy Davis	11	511	22,833	44.7	82	2
Yale Lary	11	503	22,279	44.3	74	4
Horace Gillom	7	385	16,872	43.8	80	5
Jerry Norton	11	358	15,671	43.8	78	2
Don Chandler	12	660	28,678	43.5	90	4
Rich Camarillo	5	317	13,687	43.2	76	0
Jerrel Wilson	16	1,072	46,139	43.0	72	12
Norm Van Brocklin	12	523	22,413	42.9	72	3

300 or more punts.

TOP 10 PUNT RETURNERS

Player	Years	No.	Yards	Avg.	Long	TD
Henry Ellard	3	83	1,121	13.5	83	4
George McAfee	8	112	1,431	12.8	74	2
Jack Christiansen	8	85	1,084	12.8	89	8
Claude Gibson	5	110	1,381	12.6	85	3
Louis Lipps	2	89	1,093	12.3	76	3
Bill Dudley	9	124	1,515	12.2	96	3
Billy Johnson	11	250	3,036	12.1	87	6
Rick Upchurch	9	248	3,008	12.1	92	8
Mack Herron	3	84	982	11.7	66	0
Bill Thompson	13	157	1,814	11.6	60	0

75 or more returns.

TOP 10 KICKOFF RETURNERS

Player	Years	No.	Yards	Avg.	Long	TD
Gale Sayers	7	91	2,781	30.6	103	6
Lynn Chandnois	7	92	2,720	29.6	93	3
Abe Woodson	9	193	5,538	28.7	105	5
Claude (Buddy) Young	6	90	2,514	27.9	104	2
Travis Williams	5	102	2,801	27.5	105	6
Joe Arenas	7	139	3,798	27.3	96	1
Clarence Davis	8	79	2,140	27.1	76	0
Lenny Lyles	12	81	2,161	26.7	103	3
Steve Van Buren	8	76	2,030	26.7	98	3
Eugene (Mercury) Morris	8	111	2,947	26.5	105	3

75 or more returns.

TOP 10 COMBINED YARDS GAINED

	Tot.	Rush.	Rec.	Int. Ret.	Punt Ret.	Kickoff Ret.	Fumble
Walter Payton	19,338	14,860	3,939	0	0	539	0
Jim Brown	15,459	12,312	2,499	0	0	648	0
Franco Harris	14,622	12,120	2,287	0	0	233	−18
O.J. Simpson	14,368	11,236	2,142	0	0	990	0
Bobby Mitchell	14,078	2,735	7,954	0	699	2,690	0
Tony Dorsett	13,853	10,832	2,988	0	0	0	33
John Riggins	13,435	11,352	2,090	0	0	0	−7
Greg Pruitt	13,262	5,672	3,069	0	2,007	2,514	0
Ollie Matson	12,884	5,173	3,285	51	595	3,746	34
Tim Brown	12,684	3,862	3,399	0	639	4,781	3

YEARLY STATISTICAL LEADERS

ANNUAL SCORING LEADERS

Year	Player, Team	TD	FG	PAT	TP
1985	*Kevin Butler, Chicago, NFC	0	31	51	144
	Gary Anderson, Pittsburgh, AFC	0	33	40	139
1984	Ray Wersching, San Francisco, NFC	0	25	56	131
	Gary Anderson, Pittsburgh, AFC	0	24	45	117
1983	Mark Moseley, Washington, NFC	0	33	62	161
	Gary Anderson, Pittsburgh, AFC	0	27	38	119
1982	*Marcus Allen, L.A. Raiders, AFC	14	0	0	84
	Wendell Tyler, L.A. Rams, NFC	13	0	0	78
1981	Ed Murray, Detroit, NFC	0	25	46	121
	Rafael Septien, Dallas, NFC	0	27	40	121
	Jim Breech, Cincinnati, AFC	0	22	49	115
	Nick Lowery, Kansas City, AFC	0	26	37	115
1980	John Smith, New England, AFC	0	26	51	129
	*Ed Murray, Detroit, NFC	0	27	35	116
1979	John Smith, New England, AFC	0	23	46	115
	Mark Moseley, Washington, NFC	0	25	39	114
1978	*Frank Corral, Los Angeles, NFC	0	29	31	118
	Pat Leahy, N.Y. Jets, AFC	0	22	41	107
1977	Errol Mann, Oakland, AFC	0	20	39	99
	Walter Payton, Chicago, NFC	16	0	0	96
1976	Toni Linhart, Baltimore, AFC	0	20	49	109
	Mark Moseley, Washington, NFC	0	22	31	97
1975	O.J. Simpson, Buffalo, AFC	23	0	0	138
	Chuck Foreman, Minnesota, NFC	22	0	0	132
1974	Chester Marcol, Green Bay, NFC	0	25	19	94
	Roy Gerela, Pittsburgh, AFC	0	20	33	93
1973	David Ray, Los Angeles, NFC	0	30	40	130
	Roy Gerela, Pittsburgh, AFC	0	29	36	123
1972	*Chester Marcol, Green Bay, NFC	0	33	29	128
	Bobby Howfield, N.Y. Jets, AFC	0	27	40	121
1971	Garo Yepremian, Miami, AFC	0	28	33	117
	Curt Knight, Washington, NFC	0	29	27	114
1970	Fred Cox, Minnesota, NFC	0	30	35	125
	Jan Stenerud, Kansas City, AFC	0	30	26	116
1969	Jim Turner, N.Y. Jets, AFL	0	32	33	129
	Fred Cox, Minnesota, NFL	0	26	43	121
1968	Jim Turner, N.Y. Jets, AFL	0	34	43	145
	Leroy Kelly, Cleveland, NFL	20	0	0	120
1967	Jim Bakken, St. Louis, NFL	0	27	36	117
	George Blanda, Oakland, AFL	0	20	56	116
1966	Gino Cappelletti, Boston, AFL	6	16	35	119
	Bruce Gossett, Los Angeles, NFL	0	28	29	113
1965	*Gale Sayers, Chicago, NFL	22	0	0	132
	Gino Cappelletti, Boston, AFL	9	17	27	132
1964	Gino Cappelletti, Boston, AFL	7	25	36	#155
	Lenny Moore, Baltimore, NFL	20	0	0	120
1963	Gino Cappelletti, Boston, AFL	2	22	35	113
	Don Chandler, N.Y. Giants, NFL	0	18	52	106
1962	Gene Mingo, Denver, AFL	4	27	32	137
	Jim Taylor, Green Bay, NFL	19	0	0	114
1961	Gino Cappelletti, Boston, AFL	8	17	48	147
	Paul Hornung, Green Bay, NFL	10	15	41	146
1960	Paul Hornung, Green Bay, NFL	15	15	41	176
	*Gene Mingo, Denver, AFL	6	18	33	123
1959	Paul Hornung, Green Bay	7	7	31	94
1958	Jim Brown, Cleveland	18	0	0	108
1957	Sam Baker, Washington	1	14	29	77
	Lou Groza, Cleveland	0	15	32	77
1956	Bobby Layne, Detroit	5	12	33	99
1955	Doak Walker, Detroit	7	9	27	96
1954	Bobby Walston, Philadelphia	11	4	36	114
1953	Gordy Soltau, San Francisco	6	10	48	114
1952	Gordy Soltau, San Francisco	7	6	34	94
1951	Elroy (Crazylegs) Hirsch, Los Angeles	17	0	0	102
1950	*Doak Walker, Detroit	11	8	38	128
1949	Pat Harder, Chi. Cardinals	8	3	45	102
	Gene Roberts, N.Y. Giants	17	0	0	102
1948	Pat Harder, Chi. Cardinals	6	7	53	110
1947	Pat Harder, Chi. Cardinals	7	7	39	102
1946	Ted Fritsch, Green Bay	10	9	13	100
1945	Steve Van Buren, Philadelphia	18	0	2	110
1944	Don Hutson, Green Bay	9	0	31	85
1943	Don Hutson, Green Bay	12	3	36	117
1942	Don Hutson, Green Bay	17	1	33	138
1941	Don Hutson, Green Bay	12	1	20	95
1940	Don Hutson, Green Bay	7	0	15	57
1939	Andy Farkas, Washington	11	0	2	68
1938	Clarke Hinkle, Green Bay	7	3	7	58
1937	Jack Manders, Chi. Bears	5	8	15	69
1936	Earl (Dutch) Clark, Detroit	7	4	19	73
1935	Earl (Dutch) Clark, Detroit	6	1	16	55
1934	Jack Manders, Chi. Bears	3	10	31	79
1933	Ken Strong, N.Y. Giants	6	5	13	64
	Glenn Presnell, Portsmouth	6	6	10	64
1932	Earl (Dutch) Clark, Portsmouth	6	3	10	55

**First year in the league.*
#Cappelletti's total includes a two-point conversion.

ANNUAL LEADERS—MOST FIELD GOALS MADE

Year	Player, Team	Att.	Made	Pct.
1985	Gary Anderson, Pittsburgh, AFC	42	33	78.6
	Morten Andersen, New Orleans, NFC	35	31	88.6
	*Kevin Butler, Chicago, NFC	37	31	83.8
1984	*Paul McFadden, Philadelphia, NFC	37	30	81.1
	Gary Anderson, Pittsburgh, AFC	32	24	75.0
	Matt Bahr, Cleveland, AFC	32	24	75.0
1983	*Ali Haji-Sheikh, N.Y. Giants, NFC	42	35	83.3
	*Raul Allegre, Baltimore, AFC	35	30	85.7
1982	Mark Moseley, Washington, NFC	21	20	95.2
	Nick Lowery, Kansas City, AFC	24	19	79.2
1981	Rafael Septien, Dallas, NFC	35	27	77.1
	Nick Lowery, Kansas City, AFC	36	26	72.2
1980	*Ed Murray, Detroit, NFC	42	27	64.3
	John Smith, New England, AFC	34	26	76.5
	Fred Steinfort, Denver, AFC	34	26	76.5
1979	Mark Moseley, Washington, NFC	33	25	75.8
	John Smith, New England, AFC	33	23	69.7
1978	*Frank Corral, Los Angeles, NFC	43	29	67.4
	Pat Leahy, N.Y. Jets, AFC	30	22	73.3
1977	Mark Moseley, Washington, NFC	37	21	56.8
	Errol Mann, Oakland, AFC	28	20	71.4
1976	Mark Moseley, Washington, NFC	34	22	64.7
	Jan Stenerud, Kansas City, AFC	38	21	55.3
1975	Jan Stenerud, Kansas City, AFC	32	22	68.8
	Toni Fritsch, Dallas, NFC	35	22	62.9
1974	Chester Marcol, Green Bay, NFC	39	25	64.1
	Roy Gerela, Pittsburgh, AFC	29	20	69.0
1973	David Ray, Los Angeles, NFC	47	30	63.8
	Roy Gerela, Pittsburgh, AFC	43	29	67.4
1972	*Chester Marcol, Green Bay, NFC	48	33	68.8
	Roy Gerela, Pittsburgh, AFC	41	28	68.3
1971	Curt Knight, Washington, NFC	49	29	59.2
	Garo Yepremian, Miami, AFC	40	28	70.0
1970	Jan Stenerud, Kansas City, AFC	42	30	71.4
	Fred Cox, Minnesota, NFC	46	30	65.2
1969	Jim Turner, N.Y. Jets, AFL	47	32	68.1
	Fred Cox, Minnesota, NFL	37	26	70.3
1968	Jim Turner, N.Y. Jets, AFL	46	34	73.9
	Mac Percival, Chicago, NFL	36	25	69.4
1967	Jim Bakken, St. Louis, NFL	39	27	69.2
	Jan Stenerud, Kansas City, AFL	36	21	58.3
1966	Bruce Gossett, Los Angeles, NFL	49	28	57.1
	Mike Mercer, Oakland-Kansas City, AFL	30	21	70.0
1965	Pete Gogolak, Buffalo, AFL	46	28	60.9
	Fred Cox, Minnesota, NFL	35	23	65.7
1964	Jim Bakken, St. Louis, NFL	38	25	65.8
	Gino Cappelletti, Boston, AFL	39	25	64.1
1963	Jim Martin, Baltimore, NFL	39	24	61.5
	Gino Cappelletti, Boston, AFL	38	22	57.9
1962	Gene Mingo, Denver, AFL	39	27	69.2
	Lou Michaels, Pittsburgh, NFL	42	26	61.9
1961	Steve Myhra, Baltimore, NFL	39	21	53.8
	Gino Cappelletti, Boston, AFL	32	17	53.1
1960	Tommy Davis, San Francisco, NFL	32	19	59.4
	*Gene Mingo, Denver, AFL	28	18	64.3
1959	Pat Summerall, New York Giants	29	20	69.0
1958	Paige Cothren, Los Angeles	25	14	56.0
	*Tom Miner, Pittsburgh	28	14	50.0
1957	Lou Groza, Cleveland	22	15	68.2
1956	Sam Baker, Washington	25	17	68.0
1955	Fred Cone, Green Bay	24	16	66.7
1954	Lou Groza, Cleveland	24	16	66.7
1953	Lou Groza, Cleveland	26	23	88.5
1952	Lou Groza, Cleveland	33	19	57.6
1951	Bob Waterfield, Los Angeles	23	13	56.5
1950	*Lou Groza, Cleveland	19	13	68.4
1949	Cliff Patton, Philadelphia	18	9	50.0
	Bob Waterfield, Los Angeles	16	9	56.3
1948	Cliff Patton, Philadelphia	12	8	66.7
1947	Ward Cuff, Green Bay	16	7	43.8
	Pat Harder, Chi. Cardinals	10	7	70.0
	Bob Waterfield, Los Angeles	16	7	43.8
1946	Ted Fritsch, Green Bay	17	9	52.9
1945	Joe Aguirre, Washington	13	7	53.8
1944	Ken Strong, N.Y. Giants	12	6	50.0
1943	Ward Cuff, N.Y. Giants	9	3	33.3
	Don Hutson, Green Bay	5	3	60.0
1942	Bill Daddio, Chi. Cardinals	10	5	50.0
1941	Clarke Hinkle, Green Bay	14	6	42.9
1940	Clarke Hinkle, Green Bay	14	9	64.3
1939	Ward Cuff, N.Y. Giants	16	7	43.8
1938	Ward Cuff, N.Y. Giants	9	5	55.6
	Ralph Kercheval, Brooklyn	13	5	38.5
1937	Jack Manders, Chi. Bears		8	
1936	Jack Manders, Chi. Bears		7	
	Armand Niccolai, Pittsburgh		7	
1935	Armand Niccolai, Pittsburgh		6	
	Bill Smith, Chi. Cardinals		6	
1934	Jack Manders, Chi. Bears		10	
1933	*Jack Manders, Chi. Bears		6	
	Glenn Presnell, Portsmouth		6	
1932	Earl (Dutch) Clark, Portsmouth		3	

**First year in the league.*

ANNUAL RUSHING LEADERS

Year	Player, Team	Att.	Yards	Avg.	TD
1985	Marcus Allen, L.A. Raiders, AFC	380	1,759	4.6	11
	Gerald Riggs, Atlanta, NFC	397	1,719	4.3	10
1984	Eric Dickerson, L.A. Rams, NFC	379	2,105	5.6	14
	Earnest Jackson, San Diego, AFC	296	1,179	4.0	8
1983	*Eric Dickerson, L.A. Rams, NFC	390	1,808	4.6	18
	*Curt Warner, Seattle, AFC	335	1,449	4.3	13
1982	Freeman McNeil, N.Y. Jets, AFC	151	786	5.2	6
	Tony Dorsett, Dallas, NFC	177	745	4.2	5

1981	*George Rogers, New Orleans, NFC	378	1,674	4.4	13
	Earl Campbell, Houston, AFC	361	1,376	3.8	10
1980	Earl Campbell, Houston, AFC	373	1,934	5.2	13
	Walter Payton, Chicago, NFC	317	1,460	4.6	6
1979	Earl Campbell, Houston, AFC	368	1,697	4.6	19
	Walter Payton, Chicago, NFC	369	1,610	4.4	14
1978	*Earl Campbell, Houston, AFC	302	1,450	4.8	13
	Walter Payton, Chicago, NFC	333	1,395	4.2	11
1977	Walter Payton, Chicago, NFC	339	1,852	5.5	14
	Mark van Eeghen, Oakland, AFC	324	1,273	3.9	7
1976	O.J. Simpson, Buffalo, AFC	290	1,503	5.2	8
	Walter Payton, Chicago, NFC	311	1,390	4.5	13
1975	O.J. Simpson, Buffalo, AFC	329	1,817	5.5	16
	Jim Otis, St. Louis, NFC	269	1,076	4.0	5
1974	Otis Armstrong, Denver, AFC	263	1,407	5.3	9
	Lawrence McCutcheon, Los Angeles, NFC	236	1,109	4.7	3
1973	O.J. Simpson, Buffalo, AFC	332	2,003	6.0	12
	John Brockington, Green Bay, NFC	265	1,144	4.3	3
1972	O.J. Simpson, Buffalo, AFC	292	1,251	4.3	6
	Larry Brown, Washington, NFC	285	1,216	4.3	8
1971	Floyd Little, Denver, AFC	284	1,133	4.0	6
	*John Brockington, Green Bay, NFC	216	1,105	5.1	4
1970	Larry Brown, Washington, NFC	237	1,125	4.7	5
	Floyd Little, Denver, AFC	209	901	4.3	3
1969	Gale Sayers, Chicago, NFL	236	1,032	4.4	8
	Dickie Post, San Diego, AFL	182	873	4.8	6
1968	Leroy Kelly, Cleveland, NFL	248	1,239	5.0	16
	*Paul Robinson, Cincinnati, AFL	238	1,023	4.3	8
1967	Jim Nance, Boston, AFL	269	1,216	4.5	7
	Leroy Kelly, Cleveland, NFL	235	1,205	5.1	11
1966	Jim Nance, Boston, AFL	299	1,458	4.9	11
	Gale Sayers, Chicago, NFL	229	1,231	5.4	8
1965	Jim Brown, Cleveland, NFL	289	1,544	5.3	17
	Paul Lowe, San Diego, AFL	222	1,121	5.0	7
1964	Jim Brown, Cleveland, NFL	280	1,446	5.2	7
	Cookie Gilchrist, Buffalo, AFL	230	981	4.3	6
1963	Jim Brown, Cleveland, NFL	291	1,863	6.4	12
	Clem Daniels, Oakland, AFL	215	1,099	5.1	3
1962	Jim Taylor, Green Bay, NFL	272	1,474	5.4	19
	*Cookie Gilchrist, Buffalo, AFL	214	1,096	5.1	13
1961	Jim Brown, Cleveland, NFL	305	1,408	4.6	8
	Billy Cannon, Houston, AFL	200	948	4.7	6
1960	Jim Brown, Cleveland, NFL	215	1,257	5.8	9
	*Abner Haynes, Dall. Texans, AFL	156	875	5.6	9
1959	Jim Brown, Cleveland	290	1,329	4.6	14
1958	Jim Brown, Cleveland	257	1,527	5.9	17
1957	*Jim Brown, Cleveland	202	942	4.7	9
1956	Rick Casares, Chi. Bears	234	1,126	4.8	12
1955	*Alan Ameche, Baltimore	213	961	4.5	9
1954	Joe Perry, San Francisco	173	1,049	6.1	8
1953	Joe Perry, San Francisco	192	1,018	5.3	10
1952	Dan Towler, Los Angeles	156	894	5.7	10
1951	Eddie Price, N.Y. Giants	271	971	3.6	7
1950	*Marion Motley, Cleveland	140	810	5.8	3
1949	Steve Van Buren, Philadelphia	263	1,146	4.4	11
1948	Steve Van Buren, Philadelphia	201	945	4.7	10
1947	Steve Van Buren, Philadelphia	217	1,008	4.6	13
1946	Bill Dudley, Pittsburgh	146	604	4.1	3
1945	Steve Van Buren, Philadelphia	143	832	5.8	15
1944	Bill Paschal, N.Y. Giants	196	737	3.8	9
1943	*Bill Paschal, N.Y. Giants	147	572	3.9	10
1942	*Bill Dudley, Pittsburgh	162	696	4.3	5
1941	Clarence (Pug) Manders, Brooklyn	111	486	4.4	5
1940	Byron (Whizzer) White, Detroit	146	514	3.5	5
1939	*Bill Osmanski, Chicago	121	699	5.8	7
1938	*Byron (Whizzer) White, Pittsburgh	152	567	3.7	4
1937	Cliff Battles, Washington	216	874	4.0	5
1936	*Alphonse (Tuffy) Leemans, N.Y. Giants	206	830	4.0	2
1935	Doug Russell, Chi. Cardinals	140	499	3.6	0
1934	*Beattie Feathers, Chi. Bears	101	1,004	9.9	8
1933	Jim Musick, Boston	173	809	4.7	5
1932	*Cliff Battles, Boston	148	576	3.9	3

**First year in the league.*

ANNUAL PASSING LEADERS

Year	Player, Team	Att.	Comp.	Yards	TD	Int.
1985	Ken O'Brien, N.Y. Jets, AFC	488	297	3,888	25	8
	Joe Montana, San Francisco, NFC	494	303	3,653	27	13
1984	Dan Marino, Miami, AFC	564	362	5,084	48	17
	Joe Montana, San Francisco, NFC	432	279	3,630	28	10
1983	Steve Bartkowski, Atlanta, NFC	432	274	3,167	22	5
	*Dan Marino, Miami, AFC	296	173	2,210	20	6
1982	Ken Anderson, Cincinnati, AFC	309	218	2,495	12	9
	Joe Theismann, Washington, NFC	252	161	2,033	13	9
1981	Ken Anderson, Cincinnati, AFC	479	300	3,754	29	10
	Joe Montana, San Francisco, NFC	488	311	3,565	19	12
1980	Brian Sipe, Cleveland, AFC	554	337	4,132	30	14
	Ron Jaworski, Philadelphia, NFC	451	257	3,529	27	12
1979	Roger Staubach, Dallas, NFC	461	267	3,586	27	11
	Dan Fouts, San Diego, AFC	530	332	4,082	24	24
1978	Roger Staubach, Dallas, NFC	413	231	3,190	25	16
	Terry Bradshaw, Pittsburgh, AFC	368	207	2,915	28	20
1977	Bob Griese, Miami, AFC	307	180	2,252	22	13
	Roger Staubach, Dallas, NFC	361	210	2,620	18	9
1976	Ken Stabler, Oakland, AFC	291	194	2,737	27	17
	James Harris, Los Angeles, NFC	158	91	1,460	8	6
1975	Ken Anderson, Cincinnati, AFC	377	228	3,169	21	11
	Fran Tarkenton, Minnesota, NFC	425	273	2,994	25	13
1974	Ken Anderson, Cincinnati, AFC	328	213	2,667	18	10
	Sonny Jurgensen, Washington, NFC	167	107	1,185	11	5
1973	Roger Staubach, Dallas, NFC	286	179	2,428	23	15
	Ken Stabler, Oakland, AFC	260	163	1,997	14	10
1972	Norm Snead, N.Y. Giants, NFC	325	196	2,307	17	12
	Earl Morrall, Miami, AFC	150	83	1,360	11	7
1971	Roger Staubach, Dallas, NFC	211	126	1,882	15	4
	Bob Griese, Miami, AFC	263	145	2,089	19	9
1970	John Brodie, San Francisco, NFC	378	223	2,941	24	10
	Daryle Lamonica, Oakland, AFC	356	179	2,516	22	15
1969	Sonny Jurgensen, Washington, NFL	442	274	3,102	22	15
	*Greg Cook, Cincinnati, AFL	197	106	1,854	15	11
1968	Len Dawson, Kansas City, AFL	224	131	2,109	17	9
	Earl Morrall, Baltimore, NFL	317	182	2,909	26	17
1967	Sonny Jurgensen, Washington, NFL	508	288	3,747	31	16
	Daryle Lamonica, Oakland, AFL	425	220	3,228	30	20
1966	Bart Starr, Green Bay, NFL	251	156	2,257	14	3
	Len Dawson, Kansas City, AFL	284	159	2,527	26	10
1965	Rudy Bukich, Chicago, NFL	312	176	2,641	20	9
	John Hadl, San Diego, AFL	348	174	2,798	20	21
1964	Len Dawson, Kansas City, AFL	354	199	2,879	30	18
	Bart Starr, Green Bay, NFL	272	163	2,144	15	4
1963	Y.A. Tittle, N.Y. Giants, NFL	367	221	3,145	36	14
	Tobin Rote, San Diego, AFL	286	170	2,510	20	17
1962	Len Dawson, Dall. Texans, AFL	310	189	2,759	29	17
	Bart Starr, Green Bay, NFL	285	178	2,438	12	9
1961	George Blanda, Houston, AFL	362	187	3,330	36	22
	Milt Plum, Cleveland, NFL	302	177	2,416	18	10
1960	Milt Plum, Cleveland, NFL	250	151	2,297	21	5
	Jack Kemp, L.A. Chargers, AFL	406	211	3,018	20	25
1959	Charlie Conerly, N.Y. Giants	194	113	1,706	14	4
1958	Eddie LeBaron, Washington	145	79	1,365	11	10
1957	Tommy O'Connell, Cleveland	110	63	1,229	9	8
1956	Ed Brown, Chi. Bears	168	96	1,667	11	12
1955	Otto Graham, Cleveland	185	98	1,721	15	8
1954	Norm Van Brocklin, Los Angeles	260	139	2,637	13	21
1953	Otto Graham, Cleveland	258	167	2,722	11	9
1952	Norm Van Brocklin, Los Angeles	205	113	1,736	14	17
1951	Bob Waterfield, Los Angeles	176	88	1,566	13	10
1950	Norm Van Brocklin, Los Angeles	233	127	2,061	18	14
1949	Sammy Baugh, Washington	255	145	1,903	18	14
1948	Tommy Thompson, Philadelphia	246	141	1,965	25	11
1947	Sammy Baugh, Washington	354	210	2,938	25	15
1946	Bob Waterfield, Los Angeles	251	127	1,747	18	17
1945	Sammy Baugh, Washington	182	128	1,669	11	4
	Sid Luckman, Chi. Bears	217	117	1,725	14	10
1944	Frank Filchock, Washington	147	84	1,139	13	9
1943	Sammy Baugh, Washington	239	133	1,754	23	19
1942	Cecil Isbell, Green Bay	268	146	2,021	24	14
1941	Cecil Isbell, Green Bay	206	117	1,479	15	11
1940	Sammy Baugh, Washington	177	111	1,367	12	10
1939	*Parker Hall, Cleveland	208	106	1,227	9	13
1938	Ed Danowski, N.Y. Giants	129	70	848	7	8
1937	*Sammy Baugh, Washington	171	81	1,127	8	14
1936	Arnie Herber, Green Bay	173	77	1,239	11	13
1935	Ed Danowski, N.Y. Giants	113	57	794	10	9
1934	Arnie Herber, Green Bay	115	42	799	8	12
1933	*Harry Newman, N.Y. Giants	136	53	973	11	17
1932	Arnie Herber, Green Bay	101	37	639	9	9

**First year in the league.*

ANNUAL PASS RECEIVING LEADERS

Year	Player, Team	No.	Yards	Avg.	TD
1985	Roger Craig, San Francisco, NFC	92	1,016	11.0	6
	Lionel James, San Diego, AFC	86	1,027	11.9	6
1984	Art Monk, Washington, NFC	106	1,372	12.9	7
	Ozzie Newsome, Cleveland, AFC	89	1,001	11.2	5
1983	Todd Christensen, L.A. Raiders, AFC	92	1,247	13.6	12
	Roy Green, St. Louis, NFC	78	1,227	15.7	14
	Charlie Brown, Washington, NFC	78	1,225	15.7	8
	Earnest Gray, N.Y. Giants, NFC	78	1,139	14.6	5
1982	Dwight Clark, San Francisco, NFC	60	913	15.2	5
	Kellen Winslow, San Diego, AFC	54	721	13.4	6
1981	Kellen Winslow, San Diego, AFC	88	1,075	12.2	10
	Dwight Clark, San Francisco, NFC	85	1,105	13.0	4
1980	Kellen Winslow, San Diego, AFC	89	1,290	14.5	9
	*Earl Cooper, San Francisco, NFC	83	567	6.8	4
1979	Joe Washington, Baltimore, AFC	82	750	9.1	3
	Ahmad Rashad, Minnesota, NFC	80	1,156	14.5	9
1978	Rickey Young, Minnesota, NFC	88	704	8.0	5
	Steve Largent, Seattle, AFC	71	1,168	16.5	8
1977	Lydell Mitchell, Baltimore, AFC	71	620	8.7	4
	Ahmad Rashad, Minnesota, NFC	51	681	13.4	2
1976	MacArthur Lane, Kansas City, AFC	66	686	10.4	1
	Drew Pearson, Dallas, NFC	58	806	13.9	6
1975	Chuck Foreman, Minnesota, NFC	73	691	9.5	9
	Reggie Rucker, Cleveland, AFC	60	770	12.8	3
	Lydell Mitchell, Baltimore, AFC	60	544	9.1	4
1974	Lydell Mitchell, Baltimore, AFC	72	544	7.6	2
	Charles Young, Philadelphia, NFC	63	696	11.0	3
1973	Harold Carmichael, Philadelphia, NFC	67	1,116	16.7	9
	Fred Willis, Houston, AFC	57	371	6.5	1
1972	Harold Jackson, Philadelphia, NFC	62	1,048	16.9	4
	Fred Biletnikoff, Oakland, AFC	58	802	13.8	7
1971	Fred Biletnikoff, Oakland, AFC	61	929	15.2	9
	Bob Tucker, N.Y. Giants, NFC	59	791	13.4	4
1970	Dick Gordon, Chicago, NFC	71	1,026	14.5	13
	Marlin Briscoe, Buffalo, AFC	57	1,036	18.2	8
1969	Dan Abramowicz, New Orleans, NFL	73	1,015	13.9	7
	Lance Alworth, San Diego, AFL	64	1,003	15.7	4
1968	Clifton McNeil, San Francisco, NFL	71	994	14.0	7
	Lance Alworth, San Diego, AFL	68	1,312	19.3	10
1967	George Sauer, N.Y. Jets, AFL	75	1,189	15.9	6
	Charley Taylor, Washington, NFL	70	990	14.1	9
1966	Lance Alworth, San Diego, AFL	73	1,383	18.9	13
	Charley Taylor, Washington, NFL	72	1,119	15.5	12
1965	Lionel Taylor, Denver, AFL	85	1,131	13.3	6
	Dave Parks, San Francisco, NFL	80	1,344	16.8	12

1964	Charley Hennigan, Houston, AFL	101	1,546	15.3	8
	Johnny Morris, Chicago, NFL	93	1,200	12.9	10
1963	Lionel Taylor, Denver, AFL	78	1,101	14.1	10
	Bobby Joe Conrad, St. Louis, NFL	73	967	13.2	10
1962	Lionel Taylor, Denver, AFL	77	908	11.8	4
	Bobby Mitchell, Washington, NFL	72	1,384	19.2	11
1961	Lionel Taylor, Denver, AFL	100	1,176	11.8	4
	Jim (Red) Phillips, Los Angeles, NFL	78	1,092	14.0	5
1960	Lionel Taylor, Denver, AFL	92	1,235	13.4	12
	Raymond Berry, Baltimore, NFL	74	1,298	17.5	10
1959	Raymond Berry, Baltimore	66	959	14.5	14
1958	Raymond Berry, Baltimore	56	794	14.2	9
	Pete Retzlaff, Philadelphia	56	766	13.7	2
1957	Billy Wilson, San Francisco	52	757	14.6	6
1956	Billy Wilson, San Francisco	60	889	14.8	5
1955	Pete Pihos, Philadelphia	62	864	13.9	7
1954	Pete Pihos, Philadelphia	60	872	14.5	10
	Billy Wilson, San Francisco	60	830	13.8	5
1953	Pete Pihos, Philadelphia	63	1,049	16.7	10
1952	Mac Speedie, Cleveland	62	911	14.7	5
1951	Elroy (Crazylegs) Hirsch, Los Angeles	66	1,495	22.7	17
1950	Tom Fears, Los Angeles	84	1,116	13.3	7
1949	Tom Fears, Los Angeles	77	1,013	13.2	9
1948	*Tom Fears, Los Angeles	51	698	13.7	4
1947	Jim Keane, Chi. Bears	64	910	14.2	10
1946	Jim Benton, Los Angeles	63	981	15.6	6
1945	Don Hutson, Green Bay	47	834	17.7	9
1944	Don Hutson, Green Bay	58	866	14.9	9
1943	Don Hutson, Green Bay	47	776	16.5	11
1942	Don Hutson, Green Bay	74	1,211	16.4	17
1941	Don Hutson, Green Bay	58	738	12.7	10
1940	*Don Looney, Philadelphia	58	707	12.2	4
1939	Don Hutson, Green Bay	34	846	24.9	6
1938	Gaynell Tinsley, Chi. Cardinals	41	516	12.6	1
1937	Don Hutson, Green Bay	41	552	13.5	7
1936	Don Hutson, Green Bay	34	536	15.8	8
1935	*Tod Goodwin, N.Y. Giants	26	432	16.6	4
1934	Joe Carter, Philadelphia	16	238	14.9	4
	Morris (Red) Badgro, N.Y. Giants	16	206	12.9	1
1933	John (Shipwreck) Kelly, Brooklyn	22	246	11.2	3
1932	Ray Flaherty, N.Y. Giants	21	350	16.7	3

First year in the league.

ANNUAL INTERCEPTION LEADERS

Year	Player, Team	No.	Yards	TD
1985	Everson Walls, Dallas, NFC	9	31	0
	Albert Lewis, Kansas City, AFC	8	59	0
	Eugene Daniel, Indianapolis, AFC	8	53	0
1984	Ken Easley, Seattle, AFC	10	126	2
	*Tom Flynn, Green Bay, NFC	9	106	0
1983	Mark Murphy, Washington, NFC	9	127	0
	Ken Riley, Cincinnati, AFC	8	89	2
	Vann McElroy, L.A. Raiders, AFC	8	68	0
1982	Everson Walls, Dallas, NFC	7	61	0
	Ken Riley, Cincinnati, AFC	5	88	1
	Bobby Jackson, N.Y. Jets, AFC	5	84	1
	Dwayne Woodruff, Pittsburgh, AFC	5	53	0
	Donnie Shell, Pittsburgh, AFC	5	27	0
1981	*Everson Walls, Dallas, NFC	11	133	0
	John Harris, Seattle, AFC	10	155	2
1980	Lester Hayes, Oakland, AFC	13	273	1
	Nolan Cromwell, Los Angeles, NFC	8	140	1
1979	Mike Reinfeldt, Houston, AFC	12	205	0
	Lemar Parrish, Washington, NFC	9	65	0
1978	Thom Darden, Cleveland, AFC	10	200	0
	Ken Stone, St. Louis, NFC	9	139	0
	Willie Buchanon, Green Bay, NFC	9	93	1
1977	Lyle Blackwood, Baltimore, AFC	10	163	0
	Rolland Lawrence, Atlanta, NFC	7	138	0
1976	Monte Jackson, Los Angeles, NFC	10	173	3
	Ken Riley, Cincinnati, AFC	9	141	1
1975	Mel Blount, Pittsburgh, AFC	11	121	0
	Paul Krause, Minnesota, NFC	10	201	0
1974	Emmitt Thomas, Kansas City, AFC	12	214	2
	Ray Brown, Atlanta, NFC	8	164	1
1973	Dick Anderson, Miami, AFC	8	163	2
	Mike Wagner, Pittsburgh, AFC	8	134	0
	Bobby Bryant, Minnesota, NFC	7	105	1
1972	Bill Bradley, Philadelphia, NFC	9	73	0
	Mike Sensibaugh, Kansas City, AFC	8	65	0
1971	Bill Bradley, Philadelphia, NFC	11	248	0
	Ken Houston, Houston, AFC	9	220	4
1970	Johnny Robinson, Kansas City, AFC	10	155	0
	Dick LeBeau, Detroit, NFC	9	96	0
1969	Mel Renfro, Dallas, NFL	10	118	0
	Emmitt Thomas, Kansas City, AFL	9	146	1
1968	Dave Grayson, Oakland, AFL	10	195	1
	Willie Williams, N.Y. Giants, NFL	10	103	0
1967	Miller Farr, Houston, AFL	10	264	3
	*Lem Barney, Detroit, NFL	10	232	3
	Tom Janik, Buffalo, AFL	10	222	2
	Dave Whitsell, New Orleans, NFL	10	178	2
	Dick Westmoreland, Miami, AFL	10	127	1
1966	Larry Wilson, St. Louis, NFL	10	180	2
	Johnny Robinson, Kansas City, AFL	10	136	1
	Bobby Hunt, Kansas City, AFL	10	113	0
1965	W.K. Hicks, Houston, AFL	9	156	0
	Bobby Boyd, Baltimore, NFL	9	78	1
1964	Dainard Paulson, N.Y. Jets, AFL	12	157	1
	*Paul Krause, Washington, NFL	12	140	1
1963	Fred Glick, Houston, AFL	12	180	1
	Dick Lynch, N.Y. Giants, NFL	9	251	3
	Roosevelt Taylor, Chicago, NFL	9	172	1
1962	Lee Riley, N.Y. Titans, AFL	11	122	0
	Willie Wood, Green Bay, NFL	9	132	0
1961	Billy Atkins, Buffalo, AFL	10	158	0
	Dick Lynch, N.Y. Giants, NFL	9	60	0
1960	*Austin (Goose) Gonsoulin, Denver, AFL	11	98	0
	Dave Baker, San Francisco, NFL	10	96	0
	Jerry Norton, St. Louis, NFL	10	96	0
1959	Dean Derby, Pittsburgh	7	127	0
	Milt Davis, Baltimore	7	119	1
	Don Shinnick, Baltimore	7	70	0
1958	Jim Patton, N.Y. Giants	11	183	0
1957	*Milt Davis, Baltimore	10	219	2
	Jack Christiansen, Detroit	10	137	1
	Jack Butler, Pittsburgh	10	85	0
1956	Lindon Crow, Chi. Cardinals	11	170	0
1955	Will Sherman, Los Angeles	11	101	0
1954	Dick (Night Train) Lane, Chi. Cardinals	10	181	0
1953	Jack Christiansen, Detroit	12	238	1
1952	*Dick (Night Train) Lane, Los Angeles	14	298	2
1951	Otto Schnellbacher, N.Y. Giants	11	194	2
1950	*Orban (Spec) Sanders, N.Y. Yanks	13	199	0
1949	Bob Nussbaumer, Chi. Cardinals	12	157	0
1948	*Dan Sandifer, Washington	13	258	2
1947	Frank Reagan, N.Y. Giants	10	203	0
	Frank Seno, Boston	10	100	0
1946	Bill Dudley, Pittsburgh	10	242	1
1945	Roy Zimmerman, Philadelphia	7	90	0
1944	*Howard Livingston, N.Y. Giants	9	172	1
1943	Sammy Baugh, Washington	11	112	0
1942	Clyde (Bulldog) Turner, Chi. Bears	8	96	1
1941	Marshall Goldberg, Chi. Cardinals	7	54	0
	*Art Jones, Pittsburgh	7	35	0
1940	Clarence (Ace) Parker, Brooklyn	6	146	1
	Kent Ryan, Detroit	6	65	0
	Don Hutson, Green Bay	6	24	0

First year in the league.

ANNUAL PUNTING LEADERS

Year	Player, Team	No.	Avg.	Long
1985	Rohn Stark, Indianapolis, AFC	78	45.9	68
	*Rick Donnelly, Atlanta, NFC	59	43.6	68
1984	Jim Arnold, Kansas City, AFC	98	44.9	63
	*Brian Hansen, New Orleans, NFC	69	43.8	66
1983	Rohn Stark, Baltimore, AFC	91	45.3	68
	*Frank Garcia, Tampa Bay, NFC	95	42.2	64
1982	Luke Prestridge, Denver, AFC	45	45.0	65
	Carl Birdsong, St. Louis, NFC	54	43.8	65
1981	Pat McInally, Cincinnati, AFC	72	45.4	62
	Tom Skladany, Detroit, NFC	64	43.5	74
1980	Dave Jennings, N.Y. Giants, NFC	94	44.8	63
	Luke Prestridge, Denver, AFC	70	43.9	57
1979	*Bob Grupp, Kansas City, AFC	89	43.6	74
	Dave Jennings, N.Y. Giants, NFC	104	42.7	72
1978	Pat McInally, Cincinnati, AFC	91	43.1	65
	*Tom Skladany, Detroit, NFC	86	42.5	63
1977	Ray Guy, Oakland, AFC	59	43.3	74
	Tom Blanchard, New Orleans, NFC	82	42.4	66
1976	Marv Bateman, Buffalo, AFC	86	42.8	78
	John James, Atlanta, NFC	101	42.1	67
1975	Ray Guy, Oakland, AFC	68	43.8	64
	Herman Weaver, Detroit, NFC	80	42.0	61
1974	Ray Guy, Oakland, AFC	74	42.2	66
	Tom Blanchard, New Orleans, NFC	88	42.1	71
1973	Jerrel Wilson, Kansas City, AFC	80	45.5	68
	*Tom Wittum, San Francisco, NFC	79	43.7	62
1972	Jerrel Wilson, Kansas City, AFC	66	44.8	69
	Dave Chapple, Los Angeles, NFC	53	44.2	70
1971	Dave Lewis, Cincinnati, AFC	72	44.8	56
	Tom McNeill, Philadelphia, NFC	73	42.0	64
1970	*Dave Lewis, Cincinnati, AFC	79	46.2	63
	*Julian Fagan, New Orleans, NFC	77	42.5	64
1969	David Lee, Baltimore, NFL	57	45.3	66
	Dennis Partee, San Diego, AFL	71	44.6	62
1968	Jerrel Wilson, Kansas City, AFL	63	45.1	70
	Billy Lothridge, Atlanta, NFL	75	44.3	70
1967	Bob Scarpitto, Denver, AFL	105	44.9	73
	Billy Lothridge, Atlanta, NFL	87	43.7	62
1966	Bob Scarpitto, Denver, AFL	76	45.8	70
	*David Lee, Baltimore, NFL	49	45.6	64
1965	Gary Collins, Cleveland, NFL	65	46.7	71
	Jerrel Wilson, Kansas City, AFL	69	45.4	64
1964	*Bobby Walden, Minnesota, NFL	72	46.4	73
	Jim Fraser, Denver, AFL	73	44.2	67
1963	Yale Lary, Detroit, NFL	35	48.9	73
	Jim Fraser, Denver, AFL	81	44.4	66
1962	Tommy Davis, San Francisco, NFL	48	45.6	82
	Jim Fraser, Denver, AFL	55	43.6	75
1961	Yale Lary, Detroit, NFL	52	48.4	71
	Billy Atkins, Buffalo, AFL	85	44.5	70
1960	Jerry Norton, St. Louis, NFL	39	45.6	62
	*Paul Maguire, L.A. Chargers, AFL	43	40.5	61
1959	Yale Lary, Detroit	45	47.1	67
1958	Sam Baker, Washington	48	45.4	64
1957	Don Chandler, N.Y. Giants	60	44.6	61
1956	Norm Van Brocklin, Los Angeles	48	43.1	72
1955	Norm Van Brocklin, Los Angeles	60	44.6	61
1954	Pat Brady, Pittsburgh	66	43.2	72
1953	Pat Brady, Pittsburgh	80	46.9	64
1952	Horace Gillom, Cleveland	61	45.7	73
1951	Horace Gillom, Cleveland	73	45.5	66
1950	*Fred (Curly) Morrison, Chi. Bears	57	43.3	65
1949	*Mike Boyda, N.Y. Bulldogs	56	44.2	61
1948	Joe Muha, Philadelphia	57	47.3	82

1947	Jack Jacobs, Green Bay	57	43.5	74
1946	Roy McKay, Green Bay	64	42.7	64
1945	Roy McKay, Green Bay	44	41.2	73
1944	Frank Sinkwich, Detroit	45	41.0	73
1943	Sammy Baugh, Washington	50	45.9	81
1942	Sammy Baugh, Washington	37	48.2	74
1941	Sammy Baugh, Washington	30	48.7	75
1940	Sammy Baugh, Washington	35	51.4	85
1939	*Parker Hall, Cleveland	58	40.8	80

First year in the league.

ANNUAL PUNT RETURN LEADERS

Year	Player, Team	No.	Yards	Avg.	Long	TD
1985	Irving Fryar, New England, AFC	37	520	14.1	85	2
	Henry Ellard, L.A. Rams, NFC	37	501	13.5	80	1
1984	Mike Martin, Cincinnati, AFC	24	376	15.7	55	0
	Henry Ellard, L.A. Rams, NFC	30	403	13.4	83	2
1983	*Henry Ellard, L.A. Rams, NFC	16	217	13.6	72	1
	Kirk Springs, N.Y. Jets, AFC	23	287	12.5	76	1
1982	Rick Upchurch, Denver, AFC	15	242	16.1	78	2
	Billy Johnson, Atlanta, NFC	24	273	11.4	71	0
1981	LeRoy Irvin, Los Angeles, NFC	46	615	13.4	84	3
	*James Brooks, San Diego, AFC	22	290	13.2	42	0
1980	J. T. Smith, Kansas City, AFC	40	581	14.5	75	2
	*Kenny Johnson, Atlanta, NFC	23	281	12.2	56	0
1979	John Sciarra, Philadelphia, NFC	16	182	11.4	38	0
	*Tony Nathan, Miami, AFC	28	306	10.9	86	1
1978	Rick Upchurch, Denver, AFC	36	493	13.7	75	1
	Jackie Wallace, Los Angeles, NFC	52	618	11.9	58	0
1977	Billy Johnson, Houston, AFC	35	539	15.4	87	2
	Larry Marshall, Philadelphia, NFC	46	489	10.6	48	0
1976	Rick Upchurch, Denver, AFC	39	536	13.7	92	4
	Eddie Brown, Washington, NFC	48	646	13.5	71	1
1975	Billy Johnson, Houston, AFC	40	612	15.3	83	3
	Terry Metcalf, St. Louis, NFC	23	285	12.4	69	1
1974	Lemar Parrish, Cincinnati, AFC	18	338	18.8	90	2
	Dick Jauron, Detroit, NFC	17	286	16.8	58	0
1973	Bruce Taylor, San Francisco, NFC	15	207	13.8	61	0
	Ron Smith, San Diego, AFC	27	352	13.0	84	2
1972	*Ken Ellis, Green Bay, NFC	14	215	15.4	80	1
	Chris Farasopoulos, N.Y. Jets, AFC	17	179	10.5	65	1
1971	Les (Speedy) Duncan, Washington, NFC	22	233	10.6	33	0
	Leroy Kelly, Cleveland, AFC	30	292	9.7	74	0
1970	Ed Podolak, Kansas City, AFC	23	311	13.5	60	0
	*Bruce Taylor, San Francisco, NFC	43	516	12.0	76	0
1969	Alvin Haymond, Los Angeles, NFL	33	435	13.2	52	0
	*Bill Thompson, Denver, AFL	25	288	11.5	40	0
1968	Bob Hayes, Dallas, NFL	15	312	20.8	90	2
	Noland Smith, Kansas City, AFL	18	270	15.0	80	1
1967	Floyd Little, Denver, AFL	16	270	16.9	72	1
	Ben Davis, Cleveland, NFL	18	229	12.7	52	1
1966	Les (Speedy) Duncan, San Diego, AFL	18	238	13.2	81	1
	Johnny Roland, St. Louis, NFL	20	221	11.1	86	1
1965	Leroy Kelly, Cleveland, NFL	17	265	15.6	67	2
	Les (Speedy) Duncan, San Diego, AFL	30	464	15.5	66	2
1964	Bobby Jancik, Houston, AFL	12	220	18.3	82	1
	Tommy Watkins, Detroit, NFL	16	238	14.9	68	2
1963	Dick James, Washington, NFL	16	214	13.4	39	0
	Claude (Hoot) Gibson, Oakland, AFL	26	307	11.8	85	2
1962	Dick Christy, N.Y. Titans, AFL	15	250	16.7	73	2
	Pat Studstill, Detroit, NFL	29	457	15.8	44	0
1961	Dick Christy, N.Y. Titans, AFL	18	383	21.3	70	2
	Willie Wood, Green Bay, NFL	14	225	16.1	72	2
1960	*Abner Haynes, Dall. Texans, AFL	14	215	15.4	46	0
	Abe Woodson, San Francisco, NFL	13	174	13.4	48	0
1959	Johnny Morris, Chi. Bears	14	171	12.2	78	1
1958	Jon Arnett, Los Angeles	18	223	12.4	58	0
1957	Bert Zagers, Washington	14	217	15.5	76	2
1956	Ken Konz, Cleveland	13	187	14.4	65	1
1955	Ollie Matson, Chi. Cardinals	13	245	18.8	78	2
1954	*Veryl Switzer, Green Bay	24	306	12.8	93	1
1953	Charley Trippi, Chi. Cardinals	21	239	11.4	38	0
1952	Jack Christiansen, Detroit	15	322	21.5	79	2
1951	Claude (Buddy) Young, N.Y. Yanks	12	231	19.3	79	1
1950	*Herb Rich, Baltimore	12	276	23.0	86	1
1949	Verda (Vitamin T) Smith, Los Angeles	27	427	15.8	85	1
1948	George McAfee, Chi. Bears	30	417	13.9	60	1
1947	*Walt Slater, Pittsburgh	28	435	15.5	33	0
1946	Bill Dudley, Pittsburgh	27	385	14.3	52	0
1945	*Dave Ryan, Detroit	15	220	14.7	56	0
1944	*Steve Van Buren, Philadelphia	15	230	15.3	55	1
1943	Andy Farkas, Washington	15	168	11.2	33	0
1942	Merlyn Condit, Brooklyn	21	210	10.0	23	0
1941	Byron (Whizzer) White, Detroit	19	262	13.8	64	0

First year in the league.

ANNUAL KICKOFF RETURN LEADERS

Year	Player, Team	No.	Yards	Avg.	Long	TD
1985	Ron Brown, L.A. Rams, NFC	28	918	32.8	98	3
	Glen Young, Cleveland, AFC	35	898	25.7	63	0
1984	*Bobby Humphery, N.Y. Jets, AFC	22	675	30.7	97	1
	Barry Redden, L.A. Rams, NFC	23	530	23.0	40	0
1983	Fulton Walker, Miami, AFC	36	962	26.7	78	0
	Darrin Nelson, Minnesota, NFC	18	445	24.7	50	0
1982	*Mike Mosley, Buffalo, AFC	18	487	27.1	66	0
	Alvin Hall, Detroit, NFC	16	426	26.6	96	1
1981	Mike Nelms, Washington, NFC	37	1,099	29.7	84	0
	Carl Roaches, Houston, AFC	28	769	27.5	96	1
1980	Horace Ivory, New England, AFC	36	992	27.6	98	1
	Rich Mauti, New Orleans, NFC	31	798	25.7	52	0
1979	Larry Brunson, Oakland, AFC	17	441	25.9	89	0
	*Jimmy Edwards, Minnesota, NFC	44	1,103	25.1	83	0
1978	Steve Odom, Green Bay, NFC	25	677	27.1	95	1
	*Keith Wright, Cleveland, AFC	30	789	26.3	86	0
1977	*Raymond Clayborn, New England, AFC	28	869	31.0	101	3
	*Wilbert Montgomery, Philadelphia, NFC	23	619	26.9	99	1
1976	*Duriel Harris, Miami, AFC	17	559	32.9	69	0
	Cullen Bryant, Los Angeles, NFC	16	459	28.7	90	1
1975	*Walter Payton, Chicago, NFC	14	444	31.7	70	0
	Harold Hart, Oakland, AFC	17	518	30.5	102	1
1974	Terry Metcalf, St. Louis, NFC	20	623	31.2	94	1
	Greg Pruitt, Cleveland, AFC	22	606	27.5	88	1
1973	Carl Garrett, Chicago, NFC	16	486	30.4	67	0
	*Wallace Francis, Buffalo, AFC	23	687	29.9	101	2
1972	Ron Smith, Chicago, NFC	30	924	30.8	94	1
	*Bruce Laird, Baltimore, AFC	29	843	29.1	73	0
1971	Travis Williams, Los Angeles, NFC	25	743	29.7	105	1
	Eugene (Mercury) Morris, Miami, AFC	15	423	28.2	94	1
1970	Jim Duncan, Baltimore, AFC	20	707	35.4	99	1
	Cecil Turner, Chicago, NFC	23	752	32.7	96	4
1969	Bobby Williams, Detroit, NFL	17	563	33.1	96	1
	*Bill Thompson, Denver, AFL	18	513	28.5	63	0
1968	Preston Pearson, Baltimore, NFL	15	527	35.1	102	2
	*George Atkinson, Oakland, AFL	32	802	25.1	60	0
1967	*Travis Williams, Green Bay, NFL	18	739	41.1	104	4
	*Zeke Moore, Houston, AFL	14	405	28.9	92	1
1966	Gale Sayers, Chicago, NFL	23	718	31.2	93	2
	*Goldie Sellers, Denver, AFL	19	541	28.5	100	2
1965	Tommy Watkins, Detroit, NFL	17	584	34.4	94	0
	Abner Haynes, Denver, AFL	34	901	26.5	60	0
1964	*Clarence Childs, N.Y. Giants, NFL	34	987	29.0	100	1
	Bo Roberson, Oakland, AFL	36	975	27.1	59	0
1963	Abe Woodson, San Francisco, NFL	29	935	32.2	103	3
	Bobby Jancik, Houston, AFL	45	1,317	29.3	53	0
1962	Abe Woodson, San Francisco, NFL	37	1,157	31.3	79	0
	*Bobby Jancik, Houston, AFL	24	826	30.3	61	0
1961	Dick Bass, Los Angeles, NFL	23	698	30.3	64	0
	*Dave Grayson, Dall. Texans, AFL	16	453	28.3	73	0
1960	*Tom Moore, Green Bay, NFL	12	397	33.1	84	0
	Ken Hall, Houston, AFL	19	594	31.3	104	1
1959	Abe Woodson, San Francisco	13	382	29.4	105	1
1958	Ollie Matson, Chi. Cardinals	14	497	35.5	101	2
1957	*Jon Arnett, Los Angeles	18	504	28.0	98	1
1956	*Tom Wilson, Los Angeles	15	477	31.8	103	1
1955	Al Carmichael, Green Bay	14	418	29.9	100	1
1954	Billy Reynolds, Cleveland	14	413	29.5	51	0
1953	Joe Arenas, San Francisco	16	551	34.4	82	0
1952	Lynn Chandnois, Pittsburgh	17	599	35.2	93	2
1951	Lynn Chandnois, Pittsburgh	12	390	32.5	55	0
1950	Verda (Vitamin T) Smith, Los Angeles	22	742	33.7	97	3
1949	*Don Doll, Detroit	21	536	25.5	56	0
1948	*Joe Scott, N.Y. Giants	20	569	28.5	99	1
1947	Eddie Saenz, Washington	29	797	27.5	94	2
1946	Abe Karnofsky, Boston	21	599	28.5	97	1
1945	Steve Van Buren, Philadelphia	13	373	28.7	98	1
1944	Bob Thurbon, Card.-Pitt.	12	291	24.3	55	0
1943	Ken Heineman, Brooklyn	16	444	27.8	69	0
1942	Marshall Goldberg, Chi. Cardinals	15	393	26.2	95	1
1941	Marshall Goldberg, Chi. Cardinals	12	290	24.2	41	0

First year in the league.

POINTS SCORED

Year	Team	Points
1985	San Diego, AFC	467
	Chicago, NFC	456
1984	Miami, AFC	513
	San Francisco, NFC	475
1983	Washington, NFC	541
	L.A. Raiders, AFC	442
1982	San Diego, AFC	288
	Dallas, NFC	226
	Green Bay, NFC	226
1981	San Diego, AFC	478
	Atlanta, NFC	426
1980	Dallas, NFC	454
	New England, AFC	441
1979	Pittsburgh, AFC	416
	Dallas, NFC	371
1978	Dallas, NFC	384
	Miami, AFC	372
1977	Oakland, AFC	351
	Dallas, NFC	345
1976	Baltimore, AFC	417
	Los Angeles, NFC	351
1975	Buffalo, AFC	420
	Minnesota, NFC	377
1974	Oakland, AFC	355
	Washington, NFC	320
1973	Los Angeles, NFC	388
	Denver, AFC	354
1972	Miami, AFC	385
	San Francisco, NFC	353
1971	Dallas, NFC	406
	Oakland, AFC	344
1970	San Francisco, NFC	352
	Baltimore, AFC	321
1969	Minnesota, NFL	379
	Oakland, AFL	377
1968	Oakland, AFL	453
	Dallas, NFL	431
1967	Oakland, AFL	468
	Los Angeles, NFL	398
1966	Kansas City, AFL	448
	Dallas, NFL	445
1965	San Francisco, NFL	421
	San Diego, AFL	340
1964	Baltimore, NFL	428
	Buffalo, AFL	400
1963	N.Y. Giants, NFL	448
	San Diego, AFL	399
1962	Green Bay, NFL	415
	Dall. Texans, AFL	389
1961	Houston, AFL	513
	Green Bay, NFL	391
1960	N.Y. Titans, AFL	382
	Cleveland, NFL	362
1959	Baltimore	374
1958	Baltimore	381
1957	Los Angeles	307
1956	Chi. Bears	363
1955	Cleveland	349
1954	Detroit	337
1953	San Francisco	372
1952	Los Angeles	349
1951	Los Angeles	392
1950	Los Angeles	466
1949	Philadelphia	364
1948	Chi. Cardinals	395
1947	Chi. Bears	363
1946	Chi. Bears	289
1945	Philadelphia	272
1944	Philadelphia	267
1943	Chi. Bears	303
1942	Chi. Bears	376
1941	Chi. Bears	396
1940	Washington	245
1939	Chi. Bears	298
1938	Green Bay	223
1937	Green Bay	220
1936	Green Bay	248
1935	Chi. Bears	192
1934	Chi. Bears	286
1933	N.Y. Giants	244
1932	Green Bay	152

TOTAL YARDS GAINED

Year	Team	Yards
1985	San Diego, AFC	6,535
	San Francisco, NFC	5,920
1984	Miami, AFC	6,936
	San Francisco, NFC	6,366

1983	San Diego, AFC	6,197
	Green Bay, NFC	6,172
1982	San Diego, AFC	4,048
	San Francisco, NFC	3,242
1981	San Diego, AFC	6,744
	Detroit, NFC	5,933
1980	San Diego, AFC	6,410
	Los Angeles, NFC	6,006
1979	Pittsburgh, AFC	6,258
	Dallas, NFC	5,968
1978	New England, AFC	5,965
	Dallas, NFC	5,959
1977	Dallas, NFC	4,812
	Oakland, AFC	4,736
1976	Baltimore, AFC	5,236
	St. Louis, NFC	5,136
1975	Buffalo, AFC	5,467
	Dallas, NFC	5,025
1974	Dallas, NFC	4,983
	Oakland, AFC	4,718
1973	Los Angeles, NFC	4,906
	Oakland, AFC	4,773
1972	Miami, AFC	5,036
	N.Y. Giants, NFC	4,483
1971	Dallas, NFC	5,035
	San Diego, AFC	4,738
1970	Oakland, AFC	4,829
	San Francisco, NFC	4,503
1969	Dallas, NFL	5,122
	Oakland, AFL	5,036
1968	Oakland, AFL	5,696
	Dallas, NFL	5,117
1967	N.Y. Jets, AFL	5,152
	Baltimore, NFL	5,008
1966	Dallas, NFL	5,145
	Kansas City, AFL	5,114
1965	San Francisco, NFL	5,270
	San Diego, AFL	5,188
1964	Buffalo, AFL	5,206
	Baltimore, NFL	4,779
1963	San Diego, AFL	5,153
	N.Y. Giants, NFL	5,024
1962	N.Y. Giants, NFL	5,005
	Houston, AFL	4,971
1961	Houston, AFL	6,288
	Philadelphia, NFL	5,112
1960	Houston, AFL	4,936
	Baltimore, NFL	4,245
1959	Baltimore	4,458
1958	Baltimore	4,539
1957	Los Angeles	4,143
1956	Chi. Bears	4,537
1955	Chi. Bears	4,316
1954	Los Angeles	5,187
1953	Philadelphia	4,811
1952	Cleveland	4,352
1951	Los Angeles	5,506
1950	Los Angeles	5,420
1949	Chi. Bears	4,873
1948	Chi. Cardinals	4,705
1947	Chi. Bears	5,053
1946	Los Angeles	3,793
1945	Washington	3,549
1944	Chi. Bears	3,239
1943	Chi. Bears	4,045
1942	Chi. Bears	3,900
1941	Chi. Bears	4,265
1940	Green Bay	3,400
1939	Chi. Bears	3,988
1938	Green Bay	3,037
1937	Green Bay	3,201
1936	Detroit	3,703
1935	Chi. Bears	3,454
1934	Chi. Bears	3,900
1933	N.Y. Giants	2,973
1932	Chi. Bears	2,755

YARDS RUSHING

Year	Team	Yards
1985	Chicago, NFC	2,761
	Indianapolis, AFC	2,439
1984	Chicago, NFC	2,974
	N.Y. Jets, AFC	2,189
1983	Chicago, NFC	2,727
	Baltimore, AFC	2,695
1982	Buffalo, AFC	1,371
	Dallas, NFC	1,313
1981	Detroit, NFC	2,795
	Kansas City, AFC	2,633
1980	Los Angeles, NFC	2,799
	Houston, AFC	2,635
1979	N.Y. Jets, AFC	2,646
	St. Louis, NFC	2,582
1978	New England, AFC	3,165
	Dallas, NFC	2,783
1977	Chicago, NFC	2,811
	Oakland, AFC	2,627
1976	Pittsburgh, AFC	2,971
	Los Angeles, NFC	2,528
1975	Buffalo, AFC	2,974
	Dallas, NFC	2,432
1974	Dallas, NFC	2,454
	Pittsburgh, AFC	2,417
1973	Buffalo, AFC	3,088
	Los Angeles, NFC	2,925
1972	Miami, AFC	2,960
	Chicago, NFC	2,360
1971	Miami, AFC	2,429
	Detroit, NFC	2,376
1970	Dallas, NFC	2,300
	Miami, AFC	2,082
1969	Dallas, NFL	2,276
	Kansas City, AFL	2,220
1968	Chicago, NFL	2,377
	Kansas City, AFL	2,227
1967	Cleveland, NFL	2,139
	Houston, AFL	2,122
1966	Kansas City, AFL	2,274
	Cleveland, NFL	2,166
1965	Cleveland, NFL	2,331
	San Diego, AFL	2,085
1964	Green Bay, NFL	2,276
	Buffalo, AFL	2,040
1963	Cleveland, NFL	2,639
	San Diego, AFL	2,203
1962	Buffalo, AFL	2,480
	Green Bay, NFL	2,460
1961	Green Bay, NFL	2,350
	Dall. Texans, AFL	2,189
1960	St. Louis, NFL	2,356
	Oakland, AFL	2,056
1959	Cleveland	2,149
1958	Cleveland	2,526
1957	Los Angeles	2,142
1956	Chi. Bears	2,468
1955	Chi. Bears	2,388
1954	San Francisco	2,498
1953	San Francisco	2,230
1952	San Francisco	1,905
1951	Chi. Bears	2,408
1950	N.Y. Giants	2,336
1949	Philadelphia	2,607
1948	Chi. Cardinals	2,560
1947	Los Angeles	2,171
1946	Green Bay	1,765
1945	Cleveland	1,714
1944	Philadelphia	1,661
1943	Phil-Pitt	1,730
1942	Chi. Bears	1,881
1941	Chi. Bears	2,263
1940	Chi. Bears	1,818
1939	Chi. Bears	2,043
1938	Detroit	1,893
1937	Detroit	2,074
1936	Detroit	2,885
1935	Chi. Bears	2,096
1934	Chi. Bears	2,847
1933	Boston	2,260
1932	Chi. Bears	1,770

YARDS PASSING

Leadership in this category has been based on net yards since 1952.

Year	Team	Yards
1985	San Diego, AFC	4,870
	Dallas, NFC	3,861
1984	Miami, AFC	5,018
	St. Louis, NFC	4,257
1983	San Diego, AFC	4,661
	Green Bay, NFC	4,365
1982	San Diego, AFC	2,927
	San Francisco, NFC	2,502
1981	San Diego, AFC	4,739
	Minnesota, NFC	4,333
1980	San Diego, AFC	4,531
	Minnesota, NFC	3,688
1979	San Diego, AFC	3,915
	San Francisco, NFC	3,641
1978	San Diego, AFC	3,375
	Minnesota, NFC	3,243
1977	Buffalo, AFC	2,530
	St. Louis, NFC	2,499
1976	Baltimore, AFC	2,933
	Minnesota, NFC	2,855
1975	Cincinnati, AFC	3,241
	Washington, NFC	2,917
1974	Washington, NFC	2,978
	Cincinnati, AFC	2,804
1973	Philadelphia, NFC	2,998
	Denver, AFC	2,519
1972	N.Y. Jets, AFC	2,777
	San Francisco, NFC	2,735
1971	San Diego, AFC	3,134
	Dallas, NFC	2,786
1970	San Francisco, NFC	2,923
	Oakland, AFC	2,865
1969	Oakland, AFL	3,271
	San Francisco, NFL	3,158
1968	San Diego, AFL	3,623
	Dallas, NFL	3,026
1967	N.Y. Jets, AFL	3,845
	Washington, NFL	3,730
1966	N.Y. Jets, AFL	3,464
	Dallas, NFL	3,023
1965	San Francisco, NFL	3,487
	San Diego, AFL	3,103
1964	Houston, AFL	3,527
	Chicago, NFL	2,841
1963	Baltimore, NFL	3,296
	Houston, AFL	3,222
1962	Denver, AFL	3,404
	Philadelphia, NFL	3,385
1961	Houston, AFL	4,392
	Philadelphia, NFL	3,605
1960	Houston, AFL	3,203
	Baltimore, NFL	2,956
1959	Baltimore	2,753
1958	Pittsburgh	2,752
1957	Baltimore	2,388
1956	Los Angeles	2,419
1955	Philadelphia	2,472
1954	Chi. Bears	3,104
1953	Philadelphia	3,089
1952	Cleveland	2,566
1951	Los Angeles	3,296
1950	Los Angeles	3,709
1949	Chi. Bears	3,055
1948	Washington	2,861
1947	Washington	3,336
1946	Los Angeles	2,080
1945	Chi. Bears	1,857
1944	Washington	2,021
1943	Chi. Bears	2,310
1942	Green Bay	2,407
1941	Chi. Bears	2,002
1940	Washington	1,887
1939	Chi. Bears	1,965
1938	Washington	1,536
1937	Green Bay	1,398
1936	Green Bay	1,629
1935	Green Bay	1,449
1934	Green Bay	1,165
1933	N.Y. Giants	1,348
1932	Chi. Bears	1,013

FEWEST POINTS ALLOWED

Year	Team	Points
1985	Chicago, NFC	198
	N.Y. Jets, AFC	264
1984	San Francisco, NFC	227
	Denver, AFC	241
1983	Miami, AFC	250
	Detroit, NFC	286
1982	Washington, NFC	128
	Miami, AFC	131
1981	Philadelphia, NFC	221
	Miami, AFC	275
1980	Philadelphia, NFC	222
	Houston, AFC	251
1979	Tampa Bay, NFC	237
	San Diego, AFC	246
1978	Pittsburgh, AFC	195
	Dallas, NFC	208
1977	Atlanta, NFC	129
	Denver, AFC	148
1976	Pittsburgh, AFC	138
	Minnesota, NFC	176
1975	Los Angeles, NFC	135
	Pittsburgh, AFC	162
1974	Los Angeles, NFC	181
	Pittsburgh, AFC	189
1973	Miami, AFC	150
	Minnesota, NFC	168
1972	Miami, AFC	171
	Washington, NFC	218
1971	Minnesota, NFC	139
	Baltimore, AFC	140
1970	Minnesota, NFC	143
	Miami, AFC	228
1969	Minnesota, NFL	133
	Kansas City, AFL	177
1968	Baltimore, NFL	144
	Kansas City, AFL	170
1967	Los Angeles, NFL	196
	Houston, AFL	199
1966	Green Bay, NFL	163
	Buffalo, AFL	255
1965	Green Bay, NFL	224
	Buffalo, AFL	226
1964	Baltimore, NFL	225
	Buffalo, AFL	242
1963	Chicago, NFL	144
	San Diego, AFL	255
1962	Green Bay, NFL	148
	Dall. Texans, AFL	233
1961	San Diego, AFL	219
	N.Y. Giants, NFL	220
1960	San Francisco, NFL	205
	Dall. Texans, AFL	253
1959	N.Y. Giants	170
1958	N.Y. Giants	183
1957	Cleveland	172
1956	Cleveland	177
1955	Cleveland	218
1954	Cleveland	162
1953	Cleveland	162
1952	Detroit	192
1951	Cleveland	152
1950	Philadelphia	141
1949	Philadelphia	134
1948	Chi. Bears	151
1947	Green Bay	210
1946	Pittsburgh	117
1945	Washington	121
1944	N.Y. Giants	75
1943	Washington	137
1942	Chi. Bears	84
1941	N.Y. Giants	114
1940	Brooklyn	120
1939	N.Y. Giants	85
1938	N.Y. Giants	79
1937	Chi. Bears	100
1936	Chi. Bears	94
1935	Green Bay	96
	N.Y. Giants	96
1934	Detroit	59
1933	Brooklyn	54
1932	Chi. Bears	44

FEWEST TOTAL YARDS ALLOWED

Year	Team	Yards
1985	Chicago, NFC	4,135
	L.A. Raiders, AFC	4,603
1984	Chicago, NFC	3,863
	Cleveland, AFC	4,641
1983	Cincinnati, AFC	4,327
	New Orleans, NFC	4,691
1982	Miami, AFC	2,312
	Tampa Bay, NFC	2,442
1981	Philadelphia, NFC	4,447
	N.Y. Jets, AFC	4,871
1980	Buffalo, AFC	4,101
	Philadelphia, NFC	4,443
1979	Tampa Bay, NFC	3,949
	Pittsburgh, AFC	4,270
1978	Los Angeles, NFC	3,893
	Pittsburgh, AFC	4,168
1977	Dallas, NFC	3,213
	New England, AFC	3,638
1976	Pittsburgh, AFC	3,323
	San Francisco, NFC	3,562
1975	Minnesota, NFC	3,153
	Oakland, AFC	3,629
1974	Pittsburgh, AFC	3,074
	Washington, NFC	3,285
1973	Los Angeles, NFC	2,951
	Oakland, AFC	3,160
1972	Miami, AFC	3,297
	Green Bay, NFC	3,474
1971	Baltimore, AFC	2,852
	Minnesota, NFC	3,406
1970	Minnesota, NFC	2,803
	N.Y. Jets, AFC	3,655
1969	Minnesota, NFL	2,720
	Kansas City, AFL	3,163
1968	Los Angeles, NFL	3,118
	N.Y. Jets, AFL	3,363
1967	Oakland, AFL	3,294
	Green Bay, NFL	3,300
1966	St. Louis, NFL	3,492
	Oakland, AFL	3,910
1965	San Diego, AFL	3,262
	Detroit, NFL	3,557
1964	Green Bay, NFL	3,179
	Buffalo, AFL	3,878
1963	Chicago, NFL	3,176
	Boston, AFL	3,834
1962	Detroit, NFL	3,217
	Dall. Texans, AFL	3,951
1961	San Diego, AFL	3,726
	Baltimore, NFL	3,782
1960	St. Louis, NFL	3,029
	Buffalo, AFL	3,866
1959	N.Y. Giants	2,843
1958	Chi. Bears	3,066
1957	Pittsburgh	2,791
1956	N.Y. Giants	3,081
1955	Cleveland	2,841
1954	Cleveland	2,658
1953	Philadelphia	2,998
1952	Cleveland	3,075
1951	N.Y. Giants	3,250
1950	Cleveland	3,154
1949	Philadelphia	2,831
1948	Chi. Bears	2,931
1947	Green Bay	3,396
1946	Washington	2,451
1945	Philadelphia	2,073
1944	Philadelphia	1,943
1943	Chi. Bears	2,262
1942	Chi. Bears	1,703
1941	N.Y. Giants	2,368
1940	N.Y. Giants	2,219
1939	Washington	2,116
1938	N.Y. Giants	2,029
1937	Washington	2,123
1936	Boston	2,181
1935	Boston	1,996
1934	Chi. Cardinals	1,539
1933	Brooklyn	1,789

FEWEST YARDS RUSHING ALLOWED

Year	Team	Yards
1985	Chicago, NFC	1,319
	N.Y. Jets, AFC	1,516
1984	Chicago, NFC	1,377
	Pittsburgh, AFC	1,617
1983	Washington, NFC	1,289
	Cincinnati, AFC	1,499
1982	Pittsburgh, AFC	762
	Detroit, NFC	854
1981	Detroit, NFC	1,623
	Kansas City, AFC	1,747
1980	Detroit, NFC	1,599
	Cincinnati, AFC	1,680
1979	Denver, AFC	1,693
	Tampa Bay, NFC	1,873
1978	Dallas, NFC	1,721
	Pittsburgh, AFC	1,774
1977	Denver, AFC	1,531
	Dallas, NFC	1,651
1976	Pittsburgh, AFC	1,457
	Los Angeles, NFC	1,564
1975	Minnesota, NFC	1,532
	Houston, AFC	1,680
1974	Los Angeles, NFC	1,302
	New England, AFC	1,587
1973	Los Angeles, NFC	1,270
	Oakland, AFC	1,470
1972	Dallas, NFC	1,515
	Miami, AFC	1,548
1971	Baltimore, AFC	1,113
	Dallas, NFC	1,144
1970	Detroit, NFC	1,152
	N.Y. Jets, AFC	1,283
1969	Dallas, NFL	1,050
	Kansas City, AFL	1,091
1968	Dallas, NFL	1,195
	N.Y. Jets, AFL	1,195
1967	Dallas, NFL	1,081
	Oakland, AFL	1,129
1966	Buffalo, AFL	1,051
	Dallas, NFL	1,176
1965	San Diego, AFL	1,094
	Los Angeles, NFL	1,409
1964	Buffalo, AFL	913
	Los Angeles, NFL	1,501
1963	Boston, AFL	1,107
	Chicago, NFL	1,442
1962	Detroit, NFL	1,231
	Dall. Texans, AFL	1,250
1961	Boston, AFL	1,041
	Pittsburgh, NFL	1,463
1960	St. Louis, NFL	1,212
	Dall. Texans, AFL	1,338
1959	N.Y. Giants	1,261
1958	Baltimore	1,291
1957	Baltimore	1,174
1956	N.Y. Giants	1,443
1955	Cleveland	1,189
1954	Cleveland	1,050
1953	Philadelphia	1,117
1952	Detroit	1,145
1951	N.Y. Giants	913
1950	Detroit	1,367
1949	Chi. Bears	1,196
1948	Philadelphia	1,209
1947	Philadelphia	1,329
1946	Chi. Bears	1,060
1945	Philadelphia	817
1944	Philadelphia	558
1943	Phil-Pitt	793
1942	Chi. Bears	519
1941	Washington	1,042
1940	N.Y. Giants	977
1939	Chi. Bears	812
1938	Detroit	1,081
1937	Chi. Bears	933
1936	Boston	1,148
1935	Boston	998
1934	Chi. Cardinals	954
1933	Brooklyn	964

FEWEST YARDS PASSING ALLOWED

Leadership in this category has been based on net yards since 1952.

Year	Team	Yards
1985	Washington, NFC	2,746
	Pittsburgh, AFC	2,783
1984	New Orleans, NFC	2,453
	Cleveland, AFC	2,696
1983	New Orleans, NFC	2,691
	Cincinnati, AFC	2,828
1982	Miami, AFC	1,027
	Tampa Bay, NFC	1,384
1981	Philadelphia, NFC	2,696
	Buffalo, AFC	2,870
1980	Washington, NFC	2,171
	Buffalo, AFC	2,282
1979	Tampa Bay, NFC	2,076
	Buffalo, AFC	2,530
1978	Buffalo, AFC	1,960
	Los Angeles, NFC	2,048
1977	Atlanta, NFC	1,384
	San Diego, AFC	1,725
1976	Minnesota, NFC	1,575
	Cincinnati, AFC	1,758
1975	Minnesota, NFC	1,621
	Cincinnati, AFC	1,729
1974	Pittsburgh, AFC	1,466
	Atlanta, NFC	1,572
1973	Miami, AFC	1,290
	Atlanta, NFC	1,430
1972	Minnesota, NFC	1,699
	Cleveland, AFC	1,736
1971	Atlanta, NFC	1,638
	Baltimore, AFC	1,739
1970	Minnesota, NFC	1,438
	Kansas City, AFC	2,010
1969	Minnesota, NFL	1,631
	Kansas City, AFL	2,072
1968	Houston, AFL	1,671
	Green Bay, NFL	1,796
1967	Green Bay, NFL	1,377
	Buffalo, AFL	1,825
1966	Green Bay, NFL	1,959
	Oakland, AFL	2,118
1965	Green Bay, NFL	1,981
	San Diego, AFL	2,168
1964	Green Bay, NFL	1,647
	San Diego, AFL	2,518
1963	Chicago, NFL	1,734
	Oakland, AFL	2,589
1962	Green Bay, NFL	1,746
	Oakland, AFL	2,306
1961	Baltimore, NFL	1,913
	San Diego, AFL	2,363
1960	Chicago, NFL	1,388
	Buffalo, AFL	2,124
1959	N.Y. Giants	1,582
1958	Chi. Bears	1,769
1957	Cleveland	1,300
1956	Cleveland	1,103
1955	Pittsburgh	1,295
1954	Cleveland	1,608
1953	Washington	1,751
1952	Washington	1,580
1951	Pittsburgh	1,687
1950	Cleveland	1,581
1949	Philadelphia	1,607
1948	Green Bay	1,626
1947	Green Bay	1,790
1946	Pittsburgh	939
1945	Washington	1,121
1944	Chi. Bears	1,052
1943	Chi. Bears	980
1942	Washington	1,093
1941	Pittsburgh	1,168
1940	Philadelphia	1,012
1939	Washington	1,116
1938	Chi. Bears	897
1937	Detroit	804
1936	Philadelphia	853
1935	Chi. Cardinals	793
1934	Philadelphia	545
1933	Portsmouth	558

SUPER BOWL RECORDS

Compiled by Elias Sports Bureau

1967: Super Bowl I
1968: Super Bowl II
1969: Super Bowl III
1970: Super Bowl IV
1971: Super Bowl V
1972: Super Bowl VI
1973: Super Bowl VII
1974: Super Bowl VIII
1975: Super Bowl IX
1976: Super Bowl X
1977: Super Bowl XI
1978: Super Bowl XII
1979: Super Bowl XIII
1980: Super Bowl XIV
1981: Super Bowl XV
1982: Super Bowl XVI
1983: Super Bowl XVII
1984: Super Bowl XVIII
1985: Super Bowl XIX
1986: Super Bowl XX

INDIVIDUAL RECORDS

SERVICE

Most Games
5 Marv Fleming, Green Bay, 1967-68; Miami, 1972-74
Larry Cole, Dallas, 1971-72, 1976, 1978-79
Cliff Harris, Dallas, 1971-72, 1976, 1978-79
D. D. Lewis, Dallas, 1971-72, 1976, 1978-79
Preston Pearson, Baltimore, 1969; Pittsburgh, 1975; Dallas, 1976, 1978-79
Charlie Waters, Dallas, 1971-72, 1976, 1978-79
Rayfield Wright, Dallas, 1971-72, 1976, 1978-79
4 By many players

Most Games, Winning Team
4 By many players

Most Games, Coach
6 Don Shula, Baltimore, 1969; Miami, 1972-74, 1983, 1985
5 Tom Landry, Dallas, 1971-72, 1976, 1978-79
4 Bud Grant, Minnesota, 1970, 1974-75, 1977
Chuck Noll, Pittsburgh, 1975-76, 1979-80

Most Games, Winning Team, Coach
4 Chuck Noll, Pittsburgh, 1975-76, 1979-80
2 Vince Lombardi, Green Bay, 1967-68
Tom Landry, Dallas, 1972, 1978
Don Shula, Miami, 1973-74
Tom Flores, Oakland, 1981; L.A. Raiders, 1984
Bill Walsh, San Francisco, 1982, 1985

Most Games, Losing Team, Coach
4 Bud Grant, Minnesota, 1970, 1974-75, 1977
Don Shula, Baltimore, 1969; Miami, 1972, 1983, 1985
3 Tom Landry, Dallas, 1971, 1976, 1979

SCORING

POINTS

Most Points, Career
24 Franco Harris, Pittsburgh, 4 games (4-td)
22 Ray Wersching, San Francisco, 2 games (7-pat, 5-fg)
20 Don Chandler, Green Bay, 2 games (8-pat, 4-fg)

Most Points, Game
18 Roger Craig, San Francisco vs. Miami, 1985 (3-td)
15 Don Chandler, Green Bay vs. Oakland, 1968 (3-pat, 4-fg)
14 Ray Wersching, San Francisco vs. Cincinnati, 1982 (2-pat, 4-fg)
Kevin Butler, Chicago vs. New England, 1986 (5-pat, 3-fg)

TOUCHDOWNS

Most Touchdowns, Career
4 Franco Harris, Pittsburgh, 4 games (4-r)
3 John Stallworth, Pittsburgh, 4 games (3-p)
Lynn Swann, Pittsburgh, 4 games (3-p)
Cliff Branch, Oakland-L.A. Raiders, 3 games (3-p)
Roger Craig, San Francisco, 1 game (1-r, 2-p)
2 By many players

Most Touchdowns, Game
3 Roger Craig, San Francisco vs. Miami, 1985 (1-r, 2-p)
2 Max McGee, Green Bay vs. Kansas City, 1967 (2-p)
Elijah Pitts, Green Bay vs. Kansas City, 1967 (2-r)
Bill Miller, Oakland vs. Green Bay, 1968 (2-p)
Larry Csonka, Miami vs. Minnesota, 1974 (2-r)
Pete Banaszak, Oakland vs. Minnesota, 1977 (2-r)
John Stallworth, Pittsburgh vs. Dallas, 1979 (2-p)
Franco Harris, Pittsburgh vs. Los Angeles, 1980 (2-r)
Cliff Branch, Oakland vs. Philadelphia, 1981 (2-p)
Dan Ross, Cincinnati vs. San Francisco, 1982 (2-p)
Marcus Allen, L.A. Raiders vs. Washington, 1984 (2-r)
Jim McMahon, Chicago vs. New England, 1986 (2-r)

POINTS AFTER TOUCHDOWN

Most Points After Touchdown, Career
8 Don Chandler, Green Bay, 2 games (8 att)
Roy Gerela, Pittsburgh, 3 games (9 att)
Chris Bahr, Oakland-L.A. Raiders, 2 games (8 att)
7 Ray Wersching, San Francisco, 2 games (7 att)
5 Garo Yepremian, Miami, 3 games (5 att)
Kevin Butler, Chicago, 1 game (5 att)

Most Points After Touchdown, Game
5 Don Chandler, Green Bay vs. Kansas City, 1967 (5 att)
Roy Gerela, Pittsburgh vs. Dallas, 1979 (5 att)
Chris Bahr, L.A. Raiders vs. Washington, 1984 (5 att)
Ray Wersching, San Francisco vs. Miami, 1985 (5 att)
Kevin Butler, Chicago vs. New England, 1986 (5 att)
4 Rafael Septien, Dallas vs. Pittsburgh, 1979 (4 att)
Matt Bahr, Pittsburgh vs. Los Angeles, 1980 (4 att)

FIELD GOALS

Field Goals Attempted, Career
7 Roy Gerela, Pittsburgh, 3 games
6 Jim Turner, N.Y. Jets-Denver, 2 games
5 Efren Herrera, Dallas, 1 game
Ray Wersching, San Francisco, 2 games

Most Field Goals Attempted, Game
5 Jim Turner, N.Y. Jets vs. Baltimore, 1969
Efren Herrera, Dallas vs. Denver, 1978
4 Don Chandler, Green Bay vs. Oakland, 1968
Roy Gerela, Pittsburgh vs. Dallas, 1976
Ray Wersching, San Francisco vs. Cincinnati, 1982

Most Field Goals, Career
5 Ray Wersching, San Francisco, 2 games (5 att)
4 Don Chandler, Green Bay, 2 games (4 att)
Jim Turner, N.Y. Jets-Denver, 2 games (6 att)
Uwe von Schamann, Miami, 2 games (4 att)
3 Mike Clark, Dallas, 2 games (3 att)
Jan Stenerud, Kansas City, 1 game (3 att)
Chris Bahr, Oakland-L.A. Raiders, 2 games (4 att)
Mark Moseley, Washington, 2 games (4 att)
Kevin Butler, Chicago, 1 game (3 att)

Most Field Goals, Game
4 Don Chandler, Green Bay vs. Oakland, 1968
Ray Wersching, San Francisco vs. Cincinnati, 1982
3 Jim Turner, N.Y. Jets vs. Baltimore, 1969
Jan Stenerud, Kansas City vs. Minnesota, 1970
Uwe von Schamann, Miami vs. San Francisco, 1985
Kevin Butler, Chicago vs. New England, 1986

Longest Field Goal
48 Jan Stenerud, Kansas City vs. Minnesota, 1970
47 Jim Turner, Denver vs. Dallas, 1978
46 Chris Bahr, Oakland vs. Philadelphia, 1981

SAFETIES

Most Safeties, Game
1 Dwight White, Pittsburgh vs. Minnesota, 1975
Reggie Harrison, Pittsburgh vs. Dallas, 1976
Henry Waechter, Chicago vs. New England, 1986

RUSHING

ATTEMPTS

Most Attempts, Career
101 Franco Harris, Pittsburgh, 4 games
64 John Riggins, Washington, 2 games
57 Larry Csonka, Miami, 3 games

Most Attempts, Game
38 John Riggins, Washington vs. Miami, 1983
34 Franco Harris, Pittsburgh vs. Minnesota, 1975
33 Larry Csonka, Miami vs. Minnesota, 1974

YARDS GAINED

Most Yards Gained, Career
354 Franco Harris, Pittsburgh, 4 games
297 Larry Csonka, Miami, 3 games
230 John Riggins, Washington, 2 games

Most Yards Gained, Game
191 Marcus Allen, L.A. Raiders vs. Washington, 1984
166 John Riggins, Washington vs. Miami, 1983
158 Franco Harris, Pittsburgh vs. Minnesota, 1975

Longest Run From Scrimmage
74 Marcus Allen, L.A. Raiders vs. Washington, 1984 (TD)
58 Tom Matte, Baltimore vs. N.Y. Jets, 1969
49 Larry Csonka, Miami vs. Washington, 1973

AVERAGE GAIN

Highest Average Gain, Career (20 attempts)
9.6 Marcus Allen, L.A. Raiders, 1 game (20-191)
5.3 Walt Garrison, Dallas, 2 games (26-139)
5.2 Tony Dorsett, Dallas, 2 games (31-162)

Highest Average Gain, Game (10 attempts)
10.5 Tom Matte, Baltimore vs. N.Y. Jets, 1969 (11-116)
9.6 Marcus Allen, L.A. Raiders vs. Washington, 1984 (20-191)
8.6 Clarence Davis, Oakland vs. Minnesota, 1977 (16-137)

TOUCHDOWNS

Most Touchdowns, Career
4 Franco Harris, Pittsburgh, 4 games
2 Elijah Pitts, Green Bay, 1 game
Jim Kiick, Miami, 3 games
Larry Csonka, Miami, 3 games
Pete Banaszak, Oakland, 2 games
Marcus Allen, L.A. Raiders, 1 game
John Riggins, Washington, 2 games
Jim McMahon, Chicago, 1 game

Most Touchdowns, Game
2 Elijah Pitts, Green Bay vs. Kansas City, 1967
Larry Csonka, Miami vs. Minnesota, 1974
Pete Banaszak, Oakland vs. Minnesota, 1977
Franco Harris, Pittsburgh vs. Los Angeles, 1980
Marcus Allen, L.A. Raiders vs. Washington, 1984
Jim McMahon, Chicago vs. New England, 1986

PASSING

ATTEMPTS

Most Passes Attempted, Career
98 Roger Staubach, Dallas, 4 games
89 Fran Tarkenton, Minnesota, 3 games
84 Terry Bradshaw, Pittsburgh, 4 games

Most Passes Attempted, Game
50 Dan Marino, Miami vs. San Francisco, 1985
38 Ron Jaworski, Philadelphia vs. Oakland, 1981
35 Fran Tarkenton, Minnesota vs. Oakland, 1977
Joe Theismann, Washington vs. L.A. Raiders, 1984
Joe Montana, San Francisco vs. Miami, 1985

COMPLETIONS
Most Passes Completed, Career
61 Roger Staubach, Dallas, 4 games
49 Terry Bradshaw, Pittsburgh, 4 games
46 Fran Tarkenton, Minnesota, 3 games
Most Passes Completed, Game
29 Dan Marino, Miami vs. San Francisco, 1985
25 Ken Anderson, Cincinnati vs. San Francisco, 1982
24 Joe Montana, San Francisco vs. Miami, 1985
Most Consecutive Completions, Game
8 Len Dawson, Kansas City vs. Green Bay, 1967
Joe Theismann, Washington vs. Miami, 1983

COMPLETION PERCENTAGE
Highest Completion Percentage, Career (40 attempts)
66.7 Joe Montana, San Francisco, 2 games (57-38)
63.6 Len Dawson, Kansas City, 2 games (44-28)
63.4 Bob Griese, Miami, 3 games (41-26)
Highest Completion Percentage, Game (20 attempts)
73.5 Ken Anderson, Cincinnati vs. San Francisco, 1982 (34-25)
69.6 Bart Starr, Green Bay vs. Kansas City, 1967 (23-16)
68.6 Joe Montana, San Francisco vs. Miami, 1985 (35-24)

YARDS GAINED
Most Yards Gained, Career
932 Terry Bradshaw, Pittsburgh, 4 games
734 Roger Staubach, Dallas, 4 games
489 Fran Tarkenton, Minnesota, 3 games
Most Yards Gained, Game
331 Joe Montana, San Francisco vs. Miami, 1985
318 Terry Bradshaw, Pittsburgh vs. Dallas, 1979
Dan Marino, Miami vs. San Francisco, 1985
309 Terry Bradshaw, Pittsburgh vs. Los Angeles, 1980
Longest Pass Completion
80 Jim Plunkett (to King), Oakland vs. Philadelphia, 1981 (TD)
76 David Woodley (to Cefalo), Miami vs. Washington, 1983 (TD)
75 Johnny Unitas (to Mackey), Baltimore vs. Dallas, 1971 (TD)
Terry Bradshaw (to Stallworth), Pittsburgh vs. Dallas, 1979 (TD)

AVERAGE GAIN
Highest Average Gain, Career (40 attempts)
11.10 Terry Bradshaw, Pittsburgh, 4 games (84-932)
9.62 Bart Starr, Green Bay, 2 games (47-452)
9.41 Jim Plunkett, Oakland-L.A. Raiders, 2 games (46-433)
Highest Average Gain, Game (20 attempts)
14.71 Terry Bradshaw, Pittsburgh vs. Los Angeles, 1980 (21-309)
12.80 Jim McMahon, Chicago vs. New England, 1986 (20-256)
12.43 Jim Plunkett, Oakland vs. Philadelphia, 1981 (21-261)

TOUCHDOWNS
Most Touchdown Passes, Career
9 Terry Bradshaw, Pittsburgh, 4 games
8 Roger Staubach, Dallas, 4 games
4 Jim Plunkett, Oakland-L.A. Raiders, 2 games
Joe Montana, San Francisco, 2 games
Most Touchdown Passes, Game
4 Terry Bradshaw, Pittsburgh vs. Dallas, 1979
3 Roger Staubach, Dallas vs. Pittsburgh, 1979
Jim Plunkett, Oakland vs. Philadelphia, 1981
Joe Montana, San Francisco vs. Miami, 1985
2 By many players

HAD INTERCEPTED
Lowest Percentage, Passes Had Intercepted, Career (40 attempts)
0.00 Jim Plunkett, Oakland-L.A. Raiders, 2 games (46-0)
Joe Montana, San Francisco, 2 games (57-0)
2.13 Bart Starr, Green Bay, 2 games (47-1)
4.08 Roger Staubach, Dallas, 4 games (98-4)
Most Attempts, Without Interception, Game
35 Joe Montana, San Francisco vs. Miami, 1985
28 Joe Namath, N.Y. Jets vs. Baltimore, 1969
25 Roger Staubach, Dallas vs. Denver, 1978
Jim Plunkett, L.A. Raiders vs. Washington, 1984
Most Passes Had Intercepted, Career
7 Craig Morton, Dallas-Denver, 2 games
6 Fran Tarkenton, Minnesota, 3 games
4 Earl Morrall, Baltimore-Miami, 4 games
Roger Staubach, Dallas, 4 games
Terry Bradshaw, Pittsburgh, 4 games
Joe Theismann, Washington, 2 games
Most Passes Had Intercepted, Game
4 Craig Morton, Denver vs. Dallas, 1978
3 By seven players

PASS RECEIVING

RECEPTIONS
Most Receptions, Career
16 Lynn Swann, Pittsburgh, 4 games
15 Chuck Foreman, Minnesota, 3 games
14 Cliff Branch, Oakland-L.A. Raiders, 3 games
Most Receptions, Game
11 Dan Ross, Cincinnati vs. San Francisco, 1982
10 Tony Nathan, Miami vs. San Francisco, 1985
8 George Sauer, N.Y. Jets vs. Baltimore, 1969

YARDS GAINED
Most Yards Gained, Career
364 Lynn Swann, Pittsburgh, 4 games
268 John Stallworth, Pittsburgh, 4 games
181 Cliff Branch, Oakland-L.A. Raiders, 3 games
Most Yards Gained, Game
161 Lynn Swann, Pittsburgh vs. Dallas, 1976
138 Max McGee, Green Bay vs. Kansas City, 1967
133 George Sauer, N.Y. Jets vs. Baltimore, 1969
Longest Reception
80 Kenny King (from Plunkett), Oakland vs. Philadelphia, 1981 (TD)
76 Jimmy Cefalo (from Woodley), Miami vs. Washington, 1983 (TD)
75 John Mackey (from Unitas), Baltimore vs. Dallas, 1971 (TD)
John Stallworth (from Bradshaw), Pittsburgh vs. Dallas, 1979 (TD)

AVERAGE GAIN
Highest Average Gain, Career (8 receptions)
24.4 John Stallworth, Pittsburgh, 4 games (11-268)
22.8 Lynn Swann, Pittsburgh, 4 games (16-364)
17.0 Charlie Brown, Washington, 2 games (9-153)
Highest Average Gain, Game (3 receptions)
40.33 John Stallworth, Pittsburgh vs. Los Angeles, 1980 (3-121)
40.25 Lynn Swann, Pittsburgh vs. Dallas, 1979 (4-161)
38.33 John Stallworth, Pittsburgh vs. Dallas, 1979 (3-115)

TOUCHDOWNS
Most Touchdowns, Career
3 John Stallworth, Pittsburgh, 4 games
Lynn Swann, Pittsburgh, 4 games
Cliff Branch, Oakland-L.A. Raiders, 3 games
2 Max McGee, Green Bay, 2 games
Bill Miller, Oakland, 1 game
Butch Johnson, Dallas, 2 games
Dan Ross, Cincinnati, 1 game
Roger Craig, San Francisco, 1 game
Most Touchdowns, Game
2 Max McGee, Green Bay vs. Kansas City, 1967
Bill Miller, Oakland vs. Green Bay, 1968
John Stallworth, Pittsburgh vs. Dallas, 1979
Cliff Branch, Oakland vs. Philadelphia, 1981
Dan Ross, Cincinnati vs. San Francisco, 1982
Roger Craig, San Francisco vs. Miami, 1985

INTERCEPTIONS BY
Most Interceptions By, Career
3 Chuck Howley, Dallas, 2 games
Rod Martin, Oakland-L.A. Raiders, 2 games
2 Randy Beverly, N.Y. Jets, 1 game
Jake Scott, Miami, 3 games
Mike Wagner, Pittsburgh, 3 games
Mel Blount, Pittsburgh, 4 games
Eric Wright, San Francisco, 2 games
Most Interceptions By, Game
3 Rod Martin, Oakland vs. Philadelphia, 1981
2 Randy Beverly, N.Y. Jets vs. Baltimore, 1969
Chuck Howley, Dallas vs. Baltimore, 1971
Jake Scott, Miami vs. Washington, 1973

YARDS GAINED
Most Yards Gained, Career
75 Willie Brown, Oakland, 2 games
63 Chuck Howley, Dallas, 2 games
Jake Scott, Miami, 3 games
60 Herb Adderley, Green Bay-Dallas, 4 games
Most Yards Gained, Game
75 Willie Brown, Oakland vs. Minnesota, 1977
63 Jake Scott, Miami vs. Washington, 1973
60 Herb Adderley, Green Bay vs. Oakland, 1968
Longest Return
75 Willie Brown, Oakland vs. Minnesota, 1977 (TD)
60 Herb Adderley, Green Bay vs. Oakland, 1968 (TD)
55 Jake Scott, Miami vs. Washington, 1973

TOUCHDOWNS
Most Touchdowns, Game
1 Herb Adderley, Green Bay vs. Oakland, 1968
Willie Brown, Oakland vs. Minnesota, 1977
Jack Squirek, L.A. Raiders vs. Washington, 1984
Reggie Phillips, Chicago vs. New England, 1986

PUNTING
Most Punts, Career
17 Mike Eischeid, Oakland-Minnesota, 3 games
15 Larry Seiple, Miami, 3 games
14 Ron Widby, Dallas, 2 games
Ray Guy, Oakland-L.A. Raiders, 3 games
Most Punts, Game
9 Ron Widby, Dallas vs. Baltimore, 1971
7 By seven players
Longest Punt
62 Rich Camarillo, New England vs. Chicago, 1986
61 Jerrel Wilson, Kansas City vs. Green Bay, 1967
59 Jerrel Wilson, Kansas City vs. Minnesota, 1970
Bobby Walden, Pittsburgh vs. Dallas, 1976
Ken Clark, Los Angeles vs. Pittsburgh, 1980

AVERAGE YARDAGE
Highest Average, Punting, Career (10 punts)
46.5 Jerrel Wilson, Kansas City, 2 games (11-511)
41.9 Ray Guy, Oakland-L.A. Raiders, 3 games (14-587)
41.3 Larry Seiple, Miami, 3 games (15-620)
Highest Average, Punting, Game (4 punts)
48.5 Jerrel Wilson, Kansas City vs. Minnesota, 1970 (4-194)
46.3 Jim Miller, San Francisco vs. Cincinnati, 1982 (4-185)
45.3 Jerrel Wilson, Kansas City vs. Green Bay, 1967 (7-317)

PUNT RETURNS
Most Punt Returns, Career
6 Willie Wood, Green Bay, 2 games

Jake Scott, Miami, 3 games
Theo Bell, Pittsburgh, 2 games
Mike Nelms, Washington, 1 game
5 Dana McLemore, San Francisco, 1 game
4 By seven players

Most Punt Returns, Game
6 Mike Nelms, Washington vs. Miami, 1983
5 Willie Wood, Green Bay vs. Oakland, 1968
Dana McLemore, San Francisco vs. Miami, 1985
4 By six players

Most Fair Catches, Game
3 Ron Gardin, Baltimore vs. Dallas, 1971
Golden Richards, Dallas vs. Pittsburgh, 1976
Greg Pruitt, L.A. Raiders vs. Washington, 1984

YARDS GAINED

Most Yards Gained, Career
52 Mike Nelms, Washington, 1 game
51 Dana McLemore, San Francisco, 1 game
45 Jake Scott, Miami, 3 games

Most Yards Gained, Game
52 Mike Nelms, Washington vs. Miami, 1983
51 Dana McLemore, San Francisco vs. Miami, 1985
43 Neal Colzie, Oakland vs. Minnesota, 1977

Longest Return
34 Darrell Green, Washington vs. L.A. Raiders, 1984
31 Willie Wood, Green Bay vs. Oakland, 1968
28 Dana McLemore, San Francisco vs. Miami, 1985

AVERAGE YARDAGE

Highest Average, Career (4 returns)
10.8 Neal Colzie, Oakland, 1 game (4-43)
10.2 Dana McLemore, San Francisco, 1 game (5-51)
8.8 Mike Fuller, Cincinnati, 1 game (4-35)

Highest Average, Game (3 returns)
11.3 Lynn Swann, Pittsburgh vs. Minnesota, 1975 (3-34)
10.8 Neal Colzie, Oakland vs. Minnesota, 1977 (4-43)
10.2 Dana McLemore, San Francisco vs. Miami, 1985 (5-51)

TOUCHDOWNS

Most Touchdowns, Game
None

KICKOFF RETURNS

Most Kickoff Returns, Career
8 Larry Anderson, Pittsburgh, 2 games
Fulton Walker, Miami, 2 games
7 Preston Pearson, Baltimore-Pittsburgh-Dallas, 5 games
Stephen Starring, New England, 1 game
6 Eugene (Mercury) Morris, Miami, 3 games

Most Kickoff Returns, Game
7 Stephen Starring, New England vs. Chicago, 1986
5 Larry Anderson, Pittsburgh vs. Los Angeles, 1980
Billy Campfield, Philadelphia vs. Oakland, 1981
David Verser, Cincinnati vs. San Francisco, 1982
Alvin Garrett, Washington vs. L.A. Raiders, 1984

YARDS GAINED

Most Yards Gained, Career
283 Fulton Walker, Miami, 2 games
207 Larry Anderson, Pittsburgh, 2 games
153 Stephen Starring, New England, 1 game

Most Yards Gained, Game
190 Fulton Walker, Miami vs. Washington, 1983
162 Larry Anderson, Pittsburgh vs. Los Angeles, 1980
153 Stephen Starring, New England vs. Chicago, 1986

Longest Return
98 Fulton Walker, Miami vs. Washington, 1983 (TD)
67 Rick Upchurch, Denver vs. Dallas, 1978
48 Thomas Henderson, Dallas vs. Pittsburgh, 1976 (lateral)

AVERAGE YARDAGE

Highest Average, Career (4 returns)
35.4 Fulton Walker, Miami, 2 games (8-283)
25.9 Larry Anderson, Pittsburgh, 2 games (8-207)
22.5 Jim Duncan, Baltimore, 1 game (4-90)

Highest Average, Game (3 returns)
47.5 Fulton Walker, Miami vs. Washington, 1983 (4-190)
32.4 Larry Anderson, Pittsburgh vs. Los Angeles, 1980 (5-162)
31.3 Rick Upchurch, Denver vs. Dallas, 1978 (3-94)

TOUCHDOWNS

Most Touchdowns, Game
1 Fulton Walker, Miami vs. Washington, 1983

FUMBLES

Most Fumbles, Career
5 Roger Staubach, Dallas, 4 games
3 Franco Harris, Pittsburgh, 4 games
Terry Bradshaw, Pittsburgh, 4 games
2 By five players

Most Fumbles, Game
3 Roger Staubach, Dallas vs. Pittsburgh, 1976
2 Franco Harris, Pittsburgh vs. Minnesota, 1975
Butch Johnson, Dallas vs. Denver, 1978
Terry Bradshaw, Pittsburgh vs. Dallas, 1979

RECOVERIES

Most Fumbles Recovered, Career
2 Jake Scott, Miami, 3 games (1 own, 1 opp)
Fran Tarkenton, Minnesota, 3 games (2 own)
Franco Harris, Pittsburgh, 4 games (2 own)
Roger Staubach, Dallas, 4 games (2 own)
Bobby Walden, Pittsburgh, 2 games (2 own)
John Fitzgerald, Dallas, 4 games (2 own)
Randy Hughes, Dallas, 3 games (2 opp)
Butch Johnson, Dallas, 2 games (2 own)
Mike Singletary, Chicago, 1 game (2 opp)

Most Fumbles Recovered, Game
2 Jake Scott, Miami vs. Minnesota, 1974 (1 own, 1 opp)
Roger Staubach, Dallas vs. Pittsburgh, 1976 (2 own)
Randy Hughes, Dallas vs. Denver, 1978 (2 opp)
Butch Johnson, Dallas vs. Denver, 1978 (2 own)
Mike Singletary, Chicago vs. New England, 1986 (2 opp)

YARDS GAINED

Most Yards Gained, Game
49 Mike Bass, Washington vs. Miami, 1973 (opp)
37 Mike Hegman, Dallas vs. Pittsburgh, 1979 (opp)
21 Randy Hughes, Dallas vs. Denver, 1978 (opp)

Longest Return
49 Mike Bass, Washington vs. Miami, 1973 (TD)
37 Mike Hegman, Dallas vs. Pittsburgh, 1979 (TD)
19 Randy Hughes, Dallas vs. Denver, 1978

TOUCHDOWNS

Most Touchdowns, Game
1 Mike Bass, Washington vs. Miami, 1973 (opp 49 yds)
Mike Hegman, Dallas vs. Pittsburgh, 1979 (opp 37 yds)

COMBINED NET YARDS GAINED

ATTEMPTS

Most Attempts, Career
108 Franco Harris, Pittsburgh, 4 games
66 John Riggins, Washington, 2 games
60 Larry Csonka, Miami, 3 games

Most Attempts, Game
39 John Riggins, Washington vs. Miami, 1983
35 Franco Harris, Pittsburgh vs. Minnesota, 1975
34 Matt Snell, N.Y. Jets vs. Baltimore, 1969

YARDS GAINED

Most Yards Gained, Career
468 Franco Harris, Pittsburgh, 4 games
391 Lynn Swann, Pittsburgh, 4 games
314 Larry Csonka, Miami, 3 games

Most Yards Gained, Game
209 Marcus Allen, L.A. Raiders vs. Washington, 1984
192 Stephen Starring, New England vs. Chicago, 1986
190 Fulton Walker, Miami vs. Washington, 1983

TEAM RECORDS

GAMES, VICTORIES, DEFEATS

Most Games
5 Dallas, 1971-72, 1976, 1978-79
Miami, 1972-74, 1983, 1985
4 Minnesota, 1970, 1974-75, 1977
Pittsburgh, 1975-76, 1979-80
Oakland/L.A. Raiders, 1968, 1977, 1981, 1984
3 Washington, 1973, 1983-84

Most Consecutive Games
3 Miami, 1972-74
2 Green Bay, 1967-68
Dallas, 1971-72
Minnesota, 1974-75
Pittsburgh, 1975-76, 1979-80
Washington, 1983-84

Most Games Won
4 Pittsburgh, 1975-76, 1979-80
3 Oakland/L.A. Raiders, 1977, 1981, 1984
2 Green Bay, 1967-68
Miami, 1973-74
Dallas, 1972, 1978
San Francisco, 1982, 1985

Most Consecutive Games Won
2 Green Bay, 1967-68
Miami, 1973-74
Pittsburgh, 1975-76, 1979-80

Most Games Lost
4 Minnesota, 1970, 1974-75, 1977
3 Dallas, 1971, 1976, 1979
Miami, 1972, 1983, 1985
2 Washington, 1973, 1984

Most Consecutive Games Lost
2 Minnesota, 1974-75

SCORING

Most Points, Game
46 Chicago vs. New England, 1986
38 L.A. Raiders vs. Washington, 1984
San Francisco vs. Miami, 1985
35 Green Bay vs. Kansas City, 1967
Pittsburgh vs. Dallas, 1979

Fewest Points, Game
3 Miami vs. Dallas, 1972
6 Minnesota vs. Pittsburgh, 1975
7 By four teams

Most Points, Both Teams, Game
66 Pittsburgh (35) vs. Dallas (31), 1979
56 Chicago (46) vs. New England (10), 1986
54 San Francisco (38) vs. Miami (16), 1985

Fewest Points, Both Teams, Game
21 Washington (7) vs. Miami (14), 1973

22 Minnesota (6) vs. Pittsburgh (16), 1975
23 Baltimore (7) vs. N.Y. Jets (16), 1969

Largest Margin of Victory, Game

36 Chicago vs. New England, 1986 (46-10)
29 L.A. Raiders vs. Washington, 1984 (38-9)
25 Green Bay vs. Kansas City, 1967 (35-10)

Most Points, Each Half

1st: 28 San Francisco vs. Miami, 1985
2nd: 23 Chicago vs. New England, 1986

Most Points, Each Quarter

1st: 14 Miami vs. Minnesota, 1974
Oakland vs. Philadelphia, 1981
2nd: 21 San Francisco vs. Miami, 1985
3rd: 21 Chicago vs. New England, 1986
4th: 14 Pittsburgh vs. Dallas, 1976; vs. Dallas, 1979; vs. Los Angeles, 1980
Dallas vs. Pittsburgh, 1979
Cincinnati vs. San Francisco, 1982
Washington vs. Miami, 1983

Most Points, Both Teams, Each Half

1st: 44 San Francisco (28) vs. Miami (16), 1985
2nd: 31 Dallas (17) vs. Pittsburgh (14), 1979

Fewest Points, Both Teams, Each Half

1st: 2 Minnesota (0) vs. Pittsburgh (2), 1975
2nd: 7 Miami (0) vs. Washington (7), 1973

Most Points, Both Teams, Each Quarter

1st: 17 Miami (10) vs. San Francisco (7), 1985
2nd: 27 San Francisco (21) vs. Miami (6), 1985
3rd: 21 Chicago (21) vs. New England (0), 1986
4th: 28 Dallas (14) vs. Pittsburgh (14), 1979

TOUCHDOWNS

Most Touchdowns, Game

5 Green Bay vs. Kansas City, 1967
Pittsburgh vs. Dallas, 1979
L.A. Raiders vs. Washington, 1984
San Francisco vs. Miami, 1985
Chicago vs. New England, 1986
4 Oakland vs. Minnesota, 1977
Dallas vs. Pittsburgh, 1979
Pittsburgh vs. Los Angeles, 1980
3 By many teams

Fewest Touchdowns, Game

0 Miami vs. Dallas, 1972
1 By 13 teams

Most Touchdowns, Both Teams, Game

9 Pittsburgh (5) vs. Dallas (4), 1979
6 Green Bay (5) vs. Kansas City (1), 1967
Oakland (4) vs. Minnesota (2), 1977
Pittsburgh (4) vs. Los Angeles (2), 1980
L.A. Raiders (5) vs. Washington (1), 1984
San Francisco (5) vs. Miami (1), 1985
Chicago (5) vs. New England (1), 1986

Fewest Touchdowns, Both Teams, Game

2 Baltimore (1) vs. N.Y. Jets (1), 1969
3 In five games

POINTS AFTER TOUCHDOWN

Most Points After Touchdown, Game

5 Green Bay vs. Kansas City, 1967
Pittsburgh vs. Dallas, 1979
L.A. Raiders vs. Washington, 1984
San Francisco vs. Miami, 1985
Chicago vs. New England, 1986
4 Dallas vs. Pittsburgh, 1979
Pittsburgh vs. Los Angeles, 1980

Most Points After Touchdown, Both Teams, Game

9 Pittsburgh (5) vs. Dallas (4), 1979
6 Green Bay (5) vs. Kansas City (1), 1967
San Francisco (5) vs. Miami (1), 1985
Chicago (5) vs. New England (1), 1986

Fewest Points After Touchdown, Both Teams, Game

2 Baltimore (1) vs. N.Y. Jets (1), 1969
Baltimore (1) vs. Dallas (1), 1971
Minnesota (0) vs. Pittsburgh (2), 1975

FIELD GOALS

Most Field Goals Attempted, Game

5 N.Y. Jets vs. Baltimore, 1969
Dallas vs. Denver, 1978
4 Green Bay vs. Oakland, 1968
Pittsburgh vs. Dallas, 1976
San Francisco vs. Cincinnati, 1982

Most Field Goals Attempted, Both Teams, Game

7 N.Y. Jets (5) vs. Baltimore (2), 1969
6 Dallas (5) vs. Denver (1), 1978
5 Green Bay (4) vs. Oakland (1), 1968
Pittsburgh (4) vs. Dallas (1), 1976
Oakland (3) vs. Philadelphia (2), 1981

Fewest Field Goals Attempted, Both Teams, Game

1 Minnesota (0) vs. Miami (1), 1974
2 Green Bay (0) vs. Kansas City (2), 1967
Miami (1) vs. Washington (1), 1973
Dallas (1) vs. Pittsburgh (1), 1979

Most Field Goals, Game

4 Green Bay vs. Oakland, 1968
San Francisco vs. Cincinnati, 1982
3 N.Y. Jets vs. Baltimore, 1969
Kansas City vs. Minnesota, 1970
Miami vs. San Francisco, 1985
Chicago vs. New England, 1986

Most Field Goals, Both Teams, Game

4 Green Bay (4) vs. Oakland (0), 1968
San Francisco (4) vs. Cincinnati (0), 1982
Miami (3) vs. San Francisco (1), 1985
Chicago (3) vs. New England (1), 1986
3 In seven games

Fewest Field Goals, Both Teams, Game

0 Miami vs. Washington, 1973
Pittsburgh vs. Minnesota, 1975
1 Green Bay (0) vs. Kansas City (1), 1967
Minnesota (0) vs. Miami (1), 1974
Pittsburgh (0) vs. Dallas (1), 1979

SAFETIES

Most Safeties, Game

1 Pittsburgh vs. Minnesota, 1975 vs. Dallas, 1976
Chicago vs. New England, 1986

FIRST DOWNS

Most First Downs, Game

31 San Francisco vs. Miami, 1985
24 Cincinnati vs. San Francisco, 1982
Washington vs. Miami, 1983
23 Dallas vs. Miami, 1972

Fewest First Downs, Game

9 Minnesota vs. Pittsburgh, 1975
Miami vs. Washington, 1983
10 Dallas vs. Baltimore, 1971
Miami vs. Dallas, 1972
11 Denver vs. Dallas, 1978

Most First Downs, Both Teams, Game

50 San Francisco (31) vs. Miami (19), 1985
44 Cincinnati (24) vs. San Francisco (20), 1982
41 Oakland (21) vs. Minnesota (20), 1977

Fewest First Downs, Both Teams, Game

24 Dallas (10) vs. Baltimore (14), 1971
26 Minnesota (9) vs. Pittsburgh (17), 1975
27 Pittsburgh (13) vs. Dallas (14), 1976

RUSHING

Most First Downs, Rushing, Game

16 San Francisco vs. Miami, 1985
15 Dallas vs. Miami, 1972
14 Washington vs. Miami, 1983

Fewest First Downs, Rushing, Game

1 New England vs. Chicago, 1986
2 Minnesota vs. Kansas City, 1970; vs. Pittsburgh, 1975; vs. Oakland, 1977
Pittsburgh vs. Dallas, 1979
Miami vs. San Francisco, 1985
3 Miami vs. Dallas, 1972
Philadelphia vs. Oakland, 1981

Most First Downs, Rushing, Both Teams, Game

21 Washington (14) vs. Miami (7), 1983
18 Dallas (15) vs. Miami (3), 1972
Miami (13) vs. Minnesota (5), 1974
San Francisco (16) vs. Miami (2), 1985
17 N.Y. Jets (10) vs. Baltimore (7), 1969

Fewest First Downs, Rushing, Both Teams, Game

8 Baltimore (4) vs. Dallas (4), 1971
Pittsburgh (2) vs. Dallas (6), 1979
9 Philadelphia (3) vs. Oakland (6), 1981
10 Minnesota (2) vs. Kansas City (8), 1970

PASSING

Most First Downs, Passing, Game

17 Miami vs. San Francisco, 1985
15 Minnesota vs. Oakland, 1977
Pittsburgh vs. Dallas, 1979
San Francisco vs. Miami, 1985
14 Philadelphia vs. Oakland, 1981

Fewest First Downs, Passing, Game

1 Denver vs. Dallas, 1978
2 Miami vs. Washington, 1983
4 Miami vs. Minnesota, 1974

Most First Downs, Passing, Both Teams, Game

32 Miami (17) vs. San Francisco (15), 1985
28 Pittsburgh (15) vs. Dallas (13), 1979
24 Philadelphia (14) vs. Oakland (10), 1981

Fewest First Downs, Passing, Both Teams, Game

9 Denver (1) vs. Dallas (8), 1978
10 Minnesota (5) vs. Pittsburgh (5), 1975
11 Dallas (5) vs. Baltimore (6), 1971
Miami (2) vs. Washington (9), 1983

PENALTY

Most First Downs, Penalty, Game

4 Baltimore vs. Dallas, 1971
Miami vs. Minnesota, 1974
Cincinnati vs. San Francisco, 1982
3 Kansas City vs. Minnesota, 1970
Minnesota vs. Oakland, 1977

Most First Downs, Penalty, Both Teams, Game

6 Cincinnati (4) vs. San Francisco (2), 1982
5 Baltimore (4) vs. Dallas (1), 1971
Miami (4) vs. Minnesota (1), 1974
4 Kansas City (3) vs. Minnesota (1), 1970

Fewest First Downs, Penalty, Both Teams, Game

0 Dallas vs. Miami, 1972
Miami vs. Washington, 1973
Dallas vs. Pittsburgh, 1976
Miami vs. San Francisco, 1985
1 Green Bay (0) vs. Kansas City (1), 1967
Miami (0) vs. Washington (1), 1983

NET YARDS GAINED RUSHING AND PASSING

Most Yards Gained, Game
537 San Francisco vs. Miami, 1985
429 Oakland vs. Minnesota, 1977
408 Chicago vs. New England, 1986
Fewest Yards Gained, Game
119 Minnesota vs. Pittsburgh, 1975
123 New England vs. Chicago, 1986
156 Denver vs. Dallas, 1978
Most Yards Gained, Both Teams, Game
851 San Francisco (537) vs. Miami (314), 1985
782 Oakland (429) vs. Minnesota (353), 1977
737 Oakland (377) vs. Philadelphia (360), 1981
Fewest Yards Gained, Both Teams, Game
452 Minnesota (119) vs. Pittsburgh (333), 1975
481 Washington (228) vs. Miami (253), 1973
Denver (156) vs. Dallas (325), 1978
497 Minnesota (238) vs. Miami (259), 1974

RUSHING

ATTEMPTS
Most Attempts, Game
57 Pittsburgh vs. Minnesota, 1975
53 Miami vs. Minnesota, 1974
52 Oakland vs. Minnesota, 1977
Washington vs. Miami, 1983
Fewest Attempts, Game
9 Miami vs. San Francisco, 1985
11 New England vs. Chicago, 1986
19 Kansas City vs. Green Bay, 1967
Minnesota vs. Kansas City, 1970
Most Attempts, Both Teams, Game
81 Washington (52) vs. Miami (29), 1983
78 Pittsburgh (57) vs. Minnesota (21), 1975
Oakland (52) vs. Minnesota (26), 1977
77 Miami (53) vs. Minnesota (24), 1974
Pittsburgh (46) vs. Dallas (31), 1976
Fewest Attempts, Both Teams, Game
49 Miami (9) vs. San Francisco (40), 1985
52 Kansas City (19) vs. Green Bay (33), 1967
56 Pittsburgh (24) vs. Dallas (32), 1979

YARDS GAINED
Most Yards Gained, Game
276 Washington vs. Miami, 1983
266 Oakland vs. Minnesota, 1977
252 Dallas vs. Miami, 1972
Fewest Yards Gained, Game
7 New England vs. Chicago, 1986
17 Minnesota vs. Pittsburgh, 1975
25 Miami vs. San Francisco, 1985
Most Yards Gained, Both Teams, Game
372 Washington (276) vs. Miami (96), 1983
337 Oakland (266) vs. Minnesota (71), 1977
332 Dallas (252) vs. Miami (80), 1972
Fewest Yards Gained, Both Teams, Game
171 Baltimore (69) vs. Dallas (102), 1971
174 New England (7) vs. Chicago (167), 1986
186 Philadelphia (69) vs. Oakland (117), 1981

AVERAGE GAIN
Highest Average Gain, Game
7.00 L.A. Raiders vs. Washington, 1984 (33-231)
6.22 Baltimore vs. N.Y. Jets, 1969 (23-143)
5.35 Oakland vs. Green Bay, 1968 (20-107)
Lowest Average Gain, Game
0.64 New England vs. Chicago, 1986 (11-7)
0.81 Minnesota vs. Pittsburgh, 1975 (21-17)
2.23 Baltimore vs. Dallas, 1971 (31-69)

TOUCHDOWNS
Most Touchdowns, Game
4 Chicago vs. New England, 1986
3 Green Bay vs. Kansas City, 1967
Miami vs. Minnesota, 1974
2 Oakland vs. Minnesota, 1977
Pittsburgh vs. Los Angeles, 1980
L.A. Raiders vs. Washington, 1984
San Francisco vs. Miami, 1985
Fewest Touchdowns, Game
0 By 14 teams
Most Touchdowns, Both Teams, Game
4 Miami (3) vs. Minnesota (1), 1974
Chicago (4) vs. New England (0), 1986
3 Green Bay (3) vs. Kansas City (0), 1967
Pittsburgh (2) vs. Los Angeles (1), 1980
L.A. Raiders (2) vs. Washington (1), 1984
Fewest Touchdowns, Both Teams, Game
0 Pittsburgh vs. Dallas, 1976
Oakland vs. Philadelphia, 1981
1 In seven games

PASSING

ATTEMPTS
Most Passes Attempted, Game
50 Miami vs. San Francisco, 1985
44 Minnesota vs. Oakland, 1977
41 Baltimore vs. N.Y. Jets, 1969
Fewest Passes Attempted, Game
7 Miami vs. Minnesota, 1974
11 Miami vs. Washington, 1973
14 Pittsburgh vs. Minnesota, 1975
Most Passes Attempted, Both Teams, Game
85 Miami (50) vs. San Francisco (35), 1985
70 Baltimore (41) vs. N.Y. Jets (29), 1969
63 Minnesota (44) vs. Oakland (19), 1977
Fewest Passes Attempted, Both Teams, Game
35 Miami (7) vs. Minnesota (28), 1974
39 Miami (11) vs. Washington (28), 1973
40 Pittsburgh (14) vs. Minnesota (26), 1975
Miami (17) vs. Washington (23), 1983

COMPLETIONS
Most Passes Completed, Game
29 Miami vs. San Francisco, 1985
25 Cincinnati vs. San Francisco, 1982
24 Minnesota vs. Oakland, 1977
San Francisco vs. Miami, 1985
Fewest Passes Completed, Game
4 Miami vs. Washington, 1983
6 Miami vs. Minnesota, 1974
8 Miami vs. Washington, 1973
Denver vs. Dallas, 1978
Most Passes Completed, Both Teams, Game
53 Miami (29) vs. San Francisco (24), 1985
39 Cincinnati (25) vs. San Francisco (14), 1982
36 Minnesota (24) vs. Oakland (12), 1977
Fewest Passes Completed, Both Teams, Game
19 Miami (4) vs. Washington (15), 1983
20 Pittsburgh (9) vs. Minnesota (11), 1975
22 Miami (8) vs. Washington (14), 1973

COMPLETION PERCENTAGE
Highest Completion Percentage, Game (20 attempts)
73.5 Cincinnati vs. San Francisco, 1982 (34-25)
68.6 San Francisco vs. Miami, 1985 (35-24)
67.9 Dallas vs. Denver, 1978 (28-19)
Lowest Completion Percentage, Game (20 attempts)
32.0 Denver vs. Dallas, 1978 (25-8)
41.5 Baltimore vs. N.Y. Jets, 1969 (41-17)
42.3 Minnesota vs. Pittsburgh, 1975 (26-11)

YARDS GAINED
Most Yards Gained, Game
326 San Francisco vs. Miami, 1985
309 Pittsburgh vs. Los Angeles, 1980
291 Pittsburgh vs. Dallas, 1979
Philadelphia vs. Oakland, 1981
Fewest Yards Gained, Game
35 Denver vs. Dallas, 1978
63 Miami vs. Minnesota, 1974
69 Miami vs. Washington, 1973
Most Yards Gained, Both Teams, Game
615 San Francisco (326) vs. Miami (289), 1985
551 Philadelphia (291) vs. Oakland (260), 1981
503 Pittsburgh (309) vs. Los Angeles (194), 1980
Fewest Yards Gained, Both Teams, Game
156 Miami (69) vs. Washington (87), 1973
186 Pittsburgh (84) vs. Minnesota (102), 1975
205 Dallas (100) vs. Miami (105), 1972

TIMES SACKED
Most Times Sacked, Game
7 Dallas vs. Pittsburgh, 1976
New England vs. Chicago, 1986
6 Kansas City vs. Green Bay, 1967
Washington vs. L.A. Raiders, 1984
5 Dallas vs. Denver, 1978; vs. Pittsburgh, 1979
Cincinnati vs. San Francisco, 1982
Fewest Times Sacked, Game
0 Baltimore vs. N.Y. Jets, 1969; vs. Dallas, 1971
Minnesota vs. Pittsburgh, 1975
Pittsburgh vs. Los Angeles, 1980
Philadelphia vs. Oakland, 1981
1 By seven teams
Most Times Sacked, Both Teams, Game
10 New England (7) vs. Chicago (3), 1986
9 Kansas City (6) vs. Green Bay (3), 1967
Dallas (7) vs. Pittsburgh (2), 1976
Dallas (5) vs. Denver (4), 1978
Dallas (5) vs. Pittsburgh (4), 1979
8 Washington (6) vs. L.A. Raiders (2), 1984
Fewest Times Sacked, Both Teams, Game
1 Philadelphia (0) vs. Oakland (1), 1981
2 Baltimore (0) vs. N.Y. Jets (2), 1969
Baltimore (0) vs. Dallas (2), 1971
Minnesota (0) vs. Pittsburgh (2), 1975
3 In three games

TOUCHDOWNS
Most Touchdowns, Game
4 Pittsburgh vs. Dallas, 1979
3 Dallas vs. Pittsburgh, 1979
Oakland vs. Philadelphia, 1981
San Francisco vs. Miami, 1985
2 By 10 teams
Fewest Touchdowns, Game
0 By 11 teams
Most Touchdowns, Both Teams, Game
7 Pittsburgh (4) vs. Dallas (3), 1979
4 Dallas (2) vs. Pittsburgh (2), 1976
Oakland (3) vs. Philadelphia (1), 1981
San Francisco (3) vs. Miami (1), 1985
3 In six games

Fewest Touchdowns, Both Teams, Game
0 N.Y. Jets vs. Baltimore, 1969
Miami vs. Minnesota, 1974
1 In five games

INTERCEPTIONS BY

Most Interceptions By, Game
4 N.Y. Jets vs. Baltimore, 1969
Dallas vs. Denver, 1978
3 By eight teams
Most Interceptions By, Both Teams, Game
6 Baltimore (3) vs. Dallas (3), 1971
4 In five games

YARDS GAINED

Most Yards Gained, Game
95 Miami vs. Washington, 1973
91 Oakland vs. Minnesota, 1977
89 Pittsburgh vs. Dallas, 1976
Most Yards Gained, Both Teams, Game
95 Miami (95) vs. Washington (0), 1973
91 Oakland (91) vs. Minnesota (0), 1977
89 Pittsburgh (89) vs. Dallas (0), 1976

TOUCHDOWNS

Most Touchdowns, Game
1 Green Bay vs. Oakland, 1968
Oakland vs. Minnesota, 1977
L.A. Raiders vs. Washington, 1984
Chicago vs. New England, 1986

PUNTING

Most Punts, Game
9 Dallas vs. Baltimore, 1971
8 Washington vs. L.A. Raiders, 1984
7 By six teams
Fewest Punts, Game
2 Pittsburgh vs. Los Angeles, 1980
3 By eight teams
Most Punts, Both Teams, Game
15 Washington (8) vs. L.A. Raiders (7), 1984
13 Dallas (9) vs. Baltimore (4), 1971
Pittsburgh (7) vs. Minnesota (6), 1975
12 In three games
Fewest Punts, Both Teams, Game
6 Oakland (3) vs. Philadelphia (3), 1981
7 In four games

AVERAGE YARDAGE

Highest Average, Game (4 punts)
48.50 Kansas City vs. Minnesota, 1970 (4-194)
46.25 San Francisco vs. Cincinnati, 1982 (4-185)
45.29 Kansas City vs. Green Bay, 1967 (7-317)
Lowest Average, Game (4 punts)
31.20 Washington vs. Miami, 1973 (5-156)
32.38 Washington vs. L.A. Raiders, 1984 (8-259)
32.40 Oakland vs. Minnesota, 1977 (5-162)

PUNT RETURNS

Most Punt Returns, Game
6 Washington vs. Miami, 1983
5 By five teams
Fewest Punt Returns, Game
0 Minnesota vs. Miami, 1974
1 By eight teams
Most Punt Returns, Both Teams, Game
9 Pittsburgh (5) vs. Minnesota (4), 1975
8 Green Bay (5) vs. Oakland (3), 1968
Baltimore (5) vs. Dallas (3), 1971
Washington (6) vs. Miami (2), 1983
7 Green Bay (4) vs. Kansas City (3), 1967
Oakland (4) vs. Minnesota (3), 1977
San Francisco (5) vs. Miami (2), 1985
Fewest Punt Returns, Both Teams, Game
2 Dallas (1) vs. Miami (1), 1972
3 Kansas City (1) vs. Minnesota (2), 1970
Minnesota (0) vs. Miami (3), 1974
4 L.A. Raiders (2) vs. Washington (2), 1984
Chicago (2) vs. New England (2), 1986

YARDS GAINED

Most Yards Gained, Game
52 Washington vs. Miami, 1983
51 San Francisco vs. Miami, 1985
43 Oakland vs. Minnesota, 1977
Fewest Yards Gained, Game
1 Dallas vs. Miami, 1972
0 By four teams
Most Yards Gained, Both Teams, Game
74 Washington (52) vs. Miami (22), 1983
66 San Francisco (51) vs. Miami (15), 1985
60 Dallas (33) vs. Pittsburgh (27), 1979
Fewest Yards Gained, Both Teams, Game
13 Miami (4) vs. Washington (9), 1973
18 Kansas City (0) vs. Minnesota (18), 1970
20 Dallas (−1) vs. Miami (21), 1972
Minnesota (0) vs. Miami (20), 1974

AVERAGE RETURN

Highest Average, Game (3 returns)
10.8 Oakland vs. Minnesota, 1977 (4-43)
10.2 San Francisco vs. Miami, 1985 (5-51)
8.8 Cincinnati vs. San Francisco, 1982 (4-35)

TOUCHDOWNS

Most Touchdowns, Game
None

KICKOFF RETURNS

Most Kickoff Returns, Game
7 Oakland vs. Green Bay, 1968
Minnesota vs. Oakland, 1977
Cincinnati vs. San Francisco, 1982
Washington vs. L.A. Raiders, 1984
Miami vs. San Francisco, 1985
New England vs. Chicago, 1986
6 By six teams
Fewest Kickoff Returns, Game
1 N.Y. Jets vs. Baltimore, 1969
L.A. Raiders vs. Washington, 1984
2 By six teams
Most Kickoff Returns, Both Teams, Game
11 Los Angeles (6) vs. Pittsburgh (5), 1980
Miami (7) vs. San Francisco (4), 1985
New England (7) vs. Chicago (4), 1986
10 Oakland (7) vs. Green Bay (3), 1968
9 In seven games
Fewest Kickoff Returns, Both Teams, Game
5 N.Y. Jets (1) vs. Baltimore (4), 1969
Miami (2) vs. Washington (3), 1973
6 In three games

YARDS GAINED

Most Yards Gained, Game
222 Miami vs. Washington, 1983
173 Denver vs. Dallas, 1978
162 Pittsburgh vs. Los Angeles, 1980
Fewest Yards Gained, Game
17 L.A. Raiders vs. Washington, 1984
25 N.Y. Jets vs. Baltimore, 1969
32 Pittsburgh vs. Minnesota, 1975
Most Yards Gained, Both Teams, Game
279 Miami (222) vs. Washington (57), 1983
231 Pittsburgh (162) vs. Los Angeles (79), 1980
224 Denver (173) vs. Dallas (51), 1978
Fewest Yards Gained, Both Teams, Game
78 Miami (33) vs. Washington (45), 1973
82 Pittsburgh (32) vs. Minnesota (50), 1975
92 San Francisco (40) vs. Cincinnati (52), 1982

AVERAGE GAIN

Highest Average, Game (3 returns)
37.0 Miami vs. Washington, 1983 (6-222)
32.4 Pittsburgh vs. Los Angeles, 1980 (5-162)
28.8 Denver vs. Dallas, 1978 (6-173)

TOUCHDOWNS

Most Touchdowns, Game
1 Miami vs. Washington, 1983

PENALTIES

Most Penalties, Game
12 Dallas vs. Denver, 1978
10 Dallas vs. Baltimore, 1971
9 Dallas vs. Pittsburgh, 1979
Fewest Penalties, Game
0 Miami vs. Dallas, 1972
Pittsburgh vs. Dallas, 1976
1 Green Bay vs. Oakland, 1968
Miami vs. Minnesota, 1974; vs. San Francisco, 1985
2 By four teams
Most Penalties, Both Teams, Game
20 Dallas (12) vs. Denver (8), 1978
16 Cincinnati (8) vs. San Francisco (8), 1982
14 Dallas (10) vs. Baltimore (4), 1971
Dallas (9) vs. Pittsburgh (5), 1979
Fewest Penalties, Both Teams, Game
2 Pittsburgh (0) vs. Dallas (2), 1976
3 Miami (0) vs. Dallas (3), 1972
Miami (1) vs. San Francisco (2), 1985
5 Green Bay (1) vs. Oakland (4), 1968

YARDS PENALIZED

Most Yards Penalized, Game
133 Dallas vs. Baltimore, 1971
122 Pittsburgh vs. Minnesota, 1975
94 Dallas vs. Denver, 1978
Fewest Yards Penalized, Game
0 Miami vs. Dallas, 1972
Pittsburgh vs. Dallas, 1976
4 Miami vs. Minnesota, 1974
10 Miami vs. San Francisco, 1985
San Francisco vs. Miami, 1985
Most Yards Penalized, Both Teams, Game
164 Dallas (133) vs. Baltimore (31), 1971
154 Dallas (94) vs. Denver (60), 1978
140 Pittsburgh (122) vs. Minnesota (18), 1975
Fewest Yards Penalized, Both Teams, Game
15 Miami (0) vs. Dallas (15), 1972
20 Pittsburgh (0) vs. Dallas (20), 1976
Miami (10) vs. San Francisco (10), 1985
43 Green Bay (12) vs. Oakland (31), 1968

FUMBLES

Most Fumbles, Game

6 Dallas vs. Denver, 1978
5 Baltimore vs. Dallas, 1971
4 In four games

Fewest Fumbles, Game

0 In six games

Most Fumbles, Both Teams, Game

10 Dallas (6) vs. Denver (4), 1978
8 Dallas (4) vs. Pittsburgh (4), 1976
7 Pittsburgh (4) vs. Minnesota (3), 1975
New England (4) vs. Chicago (3), 1986

Fewest Fumbles, Both Teams, Game

0 Los Angeles vs. Pittsburgh, 1980
1 Oakland (0) vs. Minnesota (1), 1977
Oakland (0) vs. Philadelphia (1), 1981
2 In three games

Most Fumbles Lost, Game

4 Baltimore vs. Dallas, 1971
Denver vs. Dallas, 1978
New England vs. Chicago, 1986
2 In many games

Most Fumbles Recovered, Game

8 Dallas vs. Denver, 1978 (4 own, 4 opp)
5 Chicago vs. New England, 1986 (1 own, 4 opp)
4 Pittsburgh vs. Minnesota, 1975 (2 own, 2 opp)
Dallas vs. Pittsburgh, 1976 (4 own)

TURNOVERS

(Number of times losing the ball on interceptions and fumbles.)

Most Turnovers, Game

8 Denver vs. Dallas, 1978
7 Baltimore vs. Dallas, 1971
6 New England vs. Chicago, 1986

Fewest Turnovers, Game

0 Green Bay vs. Oakland, 1968
Miami vs. Minnesota, 1974
Pittsburgh vs. Dallas, 1976
Oakland vs. Minnesota, 1977; vs. Philadelphia, 1981
1 By many teams

Most Turnovers, Both Teams, Game

11 Baltimore (7) vs. Dallas (4), 1971
10 Denver (8) vs. Dallas (2), 1978
8 New England (6) vs. Chicago (2), 1986

Fewest Turnovers, Both Teams, Game

2 Green Bay (1) vs. Kansas City (1), 1967
Miami (0) vs. Minnesota (2), 1974
3 Green Bay (0) vs. Oakland (3), 1968
Pittsburgh (0) vs. Dallas (3), 1976
Oakland (0) vs. Minnesota (3), 1977
4 In five games

POSTSEASON GAME RECORDS

Compiled by Elias Sports Bureau

Throughout this all-time postseason record section, the following abbreviations are used to indicate various levels of postseason games:

SB — Super Bowl (1966 to date)
AFC — AFC Championship Game (1970 to date) or AFL Championship Game (1960-69)
NFC — NFC Championship Game (1970 to date) or NFL Championship Game (1933-69)
AFC-D — AFC Divisional Playoff Game (1970 to date), AFC Second-Round Playoff Game (1982), AFL Inter-Divisional Playoff Game (1969), or special playoff game to break tie for AFL Division Championship (1963, 1968)
NFC-D — NFC Divisional Playoff Game (1970 to date), NFC Second-Round Playoff Game (1982), NFL Conference Championship Game (1967-69), or special playoff game to break tie for NFL Division or Conference Championship (1941, 1943, 1947, 1950, 1952, 1957, 1958, 1965)
AFC-FR — AFC First-Round Playoff Game (1978 to date)
NFC-FR — NFC First-Round Playoff Game (1978 to date)

Year references are to the season following which the postseason game occurred, even if the game was played in the next calendar year.

POSTSEASON GAME COMPOSITE STANDINGS

	W	L	Pct.	Pts.	OP
Green Bay Packers	13	5	.722	416	259
Pittsburgh Steelers	15	8	.652	533	447
Kansas City Chiefs**	5	3	.625	144	147
Los Angeles Raiders*	19	12	.613	761	535
Detroit Lions	6	4	.600	221	208
San Francisco 49ers	9	6	.600	331	288
Seattle Seahawks	3	2	.600	95	95
Miami Dolphins	14	10	.583	535	468
Philadelphia Eagles	7	5	.583	219	173
Chicago Bears	11	8	.579	444	348
Dallas Cowboys	20	16	.556	805	640
Baltimore Colts	8	7	.533	264	262
Houston Oilers	6	6	.500	168	267
New York Jets	4	4	.500	151	145
Washington Redskins***	11	11	.500	443	449
Minnesota Vikings	10	12	.455	378	427
New England Patriots††	4	5	.444	178	236
Los Angeles Rams****	11	17	.393	434	600
Buffalo Bills	3	5	.375	138	171
Cleveland Browns	7	14	.333	375	457
San Diego Chargers†	4	8	.333	230	279
New York Giants	7	16	.304	325	462
Cincinnati Bengals	2	5	.286	137	180
Denver Broncos	2	5	.286	105	166
Atlanta Falcons	1	3	.250	85	100
Tampa Bay Buccaneers	1	3	.250	41	94
St. Louis Cardinals†††	1	4	.200	81	134

**24 games played when franchise was in Oakland. (Won 15, lost 9, 587 points scored, 435 points allowed)*
***One game played when franchise was in Dallas (Texans). (Won 20-17)*
****One game played when franchise was in Boston. (Lost 21-6)*
*****One game played when franchise was in Cleveland. (Won 15-14)*
†One game played when franchise was in Los Angeles. (Lost 24-16)
††Two games played when franchise was in Boston. (Won 26-8, lost 51-10)
†††Two games played when franchise was in Chicago. (Won 28-21, lost 7-0)

INDIVIDUAL RECORDS

SERVICE

Most Games, Career
27 D. D. Lewis, Dallas (SB-5, NFC-9, NFC-D 12, NFC-FR 1)
26 Larry Cole, Dallas (SB-5, NFC-8, NFC-D-12, NFC-FR 1)
25 Charlie Waters, Dallas (SB-5, NFC-9, NFC-D 10, NFC-FR 1)

SCORING

POINTS
Most Points, Career
115 George Blanda, Chi. Bears-Houston-Oakland, 19 games (49-pat, 22-fg)
102 Franco Harris, Pittsburgh, 19 games (17-td)
95 Rafael Septien, L.A. Rams-Dallas, 15 games (41-pat, 18-fg)
Most Points, Game
19 Pat Harder, NFC-D: Detroit vs. Los Angeles, 1952 (2-td, 4-pat, 1-fg)
Paul Hornung, NFC: Green Bay vs. N.Y. Giants, 1961 (1-td, 4-pat, 3-fg)
18 By 15 players

TOUCHDOWNS
Most Touchdowns, Career
17 Franco Harris, Pittsburgh, 19 games (16-r, 1-p)
12 John Riggins, Washington, 9 games (12-r)
John Stallworth, Pittsburgh, 18 games (12-p)
10 Fred Biletnikoff, Oakland, 19 games (10-p)
Larry Csonka, Miami, 12 games (9-r, 1-p)
Tony Dorsett, Dallas, 17 games (9-r, 1-p)
Marcus Allen, L.A. Raiders, 7 games (8-r, 2-p)
Most Touchdowns, Game
3 Andy Farkas, NFC-D: Washington vs. N.Y. Giants, 1943 (3-r)
Tom Fears, NFC-D: Los Angeles vs. Chi. Bears, 1950 (3-p)
Otto Graham, NFC: Cleveland vs. Detroit, 1954 (3-r)
Gary Collins, NFC: Cleveland vs. Baltimore, 1964 (3-p)
Craig Baynham, NFC-D: Dallas vs. Cleveland, 1967 (2-r, 1-p)
Fred Biletnikoff, AFC-D: Oakland vs. Kansas City, 1968 (3-p)
Tom Matte, NFC: Baltimore vs. Cleveland, 1968 (3-r)
Larry Schreiber, NFC-D: San Francisco vs. Dallas, 1972 (3-r)
Larry Csonka, AFC: Miami vs. Oakland, 1973 (3-r)
Franco Harris, AFC-D: Pittsburgh vs. Buffalo, 1974 (3-r)
Preston Pearson, NFC: Dallas vs. Los Angeles, 1975 (3-p)
Dave Casper, AFC-D: Oakland vs. Baltimore, 1977 (OT) (3-p)
Alvin Garrett, NFC-FR: Washington vs. Detroit, 1982 (3-p)
John Riggins, NFC-D: Washington vs. L.A. Rams, 1983 (3-r)
Roger Craig, SB: San Francisco vs. Miami, 1984 (1-r, 2-p)
Most Consecutive Games Scoring Touchdowns
8 John Stallworth, Pittsburgh, 1978-83
7 John Riggins, Washington, 1982-84 (current)
Marcus Allen, L.A. Raiders, 1982-85 (current)
5 Duane Thomas, Dallas, 1970-71
Franco Harris, Pittsburgh, 1974-75
Franco Harris, Pittsburgh, 1977-79

POINTS AFTER TOUCHDOWN
Most Points After Touchdown, Career
49 George Blanda, Chi. Bears-Houston-Oakland, 19 games (49 att)
41 Rafael Septien, L.A. Rams-Dallas, 15 games (41 att)
38 Fred Cox, Minnesota, 18 games (40 att)
Most Points After Touchdown, Game
8 Lou Groza, NFC: Cleveland vs. Detroit, 1954 (8 att)
Jim Martin, NFC: Detroit vs. Cleveland, 1957 (8 att)
George Blanda, AFC-D: Oakland vs. Houston, 1969 (8 att)
7 Danny Villanueva, NFC-D: Dallas vs. Cleveland, 1967 (7 att)
6 George Blair, AFC: San Diego vs. Boston, 1963 (6 att)
Mark Moseley, NFC-D: Washington vs. L.A. Rams, 1983 (6 att)
Uwe von Schamann, AFC: Miami vs. Pittsburgh, 1984 (6 att)
Most Points After Touchdown, No Misses, Career
49 George Blanda, Chi. Bears-Houston-Oakland, 19 games
41 Rafael Septien, L.A. Rams-Dallas, 14 games
33 Chris Bahr, Oakland-L.A. Raiders, 11 games

FIELD GOALS
Most Field Goals Attempted, Career
39 George Blanda, Chi. Bears-Houston-Oakland, 19 games
27 Roy Gerela, Houston-Pittsburgh, 15 games
25 Toni Fritsch, Dallas-Houston, 14 games
Most Field Goals Attempted, Game
6 George Blanda, AFC: Oakland vs. Houston, 1967
David Ray, NFC-D: Los Angeles vs. Dallas, 1973
5 Jerry Kramer, NFC: Green Bay vs. N.Y. Giants, 1962
Gino Cappelletti, AFC-D: Boston vs. Buffalo, 1963
Pete Gogolak, AFC: Buffalo vs. San Diego, 1965
Jan Stenerud, AFC-D: Kansas City vs. N.Y. Jets, 1969
George Blanda, AFC-D: Oakland vs. Pittsburgh, 1973
Ed Murray, NFC-D: Detroit vs. San Francisco, 1983
Mark Moseley, NFC: Washington vs. San Francisco, 1983
Tony Franklin, AFC-FR: New England vs. N.Y. Jets, 1985
4 By many players
Most Field Goals, Career
22 George Blanda, Chi. Bears-Houston-Oakland, 19 games
20 Toni Fritsch, Dallas-Houston, 14 games
18 Rafael Septien, L.A. Rams-Dallas, 15 games
Most Field Goals, Game
4 Gino Cappelletti, AFC-D: Boston vs. Buffalo, 1963
George Blanda, AFC: Oakland vs. Houston, 1967
Don Chandler, SB: Green Bay vs. Oakland, 1967
Curt Knight, NFC: Washington vs. Dallas, 1972
George Blanda, AFC-D: Oakland vs. Pittsburgh, 1973
Ray Wersching, SB: San Francisco vs. Cincinnati, 1981
Tony Franklin, AFC-FR: New England vs. N.Y. Jets, 1985
3 By many players
Most Consecutive Field Goals
15 Rafael Septien, Dallas, 1978-82
Longest Field Goal
54 Ed Murray, NFC-D: Detroit vs. San Francisco, 1983
52 Lou Groza, NFC: Cleveland vs. Los Angeles, 1951
Curt Knight, NFC-D: Washington vs. Minnesota, 1973
Matt Bahr, AFC-FR: Cleveland vs. L.A. Raiders, 1982
51 Fuad Reveiz, AFC-D: Miami vs. Cleveland, 1985
Highest Field Goal Percentage, Career (10 field goals)
85.7 Rafael Septien, L.A. Rams-Dallas, 15 games (21-18)
80.0 Toni Fritsch, Dallas-Houston, 14 games (25-20)
78.9 Chris Bahr, Oakland-L.A. Raiders, 11 games (19-15)

SAFETIES
Most Safeties, Game
1 Bill Willis, NFC-D: Cleveland vs. N.Y. Giants, 1950
Carl Eller, NFC-D: Minnesota vs. Los Angeles, 1969
George Andrie, NFC-D: Dallas vs. Detroit, 1970
Alan Page, NFC-D: Minnesota vs. Dallas, 1971
Dwight White, SB: Pittsburgh vs. Minnesota, 1974
Reggie Harrison, SB: Pittsburgh vs. Dallas, 1975
Jim Jensen, NFC-D: Dallas vs. Los Angeles, 1976
Ted Washington, AFC: Houston vs. Pittsburgh, 1978
Randy White, NFC-D: Dallas vs. Los Angeles, 1979
Henry Waechter, SB: Chicago vs. New England, 1985

RUSHING

ATTEMPTS
Most Attempts, Career
400 Franco Harris, Pittsburgh, 19 games
302 Tony Dorsett, Dallas, 17 games
251 John Riggins, Washington, 9 games

Most Attempts, Game
38 Ricky Bell, NFC-D: Tampa Bay vs. Philadelphia, 1979
John Riggins, SB: Washington vs. Miami, 1982
37 Lawrence McCutcheon, NFC-D: Los Angeles vs. St. Louis, 1975
John Riggins, NFC-D: Washington vs. Minnesota, 1982
36 John Riggins, NFC: Washington vs. Dallas, 1982
John Riggins, NFC: Washington vs. San Francisco, 1983

YARDS GAINED
Most Yards Gained, Career
1,556 Franco Harris, Pittsburgh, 19 games
1,383 Tony Dorsett, Dallas, 17 games
996 John Riggins, Washington, 9 games
Most Yards Gained, Game
248 Eric Dickerson, NFC-D: L.A. Rams vs. Dallas, 1985
206 Keith Lincoln, AFC: San Diego vs. Boston, 1963
202 Lawrence McCutcheon, NFC-D: Los Angeles vs. St. Louis, 1975
Freeman McNeil, AFC-FR: N.Y. Jets vs. Cincinnati, 1982
Most Games, 100 or More Yards Rushing, Career
6 John Riggins, Washington, 9 games
5 Franco Harris, Pittsburgh, 19 games
4 Larry Csonka, Miami, 12 games
Chuck Foreman, Minnesota, 13 games
Marcus Allen, L.A. Raiders, 7 games
Most Consecutive Games, 100 or More Yards Rushing
6 John Riggins, Washington, 1982-83
3 Larry Csonka, Miami, 1973-74
Franco Harris, Pittsburgh, 1974-75
Marcus Allen, L.A. Raiders, 1983
Longest Run From Scrimmage
74 Marcus Allen, SB: L.A. Raiders vs. Washington, 1983 (TD)
71 Hugh McElhenny, NFC-D: San Francisco vs. Detroit, 1957
James Lofton, NFC-D: Green Bay vs. Dallas, 1982 (TD)
70 Elmer Angsman, NFC: Chi. Cardinals vs. Philadelphia, 1947 (twice, 2 TDs)

AVERAGE GAIN
Highest Average Gain, Career (50 attempts)
6.67 Paul Lowe, L.A. Chargers-San Diego, 5 games (57-380)
5.86 Marcus Allen, L.A. Raiders, 7 games (129-756)
5.68 Roger Staubach, Dallas, 20 games (76-432)
Highest Average Gain, Game (10 attempts)
15.90 Elmer Angsman, NFC: Chi. Cardinals vs. Philadelphia, 1947 (10-159)
15.85 Keith Lincoln, AFC: San Diego vs. Boston, 1963 (13-206)
10.90 Bill Osmanski, NFC: Chi. Bears vs. Washington, 1940 (10-109)

TOUCHDOWNS
Most Touchdowns, Career
16 Franco Harris, Pittsburgh, 19 games
12 John Riggins, Washington, 9 games
9 Larry Csonka, Miami, 12 games
Tony Dorsett, Dallas, 17 games
Most Touchdowns, Game
3 Andy Farkas, NFC-D: Washington vs. N.Y. Giants, 1943
Otto Graham, NFC: Cleveland vs. Detroit, 1954
Tom Matte, NFC: Baltimore vs. Cleveland, 1968
Larry Schreiber, NFC-D: San Francisco vs. Dallas, 1972
Larry Csonka, AFC: Miami vs. Oakland, 1973
Franco Harris, AFC-D: Pittsburgh vs. Buffalo, 1974
John Riggins, NFC-D: Washington vs. L.A. Rams, 1983
Most Consecutive Games Rushing for Touchdowns
7 John Riggins, Washington, 1982-84 (current)
5 Franco Harris, Pittsburgh, 1974-75
Franco Harris, Pittsburgh, 1977-79
3 By many players

PASSING

PASS RATING
Highest Pass Rating, Career (100 attempts)
104.8 Bart Starr, Green Bay, 10 games
93.3 Ken Anderson, Cincinnati, 6 games
91.4 Joe Theismann, Washington, 10 games
ATTEMPTS
Most Passes Attempted, Career
456 Terry Bradshaw, Pittsburgh, 19 games
410 Roger Staubach, Dallas, 20 games
360 Danny White, Dallas, 18 games
Most Passes Attempted, Game
53 Dan Fouts, AFC-D: San Diego vs. Miami, 1981 (OT)
Danny White, NFC-FR: Dallas vs. L.A. Rams, 1983
51 Richard Todd, AFC-FR: N.Y. Jets vs. Buffalo, 1981
Neil Lomax, NFC-FR: St. Louis vs. Green Bay, 1982
50 Dan Marino, SB: Miami vs. San Francisco, 1984

COMPLETIONS
Most Passes Completed, Career
261 Terry Bradshaw, Pittsburgh, 19 games
223 Roger Staubach, Dallas, 20 games
206 Danny White, Dallas, 18 games
Most Passes Completed, Game
33 Dan Fouts, AFC-D: San Diego vs. Miami, 1981 (OT)
32 Neil Lomax, NFC-FR: St. Louis vs. Green Bay, 1982
Danny White, NFC-FR: Dallas vs. L.A. Rams, 1983
29 Don Strock, AFC-D: Miami vs. San Diego, 1981 (OT)
Dan Marino, SB: Miami vs. San Francisco, 1984

COMPLETION PERCENTAGE
Highest Completion Percentage, Career (100 attempts)
66.3 Ken Anderson, Cincinnati, 6 games (166-110)
61.2 Dan Pastorini, Houston, 5 games (116-71)
61.0 Bart Starr, Green Bay, 10 games (213-130)
Highest Completion Percentage, Game (15 completions)
84.2 David Woodley, AFC-FR: Miami vs. New England, 1982 (19-16)
78.9 Norm Van Brocklin, NFC-D: Los Angeles vs. Detroit, 1952 (19-15)
78.3 Joe Theismann, NFC-D: Washington vs. L.A. Rams, 1983 (23-18)

YARDS GAINED
Most Yards Gained, Career
3,833 Terry Bradshaw, Pittsburgh, 19 games
2,791 Roger Staubach, Dallas, 20 games
2,641 Ken Stabler, Oakland-Houston, 13 games
Most Yards Gained, Game
433 Dan Fouts, AFC-D: San Diego vs. Miami, 1981 (OT)
421 Dan Marino, AFC: Miami vs. Pittsburgh, 1984
403 Don Strock, AFC-D: Miami vs. San Diego, 1981 (OT)
Most Games, 300 or More Yards Passing, Career
5 Dan Fouts, San Diego, 7 games
4 Joe Montana, San Francisco, 8 games
3 Terry Bradshaw, Pittsburgh, 19 games
Danny White, Dallas, 17 games
Dan Marino, Miami, 4 games
Most Consecutive Games, 300 or More Yards Passing
4 Dan Fouts, San Diego, 1979-81
2 Daryle Lamonica, Oakland, 1968
Ken Anderson, Cincinnati, 1981-82 (current)
Terry Bradshaw, Pittsburgh, 1979-82
Joe Montana, San Francisco, 1983-84
Dan Marino, Miami, 1984
Longest Pass Completion
93 Daryle Lamonica (to Dubenion), AFC-D: Buffalo vs. Boston, 1963 (TD)
88 George Blanda (to Cannon), AFC: Houston vs. L.A. Chargers, 1960 (TD)
86 Don Meredith (to Hayes), NFC-D: Dallas vs. Cleveland, 1967 (TD)

AVERAGE GAIN
Highest Average Gain, Career (100 attempts)
8.45 Joe Theismann, Washington, 10 games (211-1,782)
8.43 Jim Plunkett, Oakland-L.A. Raiders, 10 games (272-2,293)
8.41 Terry Bradshaw, Pittsburgh, 19 games (456-3,833)
Highest Average Gain, Game (20 attempts)
14.71 Terry Bradshaw, SB: Pittsburgh vs. Los Angeles, 1979 (21-309)
13.33 Bob Waterfield, NFC-D: Los Angeles vs. Chi. Bears, 1950 (21-280)
13.16 Dan Marino, AFC: Miami vs. Pittsburgh, 1984 (32-421)

TOUCHDOWNS
Most Touchdown Passes, Career
30 Terry Bradshaw, Pittsburgh, 19 games
24 Roger Staubach, Dallas, 20 games
19 Daryle Lamonica, Buffalo-Oakland, 13 games
Ken Stabler, Oakland-Houston, 13 games
Most Touchdown Passes, Game
6 Daryle Lamonica, AFC-D: Oakland vs. Houston, 1969
5 Sid Luckman, NFC: Chi. Bears vs. Washington, 1943
Daryle Lamonica, AFC-D: Oakland vs. Kansas City, 1968
4 Otto Graham, NFC: Cleveland vs. Los Angeles, 1950
Tobin Rote, NFC: Detroit vs. Cleveland, 1957
Bart Starr, NFC: Green Bay vs. Dallas, 1966
Ken Stabler, AFC-D: Oakland vs. Miami, 1974
Roger Staubach, NFC: Dallas vs. Los Angeles, 1975
Terry Bradshaw, SB: Pittsburgh vs. Dallas, 1978
Don Strock, AFC-D: Miami vs. San Diego, 1981 (OT)
Lynn Dickey, NFC-FR: Green Bay vs. St. Louis, 1982
Dan Marino, AFC: Miami vs. Pittsburgh, 1984
Most Consecutive Games, Touchdown Passes
10 Ken Stabler, Oakland, 1973-77
8 Terry Bradshaw, Pittsburgh, 1977-82
Joe Montana, San Francisco, 1981-84
6 Bart Starr, Green Bay, 1965-67
Terry Bradshaw, Pittsburgh, 1972-74
Dan Fouts, San Diego, 1980-82 (current)
Joe Theismann, Washington, 1982-83
Dan Marino, Miami, 1983-85 (current)

HAD INTERCEPTED
Lowest Percentage, Passes Had Intercepted, Career (100 attempts)
1.41 Bart Starr, Green Bay, 10 games (213-3)
2.13 Phil Simms, N.Y. Giants, 4 games (141-3)
3.32 Joe Theismann, Washington, 10 games (211-7)
Most Attempts Without Interception, Game
47 Daryle Lamonica, AFC: Oakland vs. N.Y. Jets, 1968
42 Dan Fouts, AFC-FR: San Diego vs. Pittsburgh, 1982
39 Daryle Lamonica, AFC-D: Oakland vs. Kansas City, 1968
Ron Jaworski, NFC-D: Philadelphia vs. Tampa Bay, 1979
Tommy Kramer, NFC-D: Minnesota vs. Washington, 1982
Most Passes Had Intercepted, Career
26 Terry Bradshaw, Pittsburgh, 19 games
19 Roger Staubach, Dallas, 20 games
17 George Blanda, Chi. Bears-Houston-Oakland, 19 games
Fran Tarkenton, Minnesota, 11 games
Most Passes Had Intercepted, Game
6 Frank Filchock, NFC: N.Y. Giants vs. Chi. Bears, 1946
Bobby Layne, NFC: Detroit vs. Cleveland, 1954
Norm Van Brocklin, NFC: Los Angeles vs. Cleveland, 1955
5 Frank Filchock, NFC: Washington vs. Chi. Bears, 1940
George Blanda, AFC: Houston vs. San Diego, 1961
George Blanda, AFC: Houston vs. Dall. Texans, 1962 (OT)
Y.A. Tittle, NFC: N.Y. Giants vs. Chicago, 1963
Mike Phipps, AFC-D: Cleveland vs. Miami, 1972
Dan Pastorini, AFC: Houston vs. Pittsburgh, 1978
Dan Fouts, AFC-D: San Diego vs. Houston, 1979
Tommy Kramer, NFC-D: Minnesota vs. Philadelphia, 1980
Dan Fouts, AFC-D: San Diego vs. Miami, 1982
Richard Todd, AFC: N.Y. Jets vs Miami, 1982
Gary Danielson, NFC-D: Detroit vs. San Francisco, 1983
4 By many players

PASS RECEIVING

RECEPTIONS

Most Receptions, Career
73 Cliff Branch, Oakland-L.A. Raiders, 22 games
70 Fred Biletnikoff, Oakland, 19 games
67 Drew Pearson, Dallas, 22 games

Most Receptions, Game
13 Kellen Winslow, AFC-D: San Diego vs. Miami, 1981 (OT)
12 Raymond Berry, NFC: Baltimore vs. N.Y. Giants, 1958
11 Dante Lavelli, NFC: Cleveland vs. Los Angeles, 1950
Dan Ross, SB: Cincinnati vs. San Francisco, 1981
Franco Harris, AFC-FR: Pittsburgh vs. San Diego, 1982
Steve Watson, AFC-D: Denver vs. Pittsburgh, 1984

Most Consecutive Games, Pass Receptions
22 Drew Pearson, Dallas, 1973-83
18 Paul Warfield, Cleveland-Miami, 1964-74
Cliff Branch, Oakland-L.A. Raiders, 1974-83
17 John Stallworth, Pittsburgh, 1974-84 (current)

YARDS GAINED

Most Yards Gained, Career
1,289 Cliff Branch, Oakland-L.A. Raiders, 22 games
1,167 Fred Biletnikoff, Oakland, 19 games
1,121 Paul Warfield, Cleveland-Miami, 18 games

Most Yards Gained, Game
198 Tom Fears, NFC-D: Los Angeles vs. Chi. Bears, 1950
190 Fred Biletnikoff, AFC: Oakland vs. N.Y. Jets, 1968
186 Cliff Branch, AFC: Oakland vs. Pittsburgh, 1974

Most Games, 100 or More Yards Receiving, Career
5 John Stallworth, Pittsburgh, 18 games
4 Fred Biletnikoff, Oakland, 19 games
Dwight Clark, San Francisco, 7 games
3 Tom Fears, L.A. Rams, 6 games
Cliff Branch, Oakland-L.A. Raiders, 22 games
Tony Nathan, Miami, 10 games

Most Consecutive Games, 100 or More Yards Receiving, Career
3 Tom Fears, Los Angeles, 1950-51
2 Lenny Moore, Baltimore, 1958-59
Fred Biletnikoff, Oakland, 1968
Paul Warfield, Miami, 1971
Charlie Joiner, San Diego, 1981
Dwight Clark, San Francisco, 1981
Cris Collinsworth, Cincinnati, 1981-82
John Stallworth, Pittsburgh, 1979-82
Wesley Walker, N.Y. Jets, 1982
Charlie Brown, Washington, 1983

Longest Reception
93 Elbert Dubenion (from Lamonica), AFC-D: Buffalo vs. Boston, 1963 (TD)
88 Billy Cannon (from Blanda), AFC: Houston vs. L.A. Chargers, 1960 (TD)
86 Bob Hayes (from Meredith), NFC: Dallas vs. Cleveland, 1967 (TD)

AVERAGE GAIN

Highest Average Gain, Career (20 receptions)
22.8 Harold Jackson, L.A. Rams-New England-Minnesota-Seattle, 14 games (24-548)
20.7 Charlie Brown, Washington, 8 games (31-643)
20.5 Frank Lewis, Pittsburgh-Buffalo, 12 games (27-553)

Highest Average Gain, Game (3 receptions)
46.3 Harold Jackson, NFC: Los Angeles vs. Minnesota, 1974 (3-139)
42.7 Billy Cannon, AFC: Houston vs. L.A. Chargers, 1960 (3-128)
42.0 Lenny Moore, NFC: Baltimore vs. N.Y. Giants, 1959 (3-126)

TOUCHDOWNS

Most Touchdowns, Career
12 John Stallworth, Pittsburgh, 18 games
10 Fred Biletnikoff, Oakland, 19 games
9 Lynn Swann, Pittsburgh, 16 games

Most Touchdowns, Game
3 Tom Fears, NFC-D: Los Angeles vs. Chi. Bears, 1950
Gary Collins, NFC: Cleveland vs. Baltimore, 1964
Fred Biletnikoff, AFC-D: Oakland vs. Kansas City, 1968
Preston Pearson, NFC: Dallas vs. Los Angeles, 1975
Dave Casper, AFC-D: Oakland vs. Baltimore, 1977 (OT)
Alvin Garrett, NFC-FR: Washington vs. Detroit, 1982

Most Consecutive Games, Touchdown Passes Caught
8 John Stallworth, Pittsburgh, 1978-83
4 Lynn Swann, Pittsburgh, 1978-79
Harold Carmichael, Philadelphia, 1978-80
Fred Solomon, San Francisco, 1983-84
3 By many players

INTERCEPTIONS BY

Most Interceptions, Career
9 Charlie Waters, Dallas, 25 games
Bill Simpson, Los Angeles-Buffalo, 11 games
8 Lester Hayes, Oakland-L.A. Raiders, 13 games
7 Willie Brown, Oakland, 17 games
Dennis Thurman, Dallas, 14 games

Most Interceptions, Game
4 Vernon Perry, AFC-D: Houston vs. San Diego, 1979
3 Joe Laws, NFC: Green Bay vs. N.Y. Giants, 1944
Charlie Waters, NFC-D: Dallas vs. Chicago, 1977
Rod Martin, SB: Oakland vs. Philadelphia, 1980
Dennis Thurman, NFC-D: Dallas vs. Green Bay, 1982
A.J. Duhe, AFC: Miami vs. N.Y. Jets, 1982
2 By many players

YARDS GAINED

Most Yards Gained, Career
196 Willie Brown, Oakland, 17 games
151 Glen Edwards, Pittsburgh-San Diego, 17 games
149 Bill Simpson, Los Angeles-Buffalo, 11 games
LeRoy Irvin, L.A. Rams, 6 games

Most Yards Gained, Game
98 Darrol Ray, AFC-FR: N.Y. Jets vs. Cincinnati, 1982
94 LeRoy Irvin, NFC-FR: L.A. Rams vs. Dallas, 1983
88 Walt Sumner, NFC-D: Cleveland vs. Dallas, 1969

Longest Return
98 Darrol Ray, AFC-FR: N.Y. Jets vs. Cincinnati, 1982 (TD)
94 LeRoy Irvin, NFC-FR: L.A. Rams vs. Dallas, 1983
88 Walt Sumner, NFC-D: Cleveland vs. Dallas, 1969 (TD)

TOUCHDOWNS

Most Touchdowns, Career
3 Willie Brown, Oakland, 17 games
2 Lester Hayes, Oakland-L.A. Raiders, 13 games

Most Touchdowns, Game
1 By 38 players

PUNTING

Most Punts, Career
111 Ray Guy, Oakland-L.A. Raiders, 22 games
84 Danny White, Dallas, 18 games
73 Mike Eischeid, Oakland-Minnesota, 14 games

Most Punts, Game
12 David Lee, AFC-D: Baltimore vs. Oakland, 1977 (OT)
11 Ken Strong, NFC: N.Y. Giants vs. Chi. Bears, 1933
Jim Norton, AFC: Houston vs. Oakland, 1967
Dale Hatcher, NFC: L.A. Rams vs. Chicago, 1985
10 Keith Molesworth, NFC: Chi. Bears vs. N.Y. Giants, 1933
Riley Smith, NFC: Boston vs. Green Bay, 1936
Len Younce, NFC: N.Y. Giants vs. Green Bay, 1944
Curley Johnson, AFC: N.Y. Jets vs. Oakland, 1968
Tom Orosz, AFC: Miami vs. N.Y. Jets, 1982
Maury Buford, NFC: Chicago vs. L.A. Rams, 1985

Longest Punt
76 Ed Danowski, NFC: N.Y. Giants vs. Detroit, 1935
72 Charlie Conerly, NFC-D: N.Y. Giants vs. Cleveland, 1950
71 Ray Guy, AFC: Oakland vs. San Diego, 1980

AVERAGE YARDAGE

Highest Average, Career (20 punts)
43.4 Jerrel Wilson, Kansas City-New England, 8 games (43-1,866)
43.1 Don Chandler, N.Y. Giants-Green Bay, 14 games (53-2,282)
42.6 Rich Camarillo, New England, 5 games (26-1, 107)

Highest Average, Game (4 punts)
56.0 Ray Guy, AFC: Oakland vs. San Diego, 1980 (4-224)
52.5 Sammy Baugh, NFC: Washington vs. Chi. Bears, 1942 (6-315)
51.4 John Hadl, AFC: San Diego vs. Buffalo, 1965 (5-257)

PUNT RETURNS

Most Punt Returns, Career
25 Theo Bell, Pittsburgh-Tampa Bay, 10 games
19 Willie Wood, Green Bay, 10 games
Butch Johnson, Dallas-Denver, 18 games
18 Neal Colzie, Oakland-Miami-Tampa Bay, 10 games

Most Punt Returns, Game
7 Ron Gardin, AFC-D: Baltimore vs. Cincinnati, 1970
Carl Roaches, AFC-FR: Houston vs. Oakland, 1980
6 George McAfee, NFC-D: Chi. Bears vs. Los Angeles, 1950
Eddie Brown, NFC-D: Washington vs. Minnesota, 1976
Theo Bell, AFC: Pittsburgh vs. Houston, 1978
Eddie Brown, NFC: Los Angeles vs. Tampa Bay, 1979
John Sciarra, NFC: Philadelphia vs. Dallas, 1980
Kurt Sohn, AFC: N.Y. Jets vs. Miami, 1982
Mike Nelms, SB: Washington vs. Miami, 1982
5 By many players

YARDS GAINED

Most Yards Gained, Career
221 Neal Colzie, Oakland-Miami-Tampa Bay, 10 games
208 Butch Johnson, Dallas-Denver, 18 games
204 Theo Bell, Pittsburgh-Tampa Bay, 10 games

Most Yards Gained, Game
141 Bob Hayes, NFC-D: Dallas vs. Cleveland, 1967
102 Charley Trippi, NFC: Chi. Cardinals vs. Philadelphia, 1947
101 Bosh Pritchard, NFC-D: Philadelphia vs. Pittsburgh, 1947

Longest Return
81 Hugh Gallarneau, NFC-D: Chi. Bears vs. Green Bay, 1941 (TD)
79 Bosh Pritchard, NFC-D: Philadelphia vs. Pittsburgh, 1947 (TD)
75 Charley Trippi, NFC: Chi. Cardinals vs. Philadelphia, 1947 (TD)

AVERAGE YARDAGE

Highest Average, Career (10 returns)
12.6 Bob Hayes, Dallas, 15 games (12-151)
12.4 Mike Fuller, San Diego-Cincinnati, 7 games (13-161)
12.3 Neal Colzie, Oakland-Miami-Tampa Bay, 10 games (18-221)

Highest Average Gain, Game (3 returns)
47.0 Bob Hayes, NFC-D: Dallas vs. Cleveland, 1967 (3-141)
29.0 George (Butch) Byrd, AFC: Buffalo vs. San Diego, 1965 (3-87)
25.3 Bosh Pritchard, NFC-D: Philadelphia vs. Pittsburgh, 1947 (4-101)

TOUCHDOWNS

Most Touchdowns
1 Hugh Gallarneau, NFC-D: Chicago Bears vs. Green Bay, 1941
Bosh Pritchard, NFC-D: Philadelphia vs. Pittsburgh, 1947
Charley Trippi, NFC: Chicago Cardinals vs. Philadelphia, 1947
Verda (Vitamin T) Smith, NFC-D: Los Angeles vs. Detroit, 1952
George (Butch) Byrd, AFC: Buffalo vs. San Diego, 1965
Golden Richards, NFC: Dallas vs. Minnesota, 1973
Wes Chandler, AFC-D: San Diego vs. Miami, 1981 (OT)
Shaun Gayle, NFC-D: Chicago vs. N.Y. Giants, 1985

KICKOFF RETURNS

Most Kickoff Returns, Career

29 Fulton Walker, Miami-L.A. Raiders, 10 games
19 Preston Pearson, Baltimore-Pittsburgh-Dallas, 22 games
18 Charlie West, Minnesota, 9 games

Most Kickoff Returns, Game

7 Don Bingham, NFC: Chi. Bears vs. N.Y. Giants, 1956
Reggie Brown, NFC-FR: Atlanta vs. Minnesota, 1982
David Verser, AFC-FR: Cincinnati vs. N.Y. Jets, 1982
Del Rodgers, NFC-D: Green Bay vs. Dallas, 1982
Henry Ellard, NFC-D: L.A. Rams vs. Washington, 1983
Stephen Starring, SB: New England vs. Chicago, 1985
6 Wallace Francis, AFC-D: Buffalo vs. Pittsburgh, 1974
Eddie Brown, NFC-D: Washington vs. Minnesota, 1976
Eddie Payton, NFC-D: Minnesota vs. Philadelphia, 1980
Alvin Hall, NFC-FR: Detroit vs. Washington, 1982
Fulton Walker, AFC-D: Miami vs. Seattle, 1983
Johnny Hector, AFC-FR: N.Y. Jets vs. New England, 1985
Lorenzo Hampton, AFC: Miami vs. New England, 1985
5 By many players

YARDS GAINED

Most Yards Gained, Career

677 Fulton Walker, Miami-L.A. Raiders, 10 games
481 Carl Garrett, Oakland, 5 games
458 Cullen Bryant, L.A. Rams-Seattle, 19 games

Most Yards Gained, Game

190 Fulton Walker, SB: Miami vs. Washington, 1982
170 Les (Speedy) Duncan, NFC-D: Washington vs. San Francisco, 1971
169 Carl Garrett, AFC-D: Oakland vs. Baltimore, 1977 (OT)

Longest Return

98 Fulton Walker, SB: Miami vs. Washington, 1982 (TD)
97 Vic Washington, NFC-D: San Francisco vs. Dallas, 1972 (TD)
89 Nat Moore, AFC-D: Miami vs. Oakland, 1974 (TD)
Rod Hill, NFC-D: Dallas vs. Green Bay, 1982

AVERAGE YARDAGE

Highest Average, Career (10 returns)

30.1 Carl Garrett, Oakland, 5 games (16-481)
27.9 George Atkinson, Oakland, 16 games (12-335)
24.2 Larry Anderson, Pittsburgh, 6 games (16-387)

Highest Average, Game (3 returns)

56.7 Les (Speedy) Duncan, NFC-D: Washington vs. San Francisco, 1971 (3-170)
51.3 Ed Podolak, AFC-D: Kansas City vs. Miami, 1971 (OT) (3-154)
49.0 Les (Speedy) Duncan, AFC: San Diego vs. Buffalo, 1964 (3-147)

TOUCHDOWNS

Most Touchdowns

1 Vic Washington, NFC-D: San Francisco vs. Dallas, 1972
Nat Moore, AFC-D: Miami vs. Oakland, 1974
Marshall Johnson, AFC-D: Baltimore vs. Oakland, 1977 (OT)
Fulton Walker, SB: Miami vs. Washington, 1982

FUMBLES

Most Fumbles, Career

13 Tony Dorsett, Dallas, 17 games
10 Franco Harris, Pittsburgh, 19 games
Terry Bradshaw, Pittsburgh, 19 games
Roger Staubach, Dallas, 20 games
9 Chuck Foreman, Minnesota, 13 games

Most Fumbles, Game

4 Brian Sipe, AFC-D: Cleveland vs. Oakland, 1980
3 Y.A. Tittle, NFC-D: San Francisco vs. Detroit, 1957
Bill Nelsen, AFC-D: Cleveland vs. Baltimore, 1972
Chuck Foreman, NFC: Minnesota vs. Los Angeles, 1974
Lawrence McCutcheon, NFC-D: Los Angeles vs. St. Louis, 1975
Roger Staubach, SB: Dallas vs. Pittsburgh, 1975
Terry Bradshaw, AFC: Pittsburgh vs. Houston, 1978
Earl Campbell, AFC: Houston vs. Pittsburgh, 1978
Franco Harris, AFC: Pittsburgh vs. Houston, 1978
Chuck Muncie, AFC: San Diego vs. Cincinnati, 1981
Andra Franklin, AFC-FR: Miami vs. New England, 1982
2 By many players

RECOVERIES

Most Own Fumbles Recovered, Career

5 Roger Staubach, Dallas, 20 games
4 Fran Tarkenton, Minnesota, 11 games
3 Alex Webster, N.Y. Giants, 7 games
Don Meredith, Dallas, 4 games
Franco Harris, Pittsburgh, 19 games
Gerry Mullins, Pittsburgh, 18 games
Ron Jaworski, Los Angeles-Philadelphia, 10 games
Lyle Blackwood, Cincinnati-Baltimore-Miami, 14 games

Most Opponents' Fumbles Recovered, Career

4 Cliff Harris, Dallas, 21 games
Harvey Martin, Dallas, 22 games
Ted Hendricks, Baltimore-Oakland-L.A. Raiders, 21 games
3 Paul Krause, Minnesota, 19 games
Jack Lambert, Pittsburgh, 18 games
Fred Dryer, Los Angeles, 14 games
Charlie Waters, Dallas, 25 games
Jack Ham, Pittsburgh, 16 games
Mike Hegman, Dallas, 16 games
Tom Jackson, Denver, 7 games
Mike Singletary, Chicago, 5 games

Most Fumbles Recovered, Game, Own and Opponents'

3 Jack Lambert, AFC: Pittsburgh vs. Oakland, 1975 (3 opp)
Ron Jaworski, NFC-FR: Philadelphia vs. N.Y. Giants, 1981 (3 own)
2 By many players

YARDS GAINED

Longest Return

93 Andy Russell, AFC-D: Pittsburgh vs. Baltimore, 1975 (opp, TD)
60 Mike Curtis, NFC-D: Baltimore vs. Minnesota, 1968 (opp, TD)
Hugh Green, NFC-FR: Tampa Bay vs. Dallas, 1982 (opp, TD)
52 Wilber Marshall, NFC: Chicago vs. L.A. Rams, 1985 (opp, TD)

TOUCHDOWNS

Most Touchdowns

1 By 22 players

TEAM RECORDS

GAMES, VICTORIES, DEFEATS

Most Consecutive Seasons Participating in Postseason Games

9 Dallas, 1975-83
8 Dallas, 1966-73
Pittsburgh, 1972-79
Los Angeles, 1973-80
6 Cleveland, 1950-55
Oakland, 1972-77
Minnesota, 1973-78

Most Games

36 Dallas, 1966-73, 1975-83, 1985
31 Oakland/L. A. Raiders, 1967-70, 1973-77, 1980, 1982-85
28 Cleveland/L. A. Rams, 1945, 1949-52, 1955, 1967, 1969, 1973-80, 1983-85

Most Games Won

20 Dallas, 1967, 1970-73, 1975, 1977-78, 1980-82
19 Oakland/L. A. Raiders, 1967-70, 1973-77, 1980, 1982-83
15 Pittsburgh, 1972, 1974-76, 1978-79, 1984

Most Consecutive Games Won

9 Green Bay, 1961-62, 1965-67
7 Pittsburgh, 1974-76
6 Miami, 1972-73
Pittsburgh, 1978-79
Washington, 1982-83

Most Games Lost

17 L.A. Rams, 1949-50, 1952, 1955, 1967, 1969, 1973-80, 1983-85
16 Dallas, 1966-70, 1972-73, 1975-76, 1978-83, 1985
N. Y. Giants, 1933, 1935, 1939, 1941, 1943-44, 1946, 1950, 1958-59, 1961-63, 1981, 1984-85
14 Cleveland, 1951-53, 1957-58, 1965, 1967-69, 1971-72, 1980, 1982, 1985

Most Consecutive Games Lost

6 N. Y. Giants, 1939, 1941, 1943-44, 1946, 1950
Cleveland, 1969, 1971-72, 1980, 1982, 1985 (current)
5 N. Y. Giants, 1958-59, 1961-63
Los Angeles, 1952, 1955, 1967, 1969, 1973
Denver, 1977-79, 1983-84 (current)
4 Washington, 1972-74, 1976
Baltimore, 1971, 1975-77 (current)
Miami, 1974, 1978-79, 1981
Chi. Cards/St. Louis, 1948, 1974-75, 1982 (current)
Boston/New England, 1963, 1976, 1978, 1982

SCORING

Most Points, Game

73 NFC: Chi. Bears vs. Washington, 1940
59 NFC: Detroit vs. Cleveland, 1957
56 NFC: Cleveland vs. Detroit, 1954
AFC-D: Oakland vs. Houston, 1969

Most Points, Both Teams, Game

79 AFC-D: San Diego (41) vs. Miami (38), 1981 (OT)
73 NFC: Chi. Bears (73) vs. Washington (0), 1940
NFC: Detroit (59) vs. Cleveland (14), 1957
AFC: Miami (45) vs. Pittsburgh (28), 1984
68 AFC-D: Oakland (37) vs. Baltimore (31), 1977 (OT)

Fewest Points, Both Teams, Game

5 NFC-D: Detroit (0) vs. Dallas (5), 1970
7 NFC: Chi. Cardinals (0) vs. Philadelphia (7), 1948
9 NFC: Tampa Bay (0) vs. Los Angeles (9), 1979

Largest Margin of Victory, Game

73 NFC: Chi. Bears vs. Washington, 1940 (73-0)
49 AFC-D: Oakland vs. Houston, 1969 (56-7)
46 NFC: Cleveland vs. Detroit, 1954 (56-10)

Most Points, Shutout Victory, Game

73 NFC: Chi. Bears vs. Washington, 1940
38 NFC-D: Dallas vs. Tampa Bay, 1981
37 NFC: Green Bay vs. N.Y. Giants, 1961

Most Points Overcome to Win Game

20 NFC-D: Detroit vs. San Francisco, 1957 (trailed 7-27, won 31-27)
18 NFC-D: Dallas vs. San Francisco, 1972 (trailed 3-21, won 30-28)
AFC-D: Miami vs. Cleveland, 1985 (trailed 3-21, won 24-21)
14 NFC-D: Philadelphia vs. Minnesota, 1980 (trailed 0-14, won 31-16)
NFC-D: Dallas vs. Atlanta, 1980 (trailed 10-24, won 30-27)

Most Points, Each Half

1st: 38 NFC-D: Washington vs. L.A. Rams, 1983
35 NFC: Cleveland vs. Detroit, 1954
AFC-D: Oakland vs. Houston, 1969
34 NFC: N. Y. Giants vs. Chi. Bears, 1956
2nd: 45 NFC: Chi. Bears vs. Washington, 1940
28 NFC: Chi. Bears vs. N. Y. Giants, 1941
NFC: Detroit vs. Cleveland, 1957
NFC-D: Dallas vs. Cleveland, 1967
NFC-D: Dallas vs. Tampa Bay, 1981
27 NFC: N. Y. Giants vs. Chi. Bears, 1934
NFC: Chi. Bears vs. Washington, 1943
NFC: Cleveland vs. Baltimore, 1964

Most Points, Each Quarter

1st: 28 AFC-D: Oakland vs. Houston, 1969
24 AFC-D: San Diego vs. Miami, 1981 (OT)
21 NFC: Chi. Bears vs. Washington, 1940
AFC: San Diego vs. Boston, 1963

AFC-D: Oakland vs. Kansas City, 1968
AFC: Oakland vs. San Diego, 1980

2nd: 26 AFC-D: Pittsburgh vs. Buffalo, 1974
24 NFC-D: Chi. Bears vs. Green Bay, 1941
NFC: Green Bay vs. N. Y. Giants, 1961
21 NFC: Cleveland vs. Detroit, 1954
NFC: N. Y. Giants vs. Chi. Bears, 1956
AFC-D: Houston vs. New England, 1978
NFC-FR: Green Bay vs. St. Louis, 1982
NFC-D: Washington vs. L.A. Rams, 1983
SB: San Francisco vs. Miami, 1984

3rd: 26 NFC: Chi. Bears vs. Washington, 1940
21 NFC-D: Dallas vs. Cleveland, 1967
NFC-D: Dallas vs. Tampa Bay, 1981
AFC-D: L.A. Raiders vs. Pittsburgh, 1983
SB: Chicago vs. New England, 1985
17 NFC: Cleveland vs. Baltimore, 1964
NFC-D: Dallas vs. Chicago, 1977

4th 27 NFC: N.Y. Giants vs. Chi. Bears, 1934
24 NFC: Baltimore vs. N. Y. Giants, 1959
21 AFC: Pittsburgh vs. Oakland, 1974
NFC: Dallas vs. Los Angeles, 1978
AFC-FR: N. Y. Jets vs. Cincinnati, 1982
NFC: San Francisco vs. Washington, 1983

OT: 6 NFC: Baltimore vs. N.Y. Giants, 1958
AFC-D: Oakland vs. Baltimore, 1977

TOUCHDOWNS

Most Touchdowns, Game

11 NFC: Chi. Bears vs. Washington, 1940
8 NFC: Cleveland vs. Detroit, 1954
NFC: Detroit vs. Cleveland, 1957
AFC-D: Oakland vs. Houston, 1969
7 AFC: San Diego vs. Boston, 1963
NFC-D: Dallas vs. Cleveland, 1967

Most Touchdowns, Both Teams, Game

11 NFC: Chi. Bears (11) vs. Washington (0), 1940
10 NFC: Detroit (8) vs. Cleveland (2), 1957
AFC-D: Miami (5) vs. San Diego (5), 1981 (OT)
AFC: Miami (6) vs. Pittsburgh (4), 1984
9 NFC: Chi. Bears (6) vs. Washington (3), 1943
NFC: Cleveland (8) vs. Detroit (1), 1954
NFC-D: Dallas (7) vs. Cleveland (2), 1967
AFC-D: Oakland (8) vs. Houston (1), 1969
AFC-D: Oakland (5) vs. Baltimore (4), 1977 (OT)
SB: Pittsburgh (5) vs. Dallas (4), 1978

Fewest Touchdowns, Both Teams, Game

0 NFC-D: N.Y. Giants vs. Cleveland, 1950
NFC-D: Dallas vs. Detroit, 1970
NFC: Los Angeles vs. Tampa Bay, 1979
1 NFC: Chi. Cardinals (0) vs. Philadelphia (1), 1948
AFC: San Diego (0) vs. Houston (1), 1961
AFC-D: N. Y. Jets (0) vs. Kansas City (1), 1969
NFC-D: Green Bay (0) vs. Washington (1), 1972
2 In many games

POINTS AFTER TOUCHDOWN

Most Points After Touchdown, Game

8 NFC: Cleveland vs. Detroit, 1954
NFC: Detroit vs. Cleveland, 1957
AFC-D: Oakland vs. Houston, 1969
7 NFC: Chi. Bears vs. Washington, 1940
NFC-D: Dallas vs. Cleveland, 1967
6 AFC: San Diego vs. Boston, 1963
NFC-D: Washington vs. L.A. Rams, 1983
AFC: Miami vs. Pittsburgh, 1984

Most Points After Touchdown, Both Teams, Game

10 NFC: Detroit (8) vs. Cleveland (2), 1957
AFC-D: Miami (5) vs. San Diego (5), 1981 (OT)
AFC: Miami (6) vs. Pittsburgh (4), 1984
9 NFC: Cleveland (8) vs. Detroit (1), 1954
NFC-D: Dallas (7) vs. Cleveland (2), 1967
AFC-D: Oakland (8) vs. Houston (1), 1969
8 In many games

Fewest Points After Touchdown, Both Teams, Game

0 NFC-D: N.Y. Giants vs. Cleveland, 1950
NFC-D: Dallas vs. Detroit, 1970
NFC: Los Angeles vs. Tampa Bay, 1979

FIELD GOALS

Most Field Goals, Game

4 AFC-D: Boston vs. Buffalo, 1963
AFC: Oakland vs. Houston, 1967
SB: Green Bay vs. Oakland, 1967
NFC: Washington vs. Dallas, 1972
AFC-D: Oakland vs. Pittsburgh, 1973
SB: San Francisco vs. Cincinnati, 1981
AFC-FR: New England vs. N.Y. Jets, 1985
3 By many teams

Most Field Goals, Both Teams, Game

5 NFC: Green Bay (3) vs. Cleveland (2), 1965
AFC: Oakland (3) vs. N.Y. Jets (2), 1968
NFC: Washington (4) vs. Dallas (1), 1972
AFC-D: Cincinnati (3) vs. Miami (2), 1973
NFC-D: Los Angeles (3) vs. Dallas (2), 1973
NFC-D: Dallas (3) vs. Green Bay (2), 1982
NFC-FR: N.Y. Giants (3) vs. L.A. Rams (2), 1984
4 In many games

Most Field Goals Attempted, Game

6 AFC: Oakland vs. Houston, 1967
NFC-D: Los Angeles vs. Dallas, 1973
5 By many teams

Most Field Goals Attempted, Both Teams, Game

8 NFC-D: Los Angeles (6) vs. Dallas (2), 1973
NFC-D: Detroit (5) vs. San Francisco (3), 1983
7 In many games

SAFETIES

Most Safeties, Game

1 By 13 teams

FIRST DOWNS

Most First Downs, Game

34 AFC-D: San Diego vs. Miami, 1981 (OT)
31 SB: San Francisco vs. Miami, 1984
29 AFC-D: Pittsburgh vs. Buffalo, 1974
AFC-D:,Pittsburgh vs. Baltimore, 1976
NFC-FR: Dallas vs. Los Angeles, 1980
NFC-FR: Dallas vs. Tampa Bay, 1982
AFC-FR: San Diego vs. Pittsburgh, 1982
AFC-D: Miami vs. San Diego, 1982

Fewest First Downs, Game

6 NFC: N.Y. Giants vs. Green Bay, 1961
7 NFC: Green Bay vs. Boston, 1936
NFC-D: Pittsburgh vs. Philadelphia, 1947
NFC: Chi. Cardinals vs. Philadelphia, 1948
NFC: Los Angeles vs. Philadelphia, 1949
NFC-D: Cleveland vs. N. Y. Giants, 1958
AFC-D: Cincinnati vs. Baltimore, 1970
NFC-D: Detroit vs. Dallas, 1970
8 By many teams

Most First Downs, Both Teams, Game

59 AFC-D: San Diego (34) vs. Miami (25), 1981 (OT)
55 AFC-FR: San Diego (29) vs. Pittsburgh (26), 1982
50 AFC: Oakland (28) vs. Baltimore (22), 1977 (OT)
NFC-FR: St. Louis (28) vs. Green Bay (22), 1982
AFC-FR: N. Y. Jets (27) vs. Cincinnati (23), 1982
AFC: Miami (28) vs. Pittsburgh (22), 1984
SB: San Francisco (31) vs. Miami (19), 1984

Fewest First Downs, Both Teams, Game

15 NFC: Green Bay (7) vs. Boston (8), 1936
19 NFC: N. Y. Giants (9) vs. Green Bay (10), 1939
NFC: Washington (9) vs. Chi. Bears (10), 1942
20 NFC-D: Cleveland (9) vs. N. Y. Giants (11), 1950

RUSHING

Most First Downs, Rushing, Game

19 NFC-FR: Dallas vs. Los Angeles, 1980
18 AFC-D: Miami vs. Cincinnati, 1973
AFC-D: Pittsburgh vs. Buffalo, 1974
16 NFC: Philadelphia vs. Chi. Cardinals, 1948
NFC: Dallas vs. San Francisco, 1970

Fewest First Downs, Rushing, Game

0 NFC: Los Angeles vs. Philadelphia, 1949
AFC-D: Buffalo vs. Boston, 1963
AFC: Oakland vs. Pittsburgh, 1974
1 NFC: N. Y. Giants vs. Green Bay, 1961
AFC-D: Houston vs. Oakland, 1969
NFC: Los Angeles vs. Dallas, 1975
AFC-FR: Cleveland vs. L. A. Raiders, 1982
NFC-D: N.Y. Giants vs. Chicago, 1985
SB: New England vs. Chicago, 1985
2 By many teams

Most First Downs, Rushing, Both Teams, Game

25 NFC-FR: Dallas (19) vs. Los Angeles (6), 1980
23 NFC: Cleveland (15) vs. Detroit (8), 1952
AFC-D: Miami (18) vs. Cincinnati (5), 1973
AFC-D: Pittsburgh (18) vs. Buffalo (5), 1974
22 AFC: Miami (18) vs. Oakland (4), 1973
AFC-D: Buffalo (11) vs. Cincinnati (11), 1981
AFC-D: L.A. Raiders (13) vs. Pittsburgh (9), 1983

Fewest First Downs, Rushing, Both Teams, Game

5 AFC-D: Buffalo (0) vs. Boston (5), 1963
6 NFC: Green Bay (2) vs. Boston (4), 1936
NFC-D: Baltimore (2) vs. Minnesota (4), 1968
AFC-D: Houston (1) vs. Oakland (5), 1969
7 NFC-D: Washington (2) vs. N. Y. Giants (5), 1943
NFC: Baltimore (3) vs. N. Y. Giants (4), 1959
NFC: Washington (3) vs. Dallas (4), 1972
AFC-FR: N. Y. Jets (3) vs. Buffalo (4), 1981

PASSING

Most First Downs, Passing, Game

21 AFC-D: Miami vs. San Diego, 1981 (OT)
AFC-D: San Diego vs. Miami, 1981 (OT)
20 NFC-FR: Dallas vs. L.A. Rams, 1983
19 NFC-FR: St. Louis vs. Green Bay, 1982
NFC-FR: Dallas vs. Tampa Bay, 1982
AFC-FR: Pittsburgh vs. San Diego, 1982
AFC-FR: San Diego vs. Pittsburgh, 1982
NFC: Dallas vs. Washington, 1982

Fewest First Downs, Passing, Game

0 NFC: Philadelphia vs. Chi. Cardinals, 1948
1 NFC-D: N. Y. Giants vs. Washington, 1943
NFC: Cleveland vs. Detroit, 1953
SB: Denver vs. Dallas, 1977
2 By many teams

Most First Downs, Passing, Both Teams, Game

42 AFC-D: Miami (21) vs. San Diego (21), 1981 (OT)
38 AFC-FR: Pittsburgh (19) vs. San Diego (19), 1982
32 NFC-FR: St. Louis (19) vs. Green Bay (13), 1982
AFC: Miami (18) vs. Pittsburgh (14), 1984
SB: Miami (17) vs. San Francisco (15), 1984

Fewest First Downs, Passing, Both Teams, Game

2 NFC: Philadelphia (0) vs. Chi. Cardinals (2), 1948

4 NFC-D: Cleveland (2) vs. N. Y. Giants (2), 1950
5 NFC: Detroit (2) vs. N. Y. Giants (3), 1935
NFC: Green Bay (2) vs. N. Y. Giants (3), 1939

PENALTY

Most First Downs, Penalty, Game
7 AFC-D: New England vs. Oakland, 1976
5 AFC-FR: Cleveland vs. L. A. Raiders, 1982
4 By many teams

Most First Downs, Penalty, Both Teams, Game
9 AFC-D: New England (7) vs. Oakland (2), 1976
8 NFC-FR: Atlanta (4) vs. Minnesota (4), 1982
7 AFC-D: Baltimore (4) vs. Oakland (3), 1977 (OT)

NET YARDS GAINED RUSHING AND PASSING

Most Yards Gained, Game
610 AFC: San Diego vs. Boston, 1963
569 AFC: Miami vs. Pittsburgh, 1984
564 AFC-D: San Diego vs. Miami, 1981 (OT)

Fewest Yards Gained, Game
86 NFC-D: Cleveland vs. N.Y. Giants, 1958
99 NFC: Chi. Cardinals vs. Philadelphia, 1948
114 NFC-D: N.Y. Giants vs. Washington, 1943

Most Yards Gained, Both Teams, Game
1,036 AFC-D: San Diego (564) vs. Miami (472), 1981 (OT)
1,024 AFC: Miami (569) vs. Pittsburgh (455), 1984
912 AFC-FR: N. Y. Jets (517) vs. Cincinnati (395), 1982

Fewest Yards Gained, Both Teams, Game
331 NFC: Chi. Cardinals (99) vs. Philadelphia (232), 1948
332 NFC-D: N.Y. Giants (150) vs. Cleveland (182), 1950
336 NFC: Boston (116) vs. Green Bay (220), 1936

RUSHING

ATTEMPTS

Most Attempts, Game
65 NFC: Detroit vs. N.Y. Giants, 1935
61 NFC: Philadelphia vs. Los Angeles, 1949
59 AFC: New England vs. Miami, 1985

Fewest Attempts, Game
9 SB: Miami vs. San Francisco, 1984
11 SB: New England vs. Chicago, 1985
12 AFC-D: Buffalo vs. Boston, 1963

Most Attempts, Both Teams, Game
109 NFC: Detroit (65) vs. N.Y. Giants (44), 1935
97 AFC-D: Baltimore (50) vs. Oakland (47), 1977 (OT)
91 NFC: Philadelphia (57) vs. Chi. Cardinals (34), 1948

Fewest Attempts, Both Teams, Game
45 AFC-FR: N.Y. Jets (22) vs. Buffalo (23), 1981
46 AFC: Buffalo (13) vs. Kansas City (33), 1966
48 AFC-D: Buffalo (12) vs. Boston (36), 1963
AFC: Boston (16) vs. San Diego (32), 1963

YARDS GAINED

Most Yards Gained, Game
382 NFC: Chi. Bears vs. Washington, 1940
338 NFC-FR: Dallas vs. Los Angeles, 1980
318 AFC: San Diego vs. Boston, 1963

Fewest Yards Gained, Game
7 AFC-D: Buffalo vs. Boston, 1963
SB: New England vs. Chicago, 1985
17 SB: Minnesota vs. Pittsburgh, 1974
21 NFC: Los Angeles vs. Philadelphia, 1949

Most Yards Gained, Both Teams, Game
430 NFC-FR: Dallas (338) vs. Los Angeles (92), 1980
426 NFC: Cleveland (227) vs. Detroit (199), 1952
404 NFC: Chi. Bears (382) vs. Washington (22), 1940

Fewest Yards Gained, Both Teams, Game
90 AFC-D: Buffalo (7) vs. Boston (83), 1963
106 NFC: Boston (39) vs. Green Bay (67), 1936
128 NFC-FR: Philadelphia (53) vs. Atlanta (75), 1978

AVERAGE GAIN

Highest Average Gain, Game
9.94 AFC: San Diego vs. Boston, 1963 (32-318)
9.29 NFC-D: Green Bay vs. Dallas, 1982 (17-158)
7.35 NFC-FR: Dallas vs. Los Angeles, 1980 (46-338)

Lowest Average Gain, Game
0.58 AFC-D: Buffalo vs. Boston, 1963 (12-7)
0.64 SB: New England vs. Chicago, 1985 (11-7)
0.81 SB: Minnesota vs. Pittsburgh, 1974 (21-17)

TOUCHDOWNS

Most Touchdowns, Game
7 NFC: Chi. Bears vs. Washington, 1940
5 NFC: Cleveland vs. Detroit, 1954
4 NFC: Detroit vs. N.Y. Giants, 1935
AFC: San Diego vs. Boston, 1963
NFC-D: Dallas vs. Cleveland, 1967
NFC: Baltimore vs. Cleveland, 1968
NFC-FR: Dallas vs. Los Angeles, 1980
AFC-D: L.A. Raiders vs. Pittsburgh, 1983
SB: Chicago vs. New England, 1985

Most Touchdowns, Both Teams, Game
7 NFC: Chi. Bears (7) vs. Washington (0), 1940
6 NFC: Cleveland (5) vs. Detroit (1), 1954
5 NFC: Chi. Cardinals (3) vs. Philadelphia (2), 1947
AFC: San Diego (4) vs. Boston (1), 1963
AFC-D: Cincinnati (3) vs. Buffalo (2), 1981

PASSING

ATTEMPTS

Most Attempts, Game
54 AFC-D: San Diego vs. Miami, 1981 (OT)
53 NFC-FR: Dallas vs. L.A. Rams, 1983
51 NFC: Washington vs. Chi. Bears, 1940
AFC-FR: N.Y. Jets vs. Buffalo, 1981
NFC-FR: St. Louis vs. Green Bay, 1982

Fewest Attempts, Game
5 NFC: Detroit vs. N.Y. Giants, 1935
6 AFC: Miami vs. Oakland, 1973
7 SB: Miami vs. Minnesota, 1973

Most Attempts, Both Teams, Game
102 AFC-D: San Diego (54) vs. Miami (48), 1981 (OT)
96 AFC: N.Y. Jets (49) vs. Oakland (47), 1968
85 AFC-FR: N.Y. Jets (51) vs. Buffalo (34), 1981
SB: Miami (50) vs. San Francisco (35), 1984

Fewest Attempts, Both Teams, Game
18 NFC: Detroit (5) vs. N.Y. Giants (13), 1935
21 NFC: Chi. Bears (7) vs. N.Y. Giants (14), 1933
23 NFC: Chi. Cardinals (11) vs. Philadelphia (12), 1948

COMPLETIONS

Most Completions, Game
33 AFC-D: San Diego vs. Miami, 1981 (OT)
32 NFC-FR: St. Louis vs. Green Bay, 1982
NFC-FR: Dallas vs. L.A. Rams, 1983
31 AFC-D: Miami vs. San Diego, 1981 (OT)

Fewest Completions, Game
2 NFC: Detroit vs. N.Y. Giants, 1935
NFC: Philadelphia vs. Chi. Cardinals, 1948
3 NFC: N.Y. Giants vs. Chi. Bears, 1941
NFC: Green Bay vs. N.Y. Giants, 1944
NFC: Chi. Cardinals vs. Philadelphia, 1947
NFC: Chi. Cardinals vs. Philadelphia, 1948
NFC-D: Cleveland vs. N.Y. Giants, 1950
NFC-D: N.Y. Giants vs. Cleveland, 1950
NFC: Cleveland vs. Detroit, 1953
AFC: Miami vs. Oakland, 1973
4 NFC-D: Dallas vs. Detroit, 1970
AFC: Miami vs. Baltimore, 1971
SB: Miami vs. Washington, 1982
AFC-FR: Seattle vs. L.A. Raiders, 1984

Most Completions, Both Teams, Game
64 AFC-D: San Diego (33) vs. Miami (31), 1981 (OT)
55 AFC-FR: Pittsburgh (28) vs. San Diego (27), 1982
53 SB: Miami (29) vs. San Francisco (24), 1984

Fewest Completions, Both Teams, Game
5 NFC: Philadelphia (2) vs. Chi. Cardinals (3), 1948
6 NFC: Detroit (2) vs. N.Y. Giants (4), 1935
NFC-D: Cleveland (3) vs. N.Y. Giants (3), 1950
11 NFC: Green Bay (3) vs. N.Y. Giants (8), 1944
NFC-D: Dallas (4) vs. Detroit (7), 1970

COMPLETION PERCENTAGE

Highest Completion Percentage, Game (20 attempts)
80.0 NFC-D: Washington vs. L.A. Rams, 1983 (25-20)
79.2 AFC-D: Pittsburgh vs. Baltimore, 1976 (24-19)
78.3 AFC-D: Miami vs. San Diego, 1982 (23-18)

Lowest Completion Percentage, Game (20 attempts)
18.5 NFC: Tampa Bay vs. Los Angeles, 1979 (27-5)
20.0 NFC-D: N.Y. Giants vs. Washington, 1943 (20-4)
25.8 NFC: Chi. Bears vs. Washington, 1937 (31-8)

YARDS GAINED

Most Yards Gained, Game
435 AFC: Miami vs. Pittsburgh, 1984
415 AFC-D: San Diego vs. Miami, 1981 (OT)
394 AFC-D: Miami vs. San Diego, 1981 (OT)

Fewest Yards Gained, Game
3 NFC: Chi. Cardinals vs. Philadelphia, 1948
7 NFC: Philadelphia vs. Chi. Cardinals, 1948
9 NFC-D: N.Y. Giants vs. Cleveland, 1950
NFC: Cleveland vs. Detroit, 1953

Most Yards Gained, Both Teams, Game
809 AFC-D: San Diego (415) vs. Miami (394), 1981 (OT)
747 AFC: Miami (435) vs. Pittsburgh (312), 1984
658 AFC-FR: San Diego (333) vs. Pittsburgh (325), 1982

Fewest Yards Gained, Both Teams, Game
10 NFC: Chi. Cardinals (3) vs. Philadelphia (7), 1948
38 NFC-D: N.Y. Giants (9) vs. Cleveland (29), 1950
102 NFC-D: Dallas (22) vs. Detroit (80), 1970

TIMES SACKED

Most Times Sacked, Game
9 AFC: Kansas City vs. Buffalo, 1966
NFC: Chicago vs. San Francisco, 1984
8 NFC: Green Bay vs. Dallas, 1967
7 NFC-D: Dallas vs. Los Angeles, 1973
SB: Dallas vs. Pittsburgh, 1975
AFC-FR: Houston vs. Oakland, 1980
NFC-D: Washington vs. Chicago, 1984
SB: New England vs. Chicago, 1985

Most Times Sacked, Both Teams, Game
13 AFC: Kansas City (9) vs. Buffalo (4), 1966
12 NFC-D: Dallas (7) vs. Los Angeles (5), 1973
NFC-D: Washington (7) vs. Chicago (5), 1984
NFC: Chicago (9) vs. San Francisco (3), 1984
10 AFC-FR: Houston (7) vs. Oakland (3), 1980
NFC-D: N.Y. Giants (6) vs. San Francisco (4), 1984
SB: New England (7) vs. Chicago (3), 1985

Fewest Times Sacked, Both Teams, Game
0 AFC-D: Buffalo vs. Pittsburgh, 1974
AFC-FR: Pittsburgh vs. San Diego, 1982
1 In many games

TOUCHDOWNS
Most Touchdowns, Game
6 AFC-D: Oakland vs. Houston, 1969
5 NFC: Chi. Bears vs. Washington, 1943
NFC: Detroit vs. Cleveland, 1957
AFC-D: Oakland vs. Kansas City, 1968
4 NFC: Cleveland vs. Los Angeles, 1950
NFC: Green Bay vs. Dallas, 1966
AFC-D: Oakland vs. Miami, 1974
NFC: Dallas vs. Los Angeles, 1975
SB: Pittsburgh vs. Dallas, 1978
AFC-D: Miami vs. San Diego, 1981 (OT)
NFC-FR: Green Bay vs. St. Louis, 1982
AFC: Miami vs. Pittsburgh, 1984
Most Touchdowns, Both Teams, Game
7 NFC: Chi. Bears (5) vs. Washington (2), 1943
AFC-D: Oakland (6) vs. Houston (1), 1969
SB: Pittsburgh (4) vs. Dallas (3), 1978
AFC-D: Miami (4) vs. San Diego (3), 1981 (OT)
AFC: Miami (4) vs. Pittsburgh (3), 1984
6 NFC-FR: Green Bay (4) vs. St. Louis (2), 1982
5 In many games

INTERCEPTIONS BY
Most Interceptions By, Game
8 NFC: Chi. Bears vs. Washington, 1940
7 NFC: Cleveland vs. Los Angeles, 1955
6 NFC: Green Bay vs. N.Y. Giants, 1939
NFC: Chi. Bears vs. N.Y. Giants, 1946
NFC: Cleveland vs. Detroit, 1954
AFC: San Diego vs. Houston, 1961
Most Interceptions By, Both Teams, Game
10 NFC: Cleveland (7) vs. Los Angeles (3), 1955
AFC: San Diego (6) vs. Houston (4), 1961
9 NFC: Green Bay (6) vs. N.Y. Giants (3), 1939
8 NFC: Chi. Bears (8) vs. Washington (0), 1940
NFC: Chi. Bears (6) vs. N.Y. Giants (2), 1946
NFC: Cleveland (6) vs. Detroit (2), 1954
AFC-FR: Buffalo (4) vs. N.Y. Jets (4), 1981
AFC: Miami (5) vs. N.Y. Jets (3), 1982

YARDS GAINED
Most Yards Gained, Game
138 AFC-FR: N.Y. Jets vs. Cincinnati, 1982
136 AFC: Dall. Texans vs. Houston, 1962 (OT)
130 NFC-D: Los Angeles vs. St. Louis, 1975
Most Yards Gained, Both Teams, Game
156 NFC: Green Bay (123) vs. N.Y. Giants (33), 1939
149 NFC: Cleveland (103) vs. Los Angeles (46), 1955
141 AFC-FR: Buffalo (79) vs. N.Y. Jets (62), 1981

TOUCHDOWNS
Most Touchdowns, Game
3 NFC: Chi. Bears vs. Washington, 1940
2 NFC-D: Los Angeles vs. St. Louis, 1975
1 In many games

PUNTING
Most Punts, Game
13 NFC: N.Y. Giants vs. Chi. Bears, 1933
AFC-D: Baltimore vs. Oakland, 1977 (OT)
11 AFC: Houston vs. Oakland, 1967
AFC-D: Houston vs. Oakland, 1969
NFC: L.A. Rams vs. Chicago, 1985
10 In many games
Fewest Punts, Game
0 NFC-FR: St. Louis vs. Green Bay, 1982
AFC-FR: N.Y. Jets vs. Cincinnati, 1982
1 NFC-D: Cleveland vs. Dallas, 1969
AFC: Miami vs. Oakland, 1973
AFC-D: Oakland vs. Cincinnati, 1975
AFC-D: Pittsburgh vs. Baltimore, 1976
AFC: Pittsburgh vs. Houston, 1978
NFC-FR: Green Bay vs. St. Louis, 1982
AFC-FR: Miami vs. New England, 1982
AFC-FR: San Diego vs. Pittsburgh, 1982
2 In many games
Most Punts, Both Teams, Game
23 NFC: N.Y. Giants (13) vs. Chi. Bears (10), 1933
21 AFC-D: Baltimore (13) vs. Oakland (8), 1977 (OT)
NFC: L.A. Rams (11) vs. Chicago (10), 1985
20 NFC: Green Bay (10) vs. N.Y. Giants (10), 1944
AFC: Miami (10) vs. N.Y. Jets (10), 1982
Fewest Punts, Both Teams, Game
1 NFC-FR: St. Louis (0) vs. Green Bay (1), 1982
2 AFC-FR: N.Y. Jets (0) vs. Cincinnati (2), 1982
3 AFC: Miami (1) vs. Oakland (2), 1973
AFC-FR: San Diego (1) vs. Pittsburgh (2), 1982

AVERAGE YARDAGE
Highest Average, Punting, Game (4 punts)
56.0 AFC: Oakland vs. San Diego, 1980
52.5 NFC: Washington vs. Chi. Bears, 1942
51.3 AFC: Pittsburgh vs. Miami, 1972
Lowest Average, Punting, Game (4 punts)
24.9 NFC: Washington vs. Chi. Bears, 1937
25.5 NFC: Green Bay vs. N.Y. Giants, 1962
27.8 AFC-D: San Diego vs. Buffalo, 1980

PUNT RETURNS
Most Punt Returns, Game
8 NFC: Green Bay vs. N.Y. Giants, 1944
7 NFC-D: Washington vs. N.Y. Giants, 1943
NFC-D: Chi. Bears vs. Los Angeles, 1950
AFC-D: Baltimore vs. Cincinnati, 1970
NFC: Los Angeles vs. Minnesota, 1976
AFC-FR: Houston vs. Oakland, 1980
AFC-D: Cleveland vs. Oakland, 1980
6 By many teams
Most Punt Returns, Both Teams, Game
13 AFC-FR: Houston (7) vs. Oakland (6), 1980
11 NFC: Green Bay (8) vs. N.Y. Giants (3), 1944
NFC-D: Green Bay (6) vs. Baltimore (5), 1965
10 In many games
Fewest Punt Returns, Both Teams, Game
0 NFC: Chi. Bears vs. N.Y. Giants, 1941
AFC: Boston vs. San Diego, 1963
NFC-FR: Green Bay vs. St. Louis, 1982
1 AFC: Miami (0) vs. Pittsburgh (1), 1972
AFC: Cincinnati (0) vs. San Diego (1), 1981
AFC-FR: Cincinnati (0) vs. N.Y. Jets (1), 1982
AFC-FR: San Diego (0) vs. Pittsburgh (1), 1982
NFC-D: Minnesota (0) vs. Washington (1), 1982
AFC: Seattle (0) vs. L.A. Raiders (1), 1983
2 In many games

YARDS GAINED
Most Yards Gained, Game
155 NFC-D: Dallas vs. Cleveland, 1967
150 NFC: Chi. Cardinals vs. Philadelphia, 1947
112 NFC-D: Philadelphia vs. Pittsburgh, 1947
Fewest Yards Gained, Game
−10 NFC: Green Bay vs. Cleveland, 1965
−9 NFC: Dallas vs. Green Bay, 1966
AFC-D: Kansas City vs. Oakland, 1968
−5 AFC-D: Miami vs. Oakland, 1970
NFC-D: San Francisco vs. Dallas, 1972
NFC: Dallas vs. Washington, 1972
Most Yards Gained, Both Teams, Game
166 NFC-D: Dallas (155) vs. Cleveland (11), 1967
160 NFC: Chi. Cardinals (150) vs. Philadelphia (10), 1947
146 NFC-D: Philadelphia (112) vs. Pittsburgh (34), 1947
Fewest Yards Gained, Both Teams, Game
−9 NFC: Dallas (−9) vs. Green Bay (0), 1966
−6 AFC-D: Miami (−5) vs. Oakland (−1), 1970
−3 NFC-D: San Francisco (−5) vs. Dallas (2), 1972

TOUCHDOWNS
Most Touchdowns, Game
1 By eight teams

KICKOFF RETURNS
Most Kickoff Returns, Game
10 NFC-D: L.A. Rams vs. Washington, 1983
9 NFC: Chi. Bears vs. N.Y. Giants, 1956
AFC: Boston vs. San Diego, 1963
AFC: Houston vs. Oakland, 1967
8 By many teams
Most Kickoff Returns, Both Teams, Game
13 NFC-D: Green Bay (7) vs. Dallas (6), 1982
12 AFC: Boston (9) vs. San Diego (3), 1963
NFC: Dallas (6) vs. Green Bay (6), 1966
AFC-D: Baltimore (6) vs. Oakland (6), 1977 (OT)
AFC: Oakland (6) vs. San Diego (6), 1980
AFC-D: Miami (6) vs. San Diego (6), 1981 (OT)
NFC-D: N.Y. Giants (7) vs. San Francisco (5), 1981
AFC-FR: Cincinnati (8) vs. N.Y. Jets (4), 1982
NFC-D: L.A. Rams (10) vs. Washington (2), 1983
11 In many games
Fewest Kickoff Returns, Both Teams, Game
1 NFC: Green Bay (0) vs. Boston (1), 1936
2 NFC-D: Los Angeles (0) vs. Chi. Bears (2), 1950
AFC: Houston (0) vs. San Diego (2), 1961
AFC-D: Oakland (1) vs. Pittsburgh (1), 1972
AFC-D: N.Y. Jets (0) vs. L.A. Raiders (2), 1982
AFC: Miami (1) vs. N.Y. Jets (1), 1982
3 In many games

YARDS GAINED
Most Yards Gained, Game
225 NFC: Washington vs. Chi. Bears, 1940
222 SB: Miami vs. Washington, 1982
215 AFC: Houston vs. Oakland, 1967
Most Yards Gained, Both Teams, Game
379 AFC-D: Baltimore (193) vs. Oakland (186), 1977 (OT)
321 NFC-D: Dallas (173) vs. Green Bay (148), 1982
318 AFC-D: Miami (183) vs. Oakland (135), 1974
Fewest Yards Gained, Both Teams, Game
31 NFC-D: Los Angeles (0) vs. Chi. Bears (31), 1950
32 NFC: Green Bay (0) vs. Boston (32), 1936
46 NFC-D: Philadelphia (15) vs. Pittsburgh (31), 1947
AFC-D: Baltimore (0) vs. Cincinnati (46), 1970

TOUCHDOWNS
Most Touchdowns, Game
1 NFC-D: San Francisco vs. Dallas, 1972
AFC-D: Miami vs. Oakland, 1974

AFC-D: Baltimore vs. Oakland, 1977 (OT)
SB: Miami vs. Washington, 1982

PENALTIES

Most Penalties, Game
14 AFC-FR: Oakland vs. Houston, 1980
NFC-D: San Francisco vs. N.Y. Giants, 1981
12 NFC-D: Chi. Bears vs. Green Bay, 1941
AFC-D: Pittsburgh vs. Baltimore, 1976
SB: Dallas vs. Denver, 1977
AFC-FR: N.Y. Jets vs. Cincinnati, 1982
11 NFC: N.Y. Giants vs. Green Bay, 1944
AFC-D: Oakland vs. New England, 1976
AFC-D: Pittsburgh vs. Denver, 1978
NFC-FR: Dallas vs. Los Angeles, 1980
Fewest Penalties, Game
0 NFC: Philadelphia vs. Green Bay, 1960
NFC-D: Detroit vs. Dallas, 1970
AFC-D: Miami vs. Oakland, 1970
SB: Miami vs. Dallas, 1971
NFC-D: Washington vs. Minnesota, 1973
SB: Pittsburgh vs. Dallas, 1975
1 By many teams
Most Penalties, Both Teams, Game
22 AFC-FR: Oakland (14) vs. Houston (8), 1980
NFC-D: San Francisco (14) vs. N.Y. Giants (8), 1981
21 AFC-D: Oakland (11) vs. New England (10), 1976
20 SB: Dallas (12) vs. Denver (8), 1977
Fewest Penalties, Both Teams, Game
2 NFC: Washington (1) vs. Chi. Bears (1), 1937
NFC-D: Washington (0) vs. Minnesota (2), 1973
SB: Pittsburgh (0) vs. Dallas (2), 1975
3 AFC: Miami (1) vs. Baltimore (2), 1971
NFC: San Francisco (1) vs. Dallas (2), 1971
SB: Miami (0) vs. Dallas (3), 1971
AFC-D: Pittsburgh (1) vs. Oakland (2), 1972
AFC-D: Miami (1) vs. Cincinnati (2), 1973
SB: Miami (1) vs. San Francisco (2), 1984
4 NFC-D: Cleveland (2) vs. Dallas (2), 1967
NFC-D: Minnesota (1) vs. San Francisco (3), 1970
AFC-D: Miami (0) vs. Oakland (4), 1970
NFC-D: Dallas (2) vs. Minnesota (2), 1971

YARDS PENALIZED

Most Yards Penalized, Game
145 NFC-D: San Francisco vs. N.Y. Giants, 1981
133 SB: Dallas vs. Baltimore, 1970
128 NFC-D: Chi. Bears vs. Green Bay, 1941
Fewest Yards Penalized, Game
0 By six teams
Most Yards Penalized, Both Teams, Game
206 NFC-D: San Francisco (145) vs. N.Y. Giants (61), 1981
192 AFC-D: Denver (104) vs. Pittsburgh (88), 1978
182 NFC-FR: Atlanta (98) vs. Minnesota (84), 1982
Fewest Yards Penalized, Both Teams, Game
9 NFC-D: Washington (0) vs. Minnesota (9), 1973
15 SB: Miami (0) vs. Dallas (15), 1971
20 NFC: Washington (5) vs. Chi. Bears (15), 1937
AFC-D: Pittsburgh (5) vs. Oakland (15), 1972
SB: Pittsburgh (0) vs. Dallas (20), 1975
Miami (10) vs. San Francisco (10), 1984

FUMBLES

Most Fumbles, Game
6 By nine teams
Most Fumbles, Both Teams, Game
12 AFC: Houston (6) vs. Pittsburgh (6), 1978
10 NFC: Chi. Bears (5) vs. N.Y. Giants (5), 1934
SB: Dallas (6) vs. Denver (4), 1977
9 NFC-D: San Francisco (6) vs. Detroit (3), 1957
NFC-D: San Francisco (5) vs. Dallas (4), 1972
NFC: Dallas (5) vs. Philadelphia (4), 1980
Most Fumbles Lost, Game
4 NFC: N.Y. Giants vs. Baltimore, 1958 (OT)
AFC: Kansas City vs. Oakland, 1969
SB: Baltimore vs. Dallas, 1970
AFC: Pittsburgh vs. Oakland, 1975
SB: Denver vs. Dallas, 1977
AFC: Houston vs. Pittsburgh, 1978
AFC: Miami vs. New England, 1985
SB: New England vs. Chicago, 1985
3 By many teams
Fewest Fumbles, Both Teams, Game
0 NFC: Green Bay vs. Cleveland, 1965
AFC: Buffalo vs. San Diego, 1965
AFC-D: Oakland vs. Miami, 1974
AFC-D: Houston vs. San Diego, 1979
NFC-D: Dallas vs. Los Angeles, 1979
SB: Los Angeles vs. Pittsburgh, 1979
AFC-D: Buffalo vs. Cincinnati, 1981
1 In many games

RECOVERIES

Most Total Fumbles Recovered, Game
8 SB: Dallas vs. Denver, 1977 (4 own, 4 opp)
7 NFC: Chi. Bears vs. N.Y. Giants, 1934 (5 own, 2 opp)
NFC-D: San Francisco vs. Detroit, 1957 (4 own, 3 opp)
NFC-D: San Francisco vs. Dallas, 1972 (4 own, 3 opp)
AFC: Pittsburgh vs. Houston, 1978 (3 own, 4 opp)
6 AFC: Houston vs. San Diego, 1961 (4 own, 2 opp)
AFC-D: Cleveland vs. Baltimore, 1971 (4 own, 2 opp)
AFC-D: Cleveland vs. Oakland, 1980 (5 own, 1 opp)
NFC: Philadelphia vs. Dallas, 1980 (3 own, 3 opp)
Most Own Fumbles Recovered, Game
5 NFC: Chi. Bears vs. N.Y. Giants, 1934
AFC-D: Cleveland vs. Oakland, 1980
4 By many teams

TURNOVERS

(Numbers of times losing the ball on interceptions and fumbles.)

Most Turnovers, Game
9 NFC: Washington vs. Chi. Bears, 1940
NFC: Detroit vs. Cleveland, 1954
AFC: Houston vs. Pittsburgh, 1978
8 NFC: N.Y. Giants vs. Chi. Bears, 1946
NFC: Los Angeles vs. Cleveland, 1955
NFC: Cleveland vs. Detroit, 1957
SB: Denver vs. Dallas, 1977
NFC-D: Minnesota vs. Philadelphia, 1980
7 AFC: Houston vs. San Diego, 1961
SB: Baltimore vs. Dallas, 1970
AFC: Pittsburgh vs. Oakland, 1975
NFC-D: Chicago vs. Dallas, 1977
NFC: Los Angeles vs. Dallas, 1978
AFC-D: San Diego vs. Miami, 1982
Fewest Turnovers, Game
0 By many teams
Most Turnovers, Both Teams, Game
14 AFC: Houston (9) vs. Pittsburgh (5), 1978
13 NFC: Detroit (9) vs. Cleveland (4), 1954
AFC: Houston (7) vs. San Diego (6), 1961
12 AFC: Pittsburgh (7) vs. Oakland (5), 1975
Fewest Turnovers, Both Teams, Game
1 AFC-D: Baltimore (0) vs. Cincinnati (1), 1970
AFC-D: Pittsburgh (0) vs. Buffalo (1), 1974
AFC: Oakland (0) vs. Pittsburgh (1), 1976
NFC-D: Minnesota (0) vs. Washington (1), 1982
NFC-D: Chicago (0) vs. N.Y. Giants (1), 1985
2 In many games

AFC-NFC PRO BOWL RECORDS

Compiled by Elias Sports Bureau

INDIVIDUAL RECORDS

SERVICE

Most Games

9 *Ken Houston, Houston, 1971-73; Washington, 1974-79
Joe Greene, Pittsburgh, 1971-77, 1979-80
Jack Lambert, Pittsburgh, 1976-84
8 Tom Mack, Los Angeles, 1971-76, 1978-79
*Franco Harris, Pittsburgh, 1973-76, 1978-81
Lemar Parrish, Cincinnati, 1971-72, 1975-77; Washington, 1978, 1980-81
Art Shell, Oakland, 1973-79, 1981
Ted Hendricks, Baltimore, 1972-74; Green Bay, 1975; Oakland, 1981-82; L.A. Raiders, 1983-84
*John Hannah, New England, 1977, 1979-83, 1985-86
Walter Payton, Chicago, 1977-81, 1984-86
*Randy White, Dallas, 1978, 1980-86
Mike Webster, Pittsburgh, 1979-86
7 Ron Yary, Minnesota, 1972-78
Elvin Bethea, Houston, 1972-76, 1979-80
Roger Wehrli, St. Louis, 1971-72, 1975-78, 1980
Jack Youngblood, Los Angeles, 1974-80
Ray Guy, Oakland, 1974-79, 1981
Robert Brazile, Houston, 1977-83
Randy Gradishar, Denver, 1976, 1978-80, 1982-84
Harry Carson, N.Y. Giants, 1979-80, 1982-86
*Mike Haynes, New England, 1978-81, 1983; L.A. Raiders, 1985-86
James Lofton, Green Bay, 1979, 1981-86
*Also selected, but did not play, in one additional game

SCORING

POINTS

Most Points, Career

30 Jan Stenerud, Kansas City, 1971-72, 1976; Green Bay, 1985 (6-pat, 8-fg)
18 John Brockington, Green Bay, 1972-74 (3-td)
Earl Campbell, Houston, 1979-82, 1984 (3-td)
Chuck Muncie, New Orleans, 1980; San Diego, 1982-83 (3-td)
William Andrews, Atlanta, 1981-84 (3-td)
Marcus Allen, L.A. Raiders, 1983, 1985-86 (3-td)
16 Garo Yepremian, Miami, 1974, 1979 (1-pat, 5-fg)

Most Points, Game

18 John Brockington, Green Bay, 1973 (3-td)
15 Garo Yepremian, Miami, 1974 (5-fg)
14 Jan Stenerud, Kansas City, 1972 (2-pat, 4-fg)

TOUCHDOWNS

Most Touchdowns, Career

3 John Brockington, Green Bay, 1972-74 (2-r, 1-p)
Earl Campbell, Houston, 1979-82, 1984 (3-r)
Chuck Muncie, New Orleans, 1980; San Diego, 1982-83 (3-r)
William Andrews, Atlanta, 1981-84 (1-r, 2-p)
Marcus Allen, L.A. Raiders, 1983, 1985-86 (2-r, 1-p)
2 By 10 players

Most Touchdowns, Game

3 John Brockington, Green Bay, 1973 (2-r, 1-p)
2 Mel Renfro, Dallas, 1971 (2-ret)
Earl Campbell, Houston, 1980 (2-r)
Chuck Muncie, New Orleans, 1980 (2-r)
William Andrews, Atlanta, 1984 (2-p)

POINTS AFTER TOUCHDOWN

Most Points After Touchdown, Career

6 Chester Marcol, Green Bay, 1973, 1975 (6 att)
Mark Moseley, Washington, 1980, 1983 (7 att)
Ali Haji-Sheikh, N.Y. Giants, 1984 (6 att)
Jan Stenerud, Kansas City, 1971-72, 1976; Green Bay, 1985 (6 att)

Most Points After Touchdown, Game

6 Ali Haji-Sheikh, N.Y. Giants, 1984 (6 att)
4 Chester Marcol, Green Bay, 1973 (4 att)
Mark Moseley, Washington, 1980 (5 att)
Morten Andersen, New Orleans, 1986 (4 att)

FIELD GOALS

Most Field Goals Attempted, Career

15 Jan Stenerud, Kansas City, 1971-72, 1976; Green Bay, 1985
7 Garo Yepremian, Miami, 1974, 1979
Mark Moseley, Washington, 1980, 1983
6 Ed Murray, Detroit, 1981

Most Field Goals Attempted, Game

6 Jan Stenerud, Kansas City, 1972
Ed Murray, Detroit, 1981
Mark Moseley, Washington, 1983
5 Garo Yepremian, Miami, 1974
4 Jan Stenerud, Kansas City, 1976

Most Field Goals, Career

8 Jan Stenerud, Kansas City, 1971-72, 1976; Green Bay, 1985
5 Garo Yepremian, Miami, 1974, 1979
4 Ed Murray, Detroit, 1981

Most Field Goals, Game

5 Garo Yepremian, Miami, 1974 (5 att)
4 Jan Stenerud, Kansas City, 1972 (6 att)
Ed Murray, Detroit, 1981 (6 att)
2 By many players

Longest Field Goal

48 Jan Stenerud, Kansas City, 1972
43 Gary Anderson, Pittsburgh, 1984
42 Jim Bakken, St. Louis, 1976

SAFETIES

Most Safeties, Game

1 Art Still, Kansas City, 1983
Mark Gastineau, N.Y. Jets, 1985

RUSHING

ATTEMPTS

Most Attempts, Career

76 Walter Payton, Chicago, 1977-81, 1984-86
68 O.J. Simpson, Buffalo, 1973-77
46 Franco Harris, Pittsburgh, 1973-76, 1978-81
Earl Campbell, Houston, 1979-82, 1984

Most Attempts, Game

19 O.J. Simpson, Buffalo, 1974
17 Marv Hubbard, Oakland, 1974
16 O.J. Simpson, Buffalo, 1973
Marcus Allen, L.A. Raiders, 1986

YARDS GAINED

Most Yards Gained, Career

356 O.J. Simpson, Buffalo, 1973-77
344 Walter Payton, Chicago, 1977-81, 1984-86
220 Earl Campbell, Houston, 1979-82, 1984

Most Yards Gained, Game

112 O. J. Simpson, Buffalo, 1973
104 Marv Hubbard, Oakland, 1974
77 Walter Payton, Chicago, 1978

Longest Run From Scrimmage

41 Lawrence McCutcheon, Los Angeles, 1976
30 O.J. Simpson, Buffalo, 1975
29 Franco Harris, Pittsburgh, 1973

AVERAGE GAIN

Highest Average Gain, Career (20 attempts)

5.81 Marv Hubbard, Oakland, 1972-74 (36-209)
5.71 Wilbert Montgomery, Philadelphia, 1979-80 (21-120)
5.36 Larry Csonka, Miami, 1971-72, 1975 (22-118)

Highest Average Gain, Game (10 attempts)

7.00 O.J. Simpson, Buffalo, 1973 (16-112)
Ottis Anderson, St. Louis, 1981 (10-70)
6.91 Walter Payton, Chicago, 1985 (11-76)
6.90 Earl Campbell, Houston, 1980 (10-69)

TOUCHDOWNS

Most Touchdowns, Career

3 Earl Campbell, Houston, 1979-82, 1984
Chuck Muncie, New Orleans, 1980; San Diego, 1982-83
2 John Brockington, Green Bay, 1972-74
O.J. Simpson, Buffalo, 1973-77
Walter Payton, Chicago, 1977-81, 1984-86
Marcus Allen, L.A. Raiders, 1983, 1985-86

Most Touchdowns, Game

2 John Brockington, Green Bay, 1973
Earl Campbell, Houston, 1980
Chuck Muncie, New Orleans, 1980

PASSING

ATTEMPTS

Most Attempts, Career

120 Dan Fouts, San Diego, 1980-84, 1986
88 Bob Griese, Miami, 1971-72, 1974-75, 1977, 1979
56 Ken Anderson, Cincinnati, 1976-77, 1982-83

Most Attempts, Game

32 Bill Kenney, Kansas City, 1984
30 Dan Fouts, San Diego, 1983
28 Jim Hart, St. Louis, 1976

COMPLETIONS

Most Completions, Career

63 Dan Fouts, San Diego, 1980-84, 1986
44 Bob Griese, Miami, 1971-72, 1974-75, 1977, 1979
33 Ken Anderson, Cincinnati, 1976-77, 1982-83

Most Completions, Game

21 Joe Theismann, Washington, 1984
17 Dan Fouts, San Diego, 1983
16 Dan Fouts, San Diego, 1986

COMPLETION PERCENTAGE

Highest Completion Percentage, Career (40 attempts)

68.9 Joe Theismann, Washington, 1983-84 (45-31)
58.9 Ken Anderson, Cincinnati, 1976-77, 1982-83 (56-33)
52.5 Dan Fouts, San Diego, 1980-84, 1986 (120-63)

Highest Completion Percentage, Game (10 attempts)

90.0 Archie Manning, New Orleans, 1980 (10-9)
77.8 Joe Theismann, Washington, 1984 (27-21)
71.4 Joe Montana, San Francisco, 1985 (14-10)

YARDS GAINED

Most Yards Gained, Career

890 Dan Fouts, San Diego, 1980-84, 1986
554 Bob Griese, Miami, 1971-72, 1974-75, 1977, 1979
398 Ken Anderson, Cincinnati, 1976-77, 1982-83

Most Yards Gained, Game

274 Dan Fouts, San Diego, 1983
242 Joe Theismann, Washington, 1984
212 Phil Simms, N.Y. Giants, 1986

Longest Completion

64 Dan Pastorini, Houston (to Burrough, Houston), 1976 (TD)

57 James Harris, Los Angeles (to Gray, St. Louis), 1975
Ken Anderson, Cincinnati (to G. Pruitt, Cleveland), 1977
56 Dan Marino, Miami (to Allen, L.A. Raiders), 1985

AVERAGE GAIN
Highest Average Gain, Career (40 attempts)
7.64 Joe Theismann, Washington, 1983-84 (45-344)
7.42 Dan Fouts, San Diego, 1980-84, 1986 (120-890)
7.11 Ken Anderson, Cincinnati, 1976-77, 1982-83 (56-398)
Highest Average Gain, Game (10 attempts)
11.40 Ken Anderson, Cincinnati, 1977 (10-114)
11.20 Archie Manning, New Orleans, 1980 (10-112)
11.09 Greg Landry, Detroit, 1972 (11-122)

TOUCHDOWNS
Most Touchdowns, Career
3 Joe Theismann, Washington, 1983-84
Joe Montana, San Francisco, 1982, 1984-85
Phil Simms, N.Y. Giants, 1986
2 James Harris, Los Angeles, 1975
Mike Boryla, Philadelphia, 1976
Ken Anderson, Cincinnati, 1976-77, 1982-83
Most Touchdowns, Game
3 Joe Theismann, Washington, 1984
Phil Simms, N.Y. Giants, 1986
2 James Harris, Los Angeles, 1975
Mike Boryla, Philadelphia, 1976
Ken Anderson, Cincinnati, 1977

HAD INTERCEPTED
Most Passes Had Intercepted, Career
8 Dan Fouts, San Diego, 1980-84, 1986
6 Jim Hart, St. Louis, 1975-78
5 Ken Stabler, Oakland, 1974-75, 1978
Most Passes Had Intercepted, Game
5 Jim Hart, St. Louis, 1977
4 Ken Stabler, Oakland, 1974
3 Dan Fouts, San Diego, 1986
Most Attempts, Without Interception, Game
27 Joe Theismann, Washington, 1984
Phil Simms, N.Y. Giants, 1986
26 John Brodie, San Francisco, 1971
Danny White, Dallas, 1983
21 Roman Gabriel, Philadelphia, 1974
Dan Marino, Miami, 1985

PERCENTAGE, PASSES HAD INTERCEPTED
Lowest Percentage, Passes Had Intercepted, Career (40 attempts)
0.00 Joe Theismann, Washington, 1983-84 (45-0)
3.41 Bob Griese, Miami, 1971-72, 1974-75, 1977, 1979 (88-3)
5.36 Ken Anderson, Cincinnati, 1976-77, 1982-83 (56-3)

PASS RECEIVING

RECEPTIONS
Most Receptions, Career
15 Steve Largent, Seattle, 1979, 1982, 1985-86
14 Walter Payton, Chicago, 1977-81, 1984-86
John Stallworth, Pittsburgh, 1980, 1983, 1985
James Lofton, Green Bay, 1979, 1981-86
13 William Andrews, Atlanta, 1981-84
Most Receptions, Game
8 Steve Largent, Seattle, 1986
7 John Stallworth, Pittsburgh, 1983
6 John Stallworth, Pittsburgh, 1980
Kellen Winslow, San Diego, 1982

YARDS GAINED
Most Yards Gained, Career
226 Wes Chandler, New Orleans, 1980; San Diego, 1983-84, 1986
206 James Lofton, Green Bay, 1979, 1981-86
179 Kellen Winslow, San Diego, 1981-84
Most Yards Gained, Game
114 Wes Chandler, San Diego, 1986
96 Ken Burrough, Houston, 1976
91 Alfred Jenkins, Atlanta, 1981
Longest Reception
64 Ken Burrough, Houston (from Pastorini, Houston), 1976 (TD)
57 Mel Gray, St. Louis (from Harris, Los Angeles), 1975
Greg Pruitt, Cleveland (from Anderson, Cincinnati), 1977
56 Marcus Allen, L.A. Raiders (from Marino, Miami), 1985

TOUCHDOWNS
Most Touchdowns, Career
2 Mel Gray, St. Louis, 1975-78
Cliff Branch, Oakland, 1975-78
Terry Metcalf, St. Louis, 1975-76, 1978
Tony Hill, Dallas, 1979-80, 1986
William Andrews, Atlanta, 1981-84
James Lofton, Green Bay, 1979, 1981-86
Jimmie Giles, Tampa Bay, 1981-83, 1986
Most Touchdowns, Game
2 William Andrews, Atlanta, 1984

INTERCEPTIONS BY

Most Interceptions, Career
4 Everson Walls, Dallas, 1982-84, 1986
3 Ken Houston, Houston, 1971-73; Washington, 1975-79
Jack Lambert, Pittsburgh, 1976-84
Ted Hendricks, Baltimore, 1972-74; Green Bay, 1975; Oakland, 1981-82; L.A. Raiders, 1983-84
2 By six players

Most Interceptions By, Game
2 Mel Blount, Pittsburgh, 1977
Everson Walls, Dallas, 1982, 1983
LeRoy Irvin, L.A. Rams, 1986

YARDS GAINED
Most Yards Gained, Career
77 Ted Hendricks, Baltimore, 1972-74; Green Bay, 1975; Oakland, 1981-82; L.A. Raiders, 1983-84
48 Joey Browner, Minnesota, 1986
44 Nolan Cromwell, L.A. Rams, 1981-84
Most Yards Gained, Game
65 Ted Hendricks, Baltimore, 1973
48 Joey Browner, Minnesota, 1986
44 Nolan Cromwell, L.A. Rams, 1984
Longest Gain
65 Ted Hendricks, Baltimore, 1973
48 Joey Browner, Minnesota, 1986 (TD)
44 Nolan Cromwell, L.A. Rams, 1984 (TD)

TOUCHDOWNS
Most Touchdowns, Game
1 Bobby Bell, Kansas City, 1973
Nolan Cromwell, L.A. Rams, 1984
Joey Browner, Minnesota, 1986

PUNTING

Most Punts, Career
33 Ray Guy, Oakland, 1974-79, 1981
19 Dave Jennings, N.Y. Giants, 1979-81, 1983
16 Jerrel Wilson, Kansas City, 1971-73
Tom Wittum, San Francisco, 1974-75
Most Punts, Game
10 Reggie Roby, Miami, 1985
9 Tom Wittum, San Francisco, 1974
8 Jerrel Wilson, Kansas City, 1971
Tom Skladany, Detroit, 1982
Longest Punt
64 Tom Wittum, San Francisco, 1974
61 Reggie Roby, Miami, 1985
60 Ron Widby, Dallas, 1972

AVERAGE YARDAGE
Highest Average, Career (10 punts)
45.25 Jerrel Wilson, Kansas City, 1971-73 (16-724)
44.64 Ray Guy, Oakland, 1974-79, 1981 (33-1,473)
44.63 Tom Wittum, San Francisco, 1974-75 (16-714)
Highest Average, Game (4 punts)
49.00 Ray Guy, Oakland, 1974 (4-196)
47.75 Bob Grupp, Kansas City, 1980 (4-191)
47.40 Ray Guy, Oakland, 1976 (5-237)

PUNT RETURNS

Most Punt Returns, Career
13 Rick Upchurch, Denver, 1977, 1979-80, 1983
10 Mike Nelms, Washington, 1981-83
9 Greg Pruitt, Cleveland, 1974-75, 1977-78; L.A. Raiders, 1984
Most Punt Returns, Game
6 Henry Ellard, L.A. Rams, 1985
5 Rick Upchurch, Denver, 1980
Mike Nelms, Washington, 1981
Carl Roaches, Houston, 1982
4 By six players
Most Fair Catches, Game
2 Jerry Logan, Baltimore, 1971
Dick Anderson, Miami, 1974
Henry Ellard, L.A. Rams, 1985

YARDS GAINED
Most Yards Gained, Career
183 Billy Johnson, Houston, 1976, 1978; Atlanta, 1984
138 Rick Upchurch, Denver, 1977, 1979-80, 1983
119 Mike Nelms, Washington, 1981-83
Most Yards Gained, Game
159 Billy Johnson, Houston, 1976
138 Mel Renfro, Dallas, 1971
117 Wally Henry, Philadelphia, 1980
Longest Punt Return
90 Billy Johnson, Houston, 1976 (TD)
86 Wally Henry, Philadelphia, 1980 (TD)
82 Mel Renfro, Dallas, 1971 (TD)

TOUCHDOWNS
Most Touchdowns, Game
2 Mel Renfro, Dallas, 1971
1 Billy Johnson, Houston, 1976
Wally Henry, Philadelphia, 1980

KICKOFF RETURNS

Most Kickoff Returns, Career
10 Rick Upchurch, Denver, 1977, 1979-80, 1983
Greg Pruitt, Cleveland, 1974-75, 1977-78; L.A. Raiders, 1984
8 Mike Nelms, Washington, 1981-83
6 Terry Metcalf, St. Louis, 1975-76, 1978
Most Kickoff Returns, Game
6 Greg Pruitt, L.A. Raiders, 1984
5 Les (Speedy) Duncan, Washington, 1972
Ron Smith, Chicago, 1973
Herb Mul-Key, Washington, 1974
4 By five players

YARDS GAINED

Most Yards Gained, Career

309 Greg Pruitt, Cleveland, 1974-75, 1977-78; L.A. Raiders, 1984
222 Rick Upchurch, Denver, 1977, 1979-80, 1983
175 Les (Speedy) Duncan, Washington, 1972

Most Yards Gained, Game

192 Greg Pruitt, L.A. Raiders, 1984
175 Les (Speedy) Duncan, Washington, 1972
152 Ron Smith, Chicago, 1973

Longest Kickoff Return

62 Greg Pruitt, L.A. Raiders, 1984
61 Eugene (Mercury) Morris, Miami, 1972
55 Ron Smith, Chicago, 1973

TOUCHDOWNS

Most Touchdowns, Game

None

FUMBLES

Most Fumbles, Career

6 Dan Fouts, San Diego, 1980-84, 1986
4 Lawrence McCutcheon, Los Angeles, 1974-78
Franco Harris, Pittsburgh, 1973-76, 1978-81
3 O.J. Simpson, Buffalo, 1973-77
William Andrews, Atlanta, 1981-84
Joe Montana, San Francisco, 1982, 1984-85
Walter Payton, Chicago, 1977-81, 1984-86

Most Fumbles, Game

3 Dan Fouts, San Diego, 1982
2 By nine players

RECOVERIES

Most Fumbles Recovered, Career

3 Harold Jackson, Philadelphia, 1973; Los Angeles, 1974, 1976, 1978 (3-own)
Dan Fouts, San Diego, 1980-84, 1986 (3-own)
Randy White, Dallas, 1978, 1980-86 (3-opp)
2 By many players

Most Fumbles Recovered, Game

2 Dick Anderson, Miami, 1974 (1-own, 1-opp)
Harold Jackson, Los Angeles, 1974 (2-own)
Dan Fouts, San Diego, 1982 (2-own)

YARDAGE

Longest Fumble Return

83 Art Still, Kansas City, 1985 (TD, opp)
51 Phil Villapiano, Oakland, 1974 (opp)
34 Rick Upchurch, Denver, 1980 (own)

TOUCHDOWNS

Most Touchdowns, Game

1 Art Still, Kansas City, 1985

TEAM RECORDS

SCORING

Most Points, Game

45 NFC, 1984

Fewest Points, Game

3 AFC, 1984

Most Points, Both Teams, Game

64 NFC (37) vs. AFC (27), 1980

Fewest Points, Both Teams, Game

20 AFC (7) vs. NFC (13), 1979

TOUCHDOWNS

Most Touchdowns, Game

6 NFC, 1984

Fewest Touchdowns, Game

0 AFC, 1971, 1974, 1984

Most Touchdowns, Both Teams, Game

8 AFC (4) vs. NFC (4), 1973
NFC (5) vs. AFC (3), 1980

Fewest Touchdowns, Both Teams, Game

1 AFC (0) vs. NFC (1), 1974

POINTS AFTER TOUCHDOWN

Most Points After Touchdown, Game

6 NFC, 1984

Most Points After Touchdown, Both Teams, Game

7 NFC (4) vs. AFC (3), 1973
NFC (4) vs. AFC (3), 1980
NFC (4) vs. AFC (3), 1986

FIELD GOALS

Most Field Goals Attempted, Game

6 AFC, 1972
NFC, 1981, 1983

Most Field Goals Attempted, Both Teams, Game

9 NFC (6) vs. AFC (3), 1983

Most Field Goals, Game

5 AFC, 1974

Most Field Goals, Both Teams, Game

7 AFC (5) vs. NFC (2), 1974

NET YARDS GAINED RUSHING AND PASSING

Most Yards Gained, Game

466 AFC, 1983

Fewest Yards Gained, Game

146 AFC, 1971

Most Yards Gained, Both Teams, Game

811 AFC (466) vs. NFC (345), 1983

Fewest Yards Gained, Both Teams, Game

468 NFC (159) vs. AFC (309), 1972

RUSHING

ATTEMPTS

Most Attempts, Game

50 AFC, 1974

Fewest Attempts, Game

18 AFC, 1984

Most Attempts, Both Teams, Game

80 AFC (50) vs. NFC (30), 1974

Fewest Attempts, Both Teams, Game

54 AFC (27) vs. NFC (27), 1983
AFC (18) vs. NFC (36), 1984

YARDS GAINED

Most Yards Gained, Game

224 NFC, 1976

Fewest Yards Gained, Game

64 NFC, 1974

Most Yards Gained, Both Teams, Game

425 NFC (224) vs. AFC (201), 1976

Fewest Yards Gained, Both Teams, Game

178 AFC (66) vs. NFC (112), 1971

TOUCHDOWNS

Most Touchdowns, Game

2 AFC, 1973, 1980, 1982
NFC, 1973, 1977, 1980

PASSING

ATTEMPTS

Most Attempts, Game

50 AFC, 1983

Fewest Attempts, Game

17 NFC, 1972

Most Attempts, Both Teams, Game

94 AFC (50) vs. NFC (44), 1983

Fewest Attempts, Both Teams, Game

42 NFC (17) vs. AFC (25), 1972

COMPLETIONS

Most Completions, Game

31 AFC, 1983

Fewest Completions, Game

7 NFC, 1972, 1982

Most Completions, Both Teams, Game

55 AFC (31) vs. NFC (24), 1983

Fewest Completions, Both Teams, Game

18 NFC (7) vs. AFC (11), 1972

YARDS GAINED

Most Yards Gained, Game

387 AFC, 1983

Fewest Yards Gained, Game

42 NFC, 1982

Most Yards Gained, Both Teams, Game

608 AFC (387) vs. NFC (221), 1983

Fewest Yards Gained, Both Teams, Game

215 NFC (89) vs. AFC (126), 1972

TIMES SACKED

Most Times Sacked, Game

9 NFC, 1985

Fewest Times Sacked, Game

0 NFC, 1971

Most Times Sacked, Both Teams, Game

17 NFC (9) vs. AFC (8), 1985

Fewest Times Sacked, Both Teams, Game

4 AFC (2) vs. NFC (2), 1978

TOUCHDOWNS

Most Touchdowns, Game

4 NFC, 1984

Fewest Touchdowns, Game

0 AFC, 1971, 1974, 1982, 1984
NFC, 1977

Most Touchdowns, Both Teams, Game

5 NFC (3) vs. AFC (2), 1986

Fewest Touchdowns, Both Teams, Game

1 AFC (0) vs. NFC (1), 1971
AFC (0) vs. NFC (1), 1974
AFC (0) vs. NFC (1), 1982

INTERCEPTIONS BY

Most Interceptions By, Game

6 AFC, 1977

Most Interceptions By, Both Teams, Game

7 AFC (6) vs. NFC (1), 1977

YARDS GAINED

Most Yards Gained, Game

78 NFC, 1986

Most Yards Gained, Both Teams, Game

99 NFC (64) vs. AFC (35), 1975

TOUCHDOWNS

Most Touchdowns, Game

1 AFC, 1973
NFC, 1984, 1986

PUNTING

Most Punts, Game
10 AFC, 1985
Fewest Punts, Game
2 NFC, 1984
Most Punts, Both Teams, Game
16 AFC (10) vs. NFC (6), 1985
Fewest Punts, Both Teams, Game
6 NFC (2) vs. AFC (4), 1984

AVERAGE YARDAGE
Highest Average, Game
49.00 AFC, 1974 (4-196)

PUNT RETURNS

Most Punt Returns, Game
7 NFC, 1985
Fewest Punt Returns, Game
0 AFC, 1984
Most Punt Returns, Both Teams, Game
11 NFC (7) vs. AFC (4), 1985
Fewest Punt Returns, Both Teams, Game
3 AFC (0) vs. NFC (3), 1984

YARDS GAINED
Most Yards Gained, Game
177 AFC, 1976
Fewest Yards Gained, Game
0 AFC, 1984
Most Yards Gained, Both Teams, Game
263 AFC (177) vs. NFC (86), 1976
Fewest Yards Gained, Both Teams, Game
16 AFC (0) vs. NFC (16), 1984

TOUCHDOWNS
Most Touchdowns, Game
2 NFC, 1971

KICKOFF RETURNS

Most Kickoff Returns, Game
7 AFC, 1984
Fewest Kickoff Returns, Game
1 NFC, 1971, 1984
Most Kickoff Returns, Both Teams, Game
10 AFC (5) vs. NFC (5), 1976
AFC (5) vs. NFC (5), 1986
Fewest Kickoff Returns, Both Teams, Game
5 NFC (2) vs. AFC (3), 1979

YARDS GAINED
Most Yards Gained, Game
215 AFC, 1984
Fewest Yards Gained, Game
6 NFC, 1971
Most Yards Gained, Both Teams, Game
293 NFC (200) vs. AFC (93), 1972
Fewest Yards Gained, Both Teams, Game
108 AFC (49) vs. NFC (59), 1979

TOUCHDOWNS
Most Touchdowns, Game
None

FUMBLES

Most Fumbles, Game
10 NFC, 1974
Most Fumbles, Both Teams, Game
15 NFC (10) vs. AFC (5), 1974

RECOVERIES
Most Fumbles Recovered, Game
10 NFC, 1974 (6 own, 4 opp)
Most Fumbles Lost, Game
4 AFC, 1974

YARDS GAINED
Most Yards Gained, Game
87 AFC, 1985

TOUCHDOWNS
Most Touchdowns, Game
1 AFC, 1985

TURNOVERS

(Number of times losing the ball on interceptions and fumbles.)

Most Turnovers, Game
8 AFC, 1974
Fewest Turnovers, Game
1 AFC, 1972, 1976, 1978, 1979, 1985
NFC, 1976, 1980, 1983
Most Turnovers, Both Teams, Game
12 AFC (8) vs. NFC (4), 1974
Fewest Turnovers, Both Teams, Game
2 AFC (1) vs. NFC (1), 1976

RULES

1986 NFL Roster of Officials
Official Signals
Digest of Rules

1986 NFL Roster of Officials

Art McNally, Supervisor of Officials
Jack Reader, Assistant Supervisor of Officials
Nick Skorich, Assistant Supervisor of Officials
Joe Gardi, Assistant Supervisor of Officials
Tony Veteri, Assistant Supervisor of Officials

No.	Name	Position	College
115	Ancich, Hendi	Umpire	Harbor College
81	Anderson, Dave	Head Linesman	Salem College
34	Austin, Gerald	Side Judge	Western Carolina
22	Baetz, Paul	Back Judge	Heidelberg
55	Barnes, Tom	Back Judge	Minnesota
14	Barth, Gene	Referee	St. Louis
59	Beeks, Bob	Line Judge	Lincoln
17	Bergman, Jerry	Head Linesman	Duquesne
83	Blum, Ron	Line Judge	Marin College
110	Botchan, Ron	Umpire	Occidental
101	Boylston, Bob	Umpire	Alabama
43	Cashion, Red	Referee	Texas A&M
16	Cathcart, Royal	Side Judge	UC Santa Barbara
24	Clymer, Roy	Back Judge	New Mexico State
27	Conway, Al	Umpire	Army
61	Creed, Dick	Side Judge	Louisville
78	Demmas, Art	Umpire	Vanderbilt
45	DeSouza, Ron	Line Judge	Morgan State
74	Dodez, Ray	Line Judge	Wooster
31	Dolack, Dick	Field Judge	Ferris State
6	Dooley, Tom	Referee	VMI
113	Dorkowski, Don	Field Judge	Cal State-L.A.
102	Douglas, Merrill	Side Judge	Utah
12	Dreith, Ben	Referee	Colorado State
39	Fette, Jack	Line Judge	No College
57	Fiffick, Ed	Umpire	Marquette
47	Fincken, Tom	Side Judge	Kansas State
111	Frantz, Earnie	Head Linesman	No College
71	Frederic, Bob	Referee	Colorado
62	Gandy, Duwayne	Side Judge	Tulsa
50	Gereb, Neil	Umpire	California
72	Gierke, Terry	Head Linesman	Portland State
15	Glass, Bama	Line Judge	Colorado
85	Glover, Frank	Head Linesman	Morris Brown
23	Grier, Johnny	Field Judge	D.C. Teachers
75	Habel, Don	Field Judge	Western Oregon
63	Hagerty, Ligouri	Head Linesman	Syracuse
40	Haggerty, Pat	Referee	Colorado State
96	Hakes, Don	Field Judge	Bradley
104	Hamer, Dale	Head Linesman	Calif. State, Pa.
42	Hamilton, Dave	Umpire	Utah
105	Hantak, Dick	Referee	Southeast Missouri
66	Hawk, Dave	Side Judge	Southern Methodist
112	Haynes, Joe	Line Judge	Alcorn State
19	Hensley, Tom	Umpire	Tennessee
54	Johnson, Jack	Line Judge	Pacific Lutheran
114	Johnson, Tom	Head Linesman	Miami, Ohio
97	Jones, Nathan	Side Judge	Lewis & Clark
60	Jorgensen, Dick	Referee	Wisconsin
106	Jury, Al	Back Judge	San Bernardino Valley
107	Kearney, Jim	Back Judge	Pennsylvania
67	Keck, John	Umpire	Cornell College
25	Kelleher, Tom	Back Judge	Holy Cross
108	Kemp, Stan	Side Judge	Michigan
65	Kragseth, Norm	Head Linesman	Northwestern
86	Kukar, Bernie	Field Judge	St. John's
120	Lane, Gary	Side Judge	Missouri
18	Lewis, Bob	Field Judge	No College
21	Liske, Pete	Back Judge	Penn State
49	Look, Dean	Side Judge	Michigan State
90	Mace, Gil	Side Judge	Westminster
82	Mallette, Pat	Field Judge	Nebraska
26	Marion, Ed	Head Linesman	Pennsylvania
9	Markbreit, Jerry	Referee	Illinois
94	Marshall, Vern	Line Judge	Linfield
48	McCarter, Gordon	Referee	Western Reserve
95	McElwee, Bob	Referee	Navy
41	McKenzie, Dick	Line Judge	Ashland
76	Merrifield, Ed	Field Judge	Missouri
35	Miles, Leo	Head Linesman	Virginia State
117	Montgomery, Ben	Umpire	Morehouse
36	Moore, Bob	Back Judge	Dayton
88	Moss, Dave	Umpire	Dartmouth
20	Nemmers, Larry	Side Judge	Upper Iowa
51	Orem, Dale	Line Judge	Louisville
77	Orr, Don	Field Judge	Vanderbilt
64	Parry, Dave	Side Judge	Wabash
10	Phares, Ron	Head Linesman	Virginia Tech
92	Poole, Jim	Back Judge	San Diego State
58	Quinby, Bill	Side Judge	Iowa State
53	Reynolds, Bill	Line Judge	West Chester State
80	Rice, Bob	Side Judge	Denison
68	Richard, Louis	Back Judge	Southwest Louisiana
33	Roe, Howard	Line Judge	Wichita State
98	Rosser, Jimmy	Back Judge	Auburn
70	Seeman, Jerry	Referee	Winona State
109	Semon, Sid	Head Linesman	So. California
118	Sifferman, Tom	Back Judge	Seattle
7	Silva, Fred	Referee	San Jose State
73	Skelton, Bobby	Field Judge	Alabama
3	Smith, Boyce	Line Judge	Vanderbilt
119	Spitler, Ron	Field Judge	Panhandle State
91	Stanley, Bill	Field Judge	Redlands
103	Stuart, Rex	Umpire	Appalachian State
37	Toler, Burl	Head Linesman	San Francisco
52	Tompkins, Ben	Back Judge	Texas
32	Tunney, Jim	Referee	Occidental
93	Vaughan, Jack	Field Judge	Mississippi State
100	Wagner, Bob	Umpire	Penn State
28	Wedge, Don	Back Judge	Ohio Wesleyan
87	Weidner, Paul	Head Linesman	Cincinnati
89	Wells, Gordon	Umpire	Occidental
30	Wilford, Dan	Line Judge	Mississippi
99	Williams, Banks	Back Judge	Houston
8	Williams, Dale	Head Linesman	Cal St.-Northridge
84	Wortman, Bob	Field Judge	Findlay
11	Wyant, Fred	Referee	West Virginia

Numerical Roster

No.	Name	Position
3	Boyce Smith	LJ
6	Tom Dooley	R
7	Fred Silva	R
8	Dale Williams	HL
9	Jerry Markbreit	R
10	Ron Phares	HL
11	Fred Wyant	R
12	Ben Dreith	R
14	Gene Barth	R
15	Bama Glass	LJ
16	Royal Cathcart	SJ
17	Jerry Bergman	HL
18	Bob Lewis	FJ
19	Tom Hensley	U
20	Larry Nemmers	SJ
21	Pete Liske	BJ
22	Paul Baetz	BJ
23	Johnny Grier	FJ
24	Roy Clymer	BJ
25	Tom Kelleher	BJ
26	Ed Marion	HL
27	Al Conway	U
28	Don Wedge	BJ
30	Dan Wilford	LJ
31	Dick Dolack	FJ
32	Jim Tunney	R
33	Howard Roe	LJ
34	Gerald Austin	SJ
35	Leo Miles	HL
36	Bob Moore	BJ
37	Burl Toler	HL
39	Jack Fette	LJ
40	Pat Haggerty	R
41	Dick McKenzie	LJ
42	Dave Hamilton	U
43	Red Cashion	R
45	Ron DeSouza	LJ
47	Tom Fincken	SJ
48	Gordon McCarter	R
49	Dean Look	SJ
50	Neil Gereb	U
51	Dale Orem	LJ
52	Ben Tompkins	BJ
53	Bill Reynolds	LJ
54	Jack Johnson	LJ
55	Tom Barnes	BJ
57	Ed Fiffick	U
58	Bill Quinby	SJ
59	Bob Beeks	LJ
60	Dick Jorgensen	R
61	Dick Creed	SJ
62	Duwayne Gandy	SJ
63	Ligouri Hagerty	HL
64	Dave Parry	SJ
65	Norm Kragseth	HL
66	Dave Hawk	SJ
67	John Keck	U
68	Louis Richard	BJ
70	Jerry Seeman	R
71	Bob Frederic	R
72	Terry Gierke	HL
73	Bobby Skelton	FJ
74	Ray Dodez	LJ
75	Don Habel	FJ
76	Ed Merrifield	FJ
77	Don Orr	FJ
78	Art Demmas	U
80	Bob Rice	SJ
81	Dave Anderson	HL
82	Pat Mallette	FJ
83	Ron Blum	LJ
84	Bob Wortman	FJ
85	Frank Glover	HL
86	Bernie Kukar	FJ
87	Paul Weidner	HL
88	Dave Moss	U
89	Gordon Wells	U
90	Gil Mace	SJ
91	Bill Stanley	FJ
92	Jim Poole	BJ
93	Jack Vaughan	FJ
94	Vern Marshall	LJ
95	Bob McElwee	R
96	Don Hakes	FJ
97	Nathan Jones	SJ
98	Jimmy Rosser	BJ
99	Banks Williams	BJ
100	Bob Wagner	U
101	Bob Boylston	U
102	Merrill Douglas	SJ
103	Rex Stuart	U
104	Dale Hamer	HL
105	Dick Hantak	R
106	Al Jury	BJ
107	Jim Kearney	BJ
108	Stan Kemp	SJ
109	Sid Semon	HL
110	Ron Botchan	U
111	Earnie Frantz	HL
112	Joe Haynes	LJ
113	Don Dorkowski	FJ
114	Tom Johnson	HL
115	Hendi Ancich	U
117	Ben Montgomery	U
118	Tom Sifferman	BJ
119	Ron Spitler	FJ
120	Gary Lane	SJ

1986 Officials at a Glance

Referees

Gene Barth, No. **14,** St. Louis, president, oil company, 16th year.

Red Cashion, No. **43,** Texas A&M, chairman of the board, insurance company, 15th year.

Tom Dooley, No. **6,** VMI, general contractor, 9th year.

Ben Dreith, No. **12,** Colorado State, teacher-counselor, 27th year.

Bob Frederic, No. **71,** Colorado, president, printing and lithographing company, 19th year.

Pat Haggerty, No. **40,** Colorado State, teacher and coach, 22nd year.

Dick Hantak, No. **105,** S.E. Missouri, high school department chairman, 9th year.

Dick Jorgensen, No. **60,** Wisconsin, president, commercial bank, 19th year.

Jerry Markbreit, No. **9,** Illinois, trade and barter manager, 11th year.

Gordon McCarter, No. **48,** Western Reserve, industrial sales, 20th year.

Bob McElwee, No. **95,** U.S. Naval Academy, owner, construction company, 11th year.

Jerry Seeman, No. **70,** Winona State, assistant superintendent, 12th year.

Fred Silva, No. **7,** San Jose State, consultant, 20th year.

Jim Tunney, No. **32,** Occidental, president of motivation company and professional speaker, 27th year.

Fred Wyant, No. **11,** West Virginia, regional manager, life insurance company, former NFL player, 21st year.

Umpires

Hendi Ancich, No. **115,** Harbor, longshoreman, 5th year.

Ron Botchan, No. **110,** Occidental, college professor, former AFL player, 7th year.

Bob Boylston, No. **101,** Alabama, stockbroker, 9th year.

Al Conway, No. **27,** Army, national director, industrial sales, 18th year.

Art Demmas, No. **78,** Vanderbilt, investments and financial planning, insurance company, 19th year.

Ed Fiffick, No. **57,** Marquette, podiatric physician, 8th year.

Neil Gereb, No. **50,** California, supervisor, aircraft company, 6th year.

Dave Hamilton, No. **42,** Utah, hospital administrator, 12th year.

Tommy Hensley, No. **19,** Tennessee, owner, land development and management company, 20th year.

John Keck, No. **67,** Cornell, petroleum distributor, 15th year.

Ben Montgomery, No. **117,** Morehouse, school administrator, 5th year.

Dave Moss, No. **88,** Dartmouth, insurance, 7th year.

Rex Stuart, No. **103,** Appalachian State, agency manager, life & health insurance, 3rd year.

Bob Wagner, No. **100,** Penn State, business administrator, 2nd year.

Gordon Wells, No. **89,** Occidental, college professor, physical education, 15th year.

Head Linesmen

Dave Anderson, No. **81,** Salem, senior account executive, health insurance, 3rd year.

Jerry Bergman, No. **17,** Duquesne, executive director, pension fund, 21st year.

Earnie Frantz, No. **111,** vice-president and manager, land title company, 6th year.

Terry Gierke, No. **72,** Portland State, real estate broker, 6th year.

Frank Glover, No. **85,** Morris Brown, assistant area superintendent, 15th year.

Ligouri Hagerty, No. **63,** Syracuse, manager, sporting goods company, 11th year.

Dale Hamer, No. **104,** California State, Pa., manager, leasing and equipment finance, 9th year.

Tom Johnson, No. **114,** Miami, Ohio, teacher, vice-president protection service, 5th year.

Norm Kragseth, No. **65,** Northwestern, chairman, physical education department, 13th year.

Ed Marion, No. **26,** Pennsylvania, regional pension manager, insurance company, 27th year.

Leo Miles, No. **35,** Virginia State, university athletic director, former NFL player, 18th year.

Ron Phares, No. **10,** Virginia Tech, vice-president, general contracting firm, 2nd year.

Sid Semon, No. **109,** Southern California, chairman, physical education department, 9th year.

Burl Toler, No. **37,** San Francisco, director of personnel, San Francisco Community College District, 22nd year.

Paul Weidner, No. **87,** Cincinnati, general sales manager and assistant treasurer, major appliances, 1st year.

Dale Williams, No. **8,** Cal State-Northridge, coordinator, athletic officials, 7th year.

Line Judges

Bob Beeks, No. **59,** Lincoln, law enforcement officer, 19th year.

Ron Blum, No. **83,** Marin College, manager, golf course, 2nd year.

Ron DeSouza, No. **45,** Morgan State, vice-president, student affairs, 7th year.

Ray Dodez, No. **74,** Wooster, communications consultant, 19th year.

Jack Fette, No. **39,** district sales manager, sporting goods company, 22nd year.

Bama Glass, No. **15,** Colorado, owner, consumer products, 8th year.

Joe Haynes, No. **112,** Alcorn State, public schools deputy superintendent, 3rd year.

Jack Johnson, No. **54,** Pacific Lutheran, president, sports promotions, 11th year.

Vern Marshall, No. **94,** Linfield College, counseling coordinator, 11th year.

Dick McKenzie, No. **41,** Ashland, treasurer, Wellington schools, 9th year.

Dale Orem, No. **51,** Louisville, public official and owner, sporting goods company, 7th year.

Bill Reynolds, No. **53,** West Chester State, teacher and athletic director, 12th year.

Howard Roe, No. **33,** Wichita State, manager and administrator, human resources, 3rd year.

Boyce Smith, No. **3,** Vanderbilt, executive vice-president, steel company, 6th year.

Dan Wilford, No. **30,** Mississippi, hospital executive, 4th year.

Back Judges

Paul Baetz, No. **22,** Heidelberg, financial consultant, 9th year.

Tom Barnes, No. **55,** Minnesota, president, manufacturer's rep. agency, 1st year.

Roy Clymer, No. **24,** New Mexico State, area manager, gas company, 7th year.

Al Jury, No. **106,** San Bernardino Valley, state traffic officer, 9th year.

Jim Kearney, No. **107,** Pennsylvania, marketing manager, 9th year.

Tom Kelleher, No. **25,** Holy Cross, president, marketing company, 27th year.

Pete Liske, No. **21,** Penn State, assistant athletic director, former NFL player, 4th year.

Bob Moore, No. **36,** Dayton, attorney, 3rd year.

Jim Poole, No. **92,** San Diego State, college physical education professor, 12th year.

Louis Richard, No. **68,** Southwest Louisiana, owner/president, weed control company, 1st year.

Jimmy Rosser, No. **98,** Auburn, president, employee leasing company, 10th year.

Tom Sifferman, No. **118,** Seattle, district sales manager, architectural engineering products, 1st year.

Ben Tompkins, No. **52,** Texas, attorney, 16th year.

Don Wedge, No. **28,** Ohio Wesleyan, regional sales manager, 15th year.

Banks Williams, No. **99,** Houston, vice-president sales, concrete company, 9th year.

Side Judges

Gerald Austin, No. **34,** Western Carolina, high school principal, 5th year.

Royal Cathcart, No. **16,** UC-Santa Barbara, commercial real estate broker, former NFL player, 16th year.

Richard Creed, No. **61,** Louisville, real estate management, 9th year.

Merrill Douglas, No. **102,** Utah, deputy sheriff, former NFL player, 6th year.

Tom Fincken, No. **47,** Emporia State, high school teacher, 3rd year.

Duwayne Gandy, No. **62,** Tulsa, regional sales manager, educational publishing, 6th year.

Dave Hawk, No. **66,** Southern Methodist, co-owner, warehousing company, 15th year.

Nate Jones, No. **97,** Lewis and Clark, high school principal, 10th year.

Stan Kemp, No. **108,** Michigan, vice president, commercial insurance, 1st year.

Gary Lane, No. **120,** Missouri, marketing consultant, former NFL player, 5th year.

Dean Look, No. **49,** Michigan State, vice-president, medical equipment company, former AFL player, 15th year.

Gil Mace, No. **90,** Westminster, national accounts manager, 13th year.

Larry Nemmers, No. **20,** Upper Iowa, high school principal, 2nd year.

Dave Parry, No. **64,** Wabash, high school athletic director, 12th year.

Bill Quinby, No. **58,** Iowa State, director, personnel services, 9th year.

Bob Rice, No. **80,** Denison, automobile leasing manager, 18th year.

Field Judges

Dick Dolack, No. **31,** Ferris State, pharmacist, 21st year.

Don Dorkowski, No. **113,** Cal State-Los Angeles, department head/teacher, 1st year.

Johnny Grier, No. **23,** D.C. Teachers, planning engineer, telephone company, 6th year.

Don Habel, No. **75,** Western Oregon, auto claim superintendent, 3rd year.

Don Hakes, No. **96,** Bradley, high school dean of students, 10th year.

Bernie Kukar, No. **86,** St. John's, health insurance representative, 3rd year.

Bob Lewis, No. **18,** supervisor, air force base, 11th year.

Pat Mallette, No. **82,** Nebraska, real estate broker, 18th year.

Ed Merrifield, No. **76,** Missouri, sales manager, heavy equipment, 12th year.

Don Orr, No. **77,** Vanderbilt, president, machine company, 16th year.

Bobby Skelton, No. **73,** Alabama, industrial representative, 2nd year.

Ron Spitler, No. **119,** Panhandle State, vice-president, special services, 5th year.

Bill Stanley, No. **91,** Redlands, college athletic director, 13th year.

Jack Vaughan, No. **93,** Mississippi State, insurance-field underwriter, 11th year.

Bob Wortman, No. **84,** Findlay, owner, insurance company, 21st year.

1

TOUCHDOWN, FIELD GOAL, or SUCCESSFUL TRY
Both arms extended above head.

2

SAFETY
Palms together above head.

3

FIRST DOWN
Arms pointed toward defensive team's goal.

4

DEAD BALL or NEUTRAL ZONE ESTABLISHED
One arm above head with an open hand.
With fist closed: **Fourth Down.**

5

BALL ILLEGALLY TOUCHED, KICKED, OR BATTED
Fingertips tap both shoulders.

6

TIME OUT
Hands crisscrossed above head.

Same signal followed by placing one hand on top of cap: **Referee's Time Out.**

Same signal followed by arm swung at side: **Touchback.**

7

NO TIME OUT or TIME IN WITH WHISTLE
Full arm circled to simulate moving clock.

8

DELAY OF GAME, ILLEGAL SUBSTITUTION OR EXCESS TIME OUT
Folded arms.

9

FALSE START, ILLEGAL SHIFT, ILLEGAL PROCEDURE, ILLEGAL FORMATION, or KICKOFF OR SAFETY KICK OUT OF BOUNDS
Forearms rotated over and over in front of body.

10

PERSONAL FOUL
One wrist striking the other above head.
Same signal followed by swinging leg: **Running Into or Roughing Kicker.**
Same signal followed by raised arm swinging forward: **Running Into or Roughing Passer.**
Same signal followed by hand striking back of calf: **Clipping.**

11

HOLDING
Grasping one wrist, the fist clenched, in front of chest.

12

ILLEGAL USE OF HANDS, ARMS, OR BODY
Grasping one wrist, the hand open and facing forward, in front of chest.

13

PENALTY REFUSED, INCOMPLETE PASS, PLAY OVER or MISSED GOAL
Hands shifted in horizontal plane.

14

PASS JUGGLED INBOUNDS AND CAUGHT OUT OF BOUNDS
Hands up and down in front of chest (following incomplete pass signal).

15

ILLEGAL FORWARD PASS
One hand waved behind back followed by loss of down signal.

16

INTENTIONAL GROUNDING OF PASS
Parallel arms waved in a diagonal plane across body. Followed by loss of down signal (23).

17

INTERFERENCE WITH FORWARD PASS or FAIR CATCH
Hands open and extended forward from shoulders with hands vertical.

18

INVALID FAIR CATCH SIGNAL
One hand waved above head.

19

INELIGIBLE RECEIVER or INELIGIBLE MEMBER OF KICKING TEAM DOWNFIELD
Right hand touching top of cap.

20

ILLEGAL CONTACT
One open hand extended forward.

21

OFFSIDE or ENCROACHING
Hands on hips.

22

ILLEGAL MOTION AT SNAP
Horizontal arc with one hand.

23

LOSS OF DOWN
Both hands held behind head.

24

CRAWLING, INTERLOCKING INTERFERENCE, PUSHING, or HELPING RUNNER
Pushing movement of hands to front with arms downward.

25

TOUCHING A FORWARD PASS OR SCRIMMAGE KICK
Diagonal motion of one hand across another.

26

UNSPORTSMANLIKE CONDUCT (Non-contact fouls)
Arms outstretched, palms down. (Same signal means continuous action fouls are disregarded.)

27

ILLEGAL CUT or BLOCKING BELOW THE WAIST
Hand striking front of thigh preceded by personal foul signal (10).

28

ILLEGAL CRACKBACK
Strike of an open right hand against the right mid thigh preceded by personal foul signal (10).

29

PLAYER DISQUALIFIED
Ejection signal.

30

TRIPPING
Repeated action of right foot in back of left heel.

NFL Digest of Rules

This Digest of Rules of the National Football League has been prepared to aid players, fans, and members of the press, radio, and television media in their understanding of the game.

It is not meant to be a substitute for the official rule book. In any case of conflict between these explanations and the official rules, the rules always have precedence.

In order to make it easier to coordinate the information in this digest the topics discussed generally follow the order of the rule book.

Officials' Jurisdictions, Positions, and Duties

Referee—General oversight and control of game. Gives signals for all fouls and is final authority for rule interpretations. Takes a position in backfield 10 to 12 yards behind line of scrimmage, favors right side (if quarterback is right-handed passer). Determines legality of snap, observes deep back(s) for legal motion. On running play, observes quarterback during and after handoff, remains with him until action has cleared away, then proceeds downfield, checking on runner and contact behind him. When runner is downed, Referee determines forward progress from wing official and if necessary, adjusts final position of ball.

On pass plays, drops back as quarterback begins to fade back, picks up legality of blocks by near linemen. Changes to complete concentration on quarterback as defenders approach. Primarily responsible to rule on possible roughing action on passer and if ball becomes loose, rules whether ball is free on a fumble or dead on an incomplete pass.

During kicking situations, Referee has primary responsibility to rule on kicker's actions and whether or not any subsequent contact by a defender is legal.

Umpire—Primary responsibility to rule on players' equipment, as well as their conduct and actions on scrimmage line. Lines up approximately four to five yards downfield, varying position from in front of weakside tackle to strongside guard. Looks for possible false start by offensive linemen. Observes legality of contact by both offensive linemen while blocking and by defensive players while they attempt to ward off blockers. Is prepared to call rule infractions if they occur on offense or defense. Moves forward to line of scrimmage when pass play develops in order to insure that interior linemen do not move illegally downfield. If offensive linemen indicate screen pass is to be attempted, Umpire shifts his attention toward screen side, picks up potential receiver in order to insure that he will legally be permitted to run his pattern and continues to rule on action of blockers. Umpire is to assist in ruling on incomplete or trapped passes when ball is thrown overhead or short.

Head Linesman—Primarily responsible for ruling on offside, encroachment, and actions pertaining to scrimmage line prior to or at snap. Keys on closest setback on his side of the field. On pass plays, Linesman is responsible to clear this receiver approximately seven yards downfield as he moves to a point five yards beyond the line. Linesman's secondary responsibility is to rule on any illegal action taken by defenders on any delay receiver moving downfield. Has full responsibility for ruling on sideline plays on his side, e.g., pass receiver or runner in or out of bounds. Together with Referee, Linesman is responsible for keeping track of number of downs and is in charge of mechanics of his chain crew in connection with its duties.

Linesman must be prepared to assist in determining forward progress by a runner on play directed toward middle or into his side zone. He, in turn, is to signal Referee or Umpire what forward point ball has reached. Linesman is also responsible to rule on legality of action involving any receiver who approaches his side zone. He is to call pass interference when the infraction occurs and is to rule on legality of blockers and defenders on plays involving ball carriers, whether it is entirely a running play, a combination pass and run, or a play involving a kick.

Line Judge—Straddles line of scrimmage on side of field opposite Linesman. Keeps time of game as a backup for clock operator. Along with Linesman is responsible for offside, encroachment, and actions pertaining to scrimmage line prior to or at snap. Line Judge keys on closest setback on his side of field. Line Judge is to observe his receiver until he moves at least seven yards downfield. He then moves toward backfield side, being especially alert to rule on any back in motion and on flight of ball when pass is made (he must rule whether forward or backward). Line Judge has primary responsibility to rule whether or not passer is behind or beyond line of scrimmage when pass is made. He also assists in observing actions by blockers and defenders who are on his side of field. After pass is thrown, Line Judge directs attention toward activities that occur in back of Umpire. During punting situations, Line Judge remains at line of scrimmage to be sure that only the end men move downfield until kick has been made. He also rules whether or not the kick crossed line and then observes action by members of the kicking team who are moving downfield to cover the kick.

Back Judge—Operates on same side of field as Line Judge, 17 yards deep. Keys on wide receiver on his side. Concentrates on path of end or back, observing legality of his potential block(s) or of actions taken against him. Is prepared to rule from deep position on holding or illegal use of hands by end or back or on defensive infractions committed by player guarding him. Has primary responsibility to make decisions involving sideline on his side of field, e.g., pass receiver or runner in or out of bounds.

Back Judge makes decisions involving catching, recovery, or illegal touching of a loose ball beyond line of scrimmage; rules on plays involving pass receiver, including legality of catch or pass interference; assists in covering actions of runner, including blocks by teammates and that of defenders; calls clipping on punt returns; and, together with Field Judge, rules whether or not field goal attempts are successful.

Side Judge—Operates on same side of field as Linesman, 17 yards deep. Keys on wide receiver on his side. Concentrates on path of end or back, observing legality of his potential block(s) or of actions taken against him. Is prepared to rule from deep position on holding or illegal use of hands by end or back or on defensive infractions committed by player guarding him. Has primary responsibility to make decisions involving sideline on his side of field, e.g., pass receiver or runner in or out of bounds.

Side Judge makes decisions involving catching, recovery, or illegal touching of a loose ball beyond line of scrimmage; rules on plays involving pass receiver, including legality of catch or pass interference; assists in covering actions of runner, including blocks by teammates and that of defenders; and calls clipping on punt returns.

Field Judge—Takes a position 25 yards downfield. In general, favors the tight end's side of field. Keys on tight end, concentrates on his path and observes legality of tight end's potential block(s) or of actions taken against him. Is prepared to rule from deep position on holding or illegal use of hands by end or back or on defensive infractions committed by player guarding him.

Field Judge times interval between plays on 30-second clock plus intermission between two periods of each half; makes decisions involving catching, recovery, or illegal touching of a loose ball beyond line of scrimmage; is responsible to rule on plays involving end line; calls pass interference, fair catch infractions, and clipping on kick returns; and, together with Back Judge, rules whether or not field goals and conversions are successful.

Definitions

1. **Chucking:** Warding off an opponent who is in front of a defender by contacting him with a quick extension of arm or arms, followed by the return of arm(s) to a flexed position, thereby breaking the original contact.
2. **Clipping:** Throwing the body across the back of an opponent's leg or hitting him from the back below the waist while moving up from behind unless the opponent is a runner or the action is in close line play.
3. **Close Line Play:** The area between the positions normally occupied by the offensive tackles, extending three yards on each side of the line of scrimmage.
4. **Crackback:** Eligible receivers who take or move to a position more than two yards outside the tackle may not block an opponent below the waist if they then move back inside to block.
5. **Dead Ball:** Ball not in play.
6. **Double Foul:** A foul by each team during the same down.
7. **Down:** The period of action that starts when the ball is put in play and ends when it is dead.
8. **Encroachment:** When a player enters the neutral zone and makes contact with an opponent before the ball is snapped.
9. **Fair Catch:** An unhindered catch of a kick by a member of the receiving team who must raise one arm a full length above his head while the kick is in flight.
10. **Foul:** Any violation of a playing rule.
11. **Free Kick:** A kickoff, kick after a safety, or kick after a fair catch. It may be a placekick, dropkick, or punt, except a punt may not be used on a kickoff.
12. **Fumble:** The loss of possession of the ball.
13. **Impetus:** The action of a player that gives momentum to the ball.
14. **Live Ball:** A ball legally free kicked or snapped. It continues in play until the down ends.
15. **Loose Ball:** A live ball not in possession of any player.
16. **Muff:** The touching of a loose ball by a player in an unsuccessful attempt to obtain possession.
17. **Neutral Zone:** The space the length of a ball between the two scrimmage lines. The offensive team and defensive team must remain behind their end of the ball.
    Exception: The offensive player who snaps the ball.
18. **Offside:** A player is offside when any part of his body is beyond his scrimmage or free kick line when the ball is snapped.
19. **Own Goal:** The goal a team is guarding.
20. **Pocket Area (Pass):** Applies from a point two yards outside of either offensive tackle and includes the tight end if he drops off the line of scrimmage to pass protect. Pocket extends longitudinally behind the line back to offensive team's own end line.
21. **Pocket Area (Run):** Applies from a point two yards outside of either offensive tackle (five normally spaced down linemen) and extends three yards beyond the line of scrimmage when contact is made. This area remains constant and could be shifted by an unbalanced line but cannot be expanded through use of an additional lineman.
22. **Possession:** When a player controls the ball throughout the act of clearly touching both feet, or any other part of his body other than his hand(s), to the ground inbounds.
23. **Punt:** A kick made when a player drops the ball and kicks it while it is in flight.
24. **Safety:** The situation in which the ball is dead on or behind a team's own goal if the impetus comes from a player on that team. Two points are scored for the opposing team.
25. **Shift:** The movement of two or more offensive players at the same time before the snap.
26. **Striking:** The act of swinging, clubbing, or propelling the arm or forearm in contacting an opponent.
27. **Sudden Death:** The continuation of a tied game into sudden death overtime in which the team scoring first (by safety, field goal, or touchdown) wins.
28. **Touchback:** When a ball is dead on or behind a team's own goal line, provided the impetus came from an opponent and provided it is not a touchdown or a missed field goal.

29. **Touchdown:** When any part of the ball, legally in possession of a player inbounds, is on, above, or over the opponent's goal line, provided it is not a touchback.
30. **Unsportsmanlike Conduct:** Any act contrary to the generally understood principles of sportsmanship.

Summary of Penalties

Automatic First Down

1. Awarded to offensive team on all defensive fouls with these exceptions:
   (a) Offside.
   (b) Encroachment.
   (c) Delay of game.
   (d) Illegal substitution.
   (e) Excessive time out(s).
   (f) Incidental grasp of facemask.
   (g) Prolonged, excessive or premeditated celebrations by individual players or groups of players.

Loss of Down (No yardage)

1. Second forward pass behind the line.
2. Forward pass strikes ground, goal post, or crossbar.
3. Forward pass goes out of bounds.
4. Forward pass is first touched by eligible receiver who has gone out of bounds and returned.
5. Forward pass touches or is caught by an ineligible receiver on or behind line.
6. Forward pass thrown from behind line of scrimmage after ball once crossed the line.

Five Yards

1. Crawling.
2. Defensive holding or illegal use of hands (automatic first down).
3. Delay of game.
4. Encroachment.
5. Too many time outs.
6. False start.
7. Illegal formation.
8. Illegal shift.
9. Illegal motion.
10. Illegal substitution.
11. Kickoff out of bounds between goal lines and not touched.
12. Invalid fair catch signal.
13. More than 11 players on the field at snap for either team.
14. Less than seven men on offensive line at snap.
15. Offside.
16. Failure to pause one second after shift or huddle.
17. Running into kicker (automatic first down).
18. More than one man in motion at snap.
19. Grasping facemask of opponent.
20. Player out of bounds at snap.
21. Ineligible member(s) of kicking team going beyond line of scrimmage before ball is kicked.
22. Illegal return.
23. Failure to report change of eligibility.
24. Prolonged, excessive or premeditated celebrations by individual players or groups of players.

10 Yards

1. Offensive pass interference.
2. Ineligible player downfield during passing down.
3. Holding, illegal use of hands, arms or body by offense.
4. Tripping by a member of either team.
5. Helping the runner.
6. Illegal batting or punching a loose ball.
7. Deliberately kicking a loose ball.

15 Yards

1. Clipping below the waist.
2. Fair catch interference.
3. Illegal crackback block by offense.
4. Piling on (automatic first down).
5. Roughing the kicker (automatic first down).
6. Roughing the passer (automatic first down).
7. Twisting, turning, or pulling an opponent by the facemask.
8. Unnecessary roughness.
9. Unsportsmanlike conduct.
10. Delay of game at start of either half.
11. Illegal blocking below the waist.
12. A tackler using his helmet to butt, spear, or ram an opponent.
13. Any player who uses the top of his helmet unnecessarily.
14. A punter, placekicker or holder who simulates being roughed by a defensive player.
15. A defender who takes a running start from beyond the line of scrimmage in an attempt to block a field goal or point after touchdown.

Five Yards and Loss of Down

1. Forward pass thrown from beyond line of scrimmage.

10 Yards and Loss of Down

1. Intentional grounding of forward pass (safety if passer is in own end zone). If foul occurs more than 10 yards behind line, play results in loss of down at spot of foul.

15 Yards and Loss of Coin Toss Option

1. Team's late arrival on the field prior to scheduled kickoff.

15 Yards (and disqualification if flagrant)

1. Striking opponent with fist.
2. Kicking or kneeing opponent.
3. Striking opponent on head or neck with forearm, elbow, or hands whether or not the initial contact is made below the neck area.
4. Roughing kicker.
5. Roughing passer.
6. Malicious unnecessary roughness.
7. Unsportsmanlike conduct.
8. Palpably unfair act. (Distance penalty determined by the Referee after consultation with other officials.)

15 Yards and Automatic Disqualification

1. Using a helmet that is not worn as a weapon.

Suspension From Game

1. Illegal equipment. (Player may return after one down when legally equipped.)

Touchdown

1. When Referee determines a palpably unfair act deprived a team of a touchdown. (Example: Player comes off bench and tackles runner apparently en route to touchdown.)

Field

1. Sidelines and end lines are out of bounds. The goal line is actually in the end zone. A player with the ball in his possession scores when the ball is on, above, or over the goal line.
2. The field is rimmed by a white border, a minimum six feet wide, along the sidelines. All of this is out of bounds.
3. The hashmarks (inbound lines) are 70 feet, 9 inches from each sideline.
4. Goal posts must be single-standard type, offset from the end line and painted bright gold. The goal posts must be 18 feet, 6 inches wide and the top face of the crossbar must be 10 feet above the ground. Vertical posts extend at least 30 feet above the crossbar. A ribbon 4 inches by 42 inches long is to be attached to the top of each post. The actual goal is the plane extending indefinitely above the crossbar and between the outer edges of the posts.
5. The field is 360 feet long and 160 feet wide. The end zones are 30 feet deep. The line used in try-for-point plays is two yards out from the goal line.
6. Chain crew members and ball boys must be uniformly identifiable.
7. All clubs must use standardized sideline markers. Pylons must be used for goal line and end line markings.
8. End zone markings and club identification at 50 yard line must be approved by the Commissioner to avoid any confusion as to delineation of goal lines, sidelines, and end lines.

Ball

1. The home club must have 24 balls available for testing by the Referee one hour before game time. In case of bad weather, a playable ball is to be substituted on request of the offensive team captain.

Coin Toss

1. The toss of coin will take place within three minutes of kickoff in center of field. The toss will be called by the visiting captain. The winner may choose one of two privileges and the loser gets the other:
   (a) Receive or kick
   (b) Goal his team will defend
2. Immediately prior to the start of the second half, the captains of both teams must inform the officials of their respective choices. The loser of the original coin toss gets first choice.

Timing

1. The stadium clock is official. In case it stops or is operating incorrectly, the Line Judge takes over the official timing on the field.
2. Each period is 15 minutes. The intermission between the periods is two minutes. Halftime is 15 minutes, unless otherwise specified.
3. On charged team time outs, the Field Judge starts watch and blows whistle after 1 minute 30 seconds, unless it is during the last two minutes of a half when the time is reduced to 60 seconds. However, Referee may allow two minutes for injured player and three minutes for equipment repair.
4. Each team is allowed three time outs each half.
5. Offensive team has 30 seconds to put the ball in play. The time is displayed on two 30-second clocks, which are visible to the players, officials, and fans. Field Judge is to call a delay of game penalty (five yards) when the time limit is exceeded. In case 30-second clocks are not operating, Field Judge takes over the official timing on the field.
6. Clock will start running when ball is snapped following all changes of team possession.

Sudden Death

1. The sudden death system of determining the winner shall prevail when score is tied at the end of the regulation playing time of all NFL games. The team scoring first during overtime play shall be the winner and the game automatically ends upon any score (by safety, field goal, or touchdown) or when a score is awarded by Referee for a palpably unfair act.
2. At the end of regulation time the Referee will immediately toss coin at center of field in accordance with rules pertaining to the usual pregame toss. The captain of the visiting team will call the toss.
3. Following a three-minute intermission after the end of the regulation game, play will be continued in 15-minute periods or until there is a score. There is a two-minute intermission between subsequent periods. The teams change goals at the start of each period. Each team has three time outs and general provisions for play in the last two minutes of a half shall prevail. Disqualified players are not allowed to return.
   Exception: In preseason and regular season games there shall be a maximum of 15 minutes of sudden death with two time outs instead of three. General provisions for play in the last two minutes of a half will be in force.

Timing in Final Two Minutes of Each Half

1. On kickoff, clock does not start until the ball has been legally touched by player of either team in the field of play. (In all other cases, clock starts with kickoff.)
2. A team cannot "buy" an excess time out for a penalty. However, a fourth time out is allowed without penalty for an injured player, who must be removed immediately. A fifth time out or more is allowed for an injury and a five-yard penalty is assessed if the clock was running. Additionally, if the clock was running and the score is tied or the team in possession is losing, the ball cannot be put in play for at least 10 seconds on the fourth or more time out. The half or game can end while those 10 seconds are run off on the clock.
3. If the defensive team is behind in the score and commits a foul when it has no time outs left in the final 30 seconds of either half, the offensive team can decline the penalty for the foul and have the time on the clock expire.

Try-for-Point

1. After a touchdown, the scoring team is allowed a try-for-point during one scrimmage down. The ball may be spotted anywhere between the inbounds lines, two or more yards from the goal line. The successful conversion counts one point, whether by run, kick, or pass.
2. The defensive team never can score on a try-for-point. As soon as defense gets possession, or kick is blocked, ball is dead.
3. Any distance penalty for fouls committed by the defense that prevent the try from being attempted can be enforced on the succeeding kickoff. Any foul committed on a successful try will result in a distance penalty being assessed on the ensuing kickoff.

Players-Substitutions

1. Each team is permitted 11 men on the field at the snap.
2. Unlimited substitution is permitted. However, players may enter the field only when the ball is dead. Players who have been substituted for are not permitted to linger on the field. Such lingering will be interpreted as unsportsmanlike conduct.
3. Players leaving the game must be out of bounds on their own side, clearing the field between the end lines, before a snap or free kick. If player crosses end line leaving field, it is delay of game (five-yard penalty).

Kickoff

1. The kickoff shall be from the kicking team's 35 yard line at the start of each half and after a field goal and try-for-point. A kickoff is one type of free kick.
2. Either a one-, two-, or three-inch tee may be used (no tee permitted for field goal or try-for-point plays). The ball is put in play by a placekick or dropkick.
3. If kickoff clears the opponent's goal posts it is not a field goal.
4. A kickoff is illegal unless it travels 10 yards OR is touched by the receiving team. Once the ball is touched by the receiving team it is a free ball. Receivers may recover and advance. Kicking team may recover but NOT advance UNLESS receiver had possession and lost the ball.
5. When a kickoff goes out of bounds between the goal lines without being touched by the receiving team, it must be kicked again. There is a five-yard penalty for a short kick or an out-of-bounds kick.
6. When a kickoff goes out of bounds between the goal lines and is touched last by receiving team, it is receiver's ball at out-of-bounds spot.

Free Kick

1. In addition to a kickoff, the other free kicks are a kick after a safety and a kick after a fair catch. In both cases, a dropkick, placekick, or punt may be used (a punt may not be used on a kickoff).
2. On free kick after a fair catch, captain of receiving team has the option to put ball in play by punt, dropkick, or placekick without a tee, or by snap. If the placekick or dropkick goes between the uprights a field goal is scored.
3. On a free kick after a safety, the team scored upon puts ball in play by a punt, dropkick, or placekick without tee. No score can be made on a free kick following a safety, even if a series of penalties places team in position. (A field goal can be scored only on a play from scrimmage or a free kick after a fair catch.)

Field Goal

1. All field goals attempted and missed from scrimmage line beyond the 20 yard line will result in the defensive team taking possession of the ball at the scrimmage line. On any field goal attempted and missed from scrimmage line inside the 20 yard line, ball will revert to defensive team at the 20 yard line.

Safety

1. The important factor in a safety is impetus. Two points are scored for the opposing team when the ball is dead on or behind a team's own goal line if the impetus came from a player on that team.

Examples of Safety:

(a) Blocked punt goes out of kicking team's end zone. Impetus was provided by punting team. The block only changes direction of ball, not impetus.
(b) Ball carrier retreats from field of play into his own end zone and is downed. Ball carrier provides impetus.
(c) Offensive team commits a foul and spot of enforcement is behind its own goal line.
(d) Player on receiving team muffs punt and, trying to get ball, forces or illegally kicks it into end zone where he or a teammate recovers. He has given new impetus to the ball.

Examples of Non-Safety:

(a) Player intercepts a pass and his momentum carries him into his own end zone. Ball is put in play at spot of interception.
(b) Player intercepts a pass in his own end zone and is downed. Impetus came from passing team, not from defense. (Touchback)
(c) Player passes from behind his own goal line. Opponent bats down ball in end zone. (Incomplete pass)

Measuring

1. The forward point of the ball is used when measuring.

Position of Players at Snap

1. Offensive team must have at least seven players on line.
2. Offensive players, not on line, must be at least one yard back at snap. (**Exception:** player who takes snap.)
3. No interior lineman may move after taking or simulating a three-point stance.
4. No player of either team may invade neutral zone before snap.
5. No player of offensive team may charge or move, after assuming set position, in such manner as to lead defense to believe snap has started.
6. If a player changes his eligibility, the Referee must alert the defensive captain after player has reported to him.
7. All players of offensive team must be stationary at snap, except one back who may be in motion parallel to scrimmage line or backward (not forward).
8. After a shift or huddle all players on offensive team must come to an absolute stop for at least one second with no movement of hands, feet, head, or swaying of body.
9. Quarterbacks can be called for a false start penalty (five yards) if their actions are judged to be an obvious attempt to draw an opponent offside.

Use of Hands, Arms, and Body

1. No player on offense may assist a runner except by blocking for him. There shall be no interlocking interference.
2. A runner may ward off opponents with his hands and arms but no other player on offense may use hands or arms to obstruct an opponent by grasping with hands, pushing, or encircling any part of his body during a block.
3. Pass blocking is the obstruction of an opponent by use of that part of the body above the knees. During a legal block, hands (open or closed) must be inside the blocker's elbows and can be thrust forward to contact an opponent as long as the contact is inside the frame. Hands cannot be thrust forward above the frame to contact an opponent on the neck, face, or head. (**Note:** The frame is defined as that part of the opponent's body below the neck that is presented to the blocker.) Blocker cannot use his hands or arms to push from behind, hang onto, or encircle an opponent in a manner that restricts his movements as the play develops. By use of up and down action of arm(s), the blocker is permitted to ward off the opponent's attempt to grasp his jersey or arm(s) and prevent legal contact to the head.
4. Run blocking is an aggressive action by a blocker to obstruct an opponent from the ball carrier. During a legal block, contact can be made with the head, shoulders, hands, and/or outer surface of the forearm, or any other part of the body. Hands with extended arms can be thrust forward to contact an opponent as long as the contact is inside the frame and inside the pocket area. [See Pocket Area (Run) Definitions, page 322.] As the play develops, a blocker is permitted to work for and maintain position on an opponent as long as he does not push from behind or clip (outside legal clip zone). A blocker who makes contact with extended arms within the pocket area may maintain such contact outside of the pocket area as long as the action is continuous. A blocker cannot make initial contact with extended arms outside the pocket area. A blocker lined up more than two yards outside the tackle is subject, also, to the crackback rule.
5. A defensive player may not tackle or hold an opponent other than a runner. Otherwise, he may use his hands, arms, or body only:
   (a) To defend or protect himself against an obstructing opponent.
   Exception: An eligible receiver is considered to be an obstructing opponent ONLY to a point five yards beyond the line of scrimmage unless the player who receives the snap clearly demonstrates no further intention to pass the ball. Within this five-yard zone, a defensive player may make contact with an eligible receiver that may be maintained as long as it is continuous and unbroken. The defensive player cannot use his hands or arms to push from behind, hang onto, or encircle an eligible receiver in a manner that restricts movement as the play develops. Beyond this five-yard limitation, a defender may use his hands or arms ONLY to defend or protect himself against impending contact caused by a receiver. In such reaction, the defender may not contact a receiver who attempts to take a path to evade him.
   (b) To push or pull opponent out of the way on line of scrimmage.
   (c) In actual attempt to get at or tackle runner.
   (d) To push or pull opponent out of the way in a legal attempt to recover a loose ball.
   (e) During a legal block on an opponent who is not an eligible pass receiver.
   (f) When legally blocking an eligible pass receiver above the waist.
   Exception: Eligible receivers lined up within two yards of the tackle, whether on or immediately behind the line, may be blocked below the waist at or behind the line of scrimmage. NO eligible receiver may be blocked below the waist after he goes beyond the line.
   Note: Once the quarterback hands off or pitches the ball to a back, or if the quarterback leaves the pocket area, the restrictions on the defensive team relative to the offensive receivers will end, provided the ball is not in the air.
6. A defensive player must not contact an opponent above the shoulders with the palm of his hand except to ward him off on the line. This exception is permitted only if it is not a repeated act against the same opponent during

any one contact. In all other cases the palms may be used on head, neck, or face only to ward off or push an opponent in legal attempt to get at the ball.

7. Any offensive player who pretends to possess the ball or to whom a teammate pretends to give the ball may be tackled provided he is crossing his scrimmage line between the ends of a normal tight offensive line.
8. An offensive player who lines up more than two yards outside his own tackle or a player who, at the snap, is in a backfield position and subsequently takes a position more than two yards outside a tackle may not clip an opponent anywhere nor may he contact an opponent below the waist if the blocker is moving toward the ball and if contact is made within an area five yards on either side of the line.
9. A player of either team may block at any time provided it is not pass interference, fair catch interference, or unnecessary roughness.
10. A player may not bat or punch:
    (a) A loose ball (in field of play) toward his opponent's goal line or in any direction in either end zone.
    (b) A ball in player possession or attempt to get possession.
    (c) A pass in flight forward toward opponent's goal line.
    Exception: A forward or backward pass may be batted in any direction at any time by the defense.
11. No player may deliberately kick any ball except as a punt, dropkick, or placekick.

Forward Pass

1. A forward pass may be touched or caught by any eligible receiver. All members of the defensive team are eligible. Eligible receivers on the offensive team are players on either end of line (other than center, guard, or tackle) or players at least one yard behind the line at the snap. A T-formation quarterback is not eligible to receive a forward pass during a play from scrimmage.
   Exception: T-formation quarterback becomes eligible if pass is previously touched by an eligible receiver.
2. An offensive team may make only one forward pass during each play from scrimmage (Loss of down).
3. The passer must be behind his line of scrimmage (Loss of down and five yards, enforced from the spot of pass).
4. Any eligible offensive player may catch a forward pass. If a pass is touched by one offensive player and touched or caught by a second eligible offensive player, pass completion is legal. Further, all offensive players become eligible once a pass is touched by an eligible receiver or any defensive player.
5. The rules concerning a forward pass and ineligible receivers:
   (a) If ball is touched accidentally by an ineligible receiver on or behind his line: loss of down.
   (b) If ineligible receiver is illegally downfield: loss of 10 yards.
   (c) If touched or caught (intentionally or accidentally) by ineligible receiver beyond the line: loss of 10 yards.
   (d) If ineligible receiver is illegally downfield: loss of 10 yards.
6. If a forward pass is caught simultaneously by eligible players on opposing teams, possession goes to passing team.
7. Any forward pass becomes incomplete and ball is dead if:
   (a) Pass hits the ground or goes out of bounds.
   (b) Hits the goal post or the crossbar of either team.
   (c) Is caught by offensive player after touching ineligible receiver.
   (d) An illegal pass is caught by the passer.
8. A forward pass is complete when a receiver clearly touches the ground with both feet inbounds while in possession of the ball. If a receiver would have landed inbounds with both feet but is carried or pushed out of bounds while maintaining possession of the ball, pass is complete at the out-of-bounds spot.
9. If an eligible receiver goes out of bounds accidentally or is forced out by a defender and returns to catch a pass, the play is regarded as a pass caught out of bounds. (Loss of down, no yardage.)
10. On a fourth down pass—when the offensive team is inside the opposition's 20 yard line—an incomplete pass results in a loss of down at the line of scrimmage.
11. If a personal foul is committed by the defense prior to the completion of a pass, the penalty is 15 yards from the spot where ball becomes dead.
12. If a personal foul is committed by the offense prior to the completion of a pass, the penalty is 15 yards from the previous line of scrimmage.

Intentional Grounding of Forward Pass

1. Intentional grounding of a forward pass is a foul: loss of down and 10 yards from previous spot if passer is in the field of play or loss of down at the spot of the foul if it occurs more than 10 yards behind the line or safety if passer is in his own end zone when ball is released.
2. It is considered intentional grounding of a forward pass when the ball strikes the ground after the passer throws, tosses, or lobs the ball to prevent a loss of yards by his team.

Protection of Passer

1. By interpretation, a pass begins when the passer—with possession of ball—starts to bring his hand forward. If ball strikes ground after this action has begun, play is ruled an incomplete pass. If passer loses control of ball prior to his bringing his hand forward, play is ruled a fumble.
2. No defensive player may run into a passer of a legal forward pass after the ball has left his hand (15 yards). The Referee must determine whether opponent had a reasonable chance to stop his momentum during an attempt to block the pass or tackle the passer while he still had the ball.
3. Officials are to blow the play dead as soon as the quarterback is clearly in the grasp of any tackler.

Pass Interference

1. There shall be no interference with a forward pass thrown from behind the line. The restriction for the passing team starts with the snap. The restriction on the defensive team starts when the ball leaves the passer's hand. Both restrictions end when the ball is touched by anyone.
2. The penalty for defensive pass interference is an automatic first down at the spot of the foul. If interference is in the end zone, it is first down for the offense on the defense's 1 yard line. If previous spot was inside the defense's 1 yard line, penalty is half the distance to the goal line.
3. The penalty for offensive pass interference is 10 yards from the previous spot.
4. It is pass interference by either team when any player movement beyond the offensive line significantly hinders the progress of an eligible player or such player's opportunity to catch the ball during a legal forward pass. When a player establishes a position to catch the ball in which an opponent cannot reach the ball without first contacting the player in a manner that prevents the player from catching the ball, such action by the opponent shall be considered interference. Provided an eligible player is not interfered with in such a manner, the following exceptions to pass interference will prevail:
   (a) If neither player is looking for the ball and there is incidental contact in the act of moving to the ball that does not materially affect the route of an eligible player, there is no interference. If there is any question whether the incidental contact materially affects the route, the ruling shall be no interference.
   Note: Inadvertent tripping is not a foul in this situation.
   (b) Any eligible player looking for and intent on playing the ball who initiates contact, however severe, while attempting to move to the spot of completion or interception will not be called for interference.
   (c) Any eligible player who makes contact, however severe, with one or more eligible players while looking for and making a genuine attempt to catch or bat a reachable ball, will not be called for interference.
   (d) It must be remembered that defensive players have as much right to the ball as offensive eligible receivers.
   (e) Pass interference by the defense is not to be called when the forward pass is clearly uncatchable.
   (f) Note: There is no defensive pass interference behind the line.

Backward Pass

1. Any pass not forward is regarded as a backward pass or lateral. A pass parallel to the line is a backward pass. A runner may pass backward at any time. Any player on either team may catch the pass or recover the ball after it touches the ground.
2. A backward pass that strikes the ground can be recovered and advanced by offensive team.
3. A backward pass that strikes the ground can be recovered but cannot be advanced by the defensive team.
4. A backward pass caught in the air can be advanced by the defensive team.

Fumble

1. The distinction between a fumble and a muff should be kept in mind in considering rules about fumbles. A fumble is the loss of possession of the ball. A muff is the touching of a loose ball by a player in an unsuccessful attempt to obtain possession.
2. A fumble may be advanced by any player on either team regardless of whether recovered before or after ball hits the ground.
3. A fumble that goes forward and out of bounds will return to the fumbling team at the spot of the fumble unless the ball goes out of bounds in the opponent's end zone. In this case, the defensive team is to take possession at the spot of the fumble.
4. If an offensive player fumbles anywhere on the field during a fourth down play, or if a player fumbles on any down after the two-minute warning in a half, only the fumbling player is permitted to recover and/or advance the ball. If recovered by any other offensive player, the ball is dead at the spot of the fumble unless it is recovered behind the spot of the fumble. In that case, ball is dead at spot of recovery. Any defensive player may recover and/or advance any fumble.
   Exception: The fourth-down fumble rule does not apply if a player touches, but does not possess, a direct snap from center, i.e., a snap in flight as opposed to a hand-to-hand exchange.

Kicks From Scrimmage

1. Any punt or missed field goal that touches a goal post is dead.
2. During a kick from scrimmage, only the end men, as eligible receivers on the line of scrimmage at the time of the snap, are permitted to go beyond the line before the ball is kicked.
   Exception: An eligible receiver who, at the snap, is aligned or in motion behind the line and more than one yard outside the end man on his side of the line, clearly making him the outside receiver, REPLACES that end man as the player eligible to go downfield after the snap. All other members of the kicking team must remain at the line of scrimmage until the ball has been kicked.
3. Any punt that is blocked and does not cross the line of scrimmage can be recovered and advanced by either team. However, if offensive team recovers it must make the yardage necessary for its first down to retain possession if punt was on fourth down.
4. The kicking team may never advance its own kick even though legal recovery is made beyond the line of scrimmage. Possession only.
5. A member of the receiving team may not run into or rough a kicker who kicks from behind his line unless contact is:
   (a) Incidental to and after he had touched ball in flight.

(b) Caused by kicker's own motions.
(c) Occurs during a quick kick, or a kick made after a run, or after kicker recovers a loose ball. Ball is loose when kicker muffs snap or snap hits ground.
(d) Defender is blocked into kicker.

The penalty for running into the kicker is 5 yards and an automatic first down. For roughing the kicker: 15 yards and disqualification if flagrant.

6. If a member of the kicking team attempting to down the ball on or inside opponent's 5 yard line carries the ball into the end zone, it is a touchback.
7. Fouls during a punt are enforced from the previous spot (line of scrimmage). **Exception:** Illegal touching, illegal fair catch, invalid fair catch signal, and fouls by the receiving team during loose ball after ball is kicked.
8. While the ball is in the air or rolling on the ground following a punt or field goal attempt and receiving team commits a foul before gaining possession, receiving team will retain possession and will be penalized for its foul.
9. It will be illegal for a defensive player to jump or stand on any player, or be picked up by a teammate or to use a hand or hands on a teammate to gain additional height in an attempt to block a kick (Penalty 15 yards, unsportsmanlike conduct).
10. A punted ball remains a kicked ball until it is declared dead or in possession of either team.
11. Any member of the punting team may down the ball anywhere in the field of play. However, it is illegal touching (Official's time out and receiver's ball at spot of illegal touching). This foul does not offset any foul by receivers during the down.
12. Defensive team may advance all kicks from scrimmage (including unsuccessful field goal) whether or not ball crosses defensive team's goal line. Rules pertaining to kicks from scrimmage apply until defensive team gains possession.

Fair Catch

1. The member of the receiving team must raise one arm a full length above his head and wave it from side to side while kick is in flight. (Failure to give proper sign: receivers' ball five yards behind spot of signal.)
2. No opponent may interfere with the fair catcher, the ball, or his path to the ball. Penalty: 15 yards from spot of foul and fair catch is awarded.
3. A player who signals for a fair catch is not required to catch the ball. However, if a player signals for a fair catch, he may not block or initiate contact with any player on the kicking team until the ball touches a player. Penalty: snap 15 yards behind spot of foul.
4. If ball hits ground or is touched by member of kicking team in flight, fair catch signal is off and all rules for a kicked ball apply.
5. Any undue advance by a fair catch receiver is delay of game. No specific distance is specified for "undue advance" as ball is dead at spot of catch. If player comes to a reasonable stop, no penalty. For violation, five yards.
6. If time expires while ball is in play and a fair catch is awarded, receiving team may choose to extend the period with one free kick down. However, placekicker may not use tee.

Foul on Last Play of Half or Game

1. On a foul by defense on last play of half or game, the down is replayed if penalty is accepted.
2. On a foul by the offense on last play of half or game, the down is not replayed and the play in which the foul is committed is nullified.
   Exception: Fair catch interference, foul following change of possession, illegal touching. No score by offense counts.
3. On double foul on last play of half or game, down is replayed.

Spot of Enforcement of Foul

1. There are four basic spots at which a penalty for a foul is enforced:
   (a) Spot of foul: The spot where the foul is committed.
   (b) Previous spot: The spot where the ball was put in play.
   (c) Spot of snap, pass, fumble, return kick, or free kick: The spot where the act connected with the foul occurred.
   (d) Succeeding spot: The spot where the ball next would be put in play if no distance penalty were to be enforced.
   Exception: If foul occurs after a touchdown and before the whistle for a try-for-point, succeeding spot is spot of next kickoff.
2. All fouls committed by offensive team behind the line of scrimmage and in the field of play shall be penalized from the previous spot.
3. When spot of enforcement for fouls involving defensive holding or illegal use of hands by the defense is behind the line of scrimmage, any penalty yardage to be assessed on that play shall be measured from the line if the foul occurred beyond the line.

Double Foul

1. If there is a double foul during a down in which there is a change of possession, the team last gaining possession may keep the ball unless its foul was committed prior to the change of possession.
2. If double foul occurs after a change of possession, the defensive team retains the ball at the spot of its foul or dead ball spot.
3. If one of the fouls of a double foul involves disqualification, that player must be removed, but no penalty yardage is to be assessed.
4. If the kickers foul during a punt before possession changes and the receivers foul after possession changes, penalties will be offset and the down is replayed.

Penalty Enforced on Following Kickoff

1. When a team scores by touchdown, field goal, extra point, or safety and either team commits a personal foul, unsportsmanlike conduct, or obvious unfair act during the down, the penalty will be assessed on the following kickoff.

NOTES

NOTES

NOTES

NOTES

NOTES

NOTES